The Oxford Encyclopedia of the Reformation

The Oxford Encyclopedia
of the
Reformation

HANS J. HILLERBRAND

EDITOR IN CHIEF

Volume 1

New York   Oxford
OXFORD UNIVERSITY PRESS
1996

OXFORD UNIVERSITY PRESS

Oxford   New York
Athens   Auckland   Bangkok   Bombay
Calcutta   Cape Town   Dar es Salaam   Delhi
Florence   Hong Kong   Istanbul   Karachi
Kuala Lumpur   Madras   Madrid   Melbourne
Mexico City   Nairobi   Paris   Singapore
Taipei   Tokyo   Toronto

and associated companies in
Berlin   Ibadan

Published by Oxford University Press, Inc.,
198 Madison Avenue, New York, New York 10016

Oxford is a registered trademark of Oxford University Press

Library of Congress Cataloging-in-Publication Data
The Oxford encyclopedia of the Reformation / Hans J. Hillerbrand, editor in chief
p.   cm.
Includes bibliographical references and index.
ISBN 0-19-506493-3 (set : alk. paper)
1. Reformation—Encyclopedias.   2. Reformation—Biography—Encyclopedias.
3. Theology, Doctrinal—Europe—History—16th century—Encyclopedias.
4. Europe—Church history—16th century—Encyclopedias.
I. Hillerbrand, Hans J.
BR302.8.093   1996   270.6'03—dc20   95-24520   CIP

ISBN-13 978-0-19-506493-3
ISBN 0-19-506493-3 (set)
ISBN 0-19-510362-9 (vol. 1)

EDITORIAL AND PRODUCTION STAFF

COMMISSIONING EDITOR: Claude Conyers
DEVELOPMENT EDITOR: Mark D. Cummings

PROJECT EDITOR: Stephen Chasteen
EDITORIAL ASSISTANT: Christopher Reiter
COPYEDITORS AND PROOFREADERS: Diane Foster, Karen Fraley,
David Gombac, Gary Lee, Thomas Riggs, Sally Steinberg
BIBLIOGRAPHIC AND TECHNICAL RESEARCHERS:
Jeff Bach, Barbara Pollock, Lisa A. Tirone
INDEXER: Stephen R. Ingle
PRODUCTION COORDINATOR: Tom Kieran
MANUFACTURING CONTROLLER: Michelle Levesque
BOOK DESIGNER: Joan Greenfield

Printing (last digit): 9 8 7 6 5 4

Printed in the United States of America
on acid-free paper

CONTENTS

EDITORIAL BOARD

PREFACE

The Reformation of the sixteenth century, the subject of this encyclopedia, has a long and impressive history of scholarship. Until fairly recently, it had always been easy to define. "Reformation" meant the mainstream Protestant Reformation, and the argument ran that this Reformation was, regarding both religion and European society as a whole, the single most critical phenomenon of the sixteenth century. Scholarship on the Reformation was dominated by Protestant historians, who saw in the events of the sixteenth century the unfolding of eternal truth as revealed in the teachings of the Protestant reformers. Moreover, since much of this scholarship was carried out in Germany, German Reformation scholars were predisposed to make a connection between such truth and subsequent German history: the nineteenth and twentieth centuries were seen as the glorious unfolding of what, in fact, had begun in the sixteenth century—until the specter of Nazi totalitarianism prompted the nagging thought that this connection might be true in a completely different way. In addition, the time before the Reformation was labeled a period of perversion and superstition, and no authentic Christianity was said to have existed between Patmos (where John is said to have written *Revelation*) and Wittenberg. Catholic scholars, much like the Catholic protagonists of the sixteenth century, found themselves on the defensive, and their emphasis on the existence of a vibrant Roman Catholic church on the eve of the Reformation did not gain widespread acceptance.

Scholarly Background

Much has happened in twentieth-century Reformation scholarship, as the article on that subject in this encyclopedia readily attests. A variety of new perspectives has emerged, making the study of the Reformation a rewarding, if at times bewildering, effort. The scholarly literature is substantial. The inventory taking represented by The Oxford Encyclopedia of the Reformation is thus an altogether timely and appropriate endeavor. It is characterized by a number of important features.

First, Reformation scholarship has advanced beyond a narrow focus on religion in the sixteenth century. While it has long been acknowledged that the sixteenth century also witnessed the beginnings of capitalism, the Renaissance, and European discoveries in the New World, not to mention the rise of the nation-state, recent scholarship manifests a greater openness to examining all these phenomena in relationship to one another. Second, the understanding of religion itself has evolved. Traditionally, religion meant the thought of the major reformers, notably, of course, Luther and Calvin, but also Zwingli, Bucer, Cranmer, Melanchthon, and even Michael Sattler and Bernhard Rothmann. Scholars also concentrated on the confessional documents of the Reformation, such as the Augsburg Confession, and the great theological controversies, such the Communion controversy of the late 1520s. For these scholars, the Reformation was one chapter in the history of Christian thought; the reformers' thoughts about justification, the church, and the sacraments were the heart of the Reformation. In the second half of the twentieth century, this traditional understanding has been augmented by greater attention to popular religion and to the publications of lesser known lay authors. This broadening of the definition of the Reformation has enriched our understanding of what religion meant in the sixteenth century. Third, social historians have begun to examine the structures of sixteenth-century society, yielding a rich harvest of new insights—such as the role of women in the Reformation—even though some conclusions remain controversial. Greater attention also has been paid to Catholic life in the sixteenth century.

One theme has persisted, even in recent Reformation historiography: the Reformation was a major event in European history. Whether viewed negatively as a disaster for flourishing medieval Christianity, or positively as the incisive liberating birth of modernity, with its appeal to conscience, the scholarly bottom line has remained clear: the events of the sixteenth century were of major import.

The traditional understanding of the Reformation had it that everything began with Martin Luther's Ninety-five Theses in 1517, triggering the controversy that constituted (or led to) the Reformation. The sites of activity, first in Germany, soon spread, making the Reformation a pan-European phenomenon. Everywhere the issue of religious reform and renewal, frequently accompanied by a concern for societal reform and renewal, stood at the core of extensive agitation. This agitation reached its formal conclusion—scholars have used such phrases as "the Reformation was introduced," "the Reformation was successful," or, for that matter, "the Reformation failed"—when a decision was made for or against the official introduction of the new Protestant religion. This occurred at different places at different times, but throughout Europe that decision had to be faced by the political authorities.

If the points of departure and conclusions thus seem fairly clear, even though anything but uniform as far as Europe is concerned, questions remain. What was the inner momentum of this quest for reform and renewal? Was it religion? Were the governmental decisions regarding the Reformation uniformly religious decisions? Moreover, the chronological parameters of 1517 and 1555, once deemed sacrosanct, have been challenged by two generations of scholars. We now understand the process of reform and renewal to have been far more extensive than such arbitrary dates as 1517 and 1555 (or 1559, or 1598) might indicate.

This scholarly development also means that the time-honored nomenclature that distinguished between a "Reformation" and a "Catholic reform and Counter-Reformation" is being reexamined. The underlying implication of these terms was simple: not only were all reform impulses in the sixteenth century associated with the Protestant Reformation, with Catholics both appropriating and reacting against these Protestant impulses, but also the motif of reform was thereby declared to be the overriding concern of the sixteenth century.

Recently, John W. O'Malley introduced another perspective. Arguing the liveliness of religious life carried on in confraternities and other institutions outside strictly parochial confines on the eve of the Reformation, O'Malley contends that Catholic reform and Counter-Reformation do not fully express the richness of Catholic life in the sixteenth century, a richness that at times stood quite apart from any notion of reform. Moreover, the terms "Catholic reform and Counter-Reformation" intimate officialdom, that is, modification of church life and theology from above.

This issue has bearing on how *The Oxford Encyclopedia of the Reformation* was conceptualized. The question posed was "What do we mean when we speak of the Reformation?" This reference work was not conceived as an encyclopedia of the sixteenth century nor an encyclopedia of a Protestant Reformation narrowly defined. As used in the title, "Reformation" is a convenient label to denote nothing more, but also nothing less, than the rich diversity of all religious life in sixteenth-century Europe. At the same time, the term is meant to entail something else of importance. Many of the entries included in this encyclopedia—such as those on time, discoveries in the New World, and even prostitution—would appear, on the surface, to have nothing to do with religion, yet their inclusion is not simply a matter of serendipity.

There were abundant expressions of religious life in the sixteenth century that are not captured by the term "reform" or by the term "Counter-Reformation." Such "indigenous" elements of European religion were neither characterized by the intentionality associated with the term "reform" in general nor very much affected by the Protestant Reformation in particular. This observation may be linked to Catholicism in the sixteenth century, but goes, in fact, far beyond it. What we have come to call "popular religion" in recent years undoubtedly went its own course, little touched by those events that are generally narrated in the textbooks.

The Oxford Encyclopedia of the Reformation seeks to do justice to the whole range of events and happenings of the sixteenth century. It uses the broadest possible definition of the Reformation in order to depict not only religious life but also the related societal phenomena that in one way or another had bearing on religion. *The Oxford Encyclopedia of the Reformation* employs the term "Reformation" as time-honored nomenclature, but broadly defined indeed.

The working assumption for *The Oxford Encyclopedia of the Reformation* was that the Reformation consisted of the broad phenomenon of religion and all its societal ramifications in the sixteenth century. The encyclopedia does not, therefore, confine itself to what is commonly called the "Protestant Reformation." It should be clear that the cohesiveness of the encyclopedia depends not so much on a traditional understanding of the Reformation as on the fact that the very importance of the Reformation as traditionally defined also increases the significance of a wealth of other phenomena in the sixteenth century whose ties to the Reformation may be indistinct and obscure. The sixteenth century was a singularly rich time. It may well be that future scholars will employ new terms to denote that richness; nevertheless, in its substance, *The Oxford Encyclopedia of the Reformation* will remain timeless, as the wealth of scholarship must not be allowed to obscure the centrality of *the* Reformation in the sixteenth century.

A further issue the editors faced in conceptualizing the encyclopedia pertains to the European dimension of this phenomenon of religious and societal change. If one thing is clear, then it is that the Reformation was not confined to Germany, that it occurred throughout Europe. An analysis of the Reformation in Sweden, England, or Italy, for that matter, reveals significant differences as well as similarities that exist alongside the course of events in Germany.

The historian of the Reformation must be careful not to see the Reformation as what has been facetiously called a "trip up and down the Rhine," so as to let events in Germany overshadow a larger European perspective. This eventuality is the fateful legacy of a Reformation historiography that once was dominated by German scholars, who understandably considered Germany the navel of the universe. Until recently, the sheer quantity of Reformation scholarship coming from Germany has been more formidable than that of other countries. Quantity has had a suffocating effect. In a subtle way this perspective persists, not so much in terms of amount of space and attention devoted to the chronological narratives as in the notion that the important ideological and theological issues were fully rehearsed in Germany by German personalities.

The principal legacy of the Reformation was the fundamental division of what had previously been understood as Christendom. The ecumenical spirit that prevails at the end of the twentieth century belies the hostility that existed in the sixteenth century between Protestants and Roman Catholics. Martin Luther's early claim that the pope was the Antichrist was formalized in many Protestant creedal statements. To be sure, such Christendom had never been a monolithic unity—not at the very beginning, not during the theological controversies of the early church, and not during the Middle Ages. There always was awareness of an "Eastern" as well as a "Western" Christendom, but the "East" was far away and did not enter the conscious mentality of central and western Europe. In the West, at any rate, Christendom was one.

The Reformation changed this—and did so quite dramatically. Not only was there a division that sank deep into the public consciousness, everybody was aware by the end of the sixteenth century that the Christian religion was divided among no fewer than six claimants to truth, and the differences were seen as categorical and profound. These differences were obscured for the common people because in a given political entity only one form of religion was officially enjoined, continuing the state of affairs that had prevailed before the sixteenth century. But the fierce disagreements among the religious parties were a matter of record, and for educated Europeans this state of affairs was a different matter, since the multiplicity of truth claims was problematic.

Today we doubt whether—as an earlier generation of Reformation scholars believed—the differences between Catholic and Protestant theology (for example, the anchoring of theology in dogma and tradition by the former and in faith and the Bible by the latter) were crucial for the course of events. Undeniably, the principle of authority in Protestantism *is* different from that in Catholicism. But, profound as the difference may have been, it was practically obliterated by Protestant orthodoxy, for which adherence to creedal statements and confessions became every bit as important as it was for Catholicism, despite the claim that the creedal formulations represented nothing more than summaries of sacred scripture. It seems fair to summarize current scholarship as no longer considering theological differences quite so divisive.

The Protestant creeds and confessions, whether Lutheran, Calvinist, or Anglican, breathed the breath of newness. They were recently composed, were written by contemporaries, and represented the outgrowth of current debates and discussions, while the Catholic stance echoed, with the exception of the canons of the Council of Trent, centuries long past. In a striking way, in other words, the confrontation between Catholicism and Protestantism in all its forms was a confrontation between the old and the new. The period of orthodoxy (or confessionalism) that followed the Reformation constitutes a splendid proof of the intentionality of the Reformation. The events of the early seventeenth century make the consequences flowing from the Reformation quite evident: none of the religious factions was able to perceive of the others as equals.

Editorial Principles and Practices

The original idea for *The Oxford Encyclopedia of the Reformation* had its beginnings in 1989, when it became obvious that no matter how defined, the Reformation of the sixteenth century leant itself as the topic for a cohesive reference work. This was supported by an awareness that American Reformation scholarship had come of age. There is, in North America, a substantial reserve of scholarly expertise in the field of Reformation studies, and some fields, such as the radical Reformation, are clearly dominated by North American scholars. As a reflection of this, the board of editors of the encyclopedia—senior editors, associate editors, and consulting editors—consists entirely of American scholars, a constellation of talent and expertise that would no doubt have been impossible to come by as recently as fifty years ago. It would be a narrow provincialism, all the same, had not the editors of this project sought the expert guidance of an international board of advisers, whose suggestions inestimably enriched the substance and coverage of the encyclopedia. Likewise, the roster of contributors encompasses scholars not only from the United States and Canada but the United Kingdom, Norway, Hungary, the Netherlands, Denmark, Italy, Finland, Poland, and Australia, to mention but a few nations at random. If nothing else, the encyclopedia represents the creative international guild of Reformation scholars.

There was never any doubt that this encyclopedia should be as all-inclusive as possible and accommodate both long-standing and more recent scholarly conventions. As befits a reference work, the encyclopedia strives to take no position—although individual authors do. The important principle of parity was sought throughout, giving, for example, the entry on Anglicanism the same space as that on Calvinism. However, the reader should be cautioned not to read too much into such quantitative issues: some authors stayed below their assigned word lengths, while others went far beyond them; despite all editorial intervention, some unavoidable unevenness remains. Because of its inclusiveness, the encyclopedia will be of use to those whose interest is theology no less than to those interested in social history.

Another fundamental guiding principle employed during the planning stages of the project was the idea of "resurrection." For far too long, many interesting and important personalities of the sixteenth century, because they were not major reformers, theologians, or rulers, have fallen into scholarly obscurity, having been repeatedly relegated to footnotes and bibliographical entries out of habit. One of our major intentions was to shed new light on these fascinating figures. Hence, what may at first seem to be an inordinate preponderance of biographical entries in the encyclopedia is, in fact, one of its reasons for being. We hope that new and significant research will be sparked by our attempts to rescue a number of personalities from undeserved obscurity.

A further caution that readers should bear in mind in searching for individuals in the encyclopedia is the proliferation of personal onomastics that occurred during the sixteenth century. Because a single individual might well use three or four different names (for example, one Latin, one German, one in a local dialect, and one a pseudonym) depending on the circumstance, readers are encouraged to consult the index for alternative names as well as alternative spellings of the names of individuals. It was our editorial policy to standardize personal names as much as possible; clearly, however, with more than 1,200 articles deriving from more than 450 authors, each of whom used his or her own preferred form and spelling for personal names, to standardize each and every name would have been impossible.

Entries in the encyclopedia are alphabetically arranged, strictly letter by letter. In order to make use of the specialized expertise of individual scholars while ensuring that all aspects of larger topics were fully covered, "composite entries" group together several articles under one headword. For example, the entry "Mariology" consists of two articles, one on popular piety and one on theology. Each composite entry begins with a headnote explaining its division.

To guide readers from one article to related discussions elsewhere in the encyclopedia, there is an extensive system of cross-references at the ends of many articles. In addition, "blind entries" of alternative spellings and synonyms occur throughout the alphabetical range of headwords, providing cross-references to relevant articles. For example, the reader looking up "Poverty" will be directed to two entries, "Begging" and "Social Welfare." A comprehensive index is a further resource, containing a wealth of topics that are not headwords themselves. Readers interested in finding all the articles on a particular subject (e.g., historical events, religious groups and movements) are encouraged to consult the Synoptic Outline of Contents in volume 4.

A special word about the bibliographies is appropriate. The advent of electronic on-line bibliographical databases has increasingly provided both the specialist and the general reader a wealth of information. In a real sense, this new technology has called into question the traditional way of providing bibliographical information. For example, *Religion Index* and the OCLC bibliography quickly provide information that only a few years ago required special research trips and endless hours to compile. For virtually all the bibliographical entries in the encyclopedia, the OCLC listings conveyed information about the availability of primary source material in the United States. The Internet also provides access to the on-line catalogs of many major libraries throughout the world, as well as to the catalog of the Library of Congress. The function of the bibliographies in *The Oxford Encyclopedia of the Reformation*, then, is to provide the reader with a qualitatively select bibliography deemed in the judgment of the authors and editors to be the best available literature on the subject.

Finally, we owe readers a few words of explanation concerning the lack of illustrations in the pages that follow. Early in the planning stages of the encyclopedia, we considered whether it should include illustrations and, if so, whether the program should be extensive, moderate, or minimal. Eventually it became clear to us that there exist numerous resources documenting the imagery, iconography, and architecture of the sixteenth century and that any attempt to represent the visual richness of the period within the pages of the encyclopedia would of necessity remain a cursory sampling. Likewise, we considered the advisability of including a map program. Although we decided to forego graphic images without undue editorial concern, we could not abandon quite so easily the idea of including a few simple but useful maps. Interested readers will find them in an appendix immediately following the final entry in volume 4. We were, however, obliged to limit our map program to depictions of phenomena associated with the Reformation that readily lend themselves to cartographic display. Map lovers who wish to see greater detail are referred especially to the *Atlas zur Kirchengeschichte* (Freiburg: Herder, 1970) and to the multivolume *Geschichte des Christentums* (Stuttgart: Kohlhammer, 1975–).

Acknowledgments

It remains for me to express the obligatory yet heartfelt word of appreciation to all those whose stamp is in one way or another on this encyclopedia. The enthusiastic support of the editorial staff of Oxford University Press accompanied the work from the beginning. First and foremost, a word of gratitude to Claude Conyers of Oxford University Press, whose support and encouragement for the project were always accompanied by humor and expertise. Mark Cummings served as development editor; later Stephen Chasteen served as project editor at Oxford University Press. Both provided expertise to propel this project forward.

I also salute my colleagues and friends, members of the editorial board, who surely did not realize what they were getting into when they kindly agreed to join me in this undertaking. They have been unfailingly helpful, conscientious, and cooperative; *The Oxford Encyclopedia of the Reformation* owes its quality in large measure to their rich and extensive contribution. Jeff Bach served for four years as research assistant on this project while he was pursuing his doctoral studies at Duke University. The dean of the graduate school and the dean of the faculty at Duke University provided financial support for the project, which I sincerely acknowledge. Finally, I thank Barbara Pollock, who served as office manager for my department here at Duke University. Her administrative skills, keen eye for errors, and sharp sense of deadlines spared me from many a mistake. They all have greatly enhanced the project. I stand in their debt.

Hans J. Hillerbrand
Durham, North Carolina
August 1995

The Oxford Encyclopedia of the Reformation

A

ABSTEMIUS. *See* Bornemisza, Péter.

ACADEMIES. *See* Geneva Academy; Universities; Zurich Academy.

ACONTIUS, Jacobus (also Jacob; Ital, Giacomo Aconcio; c.1520–1567), one of the most influential proponents of the idea of toleration in sixteenth-century Europe. Born in Trent, Acontius spent his early life in Italy. He surfaces in the documentation in 1557, when he embraced the Reformation and emigrated to Basel. There he became friendly with Sébastien Castellion and the Basel circle of thinkers. He next went to Zurich, where he met other Italian émigrés, including Bernardino Ochino, and then moved to Strasbourg before finally settling down in 1559 in England, where he died in 1567. A rigorously logical freethinker, he published in Basel in 1558 a treatise on knowledge, *De methodo*, which has been seen as a direct forerunner of Descartes's work. In England he was employed by the queen as a military engineer (1560), became a naturalized citizen (1561), and bought a house and land in Kent. He became a member of the refugee churches in London and actively defended a Dutch freethinker, Adriaan Corneliszoon van Haemstede (1560), who was accused of heresy by the Anglican authorities.

His fame rests chiefly on his highly successful *Satanae Stratagemata*, which he dedicated to the queen and published in Basel in 1565. It was reprinted a dozen times during the next century and immediately translated into French (1565). Although not published in English until much later (1647), the work was exceptionally influential among liberal theologians in England; it was also issued in German (1647) and Dutch (1662).

A pioneer freethinker, Acontius looked on religious discord as a stratagem by which Satan succeeded in sowing confusion among Christians. He condemned as self-defeating the use of violence to defend truth. The magistrate, he thought, had a legitimate authority in church affairs but no power to use force. Conflict in religion could be reduced if men would reach agreement on a number of fundamental articles, among which he did not include either the real presence or the doctrine of the Trinity. English latitudinarian theologians of the seventeenth century were to draw heavily on this doctrine of nonessential beliefs (adiaphora) in religion. Supporting complete liberty of choice in religion (he accepted none of the mainstream Protestant churches), Acontius conceded that freedom might lead to chaos, but the emergence of error was itself beneficial because it would compel diligent Christians to search out the truth. The scriptural word of God alone was a guide, and all "authorities" had to be rejected in its favor. Once free inquiry was allowed and all coercion of conscience removed, the truth would emerge triumphant.

BIBLIOGRAPHY

Primary Sources

Aconcio, Iacopo. *Jacobi Acontii Satanae Stratagematum libri octo.* Edited by Walther Köhler. Munich, 1927. Reprint edited by Giorgio Radetti, 1946.
———. *Acontiana: Abhandlungen und Briefe des Jacobus Acontius.* Edited by Walther Köhler and Erich Hassinger. Heidelberg, 1932.
———. *De Methodo e opuscoli religiosi e filosofici.* Edited by Giorgio Radetti. Florence, 1944. Reprint, 1983.

Secondary Sources

Cantimori, Delio. *Italian Heretics of the Sixteenth Century.* Cambridge, Mass., 1979. The standard introduction to the history of Italian reformers.
Jordan, W. K. *The Development of Religious Toleration in England.* Vol. 1. Reprint, Gloucester, Mass., 1965. Definitive on Acontius's influence in England.
Lecler, Joseph. *Toleration and the Reformation.* 2 vols. London and New York, 1960. Contains excellent chapter on the Italian refugees.

HENRY KAMEN

ACQUAVIVA, Claudio (Lat., Aquaviva; 1543–1615), fifth general of the Society of Jesus, 1581–1615. A younger son of the Neapolitan duke of Atri, Acquaviva was early destined to a clerical career. Several of his relatives were cardinals, but after studies in humanities, philosophy, theology, and law he entered the Jesuits in 1567. He was appointed rector of the Jesuit college at Naples in 1575 and provincial superior at Naples in 1577 and at Rome in 1579. In 1581 he was elected general of the Society of Jesus; his thirty-four years as general is the longest tenure in Jesuit history and coincided with the zenith of Jesuit influence and prestige. Under Acquaviva the Jesuits grew from 5,000 to

13,000, from 21 provinces to 32, from directing 144 schools to 372. He presided over the difficult transition that religious orders undergo when the first charismatic generation passes away and a phase of consolidation takes over.

Acquaviva's role in Jesuit history parallels that of Bonaventura in Franciscan history. Because candidates to the Jesuits under Acquaviva tended to be younger, he introduced a more fixed training in philosophy and theology. He also established tertianship—a sort of second novitiate for young Jesuit priests. He began sending Jesuits on rural missions to spread the spirituality of the Counter-Reformation to the countryside. Under his eye the first Sodality of the Blessed Virgin, a sort of Jesuit third order, was set up in Rome. Sodalities soon spread to most Jesuit colleges and enrolled tens of thousands of members.

Acquaviva's personality remains in shadows despite or perhaps because of his enormous extant correspondence. There is no biography of this quiet, efficient, authoritarian bureaucrat, who spent his work days dictating letters to relays of secretaries, each day handling the problems of Jesuits in a different country. His leisure was devoted to reading the church fathers. Only rarely did he leave the Jesuit headquarters in Rome next to the Gesu church. His only book, *Industriae ... ad curandos animae morbos* (Florence, 1600), taught superiors how to deal with their subjects's spiritual problems. He supervised and issued two major documents: the *Directorium* (1599), which codified Jesuit use of Layola's *Spiritual Exercises,* and the *Ratio studiorum* (1599), which laid down directives for Jesuit education and remained in force for four centuries.

Acquaviva had to outmaneuver kings and popes to retain the *Constitutions* of Loyola. Philip II wanted virtual autonomy for the Spanish Jesuits—in effect, control from Madrid rather than from Rome. Sixtus V wanted communities to elect their superiors. Clement VIII wanted periodic Jesuit general congregations. These battles Acquaviva won. But assassination attempts against Henry IV twice resulted in partial expulsion of the Jesuits from France. There were severe persecutions of Catholics, and especially Jesuits, in England. Acquaviva managed to prevent a papal condemnation, urged by Dominican theologians, of Jesuit teaching on grace and predestination as Pelagian. Under Acquaviva Jesuit missionaries such as Alessandro Valignano and Matteo Ricci developed new approaches to non-Christian cultures.

BIBLIOGRAPHY

"Acquaviva, Claudio." In *Encyclopedia of Jesuit History*. Rome, forthcoming.

Bangert, William V. *A History of the Society of Jesus*. 2d ed. St. Louis, 1986. This standard Jesuit history devotes pp. 97–175 to Acquaviva's years as general.

Guibert, Joseph de. *The Jesuits: Their Spiritual Doctrine and Practice.* St. Louis, 1964. Traces Jesuit spirituality under Acquaviva, pp. 230–280.

Rosa, M. "Acquaviva, Claudio." In *Dizionario biografico degli italiani,* pp. 168–178. Contains a bibliography.

JOHN PATRICK DONNELLY

ACRONIUS, Ruardus (d. 1611), prominent theologian in the Netherlands and defender of the Reformed faith. Before joining ranks with the Reformation in 1570, Acronius probably belonged to the Roman Catholic clergy. After his conversion, he served the Reformed churches of Friesland from 1572 to 1599 (Franeker, 1572–1573; Wijdenes, 1573–1574; Bolsward, 1579–1580; Kornjum, 1580; Leeuwarden, 1580–1590; Kornjum, 1590–1599) with the exception of a five-year pastorate in Alkmaar, Noord-Holland (1574–1579). His longest pastorate was in Schiedam, Zuid-Holland, where he served for twelve years until his death in 1611. Acronius's leadership was acknowledged by the church throughout his ministry. Among the many posts to which he was chosen by his peers, he was four times elected president of "particular" or provincial synods: in Noord-Holland (1579), Friesland (1586, 1593), and Zuid-Holland (1607).

Acronius was best known for his staunch defense of Reformed truth. In 1588 he came into conflict with fellow ministers Isbrandus Balck and Antonius Nicolai. Grievances were filed against these ministers for attacking one another publicly, resulting in a synodical request that they leave Leeuwarden. Acronius refused to do so and was supported in this decision by Friesland's governor, Willem Lodewijk, who was instrumental in bringing about reconciliation among the ministers in 1592. Since the 1592 synod decided to burn all documents pertaining to these conflicts, the point of controversy is unknown. Notwithstanding these five years of conflict, Acronius was again elected synodical president already in 1593.

Acronius also aggressively defended the Reformed faith against the Anabaptists. In 1596 he held a debate with Anabaptist spokesman Pieter van Ceulen. This debate was a direct result of Acronius's forcing his way into several Anabaptist meetings in order to challenge their speakers. Government intervention led to a public debate that consisted of 156 sessions lasting from 16 August to 17 November 1596. As a result of Acronius's influence, the synod, on 27 May 1598, forbade van Ceulen to preach in Friesland. In 1599 Acronius published a polemical work against the Anabaptists.

Acronius also battled the Remonstrants. In 1609 he supported Franciscus Gomarus in his conference with Jacobus Arminius; he was instrumental in the splitting of the classis of Schieland after Simon Episcopius accepted a call to Bleiswijk; in 1610 and thereafter he presided over the classis of protesting churches; he responded to Johannes Wtenbogaert's *Tractaet* in 1610 by republishing the author's sermon on *John* 10:3; and he published two writings against the appointment of Conradus Vorstius. While in the midst of this turmoil, Acronius died unexpectedly in 1611. None of his writings has been translated into English.

BIBLIOGRAPHY

Primary Sources

Acronius, Ruardus. *Van het onderhold der dienaren: Seer grondighe ende wt Godes woordt wel ghefundeerde onderrichting, teghens de lasteringhe ende het geschrey der wederdoperen ende andere quaetwillige.* Franeker, 1599. A polemical work against the Anabaptists.

————. *Enarrationes catecheticae: Quibus quaestiones et responsiones Catechismi Ecclesiarum Belgicarum et Palatinatus, methodice, compendiose et dilucide explicantur, ac brevis sed integra purioris doctrinae hypotyposis, continetur.* Schiedam, 1606. An explanation of the Heidelberg Catechism.

Secondary Sources

Bie, J. P. de, and J. Loosjes, eds. *Biographisch Woordenboek der Protestantsche Godgeleerden in Nederland.* Vol. 1. The Hague, 1907. See pp. 29–38 for a valuable but somewhat outdated summary of Acronius's life and theology.
Nauta, D. "Acronius, Ruardus." In *Biografisch Lexicon voor de Geschiedenis van het Nederlandse Protestantisme,* vol. 2, pp. 15–18. Kampen, Netherlands, 1983. Updated overview of Acronius's life and theology.
Platt, John. *Reformed Thought and Scholasticism.* Leiden, 1982. See pp. 72–75 for Acronius's views on the existence of God in his *Enarrationes catecheticae.*

JOEL R. BEEKE

ACTS OF SUPREMACY. By giving control of the English church to the monarch, the Act of Supremacy of 1534 (26 Henry VIII, c. 1) and its partner of 1559 (1 Eliz. I, c. 1) clearly established England's independence from the papacy and recognized the monarch's God-given right to be supreme head of the Church of England with authority to reform and redress all errors, heresies, and abuses in it. By the act of 1534 Henry VIII was publicly admitted to own all the honors, jurisdictions, authorities, profits, and dignities that belonged to the church.

The 1534 act was one of a series of acts that established the Reformation in England. The way for the supremacy was prepared by the Act in Restraint of Annates (23 Henry VIII, c. 20), the Act in Restraint of Appeals (24 Henry VIII, c. 12), and the 1532 Submission of the Clergy, which was given statutory force by a further act (25 Henry VIII, c. 19). The Act of Supremacy borrowed the concept that England was an empire from the Act in Restraint of Appeals, a justification for the king's claim to control the church. The Act of Supremacy was reinforced by the Treason Act of 1534 (26 Henry VIII, c. 13), which made it treason to challenge the supremacy. Of course, all of these statutes were linked to Henry's divorce from Catherine of Aragon and his marriage to Anne Boleyn, so they were resisted by the Aragonese faction and by devout Catholics, such as Thomas More.

Henry VIII and his viceregent, Thomas Cromwell (the apparent architect of these laws), used the supremacy to dissolve the monasteries and make other changes in the operation of the church. Edward VI's regents made use of it as well, especially to remove objectionable bishops. When Mary became queen in 1554, she used the supremacy to remove Protestant bishops but pretended not to have the power until it could be repealed by 1 & 2 Philip & Mary, c. 8.

When Elizabeth came to the throne in November 1558, she immediately moved to reestablish the supremacy. Because Parliament had repealed it, she needed Parliament to reaffirm it. Her act, although recognizing that the monarch by right controlled the national church, did not call her supreme head. Instead, bowing to criticism from both Protestants and Catholics, she took the title supreme governor of the church. The 1559 act also established the manner in which the supreme governor was to manage the church, giving her the power to create the Ecclesiastical High Commission. Moreover, the act incorporated an oath of supremacy that every ecclesiastical officer was to swear, declaring that no foreign power had any authority in the realm. Another clause declared that anyone who defamed the supremacy was, on the third conviction, guilty of treason.

Elizabeth's act was used to remove the Marian bishops and to appoint Protestant ones. Until abolished in 1641, the ecclesiastical commissions of the provinces of York and Canterbury were powerful courts primarily concerned with enforcing church law. Because the Acts of Supremacy recognized the inherent right of the English Crown to govern the church in the realm, the monarchs were key players in the English Reformation.

[*See also* Acts of Uniformity; Cromwell, Thomas; Elizabethan Settlement; Henry VIII; *and* Parliament.]

BIBLIOGRAPHY

Cross, Claire. *The Royal Supremacy in the Elizabethan Church.* London, 1969. Reviews the uses and impact of the supremacy in Elizabeth's reign.
Elton, G. R. *Reform and Reformation: England, 1509–1558.* London, 1977. Gives a narrative of the creation, use, and repeal of the first act. Argues that Cromwell was its architect.
————. *The Tudor Constitution.* 2d ed. Cambridge, 1982. Provides a summary of the constitutional issues surrounding the supremacy and prints extracts from the acts.
Jones, Norman L. *Faith by Statute: Parliament and the Settlement of Religion, 1559.* London, 1982. Provides a close analysis of the passage of the Act of 1559.
Lehmberg, Stanford. *The Reformation Parliament, 1529–1536.* Cambridge, 1970. Best account of the passage of the first Act of Supremacy.
Scarisbrick, J. J. *Henry VIII.* Reprint, London, 1981. Devotes several chapters to the creation of the supremacy.

NORMAN JONES

ACTS OF UNIFORMITY.

ACTS OF UNIFORMITY. These acts represent the successive efforts of Edward VI and Elizabeth I to impose a standardized form of Protestant worship on the Church of England. Each incorporated a prayer book, and each required the entire realm to use it in worship.

The First Act of Uniformity (2 & 3 Edward VI, c. 1) was passed in 1549. Legally it rested on the royal supremacy, which gave the monarch the right to determine rites and ceremonies for the English church, as Henry VIII had done in 1539 when he requested the Act of Six Articles. In 1547 Edward VI's first Parliament had overturned the Act of Six Articles and abolished the heresy laws. In his next Parliament Edward Seymour, duke of Somerset—acting as the king's regent—requested it establish the first *Book of Common Prayer,* written by Archbishop Thomas Cranmer, as the single, Protestant form of worship.

The bill for uniformity broke new constitutional ground because it made the text of the prayer book statutory, giving Parliament the right to amend it and establishing Parliament's right to determine, with the king, the form of English religion. This limitation on the royal supremacy became immediately obvious when the denial of transubstantiation contained in the bill was muddled by amendments.

The introduction of a Protestant service caused some disturbance among conservatives—as, for example, during the Prayer Book Revolt of 1549 in the West Country—and some Protestants were unhappy with it, too. Though Protestant, it incorporated many Catholic elements, such as the commemoration of the saints and the Virgin Mary. Consequently, a reform of the first prayer book was prepared, aligning its theology more clearly with Swiss Protestantism. It was enacted in 1552 (5 & 6 Edward VI, c. 1). The act also made statutory the Ordinal of 1550. The second *Book of Common Prayer* was defended by the act's penal provisions, which culminated in life imprisonment. When Mary Tudor came to the throne in 1553, she repealed the uniformity, declaring all English churches free to use any service legal when Henry VIII died (1 Mary, st. 2, c. 2).

Elizabeth I acceded in November 1558 and began returning England to Protestantism. A bill for a uniform order of service was introduced in the second week of her first Parliament. It had a stormy passage because of Catholic opposition, passing by only three votes in the House of Lords.

This new Act of Uniformity (1 Eliz. I, c. 2) reinstated the 1552 prayer book—but not the Ordinal of 1550—with minor changes. Most importantly, it combined the words of institution from the 1549 and 1552 books, seeming to embrace both memorialist and real presence theologies. It imposed the Ornaments Rubric that required the decor of churches and the dress of ministers to be those used in the second year of Edward VI's reign. The act reserved to the monarch the right to change rites and ceremonies for the edification of the people. Although minor alterations were made in later centuries, the act of 1559 permanently determined the form of Anglican worship.

[*See also* Acts of Supremacy; Cromwell, Thomas; Elizabethan Settlement; Henry VIII; and Parliament.]

BIBLIOGRAPHY

Booty, John E. "Communion and Commonweal: *The Book of Common Prayer.*" In *The Godly Kingdom of Tudor England: Great Books of the English Reformation,* edited by John E. Booty, pp. 139–218. Wilton, Conn., 1981. Concise discussion of the prayer books and the acts.

Brightman, F. E. *The English Rite: Being a Synopsis of the Sources and Revisions of the Book of Common Prayer.* 2 vols., 2d rev. ed. Amersham, England, 1983–1984. Comprehensive treatment of the origins of *The Book of Common Prayer.*

Gee, Henry. *The Elizabethan Prayer-Book and Ornaments.* London, 1902. Detailed study of the prayer book of 1549 in relation to the book of 1552. Has an appendix of documents.

Jones, Norman L. *Faith by Statute: Parliament and the Settlement of Religion, 1559.* London, 1982. Provides a detailed account of the passage of the 1559 act.

NORMAN JONES

ADAM OF FULDA.

ADAM OF FULDA. *See* Krafft, Adam.

ADIAPHORA.

ADIAPHORA. A concept derived from the Stoics, adiaphora denotes conditions in life that are neither virtues nor vices and thus tend toward neither good nor evil. The related Greek term, *mesa,* describes actions that have no intrinsic ethical worth apart from their final purpose. Brought into Latin from Greek by Cicero, who translated adiaphora as *indifferentia,* medieval theologians used it for actions Christians were not duty-bound to perform, such as works of supererogation. Thomas Aquinas (*Summa Theologiae,* I–II, q. 18, a. 8 & 9) reduced *indifferentia* to a theoretically possible species of actions inapplicable to individuals since all their actions have moral worth.

Martin Luther's fundamentally different approach to justification and law renewed discussion of the concept. Works, especially ceremonial ones, merited nothing before God and thus were matters of indifference in themselves. Christians, intent only on pleasing God and helping the neighbor, could exercise freedom regarding such works. In the Wittenberg unrest of 1521–1522, Luther argued that outmoded ceremonies not specifically forbidden or commanded by God—even Communion in one kind—could remain for the sake of the weak neighbor and good order. Already in the first edition of the *Loci communes* (1521), Philipp Melanchthon (1497–1560) discusses *indifferentia,* permitting violation of human traditions only before "Pharisees" but not in the presence of the weak. During the negotiations at Augsburg in 1530, however, Luther rejected Johann Eck's reference to

Communion in one kind as adiaphora, claiming it flew in the face of Christ's specific command.

The Peasants' War of 1525, in which claims for Christian freedom were applied to political revolution, forced Melanchthon to exclude civil regulations from the discussion. In the third edition of his *Colossians* commentary (1534), Melanchthon complained that some used the term to excuse their own licentiousness. By that time he had also used the term in the Latin version of the Visitation Articles (1527) and in the Apology of the Augsburg Confession (1531), where he referred to certain human practices and ceremonies that Christians could observe or omit without sin for the sake of order in the church, providing that they neither affected political order nor were attached to merit or satisfaction.

The Adiaphorist Controversy (1548–1552). With the defeat of the Schmalkald League in 1547, the emperor, Charles V, found himself in a position to enforce the religious unity of the empire. The Diet of Augsburg (1 September 1547 to 30 June 1548) formulated an ordinance for such unity until a general council of the church could resolve disputed matters. This provisional agreement, nicknamed the Augsburg Interim, was to be applied only in former evangelical territories and, besides permitting married priests and Communion in both kinds, demanded a return to pre-Reformation ceremonies. Among those who assisted in its formulation was Johann Agricola (1492?–1566), court preacher for Elector Joachim II of Brandenburg and the Interim's chief champion among Protestant theologians.

Theologians from the University of Wittenberg under the leadership of Melanchthon wrote various opinions on the Interim for their new lord, Moritz, the victorious and newly installed elector of Saxony. They sharply criticized the Interim's understanding of justification, invocation of the saints, and the Mass, while trying to maintain political obedience by appearing flexible in matters they considered adiaphora. One of these opinions was surreptitiously published in July 1547 under Melanchthon's name and caused Agricola to attack him publicly.

The Interim was ruthlessly enforced where Charles's Spanish forces were in control. Some cities farther north, such as the besieged Magdeburg, ignored the Interim. In electoral Saxony Moritz and his theologians tried to work out an ordinance that defended evangelical theology while appearing not to be seditious. In November 1548 the elector's counselors and his theologians, including Melanchthon, worked out a carefully worded statement in Altzella (the former Cistercian abbey near Nossen) that insisted on an evangelical understanding of justification and the Mass but allowed for the reintroduction of ceremonies deemed *Mitteldinge,* such as the bishop's power to ordain, baptism with exorcism, confirmation, anointing with oil, the Latin Mass (without the Canon of the Mass, its invocation of the

saints, or references to the Mass as a sacrifice), images, Latin hymns, and Corpus Christi day worship (without processions). In mid-December Joachim II of Brandenburg and Moritz agreed in Jüterbog to the gist of this statement as the basis of religious life in their territories and hence as an answer to the Augsburg Interim.

Melanchthon and the other Wittenberg theologians presented a similarly worded statement to the Saxon estates meeting in Leipzig at the end of December. It again counseled compromise in adiaphora. Though recognizing that changing adiaphora could upset the common people and be viewed as the first step toward the reintroduction of erroneous doctrine, the theologians nevertheless counseled acceptance of these concessions lest war break out again and cause even more harm and lest evangelicals be driven from their churches and replaced by priests loyal to Rome. The estates gathered in Leipzig gave only halfhearted approval to the proposal, named by detractors the "Leipzig Interim." Agricola, however, used a version of the Jüterbog agreement as proof that both Brandenburg and Saxony had accepted the Augsburg Interim. Thus, a proposal for avoiding the hated Augsburg Interim while still maintaining peace had become its imprimatur. Relegation of certain practices to adiaphora as a way of concentrating on the major differences in the doctrine of justification and the Mass became a sign of weakness and capitulation.

The statements in Altzella, Jüterbog, and Leipzig undermined Wittenberg's own theological allies. In January 1549 George Buchholzer (1503–1566), an evangelical preacher in Berlin opposed to Agricola, appealed to Melanchthon for a clearer explanation of Wittenberg's position on adiaphora and of the relation between the Jüterbog agreement, the Augsburg Interim, and the Brandenburg church order of 1540, which Buchholzer had written. Melanchthon insisted that while practices based on incorrect teaching must be rejected, the true church had to bear its present servitude regarding adiaphora.

In this confused situation a predominantly younger generation of Wittenberg-trained pastors and theologians attacked Melanchthon and his colleagues for having capitulated to the anti-Christian forces of the pope and the emperor. They were led by Matthias Flacius Illyricus (1520–1575), in 1548 teacher of Hebrew in Wittenberg, who had already attacked the Augsburg Interim and, in the face of the changing theological climate, had fled to Magdeburg. He claimed that in the Leipzig Interim the Wittenberg theologians erred by conceding authority to bishops in communion with the Roman "Antichrist," by destroying Christian freedom, by reinstituting confirmation and extreme unction as sacraments, by insisting the Mass was a work, and by failing to defend justification by faith alone. Although in times of peace church practices could be viewed as adiaphora, the present situation called for confession, not compromise. In times of persecution true worship of God included externals. "Nothing is adiaphora in the case of confession and scandal." Moreover, changes in church practice could not be legislated by civil authorities without the consent of the church. The Leipzig Interim, far from preventing Roman influence, avoiding fights over nonessentials, and serving the neighbor by making concessions, as its defenders claimed, resulted in the opposite. A number of theologians, including Nikolaus von Amsdorf (1483–1565), Johann Wigand (1523–1587), and Nicholas Gallus (1516–1570), joined with Flacius and earned the sobriquet Gnesio-Lutherans ("genuine Lutherans") for their opposition.

Pastoral concerns motivated both sides in the dispute. Whereas Melanchthon's defenders, called Philippists, wanted to save parishes from Spanish occupation, Gnesio-Lutherans wanted to protect their parishioners from the offense that results when externals that have come to represent a confession of faith are changed in such a way as to give the impression that the original reform need not be taken seriously. For them, rite carried doctrine, and there was no such thing as mere liturgy. Liturgy was intimately connected with theology and practice.

The debate over the Interim and adiaphora ended for all practical purposes in 1552 with the Treaty of Passau and the changed political situation for Protestants that treaty and the Peace of Augsburg (1555) represented. Even Melanchthon, who had separated the externals of worship from pure doctrine, later admitted that his stand on adiaphora had been incorrect. The initial dispute, however, renewed questions of Melanchthon's reliability and led to a series of divisive debates throughout the 1550s and 1560s between Gnesio-Lutherans and Philippists over justification, Original Sin, free will, and law and gospel.

In 1580 publication of the *Book of Concord* brought the dispute formally to an end. Article 10 of the Formula of Concord accepted the general definition of adiaphora as rites neither commanded nor forbidden by God's word nor opposed to good doctrine. Nevertheless, siding with the Gnesio-Lutherans against Melanchthon and the Wittenberg theologians, it stated that in times of persecution church practices and ceremonies, which in other situations were matters of Christian freedom and hence adiaphora, became matters of confession and could not be conceded to persecutors.

Controversies in England (1550–1573). The question of indifferent matters also arose within the Church of England. Already under Edward VI, John Hooper (d. 1555) and Nicholas Ridley (1502?–1555) debated the issue. Hooper limited adiaphora to those things in general accord with the scripture and useful to the Christian people. As a result, he at first refused to be consecrated bishop of Gloucester wearing a surplice as prescribed in *The Book of Common Prayer* of 1549. Only after considerable pressure from Thomas

Cranmer (1489–1556) and on the basis of opinions by Martin Bucer (1491–1551) and Peter Martyr Vermigli (1499–1562) did Hooper relent.

In the wake of the Elizabethan Settlement of 1559, the Vestiarian Controversy flared again. This time it began among some returning exiles of the Marian persecutions, who, under the influence of John Knox (1513–1572) and others on the Continent, had hoped for more "precision" in religious matters than was afforded in the settlement, especially regarding vestments and other "popish" ceremonies. Matters came to a head over the wearing of the surplice by the clergy. In January 1565 Elizabeth I expressed concern over nonconformity in a letter to the archbishop of Canterbury, Matthew Parker (1504–1575). In an effort to enforce conformity, Parker issued a set of regulations under the title *Advertisements,* which never gained official approval from either the sovereign or Parliament. To these a group of "hotter Protestants," including Miles Coverdale (1488–1568) and John Foxe (1517–1587), dissented in March 1565, requesting forbearance from the authorities. Most later conformed.

A year later Edmund Grindal (c.1519–1583), bishop of London, faced a similar dissent among the city's clergy. During the fray portions of Flacius's tract on adiaphora were published, and the opinions of Swiss theologians were sought. A first "Puritan" tract, *A Briefe Discourse against the Outwarde Apparell and Ministring Garmentes of the Popishe Church,* also appeared. Parker himself may have prepared the answer, *A Briefe Examination for the Time of a Certain Declaration.* To the cry that matters that may per se be adiaphora must be judged in the light of scripture and the church's edification, there came from Parker and others the demand for obedience to the civil magistrates regarding indifferent matters since magistrates are charged with determining what edifies. Thus, this dispute turned as much on the question of civil authority in ecclesiastical ordinance as on the definition of adiaphora. The rejection by Heinrich Bullinger (1504–1575) of the radicals' arguments and his appeal for public order helped, along with the removal from London of certain ringleaders, to break the back of this early resistance.

When attempts to reform *The Book of Common Prayer* in Parliament were thwarted by Elizabeth I in 1572, an anonymous pamphlet, *Admonition to the Parliament,* appeared, attacking both vestiges of Roman practice (vestments, the sign of the cross, baptisms by midwives, and kneeling and using wafers at Holy communion) and episcopal polity of the Church of England, including its "supreme governor," the queen. When the probable authors, John Field (1545–1588) and Thomas Wilcox (1549–1608), attempted to present the *Admonition* to Parliament, they were arrested. Parker's successor, John Whitgift (c.1530–1604), answered this tract, only to provoke a spirited defense entitled *Second Ad-*

monition, a work ascribed to Thomas Cartwright (1535–1603). With the royal suppression of both admonitions in 1573, Cartwright fled England and remained in exile fifteen years. This Admonition Controversy sparked Richard Hooker (1554–1600) to produce a defense of episcopal authority in his famous *Ecclesiastical Polity*. With this dispute the question of adiaphora receded into the background, replaced by the ecclesiological and polity concerns over which Puritans would debate into the next century.

BIBLIOGRAPHY

Brecht, Martin, and Reinhard Schwarz, eds. *Bekenntnis und Einheit der Kirche: Studien zum Konkordienbuch.* Stuttgart, 1980. Includes a thorough and well-documented article on the adiaphoristic controversy by Joachim Mehlhausen.

Collinson, Patrick. *The Elizabethan Puritan Movement.* Reprint, Oxford, 1990. A thorough description of the English controversies.

McGinn, Donald J. *The Admonition Controversy.* New Brunswick, N.J., 1949. Still the best analysis of this phase of the English conflicts; includes lengthy excerpts from contemporary tracts.

Phillips, Walter. "Heinrich Bullinger and the Elizabethan Vestiarian Controversy." *Journal of Religious History* 11 (1981), 363–384. A reexamination of the Swiss role in the English Vestiarian Controversy.

Primus, John H. *The Vestments Controversy.* Kampen, 1960. A look at the entire English controversy with helpful synopses of the most important letters and tracts.

Rosin, Wilbert, and Robert D. Preus, eds. *A Contemporary Look at the Formula of Concord.* Saint Louis, 1978. Among its essays is an excellent summary by Robert Kolb of the history of the adiaphoristic controversy and the related struggles that shaped the Formula of Concord.

Scheible, Heinz. "Melanchthons Brief an Carlowitz." *Archiv für Reformationsgeschichte* 57 (1966), 102–130. Scheible's reconstruction of the events around the Augsburg and Leipzig interims provides new clarity to the history of these complicated negotiations.

Schöne, Jobst, ed. *Bekenntnis zur Wahrheit: Aufsätze über die Konkordienformel.* Erlangen, 1978. Includes an article by Schöne that examines the relation of adiaphora to the Formula of Concord.

Verkamp, Bernard J. *The Indifferent Mean: Adiaphorism in the English Reformation to 1554.* Athens, Ohio, 1977. An examination of the early debate over adiaphora among the English and a correction of Primus's work.

TIMOTHY J. WENGERT

ADMONITION CONTROVERSY. A catchall term for the first large-scale debate about the government of the church in post-Reformation England, the Admonition Controversy took its name from *An Admonition to the Parliament*, which, together with *A View of Popish Abuses*, was published in 1572 by two young Oxford graduates, John Field and Thomas Wilcox. The *Admonition* contained the first full-scale assertion of *iure divino* presbyterianism in print in England. This represented a significant escalation in Puritan rhetoric, as previous Puritan complaint had concerned the ceremonies, liturgy, and *de facto* abuses rather than the formal structure of government of the church. John Whitgift replied and was in turn answered by Thomas Cartwright. Cartwright had been a fellow of Trinity College, Cambridge, when Whitgift was master. Whitgift as vice-chancellor had expelled him from the Lady Margaret chair of divinity and then from his fellowship, in large part because of lectures on the *Acts of the Apostles*, which had contained a number of proto-presbyterian assertions. Their extremely acrimonious exchange, pursued through a number of replies and counterreplies published in the early 1570s, was thus a continuation of an earlier very personal rivalry. It is this exchange that constitutes the Admonition Controversy proper.

The controversy petered out in 1577 with the publication of Cartwright's *The Rest of the Seconde Replie*. This remained unanswered, but the confrontation between presbyterians and conformists continued through a second round in the 1580s and a final showdown in the early 1590s. On the Puritan side the fight was continued by the likes of Walter Travers, William Fulke, Lawrence Chaderton, and, less respectably, Martin Marprelate. For the conformists the leading spokesmen were John Bridges and Thomas Cooper and later Richard Bancroft, Matthew Sutcliffe, and, most famously, Richard Hooker.

The argument centered on whether there was a form of government established in scripture that the church was bound to adopt. The Puritans argued that there was and claimed the authority of scripture for the presbyterian platform; the adoption of this platform was said to represent the completion of the reform process, whereby both the doctrine and discipline of the church were to be purged of all popish remnants and reformed according scripture.

The conformists contended that scripture prescribed no system of government for the church. Church polity and ceremony were matters inherently indifferent and were to be decided by the relevant human authorities; in England that meant the Crown. Episcopacy was praised as the form of church government most similar to and compatible with the monarchy, and the current ceremonial and jurisdictional arrangements of the church were justified in terms of the authority of the Crown and the demands of order, unity, uniformity, and obedience. Whitgift left the positive case for the status quo there and spent a good deal of time lambasting the Puritans as subversives and as potential sectaries and opponents of monarchical authority. Much of his debate with Cartwright was conducted within a common reformed culture. Doctrinally the two men had much in common, and they spent a good deal of their time manipulating the same polemical bugbears of popery and Anabaptism against one another. It was only later, in the persons of Bridges, Bancroft, and Adrianus Saravia, that the conformists turned the tables and claimed direct scriptural warrant for episcopacy, and it was even later, with Richard Hooker, that they developed a positive religious rationale for the ritual and ceremonial status quo.

BIBLIOGRAPHY

Ayre, J., ed. *The Works of John Whitgift*. 3 vols. Parker Society. Cambridge, 1851–1853.
Lake, Peter. *Anglicans and Puritans? Presbyterianism and English Conformist Thought from Whitgift to Hooker*. London, 1988.
Pearson, A. F. Scott. *Church and State: Political Aspects of Sixteenth-Century Puritanism*. Cambridge, 1928.

PETER LAKE

ADRIAN VI (born Adriaan Floriszoon Dedel; 1454–1523), Louvain theologian, administrator in Spain, and pope (1522–1523). Born in Utrecht, the son of Florens, a shipbuilder, and his wife, Gertruid, he studied with the Brethren of the Common Life, apparently at Zwolle, and then attended the University of Louvain (1476–1491), where he received his doctorate in theology, joined its theology faculty (1491–1515), and served as its rector (1493, 1500–1501) and vice-chancellor (from 1497 onward). He was a popular teacher who drew on the scholastic tradition (Thomism, Scotism, and nominalism), the church fathers, and canon law and saw two of his works (*Quaestiones quotlibeticae* and *Quaestiones in quartum Sententiarum librum*) published by his admirers. Given his reputation as an excellent and pious teacher, he was appointed in 1507 together with Guillaume de Croy as tutor of the future Charles V and in 1512 as his councillor. From 1515 to 1522 Adrian was in Spain, at first preparing for Charles's succession to the thrones of Castile and Aragon, then as coregent with Cardinal Francisco Jiménez de Cisneros until the young king's arrival in 1517, and finally as viceroy of Spain (1520–1522) while Charles went to Germany for his imperial coronation. During these years in Spain his ecclesiastical career advanced quickly: bishop of Tortosa and inquisitor of Aragon and Navarre (1516), cardinal (1517), and inquisitor of Castile and Léon (1518). On 9 January 1522 he was unexpectedly but unanimously elected pope by a previously deadlocked conclave, though he did not arrive in Rome until almost eight months later and was crowned on 31 August.

His opposition to Martin Luther was well known. He supported Louvain's condemnation of his teachings in 1519, urged Charles V in 1521 to turn Luther over to Leo X for punishment, and exhorted the Diet of Nuremberg in 1523 to enforce the Edict of Worms. He hoped to diminish Luther's support by initiating a true reform of curial practices and personnel.

For a variety of reasons Adrian's efforts at reform failed. Most of the cardinals and curialists opposed any curtailment of their privileges and revenues. Those to whom Adrian looked for assistance were not equal to the task, and the pope himself lacked any program of reform other than the avoidance of abuses. His piecemeal approach and extreme caution led to intolerable delays in making decisions and appointing worthy men. In addition, his attention was diverted by efforts to keep the peace between Charles V and Francis I and to prevent further expansion of the Turks, who took Rhodes in 1522. Moreover, the papacy was left deeply in debt by his predecessor, Leo X. The chief reason for his failure, however, was the shortness of his reign—he was in Rome but for a year. As the inscription on his tomb laments, "Alas, how much does the skillful effort, even of the best of men, depend upon favorable times."

BIBLIOGRAPHY

Primary Sources

Adrian VI. *Correspondence de Charles Quint et d'Adrien VI* (1859). Edited by L. P. Gachard. Reprint, Rome, 1970.
Dedel, Adriaan. *Quaestiones quotlibeticae*. Edited by Maarten van Dorp. Louvain, 1515. A collection of Adrian's opinions on academic topics debated at Louvain in the years 1488–1507.
———. *Quaestiones in quartum Sententiarum librum*. Edited by Jacques Dassoneville. Paris, 1516. A commentary on the fourth book of Peter Lombard's *Sentences* that treats the seven sacraments, based on notes from Adrian's public lectures probably from 1499–1509. Two sermons from the time he was bishop of Totorsa (*Sermo pareneticus in computum hominis Christiani agonizantis quo nihil saluti animarum proficuum magis excogitari potest* and *Sermo de pertuso sacculo sive de superbia*) were appended to the 1522 Rome edition.

Secondary Sources

Ducke, Karl-Heinz. "Pope Adrian VI, 2 March 1454–14 September 1523." In *Contemporaries of Erasmus: A Biographical Register of the Renaissance and Reformation*, vol. 1, pp. 5–9. Toronto, 1985.
McNally, Robert E. "Pope Adrian VI (1522–23) and Church Reform." *Archivum Historiae Pontificiae* 7 (1969), 253–285. Seeks the reasons for Adrian's failure to effect a sweeping reform.
Pastor, Ludwig. *The History of the Popes from the Close of the Middle Ages*. 40 vols. London, 1891–1954. See vol. 9, pp. 1–230, for the fullest account in English of Adrian's pontificate.
Roey, Josef Ernest van, et al., eds. *Adrien VI, le premier pape de la Contre-Réforme*. Bibliotheca Ephemeridum Theologicarum Louviensium, 14. Gembloux, 1959. An excellent collection of articles on Adrian, together with an ample bibliography.
Rosa, Mario. "Adriano VI." In *Dizionario biografico degli Italiani*, vol. 1, pp. 337–342. Rome, 1960.

NELSON H. MINNICH

AEMILIANI, Girolamo. *See* Somaschi.

AEPINUS, Johannes (Ger., Hoeck; 1499–1553), north German Lutheran educator, preacher, and controversial theologian. Aepinus was born in the Saxon town of Ziesar and studied at Wittenberg under Martin Luther, Johannes Bugenhagen, and Philipp Melanchthon, receiving his doctorate in theology in 1533. In the mid-1520s he was dismissed from his first teaching post and briefly imprisoned in the Mark Brandenburg for his Lutheran convictions. He fled to Stralsund (Pomerania), where he served as school principal and theological adviser to the municipal authorities. In 1529 he was called as preacher to Saint Peter's church in Hamburg, where he served as superintendent until his death. His first publication, *Pinnacidion de Romanae ecclesiae imposturis*, appeared in Hamburg in 1530. His *Bekenntnisse und Erkleringe* of 1548 was an insightful commentary against the Interim.

In 1534 Aepinus journeyed to England as theological adviser with a diplomatic mission from the cities of Hamburg and Lübeck. Although he failed to persuade Henry VIII to adopt the Augsburg Confession as a model for the English Reformation, Aepinus earned the high regard of Thomas Cromwell and English divines looking to give the English church a distinctly Protestant orientation.

Aepinus is best known as a theologian for his insistence that Christ suffered the tortures of the damned after his crucifixion, a belief anathema to those holding that Christ's sacrifice was complete at his death (Consummatists). In 1550, after Aepinus and his followers (Infernalists) demanded official recognition for their doctrine, the Hamburg city council appealed to Wittenberg for a resolution of the conflict. Melanchthon sent a noncommittal response mainly enjoining peace between the warring factions. Although Aepinus prevailed over his opponents in Hamburg, Lutheran theology has remained neutral on the question of the significance of Christ's sojourn in hell.

BIBLIOGRAPHY

Albrecht, D. "Aepinus." In *Lexicon für Theologie und Kirche*, vol. 1, p. 690. Freiburg, 1957.

Düfel, Hans. "Aepinus, Johannes." In *Theologische Realenzyclopedie*, vol. 1, pp. 535–544. Berlin, 1977. Informative, recent account of Aepinus's life, writings, and significance, with extensive bibliography.

Knolle, Theodor. "Aepinus, Johannes." In *Neue Deutsche Biographie*, vol. 1, p. 91. Berlin, 1953.

Staphorst, Nicolaus. *Hamburgische Kirchengeschichte*. Hamburg, 1729. Several of Aepinus's writings are reprinted in vol. 2.

KARIN BRINKMANN BROWN

AGRICOLA, Georgius (Ger., Georg Bauer; 1494–1555), German humanist and scientist. Born in Saxony, he entered the University of Leipzig in 1514, and received his B.A. in 1515. Afterward, he remained as lecturer in Greek. From 1517 he taught at Zwickau and published a humanistic manual of Latin grammar (1520). In 1522 he returned to Leipzig to study medicine, and in 1523 he moved to Bologna and almost certainly received a medical doctorate from an Italian university. His most valuable medical training, however, occurred at Venice: he assisted Giambattista Oppizoni with the first Greek edition of Galen's medical works, published in 1525 by the Aldine press.

In 1526 he returned to Germany and in 1527 became town physician at Jáchymov (Sankt Joachimsthal), a mining town in the Saxon Erzgebirge. His surroundings aroused his curiosity about mining. He had a remarkable gift for integrating the knowledge and terminology of the miners with the knowledge he had acquired from ancient and medieval books. He recognized the problem of relating the Latin terms found in ancient authors to the substances actually known to contemporary miners and physicians, a problem particularly acute in pharmacology.

The first product of these studies was a Renaissance dialogue, *Bermannus* (1530), that described Saxon mining. A friend sent the manuscript to Desiderius Erasmus, who arranged for publication by his own publisher, Johann Froben of Basel. Since Agricola's duties at Jáchymov were heavy, he resigned and in 1531 became town physician at Chemnitz, where he had more time for writing. He produced a book against the Turks (1531) and an influential study of ancient and modern weights and measures (1533). Most of his later writings were about mining, but he also produced a book on the plague (1554) and even one on subterranean elves (1549). From the early 1530s he worked on his masterpiece, *De re metallica libri XII*, a survey of the whole field of mining and metallurgy.

When it was completed in 1550, he commissioned a series of remarkable illustrations. He died on 21 November 1555, four months before its publication at Basel. Agricola also wrote a vernacular history of the Saxon dynasty, not published until 1963.

Although Agricola favored the humanist reform program of Erasmus, he was a firm opponent of heresy. The strongly Catholic Duke George of Saxony named him historiographer in 1534. The accession of Protestant dukes after 1539 did not destroy his favor at court. In 1543 Duke Moritz granted him valuable tax and legal privileges. When Moritz sided with Emperor Charles V during the Schmalkald War (1546–1547), such a prominent Catholic councillor became especially valuable to a Lutheran regime. Moritz repeatedly appointed him burgomaster of Chemnitz. He became an active agent of Saxon diplomacy, participating in the imperial government's vain effort to reunite all Germans within a single church. He survived by only a few months the conclusion of the Peace of Augsburg, which marked the failure of his hope for a reunited German Christendom.

BIBLIOGRAPHY

Primary Sources

Agricola, Georgius. *De re metallica libri XII*. Translated by Herbert Clark Hoover and Lou Henry Hoover. Reprint, New York, 1950. Classic translation of Agricola's principal work. Contains useful introduction, helpful footnotes, and reproductions of original woodcuts.

——. *De natura fossilium* (Textbook of Mineralogy). Translated by Mark Chance Bandy and Jean A. Bandy. New York, 1955. Useful introductory material, though the views on medieval scientific learning are painfully outdated.

——. *Ausgewählte Werke*. 10 vols. and 1 suppl. Edited by Hans Prescher. Berlin, 1955–1974. Appears to include all or nearly all of Agricola's works despite title. All Latin texts have been replaced by German translations.

——. *Bermannus (Le Mineur): Un dialogue sur les mines*. Edited and translated by Robert Halleux and Albert Yans. Paris, 1990. French translation of Agricola's first work on mineralogy. Contains a useful biography to 1530 and an analysis of the dialogue.

Secondary Source

Wilsdorf, Helmut. *Georg Agricola und seine Zeit.* Vol. 1 of the Prescher edition of *Ausgewählte Werke.* Berlin, 1956. Despite signs of a painstaking Marxist orthodoxy, a useful and detailed biography.

CHARLES G. NAUERT, JR.

AGRICOLA, Johann (Ger., Schneider; 1492?–1566), influential German reformer in Wittenberg, Eisleben, and Berlin; Luther's adversary in the antinomian controversy; called Magister Eisleben or (Eis-)Islebius after his native town, eventually nicknamed Grickel by Luther. His early biography is poorly known. He went to school in Braunschweig and visited the University of Leipzig before resuming his studies in Wittenberg in 1515/16. Here he soon established a relationship with Luther that was to prove momentous. With a master's degree from the faculty of arts and a bachelor's degree in theology (1519) he lectured in both faculties. For a time he turned to medicine, but from 1523 through 1525 he worked in Wittenberg as a catechist, preacher, and lecturer in biblical exegesis, activities reflected clearly in his printed writings (e.g., *In evangelium Lucae annotationes*; 1525). Most of the manuscripts from his exegetical writings still await scholarly examination.

Agricola's participation in such reformist events as the Leipzig Disputation (1519) and the burning of the papal bull (1520) contributed to his early image as a loyal Luther disciple. He assisted in the literary defeat of Thomas Müntzer, protesting against spiritualistic reference to inner experience and legalistic biblical interpretation, but missing the essence of Luther's distinction between law and gospel. Between 1525 and 1536 Agricola lived in Eisleben as head of a new grammar school and preacher at the church of Saint Nicolai. Catechetical and exegetical writings and collections of German proverbs stem from this period. That he was appointed preacher of electoral Saxony's delegation at the diets in Speyer (1526 and 1529) and Augsburg (1530) shows that he was held in high esteem.

Though Agricola objected to Philipp Melanchthon's *Articuli de quibus egerunt per Visitatores in regione Saxoniae* (1527) and though it was rumored that faith, in his opinion, could exist without good works, Luther was not suspicious of his theology. Only after Agricola's headlong return to Wittenberg in late 1536 did his deviating view attract Luther's attention. Thus Agricola referred recognition of sin and penance in the life of a Christian to the gospel and not to the law. To Luther that implied the annulment of the gospel. Late in 1537 Luther published anonymously circulating antinomian theses *(Ad incerti cuiusdam autoris positiones D. Martini Lutheri responsio)*, and then turned directly

against their alleged author, Agricola, in a series of disputations and in his pamphlet *Wider die Antinomer* (1539). Agricola also suffered accusations from other parties, as well as censorship and restricted freedom of movement.

In August 1540 he escaped his troubles and moved to Berlin to become court chaplain to Elector Joachim II Hektor of Brandenburg and later also "general superintendent" and visitator. A settlement with Wittenberg was achieved, though Luther remained adamant in his rejection and defamation of his former disciple. Agricola, however, maintained his veneration for Luther. In Brandenburg Agricola soon became entangled in new quarrels, but Joachim never failed to support him. His collaboration on and recommendation of the Augsburg Interim (1548) renewed animosity against him and further damaged his reputation among Lutherans. Yet, true to the basic convictions of his earliest writings, he sided with the Gnesio-lutherans against the Philippists. He died during a plague epidemic. Some of his hymns are still found in Lutheran hymnals.

BIBLIOGRAPHY

Primary Sources

Agricola, Johann. "Auslegung des XIX. Psalm." In *Die lutherischen Pamphlete gegen Thomas Müntzer*, edited by Ludwig Fischer, pp. 43–78. Tübingen, 1976. See also the anonymous *Ein nutzlicher Dialogus* (pp. 79–95), which was probably written by Agricola.
———. *Die Sprichwörtersammlungen.* 2 vols. Edited by Sander L. Gilman. Berlin and New York, 1971.

Secondary Sources

Kawerau, Gustav. *Johann Agricola von Eisleben: Ein Beitrag zur Reformationsgeschichte* (1881). Reprint, Hildesheim and New York, 1977. The only scholarly biography.
Kjeldgaard-Pedersen, Steffen. *Gesetz, Evangelium und Busse: Theologiegeschichtliche Studien zum Verhältnis zwischen dem jungen Johann Agricola (Eisleben) und Martin Luther.* Acta Theologica Danica, vol. 16. Leiden, 1983.
Koch, Ernst. "Johann Agricola neben Luther: Schülerschaft und theologische Eigenart." In *Lutheriana: Zum 500. Geburtstag Martin Luthers von den Mitarbeitern der Weimarer Ausgabe*, edited by Gerhard Hammer and Karl-Heinz zur Mühlen, pp. 131–150. Cologne, 1984. Introduces a new perspective by focusing on Agricola's theology of spiritual experience under the influence of Tauler.
Rogge, Joachim. *Johann Agricolas Lutherverständnis: Unter besonderer Berücksichtigung des Antinomismus.* Edited by Hans Urner. Theologische Arbeiten, vol. 14. Berlin, 1960. Not a regular biography, but a vivid presentation of Agricola's life and work in the light of his relationship with Luther. Contains a full bibliography including manuscripts.

STEFFEN KJELDGAARD-PEDERSEN

AGRICOLA, Michael (1510–1557), Finnish reformer and bishop in Turku (Åbo). Born in the south of Finland, he came to Turku after schooling at Viborg. In Turku he early met Reformation ideas through a preacher at the cathedral. The first bishop after the Swedish Reformation, the humanist Martin Skytte, gave him employment as a secretary. Owing to Skytte Agricola became a student at Wittenberg between 1536 and 1539. There he took his master's degree. Besides studies in theology he devoted himself to humanist subjects. Provided with a letter of recommendation from Luther and Philipp Melanchthon he became headmaster of the school at Turku, the foremost in Finland. At the same time he worked hard as a reformer. The 1540s in Finland involved not so much a violation of the Catholic tradition as a renewal of the inner life in the spirit of the Reformation. The reform activity was practiced in cooperation with the bishop, but not until after his death did Agricola actually serve as a bishop, even though he was appointed before 1554. During Agricola's time as bishop the Swedish king used him for peace negotiations between Sweden and Russia.

Through his extensive writings Agricola laid the foundation of Finnish orthography. He has been called the father of Finnish literature. In Finland as in so many other countries Reformation and vernacular language and culture worked together. The first printed publication by Agricola (1542 or 1543) was an alphabet book (*ABC-kiria*). It testifies to his wide interests. His work *Rucouskiria Bibliasta* (Biblical Prayer Book; 1544) carries an independent character. The prayer book begins with a short calendar together with notices on astronomy, meteorology, and theology; he adds instructions in hygiene. But the predominant content is of prayers. Of these about one-third are taken directly from the Bible, the rest from the books of Luther or other reformers. Even humanists such as Desiderius Erasmus are represented, as well as prayers of Catholic mystics such as Thomas à Kempis and prayers from *Missale Aboense*. It is significant, given the cautious attitude of Agricola, that he calls the medieval authors "saints."

As early as his time at Wittenberg Agricola worked on a translation of the New Testament into Finnish. The translation was completed in 1543 but could not be printed before 1548 (*Se Wsi Testamenti*). He used the Greek text as his basis but the translation by Luther as a guide. From Luther Agricola took some prefaces and explanations; for example, he directly translated Luther's preface to *Romans*. But often Agricola arranged the texts in an independent fashion, and he did not share Luther's estimation of some books of the Bible. He translated parts of the Old Testament that had great religious significance or were used in worship. The most important of these was the translation of *Psalms* (*Dauidin Psaltari*). For this translation Agricola built on earlier translations that had been carried out in Turku. For the needs of worship he produced in 1549 a manual (*Käsikiria Castesta ja muista Christikunnan Menoista*) and a missal (*Messu eli Herran Echtolinen*). These works consist of translations of the Swedish reformer Olaus Petri. They were extremely important for Finnish church life; heretofore the Finns had celebrated the service with handwritten documents.

As a reformer Agricola laid the foundation for the national development and independence of the church of Finland even though the country was part of Sweden until 1809. Swedish was the official language, and all books by Agricola were printed in Stockholm. His personality was to a great degree characterized by his humanist interests. His translations of Luther tone down or exclude Luther's violent attacks against the papacy, because they had no relevance to the Finnish situation. In his prefaces Agricola often gives information of sheerly historical interest. Thus his translation of the New Testament begins with information on how Finland was Christianized, how old the Swedish settlement was, and information on the Finnish provinces, tribes, and dialects. In the preface to the translation of *Psalms* he listed the pagan gods of old Finland. This remains an important source for knowledge of the pagan religion.

From a purely evangelical way of thinking, with scripture as the grounds for doctrine, Agricola developed his theology in order to show the way of salvation. The way is open for the sinner to the mercy of God only through Jesus Christ. Christ is more the savior than the judge of the world. Faith is totally the work of God. Masses and pilgrimages, relics, and prayers before shrines are of no value. God makes use of his word as an instrument to give faith. Therefore Bible study and preaching are the foundation for the congregation. But the word of God calls for a humble heart. When the human heart by faith is perfect, service to neighbor will follow; in the love for the neighbor faith will be confirmed. From this way of thinking Agricola was filled with a reverent attitude toward traditional customs and ideas in the church. His mission was more to forestall misunderstanding and abuse than to abolish customs. In his explanation of the Ave Maria he warned explicitly against depending on the Mother of God or her merits. There is no mediator between God and humanity but Christ. The Ave Maria is not a prayer to Mary, but a song of praise concerning the deeds of God. Likewise, the person in prayer must thank God for what he has done through good people.

All reform had to proceed cautiously during this period in Finland. Reform Catholicism gained strong support in Finland during the course of the entire sixteenth century, especially among the upper classes. Agricola stands out as a leading figure for both Finnish culture and the church. From the viewpoint of Reformation history he can be characterized as a cautious reformer with strong humanist, or Philippist, interests. He saw his task as deeply rooting the Christian creed and Lutheran worship in the vernacular culture.

BIBLIOGRAPHY

Gummerus, Jakko. *Mikael Agricola: Der Reformator Finnlands*. Helsingfors, 1941.

————. *Mikael Agricolan rukouskirja ja sen lähteet.* Helsingfors, 1941–1947.

HARRY LENHAMMAR

AGRICOLA, Stephan (also Castenpaur, Kastenbauer; 1491–1547), German Augustinian monk and Lutheran convert active as a preacher, writer, and translator. Born in Bavaria, Agricola entered the Augustinian order in Regensburg and studied in Vienna, where he was granted a doctorate in theology in 1519. Although highly regarded by his superiors and a favored confessor at the Habsburg court, Agricola began to display Lutheran sympathies in his preaching and writing by 1520. In 1522 he was arrested under orders of his former patron. Archbishop Matthäus Lang of Salzburg, and charged with writing and preaching against Catholic doctrine and practice. While in prison Agricola published his defense, denying he wished to break with the Catholic church yet holding to holy scripture as the lone source of faith.

In 1524 the peasant disturbances allowed Agricola to escape to Augsburg, where he married and took a leading place among the Lutheran preachers there. For five years he engaged in a vigorous yet ultimately futile battle against the spread of Zwinglian doctrines in the city, losing even his friend Urbanus Rhegius to the radical reformers. In 1531 Agricola accepted a call to serve as pastor in the more congenial town of Hof in Brandenburg-Ansbach.

He attended the Colloquy of Marburg in 1529, as well as the Diet of Augsburg in 1530, and in 1537 he signed the Schmalkald Articles. From 1542 to 1543 he assisted in the reformation of Neuburg and Sulzbach and ended his days as court preacher to Albrecht von Mansfeld in Eisleben.

Although primarily a preacher, Agricola also translated into German a number of Latin writings by Martin Luther and other prominent reformers. His son, Stephan (1526–1562), followed him in this avocation and was likewise a highly regarded Lutheran pastor until, wearied by rebukes for his adherence to the Majorist position, he converted to Catholicism.

BIBLIOGRAPHY

Datterer, F. P. *Des Cardinals Lang Verhalten zur Reformation.* Freising, 1890. A brief account of Agricola's heresy trial.

Floss. "Agricola, (Castenpaur) Stephan, sen." In *Wetzer und Welte's Kirchenlexicon,* vol. 1, pp. 360–362. Freiburg, 1882.

————. "Agricola, Stephan, jun." In *Wetzer und Welt's Kirchenlexicon,* vol. 1, pp. 362–364. The Catholic version of the son's story. Freiburg, 1882.

Hamman, Gustav. "Agricola." In *Neue Deutsche Biographie,* vol. 1, pp. 104–105. Berlin, 1953.

Paulus, N. "Agricola (der Ältere)." In *Lexicon für Theologie und Kirche,* vol. 1, p. 150. Freiburg, 1938.

————. "Agricola (der Jüngere)." In *Lexicon für Theologie und Kirche,* vol. 1, p. 150. Freiburg, 1938. The Protestant version of the son's story.

Roth, Friedrich. *Augsburger Reformationsgeschichte, 1517–1527.* Munich, 1901.

Schottenloher, Karl, ed. *Bibliographie zur deutschen Geschichte im Zeitalter der Glaubensspaltung.* Stuttgart, 1957.

Smolinsky, Heribert. "Agricola, Stephan." In *Lexicon für Theologie und Kirche,* vol. 1, p. 251. Freiburg, 1993. Most recent bibliography.

KARIN BRINKMANN BROWN

AGRIPPA, Heinrich Cornelius (also Agrippa von Nettesheim; 1486–1535), German humanist and occultist. Born in Cologne, he matriculated at the local university in 1499 and graduated in 1502. He then studied in Paris and traveled extensively. In 1509 he lectured at Dôle on the Cabbalistic work of Johannes Reuchlin. About 1512 he went to Italy, where he lectured at Pavia and possibly obtained the doctorates he claimed in law and medicine. Early in 1518 he left Italy. After working at Metz, Cologne, Geneva, and Fribourg, he became physician (1524–1526) to the queen mother of France, Louise of Savoy. In 1527 he moved to Antwerp and in 1529 became imperial historiographer. In 1532–1535 he lived at the court of the reformist archbishop of Cologne, Hermann von Wied. In 1535 he moved to France and probably died at Grenoble. Wherever he lived, he formed friendships (and enmities) based on his interests in humanist learning, occult philosophy, and a vaguely evangelical religious reform.

Agrippa's relationship to Protestantism is marginal. Although he returned north just as Martin Luther's influence was beginning to spread and closely followed the reformer's publications, he never repudiated the traditional church. He was hostile to the friars and scholastic theologians, whom he perceived as hypocritical foes of a new learning that would regenerate the church without destroying unity. Some of his friends became Protestants, but many others remained (like himself and Desiderius Erasmus) awkwardly but stubbornly loyal to the old church.

Agrippa's importance thus stands outside the main lines of the Reformation. It rests on his Renaissance dream of rediscovering a submerged but divinely ordained wisdom that would both confirm and revivify Christianity. The sources of this "ancient theology" purported to go back to the earliest times: the Orphic hymns, the Hermetic treatises, Jewish Cabbala, the works of Plato, and the Neoplatonists. Previous generations' familiarity with these texts was revolutionized by the work of the Florentine Neoplatonists Marsilio Ficino and Giovanni Pico della Mirandola. Even in its refined Florentine representatives, this esoterism implied a desire to control people and things through magic. Agrippa's *De occulta philosophia* openly embraces both the philosophical and the magical aspects of this tradition, which sought to restore the quasi-divine status possessed by Adam before the Fall.

A difficult problem is that *De incertitudine et vanitate scien-*

tiarum et artium (1530) seems to repudiate this esoteric tradition and to adopt a worldview in which all human learning is ultimately worthless and only simple faith in the gospel has any value. This viewpoint has been variously described as skeptical, anti-intellectual, paradoxical, and satirical. Still more puzzling, he wrote *De vanitate* while continuing to revise his magical treatise for publication. Yet *De vanitate* explicitly renounces his earlier interest in magic, and the first full edition of *De occulta philosophia* (1533) reprints the antimagical chapters of *De vanitate*. The difficulty of understanding Agrippa's beliefs underlines the peculiarly ambivalent position that not only he but many Renaissance thinkers took on the question of how (and whether) the human mind can attain truth. *De vanitate* influenced many later skeptics, notably Michel Eyquem de Montaigne. The impassioned tone of Agrippa's thought, with its peculiar combination of magic and doubt, also explains why he was a principal source for the legend of Faust.

BIBLIOGRAPHY

Primary Source

Agrippa von Nettesheim, Heinrich Cornelius. *Opera.* 2 vols. Lugduni, n.d. (a false imprint; several nearly identical editions of the late sixteenth and early seventeenth centuries bear it.) Virtually complete collection of Agrippa's works and correspondence in the original Latin. A modern reprint, with introduction by Richard H. Popkin, appeared at Hildesheim, 1970. See also the modern critical edition of *De occulta philosophia* by Vittoria Perrone Compagni, Leiden, 1992, with a valuable introduction.

Secondary Sources

Keefer, Michael H. "Agrippa's Dilemma: Hermetic 'Rebirth' and the Ambivalences of *De vanitate* and *De occulta philosophia*." *Renaissance Quarterly* 41.4 (1988), 614–653. A challenging attempt to integrate the magical and the skeptical elements in Agrippa's thought on the basis of Hermetic influences. Cites most of the literature that appeared since Nauert's book of 1965.
Nauert, Charles G., Jr. *Agrippa and the Crisis of Renaissance Thought.* Urbana, Ill., 1965. The most comprehensive modern study, both biographical and interpretive, with extensive bibliography.
Popkin, Richard H. *The History of Scepticism from Erasmus to Descartes.* Assen, 1960. More recent editions continue the story to Spinoza's time; pp. 22–25 relate Agrippa to the skeptical currents of the sixteenth century.
Walker, Daniel Pickering. *Spiritual and Demonic Magic from Ficino to Campanella.* Reprint, Notre Dame, Ind., 1969. An epoch-making study of the role of magic in the Neoplatonic revival of the fifteenth and sixteenth centuries, with much attention to Agrippa.
Yates, Frances A. *Giordano Bruno and the Hermetic Tradition.* Chicago, 1964. Influential interpretation of Bruno as the end product of Renaissance magical-hermetic learning, attributing an important role to Agrippa.
Zambelli, Paola. "Magical and Radical Reformation in Agrippa of Nettesheim." *Journal of the Warburg and Courtauld Institutes* 39 (1976), 69–103. Relates Agrippa to radical Nicodemite tendencies in Reformation thought. The principal English-language publication of a major Agrippan scholar, citing her other publications in German, French, and Italian, and her editions of lost or rare Agrippan works.

CHARLES G. NAUERT, JR.

ALBA, DUKE OF *See* Álvarez de Toledo, Fernando.

ALBER, Erasmus (1500?–1553), Lutheran pastor, reformer, hymnist, poet, and writer. Following Latin school, Alber studied at Mainz, then at Wittenberg beginning in 1520, first under Andreas Bodenstein von Karlstadt and then under Luther. Initially a schoolmaster, he served as Lutheran pastor in Sprendlingen from 1528 to 1539, during which time he reformed the district of Dreieich and participated in reforming the duchy of Kustrin. Many-faceted, lively, and outspoken, he was controversial as a fervent propagandist for Luther against Rome, Calvinism, and other German reformers. As his writings grew increasingly sharp, he assumed a transient pastoral life after 1539, including stays in Brandenburg, Rothenburg ob der Tauber, and the Wetterau, with Wittenberg a frequent refuge. In Magdeburg he was outspoken against the Interim in 1548 and subsequent years and was forced to leave in 1551. He died only a few weeks after entering his last position, as pastor and superintendent in Neubrandenburg.

Alber's poetry placed him among the most highly regarded German writers of his day. His principal works are Lutheran retellings of Aesop's fables enriched with accounts of personal incidents and comments on the times, customs, music, and instruments, published 1534–1550. His rhyming lexicon, *Novum dictionarii genus* (1540), is authoritative as a German-Latin lexicon.

Alber wrote many Lutheran hymns, of which twenty-three are positively identified. They frequently appeared in contemporary anthologies and a few persist in evangelical usage, most notably "Christe, du bist der helle Tag" and "Wir danken Gott für seine Gaben." Some melodies and settings are his own; he freely adopted others as contrafacta.

BIBLIOGRAPHY

Körner, Emil. *Erasmus Alber.* Leipzig, 1910. Standard biography.
Uhl, Lotte. *Alberus und die Musik: Eine volkskundliche Untersuchung.* Giessen, Germany, 1937. Meets title claim.
Verzeichnis der im deutschen Sprachbereich erschienenen Drucke des XVI. Jahrhunderts. Stuttgart, 1983–. Vol. 1, nos. 1468–1565.

KYLE C. SESSIONS

ALBER, Matthäus (1495–1570), reformer of Reutlingen, an imperial city of southwestern Germany. He came from a once wealthy middle-class Reutlingen family that was reduced to poverty in 1503. He attended Latin grammar school in his hometown, in Schwäbisch-Hall, in Rothenburg ob der Tauber, and in Strasbourg. From 1511 to 1513 he served as assistant at the elementary school in Reutlingen. Alber studied in Tübingen from November 1513 until June 1520 and taught there at the elementary school. In May 1516 he received a bachelor of arts and in 1518 a master of arts degree. Thereafter he transferred to the faculty of theology, where he studied Greek and classical writers under Philipp Melanchthon, among others. He himself taught music. In June 1520 he moved to the University of Freiburg. After giving lectures on biblical books, he received the degrees of *baccalaureus biblicus* (5 June 1521), *baccalaureus sententiarius* (August 1521), and then *baccalaureus formatus*.

After his ordination to the priesthood in Constance, Alber served from November 1521 until 1548 as a priest in Reutlingen, where his activities in the spirit of Martin Luther met a warm response from the town council and the people. From 1523 until 1548 they protected their preacher from papal demands made through the Habsburg government in Stuttgart, Archduke Ferdinand in Vienna, and the district supervisor in Constance. From 1524 until 1531 Alber introduced the German Mass, did away with auricular confession, administered Holy Communion in both kinds, married (1524), and finally, under the influence of Huldrych Zwingli, put through a prohibition of images. Ultimately his church service was limited to the reading of the scripture, the sermon, the reading of the psalms, and hymns.

On the subject of Communion, Alber, who affirmed the real presence, sided with Luther and opposed Zwingli. Alber's liturgy has, all in all, south German characteristics. In 1525 he countered effectively with sermons and disputations against the rebellious efforts of the "common man" and the Anabaptists. On 9 May 1528 he was excommunicated, an act followed in 1531 by the imperial ban for Reutlingen and its preachers, the result of the city having signed the Augsburg Confession (1530). From 1531 the churches of Reutlingen were ruled by a *senatus ecclesiae*—three counselors, three clergy, and six members of the community.

In December 1539 Alber received his doctorate in theology in Tübingen. In 1548, when Reutlingen accepted the Interim against strong opposition within the community, Alber resigned his post. Under the protection of Duke Ulrich of Würtemberg, he probably moved to the nearby town of Pfullingen. From July 1549 until April 1563 he was minister in Stuttgart and superintendent of one of the four districts of Württemberg. From 1551 he worked together with Johannes Brenz, his colleague on the church council, on a *Confessio Wirtembergica*, as well as on church organization and visitation regulations, which were published in 1559. From April 1563 until 1570 Alber was the first Protestant abbot of Blaubeuren (and, as such, became the leader of the convent school there) and a member of the regional diet. He died on 1 December 1570 holding these offices.

BIBLIOGRAPHY

Bautz, Friedrich Wilhelm. "Alber, Matthäus." In *Biographisch-biblio-graphisches Kirchenlexikon,* vol. 1, pp. 77ff. Herzberg, 1990. Extensive bibliography.

Bubenheimer, Ulrich. "Reformation in Reutlingen." In *Religionspädo-gogische Mitteilungen* 3 (1982), 26–28, 30–41.

Duncker, Christoph. *Matthäus Alber: Reformator von Reutlingen.* Weinsberg, 1970. The only recent monograph on Alber, offering sources as well as commentaries on Alber's time in Reutlingen.

Rublack, Hans-Christoph. "Albert, Matthäus." In *Theologische Realenzyklopädie,* vol. 2, pp. 170–177. Berlin and New York, 1978. The best historical-critical portrayal, offering a comprehensive bibliography to 1978.

DIETER FAUTH
Translated from German by Susan M. Sisler

ALBERT VII OF AUSTRIA (also Albert the Pious; 1559–1621), governor-general and then sovereign ruler of the Netherlands. Son of Emperor Maximilian II and Maria (daughter of Emperor Charles V and Isabella of Portugal), Albert was born on 13 November 1559 in Wiener Neustadt, Austria. After the marriage of his sister Anna in 1570 to King Philip II of Spain, he was raised at the Spanish court and destined for a clerical career. Thus, he was appointed cardinal in 1577 and archbishop of Toledo in 1594.

In 1581 Albert became the Spanish viceroy in Portugal, a function he exchanged in 1595 for that of governor of the Netherlands. As a convinced and pious Catholic and an Hispanicized Habsburg, Albert provided Philip II sufficient guarantees to secure both Spanish authority and the Catholic religion in the Netherlands. After Albert's marriage in 1599 to Isabella Clara Eugenia (the beloved daughter of Philip II), these two archdukes by virtue of a disposition of the king (6 May 1598) became sovereign rulers over the Netherlands. Under their administration a time of peace commenced, commerce and industry revived, and arts and letters flourished in the service of prince and church. The Peace of Vervins (1598) ended the war between Spain and France, and following the death of Queen Elizabeth I, Albert sought peace with England (Treaty of London, 1604). After the capture of Oostende from the rebel Dutch, both sides moved cautiously to discussions that ended on 9 April 1609 with the Twelve-Year Truce, whereby the Republic of the United Provinces was recognized as an independent state without political or religious restrictions. The *de facto* recognition of the United Provinces as an independent state was a severe blow to the Spanish monarchy, but it reflected the realistic policy of Albert. In the Catholic Netherlands, however, there was no freedom of conscience for followers of religions other than Catholicism, and Spanish troops remained. In the reconversion of the country to Catholicism, the ecclesiastical and secular authorities worked closely together. The time of bloody persecution of heretics had passed. In some cities (Antwerp and Ghent, for example) and in some regions in Flanders (for example, in the region of Sint-Maria-Horebeke), small groups of Protestants had survived because they constituted no threat to public order.

But on 31 December 1609 the archdukes stipulated in an edict that it was prohibited to attend meetings at which doctrine other than Catholic doctrine was taught. Non-Catholic residents were not obliged to attend Catholic services but had to behave discreetly and respectfully toward the Catholic religion. Migrants who wanted to settle in the Spanish Netherlands had to confess and practice the Catholic religion. In practice there was unofficial tolerance despite the edict, but this situation did not detract from the fact that Catholicism was the state religion. Thus, a non-Catholic could not hold public office or contract a valid marriage, and the laity were forbidden by the state from discussing religious questions in public (edict of 13 July 1609). Of course, government supervision of the printing and dissemination of books remained in force. This Catholic offensive was supported personally by the archdukes by means of financial subsidies to monasteries and religious orders (particularly to the Jesuits) and by the propagation of Marian pilgrimages (for example, to Scherpenheuvel and Halle). During the reign of the archdukes, the government acquired a certain authority over the University of Louvain: the archiducal visitation of 1617 contained clear instructions about the structure and the operation of the university.

As sovereign ruler—though in practice taking account of Spanish political sensitivities and also much attached to Habsburg and Catholic interests—Archduke Albert was not a mere tool in the hands of the Spanish king. Indeed, in the negotiations with England and with the United Provinces, the Netherlands had its own policy. As for ecclesiastical affairs, the establishment of a papal nunciature in Brussels (1596) promoted a national ecclesiastical policy, which was manifested in such things as the striving to shield monasteries and religious orders as much as possible from non-Netherlands influence. After the death of Albert (Brussels, 13 July 1621), Archduchess Isabella became governess general of the Spanish Netherlands, a position she held until her own death in 1633. Since the marriage of the archdukes was childless, the Catholic Netherlands lost the status of sovereign state in 1621 in accordance with the terms of 6 May 1589. The period of the archdukes was, in many respects, a new beginning. During their reign the basis was laid for further political, social, and religious development in the Catholic Netherlands lasting until the end of the ancien régime.

BIBLIOGRAPHY

Primary Sources

Correspondance de la Cour d'Espagne sur les affaires des Pays-Bas au 17e siècle. 6 vols. Edited by Henri Lonchay, Joseph Cuvelier and Joseph Lefèvre. Brussels, 1923–1937. Covers correspondence between Spain and the Netherlands, 1598–1633.

Correspondance de Philippe II d'Espagne sur les affaires des Pays-Bas, Deuxième partie: Recueil destiné à faire suite aux travaux de L.-P. Gachard. Vol. 4. Edited by Joseph Lefèvre. Brussels, 1960. Covers the correspondence of 1592–1598.

Recueil des ordonnances des Pays-Bas: Règne d'Albert et d'Isabelle. Edited by Victor Brants. Brussels, 1900–1912. Edition of the ordinances of the archdukes.

Secondary Sources

Elias, Hendrik-Jozef. *Kerk en Staat in de Zuidelijke Nederlanden onder de regeering der aartshertogen Albrecht en Isabella, 1598–1621.* Louvain, 1931. Excellent study about the relationship between church and state in the Catholic Netherlands under the archdukes.

Israel, Jonathan I. *The Dutch Republic and the Hispanic World, 1606–1661.* Oxford, 1986.

Parker, Geoffrey. *The Army of Flanders and the Spanish Road, 1569–1659: The Logistics of Spanish Victory and Defeat in the Low Countries' Wars.* Cambridge, 1972.

Pasture, Alexandre. *La restauration religieuse aux Pays-Bas catholiques sous les archiducs Albert et Isabelle (1596–1633) Principalement d'après les Archives de la Nonciature et de la Visite ad limina.* Louvain, 1925. Excellent study about the Catholic restoration in the Catholic Netherlands under the archdukes.

Schepper, Hugo de, and Geoffrey Parker. "The Decision-making Process in the Government of the Catholic Netherlands under 'the Archdukes,' 1596–1621." In *Spain and the Netherlands, 1559–1659: Ten Studies,* rev. ed., edited by Geoffey Parker, pp. 164–176. London, 1990.

GUSTAAF JANSSENS

ALBERT OF BRANDENBURG (1490–1545),

elector of the Holy Roman Empire, archbishop of Mainz and Magdeburg, and administrator of Halberstadt. He was the younger son (b. 28 June 1490) of John Cicero, elector of Brandenburg, and Magareth, daughter of Duke William III of Saxony. His brother, Joachim I, succeeded to the electorate upon his father's death. Through family influence Albert became archbishop of Magdeburg (1513) and administrator of Halberstadt. A special papal dispensation cleared the way for his acquisition of the archbishopric of Mainz (1514), which carried with it the title of elector. In return Albert agreed to pay Pope Leo X the sum of twenty-four thousand ducats (fourteen thousand for the pallium and ten thousand to receive the needed exemption for the plural holding of sees). The money was raised through the sale of indulgences in the Magdeburg archdiocese, with half of the receipts going to the papacy and half to Albert to enable him to repay a loan from the Fugger banking house. The sale of indulgences, notably by Johann Tetzel, led Martin Luther to send a letter to Albert in which he enclosed ninety-five theses calling for a debate of current practices (31 October 1517). The archbishop, who did not wish to be troubled, left Luther's letter unanswered for more than two years (though he did promptly report the matter to Rome); when he finally did respond, his influence in German ecclesiastical affairs was largely gone, while Luther's had grown.

A true Renaissance prince, Albert was a lover of art and music, a connoisseur of fine architecture, and a patron of the new humanist learning and literature. With his brother, Joachim I, he founded the University of Frankfurt an der Oder (1506). He admired Erasmus, supported Johannes Reuchlin, drew Ulrich von Hutten and Wolfgang Capito to his court, and patronized the leading artists of his age, among them Peter Vischer, Lucas Cranach, Matthias Grünewald, and Albrecht Dürer. In 1520 he founded the cathedral church at Halle, his favored residential city, and furnished it with splendid artworks and precious reliquaries; he also renovated the Mainz cathedral and the abbey church at Aschaffenburg.

Albert was made a cardinal in 1518. He supported the election of Emperor Charles V (1519). After the Diet of Worms (1521) he refused to certify the edict against Luther because of doubts about its legality. As the Reformation spread, he considered emulating the example of his cousin Albert of Prussia, grand master of the Teutonic Order, and secularizing his archbishopric—a course that Luther openly encouraged. Franz von Sickingen's abortive campaign against Trier (1523), in which he had remained a neutral bystander and, even more so, the upheaval created by the Peasants' Revolt, led Albert to abandon his earlier Erasmian position and align himself openly with the pro-papal policies of his brother Joachim I. He joined him, Duke George of Saxony, and other Catholic princes in the anti-Lutheran leagues of Dessau (1525) and Halle (1533).

This more conservative stance, however, did not prevent Albert's nephew Joachim II, Brandenburg's new elector, from introducing the Reformation in his lands (1539), nor could it forestall the advance of Luther's message into Magdeburg. The cardinal anticipated these events by removing his valuable collection of art objects and reliquaries to Mainz. In 1541 he left Halle forever; shortly afterward the estates of Magdeburg and Halberstadt voted to introduce the Reformation. Albert now fell increasingly under the influence of Jesuit advisers (notably Petrus Faber) and spent his last years as a leading champion of the Catholic Counter-Reformation. He died on 24 September 1545 and was buried in the Mainz cathedral.

BIBLIOGRAPHY

Benrath, Gustav A. "Albrecht von Mainz." In *Theologische Realenzyklopädie*, edited by Gerhard Krause and Gerhard Müller, vol. 1, pp. 184–187. Berlin, 1977. Good summary of Albert's ecclesiastical policies, but ignores his dynastic interests.

Brück, Anton P. "Kardinal Albrecht von Brandenburg, Kurfürst und Erzbischof von Mainz." In *Der Reichstag zu Worms von 1521: Reichspolitik und Luthersache*, edited by Fritz Reuter, pp. 257–270. 2d ed. Cologne, 1981. Stresses Albert's moderating influence at the Diet of Worms.

Jürgensmeier, Friedhelm, ed. *Erzbischof Albrecht von Brandenburg 1490–1545: Ein Kirchen- und Reichsfürst der Frühen Neuzeit.* Frankfurt a.M., 1991. Excellent collection of papers by historians, theologians, and art historians presented at a 1990 conference.

May, Jakob. *Der Kurfürst, Cardinal und Erzbischof Albrecht II. von Mainz und Magdeburg, Administrator des Bisthums Halberstadt, Markgraf von Brandenburg und seine Zeit.* 2 vols. Munich, 1865–1875. Still the most thorough and concise biography of the cardinal.

Roland, Berthold, ed. *Albrecht von Brandenburg: Kurfürst, Erzkanzler, Kardinal, 1490–1545.* Mainz, 1990. Exhibition catalog (on the occasion of the five-hundredth anniversary of Albert's birth) with magnificent illustrations and useful introductory essays that place the cardinal in the context of the late medieval church and German Renaissance.

BODO NISCHAN

ALCHEMY. That alchemy reached its apogee during the sixteenth and seventeenth centuries raises interesting questions. How could an occult science predicated on the belief that both matter and the alchemist could be made perfect coexist with the Protestant notion of human depravity or withstand the Counter-Reformation assault on magic? Furthermore, how could an occult and vitalist philosophy gain adherents such as Newton and Leibniz in an age supposedly characterized by Cartesian rationalism and a "mechanical philosophy"?

Alchemy flourished because no other scientific theory explained physical transformations with such plausibility. In addition, it flourished because of the very ideal of perfectionism that led to the censure and execution of some of its practitioners. In an age of bitter sectarian warfare, alchemy provided a refuge for those who clung to the Renaissance concept of a universal philosophy, or *prisca theologia*, which would unite people in a common quest to restore the world to its prelapsarian perfection. Alchemists were essentially a fifth column within the various denominations; they carried forward the optimistic ideals of Renaissance humanists into the age of the Enlightenment. As a largely educated fifth column, they escaped the worst forms of persecution directed at healers, magicians, and witches. The popularity of alchemy during the scientific revolution supports the increasingly accepted view that one cannot separate science and the occult during this period.

Alchemical theory developed from a mixture of Aristotelian, Neoplatonic, and gnostic philosophy. According to Aristotle every substance consisted of prime matter and a "form." The form determined the characteristics of the substance, including the proportion of the four elements (earth, air, fire, water), the basic building blocks of matter. Thus an alchemist had only to vary the proportions of the elements or find the "form" of gold to transmute base metal. Alchemists accepted Aristotle's belief that everything in nature has an end (*telos*). This concept was reinforced by Neoplatonic and gnostic ideas that led many alchemists to envision themselves as saviors of an imperfect world. These "spiritual" alchemists modeled themselves on Hermes Trismegistus, the legendary founder of Western alchemy (hence alchemists were called "hermeticists"). The most famous document supposedly written by Hermes Trismegistus was the *Emerald Tablet*. The basic message of this enigmatic text is that all things come from one divine nature and will return to it. This idea was enshrined in the alchemical commonplace "All in One" and symbolized by the tail-eating serpent (*ouroboros*).

European alchemists had little difficulty adopting gnostic ideas because of their apparent compatibility with Christianity. Both are concerned with salvation and describe the experience in terms of death and rebirth. The basic color sequence in alchemy therefore went from black (death) to white (regeneration) to red, the final stage marking the creation of the "royal" stone, which could give perfect life (hence the color of blood) to imperfect substances.

Paracelsus (1493–1541) was the most famous alchemist in the period. While his supporters dubbed him the "Luther of the sciences," his detractors condemned him as a black magician and gnostic heretic. The mixture of mysticism and practical chemistry in Paracelsus's writings reveals both the heretical nature of alchemy and its importance in the development of modern chemistry. Such a mixture scandalized orthodox Christians. For all their differences, Catholics and Protestants agreed that humans were innately depraved as a result of original sin. The idea that they could redeem themselves and the world was simply heresy.

On a theoretical level, orthodox Christians rejected alchemy and all magic. On a practical level, however, it was not always easy to differentiate black magic from legitimate "natural" magic, or science. The Catholic Church had especial difficulty because some Catholic rituals (exorcism, the blessing of fields, etc.) seemed so close to magic. While the situation should have been easier for Protestants, who considered all forms of magic diabolical attempts to appropriate superhuman powers, they too exempted good, "natural" magic.

For good reasons many Christians ignored the real incompatibility between Christian and alchemical thought. Catholic alchemists identified their transmutations with that of the Eucharist. Lutherans relied on the doctrine of justification by faith to legitimize their role as alchemical saviors. The Calvinist doctrine of election allowed Calvinists to do the same.

Thus the gnostic conviction that humans were sparks of divinity with the power to regenerate themselves and the world led Christian alchemists well beyond the borders of heresy. But it was an idea that could not be eradicated. The gnostic belief in innate human goodness and power, a belief nurtured by alchemists, reached its full development during the Enlightenment and has provided the rationale for liberal and progressive thinking ever since.

[*See also* Magic.]

BIBLIOGRAPHY

Coudert, Allison P. *Alchemy: The Philosopher's Stone.* Boulder, 1980. Provides a general account of the history of alchemy and the emergence of chemistry as does Debus.

Debus, Allen G. *The Chemical Philosophy: Paracelsian Science and Medicine in the Sixteenth and Seventeenth Centuries.* 2 vols. New York, 1977.

Dobbs, Betty Jo Teeter. *The Foundations of Newton's Alchemy.* Reprint, Cambridge, 1983. Describes the influence of alchemy on Newton's thought.

Montgomery, J. W. "Cross, Constellation and Crucible: Lutheran Astrology and Alchemy in the Age of Reformation." *Ambix* 11 (1963): 65–86. Discusses Lutheran attitudes toward science and the occult.

Pagel, Walter. *Paracelsus: An Introduction to Philosophical Medicine in the Era of the Renaissance.* 2d rev. ed. Basel and New York, 1982. The best analysis of Paracelsus's thought available.

———. *Religion and Neoplatonism in Renaissance Medicine.* London, 1985. Analyzes the Neoplatonic and gnostic aspects of alchemy.

Schuler, Robert. "Spiritual Alchemies of Seventeenth-Century England." *Journal of the History of Ideas* 41 (1980), 293–318. Analyzes the way Protestants legitimized their interest in alchemy.

Thomas, Keith. *Religion and the Decline of Magic.* London, 1971. Describes the various religious objections to alchemy and magic; see also Walker.

Walker, D. P. *Spiritual and Demonic Magic.* Reprint, Notre Dame, Ind., 1975, and Nendeln, 1976.

Yates, Frances A. *The Rosicrucian Enlightenment.* Reprint, London, 1986. Discusses the importance of alchemy in preparing the way for modern science.

———. *Giordano Bruno and the Hermetic Tradition.* Reprint, Chicago, 1991.

ALLISON P. COUDERT

ALEANDRO, Girolamo (1480–1542), Italian humanist, papal diplomat, and cardinal. Born of reportedly noble lineage at Motta di Livenza in the Venetian Republic, he was trained in the humanities at Motta, Venice, Pordenone, and Padua and demonstrated a great facility with languages, eventually learning Latin, Greek, Hebrew, Syriac, and Chaldean. He taught Latin and Hebrew in Venice, where he briefly served in 1501 as secretary to the papal nuncio and joined the academy of Aldo Manuzio. At the academy in 1508 he became a friend of Erasmus of Rotterdam, who urged him to seek his academic fortunes in France. His public lectures in Greek (1509–1513) drew large numbers of students in Paris, where he was elected principal of Lombard College (1511) and eventually rector of the university (1513). Unhappy with his income as a teacher, he decided to pursue an ecclesiastical career.

Aleandro advanced his career by serving important churchmen. In 1513–1514 he was secretary to Etienne Poncher, bishop of Paris. He then transferred his services to Erard de le Marck, prince-bishop of Liège, who in 1516 sent him to Rome to secure for Erard promotion to the cardinalate, which he obtained in 1520. In Rome Aleandro became in 1517 secretary to cardinal Giulio dei Medici (later Clement VII) and two years later papal librarian, a post he held under both Leo X and Adrian VI. In 1524 Gian Pietro Carafa (later Paul IV) resigned to him his archbishopric of Brindisi, in which Aleandro resided only from 1527 to 1529. Paul III named him a cardinal *in pectore* in 1536 and published the appointment in 1538 with the title cardinal-priest of S. Ciriaco. He owed this promotion to his many years of service—next to Lorenzo Campeggio, he was considered the most important papal diplomat of his generation.

Aleandro was entrusted with a number of important nunciatures. In 1520 Leo X charged him with publishing and enforcing the bull *Exsurge Domine* against Luther and his followers in the Rhineland and Low Countries. He won Charles V's support for the condemnation, helped to write the Edict of Worms, and secured its approbation and finally its publication on 26 May 1521. He suspected Erasmus of supporting Luther, and their relationship became one of guarded suspicion and hostility. In 1524–1525 Clement VII appointed him as nuncio to Francis I, and he was captured with the French king at the Battle of Pavia on 24 February 1525. The same pope sent him in 1531–1532 to Charles V to assist the sickly papal legate Lorenzo Campeggio in urging the emperor to be vigorous in his opposition to the Lutherans and Turks. As nuncio in Venice (1533–1535) Aleandro also worked to combat Protestant influences. In 1538 Paul III dispatched him to Vienna to watch over the negotiations between the emperor, supporting the Catholic party, and the Protestants. Rome considered Aleandro knowledgeable on Protestant affairs because of his contacts in the north and his large library of Protestant writings. Aleandro's opposition to Protestantism was apparently based on his conviction that it was a threat to traditional church order and that its political leaders were eager to confiscate church property. He was unsympathetic to its particular piety and sought to combat it by a combination of repressive measures, support of Catholic rulers, ecclesiastical politics (including a council), and the elimination of scandalous abuses in the church.

Under Paul III, Aleandro often sat on commissions to reform the church. He was a member of the group of reform-minded prelates that drew up the famous *Consilium de emendanda ecclesia* (1537). He then worked on a reform of the datary (1537) and of the chancellery (1539) and was part of the planning for the abortive council called to meet in Vicenza. Never enjoying robust health, he died in Rome on 1 February 1542, having resigned his diocese of Brindisi to his nephew Francesco and having provided in his will for his only surviving, illegitimate son, Claudio.

BIBLIOGRAPHY

Primary Sources

Aleandro, Girolamo. "Journal autobiographique du cardinal Jérôme Aléandre, 1480–1530." In *Notice et extraits des manuscrits de la Bibliothèque Nationale [de Paris] et autres bibliothèques*, edited by H. Omont, vol. 35, pt. 1, pp. 1–116. Paris, 1896.

———. *Die Depeschen des Nuntius Aleander vom Wormser Reichstage 1521*. Translated by Paul Kalkoff. 2d ed. Halle, 1897. Aleandro's reports to cardinal Giulio dei Medici on his efforts to secure Luther's condemnation and Erasmus's support.

———. *Legation Aleanders 1538–1539*. In *Nuntiaturberichte aus Deutschland*, edited by Walter Friedensburg, section 1, vols. 3 and 4. Gotha, 1893.

———. *Legation Lorenzo Campeggios, 1530–1531, und Nuntiatur Girolamo Aleandros 1531*. In *Nuntiaturberichte aus Deutschland*, edited by Gerhard Müller, section 1, supplemental vol. 1 (1530–1531). Tübingen, 1963. Müller provides a biographical sketch of Aleandro.

———. *Legation Lorenzo Campeggios, 1532, und Nuntiatur Girolamo Aleandros 1532*. In *Nuntiaturberichte aus Deutschland*, edited by Gerhard Müller, section 1, vol. 2. (1532). Tübingen, 1969.

———. *Lettres familières de Jérôme Aléandre, 1510–1540*. Edited by Jules Paquier. Paris, 1909.

———. *Nunziature di Venezia, 1533–1535*. Edited by Franco Gaeta. Rome, 1958.

Secondary Sources

Alberigo, Giuseppe. "Aleandro, Girolamo." In *Dizionario biografico degli Italiani*, vol. 2, pp. 128–135. Rome, 1960.

Friedensburg, Walter. "Zur Biographie Aleanders, 1529–1538." In *Nuntiaturberichte aus Deutschland*, vol. 1, pt. 4, pp. 421–444. Gotha, 1893.

Gaeta, Franco. *Un nunzio pontificio a Venezia nel cinquecento (Girolamo Aleandro)*. Civiltà veneziana, saggi 9. Venice and Rome, 1960.

Lowry, Martin John Clement. "Girolamo Aleandro." In *Contemporaries of Erasmus: A Biographical Register of the Renaissance and Reformation*, vol. 1, pp. 28–32. Toronto, 1985.

Paquier, Jules. *Jérôme Aléandre de sa naissance à la fin de son séjour à Brindes, 1480–1529*. Reprint, Geneva, 1977. Pp. v–lxxiii of this work provide an ample bibliography of Aleandro's printed and manuscript writings.

NELSON H. MINNICH

ALESIUS, Alexander (also Alexander Alan; Alane; 1500?–1565), Scottish-German theologian. He was among those theologians of the sixteenth century who converted to Reformation convictions after long inner struggles. More than any other, he influenced theological and ecclesiastical renewal in Scotland, England, and Germany by means of his experiences.

Born around 1500 in Edinburgh, he matriculated in 1512 at the University of Saint Andrews. In 1515 he turned to the Augustinian order and chose the career of a theologian. The martyrdom of Patrick Hamilton at the end of February 1528 so agitated the defender of late medieval theology that in 1529 Alesius, as a sharp critic of the lifestyle of the clergy, was threatened with imprisonment and had to flee. Traveling via Malmö, Brussels, and Cologne, Alesius arrived in Wittenberg in the fall of 1532.

His instruction from Martin Luther and Philipp Melanchthon now began, and their theology and methods would shape him for life. His treatise against the prohibition of Scottish bishops' reading the New Testament in the vernacular brought about the protest of Johannes Cochlaeus. In 1553 he traveled as an emissary of the Wittenberg theologians to Henry VIII. Until he had to flee in 1539, Alesius worked in Cambridge and London as an intermediary of the Wittenberg Reformation. Among his friends were John Bale, Hugh Latimer, and Thomas Cranmer. In particular, he supported the reform efforts of Thomas Cromwell. In the summer of 1539, when the conservative forces gained control with the Act of Six Articles, Alesius fled from England and returned to Wittenberg.

Melanchthon recommended him to Frankfurt an der Oder. There he took part intensively in the reform of the university. A struggle with Christoph von der Straasen, lawyer and confidant of Elector Joachim II, led him in 1542 to Leipzig, the most important station of his life. He strongly supported the overdue reformation of the theology faculty. Appearing under his name were more than forty exegetical, dogmatic, and controversial theological writings, such as commentaries on the gospel of John, on *Romans,* on the pastoral letters, and on *Psalms.* He was hesitant to take part in internal Protestant controversies and thus rejected both the Interim and Andreas Osiander's doctrine of justification. In the argument over the Eucharist he favored in 1559 the Heidelberg theologians, but without publicly expressing himself.

Alesius died 17 March 1565 in Leipzig. Although he remained close to Melanchthon all his life, he nevertheless maintained his theological and methodological independence. A thorough knowledge of late medieval theology, his own life experiences, and rootedness in Reformation doctrine determined his life's work, which together with apologetics was characterized by the wish to regain and reform the unity of the church—the *consensus ecclesiae*—that was founded in the gospels.

BIBLIOGRAPHY

Kawerau, Gustav. "Alexander Alesius' Fortgang von der Frankfurter Universität." *Jahrbuch für brandenburgische Kirchengeschichte* 14 (1916), 89–100.

Macpherson, John. "Alesius: The First Reformed Scottish Theologian." *Theological Review* 3 (1888), 97–114.

McNeill, John T. "Alexander Alesius: Scottish Lutheran, 1500–1565." *Archiv für Reformationsgeschichte* 55 (1964), 161–191.

Siegmund-Schultze, Ernst. "Alesius Alexander." In *Theologische Realenzyklopädie,* vol. 2, pp. 231–235. Berlin and New York, 1978.

Wartenberg, Günther. "Zum Kommentar des Alexander Alesius zum Johannesevangelium." In *Théorie et pratique de l'exégèse,* edited by Irena Backus and Francis M. Higman, pp. 329–342. Geneva, 1990.

Wiedemann, Gotthelf. "Der Reformator Alexander Alesius als Ausleger der Psalmen." D. Theol. diss., Friedrich-Alexander-Universität Erlangen-Nürnberg, 1988.

GÜNTHER WARTENBERG
Translated from German by Walter D. Morris

ALEXANDER VI (Ital., Rodrigo Borgia; 1431–1503), pope (1492–1503). Nephew of the Spanish pope Alonso Borgia (Calixtus III; 1455–1458), Rodrigo Borgia was made a cardinal by his uncle in 1456 and shortly afterward vicechancellor of the church. This position at the head of the papal chancery, together with the considerable wealth derived from the rich benefices bestowed on him by Calixtus and his own political acumen, made him a leading cardinal.

His wealth was instrumental in securing his election to the papacy in 1492, overcoming his dubious moral reputation. A sensual man, he fathered nine children, two of them while pope. Devotion to his children led to his lavishing ecclesiastical benefices, lands, titles, and the revenues of the papacy on them. The arrogance, rapacity, and brutality of his son Cesare (1475–1507), who was originally made a cardinal in 1493 but renounced his clerical status in 1498 to become the main instrument and beneficiary of Alexander's dynastic ambitions, did much to darken the pope's reputation.

While he was recognized as an intelligent, astute, and eloquent politician, a person with considerable charm, Alexander's failings outweighed his gifts in the eyes of contemporaries. They were not deluded, as some historians have been, into seeing the campaigns Alexander's sons Juan (1476–1497) and Cesare waged in the Papal States against long-established baronial and seigniorial families as primarily attempts to strengthen the papacy rather than the Borgia. Conventional piety, a special devotion to the Virgin Mary, some interest in promoting a crusade against the Turks, and sympathy for the reform of monastic orders could not make him a convincing moral head of the church. Grief at the murder of his son Juan led to the appointment of a commission of six cardinals in 1497 to propose reforms in the church, including the papal administration, but his interest waned, and their recommendations were never promulgated.

BIBLIOGRAPHY

Mallett, Michael. *The Borgias: The Rise and Fall of a Renaissance Dynasty.* Chicago, 1987. The most balanced recent account of this controversial family (though perhaps still too inclined to give them the benefit of the doubt), with a useful bibliography.

CHRISTINE SHAW

ALLEN, William (1532–1594), English Catholic theologian, administrator, and cardinal. A Lancashire native, Allen was appointed principal of Saint Mary's Hall, Oxford, in 1556, a position he resigned for religious reasons shortly after the accession of Elizabeth I in 1559. He joined the circle of Oxford religious exiles in Louvain in 1561 but returned to England a year later for reasons of health. Between 1562 and 1565, although not yet ordained, he worked to strengthen the resolve of the English Catholics against attendance at Anglican services. By 1565 he was back in Flanders, and he was ordained at Malines. His friendship with Jean Vendville, professor of canon law at the recently founded University of Douai and later bishop of Tournai (1588), led to the establishment of the English Douai College with Allen as its president (1568). Allen hoped Douai College would be an intellectual center that would attract the best men from Oxford and Cambridge and prepare them for their return to England as priests. Despite occasional absences (Rome in 1567 and 1579 and Milan in 1569) Allen presided over the growth of Douai College for eighteen years until his final move to Rome in 1585. Despite a chronic shortage of funds, the college increased in size, and from its faculty came controversial works and an authorized English translation of the Bible.

A royal proclamation of 10 January 1581 asserted that the English college in Douai, as well as its sister institution in Rome, were founded to seduce English subjects from their allegiance to their rightful monarch. Allen's *An Apologie and True Declaration of the Institution and Endeavours of the Two English Colleges* (Reims, 1581) repudiated the charge. Catholics may make more loyal subjects, as Allen explained in the defense, but his personal involvement in a number of intrigues eventually forced him to abandon that position. From the mid-1570s Allen—in association with successive popes, Philip II of Spain, the Guise family in France, and, after 1581, the Jesuit Robert Parsons—was involved in launching a number of schemes aimed at either the outright overthrow of Elizabeth or the securing of her recognition of a Catholic successor, originally Mary Stuart but, after her execution in 1587, the princess Isabella of Spain. The priests produced by the seminary would fortify the Catholicism of the people, but Allen realized that the ultimate preservation of the faith depended on the Catholic powers of Europe.

Allen's increased involvement in the political sphere can be seen in his defense of Sir William Stanley's actions at Deventer (*The copy of a letter written by M. doctor Allen concerning the yielding up of the city of Daventrie*, Antwerp, 1587) and his exhortation to support the Spanish invasion of England of 1588 (*An admonition to the nobility and people of England and Ireland concerning the present wars*, Antwerp, 1588 and its broadside summary, *A declaration of the sentence and deposition of Elizabeth, the usurper and pretended queen of England*, Antwerp, 1588). At the request of Philip II, Allen was named cardinal on 7 August 1587 in preparation for his appointment as archbishop of Canterbury after the hoped-for victory by the Spanish Armada. Named archbishop of Malines in 1589, he never took possession of the see but remained in Rome until his death on 16 October 1594.

BIBLIOGRAPHY

Primary Sources

Allison, A. F., and D. M. Rogers. *The Contemporary Printed Literature of the English Counter-Reformation between 1558–1640.* Vol. 1, *Languages other than English*; vol. 2, *English.* London, 1989, 1994. Contains full bibliographical account of Allen's writing.

Knox, T. F., ed. *Letters and Memorials of William Cardinal Allen.* London, 1882.

Renold, P., ed. *Letters of William Allen and Richard Barret, 1572–1598.* London, 1967.

Secondary Sources

Camm, B. *Cardinal William Allen.* New York, 1908. A dated and confessional biography.

Clancy, Thomas H. *Papist Pamphleteers: The Allen-Persons Party and the Political Thought of the Counter-Reformation in England, 1572–1615.* Chicago, 1964. Survey of the political writings of Allen and Parsons.

Haile, M. *An Elizabethan Cardinal.* New York and London, 1914. Another dated and confessional biography.

THOMAS M. McCOOG, S.J.

ALTENSTAIG, Johannes (c.1480–c.1525), German humanist and anti-Reformation publicist. Altenstaig was probably born in Mindelheim around 1480. The earliest affirmed date of his life is 1497, the year of his matriculation at the University of Tübingen, where he prepared for a life of teaching and scholarship. Under the sway of the humanist faculty there, he adopted an essentially moral concept of Christianity and joined with the "moderns" to rescue classical Latin from the corruptions of contemporary usage.

An Augustinian Eremite, Altenstaig taught philosophy and theology at his order's school in Polling from 1509 to 1512, when he was called to Mindelheim as chaplain to the Saint Sebastian Brotherhood. He also taught Latin at the Augustinian monastery there. He was a friend of Johann Eck and enjoyed the confidence of Bishop Christoph von Stadion, under whose auspices he conducted a visitation of the Augsburg diocese in 1518.

Thoughtful and peaceable, Altenstaig viewed Luther's Reformation with fear and dismay. Although a sharp critic of the church hierarchy for its inattention to clerical avarice and pastoral neglect, Altenstaig shrank from any break with Catholic tradition and authority. His writings against the Reformation—including *Ain nutzlich vnnd in hailiger geschrifft gegründte vnderricht* (Augsburg, 1523) and *Von der Füllerey ein müter aller vbel vnd laster* (Strasbourg, 1525)—dealt primarily with external rather than deeper religious/theological points of contention and warned the common people against the dangers of following "false prophets" who held only to the Bible and denied man's free will to choose good over evil.

While calling for reforms, Altenstaig remained convinced of the spiritual benefits of a well-ordered monastic life. This, he believed, should be dedicated to teaching and theological scholarship, the key to moral reform and God's greatest gift to mankind.

Altenstaig's scholarly treatises such as *Opusculum de amicitia* and *De felicitate triplici*, both published at Hagenau in 1519, were based primarily on maxims and reflections culled from his reading in classical and Christian literature. Neither a profound thinker nor an innovator, he may be categorized among those who, while staying their ground, gave substance to the cause of Catholic reform.

BIBLIOGRAPHY

Schottenloher, Karl, ed. *Bibliographie zur deutschen Geschichte im Zeitalter der Glaubensspaltung, 1517–1518.* Stuttgart, 1957. See vol. 1.
Stegemann, Victor. "Altenstaig." In *Neue Deutsche Biographie,* vol. 1, pp. 215–216. Berlin, 1953.
Zoepfl, Friedrich. *Johannes Altenstaig: Ein Gelehrtenleben aus der Zeit des Humanismus und der Reformation.* Münster, 1918.
———. "Altenstaig." In *Lexicon für Theologie und Kirche,* vol. 1, p. 315. Freiburg, 1930.

KARIN BRINKMANN BROWN

ALTHAMER, Andreas (1500?–1539), German humanist and reformer. Born of a peasant family in Brenz, Württemberg, Althamer attended school in Augsburg and studied in Leipzig and Tübingen (matriculating, respectively, in 1516 and 1518). In 1519 he returned to Leipzig, where he studied ancient languages, was influenced by Petrus Mosellanus, and took a particular interest in Tacitus. He worked as school assistant in Schwäbisch-Hall (1521) and later in Reutlingen. He sent the first version of his Tacitus commentary to Philipp Melanchthon, who recommended a revision. This work became a lifelong preoccupation.

Having preached evangelical reform as chaplain in Schwäbisch-Gmünd (1524), he was dismissed. After his engagement to a young woman of Gmünd, he applied for citizenship there but was rejected. He matriculated at the University of Wittenberg on 18 October 1525. In 1526 he was in Nuremberg and became pastor in Eltersdorf, near Erlangen in 1527. A deacon at Saint Sebaldus in Nuremberg from early 1528, he took part in the religious colloquy at Bern (January 1528). From 1526 onward, he defended Lutheran positions against the old church—as well as Zwinglians, Anabaptists, and others—in his publications. The first of these, on the Eucharist, he dedicated to Georg Vogler, secretary to the margrave of Ansbach. There, the Reformation was initiated upon the succession of George of Brandenburg-Ansbach, and Althamer was appointed pastor in Ansbach (May 1528). When Margrave George decreed a visitation in his territory based on the church order for Brandenburg and Nuremberg (1528/29), it was largely conducted by Althamer and his colleague Johann Rurer. Because the church order had not yet been published, he wrote an instruction—*Catechismus: Das ist vnterricht zum Christlichen Glauben . . .*—printed in Nuremberg in 1528 by Friedrich Peypus (the first work of this kind expressly called a catechism). It was meant for pastors, deacons, catechists, and fathers in the principality of Margrave George. Later it was replaced by Martin Luther's catechisms. In 1537 Althamer was called to Neumarkt by Margrave John of Brandenburg-Küstrin. As a visitor he helped to introduce the Reformation in that Hohenzollern territory in northern Germany.

BIBLIOGRAPHY

Primary Source

Cohrs, Ferdinand, ed. *Die evangelischen Katechismusversuche vor Luthers Enchiridion.* Vol. 3, *Die evangelischen Katechismusversuche aus den Jahren 1528–1529.* Monumenta Germaniae Paedagogica 22.3. Berlin, 1901.

Secondary Sources

Fraas, Hans-Jürgen. "Katechismus." In *Theologische Realenzyklopädie,* vol. 17, pp.711–722. Berlin and New York, 1988.
Kolde, Th. *Andreas Althamer, der Humanist und Reformator in Brandenburg-Ansbach.* Erlangen, 1895; reprint, Nieuwkoop, 1967. A facsimile of the original title page has been added as the frontispiece to the reprinted text of the catechism.
Pfeiffer, Gerhard. "Brandenburg-Ansbach/Bayreuth." In *Theologische Realenzyklopädie,* vol. 7, pp. 131–136. Berlin and New York, 1981.
Westermayer, Hermann. *Die Brandenburgisch-Nürnbergische Kirchenvisitation und Kirchenordnung, 1528–1533.* Erlangen, 1894.

IRMGARD HÖß
Translated from German by Anna-D. Henning

Tuesday Oct 03 03:47 PM

ALUMBRADOS. The term *alumbrados* is today a linguistic stereotype whose philological origin is certain: from Latin *illuminati, illuminatio, illuminare.* Its semantic root signifies spiritual or interior illumination, which is attributed to the Holy Spirit in the New Testament. In its Spanish form—*alumbrados*—it has a negative and even malicious connotation: it was coined at the dawn of the sixteenth century among spiritual groups who considered themselves "illuminated by the Holy Spirit," hence privileged or superior to other Christians; the common people appropriated the term to give it a pejorative meaning of fantasists, hypocrites, or false mystics. The intensity of religious sentiment, typical of what is considered the apex of mysticism, explains the appearance of the phenomenon of the *alumbrados* as the converse of the genuine mystics: they appear or have appeared in all the locales of religious enthusiasm, but in religious historiography the term is applied especially to Spaniards.

Five historical Spanish groups of *Alumbrados* have been distinguished or classified: (1) those of Toledo, in the first decades of the sixteenth century; (2) those of Estremadura, circa 1575; (3) those of upper Andalusia, at the end of the sixteenth century; (4) those of Latin America (viceroyalties of Mexico and Peru), in the late sixteenth century and early seventeenth century; and (5) those of Seville, 1520–1530. Because of the many different types of *Alumbrados* and, at times, their ambiguity, there is no doctrinal core or common denominator of content or doctrine, beyond religiosity. Those of Toledo offer, with their scant numbers, a higher level of doctrine; their fundamental dogma was "the love of God makes man God." From this principle, held unanimously and without qualifications, they inferred the ethical principle that the *Alumbrado,* being deified, does not sin, do what he might: he is impeccable. Those of Estremadura insisted on this impeccability; and in a passionate region, short of men because of the outflow of young men to America, it gave to the groups of *Alumbrados* a marked erotic tinge. Among those of upper Andalusia, in provincial centers like Baeza, Ubeda, and Jaén, the dogma of deification was as prominent as the erotic aspects. Hispanic-American illuminism (*Alumbradismo*) had, in its two great geographical spheres, different shadings: apocalyptic and millenarian in Mexico, anxious for political-religious liberation in Peru. Finally, Sevillian illuminism, which recruited the greatest number of adherents, was characterized by its folkloric manifestations, including popular superstition.

From a social perspective, it is customary to emphasize the similarity of the *Alumbrados* with the Protestant reformers and with the Erasmian spiritualists, in order to put into relief their eagerness to return to a noninstitutionalized spirituality. It is also customary to regard them socially as marginal groups, as groups of protest and social denunciation, and (more insistently) as New Christians (*Conversos*) of Sephardic or Spanish Judaic origin. The analysis of the phenomenon of the *Alumbrados* does not allow this sort of generalization: if in upper Andalusia the New Christians were many, in America they were extremely rare. One commonality, however, was the high number of *beatas* (women, generally single, who professed a distinctive spiritual life and wore distinguishing habits without belonging to a religious order approved by the church), obedient and following various leaders, usually priests but occasionally laymen. These priest-leaders generally achieved a relatively high level of learning, given their curriculum of studies; most *beatas*, however, were illiterate. The relationship of the *Alumbrados* with other currents of reform—Erasmian spirituality, Lutheranism, Crypto-Judaism, and so on—remains ambiguous; similarities did not originate from doctrinal exchange, but rather from a common religious background and from reaction to the Inquisition, which measured all religious deviations by the yardstick of orthodoxy.

The Inquisition tried to extirpate, in their respective periods, the five groups of *Alumbrados*. Thanks to the documentation conserved in archives about the trials of *Alumbrados*, the phenomenon of illuminism can be known and outlined. Of the several hundred trials of *Alumbrados*, the penalties or punishments imposed by the Inquisition on those convicted of this crime of "heretical depravity" were generally those of exile and abjuration: there were no death sentences (called "relaxation to the secular arm"). Their code of doctrine and practices can be found in the edicts of faith—the regular, publicly posted or announced summons to denunciation and self-denunciation in accordance with a list of current heresies—which extract, based on the indictments or trials, the dogmatic and moral ideology that the *Alumbrados* taught and practiced.

[*See also* New Christians.]

BIBLIOGRAPHY

Dominguez Ortiz, Antonio. *Los judeo-conversos en España y América.* Madrid, 1988.

Huerga, Alvaro. *Historia de los Alumbrados, 1572–1630.* 5 vols. Madrid, 1978–1992.

Llorca, B. *Die Spanische Inquisition und die Alumbrados, 1508–1667.* Berlin, 1934.

Marquez, Antonio. *Los Alumbrados: Orígenes y filosofía, 1525–1559.* 2d corr. ed. Madrid, 1980.

Peers, E. Allison. *Studies of the Spanish Mystics.* 3 vols. London, 1927–1940.

ALVARO HUERGA

ÁLVAREZ DE TOLEDO, Fernando (1507–1582), third duke of Alba (also Alva), Spanish general and statesman. Fernando Álvarez de Toledo was born on his family's estate at Piedrahita on 29 October 1507. Three years later his father was killed in a skirmish with the Muslims on the island of Jerba. The child was given a military upbringing by his grandfather, Fadrique, second duke of Alba, whose title he inherited in 1531. At sixteen he had fought at Fuenterrabía and thereafter served the Emperor, Charles V, in the campaigns of Vienna, Tunis, Provence, and Algiers. By the outbreak of the Schmalkald War in 1546, Alba had emerged as the emperor's chief military adviser and was largely responsible for the victory at Mühlberg in the following year.

In 1548 Alba was named majordomo to Prince Philip, a position that he retained after the latter's accession to the Spanish throne as Philip II. This enabled him to become patron of an aristocratic faction that included not only Alba's many relatives and their retainers but also several of the more important royal secretaries. His chief political rival was the royal chamberlain, Ruy Gómez de Silva, a man associated with the Mendoza family and with the secretarial "school" founded by Cardinal Espinosa.

Alba accompanied Philip to England in 1554, served briefly as viceroy of Milan and then of Naples, and in 1556–1557 commanded the royal forces in their successful war against Pope Paul IV and Henri, duke of Guise. He played a major role in the negotiations at Cateau-Cambrésis in 1559 and returned to Spain in 1560 as a member of the council of state who claimed special expertise on the affairs of France and England.

Tall, saturnine, and deeply religious, Alba was known for his sharp tongue and limitless arrogance. Philip found him trying but useful, not only in military and diplomatic affairs but also in reviewing ecclesiastical appointments. The duke's unbending orthodoxy and long association with the policies of the late emperor made him the king's conscience in the years leading up to the Revolt of the Netherlands. His innate regalism and a passionate hatred of heretics caused him to oppose all compromise with the Netherlanders, and when rioting and iconoclasm broke out in 1566, he was the natural choice to suppress what the king perceived as rebellion.

The plan was that Alba would go to the Netherlands and purge the country of heretics and rebels. The king would then come in person, repudiate his captain-general's excesses, and issue a general pardon. The scheme was supported by Alba's enemies, who until now had favored a policy of reconciliation. They wanted Alba away from court so that they could discredit him and undermine his influence.

In 1567 the duke marched to the Low Countries with an army of Spanish veterans. He immediately arranged the execution of Lamoraal, count of Egmont, and Filips van Montmorency, count of Hoorne, on charges of treason and established the Council of Troubles, a political court designed to root out enemies of the crown. At this point William of Orange assumed leadership of the revolt and invaded the Netherlands with a force composed largely of German mercenaries. Alba defeated him with ease and by the end of 1568 had achieved pacification of all seventeen provinces. The king, however, did not come. The death of his only heir, Don Carlos, followed by a revolt of the Moriscos in southern Spain, made it impossible for Philip to leave Spain, and Alba was left to reap the consequences of his own repressive policies.

In the next four years the duke installed fourteen new bishops whose appointments had been blocked since 1560 and reformed the legal code, but the alien and unsympathetic character of his regime aroused resentment. When he tried to impose perpetual taxation in the form of the Tenth Penny, a generalized revolt broke out in 1572. In trying to suppress it, Alba began a deliberate policy of terror, which encouraged bitter resistance at Haarlem and Alkmaar, and the king, urged on by Ruy Gómez, recalled him. Though Ruy Gómez died in the following year, Alba's position at court was now seriously weakened, and the king actually imprisoned him for a time in the royal castle at Uceda. In 1580 he was recalled to lead the royal armies in the annexation of Portugal, where he died in 1582.

Alba was generally acknowledged as the greatest soldier of his day, and his concept of warfare was preserved by an entire school of military writers who had served under him. He was also an able, if unpopular, diplomat, but his political legacy in the Netherlands, the most important command of his career, was entirely negative. His harsh policies provoked unified opposition to Spanish rule and may be said to have precipitated the movement toward Dutch independence.

BIBLIOGRAPHY

Alba Jacobo Stuart Fitz-James y Falco, duque de, ed. *Epistolario.* 3 vols. Madrid, 1952.

Maltby, William S. *Alba: A Biography of Fernando Alvarez de Toledo, Third Duke of Alba.* Berkeley, 1983.

WILLIAM S. MALTBY

ALVELDT, Augustin (c.1480–1535), German Franciscan and early anti-Luther polemicist. Almost nothing is known of Alveldt's early life and education aside from his birthplace in the Hannovarian town of Alveldt and his claim to have been enthralled by holy scripture from childhood. In 1520, when he was an observant Franciscan lecturing at his order's monastery in Leipzig, Bishop Adolf von Anhalt asked him to respond to Martin Luther's attacks against the papacy. Alveldt had already attracted attention by charging Luther with seven counts of heresy in a public lecture the previous year, providing Luther the first of many occasions to label him "that ass."

Alveldt never agreed with those who believed that good could come from Luther's uncompromising hostility, and he counts as the most prolific and outspoken of the reformer's early opponents. *Super apostolica sede . . .* (Leipzig, 1520), Alveldt's carefully reasoned treatise defending the primacy of the pope, signaled the opening round of a polemical battle between Alveldt and the reformers. Luther deemed the work unworthy of his personal attention and assigned Johannes Lonicer to draft a response, *Contra Romanistam fratrem Augustiniu . . .* (Wittenberg, 1520), which was a vicious personal attack designed to refute Alveldt's arguments by ridiculing his pretensions to theological expertise.

In his rebuttal, *Malagma optimum . . .* (Leipzig, 1520), Alveldt listed alphabetically the offending names he had been called, designating them "Luther's Evangel." He went on to attack Luther's recently issued *An den christlichen Adel deutscher Nation* (Address to the Christian Nobility of the German Nation) for defaming the holy church and leading pious Christians into error. At the same time, Alveldt published in German a defense of the papacy and a tract against Communion in both kinds. Luther countered with his *Von dem Papsttum zu Rom wider den hochberühmten Romanisten zu Leipzig,* followed by his great 1520 treatise *De captivitate Babylonica ecclesiae praeludium* (A Prelude Concerning the Babylonian Captivity of the Church).

Alveldt wrote in 1520 no fewer than nine polemical tracts, including a justification of the seven sacraments and a defense of monastic life. His readers were urged to shun Luther as a "son of perdition" and his movement as the ultimate heresy and a "church of the wicked."

In 1529 Alveldt was named provincial head of his order and turned his attention to preserving the Franciscan community as the Reformation swept over Germany. His last published work, *Ein Sermon vom Christlichen begräbnis* (Sermon on Christian Burial), appeared in 1530.

BIBLIOGRAPHY

Hammann, Konrad. "Ecclesia spiritualis: Luthers Kirchenverständnis in den Kontroversen mit Augustin von Alveldt und Ambrosius Catharinus." *Theologische Literaturzeitung* 116 (1991), 678–680.

Hesse, Gerold. "Augustin v. Alfeld, Verteidiger des Apostolischen Stuhles." *Franziskanische Studien* 17 (1930), 160–178.

Lau, F. "Alvelt, Augustinus von." In *Die Religion in Geschichte und Gegenwart*, vol. 1, p. 302. Tübingen, 1962.

Lehmann, Paul. "Alveldt." In *Neue Deutsche Biographie*, vol. 1, pp. 230–231. Berlin, 1953.

Lemmens, Leonhard. *Pater Augustin von Alfeld*. Freiburg, 1899. A detailed scholarly account of Alfeld's confrontation with the Lutheran Reformation.

———. "Alveldt, Augustin." In *Lexicon für Theologie und Kirche*, vol. 1, p. 329, Freiburg, 1930.

Schottenloher, Karl, ed. *Bibliographie zur deutschen Geschichte im Zeitalter der Glaubensspaltung*. Stuttgart, 1957. See vol. 1, p. 13.

Smolinsky, H. "Augustin von Alveldt (d. 1535)." In *Katholische Theologen der Reformationszeit*, edited by E. Iserloh, vol. 1, pp. 47–55. Münster, 1984.

KARIN BRINKMANN BROWN

AMANDI, Johannes (Lat., Amandus; d. 1530), Protestant preacher and reformer in Goslar. Little is known of Amandi's early life. He was most likely born in Westphalia and first appears in the records as a priest and indulgence preacher around 1520. He was an early and enthusiastic follower of Luther, and in 1523, on Luther's recommendation, was appointed the first evangelical preacher in Königsberg in East Prussia.

Amandi was typical of many popular preachers of the early Reformation. In his sermons he pressed for more rapid and more thorough establishment of an evangelical church order. Amandi apparently had strong supporters among the people of Königsberg, and his criticism of the local authorities and encouragement of an outburst of iconoclasm in the spring of 1524 led to his expulsion from the city. His reputation as a demagogue and religious fanatic followed him to Danzig, Stolp, and Stettin, where he was arrested (and later released) by the local authorities.

In 1526 Amandi defended his evangelical credentials in Wittenberg and, having received Luther's endorsement, was appointed pastor and superintendent in Goslar, a free imperial city in lower Saxony. Here, too, Amandi preached to the common people of the town, arousing fears of urban unrest in the city council. Furthermore, the authorities in Goslar, as in many other imperial cities, struggled to balance the demands of much of the population for reforms and the need to maintain good relations with the Catholic emperor. Goslar, too, had reason to fear that religious conflict and political insecurity could aid the territorial ambitions of neighboring princes, in this case the duke Heinrich of Brunswick. Between 1526 and 1530, the council of Goslar pursued a cautious religious policy, abolishing the Mass only in 1528 and resisting popular demands to abolish the monasteries until the 1530s.

Amandi preached and agitated for more rapid religious change in Goslar. The friction in Goslar, especially in 1528–1529, took on aspects of a social conflict, as economic difficulties added to the tension. As in many north German cities, the possibility of political upheaval was real. Conflicts were personal as well as political; Amandi and his fellow preachers criticized the personal lives of some of the local elite, while the council openly boycotted his sermons. Amandi had to defend himself against accusations of secretly favoring Zwinglian theological positions, especially on the Eucharist, as well as the usual charges that he encouraged public disorder. Amandi died in 1530, before the conflicts in Goslar could be resolved.

BIBLIOGRAPHY

Hölscher, L. *Die Geschichte der Reformation in Goslar*. Hannover, 1902. Older survey of the Reformation in Goslar with an emphasis on religious developments.

Stupperich, Robert. *Reformatorenlexikon*. Gütersloh, 1984. See pp. 24–25.

MARC R. FORSTER

AMBOISE, CONSPIRACY OF. The Conspiracy of Amboise erupted in March 1560 from circumstances of multiple crisis following the accidental death of Henry II in July 1559, and had far-reaching consequences. Its total failure proved disastrous for the Reformation in France because the fate of the burgeoning churches depended on the outcome of the power struggle unleashed by Henry's death. Frequent bloody affrays, involving the nobility, and violent religious conflict had already reached crisis proportions, coinciding with other causes of disaffection. Persecution was extreme, heresy being a capital crime, and Henry II had proclaimed a war of extermination. He was strongly supported by Charles, cardinal of Lorraine—one of three cardinal inquisitors—and his brother François, duke of Guise. From Geneva Calvin tried to intervene, insisting that Protestants were neither heretics nor rebels. He sought the intercession of German princes and of Antoine of Navarre, first prince of the blood. As the turmoil mounted, Calvin's exhortations to prayer and patience provoked a caustic demand for some solution less sublime, which gradually elicited Calvin's unhelpful philosophy of resistance.

When Henry II died, the hated Guise persecutors seized control of the government, defying Navarre's prescriptive right to direct the council. Those who desired a change of government advanced the legitimacy of supporting him in action to remove the Guises. Legitimate resistance required princely sanction; thus, when Navarre deftly evaded leadership, pastors and malcontents turned to his brother Louis Condé. A potential beneficiary, Condé is habitually described as the *chef muet* of the conspiracy. While this charge is unproved, it was inevitable that the Guises would condemn him.

The precise origins of the Conspiracy of Amboise are obscure; plots and plotting were endemic. The conspiracy matured through different stages and embraced disparate elements. Ultimately the churches were not involved, because Calvin withheld consent. The provincial gentry took over, led by a Périgordin, Jean du Barry, seigneur of La Renaudie, an enemy of the Guises. After traveling extensively, La Renaudie convened an assembly at Nantes in February 1560. A council was elected that arranged for small provincial contingents to support their leader. They envisaged a bloodless coup to remove the Guises, present a petition, and summon an estates-general. But practical problems turned the movement into a conspiracy for tumultuous petitioning, and the search for legitimacy undermined a potentially powerful rebellion. All theorizing was, however, specious, since the detested Guise government was not technically illegal. The plot was betrayed and preempted as small groups assembled around Amboise, where the court was in residence. La Renaudie perished and the many captives received neither justice nor mercy.

Pamphlet warfare ensued in which the Protestants denied having assumed arms for religion—which was forbidden—and the restraint of the churches probably went unrecognized. The once purely religious cause was both tainted and beyond control; henceforth Protestantism was equated with sedition. Thus religion and politics had become inextricably entangled and the springs of civil war were released. The simmering Guise-Bourbon conflict flared; both Guise and Condé were soon to be murdered and assassination became an instrument of policy.

[See also Bourbon, House of; Calvin, John; Condé, Louis I; Francis II of France; Lorraine-Guise, House of; and Wars of Religion.]

BIBLIOGRAPHY

Naef, Henri. La Conjuration d'Amboise et Genève. New York, 1967.
Sutherland, N. M. The Huguenot Struggle for Recognition. New Haven and London, 1980. See chapter 3, "Calvinism and the Conspiracy of Amboise, March 1560."

N. M. SUTHERLAND

AMERBACH, Bonifacius

AMERBACH, Bonifacius (Eng., Boniface; 1495–1562), Swiss jurist and humanist. The third son of Johannes Amerbach, Bonifacius obtained his master of arts degree at the University of Basel in 1513. He studied law in Freiburg under Ulrich Zasius and in Avignon under Andrea Alciato. Appointed to a professorship of civil law at Basel in 1524, he returned to Avignon to receive a doctorate in that field in 1525. In 1527 he married Martha Fuchs; the couple had five children. In 1535 he became a syndic of Basel's council. Amerbach became an heir and executor of Desiderius Erasmus's estates upon the latter's death in 1536. He served as rector of the University of Basel five times.

In his approach to the law, Amerbach rejected the extreme position of some humanists who condemned medieval commentators and who held that an understanding of a text was gained through grammatical and philological analysis. Amerbach maintained that understanding could not be gained by skipping over centuries of interpretation. Unbothered by the diversity of opinion among medieval legal commentators, Amerbach argued that dialogue between opinions furthered the search for truth.

Initially enthusiastic about Martin Luther, Amerbach had doubts about the theology and practices of the reformers as the 1520s progressed. In the controversy between Luther and Erasmus concerning the freedom of the will, he supported Erasmus. After Basel's adoption of the Reformation (1529), Amerbach was faced with the prospect of banishment in 1531 for failure to conform. In a defense before the city council, he held to the notion of real presence and rejected Johannes Oecolampadius's interpretation of the Lord's Supper. Action against him was delayed several times, and by 1534 Amerbach, asserting a doctrine of a real spiritual presence, was able to reconcile his beliefs with those of the Basel reformation and again received the Sacrament.

Amerbach's intellectual interests were wide. His correspondence with his many friends provides a unique record of the intellectual history of his time.

BIBLIOGRAPHY

Gilmore, Myron P. "Boniface Amerbach" In Humanists and Jurists: Six Studies in the Renaissance, pp. 146–177. Cambridge, Mass., 1963. The best source in English on the life of Amerbach; describes well the religious and academic conflicts in which he was involved.
Hartmann, Alfred. "Amerbach, Bonifacius." In Neue Deutsche Biographie, vol. 1. Berlin, 1953. A short biography giving the basic facts of Amerbach's life and some bibliography.
Hartmann, Alfred, and Beat Rudolf Jenny, eds. Die Amerbachkorrespondenz. 10 vols. Basel, 1942–1991. A critical comprehensive collection of the correspondence of the Amerbach family. Most of the collection is devoted to Bonifacius Amerbach. Each volume contains a general introduction describing the years in Amerbach's life that the volume covers.

MARY JANE HAEMIG

AMERBACH, Johannes

AMERBACH, Johannes (1443?–1513), Swiss printer of patristic and humanist texts. He earned his master of arts degree in Paris in 1462, where he studied with Johannes Heynlin de Lapide. After traveling to Rome and Venice, he returned to Basel and began printing there in 1478. Married to Barbara Ortenberg in 1483, he had five children, including Bonifacius (1495–1562). In the early years he worked with Jakob von Pforzheim, but after 1500 he printed in collaboration with Johannes Petri and Johann Froben. He had business connections with the Nuremberg printer Koberger and the Strasbourg printer Rusch. Amerbach printed editions of the Vulgate and canon law, as well as texts by various church fathers and classical writers. His first major work was a Latin vocabulary by Johannes Reuchlin (1478). He also published works by, among others, Cato (1489), Cassianus (1485), Cassiodorus (1491), Petrach (1496), and Anselm (1497). He finished a three-volume edition of Ambrose in 1492 and completed an eleven-volume collection of Augustine in 1506 in collaboration with Petri and Froben. He organized an edition of Jerome that was published after his death by Froben.

Amerbach was the most learned printer of Basel in his time. Influenced by humanists who sought to return to the sources, he strove to make accurate texts of the Bible and of the church fathers easily available. His editions encourage consideration of source and text-critical problems. Those of the Bible show evidence of reference to the Greek and Hebrew texts; they also contain a list of parallel verses in the margin. Bringing together widely scattered manuscripts of the church fathers, Amerbach emphasized the careful comparison, reproduction, and editing of texts. His editions of the church fathers contain marginal notes on the origin of quotations. Amerbach was aided in his work by de Lapide and other Basel humanists. His editions of the Bible and of texts by the church fathers were widely influential and used by, among others, Martin Luther.

BIBLIOGRAPHY

Benzing, Josef. *Die Buchdrucker des 16. und 17. Jahrhunderts im Deutschen Sprachgebiet.* 2d ed. Wiesbaden, 1982. Little information but includes a bibliography citing several lesser-known sources.

Catalogue of Books Printed in the XVth Century Now in the British Museum. Pt. 3, *Germany: Leipzig-Pforzheim, German-Speaking Switzerland and Austria-Hungary.* Reprint, London, 1963. On pp. 742–759 this catalog provides a complete description of seventy books printed by Amerbach and owned by the British Museum. Additional works are listed under Johann Froben.

Hartmann, Alfred, ed. *Die Amerbachkorrespondenz.* Basel, 1942. Vol. 1 of the collected correspondence of the Amerbach family contains letters from the time of Johannes Amerbach. Also provides a general introduction to the collection as well as a biography of Johannes Amerbach.

Junghans, Helmar. *Der junge Luther und die Humanisten.* Göttingen and Weimar, 1985. Pages 109–114 in particular discuss Amerbach's contributions in publishing the church fathers and the influence of these editions on Luther.

Voullième, E. *Die deutschen Drucker des fünfzehnten Jahrhunderts.* Berlin, 1922. Pages 25–26 give a short biography of Amerbach and briefly discuss the works he printed.

MARY JANE HAEMIG

AMERICA. For the conquerors America meant gold for themselves, subjects for the Crown, and souls for God, most fundamentally the conversion and labor of its peoples. Initially justifying their rule over America by papal bulls granting dominion in order to Christianize the natives, sixteenth-century Spanish leaders often saw their role in America as a divinely authorized mission. The importance of this commitment would be tested early in the century.

On an Advent Sunday morning in 1511 Fray Antonio Montesinos castigated the leading citizens of Hispaniola (and their Franciscan allies) for their neglect of missionizing. Declaiming "are these [Indians] not also men?" he ignited a political controversy that would rage with varying degrees of intensity in Spain for the next four decades. Insisting upon the Indians' "humanity," Montesinos and his fellow Dominicans were demanding that the Spanish Crown stand by its formal political commitments to evangelization—because the Indians were human, and hence capable of Christianity. Since converting natives justified Spanish sovereignty in the Americas, conversion was a matter neither of belief nor of private initiative (as in the English colonies) but of public (imperial) policy.

In testing the strength of the Crown's commitment to evangelization, Montesinos and his fellow Dominican Bartolomé de Las Casas accused their opponents of treating the natives as "animals," relying upon a fundamentally Christian distinction. Beginning with Augustine, Christianity had affirmed possession of "reason" as a defining characteristic of humanity. "Reason," which "humans" were classified as having and animals as lacking, demarcated an absolute difference between humans and animals. To the Dominican Thomas Aquinas everyone who was baptized or who could potentially be baptized was "human," that is, having a "rational soul," while all those not capable of being Christians were "brute animals." The category "animal" marked a difference that could not be overcome; "animals" could not become "humans." Montesinos insinuated that Spanish settlers who treated or labeled the Indians as "animals" were undermining their status as potential Christians who could be legitimately brought under authority of the Spanish Crown. Phrasing the issue in those terms proved effective, since shortly thereafter the Crown revised its guidelines for treatment of the Indians and instituted a new political ritual (the Requirement) by which authority over the New World was to be established.

Nearly a quarter of a century later, the identical issue resurfaced as rumors of a highly placed friar's statement that the natives resembled animals once again appeared to threaten or minimize the role of clergy in the conquest of America. To counter any threat that the Spanish Crown might alter its political justification for rule, the Dominicans sought support from the pontiff. Bernardino Minaya was sent to obtain a papal declaration of the natives' "humanity." In 1537 Pope Paul III responded by issuing *Sublimus deus*, establishing the official opinion of the Catholic church that "the Indians are truly men and that they are . . . capable of understanding the Catholic faith."

The terms of the debate were ecclesiastical. The principal proponents of the "rationality" of the Indians were clerics. The instigators of the controversy—Montesinos and Las Casas—were priests, as were nearly all the respondents—Bernardino Minaya, Domingo de Betanzos, and Pope Paul

III. Furthermore, most were Dominicans familiar with Thomas's definition of humanity as "potential for Christianity." Even the pope's resolution of the issue of the natives' humanity related it to natives' potential for evangelization. While securing the pope's support had pleased the friars of the New World, it caused the Spanish Crown to react by forbidding any further papal bulls to be sent to the New World without formal royal authorization.

Shortly after this incident, Francisco de Vitoria declared that the papal bull was an invalid foundation of Spanish claims to the New World; instead he suggested that the guiding principle of Hispanic expansion overseas should be "go forth and teach." Thus the closing lines of *Matthew* (28:19–20) eventually became the opening for the seventeenth-century Hispanic colonial legal code *Recopilación de leyes de las Indias*. Like the papal bull, it was a religious justification for political colonization.

In 1542 the "New Laws" transformed the political status of all natives of the New World. Existing native political systems were subordinated to Spanish ones, as all natives were incorporated as subjects and vassals of the Crown. Like all Spanish subjects, Indians owed political and religious obedience to the Spanish Crown. This move strengthened the role of clerics in the New World and marked an important victory for those who argued for the Indians' humanity. If the Indians were "like brute animals" (in the language of Thomas), then they were incapable of becoming Christians and also unable to be obedient subjects and vassals of the Crown of Castile. Since the labels "animal" and "human" stood for opposing poles in a debate over the potential for Christianity, it is not surprising that no other European powers would debate the issue. No other powers legitimated their rule over America chiefly by virtue of the authority to convert.

But it would be a mistake to confuse this debate with humanitarianism. Indigenous peoples of the Spanish New World did not have the right to choose to become vassals or to remain independent. Nor did they have the right to reject or resist the imposition of Spanish religious beliefs. Spanish colonization incorporated natives as "subjects and as vassals" of the Crown by unilaterally eliminating both their political independence and their religious liberty. While critical of their fellow Spaniards who tended to treat indigenous peoples as commodities, the ecclesiastical partisans of native "humanity" demanded the Indians' political and religious submission. Furthermore, those asserting the Indian's humanity were not natives themselves, but Spaniards who claimed the privilege of speaking for the natives. And their political relationship with those for whom they claimed to speak was that of ruler to subject.

In America, Spain and England pursued distinctly different economic and political objectives. When the English conquered, they aimed to conquer space; and when they took over a territory, they sought to possess the land, not the people. They measured their political progress across America by maps, successively erasing indigenous presence, reinventing America as a blank space, a "virgin" land. When Spaniards conquered, they enacted authority over persons rather than space, constituting dominion chiefly over bodies and minds of natives, as subjects to colonize, labor to exploit, and pagans to convert. The cultural priorities of colonization differed between the two European societies: the conquest of land and the conquest of peoples.

[*See also* Discoveries in the New World.]

BIBLIOGRAPHY

Friede, Juan, and Benjamin Keen, eds. *Bartolomé de Las Casas in History: Toward an Understanding of the Man and His Work*. De Kalb, Ill., 1971.

Hanke, Lewis. *Aristotle and the American Indian: A Study in Race Prejudice in the Modern World*. London, 1959.

Pagden, Anthony. *The Fall of Natural Man: The American Indian and the Origins of Comparative Ethnology*. 2d ed. Cambridge, 1986.

Seed, Patricia. "Taking Possession and Reading Texts: Establishing the Authority of Overseas Empires." *William and Mary Quarterly* 49.2 (1992), 183–209.

———. " 'Are These Not Also Men?': The Indian's Humanity and Capacity for Spanish Civilization." *Journal of Latin American Studies* 25 (1993), 629–652.

PATRICIA SEED

AMSDORF, Nikolaus von (1483–1565), German Lutheran churchman and bishop of Naumburg-Zeitz. Grandson and son of noblemen who had served at th electoral Saxon court and nephew of Johannes von Staupitz, Amsdorf was born at Torgau on 3 December 1483 and studied at Leipzig and Wittenberg before becoming an instructor at Wittenberg. Scotist influences in his training may have helped shape his theology. One of Luther's first "converts" (1516) and closest friends, he accompanied Luther to the Leipzig Debate (1519) and to the Diet of Worms (1521). With his friend Philipp Melanchthon he helped lead Luther's movement while Luther was at the Wartburg. At this time Amsdorf developed deep-seated eschatological convictions regarding the papacy as Antichrist and looked for the end of the world to come soon. He counseled the propriety of armed resistance by inferior magistrates against the emperor in defense of evangelical belief while others were rejecting any theory justifying such resistance (1523).

At Luther's suggestion Amsdorf became pastor in Magdeburg in 1524, where he led the introduction of the Reformation and battled not only the Roman Catholic establishment but also the sacramentarian physician Wolf Cyclop, Zwinglian sympathizers Heinrich Knigge and Johann Grawert, and Anabaptist Melchior Hoffmann. From Magdeburg he assisted in the reformations of Goslar and

Einbeck (composing church orders for both), as well as of Hannover, ducal Saxony, and other places, as he supported the ecclesiastical and political program of Elector John Frederick of Saxony. In 1542 the elector imposed Amsdorf upon the episcopal canons of the bishopric of Naumburg-Zeitz as their new bishop. Frustrated by political aides appointed by the elector, opposition from the canons and nobility, and independent Lutheran pastors in Naumburg, Amsdorf accomplished little in his four years as bishop. He went into exile when imperial forces triumphed over the Schmalkald League in the Schmalkald War of 1547.

In the troubled period created by the Schmalkald War, Amsdorf emerged as a radical interpreter of Luther's legacy. He had disagreed with his friend Melanchthon over a series of issues in the 1530s and 1540s—over the role of good works in salvation (in the Cordatus Affair, 1536), the role of the will in conversion, the relationship of the Lutheran churches to Rome (at the Colloquy of Regensburg, 1541), and the real presence of Christ's body and blood in the Lord's Supper (in his critiques of the Wittenberg Concord and of the reform of Archbishop Hermann von Wied in Cologne). These largely private disagreements foreshadowed the disputes that engulfed the Lutheran churches in the wake of the Schmalkald War. Amsdorf wrote a stinging critique of the Augsburg Interim (1548). He publicly criticized both the failure of Melanchthon and his colleagues to oppose it strongly and their role in composing the Leipzig Interim. Beginning in 1550, his attacks on the principle of concession in adiaphora in the Leipzig Interim reflected the principle "when confession of the faith is necessary, there are no adiaphora."

Amsdorf returned to Magdeburg after his exile from Zeitz (1548) and there helped initiate the Gnesio-Lutheran movement. Although not its author, Amsdorf supported and probably influenced the Magdeburg Confession of 1550, with its classic expression of Lutheran resistance theory. Returning to the lands of Elector John Frederick, Amsdorf moved to Eisenach in 1552 and in retirement served as "general inspector and ecclesiastical counselor" for the elector's sons. He also assisted in launching the Jena edition of Luther's works.

He criticized his former Magdeburg colleague Georg Major, then professor at the University of Wittenberg, for defending the Leipzig Interim's proposition that "good works are necessary for salvation," a concept that both men had opposed while battling Roman Catholics twenty years earlier. Amsdorf embraced Luther's proposition that "good works are harmful to salvation" (when relied upon for salvation) in opposing Major. He also criticized Justus Menius, superintendent in ducal Saxon Gotha, for defending Major. At a synod in Eisenach in 1556 Amsdorf rejected the concept that "in the doctrine of the law good works are theoretically necessary for salvation," perhaps because it seemed impractically scholastic to him or because, in Scotist fashion,

he believed that, as the grace of God established human life itself apart from human performance, good works could in no way contribute to salvation.

Amsdorf also rejected the synergism of Johann Pfeffinger and Viktorin Strigel without developing his earlier doctrine of double predestination in his published tracts against them. He opposed government interference in ecclesiastical affairs, objecting to the establishment of a ducal Saxon consistory in 1561. Although not an original thinker, his polemic and pastoral spirit helped launch and establish the Gnesio-Lutheran movement and its radical interpretation of Luther's legacy.

BIBLIOGRAPHY

Brunner, Peter. *Nikolaus von Amsdorf als Bischof von Naumburg.* Gütersloh, 1961. Critical examination of Amsdorf's performance as bishop of Naumburg-Zeitz.

Kolb, Robert. *Nikolaus von Amsdorf (1483–1565): Popular Polemics in the Preservation of Luther's Legacy.* Nieuwkoop, 1978. Biographical overview, concentrating on Amsdorf's participation in the adiaphoristic, Majoristic, and synergistic controversies.

Lerche, Otto. *Amsdorf und Melanchthon: Eine kirchengeschichtliche Studie.* Berlin, 1937. Helpful information but incomplete study.

Nebe, Otto Henning. *Reine Lehre: Zur Theologie des Niklas von Amsdorff.* Göttingen, 1935. Basic introduction to Amsdorf's thought.

Steinmetz, David C. "Nikolaus von Amsdorf, 1483–1565: Set for the Defense of the Gospel." In *Reformers in the Wings,* pp. 100–108. Philadelphia, 1971. Popular summary, based on current scholarship.

Stille, Hans. *Nikolaus von Amsdorf: Sein Leben bis zu seiner Einweihung als Bischof in Naumburg, 1483–1542.* Zeulenroda, Germany, 1937. Competent, well-researched biographical overview.

ROBERT KOLB

AMSTERDAM. Luther's theology reached the Low Countries in the 1520s in the wake of Christian humanism. The ideas of Lutheranism, along with other calls for church reform, gained a sympathetic hearing, especially among the intelligentsia. The early dissidents, who had no well-defined confession and did not yet constitute a genuine movement, gathered in secret conventicles to read and discuss the Bible. These conventicles, which were meant not as a substitute for the Mass but as an adjunct to it, were held in Amsterdam from 1523 onward, and at least five evangelically minded priests and two learned humanists (Jan Sartorius and Wouter Deelen) were involved. Initially the Amsterdam town council, contrary to the wishes of the imperial central government of Charles V, adopted a moderate attitude toward these developments on the grounds that persecutions would interfere with the maintenance of peace and order. There were limits to official tolerance, however, and evangelical priests and humanists, fearing persecution, fled the city one by one.

The conventicles continued, but now were led by lay dissidents. The Catholic Mass and elements of Catholic popular belief came under increasing attack. Also, from about

1525 onward, a growing number of evangelicals, abandoning the doctrine of real presence as expressed by Luther, came to see Holy Communion as a remembrance meal and thus moved toward Sacramentarianism. In Amsterdam, too, skepticism regarding the Mass was already widespread, and traditionalists were shocked at how easily the populace abandoned common religious usage and ridiculed the Eucharist and the clergy. At first most evangelicals remained members of the Catholic church; in consideration of their preferences, however, the city government obtained the services of at least four evangelically minded clergymen between 1530 and 1534.

Unlike the evangelicals, Anabaptists formed genuine (if rudimentary) congregations of their own. They did not share the evangelicals' confusion concerning whether it was allowed to break away from the Catholic church. Salvation for them actually lay in secession from the Catholic church and from the world. It is generally agreed that the Dutch Anabaptist movement began with the arrival of Melchior Hoffman in Emden in 1530. After Hoffman's departure and the expulsion of his followers, a congregation was established in Amsterdam, and the movement spread quickly through the northern parts of the Netherlands. Melchior Hoffman announced the Second Coming, at which time only the born-again would be saved.

The size of the Anabaptist congregation at this date is difficult to determine. Estimates vary from 1,000 to 3,500, including quite a few evangelicals who had been radical Sacramentarians. At any rate the Anabaptists believed in the strength of their own following, so that on 10 May 1535 some forty Anabaptists assaulted the city hall in Amsterdam in hopes of establishing the New Jerusalem. The coup, in which many local Anabaptists refused to join, was easily suppressed. Movements of this sort aggravated persecutions all over Holland; in Amsterdam, too, the city government began to change its moderate attitude. Between February and July 1535 no less than sixty-two Anabaptists were executed in Amsterdam. (The records show that many of those condemned came from the artisan class, which had suffered badly during the economic depression of the 1530s—thus, apparently, becoming more susceptible to the Anabaptists' message of salvation.) Nonetheless, the current ruling faction came under pressure both from the central government and from those in the city who blamed the 1535 uprising on the leniency of the magistrates. A staunchly Catholic ruling faction took over by 1538 and held power for the next forty years. The ruling classes in Holland did not overcome their fear of heresy until about 1550, when persecution slackened. This was partly due to the changing character of the Anabaptist movement itself, which by now was dominated by Menno Simons's pacifism. This new variant spread in Amsterdam during the 1550s.

Meanwhile, the evangelicals had not started counter-churches of their own until the middle of the century; until then the conventicles had so far been felt to suffice. Owing to persecution, the movement lacked central leadership and was of a multiform nature. Persecutions in the Netherlands led to refugee churches springing up abroad, most notably in Emden and London, with Emden in particular the scene of various attempts to give guidance to the oppressed churches at home. It was from here that the "Holland mission" was coordinated in the late 1550s. Jan Arentsz, a lay preacher from Alkmaar who died in 1573, was assigned to serve the congregations in Holland. Perhaps he also visited Amsterdam, where a Reformed congregation had existed from 1558.

There were as yet no fully organized churches during this period. Instead small groups of individuals gathered when possible, and in the face of competition, in Amsterdam and elsewhere, from the better-organized Anabaptist groups. The real centers of reform during the 1550s and 1560s were in the southern Netherlands where the Reformed held their first sermons, in fields outside town walls (hedge preaching), in May 1566, and where the first outbreaks of iconoclasm occurred in August.

On 8 July 1566 a group of prominent citizens of Amsterdam decided to hold field sermons outside the town. Jan Arentsz preached his first sermon right outside the town gate on 31 July, with many well-known citizens of Amsterdam attending. Pieter Gabriel had already been minister in the city before July 1566, and was from that month onward assisted by Arentsz. During these months the situation was tense; following reports arriving from Antwerp and elsewhere, Amsterdam saw its first iconoclastic fury on 23 August, and another late in September. After the second outburst the Reformed acquired the Minorites' church, the Minderbroederskerk. A consistory and a diaconate were installed in October, and on 15 December the Lord's Supper was celebrated for the first time, with one thousand people communing. Contacts between the fledgling congregations in Holland intensified under the guidance of Amsterdam.

Factors other than religion—namely, the grievances of the local economic elite, who chafed at being denied political power by the staunchly Catholic oligarchy—accounted in part for the success of the reformers. By early 1567, however, Spanish groups were en route to the Netherlands; the political leaders of the Revolt of the Netherlands, William of Orange and Hendrik van Brederode, soon took refuge in Germany, followed by many ministers and members of consistories. On 17 April 1567 the Amsterdam city government banned Reformed worship services, and here too a large exodus began, most of it heading for Emden.

The exiles were not idle. Assemblies at Wesel (1568) and Emden (1571) aimed at producing a binding confession of faith and a church order as a means to close the ranks and build a church organization as soon as political conditions would permit. The tone for these refugee synods was set by the orthodox exiles from the southern Netherlands. Those from Holland, including the Amsterdam ministers, though more moderate, conformed to the will of the majority. But this divergence of views was later to recur with great vehemence.

In the spring and summer of 1572 the struggle against Spain entered a new phase as the so-called *Geuzen* ("beggars") established themselves in the towns of Holland. In these towns the Reformed organization was rapidly rebuilt with the help of exiles who had come home. However, the battle was not won yet, and Amsterdam especially, with the Catholic ruling faction in firm control again since 1567, long continued to side with the Spaniards. Only on 8 February 1578 was a treaty concluded with William of Orange. The city took the side of the rebellious provinces but stipulated that Reformed services were not to be permitted within the town, though the exiles could come home. Frustrated by this limitation, the Reformed undermined the authority of the still-Catholic town council. They were finally able to take control of the city on 26 May 1578. The Catholic rulers and part of the clergy were now expelled.

Under preachers like Johannes Cuchlinus (who was in Amsterdam from 1585 to 1595), Martinus Lydius (1580 to 1585), and Petrus Plancius (1585 to 1622), Amsterdam resolved its prominent role in the Reformed church organization in- and outside Holland. Still, the creation of a Reformed church in Amsterdam itself was not without problems. For one thing, the number of Reformed church members, in Amsterdam as elsewhere, was still very small at the end of the sixteenth century (nowhere exceeding ten percent of the population). This tardy growth was partly due to the continuing struggle against Spain, which made discretion in the matter of religious affiliations advisable, and also to the heavy demands the Reformed church placed on its members. Yet some growth was achieved, probably as a result of the stream of refugees coming from the southern Netherlands. After the conquest of Antwerp (1585) and its return to Catholicism, the stream assumed vast proportions. The Lutheran, Mennonite, and French-speaking Calvinist communities also gained from this influx. The local Reformed church moved toward greater orthodoxy under the guidance of men from the south such as Plancius.

Consequently, the concord achieved in May 1578 between the new town council and the consistory did not last. Even national synods were not able to resolve disputes about the precise meaning of predestination, nor the debate between moderates who understood the church as a broad community open to everyone and the firmly orthodox defenders of a Calvinist church discipline. These controversies often took on political overtones, especially following the conclusion of the Twelve Years' Truce with Spain in 1612, when Holland was divided by the bitter strife between Remonstrants and Contra-Remonstrants. The Amsterdam consistory, led by Plancius and Jacobus Triglandus (minister there from 1610 to 1634), opted for Contra-Remonstrant orthodoxy. Only a small minority, comprising mainly prominent citizens, opted for the moderate Remonstrant line. From about 1611 onward the city government of Amsterdam was of predominantly Contra-Remonstrant sympathies, led by Reijnier Pauw, the adversary of the one-time influential moderate Cornelis Pieterszoon Hooft. Within Holland, the Amsterdam consistory led the struggle against the Remonstrants, who for their part were supported by the provincial government (the States of Holland).

When the States of Holland and their leader, Oldenbarnevelt, were overthrown by a coup d'état led by Maurits van Nassau, the orthodox party was enabled to organize the Synod of Dordrecht (1618–1619), in which Amsterdammers played a prominent role. All the disputed issues were decided in favor of orthodoxy. Denominational strife was thus brought to a temporary conclusion, whereupon the Reformed church began to concentrate on bringing about a Christian society. However, the Reformed church was never to become the church of the majority among the Dutch, as it stuck to its beliefs about the strict discipline required of communicants. In the years after 1618 a firm line was taken with the Remonstrant leaders, some of whom returned to the Reformed church; others broke away definitively, and so in 1621 a Remonstrant congregation was founded in Amsterdam. In Amsterdam, too, the Reformed church was never to obtain the support of the majority of the people. Lutherans, Mennonites, and Remonstrants remained active, and Catholic life went on as well, albeit mainly underground until 1630.

[*See also* Hooft, Cornelis Pieterszoon; Lydius, Martinus; *and* Plancius, Petrus.]

BIBLIOGRAPHY

Briels, J. G. C. A. *De Zuidnederlandse immigratie in Amsterdam en Haarlem, omstreeks 1572–1630*. Utrecht, 1976. Analysis of the impact of the refugees from the southern parts of the Low Countries on the society of Amsterdam.

Deursen, A. Th. van. *Bavianen en slijkgeuzen: Kerk en kerkvolk ten tijde van Maurits en Oldebarnevelt*. Assen, 1974. Well-documented study concerning the development of the Reformed church in Holland and the struggle between Remonstrants and Contra-Remonstrants.

Duke, Alastair. *Reformation and Revolt in the Low Countries*. London, 1990. Collection of essays, most of them published before, on the reception and impact of the Reformation in the Netherlands in the sixteenth century.

Evenhuis, R. B. *Ook dat was Amsterdam: De kerk der hervorming in de gouden eeuw*. Vols. 1 and 2. Amsterdam, 1965 and 1967. Detailed (if not very objective) description of the development of the Reformed church in Amsterdam in the sixteenth and seventeenth centuries.

Grosheide, G. "Verhooren en Vonnissen der wederdoopers, betrokken bij de aanslagen op Amsterdam." *Bijdragen en mededeelingen van het historisch genootschap* 41 (1920), 1–232. Regarding the sentencing of the Anabaptists involved in the attacks on Amsterdam in 1534–1535.

Nierop, Henk van. *Beeldenstorm en burgerlijk verzet in Amsterdam, 1566–1567*. Nijmegen, 1978. A study of the outbreaks of iconoclasm in Amsterdam and the social backgrounds of the participants.

Pettegree, Andrew. *Emden and the Dutch Revolt: Exile and the Development of Reformed Protestantism*. Oxford, 1992.

Roodenburg, Herman Willem. *Onder censuur: De kerkelijke tucht in de gereformeerde gemeente van Amsterdam, 1578–1700.* Hilversum, 1990. Quantitative and qualitative study of the impact of church discipline on the Reformed church of Amsterdam.

Vis, G. N. M. *Jan Arentsz, de mandemaker van Alkmaar, voorman van de Hollandse reformatie.* Alkmaar, 1992. About the role of Jan Arentsz, one of the first ministers of Amsterdam, in the development of Reformed Protestantism in Holland.

Waite, G. K. "The Anabaptist Movement in Amsterdam and the Netherlands, 1531–1535: An Initial Investigation into Its Genesis and Social Dynamics." *Sixteenth Century Journal* 18 (1987), 249–268.

Woltjer, J. J. "Het Conflict tussen Willem Bardes en Hendrick Dirckszoon." *Bijdragen en mededelingen betreffende de geschiedenis der Nederlanden* 86 (1971), 178–199. A study of Amsterdam's Catholic ruling faction and its prominent opponents.

ELIZABETH GEUDEKE
Translated from Dutch by Arend Smilde

ANABAPTISTS were groups organized around the baptism of mature believers and the major representatives of Christian nonconformity in opposition to the Roman church, the established Protestant churches, and temporal governments in the German-speaking Reformation. Even this loose description does not totally encompass the heterogeneity of the Anabaptists: small numbers of French, Italians, English, and Slavs joined Anabaptist groups, and the commitment to baptism was unsteady among the followers of Melchior Hoffman and some of their successor sects, such as Jorites and Batenburgers.

General characteristics among Anabaptists were social radicalism centering on a desire for restoration of the practices of the New Testament church and an expectation of the end of the world, commitment to individual holiness of conduct, and aversion to clerical, scholarly, mercantile, and governmental elites. Even Latin-educated Anabaptists and former clerics joined those who could read only German and those who could not read at all in proclaiming a nonscholarly vernacular biblicism as their authority, using biblicism together with, not in opposition to, beliefs in the direct inspiration of ordinary people by the Holy Spirit in the last days of the world. Hence the cultural gap between educated leadership and uneducated clergy and laity characteristic of the Roman church and the Protestant established churches was narrowed drastically among Anabaptists. But the patriarchal principle of the domination of men over women was sometimes articulated and generally practiced among Anabaptists. Women did have somewhat wider opportunities for prominence among early Anabaptists than in the established Protestant churches (for instance, when they were the overwhelming majority of Anabaptists in besieged Münster, 1534–1535), but these opportunities shrank with sect formation and organization; male predominance was the rule among Anabaptists from the beginning.

There were three primary, overlapping expressions of the popular Reformation: the popularly directed Reformation pamphlets (*Flugschriften*), the German Peasants' War of 1525, and the Anabaptists. The lines between Reformation pamphlet, Peasants' War program, and Anabaptist tract are fluid. In Switzerland, the Tirol, Franconia, Thuringia, and Hesse the commoners' resistance of 1525 had significant connections with Anabaptism: quite a few important Anabaptist leaders had formerly participated in the Peasants' War, and the experience of the Peasants' War often turned commoners against the established churches and made them receptive to Anabaptist missionaries. In addition, resistance to tithes and rents was an issue that connected the *Flugschriften*, the Peasants' War programs, and early Anabaptism.

Reformation nonconformity began when radical supporters of the Reformation found their anticlerical projects and activities opposed not only by the Roman clergy and the governments but also by major reformers who had come into increasingly friendly and settled connections with governments of the sort that led to the gradual establishment of Protestant confessions. Among Luther's radical opponents in Saxony, persons such as Andreas Bodenstein Karlstadt, Jakob Strauss, Thomas Müntzer, and Nicholas Storch attacked infant baptism as a glaring example of the empty ceremonialism that distracted the laity from a genuine experience of the Holy Spirit, but they did not organize their followers around a renewed baptism of mature believers. The antipedobaptism of Karlstadt and Müntzer did, however, become known to radical adherents of the Zurich reformation, persons already estranged from Huldrych Zwingli because he supported and they rejected the continued collection of clerical tithes in the villages around Zurich.

Mennonite and Hutterite tradition assigns the beginning of Anabaptism, correctly, to an adult baptism in Zurich in early 1525 involving Conrad Grebel, a Zurich patrician with a humanist education, and Georg Blaurock, a priest from Chur. This event probably occurred at Felix Mantz's house on 21 January 1525; besides Mantz, Wilhelm Reublin and Johannes Brötli, priests serving the villages of Witikon and Zollikon, and Andreas Castelberger, a peddler of Reformation pamphlets, were almost certainly participants. The adult baptisms occurred immediately following the Zurich government's decision that this group's objections to infant baptism were unfounded, and they were followed by household Communions, at a time when the Zurich council and pastors had not yet instituted a Protestant Lord's Supper. Accordingly the household baptisms and Communions were acts of defiance against the Zurich council and the Zurich church, which under Zwingli's leadership had been in the process of throwing off Roman obedience since 1522.

Zwingli accused Grebel and his followers of aiming at a schism among the followers of the Reformation and the creation of a separate church. But the symbolic interpretation of the Lord's Supper advanced by Zwingli was as equally radical a departure from Catholic sacramental theology as was adult believers' baptism, and the Reformed churches had no intrinsic theological reason to continue infant baptism. The dispute over baptism in the Zurich reformation was not intentionally schismatic but part of a struggle over the forms of Reformed Protestantism. Similarly the issue of whether the civil government or an independent church should control the ecclesiastical ban was settled differently by Zwingli in Zurich than by Johann Oecolampadius in Basel or Calvin in Geneva. In the late sixteenth century the Reformed church of the northern Netherlands was more a believers' church with government sponsorship (such as Balthasar Hubmaier tried to establish in Anabaptism) than an established church as in Geneva and Scotland. Community chests, ostensibly to assist the poor, were a common feature of all Protestant congregations, but they had different social functions: to consolidate the wealth of the conciliar elite in Lutheran Zwickau, to enforce social discipline against "sturdy beggars" in Reformed Zurich, and to expropriate the wealth of *rentiers*, who were henceforth to live from their trades, among the Swiss Anabaptists.

Anabaptism began, then, as a struggle over the character of Reformed churches, and traditional scholarship has overlooked the continuing affinity between Anabaptist and Reformed. The later English observation that a disestablished Calvinist was a Baptist and an established Baptist a Calvinist applies as well to the earlier Reformation in central Europe. Sectarian Protestantism was not a doctrine of the church that inspired the first baptisms of 1525 but an accidental product of disestablishment and persecution.

The aim of the first Anabaptists in Zurich was to restore the practices of the church of the apostles, but it is a mistake to try to derive the character of Anabaptism generally from what we know of the first Swiss Anabaptists. The Anabaptist congregations were radically decentralized. Claus-Peter Clasen enumerates twenty Anabaptist groups in a study that does not even include the numerous groups in northern Germany and the Netherlands; there were in fact many Anabaptist groups, most of them making exclusivist claims and condemning the others. Current scholarship distinguishes three major historical families among sixteenth-century Anabaptists: those stemming from Conrad Grebel and Michael Sattler, those from Hans Denck and Hans Hut, and those from Melchior Hoffman and Jan Matthijs. The Hut-Denck grouping are the heirs of Thomas Müntzer, who might well himself have become an Anabaptist had he survived the Peasants' War. Before his Anabaptist career Hoffman was a radical apocalyptic lay preacher in the Baltic lands.

Until the 1960s scholars thought Anabaptism had spread from Zurich throughout the German-speaking lands. In fact we do not know who baptized Denck, although he may have received baptism in Switzerland in 1525 after fleeing from Mühlhausen at the end of the Peasants' War. Nor do we know who baptized Hoffman, although he had contacts with Hut-Denck Anabaptists in Strasbourg in 1529 and may have

been baptized there. What is more important is that Denck, Hut, and Hoffman set a markedly different tone for Anabaptists in most of south and central Germany, north Germany, and the Netherlands. The piety of Anabaptists in these regions differed widely from that of Swiss Anabaptists, whose influence was predominant in neighboring Alsace, the Palatinate, and parts of Swabia. So it has become conventional to regard Anabaptism as having had three beginnings: at Zurich in 1525, at Augsburg in 1526 when Denck baptized Hut, and at Emden in 1530, when Hoffman brought Anabaptism to north Germany. But this classification is not entirely satisfactory in accounting for the Anabaptism of the Hutterites in Moravia, who organized refugees from Swiss and south German Anabaptism into communities that blended the piety of the various Anabaptist regions from which their followers originated. Nor does it allow a place for the Marpeck brotherhood, led by the civil engineer and lay theologian Pilgram Marpeck, whose eclectic theology combined ideas taken from Luther, Kaspar von Schwenckfeld, and Bernhard Rothmann, the spokesman of the Münster Anabaptists.

Anabaptist groups differed in both belief and practice. Although all thought of themselves as living in the last days, the apocalyptic urgency (and latent violence) of the followers of Hut, Hoffman, and Matthijs, the prophet of Münster, far surpassed that of the first Swiss Anabaptists, the Marpeck brotherhood, and the followers of Menno Simons. (The Hutterites, the group around Melchior Rinck, and the adherents of David Joris occupied an intermediate position.) Adult baptism was for the Swiss Anabaptists a ceremony handed down from Christ and the apostles, to be literally observed. For Hut's followers it was the sign of the covenant of the apocalyptic elect, protecting them from the wrath of Christ returning in judgment. Hoffman suspended believers' baptism in 1531 when it led to the persecution of his followers, and although it was resumed by the Münster Anabaptists and the Mennonites it was abandoned by the Batenburgers and Joris's followers. Hence the Melchiorite sects were less firm in their commitment to believers' baptism than the Anabaptists of the south. Belief in direct inspiration by the Spirit was strong in Hut-Denck Anabaptism and in the Melchiorite-Münsterite-Jorite tradition, but it was eclipsed by a more prosaic biblicism among the Swiss Anabaptists, the Mennonites, and the Hutterites; only the Marpeck brotherhood became self-consciously antispiritualist. The Melchiorite belief that Christ's flesh came directly from heaven was a theological signature for all north German and Dutch Anabaptist groups until the Waterlanders abandoned it in the second half of the sixteenth century. In Anabaptism it was opposed forcefully only by Marpeck, who developed a more orthodox Christology that emphasized the reality of Christ's human nature. Denck and Hubmaier articulated a soteriology of synergism, a belief in the cooperation of the will of God and the human will in the salvation process; this belief was implicit among all Anabaptist sects, which in the manner of lay religion avoided the paradoxes about predestination so dear to the theologically sophisticated major reformers.

Among Anabaptists, however, theology was rudimentary and differences of religious ideas were secondary to differences of practice, which were more widely understood. Relations to rulers combined belief and practice. Aversion to temporal governments, which protected the established churches and persecuted Anabaptists, expressed itself most commonly in the declaration that rulers could not be Christians (Sattler and the Schleitheim Articles) or that they could be Christians only with great difficulty (Marpeck and Simons). But the hostility to government could take militant forms among Münsterites and Batenburgers, the "covenanters of the sword," who convinced themselves that they were unsheathing their swords for apocalyptic vengeance, a possibility that Hans Hut had earlier held before his followers. Only when Anabaptists lived under friendly, nonpersecuting governments, as in Moravia and in the Dutch Republic in the late sixteenth century, could "nonresistance" exhaust itself in exemption from military service and other civic duties thought to be religiously prohibited.

Restoration of the Christian community of goods described in *Acts* 2 and 4 was a common ideal differently expressed among the early Anabaptist groups. At first in Switzerland and south and central Germany community of goods was assumed to be compatible with the continuance of the single-family household as the focus of living and working. Among the Swiss Anabaptists the rule of community of goods was that everyone should work and that the wealthy should distribute their property among the needy and eschew all profit from usury. Among south and central German Anabaptists Müntzer's mystical piety of *Gelassenheit* ("yieldedness") was focused on renunciation of ties to material possessions, a communist spirituality. The two traditions blended in the highly organized Hutterite settlements in Moravia, which went beyond the economics of the family to create economic units of about five hundred people living from the profits of advanced craft production. By contrast, in Münster, community of goods was proclaimed but distorted by the prominence among the Anabaptists of civic notables who continued in possession of their houses, by the lavish royal court, and by the necessities of the constant siege. In reaction against Münster and the Hutterites, the Marpeck brotherhood and the Mennonites abandoned the ideal of imitating the communism of the early church, but the Dutch Mennonites for centuries maintained a strong tradition of philanthropy toward needy groups, some of them non-Anabaptist. The Swiss Brethren, as the Grebel-Sattler heirs came to be called (c.1540), were the most radically laicist of the Anabaptists, repeatedly humbling and disciplining their would-be leaders. Their religion centered on distinctive practices rather than on ideas or emotive piety.

Throughout the spectrum of Anabaptist groups the administration of the ban, which led to shunning of the excommunicated, was a source of unending controversy. Particularly the issue of "marital avoidance," that is, whether a banned member should be shut off from family intimacies, aroused strong emotions and led to schisms. This and the closely associated matter of whether Anabaptists should separate from non-Anabaptist spouses, and whether separated Anabaptists were permitted to remarry in the lifetime of their spouses, were the questions most productive of sectarian division. This issue of "mixed marriages" arose in Moravia and Münster, where many Anabaptists, in seeking refuge, had abandoned their spouses, and in central Germany among the Anabaptist heirs of Müntzer. In the Netherlands in the last years of the sixteenth century, when the Mennonites splintered into a half-dozen groups, the divisions began over the subject of marital avoidance. Quarrels over the ban and marriage required no theological acumen. Like the controversies over the proper form of community of goods that divided Anabaptists in Moravia, they fully involved ordinary Anabaptists as well as aspiring leaders.

The social composition of Swiss–south German Anabaptism has been studied more carefully than that of Dutch-north German Anabaptism. The Anabaptism of the southern sects was a religion of commoners, including only 2 percent who were of aristocratic birth or who had higher education. The majority of Swiss–south German Anabaptists were peasants, although their leaders tended to be craftsmen, particularly after the persecutions of the late 1520s killed so many educated leaders. At first, in the 1520s, 40 percent of Swiss–south German Anabaptists of known residence lived in cities, the rest in the small towns, villages, and farms from which the Peasants' War rebels came. But Anabaptism was more rapidly suppressed in the cities than in the countryside, so that in the later sixteenth century only one in twelve Swiss–south German Anabaptists was a town dweller. The limited studies of north German-Dutch Anabaptism suggest that townspeople were proportionately more numerous than in the south. It was above all a religion of craftsmen, although urban patricians joined the Anabaptists, not only in Münster but in the cities of the Netherlands. Joris was especially successful in attracting aristocratic supporters. The wave of apocalyptic fright that spread Anabaptism in the Netherlands in 1534 apparently affected all classes, while the social polarization created by the Peasants' War in 1525 hardened the south German elites against popular initiatives in religion.

Because of their defiance of governmental control over religion, their real and imagined connection with the Peasants' War, and their insurrectionary militance in Münster and the Netherlands (1534–1535), the Anabaptists were severely persecuted. Catholic governments, such as the Habsburgs in the Netherlands and in the Tirol and the Bavarian dukes, were particularly brutal, while many Protestant rulers evaded the imperial mandate of Speyer of 1529, which, with their agreement, had made Anabaptism a crime punishable by death. But Zwinglian Zurich and Bern and Lutheran Saxony have prominent Anabaptist martyrs to their account; Zwingli and Melanchthon showed particular enthusiasm for using the executioner to silence nonconformists. The Dutch Mennonites compiled martyrologies, *Het Offer des Heeren* and the subsequent *Martyrs' Mirror*, which embedded memories of persecution at the center of their piety.

Claus-Peter Clasen has raised the question of actual numbers: he has been able to document 845 certain and probable executions of Anabaptists in Switzerland, south and central Germany, and Austria in the period between 1525 and the Thirty Years' War, and he concedes the possibility of two or three hundred additional executions. Estimates by twentieth-century Dutch scholars of the number of Anabaptist martyrs in the Netherlands vary from about fifteen hundred (Samuel Cramer and W. J. Kuhler) to at least twenty-five hundred (N. van der Zijpp). More recently Alastair Duke writes that up to the beginning of the Revolt of the Netherlands the total number of executed heretics in the Netherlands, including Calvinists, "exceeded 1300." In the *Mennonite Encyclopedia* in the 1950s Paul Schowalter made what was for that time a restrained estimate when he guessed that the number of Anabaptist martyrs "would probably exceed rather than fall below 4,000." The more recent studies of Clasen and Duke suggest that that figure may be too high.

Pursuing his quantitative research, Clasen concluded that the sixteenth-century Anabaptists were numerically insignificant, and therefore insignificant historically. He identified 12,522 Anabaptists in Switzerland, south and central Germany and Austria between 1525 and 1618, conceding that the aggregate number may have been as high as thirty thousand—still insignificant. It can be retorted that he studied the wrong regions. Anabaptism, to be sure, began in the Swiss–south German area, but it was severely reduced in those regions (despite the importance of the Swiss remnant in the Pennsylvania German settlements in America). Eighty percent of the Anabaptist executions that Clasen documented in his area of study occurred before the beginning of 1534; after that the flames of persecution ebbed because their tinder was exhausted. Thereafter Anabaptism continued predominantly in the refugee communities of Moravia and in north Germany and the Netherlands. At the end of the sixteenth century Anabaptists constituted about 10 percent of the population of southeastern Moravia and a similar percentage of the population of the Dutch Republic, roughly as numerous as the officially favored and politically influential Calvinists. According to Alastair Duke they outnumbered the Reformed in some parts of the Netherlands (for instance, Frisia, where another estimate puts them at one-quarter of the population). While not as prominent in the German Reformation as in the seventeenth-century struggles in England, Protestant nonconformity was not numerically insignificant in sixteenth-century central Europe.

There are measures of significance other than numbers of adherents. The Anabaptists give us a window on the popular experience of the Reformation, because theirs was a movement initiated by ordinary laity free of the direction of clerical, political, and university elites. The court interrogations that constitute much of the Anabaptist source materials are what Arnold Snyder calls "oral deposits"—a sort of oral history of the Reformation of the common people of town and village. Even these sources underrepresent the role that women must have played in sixteenth-century Anabaptism. Beyond more attention to prominent Anabaptist women such as Anna Jansz or Hille Feiken and more ingenious quantitative research, some of the history of Anabaptist women is no doubt irrecoverable, if one maintains the distinction between historical writing and fiction. But sixteenth-century Anabaptism as revealed in the sources gives the purest expression of the popular anticlericalism that animated the Reformation as a whole. Anabaptism preserved the radicalism of the early Reformation after it began to ebb in the established Lutheran and Reformed churches.

[*See also* Hutterites; Melchiorites; Mennonites; Münster; Radical Reformation; *and* Zwickau Prophets.]

BIBLIOGRAPHY

Primary Sources

Harder, Leland, ed. *The Sources of Swiss Anabaptism: The Grebel Letters and Related Documents.* Classics of the Radical Reformation, vol. 4. Scottdale, Pa., 1985. English translation of the documents of Swiss Anabaptism until Grebel's death in 1526.

Hutterian Brethren, eds. *The Chronicle of the Hutterian Brethren.* Rifton, N.Y., 1987. English translation of the "Great Chronicle" by a neo-Hutterite community.

Klassen, William, and Walter Klaassen, eds. and trans. *The Writings of Pilgram Marpeck.* Classics of the Radical Reformation, vol. 2. Scottdale, Pa., 1978. A partial English translation of Marpeck's works, including letters, most of which are not yet published in German.

Pipkin, H. Wayne, and John H. Yoder, eds. and trans. *Balthasar Hubmaier: Theologian of Anabaptism.* Classics of the Radical Reformation, vol. 5. Scottdale, Pa., 1989. An English translation of Hubmaier's complete works, more extensive than the standard German edition by Westin and Bergsten.

Quellen zur Geschichte der Täufer. Quellen und Forschungen zur Reformationsgeschichte, vols. 1–17. Gütersloh, 1930–.

Wenger, John C., ed. *Complete Writings of Menno Simons.* Translated by Leonard Verduin. Scottdale, Pa., 1956.

Yoder, John H., ed. and trans. *The Legacy of Michael Sattler.* Classics of the Radical Reformation, vol. 1. Scottdale, Pa., 1973. Besides letters by and about Sattler, accounts of his martyrdom, and the Schleitheim Articles, these English translations include documents traditionally associated with Sattler.

Secondary Sources

Armour, Rollin S. *Anabaptist Baptism: A Representative Study.* Scottdale, Pa., 1966. A comparative study of the baptismal theologies of Balthasar Hubmaier, Hans Hut, Melchior Hoffman, and Pilgram Marpeck.

Bender, Harold S. *Conrad Grebel, c.1498–1526: The Founder of the Swiss Brethren Sometimes Called Anabaptists.* Goshen, Ind., 1950. The classic biography of the first Anabaptist leader, still regarded as substantially accurate.

Boyd, Stephen. *Pilgram Marpeck: His Life and Social Theology.* Durham, N.C., 1992. Meticulously researched, this study produces significant new data on Marpeck.

Clasen, Claus-Peter. *Anabaptism: A Social History, 1525–1618; Switzerland, Austria, Moravia, and South and Central Germany.* Ithaca, N.Y., 1972. A quantitative study that minimizes the significance of Anabaptism but continues the emphases of earlier Mennonite scholarship: rejecting connections between Anabaptism and the Peasants' War, finding Anabaptism originally urban rather than rural, and describing the movement as sectarian.

Davis, Kenneth R. *Anabaptism and Asceticism.* Scottdale, Pa., 1974. Describes Anabaptism as a laicized movement for ascetic holiness; the last major defense of a separate study of evangelical Anabaptism.

Depperman, Klaus. *Melchior Hoffman: Social Unrest and Apocalyptic Visions in the Age of Reformation.* Edinburgh, 1987. English translation of *Melchior Hoffman: Soziale Unruhen und apokalyptische Visionen im Zeitalter der Reformation,* Göttingen, 1979. The best, most thorough treatment of Hoffman and his movement, especially strong on Hoffman's connection to the Strasbourg dissenter community.

Deppermann, Klaus, Werner O. Packull, and James M. Stayer. "From Monogenesis to Polygenesis: The Historical Discussion of Anabaptist Origins." *Mennonite Quarterly Review* 49 (1975); 83–122. A historiographical survey contending for the distinct origins and character of Anabaptism in Switzerland, south Germany, and the Netherlands.

Dyck, Cornelius J., ed. *An Introduction to Mennonite History.* 3d ed. Scottdale, Pa., 1993. A cooperative work of Mennonite scholars. The first edition of 1967 moved toward a pluriform view of Anabaptism but maintained the primary interpretations of H. S. Bender and J. H. Yoder.

Friedmann, Robert. *The Theology of Anabaptism.* Scottdale, Pa., 1973. An effort at systematic statement of the New Testament–oriented "kingdom theology" of the Anabaptists.

Goertz, Hans-Jürgen. *Die Täufer: Geschichte und Deutung.* 2d ed. Munich, 1988. Soon to be published in English translation; the excellence of the book lies in the author's theological acumen in distinguishing the several Anabaptist traditions. In the forthcoming edition he adds a chapter on ordinary Anabaptists and Anabaptist women, contending that their piety was uniform throughout the Anabaptist sects.

Goertz, Hans-Jürgen, ed. *Profiles of Radical Reformers.* Scottdale, Pa., 1982. Introduced by an important discussion of Reformation radicalism, containing twenty-one biographical sketches from Thomas Müntzer to Paracelsus. Translation of *Radikale Reformatoren,* Munich, 1978; English edition edited by Walter Klaassen.

Hillerbrand, Hans J., ed. *Anabaptist Bibliography, 1520–1630.* Saint Louis, 1991. Supersedes Hillerbrand's Anabaptist bibliographies of 1962 and 1975; includes over 6,100 titles.

Klaassen, Walter. *Living at the End of the Ages: Apocalyptic Expectation in the Radical Reformation.* Lanham, Md., 1992. The apocalyptic beliefs of Reformation radicals in the context of ancient and medieval Christian thought and broader Reformation eschatology.

Krahn, Cornelius. *Dutch Anabaptism: Origin, Spread, Life and Thought.* 2d ed. Scottdale, Pa., 1981. A survey of the sixteenth-century movement from the Sacramentarian precursors through the Melchiorites to the Mennonites.

Oyer, John S. *Lutheran Reformers Against Anabaptists: Luther, Melanchthon, and Menius and the Anabaptists of Central Germany.* The Hague, 1964. An irenic presentation of the Lutheran controversialists and a recognition of the distinct character of central German Anabaptism.

Packull, Werner O. *Mysticism and the Early South German–Austrian Anabaptist Movement, 1525–1531.* Scottdale, Pa., 1977. Traces south German Anabaptism from its beginning among followers of Thomas Müntzer to its division into individualistic spiritualism and sectarian congregations.

Snyder, Arnold. "Orality, Literacy and the Study of Anabaptism." *Mennonite Quarterly Review* 65 (1991), 371–392. Programmatic statement of Snyder's undertaking to uncover the "oral texts" that circulated among illiterate Anabaptists.

Stayer, James M. *Anabaptists and the Sword.* 2d ed. Lawrence, Kans., 1976. A description of the variety of standpoints taken by Anabaptist groups toward government and war.

———. *The German Peasants' War and Anabaptist Community of Goods.* Montreal, 1991. Argues the importance of the Peasants' War for Anabaptism and traces the various attempts to restore the apostolic communism of *Acts* 2 and 4.

Waite, Gary K. *David Joris and Dutch Anabaptism, 1524–1543.* Waterloo, Ont., 1990. Focusing on Joris's career as an Anabaptist, Waite argues convincingly that Joris was the most prominent Anabaptist leader in the Netherlands after the fall of Münster, 1536–1539.

Williams, George H. *The Radical Reformation.* 2d English ed. Kirksville, Mo., 1992. A thorough revision and updating of the encyclopedic classic on Anabaptist and related movements in central and eastern Europe.

JAMES M. STAYER

ANCHORITES.

Persons who enclosed themselves and chose a life of seclusion as the most direct route to establishing and furthering a personal relationship to God are known as anchorites. They were individuals, men as well as women, from lay as well as religious backgrounds. They elected to enter into an anchorhold and remain within it for the remainder of their lives. They made this choice under the spiritual guidance and with the permission of their bishops. The anchorhold to which they retired was most often a cell attached to a parish church. Anchorholds also were found in monasteries and in hospitals, in chapels within cities and towns, nesting on the bridges of tiny villages, and dotting the countryside.

Anchoritism, which had developed in antiquity as a largely male phenomenon, became feminized in the high Middle Ages. A combination of demographic and religious factors created a pool of upper- and middle-class women who welcomed the opportunity to become anchorites, especially in England, where the ratio of women to men recluses was six to one in the thirteenth century. This sexual imbalance gradually equalized in succeeding centuries. By the sixteenth century, when the reforms of Henry VIII ended anchoritism along with monastic vocations, the ratio of men to women was approaching parity.

Even as anchoritism originally had developed as a male vocation, so also it had been conceived as an advanced stage of communal life for proven and stalwart monks. The infusion of women into the profession was paralleled by a growth in the numbers of laypersons. Most medieval anchorites came directly to the anchorhold from lay life. This pattern too was moderating in the later medieval period as the percentage of religious in the anchorhold grew.

Ideally persons entered the anchorhold seeking the most intimate relationship with God. The tradition that fostered this ideal assumed that it could best be achieved in a wilderness or desert or in symbolic substitutes for such places. The ideal supported, promoted, and sanctified those who attempted to sustain the rigors of an ascetic life limited by minimal human intercourse and the loss of physical freedom.

The anchoritic ideal was particularly powerful in late medieval England, especially among a group of persons generally called the "Fourteenth-century English Mystics," including Julian of Norwich, Walter Hilton, Richard Rolle, and the author of *The Cloud of Unknowing*. Julian was an anchoress and wrote her *Revelations* while living in her cell, attached to a parish church in Norwich. Both Rolle's *Fire of Love* and Hilton's *Scale of Perfection* were rules written for specific anchoresses for whom Rolle and Hilton were spiritual advisers. The *Cloud* author also was a solitary and wrote his treatise to benefit others secluded as he was. Continental mystics of the same period—Johannes (Meister) Eckehart, Johannes Tauler, Heinrich Süse, Jan van Ruysbroeck, and Catherine of Siena—shared no such commitment to anchoritism.

Anchoritism ended abruptly in those countries and areas that adopted Protestantism, including England. In Catholic countries it persisted for a while in the post-Tridentine era. But as religious movements of the early modern period increasingly encouraged action in this world, a theological ideal extolling extreme social abnegation grew less appealing. Anchoritism then essentially disappeared as an alternative religious vocation, and the concept itself became identified with an "archaic" or "medieval" church.

BIBLIOGRAPHY

Clay, Rotha Mary. *The Hermits and Anchorites of England* (1914). Reprint, Detroit, 1968.
———. "Further Studies on Medieval Recluses." *Journal of the British Archaeological Association* 3d ser. 16 (1953), 74–86.
———. "Some Northern Anchorites." *Archaeologia Aeliana* 4th ser. 33 (1955), 202–217. The seminal studies of English anchoritism now somewhat replaced by Warren, *Anchorites*.
Gougaud, Louis. *Ermites et reclus: Etudes sur d'anciennes formes de vie religieuse.* Moines et monasteres, 5. Vienna, 1928. A glimpse of the Continental experience; useful for comparison with the English.
Warren, Ann K. *Anchorites and Their Patrons in Medieval England.* Berkeley, 1985. The definitive work on English anchoritism.
———. "The Nun as Anchoress: England, 1100–1500." In *Distant Echoes: Medieval Religious Women I*, edited by John A. Nichols and Lilian T. Shank, pp. 197–212. Cistercian Studies Series, 71. Kalamazoo, Mich., 1984.

ANN K. WARREN

ANDERSON, Lars. *See* Andreae, Laurentius.

ANDREAE, Jakob (1528–1590), German Lutheran professor at the University of Tübingen and codrafter of the Formula of Concord. Son of a smith in the Swabian town of Waiblingen, Andreae studied on a ducal scholarship in Stuttgart and at the University of Tübingen (1541–1546). He remained fiercely loyal to the ducal family his entire life. The university's weak theology faculty gave him a barely adequate foundation for his career as doctrinal arbiter within Lutheranism. He was called to be a deacon in Stuttgart in 1546 and married Johanna Entringer, a member of a prominent Tübingen family. She bore him eighteen children. During the imperial occupation of Württemberg (1548) Duke Ulrich of Württemberg returned him to Tübingen, where he worked to subvert the enforcement of the Augsburg Interim and completed his doctoral studies. In 1553 Duke Christoph of Württemberg had him called to be ecclesiastical superintendent of Göppingen. Andreae soon became active in the affairs of the Württemberg church. He promoted a plan for decentralized, presbyterian church discipline that developed while he was in correspondence with John Calvin. Defeated in this effort by Johannes Brenz and others, Andreae wholeheartedly accepted Brenz's subjection of the church to princely control.

The duke used him frequently as an ecclesiastical diplomat. In 1556 Andreae was sent to assist the reformation of Wiesensteig, the Palatinate-Neuburg, and Baden-Durlach. The next year he served as notary for the evangelical theologians at the Colloquy of Worms and sided with the Philippist representatives from electoral Saxony against the Gnesio-Lutherans' insistence on explicit condemnation of false teachers and false teaching. He engaged Kaspar von Schwenkfeld in an epistolary exchange on ecclesiology and related issues in the early 1550s and aided Elector Ottheinrich of the Palatinate in refuting Anabaptists in a colloquy at Pfedersheim in 1557. In subsequent years he participated in the reformation or visitation of other towns and principalities in southern Germany. Andreae entered into mediating discussions on the doctrine of the Lord's Supper with Reformed theologians, including Théodore de Bèze (1557); however, at a synod in Stuttgart in 1559 he took the lead in formulating the *Bekantnus und Bericht der Theologen . . . im . . . Wurtemberg*, which explicitly taught Brenz's doctrines of the Lord's Supper and Christology (antithetical to a Reformed view).

In 1561 he represented Duke Christoph at a meeting in Erfurt, which discussed a united evangelical approach to the Council of Trent, and at the Colloquy of Poissy. (Christoph's delegation arrived too late to take part, but Andreae and his colleagues held informal discussions with political leaders of both sides.) He pursued negotiations with the Guise family on behalf of the duke the following year, when he also attempted to settle a controversy over synergism in ducal Saxony, alienating its Gnesio-Lutheran ministerium in the process. They had already objected to his and Brenz's conciliatory attitude toward Andreas Osiander. In 1563 he mediated the dispute between Johannes Marbach and Girolamo Zanchi in Strasbourg, concluding an agreement that favored the former's positions on the Lord's Supper and election. In 1564 he joined Brenz and others in defending the "Swabian Christology"—the doctrine that Christ's human nature is omnipresent through the communication of attributes—in a colloquy at Maulbronn with the Reformed theologians of the Palatinate. They labeled the Andreae-Brenz teaching "ubiquitist," and a bitter controversy arose over this issue.

In 1561 Andreae was called to serve as professor of theology and chancellor of the University of Tübingen and as provost there. His loyal pursuit of ducal policies as chancellor led him into bitter controversies with his professorial colleagues as he strove to subject the university to ducal control, a model he later imposed on electoral Saxon schools. Throughout this period Andreae engaged in polemics against foes of his Lutheran convictions, attacking in print Roman Catholics, such as Friedrich Staphylus, as well as "Zwinglians, Schwenckfelders, and Anabaptists." He favored a popular approach couching his case in a homiletic style or in argument from the catechism.

From his accession in 1550 Duke Christoph had worked politically for unity among the strife-torn Lutherans of Germany. In 1568 he dispatched Andreae to join a team (which included Martin Chemnitz and Nicholas Selnecker) assembled to aid his cousin, Duke Julius of Braunschweig-Wolfenbüttel, in introducing the Reformation to his lands. At Christoph's behest and in accord with the duke's program for Lutheran unity drafted some twelve years earlier, Andreae also visited Lutheran princely courts, city councils, ministeriae, and theology faculties in 1569 and 1570, attempting to elicit support for a brief statement of doctrinal agreement. He hoped that his proposals would draw the Lutheran disputants together under a broad agreement lacking detail and specifics. His efforts were scorned by the Gnesio-Lutheran party, but he gathered Philippists and others together in a colloquy at Zerbst in May 1570. Although harmony prevailed outwardly among those invited, Andreae's agreement was not signed by the participants, and his relationship with the Philippist party, and particularly his relationship with the theologians of Wittenberg, broke apart soon thereafter over christological issues. Agreement among the parties had proved elusive.

Andreae continued to search for ways to establish Lutheran unity in private correspondence and conversation. In 1573 he published *Sechs christliche Predigten von den Spaltungen, so sich zwischen den Theologen Augsburgischer Konfession . . . erhoben* (Six Christian Sermons on the Divisions Which Have Continued to Surface among the Theologians of the Augsburg Confession). In his homiletically cast analysis of ten disputed issues among the Lutherans, he followed the style he had developed six years earlier in treating differences between Lutherans and Christians of other confessions: he analyzed each issue in terms of the catechism, at a level at which lay people could understand. Here Andreae rejected the position of the Wittenberg Philippists on the Lord's Supper and Christology. He also accepted the views of the main body of the Gnesio-Lutherans and affirmed their condemnation of Matthias Flacius Illyricus's doctrine of original sin. He met Flacius (1571), his followers in Lindau (1575), and his chief defender, Cyriakus Spangenberg (1577), in colloquies but failed to grasp their central concern. In addition, he laid aside his earlier method of seeking concord by avoiding careful doctrinal analysis of issues, adopting instead the Gnesio-Lutheran method of explicit condemnation; he assessed in detail the contrary positions of the disputants and named those whose positions he rejected (usually in the margins, though naming the Wittenbergers in the text). Andreae proposed that this work be the basis of a doctrinal agreement among all Lutherans. His colleagues in northern Germany rejected his approach as too simplistic; they were suspicious of Andreae and offended by his arrogance. They urged that his colleagues in Württemberg recast the *Predigten* into a formal proposal for concord. He assumed that task himself, sending out his "Swabian Concord" in March 1574. Chemnitz and David Chytraeus took up the task on the basis of this document. Others pursued different routes toward Lutheran concord. In one of the most important of these, the Maulbronn Formula, Andreae's influence is evident, even though it was his Württemberg colleagues, not Andreae himself, who participated in its drafting.

Later in 1574 political-ecclesiastical developments in Saxony laid the basis for further work on a formula for Lutheran concord as Elector August discovered and removed the leading members of the so-called "crypto-Calvinist" party from his church. In 1576 he invited Andreae and others to help reorganize the church in his land. Andreae spent four years in Saxony carrying out a reorganization of the church and giving leadership to the drive to draft the Formula of Concord, win adherence to it, publish it, and make it the standard for teaching in electoral Saxony. Andreae participated in the meetings at Torgau and Bergen in 1576 and 1577, which completed work on the Formula of Concord's Solid Declaration. He composed its epitome, drafted its preface, and arranged its publication with other Lutheran confessional documents in the *Corpus doctrinae* called the *Book of Concord*. He met with a number of individuals and groups of theologians in several principalities, attempting to overcome objections and win their subscription, with varying success.

The mature Andreae favored close princely supervision of the church and worked to enforce a model for "state church" Lutheranism in Saxony during his sojourn there. He actively worked to gain the support of pastors and lay people for the theology of the Formula of Concord, and he wrote guidelines for the conduct of the Saxon clergy and schools before his relationship with Elector August cooled in 1580 and he returned to Tübingen.

Upon his return to Württemberg Andreae resumed his former duties at the university and his polemics against Calvinists (e.g., Lambert Daneau and Théodore de Bèze), Roman Catholics (e.g., Gregory de Valentia), and opponents of the *Book of Concord* (e.g., Christoph Herdesian, Johannes Sturm, and Christoph Pezel). In 1586 he led the Lutheran delegation to the Colloquy of Montbéliard, where he and Bèze confirmed Lutheran-Reformed divisions on the Lord's Supper, the person of Christ, baptism, the use of images, and predestination. He died on 7 January 1590.

Throughout his career Andreae's personality irritated others and brought to an end countless friendships, including those with Chemnitz, Chytraeus, and Selnecker, his codrafters of the Formula of Concord. He successfully aided the adoption of Brenz's understanding of the relationship of church and state within seventeenth-century Lutheranism, placing the church under civil administration. In spite of his early attempts to bridge the gap between Lutherans and Calvinists on the Lord's Supper, he became a staunch advocate of Johannes Brenz's Christology and his christological argument in defense of the real presence, thus alienating both Calvinists and Philippists with spiritualizing tendencies, as well as some who held a Lutheran doctrine of the real presence but defended it with other argumentation. Not an independent thinker or gifted theologian himself, he represented the views of Brenz and Luther as faithfully as he could, and he communicated his theology simply but effectively in his many published sermons. His influence on the content of the Formula of Concord is overshadowed by the work of Chemnitz; the metaphysical elements of his Christology were largely laid aside in its eighth article. But without his tireless diplomatic efforts and skills, the settlement of the Formula of Concord and *Book of Concord* would probably not have been accomplished.

BIBLIOGRAPHY

Ebel, Jobst. "Jacob Andreae (1528–1590) als Verfasser der Konkordienformel." *Zeitschrift für Kirchengeschichte* 89 (1978), 78–119. A careful analysis of the sources and insightful assessment of Andreae's role in the Formula of Concord.

Jungkuntz, Theodore R. "Jakob Andreae: The Supplanter?" In *Formulators of the Formula of Concord: Four Architects of Lutheran Unity*, pp. 19–45. Saint Louis, 1977. A brief biographical overview based on extant published sources and analyses.

Kolb, Robert. *Andreae and the Formula of Concord: Six Sermons on the Way to Lutheran Unity*. Saint Louis, 1977. Translation of the six sermons of 1573, with an extensive introduction to Andreae's life and the controversies on which he wrote.

―――. "Jakob Andreae, 1528–1590." In *Shapers of Religious Traditions in Germany, Switzerland, and Poland, 1560–1600*, edited by Jill Raitt, pp. 53–68. New Haven, 1981.

Müller-Streisand, Rosemarie. "Theologie und Kirchenpolitik bei Jacob Andreae bis zum Jahr 1568." *Blätter für württembergische Kirchenge-*

schichte 60/61 (1960–1961), 224–395. Carefully researched, analytical assessment of Andreae's life and work to 1578.

ROBERT KOLB

ANDREAE, Laurentius (c.1470–1552), Swedish reformer and statesman. After preparatory studies in Skara and Uppsala in Sweden, he obtained his master's degree at the University of Rostock in 1498. He visited Rome three times. Returning home, he became archdeacon in Strängnäs and took charge of the diocese after the execution of Bishop Mattias in 1520.

Andreae made contact with Gustavus Vasa, who liberated Sweden from Danish hegemony, and proclaimed him the elected king of Sweden in 1523. Andreae was appointed as his "secretary," (i.e., adviser). In 1524 he became a member of the council of the state and archdeacon of the archbishopric of Uppsala. In his endeavors to develop an independent Lutheran national church in Sweden he cooperated with Sweden's great reformer, Olaus Petri. Andreae expressed his reformed way of thinking in a letter to the convent of Vadstena in 1524, in which he argued that the church did not exist for the sake of the clergy but for the local congregation, which was thus entitled to administer the property of the church. Andreae inspired and directed the king's ecclesiastical policy. His signature is found on most of the royal documents concerning ecclesiastical matters.

In the early 1530s Andreae lost the king's favor. The reason for disgrace was his opposition to the king's effort to gain full power over the church. The culmination of disfavor was reached in the Diet of Örebro of 1539–1540, where he and Olaus Petri were sentenced to death for high treason. They were both reprieved but charged a heavy fine. Andreae spent his last years in retirement in Strägnäs.

His work as a statesman was of vital importance to the molding of Sweden as a free Lutheran state. In addition, he supervised the translation into Swedish of the New Testament, which appeared in 1526. He is the author of *Een kort undervisning om troona och godha gerningar* (A Short Introduction to the Creed and Good Deeds), printed in 1528. In this work he made use of his linguistic talent.

BIBLIOGRAPHY

Svart, Peder. *Gustav Vasas krönika*. Edited by Gunnar T. Westin. Malmö, 1964.

INGUN MONTGOMERY

ANDREAS, Joachim. *See* Schlick of Passauni, Joachim Andreas.

ANGLICANISM. As a distinct term, *Anglicanism* has its origins in nineteenth-century England. According to the

Oxford English Dictionary (1933, vol. l, p. 327) it means: "Adherence to the doctrine and discipline of the reformed Church of England (and other churches in communion therewith) as the genuine representative of the Catholic Church." The word *Anglican* on which it is based means simply "English" and in combination with *Ecclesia* refers to the Church of England, terminology dating from the twelfth century. In 1215 the *Magna Carta* stated, "*Quod Anglicana ecclesia libra sit*," that is, that the English church shall be free. In that early usage the word *Anglican* simply referred to a geographical entity and did not, as it did later, involve doctrinal considerations (see J. R. Wright, "Anglicanism, Ecclesia Anglicana and Anglican: An Essay in Terminology," in *The Study of Anglicanism*, edited by S. W. Sykes and J. E. Booty, London and Minneapolis, 1988, pp. 424–428). The phenomenon of "Anglicanism" emerged historically with the development of the nineteenth-century quest for the uniqueness of the doctrine and discipline of the English church and with the spread of that church beyond Britain to other parts of the world forming the Anglican communion of autonomous churches voluntarily adhering to the doctrine and discipline of the English church. The bishops of the Anglican Communion, assembled in the Lambeth Conference of 1930, recognized that the term *Anglican* at one time had a "purely local connotation," but now referred to the doctrine of the Catholic faith as contained in scripture, stated in creeds, "expressed in the Sacraments of the Gospel and rites of the Primitive Church as set forth in the Book of Common Prayer, with its various local adaptations; and safeguarded by the historic threefold Order of the Ministry" (*Lambeth Conference*, London, 1930). This statement reflects the influence of the Chicago-Lambeth Quadrilateral with its emphasis on scripture, creeds, sacraments, and historic episcopacy. It goes on to emphasize the freedom of its member churches to agree or disagree on nonessentials and to interpret such essentials as have been mentioned with some degree of latitude. That Anglicanism has set limits to freedom in the past is evident from the ways in which it has excluded those who refused to use *The Book of Common Prayer* and to accept an episcopal polity. That it has been comprehensive is revealed by its ability in the past to hold together widely differing groups, such as Anglo-Catholics, evangelicals, and liberals, in one communion and fellowship.

It is on the basis of understandings of Anglicanism dating from the nineteenth century that the quest for Anglican identity and Anglican roots has been conducted. Some, such as J. R. Wright, have argued for reaching back to New Testament doctrine and the continuous history of the Church of England beginning with the Anglo-Saxon church. Others have pointed to the sixteenth century as the critical time in the formation of Anglicanism, and still others to the seventeenth century. John Spurr argues that Anglicanism was invented between 1646 and 1689, in the era of the Restoration of the Stuart monarchy and the Church of England, "which

then found a heritage to be re-appropriated, cannibalized, or transformed into other 'Anglicanisms'" (*The Restoration Church of England*, New Haven, 1991, p. 396). Here a case will be made for locating the roots of what subsequent generations called "Anglicanism" in sixteenth-century England, in the development of the English Reformation, and especially in the reign of Queen Elizabeth I, without denying the existence of roots prior to that time and without arguing that present understandings have not been influenced by events following the sixteenth century.

The formative influences in the development of "Anglicanism" in the sixteenth century were (1) political and intellectual and (2) theological and ecclesiological, which at any given time were to be seen interacting and not altogether separable. The political context was dominated by the emergence of a national or patriotic consciousness under the Tudor monarchs and their parliaments. The understanding that "this realm of England is an empire . . . governed by one supreme head and king" (24 Henry VIII, c. l) was modified under Queen Elizabeth I. As supreme "governor" of the Church of England she prevented foreign interference, such as that of the Church of Rome, and reformed the church, correcting "errors, heresies, schisms, abuses, offenses, contempt and enormities." In her reforming activities she was to look not to the example of the Church of Rome or any other church but to the scriptures, the first four general councils, and any other council that identified heresy "by the express and plain words of the canonical Scriptures," or Parliament with the "assent of the clergy in their convocation" (1 Eliz. I, c.l).

Anglicanism began with the supposition that a national state is an independent political entity, that a national church rightfully takes charge of its own affairs, and that it does so while maintaining continuity with the earliest church, with scripture and the first four general councils, and with the early church fathers, revered for their adherence to scripture in unity with the church catholic. The Church of England was the one, holy, catholic, and apostolic church in England. The national concept as enunciated by statutes and in the preaching and teaching of scholars, lay and ecclesiastic, reflected the influence of the Continental Reformation but also that of Erasmian humanism and the medieval understanding of the commonwealth. The unity of church and state was affirmed by the theologian Richard Hooker (1554–1600), who said, "We hold that . . . there is not any man of the Church of England, but the same is also a member of the Commonwealth, nor any man a member of the Commonwealth which is not also of the Church of England" (Richard Hooker, *Of the Laws of Ecclesiastical Polity* [1953], book 8, chapter 1, section 2; hereafter, *Laws*). This was stated against the Puritan claim that church and state were two separate corporations. The basic meaning of this for developing Anglicanism was not so much in the implication that there could be only one church in England: Even in the sixteenth century there were Roman Catholics, extreme Puritans, sectaries, and representatives of the Continental church worshiping apart from the established church. Rather the meaning was that the church was rightly concerned with affairs of state and that the church was committed to the comprehension not just of the elect but of all people in one communion and fellowship.

The commitment to comprehension was notably expressed as the Crown in Parliament pursued uniformity as well as supremacy. The process began with statutes enacted under Henry VIII and was completed in statutes enacted under Edward VI and Elizabeth I. Uniformity was to be pursued and maintained not through subscription to a set of doctrines, although the Thirty-nine Articles of Religion (1563, 1571) provided for that possibility, and not through allegiance to a pope, but rather through the use of a book of common prayer. The Elizabethan statute, the centerpiece of the Elizabethan Settlement of Religion, revived the Edwardian statute (5 and 6 Edward VI, c. 1) that enforced the use of *The Second Book of Common Prayer*, with a few significant revisions. The Church of England (including all citizens) was required "to say and use matins, evensong, celebration of the Lord's Supper and administration of each of the sacraments, and all their common and open prayers, in such order and form" as were found in the 1559 prayer book. Penalties for nonuse were provided, culminating in "forfeiture of goods and imprisonment for life" (1 Eliz. I, c. 2). "Outward conformity" and the continuity of worship were emphasized, along with the example of the early church (albeit that the church of the Middle Ages was recognized for its positive influence as well).

In a document called "A Declaration of the Queen's Proceedings Since Her Reign," written in 1569 at the time of the rebellion in the north, and intended to refute rumors and slanders concerning the queen, the principles of comprehension and outward conformity were emphasized. Defending royal supremacy, the queen is represented as saying that the only authority she knew was that provided by the laws of the realm of England, authority recognized by all estates, clerical as well as temporal. She said that she neither challenged nor took to herself "(as malicious persons do untruly surmise) any superiority . . . to define, decide or determine any article or point of the Christian faith and religion, or to change any ancient ceremony of the Church from the form before received and observed by the Catholic and Apostolic Church, or the use of any function belonging to any ecclesiastical person being a minister of the Word and Sacraments of the Church." By such authority as she rightly possessed she was so to govern that her subjects would "live in the faith and obedience of the Christian religion . . . and consequently provide, that the Church may be governed and taught by archbishops, bishops, and ministers according to the ecclesiastical ancient policy of the realm." She further explained: "we know not, nor have any meaning to allow that any our subjects should be molested either by examination or inquisition in any matter, either of faith, as long as they shall profess the Christian faith, not gainsaying the authority of the holy Scriptures and of the articles of our faith contained in the Creeds Apostolic and Catholic, or for matter of ceremonies, or any other external matters appertaining to Christian religion, so long as they shall by outward conversation [i.e., manner of living] show themselves quiet and comfortable, and not manifestly repugnant and obstinate to the laws of the realm, which are established for frequentation or divine service in ordinary churches" (*Queen Elizabeth's Defence of Her Proceedings in Church and State*, W. E. Collins, ed., London, 1958, pp. 45–47).

The policy enunciated here was not always observed, but it included principles based upon political necessities that were formative in the development of Anglicanism. Thus the church was to be not a body of an elect few but of all the people who outwardly conformed, chiefly by joining in public worship at their parish churches. They might be heretics, immoral, doubters, but as long as they presented themselves in orderly fashion week by week at common prayer they were to be accounted members of the church visible, which is the church catholic (*Laws*, book 3, chapter 1, section 7).

The ideal of the national church was to be tested and found impractical in the seventeenth century and beyond. As in other countries there were to be churches, sects, and denominations contending against one another for the allegiance of the citizenry. Yet the ideal of comprehension was to persist, and the conviction that church and state were involved in one another and not ultimately separable was to live on as church leaders such as Coleridge, Arnold, Maurice, Gore, and Temple found the church serving different but equally vital needs in the life of the body politic. Furthermore, the reserve evidence in the official documents of the sixteenth century was to remain. Paul Avis has written, "It was no doubt for reasons of political expediency, that Elizabeth I declined 'to make windows into men's souls,' but that policy came to acquire theological legitimation as the expression of a principle of spiritual reticence" ("What is Anglicanism?" in *The Study of Anglicanism*, edited by Sykes and Booty, p. 421).

Such political and intellectual considerations were to be developed theologically as the Elizabethan Settlement of Religion was challenged by Roman Catholics and Puritans. Against the Roman Catholics John Jewel (1522–1571), writing the official *Apology of the Church of England* (1562, 1564), asserted: ". . . we have searched out of the Holy Bible, which we are sure cannot deceive, one sure form of religion, and have returned again unto the primitive church of the ancient fathers and apostles, that is to say, to the first ground and beginning of things, as unto the very foundation and headsprings of Christ's church" (J. E. Booty, ed., Ithaca, N.Y., 1963, p. 135), and in his Challenge Sermon (1559, 1560) claimed that Roman Catholic teachings such as those on transubstantiation and papal authority were innovations unknown to scripture, the early church fathers, or councils. In doing this Jewel was asserting the authority of scripture (with the tradition of the early church) while through the use of reason distinguishing between essentials and nonessentials, the latter being alterable by a national church (see the Thirty-nine Articles of Religion, Article 6, on scripture, and Article 20, on the authority of the church), and allowing for some differences on lesser matters not only among churches but within a church. The concern was for what a later age would name "unity in diversity," as well as for communion and community in church and commonwealth. Thomas Cranmer, the architect of *The Book of Common Prayer*, regarded the chief end of the church through word and sacraments to be the initiation and maintenance of communion between individuals and Christ, and among the people and peoples for the sake of the commonweal.

The year after the appearance of *The First Book of Common Prayer* (1549), Cranmer stated that the sacrament, which he preferred to call "the Lord's supper and holy Communion," was ordained by Christ "to move and stir all men to friendship, love, and concord, and to put away all hatred, variance, and discord, and to testify a brotherly and unfeigned love between all that be members of Christ" (*Writings and Disputations of Thomas Cranmer*, edited by J. E. Cox, Cambridge, 1844, vol. 1, p. 30). This presumes a deeper or prior meaning, that persons should be in communion with Christ, whereby they have salvation from sin and victory over death in everlasting life. Word and sacrament together effect such a communion. Cranmer wrote: "as the word of God preached putteth Christ into our ears, so likewise these elements of water, bread, and wine, joined to God's word, do after a sacramental manner put Christ into our eyes, hands, and all our senses" (*Writings*, p. 41). Cranmer denied that Christ was corporally in water, bread, and wine, but affirmed that through word and sacraments Christ was in the worthy receivers, word and sacraments being instrumental to change people, bringing them into communion with Christ and with one another in Christ. As Jewel said, "that was not Christ's meaning that the wheaten bread shall lay apart his own nature and receive a certain new divinity, but that he might rather change us, and (to use Theophylact's words) might transform us into his body" (*Apology of the Church of England*, Booty ed., p. 33).

Richard Hooker reflected the influence of Cranmer, *The Book of Common Prayer*, and Jewel in arguing that the purpose of the sacrament is to change people, not things, the things (bread and wine), being instrumental to that purpose. The reasonable person of faith is content to know the purpose of the sacrament and does not speculate on the manner in which Christ is present, in the way that Roman Catholic, Lutheran, and Reformed theologians do: "What these elements are in themselves it skilleth not, it is enough that to me which take them they are the bodie and blood of Christ." Of the purpose and effect of the elements he said: ". . .they are . . . such instruments as mysticallie yeat trulie, invisiblie yeat reallie worke our communion or fellowship with the person of Jesus Christ" (*Laws*, book 5, chapter 67, sections 11–12).

The reticence (or purpose) expressed here is related to the emphasis on worship in the Elizabethan Settlement and the sense of awe and wonder at the heart of that worship: the dynamic of angels descending with doctrine and angels ascending with prayer (*Laws*, book 5, chapter 23, section 1); George Herbert's "God's breath in man returning to his birth"; and the mystical understanding of mutual participation ("that mutuall inward hold which Christ hath of us and wee of him"; *Laws*, book 5, chapter 56, section 1). Thus it is that behind the reticence to spell out more than is essential in understanding the purpose of any doctrine is the realization of human limitations in describing God's being and activities and an overwhelming sense of divine beneficence and grace. A later age would look back to Hooker as the inventor of the three-strand theory of scripture, tradition, and reason. Others have discerned this theory in the writings of Cranmer and Jewel as well. And Hooker does speak of scripture, reason, and "the voice of the Church" (*Laws*, book 5, chapter 8, section 2). But when considering the ways by which God communicates, he expressed awe and wonder: our knowledge "is as a drop of that unemptiable fountaine of wisdom, which wisdom hath diversely imparted her treasures into the world." The ways by which we receive wisdom are not limited to scripture and tradition but are beyond number (*Laws*, book 2, chapter 1, section 4), although scripture, confirmed by the example of the early church, indicates to us all that is necessary to salvation. All knowledge is precious "whereby any part of truth is seen, . . . yea that principal truth [God's word in Scripture]. . . may receive from it some kind of light" (*Laws*, book 3, chapter 8, section 9).

Hooker was responding to what he saw as the Puritan overemphasis on scripture and on human depravity, the implication being that nothing could be done without the express warrant of scripture. Hooker viewed the world, as others had done before and have since, as the theater of God's gracious works and the creation as a whole as fundamentally good, though flawed. There was no great gulf fixed between grace and nature. In his sermon on pride he stated: "God hath created nothing simply for itself, but each thing in all things, and of everything each part in other hath such interest that in the whole world nothing is found whereunto any thing created can say, 'I need thee not'" (*Works*, vol. 5, Cambridge, Mass., 1990, p. 333). Furthermore, scripture is illumined by non-Christian teachings, such as those of the Egyptians and the Chaldeans, the Greeks and the Jews (*Laws*, book 3, chapter 8, section 9).

Thus, in its formative stages, Anglicanism was marked by

spiritual reticence but also by a spiritual and intellectual openness imbued with an atmosphere of awe and wonder. This openness was expressed in diverse ways: by Cranmer and his quest for a central council of the non-Roman churches, by Lancelot Andrewes (1555–1616) in his prayers for the church of the East as well as of the West, by Richard Field (1561–1616), dean of Gloucester, in his fervent ecumenicity, and by Richard Hooker in his controversial statement that the Church of Rome was a true church, albeit an imperfect one (*Laws*, book 5, chapter 68, section 9). This attitude or openness involves a relatively high estimation of humanity as made in the image of God, of persons who, although incapable of salvation without the grace of revelation, are by the grace of creation capable of discerning good from evil and much else. Reason, or "right reason," as the Christian humanists spoke of it, could disclose much about God and moral law. Said John Wilkins (1614–1672), bishop of Chester and warden of Wadham College, Oxford, "The nature of man . . . consists in that faculty of reason whereby he is made capable of religion, of apprehending a Deity, and of expecting a future state of rewards and punishments" (*Principles and Duties of Natural Religion*, London, 1675, pp. 18–19). Openness toward creation led persons such as the naturalist-clergyman John Ray to write of *The Wisdom of God Manifested in the Works of Creation* (1691). Anglicanism was to maintain a lively interest in natural religion and a seeking spirit in regard to all of creation.

This openness was tempered by an insistence upon fundamentals and by the conviction that sin dulls reason and inhibits the will from doing the good that reason illumines. Fundamentals were variously defined by the doctrinal articles of the Thirty-nine Articles of Religion, by part 2 of Jewel's *Apology*, and by Hooker's emphasis on "one Lord, one faith, one baptism," the one faith defined by the creeds as found in rules of faith in the ancient church and in the sacraments of *The Book of Common Prayer* (S. W. Sykes, "Fundamentals of Christianity," in *The Study of Anglicanism*, pp. 235–236). When accused of teaching freedom of the will without qualification, Hooker distinguished between aptness and ability. While insisting upon aptness to choose the good, he denied ability to do good without the assistance of divine grace (*Works*, vol. 4, pp. 18, 101). Lancelot Andrewes taught, with the Schoolmen, that "grace does not abolish nature but perfects it." Humans, he believed, are fallen sinners, but they are not totally corrupt. Their defect is corrected by grace, grace working to perfect that which is imperfect (H. C. Porter, *Reformation and Reaction in Tudor Cambridge*, Cambridge, 1958, p. 393), and the means of grace are the sacraments in which the word works and fallible humans are brought to saving belief in the fundamentals: one Lord, one faith, one baptism.

The attitude being explored here influenced the theological understanding of Anglican ecclesiology. First, the church was viewed as essential in every detail. To be in Christ was to be in the church, his body, to be baptized in the sacrament of justification, and to be a participant in the Holy Communion, the sacrament of sanctification. Hooker said that the church "is in Christ as Eve was in Adam . . . his church he frameth out of the verie flesh, the verie wounded and bleeding side of the Sonne of man" (*Laws*, book 5, chapter 56, section 7). Anglicans were to emphasize ecclesiology and revere the church, but they also, as did others, distinguished between the invisible church and the visible, the former perfect and known only to God, the latter of mixed character, composed, as Saint Augustine taught, of a mixture of wheat and tares. Anglican theologians did not dwell on the invisible church but focused on the visible. In tune with their commitment to a national, comprehensive, inclusive church, the early Anglican theologians believed that the church was composed, as Hooker said, of those who are signed with the marks "One Lord, one faith, one baptism. In whomsoever these things are, the church doth acknowledge them for his children. . . . Christians by external profession they are all, whose marks of recognizance hath in it things, which wee have mentioned, yea, although they be impious idolaters, wicked heretiques, persons excommunicable, yea, and cast out for notorious improbitie" (*Laws*, book 3, chapter 1, section 7). Hooker further said, "Manie things exclude from the Kingdom of God although from the Church they separate not" (*Laws*, book 5, chapter 68, section 6). Richard Field, who wrote the first great study of ecclesiology for nascent Anglicanism, agreed with Hooker, stating that heretics, schismatics, hypocrites, and "wicked men, not outwardly divided from the people of God," are all, with the sanctified ones, "in some degree and sort of that society of men, whom God calleth out to Himself, and separateth from infidels, which is rightly named the Church" (*Of the Church*, vol. 1, Cambridge, 1847, pp. 25–26). In refuting the claims of the sectaries that the church is composed only of the elect, the perfect and pure, these Anglicans, stressing the importance of the church, believed that those whose attachment was by outward observance only, were participants in a holy routine powerful enough to change lives.

That holy routine was, as was true of late medieval religion in general, strongly penitential. Such an emphasis on penitence in nascent Anglicanism was defended in part on the basis of the conviction that God's first will is that all be saved; that God, whose righteous judgment is made known through grace, is loving and merciful; and that by grace the mixed lot of people composing the church in any given place is capable of repentance and new life. The traditional understanding of penitence in terms of contrition, confession, and satisfaction (newness of life) was maintained. There was no sacrament of penance in *The Book of Common Prayer*, although allowance was made for those having difficulty confessing their sins in public worship and alone. They were urged to seek help from the clergy. As some have taught, the confessional was replaced by pulpit and pew, the presentation of the word and the application of it to the lives of clergy and people, resulting in repentance and forgiveness (H. R. McAdoo, *The Structure of Caroline Moral Theology*, London, 1949). It was also taught that although a holy fear was needed in order for repentance to occur, "feare worketh no mans inclination to repentance, till somewhat else have wrought in us love also" (*Laws*, book 6, chapter 3, section 5). This suggests that nascent Anglicanism was marked by a salvific rhythm of contrition and praise with the recognition that there can be no true praise without contrition and no true contrition without praise, which is the recognition of the mercy of God (J. E. Booty, *Three Anglican Divines on Prayer: Jewel, Hooker, Andrewes*, Cambridge, Mass., 1977).

Anglican piety was focused on the God of love whose love is made known through all creation and all history, but chiefly in the revelation of the sacrificial love of God in Christ on the cross. Thus, while sixteenth-century Anglicanism gave serious attention to the Incarnation (see Andrewes's nativity sermons and Hooker's *Laws*, book 5, chapters 50–56), the Crucifixion and Resurrection were ever before ordinary people in liturgy and preaching and in works of theology, beginning with Cranmer. Cramer's *Pascha nostrum* ("Christ our Passover is Sacrificed for Us") sets forth the fundamental theme in the second section of the anthem drawn from Paul's letter to the Romans:

Christ being raised from the dead dieth no more;
  death hath no more dominion over him.
For in that he died, he died unto sin once:
  but in that he liveth, he liveth unto God.
Like wise reckon ye also yourselves to be dead indeed unto
  sin, but alive unto God through Jesus Christ our Lord.

The same theme is found in a sermon of Jewel's in which Christ speaks through him to the congregation, in the holy sonnets of John Donne ("What If This Present Were the World's Last Night"), in poems of Herbert ("The Altar," "The Sacrifice"), and in such sermons as that of Lancelot Andrewes on *Zechariah* 12:10 ("And they shall look upon him whom they have pierced") with reference to *John* 19:37, preached at the court of Queen Elizabeth I. This sermon, which like many others at the time (and like some of the poems of Donne and Herbert) was composed in a meditative style, pictures Christ on the cross, his side pierced, water and blood flowing down, the water of baptism and the blood of the Holy Communion. The preacher asks the congregation to look upon him whom we pierce with our sins, look upon him who pierces us with his love, look and receive the water of baptism and the blood of the sacrament of his body and blood, look and respond in humility, so receiving that we partake of mutual love and learn to love (*Ninety-Six Sermons*, Liturgy of Anglo-Catholic Theology, Oxford, 1841, vol. 2, pp. 134–137).

The political/intellectual and theological/ecclesiological

influences converged in the production of a piety whose nature was expressed in the concept of participation. The outward conformity insisted upon by the queen and statutory law aimed at the comprehension of the greatest possible number of English citizens and involved participation in the church and its organic complex of ministry, word, and sacraments. Such participation had as its purpose participation in Christ, in that essence of Christianity, "One Lord, one faith, one baptism," and was carefully defined by Hooker and others to emphasize communication and not annihilation of the faithful in Christ. The model for mutual participation was found in the doctrine of the Trinity, three in one and one in three. This participation of the faithful in Christ, "that mutual hold which Christ hath of us and we of him" (*Laws*, book 5, chapter 56, section 1), changes the sinful, bringing forgiveness and new life, life eternal. Participation is a mystical reality known by its fruits.

This piety is mystical, but it is not irrational. The Holy Spirit ordinarily operates by means of human reason. Against some Puritans who believed that what they professed they learned directly from the Holy Spirit, Hooker argued that the Spirit has its reasons. It is not enough to be zealous in one's convictions, as are those who claim the direct influence of the Holy Spirit. One must have sound reasons to support one's beliefs (*Laws*, preface, chapter 3, section 10). Such reason is not that of Newtonian physics, limited to quasimathematical deduction and to quantitative inductive reasoning, but rather, as Jeremy Taylor argued, "a transcendent that runs through all topics," or, as Raymond Peterson puts it, "the entire human mind, operating upon the complex and manifold data of human experience" ("The Theology of Jeremy Taylor: An Investigation of the Temper of Caroline Anglicanism," unpublished dissertation, Union Theological Seminary, New York, 1960, p. 60). The implication was that, as in Joseph Hall's *Divine Arte of Meditation* (1606), intellect, memory, and the affections were interactive and interdependent. Therefore, to counteract what some saw as an overemphasis on intellect, the affections were cultivated; and to counteract an overemphasis on the affections, intellect was cultivated. The spirit of *The Book of Common Prayer* may be characterized as "emotion controlled by reason or intellect." The standard Anglican divine is identified as a bishop or priest of the Church of England, or one of the churches of the Anglican communion, "a learned theologian" whose writings include "a wide range of materials: theological treatises, polemical or apologetical tracts, catechetical works . . ., books and essays designed to counsel the faithful in making moral-ethical decisions, sermons, liturgical forms, prayers and meditations for personal devotions" (J. E. Booty, "Standard Divines," in *The Study of Anglicanism*, pp. 163–164). The standard divines include Hooker, Andrewes, Taylor, and others. And in line with the concern for intellect, memory, and affections working in conjunction with one another, with early formative influences emanating from the Universities of Oxford and Cambridge, and the Inns of Court, there has been in Anglicanism a strong emphasis on education, presuming an intimate relationship between theology and prayer and what T. S. Eliot identified as unified sensibility whereby a thought is also a feeling and a feeling a thought. The emphasis on word and sacraments, and thus on sacramentality which includes the word, is both influenced by this theme in Anglicanism and influences it. In all of this there is a strong insistence that the individual be placed at the locus of salvation, the community that is the church, there to be wooed into participation and not coerced.

Here is expressed an ideal, rooted in historical events, extracted and transferred to widely differing contexts, never fully realized, never altogether the same in its various manifestations, rooted and yet always changing, holding firm to a few things ("One Lord, one faith, one baptism") but flexible in the many things (adiaphora), committed to the worship of the one God in whom all is interdependent, through whose incarnate word and living spirit all are made participants of saving grace and live in the world as conduits of grace. The ideal and those who espouse it stand in danger of a simplistic comprehensiveness without clear agreement on fundamentals, or, as W. S. F. Pickering has put it, they are in danger of "flabbiness," uncertain where authority is to be located and wavering in conviction. This accusation was made in the sixteenth century, and it has been made in subsequent centuries. There were times when Anglicanism was viewed as being harshly authoritarian, as in the Hampton Court and Savoy Conferences. But its survival in the sixteenth century was dependent in large part upon its ability to maintain certain delicate balances: between church and state in one commonwealth, between outward conformity and life-changing piety, between grace and nature, between fundamentals and adiaphora, between revelation and reason, between word and sacraments, between authority and freedom, and between intellect and the affections. Its identity is to be located not in a formula but rather in the midst of vital tensions.

[See also Hooker, Richard; Jewel, John; Nonconformity; Presbyterianism; Puritans; and Separatists.]

BIBLIOGRAPHY

Avis, Paul. *Anglicanism and the Christian Church: Theological Resources in Historical Perspective*. Edinburgh and Minneapolis, 1989. A valuable study with a solid section on the sixteenth century.

Holmes, Urban T. III. *What is Anglicanism?* Wilton, Conn., 1982. A general consideration of the identity of Anglicanism with historical reflections.

McAdoo, Henry. *The Spirit of Anglicanism*. London, 1965. Specifically concerned with seventeenth-century theology; nevertheless, important for an understanding of the formation of Anglicanism in the sixteenth century.

Neill, Stephen. *Anglicanism*. 3d rev. ed. London, 1977. Most widely read modern study of the subject. First six chapters present historical review through the seventeenth century.

Sykes, Stephen W. *The Integrity of Anglicanism*. London, 1978. This book marks a turning point in the discussion of Anglicanism. Most important.

Wolf, William J. *Anglican Spirituality*. Wilton, Conn., 1982. Essays, mostly historical, by various scholars on a subject of growing importance in the discussion of Anglicanism.

Wolf, William J., ed. *The Spirit of Anglicanism: Hooker, Maurice, Temple*. Reprint, Edinburgh, 1982. The essay on Hooker is by John Booty.

JOHN E. BOOTY

ANNE OF CLEVES (1515–1557), fourth consort of Henry VIII. The second of three daughters of John, duke of Cleves, and Mary of Juliers, Anne was provided with a limited education. She learned no foreign language and was unable to play on instruments or sing, although she did become proficient in needlework. With the death of Queen Jane in 1537, Henry VIII's councilors, led by Thomas Cromwell, began for diplomatic reasons to search seriously for a new queen among the German candidates. In late 1538 Paul III put into effect the suspended bull of excommunication against Henry; and in early 1539, with the withdrawal of their ambassadors from England, Charles V and Francis I signaled their mutual hostility toward the kingdom. Cromwell narrowed the search to Anne, whose brother William had succeeded as duke of Cleves. The duke denied the papal supremacy, but, despite his strong connections with Protestants, he was not a Lutheran. After viewing a portrait of Anne by Hans Holbein the Younger, Henry agreed to the marriage. On New Year's eve, 1540, she arrived at Rochester, where Henry, conforming to the welcoming practice of contemporary monarchs, visited her privately in disguise. They were married at Greenwich on 12 January.

Cromwell's fall and execution have been blamed on a factional struggle at court in which the Catholics, headed by Thomas, duke of Norfolk, emerged victorious. The softening of the rapprochement between France and the empire seems also to have made this ministerial change possible. In July convocation annulled the marriage on the ground of her precontract with the duke of Lorriane's son and of the king's selective impotence toward her, an inability then usually blamed on witchcraft. Known as the king's sister, she received considerable estates and agreed to reside in England. At her death in 1557 she was buried in Westminster Abbey.

BIBLIOGRAPHY

MacEntegart, Roy. "Fatal Matrimony: Henry VIII and the Marriage to Anne of Cleves." In *Henry VIII: A European Court in England*, edited by David Starkey, pp. 140–143. London, 1991. No standard biography of her exists, but this is a recent, useful evaluation.

Scarisbrick, J. J. *Henry VIII*. Los Angeles, 1968. Standard biography of the king with insights into the diplomatic maneuverings of 1539 and 1540.

RETHA M. WARNICKE

ANTICHRIST. The notion of the Antichrist, or "anti-Messiah," is based on several New Testament passages (*1 Jn.* 2, 4; *2 Jn.* 2) and refers to a formidable human antagonist of Christ and his gospel who will make his appearance toward the end of time. The notion has a history reaching from the early church to the present. It is part of the drama of eschatology and the apocalyptic concept that the return of Jesus will be preceded by unprecedented catastrophes and a period of hostility to the Christian church. During that time the Antichrist will appear, a man inspired and controlled by Satan. The Antichrist will not be an open enemy of Christ (therein lies his perniciousness), but will pretend to be the returning Messiah and will gather followers while oppressing and persecuting the true believers. Deceit, false teaching, persecution, apostasy, tyranny, but also miracles will be his hallmarks. It should be noted that the Antichrist is only one of several prominent antagonists of Jesus mentioned in the New Testament.

This rudimentary New Testament notion, which surely bore traces of Jewish and other influences, was increasingly systematized from the early Middle Ages on (by, among others, Augustine and Adso of Martin-en-Der). In the thirteenth century, theological reflection took on practical significance when emperor and pope were identified as the Antichrist by the Spiritual Franciscans; in the following century John Wycliffe in *De Christo et adversario suo Antichristo* repeated the charge against the pope.

The sixteenth century was thus heir to a rich, if evasive, tradition (evasive in the sense that identifications of the Antichrist differed). It is not at all surprising that it was explicitly utilized by Martin Luther in the early phase of the German Reformation, both in his tract on *The Babylonian Captivity of the Church* and in his response to the papal bull that threatened him with excommunication, *Against the Damned Bull of the Antichrist.* In appropriating the medieval tradition of the Antichrist, Luther took a fundamental stance of opposition against the papacy, countering the church's weapon of excommunication with his own weapon of identifying the pope as the Antichrist.

The theme that the pope was the Antichrist was echoed by other reformers and became the hallmark of the Antichrist theme in the Reformation. The German pamphlet *Passional of Christ and Antichrist,* which drew on Wycliffe's comparison between pope and Antichrist by means of a series of parallel woodcuts (by Cranach), depicted the radically different demeanors of pope and Jesus, leaving to the reader (and viewer) the inevitable conclusion—embodied in the title—that the pope was indeed the Antichrist. Luther's own view evolved to include elements not found in the medieval tradition (such as his attack on the institution of the papacy rather than individual popes and on papal teaching rather than issues of personal morality), but these were nuances and, moreover, were not always consistently pursued by him. Still, two themes remained prominent in Luther's writings: that the Antichrist epitomized enmity to the true gospel, and that he camouflaged himself with the mantle of Christian teaching. Luther's "theology of the cross" (the notion that divine truth always appears in hiding) thereby appeared in splendid harmony with his understanding of the Antichrist.

This new theological conceptualization (found also in the writings of most other Protestant reformers, including Andreas Osiander, Philipp Melanchthon, Huldrych Zwingli, Johannes Oecolampadius, and John Calvin) was echoed in a wide array of popular literature, stage plays, and so on. While theologically a secondary issue, the theme of pope as Antichrist was effective propaganda, a convenient rallying cry for the Protestant reformers. It even found its way into official documents, such as the Apology of the Augsburg Confession, the Scottish Confession of 1560, and the Westminster Confession of 1647.

One aspect of the Antichrist theme—the Antichrist's usurpation of a Christian mantle—became blurred in some sixteenth-century polemics in that occasionally "the Turk," the military power threatening to overrun central Europe, was identified as the Antichrist. From the Protestant perspective, pope and Turk had in common that both were enemies of the gospel. In either case the Antichrist was not a specific individual, but a group of individuals.

Intra-Reformation polemics extended the concept. The Reformation radicals (for example, Thomas Müntzer, Bernhard Rothmann, and Michael Servetus) saw Luther no less than the pope as the Antichrist, and in so arguing reiterated the traditional notion of the "Christian" pretension of the Antichrist. When, in the second half of the sixteenth century, confessional polemics intensified among the various Protestant factions, all sides found it easy to label the others as Antichrist, now defining the Antichrist as a category rather than an individual. According to Catholic polemists, this definition conflicted with the biblical record, which spoke of the Antichrist in the singular and confined his rule to three and a half years (*Dn.* 7:25, 12:7, 12:11). Relatively late in the Reformation, Roberto Bellarmino offered a systematic Catholic repudiation of the Protestant notion in book 3 of his magnum opus, *Disputationes de controversiis Christianae* (1586–1593), in which he declares the Antichrist to be of Jewish origin.

References to the Antichrist continued to appear in theological and political discourse until the middle of the seventeenth century. The concept figured especially prominently in polemics occasioned by the English Revolution. Not only was the pope identified with the Antichrist; in response to the Catholicizing notions of Archbishop Laud, Puritans attacked the English bishops and the king as the pope's helpers. (The convergence of theological and political opponents is noteworthy.) Hugo Grotius had explored the subject of the Antichrist in his *Commentatio ad loca N. Testamenti quae de Antichristo agunt* (1640), and by highlighting the ambiguity of the concept and the source he eventually succeeded in banishing it from mainstream theological reflection.

The Antichrist literature of the late sixteenth and early seventeenth century must be considered in the broader context of the intellectual currents of the time. Christian theologians had incorporated the Antichrist into a sweeping view of history as outlined in *Daniel* and *Revelation*; the appearance of the Antichrist was taken seriously because the biblical prophecies were taken seriously as history. When, during the course of the seventeenth century, the evidentiary authority of the Bible began to be challenged, the Antichrist as an actor in human history ceased to be an object of widespread theological reflection.

All in all, the Reformation brought a dramatic intensification of the Antichrist polemic. While by no means central for any of the theologians of the time, the concept became an important peg in a more general argument. Always, however, the Antichrist was identified with one's opponent—usually in matters of theology, but sometimes, as in seventeenth-century England, in matters of politics. The Antichrist thus may be seen as serving a political no less than a theological function.

[*See also* Apocalypticism *and* Millenarianism.]

BIBLIOGRAPHY

Hill, Christopher. *Antichrist in Seventeenth-Century England.* Rev. ed. London and New York, 1990. The standard work for England.
Hillerbrand, Hans J. "The Antichrist in the Early German Reformation: Reflections on Theology and Propaganda." In *Germania Illustrata*, edited by Andrew C. Fix and Susan Karant-Nunn, pp. 3–17. Kirksville, Mo., 1992. Seeks to put theology into the context of politics.
McGinn, Bernard. *Antichrist: Two Thousand Years of the Human Fascination with Evil.* San Francisco, 1994.
Preuß, Hans. *Die Vorstellungen vom Antichrist im späten Mittelalter, bei Luther und in der konfessionellen Polemik.* Leipzig, 1906. Continues to be the standard monograph.
Seebass, Gottfried. "Antichrist." In *Theologische Realenzyklopädie*, vol. 3, pp. 28–43. Berlin and New York, 1978.

HANS J. HILLERBRAND

ANTICLERICALISM. As a concept, anticlericalism arose in the nineteenth century during the debate about the political and cultural influence that the Roman Catholic clergy continued to exert or sought to recover in numerous European states (Elm, 1992). In France this occurred during the debate about the heritage of the French Revolution of 1789; in Austria, as a reaction to the massive efforts of the "clericals" to secure the preeminence of the Habsburg monarchy in Europe; and, in Germany, during the *Kulturkampf*, which was carried out between the state and the Roman Catholic church in the period 1872–1879. Where anticlericalism was linked to an atheistic criticism of religion, it became not only an energetic challenge to the church hierarchy

but also an attack on the theology and beliefs that the clergy represented. Here, anticlericalism was a matter of a general triumph over church and religion. "The swindle of the priests" (Holbach), "the opium of the people" (Marx), and "God is dead" (Nietzsche) were the battle cries produced in a climate that was hostile to religion. These slogans implicated the clergy in particular and made it the object of a political-journalistic polemic that was also of significance for cultural history.

This modern concept of anticlericalism cannot be simply applied to social relations in the late medieval and early modern periods. During the age of the Reformation, for example, anticlericalism was not a matter of eradicating religious influence from public life and of relegating religion to the sphere of private life. Anticlericalism then was much more a matter of criticizing those holding office in the church out of a deep, fundamental religious need. The clergy was mocked, insulted, threatened, and actually attacked because it neglected the duties of its offices and generated among the laity an anger that was morally based. The spiritual estate was "totally negligent" (M. Luther, *An den christlichen Adel*, 1520). The laity's trust in the clergy as mediators of salvation declined and was transformed into an aggressive mistrust of the clergy in general. It is appropriate to use the concept of anticlericalism in historical studies as the expression, not of a radical criticism of religion per se, but of a withering criticism that was directed against the clergy as a spiritual estate in society and as the expression of the tensions that arose between the laity and the clergy in the late Middle Ages and the Reformation. In this sense the concept of anticlericalism—which has already been tested in the historiography of the Reformation in England (e.g., by G. Elton, C. Haigh, J. J. Scarisbrick, and A. G. Dickens)—has begun to be applied to the investigation of the Reformation in Germany. The most impressive evidence thus far of the increasing importance of anticlericalism as an interpretive category and explanatory model is the collective volume edited by P. A. Dykema and H. A. Oberman, *Anticlericalism in Late Medieval and Early Modern Europe* (1992).

Before the Reformation. A gradual separation between the laity and the clergy developed after the "peace of God" of the eleventh century (Duby, 1986). This separation received its legal articulation in the twelfth century (Gratian) in the *Codex iuris canonici*: the clergy is called to lead the church, and the laity is obligated to accept this leadership. The sacrament of ordination was a distinctive manifestation of this division; ordination gave the priest a *character indelebilis* that, in comparison with the laity, elevated him to a higher level of participation in divine being and that empowered him to repeat the sacrifice of Christ in the Mass. The spiritual estate alone, not the laity, lived in a condition of "perfection" and was entitled to mediate salvation: it constituted *homo religiosus*. Initially the intermixture of spiritual and temporal estates may have been unproblematic, although already in 1157 Frederick Barbarossa complained of the corrupting attitude of the pope and feared a split between "monarchy and priesthood" (Elm, 1992). Tensions between these estates along a broad front emerged in the late Middle Ages in the wake of the movements of apostolic poverty and heresy. Walther von der Vogelweide complained of the misery that began as "priest and lay began to split" (Maurer, 1972). Johannes Tauler was certainly no longer convinced that every priest was perfect and thought that, in a "spiritual way," every man, or even a woman, was capable of making the priestly sacrifice. Anticlerical hostility radiates from the writings of William Langland, John Wycliffe, and Geoffrey Chaucer in England, and the rebellions of 1381 and 1450 featured anticlerical agitation (Dickens, 1987). Anticlerical resentment is found in Jan Hus and the Hussite Wars, in the *Defensor pacis* of Marsilius of Padua, and in the *Reformatio Sigismundi*. It is even more extreme in the work of the anonymous Upper Rhine revolutionary, in Girolamo Savonarola's apocalyptic calls to repent, and in the reform sermons of Johann Geiler von Kaysersberg, who traced the laity's hatred of the parsons back to the greed of the clergy (*De emeis*, 1516, 28 b). In Sebastian Brant's *Ship of Fools*, in numerous astrological tracts, and in the writings of the humanists (Desiderius Erasmus of Rotterdam, Poggio Bracciolini, and Ulrich von Hutten), there were complaints about the clergy at all levels—in some cases sharp attacks—not only by learned authors but also by the "common man" in urban and rural areas, in city council chambers, in the chancelleries of the territorial princes, and at meetings of the Reichstag (e.g., *Gravamina nationis germaniae*). The theme of anticlericalism was also taken up in literary works and the visual arts, as well as in popular songs, jokes, moral sayings, mocking verses, and fairy tales.

Anticlericalism can be traced to various causes: (1) to the moral failure of those who, in their own minds, represented Christian perfection; (2) to the privileges of legal immunity, freedom from taxation, and supervisory rights over schools and hospitals (citizens were offended that the spiritual estate, despite their legal immunities, enjoyed the advantages of the city and claimed a right to them); (3) to the clergy's release from military, defense, and watch duties; (4) to the clergy's economic activities (credit businesses, beer selling, viticulture, and weaving) that had developed into a burdensome source of competition for lay artisans; (5) to the church's legal system, which increasingly concerned itself with worldly matters, attempted to enforce its judgments with ecclesiastical sanctions (such as excommunication, the ban, and interdiction), and denied that the spiritual estate was subject to secular courts; and (6) to pluralism, begging (mendicant orders), legacy hunting, and luxurious living, especially on the part of prelates, superiors, and noble canons in the cities who charged fees for the performance of ecclesiastical services (stole fees) and neglected the duties of their office. Thus, the causes of anticlericalism were moral,

spiritual, ecclesiastical, fiscal, economic, and cultural. The anticlerical opposition of the laity, from the princes to the burghers and peasants, indicates how intensively and dominantly the ecclesiastical hierarchy had penetrated late medieval social life, so much so that the pressure that the clergy exerted as a ruling elite could be said to be the actual cause of anticlericalism. Only in this way can one explain such phenomena as the storming of cloisters, the "mad years" (*tolle Jahre*) in Erfurt (1509–1516), and the "parson wars" (*Pfaffenkriege*) of some Hansa cities.

From the manifestations of anticlericalism, however, it is not possible to draw firm conclusions about the actual condition of the clergy. These manifestations frequently presented stereotyped arguments (catalogs of vice, satires) and involved ritualized forms of protest and exaggerated and provocative agitation. The massive evidence of anticlericalism, however, expresses similar complaints, as well as similar forms of response to these complaints in various regions and countries (for England, see Dickens, 1987; for Italy, Seidel-Menchi, 1992; and for inner Switzerland, Blickle, 1992). The similarities in the evidence clearly show that the laity did not make up its protests against the clergy from thin air. Rather, they either stemmed from actual experience with the clergy or developed out of a certain mood and movement against the clergy—against the papacy, the upper ranks of the clergy, and the "common parsons." In the course of constructing territorial principalities and in the context of the ascendant communalism in both cities and rural areas, the clergy, with its estate privileges and its hierarchical, lordly forms of conduct, was a hindrance. It was not only tensions between the clergy and the laity, however, that generated anticlericalism. The tensions between regular and secular clergy, the so-called antifraternalism (Szittya, 1986), as well as conflicts concerning the strict or lax observance of an order's rule, contributed to the growth of criticism of the clergy and provided it with additional arguments. For, in general, it was members of the clergy who provided the laity with their language and who made the laity the protagonists of anticlerical articulation.

The observation that the general level of piety on the eve of the Reformation was unusually high does not contradict the presence of a deep anticlericalism in society. To the extent that the lay people of the church felt incapable of renouncing the idea that the clergy mediated their salvation, the "laity's feeling of responsibility for ecclesiastical order clearly increased" (Moeller, 1965). The laity measured the clergy according to the ideal of the *homo religiosus*, and out of concern for their salvation they turned against the spiritual estate, which had left them in the lurch. "Anticlericalism" in the late Middle Ages should be understood as a long struggle of the laity against the clergy—here concealed and there open; here criticism, mockery, and insult, there refusal, aggressive agitation, and violence (including the murder of bishops and priests). Behind this variety of forms stood the laity's intention to free itself from the accumulated complaints against the clergy, but above all the laity sought in these ways to call popes, bishops, priests, and monks to their senses. In sum, concern for salvation, which was deeply rooted in the lives of people, may have been the cause of their hatred of the clergy. It was certainly no "principled anticlericalism" that was expressed in hostility to the church (Borgolte, 1992); rather, it was an anticlericalism that was concerned with a fundamental reform of the clergy and the church.

Reformation Anticlericalism. Late medieval anticlericalism was extremely diverse. Its specific character in individual cases depended on whether its criticism was directed against popes, cardinals, cathedral canons, and prelates or against priests, chaplains, nuns, and monks. It also depended on who was making the criticism, whether members of the clergy itself (e.g., lower clergy against prelates or the reverse) or such members of the laity as peasants, artisans, city councilors, the learned, and princely councillors. Anticlericalism was a complex phenomenon that requires a differentiated analysis. It was also a diffuse phenomenon. On one occasion the protest might be radical, while on another it might be moderate; it might be directed against a specific cleric or order or against the whole estate of the clergy. All the forms of anticlericalism found in late medieval protests are also found in the Reformation, but during the Reformation it became increasingly clear that the estate of the clergy was the object of a radical criticism that called for its abolition. People no longer expected a mere reform of the clergy to accomplish anything. People rapidly became convinced that the papacy was the Antichrist at Rome and that priests as mediators of salvation could be dispensed with. With equal speed, people accepted the slogan of the "priesthood of all believers," which unleashed a powerful impulse that mobilized the laity in favor of the Reformation. In this way a specifically Reformation anticlericalism emerged, one directed toward the complete abolition of the clergy as a social estate. This form of anticlericalism was initially developed in Martin Luther's *An den Christlichen Adel Deutscher Nation* (Address to the Christian Nobility of the German Nation) and was carried further by his *De votis monasticis iudicium* (On Monastic Vows) and his Epiphany sermon from the *Kirchenpostille* of 1522. It contained a "catalog of anticlerical complaints" that found broad resonance (Rublack, 1992). Luther's attacks on the papacy and on monasticism were especially sharp; he described cloisters as "the filthy cunts and whore houses of the devil" (WA 8, 325), and priests as "the trail blazers of the Antichrist" and "the devil's staghounds" (WA 19, 11). It has been debated precisely when Luther's thought began to be suffused by a general anticlericalism (Goertz, 1987, especially pp. 84–90; Brecht, 1992; and Moeller, 1992). But it is indisputable that with his writings of 1520 Luther contributed decisively to a

suspension of the sale of indulgences and that the authority of the papacy continued to collapse, monks and nuns began to leave their cloisters and orders, and priests began to marry. Luther intensified the anticlerical atmosphere—not accidently but very deliberately—and his anticlerical orientation was anchored at the center of the Reformation he inaugurated. In Luther's view the works righteousness of the priests and cloistered clergy, who worked hand in hand with the Antichrist, stood in glaring contradiction to justification by faith alone which was valid before God (Goertz, 1992). Anticlerical agitation with an evangelical intent is already observable in the Erfurt "parsons storm" (*Pfaffensturm*) of 1521 and in the Wittenberg unrest of 1521–1522. It had, in fact, made its appearance even earlier in Jüterbog and Zwickau, where Thomas Müntzer was first active in the Reformation cause. In the following period there was scarcely a city in which anticlerical agitation did not appear with the initial preaching of the evangelical message (Scribner, 1992). This agitation, which above all served the purposes of propagating Reformation ideas among the people and of forcing a political decision in favor of the Reformation, belongs to the general etiology of the Reformation. Anticlerical agitation, whose forms of expression were filled with manifold fantasies and which was often highly ritualistic (Scribner, 1987, pp. 103–122), continued to occur even after Luther, who was shocked by the first great anticlerical upheavals, warned against it in his *Treuen Vermahnung sich zu hüten vor Aufruhr* (True Warning to Guard Against Insurrection; 1522), and curtailed his own anticlerical polemic. Luther certainly hoped that events would not lead to an open insurrection against the clergy, but he could not entirely discount this possibility.

Too many voices had already entered the struggle over the Reformation for Luther alone to prevail in his warning. Anticlerical sermons and agitation continued—spontaneously or with a prepared dramaturgy (e.g., the *Fastnacht* plays of Niklaus Manuel). Sermons were disrupted; images and cloisters were attacked; the old believers among the priests were mocked, threatened, and actually attacked; the tithe was refused; and Communion hosts were destroyed. Occasionally the clergy had to be placed under the protection of secular authorities. But above all the swelling flood of pamphlets and leaflets propagandized for the Reformation, and in this literature the anticlerical argument dominated the content: "A rage for battle against the spiritual estate penetrates these pages" (Störmann, 1916). One can speak of anticlericalism reaching a culmination in the age of the Reformation not only with respect to visual propaganda (Goertz, 1991), but also with respect to pamphlet literature in general (Rublack, 1992). The anticlerical argument—in its assumptions, development, and application by various means—is especially prominent in writings by monks who had fled their cloisters and among the famous pamphlet authors Johann Eberlin von Günzburg, Heinrich von Kettenbach, and Johann Rot-Locher, who combined anticlerical and antifraternalistic arguments (Dipple, 1991). The transition from late medieval to Reformation anticlericalism is especially evident in the developmental phases that Günzburg passed through.

Anticlericalism also played an important role in the effort of the radical reformers to bring about a renewal of Christianity. Andreas Bodenstein von Karlstadt, the leading figure of the Wittenberg unrest, gained prominence through symbolic actions that were bound to provoke the traditional clergy: he set aside priestly vestments, distributed the Lord's Supper in the forms of both bread and wine, renounced his offices, and moved to the country as a "new layman." His anticlericalism was directed toward a communal orientation for the Reformation. Thomas Müntzer, who already at Zwickau in 1520–1521 was involved in a conflict with the Franciscans, expressed anticlerical insults in his writings and missed no opportunity to contest the clergy's right of existence and to demand that, in fact, the laity should be "our prelates and pastors." He coupled his anticlerical argument with mystical piety and apocalyptic expectations. He contrasted the parson, negligent and lacking the divine spirit, with the layman, filled with the spirit and yielding to God; he relegated both to the Last Judgment, in which the separation of the damned and the elect that had already begun would be completed. Not only the Roman clergy but also the Wittenberg reformers and worldly authorities who stood in the way of his "future Reformation" must be conquered—and annihilated (Goertz, 1989).

A violent anticlericalism also emerged in the Peasants' War in 1525. Their demands for the right to elect their own pastors and for communal self-determination in religious matters, both of which were expressed in the Twelve Articles, were among the mildest forms of anticlerical rebelliousness. The peasants also went after priests, abbots, and monks. They refused to pay dues owed to the clergy, plundered their storage cellars, drove out monks and nuns, and destroyed their cloisters (Cohn, 1979).

Anticlericalism could not be repressed. After the defeat of the peasants, it appeared again in the movements of the Anabaptists. The proto-Anabaptists had been active earlier on the general Reformation-anticlerical scene, and after 1525 they found their own sense of religious identity by inverting the features of the image of the Roman Catholic priest. They disrupted sermons and masses; refused to pay the tithe (Stayer, 1992); destroyed images and crucifixes; and mocked the clergy, women as well as men. The practice of Anabaptist piety—in the concrete, lived experience of the imitation of Christ—can be understood as an anticlerical reflex, as can the fraternally oriented constitution of their communities (above all in Switzerland), in which the power of the ban lay more with the members of the community than

with the leadership. Anticlerical components also entered their Communion liturgy and baptismal practices. These rituals were now practiced without priests, without cult ceremony and paraphernalia, and at profane places. The Anabaptists loathed "antichristian customs" (Goertz, 1988). Anticlericalism was expressed in their various movements in various ways, but it was present everywhere—in Switzerland, in central and upper Germany, in the Tirol and Moravia, in the Netherlands, in Münster, and in East Friesia. Occasionally the Anabaptists took the reanimation of the ideal of the *homo religiosus* so seriously that contemporaries feared the development of a "new monasticism." One explanation for this anticlericalism is that most Anabaptist spokesmen were former clerics who had decisively turned their backs on their own previous lives. Another explanation is that the dualistic way of arguing, which was inherent in anticlericalism, had great persuasive power among the commoners in the Anabaptist movements, and the moral integrity of the Anabaptist leadership facilitated the recruitment of many followers.

A Sociohistorical Explanatory Model. Anticlerical emotions and arguments were also present among spiritualists, antitrinitarians, and all who attempted to escape the influence of the church hierarchy. Anticlericalism meant criticism, on the basis of their membership in a definite social estate, of those who held office in the church; it was criticism of persons who exercised spiritual and, in part, temporal power but who, if they were going to imitate Christ, should be servants rather than rulers. Luther relied entirely on the abolition of the estate of the clergy; he did not intend to bring a new church into existence but to maintain the old church and to use its original power to renew it. Thus, anticlericalism was not synonymous with criticism of the church, or was so only insofar as the Roman church defined itself in terms of a clerical hierarchy. The dynamic of Reformation controversies is best explained by maintaining the distinction between anticlericalism and criticism of the church. On the one hand, the object of criticism was restricted to a social estate; on the other, criticism widened out to encompass society as a whole. With respect to Protestantism, anticlericalism removed the "first estate." Finally, one may speak of a post-Reformation anticlericalism (Scribner, 1987), but with the qualification that it was no longer a matter of criticizing a social estate to whom the laity of the church were contrasted as estate members (as was once the case for the clergy of the old church) but rather of criticizing ecclesiastical functionaries.

In the period of the Reformation, anticlericalism had many faces. Its forms of expression and justifications were diverse, as were its instrumentalities, its intensity, and its degree of radicalism. Common to all forms, however, was the intention of setting aside the clergy as a social estate. To a considerable extent this was attained—monks and nuns left their cloisters, priests became laypeople, the clergy lost its estate representation in territorial diets, and spiritual power was secularized. The process leading to this outcome occasionally bore features that were revolutionary, so that the Reformation is sometimes interpreted as an "anticlerical revolution" (Kingdon, 1974). Certainly it would be inappropriate to regard anticlericalism as *the* cause of the Reformation, but, equally, it is not a fiction (Haigh, 1983). Rather, anticlericalism molded the socioreligious milieu in which Reformation ideas and actions found their form and direction. In this milieu anticlericalism obviously could become one among several causes and one among several goals—above all, in Germany, Switzerland, the Netherlands, and England. In Italy the situation was different. Here anticlericalism was not an agent of religious and social transformation as it was elsewhere in the late Middle Ages and the Reformation. Rather, it was an escape valve that gave people the opportunity to release their rage and anger against a clergy with whom they had to live in close contact. In the last analysis, anticlericalism in Italy worked to stabilize the *corpus Christianum*, whereas elsewhere it broke it apart, dissolved it, or destroyed it (Seidel-Menchi, 1992). In the concept of anticlericalism, religious, cultural, social, economic, and political factors combine to form a model of historical explanation that helps clarify and analyze in a differentiated way the processes surrounding the origins of the Reformation.

[*See also* Clergy; Common Man; Concubinage; *and* Riots, Religious.]

BIBLIOGRAPHY

Arnold, Klaus. *Niklashausen 1476*. Baden-Baden, 1980.

Blickle, Peter. "Antiklerikalismus um den Vierwaldstätter See 1300–1500: Von der Kritik der Macht der Kirche." In *Anticlericalism in Late Medieval and Early Modern Europe*, edited by Peter A. Dykema and Heiko A. Oberman, pp. 115–132. Leiden, 1992.

Borgolte, Michael. *Die mittelalterliche Kirche*. Munich, 1992.

Cohn, Henry J. "Reformatorische Bewegungen und Antiklerikalismus in Deutschland und England." In *Sozialgeschichte der Reformation in England und Deutschland*, edited by Wolfgang J. Mommsen et al., pp. 309–329. Stuttgart, 1979.

Corvin(-Wiersbitzki), Otto Julius Bernhard von. *Pfaffenspiegel*. Reprint, Schwerte, 1974.

Dickens, A. G. "The Shape of Anti-Clericalism and the English Reformation." In *Politics and Society in Reformation Europe*, edited by E. J. Kouri and Tom Scott, pp. 379–410. Houndmills and London, 1987.

Dipple, Geoffrey Luke. "'Woe unto you Stomachpreachers, Cheesebeggars, and Hypocrites!': Antifraternalism and Reformation Anticlericalism." Ph.D. diss., Queen's University, Kingston, Ont., 1991.

Duby, Georges. "Die Laien und der Gottesfrieden." In *Wirklichkeit und höfischer Traum: Zur Kultur des Mittelalters*, pp. 117–132. Berlin, 1986.

Dykema, Peter A., and Heiko A. Oberman, eds. *Anticlericalism in Late Medieval and Early Modern Europe*. Leiden, 1993.

Elton, G. R. *Star Chamber Stories*. Reprint, London and New York, 1974.

Faguet, Émile. *Anticléricalisme*. Paris, 1905.

Fast, Heinold. "Reformation durch Provokation: Predigtstörungen in den ersten Jahren der Reformation in der Schweiz." In *Umstrittenes Täufertum, 1525–1975: Neue Forschungen*, edited by Hans-Jürgen Goertz, 2nd ed., pp. 79–110. Göttingen, 1977.

Franz-Willing, Georg. *Kulturkampf: Staat und katholische Kirche in Mitteleuropa von der Säkularisation bis zum Abschluss des Preussischen Kulturkampfes*. Munich, 1954.

Fubini, Riccardo. *Umanesimo e secolarizzazione da Petrarca a Valla*. Rome, 1990.

Gebhardt, Paul. *Die Gravamina der deutschen Nation gegen den römischen Hof*. 2d ed. Breslau, 1895.

Geiler von Kaysersberg, Johann. *Die Emeis*. Strasbourg, 1516.

Goertz, Hans-Jürgen. "Aufstand gegen den Priester: Antiklerikalismus und reformatorische Bewegungen." In *Bauer, Reich und Reformation*, edited by Peter Blickle, pp. 182–200. Stuttgart, 1982.

———. "Der fremde Menno Simons: Antiklerikale Argumentation im Werk eines melchioritischen Täufers." In *The Dutch Dissenters: A Critical Companion to Their History and Ideas*, edited by Irvin B. Horst, pp. 160–176. Leiden, 1986.

———. *Pfaffenhaß und groß Geschrei: Die reformatorischen Bewegungen in Deutschland, 1517–1529*. Munich, 1987.

———. *Die Täufer: Geschichte und Deutung*. 2d ed. Munich, 1988.

———. *Thomas Müntzer: Mystiker, Apokalyptiker, Revolutionär*. Munich, 1989.

———. "'Bannwerfer des Antichrist' und 'Hetzhunde des Teufels': Die antiklerikale Spitze der Bildpropaganda in der Reformation." *Archive for Reformation History* 82 (1991), 5–38.

———. "'What a Tangled and Tenuous Mess the Clergy Is': Clerical Anticlericalism in the Reformation Period." In *Anticlericalism in Late Medieval and Early Modern Europe*, edited by Peter A. Dykema and Heiko A. Oberman, pp. 499–520. Leiden, 1992.

———. *Religiöse Bewegungen in der frühen Neuzeit*. Munich, 1993.

Goertz, Hans-Jürgen, ed. *Umstrittenes Täufertum, 1525–1975: Neue Forschungen*. 2d ed. Göttingen, 1977.

Haas, Martin. "Der Weg der Täufer in die Absonderung: Zur Interdependenz von Theologie und sozialem Verhalten." In *Umstrittenes Täufertum, 1525–1975: Neue Forschungen*, edited by Hans-Jürgen Goertz, 2d ed., pp. 50–78. Göttingen, 1977.

Haigh, Christopher. "The Reformation Historiography of the English Reformation." *Historical Journal* 25 (1982), 995–1007.

———. "Anticlericalism and the English Reformation." *History* 68 (1983), 391–407.

Heimpel, Hermann. "Das fünfzehnte Jahrhundert in Krise und Beharrung." *Vorträge und Forschungen* 9 (1965), 9–29.

Hergemöller, Bernd-Ulrich. "Pfaffenkriege" im spätmittelalterlichen Hanseraum. Cologne, 1988.

Hörger, Marlies. *Märchen von Ketzern*. Frankfurt a.M., 1986.

Kingdon, Robert M. "Was the Protestant Reformation a Revolution?" In *Transition and Revolution: Problems and Issues of European Renaissance and Reformation History*, edited by Robert M. Kingdon, pp. 53–77. Minneapolis, 1974.

Kobelt-Groch, Marion. "Frauen gegen Geistliche: Weiblicher Antiklerikalismus in frühreformatorischen und täuferischen Bewegungen." *Mennonitische Geschichtsblätter* 49 (1992), 21–31.

Kurze, Dieter. "Der niedere Klerus in der sozialen Welt des späteren Mittelalters." In *Beiträge zur Wirtschafts- und Sozialgeschichte des Mittelalters*, edited by Knut Schulz, pp. 273–305. Cologne, 1976.

Lortz, Josef. "Zur Problematik der kirchlichen Missstände im Spätmittelalter." *Trierer theologische Zeitschrift* 58 (1949), 1–26, 212–227, 257–279, 347–357.

Maurer, Ferdinand. *Die politischen Lieder Walthers von der Vogelweide*. 3d rev. ed. Tübingen, 1972.

Moeller, Bernd. "Frömmigkeit in Deutschland um 1500." *Archive for Reformation History* 56 (1965), 5–31.

———. "Kleriker als Bürger." In *Festschrift für Hermann Heimpel*, vol. 2, pp. 195–224. Göttingen, 1972.

Moser, Dietz-Rüdiger. *Verkündigung durch Volksgesang: Studien zur Liedpropaganda und Katechese der Gegenreformation.* Berlin, 1981.

Oberman, Heiko A. "Tumultus rusticorum: Von 'Klosterkrieg' zum Fürstensieg." In *Deutscher Bauernkrieg 1525*, edited by Heiko A. Oberman, pp. 301–306. Stuttgart, 1974.

Oexle, Otto G. "Die funktionale Dreiteilung als Deutungsschema der sozialen Wirklichkeit in der ständischen Gesellschaft des Mittelalters." In *Ständische Gesellschaft und soziale Mobilität*, edited by Winfried Schulze, pp. 19–51. Munich, 1988.

Owst, G. R. *Literature and the Pulpit in Medieval England.* 2d rev. ed. New York, 1966.

Pfrunder, Peter. *Pfaffen, Ketzer, Totenfresser: Fastnachtskultur der Reformationszeit; Die Berner Spiele des Niklaus Manuel.* Zurich, 1989.

Rosenow, Emil. *Wider die Pfaffenherrschaft: Kulturbilder aus den Religionskämpfen des 16. und 17. Jahrhunderts (1904–1905).* 2 vols. Reprint, Menden, 1987.

Scarisbrick, J. J. *The Reformation and the English People.* Oxford, 1984.

Schmidt, Heinrich Richard. *Reichsstädte, Reich und Reformation: Korporative Religionspolitik, 1521–1529/30.* Stuttgart, 1986.

Schulze, Manfred. *Fürsten und Reformation: Geistliche Reformpolitik weltlicher Fürsten vor der Reformation.* Tübingen, 1990.

Scribner, Bob (Robert W.), ed. *Bilder und Bildersturm im Spätmittelalter und in der frühen Neuzeit.* Wiesbaden, 1990.

Scribner, Robert W. *For the Sake of Simple Folk: Popular Propaganda for the German Reformation.* Cambridge, 1981.

———. *Popular Culture and Popular Movements in Reformation Germany.* London and Ronceverte, 1987. See "Reformation, Carnival and the World Turned Upside Down," pp. 71–102; "Ritual and Reformation," pp. 103–122; and "Anticlericalism and the German Reformation," pp. 243–256.

Snyder, C. Arnold. "Biblical Text and Social Context: Anabaptist Anticlericalism in Reformation Zürich." *Mennonite Quarterly Review* 65 (1991), 169–191.

Störmann, Anton. *Die städtischen Gravamina gegen den Klerus.* Münster, 1916.

Strauss, Gerald, ed. *Manifestations of Discontent in Germany on the Eve of the Reformation.* Bloomington, Ind., 1971.

Szittya, Penn R. *The Antifraternal Tradition in Medieval Literature.* Princeton, 1986.

Talkenberger, Heike. *Sintflut: Prophetie und Zeitgeschehen in Texten und Holzschnitten astrologischer Flugschriften, 1488–1528.* Tübingen, 1990.

Tauler, Johannes. *Predigten.* Edited by Georg Hofmann. Freiburg, 1961.

Weiss, Ulman. *Die frommen Bürger von Erfurt: Die Stadt und ihre Kirche im Spätmittelalter und in der Reformationszeit.* Weimar, 1988.

HANS-JÜRGEN GOERTZ
Translated from German by Michael G. Baylor

ANTIJUDAISM. *See* Antisemitism; Jews.

ANTINOMIANISM.

Throughout the sixteenth century disputes occurred over the place of the law in Protestant theology and practice. In its broadest application antinomianism means simply license. John Calvin accused his libertine opponents of wanting to do away with the law (*Institutes*, II.vii.13). This same usage occurred in Puritan disputes in early seventeenth-century England and surfaced at nearly the same time in clashes between Anne Hutchinson and John Cotton in New England. In its narrower definition, antinomianism describes one set of disputes involving Martin Luther, Philipp Melanchthon, and Johann Agricola over whether the law played any significant role in repentance and salvation, and a second, separate set involving Luther's theological heirs that focused on the role of the law in justification and on the relation between law and gospel.

Prelude: Melanchthon's Visitation Articles. In June 1527 Elector John of Saxony authorized a visitation of the churches in his realm. The visitors included a theologian, Melanchthon, who drafted an outline of evangelical theology to serve as a guide and catechism for Saxony's pastors and preachers. These *Articuli Visitatorum* occasioned two waves of opposition. In August 1527 Caspar Aquila, preacher in Saalfeld, and Johann Agricola, rector of the Latin school in Eisleben, objected to Melanchthon's criticism of antipapal preaching and accused him of returning to Rome by dividing repentance into contrition, confession, and satisfaction. When the elector himself voiced concerns, Luther reassured him that the *Articuli Visitatorum*, having been translated into German and edited by Luther, did not spell a return to papal doctrine, despite the use of old terminology.

After the unauthorized publication in October 1527 of an unrevised Latin version of the articles, Agricola leveled substantive theological charges against them for teaching that sorrow for sin arose not from the gospel and the love of God but rather from the fear of punishment incited by the law. As he had already argued in his *In Evangelium Lucae annotationes* (Annotations on Luke; 1525; 2d ed. 1526), in his catechism (*Elementa pietatis*, 1527), and in his sermons on *Colossians* (*Die Epistel an die Colosser, S. Pauls, zu Speier gepredigt*, 1527), Agricola insisted that the law did not lead to true repentance but only to pride or despair, as in the cases of King Saul and Judas. Only those who, like Peter before his denial, had believed the promise of Christ could come to true repentance.

The feuding parties met at the Torgau Castle November 26–29, where Luther achieved reconciliation by proposing a compromise to what he labeled a war of words. To be sure, general faith preceded repentance, since one must believe that there is a God who threatens, but only justifying faith, which arose after the law had condemned, made a person righteous through the forgiveness of sin. Sinners under God's wrath could scarcely determine whether their sorrow over sin arose out of fear or love.

While this compromise is reflected both in the second edition of Melanchthon's commentary on *Colossians* (*Scholia in Epistolam Pauli ad Colosseuses*, 1528), in the third edition of Agricola's commentary on *Luke* (1529), and in the German edition of the *Articuli Visitatorum* (1528), the basic theology of neither man was affected. Thus, Agricola's 1528 catechism (*130 Fragestücke*) downplayed the role of the Ten Commandments and insisted that the best penitence was to refrain from sinning. Melanchthon made the law the basis of humanity's relation to God, developing in the third edition of his *Colossians* commentary (1534) the notion of a "third use" of the law, as a guide for Christians. Luther's catechisms of 1529 answered Agricola by stressing the commandments and joining fear and love in their fulfillment.

The First Antinomian Controversies, 1537–1540. At the end of 1536 Agricola abruptly left Eisleben in an attempt to become a teacher in Wittenberg. He moved his large family into Luther's house and at about the same time subscribed to the Schmalkald Articles. By June 1537, however, charges of antinomianism against Agricola had surfaced among members of Luther's inner circle, who complained of innovations in Agricola's sermons. Johannes Bugenhagen, anticipating a prolonged absence in Denmark, even refused to allow Agricola to replace him as preacher at the city church. At the same time some theses, which attacked both Luther and Melanchthon for abandoning their own theology in favor of legalism, circulated anonymously.

As in the earlier controversy, the dispute centered on the role of the law in justification and preaching. For Agricola the true preaching of repentance did not focus on the violation of the law but upon the violation of the Son of God, to whom one was bound by the promise of baptism. Thus, according to his interpretation of *Luke* 24:47, the gospel, not the law, worked faith and thereby repentance. Melanchthon regarded this view as an attack on his own theology, which stressed the law's "third use" to guide believers, and argued that good works were a "*causa sine qua non*" of salvation. (This latter position had been debated in the so-called Cordatus Controversy of 1536 between Conrad Cordatus and Caspar Cruciger.) While not placing the law in as central a position as Melanchthon, Luther also attacked the antinomians. God had given the law to put the old creature to death. To eliminate the law from the preaching of repentance was a fraud that simply turned the gospel itself into law and, rather than avoiding the law, increased God's wrath. Instead, preaching must move the penitent from law, which works death, wrath, and punishment in the old creature, to gospel, which creates faith, consolation, and forgiveness for the new—never the other way around.

An early reconciliation between Agricola and Luther in September 1537 was shattered in October when the former tried to publish his *Summarien über die Evangelien*, in which he insisted that the law could not effect true repentance. This view provoked Luther into banning its publication. In December Luther published the theses anonymously, with his responses. The theses argued among other things that the law belonged in the courthouse, not God's house. Luther then debated them at the University of Wittenberg in a disputation from which Agricola was conspicuously absent. Threatened with being banned from lecturing, Agricola at-

tended another disputation (12 January 1538) and, through the entreaties of his wife, Elsa, again was reconciled with Luther. In a third disputation on the subject (September 1538), Luther admitted to having used some of the same formulae as the antinomians but claimed that this occurred because the audience was different. Frightened consciences needed comfort; self-assured ones needed the law. By failing to preach law before gospel, the antinomians made secure consciences feel more secure and fostered licentiousness. Like many epigoni, Agricola had caught part of Luther's idea—the centrality of the gospel and Christian freedom in criticizing the late medieval church—without finally understanding the crucial distinction between law and gospel.

Melanchthon effected another reconciliation between the two that resulted in Agricola's request that Luther write on the subject, which Luther did in *Wider die Antinomer* (Against the Antinomians; 1539). There, dismissing the charge that he rejected the law, Luther argued that antinomianism attempted to remove Christ from the Christian and to avoid God's wrath. Avoiding the word *law* in theology did not lessen its effects. When the controversy flared yet again in 1539, Agricola appealed first to the rector of the university and, when that failed, filed a formal complaint with the elector in March 1540. Luther and the other theologians at Wittenberg dismissed Agricola's charges and counterattacked. Formal proceedings were begun against Agricola in Wittenberg's consistory, culminating in his hasty flight to Berlin in August 1540. A formal reconciliation was reached when Agricola withdrew his complaint against Luther and in December published a retraction of his understanding of law.

The Second Antinomian Controversies, 1550–1580. After Luther's death (1546) a second wave of controversies over the law arose among Lutherans as they attempted to reconcile Luther's theology to Melanchthon's. By the late 1540s Melanchthon had come to view the law increasingly in moral categories and thus became convinced that the gospel, not the law, was alone capable of bringing about true repentance. His definition of the gospel as "the entire doctrine of Christ" brought him into conflict with Matthias Flacius Illyricus and other Gnesio-Lutherans, who defined the gospel narrowly as consolation and who suspected Melanchthon of confusing law and gospel.

Besides early disputes between Flacius and Melanchthon and later between Flacius and Viktorin Strigel, the same conflict arose in the 1570s between Johann Wigand on the Gnesio-Lutheran side and Paul Crell on the Philippist side. Following Melanchthon, Crell argued that only the gospel could reveal the sin of unbelief. The Gnesio-Lutherans insisted that this was an antinomian confusion of law and gospel. Article 5 of the Formula of Concord addressed this dispute by granting validity to Melanchthon's broader definition of gospel but insisting that, strictly speaking, the gospel comforts transgressors of the law with God's mercy.

A second dispute also arose in the aftermath of disputes over the so-called Leipzig Interim, but among Gnesio-Lutherans. To counteract the proposal of Melanchthon's students Georg Major and Justus Menius that good works were necessary for salvation, a synod was called in Eisenach in 1556. The theses to which Menius was forced to subscribe included a statement that good works were hypothetically necessary for salvation but that human sin prevented using the law and good works actually to obtain salvation. While Flacius, Wigand, and another Gnesio-Lutheran, Joachim Mörlin, were willing to defend this statement, Andreas Poach, who served a congregation in Erfurt, and Anton Otto, preacher in Nordhausen, were not. Poach rejected any notion that God was obligated to human beings through their performing the law. Even perfect obedience earned nothing from God. Mörlin responded that Jesus himself had upheld the law as a way of salvation and that Poach's approach, by undermining the third use of the law, was at heart antinomian. Otto insisted that the law, while accusing sinners and ordering society, had no positive use regarding either justification or good works, since the former arose from grace and the latter were spontaneous fruit of the Holy Spirit. These views and some radical antinomian theses written by Otto's supporters were discussed at the Altenburg Colloquy of 1568–1569. Article 6 of the Formula of Concord addressed this debate.

A third dispute also had its roots in the Majoristic controversy and erupted between Agricola's student and brother-in-law, Andreas Musculus, and the Philippist Abdias Praetorius, both of Frankfurt an der Oder. Musculus argued that good works flow from faith naturally and spontaneously, not through the threats of the law. Praetorius again insisted upon a third use of the law (to which Musculus objected), but denied that this implied any coercion. This dispute was far more bitter than the others, ending publicly only when Praetorius moved back to Wittenberg in 1563, but simmering even after that time among the clergy of Brandenburg. Although branded as an antinomian, Musculus contributed to the final draft of the Formula of Concord. Article 6 attempted to incorporate their conflicting views, emphasizing the necessity of good works and the third use of the law alongside the spontaneity of good works and the law's singularly coercive powers.

All the articles of the formula dealing with these issues wrestled with Luther's insistence on the gospel and faith as central to justification and Melanchthon's assumption that the law outlines the eternal structure of the creature's relation to the creator. In this view Melanchthon and Agricola stand united against Luther. Agricola would end the law's threat by theological fiat, decreeing that it had no place in the gospel or the believer's life. Melanchthon and his students would end its threat by theological definition: narrowing justification to the forensic declaration of God, broadening the gospel to include the law, and making the law

central at every other stage of a human being's relation to God. By contrast, Luther insisted that the threat of the law continues unless and until God brings it to its end through the gospel, effecting the death of the old creature and creating the new life of faith.

The antinomian disputes were among several that raged among Protestants over the nature of justification. They indicate the struggles in understanding Christian freedom from an evangelical perspective, especially when many defined the Christian's relation to God in moral categories. That these disputes dominated especially Lutheran circles shows the tension within Luther's own thought and the interaction between a Lutheran doctrine of justification and a hermeneutic based on the relation between law and gospel.

[*See also* Law, *article on* Theological Understanding of Law.]

BIBLIOGRAPHY

Baker, J. Wayne. "Sola fide, sola gratia: The Battle for Luther in Seventeenth-Century England." *Sixteenth Century Journal* 16.1 (1985), 115–133. This article helps acquaint the reader with antinomian controversies in England after the Reformation.

Battis, Emery. *Saints and Sectaries: Anne Hutchinson and the Antinomian Controversy in the Massachusetts Bay Colony.* Chapel Hill, N.C., 1962. A social analysis, dependent on Perry Miller's work, of this post-Reformation controversy in North America.

Brecht, Martin, and Reinhard Schwarz, eds. *Bekenntnis und Einheit der Kirche: Studien zum Konkordienbuch.* Stuttgart, 1980. One of several German volumes marking the four-hundredth anniversary of the *Book of Concord*, it includes an article by Oswald Bayer on law and gospel.

Edwards, Mark U. *Luther and the False Brethren.* Stanford, Calif., 1975. This rewritten doctoral dissertation includes one chapter on Luther's conflict with Agricola.

Nestingen, James A. "Luther: The Death and Resurrection of Moses." *Dialog* 22 (1983), 275–279. Growing out of the author's doctoral dissertation on an aspect of antinomianism, this article focuses on the theological import of Luther's position in the antinomian dispute with Agricola.

Rogge, Joachim. *Johann Agricolas Lutherverständnis unter besonderer Berücksichtigung des Antinomismus.* Berlin, 1960. This book is by far the most complete analysis of Johann Agricola and his relation to Luther and Melanchthon.

Rosin, Wilbert, and Robert D. Preus, eds. *A Contemporary Look at the Formula of Concord.* Saint Louis, 1978. This collection of essays includes a thorough historical overview by Robert Kolb as well as analyses of articles 5 and 6 of the formula by Henry Hamann and Eugene Klug, respectively.

TIMOTHY J. WENGERT

ANTISEMITISM, hatred of the Jewish people, must be distinguished from "anti-Judaism," which is the religious opposition to Jewish religious teachings, views, or scriptural methods. Whereas the latter is a legitimate Christian perception of Judaism's soteriological and religious deficiencies, the former is the irrational hatred of the Jewish people as human entities and the belief that tolerating Jews will harm the larger society. Antisemitism reached its apogee in the

Holocaust of the twentieth century with the systematic murder of more than six million Jews, but the hatred of Jews provided a powerful social motive for many centuries before that.

Perhaps the most significant historical foundation for antisemitism has been the traditional Christian teaching that Jews remain collectively responsible for the crucifixion of Jesus. Several New Testament writings, especially the gospel of John, exhibit hostility toward Jews, and many early church fathers expressed anti-Jewish sentiments. Among others, Gregory of Nyssa considered Jews "murderers of the Lord, assassins of the prophets, rebels and detesters of God . . . companions of the devil, race of vipers, informers and calumniators, darkeners of the mind . . . and enemies of all that is beautiful." John Chrysostom believed that "living for their belly, mouths forever gaping, the Jews behave no better than hogs and goats in their lewd grossness." Through Carolingian times, church officials and council meetings repeatedly demanded the separation of Jews from Christian society. Before the Crusades, however, Jews seem to have mingled easily with other Europeans since Jewish communities in Italy, France, and Germany predated Teutonic Europe and represented a vital link to Roman times and skills. Between the eleventh and fourteenth centuries overpopulation and other severe demographic problems led to deteriorating economic conditions that were increasingly blamed upon Jews. Indeed, by the twelfth century it was common to hold Jews accountable for most local misfortunes, from poor weather and bad harvests to the untimely death of children and ill health among adults. The most extreme form of hatred of Jews took the form of the "blood libel" and accusations of "ritual murder," which maintained that Jews executed Christian children in order to drain their blood for the baking of Passover bread or for use in other Jewish rituals. Jews were also charged with "host desecration," the theft of eucharistic wafers in order to destroy them in private and thereby reenact the killing of Jesus. Whenever Jews were charged with these crimes, local passions led to pogroms and expulsion. Periods of Christian religious enthusiasm were particularly troubling. During the Crusades, for instance, armies en route to the Holy Land led by Guillaume le Charpentier, Thomas de Feria, and, especially, Emicho von Leiringen devastated entire Jewish communities in the Rhineland. Thereafter, local popular celebrations in many parts of Europe often included annual public humiliations of Jews, and attacking Jewish merchants and houses of worship during Easter week processions became common.

As a result of increasingly hostile anti-Jewish sentiment, the Fourth Lateran Council of 1215 demanded that Jews wear distinctive signs specifically identifying them as Jews. In Germany Jews were often required to wear pointed green hats, while in Latin Europe the general rule was for Jews to affix to their clothing yellow patches in the shape of a disk or the Star of David. Jews were also forbidden to own land, participate in feudal or guild relations, or otherwise compete with Christians. As a result, they dealt with the resale of used clothing or were involved in short-term money lending. Primarily, Jews practiced medicine or commerce or traded within their own communities or with other Jewish communities. In urban areas Jewish residence was usually proscribed to specific neighborhoods, and special taxes were levied upon the community as reparations for Jewish "anti-Christian" behavior.

Despite prohibitions regulating most aspects of Jewish life and the growing isolation of Jewry within Christian society, Jews were increasingly feared as sources of demonic power and malicious intent. During the fourteenth century, for instance, Jews were blamed for spreading the Great Plague by poisoning wells, charges which led to much local violence and widespread expulsions. As a result, from the twelfth to the sixteenth century, most of Europe's ancient Jewish communities were expelled from one country after another: from England in 1215 and 1290, from France in 1315 and 1348, and from most German free imperial cities and states from 1480 to 1500. Finally, in 1492, the largest and oldest Jewish community was expelled from Spain and from Portugal shortly thereafter. Only in Italy, particularly in the Papal States and Venice, were Jews able to maintain some measure of tolerable existence because of their perceived economic value to the local Christian community. Even so, the isolation of Jews from Christians was rigidly maintained, and in 1516 Venice established the first official walled ghetto. Jews were permitted to leave the ghetto during the day but had to return at sunset, when gates were locked until the following sunrise. This residential and legal pattern would soon find its way into other areas of Europe, wherever Jews were tolerated.

In addition to deicide, the usual justification for antisemitism was the charge that Jews refused to convert and thus continued to harm Christianity. Indeed, popular myths such as that of the "Wandering Jew" actually provided justification for Christian ill-treatment of Jews. According to this story, when Jesus labored in the Valley of the Cross, he asked a Jewish bystander for a cup of water. The Jew refused even this small favor, and Jesus cursed him to wander the face of the earth as a perpetual foreigner until he returned. Hence, if Jesus cursed and isolated Jews, Christian society could do no less. Still, before the fifteenth century potential Jewish converts were often offered economic incentives to embrace Christianity, and Jewish communities were required to provide for a "house of converts" where such *Conversos* (New Christians) might reside. After the fifteenth century, however, it became common to assume that racial differences separating Jews from Christians made Jewish conversion unlikely. Indeed, Spanish "purity of blood" statutes assumed that Jews were biologically corrupt and denied the admission of *Conversos* into Christian society for three to seven generations, and often longer, depending upon their biological distance from an earlier Jewish ancestry, lest their blood mix with Christian blood and thereby pollute society. Indeed, contemporary debates regarding the taints of Jewishness attempted to determine whether Christians might also become infected through such nongenerative practices as nursing, kissing, and through the handling of money. Hence, the records of the Spanish Inquisition from Toledo devote four times more space to determining whether *Conversos* were one-fourth, one-sixteenth, one thirty-second, or one sixty-fourth Jewish than to alleged instances of religious irregularity among *Conversos*. Some institutions, such as the Society of Jesus, even imposed "Aryan" laws which forbade descendants of *Conversos* from joining the society despite the fact that Diego Laínez, Juan Alonso de Polanco, and Antonio Possevino, among other important early members of the order, were of Jewish ancestry. These restrictions were removed only in 1945.

The Protestant Reformation brought an intensification of antisemitism since it was assumed that Jews were responsible for all problems of religious dissent. Catholic authorities blamed Jews for exhorting Jan Hus to rebel and then for teaching and spreading Luther's ideas all over Europe. Moreover, the court of Charles V believed Jews aided and abetted the Turkish offensive into eastern Europe. In turn, many Protestants feared "Judaizing tendencies," and Calvinists and Lutherans accused each other of being secret Jews, in league with Jews, or of actually attempting to revive Judaism. Even normally judicious Protestant leaders such as Martin Bucer, author of the precedent-setting *Cassel Advice* of 1538, believed the new Protestant state should enact a hostile social policy for dealing with Jews. Leaders of the Peasants' War such as Thomas Müntzer blamed Jews for the peasant's poor condition, and radicals such as Melchior Hoffman and Balthasar Hubmaier made antisemitism a concomitant feature of their religious systems. As Erasmus quipped, "If to hate Jews is to be a good Christian, we are all abundantly Christian." In this sense, as in so many others, Erasmus was also a man of his times.

While antisemitic writings during the sixteenth century are common, those by Catholic polemicist Johann Eck are possibly the most extreme. Among Protestants, only Luther wrote a considerable number of inflammatory works against Jews, some of which were banned from publication in many German cities and have been deleted from modern collections of Luther's writings. Of major Continental reformers, only Andreas Osiander expressed outrage at German Protestant expressions of antisemitic ideas. Calvin remained silent on this subject, perhaps because Jews had been expelled from Switzerland in the 1490s. By the 1560s, there were virtually no Jews in Germany. Hence, the Reformation witnessed the conclusion of the process of eliminating Jews from western and central Europe begun centuries earlier in England. Jewish communities moved to eastern Europe, especially Poland, Lithuania, and Russia, and to Turkey and the Arab world, already the locus of large Jewish settlement. In turn, this pattern ended in the twentieth century. Eastern European Jewry was entirely eliminated in the Holocaust, and the large Jewish communities in Arab lands were virtually all expelled after 1948, leaving large Jewish population centers only in the United States, Russia, and Israel. Most recently, strident antisemitism in Russia and eastern Europe has led to the migration of several hundred thousand Jews to Israel and the United States.

[*See also* Jews.]

BIBLIOGRAPHY

Hsia, R. Po-Chia. *The Myth of Ritual Murder: Jews and Magic in Reformation Germany.* New Haven, 1988. The most recent and certainly the best treatment of the subject.

Lewin, Reinhold. *Luthers Stellung zu den Juden* (1911). Reprint, Aalen, 1973. A classic study of Luther's writings.

Nijenhuis, Willem. *Bucer and the Jews.* Leiden, 1972. The best study of Bucer's attitudes toward Jews.

Oberman, Heiko A. *The Roots of Antisemitism in the Age of Renaissance and Reformation.* Translated by J. I. Porter. Philadelphia, 1981. The most recent and most provocative treatment of Erasmus, Reuchlin, and Luther by a dean of Reformation studies.

Parkes, James. *The Jew in the Medieval Community.* Reprint, New York, 1976. A standard treatment by antisemitism's most sensitive analyst.

Poliakov, Léon. *The History of Antisemitism.* Translated by R. Howard. New York, 1974. An excellent general summary of the subject.

Sicroff, Albert A. *Les controverses des statuts de "pureté de sang" en Espagne du XVe au XVIIe siècle.* Paris, 1960. The best treatment of the purity-of-blood laws.

Stow, Kenneth R. *Catholic Thought and Papal Jewish Policy, 1555-1593.* New York, 1977. A good recent analysis of post-Tridentine papal Jewish policy.

Sucher, C. Bernd. *Luthers Stellung zu Juden.* Munich, 1977. Along with Lewin, a very good analysis of Luther's writings.

Trachtenberg, Joshua. *The Devil and the Jews.* Reprint, Philadelphia, 1993. The very best treatment of antisemitism from the vantage point of medieval Christian ideas of the demonic and satanic.

JEROME FRIEDMAN

ANTITRINITARIANISM.

A religious doctrine opposed to the dogma on the Holy Trinity as formulated by the Council of Nicea (AD 325) and the Council of Constantinople (AD 381), antitrinitarianism was severely attacked by both Catholics and Protestants (Lutherans, Zwinglians, Calvinists, and Anglicans) during the Reformation. They usually viewed it as a return to the ancient heresies of Arius (256–336), Paul of Samosata (d. around 272), Photinus (4th century), Sabellius (2d–3d century), and still other authors of earlier trinitarian or christological heresies. Hence Catholic and Protestant theologians called the sixteenth-century adherents to antitrinitarianism "Arians," "Samosatenians," "Photinians," "Sabellians," and so on.

The Early Reformation. At the beginning of the Reformation, when there was great doctrinal flexibility, antitrinitarianism and the unorthodox christological formulations inseparable from it found many followers among adherents to Anabaptism, because the latter represented an extreme biblical position that counteracted all speculation as being inimical to the simplicity and directness of the message contained in holy scriptures. On the other hand, early Anabaptism directed to the pursuit of the practical ethical goal of following Christ was often tolerant of doctrinal statements of a "revisionist" nature and treated them as an indispensable element of collective religious life.

One of the pioneers of antitrinitarianism in the Anabaptist camp was the Swiss Ludwig Hätzer (d. 1529), who stated that there is only one God, but Christ is not equal to God and is not of the same essence as God. Christian Entfelder (d. after 1536), who was active in Moravia, Strasbourg, and Königsberg (Kaliningrad), was well read in the writings of the fathers of the church and German mystics. He formulated his conception of God as a triune power: essence, which lay at the root of all things, the Father; action, which was manifested in the creation of the world, the Son; and the godly spirit of love present in all created things, the Holy Spirit. Adam Pastor (Roelof Martens, c.1510–c.1552) was active in the Mennonite church in the Netherlands. His views could be called "adoptionist tritheism." God the Father acts through his miraculously born son, who shares his power, wisdom, and will, but Christ is later in time than the Father and less than the Father, while the Holy Spirit is merely divine breath that inspires us to a good life. Pastor's doctrine was condemned in 1547, and he himself was excommunicated and dismissed from his position as minister.

Antitrinitarianism also appeared among the spiritualists. The chief proponent here was the Belgian Johannes Campanus (d. about 1574). He was especially popular among the revolutionary Anabaptists. Among his works was *Göttlicher und heiligen Schrift . . . Restitution* (Divine and Holy Scripture . . . Restitution; 1532), in which he showed that God the Father and Christ have one and the same essence and nature and, like husband and wife, are two people in a single body, but the Son is subordinate to the Father, being born through the Father before the creation of the world. The Holy Spirit is not a person but a common bond linking Father and Son, a divine power that inspires the faithful to live in true faith and holiness.

Italy and Switzerland. The genesis of sixteenth-century Italian antitrinitarianism has not yet been fully explained, although numerous historians are inclined to the view that the beginnings of this movement in Italy were associated with the followers of the Spanish religious thinker Juan de Valdés (c.1500–1541), who attracted a group of disciples to him while he was in Naples between 1535 and 1541. Valdés does not appear to have been an antitrinitarian, but his individualistic doctrine, which emphasized the fulfillment of the ethical commands of Christianity and minimized the significance of dogmatic teaching, played an important role in the history of Italian religious radicalism.

The first Italian antitrinitarians, under the leadership of

Girolamo Busale, appeared during the 1540s in the milieu of Valdés in Naples and Padua. Busale rejected the doctrine of the Trinity and the preexistence of Christ, teaching that Christ was only human, being the son of Mary and Joseph, but filled with divine power. He preached that the souls of the ungodly died, and he questioned the authenticity of a number of books of the New Testament. Energetic and well educated, around 1548 Busale attached himself to the Anabaptists who were particularly active in central northern Italy, managing to convince some of them to adopt his own radical views, but the "new doctrine" that Busale's group proclaimed aroused vehement protests. Italian Anabaptism was shattered in 1551, after Pietro Manelfi, one of its leaders who was in fact sympathetic to Busale's views, denounced himself before the tribunal of the Inquisition.

From this point on, Switzerland became the Italian antitrinitarians' center of operations. Discussions and pronouncements concerning issues that dealt mainly with teachings on the Trinity sprang up during the latter half of the 1550s on the very grounds of the *ecclesiolae* of the Italian immigrants scattered throughout Switzerland and formally affiliated with the Reformed churches. Although the elite among the Italian immigrants were scattered, they formed a solid, tenacious group, despite sometimes considerable differences in their views. Moreover, this group was well informed of European political, religious, and intellectual issues of the day. One of its most prominent exponents was Matteo Gribaldi (d. 1564), a renowned jurist and university professor, first in Padua and then in Tübingen, who was a frequent visitor to Switzerland, where he had family property. The philologist Giovanni Valentino Gentile (d. 1566), as well as the physician Giorgio Biandrata (1516–1588), who had extensive contacts in central eastern Europe, where he practiced medicine for several years, were also prominent members.

This group attacked the dogma of the Trinity, influenced by the early works of Michael Servetus (*De Trinitatis erroribus* [On the Errors of the Trinity], 1531), stating that the dogma was constructed using terms that did not occur in holy scripture and that it was contrary to sound thinking. The positive result of this criticism, in which one can also find a link to late Medieval nominalism and Renaissance philology (Lorenzo Valla, Desiderius Erasmus), was the conception of three separately existing divine beings. They are joined in a single nature and come from one eternal God the Father, who is God in and of himself. (This primary nature of God the Father was also to be a guarantee of monotheism.) Christ, who indeed has an eternal nature but does not exist coeternally with God the Father, depends on the Father, as does the Holy Spirit. The Spirit's role in the system of the three was never completely explained, although one may imagine the Spirit to have been treated as an eternal divine power. As we shall see, this subordinationist theory, which Calvinist opponents called "tritheism," played an important role during the initial period of Polish and Transylvanian antitrinitarianism.

Lelio Sozzini (also Socinus; 1525–1562) was perhaps the most original thinker within the circle of the Italian expatriates operating in Switzerland. His commentary on the prologue to John's gospel, written at the beginning of the 1560s, presented a radical interpretation of the traditional christological doctrine. He stated that Christ was not God, who had existed from all eternity. Instead Christ was a man who, by virtue of his merits, was elevated to the rank of divine son; Christ is a divine speech (*sermo*), that is, the teacher of divine truth who created a new world of purely spiritual values. Sozzini's commentary, which was circulated in manuscript form and did not see print until 1568, when it was published anonymously, had a fundamental impact on the christological notions of Italian, Polish, and Transylvanian antitrinitarians during the late 1560s.

The statements that the Italian antitrinitarians made elicited vehement reaction from Helvetic orthodoxy, which, after the trial of Servetus, had become sensitive to any hint of antitrinitarian doctrine. Gribaldi was thus forced to undergo the humiliation of recanting in Bern in 1557. Gentile met a similar fate in Geneva and had an action brought against him in 1558. Biandrata and Gianpaolo Alciati, another Italian antitrinitarian, left Bern in 1558 in order to avoid signing the declaration of faith that the Calvinist theologians put to them. These events greatly weakened any possibilities the Italian antitrinitarians might have had for action and caused them to begin emigrating from Switzerland to central eastern Europe (Moravia, Poland, and Transylvania). Basel remained the center of liberal religious thought. Celio Secondo Curione (1503–1569) and Sébastien Castellion (1515–1563), two well-known humanist professors of the local university were closely connected to the Italian "heretics."

Poland and Lithuania. The Reformation movement in Poland, which developed at the end of the 1540s and during the 1550s, was not uniform. Alongside Lutheranism, which encompassed mainly the northern and western parts of the area and had the largest number of followers among residents of cities and towns, there were also the Bohemian Brethren, who were concentrated mainly in Great Poland (Wielkopolska), while the Calvinists gained noteworthy influence in Little Poland (Malopolska), Lithuania, and the eastern lands, especially among the nobility, because nearly all the leaders of the noble reform groups hoping to form a national church independent of Rome were adherents of Calvinism. The preponderance of the noble supporters of Calvinism in Poland and Lithuania fomented frequent disputes with the clergy of that faith, who were for the most part common folk. These disputes undermined the young church's unity and at the same time helped to create various factions, which were often dependent on the will of the Polish and Lithuanian nobles and magnates.

The first clear declaration against the dogma of the Trinity in the form of a public statement at a Calvinist synod (1556) was made by Peter of Goniądz (d. 1573), a student of the Italian antitrinitarian Gribaldi, who was also influenced by the social doctrine of the Moravian Anabaptists (Hutterite Brethren), whose community he visited. Despite condemnation and repression, during the latter half of the 1550s he continued his semiconspiratorial activity in the Lithuanian Calvinist churches and attracted a number of followers. These supporters did not become active, however, until the beginning of the 1560s, when trinitarian and christological discussions became a major theme in Calvinist churches in both Poland and Lithuania. The arrival of Francis Stancarus (1501–1574) in Poland in 1559 was a direct cause of these discussions. Stancarus, an Italian theologian, presented the thesis that Christ was an intermediary to the Father only by virtue of his human nature. The dispute concerning Stancarus's theory also encompassed many famous western European Reformation theologians and even led to a schism with the church in Little Poland. It also presented a convenient occasion for opponents of the dogma of the Trinity to advance their own theories, under the pretext of combating Stancarus's views.

Most prominent here was the activity of the Italian antitrinitarian Giorgio Biandrata. He came to Poland in 1558 and began to play an important role in the Calvinist community in Little Poland, despite the warnings and exhortations of the Helvetic reformers. Having gained the support of a few key Calvinist pastors, Biandrata succeeded in spreading the view that, in order to be victorious over Stancarus, it was essential to reject "foreign" terms not present in the holy scriptures, especially the term "Trinity." This struggle over "scholastic" terminology involved rejecting a significant part of church tradition, now limited to the writings of early Christian authors (Hilary of Poitiers, Irenaeus, Tertullian) who were considered to be close to "apostolic purity." The Trinity was replaced by "the three": God the Father, the Son, and the Holy Spirit, existing separately, with the Son and the Holy Spirit subordinate to God the Father.

The acceptance of Biandrata at the synod in Pinczów on 2 April 1562 was a turning point in the history of Polish Calvinism, because it involved the creation of a separate group that accepted views contrary to the official confession. Advocates of the latter, strongly supported by Swiss theologians who were deeply disturbed by the whole controversy and by the arrival in 1562 of Gentile and Alciati, took decisive counteraction: in 1563 they set up a separate church, which they called the "major church" (*ecclesia maior*) to distinguish it from the antitrinitarian "minor church" (*ecclesia minor*). The Calvinists also tried to annihilate "the Arians" with the help of government officials. In 1564 King Sigismund August even issued a special decree against the antitrinitarians, but the decree led only to having several of their foreign representatives leave Poland. The Calvinists' action was effectively paralyzed by the Catholic hierarchy, who thought that the persecution of only one of the dissident groups would be tantamount to legalizing the activities of the others.

Only with great difficulty did the young minor church develop some internal unity and become in reality a loose federation of local groups that sometimes varied greatly on doctrinal matters. The basic dividing line was the approach to christological questions, because during the latter half of the 1560s, a discussion arose in the *ecclesia minor* of Little Poland concerning Christ's preexistence. The commentaries on the prologue to John's Gospel by Lelio Sozzini and his nephew Fausto, and a letter of Biandrata to Gregory Paul (1565), who was then in Transylvania, played a critical role. A further split occurred when some of the members of the antitrinitarian church rejected Christ's preexistence and claimed that he was only a man who had been eternally predestined to the role of Son of God, a doctrine called *Unitarianism*. Led by Peter of Goniądz in Lithuania and Stanisław Farnowski in Little Poland, believers in Christ's preexistence, called *Ditheists*, created a separate group that lasted until the beginning of the seventeenth century.

The Anabaptist issue also stirred many debates. Peter of Goniądz's campaign against the baptism of children, which he inaugurated in Lithuania, later came to encompass the issue of rebaptism of adults and ventured into the area of Anabaptist social doctrine, which he treated in his now lost work *De primatu ecclesiae Christianae* (On the Primacy of the Christian Church) around 1562–1564. The eminent writer and polemicist Marcin Czechowic (1532–1613) was next to take up the issue. At the end of the 1560s, baptism by immersion in water was approved, although chiefly in theory, because there was no mass practice of immersion in either the Unitarian or Ditheistic churches until the 1570s.

Some Unitarian believers also proclaimed the typically Anabaptist doctrine of social egalitarianism, calling for the practice of physical labor and demanding that the nobility sell their estates, although only a few such instances are documented. Under the influence of these ideas, a "New Jerusalem" was even created in the newly founded town of Raków in 1569. This egalitarian religious community included many Unitarian believers from Poland and Lithuania. This Racovian experiment, however, did not succeed, because efforts to establish union with the Hutterite Anabaptists failed completely. At the same time, the radical spiritualist trend opposed to any form of church hierarchy or organization prevailed. It was defeated only in 1572. From that time on, the tone of the Unitarian movement in Poland was set by the dynamic center in Lublin, directed by Czechowic and his noble patron Jan Niemojewski (d. 1598). Alongside Lublin, Kraków, too, with Jerzy Szoman (also Schoman; d. 1591) as pastor, occupied an important place.

The Unitarian movement's doctrinal and organizational stability was expressed in the publication of two catechisms.

The first, modest in size and written in Latin, was the joint effort of Grzegorz Paweł of Brzeziny and Szoman (*Catechesis . . .*, 1574), and the second, very extensive and in Polish, was written by Czechowic (*Rozmowy chrystyiańskie* [Christian Dialogues], 1575), who also issued a Polish translation of the New Testament in 1577. The antitrinitarians also used their own print shop in Kraków, run by Aleksy Rodecki. Between 1574 and 1600 it produced more than eighty titles, the overwhelming majority of which were polemical theological works. Beginning in 1572, synods were also held systematically, usually once a year; they resolved the most important questions.

During the period following the end of the experiment in Raków, the religious doctrine of the Polish Unitarians maintained many Calvinist elements, which were especially obvious in the theory of justification, the concept of predestination, and the Lord's Supper. It decisively parted ways with Calvinism, however, on the matter of church tradition, which was rejected in favor of "strict scripturalism," wherein the New Testament played a primary, normative role and was antithetically contrasted to the Old Testament. At the same time scripturalism served as the basis for rejecting the dogma of the Trinity and the preexistence of Christ. The Unitarians said that Christ was human and that he had been designated by God the Father to fulfill his mission and henceforward to serve as intermediary between God and human beings. Unitarian Christology is inseparably connected to ethics, because the nucleus of ethics is the following of Christ. This ethic, which shows a basic similarity to Anabaptist doctrine, is heroic. It refers continually to the principle of nonresistance in the face of evil, and in this connection it proclaims absolute pacifism and neutrality toward the state and its interests. Those who were truly faithful should carry out the commands of the state authority, such as paying taxes, but they must not perform any "office of the sword" or take part in war.

The pacifism and egalitarianism of Polish Unitarians provoked numerous reservations, expressed not only by Catholic polemicists—during the 1570s the Counter-Reformation camp began to mount an offensive against dissidents in general and antitrinitarians in particular—but also among their Lithuanian co-religionists. The eminent philologist and biblical scholar Szymon Budny (1530/35–1593), who was active in Lithuania, played an especially important role in this debate. On dogmatic issues, he diverged from the Polish minor church and especially upset it with his naturalist notion of the conception of Jesus from the seed of Joseph and the view that Christ should not be invoked in prayers (nonadorantism). He treated the Polish Unitarians' social doctrine as a dangerous fantasy. In *O urzędzie miecza używającym* (On the Office of Employing the Sword; 1583) Budny presented a fundamental criticism of the social and political radicalism, stating that the nobility should take part in warfare and public life and defending the nobility's right to own land and have serfs. His radical religious views, however, brought about his defeat; he was excommunicated in 1584. But his ideas of an "open church" free of sectarianism were adopted by the Italian religious emigrant Fausto Sozzini (1539–1604), although in a different way and based on different assumptions.

Fausto Sozzini settled in Poland in 1579, applied to join the Unitarian church, but was not formally accepted because of his doctrinal beliefs. Sozzini's religious doctrine had been fundamentally shaped while he was in Switzerland between 1575 and 1578. During his stay in Switzerland he had written his two great works, *De Iesu Christo Servatore* (On Jesus Christ, the Savior) and *De statu primi hominis ante lapsum* (On the Condition of the First Man before the Fall), but they were not published until 1594 and 1610, respectively, in Poland. He differed from the Polish Unitarians' official confession on many points. He attacked the traditional view that Christ offered satisfaction through his sacrifice on the cross, stating that Christ's mission of redemption consisted of exemplifying for human beings the model of life and holiness and confirming the truth of his teaching through the resurrection. Sozzini also rejected the concept of original sin, regarding it as contrary to reason and justice, because he said that Adam's sin could be charged only to Adam himself, not to his descendants. He therefore considered human beings capable through their own efforts of reaching moral perfection and of thus earning the right to the prize of immortality. Sozzini did not consider baptism necessary but deemed it indifferent to salvation; and, in the case of the Lord's Supper, he was inclined to Zwingli's view that it was a purely symbolic rite.

Despite these differences, Sozzini soon gained great authority among the Polish and Lithuanian Unitarians. His work *Ad Iacobi Palaeologi librum responsio* (Response to Jacobus Palaeologus's Book; 1581) played an important role. In his work Sozzini supported almost without reservation the pacifism of his Polish co-religionists. At their request he also supported attacks against both the Jesuits, in his *Assertiones theologicae . . . cum animadversionibus* (Theological Assertions . . . with Comments; 1583), and *Refutatio libelli, quem Iacobus Wuiekus edidit* (Refutation of the Book that Jacob Wuiek Produced; 1594), and the Calvinists, in *De Iesu Christi Filii Dei natura* (On the Nature of Jesus Christ, Son of God), which was written in 1583 but not published until 1588.

Sozzini's statements against the nonadorantists also played an important role. He had a dispute with Christian Francken (1584) and Szymon Budny (1588). As a result, Budny recanted his views.

At the same time, Sozzini held discussions with leaders of the church in Lublin, especially with Jan Niemojewski, trying to convert them, without success, to his views. Not until the Lublin synod in 1593, however, did Sozzini succeed in driving home his theories on justification, redemption, and the Lord's Supper. During the next half decade he managed to soften the rigid, Anabaptist-like ethics of the Polish minor church. Sozzini therefore approved of the nobility's possession of serfs, serving in office, and bringing actions for judgment. A decree of the 1598 Lublin synod removed Marcin Czechowic from his position as the pastor of this city and allowed the bearing of arms, thus closing the period of Anabaptist Unitarianism and beginning the period of Socinianism.

Transylvania and Hungary. Antitrinitarianism in Transylvania developed in a manner similar to that in Poland and Lithuania, at more or less the same time and under the influence of a similar ideological impetus. Nevertheless, unlike Poland, where the Catholic church maintained its power even at the height of the Reformation, Transylvania was, practically speaking, a Protestant country during the latter half of the sixteenth century, inasmuch as the country did not regain any real Catholic shape until the end of the century.

The advent of antitrinitarianism in Transylvania was related to discussions carried on within the Calvinist church. The Italian physician Biandrata played a major role here, just as he had in Poland. Arriving in Transylvania in 1563, he quickly became a trusted adviser to János Zsigmond Zápolya, the country's ruler. Between 1564 and 1566 Biandrata and Francis Dávid (c.1520–1579), the famous author, preacher, and Calvinist church superintendent, managed to bring about the rejection of the scholastic terminology that had buttressed the dogma on the Holy Trinity. This sort of subordinational tritheism was, however, a transitional phase in the doctrinal development of Transylvanian antitrinitarianism, which during the next two years came to accept the christological doctrine developed by Fausto Sozzini and his uncle Lelio, thus rejecting the preexistence of Christ. (Commentaries on the prologue to John's gospel by both of them were printed in Alba Iulia in 1568.)

The ultimate confirmation, as it were, of the split within the Calvinist camp and therefore the onset of Transylvanian Unitarianism was the great dispute in Alba Iulia in 1568, which ended with the success of the antitrinitarians. Up until then, Zápolya had openly supported Unitarianism, and Dávid had been his court pastor. Unitarianism was legally recognized as one of the four faiths accepted in the country, along with Calvinism, Lutheranism, and Roman Catholicism, and gained for itself a great number of followers, as it did in Lower Hungary, which was under Turkish occupation.

In contrast to the antitrinitarian churches in Poland, those in Transylvania showed no great interest concerning the issue of Anabaptism, in the realm of either social doctrine or rebaptism. By the end of the 1560s, however, declarations were being made against the baptism of children. As a result, this practice seems to have died out in most of the churches in Transylvania.

What is called Transylvania's "golden age of Unitarianism," which is traditionally linked to the reign of János Zsigmond Zápolya, bore fruit in plentiful writings in Hungarian, along with even more copious works in Latin. The major work in Latin was a joint one entitled *De falsa et vera unius Dei . . . cognitione* (On the False and True Knowledge of the One God; 1568), edited by Biandrata and Dávid. It incited a great polemical reaction among western European Calvinist and Lutheran theologians, such as Georg Major (1502–1574), Johann Simler (1505–1572), and Girolamo Zanchi (1516–1590). During this period, Transylvania was the second—along with Poland—center of organized antitrinitarianism. It also served simultaneously as a temporary or permanent refuge for religious radicals from various countries, chiefly Germany and Italy.

When Zápolya died in 1571 and Stephen Báthory, a Catholic, replaced him on the throne, however, Unitarianism irrevocably lost its privileged position as the "faith of the monarch." Báthory began controlling the printing of books in an ordinance upheld by his successors that basically limited the possibility of printing Unitarian theological works. Báthory's election also divided the Unitarians politically, because some of them supported another pretender to the throne, their coreligionist Gáspár Bekes.

Despite these difficulties, the 1560s were the most creative period for Unitarian theology in Transylvania, with attempts being made to adapt the Unitarian confession in a spirit of naturalism, rationalism, and dogmatic minimalism. The chief instigators of this trend were Johann Sommer (d. 1574), the distinguished Greek scholar and theologian, who was rector of the Unitarian college in Kolozsvár (Cluj); and Jacobus of Chios, who called himself Palaeologus (c.1520–1585), a Greek-Italian antitrinitarian who was an original thinker and an exceptionally prolific writer. Palaeologus's works, which circulated in manuscript form, made a significant impact on Transylvanian Unitarianism.

According to Palaeologus, Christianity was an organic development of Mosaic doctrine. The Old and New Testaments are entirely consistent and complementary to one another. The New Testament takes nearly all its teachings from the Old Testament. Like other prophets, Christ, who was human but endowed with divine power, managed first of all to bring atonement to the Jews and be acknowledged as the king of Israel. It was only after his death that he commanded the apostles to bring the Gospel to all people. The period after Christ's death was crucial solely because from then on the heathens had gained through faith in one God and Christ the possibility of being "children of God," and their offspring also gained this status automatically. Palaeologus also emphasized strongly that the killing of Christ provoked the disgrace of the Jews, suspending their "divine sonship," which they had previously gained through Abraham's faith. The Jews, however, could also free themselves from disgrace through faith that Jesus, the son of Mary, was

the Christ, the anointed one of God. Even then, unlike "uncircumcised Christians," they were obliged to respect all the precepts of the old law. The truths necessary to salvation were reduced to two basic commands: faith in one God and in Christ. At the same time, the traditional Trinity, Christology, the teachings on original sin, and the sacraments were rejected, although Palaeologus favored eliminating baptism and the Lord's Supper from church life prudently and gradually, in consideration of the traditionalism of the faithful. This approach had as its aim the future unification of the two great religions, Judaism and Christianity, and the Unitarian confession here was to serve as the basis for such a union. Palaeologus's universalist program included Islam, too (*De tribus gentibus* [On the Three Peoples], 1571). He considered followers of Muhammad to be the heirs of Christians, that is, endowed with "divine sonship" and given access to God's law, through the Qur'an, which, imperfect as it was, in essence came from God. It is nonetheless significant that Palaeologus considered this subject to be too controversial and shocking, and he never mentioned the Islamic religion at all in his *Catechesis Christiana* (Christian Catechism; 1574), a work that summed up his radical theology.

The doctrinal debates and disputes at the core of Transylvanian Unitarianism reached their peak at the end of the 1570s, when they were brought to the forum of the synods. They were sparked by the controversy over the questions of the adoration and invocation of Christ, against which Dávid took a stand, maintaining that after carrying out his mission, Christ the man was made completely subordinate to God the Father. The invocation of Christ therefore not only contradicted holy writ but also threatened monotheism itself, because such a practice would lead to adoption of the view that Christ was acting as a divine coregent. On this point Dávid and Biandrata came into open conflict.

Biandrata continued to serve as one of the church elders and had great influence at the court of Christopher Báthory, the Transylvanian ruler. Biandrata feared that the whole dispute would have adverse political repercussions for the Unitarian church, which was under constant attack from Lutherans and Calvinists and was viewed unfavorably by the Catholic ruler. He attempted first to win Dávid over to his views. When he found Dávid's resistance to be unbreakable, he accused him before state officials of having implemented doctrinal innovations, a practice that a parliamentary resolution of 1572 had prohibited. In April 1579, after a short trial, Dávid was convicted and sent to prison, where he died soon thereafter. Then in 1579 and 1580, Biandrata reorganized the Unitarian church. Striving to eliminate Dávid's followers, he placed the conservative theologian Demeter Hunyady (d. 1592) in the position of superintendent and edited the christological confession so as to counter Dávid's views. Most of the pastors signed it. At this time the baptism of children and the Lord's Supper were also restored.

Radical currents of Transylvanian Unitarianism continued to develop, however, despite official prohibitions and sometimes even repression. In Lower Hungary, which at that time was under Turkish occupation, the Unitarian churches remained a dynamic center of these radical tenets, and Dávid's followers frequently took refuge in them. The superintendent of these churches was Pál Karádi (d. 1592), author of a commentary on *Revelation,* and a decided advocate of nonadorantism. Miklós Fazakas Bogáti (d. 1588 or 1593), a poet, Bible translator, and commentator on *Revelation,* was strongly influenced by the ideas of Sommer and Palaeologus and played an important role in the nonadorantist group headed by magnate János Gerendi.

Sabbatarianism also occupied a special place among the radical groups operating on the fringes of the "official" Unitarian church. Matthias Vehe-Glirius (d. 1590), a German hebraicist and antitrinitarian who came to Kolozsvár in 1578 or 1579, was a chief founder of Sabbatarianism. This movement, which had many followers among the Unitarians of various social groups, took root especially in eastern Transylvania, where it was championed by the wealthy landowner András Eössi (d. 1599). The movement's doctrine contained elements of radical Unitarianism (negation of the Trinity and the divinity of Christ) and Old Testament legalism, inasmuch as it proclaimed that Christians must follow the law of Moses (except for circumcision), that is, the Sabbath (Saturday) must be observed (hence the name). Accused of Judaism and often persecuted, the Sabbatarians were expelled from the Unitarian church in 1618, and in the 1620s and 1630s they were transformed into an independent Mosaic sect, the remnants of which persevered until as late as 1944.

Toward the end of the sixteenth century, Transylvanian Unitarianism entered again into close relations (which had been practically broken after the trial of Dávid) with its Polish counterpart. Visible proof of this close relationship was the work of the distinguished theologian György Enyedi (1554–1597), *Explicationes locorum Veteris et Novi Testamenti ex quibus Trinitatis dogma stabiliri solet* (Explication of the Places in the Old and New Testaments upon Which the Dogma of the Trinity Is Usually Based; 1598), which was strongly influenced by the doctrine of Fausto Sozzini.

[*See also* Socinianism.]

BIBLIOGRAPHY

Balázs, Mihály. *Az erdélyi antitrinitarizmus az 1560-as évek végén.* Budapest, 1988. An authoritative study on antitrinitarianism in Transylvania in the 1560s.

Cantimori, Delio. *Eretici italiani del Cinquecento.* 3d ed. Edited by Adriano Prosperi. Turin, 1992. (An earlier edition is available in English translation: *Italian Heretics of the Sixteenth Century,* Cambridge, Mass., 1979.) The most complete work on the history and doctrines of Italian antitrinitarianism; a classic.

Chmaj, Ludwik, ed. *Studia nad arianizmem.* Warsaw, 1959. A series of important studies, some in western European languages, on the history and doctrines of antitrinitarianism during the sixteenth and seventeenth centuries.

———. *Faust Socyn, 1539–1604.* Warsaw, 1963. The first thorough guide to Fausto Sozzini's literary legacy.

Dán, Róbert. *Matthias Vehe-Glirius: Life and Work of a Radical Antitrinitarian, with His Collected Writings.* Budapest, 1982.

Dán, Róbert, and Antal Pirnát, eds. *Antitrinitarianism in the Second Half of the Sixteenth Century.* Budapest, 1982.

Firpo, Massimo. *Antitrinitari nell'Europa orientale del'500: Nuovi testi di Szymon Budny, Niccolò Paruta e Iacopo Paleologo.* Florence, 1977.

Górski, Konrad. *Grzegorz Paweł z Brzezin: Monografia z dziejów polskiej literatury ariańskiej XVI wieku.* Kraków, 1929. A work still unsurpassed on the theological doctrine of early Polish antitrinitarianism.

Kawecka-Gryczowa, Alodia. *Les imprimeurs des antitrinitaires polonais Rodecki et Sternacki: Historie et bibliographie.* Geneva, 1974.

Kot, Stanislas. *Socinianism in Poland: The Social and Political Ideas of the Polish Antitrinitarians in the Sixteenth and Seventeenth Centuries.* Translated by Earl Morse Wilbur. Boston, 1957. The best treatise on Polish antitrinitarian sociopolitical doctrine, it might well serve as an introduction to further study.

Pirnát, Antal. *Die Ideologie der siebenbürger Antitrinitarier in den 1570er Jahren.* Budapest, 1961.

Rotondó, Antonio. *Studi e ricerche di storia ereticale italiana del Cinquecento.* Turin, 1974.

Stella, Aldo. *Dall'anabattismo al socinianesimo nel Cinquecento veneto.* Padua, 1967. Both books by Stella are worth noting owing to their new source material, among other things.

———. *Anabattismo e antitrinitarismo in Italia nel XVI secolo.* Padua, 1969.

Szczucki, Lech. *Marcin Czechowic, 1532–1613: Studium z dziejów antytrynitaryzmu polskiego XVI wieku.* Warsaw, 1964.

———. *W kręgu myślicieli heretyckich.* Wrocław, 1972. (Revised translation: *Két XVI. sázadi eretnek gondolkodó: Jacobus Palaeologus és Christian Francken.* Budapest, 1980.)

Urban, Wacław. *Der Antitrinitarismus in den böhmischen Ländern und in der Slowakei im 16. und 17. Jahrhundert.* Baden-Baden, 1986.

Wilbur, Earl Morse. *A History of Unitarianism in Transylvania, England and America.* Cambridge, Mass., 1952.

———. *A History of Unitarianism: Socinianism and Its Antecedents.* Reprint, Boston, 1977. These works by Wilbur are somewhat outdated today, but they provide information that has been presented with great thoroughness and care, especially the historical and biographical material.

Williams, George H. *The Radical Reformation.* 3d ed., rev. and enl. Kirksville, Mo., 1992. The best exposition of antitrinitarian doctrine and history in English.

LECH SZCZUCKI
Translated from Polish by AnnMarie Mitchell

ANTOINE OF NAVARRE (1518–1562), duke of Vendôme and king of Navarre. Owing to his direct descent from Louis IX in the Bourbon branch, next in line for the French crown after the reigning Valois, Antoine of Bourbon was first prince of the blood. His father, Charles of Bourbon, had distinguished himself in the earlier wars against the Habsburgs, so his heirs had escaped the disgrace that had fallen on others after the defection of the constable of Bourbon in 1523. Antoine was made governor of Picardy in 1537 by Francis I and campaigned extensively against Charles V for twenty years. He acquired a brilliant military reputation that was emphasized by contemporaries prior to the crisis (1559–1562) that precipitated the Wars of Religion (1562–

1598). Royalist and nationalist historians since have focused almost exclusively on his paternal role. In Brantôme's words, "if in his time he had done nothing but procreate our great King of today [Henry IV, b. 1553, r. 1589–1610] he would have done much and is worthy of great and incomparable praise. To him France owes all her good fortune" (Pierre de Bourdeille, *Oeuvres complètes*, vol. 4, pp. 361–373). Aside from its expression of national gratitude for a strong king after two generations of civil war, this interpretation helps to offset Antoine's near-treasonable role in the final months of his life (January-November 1562) when he accepted Philip II's lure of a kingdom to replace Navarre—most of which had been conquered by Ferdinand of Aragon in 1512—as a quid pro quo for his adherence to the ultra-Catholic party. In reality, Antoine was only the consort of the true sovereign of the remaining part, his wife, Jeanne of Navarre, who had inherited it from her father along with the *vicomté* of Béarn.

In the 1550s Calvin and his French followers sought Antoine's conversion and leadership of the Reformed movement in France, believing, justifiably, that their best chance for success lay in winning over the royal family. They were repeatedly disillusioned as Antoine lost credibility by vain attempts to play off the Protestant and Catholic parties against each other. This was in marked contrast to the actions of Jeanne, who, after some years of reserved conventional Catholic practice, made a clear-cut conversion in December 1560. This act ended her outward acceptance of Antoine's unreliable behavior in both the personal and the political spheres. He was a notorious womanizer. While constantly shifting the means according to apparent advantage, his "end" remained to regain the kingdom and to retain the title of king in Navarre, or failing that, a substitute kingdom. After Jeanne's definitive espousal of Calvinism their separation became public and irreparable. Among Philip II's conditions for granting a substitute kingdom was the Catholic education of Henry of Navarre (age nine), who had previously been brought up as a Calvinist by tutors chosen by his mother. Another was the requirement that Antoine cease all connections with the Huguenot party and bring about the exile of the pastors.

Understandably, Antoine has figured among the chief villains of French Protestant history. His younger brother, Louis of Bourbon, prince of Condé (1530–1569), became titular head of the French Protestant movement until his death but was ineffective except in the military field. After 1569 the military leadership was assumed by Admiral Gaspard II de Coligny and the political leadership passed to his brother, Odet de Coligny, cardinal of Châtillon, and Jeanne of Navarre, *Dame souveraine*, as she styled herself in one of the early assertions of divine-right monarchy.

Antoine's place in Reformation history is a negative one: the ultra-Catholic party was much strengthened by his adherence and the Protestant cause suffered a near-fatal blow.

In the autumn of 1561 the Huguenot leaders were Catherine de Médicis's closest advisers; by February 1562 they had been obliged to leave court, and she turned to Spain's Counter-Reformation allies in the House of Guise-Lorraine.

BIBLIOGRAPHY

Balteau, J., et al. *Dictionnaire de biographie française.* Paris, 1933–. See vol. 3, cols. 35–37, for a biographical entry on Antoine.
Haag, Eugène, and Émile Haag. *La France Protestante.* 10 vols. 2d ed. Reprint, Geneva, 1966. See vol. 2, pp. 429–437, for a biography of Antoine.
Roelker, Nancy Lyman. *Queen of Navarre, Jean d'Albret, 1528–1572.* Cambridge, Mass., 1968. See especially chaps. 3 and 4.
Ruble, Alphonse de. *Le Mariage de Jeanne d'Albret.* Paris, 1877.
———. *Antoine de Bourbon et Jeanne d'Albret.* 4 vols. Paris, 1881–1886.
———. *Jeanne d'Albret et la guerre civile.* Paris, 1897.

NANCY LYMAN ROELKER

ANTWERP. In the early sixteenth century anticlerical agitation and propaganda were clearly at work in Antwerp, but they did not receive wide support until the general economic crisis of the 1520s. The strong German connection of the Antwerp economy, large-scale immigration, and the direct influence of Augustinians like Hendrik Voes and Jan van Esschen also favored the rapid spread of Lutheran books and ideas. Other ideas of reform included the hedonist principles of the libertine Loy Pruystinck—designated as diabolic by Luther in 1525—who aimed at liberating individual craftsmen and merchants from the burden and obligations of late medieval religion. From about 1534 chiliast, revolutionary, and subversive Anabaptist influences originating from Amsterdam, Münster, Maastricht, and Liège led to more drastic government measures and a series of executions in Antwerp. No less than four-fifths of all heretics executed between the mid-1530s and the early 1560s were Anabaptists, and some two-thirds of these martyrs were immigrants. The fact that most victims were poor immigrants no doubt made it easier for the magistrates to enforce Habsburg heresy laws, although they had no love for the Inquisition. Antwerp's rulers succeeded in putting off the appointment of the first Antwerp bishop from 1559 until 1570, and they often used an elevated humanist language of toleration to shield foreign merchants from persecution. (In the early 1560s the Antwerp community of eleven hundred foreign merchants included some three hundred German Lutherans, along with a hundred French and fifty English Calvinists.) The growing success of Calvinism from the early 1550s was mainly due to the immigration of merchants as well as industrial entrepreneurs and workers, particularly from Hainaut, Artois, and Flanders.

After the Antwerp iconoclasm (1566), heterodox propaganda, underground organization, and persecution all reached a climax. Whereas 285 citizens were condemned and 130 executed in the years 1550–1566, the number of judgments and executions rose to 810 and 159, respectively, in the years 1567–1577, a period, however, in which Protestant emigration to England, Germany, Holland, and Zeeland already had started. Religious repression in particular added a revolutionary dimension to Protestantism. Moreover, as severe economic contraction hit a large share of the Antwerp population, many merchants believed that the only means by which the closing of the river Scheldt (Antwerp's maritime lifeline) could be avoided was through alignment with the rebels of the north. As a result of the disintegration of central political authority and military unrest (e.g., the Spanish Fury, 1576), people became increasingly sympathetic to the revolt and its Protestant leaders. After the withdrawal of the Spanish troops in 1577, Antwerp came under the control of the rebel States-General and William of Orange. The city soon became a Calvinist republic, and Catholic church practices were suspended temporarily from 1581. Nevertheless, estimates are that among Antwerp's eighty thousand people at the time of the Spanish reconquest (1585), 55 to 60 percent were Catholic, 26 to 30 percent Calvinist, 13 to 15 percent Lutheran, and 2 percent Anabaptist.

The Protestant community had a relatively greater share of the more literate and well-to-do burghers, those with interests beyond the city walls; the city's Calvinist rulers also did much to finance the revolt, and they engaged the support of the lower and middle classes by exploiting their distrust of absolutist rule. The religious policy of the Spanish government was moderate in the immediate aftermath of the reconquest (1585–1589), but the Antwerp population was soon split for reasons extending beyond religion; in 1590, only six thousand Protestants had reconciled with the Catholic church. Protestants gradually became a fringe group; within a few decades the new organizational framework of the Counter-Reformation, with the support of the state and religious orders in particular, turned Antwerp into a Catholic bastion and gave a strong impetus to its luxury industries. This Catholic success was largely based upon an impressive revalorization of traditional ritual and belief, one that had remained meaningful to a "silent" (to us) majority of Antwerp citizens.

BIBLIOGRAPHY

Antwerpen in de XVIde eeuw. Genootschap voor Antwerpse Geschiedenis. Antwerp, 1975.

Antwerpen in de XVIIde eeuw. Genootschap voor Antwerpse Geschiedenis. Antwerp, 1989.

Boumans, R. "De getalsterkte van katholieken en protestanten te Antwerpen in 1585." In *Belgisch Tijdschrift voor Filologie en Geschiedenis* 30 (1952), 741–798.

Briels, J. *Zuid-Nederlanders in de Republiek, 1572–1630. Een demografische en cultuurhistorische studie*. Sint-Niklaas, 1985.

———. "Handelingen van het colloquium "Religieuze stromingen te Antwerpen voor en na 1585." In *Bijdragen tot de Geschiedenis* 70 (1987), 3–137.

Hendrickx, M. "Enkele cijfers in verband met de bekering van de protestanten te Antwerpen in 1585–1589." In *Ons Geestelijk Erf*, 41 (1967), 302–309.

Isacker, K. van, and R. van Uytven, eds. *Antwerpen: Twaalf eeuwen geschiedenis en cultuur*. Antwerp, 1986. (Also available in English: *Antwerp: Twelve Centuries of History and Culture*, Antwerp, 1986.)

Marinus, Marie Juliette. *Laevinus Torrentius als tweede bisschop van Antwerpen, 1587–1595*. Brussels, 1989.

Marnef, G. "Protestanten in 'Noord' en 'Zuid': Kerkhistorische beschouwingen n. a. v. een recente studie." *Bijdragen tot de Geschiedenis* 70 (1987), 139–145.

Materné, J. "The Officina Plantiniana and the Dynamics of the Counter-Reformation, 1590–1650." Paper presented at the XXIII Settimana di Studi: *Produzione e commercio della carta e del libro* (secc. XIII–XVIII) Prato 15–20 aprile 1991.

Roey, J. van. "De correlatie tussen het sociale beroepsmilieu en de godsdienstkeuze te Antwerpen op het einde der XVIde eeuw." In *Bronnen voor de religieuze geschiedenis van Belgie. Middeleeuwen en moderne tijden*, pp. 239–258. Louvain, 1968.

Thijs, A. K. L. *Van Geuzenstad tot katholiek bolwerk: Maatschappelijke betekenis van de Kerk in contrareformatorisch Antwerpen*. Antwerp, 1990.

JAN MATERNÉ

APOCALYPTICISM.

APOCALYPTICISM. Like Christianity itself, the Reformation was spawned in and nurtured by an atmosphere of intense hopes and fears about impending universal upheaval, disaster, transformation, judgment, and the end of the world. The term *apocalypticism* refers generally to this expectancy. More specifically, apocalypticism is best understood as a pattern of eschatological beliefs—beliefs about the final fate of the world and of souls—that sees history as a divinely predetermined drama in which the present is a time of crisis and in which a triumph of good over evil is imminent. The concept thus includes a highly varied array of convictions about the nearing end of history, as well as millenarian expectations of God's kingdom on earth. Apocalyptic thinking is "prophetic" in a twofold sense: it undertakes to warn evildoers and to console the righteous, and it seeks definite insight into God's plan for the world.

This pattern of beliefs appeared among the ancient Jews around the beginning of the second century BC, and has influenced the Judeo-Christian tradition in varying degrees ever since. While early Christianity was characterized by widespread expectations of Christ's second advent, the Western church followed the theologians Tyconius (c.330–390) and Augustine (fl. c.400) in playing down concrete prophetic hopes and fears; God's kingdom was to be sought not on or over the historical horizon but through the institutional avenues of the church. Such teachings complemented the generally ahistorical culture of the early Middle Ages.

In the high Middle Ages, the prevailing culture of Scholasticism continued to be governed by an outlook that deemphasized the historical interpretation of prophecy. Yet a growing sense of historical change was manifest in a proliferation of speculations about great worldly upheavals, the advent of the Antichrist (Satan's final and most dangerous earthly agent), the coming of a new age, and the Last Judgment. The most radical challenge to the inherited static vision came from the Calabrian abbot Joachim of Fiore (c.1135–1202), who interpreted history as an unfolding of three stages corresponding to the three persons of the Trinity. Joachim saw his own time as the dawning of the age of the Holy Spirit, a final historical epoch of love and freedom. Joachimite expectations contributed to a powerful groundswell of apocalypticism that followed during the later Middle Ages.

While apocalyptic imagery often played a role in the widespread social and political unrest of the fourteenth and fifteenth centuries, it is misleading to conceive of apocalyptic notions as an extreme and inherently revolutionary reaction to troubled times. Such assumptions and ideas were by no means a preserve of the poor, the oppressed, or the disaffected; indeed literate and well-established clergy and townspeople often led the way in viewing the present as a critical moment within a transcendent scheme of meaning. Many late medieval apocalyptic schemes—those of the Taborites in Bohemia, for example—showed hostility toward the powers of the pope, the higher clergy, religious orders, and princes and magistrates, but many others defended such groups and institutions. What mattered was who was on God's side in the cosmic struggle that was coming to a head.

The main sources of apocalyptic thought lay in the Bible, above all in *Daniel* and *Revelation*. Increasingly, however, both lay and clerical thinkers of the late Middle Ages sought out and used a wide variety of other prophetic sources, including the ancient *Sibylline Oracles*, the Byzantine Pseudo-Methodius, the predictions of visionaries such as Birgitta of Sweden (d. 1373), and powerful divinatory traditions such as astrology. By the end of the fifteenth century, the combination of such traditions was contributing to a widespread sense of historical crisis and fearful apprehension of the future. At the same time, apocalyptic notions about God's plan for the culminating stages of world history lay behind some of the most hopeful and expansive enterprises of the age, including the voyages of Christopher Columbus.

From the perspective of traditional religious institutions and culture, the sense of culminating universal drama was deeply corrosive. Earthshaking changes seemed inevitable; the present world, with all its troubled human structures, appeared ever further removed from the perfection of the coming heavenly or millennial kingdom. In the decades around 1500, printed prophetic writings such as the *Prognostication* of Johannes Lichtenberger, a veritable grab bag of medieval prophecy, reflected the common assumption that the ship of Saint Peter—the church—would soon be buffeted by terrible storms. There can be little doubt that by fueling expectations of social and religious change, the apocalyptic currents in late medieval culture helped to pre-

pare the way for the sixteenth-century revolt against the Roman church as well as for the positive teachings of the evangelical reformers.

Attention to apocalypticism in the early Reformation era has traditionally concentrated on the so-called left-wing groups. Thus figures such as the revolutionary preacher Thomas Müntzer, Anabaptists such as Hans Hut and Melchior Hoffman, and spiritualists such as Sebastian Franck have been studied intensively as examples of thinkers whose apocalyptic notions set them clearly apart from the mainstream. In fact, however, the assumption that such figures were "radical" mainly by virtue of the intensity of their apocalyptic convictions has little basis, for genuinely apocalyptic conceptions of the struggle between defenders and perverters of the gospel were widely shared among proponents and adherents of the early evangelical movement.

Moreover, the figures most commonly associated with Reformation-era radicalism varied greatly in their eschatological outlooks. Some, such as Hans Denck, generally avoided explicitly apocalyptic language. Others, such as Hans Hut, adopted medieval Joachimite teachings of a final age of purity and viewed themselves as God's chosen executors in the all-important cleansing of the world. Chiliasm in the sense of explicit belief in a thousand-year reign of Christ on earth (*Revelation* 20) was rare but did surface in a few figures such as Augustin Bader, an early disciple of Hut. The Anabaptist uprising at Münster in 1534–1535 is widely recognized as the most sensational expression of popular apocalypticism in the sixteenth century; here the teachings of Melchior Hoffman about a final Davidic kingdom to precede the Last Judgment led to disaster under the leadership of Jan Matthijs, Bernhard Rothmann, and John of Leiden.

More fruitful than the effort to link "radicalism" with apocalypticism is an approach that distinguishes between what one might call activist and contemplative forms of apocalypticism. For example, the differences between Müntzer and Luther consisted far less in the intensity of their apocalyptic expectations than in their conceptions of human participation in the events of the end time. It is difficult to call Müntzer a millenarian, at least in the traditional sense, for it is not clear that he actually envisioned a realization of God's kingdom within history. Like many others who are typically labeled "radicals," however, he did believe that among the living, the righteous had an active role to play in the final triumph over evil. This sort of activist apocalypticism had roots in medieval mysticism, with its emphasis on purification of the soul, as well as in Old Testament visions of the triumph of God's people.

The most significant forms of Reformation apocalypticism were the broadly shared expectations that reflected the attitudes of a larger culture and that persisted throughout the era. In general, early Protestant piety directed the religious imagination away from traditional rituals and turned it toward prayer and prophecy. This shift concentrated and focused religious attention on a future-directed hope and the avenues by which the promise of salvation was revealed. Medieval piety had offered countless forms of mediate contact between humanity and the divine through which believers could to some extent assuage their fears of judgment. While evangelical teachings brought in one sense a liberation from the oppressive aspects of this spiritual bureaucracy, they also did away with the security afforded by these traditional forms. Thus one cannot say that the Reformation dissolved the tense prophetic atmosphere of the late Middle Ages; rather it brought the final great reorientation and focusing of the medieval apocalyptic imagination. The German Reformation particularly tended to legitimize and intensify the sense of world-historical crisis that had been building for several centuries in Western Christendom.

Among the major reformers, Luther showed the most pronounced apocalyptic tendencies. Other leading figures such as the urban reformers Huldrych Zwingli and John Calvin were more deeply influenced by Erasmian humanism, which assumed an integration of the sacred and the social realms that worked against the apocalyptic tendency to distinguish sharply between this fallen world and the perfection of the coming kingdom. Although virtually all of Western Christendom was affected by the heightened expectancy of the age, the authority of the Wittenberg reformer helped to sanction in Lutheran Germany the most consistently pronounced apocalyptic atmosphere in sixteenth-century Europe.

Luther's expectancy was shaped in basic ways by prophetic ideas and assumptions of the late Middle Ages. For example, his vision of world history was clearly influenced by inherited notions of universal decline and degeneracy. Yet his original readings of scripture and his re-visioning of prophetic truth became the main basis for a long tradition of Protestant apocalypticism both in Germany and elsewhere. Luther's revival of the New Testament hope included the apocalyptic conviction of imminent universal judgment. For him the basic reality was an all-encompassing struggle between God and the devil. Luther saw his own movement to revive the gospel as the last act in this great conflict. God was allowing the light of truth to flash over the world with a final burst of clarity. At the same time, true believers were subject to unprecedented threats and persecutions.

Central to Luther's prophetic understanding was his discovery of the Antichrist in the Roman papacy. Unlike the many medieval interpreters who had identified the popes as Antichrist because of their immoral lives, Luther identified the institution of the papacy itself as the embodiment of a perverted gospel. This discovery indicated clearly that the last days had arrived. The struggle was now out in the open; nothing more was to be awaited before the end. Believers were simply to bear the multiplying horrors on earth as they joyfully awaited the Day of Redemption. The basic shape of Luther's prophetic outlook did not change after his break from Rome. But in his later years his tone became more markedly and consistently apocalyptic as his interest in the historical dimension grew, and also as he perceived this world's plight becoming more desperate.

Although Luther's biblical discoveries and outlook were of central influence in shaping the Protestant apocalyptic tradition both in Germany and elsewhere, inherited hopes and fears persisted, and often took on new dimensions in the early years of the evangelical movement. There is evidence, for example, of widespread fears, based on popular astrological forecasts, of a universal flood and the Last Judgment to come in 1524. While some preachers of reform tried to discredit these predictions, such scenarios of doom certainly contributed to the common perception that the crucial hour of decision was at hand. The nightmare of an invasion by the Turks, which would come as a final punishment on a sinful world, had never seemed closer to realization than it did by the late 1520s; such a feeling spurred Luther to complete his vernacular translation of the Bible so that the word might spread as widely as possible in whatever brief time remained.

Evangelical propaganda continued to draw on the large stock of medieval apocalyptic lore and imagery. Thus, for instance, popular expectations of a final great prophet, a last Elijah who would come to prepare the way for the Lord's return, were commonly applied to Luther himself. Other prophecies with a long history, such as the so-called Cedar of Lebanon vision, were adapted to support the Protestant convictions that Luther's movement was of divine origin, that the faithless would soon be punished, and that the deliverance of believers was imminent. In 1527 Andreas Osiander of Nuremberg updated and published an old Joachimist prophecy and a prediction of Hildegard of Bingen, both of which looked to a recovery of the true church before the end of the world.

Other common medieval beliefs played a role in Reformation expectancy. Monstrous births and other natural wonders were commonly viewed as divine signs and warnings; Luther and Philipp Melanchthon sanctioned such interpretations with publications about the prophetic significance of grotesque appearances in nature. Although 1524 had passed without a flood, the signs in the heavens continued to draw intense interest; the appearance of a great comet in 1531 (Halley's) claimed the rapt attention of many observers as an almost certain warning of divine wrath. But one certainly did not need to depend on such signs when the evidence of scripture itself seemed clear. Among fervent evangelicals the excitement sometimes reached a fever pitch, as it did in a village near Wittenberg when Luther's friend Michael Stifel predicted from his pulpit that the world would end at 8 A.M. on 19 October 1533.

While evangelical leaders generally sought to discourage

this sort of precise calculation, the conviction that judgment and deliverance were nigh did not wane as the sixteenth century progressed. Indeed the decades after Luther's death (1546) saw the emergence of an increasingly explicit, eclectic, and strident apocalypticism among many Protestants, especially in Germany. Under the influence of factional strife among Luther's heirs, the rise of Calvinism and other competing confessions, and the ongoing social ferment of the age, evangelical preachers and writers such as Andreas Musculus (d. 1581) at Frankfurt an der Oder expressed a growing sense that the plight of this world was hopeless. Everywhere there was evidence of the drying up of true faith and love, of unparalleled religious and moral decay that could only be resolved at the last day. The devil appeared to be more active than ever before. The possible connections between this apocalyptic perception and the intensification of witch hunting in the later sixteenth century remain largely unexplored.

In a society rapidly learning to articulate its hopes and fears through the mass medium of vernacular literature, burghers as well as pastors witnessed eagerly to the multiplying signs of the coming end. The second half of the sixteenth century was a golden age of popularity for the genre of wonder-books, which recorded every apparent anomaly in nature as testimony to the imminent collapse of the old creation; among the most prolific writers of such collections was the pastor Job Fincel. But apocalyptic assumptions carried observers far beyond the mere recording of wonders. Broadly inspired by the humanist interests in nature and in history encouraged by Melanchthon at Wittenberg, students of prophecy eagerly applied the tools of chronology, mathematics, and astrology to this broad field of inquiry.

The traditional historical scheme of the four world monarchies from the book of Daniel was now commonly supplemented by the so-called Prophecy of Elias, according to which the world was allotted two thousand years before the Law, two thousand years under the Law (roughly the age of the Old Testament), and two thousand years after the coming of the Messiah. *Matthew* 24:22 made clear that the last age would be cut short, for "except those days should be shortened, there should no flesh be saved." Over fifteen hundred years of that epoch had already passed; when one added the testimony of astrologers about the heavenly signs, including unusual conjunctions of the planets and the shocking new star of 1572, it was difficult indeed to escape the common conclusion. There was a major buildup of expectations for 1588, but that year brought only one peak, and by no means the last, in the apocalyptically charged atmosphere of the late Reformation era.

The era around 1600 brought a host of especially excited but confused efforts to unlock the all-important secrets of the last times. The strong sense of dualism between the fallen present and the redeemed future, and the belief that divine truths would be revealed to the faithful in the last times, provided impetus to the spread of magical efforts to discover the ultimate secrets of creation. Such trends were again most evident in Lutheran Germany, where apocalyptic astrology, alchemy, number mysticism, and related arts buoyed dreams of a new and truly universal Reformation. The widespread destruction and the sordid realities of the Thirty Years' War (1618–1648) contributed to the dissipation of such overblown hopes and apocalyptic fears, and thus appears to have accelerated in Germany the general seventeenth-century trend toward a more purely personal or subjective religious faith.

Although the historical and prophetic outlook of Reformed Protestants tended less toward worldly pessimism and apocalypticism than did Luther's heirs, during the era of the Wars of Religion (c.1550–1650) a significant tradition of Reformed prophecy developed, which included numerous expressions of apocalyptic conviction. The leaders of Swiss-German Protestantism in Zurich adopted a prophetic orientation that was far more historical and focused in its expectancy than Zwingli had been. Heinrich Bullinger helped establish this new tone in his *In Apocalypsim Iesu Christi, reuelatam quidem per angelum Domini, uisam uero uel Exceptam Atque Conscriptam a Ioanne Apostolo & euangelista, Conciones centum* (One Hundred Sermons on the Apocalypse), first published in 1557. Reformed prophecy tended increasingly to be hopeful about the progress of God's kingdom within history; Calvinism in particular proved fertile for the appearance of a forward-looking millenarianism, often bordering on historical meliorism. Calvin himself was perhaps less inclined to apocalyptic thought than any other early Protestant leader, and early Calvinist thinkers tended to avoid the explicit interpretation of current events in prophetic terms. But many followers would soon find use in prophecies regarding a culmination of the current struggle against evil and the hope for swift progress toward the rule of Christ.

Already in the middle decades of the sixteenth century, English Calvinists were translating and adapting German apocalyptic ideas showing the crucial significance of the struggle against the Roman Antichrist and of the current preaching of the purified gospel. Many English prophetic writings echoed the worldly pessimism characteristic of Lutheran Germany, but a different note is discernible quite early on. The works of John Bale (d. 1563) and John Foxe (d. 1587) placed the events of the English Reformation clearly within the context of providential history; in his famous *Actes and Monuments* (English ed. 1563), Foxe gave England an explicit and central role in the advance of Christ's kingdom. These thinkers were not openly millenarian in outlook, but they helped prepare the way for the approach popularized above all by Thomas Brightman (d. 1607), which led many English to see their own time as directly preparatory to the earthly millennium.

The development of English Protestant millenarianism

continued in the decades preceding the Civil War, and reached a peak of excitement during the years of the war and interregnum (1642–1660). Popular millenarianism became an integral element of propaganda for a cause that linked strident Protestantism with parliamentary or republican government and the establishment of a "godly kingdom." The most famous case of radical millenarianism in this period was that of the Fifth Monarchy Men, who saw it as the responsibility of believers to help bring on the final and most perfect historical age through militant action. The more general hope for a godly society among English Protestants expressed itself most clearly in the Puritan migration to the New World, where the elect might yet properly prepare the way of the Lord.

Apocalyptic themes continued in Catholic Europe during the age of the Reformation as well, although here the greater traditional integration of the sacred and the social, as well as heavy official discouragement of prophetic speculation, made for a considerably more muted atmosphere. Through the 1520s, Italy teemed with popular prophecies, many of which had an apocalyptic aspect; after around 1530 this popular discourse was effectively suppressed by a deeply defensive clerical establishment. Such clerical suppression was apparently less successful in France, where the violence of the Wars of Religion (c.1562–1595) was often driven by popular Catholic prophecies about the leagues of God and Satan. The famous French astrologer Michel Nostradamus was among those who suggested that a major planetary conjunction in 1565 might herald the Second Coming. In general, however, the prophetic atmosphere in France was less pervasively and consistently apocalyptic than it was among German Protestants.

Not surprisingly, Catholic propaganda sometimes identified Luther (among other Protestant leaders) as the Antichrist; the open spread of heresy could easily be seen as a sign of the last days. Apocalyptic ideas held a more positive role among various religious orders; for example, many Jesuits adopted Joachimite assumptions about their order as a prophetic elite with a special role to play in the final acts of the divine drama. Guillaume Postel's breathtaking visions of a return to universal harmony after the present time of crisis proved to be too much even for his own Jesuit order, but they are clear reflections of persistent strains of hopeful apocalypticism within the broader Catholic world. Thus too the New World missions of groups such as the Franciscans were charged with beliefs about the final earthly flowering of Christian truth and the establishment of the millennial kingdom.

On balance, the apocalyptic outlook appears generally most pronounced among Protestants in the age of the Reformation. The apocalyptic imagery of the Bible proved a key ingredient in the self-definition of the Protestant cultures of northern and northwestern Europe, and could be adapted to a wide variety of Protestant uses. Historians have long seen links between the forward-looking Protestant millenarianism of the seventeenth century and modern notions of historical progress, although the process by which such a "secularization" occurred is by no means well understood. On the other hand, there is evidence that among some radical Dutch Protestants of the seventeenth century, belief in the decay of the world, and in the impossibility of establishing the true church before the coming of the millennial kingdom, contributed to a self-conscious reliance on reason as a necessary if provisional guide in human affairs.

Whether hope or disillusionment played the more important historical role, what is clear in either case is that the apocalyptic conceptions of the Reformation era did not simply lose all significance with the development of Enlightenment thought. Rather, by raising fundamental questions about the orientation of human beings in the cosmos and in time, those conceptions marked a crucial stage in the evolution of Western attitudes toward both nature and history.

[*See also* Antichrist *and* Millenarianism.]

BIBLIOGRAPHY

Asendorf, Ulrich. *Eschatologie bei Luther.* Göttingen, 1967.
Ball, Bryan W. *A Great Expectation: Eschatological Thought in English Protestantism to 1660.* Leiden, 1975.
Barnes, Robin Bruce. *Prophecy and Gnosis: Apocalypticism in the Wake of the Lutheran Reformation.* Stanford, 1988.
Cohn, Norman. *The Pursuit of the Millennium: Revolutionary Millenarians and Mystical Anarchists in the Middle Ages.* 3d ed. Reprint, London, 1984. A fascinating but dated interpretation of popular millenarianism through the early Reformation period.
Crouzet, Denis. *Les guerriers de Dieu: La violence des troubles de religion, vers 1525-vers 1610.* 2 vols. Seyssel, 1990. Includes an extended treatment of popular apocalypticism in France.
Deppermann, Klaus. *Melchior Hoffman: Social Unrest and Apocalyptic Visions in the Age of the Reformation.* Edited by Benjamin Drewery, translated by Malcolm Wren. Edinburgh, 1987. The best study of radical Anabaptist apocalypticism.
Edwards, Mark U., Jr. *Luther's Last Battles: Politics and Polemics, 1531–46.* Ithaca, N.Y., and London, 1983.
Firth, Katharine R. *The Apocalyptic Tradition in Reformation Britain, 1530-1645.* Oxford, 1979. The best among many works on the British tradition.
Fix, Andrew. *Prophecy and Reason: The Dutch Collegiants in the Early Enlightenment.* Princeton, 1991. A stimulating argument regarding prophecy and the Enlightenment appeal to reason.
Headley, John M. *Luther's View of Church History.* New Haven, 1963.
Lerner, Robert E. *The Powers of Prophecy: The Cedar of Lebanon Vision from the Mongol Onslaught to the Dawn of the Enlightenment.* Berkeley, 1983. Shows the transformations of a particular prophetic tradition.
McGinn, Bernard. *Visions of the End: Apocalyptic Traditions in the Middle Ages.* New York, 1979. Does not cover the Reformation era, but provides essential historical and conceptual background.
Niccoli, Ottavia. *Prophecy and People in Renaissance Italy.* Princeton, 1990.
Oberman, Heiko A. *Luther: Man between God and the Devil.* New Haven and London, 1989. The best comprehensive treatment of Luther's apocalyptic world-view.
Peterson, Rodney L. *Preaching in the Last Days: The Theme of 'Two Witnesses' in the Sixteenth and Seventeenth Centuries.* New York and Oxford, 1993.

Peuckert, Will-Erich. *Die Grosse Wende: Das apokalyptische Saeculum und Luther*. 2 vols. Reprint, Darmstadt, 1976. A highly colorful and somewhat eccentric picture.

Phelan, John Leddy. *The Millennial Kingdom of the Franciscans in the New World: A Study of the Writings of Geronimo de Mendieta, 1525–1604*. Berkeley, 1970.

Reeves, Marjorie. *Joachim of Fiore and the Prophetic Future*. London, 1976. Joachimism in the sixteenth and seventeenth centuries.

Scribner, Robert W. *For the Sake of Simple Folk: Popular Propaganda for the German Reformation*. Cambridge, 1981.

Tuveson, Ernest Lee. *Millennium and Utopia: A Study in the Background of the Idea of Progress*. Reprint, Gloucester, Mass., 1972. An older but still useful study.

ROBIN B. BARNES

AQUAVIVA, Claudio. *See* Acquaviva, Claudio.

ARCHITECTURE. The history of religious architecture from about 1520 until the end of the Thirty Years' War in 1648 offers a fascinating story about conflicting attitudes over the true function of the church. Throughout the Middle Ages the Roman Catholic church argued that the actual building was invested with complex symbolic and liturgical meanings. It provided a microcosmic anticipation of heavenly Jerusalem. Here its clerics mediated between heaven and earth and between God and humanity. Thousands of remarkably elaborate churches were built from the twelfth through the early sixteenth century. The desire to honor God was often mixed with local pride. For instance, the attractive Saint-Annen-Kirche in Annaberg, then a booming silver-mining center, celebrated the town's patron saint and its newly found affluence. Everywhere the number of churches proliferated. A city such as Nuremberg could boast two imposing parish churches and fifteen other religious establishments.

The expense of these churches, their decorations, and the upkeep of their clerical communities inspired many Protestant and Catholic critics, including Desiderius Erasmus. In his *Epistel zur Messe in der Christnacht* of 1522, Martin Luther exclaimed: "See, that is the proper worship, for which a person needs no bells, no churches, no vessels or ornaments, no lights or candles, no organs or singing, no paintings or images, no panels or altars. . . . For these are all human inventions and ornaments, which God does not heed, and which obscure the correct worship, with their glitter." For him the true church was wherever the word of God was spoken, even if this occurred while standing outdoors on a bridge over the Elbe River. The church could no longer be limited to a specific physical place. Luther, Huldrych Zwingli, and John Calvin, among others, concurred that a meeting hall was useful, but it should be neither costly nor adorned with art that might distract the worshiper or even promote idolatry. Zwingli lauded the "positively luminous"

character of the whitewashed walls of Zurich's churches following their artistic cleansing in 1524. With the advent of the Reformation, a fundamental aesthetic and conceptual change occurred. Protestant criticisms of religious art and architecture, coupled with their political successes, produced a chilling effect upon the construction of new houses of worship in both evangelical and Catholic territories. Only at the turn of the century did the number of new buildings increase dramatically in northern Europe.

Protestants and Their Churches. Protestant church architecture is characterized first by adaptation and then by experimentation. In the German-speaking lands between 1520 and 1600, there was virtually no significant new church construction, other than a handful of palace chapels. The same is true in the Netherlands in the immediate decades after the revolt from Spain in the 1570s. The Lutherans, Zwinglians, and Calvinists, including the Dutch Reformed church, had scant need for new buildings since they took control of an ample stock of former Catholic structures. Alterations to individual buildings varied from town to town and from confession to confession. After the initial wave of iconoclasm, the Lutheran towns tended to be far more tolerant of preexisting decorations than those under either Zwinglian or Calvinist control. Since each group stressed the word of God, a fundamental shift in priorities occurred. The pulpit replaced the high altar and the choir as the congregation's focus. Pulpits were often constructed at or moved to more central locations in the middle of the nave. As early as 1536–1537, wooden tribunes were appended to some existing churches, such as the Wolfgangskirche in Schneeberg, to bring worshipers closer to the pulpit. This became a common feature in the seventeenth and eighteenth century Protestant churches in both Europe and North America. Choirs were often no longer needed. Their stalls and screens were frequently removed. Creative new uses for choirs included serving as baptismal chapels, settings for Last Supper celebrations, and burial sites. The Stiftskirche in Tübingen and the Marienkirche (cathedral) in Freiberg, Saxony, were converted into princely mausoleums. The choir of the Nieuwe Kerk in Delft was transformed into a national shrine honoring William of Orange, the slain leader of the Dutch revolt. Lutheran churches did retain a single altar, sometimes decorated with a painted or carved altarpiece, and a baptismal font.

Gerrit Berckheyde's painting *Interior of St. Bavo's in Haarlem* (1673; London, National Gallery) offers a valuable glimpse into the late Gothic church as adapted to Reformed services. A large crowd sits facing a simple yet imposing pulpit that is now located on a pier in the center of the nave. The choir, separated by its brass grille, stands empty. The only ornament other than the candelabra and painted family crests is the massive Renaissance organ with its painted shutters, observed in the south aisle. Music retained an important role in most Protestant services.

For most communities there was no reason to build new Protestant churches. Houses of worship under construction at the time of a confessional change, such as the Stadtkirche in Halle or the Neupfarrkirche in Regensburg, were slowly completed. The earliest new Protestant structures in the German-speaking lands were a series of palace chapels erected for Lutheran princes at Dresden, Gotha, Schwerin, Schmalkalden, and Augustusburg, among others. The most influential of these was the chapel that John Frederick, elector of Saxony, erected between 1540 and 1544 at Schloss Hartenfels in Torgau. The four-bay rectangular building, designed by Nickel Gromann in a late Gothic style, is without an apse. Entering through the simple courtyard portal, one is drawn first to the elevated pulpit in the center of the long eastern wall. A two-story stone gallery surmounts this simple core. The form certainly reflected the ideas of Luther, who, in his inaugural sermon on 5 October 1544, reminded his august audience that "the purpose of this new house may be such that nothing else may ever happen in it except that our dear Lord himself may speak to us through his holy Word and we respond to him through prayer and praise" (*Luther's Works*, vol. 51: *Sermons I*, edited and translated by John W. Doberstein [Philadelphia, 1959], p. 333.) The only major decoration other than the carved pulpit was a simple altar stone resting upon four sculpted angels. A similar architectural form was employed at Schmalkalden (1586–1590); however, here the pulpit, altar stone, and organ are arranged together along one vertical axis. Torgau's simple rectangular plan with its galleries likely influenced Trinity Church in Klagenfurt (Carinthia) of 1582–1591. With the suppression of the Lutheran community here in 1604, this parish church passed to the Jesuits, who decades later added a deep choir.

Major new Protestant churches, typically sponsored by princes, began to appear in the early seventeenth century. Some were initiated as evangelical responses to the Catholics' aggressive building campaigns. In 1599 Duke Frederick of Württemberg founded Freudenstadt, a planned town at the site of a new silver mine that was populated mainly by Lutherans expelled from southern Austria. Architect Heinrich Schickhardt laid out the major buildings, including the Stadtkirche (1601–1609), at the corners of the central square. The resulting church has an L-shape. This ingenious solution permitted the congregation downstairs and in the second-floor gallery to have an unimpeded view of the altar, font, and pulpit, which are located at the juncture of the two arms. Frederick and his architect also collaborated on the more conventional Saint Martin in Montbéliard (Mömpelgard [Doubs]; 1601–1607). The two most imposing Protestant edifices are the Hauptkirche in Wolfenbüttel (begun in 1608), commissioned by Duke Henry Julius of Braunschweig-Lüneburg, and the Stadtkirche in Bückeburg (1610–1615), ordered by Count Ernest of Schaumburg. Architect Paul Francke and the unknown master of the Stadt-

kirche revived the longitudinal, hall-church formula, one that permits excellent lighting and clear visibility across the structure. In both instances an elaborate veneer of mannerist ornamentation was used. The imposing facade of Bückeburg is prominently inscribed EXEMPLUM RELIGIONIS NON STRUCTURAE ("an example for piety not architecture"), with the patron's name highlighted in gold letters. This disclaimer might have been intended to disarm potential critics of the church's opulence. During these years two churches were built in Prague for the city's extensive German Lutheran community. Duke Henry Julius contributed greatly to the construction costs of Trinity Church (1611–1613), another hall-style building. In the aftermath of the Battle of White Mountain (1620) and the suppression of Prague's Protestants, its altar was shipped to Wolfenbüttel, and the building ultimately passed to the Carmelites. The most notable community-sponsored project was Trinity Church in Regensburg (1627–1631), whose progress, like that of Wolfenbüttel, was interrupted by the war. The single nave, bound on three sides by a gallery, facilitated its function as a preaching church.

The situation in France developed later and rather differently than in the German lands. Physical evidence of the Reformed churches, or temples, as they were called, does not survive. Upwards of two thousand small temples may have been constructed by the 1560s. These were generally insignificant structures. Best known was the Paradise Temple in Lyon, a two-story circular edifice with a central pulpit, which stood only from 1564 to 1566. Other notable centrally planned temples made primarily of wood stood in Le Petit-Quevilly near Rouen (1599), in Dieppe (1606), and in Caen (1612). The sole monumental stone church was Salomon de Brosse's temple at Charenton-sur-Marne. Paris's Huguenot community, prevented by the Edict of Nantes (1598) from building within the city, selected a site just outside its walls. Inspired by Vitruvius's description of his basilica at Fano, Brosse devised an "unobstructed auditorium," one that could accommodate between four thousand and five thousand worshippers. The rectangular building, measuring about 30 by 15 meters, consisted of a large open space bordered by a ground-floor ambulatory and a two-story gallery. Its simple, austere form would influence English churches, including Inigo Jones' Covent Garden Church in London, and the famous Jewish synagogues in Amsterdam and the Hague. The Charenton temple, like so many others, was pulled down in 1685 after the revocation of the Edict of Nantes.

The Calvinist community in the Low Countries, like the German Protestants before them, rarely built any churches between 1560 and 1620, as they converted existing buildings to their use. Between 1596 and 1603 Konrad van Noremburch the Younger constructed the simple octagonal church in Willemstad (North Brabant), the star-shaped fortress that William of Orange had founded in 1583 to guard the strategic Hollands Diep on the delta of the Meuse and Rhine rivers. This project, funded by Prince Maurice, was the first of the centralized churches favored by the Dutch. Its finest heirs include the Marekerk in Leiden (1639–1649), a graceful octagonal building by Arent van 's-Gravesande; the octagonal Oosterkerk in Middelburg (1647–1667); and Adriaen Dortsman's domed New Lutheran Church in Amsterdam (1668). Hendrick de Keyser, who designed three of Amsterdam's four new Reformed churches, explored other alternatives. His Zuiderkerk (1603–1611) employs a Gothic hall-church formula minus a choir. Subsequently he devised his much larger Westerkerk (1620–1631) with its elegantly balanced basilica form—a rectangle with a double transept. Windows on both floors make this church far airier than the Zuiderkerk. The building's 86-meter-tall tower, Amsterdam's highest, provides an imposing symbol of the city's Calvinist faith. Keyser's final structure was the Noorderkerk (1620–1622), which has a Greek-cross plan. In all three churches Keyser ensured the pulpit's centrality. Jacob van Campen also utilized a Greek cross, now inscribed within a square, in his Nieuwe Kerk in Haarlem (1645–1649). Again his attempt was to devise an aesthetically pleasing yet highly practical space for the congregation and its preachers. The most complex church in the Netherlands is the Nieuwe Kerk in the Hague (1649–1656), which has two centralized spaces united by a common longitudinal axis. At the juncture of the two, the architects Bartholomeus van Bassen and Pieter Noonwits located the pulpit and the baptismal screen.

Catholics and Their Churches. The challenge of the evangelical movement affected northern Europe's Catholics. Few communities or orders were willing to invest in new churches when the religious situation was so unsettled. Confessional allegiances of entire regions could switch almost overnight, as in the case of the duchy of Saxony in 1539. The fate of the Neue Stift in Halle also may have provided a cautionary model. In 1519 Cardinal Albert of Brandenburg (1490–1545), archbishop of Mainz and Magdeburg, started transforming an existing though virtually bare Dominican church into one of the most sumptuous structures in all of Europe. It housed 21,384 holy relics and was decorated by Germany's foremost artists. He conceived of the Neue Stift as a glorious reaffirmation of traditional Catholic practices and doctrines, most notably the power of saints. Yet Albert lost control of Halle. What had taken two decades to conceive was dispersed overnight by 1541. If the cardinal, the empire's most powerful cleric, could not hold his own territories, what chance did others have? Churches under construction were quietly finished and modestly outfitted. Only a few new ones, such as the Hofkirche in Innsbruck (1553–1563), were initiated by Catholic nobles. In this instance Ferdinand I devised the monument expressly as a Habsburg family shrine, the burial site for Emperor Maximilian I, not for community use.

The Peace of Augsburg (1555) and the conclusion of the Council of Trent (1563) altered the religious situation. The first provided the Catholics with time to reassess their future without fear of further territorial losses. The second inspired a renewed sense of identity. Fueled by the union of militant orders (especially the Jesuits), a set of ambitious bishops and clerics, and the growing political strength of such noble families as the Wittelsbachs, an astounding surge of new Catholic architecture began in the late 1570s.

Most significant were the activities of the Jesuits. Between the late 1570s and 1640, they erected no fewer than twenty-six major and dozens of minor churches just in the Upper and Lower German provinces. The same energy can also be observed in the southern Netherlands, France, Bohemia, and Austria. Their buildings reveal a stylistic pluralism linked to the resources, scale, and activities of their individual communities. Some, such as the Saint Petrikirche in Münster (1590–1597), borrowed heavily from older Gothic buildings; others, notably the monumental Saint Michael in Munich (1583–1597) or Unserer Lieben Frau in Neuburg (1605/1607–18), offer late Renaissance formulas; and a few, such as the Dreifaltigkeitskirche in Molsheim (1615–1617/18), present a curious blending of Gothic and classical features. There are, nonetheless, some common characteristics. Virtually all were built as preaching churches, and thus naves tend to be quite wide and not overly long. The Konradskirche in Constance (1604–1607) or the Allerheiligenkirche in Hall, Tirol (1607/08–10), recall the intimacy of comfortable audience halls. Simple, ambulatory-less choirs retained their liturgical focus. Eucharist tabernacles now stand on the high altar. Communion rails help bind the choir and congregation. Transepts, where these exist at all, are commonly no deeper than the aisles or side chapels. A large, prominently situated pulpit was essential to the Jesuits' educational mission. Clear artistic programs, often depicting the catechism or litany, link the different parts of these buildings. The scale and sumptuousness of the Wittelsbach-sponsored Munich church, which is arguably the finest Renaissance building in northern Europe, provided a model for many Jesuit and non-Jesuit buildings. Interestingly, the church in Neuburg was initiated as a Protestant response to Saint Michael; however, during the course of its construction, the new prince, Wolfgang Wilhelm, converted to Catholicism and presented the church to the Jesuits. No other order had as strong a role as the Jesuits. Nevertheless, the Augustinians, Franciscans, Benedictines, and, later, the Carmelites, among others, renovated existing or erected new churches.

As a result of the religious wars and other political upheavals, many bishoprics were in severe disrepair by the 1570s. In the aftermath of the Council of Trent, a generation of industrious reforming bishops struggled to reverse this trend. Foremost among these was Julius Echter von Mespelbrunn, prince-bishop of Würzburg. Subsequently dubbed the "father of the fatherland," the bishop built or restored an estimated three hundred churches during his reign from 1573 to 1617. The majority were small parish churches done in the so-called Echter Gotik style. For the bishop the Gothic style, with its ribbed vaults and pointed arches, offered a means of historical legitimation, a symbolic reconnection with the pre-Reformation Catholic church. This conscious archaism may be observed in such structures as the famed Marian pilgrimage church at Dettelbach (1608–1613). Bishop Echter's finest building was the University Church in Würzburg (1583–1591), which was heavily damaged by the Swedes in 1631 and again in 1945. Reminiscent of some Protestant churches, this structure includes a two-story gallery though here linked with a longitudinal axis and short apse. Its form is still largely Gothic, but the decorative vocabulary, perhaps in a salute to the new university, is late Renaissance in character.

In the southern Netherlands, or modern Belgium, the story was much the same. The turmoil of the 1560s through the 1580s was hardly conducive to new building projects. Under the joint regency of Archduke Albert (r. 1596–1621) and Archduchess Isabella (r. 1596–1633), the region was transformed into a bulwark of the Counter-Reformation. Most Protestants had emigrated northward or to Germany. With the sharp decline in population, new parish churches were unneeded. Instead, it was the religious orders, most notably the Jesuits, Augustinians, and Carmelites, that commissioned new buildings in the opening decades of the seventeenth century. The Jesuits possessed either new or renovated churches in Antwerp, Brugge, Brussels, Ghent, Louvain, Maastricht, Mons, Namur, Tournai, and Valenciennes, among other towns. Their configuration to emphasize preaching and most other essential characteristics repeat patterns already observed in Germany. Most offer a melange of Gothic and classical architectural forms. The finest examples, such as Saint Ignatius (now Saint Charles Borromeo) in Antwerp (1615–1621), incorporate single galleries. The apse of this once sumptuous church is dominated by a monumental altarpiece designed and originally painted by Peter Paul Rubens. The scale of the altar draws the worshiper toward the sanctuary. Here, as in most Jesuit churches, wooden confessionals line the side walls.

Not surprisingly, there was no new church construction by the sizable Catholic community in the Northern Netherlands. Catholics worshiped clandestinely, normally in private homes. Tolerant civic officials in Amsterdam did condone so-called attic churches, structures situated in the upper floors of houses that, from the street, could not be distinguished as religious meeting places. The best known of these is the Ons' Lieve Heer op Solder (Our Lord in the Attic; 1661–1663), which is located on the Oude Zijds Voorburgwal, one of the city's main canals. To maximize its limited space, two galleries rise above the simple rectangular nave that terminates in the single altar.

France's situation was somewhat analogous to that of the southern Netherlands. The Wars of Religion from 1560 to 1598 discouraged new architectural projects. Only with royal leadership during the reign of Louis XIII (r. 1610–1643) and his minister Cardinal Richelieu (Armand-Jean du Plessis) were grand building campaigns again commissioned. The most imposing of the Parisian churches are François Derand's Saint Paul–Saint Louis (1634), Jacques Lemercier's church of the Sorbonne (begun 1635), and François Mansart's great domed Val-de-Grace, founded by Queen Anne in 1645.

Between 1520 and 1648 an animated debate about the function and appearance of religious architecture occurred in northern Europe. The resulting solutions, some deviating radically from the pre-Reformation canon, have continued to define the basic character of Protestant and Catholic churches into the twentieth century.

England. Like the countries on the Continent, England was well supplied with parish churches, cathedrals, and monasteries by the beginning of the sixteenth century. The Perpendicular Gothic style, which had come into use about 1350, was unique to England, although it had some similarities to Flamboyant Gothic in France. English Perpendicular buildings were characterized by large windows, divided into sections by stone tracery bars meeting each other at perpendicular angles. Cathedrals and the most elaborate parish churches had fan-vaulted ceilings of stone, while the usual church had a timber roof, sometimes ornamented with figures of angels or saints. Many fine buildings were still under construction in the 1530s; these included some grand parish churches, such as Lavenham in Suffolk, and larger buildings like Bath Abbey and the chapel of King's College, Cambridge.

Building activity generally ceased with the Reformation, and some great buildings fell victim to it. The dissolution of the monasteries (1536–1540) ended the useful life of hundreds of church buildings. A few were turned into cathedrals (Gloucester and Peterborough, for example), but more (like Glastonbury in Somerset and Fountains Abbey in Yorkshire) were allowed to fall into ruin. A few were remodeled into private dwellings. The dissolution of shrines under Henry VIII and of chantries under Edward VI meant demolition of significant structures in many churches and cathedrals, and successive waves of iconoclasm resulted in the smashing or defacing of much medieval statuary, including rood lofts and reredoses. Stone altars were proscribed by *The Second Book of Common Prayer* (1552), and many altars were destroyed and replaced by movable wooden Communion tables. Reformed theology, which denied transubstantiation and the notion of the Mass as a sacrifice, dictated these changes. In the late sixteenth century the east end of the church building normally displayed a table of the Ten Commandments, surmounted by the royal arms.

Archbishop William Laud's attempt to restore stone altars, together with much of the ceremony abandoned in the mid-sixteenth century, proved unpopular and was one of the factors leading to the English Civil War. During the fighting stained-glass windows were smashed in many places. Following the Puritan victory further iconoclasm took place, and Anglican churches were converted into houses of worship for Presbyterians and Independents. The restoration of the monarchy in 1660 brought with it the reestablishment of the state church, whose buildings were then restored. Major reconstruction was needed at some of the cathedrals, especially Lichfield, but many cathedrals, like Canterbury, York, and Salisbury, survived without significant damage.

The seventeenth century saw the introduction of classical and baroque architectural styles. Saint Paul's cathedral, rebuilt by Christopher Wren after the medieval building was ruined by the great fire of London (1666), is the finest example of building from this period. Wren also rebuilt many of the London churches that had been destroyed by the fire, and he established architectural forms that were widely copied throughout the British Isles as well as in the American colonies.

[*See also* Art; Cathedrals; Iconoclasm; *and* Iconography.]

BIBLIOGRAPHY

Blunt, Anthony. *Art and Architecture in France: 1500 to 1700.* 4th rev. ed. New Haven, 1993.

Braun, Joseph. *Die Kirchenbauten der deutschen Jesuiten.* 2 vols. Freiburg, 1908–1910.

Coope, Rosalys. *Salomon de Brosse and the Development of the Classical Style in French Architecture from 1565–1630.* London, 1972.

Garvan, Anthony. "The Protestant Plain Style before 1630." *Journal of the Society of Architectural Historians* 9.3 (1950), 5–13.

Gerson, Horst, and E. H. ter Kuile. *Art and Architecture in Belgium: 1600 to 1800.* Harmondsworth, 1960. See especially chap. 2.

Grossmann, Dieter. "Die Bedeutung der Schlosskapellen für den protestantischen Kirchenbau." In *Renaissance in Nord-Mitteleuropa I,* edited by G. Ulrich Grossman, pp. 127–147. Schriften des Weserrenaissance-Museums Schloss Brake, vol. 4. Munich, 1990.

Hitchcock, Henry-Russell. *German Renaissance Architecture.* Princeton, 1981.

Krause, Hans-Joachim. *Die Schlosskapellen der Renaissance in Sachsen.* Berlin, 1970.

Kuyper, W. *Dutch Classicist Architecture.* Delft, 1980. See especially chap. 3.

Lietzmann, Hildap. "Die Deutsche-Lutherische Dreifaltigkeits-, die spätere Ordenskirche St. Maria de Victoria auf der Kleinen Seite zu Prag." *Zeitschrift für Kunstgeschichte* 40 (1977), 205–226.

Lehmberg, Stanford E. *The Reformation of Cathedrals: Cathedrals in English Society, 1485–1603.* Princeton, 1988.

Mercer, Eric. *English Art, 1553–1625.* Oxford, 1962.

Möseneder, Karl. "Die Dreieinigkeitskirche in Regensburg: Ein protestantischer Kirchenbau." In *1542–1992: 450 Jahre evangelische Kirche in Regensburg,* exhibition catalog, Museum der Stadt Regensburg, pp. 109–51. Regensburg, 1992.

Rosenberg, Jakob, Seymour Slive, and E. H. ter Kuile. *Dutch Art and Architecture: 1600 to 1800.* 3d ed. Harmondsworth, 1977.

Smith, Jeffrey Chipps. *German Sculpture of the Later Renaissance, c.1520–1580: Art in an Age of Uncertainty.* Princeton, 1994.

Stone, Lawrence. *Sculpture in Britain: The Middle Ages.* Baltimore, 1955.

Summerson, John. *Architecture in Britain, 1530–1830.* 4th rev. ed. Harmondsworth, 1963.

Wagner, Karl, and Albert Keller, eds. *St. Michael in München.* Munich, 1983.

White, James F. *Protestant Worship and Church Architecture.* New York, 1964. See especially chap. 4.

JEFFREY CHIPPS SMITH

ARIAS MONTANO, Benito

ARIAS MONTANO, Benito (1527–1598), Spanish humanist, theologian, and poet born in the Extremaduran village of Fregenal de la Sierra. In the course of his studies at Seville and Alcalá, he was influenced by the example of Desiderius Erasmus and developed a fine reputation as a classical scholar. He attended the final sessions of the Council of Trent in 1562, and in 1566 Philip II named him a royal chaplain. Two years later the king sent him to Flanders to supervise the publication of the Antwerp Polyglot Bible. This volume, magnificently produced by Christophe Plantijn, appeared in 1572 but failed to win unconditional approval from the papacy. Arias went to Rome in 1575 to argue on its behalf but returned to Spain the following year when León de Castro and others accused him of Judaizing.

While in Antwerp Arias had translated some of the *Psalms,* produced a poem based on the *Song of Songs,* and written extensive commentaries on the prophets. He became intimately acquainted with the intellectual world of the Netherlands and, though his accusers did not know it, joined the Family of Love, a group whose views are usually described as spiritualist. The king, who valued his advice on the Low Countries and knew nothing of the Family of Love, protected Arias against his accusers and in 1576 appointed him curator of the library at the Escorial. While there Arias influenced several of the monks whose heterodoxy was apparently unsuspected by the Inquisition. In 1586 he retired to his home at Peña de Aracena to pursue natural history and other studies. He died at Seville on 6 July 1598.

Arias Montano was perhaps the greatest Spanish Hebraist and biblical scholar of his generation. Almost alone he carried the Erasmian tradition into the age of the Counter-Reformation and argued, albeit discreetly, for an interior faith based on scripture. Though his teachings did not long survive him, he was largely responsible for the superb collection of Protestant and Jewish books at the Escorial.

BIBLIOGRAPHY

Morales Oliver, Luis. *Arias Montano y la política de Felipe II en Flandes.* Madrid, 1927.

Rekers, B. *Benito Arias Montano.* London, 1972.

WILLIAM S. MALTBY

ARMINIUS, Jacobus

ARMINIUS, Jacobus (Dutch, Jacob Harmensen, Hermanszoon; 1559–1609), Reformed pastor in Amsterdam from 1588 to 1603 and theologian at Leiden from 1603 to

1609. He was the spokesman and symbol of resistance to strict Calvinist orthodoxy in the formative years of the Dutch Reformed church. He was born in Oudewater into a family of stature in church and financial circles in Holland. With the early death of his father and as the inheritor of property, he was put in the care of a legal guardian, the local priest, Dirck Amelgerszoon, a cousin of his mother, who saw that his charge received the Latin school education that would lead to university.

Amelgerszoon (known in Latin secondary sources as Theodorus Aemilius) died in 1574, and Arminius was placed under another guardian, also a cousin of his mother as well as a cousin of Amelgerszoon. Roelof Willebrordszoon (who Latinized his name as Rudolphus Snellius) was a mathematician and philosopher who taught first at Marburg and then at Leiden. Arminius followed Snellius to Marburg for a short time, but on the death of his mother and all his siblings at the hands of Spanish troops in the sack of Oudewater in 1575, he returned to Holland and became the twelfth student to matriculate in the new university at Leiden.

The recipient of a former mass endowment from the now Protestant merchants' guild in Amsterdam, Arminius studied theology under Théodore de Bèze and the Geneva faculty, returning to Amsterdam in 1587, where he was soon installed as a pastor and married to the daughter of a council member. During his fifteen years there he was the favorite of the merchant oligarchy, many of whom had little sympathy for the strict Calvinism of the other clergy. He showed his independence in expositions of *Romans* 7 and 9, and he wrote a lengthy critique of the Calvinism of the Cambridge Puritan William Perkins.

In 1603 Arminius was appointed *professor ordinarius* of theology at the University of Leiden, which made him a doctor of theology. Here again he was the first and only Hollander in a company of foreigners from other Calvinist centers. He received strong support in and out of the university and had a large following among the students, many of whom were among the signers of the Remonstrance of 1610.

Conflict broke out in 1604, when, in the rotation of the three theologians, it was his turn to present theses on predestination. His colleague Franciscus Gomarus attacked his views, and the university was soon polarized between Arminians and Gomarists. In 1605 he served as *rector magnificus* of the university. His rectorial address in 1606, "On Reconciling Religious Dissension among Christians," expressed many of his concerns. Dissension, he said, forces people to take sides, to fear to make the smallest concession, and to credit their opponents with base motives. Cynical rulers take advantage of this and promote disputes in order to enhance their own power. The remedy must include prayer, humility, and goodwill, with careful study replacing "learned ignorance."

He called for a conference among the disputants to be convened by the magistrates, who had such authority by divine mandate based on Old Testament practice and the precedent of the early church before the rise of the papacy. This position was explicit Erastianism, and it was rejected by the Calvinists, who wanted to keep the affairs of the church entirely in the hands of the presbytery. (Arminius had studied for a time at Basel while Thomas Lüber [Erastus] was on the faculty there.)

At issue was the authority of the Belgic Confession and the Heidelberg Catechism, which the Calvinists wanted binding on all clergy for interpreting scripture, thereby canonizing a high Calvinist doctrine of predestination. Arminius proposed a synod whose task would be to revise the confessions in the light of scripture, by which means he hoped that a less rigid doctrine of predestination would be allowed or even affirmed. Also at issue, then, were the purpose and purview of a national synod and the content of the faith itself. These views and his doctrine of predestination reached a wider public when the states of Holland and West Friesland invited him to address them on 30 May 1608. The speech, in Dutch, was soon published.

In brief, Arminius's view of predestination was that God has appointed his Son as the Savior, to receive into favor sinners who are "in Christ" by faith and who persevere in faith, and to grant to all who are helpless in sin (not just to the "elect") prevenient grace sufficient and efficacious for repentance and faith. As the work of the Holy Spirit, however, grace is not an irresistible force. God finally decrees the salvation or the damnation of particular persons on the basis of the divine foreknowledge of their faith and perseverance or the lack thereof. After the death of Arminius, when England's King James involved himself in the appointment of Arminius's successor (the Vorstius affair), international curiosity about Arminius led to a spate of posthumous publications, including the first edition of his collected *Opera theologica* (1629).

BIBLIOGRAPHY

Primary Source

Arminius, Jacob. *The Works of James Arminius*. 3 vols. Reprint, London, 1991.

Secondary Sources

Bangs, Carl. "'All the Best Bishoprics and Deaneries': The Enigma of Arminian Politics." *Church History* 42.1 (March 1973), 5–16.
———. *Arminius: A Study in the Dutch Reformation*. Reprint, with corrections and addenda, Grand Rapids, Mich., 1985.
Dekker, E. *Rijker dan Midas: Vrijheid, Genade en predestinatie in de theologie van Jacobus Arminius, 1559–1660*. Zoetermeer, Netherlands, 1993.

CARL BANGS

ARNOLDI, Bartholomew. *See* Usingen, Bartholomäus Arnoldi von.

ART. The topic of the Reformation and art can claim a long history. The Protestant movement had scarcely got under way before observers noted implications for painting and sculpture. The Nuremberg artist Albrecht Dürer in 1525 uttered warnings concerning the futility of image destruction and the difficulty of reviving the arts once they were lost. The Dutch humanist Desiderius Erasmus also alluded to some of these problems. In a 1526 letter of introduction provided for Hans Holbein the Younger to take with him to the Netherlands, Erasmus explained the painter's departure from Reformation Basel by stating that "here the arts are cold." The Wittenberg reformer Martin Luther seems to have felt sensitive to accusations of responsibility for causing this frigid atmosphere. He once protested that he was not "of the opinion that the gospel should destroy and blight all the arts."

If Luther's remark displays an element of defensiveness, subsequent events demonstrate why. Arguments over post-Reformation cultural decline became a standard theme in Protestant-Catholic polemics, one that endured down to the twentieth century. Fortunately a number of factors have combined over the past several decades to render the topic of the Reformation and art much less controversial. The improved relations between churches, resulting from the modern ecumenical movement, left their mark upon the writing of history. Perhaps even more of a moderating influence resulted from a greater participation in the discussion by two groups of secular scholars. Academic specialists in early modern European history gradually have overcome some inhibitions against systematic use of visual evidence. Art historians, for their part, appear in many instances to have laid aside earlier reservations regarding serious study of the often didactic or polemical and sometimes aesthetically mediocre artistic creations of the Reformation and Counter-Reformation. Researchers from both disciplines have begun to make more systematic use of methodological insights derived from the social sciences. All of this bodes well for the future, which should witness a continued expansion of our knowledge.

Protestant Reformers' Views on Art. The question of religious art represents an important area of disagreement among early Protestants. Luther developed his views on images largely in reaction to the attacks made on them by more radical reformers, particularly the iconoclastic teachings published from the early 1520s by his Wittenberg faculty colleague Andreas Bodenstein von Karlstadt. Unlike Karlstadt, Luther did not regard actual image idolatry as a widespread problem. Nor did Luther share the notion that the image prohibition of the Old Testament remained strictly in force for Christians, preferring to think that it formed part of the Jewish ceremonial law abrogated by the coming of Christ. Furthermore, Luther repudiated any body-spirit dualism that might seem to invalidate reliance upon physical aids in worship. Ultimately for the reformer the use or nonuse of religious images fell in the realm of Christian liberty.

Luther, in fact, viewed mental image making as a natural part of the human psyche, a necessity for humans to visualize that about which they think. Religious art follows as a natural extension of people's inherent tendency to form mental images, and the creations of the painter's and sculptor's craft possessed definite value for the evangelizing mission of the church. Luther endorsed the medieval conception of visual illustrations as forming a layperson's Bible. In his view children and simple folk are "more apt to retain the divine stories when taught by picture and parable than merely by words or instruction." The Wittenberg reformer ultimately acquired a high regard for the pedagogical potential of pictorial compositions, emphasizing their usefulness for enlivening the understanding and for refreshing the memory.

Luther's moderately positive views on religious imagery gained lasting acceptance only in those lands where his theology provided the doctrinal basis for the emerging established churches. Meanwhile, the iconoclastic ideas of Karlstadt had reached Switzerland, where, mediated through the work of another radical author, Ludwig Hätzer, they influenced the developing thought of the Zurich reformer Huldrych Zwingli.

Zwingli denied that the question of images in churches belonged to the realm of religious liberty, thus refuting the notion that Christians were free to choose whether to have them. For him the image prohibition in the Old Testament remained fully binding. This was necessary owing to the fact that, because of people's natural inclination to false worship, virtually all images placed in churches inevitably ended up becoming idols. This proved particularly true of images of Christ.

Zwingli did not totally reject the possibility of an art with religious subject matter. Pictures of Jesus and other biblical themes might be allowed—outside of churches—so long as they were regarded merely as historical representations, were not employed as devotional aids, and did not give rise to feelings of reverence.

John Calvin also made a fundamental contribution to the emerging Reformed doctrine of images. The Genevan theologian assigned to the Old Testament image prohibition the status of an independent (second) commandment within the Decalogue, allowing him to emphasize to an unprecedented degree the scriptural ban on idolatry. According to some scholars, however, of greater importance than any biblical legalism for Calvin was his concern with restoring a properly spiritual form of worship. The utter transcendence of God ruled out any attempt to bring him down to man's level through the medium of visual portraiture. Efforts directed to this end, the reformer believed, seek to domesticate God and deprive him of his glory. In place of the image he emphasized the centrality of the divine word. As a consequence, wall inscriptions from the Bible were the only embellishments allowed to adorn churches. Calvin did permit, however, the representation of narrative biblical scenes—except those with pictures of God—as long as their use was restricted to the sphere of private homes. He also recognized historical themes and landscapes as proper subjects for secular art, which was viewed as a gift from the divine creator. Because of this, some have credited him with providing one source of inspiration for the realistic Dutch painting of the following century.

Early Protestant Art. From an early stage in the Reformation, German Protestants, especially those influenced by Luther, began to employ the representational arts for the advancement of their polemical and pedagogical goals. Images printed from wood blocks offered an especially serviceable medium owing to their low cost and capacity for large-scale reproduction. Enormous numbers of these inexpensive woodcuts circulated throughout Europe. Since their use and enjoyment did not require literacy, it may be safely assumed that these visual materials appealed to an audience covering a much wider social spectrum than was the case with written texts.

Independent woodcut pictures of Luther by an assortment of artists began to appear in great quantities almost from the beginning of the Reformation movement. Most of these likenesses patterned themselves on a few basic prototypes drawn from life by Lucas Cranach the Elder, who served as court artist for Luther's prince, Frederick III of Saxony. Protestant portraits of Luther during this early period typically depicted their subject in one of the following religious roles: pious monk, doctor of theology, man of the Bible, evangelical prophet, or saint. Their intent included investing the reformer with a special spiritual authority, thereby justifying his break with Rome, as well as inducing others to follow his lead.

Many of the Reformation-era Luther portraits inevitably came to be regarded as a form of visual polemics. Indeed, polemical art constitutes the rubric under which a great number of the most effective woodcuts of the period must be grouped. In fashioning these works, Protestant propagandists freely borrowed themes from the popular beliefs and popular culture of the time, a practice that lent their creations the advantage of familiarity and accessibility. Traditional anticlericalism provided such a motif, one gaining new life in the often bitterly satiric attacks on monks and nuns found in evangelical art. Two further examples, demonology and fascination with monsters, came together in numerous woodcut compositions depicting leaders of the Catholic church in animal or bestial form in order to suggest their satanic origins.

Naturally, Reformation polemicists sought inspiration from scripture as well. For example, the Bible offered helpful resources for those hoping to show a radical antithesis between the evangelical simplicity of Christ's life and the corruption said to characterize the curia Romana. Attacks on the papacy ultimately secured their place as the dominant theme finding expression in Protestant polemical art.

Works of the graphic arts produced by early German Protestants, of course, undertook to present both positive and negative subjects; many strove to teach and promote acceptance of the evangelicals' own beliefs. This body of pedagogical art pursued two main goals—to communicate the key doctrines of the Protestant reform and to assist in the creation of a new church with a clear sense of identity and mission. Giving visual embodiment to abstract theological tenets proved difficult. Probably the most successful of the doctrinal compositions were those illustrating the polarity of law and gospel in Lutheran teaching. Cranach developed the standard iconographic formula for this purpose at the end of the 1520s, and over the next half century it found widespread use in the evangelical lands influenced by Wittenberg. The concept of a new church, on the other hand, found pictorial expression in works portraying the act of preaching to an assembly of believers or in compositions commemorating the Lutheran sacraments of baptism and the Lord's Supper.

Although Lutheran Bible and book illustrations sometimes employed the same imagery as that found in independent woodcuts and engravings, they nonetheless constitute a separate category of Reformation art meriting brief mention. Visual imagery accompanied the publication of Luther's Bible translations from the very beginning. His first German New Testament in 1522 included 21 woodcut illustrations. The initial edition of Luther's complete German Bible, published in 1534, contained 118. By the time of Luther's death in 1546 more than 500 different pictorial compositions had been created for inclusion in the various Wittenberg editions of the reformer's Bible. With regard to the selection of New Testament texts to illustrate, Luther and his publishers displayed a surprising conformity to tradition. As a result, the gospel books generally received only evangelist portraits, and the epistles fared no better. The majority of the New Testament woodcuts, in all the early Lutheran Bibles, adorned a single scriptural book, *Revelation*. Greater originality characterized the Wittenberg approach to artistic embellishment of the Old Testament. This applied most conspicuously to writings of the prophets, which now were given more attention than was common among medieval illuminators. Luther and his collaborators exercised astonishing freedom in their interpretations, placing explicitly New Testament scenes into the background of these compositions as an overt statement of their belief that the ancient Hebrew prophets already foretold the life and passion of Christ.

In addition to the Bible translations, several other early

Lutheran publications typically acquired woodcut illustrations. These included Luther's Large Catechism, prayer book, postils (sermon collections), and hymnals. Generally speaking, tradition and perhaps theological scruples exerted a less restrictive influence on the selection of pictorial matter for these works than was the case with scripture editions.

Besides employing the graphic media, German Protestants linked with Wittenberg also made fairly extensive use of certain of the more monumental art forms, particularly oil painting and relief sculpture. The following discussion focuses on panel paintings, altarpieces, decorated pulpits, and pictorial epitaphs. All four categories were well established in earlier art tradition but experienced somewhat altered treatment from the early Lutherans.

The earliest group of German paintings reflecting a distinctly Lutheran point of view consisted of independent panels produced by the Cranach workshop, beginning at the end of the 1520s. Most important among them iconographically are three groups of works entitled The Law and the Gospel, Christ and the Adulteress, and Christ Blessing the Children. The Law and Gospel motif, which simultaneously found wide use in pedagogical woodcuts, has already been noted above. The Christ and the Adulteress compositions appear to have used a familiar biblical story to advance a doctrinal message similar to that of works in the preceding group, asserting that salvation comes through divine grace and not through human deeds. Although the popularity of the Christ Blessing the Children works is customarily attributed to the possibilities it offers for the polemical defense of infant baptism, it, too, may have been intended, in part at least, as a good example of the simple, childlike trust in God implied by Luther's doctrine of salvation by faith alone.

A substantial number of Lutheran altarpieces were introduced into evangelical churches from the late 1530s. Although sometimes contributed by Protestant princes or municipal councils, these often were commissioned and installed by private donors—that is, wealthy laypersons who may have been motivated by a mixture of religious piety, family pride, and civic patriotism. Although the size and form of such works varied considerably, many proved to be large, imposing constructions. The traditional triptych design, with painted wing panels and predella, continued for a time to be popular. From the 1550s fixed altars with stone or wood relief sculpture also found increasing use.

Clearly the new Lutheran altarpieces differed from their late medieval forerunners not so much in configuration or format as in iconography. Many traditional Catholic themes, of course, were abandoned—above all, Mariological motifs and the lives of the saints. There arose an almost exclusive reliance on scriptural sources, with special emphasis upon the life, death, and resurrection of Christ. The most widely used subject of all seems to have been the Last Supper, despite the fact that the theme appeared relatively infrequently in earlier altarpiece art. Luther himself called special attention to the appropriateness of portraying this biblical event on altars designated for the sacrament of Holy Communion.

Celebration of the Sacrament was closely linked to proclamation of the word in Lutheranism, and accordingly the pulpit received fresh attention in the Reformation. Hundreds of new stone and wood preaching platforms, most of them adorned with relief sculpture or paintings, were erected in the Lutheran churches of central and northern Germany in the century following the break with Rome. The iconography displayed on these pulpits differed from that on other evangelical art works in relatively minor ways—for example, in the more frequent depiction of the four evangelists, a theme that was traditional in such settings.

The largest single group of art objects placed in Lutheran churches in sixteenth-century Germany was formed by epitaph monuments. These consisted of artistically conceived memorials honoring the deceased and normally containing three parts: a portrait, a painted or sculptured representation of a religious theme, and a commemorative inscription. Although Lutherans normally needed only one altar or pulpit in a church, there existed no fixed limit upon the number of epitaphs that might be installed. In some instances these funerary monuments may have compensated for side altars and chapels that had become superfluous with the advent of the Reformation. The iconography of the Lutheran epitaphs offers little that is new; the themes are drawn either from traditional biblical subjects or from the corpus of evangelical motifs already encountered in panel painting and altarpiece art.

In contrast, in the Protestant art of the northern Netherlands, there was a set of circumstances differing markedly from those existing in Germany. The Reformed churches that ultimately came to dominate there adopted a largely Calvinist theology and thus demonstrated little sympathy for the creation or installation of works of ecclesiastical art. Occasional exceptions—including some new stained glass, sculptured tomb monuments for a few very distinguished parishioners, and painted organ shutters—do not substantially alter the generally accepted view of a worship community devoted to simplicity and even austerity in church furnishings. Consequently, religious painting depended upon private patronage and was subject to no ecclesiastical control. These factors, however, make it all the more difficult to identify which art works should be labeled Protestant, particularly since it is now known that Dutch Calvinism grew very slowly, with the result that a confessionally mixed population endured far longer than used to be thought. Catholic artists continued to practice in the northern Netherlands even in the seventeenth century.

Despite the difficulties of evaluating Dutch religious art, it does seem possible to single out a number of iconographic motifs whose popularity in the sixteenth and seventeenth centuries probably should be linked with spiritual ideas or practices deriving from the Reformation, even if the artists involved in their creation were not in every instance orthodox Protestants. One such theme derives from the parable of the prodigal son. The immense popularity of this subject is recorded in one index of Netherlandish art that lists well over a hundred examples. Some of these depicted the biblical story in a predominantly moralistic sense. Others, however, including Rembrandt's famous painting now in Leningrad, seem to have followed Protestant commentators from Luther and Calvin onward, who interpreted the scriptural text and above all its characterization of the forgiving father as a demonstration of God's unmerited grace.

Another theme that enjoyed unprecedented favor among Netherlandish artists of the Reformation era derives from the biblical story of the calling of Matthew. In this narrative of Jesus' summoning of a sinful tax collector to Christian apostleship, Calvin had perceived a striking illustration of the grace of God. Other sixteenth-century evangelicals saw in the text a foreshadowing of their own later call to reform. It seems to have been mainly artists sympathetic to this point of view who turned their talents to reproducing the gospel story in visual form.

The Bible, of course, describes a spiritual turnabout even more famous than that experienced by the evangelist Matthew—the conversion of Paul. This dramatic Damascus road episode also offered congenial subject matter for Netherlandish artists influenced by the reform movement. Paul's scriptural writings contain the most explicit discussion of justification by faith found in the Bible, and Protestants, beginning with Luther, repeatedly had turned to them for theological confirmation of their own teachings. The apostle could scarcely avoid being regarded as a spiritual hero by evangelicals. Some, including Rembrandt, seem to have personally identified with him. This may explain the existence of almost a dozen pictures of Paul by the Dutch painter, at least one of which depicts the conversion.

Netherlandish artists inspired by the Reformation also gave new or unusual prominence to certain other iconographic motifs—the raising of Lazarus, the preaching of Jesus and John the Baptist, and the family saying grace. Like other religious themes, however, these found expression in art works destined for personal use rather than placement in churches.

The Catholic Defense of Images. The Protestant assault on ecclesiastical art naturally provoked a defense of religious imagery from the opposing side. The earliest Catholic writings of the Reformation era on this theme arose in Germany during 1522 and were stimulated by Karlstadt's major iconoclastic manifesto, which was published that year. Over the next four decades a number of authors from several countries contributed further treatises to the gradually intensifying debate over images. The most influential Catholic statements on religious art, however, appeared only after the Council of Trent had issued its ruling on the matter. By then Calvinist iconoclasm, above all in France, had become

a sufficiently serious problem that a decisive statement clearly was needed—a fact that helps explain Trent's decision finally to address this issue. For it was not until the last session of the assembly that the conciliar fathers issued their decree "De invocatione, veneratione et reliquiis sanctorum, et sacris imaginibus" (On the Invocation, Veneration, and Relics of Saints, and on Sacred Images; 3–4 December 1563).

The Council of Trent's brief declaration on images consists of two parts, the first containing a defense of ecclesiastical art and the second addressing abuses that might arise in its use. It unequivocally affirms that honor and veneration are to be given to likenesses of Christ, the Virgin Mary, and other saints, though not because of any divinity or special virtue residing in them. The honor shown to images passes to the prototypes or subjects that they represent. Further, the decree declares images to be useful because they instruct the people and remind them of God's blessings; because they provide salutary examples from the lives of the saints, in imitation of which the faithful may fashion their own lives and conduct; and because they help promote the love of God and the cultivation of piety.

Next follows a treatment of potential abuses, perhaps partly motivated by the hope that their prevention might deflect Protestant criticism. The representation of false doctrine receives censure, especially "such as might be the occasion of grave error to the uneducated." The decree also commands the elimination of any superstition that might be associated with the use of images. Finally, all lasciviousness must be avoided. Oversight is placed squarely in the hands of the bishops, under whose responsibility it falls to ensure that nothing disorderly, unbecoming, profane, or disrespectful appears in the house of God. This highly significant call for an expanded role of the bishops echoes several earlier Catholic treatises on images, as well as the previous pronouncements of provincial church councils.

The Tridentine decree on images, viewed as a whole, takes on the aspect of a concise, moderate, and practical Catholic response to one of the burning questions of the Reformation. It breaks no new doctrinal ground and leaves unaddressed certain intra-Catholic disputes of long standing—for example, that concerning the proper degrees of veneration to be accorded to various types of images. The emphasis falls upon instruction and the addressing of concrete problems. The major weakness of the pronouncement lies in its brevity, no doubt partly explained by the circumstances of its composition. The failure to furnish more details, however, made inevitable the appearance of further discussions of the topic, in which there would be provided refinement and elaboration of the conciliar decree.

In fact, a large number of important Counter-Reformation writings on religious art and the image question made their appearance in the decades following Trent. Although some of these continued in a polemical vein, the better known and more significant of them concerned themselves primarily with interpreting and augmenting the Tridentine decree for the benefit of the Catholic community itself. Among authors contributing to the latter group, the two most important were Johannes Molanus, professor of theology at the University of Louvain, and Gabriele Paleotti, a reforming cardinal and bishop of Bologna. Molanus's major work first appeared in 1570, while Paleotti's came out in 1582. Further treatises of note were contributed by G. A. Gilio da Fabriano (1564), Carlo Borromeo (1577), Raffaele Borghini (1584), and Antonio Possevino (1593). Despite individual emphases, these works develop a number of common themes.

Trent's call for doctrinal orthodoxy in religious art found agreement in the statements of later Catholic authors. This could take the form of a denunciation of specific iconographic motifs that were considered theologically objectionable. Molanus, for example, attacked the practice of depicting the preformed body of the Christ Child descending from heaven to the Virgin in paintings of the Annunciation. Orthodoxy would be preserved by the artist adhering to scripture or other approved religious sources and not indulging in uncontrolled flights of imagination. Molanus acknowledged that artists could fill in missing information not provided in the text, but they must do so intelligently and in accord with church tradition.

There existed a widespread consensus on the need for accuracy, clarity, and simplicity in religious compositions. Gilio and Borghini agreed that beauty must not take precedence over accuracy of representation, as, for example, in martyrdom scenes. Paleotti argued that historical accuracy was particularly essential in biblical pictures; there can be no credibility in a crucified Christ who shows no evidence of suffering or wounds. The saints must be portrayed true to life if they are to be effectively imitated. Paleotti coupled a strong demand for clarity with an attack on its opposite; obscurity in a visual representation constituted a sin against the essential didactic function of art. Finally, there was the need for simplicity, without which (as Borghini noted) the visual message would not be accessible to the illiterate.

Decorum and decency both received strong endorsements from all these authors. Decorum was understood to mean that everything in a composition must be appropriate to the subject matter portrayed, the intended audience, and the place where it was to be displayed. Indecency in an artwork obviously constituted a major breach of decorum; indeed, it has been asserted that following Trent the decency of images was as closely watched as their orthodoxy. The problem assumed its most notorious form with regard to the matter of nudity in paintings and sculpture. Molanus contributed important comments on this question; it was he, for example, who pointed out that indecent (nude) images represented a total distortion of the purpose of religious art, which was to arouse the pious devotion of the people. He

even opposed naked pictures of the Christ Child for fear that youthful spectators might be corrupted.

Catholic Iconography. The iconography of Catholic art as it developed in the later sixteenth and seventeenth century represented a conscientious response to the needs of the Catholic church during the post-Tridentine era. There were old doctrines to be reaffirmed and new saints to be honored. There appeared a tendency to proclaim the very teachings that had been most disputed by the Protestants, which in certain instances meant that visual motifs that had held only modest importance now took on greater prominence. Moreover, a few subjects arose that were entirely original.

Among the sacraments challenged by Protestants, two in particular figured in Catholic art—the Eucharist and penance. The former, which frequently appeared in paintings under the form of the Last Supper motif, now usually featured Jesus' consecration of the Communion wafer and asserted by implication the disputed doctrine of transubstantiation. The same dogmatic point found bold affirmation in a number of allegorical compositions dramatically celebrating the triumph of the Sacrament and including an exhibition of the elevated chalice or monstrance. Works displaying the last communion of a saint also enjoyed considerable favor.

The sacrament of penance, also the occasion of much controversy in the Reformation, now received heightened attention in Catholic art. But rather than representing the rite itself (confession and absolution), the most popular approach involved depicting the remorse of individual penitents. Most frequently portrayed were Mary Magdalene, believed to have been a converted harlot; Peter, whose tears reminded the viewer of that disciple's denial of his Lord; and the prodigal son, from Jesus' parable. All three functioned as symbols of the sacrament, as well as exemplary models of moral contrition.

A desire to provoke emulation also apparently gave rise to many of the numerous martyrdom scenes found in Counter-Reformation art. This is particularly true of the earlier and more explicit ones dating from the 1580s and 1590s, which were often the subject of either wall frescoes or altarpieces created for Jesuit churches and seminaries. Ignatius Loyola's militant followers in the Society of Jesus regarded the viewing of images of earlier Christian heroics as useful in overcoming their own impending trials and tribulations. Martyrs and martyrdom remain an important iconographic theme as one moves into the baroque art of the seventeenth century. During the later period, however, there can be detected a diminution of interest in the graphic details of physical suffering and an enlarged concern with illuminating the spiritual exaltation of those who had overcome pain and death.

The hagiographic tradition of the church, of course, included many saints who were not actually martyrs. Some of the most popular of these—for example, Francis—continued to attract frequent attention from painters and sculptors. By the 1620s their ranks had swelled to admit several newly canonized heroes of the faith—Borromeo, Teresa of Ávila, Filippo Neri, Ignatius Loyola, and Francis Xavier. All quickly found their way onto the list of most favored subjects for Catholic artists.

Among those deemed worthy of veneration, the Virgin Mary, as would be expected, continued to occupy a special position. Visual images of the Virgin's bodily assumption into heaven, alone or combined with the Immaculate Conception, gained greatly in popularity. Immaculate Conception compositions experienced extraordinary popularity, above all in Spain during the seventeenth century.

Finally, brief note should be taken of a number of additional themes, whether new or only newly emphasized, that enjoyed considerable currency in Counter-Reformation art. These include guardian angels, often shown as protectors of the young; Joseph, husband of the Virgin, depicted as a worthy example of paternal devotion; founder portraits, commemorating the origins of pre-Reformation ascetic orders; the ecstasies of the visionaries and mystics of the church; and the works of charity and mercy.

The Reformation and Counter-Reformation clearly had a considerable effect upon the visual arts, beginning with a significant impact upon demand. Large-scale works of painting and sculpture designed for churches, which previously had provided vast employment for artists, lost their markets in regions adopting Reformed Protestantism. Lutherans, to be sure, continued to commission ecclesiastical monuments, but on a greatly reduced scale. On the other hand, the graphic arts—above all, woodcuts—for a time enjoyed significantly enlarged usage, as they were called into service to advance the polemical and pedagogical purposes of the early evangelical movement.

The iconographic repertoire of European art also underwent change, expanding in some directions and contracting in others. The largest losses, of course, occurred in Protestantism through the rejection of what was regarded as nonscriptural subject matter. Nonetheless, evangelicals, to the extent that they continued to use religious images, demonstrated tendencies found also in Counter-Reformation Catholicism. Both combined a modest degree of iconographic innovation with a pronounced inclination to give new interpretations or new prominence to visual motifs already at hand in the Christian tradition.

Beyond these considerations there remains an interesting question concerning the extent to which artists were prompted to shift to more secular subject matter in order to compensate for lost opportunities in religious art. But this opens up a topic extending beyond the scope of this essay.

[See also Architecture; Baldung, Hans; Cathedrals; Cranach, Lucas the Elder; Cranach, Lucas the Younger; Dürer, Albrecht; Holbein, Hans the Younger; Iconoclasm; Iconography; and Michelangelo Buonarotti.]

BIBLIOGRAPHY

Battisti, Eugenio. "Reformation and Counter Reformation." In *Encyclopedia of World Art*, vol. 11, cols. 894–916. New York, 1966. A general survey, including architecture; the lengthy bibliography is useful for older works.

Boschloo, A. W. A. *Annibale Carracci in Bologna: Visible Reality in Art after the Council of Trent*. 2 vols. Translated by R. R. Symonds. The Hague, 1974. Informative on Catholic writers, especially Paleotti; also on Counter-Reformation art styles.

Brown, Jonathan. *The Golden Age of Painting in Spain*. New Haven and London, 1991. Illuminating on the iconography and patronage of Counter-Reformation art.

Christensen, Carl C. *Art and the Reformation in Germany*. Athens, Ohio, 1979. Covers image theology, iconoclasm, early Lutheran painting, and the decline of German art.

———. *Princes and Propaganda: Electoral Saxon Art of the Reformation*. Kirksville, Mo., 1992. Discusses use of the visual arts to promote Lutheran reform and dynastic political goals.

Eire, Carlos M. N. *War against the Idols: The Reformation of Worship from Erasmus to Calvin*. Cambridge, 1986. Views the theological attack on idolatry as the theoretical basis of Reformation iconoclasm; helpful above all for Calvin, Geneva, and developments in France.

Freedberg, David. *Iconoclasm and Painting in the Revolt of the Netherlands, 1566–1609*. New York and London, 1988. See for Catholic writers, especially Molanus, as well as the effect of iconoclasm on painting.

Garside, Charles, Jr. *Zwingli and the Arts*. New Haven and London, 1966. Provides a thorough account of Zwingli's critique of images and their removal from the Zurich churches.

Halewood, William H. *Six Subjects of Reformation Art: Preface to Rembrandt*. Toronto, 1982. Relates to the Reformation several themes in Netherlandish art, e.g., the calling of Matthew, the prodigal son, and the conversion of Paul.

Hall, Marcia B. *Renovation and Counter-Reformation: Vasari and Duke Cosimo in Santa Maria Novella and Santa Croce, 1565–1577*. Oxford, 1979. Helpful on post-Tridentine writers and Counter-Reformation art styles.

Haskell, Francis. *Patrons and Painters: A Study in the Relations between Italian Art and Society in the Age of the Baroque*. 2d ed., rev. & enl. New Haven and London, 1980. Essential for art patronage of the papacy and religious orders.

Hofmann, Werner, ed. *Luther und die Folgen für die Kunst*. Exhibition catalog, Kunsthalle, Hamburg. Munich, 1983. Examines Luther's influence on the visual arts up to the twentieth century; profusely illustrated.

Knipping, John B. *Iconography of the Counter Reformation in the Netherlands*. 2 vols. Nieuwkoop, 1974. Useful, although difficult to read; heavily illustrated, including popular prints.

Mâle, Émile. *L'art religieux après le concile de Trente*. 2d rev. & corr. ed. Paris, 1951. A classic study of Counter-Reformation iconography; summarized in the same author's *Religious Art from the Twelfth to the Eighteenth Century*, New York, 1949.

Michalski, Sergiusz. *The Reformation and the Visual Arts: The Protestant Image Question in Western and Eastern Europe*. London and New York, 1993. Includes a discussion of Protestant image theology, a comparative analysis of Reformation iconoclasm, and a consideration of the image question in East-West church relations.

Moxey, Keith P. F. *Pieter Aertsen, Joachim Beuckelaer, and the Rise of Secular Painting in the Context of the Reformation*. New York and London, 1977. Links secularization with doubts about religious art; includes a detailed discussion of the image debate.

Parshall, Linda B., and Peter W. Parshall. *Art and the Reformation: An Annotated Bibliography*. Boston, 1986. Provides comprehensive coverage of the image controversy, iconoclasm, book illustration, propaganda prints, religious iconography, individual artists, church furnishings, and portraits of the reformers.

Schmidt, Ph. *Die Illustration der Lutherbibel, 1522–1700.* Reprint, Basel, 1977. A thorough discussion of the illustrations of the early Luther Bibles; contains almost four hundred reproductions.

Scribner, R. W. *For the Sake of Simple Folk: Popular Propaganda for the German Reformation.* Cambridge, 1981. A pioneering and methodologically innovative study of popular prints as visual propaganda.

Smith, Jeffrey Chipps. *German Sculpture of the Later Renaissance, c.1520–1580: Art in an Age of Uncertainty.* Princeton, 1994. Shows the impact of the Reformation on sculpture; offers new evidence concerning secularization and the questions of art decline.

Wittkower, Rudolf, and Irma B. Jaffe, eds. *Baroque Art: The Jesuit Contribution.* New York, 1972. A collection of fundamental essays treating patronage, style, iconography, and architecture.

CARL C. CHRISTENSEN

ARTICLES OF RELIGION. Better known as the Thirty-nine Articles, the Articles of Religion of the Elizabethan Church of England, were the result of a complex process that responded to the shifting issues and influences of the Reformation and yet also had its origins in pre-Reformation academic and ecclesiastical teachings and debates about doctrine, ecclesiology, and authority. While they, and comparable Continental texts of the period, have some creedal, confessional, and catechetical aspects, they also reflect, both in structure and content, the attempts by medieval and later university faculties of theology (and those trained in them) to focus and define theological issues. (Thus in form, as well as in some other ways, they are related to Luther's Ninety-five Theses, as well as to the Augsburg Confession.) The English Articles and their companion pieces on the Continent also emerged from both theoretical and real political and social considerations of their times, especially a widespread belief in the necessity of some general national consensus on matters of religion as the crucial foundation for societal peace and avoidance of civil war.

Leaders of the Reformation, both in England and on the Continent, naturally felt that definitions of doctrine were necessary. Theologians and church authorities had to articulate, for themselves and to others, to what extent they were in continuity with the church of the past, how much of the medieval system they now repudiated, and to what degree and in what ways they could agree among themselves. Huldrych Zwingli's *Fidei Ratio* (1530) was one of the first such articulations, and marked the strong reactions of Swiss reformers. The Augsburg Confession (1530), for which Philipp Melanchthon was mainly responsible, formed the charter of those who followed Martin Luther's hermeneutic of the Christian religion. Dozens of major and minor attempts at definition and orderly presentation followed during the sixteenth and seventeenth centuries. Some tried to resolve debates into final syllogisms, catechisms, and confessions that claimed concord with the divine word. Others were, like

their scholastic predecessors, more limited. These sought focus and boundaries for the interpretation of divine mysteries and the historic faith. They were usually not so much ambiguous as minimalist: statements leaving room for interpretation, not fully realized arguments. The English Articles of Religion in their various versions fell more into the latter category, although those who issued them—monarchs, Parliament, and bishops—did intend for them to be taken seriously as guides to Christian beliefs and practices.

Although always having a certain religious impetus (whether Protestant or Catholic Christian humanist), the Reformation in England had from the first a significant political dimension. Politics and religion interacted both in Parliament and in other domestic venues, as well as in international diplomacy. Of particular interest for the development of the English Articles were the hopeful negotiations in 1535 with the Germans who brought with them the tenets of the Augsburg Confession. Partly as a result of these discussions, the first English articles of religion, known as the Ten Articles, were published in 1536. Although probably best remembered for their repudiation of papal supremacy and the establishment of the king as supreme head of the church in England, they dealt with justification, the three sacraments of baptism, penance, and the "sacrament of the altar" (with no mention of the other four Catholic sacraments), and the issues of holy images, prayers to saints, and purgatory. The Lutherans did not respond very positively. Although he was quoted and paraphrased in the Ten Articles, Melanchthon remarked that they seem to have been "put together with the greatest confusion."

In 1538, as an outcome of further negotiations between Lutheran theologians invited by Henry VIII and their English counterparts, which was intended to produce a common confession of faith, the Thirteen Articles were drawn up. These were never sanctioned by authority or even published, but are known from material found among Archbishop Thomas Cranmer's papers. They lend credence to the academic heritage of this genre of the Reformation theological debate. They are also important because much of their language was adopted, although with modifications, from the Augsburg Confession. Because they were the foundation for the later compilation of the Forty-two Articles of 1552, they formed the channel through which more of the language of the Lutheran formulary passed to the later English Articles of Religion.

Significant new theological currents emerged during the reign of Edward VI. The influence of Lutheranism waned in England. Cranmer as early as 1548 appeared in the House of Lords as the spokesman of opinions about the Eucharist held by the Geneva school of reformers. The leaders of the English reforming party were in close touch with Swiss thought through their contact with such important figures as Jan Łaski at Lambeth and Peter Martyr Vermigli and Martin Bucer at Oxford and Cambridge, respectively. Parallel to Henry VIII's earlier plan with the German Lutheran divines, Cranmer seems at this time to have cherished the idea of drawing together the reformers on the Continent and uniting them with the Church of England in the acceptance of a common confession of faith. The publication of the draft of these articles was deferred until the following year in the vain hope of inducing the various Reformed bodies to come to an agreement. In the end, England remained somewhat isolated in its attempts to blend continuity, compromise, and comprehensiveness.

The Forty-two Articles are misleadingly headed "Articles agreed on by the Bishoppes and other learned menne, in the Synode at London, in the yere of our Lorde Godde MDLII. for the auoiding of controuersie in opinions and the establishment of a godlie concorde in certeine matiers of Religion." In another important academic setting of the Reformation era, Cranmer's examination and trial held at Oxford (and involving both Oxford and Cambridge theological dons), Cranmer admitted that he had been wrong in claiming synodal authority for these articles. Still the title well indicates their ambition, purpose, and scope.

These articles do not set out a system of divinity or a creed, and in this respect they differ very much in character from many of the formularies of Continental reformers, which usually exhibited a more uniform body of doctrine and consistent line of theological reasoning. This important difference is accounted for by several causes. First, the Continental reformers had largely severed their connection with the church of the immediate past; and having thus rejected the authority and teaching previously vested in the church, they were now obliged to reconstruct the whole structure of Christian theology on a new foundation of holy scripture alone. By contrast, the aim of the English reformers was more just the reformation of some apparent mistakes in doctrine, accretions in practice, and false claims of authority that had developed in the late medieval church. The early church creeds were explicitly assumed, and patristic writings were restored to preeminence in interpretation. Some medieval views were deemed erroneous and attacked, but the organic identity of the church—past and present—was taken for granted. It was, therefore, not considered necessary to develop a new theology, but only to put forth articles dealing, as their title states, with certain matters that were in controversy. Again, this was not a new process. In different ways, it was the commonplace practice of medieval universities and their Reformation successors.

Another reason why the Continental confessions were more systematic than the English Articles lay in the personalities of the individuals who produced them. Since the English formulary was the outcome of various political and religious influences at work at various moments from the 1520s on, it did not try to evolve a logically complete theory of God and God's dealings with creation and humankind, and many important subjects in theology were not touched upon at all. On the Continent it was otherwise. The Reformation there owed a great deal to individuals of commanding minds and personalities with central theories of their own. In the English Articles, it is remarkable that distinctively Lutheran language is mostly avoided on justification; and a strictly Calvinistic vocabulary is largely absent in the treatment of predestination, with the essential point of reprobation not even being mentioned. At the same time, the growing influence in England of the Geneva school during this period may be seen in the way the Forty-two Articles dealt with the sacraments. Thus once again no mention was made of Catholic understandings of confirmation, holy orders, or matrimony as sacramental ordinances of the church, and now penance was also left out. The doctrine that sacraments take effect *ex opere operato* was explicitly repudiated. The practice of infant baptism was barely commended; and the article on the Lord's Supper expressly affirmed that a faithful believer ought not either believe in or openly confess the real presence and that transubstantiation was an impossibility.

During the reign of Mary Tudor, the articles bore no doctrinal authority or recognition, except as examples of the heretical views of Cranmer and others. For four years after Queen Elizabeth I's accession, only *The Book of Common Prayer* stood as an authoritative standard for the Church of England. But in January 1562 a text of the Forty-two Articles was presented to convocation. These articles started with the Edwardian-Cranmerian Articles, but they had been substantially revised by Archbishop Matthew Parker, an ally and admirer of Cranmer, aided principally by bishops Richard Cox of Ely and Edmund Guest of Rochester. Four of the earlier articles had been omitted: those on grace, on blasphemy against the Holy Ghost, on the moral law, and on the heretics called Millenarii. Four articles had been added by the same committee: on the Holy Ghost, on good works, on the wicked at the Lord's Supper, and on Communion in both kinds. Seventeen articles had been more or less modified. The upper house of convocation struck out three articles dealing with Anabaptist errors that no longer seemed of much importance in the controversies of the time. Thus the number of the articles was reduced to thirty-nine. Two changes of importance were further made in the Latin version of the articles sanctioned by the queen and her council in 1563: the first part of article 20, on the authority of the church, was strengthened against possible sectarian challenge; and the article on the non-participation of the wicked in the Eucharist was left out, possibly as a negotiating point with Roman Catholics. The latter was, however, reinserted in 1571, when a revision, in which Bishop John Jewel was the most prominent figure, gave us the Thirty-nine Articles in their more-or-less permanent form. The articles, in official Latin and English versions, were in that year approved by both convocation and Parliament, although Queen Elizabeth had wanted to issue them under her own authority.

The great emphasis by Renaissance Christian humanists (both Catholic and Protestant) on early church and patristic sources strongly shapes the first articles on the doctrine of the Trinity. Many of the other changes introduced by the Elizabethan revisers are traceable to the Württemberg Confession (1552), which was at the time the latest authoritative statement by Lutheran reformers. Clauses added to articles 2, 6, and 10, and the new article 5 were taken verbatim from this confession, while additions to articles 11 and 20, and the new article 12 are in close agreement with it. In general, the articles on sacramental matters bore a Swiss/Calvinist tone, although differing on many points in expression. But in some other important ways, there were also the indications in the articles of some return to a more Catholic position in the recognition of the general consent of the church as determining the canon of scripture (article 6), the emphasis on good works (article 7), the vindication of the authority of the church in matters of faith (article 20), the refusal to condemn the doctrine that sacraments take effect *ex opere operato* (article 25), the assertion that infant baptism is "most agreeable with the institution of Christ" (article 27), the substitution of the statement that "the body of Christ is given" in the Lord's Supper for a repudiation of the real presence (article 28), and the defense of the ordinal (article 36). This last article, while apparently focused on matters of liturgical rite and form, is in fact a vital defense of the traditional Catholic structure of the threefold ordained ministry (bishop, priest, and deacon) and a claim that the English episcopate remains in apostolic succession.

The basic contents of the articles may be summarized as follows: the first five articles state the fundamental Catholic principle of continuity and unity of truths accepted by all orthodox Christians. These deal with the Trinity, the incarnation and atonement, and the resurrection. The next three articles name the sources of Christian belief: holy scripture and the three ancient creeds. Articles 9–18 set forth a framework of theological anthropology and the spiritual state of sinful yet redeemed individuals. Articles 19–21, 23, and 36 outline the constitution, order, and authority of the church. Article 22 countering the "Romish doctrine" of purgatory and related beliefs and practices and article 24 mandating services and prayers in the vernacular seem somewhat out of place, but they are important in the context of the time. Articles 25–31 set out the doctrine of the sacraments. A series of somewhat miscellaneous, but quite important, articles follow on married clergy, excommunication, traditions of the church, and the doctrinal value of the *Book of Homilies* (articles 32–35). The text closes with matters of public religion (articles 37–39), treating the church and individual Christians in the relation to the state and private property (explicitly denouncing Anabaptist positions). Article 34, which argued that the traditions and ceremonies of the church have not always been the same and may vary in different countries but that no one through private judgment should break with the ceremonies ordained by appropriate authorities, proved particularly important for Anglicanism.

The Articles of Religion were intended to mark the agreement of the Church of England and the Church Catholic, to define its attitude toward contemporary Rome and the Reformed Protestant churches, to assert the power and independence of the English state in its relation to the church, and to preclude errors such as had arisen among those sectaries who had departed too far from the common Catholic heritage of Western Christianity.

Finally, to whom did the Articles of Religion apply? In 1553 subscription to the Forty-two Articles was mandated for all clergy, schoolmasters, and members of the universities of Oxford and Cambridge before they could receive their degrees. Here again were echoes of the practices of medieval theology faculties, who felt responsible to assert and control the orthodoxy of those whom they licensed to teach the faith to others. In 1571 Parliament passed legislation stating that all candidates for ordination were expected to affirm the articles. In 1581 Oxford made subscription to the Thirty-nine Articles mandatory for matriculation. In his 1628 preface to the articles, Charles I ordered all his "loving subjects to continue in the uniform profession thereof." Thus the original factors that began the path toward the articles a century earlier—first the academic and ecclesiastical ambition to articulate religious truths clearly (if always partially) and to regulate what was taught and preached by those under their control; second, the political ambition of avoiding diversity of religious opinions (beyond an acceptable limit) and the preservation of civil peace—were asserted for the populace at large. Ironically this occurred just as the reality of a widening diversity within that nation was becoming more visible to church and state alike.

Members of the laity were rarely required to assent to the articles. During the eighteenth and nineteenth centuries many Anglican clergy were reluctant to do so, and in 1865 it was decided that they would have to declare only that the doctrine in the articles is "agreeable to the word of God," something less than an oath of personal belief in each article. The Articles of Religion were revised in 1801 for use in the Protestant Episcopal Church in the United States, principally in order to delete references to royal supremacy. Subscription has never been a requirement in the American church.

The Thirty-nine Articles have traditionally been printed in *Books of Common Prayer*, both in the Church of England and in other churches of the Anglican communion. In 1977 they were relegated to an appendix of "Historical Documents of the Church" in the revised prayer book of the Episcopal church in the United States.

[*See also* Book of Common Prayer *and* Cranmer, Thomas.]

BIBLIOGRAPHY

Bicknell, E. J. *A Theological Introduction to the Thirty-Nine Articles of the Church of England.* Revised by H. J. Carpenter. London, 1955.

Gibson, Edgar C. S. *The Thirty-Nine Articles of the Church of England.* London, 1904.

Hardwick, Charles. *A History of the Articles of Religion.* Rev. ed. Cambridge, 1859.

Haugaard, William P. *Elizabeth and the English Reformation: The Struggle for a Stable Settlement of Religion.* Cambridge, 1968. Important for its account of discussion of the Articles in convocation.

Kidd, B. J. *The Thirty-Nine Articles: Their History and Explanation.* London, 1911.

GUY FITCH LYTLE III

ASCHAM, Roger

ASCHAM, Roger (1515/16–1568), English humanist scholar and Latin secretary to the Tudor queens, Mary and Elizabeth I. Ascham was a pioneer of English literary prose and an early supporter of the Reformation. He is best known for his *Toxophilus* (1545), a dialogue in praise of archery, and *The Scholemaster* (1570), a treatise on "the ready way to the Latin tongue" that has enjoyed high regard for its "plain and sensible utterance" of sound and humane principles for educating the young. He also wrote a fragmentary history, *A Report and Discourse of the State of Germany* (1570), treating the difficulties of Emperor Charles V during the early 1550s, when Ascham was secretary to the English ambassador at the imperial court. Although brief, *A Report* contains one of the earliest accounts of critical events that would eventually lead to Charles's abdication and to the recognition of Protestantism in Germany.

Ascham began supporting the Reformation as an undergraduate at Cambridge, and in 1534 his outspoken "Lutheranism" nearly cost him election to a fellowship in Saint John's College, which was religiously conservative at the time. Not a divine, during his university career he nevertheless composed several works on theological subjects. Written in the 1540s, when the English church was moving only cautiously toward reform, they were not published until 1577. They include Latin translations of Oecumenius's Greek commentaries on Paul's letters to Philemon and Titus; eleven *Themata theologica*, mainly exegeses of Scriptural verses; and *Apologia . . . pro caena Dominica . . .,* which argues that the Mass is not identical with the Lord's Supper. Though sharp attacks on "Romish abuses" of the sacrament appear in the *Apologia,* on the whole these writings show Ascham to have been a relatively conservative Protestant whose religious beliefs did not impair lifelong friendships with prominent English and continental Catholics or prevent his attaining preferment by Queen Mary Tudor.

BIBLIOGRAPHY

Primary Sources

Ascham, Roger. *Apologia . . . pro caena Dominica. . . .* Edited by Edward Grant. London, 1577. The only printing of the theological writings.

————. *The Whole Works of Roger Ascham.* Edited by J. A. Giles, 3 vols. in 4. London, 1864–1865. Out of print, but the most complete edition of the English works and of Ascham's extensive correspondence with prominent religious, political, and scholarly personages.

————. *The Schoolmaster, 1570.* Edited by Lawrence V. Ryan. Reprint, Charlottesville, Va., 1974. An annotated and modernized edition of this influential treatise on educating the young for service to religion and the state.

————. *The Letters of Roger Ascham.* Translated by Maurice Hatch and Alvin Vos. New York, 1989. A selection of sixty representative Latin epistles, including observations on Charles V's troubles and Ascham's correspondence with the Strasbourg Protestant educator Johannes Sturm.

Secondary Source

Ryan, Lawrence V. *Roger Ascham.* Stanford and London, 1963. The standard critical biography.

LAWRENCE V. RYAN

ASKE, Robert

ASKE, Robert (d. 1537), "captain" of the Pilgrims of Grace. He was the younger son of John Aske of Aughton, Yorkshire. His date of birth, together with most details of his life, is unknown. He was a lawyer at Gray's Inn in London but never achieved sufficient seniority to be added to the commission of the peace.

Aske came to sudden prominence in the rebellion of 1536, called the Pilgrimage of Grace, acting as the Pilgrims' leading spokesman and gaining the deference of such individuals as Lord Thomas Darcy. Aske's own account of how he strayed into the Lincolnshire uprising while traveling toward London is plausible enough. Returning to Yorkshire, he attempted to emulate the Lincolnshire uprising by coordinating a largely spontaneous rebellion already taking place. Aske was certainly an activist in furthering the cause of the Pilgrimage of Grace, first in the taking of York, then in the siege and capture of Pontefract castle, and finally in the compilation of the Pilgrims' articles, but there is no sign that he conspired to launch the movement, and his grip over the rank and file was far from total.

On the disbandment of the Pilgrimage of Grace after negotiations between Aske (and other rebel leaders) and Thomas Howard, duke of Norfolk, at Doncaster (Yorkshire) on 6 December 1536, Aske was invited to court and there feted by King Henry VIII. On his return to Yorkshire he revealed his commitment to the settlement achieved at Doncaster by opposing the uprising in the East Riding in January 1537. In April he and other "leaders" of the rebellion were arrested and tried on feigned charges of renewed plotting against the king. He was executed in York on 12 July 1537.

Aske's pre-trial examinations show that he was capable of formulating a persuasive (though legalistic) conservative case against the divorce, the dissolution, and other legislation of 1533–1536. In this respect his importance lies in the articulation of a rarely recorded strain of dissent to the early Henrician Reformation.

BIBLIOGRAPHY

Bateson, M. "Aske's Examination." *English Historical Review* 5 (1890), 550–573.

———. "The Pilgrimage of Grace." *English Historical Review* 5 (1890), 330–343. Prints Aske's account of the movement.

Dodds, Madeleine Hope, and Ruth Dodds. *The Pilgrimage of Grace, 1536–1537, and the Exeter Conspiracy, 1538.* 2 vols. Cambridge, 1915. The fullest narrative account of the Pilgrimage of Grace, now superseded on motivation and interpretation.

Hoyle, R. W. *The Pilgrimage of Grace.* Oxford, forthcoming. Fullest modern account including a fresh assessment of Aske's role in the Pilgrimage.

R. W. HOYLE

ASKEW, Anne

ASKEW, Anne (1521–1546), Protestant martyr. One of five children of Sir William Askew, or Ayscough, and Elizabeth Wottesley, Anne was probably born at Stallingborough, Lincolnshire. She was well educated and was known for her devotion to scripture reading. Before 1540 she married Thomas Kyme of Kelsey, who had intended to wed her older sister (now deceased), and gave birth to two children. In 1544 her husband, from whom she had become estranged because of her heretical views, evicted her from their home. After unsuccessfully attempting to obtain a divorce from the bishop's court at Lincoln, she traveled to London for a remedy at the Court of Chancery.

The first of her two arrests occurred in 1545, when the lord mayor and the bishop of London interrogated her about her religious beliefs. She was set free but seized again in the summer of 1546. After questioning by members of the king's council, including Stephen Gardiner, bishop of Winchester, she was arraigned at the Guildhall and convicted of heresy for denying the doctrine of transubstantiation. She was then racked at the Tower of London, her inquisitors apparently having hoped she would implicate members of Queen Catherine Parr's household. Anne finally did admit to having received money from Anne, countess of Hertford (the future duchess of Somerset), and Lady Joan Denny. On 16 July 1546, crippled by the torture, she had to be carried in a chair to Smithfield, where she was burned alive, providing an example to the world of the ideal martyr.

In Germany John Bale, sometime bishop of Ossory, published an account of her examinations, which was circulated in England; in 1549 Gardiner, then a prisoner himself, complained about its availability in London. This publicity seems to have been responsible for her becoming an inspiring role model for later devout female Protestants.

BIBLIOGRAPHY

Bale, John. *Select Works of John Bale.* Edited by H. Christmas. Oxford, 1849. Contains a copy of Anne Askew's examinations.

Warnicke, Retha M. *Women of the English Renaissance and Reformation.* Westport, Conn., 1983. Discusses Anne's death and its impact on other female Protestant martyrs.

Wilson, Derek. *A Tudor Tapestry: Men, Women, & Society in Reformation England.* Pittsburgh, Pa., 1972. Contains personal information about Anne's life and provides standard information.

RETHA M. WARNICKE

ASLAKSEN, Cort

ASLAKSEN, Cort (1564–1624), Norwegian theologian. Born in Bergen, Norway, he was orphaned early in life and became the foster son of Bishop Jens Skjeldrup of Bergen. He matriculated at the University of Copenhagen in 1584, where he studied theology, philosophy, law, and medicine. In 1590 he became the assistant to the famous Danish astronomer Tycho Brahe. From 1593 to 1599 he studied at various universities (Herborn, Heidelberg, Basel, Geneva) and visited intellectual centers in France, England, and Scotland. In 1597 he published a synthesis of the theories of Copernicus, Brahe, and the scriptures entitled *De natura coeli triplicis.* He was appointed professor of pedagogy in 1600 at the University of Copenhagen, and in 1603 he became professor of Greek and Hebrew and in 1607 professor of theology.

Early in his career Aslaksen opposed the practice of exorcism in church ordinances, stating that it had no biblical validity. (Exorcism was finally abolished in 1783.) In so doing, Aslaksen incurred the wrath of the Lutheran orthodox theologian Hans Resen, who saw the rite of exorcism in baptism as needed to counter the effects of sinful human nature. Aslaksen and Resen continued their theological debates at the university, with Resen accusing Aslaksen of crypto-Calvinism and the latter accusing Resen of Sabellianism.

Aslaksen was a follower of Petrus Ramus and a champion of Plato. Aslaksen contended that Aristotelian philosophy was a faulty foundation upon which to build Lutheran theology. In 1616, however, he attacked his former crypto-Calvinist position in his thoroughly orthodox *Praelectiones theologicae in Augustanam Confessionem.* His most celebrated work was his *Physica et Ethica Mosaica* (1613), in which he sought to create a synthesis between the astronomy of Brahe and the cosmology of the Pentateuch. Aslaksen epitomizes the demise of crypto-Calvinism in Denmark-Norway and the triumph of orthodoxy at the end of a century-long process of Lutheran indoctrination and education that marked the close of the Reformation era.

BIBLIOGRAPHY

Garstein, Oskar. *Cort Aslakssøn.* Oslo, 1953.

TRYGVE R. SKARSTEN

ASPER, Hans

ASPER, Hans (1499–1571), Swiss painter and politician. As a member of the inner circle of the Zurich magistrates, the Large Council (*Grossrat*), Asper was known after 1545 as "the Apelles of Zurich." Like the original Apelles, court painter of Alexander the Great (336–323 BC), Asper painted the portraits of Reformation leaders and other influential citizens. His artistic imagination was fueled by the German artist Albrecht Dürer, whose Zurich student was Asper's teacher, and all his work discloses the spirit of the late Gothic period. A member of a well-known Zurich family—his father, Heinrich, also served on the Large Council—he was subsidized by the Large Council since his painting did not provide sufficient income.

Some of his portraits that have survived include: Huldrych Zwingli and his successor, Heinrich Bullinger; Zwingli's daughter Regula and his granddaughter Anna; Zwingli's son-in-law Rudolf Gwalther; Theodor Bibliander, a professor of Hebraic studies at Zurich; Konrad Pellikan, who taught Greek and Hebrew there; and Johannes Oecolampadius, Zwingli's friend and leader of the Reformation in Basel. Paul Boesch discovered a series of letters in Latin written by the Englishman Christopher Hale to Gwalther requesting him to commission Asper to paint five Swiss reformers. When the Zwinglian reformers prohibited religious art in 1523, Asper also produced frescoes in public buildings, small fountain sculpture, and coats of arms. The Zurich city hall (*Rathaus*) still possesses Asper's depiction of the city's coat of arms—lions holding shields, flanked by a still life of animals and fruit—and the city library contains his self-portrait, painted in 1540. Zurich honored Asper in 1540 by a medal with his portrait on one side and an inscription about mortality on the other. He is still honored through exhibits of about a dozen surviving paintings in museums in Zurich, Solothurn, and Basel.

BIBLIOGRAPHY

Boesch, Paul. "Der Zürcher Apelles: Neues zu den Reformatorenbildnissen von Hans Asper." *Zwingliana* 9 (1949), 16–50. Only detailed analysis of Asper's work.
Hugelshofer, Walter. "Asper, Hans, Maler." In *Neue deutsche Biographie*, edited by Historische Kommission der bayrischen Akademie der Wissenschaften, vol. 1, pp. 417–418. Berlin, (1953-). Brief biographical sketch. This series is the successor to *Allgemeine deutsche Biographie*.
Schmid, W. "Asper, Hans." In *Allgemeine deutsche Biographie*, vol. 1, p. 620. Leipzig, 1875–1912.

ERIC W. GRITSCH

ASSEMBLY OF CLERGY. Convened in France at the initiative of the royal government, the Assembly of Clergy negotiated the financial contribution of the clergy to the government and eventually treated questions of religious order. It met with increasing regularity beginning in 1561.

The Gallican church had experienced earlier assemblies ordained by the king. Beginning with the assembly at Bourges in 1438, members of the clergy had met at Tours in 1498 to study a plan for the reform of the church. Again at Tours in 1510 and in Lyon in 1511, clerics met to prepare for the council at Pisa: in principle they expected all the bishops plus two clerical representatives from each diocese to attend, but in fact the participants were far fewer. Theologians met in Melun in 1544 to prepare for the Council of Trent, and the French prelates met at Paris in 1552 to grant extraordinary subsidies to the king.

In 1561 the convocation of the Estates-General (where there normally sat a representation of the clergy as the first order of the kingdom) permitted the regent, Catherine de Médicis, to call a meeting at Poissy (approximately thirty kilometers west of Paris) of all the bishops of France. Her purpose was twofold: to attempt to find a basis for conciliation with the Protestant theologians (the Colloquy of Poissy) and to extract from the members of the first order a sizable financial contribution.

Pressured by royal power (and menaced by the other orders of the Estates-General) the clergy agreed to conclude a sixteen-year contract. During the first six years they would pay four *décimes* (tenths of their income) per year in order to permit the amorticization of the royal debt; then during the following ten years, they would pay 1.3 million pounds *tournois* to reclaim the lost royal domain. Another assembly met in 1567 (with the expiration of the first six years), and again in 1573. Although theoretically the contract was to end in 1577, the Assembly of Clergy was reconvened in 1579 and in 1580 the Assembly agreed to a continuation of the terms of the contract. In exchange, the clergy obtained the continued right to meet regularly without any prior royal authorization. The clergy would meet every five years in "small assembly" to check the accounts and every ten years in "general assembly" in order to renegotiate the contract. The function of these assemblies was interrupted by the troubles of the Catholic League, but beginning in 1595 the Assembly of Clergy would meet regularly until the end of the ancien régime at the beginning of the French Revolution.

The representation of the clergy at the assemblies was determined by a two-staged election: diocesan assemblies would elect delegates to provincial assemblies, which would then designate their representatives to the general assembly. The number of delegates varied until 1579, when it was established that four delegates should be received from each province for the decennial assemblies. The French cardinals took part automatically by right. Royal commissioners attended the meetings. The president of a given assembly was elected to avoid disputes among the primates. The assembly would meet near the royal court in or around Paris.

Between the sessions of the assembly, business was conducted by "general agents." The monies were collected by a lay banker known as the "general accountant of the clergy." At the grass roots the diocesan assemblies would divide the financial burden among the clergymen. The monies were then collected by clerical deputies, who would be aided by one or two laypersons.

Besides fulfilling their financial responsibilities, the Assembly of Clergy early on developed the custom of addressing the king concerning demands for reform of the church. As early as 1567 the bishops urged the reception of the decrees of the Council of Trent; in 1573 they presented to the king a complete program of reform for secular clergy, regular clergy, and the universities. Only after 1579, however, were the assemblies successful in convincing the canons to join them in their efforts for reform. In addition, the spokespersons for the assemblies energetically worked to convince the king that vacant episcopal sees be supplied with qualified prelates. In 1580 the Assembly of Clergy, which met in Melun, presented "reforming constitutions" with the hope that they would be adopted by the provincial councils. (Known as the "Constitutions of Melun," they were greatly influenced by the Borromean councils of Milan.) Finally, in 1615 the Assembly of Clergy, impatient with the delay of a royal decision concerning Trent, declared that it accepted all of the decrees of the council. This was largely a symbolic act, however, and had no legal power in France.

The principal leaders of the Assembly of Clergy were initially the cardinal of Lorraine, Charles de Guise, then in 1579–1580 Pierre d'Epinac, archbishop of Lyon, and Arnaud de Pontac, bishop of Bazas; and in 1615 Cardinal François de la Rochefoucauld. Throughout the history of the assemblies, the papal nuncios worked tirelessly behind the scenes.

Little by little the Assembly of Clergy assumed the form of a national council. During the seventeenth century it would mount efforts to curtail the liberties of French Protestants and to smother Jansenism.

[See also Wars of Religion.]

BIBLIOGRAPHY

Primary Sources

Cloulas, Ivan, ed. *Correspondance du nonce en France, Anselmo Dandino, 1578–1581*. Acta Nuntiaturae Gallicae, 8. Rome, 1970.

Collection des procès-verbaux des Assemblées du Clergé de France, depuis 1560 jusqu' à présent, rédigés par ordre de matière et réduits a ce qu'ils ont d'essentiel . . . . 9 vols. Paris, 1767–1778.

Secondary Sources

Blet, Pierre. *Le clergé de France et la monarchie: Étude sur les Assemblées du Clergé de 1615–1666.* 2 vols. Rome, 1959.

Martin, Victor. *Le gallicanisme et la Réforme catholique: Essai historique sur l'introduction en France des décrets du concile de Trente, 1563–1615* (1919). Reprint, Geneva, 1975.

Michaud, Claude. *L'eglise et l'argent sous l'ancien régime: Les receveurs généraux du clergé de France aux XVIe–XVIIe siècles.* Paris, 1991.

Serbat, Louis. *Les Assemblées du Clergé de France: Origines, organisation, et développement, 1561–1615.* Paris, 1906.

MARC VENARD
Translated from French by Paul Douglas Leslie

ASTROLOGY. The age of the Reformation witnessed the climax of European interest in the ancient divinatory arts, of which the most important by far was astrology. The theory and practice of prediction from the movements of the heavens had spread quickly in the West after the translation of Arabic scientific writings began in the twelfth century. By the fifteenth century, with the rapid rise of humanist interest in all ancient traditions, astrological teachings from classical authorities such as Ptolemy melded with longstanding popular notions about the force of the sun, moon, and stars to exercise a nearly pervasive influence in European culture. Despite official theological opposition to the prediction of specific human events, and despite the long, learned debate sparked especially by Giovanni Pico's *Disputationes aduersus astrologiam divinatricem* ("Disputations Against Astrology," 1494), the prevailing cosmological beliefs of late medieval and Renaissance society included the idea of regular and predictable celestial influences in nature. In the pre-Reformation era both individual and universal forecasts were sought avidly by popes and princes, townsfolk and peasants. Astrological allusions and calculations appeared in virtually every form of expression, from art to political propaganda.

The relationship of this ferment of astrological interest to the religious and social reform movements of the sixteenth century is an issue fraught with complexity. In Germany during the early 1520s, evangelical teachings spread in an atmosphere charged with prophetic expectations that grew partly out of astrological forecasts. The famous stargazer Johannes Lichtenberger, for example, had foreseen a terrible time of troubles for the Roman church and for Germany. Most notable were fears of a universal flood to come in 1524, when major planetary conjunctions would occur in the "watery" signs of the zodiac (Cancer, Scorpio, and Pisces). It is difficult to say how great a role such apprehensions may have played in the minds of those who adopted the cause of reform, but they cannot be overlooked as a basic part of the mentality of the age.

Probably more important than any particular prediction was the rapid development, in the half-century before 1520, of a whole new genre of popular astrological literature: printed calendars and prognostications. The annual vernacular broadsheet calendar or "almanac," a practical publication virtually unique to Germany in this period, encouraged conceptions of time and of nature that were at odds with traditional ecclesiastical culture. Yearly prognostications drew on the anticipated celestial motions to make forecasts about everything from the weather to the fortunes of various lands and peoples. The astrological notions conveyed in such works, for example that the stars were the handmaidens of divine providence, may have helped undermine aspects of medieval piety such as the veneration of the saints and the mediating role of the institutional church. Both calendars and prognostications suggested a linear, prophetic conception of time that can only have contributed to a general expectancy and readiness for change.

Most of the major reformers, such as Luther and Calvin, were fundamentally hostile to sidereal predictions of human fate. In their eyes any such art implicitly undermined belief in God's omnipotence and therefore destroyed the absolute trust that was necessary to faith. Yet they neither could nor wished to deny altogether the power of the stars as "secondary causes," or the value of understanding their natural effects. Luther also believed that the heavens were filled with God's prophetic signs, which had to be read not scientifically but with the eyes of faith. For the highly influential Philipp Melanchthon, the "teacher of Germany," prophetic and natural understanding often overlapped and complemented one another; astrology could thus implicitly become a means to both kinds of insight for the true Christian. Melanchthon's lectures on physical science, first published in 1549, encouraged an intensive effort to refine the study of planetary influence in later decades. But even more important were major Lutheran reference works such as the *Chronica* of Johann Carion, edited by Melanchthon, which used astrology to interpret the history of the world and to draw out the prophetic significance of the Reformation.

By the second half of the sixteenth century, the desire for insight into the future proved so strong among many prophetically minded Protestants that astrology became a key instrument for interpreting scriptural promises. This was particularly the case among German Lutherans. Unlike Catholics or Calvinists, Lutherans felt increasingly on the defensive in this period; their outlook was typically characterized by apocalyptic convictions that left little hope for this world. As a result, they were strongly attracted to prophetic methods that suggested the inevitability of present troubles as part of a larger divine scheme. The figure of the pastor-astrologer became common, as popular astrology and Lutheran preaching both dwelt upon the need for quick repentance before the final outpouring of divine wrath. In 1566 the Catholic critic Johannes Nas denounced Lutheran almanac writers for trying to see "if they can dupe the people for a while longer, proving from the constellations that Luther's doctrine is right and steady, and will last until the end of the world, which they say will come in 1588." That year was only one of several main foci for astrological predictions of disaster; the apocalyptic use of astrology would continue until well into the following century.

German Protestants by no means had a monopoly on stargazing. By the early seventeenth century popular astrology was booming in England, although here the links between sidereal prediction and apocalyptic prophecy were less direct. The annual almanac became a staple of popular culture; such works reflected and also probably helped to shape the intense religious and political debates of the period before, during, and after the English Civil War of the 1640s.

On the Continent, Calvinists were relatively reserved toward the use of astrology; indeed in France it was largely Catholics who fell under its influence. Here popular fear of the disasters announced by the stars inflamed a widespread sense of religious anguish and a violent hatred of heretics; in this way astrology may have contributed to the background of the Wars of Religion (c.1562–1594). Elsewhere in Catholic Europe, especially in Italy, the popular Renaissance culture in which astrology had played a major role was rapidly suppressed by the 1530s. While powerful individuals, including higher clergy, often continued to have their horoscopes read and to ask for private predictions, astrology was too closely associated with heretical prophecies to remain a part of public discourse.

In both Catholic and Protestant cultures, astrological theories continued to have a place in the schemes of magical reformism that surfaced in the late Renaissance-Reformation era. Thus, for example, the hermeticism of Giordano Bruno included many elements of the supposed astrological wisdom of the ancients. But it would be misleading to associate astrology mainly with wild-eyed occultism or with the mystical mavericks of that age. The art and science of astrology was based on cosmological assumptions that were well-nigh universal. Interpretation of the heavens was the predictive method *par excellence* in premodern Europe. It appealed to countless souls, ignorant and learned alike, who sought assurance in the face of an uncertain future. Only with the larger seventeenth-century separation of religion and cosmology would astrology lose its central role.

[*See also* Magic.]

BIBLIOGRAPHY

Allen, Don Cameron. *The Star-Crossed Renaissance.* New York, 1966.

Barnes, Robin Bruce. *Prophecy and Gnosis: Apocalypticism in the Wake of the Lutheran Reformation.* Stanford, Calif., 1988.

Capp, Bernard. *English Almanacs, 1500–1800: Astrology and the Popular Press.* Ithaca, N.Y., 1979.

Curry, Patrick. *Prophecy and Power: Astrology in Early Modern England.* Cambridge, 1989.

Matthäus, Klaus. "Zur Geschichte des Nürnberger Kalenderwesens." *Archiv für Geschichte des Buchwesens* 9 (1969), cols. 965–1396.

Talkenberger, Heike. *Sintflut: Prophetie und Zeitgeschehen in Texten und Holzschnitten astrologischer Flugschriften, 1488–1528.* Tübingen, 1990.

Thomas, Keith. *Religion and the Decline of Magic.* London, 1971.

Warburg, Aby. *Heidnisch-antike Weissagungen in Wort und Bild zu Luthers Zeiten.* Heidelberg, 1920. Reprinted in *Gesammelte Schriften*, vol 2, pp. 487–558. Nendeln, Liechtenstein, 1969.

Zambelli, Paola, ed. '*Astrologi hallucinati*': *Stars and the End of the World in Luther's Time.* Berlin and New York, 1986.

ROBIN B. BARNES

ASTRONOMY. *See* Astrology; Brahe, Tycho; Copernicus, Nicolaus; Science.

AUBIGNÉ, Théodore-Agrippa d' (1552–1630), French poet, historian, military man, and companion and counselor to Henry IV. He took part in the most important French battles from 1568 to 1590 and thus became governor of Maillezais (Fontenay-le-Compte) in 1587 and vice admiral of the regions of Aunis and Saintonge in 1598. He was active in the deliberations emerging from the political assemblies of Protestants (Vendôme, Saumur, Loudun, and Châtellerault), where he displayed his opposition to the Edict of Nantes and, in general, to the attempts at concord with the Catholics. In 1611 at Saumur he opposed Henri de la Tour, duke of Bouillon, who would have been willing to relinquish the fortified places of safety. In 1615 he joined Henri II Bourbon, prince of Condé, as the leader of some malcontents, along with the duke of Bouillon and Henri, duke of Rohan. Likewise, in 1620 he took part in the revolt of the duke of Rohan, and on this account he was condemned to death in absentia in Paris.

He took refuge in Geneva, where he was to remain for the rest of his days, devoting himself to the composition and revision of his major works. As a keen polemicist in his dialogue *Le Caducée, ou l'Ange de la Paix,* he attacked the "prudent" elements of his party, who showed themselves to be too conciliatory toward the regency of Marie de Médicis, and in the same way he assailed the "tyrannical" rule of Louis XIII in his treatise *Du devoir mutuel des rois et des sujets.* In the *Confession catholique du sieur de Sancy* (1599, published in 1660), he ridicules and insults the Protestants who converted for base motives. In an attempt at impartiality in his important work *Histoire universelle,* dealing with the years 1533 to 1602, he nuances the overly one-sided descriptions of the government of Charles IX presented in his famous poems *Tragiques.* He might also be the author of *Libre discours des Églises réformées de France* (1619), which, with a degree of exactness uncommon for Aubigné, argues his basic thesis: while respecting the loyalty due to Louis XIII, the government must henceforth tolerate Reformed Christians since intolerance is the attitude of "senile and feeble minded Princes."

BIBLIOGRAPHY

Primary Sources

Aubigné, Theodore-Agrippa d'. *Oeuvres complètes de Théodore Agrippa d'Aubigné . . . d'après les manuscrits originaux.* Edited by Eugene Réaume and Françoise de Caussade. 4 vols. Paris, 1873–1877.
———. *Pages inédites de Théodore Agrippa d'Aubigné.* Edited by Pierre-Paul Plan. Geneva, 1945.
———. *Oeuvres.* Edited by Henri Weber, Jacques Bailbe, and Marguerite Soulié. Reprint, Paris, 1987.
———. *Histoire universelle.* Edited by Andre Thierry. Geneva, 1981.

Secondary Sources

Garnier, Armand. "Études." In *Agrippa d'Aubigné et le parti protestant.* 3 vols. Paris, 1928.

Soulié, Marguerite. *L'inspiration biblique dans la poésie religieuse d'Agrippa d'Aubigné.* Lille, 1980.
Thierry, Andre. *Agrippa d'Aubigné: Auteur de l'Histoire universelle.* Lille, 1982.

MARIO TURCHETTI
Translated from French by Robert E. Shillenn

AUGER, Émond (1530–1591), French Jesuit, author, and spiritual director to King Henry III. Born at Alleman in the diocese of Troyes, Auger joined the Society of Jesus at Rome in 1550 and worked in Italy before returning to France in 1559 to staff the Jesuit college at Pamiers. He was rector at Tournon (1561–1563) and provincial of Aquitaine (1565–1571), and his work as a teacher, administrator, controversialist, and preacher took him to many towns in France, most notably Lyon and Paris. His ability as a preacher earned him the title "the French Chrystostom," and his catechisms and works of controversy against the Calvinists earned him the title "the French Canisius." His catechisms were still in use in the seventeenth century, and of his works of controversy those in support of the seven sacraments were the most notable.

Auger was probably the most important and certainly the most controversial French Jesuit of the sixteenth century. Especially notorious were his early association (1568–1570) with the militant policies of Charles de Guise, cardinal of Lorraine; his work as chaplain to the Catholic soldiers led by Henri-Alexandre, duke of Anjou, during the Third War of Religion (1568–1569); his supposed role in the Saint Bartholomew's Day Massacre at Bordeaux (1572); and his work as Henry III's spiritual director (1583–1587). His support of the king's politique and gallican policies created dissension within the society; some Jesuits sided with Auger, and others favored the Catholic League and its leader, Henri de Lorraine, duke of Guise. Auger's reluctance to leave the court almost resulted in his expulsion from the society, but he retired to Lyon in 1587 and then left France in 1589 following the antiroyalist uproar that resulted from the king's assassination of the Guise brothers at Blois (December 1588). Auger died in Como on 19 January 1591.

BIBLIOGRAPHY

Martin, A. Lynn. *Henry III and the Jesuit Politicians.* Geneva, 1973. Focuses on the relationship between Henry and Auger.
———. *The Jesuit Mind: The Mentality of an Elite in Early Modern France.* Ithaca, N.Y., 1988. Contains much information on Auger.

A. LYNN MARTIN

AUGSBURG. Originally a Roman settlement, Augsburg had a bishop from the fourth century. It became a free imperial city in 1316 and enjoyed impressive economic and commercial growth in the late Middle Ages. By the early sixteenth century, it had become—through the activities of such families as the Fuggers, Welsers, and Paumgartners—a leading economic power in Europe. Renaissance ideas and humanism flourished in the city in the early sixteenth century. Some 17 monasteries and convents existed in the city in the late fifteenth century, denoting a rich ecclesiastical life, even though the chronic tensions between city and bishops prompted the transfer of the episcopal residence to Dillingen in the late fifteenth century.

When Martin Luther came to the free imperial city of Augsburg in October 1518 to face a hearing before the papal nuncio Cardinal Cajetan, he was surprised to see so many people along his way greeting him. Barely one year after his famous theses against the selling of indulgences the monk and professor of Wittenberg was celebrated as *herostratos* ("hero")—an enthusiasm that would last for years to come. The Augsburg printers, who published no less than 530 of Luther's writings (among a total of about 3,700) during his lifetime, showed not only the widespread demand for Luther's tracts but also the city's openness to new ideas. By contrast, the output of traditional Catholic books was meager during the same period.

Christoph von Stadion (1478–1543, bishop of Augsburg from 1517) had to face this reality when he wanted to publish the papal bulls against Luther. None of the eighteen printers in the city was willing to print *Exsurge Domine* (the bull threatening Luther with excommunication). So Stadion had to employ the services of a totally inexperienced printer outside Augsburg. Not until 30 December 1520 could the newly installed cathedral preacher Urbanus Rhegius (1489–1541) undertake the official publication. But the people of Augsburg resisted the stipulation in the bull that they surrender and burn all of Luther's writings.

The city council had a similar experience when it had the Edict of Worms against Luther and his followers nailed to the door of the town hall shortly after 14 September 1521. The outlawing of the Lutherans and the prohibition of their writings remained but a piece of paper. The city council was satisfied to convey the impression that it strictly followed imperial law. Its priority was to maintain law and order, and it did not want to become embroiled in theological conflict. This policy was the doing of the influential town clerk *(Stadtschreiber)*, humanist, and imperial councillor Conrad Peutinger.

In the meantime, the sentiment of the reform-minded burghers in the city turned more and more away from Luther. Especially with regard to the worship service and the Eucharist, Augsburg became sympathetic, as did other southern German cities, to the theology of Huldrych Zwingli. Soon after the Peasants' War Anabaptists from south Germany and Switzerland immigrated to Augsburg, where they met in private houses and gardens for sermons, prayer, Bible study, and the Lord's Supper, even as they were prosecuted throughout the empire. It was here that the

important Anabaptist synod, the so-called Martyrs' Synod, took place. Awaiting the imminent Second Coming, sixty leading Anabaptists held a synod on 24 August 1527 dealing with questions of secular authority, oath, and military service. The result of the deliberations was circulated to all Anabaptists in Germany, Austria, and Switzerland. The Augsburg city council did not take measures against the Anabaptists until it sensed insurrection and communitarian tendencies, which appeared to be a threat to the existing social order.

A clearer decision with respect to the religious controversy was called for by the final edict of the diet of 1530, which had taken place in Augsburg. Although strongly pressed by the imperial court, the city council refused to accept the edict. While this was a clear declaration of the Protestant leanings of the majority of the city, it was not possible to achieve religious unanimity. The clergy whom Charles V had expelled from the city during the diet, since he wanted to prohibit Protestant preaching in general, were asked by the city council to return. In addition, Wolfgang Musculus and Bonifacius Wolfart were called from Strasbourg. Another step favoring the Reformation was the founding of a municipal school in the abandoned Carmelite monastery of Saint Anne at the end of 1531. Augsburg sought to follow Strasbourg in its compromise between Luther and Zwingli, a task that Martin Bucer, who had spent a few weeks preaching in Augsburg, supported. But in time Augsburg turned definitely toward the Swiss Reformation, which even Luther, who wrote no fewer than twenty-two letters to Augsburg in less than ten years' time, could not change.

However, the basic question for the city council was not a religious one. If the rich city on the bank of the Lech were to convert to the Reformation, it could expect sanctions from its Catholic neighbors. To the west of Augsburg the Habsburgs held the margravate of Burgau, to the east were the Bavarian Wittelsbachs, and to the south was the prince bishop connected to the emperor. They all could endanger the city's survival by cutting off its supply of water and food. The Austrian and Spanish Habsburgs had been granted extensive credits by Augsburg banking houses; they protected the monopolies of Augsburg trade, and they dominated an important part of the European and the new transatlantic trade. Thus they could jeopardize the economic power of Augsburg in many ways.

The demise of the Catholic Swabian League and the formation of a Protestant League including Augsburg, Ulm, and Nuremberg prompted the city council, encouraged by the Zwinglian preachers in the city, to disregard political and economic considerations, assume control over ecclesiastical affairs in Augsburg on 22 July 1534, and prohibit Catholic priests from officiating in the city. Mass was to be celebrated only in eight churches, all held by the bishop: the cathedral; the Benedictine monastery of Saints Ulrich and Afra, which belonged to the bishop; the two collegiate churches of Saint

Maurice and Saint Peter am Perlach; the two collegiate churches of the Augustinian canons, (Saint George and Holy Cross); Saint Ursula of the Dominican tertiary nuns; and the church of the aristocratic canonesses at Saint Stephen.

The prohibition of Catholic preaching accelerated the decline of Catholic practice in the city. The Dominican and Franciscan monks left, as did nuns from several convents. The council took over full responsibility for the religious organization in the churches that had been assigned to the Protestants: Saint Anne, the monastery of the Franciscans and the chapels designed for preaching and teaching *(Predighäuser)*. Since the council held all rights, it had to cover the costs for the buildings, services, and ministers.

During the first months of 1537 the city council took another step toward establishing the Reformation: on 17 January Catholic clerics and nuns who were still living in Augsburg were forced either to become Protestants or to emigrate. All eight churches that had remained Catholic were now assigned to the Protestants, who destroyed, removed, or painted over altar pieces, sculptures, epitaphs, and frescoes. This iconoclasm as well as the simple form of religious service in the new church order *(Kirchenordnung)* of 1537 meant the definitive introduction of Zwinglianism in Augsburg.

Most of the Catholic clerics and nuns chose to go into exile. All from the cathedral chapter went to Dillingen, a small town some 65 kilometers north of Augsburg. Most of the canons, the Benedictines, the nuns of Saint Ursula, and the tertiary Franciscan nuns went to religious houses near Augsburg and stayed there for a decade, waiting for better times. The Dominican nuns of Saint Catherine, as well as the Benedictine nuns of Saint Nicolas, held citizenship in Augsburg and therefore could not be expelled. When they unswervingly refused to convert to Protestantism, they were put under Protestant prioresses. Contact with Catholic priests was forbidden, and Protestant ministers were regularly sent to the convent for preaching, prayer, and worship. These nuns were part of the small Catholic minority of citizens and patricians who remained in Augsburg until Cardinal Otto Truchsess von Waldburg (bishop of Augsburg from 1543) returned to the city as victor in the Schmalkald War in 1546/47 and had the churches that had been transferred in 1537 reassigned to Catholics. To ensure Catholic life in the city, Emperor Charles V did away with the medieval rule of the guilds on 3 August 1548, replacing it with a new constitution guaranteeing that citizens of both confessions should equally be appointed to the city's government and other leading posts, even though the Catholic minority made up only 10 percent of the population. This constitution laid the foundation for a permanent parity between Protestants and Catholics in Augsburg when the Interim dictated by Charles V failed.

The Peace of Augsburg of 1555 granted the legal basis for a permanent peace between the two confessions. Article 14 of the peace forced those imperial cities in which the two confessions coexisted in 1552 to grant equal protection for "one another's beliefs, worship, and possessions." This peace applied to Catholics and adherents of the Augsburg Confession only, but not to Zwinglians, Anabaptists, or antitrinitarians. Thus Augsburg Protestants were forced to convert from Zwinglianism to Lutheranism. Luther's Large Catechism, a manual for instructing pastors, was made obligatory for teaching in 1559, whereas not before the Thirty Years' War in 1632 was Luther's Small Catechism, an instruction manual for the faithful in the fundamentals of the Christian religion, officially introduced, imposed on the city by the victorious Swedish army.

[See also Augsburg Confession; *and* Augsburg, Peace of.]

BIBLIOGRAPHY

Broadhead, Philip. "Popular Pressure for Reform in Augsburg, 1524–1534." In *Stadtbürgertum und Adel in der Reformation: Studien zur Sozialgeschichte der Reformation in England und Deutschland,* edited by Wolfgang J. Mommsen, pp. 80–87. Stuttgart, 1979.

———. "Politics and Expediency in the Augsburg Reformation." In *Reformation Principle and Practice: Essays in Honour of Arthur Geoffrey Dickens,* edited by Peter Newman Brooks. London, 1980.

———. "International Politics and Civic Society in Augsburg during the Era of the Reformation, 1518–1537." Ph.D. diss., University of Kent at Canterbury, 1981.

Clasen, Claus-Peter. *Anabaptism: A Social History, 1525–1618.* Ithaca, N. Y., 1972.

———. *The Anabaptists in South and Central Germany, Switzerland, and Austria: Their Names, Occupations, Places of Residence and Dates of Conversion, 1525–1618.* Goshen, Ind., 1978.

Davis, Kenneth Ronald. *Anabaptism and Ascetism: A Study in Intellectual Origins.* Scottdale, Pa., 1974.

Dirr, Pius. "Zur Geschichte der Augsburger Zunftverfassung, 1368–1548." *Zeitschrift des Historischen Vereins für Schwaben* 39 (1913), 144–243.

Hege, Christian. "Augsburg." In *The Mennonite Encyclopedia,* vol. 1, pp. 182–185. Scottdale, Pa., 1955.

Immenkötter, Herbert. "Kirche zwischen Reformation und Parität." In *Geschichte der Stadt Augsburg von der Römerzeit bis zur Gegenwart,* edited by Gunther Gottlieb et al., pp. 391–412. 2d rev. ed. Stuttgart, 1985.

———. "Wahrhafte Verantwortung. Zur 'Abtuung der papistischen Abgötterey' in Augsburg, 1537." *Jahrbuch des Vereins für Augsburger Bistumsgeschichte* 21 (1987), 72–111.

———. "Die katholische Kirche in Augsburg in der ersten Hälfte des 16. Jahrhunderts." In *Die Augsburger Kirchenordnung von 1537 und ihr Umfeld,* edited by Reinhard Schwarz, pp. 9–31. Göttingen, 1988.

———. "Die Augsburger Pfarrzechen als Träger der Kirchenreform im 15. und 16. Jahrhundert." In *Papsttum und Kirchenreform: Historische Beiträge,* edited by Manfred Weitlauff and Karl Hausberger, pp. 301–323. St. Ottilien, Germany, 1990.

Klassen, Herbert. "The Life and Teachings of Hans Hut." *Mennonite Quarterly Review* 33 (1959), 171–205, 267–304.

Liebmann, Maximilian. *Urbanus Rhegius und die Anfänge der Reformation.* Münster, 1980.

Lutz, Heinrich. *Conrad Peutinger.* Augsburg, 1959.

Packull, Werner O. *Mysticism and the Early South German-Austrian Anabaptist Movement, 1525–1531.* Scottdale, Pa., 1977.

Roper, Lyndal. "Discipline and Respectability: Prostitution and the

Reformation in Augsburg." *History Workshop Journal* 19 (1985), 3–28.

———. "Work, Marriage and Sexuality: Women in Reformation Augsburg." Ph.D. diss., University of London, 1985.

———. *The Holy Household: Women and Morals in Reformation Augsburg.* Oxford, 1989.

Roth, Friedrich. *Augsburgs Reformationsgeschichte.* 4 vols. Munich, 1901–1911.

Stayer, James M. *Anabaptists and the Sword.* 3d ed. Lawrence, Kans., 1979.

Warmbrunn, Paul. *Zwei Konfessionen in einer Stadt: Das Zusammenleben von Katholiken und Protestanten in den paritätischen Reichsstädten Augsburg, Biberach, Ravensburg und Dinkelsbühl von 1548–1648.* Wiesbaden, 1983.

Wolfart, Karl. *Die Augsburger Reformation in den Jahren 1533/34* (1901). Reprint, Aalen, 1972.

Zoepfl, Friedrich. *Das Bistum Augsburg und seine Bischöfe im Reformationsjahrhundert.* Augsburg, 1969.

Zorn, Wolfgang. *Augsburg: Geschichte einer deutschen Stadt.* 2d ed. Augsburg, 1972.

HERBERT IMMENKÖTTER
Translated from German by Johanna Schmid

AUGSBURG, PEACE OF.

AUGSBURG, PEACE OF. The most important constitutional edict of early modern Germany, the Peace of Augsburg was signed on 25 September 1555. Perceived as a provisional document, it remained essentially valid imperial law for two and a half centuries until the demise of the Holy Roman Empire in 1803/05.

Before 1555 the empire had no uniform ecclesiastical law. The several sometimes mutually contradictory recesses, treaties, and edicts that had been promulgated since the beginning of the German Reformation were in fact truces, generally the result of confessional and political concessions on the part of the emperor, whose ability to influence events was limited by the demands of his involvements in Europe, notably his relations with France. Even though the youthful Emperor Charles V had managed in 1521 to issue the Edict of Worms which banned Martin Luther and his followers, the implementation of the edict was left for a full nine years to the imperial estates while Charles himself stayed in Spain and the Netherlands. The estates, after unsuccessful efforts at the diets at Nuremberg 1522/23 and 1524, agreed at Speyer in 1526 to deal with the religious controversy in such a way "as everyone hopes and trusts to be accountable before God and his Imperial Majesty." While it was the intent of the Speyer recess to petrify affairs with respect to the increasing reform sentiments, the reform minded estates took it as an endorsement of full freedom of action. As far as they were concerned, the idea of a uniform religious policy in the empire had been abandoned. When, three years later, the Catholic majority prescribed, also at Speyer, the implementation of the Edict of Worms in its territories and prohibited any further religious change by the advocates of reform, the evangelicals protested. Their protest gave them the label "Protestants," meant by Catholics as a derogatory epithet, but accepted by advocates of reform with pride.

After the followers of Luther had presented to the Diet of Augsburg the Augsburg Confession, the cities of Strasbourg, Lindau, Constance, and Memmingen their Tetrapolitan Confession, and, in addition, Huldrych Zwingli his *Ratio fidei* in the summer of 1530, the recess of the diet (19 November 1530) demanded, under the threat of the use of imperial force, the return of all adherents of reform to the teaching and practice of the old church within six months. This led in the spring of 1531 under the leadership of Saxony and Hesse to the formation of the Schmalkald League for the defense against the imperial Catholic interpretation of the legal situation. This meant that the colleges of the imperial diet—electors, nobility, and imperial cities—that had traditionally convened separately, now found a more meaningful cohesiveness according to their respective confessions of faith. A confessional dualism was added to the traditional dualism between emperor and estates.

The Ottoman empire, which in 1526 had conquered Transylvania and most of Hungary and which in October 1529 stood outside Vienna, precluded for a while a threatening religious war in the empire. The Protestants made their participation in the common defense of Europe against the Ottoman empire dependent on an advantageous domestic peace. They managed in the Peace of Nuremberg (1532), the Peace of Frankfurt (1539), and later at Regensburg (1541) and Speyer (1544), to obtain the emperor's concession for a temporary political peace. This was accomplished by the suspension of all ecclesiastical litigation before the imperial court and the suspension of the relevant recesses issued against the Lutherans by the several diets. Moreover, the emperor accepted the secularization of church property in Protestant territories. These were the initial steps in the direction of the recognition of the Lutheran Reformation by imperial law. At the same time, the emperor began, however much in a temporizing fashion, to surrender the responsibility for ecclesiastical affairs to the territorial rulers.

The Curia Romana responded angrily with a papal admonition to Charles dated 24 August 1544. Charles was declared guilty of a serious violation in canon law. The emperor was admonished to revoke all concessions to the Protestants immediately; then it became the emperor's responsibility to secure peace in the empire. To bring an end to the nagging ecclesiastical controversy, Pope Paul III promulgated (30 November 1544) the bull *Laetare Jerusalem,* which convened at long last a general council at Trent, eagerly anticipated for over two decades. The emperor appeared to agree with this decision, but at the same time he continued to pursue his ambitious plans to defeat the Schmalkald League on the battlefield and thereby to force the Protestants to recognize and attend the council. A treaty with the pope provided him with 12,500 mercenaries for a period of four months for his war against the Schmalkald League, together with 200,000 ducats and further financial support from his Spanish possessions. After the dukes of Bavaria pledged neutrality, and Duke Moritz of Saxony, with the prospect of the Saxon electorship before him, sided with the Catholics, the emperor declared the ban over electoral Saxony and Hesse. Thus Charles V defined the war of religion as "a purely secular execution of imperial law by the emperor against the lawlessness of the evangelical rulers." When the Catholic victory became evident the following winter, the pope withdrew his soldiers, much to the emperor's annoyance, before the decisive battle. Paul III clearly wanted to punish the evangelical rulers, but did not wish to enhance the power of the House of Habsburg.

In March 1547 the papal party succeeded in moving the council, which had been in session at Trent since 13 December 1535, to Bologna, the second most important city of the Papal States. This move gave the emperor no choice but to seek a resolution of the ecclesiastical controversy in Germany without the pope. That was exactly his intention with respect to the Augsburg Interim, the temporizing solution promulgated by the armed Diet of Augsburg (1547/48). The theological substance of the Interim was Catholic, but it conceded to the Protestants the Communion cup for the laity and the toleration of priests who had married. At the same time a *formula reformationis* was promulgated as imperial law, a decree concerning the reform of the Catholic clergy. Both documents were a dictate of the victor. The reform statute failed to be effective because of the lack of a well-educated clergy. Charles V's absolutist tendencies, together with his plans to tie his own dynasty permanently to the imperial office, prompted resistance.

Moritz of Saxony, the new Saxon elector, succeeded in winning King Henry II of France for his anti-Habsburg coalition and led the Princes' Rebellion of 1550/51. Imperial policy fell apart, with grave consequences for Charles's ecclesiastical policies as well. To his deepest dismay Charles V learned that the majority of the imperial estates agreed in the Treaty of Passau of 15 August 1552 to the removal of the Interim, the secularization of all church property in Protestant possession, and the convening of a national assembly to conclude a permanent religious peace. Archduke Ferdinand I acted as spokesman for the neutral estates and as mediator between the emperor and the Protestants. Ferdinand was particularly concerned about a domestic conciliation in view of the renewed Ottoman threat. Charles abdicated and transferred his realm "over which the sun never set" to his son Philip II and his brother, Archduke Ferdinand, who presided over the tedious negotiations at the Diet of Augsburg in 1555. Only a few of the territorial rulers took part; most of the negotiators were lawyers and diplomats, who agreed on a political peace and the legally guaranteed coexistence of two confessional parties in the empire. In particular, the peace had the following characteristics.

- A theological compromise of the controversy was not a concern of the feuding religious parties.
- Instead of a single Christian norm in the empire, the Roman Catholic and the Lutheran confessions were to be on equal legal footing, while the Zwinglians, Calvinists, Anabaptists, and other Protestant "sects" were excluded. However, in the emperor's Burgundian territories, existing heresy laws were to remain in force.
- This equality meant that the ecclesiastical jurisdiction of Catholic prelates (bishops and abbots who also functioned as secular rulers) over the adherents of the Augsburg Confession was suspended and the medieval laws respecting heresy were rescinded.
- "Ubi unus dominus ibi una sit religio": Catholic and Lutheran estates (electors, princes, dukes, and counts) received the right to determine the religion of their subjects. This right, quickly labeled *ius reformandi* ("right to reform"), was expressed early in the seventeenth century by the pithy phrase *cuius regio, eius religio* ("whoever the king, his religion").
- The "ecclesiastical reservation" dealt specifically with the issue of ecclesiastical rulers (bishops and abbots) turning Protestant. They did not possess the right of reform that the secular estates possessed. They were free to embrace Lutheranism, but at the loss of their ecclesiastical offices, and especially their secular authority. The evangelical estates agreed to include the "ecclesiastical reservation" in the diet's recess by King Ferdinand, who acted on behalf of the emperor.
- The knights and towns (other than imperial free cities) that, even though subjects of ecclesiastical rulers, had accepted the Augsburg Confession were guaranteed their faith through the *Declaratio Ferdinandea,* a side agreement that was not included in the official recess of the diet.
- The free exercise of religion did not extend to the subjects of the imperial estates. If they disagreed with the religious decision of their rulers, they had the right to sell their property and emigrate. "This freedom of religion, clothed in the mantle of the religious right of the nobility, was the first universal human right that the empire guaranteed as formal constitutional law to each German" (Heckel, 1983, p. 48).
- Imperial free cities that had by 1555 adherents of both religious parties were guaranteed the exercise of religion.
- The Peace of Augsburg was meant as a provisional agreement until the restoration of a common faith by an ecumenical council. This goal was anchored in imperial law. This prompted the withdrawal of the papal protest against the peace (1566).

For the Lutheran churches, the Peace of Augsburg meant the legal recognition by imperial law of a development that had begun in the 1520s. The Lutheran rulers were functioning legally as "emergency" bishops, and extendeding their power and authority over the whole range of religious and ecclesiastical affairs. This was in harmony with their absolutist claims against emperor and empire. In the course of time the Lutheran territorial churches increasingly became an institution of the state, and evangelical teaching became state doctrine.

The ecclesiastical bishoprics of south and west Germany became almost exclusively the domain of the Catholic nobility. They served henceforth to provide for sons (and daughters), especially of the houses of Habsburg and Wittelsbach. The pope, in turn, suspended the provisions of the Council of Trent concerning the qualifications of bishops with respect to theological education, personal quality, canonical age, and pluralism of office. In both Catholic and Lutheran territories confessional federalism emerged that hindered the harmonious development of the empire into a modern state and that was a cause for its international weakness in seventeenth- and eighteenth-century Europe.

The Peace of Augsburg marked the end of the Reformation in Germany. Neither side had won; the peace was a compromise between the Catholic and Lutheran estates. And as a compromise the peace quickly showed tensions that lasted until the Thirty Years' War. Specific points of tension were the complex legal situation created by the *Reservatum ecclesiasticum* and the *Declaratio Ferdinandea*, as well as the problems in south Germany, where Catholics and Lutherans lived side-by-side in fairly small territories. Calvinism, which had been excluded from recognition, found it difficult to expand in Germany, while the right to emigrate that the peace formalized was to have major economic consequences in the seventeenth and eighteenth centuries.

[*See also* Holy Roman Empire *and* Lutheranism.]

BIBLIOGRAPHY

Primary Sources

Brandi, Karl. *Der Augsburger Religionsfriede vom 25. September 1555.* 2d rev. ed. Leipzig, 1927.

Walder, Ernst. *Religionsvergleiche des 16. Jahrhunderts.* 3d rev. ed. Bern, 1974.

Secondary Sources

Blickle, Peter. *Die Reformation im Reich.* 2d ed. Stuttgart, 1992.

Bornkamm, Heinrich. "Die religiöse und politische Problematik im Verhältnis der Konfessionen im Reich." *Archiv für Reformationsgeschichte* 56 (1965), 209–218.

Cameron, Euan. *The European Reformation.* Oxford, 1991.

Decot, Rolf. *Religionsfrieden und Kirchenreform: Der mainzer Kurfürst und Erzbischof Sebastian von Heusenstamm, 1545–1555.* Wiesbaden, 1980.

Elton, G.R. *The Reformation.* London, 1962.

———. *Reformation Europe, 1517–1559.* London, 1963.

Frisch, Michael. *Das Restitutionsedikt Kaiser Ferdinands II. vom 6. März 1629.* Tübingen, 1993.

Heckel, Martin. "Autonomia, Pacis Compositio: Der Augsburger Religionsfriede in der Deutung der Gegenreformation." *Zeitschrift der Savigny-Stiftung für Rechtsgeschichte, Kanonische Abteilung* 45 (1959), 141–248.

———. *Deutschland im konfessionellen Zeitalter.* Göttingen, 1983.

———. "Augsburger Religionsfriede." In *Evangelisches Staatslexikon,* edited by Roman Herzog et al., vol. 1, pp. 111–117. 3d ed. Stuttgart, 1987.

Laufs, Adolf, ed. *Die Reichskammergerichtsordnung von 1555.* Cologne, 1976.

Lutz, Heinrich. *Christianitas afflicta.* Göttingen, 1964.

Lutz, Heinrich, ed. *Zur Geschichte der Toleranz und Religionsfreiheit.* Darmstadt, 1977.

Lutz, Heinrich, and Alfred Kohler, eds. *Das Reichstagsprotokoll des kaiserlichen Kommissars Felix Hornung vom augsburger Reichstag, 1555.* Vienna, 1971.

Oelrich, K. H. *Weltliche Obrigkeit und geistliche Jurisdiktion im 16. Jahrhundert.* Ph.D. diss., Rheinische Friedrich-Wilhelms-Universität Bonn, 1970.

Pfeiffer, Gerhard. "Der Augsburger Religionsfriede und die Reichsstädte." *Zeitschrift des Historischen Vereins für Schwaben* 61 (1955), 211–321.

———. "Augsburger Religionsfriede." In *Theologische Realenzyklopädie,* vol. 4, pp. 639–645. Berlin and New York, 1979.

Rabe, Horst. *Deutsche Geschichte, 1500–1600.* Munich, 1991.

Schilling, Heinz. " 'Konfessionsbildung' und 'Konfessionalisierung': Literaturbericht." *Geschichte in Wissenschaft und Unterricht* 42 (1991), 447–463 and 779–794.

Simon, Matthias. *Der Augsburger Religionsfriede: Ereignis und Aufgabe.* Augsburg, 1955.

Spitz, Lewis W. *The Protestant Reformation, 1517–1559.* New York, 1985.

Ströle-Bühler, Heike. *Das Restitutionsedikt von 1629 im Spannungsfeld zwischen Augsburger Religionsfrieden 1555 und dem Westfälischen Frieden.* Regensburg, 1991.

Wittenberg, Martin. *Friede im Reich: Geschichte und Probleme des Religionsfriedens von Augsburg, 1555.* Munich, 1956.

HERBERT IMMENKÖTTER
Translated from German by Hans J. Hillerbrand

AUGSBURG CONFESSION. As prince elector, John Frederick ordered visitations of schools and churches on 16 June 1527. Since his instruction was insufficient, the Wittenberg theologians, together with the councillors of the electorate, drafted the *Unterricht der Visitatoren an die Pfarrherrn im Kurfürstentum Sachsen* (Visitators' Instruction to the Pastors in the Electorate of Saxony), which appeared in mid-March 1528. Although Philipp Melanchthon had created a model with his Visitation Articles in 1527 and had largely formulated the *Unterricht der Visitatoren,* Martin Luther, Johannes Bugenhagen, Georg Spalatin, and the councillors also contributed to it.

The *Unterricht der Visitatoren* also issued organizational guidelines for church and school; it was the content of doctrine that stood in the forefront, along with "how one comes to faith." The text was to be at one and the same time a testimony and a confession of the faith of the visitators, intended to encourage imitation. The presentation of correct doctrine automatically led to the delimitation of false doctrines and their adherents.

While the *Unterricht der Visitatoren* was being edited, Luther composed *Vom Abendmahl Christi, Bekenntnis* (The Last Supper of Christ, Confession) against Huldrych Zwingli. At the end he added a personal confession of faith. He thereby sought to prevent his writings from being interpreted against his intentions after his death.

In 1529, after the majority of the imperial Diet of Speyer had voted for the enforcement of the 1521 Edict of Worms, the evangelicals redoubled their efforts to reach agreement among themselves. Margrave George of Brandenburg-Ansbach and his Franconian theologians pressed for a confession of faith as the basis for a protective alliance. On 1 July 1529 Landgrave Philipp of Hesse invited reformers from Switzerland, south Germany, and Wittenberg to Marburg for a religious discussion to resolve their differences and to create an ecclesiastical and theological agreement as the basis for a political alliance. At the order of Elector John of Saxony, the Wittenberg theologians met in Torgau in mid-September and drafted seventeen articles. Saxony and Brandenburg-Ansbach agreed on these articles in Schleiz between 3 and 7 October, and Nuremberg followed in Schwabach on 16 October. Thus, they were called the Schwabach Articles.

The Schwabach Articles served as a model for Luther, who, at the insistence of the landgrave, drafted fifteen articles on 4 October after the colloquy with the Swiss and the south Germans on 2 and 3 October. After some modifications, the first fourteen articles met with the approval of the participants, and together with the fifteenth article they are known as the Marburg Articles. Since both Luther's confession and the Schwabach and Marburg articles emerged in the context of the debate with the Swiss and the south Germans, they retained some of the differences among evangelicals, as well as points of agreement.

Preparations for the Diet of Augsburg of 1530. After the close of the Diet of Worms, Emperor Charles V signed (26 May 1521) the Edict of Worms, which made Luther and his followers outlaws in the empire. Afterward the wars with France, the Papal States, and the Turks prevented the emperor from presiding over an imperial diet. He was represented by his brother Ferdinand (later Emperor Ferdinand I), archduke of Austria, who had been king of Bohemia and Hungary since 1526. Since Charles V did not pursue the implementation of the Edict of Worms himself, the Reformation spread rapidly. In the summer of 1529 the emperor came to an agreement with Pope Clement VII (r. 1523–1534) in the Treaty of Barcelona and with the French king Francis I in the Treaty of Cambrai. On 14 October the Turks were forced to give up their siege of Vienna and to withdraw to Hungary. Now Charles V had a free hand to deal with internal affairs of the empire.

At first Charles V did not demand enforcement of the Edict of Worms; rather, in a surprisingly mild manner he announced an imperial diet to hold consultations concerning the defense against the Turks and the resolution of the divisions in the holy faith. As early as 1518 Luther had appealed for a council, and since 1521 there had been other calls for a council, which Clement VII firmly opposed. The emperor had to act. He seemed to be offering himself as an arbiter at an imperial diet between the two religious factions.

On March 14 Elector John ordered Luther, Justus Jonas, Bugenhagen, and Melanchthon to draw up a report and present it in Torgau. The resulting draft comprised articles that were not contained in the Schwabach Articles. It was reworked around 27 March with the inclusion of new questions, and consideration of Saxon diplomacy was also taken into account. Chancellor Gregor Brück (1485/86–1557) wrote the foreword. The document was later given the name the Torgau Articles. In Innsbruck in early May 1530, Hans von Dolzig (c.1485–1551) submitted the *Unterricht der Visitatoren* and the Schwabach Articles to the emperor, who reluctantly received them.

Negotiations Concerning Religion at the Diet of Augsburg. Since Luther was under the ban, he could not appear at the diet. He had to remain in Coburg and follow the proceedings from there, while Melanchthon and Jonas accompanied Elector John to Augsburg.

Probably while still on his way, Melanchthon began to work on a written defense, which he intended the Saxon politicians to transmit to the emperor. He made the Schwabach Articles the basis of articles 1 to 17 and the Torgau Articles the basis of articles 22 to 27; however, he also resorted to the *Unterricht der Visitatoren* and Luther's confession of 1528. His draft summed up the confessional development that had taken place in Saxony since 1528.

Two events exerted a strong influence on the composition of this draft. Johann Eck had published 404 articles, in which he had included 380 allegedly heretical statements culled from Reformation writings together with 24 additional theses. Against this attack the evangelicals stressed that they represented the original, true doctrine.

Soon efforts were under way to transform this Saxon defense into a confession supported by as many Protestants as possible. Margrave George of Brandenburg-Ansbach, the imperial cities of Nuremberg, Reutlingen, and Strasbourg, and Landgrave Philipp of Hesse took part in the modification. Thus, many varied interests lacking any unifying intention were eventually reflected in the text through the efforts of princes, councillors, theologians, and other scholars. With respect to Rome some articles were sharpened, while others were softened. A final stylistic editing was undertaken by Melanchthon. A foreword drafted by Melanchthon was replaced by one by Brück.

The Augsburg Confession also took account of the fact that it was being submitted to the emperor at a diet. Since 13 February 1521, when Girolamo Aleandro had charged at the diet that Luther's doctrine would lead to insurrection, the evangelicals found themselves compelled to refute this assertion. Article 16 emphasized that the secular order had been established by God, and it condemned any teachings to the contrary. In article 21 the emperor's war against the Turks was cited as an example of a good work. Article 9 condemned the Anabaptists and thus corresponded to the imperial law of 23 April 1529 that threatened all Anabaptists with the death penalty.

The conclusion of part 1 made clear how much the political situation was taken into account. The signatories emphasized that their teaching was in contradiction with neither the church fathers nor with the Roman church. Thus, they defended themselves from being considered heretics since "the confusion and strife is mainly over numerous traditions and abuses." In the introduction to the Torgau Articles, reference was made to "abuses, which had come about through human teachings and regulations." In one draft prepared in Augsburg there was still mention of a possible agreement with the Roman church, "as long as it is based on the proven and accepted teachers." The authors of the Augsburg Confession were thus aware of the doctrinal differences but downplayed them to obtain toleration of their teaching and to leave open the possibility of coming to an agreement.

On 11 May 1530 Luther received a draft of the confession, which he approved, but added on 29 June that the failure to address several disagreements suggested that too much had been conceded. On 21 July he argued that disagreements on the articles on purgatory, the veneration of saints, and the pope as Antichrist should not have been passed over.

Although the Augsburg Confession was adapted to the situation at the diet of 1530, it was in no way merely a product of ecclesiastical politics. Reformation theology was so strongly marked by an appeal to the scriptures and the church fathers that it self-consciously did not represent a new "heresy" but rather the unadulterated, common Christian doctrine, which was also the foundation of the Roman church. Its only innovation was to address Christians of the sixteenth century and take account of new questions.

In the places where the Augsburg Confession glossed over points of disagreement, it in no way agreed with its theological opponents. In light of the expectations of the emperor and of the Roman church (represented by a legate and bishops) with respect to the "heretics," silence meant simply refusal of an agreement. That was tantamount to an unspoken critique of the teachings in question.

In the afternoon of 25 June 1530 in the presence of the emperor and the members of the imperial diet, who were seated in the chapter hall of the episcopal palace, the Saxon chancellor Christian Beyer (c.1482–1535) read out the Augsburg Confession in German. With the windows of the hall open, people were standing outside and listening. Then the German and the Latin versions were handed to the emperor. The Augsburg Confession had been signed by Elector John and his son John Frederick, Philipp of Hesse,

George of Brandenburg-Ansbach, the dukes Ernst and Franz of Lüneburg, Prince Wolfgang of Anhalt, and the imperial cities of Nuremberg and Reutlingen. Because of the article on the Lord's Supper, Strasbourg did not concur but instead (along with Constance, Lindau, and Memmingen) submitted the Tetrapolitan Confession.

As a rebuttal to the Augsburg Confession, the Roman Catholic theologians—under the influence of the emperor, Cardinal Lorenzo Campeggio, and their estates—drafted the Confutatio Confessionis Augustanae, in which they responded to the individual articles of the Augsburg Confession. They stressed the points of agreement and defended their counterpositions forcefully from scripture and tradition. On 3 August the Confutatio was read aloud in German in the name of the emperor at the same place where the Augsburg Confession had been read. Charles V demanded that the evangelicals accept the Confutatio, even before its text had been conveyed to them. When this was rejected by the Protestants and negotiations to iron out differences proved fruitless, Brück and the Saxon delegation were appointed to draft a written defense, which Melanchthon polished. At a session of the diet on 22 September, Brück raised objections to the assertion that the Augsburg Confession had been refuted and sought unsuccessfully to hand the Apologia Confessionis Augustanae to the emperor. Instead, the emperor, by adjourning the diet, made it clear that the Edict of Worms was to be enforced. Charles V had not mediated as an arbiter but had sided with the Roman Catholics. He did not achieve unification, but he did contribute to the formation of a significant confessional declaration.

The Content of the Augsburg Confession. In its first part (articles 1–21) the Augsburg Confession presents almost the entirety of the doctrine that "is preached and taught in our churches for true Christian instruction and consolation of consciences and also for the improvement of believers." The second part offers a justification of the changes that have been undertaken (articles 22–28).

Article 1 affirms the belief in the doctrine of the Trinity (as promulgated by the Council of Nicea) and the condemnation of its opponents. Thus, the common foundation of theology was maintained, and the incisively trinitarian charter of Reformation theology was emphasized.

Article 2 defines Original Sin as both a lack of fear of God and a lack of trust in God, as well as evil desire, which is inborn in every person. It is real sin. The condemnation of those who deny Original Sin as real sin is also directed against scholastic theology.

Article 3 confesses belief in the Christology of the ancient church and closely follows the second article of the Apostles' Creed. It emphasizes the notion of salvation history in that Christ, through his sacrifice, appeased the wrath of God that had been caused by both Original Sin and actual sin.

Article 4 touches upon a major point of controversy with the teaching on justification. It rejects the idea that forgiveness of sin and righteousness can be attained through human effort (though without an explicit condemnation) and affirms that this takes place by grace for the sake of Christ (article 3) and through faith that believes that Christ has suffered for humans. For his sake sin is forgiven and both righteousness and eternal life are bestowed. There is no *sola* inserted before *fide*, but the concept is included in article 6 with a quote ascribed to Ambrose (339–397).

Article 5 deals with the office of preaching, which proclaims the gospel and administers the sacraments. Both are described as the means by which God bestows the Holy Spirit. Thereby the office of the minister is completely defined in terms of service to the deeds of God, and alongside the sacrament the proclamation of the gospel is given a significance unknown in the late Middle Ages.

Article 6 limits good works to those commanded by God. It is stressed that good works follow justification as the fruits of faith but contribute nothing to it.

Article 7 describes the church as the assembly of all believers, in which the pure gospel is preached and the sacraments are administered according to the gospel. It rejects the notion that uniformity in ceremonies is required for unity. Thus, the ground was laid to accept the changes made by the evangelicals. Although the late Middle Ages often equated the church with the hierarchy, the hierarchy is not mentioned even once. The Schwabach Articles had stated that the church is not bound together with laws and external splendor to places and time, persons, and rites. The Latin version of the Augsburg Confession speaks of human traditions, rites, and ceremonies. Since for the Wittenberg theologians the papacy was a human institution, they were signifying that the church exists even without hierarchy.

Article 8 maintains that the sacraments are effective independent of the qualities of the priest who administers them. It condemns the Donatists and those of like mind.

Article 9 declares baptism necessary for salvation. It affirms infant baptism and condemns the Anabaptists who reject it.

Article 10 emphasizes that the body and blood of Christ, under the form of bread and wine, are present and distributed in the Lord's Supper. The rejection—not condemnation—of the opposing notion was clearly directed against a symbolic interpretation of the words of the Lord's Supper by evangelical theologians. The Confutatio inaccurately saw this article as affirming the doctrine of transubstantiation.

Article 11 affirms private confession, while article 12 explains penance as remorse for sins committed and also as faith in forgiveness for the sake of Christ, thereby criticizing the late medieval understanding of the sacrament of penance. The article condemns perfectionism (meaning that a pious person can live without sin), the Novatianists (who denied the baptized forgiveness of sins through absolution), and those who taught that forgiveness of sins could be attained through satisfaction.

Article 13 deals with the use of the sacraments as testimony of God's will to awaken and strengthen faith; they are rightly used when they are received in faith. In this manner the Augsburg Confession distinguished itself both from Zwingli, insofar as he interpreted their use as signs by which a Christian can be recognized, and from the late medieval notion of receiving the sacraments, which neglected the significance of faith for a positive effect of the sacraments. Concerning the doctrine that there are seven sacraments, as defined in Florence in 1439 and which the Reformers rejected, the Augsburg Confession is silent.

Article 14 demands an appropriate calling for public proclamation and the administration of the Sacrament. Article 15 states that the ecclesiastical orders are useful human institutions, which, however, are not necessary for salvation and must neither burden consciences nor contradict the gospel.

Article 16 praises the secular order as a good order of God and condemns both the Anabaptists, who reject participation in it as unchristian, and the monastic flight from the world, justified by the goal of Christian perfection. The article calls for the exercise of Christian love in everyday life.

Article 17 affirms the belief in the second coming of Christ and the Last Judgment. It condemns the teaching that even the devil and the damned will not suffer everlasting punishment and affirms the expectation of a millennial reign in which the godless will be rooted out.

Article 18 recognizes free will in outward matters, such as living honorably, but denies that it is able to please God unless brought about by the Holy Spirit. Article 19 declares the will for evil as the cause of sin.

Article 20 argues against the misinterpretation that the evangelicals forbid good works and against the notion of merit. It emphasizes that through faith in forgiveness, God bestows the Holy Spirit, who enables good works.

Article 21 encourages devotion to the saints, to whom grace was given to strengthen faith. It also recognizes the saints as examples of faith but opposes calling on them for intercession.

Article 22 defends with scripture and tradition the practice of giving the Communion cup to the laity, while article 23 deals with the dangers to priests that stem from obligatory celibacy. Appealing to scripture, historical practice, and experience, it opposes the prohibition of the marriage of priests.

Article 24 defends the evangelicals against the misinterpretation that they have done away with the Mass and charges that the Mass has become an object of commerce. It also identifies abuses that have crept in, defends the reforms undertaken, and particularly attacks the late medieval notion of sacrifice associated with the Mass. Article 25 maintains that confession has not been done away with and summarizes the newly introduced practice.

Article 26 opposes the notion that fasting and other human ordinances are meritorious, though it maintains that fasting and other practices can certainly help a person to fulfill the obligations of his vocation. Article 27 thoroughly opposes the notion that monastic vows are meritorious and in contrast defines Christian perfection as fear of and trust in God.

Article 28, which is quite lengthy, discusses the power of bishops. It criticizes the fact that bishops have installed and deposed secular leaders. It stresses the distinction between the spiritual and the secular order and opposes the mixture of these two orders in the case of bishops who were at the same time imperial princes. It also disputes the bishops' right to make laws and regulations in contradiction to scripture and thereby burden consciences.

The Effects of the Augsburg Confession. In July 1530 Windsheim, Heilbronn, Kempten, and Weissenburg quickly signed the confession in Augsburg. The Homberg church order for Hesse of 1532 begins with a reference to the Augsburg Confession and its Apology. The recess of the Schmalkald League of March 1537 adopted the Augsburg Confession with its Apology and the recently drafted *Tractatus de potestate et primatu papae* (Treatise on the Power and Primacy of the Pope) as the doctrinal foundation for members of the Schmalkald League. The Peace of Augsburg of 1555 guaranteed peace only for the adherents of the Augsburg Confession, along with those who embraced the old faith, and so this confession took on a high degree of legal significance in the empire.

Melanchthon took it upon himself to rework both the Augsburg Confession and its Apology. As the Schmalkald League made preparations for a religious colloquy with Roman Catholics, the Wittenberg theologians issued a report. In the fall of 1540 Melanchthon worked this report into the Augsburg Confession, but also took into account the Wittenberg Concord of 1536 and its doctrine on justification that had been modified after 1535. This Confessio Augustana variata was submitted as an official document by the members of the Schmalkald League on 30 November 1540 at the Colloquy of Worms. Since several formulations of this text were later used to introduce Calvinist concepts into Lutheranism, the original texts of these two written confessions were adopted into the *Book of Concord* of 1580.

[*See also* Augsburg, Peace of; Formula of Concord; Gnesio-Lutherans; *and* Philippists.]

BIBLIOGRAPHY

Die Bekenntnisschriften der evangelisch-lutherischen Kirche. Edited by Deutschen Evangelischen Kirchenausschuss. Göttingen, 1930.

Burgess, Joseph A., and George Lindbeck, eds. *The Role of the Augsburg Confession: Catholic and Lutheran Views.* Philadelphia, 1980.

Forell, Wolfgang, and James McCue, with Wenzel Lohff, eds. *Confessing One Faith: A Joint Commentary on the Augsburg Confession by Lutheran and Catholic Theologians.* Minneapolis, 1982.

Grane, Leif. *Die Confessio Augustana: Einführung in die Hauptgedanken der lutherischen Reformation.* 4th rev. ed. Göttingen, 1990.

Hoffman, Fritz, and Ulrich Kühn, eds. *Die Confessio Augustana im ökumenischen Gespräch.* Berlin, 1980.

Iserloh, Erwin, ed. *Die Confessio Augustana and Confutatio: Der Augsburger Reichstag 1530 und die Einheit der Kirche.* Internationales Symposium der Gesellschaft zur Herausgabe des Corpus Catholicorum, Augsburg, 3–7 September 1979. 2d ed. Münster, 1981.

Lohse, Bernhard, and Otto Herman Pesch, eds. *Das "Augsburger Bekenntnis" von 1530: Damals und heute.* Munich, 1980.

Lohse, Bernhard, et al. "Augsburger Bekenntnis, Confutatio and Apologie." In *Theologische Realenzyklopädie*, vol. 16, pp. 616–639. Berlin and New York, 1979.

Maurer, Wilhelm. *Historischer Kommentar zur Confessio Augustana.* 2 vols. Gütersloh, 1976–1978. Also available in English as *Historical Commentary on the Augsburg Confession,* translated by H. George Anderson. Philadelphia, 1986.

Neuser, W. H. *Bibliographie der Confessio Augustana und Apologie, 1530–1580.* Nieuwkoop, 1987.

Prenter, Regin. *Das Bekenntnis von Augsburg: Eine Auslegung.* Erlangen, 1980. German translation of *Kirkens Lutherske bekendelse.*

Reinhard, Wolfgang, ed. *Bekenntnis und Geschichte: Die Confessio Augustana im historischen Zusammenhang.* Ringvorlesung der Universität Augsburg im Jubiläumsjahr 1980. Munich, 1981.

Vajta, Vilmos, ed. *Confessio Augustana, 1530–1580: Commemoration and Self-Examination.* Translated by David Lewis. Stuttgart, 1980.

HELMAR JUNGHANS
Translated from German by Robert E. Shillenn

AUGSBURG INTERIM. *See* Interims.

AUGUSTA, Jan (1500–1572), bishop of the Unity of Brethren (Bohemian Brethren) and theologian. He sought to establish cooperation between the Unity of Brethren and Martin Luther and also with the neo-Utraquists. Born in Prague in 1500, the son of an Utraquist milliner, Jan Augusta was trained in his father's craft. Around 1520 his reading of works by Bohemian reformers, especially those of Jan Hus and Thomas Štítný of Štítné, caused him to leave Prague and the Utraquists. In 1524 he joined a congregation of the Unity of Brethren in Mladá Boleslav. Five years later he was ordained a deacon in Brandýs and, in 1531, a priest. He worked in Benátky nad Jiserou, where the nobleman Friedrich of Donín was the patron of the brethren. Energetic and resolute, Augusta was elected bishop in 1532 and chose as his seat a congregation in Litomyšl in east Bohemia whose patron was Bohuš Kostka of Postupice.

From 1533 to 1542 the brethren cultivated contacts with Luther, first established in 1522 by Jan Roh of Domažlice during a journey to Wittenberg. By 1542 Augusta had visited Luther at least three times. A result of these contacts was the publication in Germany in 1538 of the confession of the brethren in Latin with an introduction by Luther. Augusta had revised the original version to make it more compatible with the views of Luther. Despite his affinity for Luther, Augusta remained loyal to the theology and practice of the Unity of Brethren. He viewed the German reformer as a colleague who stressed the Bible as the fundamental authority of the church.

As bishop, Augusta vainly sought toleration of the Unity of Brethren from Emperor Ferdinand. His efforts to broaden the contacts of the brethren led to disputes with the Utraquists, whom he reproached as inconsistent in their practice of Christianity, and with members of the brethren who criticized Augusta for his departure from their theology as it had been summarized by Luke of Prague.

After the Schmalkald War in 1547, in which nobles from the Unity of Brethren also played a role, congregations of the brethren were closed by royal command. Members were forced to join churches that were still permitted. This was true for the congregation in Litomyšl. Augusta and his assistant, Jakub Bílek, hid in the forest outside town but were betrayed and imprisoned in 1548 in Prague, where they were tortured. They were later incarcerated for many years at Křivoklát castle. Bílek later described in detail their tribulations there. Especially during the first years in prison, Augusta was allowed to produce theological works. In 1561 he appealed to the king for clemency. He was taken to Prague, where he engaged in a disputation with the Jesuits and representatives of the Utraquists. In order to gain his release Augusta declared his willingness to align with a church practicing Communion in both kinds. He did not, however, agree to join the Utraquists; nevertheless, in 1561 a synod of the Unity of Brethren denounced the artifice of Augusta. While Bílek was released from prison after accepting the Eucharist from the hands of a Utraquist priest, Augusta refused to participate and remained imprisoned until 1564. Shortly after he reconciled with leaders of the brethren at the synod in Lipník. However, the other leaders, especially Jan Blahoslav, repeatedly rebuffed Augusta's efforts to bring about a union of the brethren with the neo-Utraquists and Czech Lutherans in order to create a single Bohemian Protestant church. He tried to enlist the support of congregations in Bohemia, Moravia, and Poland for his endeavor but fell seriously ill, became paralyzed, and died on 13 January 1572 in Mladá Boleslav, where he was buried.

Augusta's first significant theological work, *Rozlouvání jedneho učného muže se sedlákam* (The Discourse of a Learned Man and a Peasant; 1532), emphasized the supremacy of God's authority, the certainty of redemption, and the fact that every believer is a theologian. The certainty of salvation was also the theme of *Knížka tato bez tytile jest o tomto: Jestli pravda by to člověk jistotně věděti mohl, že spasen bude* (This Book without a Title Is about the Following: Whether a Man Can Be Certain That He Would be Saved; 1543). His most penetrating polemic, *Pře Jana Augusty a kněžstva kališného* (The Contention of Jan Augusta and the Utraquist Priests; 1543), responded to those Utraquists who had attacked Augusta's *Zrcadlo kněžské* (The Mirror of Priesthood; 1541), a translation of *Antithesis verae et falsae ecclesiae* by Antonius Corvinus as adapted by Luther. Au-

gusta's most important work was a textbook of practical theology, *Umění díla Páné služebného* (Ways of Serving Our Lord) written in prison before 1550. It was called by its modern editor "the first practical theology of the world reformation." In prison he also began to write his *Sumovník* (Summary) and *Smysl a úmysl Kristův jako vlastní svátosti večeře jeho* (Christ's Understanding of the Sacrament of His Supper; 1562). The former reflected the strong influence of Luther on Augusta. His last significant work was *Instuce k reformaci utrakvistické konsistoře* (The Institution for the Reformation of the Utraquist Consistory; 1571), in which he urged that the Unity of Brethren and the Utraquists seek common ground on the basis of their Hussite heritage and that a new Calixtine church be established. His desire to bring together the various currents in the Czech Reformation was at least partially achieved, if only formally, by the presentation of the Bohemian Confession of 1575. It was also a theme taken up by another bishop of the brethren, Jan Amos Comenius, after the defeat of the Czech Protestants at the Battle of White Mountain in 1620.

BIBLIOGRAPHY

Bílek, Jakub. *Jan Augusta v letech samoty 1548–1564*. Edited by F. Bednář. Prague, 1942. Bílek's chronical. See the editor's important preface (pp. 5–35) for information on Augusta as well as historical background.

Hrejsa, F. *Dějiny křestanství v Československu*. Prague, 1947. See vol. 5.

Müller, J. Th. *Die Gefangenschaft des Johann Augusta Bischofs der böhmischen Brüder 1548–1564 und seines Diakonen Jakob Bílek*. Leipzig, 1895. Contains a German translation of Bílek's chronical.

———. *Geschichte der Böhmischen Brüder*. Herrnhut, 1931. See vol. 2.

Smolík, Josef. "Jan Augusta na Křivoklátě." In *Středočesky sborník historický*, p. 17off. Prague, 1957

———. "Poslední Augustova léta." In *Křestanská revue*, p. 34ff. Prague, 1972.

———. *Bratr Jan Augusta*. Prague, 1984. The basic monograph on Augusta. Contains bibliography of his writings as well as information regarding locations of manuscripts.

JAN B. LÁŠEK

AUGUSTINE (354–430), bishop and theologian. Born 13 November in Thagaste, north Africa, the son of a pagan father, Patricius, and a Christian mother, Monica, Augustine was educated in Madaura (grammar and rhetoric) and Carthage. His encounter with Cicero's *Hortensius* led him to ponder the nature of true happiness. Raised as a Christian, Augustine faulted Cicero for ignoring Christ and began to study the Bible; alienated by its style and content, however, he turned to the study of Manichaeanism (373–382). In 375 he returned to Thagaste as a teacher of grammar and a year later moved to Carthage. He lived in Rome in 383 and in the spring of 384 became a teacher of rhetoric in Milan. Fascinated by the sermons of Ambrose, he came to appreciate Catholic Christianity and abandoned Manichaeanism, with which he had been disenchanted since his days in Carthage. Thanks to the circle of Christian Neoplatonists in Milan he became acquainted with the writings of Porphyry and Plotinus. In Ambrose he had encountered a synthesis of Christianity and Neoplatonism that convinced him that the Catholic faith was consonant with philosophy, and he was confirmed in this opinion by his reading of Paul.

In a famous scene, while in a garden Augustine heard, probably on 1 August 386, a child's voice calling "take and read," and then found in *Romans* 13:13 an instruction to break with the world. This was Augustine's conversion to a monastic form of Christianity. He gave up his position and moved to a country estate where he engaged in meditation, read Virgil, and fought skepticism by looking to the teachings of the Neoplatonists.

In 387 he returned to Milan; that Easter he was baptized by Ambrose. The following year he traveled to Carthage and Thagaste. Much against his will, he was ordained in Hippo at the end of 390 or in early 391; his ministerial responsibilities began with Easter preaching. Probably in the winter of 395/396 he was consecrated coadjutor, and in 396 he succeeded Bishop Valerius. He lived for twenty-five years at Hippo and exercised an enormous influence on the church of north Africa and the West. Augustine died at Hippo as it was being besieged by the Vandals. His life to the time of his ordination as a priest is described in his *Confessiones*.

His most important writings were immensely significant to the Protestant reformers, especially to Luther, as Protestant theology is unthinkable without Augustine. Among Augustine's works are personal writings including *Confessiones* (397–401), *Soliloquia* (386), and *Retractationes* (426), as well as philosophical writings including *Contra Academicos* (386), *De ordine* (386), and *De beata vita* (396). A number of works were written in opposition to the Manichaeans, including *De moribus ecclesiae catholicae et de moribus Manichaeorum* (388–390), *Contra Adimantum Manichaei discipulum* (394), *De libero arbitrio* (388–395), *Contra epistulam (Manichaei), quam vocant fundamenti* (396), and *Contra Faustum Manichaeum* (398–404). The works *Contra epistulam Parmeniani* (404) and *De baptismo* (after 404) were anti-Donatist pieces. Still other writing were directed against the Pelagians: *De peccatorum meritis et remissione* (411), *De spiritu et littera* (412), *De natura et gratia* (413–415), *De gratia Christi et de peccato originali* (418), *De nuptiis et concupiscentia* (c.420), *Contra duas epistulas Pelagianorum* (419), *De natura et origine animae (de anima et eius origine)* (419), *Contra Iulianum* (421), *De gratia et libero arbitrio* (425), *De praedestinatione sanctorum* (429) and *De dono perseverantiae* (429). Finally, Augustine produced two major apologetic writings, *De vera religione* (c.390) and *De Civitate Dei* (413–426/427).

It can be demonstrated that all these titles were at least known by Luther, and it is conceivable that they were used by him, for a complete edition of Augustine had been published in Basel in 1506 by Johannes Amerbach. Augustine's theology, especially his teaching on grace, was the common

heritage of medieval theology, and was of course especially influential among the Augustinian Hermits, the order to which Luther belonged. Luther may have become conversant with Augustinian thought through other medieval theologians, through exegetes such as Lyra, or through canon law. Possibly he used other works as well, as evidenced by occasional citations.

No firm conclusions have been drawn regarding the reception of Augustine during the Reformation. There have been two approaches to the question. Leif Grane examined, by way of specific comparisons, Augustine's texts as used by Luther. Heiko Oberman studied Luther's thought on the basis of late medieval Augustinianism as perpetuated by Luther's monastic order, so that Luther was seen as thinking and writing as if Gregory of Rimini, Augustine Favaroni, and Jacob Perez were at his desk. Because the objective of a *via Gregorii* at Wittenberg University went unrealized, Luther never experienced an Augustinian version of the *via moderna*. Luther studied Augustine intently only at the time of the Leipzig Disputation and then looked to him merely to confirm his own theology. Luther's preoccupation with Augustine was limited primarily to questions of exegesis. He used Augustine chiefly as an avenue to gain a better understanding of Paul. The overall intention of Augustine's arguments was ignored, points were taken out of context—indeed at times Augustine was used to bolster arguments that were diametrically opposed to his own. According to Grane, Luther viewed Augustine through the lens of his own theology and his own understanding of Paul. The slowly developing anti-Pelagian Augustinianism—used during the Reformation as a support against scholasticism and Aristotle—was seen by Luther as parallel to the controversy between Augustine and Pelagius (see Bubenheimer).

As for Zwingli, the question of his reception of Augustinian tradition has not been answered. Calvin, meanwhile, appears to have made an independent study of Augustine. The influence of Augustinianism on the Reformation as a whole is a moot question, for all the reformers owed an indirect debt to Augustinian traditions in ways that today can no longer be calculated.

BIBLIOGRAPHY

Andresen, Carl. *Bibliographia Augustiniana*. Darmstadt, 1973.

Bubenheimer, Ulrich. "Augustinismus in der Reformationszeit." In *Theologische Realenzyklopädie*, edited by Gerhard Krause and Gerhard Müller vol. 4, pp. 718–721. Berlin and New York, 1979.

Delius, Hans-Ulrich. *Augustin als Quelle Luthers*. Berlin, 1984.

Grane, Leif. *Modus loquendi theologicus: Luthers Kampf um die Erneuerung der Theologie, 1515–1518*. Leiden, 1975.

Hamel, Adolf. *Der junge Luther und Augustin*. 2 vols. Reprint, New York, 1980.

Mayer, Cornelius Petrus, ed. *Augustinus-Lexikon*. Basel and Stuttgart, 1986.

Oberman, Heiko A. *The Dawn of the Reformation: Essays in Late Medieval and Early Reformation Thought*. Edinburgh, 1986.

Schindler, Alfred. "Augustin/Augustinismus I." In *Theologische Realen-*

zyklopädie, edited by Gerhard Krause and Gerhard Müller, vol. 4, pp. 646–698. Berlin and New York, 1979.

Stakemeier, Eduard. *Der Kampf um Augustin auf dem Tridentinum.* Paderborn, 1937.

HANS-ULRICH DELIUS
Translated from German by Hans J. Hillerbrand

AUGUSTINIANS. A generic term used to designate the members of several religious orders of the Catholic church, the Augustinians are so named because their community life is governed by the observance of the Rule of Saint Augustine. This text, in contrast to other monastic rules, does not take the form of a systematic set of regulations for the life of a particular religious order. Rather, it originated from a series of precepts dictated by Saint Augustine, toward the end of the fourth century, for the first male monastery in Hippo. This rule, particularly from the time of the Fourth Lateran Council in 1215, was adopted by various religious orders as their constitutional law. Today the term *Augustinian* has taken on two different meanings: in the broad sense it includes some 350 orders and congregations, of both men and women, which, from the Middle Ages to the present, observed or have observed the Rule of Saint Augustine; in the strict sense, it designates the male branches of two orders, the Canons Regular of Saint Augustine and the Hermits of Saint Augustine. It is in this strict meaning and within the limits of the sixteenth century that this topic will be discussed.

Canons Regular of Saint Augustine. The Canons Regular appeared about the eighth century; they were originally merely groups of priests bound together by the taking of vows and living in communities independent from one another, dedicated to the religious service of a given church. No bond united the individual communities to one another; starting from the time of the Second Lateran Council of 1059, however, the obligation of adopting the Rule of Saint Augustine was imposed on them. From that time on, within the religious family of the canons regular, independent religious orders in the true sense of the word began to form, such as the Canons Regular of Saint Norbert, or Premonstratensians (1120), the Gilbertines of Sempringham (1146), and the Chanoines Croisiers of Liège (1215). Of these three groups the most important is the first. In the first half of the sixteenth century, however, this group stood in need of real reform. In Spain, this reform was set in motion by the initiative of Philip II, who in 1567 entrusted its implementation to the order of the Hieronymites, while the renewal of the rest of the Premonstratensian order was undertaken by Abbot Jean Despruets after 1573.

Beginning in the fifteenth century, the trend for individual communities of canons to federate into congregations placed under the jurisdiction of a superior general introduced a profound change in the structures of the order. The birth in Italy in the fifteenth century of the Congregation of the Most Holy Savior of Bologna, also called the *Renana* Congregation (1419) and of the Lateran Congregation of the Most Holy Savior (1445) did not, however, succeed in stemming a slackening of discipline in the period before the conclusion of the Council of Trent. Despite this, the order gave to the church some men worthy of note, such as Antonio Contarini, patriarch of Venice; Lucio Vitruvio Roscio, a philosopher and man of letters; Bishop Agostino Steuco, head of the Vatican Library and the author of works on exegesis, philosophy, and apologetics; and the zealous bishop of Alba, Marco Gerolamo Vida, a reform bishop who took part in the Council of Trent and who also became well known for his religious poem *Christias*, which won for him the title of the "Christian Virgil."

Of particular relevance for the history of the order, however, was the congregation of Wildesheim (1395), whose name is linked to that expression of Catholic reform represented by the religious movement known as the *devotio moderna*. Although in the first half of the sixteenth century, as a result of the closing of numerous houses in the territories that had gone over to the Protestant Reformation, this congregation had gone through a period of crisis, a definite renewal came about through the reforming endeavors of Johannes Latomus. The reformer of the houses of the order in Lorraine at the beginning of the seventeenth century was Pierre Fourier. It was from the Congregation of Our Savior, which he founded, that the congregation of France was to emerge later in the seventeenth century.

Hermits of Saint Augustine. The order of the Hermits of Saint Augustine, a mendicant order more commonly known as the Augustinian order, owes its name from having arisen in 1244 from the merger of several hermitical groups. The slackening of discipline that subsequently became apparent led to a reaction, similar to what had occurred in other religious orders, that took the form of a return of some communities to a more rigorous following of the rule. This phenomenon became known as the observantist movement. The order was governed by a prior general and had its own governing body in the general chapter that met periodically. Toward the beginning of the sixteenth century the Hermits of Saint Augustine numbered about twenty thousand, living in about a thousand religious houses. These houses, in turn, were grouped into twenty-six provinces. Ten houses had joined the observantists; the only one of these in Germany was the congregation of Saxony, one of whose members was Martin Luther.

Although the Augustinian order had not reached the degree of decadence that prevailed in other sectors of the church, overall the order was undoubtedly going through a period of crisis. Energetic reform was initiated as a result of the election of a new prior general in 1507, Giles of Viterbo. Only in 1518 did he leave that office, when he was named a cardinal. An eminent humanist, philosopher, and theologian, Giles set his sights on restoring both the letter and the spirit of the pristine observance of the Augustinian rule, particularly with regard to the respect of cloister and the common life, that he saw as the principal means of spiritual perfection. The results of his efforts, though worthy of note, were not enough to prevent Luther's separation from the church of Rome nor to prevent other similar defections within the order, such as those of Wenceslaus Linck, Johannes Lang, and Gabriel Zwilling in Germany, those of George Browne (later the first Anglican archbishop of Dublin) and Miles Coverdale (the first to produce the entire Bible in English) in England, and those of Agostino Mainardi and Giuliano della Rovere in Italy.

Despite this crisis, Giles's work was carried forward by Girolamo Seripando, prior-general from 1539 to 1551, who also was named a cardinal. A great theologian, Seripando was the main personality to whom the order looked in the sixteenth century and one of the most important reform figures in the church of his time. As general of the order, he was the first to travel to some of the provinces outside Italy: between 1539 and 1542 he personally visited, in addition to the Italian provinces, those in France, Spain, and Portugal.

Besides Giles of Viterbo and Seripando, in the sixteenth century the order could point to a number of significant figures, such as San Tomás de Villanueva, who in 1544 became archbishop of Valencia, a diocese where he carried on intense pastoral activity that anticipated the reforms later mandated by the Council of Trent; the historian Onofrio Panvinio; the theologian Cristoforo da Padova, who was also later to hold the office of general; Gaspar Casal, bishop of Coimbra from 1579 on and the author of works of philosophy and of dogmatic and moral theology; and Luis de León, whose three books *De los nombres de Cristo* represent a masterpiece both of mystical literature and of Christocentric theology.

Of particular significance to the history of the order was the observant province of Castile, not only on account of the large number of its religious houses but also because it was responsible for the creation of provinces in mission territories: Mexico in 1568, Peru and the Philippines in 1575, Quito in 1575. The province of Castile was also the birthplace of the *recolección* movement, which promoted a more intense contemplative life; the first house that embraced it was the convent of Talavera de la Reina in 1589.

Having comparable characteristics, the congregation of the Discalced Friars of Saint Augustine of the kingdom of Naples arose in Italy. It was canonically approved by Clement VIII in 1599. It spread subsequently beyond the borders of Italy, extending as far as Vienna and Prague. Both the Discalced and the Recollect Friars remained subject to the jurisdiction of the prior general of the Augustinian Hermits, until they became independent orders during the twentieth century.

[*See also* Augustine.]

BIBLIOGRAPHY

Canonicorum Regularium Sodalitates Decimo Sexto revoluto saeculo ab ortu Sancti Augustini Episcopi Hipponensis. Vorau, 1954. A complete review of all the congregations that belong to the order of the canons regular.

Estrada Robles, Basilio. *Los Agustinos Ermitaños en España hasta el siglo XIX.* Madrid, 1988. See pp. 30–104.

Giroud, Charles. *L'ordre des chanoines réguliers de Saint-Augustin et ses diverses formes de régime interne: Essai de synthèse historico-juridique.* Martigny, Switzerland, 1961.

Goñi Gaztambide, José. "La reforma de los Premonstratenses españoles del siglo XVI." *Hispania Sacra* 13 (1960), 5–92.

Gutiérrez, David. *The Augustinians from the Protestant Reformation to the Peace of Westphalia, 1518–1648.* Villanova, Pa., 1979. The best synthesis of the history of the order during the sixteenth century.

Luijk, Benigno A. L. van. *L'ordine agostiniano e la riforma monastica dal Cinquecento alla vigilia della Rivoluzione francese: Un sommario cronologico-storico.* Heverlee, Belgium, 1973. See pp. 13–128.

Martin, Francis X. "The Augustinian Order on the Eve of the Reformation." In *Miscellanea Historiae Ecclesiasticae II: Congrès de Vienne, août–septembre 1965,* pp. 71–104. Bibliothèque de la Revue d'histoire ecclésiastique, 44. Louvain, 1967. A study of the history of the Hermits of Saint Augustine during the generalate of Giles of Viterbo.

Post, R. R. "The Windesheimer after c.1485: Confrontation with the Reformation and Humanism." In *The Reformation in Medieval Perspective,* edited by Steven E. Ozment, pp. 157–184. Chicago, 1971.

Rodríguez Rodríguez, Isacio, ed. *Agustinos en América y Filipinas.* Proceedings of an international conference, Valladolid, 16–21 April 1990. 2 vols. Valladolid and Madrid, 1990. A series of contributions on the missions of the Augustinians.

Weyns, N. J. "La réforme des Prémontrés aux XVIe et XVIIe siècles, particulièrement dans la circarie de Brabant." *Analecta Praemonstratensia* 46 (1970), 5–71.

AGOSTINO BORROMEO
Translated from Italian by Robert E. Shillenn

AUGUSTINUS, Aurelius. *See* Augustine.

AURIFABER, Johannes

(Ger., Goldschmied; 1519?–1575), German Lutheran pastor and compiler and editor of Martin Luther's writings. Aurifaber studied at Wittenberg (1537–1540), and in 1545 he became Luther's personal attendant until the reformer's death the following year. After a stint as chaplain to John Frederick of Saxony (1546–1547), Aurifaber moved to Weimar as court preacher. His fourteen years in Weimar were distinguished by taking the side of Matthias Flacius Illyricus in the various intra-Lutheran controverises. Aurifaber signed opinions opposing the Augsburg Interm (1548) and Osiander's notion of justification (1552), challenged the "Adiaphorists" and the "Majorists" (1556), and edited (with Flacius) the *Weimar Book of Confutation* (1558). When the Flacians fell out of favor at the Weimar court in 1561, Aurifaber moved to Eisleben. In 1565 Aurifaber fled the plague and became pastor at Erfurt, where he died in 1575.

Aurifaber's most enduring contribution was his effort to

collect, edit, and publish Luther's works. Aurifaber traveled throughout Germany assembling both published and unpublished documents associated with Luther. His first such publication was a volume containing Luther's last four sermons (1546). From 1553 to 1558 he collaborated with Georg Rörer on what is known as the Jena edition of Luther's works, which he completed after Rörer's death. His editing activities continued after he moved to Eisleben, where he published two volumes of Luther's German writings (1564–1565), a volume of Luther's Latin correspondence (1565), and his famous edition of Luther's *Tischreden* of 1566. (It proved to be Aurifaber's most successful and influential publication, going through twenty editions, the latest in 1968). His editing helped determine the standard characterization of Luther's personality until the nineteenth century, when scholars began to question Aurifaber's methodology. Later scholarship (e.g., Junghans), however, has come to a greater appreciation of the accuracy of Aurifaber's work.

BIBLIOGRAPHY

Bente, F. *Historical Introductions to the Book of Concord.* Reprint, Saint Louis, 1965. Interprets Aurifaber in relationship to the emerging sixteenth-century Lutheran confessional consensus.

Jauernig, Reinhold. "Johannes Aurifaber." In *Des Herren Namen Steht Uns Bei,* edited by Karl Brinkel and Herbert von Hintzenstern, pp. 147–154. Berlin, 1961. A general introduction to Aurifaber's life, for non-specialists.

Junghans, Helmar. "Aurifaber, Johannes." In *Theologische Realenzyklopädie,* edited by Gerhard Krause and Gerhard Müller, vol. 4, pp. 752–755. Berlin, 1979. The most thorough scholarly biographical sketch of Aurifaber available, with excellent bibliographies.

Kawerau, Gustav. "Aurifaber, Johannes." In *Realencyklopädie für protestantische Theologie und Kirche,* edited by Albert Hauck, vol. 2, pp. 290–293. Leipzig, 1897. An abbreviated translation of this article appears in *The New Schaff-Herzog Encyclopedia of Religious Knowledge,* edited by Samuel M. Jackson, vol. 1, pp. 374–75, Grand Rapids, Mich., 1949.

WILLIAM R. RUSSELL

AUSTRIA. In its modern form, meaning the eight federal states of Vorarlberg, the Tirol, Styria, Salzburg, Upper and Lower Austria, Carinthia, and the Burgenland, "Austria" did not exist in the sixteenth century. While contemporaries sometimes referred to Lower Austria as the archduchy of Austria, the term was more commonly associated with the dynasty that ruled many of those lands, the Habsburgs, or the "house of Austria." Even that expression was a relatively recent coinage, first used consistently by Emperor Frederick III (1415–1493). Nor did the dynasty's "Austrian" patrimony include at all times the totality of present-day Austria. The Burgenland belonged largely to the kingdom of Hungary, to be sure among the Austrian Habsburg holdings after 1526, but separate and distinct from the Austrian inheritance itself. While the Habsburgs exerted considerable influence in the archbishopric of Salz-

burg, the land was an ecclesiastical principality with its own seat in the imperial diet of the Holy Roman Empire. It did not become part of the house of Austria's holdings until 1805. On the other hand, the Habsburgs also controlled areas in the southwest of the empire which are now part of the Federal Republic of Germany, and in the southeastern regions of Europe, currently incorporated into Slovenia, Croatia, and, in the case of Trieste, Italy.

During much of the Reformation era, the "Austrian" lands of the dynasty were organized administratively under the following titles: Anterior Austria (*Vorderösterreich*), which took in Vorarlberg and the Habsburg holdings in Swabia and Alsace; Upper Austria (*Oberösterreich*), or the Tirol; Inner Austria (*Innerösterreich*) including Carinthia, Styria, and Carniola (*Krain*), now part of modern Slovenia. Beyond these was Lower Austria (*Niederösterreich*), which itself had two parts: Austria below the Enns and Austria above the Enns, the latter developing a separate political identity comparatively late. Each region had its own estates with its structural idiosyncrasies, both internally and in the relationship to the territorial ruler. In Styria and the Tirol, where vast stretches of mountain made communication difficult, certain areas had local or partial estates of their own. Spokesmen from rural peasant communes made up the fourth chamber of the Tirolean estates. A more conventional grouping of lords, knights, prelates, and towns spoke for the eastern lands. In the Tirol, the territorial ruler had extensive powers in the various types of local courts. In Lower and Inner Austria, the nobility and prelates played a far more active role in judicial affairs.

Vienna, the largest city, indeed the only city of the Habsburg Austrian patrimony, held between 20,000 and 40,000 people by 1527. Feuds and warfare in the region during the fifteenth century, the shift of finance and trade to places such as Augsburg and Nuremberg, and a general stagnation in its exports, the wine trade excepted, had much reduced the economic importance of the Habsburg capital. The only other town near it in size was the mining settlement of Schwaz in the Tirol, though as the silver deposits began to run out many of its inhabitants drifted away, not to be replaced during the course of the sixteenth century. Wiener Neustadt (Austria below the Enns), Bruck an der Mur (Styria), Judenburg (Styria), Linz (Austria above the Enns), Innsbruck (Tirol), and Hall (Tirol) served as trading centers for spices, rice, cotton, sugar, fine fabrics, tropical fruits, and glass that came from Venice.

In general, population in the Habsburg Austrian lands rose throughout the period, markedly straining peasant holdings. Many previously employed in agriculture moved into mining, trade, and crafts more lucrative when plied in (what were by contemporary standards) urban settings. Though the overwhelming mass of people, estimated to be about eighty percent, remained in the countryside, many supplemented their incomes with occasional ventures into commerce, service, or both. Some peasants became small traders; indeed those who lived along the current Slovenian border profited more from such enterprise in the sixteenth century than did their local middle-class counterparts. Others ran modest establishments such as hospices for travelers and grain depots.

The inflation of the sixteenth century, which began to make itself felt in Austria in the 1530s, increased economic burdens all around. Compelled to finance massive military undertakings against the Turks, the Habsburgs asked time and again for new revenues, both ordinary and extraordinary. The estates of the various lands cooperated, but the greater landlords covered their expenses, especially in Lower Austria, by expanding their holdings at the expense of both the lower nobility and the peasantry. Where they could pass along the costs of an evermore intrusive central government to their tenant labor they did so. Violent local resistance was commonplace, a noteworthy example being a bloody peasant eruption in Austria above the Enns between 1594 and 1599 that eventually forced Emperor Rudolph II (1552–1612) to intervene.

Like most German princes, the Habsburgs had often partitioned their Austrian lands among their sons, though the eldest among them was generally designated the head of the house. Emperor Maximilian I (1459–1519) was the first of his dynasty in over a hundred years to control the entirety of the Habsburg Austrian patrimony. Ambitious to the point of fantasy, he was always in need of funds for the wars he waged in Italy, the empire, and elsewhere. Given his far-flung responsibilities, he was not always available to argue his position in person before the various estates and the committees through which they often worked. During the 1490s as part of a systematic plan to restructure his government, he created a set of administrative and judicial organs (*Regimente*) that could act in his name during his absences. Though these bodies did indeed take shape and function, the estates much resented the loss of direct contact with their ruler. They quickly fell into a pattern of granting what their sovereign wished only if he recognized their privileges as well. The cause of central authority rarely prevailed in these negotiations. The Tirolean "Small Landbook" (*Landeslibell*) of 1511, for example, made it almost impossible for the territorial ruler to commit it to any war beyond one for local self-defense. While these provisions were unique to the Tirol, they showed the power the estates had over their needy prince and the lengths to which they could use it. Maximilian's financial woes also led him to mortgage the silver mines of the Tirol to the wealthy merchant princes of the empire, most notably the Fuggers of Augsburg. These measures did much to alienate the local population.

All these arrangements were challenged, or virtually brought to a standstill, following Maximilian's death. The Tirol excepted, estates throughout the Habsburg Austrian lands called for disbanding the administrative councils and

the restoration of what they believed was the earlier, more directly personal form of political relationship to their territorial ruler. Maximilian's successor to his German inheritance, his grandson Ferdinand (1503–1564), was plunged into this scene upon his arrival in the Austrian lands. A territorial division, agreed upon with his brother, Emperor Charles V (1500–1558), in 1522, gave him the bulk of the dynasty's Austrian possessions. The young archduke moved ruthlessly against the sedition in Austria below the Enns, where the estates had adopted a particularly dangerous policy: they claimed that, until the new prince received their oath of fealty, they were responsible for government in the territory. To fund their self-appointed charge, they appropriated the regalian incomes of their prince. Ferdinand checked this movement quickly, with his punitive action falling chiefly upon municipal leaders in Vienna, the provincial capital. Here he executed several key figures, chief among them the mayor, Martin Siebenbürger. He put the city tightly under the control of the territorial ruler, thus beginning a policy his successors would employ consistently and with great effect throughout their territories. A commission of the prince, for example, now inspected the lists of nominees to the city councils, then passed these on to the prince who made the final selection. The arrangement proved strategically advantageous, most especially during the Counter-Reformation of the seventeenth century.

Ferdinand had to master an equally threatening, though somewhat different, situation in the Tirol. Here a serious uprising of peasants and miners exploded during his first years in the Austrian lands. In 1525 the rebels called for removal of foreign managements in the mines along with some of Ferdinand's close advisers whom he had brought with him from Spain and who were thought to be profiting unduly in the region. Following the lead of the peasant rebels in other German lands, they called for religious reforms in the evangelical vein as well. The movement inspired Michael Gaismaier, the one-time secretary of the bishop of Brixen, to propose that all distinctions of order and class be abolished, to be replaced by an egalitarian commonwealth in which the mines would be publicly managed. After some initial indecisiveness, Ferdinand suppressed this as well. Gaismaier was assassinated under cloudy circumstances in Padua in 1532. Though Ferdinand could not be directly implicated, he had tried to get rid of the troublesome clerk several times and therefore remains a suspect in the entire affair.

Like his grandfather, Ferdinand viewed organizational reform as the way to more effective use of the Habsburg Austrian territories for financial and military purposes. During the 1520s he established an elaborate administrative edifice to oversee his affairs. Consisting of a court chancellory, court treasury, and the court council—a court war council was put in place in 1556—the structure served as the model upon which other German territorial princes recast their own governments during the early modern era. Though their actual operation throughout the sixteenth century was often far more casual than as formally described, these offices, with clearly defined subordinate branches, made the whole scheme easy to imitate or adapt. Some features of division of territorial responsibilities among prince and estates remained. The latter were theoretically responsible for raising all extraordinary revenues; however, Ferdinand created a series of subordinate treasuries, so-called *Raitkammern*, to receive and account for these funds. Until the 1540s, he experimented with holding general meetings of the estates or their representatives in the interests of deliberative efficiency. He was, however, often at a considerable disadvantage in such settings. This was especially true when the estates worked through committees that were prepared to deal with him over long periods of time. He eventually abandoned the practice.

The Reformation introduced a new level of fractiousness into the economic, social, and political life of the Austrian lands as a whole. Lutheran ideas spread there quickly, both by word of mouth and printed materials. Between 1519 and 1522, fifteen of the Wittenberg reformer's writings were published in Vienna alone. In January of 1522, Paul Speratus (1484–1551) preached on the subjects of monastic vows, marriage, and baptism in Saint Stephen's cathedral in the heart of the city. By 1526, the call for general reform of church conditions had reached as far to the southeast as Villach in Carinthia.

As emperors, actual and would-be, the Habsburgs were bound to uphold the doctrines of the Church of Rome. Were they to renounce Catholicism, they would have reduced themselves to just one of several German princely houses and by no means the most significant among these. The hope of increasing revenues through confiscation of church lands, so tempting to many of their counterparts in the empire, held little advantage for them. Comparatively speaking, the Austrian Habsburgs had more control over religious institutions than did many other German secular rulers. While the holdings of several independent bishoprics reached deeply into their lands—Brixen and Trent in the south and east, Passau and Salzburg in the north—the dynasty's Austrian patrimony had much leeway to draw upon the resources of church properties within the lands they actually governed. Any change in these arrangements threatened both their financial well-being and their sovereignty. This was all the more alarming when the core of support for the Lutheran movement in Austria came, as it did, from the estates, especially the nobility, whose religious sensibilities had been sharpened by the abortive Erasmian reform at the turn of the sixteenth century. Confessional convictions reinforced the political and economic self-awareness of these men, thereby further polarizing relations between the Habsburgs and the representatives of their various lands. Though Lutheranism would take root in Austrian towns as well, it

was often under noble patronage rather than municipal sponsorship, especially in the eastern regions.

Ferdinand I's government first tried to stem the movement with various punitive tactics. Following the imperial Edict of Worms issued by his brother, Charles V, in 1521, Ferdinand formally condemned Luther's ideas in 1523. Another mandate in 1527 prescribed property confiscation, exile, and death for those who refused to abandon the new teachings. The first two measures were sometimes enforced, though not consistently. Actual executions were, however, very rare.

Such policies had little apparent effect on individuals. Lutheran circles arose around important noblemen such as Christoph II Jörger (1502–1578), in Austria above the Enns and Siegmund von Dietrichstein (1480–1553) a trusted official of both Maximilian and Ferdinand in Inner Austria. However, even after 1530, when the Augsburg Confession was an established and published fact, there was no Lutheran church as such in the Austrian lands. Though the evangelical faith spread ever more widely, efforts to give it an institutional presence never went unchallenged for very long from the Habsburg territorial rulers, regardless of how intensely they were committed to the faith of Rome.

The Reformation in the Tirol developed somewhat differently. Here Lutheran teachings were crushed in 1525 along with the mass uprisings that often echoed them. Anabaptism, however, which appeared in the area about the same time, did capture the popular imagination for a while. Balthasar Hubmaier, Hans Hut, and George Blaurock all preached in the region. The practice of withdrawal from the general body politic espoused by their followers, which often encouraged some form of pacifism, made these people the target of merciless persecution by Habsburg authorities. Overall, however, the Tirol would be the most reliably Catholic part of the Habsburg Austrian lands, especially after 1564, when it passed to Ferdinand's son, Ferdinand II (1529–1595) of the Tirol, a firm supporter of the traditional church.

The devoutly Catholic Ferdinand I was well aware of the pervasive corruption in the parishes and cloisters of the Austrian lands. In 1528 and again in 1544, his reform commissions catalogued the doctrinal, moral, and structural abuses they found in these establishments. Locally and in Rome, he urged that these be corrected. His subjects, particularly the nobility of eastern and southeastern Austria, were unwilling to wait. After 1535 their sons often went to Protestant universities as part of their grand tour. The first Austrian enrolled at Wittenberg in 1539. By 1550, large numbers of Lutheran preachers were appearing in the Habsburg lands. For all their concern, Ferdinand and his successors failed to reform Catholic institutions significantly through the sixteenth century. The nobility of Austria below the Enns exercised heavy influence on religious life in Vienna; in Graz, the Styrian capital, Lutheranism flourished with the support of the estates. Where Protestants controlled substantial amounts of property, Protestant congregations flourished. By 1580, around ninety percent of the nobility of Austria below the Enns was Protestant, the lords (*Herrenstand*) being somewhat more heavily represented, the knights (*Ritterstand*) somewhat less. By 1620, with the Counter-Reformation well under way, seventy percent of the two groups still held to evangelical teaching and practice. Similar conditions prevailed in Austria above the Enns where, Protestantism, especially Lutheranism, had a wide popular as well as noble following.

However, the success of Lutheranism owed as much to the circumstances in which the Habsburgs found themselves as it did to the intrinsic appeal of the evangelical message. The forces of Sultan Süleyman I had actually besieged Vienna in 1529 and came close to doing so again in 1532; neither Ferdinand I nor Maximilian II could afford to antagonize their patrimonial estates when they needed military support against the Turks. This was all the more true as the size of mercenary armies deemed necessary to turn back the challenge from Constantinople reached proportions heretofore unknown in central Europe. Ferdinand followed a policy of religious compromise with the imperial estates in order to win their aid; he did the same in his Austrian lands. The Protestants in the latter were quick to pick up this cue. His vigorous support of the Peace of Augsburg of 1555 and his equally insistent quest in Rome for permission to extend communion in both kinds to his lands should this be tactically useful inspired many in the Austrian estates to press for free exercise of their Protestant faith.

Emperor Maximilian II (1527–1576), who succeeded his father in 1564, encouraged this behavior even more. From the middle of the 1540s until his father's death, he moved from sympathy with some Lutheran goals to something near open support of them. Once in power, however, he made known his intentions to follow his father's religious policies and to continue the search for reconciliation of the traditional and the evangelical faiths as specified in the Augsburg settlement. With Calvinism, which began to find its way into the Austrian lands in the 1560s, he would have nothing to do.

The Genevan reformation remained a marginal confession in the Austrian lands though it won some key converts within the nobility of Austria above the Enns. Among them was George von Tschernembl, the leader of the area's Protestants at the outbreak of the Thirty Years' War. However, the more rigorous reading of Lutheranism spread by Matthias Flacius Illyricus and his followers did make crucial inroads throughout the Habsburg Austrian territories. Some argue that between 1565 and 1580, this persuasion, which differed from the more moderate views of Philipp Melanchthon in matters of original sin and the distinctions between accident and substance, dominated Lutheran circles in the area.

Protestant sectarianism did much to hamper the reunification of the old and the new confessions; it also helped to sour Maximilian's attitude toward organized confessions of any kind. In fact, he never did cut his ties to Rome completely. It was he who took the first steps toward the revitalized Catholicism closely associated with his successors. In 1568 he established a *Klosterrat* charged with promoting sound moral, spiritual, and intellectual life in Austrian monastic establishments, which was crucial to the Counter-Reformation to come.

But it was also under Maximilian that Lutheranism made its most significant advances in Austria. In 1568, faced with debts of nearly two million florins, he asked the estates of Austria below the Enns to take them over. In return, he granted the lords and knights, but not the towns and markets which were Habsburg domainal property, free exercise of the Lutheran faith in their homes and in their various properties. They were not, however, to build any churches. These arrangements were also conditional upon the convening of a theological commission charged with composing an order of worship that would further confessional reunification. He came to a similar bargain with the estates of Austria above the Enns later that year. David Chytraeus, an elderly Lutheran scholar of moderate persuasions, was brought from the University of Rostock to direct the task. The panel finished its work in 1570; angered by publication of the finished product, the *Kirchenagenda*, before he sanctioned it, Maximilian refused to accept the document, though he did agree the following year to continue the concessions he had made in 1568. His youngest brother, Archduke Charles (1540–1590), who inherited the lands of Inner Austria in his father's territorial partition, made similar concessions to the nobility of those lands in the *Libell* of Bruck in 1578.

Religious privilege had therefore become a form of noble privilege. It was a relationship calculated to encourage demands for even greater public freedom, including the establishment of Lutheran churches and holding services within cities and towns. At first Protestant worship took place in public buildings designed for other uses, such as the Lower Austrian administrative building in Vienna (*Landesgebäude*) or its counterparts in Graz and Linz. Private chapels in noble town houses were opened to the general public as well. Some already-existing churches were converted to Protestant uses; indeed, during the generally tolerant years of Maximilian II's reign, Lutherans and Catholics occasionally shared the same quarters for their public devotions, often to the bewilderment of some in their congregations.

This general laissez-faire continued in Austria above and below the Enns during the early years of Emperor Rudolph II's reign. However, he gradually revealed that he understood the dangers that the interpenetration of political and religious rights brought. He announced that the disposition over religious matters was solely in the hands of the territorial ruler. With his brother Ernst (1553–1595), who had grown up with him in Spain, serving as his governor in Lower Austria, he ordered the nobility there to remove Protestant worship and their school from the provincial administration building in Vienna in 1578. Protestant members of the Vienna city council were dismissed and replaced by Catholics. In 1581 Rudolph took away the power of decision in religious matters from his Lower Austrian administration and put it in the hands of the court chancellory. Catholic conversions multiplied. Between 1610 and 1620 it became clear that the Habsburgs were no longer prepared to take Protestants into their governments. The percentage of Catholic nobility gradually increased, a development made weightier still because some Catholic lords and knights now owned very substantial properties and had ready-made confessional allies among the prelates in the estates. By 1620, more than thirty percent of the lords of Austria below the Enns were Catholic.

But the most significant turn in the Protestant cause before the Thirty Years' War came in Archduke Charles's Inner Austria. In 1579 he agreed with Ferdinand of the Tirol and Duke William of Bavaria that concessions to Protestantism must stop. Married to a devoutly Catholic Wittelsbach princess, Charles and his advisers had begun to read the *Libell* of Bruck idiosyncratically almost as soon as he issued it. Wolfgang Schranz, the vice-chancellor, insisted that the articles permitting free exercise of Lutheranism among the noble members of the estates were never included in the agreement. In 1580, Charles forbade Protestant worship in the major cities of Inner Austria; in 1585 he raised the Jesuit college in Graz, his capital, to the status of a university. He died in 1590, leaving a minor son, the future Emperor Ferdinand II (1578–1637). Upon reaching his majority, he continued his parents' vigorous attack on the reformed faiths. In 1599, the re-Catholicization of Inner Austria was declared to be an official policy—only the personal beliefs of the nobility were exempt. All others who resisted were threatened with punishment or exile. Evangelical services were to cease. Influenced by the doctrine of "suffering obedience" (*leidender Gehorsam*) that emanated from Württemberg and by the need to defend the borders of Inner Austria against a major confrontation with the Turks, the nobility of Styria offered only token opposition to these policies. Austria was on the way to becoming a land where, well into the modern era, Protestants, among others, were officially classified as "un-Catholics" (*Akatholiker*), a term first used in the seventeenth century.

However, intradynastic conflict that flared up during Rudolph's reign as emperor delayed the general re-Catholicization of the Habsburg Austrian lands. Transferring his capital from Vienna to Prague after 1583, Rudolph left the government of Austria above and below the Enns to his brothers Ernst and Matthias (1557–1619). Operating all but independently following the death of the former in 1595,

Matthias was willing to compromise his initially stern anti-Protestantism to win the support of the estates in both areas as he tried to unseat his eldest brother. Significant concessions of religious freedom made in 1609 were crucially important in Austria above the Enns, where George von Tschernembl argued that the territorial prince should govern only with the consent of the nobility—a position that would ineluctably lead such a ruler to the toleration of various confessions—and that rulers who violated such principles should be removed. It was this view that led the estates of the area to make common cause with their Bohemian counterparts in 1618, thereby setting the stage for an armed confrontation with the Habsburgs and the eventual downfall of the Protestant cause as a whole in Austria.

Catholic members of the estates never did accept Matthias's recognition of Protestant religious privileges, further straining interconfessional relations in the territories of eastern Austria. While some Protestant members of the estates in Austria below the Enns followed the lead of their counterparts in Linz, Ferdinand II, now emperor, was able to win the support of many among them at the outbreak of the Thirty Years' War. He promised to allow Lutheran practice to continue on the lands of these loyalists, even though the Counter-Reformation was making deep inroads here. Austria above the Enns was given as a fief to Maximilian I of Bavaria, who put down the rebellious estates by force. In 1624 Ferdinand ordered all Protestant pastors to leave that land and all Protestant schools closed. Though this and similar measures met with considerable resistance, most notably in the peasant uprising of 1625/26, the fate of public Protestant worship was sealed, both here and in Austria below the Enns. *Geheimprotestantismus* ("secret Protestantism") continued in the Habsburg Austrian lands through the eighteenth century, indeed until 1781, when Emperor Joseph II (1741–1790) extended public freedom to Lutheran and Calvinist practice through his Edict of Toleration.

[*See also* Ferdinand I; Habsburg, House of; *and* Maximilian II.]

BIBLIOGRAPHY

Bruckmüller, Ernst. *Sozialgeschichte Österreichs*. Vienna, 1985. Section on early modern period (pp. 133–282) incorporates latest work on topic.

Bücking, Jürgen. *Michael Gaismair: Reformer, Sozialrebell, Revolutionär*. Stuttgart, 1978. Valuable analysis of ideological issues which have emerged in social history of early modern Austrian lands, in this case the Tirol. Manuscript left unfinished at author's death.

Dörrer, Fridolin, ed. *Die Bauernkriege und Michael Gaismair*. Innsbruck, 1982. Strong on social and economic history of the Tirol.

Evans, R. J. W. *Rudolf II and His World: A Study in Intellectual History, 1576–1612*. Oxford, 1973. A rich portrait of the court and intellectual atmosphere within which Rudolf functioned.

———. *The Making of the Habsburg Monarchy, 1550–1700*. Oxford, 1979. An important cultural and social synthesis.

Grüll, Georg. *Der Bauer im Lande ob der Enns am Ausgang des 16. Jahrhunderts*. Vienna, 1969. A detailed, often heavily quantitative, picture of peasant conditions in a crucial territory.

Lhotsky, Alphons. *Das Zeitalter des Hauses Österreich: Die ersten Jahre der Regierung Ferdinands I. in Österreich, 1520–1527.* Vienna, 1971. Tells the institutional and political story with a matchless grasp of sources.

Loesche, Georg. *Geschichte des Protestantismus im vormaligen und in neuen Österreich.* 3d ed. Leipzig, 1930. Lively Protestant account written from perspective of entire Habsburg empire. Excellent bibliography of older works.

Loserth, Johann. *Die Reformation und Gegenreformation in den innerösterreichischen Ländern im 16. Jahrhundert* (1898). Reprint, Nieuwkoop, 1970. The rise and fall of Lutheranism in southeastern Austria. Written with dramatic flair and sense of appropriate anecdote. Useful documentary appendixes.

Mecenseffy, Grete. *Geschichte des Protestantismus in Österreich.* Graz, 1956. Brief and reliable introduction from Protestant standpoint.

Pickl, Othmar. *Die wirtschaftlichen Auswirkungen der Türkenkriege.* Graz, 1971. Though most of the papers at this symposium dealt with eastern and southeastern Europe, this volume makes abundantly clear the impact of Turkish wars on all the Habsburg lands.

Reingrabner, Gustav. *Adel und Reformation: Beiträge zur Geschichte des protestantischen Adels im Lande unter der Enns während des 16. und 17. Jahrhunderts.* Vienna, 1976. Condensed, but comprehensive in range. Excellent bibliography and documentation.

———. *Protestanten in Österreich: Geschichte und Dokumentation.* Graz, 1981. Pages 9–176 provide a very good introduction for those who read German. Author makes good use of excerpts from important documents.

Schragl, Friedrich. *Glaubensspaltung in Niederösterreich.* Vienna, 1973. A picture of the impact of the Reformation on local Catholic parishes.

Sturmberger, Hans. *Georg Erasmus Tschernembl.* Graz, 1953. A biography of a key Protestant leader.

———. *Adam Graf Herberstorff: Herrschaft und Freiheit im konfessionellen Zeitalter.* Vienna, 1976. A vividly written study of a key figure in Ferdinand II's Counter-Reformation in Austria above the Enns.

Tomek, Ernst. *Kirchengeschichte Österreichs.* 3 vols. Innsbruck and Vienna, 1937–1959. Catholic orientation. Volume two covers sixteenth and seventeenth centuries.

Wiedemann, Theodor. *Geschichte der Reformation und Gegenreformation im Lande unter der Enns.* 5 vols. Prague, 1879–1886. First volume presents general overview of Reformation and Counter-Reformation through 1530. Remaining volumes present parish and district history.

PAULA SUTTER FICHTNER

AVENTINUS, Johannes (Ger., Johann Turmair; 1477–1534), Bavarian humanist and historian, author of *Annales ducum Boiariae* and its German version, *Baierische Chronik.* Born in Abensberg (Lat., Aventinum, hence "Aventinus") in Lower Bavaria, he studied at the universities of Ingolstadt, Vienna, Kraków, and Paris, where he came under the influence of notable northern humanists, among them Jacques Lefèvre d'Étaples and Conradus Celtis, the latter arousing his lifelong enthusiasm for historical scholarship. Having served as tutor to the younger brothers of Duke Wilhelm IV of Bavaria, he was appointed court historiographer in 1517 and commissioned to write a major historical work on Bavaria's ancient and medieval past.

Aventinus's fame rests entirely on his two chronicles, both of which are huge productions. Based in their Bavarian sections on a firsthand and critical survey of documents, inscriptions, and monuments, the *Annales* and *Chronik* are also an exercise in comparative history, glossing the rise and fall of kingdoms and civilizations with pointed comments meant to hold a mirror to the author's own time. The German chronicle in particular reflects Aventinus's moral view of the historian's craft, expressing his resolute pessimism about human affairs. These qualities, and Aventinus's blatant anticlericalism, made the work unsuitable for publication when it was completed in 1533. Expurgated editions appeared in the 1550s and 1560s, but the *Annales* and *Chronik* as Aventinus wrote them were not printed until his collected works were published in 1881–1908.

Aventinus's biographers have disputed his relation to the Reformation. In 1528 he was arrested as a heretic but was quickly released. His violent polemics against Rome and his open contacts with Lutheran partisans in Regensburg must have put him under suspicion. His insistence on human depravity links him with Luther, but he also affirmed the freedom of the will and rejected what he thought was Wittenberg's exaggerated biblicism. His personal faith probably resembled most closely that of Erasmus, with whom he shared an insistence on separating external practices from the evangelical core, along with hopes for the preservation of Christian unity and concord. Unusual among humanists was his deep concern for the impact of great political and religious events on the ordinary person, whose fate throughout history he viewed with genuine sympathy.

BIBLIOGRAPHY

Bosl, Karl. "Johann Turmair genannt Aventinus aus Abensberg in seiner Zeit," *Zeitschrift für bayerische Landesgeschichte* 40 (1977), 325–340.

Schmid, Alois. "Die historische Methode des Johannes Aventinus," *Blätter für deutsche Landesgeschichte* 113 (1977), 338–395.

Strauss, Gerald. *Historian in an Age of Crisis. The Life and Work of Johannes Aventinus.* Cambridge, Mass., 1963.

GERALD STRAUSS

AYALA, Felipe Guamán Poma de (1534?–1619?), Peruvian Catholic chronicler and defender of native rights against Spanish abuses. A native of Peru who traced his ancestry to the pre-Inca aristocracy, Ayala produced one of the earliest commentaries on the Spanish conquest from the perspective of the indigenous population. Although a believing Catholic who accepted Spanish dominion, Ayala did not disown the indigenous culture to which he was born, seeking rather a modus vivendi between it and the colonial regime he served as a scribe and translator.

In his life's work, *Nueva corónica y buen gobierno* (New Chronicle and Good Government; 1615), which was richly illustrated with pen and ink drawings and written mostly in Spanish with a dedication to Philip III, he assumed the role of spokesman for his people against colonial exploitation, which he found to be at odds with proclaimed Christian doctrine. The two-part chronicle, covering pre-Columbian history, the Spanish conquest, and the experiences of his own time, is a strange mixture of fact and fiction clearly designed to attempt to move the king of Spain to institute new reforms in the civil and ecclesiastical administration of the viceroyalty.

Based in part on documentary sources as well as instructive Catholic literature and the writings of Dominican critics such as Bartolomé de Las Casas, and in part on native mythology and his own inventive imagination, the work is essentially a polemic denying on Christian principles the justice of the subjugation of the native population. Ayala not only condemned forced labor in the mines and confiscation of native property, but singled out the Catholic clergy for setting a bad moral example and, through its "evil life-style," hindering rather than promoting the Christianization of Andean society. He noted at one point that as a result of widespread concubinage, the clergy were reproducing faster than the local population.

Ayala's thousand-page opus came to the attention of modern scholars only on being discovered in the Royal Library of Denmark in 1908. It was first published in 1936 in France, and has since won recognition as a major work of ethnographic, linguistic, historical, and theological importance.

BIBLIOGRAPHY

Primary Source

Ayala, Felipe Guamán Poma de. *Nueva cronica y bien gobierno.* Madrid, 1987.

Secondary Sources

Adorno, Rolena. *Guaman Poma: Writing and Resistance in Colonial Peru.* Austin, Tex., 1986. A critical analysis of the ideas and sources of Ayala's chronicle by a foremost scholar of his work; useful bibliography.

Meier, Johannes. "Ayala, Felipe Guamán Poma de." In *Lexikon für Theologie und Kirche,* vol. 1, p. 1323. Freiburg, 1993.

Ossio, Juan M. "Myth and History: The Seventeenth Century Chronicle of Guamán Poma de Ayala." In *Text and Context,* pp. 51–93. Philadelphia, 1977.

Peitschmann, Richard. "Some Account of the Illustrated Chronicle by the Peruvian Indian D. Felipe Huamán Poma de Ayala." In *Proceedings of the XVIII International Congress of Americanists,* pp. 510–521. London, 1912. Abstract of Ayala's *Corónica* by its "discoverer."

Steiner, Michael. *Guamán Poma de Ayala und die Eroberer Perus: Indianischer Chronist zwischen Anpassung und Widerstand.* Saarbrücken, 1992. Examines Ayala's work in the context of his dual cultural identity; extensive bibliography.

Varallanos, Jose. *Guamán Poma de Ayala: Cronista precursur y libertario.* Lima, Peru, 1979. Examines Ayala's work in the context of his life and times.

KARIN BRINKMANN BROWN

AYTTA, Viglius Zuichemius van. *See* Viglius, Joachim van Aytta van Zuychem.

AZPILCUETA, Martín de (also Navarrus, El Doctor Navarro; 1492–1586), Spanish jurist and theologian. Martín de Azpilcueta was born 13 December 1492 at Barasoín in Navarre. He received his first benefice at the age of nine, and at eleven began the course in arts and theology at Alcalá de Henares. In 1510 he moved to Toulouse, where he received a doctorate in canon law. He took major orders in 1515 and in 1524 made his profession as a canon regular of Roncesvalles. After 1518 Azpilcueta taught canon and civil law at the universities of Toulouse, Cahors, Salamanca, and Coimbra.

Returning to Spain in 1555, he abandoned teaching for ecclesiastical politics. His mother had been a cousin of Francis Xavier, and Azpilcueta supported the Jesuits in their campaign to secure papal approval. Shortly thereafter, his work on the financial administration of monasteries attracted the attention of the regent, Juana, who employed him in the reform of several houses in Castile. Philip II then asked him to defend Archbishop Bartolomé de Carranza in what was probably the most celebrated heresy case of the century. Azpilcueta went to Rome in 1567 and secured a papal acquittal, but in the process offended the king. He did not return to Spain, and served as an advisor to both Pius V and Gregory XIII until his death in Rome on 21 April 1586.

Though admired as a canonist in his own day, Azpilcueta is now better known for his sanctity of life and for his writings on poverty, prayer, and the Mass. His *Manual de confesores* (1566) was enormously popular in Spanish and Portuguese and went through no fewer than twenty-nine Latin editions. The *Opera Omnia,* including his legal and economic treatises, appeared posthumously in 1597. Of his treatises, the best known are probably the *Tratado de las rentas de los beneficios* (1566) and the *Comentario resolutario de cambios* (new ed., Madrid, 1965).

BIBLIOGRAPHY

Arigita y Lasa, Mariano. *El doctor navarro Don Martín de Azpilcueta y sus obras.* Pamplona, 1905.

Lopez Ortiz, L. "Un canonista español del siglo xvi, el doctor na-o Don Martín de Azpilcueta." *Ciudad de Dios* 153 (1941), 271–301.

Oloriz, H. *Nueva biographia del doctor navarro Martín de Azpilcueta y enumeración de sus obras.* Pamplona, 1918.

WILLIAM S. MALTBY

B

BACON, Francis (Baron Verulam, Viscount St. Albans; 1561–1626), English statesman and philosopher known for his empirical approach to science, learning, and politics. Bacon was the son of Sir Nicholas Bacon, an eminent state official at the court of Queen Elizabeth I. At the age of twelve Bacon entered the University of Cambridge, where he developed an aversion to the syllogistic logic he would later challenge as an avenue to true knowledge of the world. In 1576 he turned to the study of law with the aim of earning a place at the highest levels of government, an ambition he achieved under James I, who appointed him to a succession of political offices culminating in the lord chancellorship in 1619. Bacon also sat in Parliament from 1584 to 1621, when he was dismissed from all his offices on charges of corruption.

Bacon's rather indecorous quest for wealth, status, and power not only tarnished his reputation but took valuable time and energy from his project to create a naturalistic and materialistic foundation for the acquisition and expansion of knowledge (*Advancement of Learning*, 1605). Although he failed to complete his lifetime work, *Great Instauration*, intended to supplant traditional thinking about the natural order, he published a vital part as *The New Organon* in 1620. Here he outlined his new inductive method of inquiry, insisting on verification of sense data through experimentation and severing science from religion and preconceived ideas about the natural order.

Bacon meant to construct a new philosophical foundation not only for science but for all of human society, which he believed would benefit greatly from man's conquest of nature and release from supernatural dominion over the conduct of temporal affairs. In his *Essays or Councels, Civil and Moral* (1597 and 1625) and his utopian fantasy *New Atlantis* (1627), Bacon goes so far as to present arguments for atheism as more conducive to human progress than Christianity's promise of an other-worldly paradise. While Bacon acknowledged the imprint of the divine in nature, he relegated revealed theology to the realm of inexplicable mystery and individual faith, thereby clearing the way for the unimpeded advance of modern science.

BIBLIOGRAPHY

Primary Sources

Bacon, Francis. *The New Organon and Related Writings*. New York, 1960.

——. *Essays*. London, 1994.
——. *Novum Organum*. Chicago, 1994.

Secondary Sources

"Baconianism." In *Dictionary of the History of Ideas*, vol. 1, pp. 172–179. New York, 1973.
Bautz, Friedrich Wilhelm, ed. *Biographisch-bibliographisches Kirchenlexikon*. Hamm, Germany, 1970–. See vol. 1, pp. 330–331.
Blumberg, Hans. *The Legitimacy of the Modern Age*. Cambridge, Mass., 1983. Explores Bacon's relevance to modern culture.
Faulkner, Robert K. *Francis Bacon and the Project of Progress*. Lanham, Md., 1993. Analyzes Bacon's approach to reform of state and society.
Jardine, Lisa. *Francis Bacon: Discovery and the Art of Discourse*. Cambridge, 1974.
Rossi, Paolo. *Francis Bacon: From Magic to Science*. Chicago, 1968.
Whitney, Charles. *Francis Bacon and Modernity*. New Haven, 1986. Bacon analyzed in the light of critical theory; useful bibliographical citations.
Wybrow, Cameron. *The Bible, Baconianism, and Mastery over Nature: The Old Testament and Its Modern Misreading*. New York, 1991.

KARIN BRINKMANN BROWN

BADER, Augustin (d. 1530), Anabaptist chiliast. A weaver by trade, Bader belonged to the first followers of Anabaptism in Augsburg. In 1526 he was baptized along with his wife. Influenced by Johannes Bünderlin and Hans Denck, Bader was especially close to Hans Hut, who introduced his apocalyptic concept to Bader. A few weeks after the failure of Hut's prediction that the Last Judgment would occur at Pentecost 1528, which prompted Bader to an uncertain life of wandering, Bader received his first visions. He proclaimed that the time of baptizing was past, thereby cutting his ties with the Anabaptists.

After the fall of 1529 he lived with his family and a few followers (the former Anabaptists Hans Koller, Gastel, Gall Vischer, and the former priest Oswald Leber) in remote mills near Ulm, one of the imperial free cities of Württemberg. Here they prepared themselves for the end, which they expected to be Easter 1530.

In January 1530 the group was arrested. The hearings conveyed to the authorities in Stuttgart the impression that Bader and his followers were plotting with the expelled Duke Ulrich of Württemberg (r. 1503–1519; 1534–1550). Bader and his followers were executed on 30 March 1530, but his wife and children were spared.

Bader was the first exponent of a clear chiliasm in the Reformation that later formed the foundation for the Anabaptist kingdom created by Bernhard Rothmann in Münster. According to Bader's conception, the Last Judgment would begin with an attack by the Turks and last for one and a half years. During that time, social relationships would be overthrown, and only the elect, who might include heathens, Turks, and Jews, would survive. Then the thousand-year reign would begin, during which there would be no "external church," rather the Spirit of Christ alone would rule. A chosen king would govern according to the rule of Christ (*Mt.* 18:15–17). Mandatory work, freedom from taxes, and communal property would rule the day.

Bader's conception, which shows harmony with the writing "Von der newen wandlung eines Christlichen lebens" (Concerning the New Conduct of a Christian Life; 1527), was an attempt to merge religious and eschatalogical social change after the Peasants' War. The repudiation of chiliasm in article 17 of the Augsburg Confession is directed against Bader.

BIBLIOGRAPHY

Bossert, Gustav. "Augustin Bader von Augsburg, der Prophet und König, und seine Genossen, nach den Prozeßakten von 1530." *Archiv für Reformationsgeschichte* 10 (1913), 110–175, 209–241, 297–349; 11 (1914), 19–64, 103–133, 176–199.

Clasen, Claus-Peter. *Die Wiedertäufer im Herzogtum Württemberg und in benachbarten Herrschaften: Ausbreitung, Geisteswelt und Soziologie.* Stuttgart, 1965. See especially pp. 114–117.

Laube, Adolf, Annerose Schneider, and Ulman Weiß, eds. *Flugschriften vom Bauernkrieg zum Täuferreich, 1526–1535.* Vol. 2. Berlin, 1992. See especially pp. 984–996.

List, Günther. *Chiliastische Utopie und radikale Reformation: Die Erneuerung der Idee vom Tausendjährigen Reich im 16. Jahrhundert.* Munich, 1973. See especially pp. 172–186.

ULMAN WEISS
Translated from German by Jeff Bach

BADER, Johannes (c.1470–1545), Protestant theologian and author of the first evangelical catechism. Bader's origins are obscure. There are no records of his birth, education, or ordination to the priesthood. He is first noted in 1509 as tutor and, from 1514, as chaplain to Duke Ludwig of Zweibrücken. In 1518 he was named priest in Landau, where he earned the displeasure of the Catholic hierarchy for preaching against church abuses and practices, such as auricular confession, which, he argued, had no basis in scripture. In 1523 he was cited to appear before the clerical court of Speyer and admonished about his reforming tendencies. Bader's opposition hardened and embraced new topics: purgatory, invocation of the Virgin and the saints, fasting, monasticism, and the church hierarchy, as well as the sacraments except baptism and the Eucharist. In 1524 he was excommunicated after failing to appear for a second hearing before the court.

Bader nonetheless remained at his post and continued his evangelical preaching under the protection of the Landau city council, which rejected all directives from the bishop and secular authorities for his dismissal and extradition. Bader was particularly concerned with religious instruction for the young and to this end he wrote the first evangelical catechism, printed as *Ein Gespräch Büchlein* (Dialogue Booklet) in 1526. It included explications on the Lord's Prayer, the Apostles' Creed, baptism, and the Ten Commandments. In 1527, to refute the teachings of the Anabaptist Hans Denck, who was seeking refuge and converts in Landau, Bader wrote *Brüderliche Warnung vor dem neuen abgöttischen Orden der Wiedertäufer* (A Brotherly Warning Against the New Heretical Order of the Anabaptists).

Bader was highly respected as a churchman of independent mind concerned with bringing clarity to theological formulations. Although his theological positions closely followed Martin Bucer, he later differed with the Strasbourg reformer over the meaning of the Lord's Supper. In 1544 Bader brought out a new summary instruction of the faith, *Katechismus* (Catechism), with a new section on the Lord's Supper affirming the influence of his close association with the spiritualist Kaspar von Schwenckfeld. Bader had become convinced that the Lord's Supper should be celebrated only by a community of upright believing Christians imbued with brotherly love. Given the practical difficulty of excluding "unworthy" Christians, Bader simply ceased to celebrate the Lord's Supper during his last years as a pastor in Landau.

BIBLIOGRAPHY

Primary Source

Bader, Johannes. "Catechismus oder Christliche Schülerstück, wie die mit der Jugent zu Landawe gehandelt werden" (1544). In *Quellen zur Geschichte des Kirchlichen Unterrichts*, edited by J. M. Reu, vol. 1. Gütersloh, 1904.

Secondary Sources

Biundo, Georg. "Bader, Johannes." In *Neue Deutsche Biographie*, vol. 1, p. 512. Berlin, 1953.

Gelbert, J. P. *Magister Johann Bader's Leben und Schriften, Nicolaus Thomae und seine Briefe.* Neustadt a.d.H., 1868.

Ney, Theodor J. "Bader, Johannes." In *Realencyklopädie für protestantische Theologie und Kirche*, vol. 2, pp. 353–357. Leipzig, 1897.

Schottenloher, Karl. *Bibliographie zur deutschen Geschichte im Zeitalter der Glaubensspaltung, 1517–1585.* Stuttgart, 1956. See vol. 1, p. 33.

KARIN BRINKMANN BROWN

BADUEL, Claude (1491?–1561), French humanist, first rector (1542–1543) of the Academy of Nîmes and the University of Arts. He received his degree in 1530 from Louvain, where he met Johannes Sturm and was exposed to Lutheranism. Completing his studies at Paris, Baduel spent 1537–1538 at Strasbourg and witnessed the foundation of its gymnasium. Returning to Paris, he became a popular and well-paid professor. In 1539 Marguerite d'Angoulême, his patron, nominated him as rector of the Nîmes school, a task he began in October 1540.

In *De Collegio et Universite Nemausensi* (1540), Baduel described the plan that made grammar and rhetoric foundations for philosophy and literature in age-graded classes for boys from age five to twenty, after which they began professional training. Annual promotions, carefully graded exercises, daily recitation in Latin and later in Greek, and imitation of classical models were basics developed by the Brethren of the Common Life and perfected by Johannes Sturm. Baduel adopted this curriculum, which was designed to enhance Christian piety even though most of the readings were classical. *Pietas literata* was the goal Baduel shared with Sturm.

Baduel's rectorship was plagued by disagreements with Guillaume Bigot (rector 1543–1547) over the emphasis philosophy should be given as opposed to grammar and rhetoric, or technical versus literary information. When Baduel regained his position as rector in 1547, Bigot exposed him as a "Lutheran" (turned Calvinist). Baduel resigned in September 1548 and in 1550 fled from Nîmes to Geneva. He spent his last decade in Switzerland as a pastor and after 1560 as professor of philosophy and mathematics at the Geneva Academy. Not an original thinker, he nevertheless helped solidify the humanist tradition in Protestant secondary education.

BIBLIOGRAPHY

Bourchenin, Pierre-Daniel. *Étude sur les académies protestantes en France au 16e et au 17e siècles.* (1882). Reprint, Geneva, 1969.

Casteel, Theodore W. *The College and University of Arts in Nîmes: An Experiment in Humanistic Education in the Age of the Reform.* Ph.D. diss., Stanford University, 1973.

Delepine, P.E. *Claude Baduel, Humaniste et pedagogue français, 1491–1561.* Nîmes, 1880.

Gaufrès, Mathieu-Jules. *Claude Baduel et la réforme des études au 16e siècle* (1880). Reprint, Geneva, 1969.

Puech, A. *La Renaissance et la Réforme à Nîmes.* Nîmes, 1893.

BARBARA SHER TINSLEY

BAER, Zacharias. *See* Ursinus, Zacharius.

BAERDES, Willem Dirkszoon (1496–1568), sheriff of Amsterdam from 1542 to 1566. A scion of Amsterdam's mercantile aristocracy, Baerdes was the son of a former burgomaster and the father of a man who was elected thirteen times to the same office. His own public career developed under circumstances that portended conflict with his social peers. In consequence of a loan to the government, since 1509 the city fathers held the important office of sheriff in pawn, meaning that the incumbent was their appointee and thus not beholden to the government of Charles V as count of Holland. Baerdes was first appointed sheriff in 1542 but continued in office after 1550, when Charles's regent in the Low Countries, Mary of Hungary and Bohemia, spent a notable sum to redeem the 1509 loan. He was vigilant in enforcing the regent's will in sensitive matters like the regulation of trade, if only up to a point, and he also lived up to his responsibilities for enforcing the government's unpopular heresy laws, though he was no zealot.

His relations with the ruling faction among the town's patricians, led by Hendrik Dirkszoon, were problematic from the start, since Baerdes had close ties to a previous ruling faction that was displaced in the wake of an Anabaptist uprising in Amsterdam (1535). This conflict was intensified in 1553, when Baerdes, along with his wife and daughter, was accused of heresy by the pastor of the Old Church, Floris Engelbrechtszoon, backed by Dirkszoon. After years of litigation Baerdes was vindicated; the principal informant, a woman of low estate, was executed for bearing false witness, and for having suborned her the pastor was permanently exiled from the city. Dirkszoon was sentenced to four years of house arrest in The Hague.

The sheriff, trusted by the government in Brussels, now became a rallying point for local opposition to the so-called Hendrik-Dirkist ruling faction in the city, especially as expressed in a formal complaint, or *Doleantie*, submitted to the government in 1564 and signed by seventy men of substance, many of them involved in the vital Baltic trade. The *Doleantie* accused the Dirkisten of sharing out offices among their kinfolk, as such ruling factions were indeed wont to do, and also came to the sheriff's defense in his various conflicts with city hall. Officials in Brussels were initially receptive to these complaints but not after the events of the Wonderyear (1566), when signatories of the *Doleantie* turned up both as leaders of the local Calvinist congregation and of the middle party that sought religious compromise. Baerdes was ousted as sheriff and joined former *Doleanten* in exile the following year. When Amsterdam's exiles returned in a bloodless coup (1578), it was again former *Doleanten* who took the lead in aligning the city with the Revolt of the Netherlands and in organizing the new church. Baerdes himself had died ten years previously, but one of the first burgomasters elected by the new regime was his son, Willem Bardesius.

BIBLIOGRAPHY

Elias, J. E. *De Vroedschap van Amsterdam* (1903–1905). 2 vols. Reprint, Amsterdam, 1963.

Tracy, James D. "Habsburg Grain Policy and Amsterdam Politics: The Career of Sheriff Willem Dirkszoon Baerdes, 1542–1566." *Sixteenth Century Journal* 14 (1983), 293–319.

Woltjer, J. J. "Het Conflict tussen Willem Baerdes en Meester Hendrik Dirkszoon." *Bildragen en Mededelingen betreffende de Geschedenis der Nederlanden* 86 (1971), 178–199.

JAMES D. TRACY

BAJUS, Michael (Fr., de Bay; 1513–1589), controversial Belgian Catholic theologian and forerunner of Jansenism. Born in Meslin in the Spanish Netherlands, Bajus was ordained in 1542 and educated at the University of Louvain, where he earned a doctorate and professorship in theology in 1550 and served as chancellor from 1578 until his death. In 1578 he was named royal grand inquisitor for the Netherlands.

In a singular quest for theological truth Bajus hoped to meet the challenge of Protestantism on its own grounds—the sources of early Christianity (scripture, the church fathers, and especially Augustine). His primary concerns were with the nature of the human condition and the metaphysical basis of justification, which he saw as the central problem of the Reformation. Bajus's denigration of scholastic theology and his exclusive reliance on scripture and the church fathers subjected him to repeated charges of holding unorthodox views on original sin, grace, and free will.

Following Augustine's anti-Pelagian writings, Bajus held that human nature is in essence corrupted, concupiscence is sin, and humans are incapable of avoiding sin through their own efforts without the help of the Holy Spirit. The forgiveness of sins is an on-going inner process in exercising virtue.

In 1560 the Faculty of Theology of Paris censured 18 propositions extracted from Bajus's lectures by some of his Belgian Franciscan students. Bajus denied responsibility for the propositions as stated, insisting that he had been misinterpreted if not deliberately slandered (*Apologia*). Rome enjoined both parties to silence in anticipation of a decision by the Council of Trent which Bajus attended in 1563. At this time Bajus published three brief tracts, *De libero arbitrio*, *De justitia et justificatione*, and *De sacrificio*, which were followed by a succession of concise, eloquent statements of his theological positions. Sentences from *De justitia et justificatione* were condemned by the universities of Alcalá and Salamanca. The council's failure to rule on the controversy brought further charges in 1567 against Bajus leading to the 1567 bull by Pius V, *Ex omnibus afflictionibus*, which addressed 76 tenets found to be in error by Bajus's critics. Bajus's extensive use of quotations from Augustine caused the bull to be cautiously worded. Moreover, the text was ambigious: depending on the placement of a comma, one could read that the sentences were condemned as interpreted by Bajus or that the sentences were orthodox as interpreted by Bajus. Arguments over the comma, which left the church's position ambiguous, resurfaced during the Jansenist controversy of the 17th century.

The church did not so much succeed in silencing as in containing Bajus's unorthodox views within the confines of papal inquiry and academic discourse. The 1567 bull was promulgated only at the University of Louvain, whose faculty agreed in 1572 to disavow the disputed propositions and proscribe Bajus's written works for its students. In 1580, at the behest of Pope Gregory XIII, Bajus finally satisfied Rome and the Louvain faculty by acknowledging responsibility for certain of the censured propositions.

Despite his formal submission, Bajus remained convinced that his propositions were true to the letter and spirit of Augustine, an opinion not shared by modern scholars. His significance was rather that he bequeathed to the Catholic church an unresolved debate on justification that was to resume in the more disruptive form of Jansenism.

BIBLIOGRAPHY

Primary Source

Bajus, Michael. *Opera M. Baji.* Edited by G. Gerberon. 2 vols. Cologne, 1696.

Secondary Sources

Donnelly, P. J. "Baius and Baianism." *In New Catholic Encyclopedia*, vol. 2, pp. 19–21. New York, 1967. Gives a clear summary of Bajus's doctrine and the modern Catholic view of his "errors."
Eijl, E. J. M. van. "Bay (Baius), Michael de" In *Nationaal Biografisch Woordenboek*, vol. 1, pp. 114–129. Brussels, 1964.
Grossi, Vittorino. "Bajus, Michael." In *Theologische Realenzklopädie*, vol.1, pp. 133–137. Berlin, 1980. A concise overview with bibliography of French and Spanish sources.
Linsemann, Franz X. *Michael Bajus und die Grundlegung des Jansenismus.* Tübingen, 1867. Still important.
Scheeben, Matthias J. "Bajus, (de Bay), Michael." In *Wetzer und Welte's Kirchenlexicon*, vol. 1, pp. 1852–1862. Freiburg, 1882. Detailed account of the controversy over Bajus's disputed theses.
Smulders, Pieter. "Bajus (De Bay), Michael." In *Lexikon für Theologie und Kirche*, vol. 1, pp. 1198–1199. Freiburg, 1957.
Tans, Joseph A. G. "Bajus (De Bay), Michael." In *Lexikon für Theologie und Kirche*, vol. 1, pp. 1360–1362. Freiburg, 1993.

KARIN BRINKMANN BROWN

BALDUNG, Hans (also called Hans Baldung Grien; 1484/85–1545), German painter and print maker. Baldung most likely was born in Schwäbisch-Gmünd, the son of a university-educated jurist. He spent much of his childhood in and around Strasbourg, where his father served as an episcopal official. He received part of his artistic training in Nuremberg, distinguishing himself as Albrecht Dürer's most gifted pupil. In 1509 he returned to Strasbourg, where he lived most of the remainder of his life. He played an active role in the politics of the city, rising to become a member of the civic senate.

As a painter, Baldung is best known for his skill as a colorist and his frequent choice of unusual—often erotic or demonic—subject matter. The more important of his hundred or so surviving paintings include, in addition to many conventional religious compositions: *Death and the Maiden* (1509–1511); *Eve, the Serpent, and Death* (1520–1525); *Two Witches* (1523); and *The Seven Ages of Woman* (1544). Baldung also made major contributions to the graphic arts. His best known single-leaf woodcuts are *Witches' Sabbath* (1510), *Wild Horses Fighting* (1534), and *Bewitched Groom* (c.1544). In addition, he designed hundreds of woodcut illustrations for use by Strasbourg printers in publications, including a catechism by Martin Bucer and a Protestant lay Bible.

Baldung's personal relationship with the Reformation nonetheless remains problematic, partly because of the lack of any direct written evidence. Most likely he accepted the new evangelical movement and conformed to the new church established in Strasbourg during the 1520s and 1530s. He fully exploited, however, the new freedom resulting from the growing separation of art and religion in the Reformation. In Baldung's case, this freedom led to an unprecedented preoccupation with female sensuality, death, and the occult.

BIBLIOGRAPHY

Brady, Thomas A., Jr. "The Social Place of a German Renaissance Artist: Hans Baldung Grien, 1484/85–1545, at Strasbourg." *Central European History* 8 (1975), 295–315. Includes discussion of Baldung's relationship to the Reformation.

Marrow, James H., and Alan Shestack, eds. *Hans Baldung Grien: Prints and Drawings.* Exhibition catalog, Washington, D.C., National Gallery of Art. New Haven, 1981. Includes three essays, one on Baldung and the Reformation.

Parshall, Linda B., and Peter W. Parshall. *Art and the Reformation: An Annotated Bibliography.* Boston, 1986. See items 827–854.

CARL C. CHRISTENSEN

BALE, John (1495–1563), Protestant dramatist, literary historian, and inventor of a powerful apocalyptic interpretation of the English Reformation. Regarded as a master stylist and major literary figure by his contemporaries, Bale's reputation was almost permanently damaged in the seventeenth century by Thomas Fuller, who, in summarizing his judgment of taste, invented the epithet "bilious Bale." A convert to Protestantism in the mid-1530s, Bale kept the ardor of a recent convert throughout his career. He produced an enormous number of controversial writings in the course of the first three major phases of the English Reformation. A protégé of Thomas Cromwell in the late 1530s, Bale went into exile during the last six years of Henry VIII's reign (1541–1547) but returned to England under Edward VI, eventually achieving the dubious honor of the bishopric of Ossory in Ireland (a story told in *The Vocation of John Bale to the Bishopric of Ossory in Ireland*, London, 1553). Under the Marian reaction Bale again went into exile to the Continent, living mainly in Switzerland and working closely

with the major Protestant publisher Johannes Oporinus. Displaying the same split-second timing as he had at Edward's accession, Bale greeted Elizabeth I in 1559 with an encomiastic preface to the final printing of his *Scriptorum Illustrium Brytanniae Catalogus*. This time he finally secured worthwhile patronage from Elizabeth's first archbishop of Canterbury, Matthew Parker, but Bale's literary career was over.

Bale is best known for one play, *King Johan*, his treatise *The Image of Both Churches after the Most Wonderfull and Heavenly Revelation of Sainct John the Evangelist* (London?, 1550?), and his catalog of English writers. The date and auspices of *King Johan* have been hotly disputed, and there is also some question about the status of the text, which Bale never published; the uncertainty arises both from lack of external documentation and Bale's own vagueness about his literary production. While cases have been made for a date as late as around 1540, Peter Happé has opted for 1533–1534, about the time Bale underwent his conversion, with revision later in that decade. Critics have disagreed as sharply about the literary and historical merit of the play. Undoubtedly an antipapal work, Bale also made a number of more specific points concerning reform, as Greg Walker has emphasized; they may help to fit the play into a specific political context. However that may be, the work's literary merit still tends to be assessed along ideological lines. (Bale undoubtedly wrote unhumanistic Latin, and his English prose style had deep medieval roots. His is another case suggesting caution in identifying humanism with reform.) It seems clear that Bale's drama, including *King Johan*, does not easily fit established categories, both then and now. Bale's drama oscillates between the same comic and tragic generic poles that John King found structuring his historical work. Bale, like other of his contemporaries of various religious persuasions, had too Pauline a view of the world to be a successful ideologue.

The Image of Both Churches, although also superficially antipapal polemic, developed a profoundly apocalyptic view of sacred history. Going beyond his apparent roots in Augustine, Bale adapted the views of Joachim of Fiore, particularly Joachim's theory (derived ultimately from Augustine) of the six ages of the church. Bale believed that the apocalypse of the sixth and final age was imminent. The herald of the end was John Wycliffe, an interpretation that Bale also stretched into a framework for his catalog of English writers. The tragicomic history Bale wrote had a deep impact on the work of his sometime collaborator, John Foxe, who probably derived most of the form of his *Acts and Monuments* from Bale.

Bale was also a scholar and editor of a large number of works. His *Catalogus*, despite its many mythical elements, was the first serious work of English literary history. Bale drew on the much more incomplete work of his friend John Leland in assembling his list of writers (he also published some of it under Leland's name) and carefully distinguished his work from Leland's. In addition, Bale contributed through his editorial work to making the link between Henrician reform and the Lollards and, among other of his martyrological efforts, to preserving the affecting case of Ann Askew. His *Vocation*, which deserves further study, is an early instance of autobiography in English.

BIBLIOGRAPHY

Primary Sources

Blatt, Thora Balslev. *The Plays of John Bale: A Study of Ideas, Technique and Style.* Copenhagen, 1968. Most balanced, comprehensive critical study.

Happé, Peter, ed. *The Complete Plays of John Bale.* 2 vols. Woodbridge, England, 1985–1986. Careful introductions. Includes *King Johan, God's Promises, Johan Baptist Preaching, The Temptation of Our Lord,* and *The Three Laws.*

Secondary Sources

Fairfield, Leslie P. *John Bale, Mythmaker for the English Reformation.* West Lafayette, Ind., 1976. Reads Bale in extrinsic typological categories, instead of as a writer drawing heavily on the Bible.

King, John N. *English Reformation Literature: The Tudor Origins.* Princeton, 1982. Most appreciative literary-historical study. Contains a bibliography of Bale's works.

McCusker, Honor. *John Bale, Dramatist and Antiquary.* Reprint, Freeport, N.Y., 1971. Best biographical study. Needs updating in light of Happé and Fairfield.

Walker, Greg. *Plays of Persuasion: Drama and Politics at the Court of Henry VIII.* Cambridge, 1991. Sometimes thinly supported, but at least suggests a political reading of *King Johan.*

THOMAS F. MAYER

BALNAVES, Henry (c.1503–1570), Scottish Protestant reformer and theologian. Balnaves was educated at Saint Salvatore's College (Saint Andrews, Scotland) and seems to have received an M.A. at Cologne. After study there he returned to Scotland and served the earl of Arran, regent for Mary Stuart (daughter of the late James V). Balnaves became a prominent Protestant during the time when Arran encouraged the evangelical reformers. When the regent returned to Catholicism and persecution of Protestants began, Balnaves joined militants who killed Cardinal David Beaton in reprisal for that prelate's execution of George Wishart, a friend of John Knox, who had brought the Helvetic Confession from the Continent. Although Balnaves was not one of the assassins, he suffered imprisonment with them from 1547 to 1550 at Rouen, France.

After returning to Scotland in 1557, Balnaves joined rebels against the regent, Mary of Guise, and obtained English aid against the French troops she had brought to Scotland. This practically ended French influence there, and Balnaves was a hero to fellow Protestants. Parliament adopted the Scottish Confession of Faith (1560), thereby embracing Protestantism officially, and Balnaves received an appointment to re-

vise the *First Book of Discipline,* a proposed plan to organize national life in accord with biblical precepts.

In addition to his leadership in the Protestant cause, Balnaves was a keen theologian. While in prison he composed his *Confession of Faith,* a systematic exposition of justification through faith alone, a doctrine he traced throughout the scriptures in the method of biblical theology. This study closely resembles Martin Luther's teachings about sin and salvation. John Knox hailed it as a learned exposition of sound doctrine. The work of Balnaves and other early Scottish Protestants reflects Luther's influence upon them, even though the Church of Scotland officially adopted the Reformed faith, and even though Balnaves himself espoused the Reformed doctrine of limited atonement, in contrast with the Lutheran belief that Christ died for everyone. It appears that Balnaves was an important figure in the transition of Scottish Protestantism from its Lutheran foundations to the Calvinism of its maturity.

BIBLIOGRAPHY

Primary Source

Balnaves, Henry. *Balnaves on Justification.* London, 1831.

Secondary Sources

McGoldrick, James Edward. *Luther's Scottish Connection.* Cranbury, N.J., 1989. Study of the early Scottish Reformation that considers the generation of Protestants before John Knox and emphasizes Luther's influence upon them.

Rogers, Charles. *Three Scottish Reformers.* London, 1876. Work contains a well documented chapter about Balnaves.

Watt, Hugh. "Henry Balnaves and the Scottish Reformation." *Records of the Scottish Church History Society* 5 (1935), 23–39. Excellent summary of the early Scottish Reformation that affirms Luther's influence upon Balnaves's doctrine of justification and upon the first generation of Scottish Protestants in general.

JAMES EDWARD MCGOLDRICK

BAÑEZ, Domingo (1528–1604), Spanish Dominican theologian and exponent of the strict Thomist account of predestination and divine grace. Born in Valladolid, Bañez became a Dominican in 1546. At Salamanca he studied under Melchior Cano and Bartolomé de Medina, both educated by Francisco de Vitoria and Domingo de Soto in the newly revived tradition of Thomism. After teaching at Ávila, Alcalá, and Valladolid, Bañez returned to Salamanca in 1577, where he held the principal chair of theology from 1580 until his death in 1604. His *Scholastica commentaria* on parts 1 and 2.2 of Thomas's *Summa theologiae* were published in four volumes at Salamanca between 1584 and 1594. Five more volumes, treating parts 2.1 and 3, have been published from manuscript by V. Beltrán de Heredia (Madrid, 1942–1953).

As early as 1582 Bañez intervened before the Inquisition as a critic of theses on redemption, grace, and free choice held by a Jesuit, Prudencio de Montemayor. After the publication of Luis de Molina's *Concordia* (1588), Bañez was the principal Dominican opponent of his account of predestination, grace, and human freedom. Bañez wrote the *Apologia Fratrum Praedicatorum* (1595), in defense against Molina's charge that the Dominican notion of grace being efficacious by its intrinsic quality veered toward Calvinism. Bañez responded that Molina attributed to fallen human beings a determining role in meriting their salvation that was redolent of Pelagianism. The dispute was transferred to Rome for hearings before the papal Congregatio de auxiliis between 1597 and 1607. Neither Molina nor Bañez appeared in person, as presentations and rebuttals were made by appointees of the respective general superiors of the Jesuit and Dominican orders. The Molinist position was assessed critically by most of the cardinals of the tribunal, but Pope Paul V decided against issuing a condemnation. Instead, both positions were permitted to be taught, but with the stipulation that neither side was to charge the other with heresy.

BIBLIOGRAPHY

Beltrán de Heredia, Vicente. *Domingo Bañez y la controversias sobre la gracia*. Madrid, 1968. After a ninety-page introduction, publishes treatises by Bañez, including the *Apologia Fratrum Praedicatorum* against Molina (pp. 115–380).
———. *Miscelánea Beltrán de Heredia*. 4 vols. Salamanca, Spain, 1971–1973. Includes studies of the life and thought of Bañez.
Llamzon, Benjamin S., ed. *The Primacy of Existence in Thomas Aquinas*. Chicago, 1966. Translation of Bañez's exposition of a central point of Thomist metaphysics.
Stöhr, Johannes. *Zur Frühgeschichte des Gnadenstreites*. Münster, 1980. Edition from manuscript of four position-papers by Bañez's allies against Molina.

JARED WICKS

BAPTISM. [*This entry comprises two articles on the sacrament of baptism. The first presents a transnational survey of the practice of baptism, popular beliefs about the rite, and the impact of both Protestant and Roman Catholic reform on baptism; the second surveys the history of baptismal theology and the learned theological controversies that arose both as a result of and a reaction to the forces of religious reform. For a more general discussion, see* Sacraments.]

Popular Practices

The practice of baptism in the sixteenth century was as varied as the Christian confessions of the age. This article examines the Roman rite of the pre-Reformation period and then looks at how the baptismal liturgy was changed to reflect the theological concerns of the Lutheran, Calvinist, Anabaptist, and Anglican traditions.

The Roman Rite. There was no uniform baptismal rite in the late medieval period. Liturgy often reflected local customs, thus precluding a baptismal rite that was universally accepted in all details. Nevertheless, a comparison of various liturgies reveals that a general pattern prevailed, allowing for minor parochial variations. Save for a few alterations in the *Rituale Romanum* of 1614, this service was used until 1964.

It should be remembered that the Roman rite had been pared considerably since the days of the early church, when baptism was administered largely to adults after a lengthy period of instruction. By the Middle Ages the baptism of infants was the norm, and the former period of catechization was now compressed into the first part of the rite itself.

The service consisted of three parts: the making of a catechumen, the blessing of the font, and the order for baptism. The ceremony usually originated at the church doors, where a series of prayers and exorcisms would be performed over the one to be baptized, often using salt to symbolize the candidate's preservation in the faith. Included in this section would be a reading of the account of Jesus blessing the children and also the *effeta*, or "opening," in which the priest would spit into his hand and touch the ears and nose of the infant, thus making him or her receptive to the word of God. The emphasis on exorcism, foreign to modern ears, reflects not only the Bible's frequent mention of the devil but also the late medieval concern with satanic forces and powers.

After the order for making a catechumen, the baptism party entered the church, where the water in the baptismal font would be blessed. This involved an elaborate ceremony with lengthy prayers, frequent invocations of the Trinity, and the mixing of oil with the water. The purpose was to "prepare" the water for the sacrament.

The baptism itself began with a renunciation of Satan by the godparents. Following a creedal affirmation by the assembled party, the priest held the child and dipped him or her three times into the water. The infant was then dressed in a white robe (signifying the innocence of Christ), anointed with chrism, and presented with a candle.

The church taught that baptism was necessary for salvation. In earthly life no person approached the lofty status of a baptized infant. Cleansed from the stain of Original Sin and yet free from the guilt of actual sin, a newly baptized infant hovered near the portals of heaven. Thus, the sacrament was held in high esteem and was typically an occasion for parents, godparents, family, and friends to gather and celebrate this significant event. A day of baptism often meant the cessation of labor and the eating of a meal in honor of the newest member of the church.

The Lutheran Rite. Martin Luther's first order for baptism (1523) is remarkably similar to its Roman predecessor. It differs in that it eliminates several (but not all) of the exorcisms of the late medieval rite, contains no blessing of the font, and includes Luther's famous Flood Prayer, which describes God's saving use of water in the Bible. The service is also said in German, reflecting Luther's concern that the common people be able to understand God's word. The similarity between this order and the Roman rite demonstrates Luther's idea that the pace of liturgical reform could be slow as long as the gospel were preached.

Luther's rite of 1526 is considerably abbreviated. He retains a single exorcism at the beginning of the service, reflecting his ardent belief that the faithful are locked in battle with Satan until death. Also kept is the Flood Prayer, the Gospel story of Jesus blessing the children, and the creedal affirmation with the corresponding renunciation of the devil. For the actual baptism itself, "dipping" in the name of the triune God is suggested, although elsewhere Luther advocated full immersion, indicative of his belief that baptism is an actual death and resurrection and not a mere washing.

This rite reflects Luther's mature sacramental theology. While never denigrating the material element, Luther is concerned with highlighting the role of God's word, which, combined with the water, creates faith in the recipient of baptism. The goal of baptism is to bring the one being baptized into a living and vital relationship with Jesus Christ, something that can only be effected by the promises of God. Thus, Luther's shortening of the medieval rite is done with an eye toward highlighting God's gracious word in the ceremony. For Luther the accretions surrounding the late medieval ceremony tended to obscure the divine promises.

The Reformed Rites. There was not only one Reformed rite when the significant theologians of this tradition developed baptism services for their own communities. Relying on the fine work of Hughes Oliphant Old (*The Shaping of the Reformed Baptismal Rite in the Sixteenth Century*, Grand Rapids, Mich., 1992), it is perhaps most useful to examine the Genevan rite of John Calvin because it is representative of the tradition and is from the hand of the Reformed theologian *par excellence*.

Calvin makes clear that his preference is for baptisms to take place during Sunday worship, although many people still hesitated to wait that long. The service itself begins with an exhortation that is essentially a homily on the meaning of baptism. Calvin describes the sacrament as a "true sign" by which Christ's redemptive work on the cross is communicated to us. He also discusses the question of infant baptism and includes the story of Jesus blessing the children.

Next comes a prayer and an admonition to parents and godparents to nurture the child in the faith. There is also a ceremony for naming the child, with a list of "approved" names provided. This suggests a strong belief in the religious significance of a name. Then follows the baptism itself, which is done with water in the name of the triune God. The rite concludes with a thanksgiving and benediction.

Several things are significant about the service. First, unlike the Roman and Lutheran rites, all reference to exorcism is omitted. Calvin viewed this as an unnecessary encumbrance of the Roman past. Second, the prominent role of the exhortation highlights the role of the word in the Reformed heritage. Third, the conflict with Anabaptism makes an apologia for infant baptism an important part of the Reformed ceremony.

The Anabaptist Rites. The Anabaptists made a radical break with church tradition, emphasizing a decision of faith prior to baptism, which led to a rejection of all infant baptism. The rite of the Anabaptist Balthasar Hubmaier reflects these concerns. Before baptism candidates were asked to demonstrate a basic understanding of Christian doctrine and to be willing to subject themselves to the discipline of the church, should that be necessary. Then, after affirming their desire to be baptized, the candidate was baptized with water in the name of the Father, Son, and Holy Spirit.

The Anglican Rites. The Church of England hoped to be a *via media* between Rome and the Continental reformers. Accordingly, Thomas Cranmer's prayer book rite of 1552 has a Reformed flavor while retaining more of the tradition. The service begins at the font and excludes all exorcisms and anointings. Like the Genevan rite, there is an exhortation that places the sacrament in the proper theological and historical context. The section for the blessing of the font is retained, but the rite curiously eliminates any reference to the hallowing of the water. Next comes the baptism itself. The sacramental act is preceded by a renunciation of Satan and the corresponding creedal affirmation. Cranmer's revision reveals the Reformation concern to trim the "unnecessary" elements of the ceremony, as well as his desire to retain the outward form of the historic rite.

[*See also* Godparentage *and* Family.]

BIBLIOGRAPHY

Armour, Rollin S. *Anabaptist Baptism: A Representative Study*. Scottdale, Pa., 1966. A helpful overview of Anabaptist views on baptism. Includes the baptismal service of Balthasar Hubmaier.

Fisher, J. D. C. *Christian Initiation: Baptism in the Medieval West*. London, 1965. Includes a translation of the *Sarum Manual*, a representative late medieval rite.

———. *Christian Initiation: The Reformation Period*. London, 1970. An invaluable collection of sixteenth-century baptismal liturgies.

Grönvik, Lorenz. *Die Taufe in der Theologie Martin Luthers*. Turku, 1968. A comprehensive study of the vital role played by baptism in the theology of Martin Luther.

Schlink, Edmund. *The Doctrine of Baptism*. Translated by Herbert J. A. Bouman. Saint Louis, 1972. A profound examination of the church's theology and practice of baptism.

Whitaker, E. C. *The Baptismal Liturgy*. 2d ed. London, 1981. A historical sketch of the Catholic and Anglican baptismal liturgy.

MARK D. TRANVIK

Theological Views

The Augsburg Confession sounded a general Reformation theme when it declared that "the church is the assembly of saints in which the gospel is taught purely and the sacraments are administered rightly." From the beginning of the

Reformation movement, the reformers had leveled a severe critique against the sacramental system of medieval Catholicism. They reduced the number of sacraments from seven to two, retaining only baptism and the Lord's Supper as biblically warranted by the institution of Christ. All the Protestant reformers, except for the Anabaptists, continued the practice of infant baptism, but they forged distinctive baptismal theologies in order to explain the role of the sacrament of initiation in their new understanding of grace, salvation, and the church.

Martin Luther's first detailed exposition of his teaching on baptism appeared in his 1519 sermon, "Ein Sermon von dem heiligen hochwürdigen Sakrament der Taufe," and in his famous treatise *De Captivitate Babylonica Ecclesiae* (1520). *In these writings Luther challenged the medieval sacramental doctrine of ex opere operato* ("that grace is conferred by the sheer performance of the act") with the opposing doctrine of *nullum sacramentum sine fide* ("without faith there is no sacrament"). Baptism conveys the word of promise proclaimed in the gospel. In his Small Catechism (1527) Luther asked, "What does baptism give or profit?" Answer: "It works forgiveness of sins, delivers from death and the devil, and gives eternal salvation to all who believe this." He went on to explain that the water itself does not have this power, but the word of God that is in and with the water and faith that trusts such a word in the water. In baptism God announces his gracious acceptance of the sinner, for those who receive baptism in faith are none other than those who have been bathed and cleansed in "the beautiful, rosy-red blood of Christ." Thus baptism is the liturgical enactment of Luther's doctrine of justification by faith alone.

Although Luther refused to elevate penance to the status of a sacrament, he realized that there was the closest possible relationship between baptism and repentance. Luther pointed out the connection between the German words *Taufe*, "baptism," and *tief*, "deep," corresponding to the Greek words for plunging or dipping, and signifying immersion as the preferred mode of baptism. Thus in baptism sinners "are to be wholly drowned by the grace of God." Although baptism is a one-time event, its salvific effect sustains the believer throughout life. The "Christian life is nothing else than a daily baptism, once begun and constantly lived in." In Lutheran piety baptism was both an incentive for godly living and a divine comfort in the face of temptation and doubt.

Luther, along with all the mainline reformers, defended infant baptism against the Anabaptists. Although he admitted that this practice lacked explicit scriptural support, he appealed to the long tradition of the church and argued that God would not have permitted a universal error on a matter of such importance. When confronted with the tension in his own thinking derived from his strict correlation of sacrament and faith, however, Luther developed his concept of "infant faith": when children below the age of reason are baptized they too believe by virtue of God's grace. Faith, as it were, is imputed to infants in baptism even though they are not aware of it. "To be sure," he wrote, "children are brought to baptism by the faith and work of others; but when they get there and the pastor baptizes them in Christ's stead, it is Christ who blesses them and grants them faith and the kingdom of heaven." That the intellective processes of the infant are in abeyance is no hindrance to the impartation of faith. If anything, it is easier to receive faith since "whorish" reason is not likely to get in the way. Luther interpreted the Anabaptist insistence upon faith as a prerequisite for baptism as a relapse into works righteousness. Rather than trying to peep into people's hearts to see whether or not they believe, it is better to trust that, in baptism, the infant is changed, cleansed, and renewed by the divine gift of faith.

Luther rejected the idea, widely believed in the Middle Ages, that unbaptized babies went to limbo, the upper level of hell, which, though not a place of severe torment, was their eternal home. Thus in the case of miscarriage, he advised that water not be sprinkled on the abdomen of the mother. Rather the endangered infant should be committed to God in prayer. In his pastoral advice Luther did not discount the salvation of infants dying before baptism, but he was reluctant to preach this publicly lest the common folk grow lax in bringing their children to the baptismal font.

The shift of emphasis in Luther's baptismal theology reflects the changing polemical fronts of his Reformation struggles. Against the sacramental objectivism of the medieval tradition, he stressed the word of promise and the necessity of faith for a proper understanding of baptism. Against the Anabaptists and other spiritualists, he emphasized the necessity of water baptism, which, in accordance with God's promise, "receives the faith" vouchsafed by divine grace.

The reformers of Switzerland and southern Germany developed a distinctive baptismal theology at odds on crucial points with both Luther and the medieval tradition. Luther's *Täufbüchlein* of 1523 offered a German translation of the Latin baptismal rite although it retained many of the ceremonies traditionally associated with the administration of baptism including exorcism, a double signing with a cross, blowing under the eyes, placement of salt in the mouth and spittle on the ears and nose, and anointment with oil that had been consecrated by a bishop. The reformers of Strasbourg rejected these baptismal accouterments in their primer on Reformed worship, *Grund und Ursach der Erneuerung* (1524). The pruning of the liturgical tradition was carried further still by Johannes Oecolampadius of Basel, Huldrych Zwingli of Zurich, and John Calvin of Geneva. All these reformers were steeped in Erasmian humanism with its preference for inward, spiritual realities over outward, material signs. For the Reformed tradition, the outward washing of water in baptism was a sign of the inward work of the Holy Spirit. Baptism was not the instrumental cause of regenerating grace, but rather a divinely appointed sign of the sovereign work of God's Spirit within one of the elect. Thus the *epiclesis*, a prayer of invocation for the Holy Spirit, assumed a prominent place in Reformed liturgies of baptism.

Erasmus had speculated that baptism might be postponed until adolescence at the discretion of the parents, and Zwingli had once harbored similar ideas. When some of his erstwhile followers began to practice adult rebaptism, however, Zwingli developed a forceful apology for the baptism of infants. Three strands of this argument, especially as elaborated by Heinrich Bullinger and Calvin, became standard features in the Reformed doctrine of infant baptism.

First, the people of Israel in the Old Testament and the visible church in the New stand in a relationship of covenantal continuity. Just as God had directed Abraham and his descendants to circumcise their male infants in the former dispensation, so in the present age infant baptism is the external, collective sign of the New Israel, the church.

Second, various New Testament texts were taken as scriptural validation of infant baptism, especially the embrace of little children by Christ (*Lk.* 18:15–17) and household baptisms in Acts and the Epistles. Although the New Testament nowhere commands infant baptism, its practice could be inferred from such passages. The reformers refused to draw a sharp distinction between the baptism inaugurated by Jesus and that practiced by John the Baptist. By submitting himself both to circumcision and to the baptism of John, Jesus joined the sacraments of the two dispensations, signifying thereby their coordinate meaning and equal value.

Third, there is no attempt to correlate the faith of the infant with the act of baptism. Rather Christian parents make a confession on behalf of their child, by proxy as it were, vowing to teach and nurture the child in the rudiments of the Christian faith. Thus infant baptism became essentially an ecclesial event. The kind of faith that it presupposed was not the personal, subjective faith of the infant, but rather that of the parents and the entire Christian community. For this reason the Reformed tradition disallowed emergency baptisms by midwives as well as private family baptisms. As an act of public worship baptism was to be administered in the presence of the church by a duly appointed minister of the word.

The Genevan Psalter of 1545 reflects these emphases with the additional note that at baptism the child is given a Christian name. This again reinforces the analogy between baptism and circumcision since the latter was also the occasion of giving names to children (*Lk.* 1:59–60; 2:21). Calvin wrote several treatises against the Anabaptists and incorporated his arguments into his *Institutio Christianae Religionis*. He claimed that the baptism of infants was a powerful sign of God's divine initiative in salvation. The effect of the sacrament was determined by the decision of predestination and its temporal unfolding through the activity of the Holy Spirit. However, Calvin's view of baptism differed from that of Zwingli, whose sacramental theology he criticized as focused too narrowly on "empty figures." Without relapsing into the kind of sacramental realism that borders on idolatry, Calvin was concerned to lessen the separation of sign and the thing signified. Like Luther he connected baptism with the lifelong process of repentance for, as the Second Helvetic Confession (1566) put it: "To be baptized is to be purged from the filthiness of sins, and to be endued with the manifold grace of God." For the later Reformed tradition baptism signifies not only the providential placement of the elect within the covenanted community but also their personal union with Christ. In the words of John Knox: "We assuredly believe that by baptism we are engrafted in Christ Jesus, to be partakers of his justice, by which our sins are covered and remitted."

The Church of England retained a strong emphasis on baptism as an efficacious means of grace. *The Book of Common Prayer* of 1549 called for the baptism of infants and referred to this sacrament as the "wholesome laver of regeneration." In agreement with Luther, the English reformers taught that baptism, as well as the Lord's Supper, had a definite effect upon all to whom it was administered, issuing in salvation for the elect and condemnation for all others. The Anglican baptismal liturgy also carried over many of the traditional practices associated with the medieval rite of infant baptism. These became a point of controversy in the Puritan struggle to bring the Church of England into closer alignment with Reformed churches elsewhere. For example, the Puritans took exception to private baptisms, baptism by midwives, signing with the cross, the custom of godparents acting as sponsors, and the tradition of asking infants, who cannot answer for themselves, a series of questions concerning their belief and intention. Whereas Thomas Cranmer had spoken of the "mystical water" of baptism, later Puritans stressed the role of baptism as a seal of God's covenant with his people, a badge of identification with Christ's church, confirmatory of faith in the elect. The Puritan baptismal ceremony was stark in its simplicity, consisting of six items: (1) the demand for the parents to teach their child "in all doctrine necessary for a true Christian"; (2) a sermon including a scriptural explanation of the purpose of baptism; (3) recitation of the Apostles' Creed by the parents; (4) prayer for grace and for the reception of the child into the kingdom of Christ, completed by the Lord's Prayer; (5) the act of baptism in the triune name; (6) thanksgiving.

The radical reformers went further than the mainline Protestants in making a break with traditional sacramental initiation. They rejected infant baptism as a devilish invention with no basis in either the Old or the New Testament. They regarded the analogy to circumcision as spurious and insisted that Jesus' own adult baptism was the normative model for New Testament Christians.

The Schleitheim Confession (1527) set forth the Anabaptist understanding of baptism as consequent to repentance, faith, and conversion: "Baptism shall be given to all who have learned repentance and amendment of life, and who believe truly that their sins are taken away by Christ and to all those who walk in the resurrection of Jesus Christ, and wish to be buried with him in death, so that they might be resurrected with him." The insistence upon "believers' baptism" among the Anabaptists was confirmed by their strict reading of Jesus' statements to his disciples in the Great Commission: Go *first* to teach all nations and *then* to baptize them (*Mt.* 28:19–20).

Despite the emphasis on individual conversion, Anabaptist baptism retained a strong covenantal connotation in that it was the public pledge of commitment that bound the repentant believer to the congregation. Anabaptist theologian Balthasar Hubmaier described this aspect of baptism thus: "In receiving water baptism, the baptized confesses publicly that he has yielded himself to live henceforth according to the rule of Christ. In the power of this confession he has submitted himself to the sisters, the brothers, and the church, so that now they have the authority to admonish him if he errs, to discipline, to ban, and to admit him." In many ways, adult baptism in the radical Reformation stood in the place of the monastic vow as a solemn pledge of commitment to an ascetic community, signifying both a radical break with one's prior life and an intention to fulfill the "councils of perfection" not in the confines of a cloister but amid the conflicts of life in the world.

Baptism was also seen as a prepatory washing for possible martyrdom. The legal strictures against the act of baptism in the ancient Code of Justinian were revived in the sixteenth century, and numerous Anabaptists were put to death by Catholic and Protestant authorities alike. Hubmaier's Catechism refers to a threefold baptism of the Spirit, of water, and of blood. Felix Mantz, one of the Anabaptists of Zurich, commented upon hearing his sentence of death by drowning: "Ah, that is real baptism."

The theology and administration of baptism varied greatly among the different traditions within the radical Reformation. Some spiritualists, such as David Joris, eliminated the outward rite altogether while others, such as Melchior Hoffman, called for its temporary suspension (*Stillstand*). For most Anabaptists, however, water baptism was an ordinance of great significance marking the public initiation of the believer into a life of radical discipleship. As an illegal act, rebaptism had to be done clandestinely. There are reports of Anabaptist baptisms in houses, barns, water towers, in fields and meadows, by rivers and creeks. The most common mode of baptism was pouring, although some, such as Michael Servetus, insisted on immersion in literal imitation of Jesus' own baptism. The antitrinitarian Polish Brethren also equated immersion with true external baptism. As the Racovian Catechism put it: "Where you don't dip or immerse into water, you can have no understanding of baptism unto

the death, burial, and resurrection of the Lord Jesus Christ." In the seventeenth century the Baptists of England also adopted immersion as the only acceptable mode of baptism, arguing that the sign must correspond to the thing signified, that is, the "putting off" of the old self and the "rising to walk in the newness of life."

The Council of Trent defended all seven sacraments of the Roman Catholic church against various criticisms of the reformers. The decrees on original sin and justification affirm the necessity of baptism for the removal of original sin so that "what is contracted by generation may be washed away by regeneration." The seventh session of the council (1547) condemned as heretical the denial of infant baptism, the teaching that baptism was not necessary for salvation, and the idea that the Roman church did not teach the true doctrine of baptism. The council thus taught that baptism conferred grace *ex opere operato*, not by faith alone. Together with confirmation and ordination, baptism conveyed an indelible character and could not be repeated. The council also reaffirmed, in the tradition of Augustine, the validity of heretical baptism, including that of Protestants, provided it was administered in the triune name and with the same "intention" as the church. With the worldwide missionary expansion led by the Society of Jesus and other orders, the Roman church of the sixteenth century faced for the first time in many years the pastoral problems associated with national conversion and mass baptisms. The publication of the Roman Catechism of 1566 provided for the training of children and uneducated adults on such matters as the sacraments, the commandments, and prayer. In this way the baptismal theology of the Catholic Reformation was placed in the larger context of Christian life and doctrine.

[*See also* Sacraments.]

BIBLIOGRAPHY

Althaus, Paul. *The Theology of Martin Luther.* Philadelphia, 1966.

Andresen, Carl, ed. *Handbuch der Dogmen- und Theologiegeschichte.* Vol. 2. Göttingen, 1980.

Armour, Rollin. *Anabaptist Baptism.* Scottdale, Pa., 1966. A basic introduction to Anabaptist thought, succinctly gives Luther's understanding.

Brecht, Martin. "Herkunft und Eigenart der Taufanschauung der Züricher Täufer." *Archiv für Reformationsgeschichte* 64 (1973), 147–165.

De Ferrari, T. M. "Theology of Baptism." In *New Catholic Encyclopedia,* pp. 62–68. Washington, D.C. 1967.

George, Timothy. "The Spirituality of the Radical Reformation." In *Christian Spirituality: High Middle Ages and Reformation,* edited by Jill Raitt, pp. 334–371. New York, 1987.

Jones, Cheslyn, et al., eds. *The Study of Liturgy.* Rev. ed. New York, 1992.

Martos, Joseph. *Doors to the Sacred.* 2d ed. New York, 1981.

Neunheuser, Burkhard. "Baptism." In *Sacramentum Mundi,* vol. 1, pp. 136–144. London, 1968.

Old, Hughes Oliphant. *Worship That Is Formed according to Scripture.* Atlanta, 1984.

Steinmetz, David. "The Baptism of John and the Baptism of Jesus: Huldrych Zwingli, Balthasar Hubmaier, and Late Medieval Theol-

ogy." In *Continuity and Discontinuity in Church History*, edited by F.
F. Church and Timothy George, pp. 169–181. Leiden, 1979.
Windhorst, Christof. *Täuferisches Taufverständnis*. Leiden, 1976.

TIMOTHY GEORGE

BAPTISTS. Two sharply contrasting views of the origins of the Baptists, so called because of their espousal of the doctrine that only believers can be baptized, have been advanced by scholars. The less widely held view attributes their origins to the sixteenth century, largely on circumstantial grounds. According to this interpretation, the General Baptists emerged out of a largely underground tradition that extended back to the 1530s, at which time an Anabaptist congregation existed in London. It in turn had probably built on Lollard foundations. During the reign of Henry VIII the Anabaptist message was propagated in England by both immigrants (notably Scottish, Dutch, and Flemish) and English citizens; of these the most notable was Joan Boucher of Kent, who was executed as a heretic in 1550. Despite the loss of their leaders in the Marian persecution, the Anabaptists survived, though records of them in the late sixteenth century are extremely meager. The possibility that the Anabaptists were linked to the emergence of the General Baptists in the early seventeenth century rests in large part on geography. Anabaptist activity in England was concentrated in the southeast, particularly London, Essex, and Kent. This region, as well as Buckinghamshire, Sussex, and Coventry, where Lollardy had been strong, was receptive to the General Baptists.

All scholars acknowledge that the General Baptists evolved from the Separatists, but most reject substantive connections with English Anabaptists or Lollards even while admitting similarities in the adherence of both groups to believers' baptism and congregations comprising believers alone. Two men played key roles in the emergence of the General Baptists: John Smyth and Thomas Helwys. Smyth, the son of a Nottinghamshire yeoman, had taken his B.A. and M.A. degrees from the University of Cambridge, been ordained as a minister of the Church of England, and served for two years as city lecturer at Lincoln. Around 1607 he adopted Separatist views and a year later emigrated to Amsterdam with the Separatist congregation of John Robinson. He soon became embroiled in a dispute with Francis Johnson, another Separatist minister, arguing for strict congregational autonomy and against the use of Bibles in worship services. Shortly thereafter, he espoused two principles that became hallmarks of the General Baptists, namely believers' baptism and a universal atonement, according to which Christ had died for all persons, not, as the Calvinists argued, for the elect alone. Smyth proceeded to baptize himself and then his followers, including Helwys, rather than seek baptism from the Waterlander Mennonites, whom he deemed apostates.

Helwys, who was also from a gentry family in Nottinghamshire, had engaged in legal studies at Gray's Inn, London, before emigrating to Amsterdam with Smyth and later following him when he broke with the Separatists. When Smyth and a majority of his congregation opted to establish close ties with the Mennonites (whom he had come to respect and with whom his followers would eventually unite in 1615), Helwys and a few others formed their own church, published *A Declaration of Faith* (1611), and returned to London in 1612, where they became the first General Baptist church in England. Although the group issued a call for toleration in *A Short Declaration of the Mystery of Iniquity*, Helwys went to prison. After his death, leadership of the church passed to John Murton, a furrier from Lincolnshire. By 1626, General Baptist churches had been founded at Lincoln, Salisbury, Coventry, and Tiverton; with the mother church in London, they had approximately 150 members.

The Particular (or Calvinistic) Baptists date their origins to the early 1630s, when John Spilsbury, a London cobbler, apparently seceded from the Separatist congregation of John Dupper to form his own church. Dupper's group had previously split from the Separatist church of John Lathrop in Southwark, from which Samuel Eaton, a London button-maker, withdrew in 1633. Spilsbury rebaptized Eaton, either because Eaton denied the legitimacy of baptism in the "false" Church of England or because he now believed in believers' baptism. Unlike Spilsbury, Eaton did not require believers' baptism for membership in the congregation he established; his was thus the first open-membership church in England. By the time the Particular Baptists issued their first confession of faith in 1644, they had seven churches in London. Both groups of Baptists drew their strength primarily from the "middling sort," such as artisans and small traders, and from those living in the countryside, though the Particular Baptists also attracted a number of wealthy London merchants.

Three areas of Baptist thought are especially significant: (1) Like the Separatists from whom they emerged, both General and Particular Baptists adhered to the notion of a "gathered" church composed of visible saints. Sound doctrine and a godly life were essential for membership. (2) The hallmark of both Baptist groups was the decision to administer baptism to believers alone, since children could not provide evidence of the saving faith that was reputedly the prerequisite for baptism. Baptists thus rejected the traditional argument that likened baptism to circumcision and made it the sign or seal of both the divine promise and the covenant of grace established with the faithful and their children. By 1642, some of the Baptists had become convinced that the proper method to administer baptism was not sprinkling but immersion, which signified the bathing of the soul in the blood of Christ, the identification of the recipient with Christ's death and resurrection, and the assurance that the believer would ultimately be resurrected to reign with Christ. (3) Unlike the Mennonites, the Baptists accepted the legitimacy of civil government as a divine ordinance and did not exclude magistrates from church membership. Nor did they object to taking legitimate oaths or to fighting in just wars.

By the end of the sixteenth century, the Anabaptist movement was on the verge of extinction in England. The emergence of the Baptists offered a radical religious alternative to the Separatists, whose ranks they split. The resulting debates between the Independents (Congregationalists), Particular Baptists, and General Baptists drew attention to baptism as well as the importance attached to experiential faith and the role of the congregation in church government. The Baptists in particular came to champion the cause of religious toleration.

[See also Anabaptists; Congregationalism; Nonconformity; Puritans; and Separatists.]

BIBLIOGRAPHY

Horst, Irvin Buckwalter. The Radical Brethren: Anabaptism and the English Reformation to 1558. Nieuwkoop, 1972. Argues the case for the importance of Anabaptist influence in England.

Tolmie, Murray. The Triumph of the Saints: The Separate Churches of London, 1616–1649. Cambridge, 1977. Superb account of the early Baptist, Separatist, and Independent congregations.

Watts, Michael R. The Dissenters: From the Reformation to the French Revolution. Oxford, 1978. Contends that the General Baptists were linked to the English Anabaptists.

White, B. R. The English Separatist Tradition: From the Marian Martyrs to the Pilgrim Fathers. London, 1971. Discusses the emergence of the General Baptists out of the Separatist movement.

———. The English Baptists of the Seventeenth Century. London, 1983. Rejects the influence of the English Anabaptists on the General Baptists. A sound survey.

RICHARD L. GREAVES

BARLOW, William (c.1500–1568), English reform bishop and author of an English account of the continental Reformation. Barlow's early career is troublesome, as nothing is known about his formal education nor where he was between about 1528 and 1534. He might have seen diplomatic service in 1528 and gone to Rome. In 1531 he published the earliest English account of the Continental Reformation, A dyaloge descrybyng the Orgynall Ground of these Lutheran Faccyons, which outlines Luther's controversies with Henry VIII, Andreas Bodenstein von Karlstadt, and Huldrych Zwingli; discusses the Lutheran and Zwinglian quarrel over the Eucharist and the meeting at Marburg (1528), and provides an early English account of the Anabaptists, the "third faction."

Barlow recanted his Catholicism and quickly rose as bishop of Saint Asaph's (1535) and Saint David's (1536), where his Protestantism clashed with the Welsh clergy. He opposed the Six Articles, participated in the welcome party for Anne of Cleves, and went to Scotland to induce James V to abandon Rome. Marrying around the time he was transferred to Bath and Wells (1548), Barlow was the first married and distinctly Protestant bishop there; he colluded with Edward Seymour, duke of Somerset, to deplete the diocesan endowment.

Recanting his Protestantism in January 1555, Barlow went into exile at Emden, possibly to Wesel, and then to Weinheim (near Heidelberg) with the duchess of Suffolk, and to Poland. Returning to England with letters from Albert of Brandenburg and Philipp Melanchthon, he was transferred to Chichester (1559). He consecrated Archbishop Matthew Parker, fought against Roman Catholic recusancy in his diocese, revised several books for the Bishops' Bible, and died 17 August 1568. When Thomas Fuller characterized Barlow as "a man of much motion and promotion," he captured much of the fervor surrounding the life of this Protestant activist who, in marrying his five daughters to five bishops, earned a unique niche in Anglican history.

BIBLIOGRAPHY

Hembry, Phyllis M. The Bishops of Bath and Wells: 1540–1640. London, 1967. Details results of collusion with Somerset.

McLean, Andrew. "'Detestynge Thabomynacyon': William Barlow, Thomas More and the Anglican Episcopacy." Moreana 49 (February 1976), 67–77.

———. "'A noughtye and a false lyeng boke': William Barlow and the Lutheran Factions." Renaissance Quarterly 31 (Summer 1978), 173–85. Establishes Barlow's authorship and political involvements.

McLean, Andrew, ed. Bishop Barlowe's Dialogue on the Lutheran Factions. Courtenay Library of Reformation Classics, no. 15. Appleford, England, 1981. A scholarly edition of the 1531 text with notes.

Rupp, E. Gordon. Studies in the Making of the Protestant Tradition. Reprint, Cambridge, 1966. Attempts to account for the lacuna of the early years.

Williams, Glanmor. Welsh Reformation Essays. Cardiff, 1967. See pp. 111–139. Details confrontations with clergy in Wales.

ANDREW M. MCLEAN

BARNABITES. The Clerics Regular of Saint Paul, popularly known as the Barnabites because of their association with the church of Saint Barnabas in Milan, were founded in 1530 as the third of ten orders of clerics regular by Antonio Maria Zaccaria (1502–1539), a nobleman from Cremona. The order received papal authorization in 1533.

Zaccaria studied philosophy and medicine at the University of Padua between 1520 and 1524. He may also have practiced medicine briefly in Cremona before organizing a group of laypeople, referred to as the Amicizia, about 1526. This organization of men and women became the nucleus of two religious orders—the Clerics Regular of Saint Paul and the Angelic Sisters of Saint Paul, who were cofounded by Ludovica Torelli (1499–1569), the countess of Guastalla—and a lay sodality, called the Married Couples of Saint Paul. Zaccaria was ordained a secular priest in 1528. Late in 1530 he joined the Oratory of Eternal Wisdom in Milan, where he met the two cofounders of the Barnabites, Giacomo Antonio Morigia (1497–1546), an architect, and Bartolomeo Ferrari (1499–1544), a notary.

Zaccaria conceived a tripartite apostolate in which priests, vowed but uncloistered sisters, and laypeople joined forces to work among the indigent, the infirm, orphans, and unwed mothers. He drafted a constitution for the Barnabites that was based on the rule of Augustine and the ideas of Zaccaria's spiritual director, Battista Carioni of Crema (c.1460–1534), a Dominican priest. Barnabite spirituality is based on the writings of Paul and devotions to Christ crucified and the Eucharist in the "forty hours."

Carlo Borromeo, archbishop of Milan, is regarded as the second founder of the Barnabites because he instructed them to rewrite their constitution in order to reflect Tridentine reforms. The papacy approved it in 1579. Following an apostolic visitation by Bishop Leonardo Marini in 1552, the Angelics were enclosed and could no longer contribute to the public ministries of the Barnabites.

The first permanent foundations of the order outside Milan were in Pavia (1557), Cremona (1570), Monza and Casale Monferrato (1571), Rome (1575), Vercelli (1576), Pisa (1595), and Bologna and Novara (1599). The Barnabites consisted of priests only until 1554, when lay brothers were admitted. Their membership remained small throughout the sixteenth century. In 1576, for example, they consisted of 45 priests, 21 brothers, and 15 professed clerics. They had no permanent houses outside Italy in the 1500s.

BIBLIOGRAPHY

Cagni, Luigi G., et al. *Barnabiti Studi.* 10 vols. Rome, 1984–1993.
DeMolen, Richard L., ed. *Religious Orders of the Catholic Reformation.* New York, 1994.
Moltedo, Francesco T. *Vita di S. Antonio Maria Zaccaria, Fondatore de' Barnabiti e delle Angeliche.* Florence, 1897.
Premoli, Orazio M. *Storia dei Barnabiti nel Cinquecento.* Rome, 1913.

RICHARD L. DEMOLEN

BARNES, Robert (1495–1540), pioneer English Lutheran reformer. About 1521 Barnes introduced humanist methods of scholarship to friars of the Augustinian house at Cambridge, where he was prior. He thereafter became a bold critic of ecclesiastical corruption and an avid student of the New Testament. He participated with other reform-minded scholars in studying Luther's writings at the White Horse Inn, the birthplace of the English Reformation. Barnes's tactless zeal produced stinging criticisms of leading churchmen, including Thomas Wolsey, and the reformer spent six months in prison and underwent subsequent house arrest in two friaries.

While in confinement Barnes promoted the circulation of William Tyndale's New Testament, for which he faced death by burning. He escaped to Germany and at Wittenberg became a Lutheran theologian and author of *A Supplication unto King Henry VIII* (1530), in which he affirmed loyalty to his monarch, whom he hoped to convert to the Protestant faith. *The Supplication* impressed Henry's chief minister, Thomas Cromwell, who convinced the suspicious king to employ Barnes on diplomatic missions to the German Lutheran states.

By 1536 Barnes despaired of Henry's conversion, but he returned to England even though his diplomacy had failed. He continued in royal service, and while he was in Germany on his last mission, Parliament passed the Act of Six Articles (1539), a reaffirmation of medieval Catholic doctrine that made Barnes a Lutheran heretic. He returned to England nevertheless and preached evangelical doctrines, especially justification through faith. He died at the stake, 30 July 1540.

Barnes was not an original thinker. He espoused Luther's teachings and spread them in England. Some of his writings are paraphrases of his German mentor. Although Lutheranism did not become the creed of the Protestant church in England, its influence upon that institution was substantial. Historic documents, such as the Ten Articles (1536), the *Bishops' Book* (1537), the Thirteen Articles (1538), and *The Book of Common Prayer* (1549), reflect the Lutheran influence that Barnes brought from Germany.

BIBLIOGRAPHY

Primary Sources

Barnes, Robert. *Sentenciae ex doctoribus collectae, quas papistae valde impudenter hodie damnant.* Wittenberg, 1530.
———. *Vitae Romanorum Pontificum, quos Papas vocamus.* Basel, 1555.
———. *The Reformation Essays of Dr. Robert Barnes.* Saint Louis, 1963.
———. *A Supplication . . . unto Henry VIII* (1534). New York, 1973.
———. *The Whole Workes of W. Tyndall, John Frith, and Doct. Barnes, Three Worthy Martyrs. . . .* London, 1983.

Secondary Sources

Clebsch, William A. *England's Earliest Protestants.* Reprint, Westport, Conn., 1980. Revisionist intrepretation that portrays Barnes and others as primarily humanist moral reformers rather than Protestant theologians.
McGoldrick, James Edward. *Luther's English Connection.* Milwaukee, 1979. Examines the works of Barnes and Tyndale on every major area of doctrine and concludes that they were primary agents for the transmission of Luther's influence to their homeland.
Tjernagel, Neelak S. *Lutheran Martyr.* Milwaukee, 1982. Only actual biography of Robert Barnes, this work maintains the traditional view of the subject as a Lutheran reformer.

JAMES EDWARD MCGOLDRICK

BARONIO, Cesare (Lat., Caesar Baronius; 1538–1607), Italian cardinal and ecclesiastical historian. He is best known for his massive, twelve-volume *Annales Ecclesiastici,* the first comprehensive compilation of church history in modern times, and for his role in the church reforms under several late sixteenth-century popes, most importantly

Clement VIII. Born in the historic Campagna town of Sora on 31 October 1538 and having completed his early education in Veroli, Baronio was sent to Naples in 1556 at the age of eighteen to pursue a legal education at the university. Because of the impending French invasion, he left Naples on 29 October 1557, and traveled to Rome.

In Rome young Baronio was soon drawn to the circle of Filippo Neri, a future saint, who opened a meeting place for churchmen and laity who were interested in intellectual discussions on religion and philosophy. The Bible, church reform, ethics, and liturgy were some of the main themes of their evening discussions. Among those who frequented the evening meetings at Neri's residence were some of the most influential church leaders of the Catholic Reformation—Carlo Borromeo, Federico Borromeo, Jacopo Sadoleto, and Gian Matteo Giberti, to name a few. Contacts with such illustrious humanist-reformers and the charismatic Neri brought about a dramatic change in the impressionable young scholar from the small town in Campagna. As a result Baronio switched his main interest from law to theology. Following the ardent request of his father, however, he continued his legal studies and obtained a doctorate in law in 1561.

Baronio considered the degree in law as something he owed his father. His real interest was in pursuing a religious vocation. He therefore moved in with Neri and his disciples, who by then formed the Oratory, at that time an unofficial religious congregation. As a member of the Oratory, Baronio had only one interest—to live an ascetic religious life—but Neri had different plans for his young disciple. Neri felt that Baronio's keen mind, strong will, and ascetic self-discipline could be put to good use in the service of the church in a critical matter—namely, to refute the *Centuriae Magdeburgenses* (Magdeburg Centuries), the massive history of the church prepared by Matthias Flacius Illyricus and his Lutheran collaborators in order to demonstrate that the hierarchical order and papal supremacy in the church were aberrations. The first volume of the *Centuriae* was published in 1559, but the year before Neri had already asked Baronio to start a series of lectures on church history to be delivered at the regular meetings of the Oratory. When the appearance of the *Centuriae* created such a consternation in the church, it was natural that Neri would assign Baronio the task of refuting it, but that was no simple task. He would spend from 1564 until the day of his death on 30 June 1607 on this grueling task.

It took Baronio from 1564 until 1588 to publish the first volume of the *Annales*. This and the succeeding eleven volumes of the work, the last of which was published in 1607, covered the history of the church from its origins to 1193. The *Annales* caused great rejoicing among Catholics. It refuted to their own satisfaction the central argument of the *Centuriae*. The reason for the effectiveness of the *Annales* was the way Baronio used excerpts of even full texts of original documents to describe history. These he presented to the reader in chronological order without much elaboration or embellishment. His position was that a historian should be concerned only with accuracy and not at all with narrative style. The historian's job is not to persuade or entertain anyone but only to present the raw data. True to this philosophy of history, Baronio collected every document available on all aspects of church history and arrayed them against the *Centuriae*. In collecting and selecting these documents, Baronio took great care. Yet his central interest in proving the primacy of the papacy caused him to be less than accurate in some key instances; for example, he accepted the authenticity of the so-called Donation of Constantine, which humanist philologists and historians, such as Lorenzo Valla, had already demonstrated to be spurious.

The *Annales*, in spite of some inaccuracies, was a veritable treasury of information and a huge success against the *Centuriae*. It was indeed one of the keys to the success of the Catholic Counter-Reformation. The author, therefore, became the beneficiary of great fame and fortune. Popes bestowed on him many honors, including the dignity of the cardinalate. Clement VIII made him his confessor and principal adviser. In that role and in his role as member or head of various papal commissions, he made his influence felt on many important decisions—revision of the calendar and the Roman martyrology, the reform of religious congregations, the reconciliation of Henry IV of France with the church, and the interdict of Venice, to name a few.

Finally, the papal office itself came within the reach of Baronio. He became a reluctant candidate for the papacy in the conclaves held after the deaths of Clement VIII and Leo XI and in the latter instance even received a two-thirds majority of votes. His election was blocked only by use of the *jus exclusivum* by the Spanish king, whom Baronio had offended by his defense of papal authority in Sicily.

Baronio's last days were spent in the Oratory at Vallicella, where his spiritual journey had begun many decades earlier. He found solace in the humble surroundings of the Oratory and in the company of his fellow religious. There he died on 30 June 1607. The Oratorians made many unsuccessful attempts to have him canonized, but his enemies succeeded in denying him that title. He has remained a "Venerable," the first step of the canonization process, an honor to which Benedict XV elevated him in 1745.

BIBLIOGRAPHY

Albericius, Raymundus. *Venerabilis Caesaris Baronii Epistolae et Opuscula.* 3 vols. Rome, 1759–1770.

Barnabeus, Hieronimus. *Vita Caesari Baronii.* Rome, 1651.

Calenzio, Generoso. *La Vita e gli Scritti del Cardinale Cesare Baronio della Congregazione del oratorio.* Rome, 1907.

Kerr, Amabel. *The Life of Cesare Cardinal Baronio of the Roman Oratory.* London, 1898.

Libero, Giuseppe de. *Cesare Baronio Padre della Storia Ecclesiastica.* Rome, 1939.

Pullapilly, Cyriac K. *Caesar Baronius: Counter-Reformation Historian.* Notre Dame, Ind., 1975.

CYRIAC K. PULLAPILLY

BARREFELT, Hendrik Jansen van (also Barrevelt; Hiël; 1520?–1594?), radical spiritual leader in the Low Countries. Born around 1520 in Barneveld (near Amersfoort), Barrefelt, a poor weaver, lived in Gelderland and was initially attracted to the teachings of Menno Simons. He became one of the first followers of Hendrik Niclaes and his Family of Love shortly after the prophet's establishment in Emden, East Frisia, in 1540. As Niclaes's first secretary and principal agent, Barrefelt carried his manuscripts and supervised the distribution of the printed editions in Friesland, Overijssel, Holland, and Brabant. A bachelor when he joined Niclaes, he must have married about 1550 and had at least two children. Barrefelt followed Niclaes when the latter decided in 1566/67 to move to the "country of peace" in or near Cologne. During the Cologne period, however, the Family of Love was afflicted by both financial misunderstandings and doctrinal differences, and in 1573 a schism occurred when Niclaes attempted to organize the Family of Love into a visible church.

A group of disaffected "Niclaesites" gathered around the less authoritarian Barrefelt, who, inspired by a divine revelation, began to act under the name "Hiël" (Life of God). The core of the so-called "Hiëlists," or second Family of Love, was formed by relatives, dependents, and business associates of the Antwerp printer Christoffel Plantijn (1520?–1589), including the cartographer Abraham Ortelius (1527–1598), the neo-Stoicist Justus Lipsius (1547–1606), and the Hebraeist and former chaplain of Philip II Benito Arias Montano (1527–1598). Little is known about Barrefelt's whereabouts in the 1570s and early 1580s, but around 1587 Barrefelt established himself at Cologne, where he died shortly after 1594. The spiritual movement characterized by conciliatory aspirations, to which both Niclaes and Barrefelt had belonged, retained its strength, particularly in the northern Netherlands, where a number of spiritual confraternities were in effect preparing the way for Arminianism.

Niclaes and Barrefelt set out with similar premises. For both men Original Sin was a breaking away from oneness with God, reincorporation into whom was possible only by imitating Christ and dying to one's own will. Both men held that ceremonies and sacraments had only a symbolic value. Both rejected solifidianism and consequently remained closer to Catholicism than to Protestantism, although Barrefelt was less outspoken in his criticism of the Reformation than Niclaes. In a true Nicodemite spirit, Barrefelt took issue with Niclaes's attempts to make the Family of Love a visible church with a visible priesthood and, above all, a visible papacy in the person of Niclaes. Barrefelt's was indeed the invisible church or mystical body of Sebastian Franck, and,

in contrast to Niclaes, he openly acknowledged the influence of the *Theologia germanica* and the *De imitatione Christi.* Against the cult of personality of Niclaes and his claims of deification, Barrefelt formulated the doctrine of personal identification with the divine being in which each man has as much right to inspiration as the next. His major works are the *Boeck der Ghetuygenissen van den verborghen Acker-schat* (c.1581), *Imagines et figurae Bibliorum* (1582), and *Sendtbrieven* (1584).

BIBLIOGRAPHY

Primary Sources

Barrefelt, Hendrik Jansen van. *Het boeck der ghetuygenissen van den verborghen Ackerschat, verklarende de verborghen wonderdaeden Godts.* Antwerp, c.1581.

———. *Een geestelyke reyse eens jonghelincks nae het landt van vreden, om daer weseralyck in Godt inne te leven.* Antwerp, 1582.

———. *Imagines et Figurae Bibliorum.* Antwerp, 1582.

———. *Sendtbrieven wt yverighe herten, ende int afvoorderinghe, schriftelyck aen de liefhebbers der waerheyt, deur den utvloedt van den Gheest des eeuwighen levens utghegeven.* 2 vols. Leiden, 1584.

———. *Historie des ouden en nieuwen testaments.* Haarlem, 1650.

———. *Das Grundstück, welches gründlich im Hertzen erklärt zwei widerwartige Wesen.* Amsterdam, 1687.

———. *Het derde deel der Epistelen, ofte Zendbrieven.* Amsterdam, 1714.

———. *Zweyter-Theil der Send-Brieffe.* Amsterdam, 1714.

———. *Geestelycke brieven: Bijbelsche figuren, vertoonende de voornaemste historien der H. Schrifture, met verklaringe van jedere figure, en zinrycke verzen.* Haarlem, c.1717.

Secondary Sources

Hamilton, Alastair. "Hiël and Hiëlists: The Doctrines and Followers of Hendrik Jansen van Barrefelt." *Quaerendo* 7.3 (Summer 1977), 243–286. A good survey of Barrefelt's teachings and of his most assiduous supporters.

———. "Seventeen Letters from Hendrik Jansen van Barrefelt (Hiël) to Jan Moretus." *De Gulden Passer* 57 (1979), 62–127. Van Barrefelt's correspondence with Jan Moretus, Plantijn's son-in-law and successor at the Officina Plantiniana, complete with editorial notes.

———. *The Family of Love.* Cambridge, 1981. The first study of the Family of Love to place it in its full context, both Continental and British.

Hamilton, Alastair, ed. *Cronica: Ordo Sacerdotis: Acta H. N.; Three Texts on the Family of Love.* Leiden, 1988. Treats the texts in the original western Low German; detailed synopses in English at the head of each chapter.

Moss, Jean Dietz. *"Godded with God": Hendrik Niclaes and His Family of Love.* Transactions of the American Philosophical Society, vol. 78, pt. 8. Philadelphia, 1981. Although focused on the growth of Familiarism in England, this work contains a valuable section on the theoretical issues at stake.

Mout, N. "The Family of Love (Huis der Liefde) and the Dutch Revolt." In *Britain and the Netherlands,* vol. 7, *Church and State since the Reformation,* edited by A. C. Duke and C. A. Tamse, pp. 76–93. The Hague, 1981. A brief discussion of the temporary influence of the Familists' conciliatory ideas in the early stages of the Revolt of the Netherlands.

La Fontaine Verwey, Herman de. "Trois Hérésiarques dans les Pays-Bas du XVIe siècle." *Bibliothèque d'Humanisme et Renaissance* 16 (1954), 312–330. For a short discussion of Niclaes, Barrefelt, and the third Familist leader David Joris.

———. "The Family of Love: Radical Spiritualism in the Low Countries." *Quaerendo* 6.3 (Summer 1976), 219–271. Detailed analysis of the origins and spread of the Family of Love in and, to a lesser extent, outside the Dutch Republic.

MARCUS P. M. VINK

BASEL. The Reformation in Basel went through several phases before the city's church assumed its final form at the end of the sixteenth century. Although the majority of the city's inhabitants accepted the evangelical gospel in the early 1520s, the magistracy did not officially adopt Protestantism until the end of the decade, when it was forced to do so by the threat of a popular revolt. The next two decades were a time of institutional establishment and consolidation for the Protestant church. The second half of the century witnessed renewed conflict as a powerful minority within the church opposed the doctrines associated with Huldrych Zwingli and John Calvin and tried to steer the church in a more Lutheran direction. These efforts failed, and by the end of the century the Basel church had adopted Reformed orthodoxy.

The years immediately preceding the Reformation witnessed two important political changes that would influence the process of religious reform in the city. In 1515 members of the urban patriciate were effectively excluded from the council. Their places were assumed by representatives of the craft guilds, thus increasing the latter's participation in the government. Six years later the council removed the last vestiges of power from the city's nominal ruler, the bishop of Basel, by unilaterally rejecting the right of the bishop and cathedral chapter to participate in the election of the council. This act gave the council more freedom to extend its control over the city's church. Members of the actual decision-making bodies of the government were chosen by co-optation, and they generally held their positions for life. Dominated by merchants and the wealthiest members of the craft guilds, the council remained more conservative than the majority of the city's population; during the 1520s it resisted popular pressure to abolish Catholic worship and instead tried to hold a mediating position between Protestants and Catholics.

Basel was an important printing center, and such humanists as Desiderius Erasmus and Beatus Rhenanus published first editions of many patristic works there during the early decades of the sixteenth century. Martin Luther's works were first printed in Basel in 1518, and by the early 1520s preachers at several of the city's churches were proclaiming the evangelical gospel. The Protestant message was particularly attractive to those belonging to the city's lower social and economic strata. Opposition to evangelical preaching was centered in the university. Both the bishop and the cathedral chapter opposed the evangelical preachers, but long-standing disputes between them prevented effective cooperation against the Protestants.

In November 1522 the prominent humanist Johannes Oecolampadius arrived in Basel. He quickly became the leader of the evangelical movement. Within a few months the council appointed him to the theology faculty of the university. His lectures, delivered in both Latin and German, further promoted the evangelical cause, as did his subsequent appointment as parish pastor. Oecolampadius became a close friend and supporter of Zwingli, particularly after the outbreak of the eucharistic controversy in late 1524.

The conflict between Catholic and Protestant factions increased gradually over the course of 1523. In an attempt to limit polemical sermons given by both parties, the council issued a mandate ordering preachers to proclaim the gospel according to the scriptures and to avoid discussion about other doctrines. The council frequently cited this edict over the next few years, as it attempted to preserve civic peace by seeking a position on doctrinal issues that would be acceptable to both Catholics and Protestants. On the other hand, the council took advantage of the religious and political disturbances to increase its control over the city's church. The threat of violence arising from the Peasants' War of 1525 prompted the Basel clergy to seek the protection of citizenship, which the council granted in exchange for clerical submission to the city's jurisdiction. The council also gradually assumed the right to appoint clergy to vacant benefices. The secularization of the city's ecclesiastical institutions began in early 1525, when the prior of the collegiate church of Saint Leonhard surrendered the foundation's property to the city. Within a few weeks the council had also extended its control over the four women's convents in the city. The nuns were allowed to remain, but the rigors of the monastic rule were relaxed, and a procedure was set up to ease the way for those who wished to leave the convent. In the spring of 1527 the council abolished the celebration of most church festivals in both the city and the surrounding territory. Later that year the council officially recognized the evangelical status of several of the city's churches by exempting their pastors from the requirement to celebrate Mass.

The Bern Disputation in early 1528 encouraged the evangelical party to even more determined action against the Catholics. At Easter a small group of artisans destroyed some of the images in two of the evangelical churches. To prevent further outbreaks of iconoclasm the council ordered the partial removal of images from all the evangelical churches. This measure did not satisfy the Protestant party, which by now greatly outnumbered the Catholics. On 23 December 1528 a large group of citizens gathered at the gardeners' guildhall and adopted a resolution calling for the prohibition of the Mass in the city and the removal of all Catholic preachers from their positions. An open revolt was averted only after the council agreed to limit the celebration of the Mass to three churches and set a date for a public disputation concerning the Mass for the coming summer.

Within a short time, however, the council was accused of reneging on its agreement. On 8 February 1529 a large crowd again assembled, repeating its earlier demands and now calling for the removal of Catholics from the council and for a constitutional revision that would allow guild members the right to elect their leaders directly. The meeting led to an iconoclastic riot in the cathedral. Under pressure of events, the council gave in to popular demands. Twelve Catholics were deprived of their positions on the council, the Mass was abolished, and all remaining images were removed from the city's churches. In addition, the council agreed to broaden the right to participate in guild elections, although not to the degree demanded by the populace. The council was able to repeal these constitutional changes in 1533.

In the wake of the Protestant victory, the cathedral chapter, the majority of the university faculty and their students, and several prominent individuals, including Erasmus, left the city. The university was closed, and its records and property were taken over by the magistrate. The university reopened as a Protestant institution at the end of 1532, although it only gradually regained its former reputation. Erasmus returned in 1535 to Basel, where he died the following year.

The council had been slow to adopt Protestantism, but it did not hesitate to act against the threat posed by the growing number of Anabaptists in its territories during the second half of the 1520s. The council's first edict against the Anabaptists, issued in 1527, was fairly effective in preventing the establishment of sectarian groups within the city, but by 1530 the movement had many followers in the city's rural territories. Successive edicts sharpened the penalties imposed on Anabaptists, culminating in the threat of exile or execution included in an edict issued at the end of 1530. The severity of this last edict proved effective in eliminating Anabaptism as a popular movement, although over the next several years officials continued to uncover individuals or family groups who adhered to Anabaptist doctrines.

On 1 April 1529 a new church ordinance was issued for the city. The ordinance divided the city into four parishes; established a procedure for examination and appointment of the clergy and specified the duties expected of them; regulated the time of worship and the manner of celebrating the sacraments; and created a civil marriage court and a moral code governing sexual offenses. In response to pressure by Oecolampadius, the council issued an additional ordinance at the end of 1530 regulating the process of church discipline. The ordinance gave the responsibility for church discipline to three laymen—two of them council members—from each parish. The pastors were not involved in the disciplinary process until the final warning before excommunication, and excommunicates who were not reconciled with the church within a month were subject to civil penalties.

Six months later the procedure was modified so that obstinate sinners were referred to the council, which now assumed the ultimate authority to impose the ban. In 1532 the council created a new commission comprised of pastors, council members, and laymen to oversee the church, but this body was eliminated in 1539. From this point on the council had direct oversight of the city's church.

Oecolampadius did not live to see the subordination of the church to the magistrate; he died in November 1531, shortly after Zwingli's death at Kappel. Oecolampadius's successor as *Antistes*, or head of the church, was Oswald Myconius, a former schoolteacher in Zurich. Largely self-taught in theology, Myconius relied greatly on the advice of Simon Grynaeus, professor of New Testament at the university, until the latter's death in 1541. Both men supported the efforts of Martin Bucer to end the eucharistic controversy, and Basel was the only Swiss city to accept the Wittenberg Concord, signed in 1536. Myconius and Grynaeus together produced the Basel Confession, which was based on a confession of faith written by Oecolampadius shortly before his death. The confession was officially adopted and published by the council in January 1534, and all guild members were required to accept it under oath. Although marginal notes gave its article on the Lord's Supper a Zwinglian cast, the confession's wording was ambiguous enough that both Reformed and Lutherans could claim that it upheld their own positions in the doctrinal conflicts of the later sixteenth century.

Myconius died in October 1552 and was succeeded as *Antistes* by Simon Sulzer. Sulzer had been the leader of a pro-Lutheran faction in the Bern church until he was expelled from that city in 1548. He had then come to Basel, where he was given both a pastorate and a professorship at the university. As leader of the Basel church, Sulzer continued to promote his Lutheran views. Although he was opposed by most of the clergy, Sulzer had the support of the magistrate and many of the humanists, some of them religious refugees, who taught at the university or worked for the city's printing houses. His opposition to Reformed doctrine made him a natural ally for those who opposed Calvin on such issues as the exercise of church discipline or the doctrine of predestination. One of the most prominent members of this group was the Savoyard humanist Sébastien Castellion, whose book *De haereticis an sint persequendi* ("Whether Heretics Ought to be Persecuted"), was published under a pseudonym in 1554, several months after the execution of the Spanish heretic Michael Servetus in Geneva. As a consequence of Sulzer's leadership, the Basel church gradually became alienated from the other Swiss Reformed churches. In 1566 Basel refused to sign the Second Helvetic Confession, stating that it preferred to retain its own confession of 1534. When conflict broke out among the pastors over the interpretation of the Lord's Supper at the end of 1570, Sulzer was able to require the clergy in both the city and territory to sign the Wittenberg Concord. Opposition to Sulzer's policies increased over the course of the 1570s, however, and he was unsuccessful in his efforts to have the Lutheran *Book of Concord* accepted by the Basel church. Upon Sulzer's death in 1585, Johann Jacob Grynaeus was chosen as his successor. As a theology professor at the university, Grynaeus had been Sulzer's chief opponent, and after his election as *antistes* he established Reformed orthodoxy as the standard for both the church and university. His efforts to enforce doctrinal orthodoxy were accompanied by the council's issuance of a new moral code for the city and rural territories that reaffirmed the magistrate's control over the church.

[*See also* Oecolampadius, Johannes.]

BIBLIOGRAPHY

Berchtold, Alfred. *Bâle et L'Europe: Une histoire culturelle.* 2 vols. 2d rev. & corr. ed. Lausanne, 1991. An account of Basel's cultural significance written for a general audience; concentrates on the sixteenth century, discussing humanism, religious reform, and heterodoxy, with brief biographical chapters on several of the most prominent figures in Basel during this period.

Burckhardt, Paul. *Basel in den ersten Jahren nach der Reformation.* Basler Neujahrsblatt 124. Basel, 1946. A general history of Basel during the 1530s, emphasizing the consequences of the Reformation on politics and on the relationship between church and state.

Guggisberg, Hans R. *Basel in the Sixteenth Century: Aspects of the City Republic before, during, and after the Reformation.* Saint Louis, 1982. Brief but excellent introduction to the most important aspects of Basel's history and culture during the period of the Reformation; includes a useful bibliographical note.

Köhler, Walther. *Zürcher Ehegericht und Genfer Konsistorium.* Vol. I, *Das Zürcher Ehegericht und seine Auswirkung in der deutschen Schweiz zur Zeit Zwinglis.* Quellen und Abhandlungen zur schweizerischen Reformationsgeschichte 7, II. Serie der Quellen zur schweizerischen Reformationsgeschichte X. Leipzig, 1932. Chapter 8 describes the workings of Basel's marriage court and the exercise of church discipline after the Reformation.

Linder, Gottfried. *Simon Sulzer und sein Antheil an der Reformation im Lande Baden, sowie an den Unionsbestrebungen.* Heidelberg, 1890. Outdated, but the only monograph on Sulzer; its title is misleading, since most of the book deals with Sulzer's leadership of the Basel church.

Plath, Uwe. *Calvin und Basel in den Jahren 1552–1556.* Basler Beiträge zur Geschichtswissenschaft 133. Basel, 1974. A detailed discussion of Calvin's supporters and opponents in Basel, particularly in the wake of Servetus's execution.

Roth, Paul. *Die Reformation in Basel.* Pt. 1, *Die Vorbereitungsjahre, 1525–1528.* Basler Neujahrsblatt 114. Basel, 1936. Difficult to obtain; a thorough treatment of events leading up to the official adoption of the Reformation.

———. *Durchbruch und Festsetzung der Reformation in Basel: Eine Darstellung der Politik der Stadt Basel im Jahre 1529 auf Grund der öffentlichen Akten.* Basler Beiträge zur Geschichtswissenschaft 8. Basel, 1942.

Staehelin, Ernst, ed. *Das Buch der Basler Reformation.* Basel, 1929. A collection of original documents illustrating the gradual victory of Protestantism in Basel, in modern German, and with accompanying commentary.

———. *Das theologische Lebenswerk Johannes Oekolampads.* Quellen und Forschungen zur Reformationsgeschichte 21. Reprint, New York, 1971. The authoritative biography of the founder of Basel's Protestant church.

Wackernagel, Rudolf. *Geschichte der Stadt Basel.* Vol. 3. Reprint Basel, 1968. Covers all aspects of Basel's history during the period 1501–1529 in great detail.

AMY NELSON BURNETT

BASTINGIUS, Jeremias (Dutch, Bastinck; 1551–1595), Dutch Reformed theologian best known for his exposition of the Heidelberg Catechism. Bastingius was trained by several prominent second-generation Reformers. He studied in Heidelberg under Zacharius Ursinus in 1573, where Peter Dathenus was his roommate, and in Geneva under Théodore de Bèze in 1574, where he boarded with Lambert Daneau. He also received instruction from Kaspar Olevianus and was graduated under Girolamo Zanchi as doctor in theology in Heidelberg (1575–1576).

His reputation was such that he was called in 1578 to Antwerp, the most prominent of the Low Countries' Reformed churches at that time. During his Antwerp pastorate (1578–1585) Bastingius enjoyed the confidence of the Dutch churches. When the provinces of Holland and Zeeland drafted a church order without involving the Reformed churches officially, Bastingius was still consulted privately by the provinces. With Jean Taffin he gave counsel to the Walloon ministers concerning this matter. Bastingius was consulted by Gaspar van der Heyden prior to his publication of a revised version of the Heidelberg Catechism in 1580. Consequently, the National Synod of Middelburg decided that Bastingius, in cooperation with Classis Walcheren, should compose exegetical studies (*Exegemata*) related to the catechism.

After the fall of Antwerp (1585), Bastingius settled temporarily in Zeeland. Shortly thereafter he accepted a call to Dordrecht (1585), where he remained for eight years. Here his renowned exposition of the Heidelberg Catechism was published in Latin, *In Catechesim religionis Christianae, quae in Ecclesiis et scholis, tum Belgii tum Palatinatus traditur, exegemata, sive commentarii* (1588). This popular work reflected the influence of Ursinus and Zanchi, as well as Calvin, to whom he refers more than thirty times. Several translations followed: an English text in 1589 (six reprints between 1592 and 1617), a Dutch version in 1591 (seven new editions printed by 1762), and a German translation in 1596. Bastingius himself translated it into Flemish. This work motivated the Synod of Friesland to express deep appreciation for Bastingius's "faithful labors toward the edification of the church of Christ."

Bastingius was a careful exegete. He preferred Calvin's hermeneutics over Melanchthon's, as he felt Calvin strove for a method that did justice to the context of all of scripture. Consequently, Bastingius persuaded Daneau to publish his *Methodus Sacrae Scripturae tractandae* in 1579.

Bastingius was a leading figure in ecclesiastical assemblies. Numerous times he was a member of the *moderamen* of his classis; he represented his provincial or particular synod at the National Synod of 1587; and he served as president (1588) and assessor (1592) of his particular synod. Though he embraced strong Calvinist convictions, he showed remarkable tolerance for those who embraced different persuasions from his own. His congenial and peace-loving disposition explains why his circle of friends included men such as Johan van Oldenbarnevelt, Johannes Wtenbogaert, and Gerardus Joannes Vossius.

Soon after his appointment to the board of regents of the University of Leiden (1593), Bastingius was honorably dismissed in 1595, as he lacked the firm hand required to guide the students. Subsequently he was appointed professor of theology. He never functioned as such, however, since shortly after his appointment he died at the age of forty-four.

BIBLIOGRAPHY

Bastingius, Jeremias. *An Exposition or Commentarie Upon the Catechisme of Christian Religion which is taught in the Schooles and churches both of the Lowe Countryes and of the dominions of the Countie Palatine.* Translated by John Legatt. Cambridge, 1589.

Gerstner, Jonathan Neil. *The Thousand Generation Covenant: Dutch Reformed Covenant Theology and Group Identity in Colonial South Africa.* Leiden, 1991. Argues that Bastingius represents in the Dutch Reformed tradition "the high water mark of optimism concerning the internal holiness of children of believers even before their baptism." See especially pp. 117–119.

Nauta, D. "Bastingius, Jeremias." In *Biografisch Lexicon voor de Geschiedenis van het Nederlandse Protestantisme,* vol. 2, pp. 46–48. Kampen, 1983. Updated overview of Bastingius's life and theology.

Platt, John. *Reformed Thought and Scholasticism.* Leiden, 1982. Focuses on Bastingius's arguments for the existence of God in his exposition of the Heidelberg Catechism. See especially pp. 62–73.

Schotel, G. D. J. *Kerkelijk Dordrecht, eene bijdrage tot de Geschiedenis der vaderlandsche Hervormde Kerk, sedert het jaar 1572.* Vol. 1. Utrecht, 1841. Basic summary of Bastingius's life and theology on pp. 205–219; includes specific quotations of his contemporaries on the value of his catechism exposition.

JOEL R. BEEKE

BATENBURG, Jan van (1495–1538), a major leader of militant Dutch and north German Anabaptists after the fall of Münster in June 1535. Apparently Batenburg, bastard son of the Guelders nobleman Dirck van Batenburg, had been mayor of the Overijssel town of Steenwijk but had lost his position early in 1535. A few months later some Anabaptists sought to convince the unemployed nobleman to become their new leader in light of the failure of the king of Anabaptist Münster, John of Leiden, to deliver his besieged city. At a meeting near Groningen in the spring of 1535, Batenburg was baptized, accepting the mission to lead the "people of God" in the punishment of their persecutors, the papal church and imperial authorities.

As the "new David," Batenburg maintained the apocalyptic ideology of Münster, along with its community of goods and polygamy. Believing that the time of grace had passed, Batenburg proclaimed the end of water baptism; further adherents could be accepted only as servants, not as full members. Women members were often harshly treated, many having been abducted into the group. Those revolutionaries who hoped that Batenburg would quickly restore the kingdom of God in another city were soon disappointed, for he avoided suicidal attacks on large centers. Instead, he organized his followers into small bands of guerrilla activists who robbed churches, cloisters, and manors; destroyed the livestock and crops of "the godless"; and occasionally committed murder. Batenburg turned down requests to participate in attacks on Emden, Amsterdam (where some Anabaptists attacked the city hall on 10 May 1535), and Groningen. He had, however, purchased some weapons for the attempt to capture the village of Hazerswoude in December 1535 but canceled his plans when the rebels were captured. There is also evidence that Batenburg was plotting with Heinrich Krechting, leader of the Münsterite refugees in Oldenburg, Westphalia, to recapture Münster in 1538. Until these larger schemes could be carried out (with the assistance of mercenaries and disgruntled noblemen), Batenburg's goal was to use small-scale brigandage to keep alive the revolutionary Anabaptist campaign. He failed, however, to win the support of nonviolent Anabaptist leaders, such as David Joris and the Dutch Anabaptist refugees in Strasbourg (to whom he had delivered in 1537 a now lost tract on marriage, deception, and the godless). Batenburg's guerrilla bands were a considerable vexation to the authorities, who, in their prosecutions, did not always discriminate between violent and peaceful groups of Anabaptists.

Batenburg was captured in the winter of 1537/38, and many of his followers joined Joris's group. In his confession of February 1538, Batenburg remarked that the goal of the Anabaptists "was to ruin cities, castles and churches, to reject and despise all ceremonies and sacraments of the church." Furthermore, he implicated many Anabaptist opponents in his schemes. Although Batenburg was executed in Vilvoorde, Brabant, in the early months of 1538, various Batenburger bands continued their lawbreaking activities throughout the Low Countries and Westphalia until about 1580.

BIBLIOGRAPHY

Jansma, Lammert. *Mechiorieten, Munstersen en Batenburgers: Een sociologische analyse van een millennistische beweging uit de 16e eeuw.* Buitenpost, 1977. The most complete study of the Batenburgers. Analyzes their ideology, organization, and development from a historical-sociological perspective.

———. "Revolutionaire Wederdopers na 1535." In *Historisch bewogen: Opstellen over de radicale reformatie in de 16e en 17e eeuw, anngeboden aan Prof. Dr. A. F. Mellink*, pp. 49–64. Groningen, 1984. A brief but important survey of the history and practices of the Batenburgers from 1535 to the 1580s.

Mellink, Albert F., ed. *Friesland en Groningen, 1530–1550.* Documenta Anabaptistica Neerlandica, 1. Leiden, 1975. Contains Batenburg's confession of 1538, the only extant source from Batenburg himself.

Stayer, James M. *Anabaptists and the Sword.* 2d ed. Lawrence, Kans., 1976. Includes a widely influential discussion of the beliefs and actions of Batenburgers and other militant Anabaptists, especially regarding their justification of violence and relationship to nonviolent Anabaptists.

Waite, Gary K. "From Apocalyptic Crusaders to Anabaptist Terrorists: Anabaptist Radicalism after Münster, 1535–1545." *Archiv für Reformationsgeschichte* 80 (1989), 173–193. Argues that Batenburger activities were linked to both the socioeconomic crises and the political-military struggles of the 1530s and 1540s.

GARY K. WAITE

BÁTHORY, István. *See* Stephen Báthory.

BATTLE OF LEPANTO. *See* Lepanto, Battle of.

BATTLE OF MOHÁCS. *See* Mohács, Battle of.

BATTLE OF WHITE MOUNTAIN. *See* White Mountain, Battle of.

BAUER, Georg. *See* Agricola, Georgius.

BAVARIA. A territorial state in Germany, Bavaria was the leading Catholic power in the Holy Roman Empire during the age of the Reformation. Although Protestantism never gained a solid foothold in Bavaria, the Reformation period was vital in Bavarian history. It enabled the duchy's rulers to exploit the troubles of the Catholic church and the threat of religious fission to make major inroads on the autonomies constituting corporate medieval society, creating in its place a state in which power was concentrated, centralized, and brought effectively to bear on the lives, including the religious lives, of their subjects. Successful in this endeavor, Bavaria became the vanguard of the Catholic revival in the empire and a major force in the European Counter-Reformation.

The opening events of the Reformation found Bavaria emerging from a troubled period of internal strife. Numerous territorial divisions had culminated in 1503–1504 in a bitter war of succession, and the victor, Albert IV of Bavaria-Munich, promulgated in 1506 the Wittelsbach duchy's first law of primogeniture intended to end territorial divisions. Albert's untimely death two years later, however, imperiled this accord, as his younger son, Ludwig, demanded a third of the realm against his older brother, William IV. He was supported in this claim by the duchy's estates who saw in fraternal strife an opportunity to expand their corporate and individual liberties. At a territorial diet in 1514, their leaders compelled the dukes to accept their participation in all aspects of government, notably in the appointment of ducal officials, but the estates' preeminence was of short duration. Reconciled, William and Ludwig agreed to rule jointly. The conduct of affairs was placed in the hands of a declared enemy of representative bodies and strong advocate of political centralization, Leonhard von Eck, a lawyer and aggressive political and diplomatic tactician who dominated the small circle of ducal advisers until his death in 1550. It was Eck's sense of the danger to state and society represented by the evangelical movement that determined Bavaria's response to Lutheranism.

Evidence of interest in the Lutheran cause is spotty for the 1520s and 1530s in Bavaria, but enough is known to indicate a wide spectrum of sympathy arising from the undoubted need for reform in the church and the reluctance of responsible prelates (the archbishop of Salzburg and the bishops of Freising, Regensburg, Passau, and Chiemsee, who formed the hierarchy of his province in Bavaria) to undertake it. One center of sympathy was the Augustinian monastery in Munich, observantist since the fifteenth century, where Johannes von Staupitz had been prior in 1500–1503 and was a frequent visitor in later years. The Augustinians' preaching seems to have spread Lutheran ideas. A sermon by Martin Luther was printed in 1519; two years later the same printer, Hans Schobser, is said to have published an edition of *An den christlichen Adel deutscher Nation* (To the Christian Nobility of the German Nation), all copies of which were seized on order of the dukes in their first official antievangelical action. More Lutheran books were printed in Landshut, however, and reports of Lutheran preaching came from Wasserburg and Ingolstadt, as well as from Munich. In 1522 a Bavarian academic who had studied in Wittenberg, Arsacius Seehofer, was denounced for giving heretical lectures at the University of Ingolstadt. He recanted after being arrested, but the incident caused the wife of a ducal official, Argula von Grumbach, to publish two combative letters, one of them addressed to Duke William in defense of the freedom to preach the gospel. There is also indication of the presence of Lutheranism in court circles and among mercantile groups. In any case, enough evidence came together to persuade Eck and his ducal masters that they must get control of the situation, particularly from 1525, when reports of Lutheran activities merged with information about Anabaptist proselytizing (mainly by way of the imperial city of Augsburg) and when the peasant uprising in other parts of the empire raised fears in Bavaria that—

as Eck warned his dukes—Luther's teachings would "strike down and overturn all established laws and all authority and government."

Official reaction took two forms. Negatively, religious mandates issued in 1522 and 1524 notified subjects of the excommunication and ban pronounced on Luther, forbade acceptance and even discussion of Luther's teachings, gave instruction for the arrest and trial of violators of these provisions, instituted censorship of books, interdicted study at Wittenberg, and prohibited clerics from making any changes in divine service. Some exemplary sentences were meted out. A baker's apprentice was beheaded in Munich in 1523, an itinerant preacher and pamphleteer was put to death in 1524, and a priest in Wasserburg was executed in 1526. Duke Ludwig's court chaplain, Georg Fabri, was arrested for advocating Lutheranism in 1528, and that same year Johannes Aventinus, court historian and tutor to the two younger dukes, was incarcerated. Also in 1528 twenty-nine Anabaptists were arrested, nine of them put to death. Substantial rewards were posted for reporting suspected heretics (thirty-two gulden for an Anabaptist and twenty for a Lutheran).

At the same time, the government sought to respond positively to the perceived threat. When demands for corrective action addressed to the bishops led nowhere (all requests for reform on the episcopal level being met with a list of the church's *gravamina contra saeculares*), the dukes, guided by Eck, proceeded on their own authority to curtail the independence of the church in their duchy so as to obviate criticism and prevent defection. Negotiations with Pope Clement VII yielded such privileges as the right to visit (i.e., inspect) monasteries and to subject clerics to criminal justice and even to taxation (amounting to a fifth of their annual income). Initiative in effecting church reform thus passed to the government almost from the beginning of the Reformation in Bavaria. It was never returned to the church.

If the direction of government policy was obvious from the outset, little is clear about the nature of the evangelical movement itself. In part it was a protest against a clergy held to be inadequate on professional, as well as moral, grounds, and there is evidence that the authorities took public displeasure with the church very seriously. It also seems to have been a quest for a more intense piety, as indicated by persistent calls for the use of German in the service; by opposition to rigid fasting rules, enumeration of sins in confession, pilgrimages, and the cult of saints; and later by the demand for Communion under both kinds and free access to Luther's writings. In its early phase in the 1520s, the movement appears to have enlisted all social strata, though no precise information is available about this. "Lutherans" were mostly found among burghers; Anabaptists seem to have come from the lower orders. In any case, the government's success in depriving the movement of a base in the population at large is impressive. By 1530 the new faith

scarcely existed in Bavaria. Leaders or potential leaders were put to death or imprisoned. Many followers emigrated. No congregations had been organized, and the few conventicles or circles that had sprung up disbanded. No distinct doctrine was formulated. Nonetheless, an inclination toward Protestantism, both as a protest and as a mode of piety, must have survived in Bavaria, which could not be entirely sealed off against the rapid spread of the Wittenberg and Zurich movements in the empire, especially in areas adjacent to the free cities of Augsburg and Regensburg (Lutheran from 1534 and 1542, respectively). Even so, it was to be twenty years before this tendency became a threat again.

Eck's policies never foreclosed collaboration with Protestants outside the duchy. Thus, his suspicions of Habsburg intentions brought Bavaria for a time into alliance with such Lutheran princes as Elector John of Saxony and Landgrave Philipp of Hesse (Alliance of Saalfelden, 1531). As civil war approached in the empire, however, he moved more decisively into the Catholic camp, affirming the anti-Protestant front with a marriage of William's son Albert to the daughter of the emperor's brother and heir, Ferdinand. When Albert V succeeded his father in 1550 (Eck having died the same year), the new ruler's initially less intransigent views toward religious deviance, along with the concessions made to Lutherans in the Augsburg Interim of 1548, encouraged a new wave of evangelical activity that, for a decade or so, was given more or less free rein. Once again opposition was voiced to unresponsive priests and to such traditional practices as fasting, listing sins *in specie*, elevating the Host, and Corpus Christi processions. Itinerant preachers read from the postils of Luther and Johann Spangenberg and led in the singing of German hymns. Central to renewed agitation was the drive for the lay cup, in which guise Protestantism in Bavaria assumed for a time the role of a coherent movement with a political center in the nobility, particularly the higher nobility of Lower Bavaria. First raised as a formal request at a territorial diet in 1553, the demand for Communion *sub utraque*, whatever its religious impulse, served a large segment of the estates as a lever with which to regain from the financially strapped duke privileges lost in the preceding reign. The extent of these nobles' doctrinal commitment to any form of Protestantism has been a matter of controversy, but their support of the cause was clearly significant, as they seem to have encouraged evangelical preaching in their respective domains, thus broadening the movement's popular base.

His request for permission to make concessions having been rebuffed by Rome, Albert, on his own, suspended all fines for the lay cup in 1556 after the estates had refused to grant revenues until their religious demands were met. At a later diet in 1563, a group of nobles went so far as to argue for official introduction of the Augsburg Confession into Bavaria. Once again, however, the assembly had reached a high point of influence from which it had to come down. In 1564

Albert, guided by Simon Thaddaeus Eck (a half brother not of Leonhard but of the famous Johann Eck, Luther's opponent at the Leipzig Disputation), arrested the spokesmen of the more radical nobles and invaded the enclave of their leader, capturing in that expedition a cache of documents that allowed him to claim (with some justification, in the view of recent scholars) the existence of an aristocratic conspiracy against him for which the lay cup served as pretext. A trial of the alleged conspirators ensued, as did stern measures to root out heterodox "confessionists." New religious mandates from 1565 raised the penalties for attending evangelical services in neighboring territories (*Auslaufen*), sharply limited the choice of universities Bavarians could attend, warned travelers to Protestant states they might not be allowed to return, ordered licensing and inspection of printing shops and booksellers, issued a *Schulordnung* to clear teaching of seditious elements, required parish priests to furnish regular reports on deviants, and encouraged spying to flush them out. A standing commission was set up in 1567–1568 to organize regular visitations not only of the clergy but also of lay folk. It was the protocols of these countrywide inspections, beginning with an earlier visitation in 1558–1560, that enabled authorities to discover and then deal with actual religious conditions in the land. In the late 1560s and early 1570s religious tribunals conducted inquisitions in Munich and elsewhere, resulting in a number of expulsions from the duchy. In 1571 the lay cup was forbidden outright.

The capstone of this policy of vigilance and enforcement was the creation in 1570 of a new consistory, the *Geistliche Rat*, a collegiate board of state councillors and theologians exercising jurisdiction "over everything that touches the preservation of the true Christian religion." Specifically, this body enforced the religious mandates, supervised clergy and school personnel, administered church finances, interrogated all individuals accused of sectarian actions, and took charge of the "social disciplining" of all subjects. In practice it also stripped the episcopal hierarchy in Bavaria of much of its authority and was meant to do so. No less important as a means of bypassing the hidebound hierarchy and concentrating control over the church was the calling to Bavaria of the Jesuits. The order took over the theology faculty at Ingolstadt in 1556 and settled in at the Augustinian monastery in Munich in 1559. Jesuits acted as confessors to Albert's successors William V and Maximilian I. Their schools and gymnasiums provided an exemplary Catholic education. In their Marian congregations (from 1577) they reached out to all social classes. Peter Canisius's catechism (1555) became the vital teaching instrument of the orthodox faith.

Although there is evidence to suggest that evangelical proclivities persisted among some nobles and well-to-do burghers at least to the end of the century, Protestantism lost most of its momentum in Bavaria owing to these measures. What had become permanent as a consequence of the Reformation was the passage of control over religion and the church into the hands of the ruler, who, in fact if not in law, became the *summus episcopus* of his territory's ecclesiastical organization. Under William V (r. 1579–1598) and Maximilian I (r. 1598–1651) Bavaria entered the age of confessionalism as the most militant Catholic state in Germany. In 1583 Bavarian troops (aided by Spain) conquered the archbishopric of Cologne, whose ruler had converted to Protestantism without, as required, relinquishing his seat. From then on younger Wittelsbach princes resided there as archbishops, securing for the dynasty its first seat in the electoral college. Under Maximilian the imperial city of Donauwörth was seized in 1607 and the entire Upper Palatinate forcibly re-Catholicized after it had fallen to Bavaria in 1621 during the Thirty Years' War, in which Bavaria also obtained for its duke the electoral dignity formerly held by the Palatinate.

A model of a Counter-Reformation ruler, Maximilian—deeply pious, Jesuit-trained and counseled but fiercely independent, and closely involved personally in all aspects of government—completed during his more than fifty-year reign the long-prepared tilt in the balance of state-church relations in Bavaria. He made full use of the prerogatives allowed by the Concordat of 1583 to supervise clerical properties and revenues and to "present" appointees to high ecclesiastical office. Religious policy was firmly lodged in his hands. Insisting on unity of faith in his duchy, he forced remaining Protestants to convert or emigrate, required all officials to make confessions of faith, and inhibited traffic to non-Catholic regions. Conscious of the social perils of heterodoxy, he saw to universal enforcement of church attendance and observances (such as fasting) and paid close attention to the quality of Catholic education countrywide. He gave strong support not only to Jesuits but to Capuchins and reform Franciscans as well. In all this his authority went virtually unchecked by the Bavarian estates, which were summoned only twice during his entire reign and from which he effectively gained financial independence through long-term tax grants. An excellent administrator and fiscal rationalizer, he governed his country with the help of his privy council and a competent staff of professional bureaucrats. His role in imperial politics was commensurate with these powers. As chief organizer and political head of the Catholic League (from 1609), Maximilian was the most prominent Catholic in the empire. Under his rule and particularly as a result of his actions in the Thirty Years' War, Bavaria gained a place among the major European states.

[*See also* Augsburg; Diet; Holy Roman Empire; *and* Nuremberg.]

BIBLIOGRAPHY

Bireley, Robert. *Maximilian von Bayern. Adam Contzen S.J. und die Gegenreformation in Deutschland, 1624–1635.* Göttingen, 1975.

Kaff, Brigitte. *Volksreligion und Landeskirche. Die evangelische Bewegung im bayerischen Teil der Diözese Passau.* Miscellanea Bavarica Monacensia, 69. Munich, 1977.

Kraus, Andreas. *Geschichte Bayerns: Von den Anfängen bis zur Gegenwart.* Munich, 1983.

Lanzinner, Maxmilian. *Fürst, Räte und Landstände: Die Entstehung der Zentralbehörden in Bayern, 1511–1598.* Göttingen, 1980.

Metzger, Edelgard. *Leonhard von Eck, 1480–1550: Wegbereiter und Begründer des frühabsolutistischen Bayern.* Munich, 1980.

Rössler, Hans. *Geschichte und Strukturen der evangelischen Bewegung im Bistum Freising, 1520–1571.* Nuremberg, 1966.

Weinfurter, Stefan. "Herzog, Adel und Reformation: Bayern im Übergang vom Mittelalter zur Neuzeit." *Zeitschrift für historische Forschung* 10 (1983), 1–39.

GERALD STRAUSS

BÉARN. The territory of the "viscounty of Béarn," as it was established in the thirteenth century, corresponds essentially to the *arrondissements* of Oloron, Orthez, and Pau in the present-day *département* of Pyrénées-Atlantiques (80 kilometers from north to south, 60 kilometers from east to west). In the strict sense (i.e., without counting Soule or Basse-Navarre), it extends essentially over the Gaves of Aspe and Osseau, which became the Gave d'Oloron at Sauveterre, and the Gave de Pau (Pau, Lescar, Orthez). In 1512 the sovereigns of Béarn, Catherine de Foix and Jean d'Albret, lost the territory of Haute Navarre (Upper Navarre), which was soon after incorporated into the kingdom of Castile. Military expeditions and negotiations failed to change this state of affairs. Later religious politics and the defense of the independence of Béarn against Spanish and French ambitions often went hand in hand. The powers of the sovereigns were traditionally counterbalanced by the prerogatives of the Estates, made up of delegates from the clergy, the nobility, and the free towns. This explains the vacillations of Jeanne of Navarre and the opposition she met between 1560 and 1571.

Henry of Navarre (1502–1555) and Marguerite d'Angoulême (1492–1569), the sister of Francis I and queen of Navarre by her second marriage (1527), allowed "evangelism" to gain a foothold in Béarn under Gérard Roussel, bishop of Oloron, whose episcopacy displeased John Calvin; other bishops imitated Roussel's pastoral activity. At the same time, there are some indications that Lutheran preachers passed through the area. Although some conventicles were formed and heretical practices introduced, they were soon repressed.

Their daughter, Jeanne of Navarre (1528–1572), and her husband Antoine Bourbon-Vendôme (1518–1562), who became the sovereigns of Béarn in 1555, allowed Calvinism to make inroads in their territories, beginning with the welcome they accorded in their court to ministers such as Pierre David, François Boisnormand, Arnaud-Guillaume Barbaste, and Pierre-Henry de Barran. From that point on, the story of the establishment of the Calvinist reform in Béarn followed the rhythm of the politico-religious situation in the kingdom of France.

Antoine of Navarre, who was eager to recover Upper Navarre or to obtain some compensation for it, continued to waver between Catholicism and the Reformed faith under the pressures to which he was subjected at the end of the reign of Henry II of France (d. July 1559) and under the reign of Francis II (d. December 1560). Neither the letters written by Calvin nor the words of encouragement offered by Théodore de Bèze were sufficient to put an end to Antoine's wavering. The Reformed had at first hoped that Antoine would become the head of the Calvinist movement in France, but they eventually turned to Louis, prince of Condé, and Admiral Gaspard II de Coligny.

Through the impetus of the ministries of Barran, Barbaste, and Boisnormand, some Béarn churches were represented at the synod of the province of Basse-Guyenne, which was held at Clairac on 19 November 1560. This assembly adopted the confession of faith drawn up by the delegates to the first national synod of the Reformed churches of the kingdom of France, which had met in Paris at the end of May 1559. At the same time some residents left Béarn to be trained at the academy of Geneva.

The course of events accelerated after the conversion of Jeanne of Navarre (December 1560), in which Bèze may have played a part. But adding to the pressures in the king's entourage, problems arose owing to Jeanne's quarrels with Antoine of Navarre, who eventually sent her back to Béarn.

Starting in July 1561 measures were taken in Béarn that stirred up the first signs of resistance. Insults were prohibited, oaths could be taken only on the Bible, and offerings for the poor became obligatory. The possibility of celebrating the Mass and Reformed worship in the same building (*simultaneum*) was instituted; priests were asked not to interfere with the preaching of the pastors, who were also to be protected; and Reformed schoolmasters opened schools. The establishment of Protestantism in Béarn benefited from the climate created, both before and after the Colloquy of Poissy (fall of 1561), by the rapid expansion of Calvinism in the kingdom of France, until 1562, when, despite the Edict of January, the tide ebbed.

In Béarn, however, the widowed Jeanne of Navarre, with support she found locally and obtained from Geneva, organized a religious reformation "from above," in spite of pressure from Pope Pius IV exerted through Cardinal Georges d'Armagnac. The minister Jean-Raymond Merlin was the main author of measures taken in the spring of 1563, while new pastors arrived from Geneva, including Jacques Spifame, who was later disgraced. Corpus Christi processions were prohibited and statues and paintings were removed from the churches, sometimes with violence and public disorder.

The first Synod of Béarn met at Pau on 20 September 1563, with thirty-nine pastors in attendance. They did not obtain the abolition of Catholicism, since the queen was at the time under summons to appear before the Roman Inquisition. They agreed on an order of discipline, and soon an ecclesiastical council was formed, charged with watching over the material affairs of the new churches. From 1564 to 1567, Jeanne of Navarre remained absent from Béarn, but the Reformed movement developed, despite some resistance, with the support of lieutenant-general Antoine de Gramont and the complacency of Louis d'Albret, bishop of Lescar, and Claude Régin, bishop of Oloron.

A second synod was held at Nay in June 1565; it demanded that "every vestige of Catholicism be removed from Béarn." From Paris, Jeanne of Navarre published new ordonnances (July 1566) particularly relating to public morality and the conferral of benefices. During these years (1564–1567) the academy of Orthez took shape; from time to time its headquarters were at Lescar. Pierre Viret, who had been pastor at Pau since 1567, contributed significantly to the life of the academy in 1571.

Three years of protests against these decisions followed, leading to rebellion and then war. Then, under the command of Terride at the request of Charles IX, Catholic armies invaded Béarn to set the stage for a full restoration of Catholicism. Jeanne managed to put together an "army of rescue" and at the end of August 1569 won back Béarn. Its commander, Gabriel de Lorges, count of Montgomery, issued an order for civil peace, "Ordonnance en faveur de la paix civile," on 22 September 1569, and then issued a second order for the confiscation of church properties, "De la confiscation des biens ecclésiastiques."

Various measures followed, gathered in the seventy-seven *Ordonnances ecclésiastiques* published on 26 November 1571. They deal with problems relating to the confession of faith and discipline (1–10), the institutional framework (11–21), the question of church property (34–67), and public morality (68–77). These Ordonnances represent the charter of Protestantism in Béarn.

Jeanne died on 9 June 1572 without knowing the outcome of the accords that had been negotiated over a long period for the marriage of her son Henry of Béarn (at her death, king of Navarre and the future Henry IV of France) to Margarete of Valois (1553–1615). Following the Saint Bartholomew's Day Massacre (23–24 August 1572), the Ordonnances were abolished for a time, but then reinstated in 1576. Once he became king in 1598, Henry IV granted to the Catholics of Béarn the Edict of Fontainebleau (15 April 1599), which should be understood in the light of the Edict of Nantes (August 1598). It allowed a restoration of Catholicism compatible with the presence of Protestants.

Béarn again experienced serious upheavals in the context of civil wars in the kingdom of France, when Louis XIII issued, on 25 June 1617, the "Édit de main levée des biens ecclésiastiques" (Edict for the Restitution of Church Property), which was intended to rescind the secularization measures taken in 1569. The resistance that ensued led to open warfare that concluded with the annexation of Béarn to the Kingdom of France in 1620.

That the Reformed churches were organized in Béarn and in the kingdom of France at the same time, the interdependence of their development, and finally their movement toward unification should not obscure some specific traits of Protestantism in Béarn. On the one hand, it was not merely a matter of French-speaking Protestantism: those who recruited pastors took account of their ability to communicate in the languages and dialects of the various territories of Béarn and its neighboring possessions (Soule, Basse-Navarre). In 1583 Arnaud de Salette translated the Psalter into the dialect of Béarn (*Les Psalmes de David metuts en rima bernesa*). On the other hand, as Nancy L. Roelker suggests, there is reason to compare the process of the establishment of Protestantism in Béarn with events in England, or in some Swiss and German territories, where the ruler or the magistrates played an important role in the development and institutionalization of a Reformed movement.

[*See also* Henry IV of France.]

BIBLIOGRAPHY

Arnaud de Salette et son temps: Le Béarn sous Jeanne d'Albret. Proceedings of an international conference, Orthez, France, 16–18 February 1983. Orthez, 1984.

Babelon, Jean-Pierre. *Henri IV.* Paris, 1982.

Bordenave, N. de. *Histoire de Béarn et Navarre.* Edited by Paul Raymond. Paris, 1873.

Bulletin de la Société des sciences, lettres et arts de Pau et du Béarn.

Bulletin du Centre d'étude du protestantisme béarnais.

Dufour, Alain. "La Réformation en Béarn d'après la lettre de Théodore de Bèze à Jeanne d'Albret de Janvier 1567." In *Actes du Colloque "L'Amiral de Coligny et son temps,"* proceedings of an international conference, Paris, 24–28 October 1972, pp. 313–322. Paris, 1974.

Forissier, Marc. *Histoire de la réforme en Béarn.* Tarbes, 1950.

Frossard, Ch.-L. *La discipline ecclésiastique du pays de Béarn publiée pour la première fois.* Paris, 1877.

Ordonnances ecclésiastiques, Pau, 26 Novembre 1571. Mont-de-Marsan, 1934. See pp. p. 145–164.

Le Protestantisme en Béarn, des origines à la Révolution, XVIe-XVIIIe siècles. Exhibition catalog. Pau, 1977.

Réformes et révocation en Béarn, XVIIe-XXe siècles. Proceedings of an international conference. Pau, 1986.

Roelker, Nancy. *Queen of Navarre: Jeanne d'Albret.* Cambridge, Mass., 1968.

Synodes de Béarn: Procès verbaux manuscrits. Bibliothèque de la Société de l'histoire du protestantisme Français, Paris. Ms 433/4.

Tucoo-Chala, Pierre. *La vicomté de Béarn et le problème de sa souveraineté des origines jusqu'à 1620.* Bordeaux, 1961.

———. *Histoire du Béarn.* Paris, 1970.

BERNARD ROUSSEL
Translated from French by Robert E. Shillenn

BEATAS. A later flowering of the Beguine movement that had peaked in northern Europe in the fifteenth century, *beatas* could be found in most early modern Spanish cities.

The term *beata* was commonly used to designate a woman who had made a private vow of celibacy, wore a habit, and observed some religious rule. These laywomen lived in a bewildering array of circumstances. The length of their commitments and their living arrangements could vary: some took temporary vows, others permanent; some lived alone in their own homes, or in hermitages, others in communal houses known as *beaterias*; some remained cloistered, others were active in society, caring for the sick and poor. Most *beatas* were under diocesan supervision and were not subject to any order, even if they followed its rule, wore its habit, or lived in an attached dwelling. Nonetheless, in some instances *beaterias* could unexpectedly evolve into convents or be deliberately established with such an evolution in mind; and third-order Franciscan women could also sometimes be called *beatas*. To complicate matters further, some women who aspired to live like *beatas* without vows, a rule, or a habit, could end up being considered *beatas* by their neighbors. This identification could also happen with women who were simply considered devout or with women who claimed to experience visions and apparitions. The social complexion of this phenomenon was also fluid. Many *beatas* were simple widows and single women who could not afford the dowries required by most religious houses, but some came from the higher social classes.

Beatas became an integral part of urban religious life in Spain during the sixteenth century, an era that witnessed an unprecedented rise in the number of highly visible and active holy women. In 1575, for instance, Madrid and Toledo each had at least six *beaterias*—some with as many as forty women—and a good number of solitary *beatas*, some of them quite famous and highly regarded by the clergy or even by the royal court. Since they prayed for others and sometimes resolved conflicts, consoled the grieving, received visions, prophesied, or healed the sick, *beatas* could become charismatic leaders within their society. Yet *beatas* also lived precariously, for the opinion expressed by Diego de Yepes, a devout admirer of Teresa of Ávila, was shared by most of his contemporaries. "Since women are more gullible and not as intelligent," he cautioned, "they can be easily fooled" (*Vida de Santa Teresa de Jésus*, 1599). Given this cultural attitude and given their relative independence, their aura of holiness, and their liminal status, it is not surprising that *beatas* came to be distrusted by church and state, especially in the second half of the sixteenth century. Though some *beatas* such as Catalina de Herrera of Toledo (d. 1616) and Mari Diaz of Ávila (d. 1572) could gain the trust of the clergy and be revered as saints, many others ran afoul of the authorities, making the *beata embaucadora* ("deceiving *beata*") a favorite target of the Inquisition and an enduring Spanish cultural stereotype.

BIBLIOGRAPHY

Bilinkoff, Jodi. "The Holy Woman and the Urban Community in Sixteenth-Century Ávila." In *Women and the Structure of Society: Selected Research from the Fifth Berkshire Conference on the History of Women*, edited by Barbara J. Harris and Jo Ann McNamara, pp. 74–80. Durham, NC, 1984.

———. *The Ávila of Saint Teresa: Religious Reform in a Sixteenth-Century City*. Ithaca, N.Y., 1989. A concise analysis of the social, political, and religious context of Teresa's life and work that highlights the role of *beatas*.

Imirazaldu, Jesús, ed. *Monjas y Beatas embaucadoras*. Madrid, 1977.

Kagan, Richard. *Lucrecia's Dreams: Politics and Prophecy in Sixteenth-Century Spain*. Berkeley, 1990. Microhistory at its best: the case of a young female visionary in Madrid is used to shed light not only on the sociopolitical dimension of *beatas* and religious women, but also on the very soul of early modern Spain.

Perry, Mary Elizabeth. "Beatas and the Inquisition in Early Modern Seville." In *Inquisition and Society in Early Modern Europe*, edited by S. Haliczer, pp. 147–168. Totowa, N.J., 1987. Assesses the gender question.

CARLOS M. N. EIRE

BEATON, David (1494?–1546), archbishop of Saint Andrews (1539–1546), abbot of Arbroath (1524), bishop of Mirepoix (1537), cardinal (1538), and papal legate *a Latere* (1544) who led the Scottish ecclesiastical establishment and Francophile party in the later reign of James V (1513–1542) and in the minority of Mary Stuart (1542–1567). Son of a small landowner, Beaton followed his uncle James as archbishop of Saint Andrews after several years as Scottish ambassador to France, where he negotiated the successive marriages of James V to Madeleine of Valois (1537) and Mary the Guise (1538). In the power struggle following James's death in 1542 Beaton was temporarily imprisoned while the anglophile party made James, second earl of Arran, governor for the infant Mary, negotiated her marriage to Prince Edward of England, and sanctioned the use of the English New Testament. Regaining power, Beaton annulled the Anglo-Scottish Treaty (1543), renewed the Franco-Scottish Alliance, and strengthened the antiheresy laws. In spite of periodic inquisitions he failed to seize the influential leaders of the Anglophile-reformist party and received only limited French military help during the invasions launched in 1544 and 1545 by Henry VIII in revenge for the annulment of the Anglo-Scottish marriage treaty. In March 1546 Beaton ordered the execution of the reformer George Wishart and was himself assassinated shortly afterwards in retaliation by members of the Anglophile party.

Some moves toward improved clerical education were made during his incumbency. Funds were raised for preachers in monasteries. He continued building a new college at Saint Andrews founded by his uncle (now Saint Mary's College), to which his cousin, the humanist scholar Archibald Hay, was appointed principal, and gave a new charter to Saint Leonard's College, Saint Andrews, which, although making it independent of the priory there, gave him closer supervision of the college, whose orthodoxy was suspect. Beaton's aggressive policy toward religious dissent and his recovery of power in 1543 may have slowed down the reform movement, as its supporters were forced to go underground for a decade.

BIBLIOGRAPHY

Hannay, Robert K., ed. *Rentale Sancti Andree, 1538–1546.* Edinburgh, 1913. Partial transcript and summaries of complete texts of the accounts of the archdiocese of Saint Andrews during the incumbency of Cardinal-Archbishop David Beaton; many references to events and personnel of the period.

Herkless, John. *Cardinal Beaton, Priest and Politician.* Edinburgh, 1891. Narrative biography, very few footnotes. Based largely on the *Letters and Papers of Henry VIII* and other calendars of documents.

Herkless, John, and Robert K. Hannay. *The Archbishops of St. Andrews.* Vol. 4, Edinburgh, 1913. Draws on Herkless's earlier work on Beaton.

Sanderson, Margaret H. B. *Cardinal of Scotland: David Beaton, c.1494–1546.* Edinburgh, 1986. First full-length study in more than 60 years; makes full use of contemporary sources including private archives. Contains list of *Acta,* itinerary, and provisional list of heretics, 1528–1546.

MARGARET H. B. SANDERSON

BEATUS RHENANUS (Ger., Rhinower; 1485–1547), German humanist textual critic and historian. This intimate friend of Erasmus was among the foremost textual critics and arguably the most sophisticated German textual editor of his age. His concentration on the reconstruction of ancient texts, judicious commentaries on them, and dispassionate historical narrative, together with his self-imposed seclusion from religious and civic affairs, rendered his influence on Reformation matters oblique, even remote. Yet by his editions and commentaries, he refined principles of textual criticism, emphasizing the philological element of Erasmus's legacy over its moral and theological aspects. With some overlapping, Beatus's career divides into three phases. Up to 1515 philosophical and pedagogical interests predominate; then until 1525/27 classical philology and religious matters are important; thereafter until his death classical philology and historical research are his main concerns.

A native of Schlettstadt (now Sélestat) in Alsace, he was educated at its celebrated Latin school before studying at Paris from 1503 to 1507 with such humanist luminaries as Jacques Lefèvre d'Étaples, Josse van Clichtove, and others. From 1511 to 1526 he worked at Basel as editor and corrector for the Froben press, especially but not exclusively in the publication of classical and patristic texts. Here he won Erasmus's scholarly respect and personal friendship. His principal accomplishments in this period were the *editio princeps* both of the Roman historian Velleius Paterculus (1520) and of the early Christian theologian and moralist Tertullian (1521), an edition of early Christian histories in *Autores historiae ecclesiasticae* (1523), and his *Annotationes* for and edition of Pliny's *Naturalis historia* (1526). His work on Pliny contains the clearest explanation of his critical principles. He initially saw in Luther a complement to Erasmus's propos-

als; he probably advocated an Alsatian edition of Luther's writings. After 1523 partisan unrest and the Peasants' War of 1524–1525 considerably muted his support.

In 1527, disposing of an adequate inheritance, unwilling to be embroiled in Basel's conversion to Protestantism, and wishing to work undisturbed by duties for Froben, he retired to scholarly seclusion in Sélestat. His greatest work, *Rerum Germanicarum libri tres* (1531), offered a judicious historical narrative of early German history revered by later Renaissance historians for its sophisticated historical techniques; therein Beatus dryly avoided the patriotic enthusiasm of earlier humanist historians. He produced editions of the Roman historians Tacitus (1533) and Livy (1535) and supervised the posthumous edition of Erasmus's complete works (1540), which he dedicated to the emperor, Charles V, with a still-famous biography of Erasmus. His reeditions of Tertullian (1528, 1539) enabled him to comment further on historical and theological points crucial to Reformation controversy and to modify his earlier support of the reformers, even to the point of acknowledging in the 1539 edition the papacy's potential role in securing religious peace. Although engaged in scholarship until his death, he published no more after 1539. At least by the Colloquy of Regensburg in 1541 he probably considered himself an evangelical but lived by the Catholic regime in Sélestat. He died at Strasbourg and is buried at Sélestat.

BIBLIOGRAPHY

Annuaire de la Société des Amis de la Bibliothèque humaniste de Sélestat. Vol. 35 (1985). Essential if somewhat inaccessible, this issue reproduces a rich variety of articles in French and German covering every aspect of Beatus in honor of the fifth centenary of his birth.

D'Amico, John, F. "Beatus Rhenanus, Tertullian, and the Reformation." *Archive for Reformation History* 71 (1980), 37–63.

———. *Theory and Practice in Renaissance Textual Criticism: Beatus Rhenanus between Conjecture and History.* Berkeley, 1988. Best available study of Beatus's life and work.

Scarpatetti, Beat von. "Beatus Rhenanus." In *Contemporaries of Erasmus: A Biographical Register of the Renaissance and Reformation,* edited by Peter G. Bietenholz, vol. 1., pp. 104–109. Toronto, 1985. Good introduction.

Weiss, James. "The Technique of Faint Praise: Johann Sturm's *Life of Beatus Rhenanus.*" *Bibliothèque d'Humanisme et Renaissance* 43 (1981), pp. 289–302. Examines the official contemporary biographer's criticism of Beatus as irresponsibly remote from civic and religious duties.

JAMES MICHAEL WEISS

BECON, Thomas (c.1512–1567), English Protestant propagandist and popular preacher. His origins in west Norfolk suggest early Lollard influences. At Cambridge (1527–1531; B.A., 1531) he enjoyed the patronage and friendship of Hugh Latimer and absorbed the Lutheranism that dominated his theological outlook until 1548. Official allegations of "heresy" drove him into obscure wanderings in disguise in Kent and the Midlands (1541–1547), and participation (under the pseudonym Theodore Basile) in an underground campaign of reformist propaganda.

As chaplain to both Edward Seymour, protector of the realm from 1547 to 1549, and Archbishop Thomas Cranmer, Becon preached at Edward VI's court (1547–1553). Mary Tudor found his preaching "seditious" and committed him to the Tower of London (16 August 1553 to 22 March 1554); in exile at Strasbourg (after March 1554) Becon prayed for her destruction. A Zwinglian (after 1548) and Erastian episcopalian, he supported Richard Cox against John Knox and the English Calvinists at Frankfurt in 1555 and was probably appointed (by the Frankfurt magistrates) one of two governors of the city's English church. Philipp of Hesse secured him a place as tutor at Marburg University, where Becon spent the remainder of his exile (1556–1558) composing Latin tracts. After Queen Elizabeth I's accession he returned to England (January 1559). He was made a canon of Canterbury Cathedral in 1559 and vicar of Christ Church, Newgate (one of London's grandest churches), in 1561. He died at Canterbury 30 June 1567, survived by his wife (of unknown identity) and three children.

Becon was acknowledged to be a remarkable preacher; the publication of his sermons and devotions in numerous editions made him in England the most widely read popular religious writer of the Reformation era. *The Sycke Mans Salue*, a guide for the ill and dying (composed before 1553), became *the* Protestant tract of the period 1550–1630. His published prayers helped shape a distinctive Protestant English piety. Becon said that he composed all such works for the common people; his genius was to translate the dicta of religion into the vigorous rhythms of everyday speech. Stylistically, his extensive use of scriptural *exempla* helped make the Bible itself seem both relevant and familiar—an important development in the popular culture of Protestantism. The invective he hurled against Catholic prelates was conventionally vicious; his critique of the contemporary "revolution of the rich" against the poor in *The Fortresse of the Faythfull* (1550) was damning and accurate; and his arguments in *A New Catechisme* (c.1560) and *The Booke of Matrimony* (c.1560) exalting wives (whom he thought often more wise than their husbands) and marriage (for him the superior earthly state) were both progressive and original.

BIBLIOGRAPHY

Bailey, Derrick Sherwin. *Thomas Becon and the Reformation of the Church of England.* Edinburgh, 1952. Establishes the facts of Becon's life and career, assesses his place in the English Reformation, and lists (with corresponding reference numbers to *A Short Title Catalogue . . . 1475–1640*, 3 vols, London, 1976–1991) all of his known works.

Becon, Thomas. *The early works of Thomas Becon . . . Being the Treatises Published by Him in the Reign of King Henry VIII.* Edited by John Ayre. Reprint, New York, 1968.

———. *The Catechism of Thomas Becon . . . with Other Pieces Written by Him in the Reign of King Edward VI.* Edited by John Ayre. Reprint, New York, 1968.

———. *Prayers and Other Pieces of Thomas Becon. . . .* Edited by John Ayre. Reprint, New York, 1968. The three Becon volumes, edited for the Parker Society by John Ayre, make Becon accessible—in contrast to the three-volume folio edition of *The Workes of Thomas Becon . . .* published by John Day in London in 1560, 1563, and 1564—but Ayre's edition omits thirty-one of the sixty-seven titles in Bailey.

DALE HOAK

BEDA, Noël (1470?–1537), French Catholic theologian. Leader of the Paris Faculty of Theology (1520–1534) and staunch opponent of the Reformation, Beda was born either in Picardy or in Normandy. As a student from about 1494 at the Collège de Montaigu in Paris, Beda embraced Jan Standonck's reforming principles of radical poverty and asceticism derived in part from the *Devotio moderna*. He directed the college from 1504 to 1514, and obtained his doctorate in the Faculty of Theology in 1508.

From 1514 Beda attacked the exegetical methods of Christian humanists as dangerous to church unity and doctrine. His *Annotations* against Jacques Lefèvre d'Étaples and Erasmus (1526), suppressed by King Francis I, were quickly reprinted in Cologne. His *Adversus clandestinos Lutheranos* (1529) depicted the humanists as laying the foundation for Luther and for the Protestant movement in general.

Beda is especially important for regimenting the Paris Faculty of Theology (Sorbonne) against the Reformation. In 1520 he suggested reviving the office of "syndic" in the Faculty of Theology in order to deal more effectively with Luther. Exercising this office during the next fourteen years, Beda streamlined faculty procedures, enforced statutes and the traditional scholastic curriculum, and kept careful records of doctrinal decisions. He pursued Paris theologians who showed sympathy for reformed views and opposed every manifestation of humanism and Reformation ideas, among them Bishop Guillaume Briconnet's evangelical reforms in the diocese of Meaux. He led the opposition to Louis de Berquin, who was executed for heresy in 1529. He engineered the condemnation of Erasmus by the entire University of Paris in 1528, evoking in response three polemical treatises and two satirical colloquies from Erasmus, as well as the satires of Rabelais and others. Spurious Protestant books were attributed to Beda in an attempt to discredit him with Catholic authorities.

Beda's indefatigable defense of church tradition, without respect of persons, incurred the vilification by his enemies that has dominated subsequent discussion of him. It also led to his downfall. In 1530, against the express wishes of Francis I, he opposed faculty approval of King Henry VIII's annulment proceedings. In 1533 he led the opposition to the reformist Lenten sermons of Gérard Roussel, which were given under the aegis of the king's sister Marguerite of Navarre; and in 1534, after royal reprieve from a six-month exile, he boldly cited the regius professors (Collège de France) before the court of the Parlement of Paris. Francis I imprisoned and then exiled Beda to Mont-Saint-Michel, where he died on 18 January 1537.

Beda had nevertheless been successful in marshaling the support of conservative leaders in France, notably Pierre Lizet, who from 1530 to 1551 was *premier président* of the Parlement. Thus, as the Reformation became more widely viewed as disruptive to church and state, the Faculty of Theology assumed a major role in ecclesio-political policy in France. In 1543, six years after Beda's death, both king and Parlement adopted the Faculty's twenty-six articles of faith and, from 1545 to 1556, approved its catalogs of prohibited books that, in a manner entirely consistent with Beda's policies, established guidelines for orthodoxy and censorship in France for the remainder of the century.

BIBLIOGRAPHY

Bense, Walter Frederick. *Noël Beda and the Humanist Reformation at Paris, 1504–1534.* Unpublished Ph.D. diss. 3 vols. Harvard University, 1967. Most complete and first unbiased study of Beda; available in some libraries on microfilm or photocopy.

———. "Noël Beda's View of the Reformation." *Occasional Papers of The American Society for Reformation Research* 1 (December 1977), 93–107. Only published synthetic treatment of Beda produced by Bense before his early death.

Farge, James K. *Biographical Register of Paris Doctors of Theology. 1500–1536.* Subsidia Mediaevalia 10. Toronto, 1980. S.v. 'Beda,' pp. 31–36. Extended treatment of Beda's career, with complete list of his works.

———. *Orthodoxy and Reform in Early Reformation France: The Faculty of Theology of Paris, 1500–1543.* Studies in Medieval and Reformation Thought, vol. 32. Leiden, 1985. History of the "Sorbonne" principally under Beda's direction.

Farge, James K., ed. *Registre des procès-verbaux de la Faculté de théologie de l'Université de Paris, de janvier 1524 à novembre 1533.* Paris, 1990. Annotated proceedings of Paris Faculty of Theology meetings, 1524–1533, compiled under Beda's direction; essential for understanding his significance in the Catholic opposition to the Reformation.

Rummel, Erika. *Erasmus and His Catholic Critics.* Nieuwkoop, 1989. Ground-breaking, dispassionate study of Beda's controversies with Erasmus; see particularly vol. 2, pp. 29–59.

JAMES K. FARGE, C.S.B.

BEGGING. In the past, begging consisted primarily in a gesture, the outstretched hand, and a demeanor of pleading. By the sixteenth century, it was a pattern of behavior shared by a variety of people in Europe: the traditional poor, widows, orphans, and the lame; those temporarily impoverished, artisans, peasants, rural and urban day laborers; marginal folk of many kinds, such as gypsies; the "sturdy beggars," who were healthy and able, yet chose to beg for their livelihood; pilgrims; and the mendicant orders, whose religious identity was anchored in the supplicating gesture of the beggar. Anyone who had fallen into poverty for any reason—from the most personal to structural fluctuations in the economy—might extend the hand to ask for help from stranger, neighbor, priest, or lord. Only the "shamefaced" poor, whose status would not allow it, did not beg when impoverished.

As early as Augustine (354–430), begging had also been a metaphor for humanity's stance before God: humanity was a beggar before God, destitute before divine majesty, a seeker of divine mercy. Francis of Assisi (1181–1226) sought to enact Augustine's metaphor and to give it expression within his order. Three centuries later, Martin Luther, while employing the metaphor to capture his sense of human dependence on and humility before God, effectively separated the natural condition of all persons from the outward gesture of begging, severing the tie Francis had set between mendicant spirituality and Augustinian theology.

Increasingly in the sixteenth and seventeenth centuries, urban populations perceived the persons of beggars with apprehension as the numbers of beggars confronted authorities with greater problems of vagrancy. Catholic authorities, recognizing the validity of mendicant and pilgrims' begging, sought to proscribe sturdy beggars and to control other beggars. Protestant authorities, however, forbade the very gesture of begging, seeking instead a new, inaudible, and passive but visible mode of poverty and eradicating those orders that had defined themselves through that gesture. The formal introduction of the Reformation was accompanied everywhere by the promulgation of "orders for the poor," which sought to provide for systematic relief for the poor and thereby do away with begging.

BIBLIOGRAPHY

Boehncke, Heiner. *Das Buch der Vaganten: Spieler, Huren, Leutbetrüger.* Cologne, 1987. A general exploration of various kinds of marginal people who begged.

Jütte, Robert. *Abbild und soziale Wirklichkeit des Bettler- und Gaunertums zu Beginn der Neuzeit: sozial-, mentalitäts-, und sprachgeschichtliche Studien zum Liber Vagatorum (1510).* Cologne, 1988. A linguistic investigation of the *Liber Vagatorum* (Book of Beggars), the terms it lists, and the kinds of beggars they denote, in comparison with other contemporary designations of such beggars.

———. *Poverty and Deviance in Early Modern Europe.* Cambridge, 1994. A general treatment of the condition of poverty and responses to it in pre-industrial Europe.

Lis, Catharina, and Hugo Soly. *Poverty and Capitalism in Pre-Industrial Europe.* Reprint, Brighton, England, 1979. A general overview of the forms and sources of poverty in Europe from 1500 to 1800.

LEE PALMER WANDEL

BEHEM, Hans. *See* Böheim, Hans.

BEKE, Lieven van der. *See* Torrentius, Laevinus.

BELGIC CONFESSION. The earliest confessional statement of the Reformed churches in the Low Countries, the Belgic Confession became one of the major doctrinal standards of the Reformed church in the Netherlands. The primary author of the Belgic, or Netherlands, Confession was Guy de Brès (d. 1567), a Calvinist minister from Mons in the southern Low Countries who himself became a victim of the Counter-Reformation. The confession, which may have been drafted as early as 1559, first appeared in 1561, published in French at Rouen; it was translated into Dutch in 1562 and quickly began to circulate among both the French- and Dutch-speaking congregations of the Reformed churches in the Low Countries. De Brès wrote this Calvinist confession as a defense of the clandestine "churches under the cross" in the southern Low Countries, and in 1562 de Brès's confession was presented to Philip II, the Habsburg ruler of the Low Countries, in order to convince Philip that the followers of the new Reformed religion were not a threat to the civil authorities or disobedient subjects of the king. The hope of toleration most likely also motivated this petition to Philip II; however, it did not secure any freedom for the Calvinists in the Low Countries.

The early textual history of the Belgic Confession is very complex and confusing. Copies of the confession circulated in French, Dutch, and Latin, and minor revisions and alterations were made to the text as early as 1566 and throughout the later sixteenth century. In the early seventeenth century the Synod of Dordrecht (1618/19) authorized a careful revision of the text based on the existing versions. But this authorized version differed from the original French text: the synod's version, which became the most influential, gave the confession more precise language, particularly with respect to the denunciation of the Anabaptists. Article 16 on the doctrine of election was also revised, and article 36 on the civil magistrate clarified the relationship between the church and the civil authority in recognition of the fact that the Reformed church in the Netherlands no longer operated in the context of persecution but now enjoyed the support of the state.

Toward the end of the sixteenth century the Belgic Confession rapidly acquired an authoritative status in the Reformed churches of the Low Countries, but it became most influential among the Dutch churches of the northern provinces; it was adopted first by the Synod of Antwerp in 1566 and again by the Synod of Emden in 1571. At this synod, the most important assembly in the early history of the Reformed church of the Netherlands, the Belgic Confession was approved as a confessional standard; this was significant in that it signaled the acceptance of a Calvinist theology in the Reformed churches of the Low Countries, gave these churches an increasing sense of unity, and also helped to link the Netherlands churches with the international Calvinist movement. In the decades following Emden, other synods—both provincial and national—continued to recommend and prescribe adherence to the Belgic Confession as a doctrinal standard for the church. For example, the Synod

of Middelburg (1581) required that all ministers and theology professors sign the confession to signal their agreement with it. One should not, however, take this fairly rapid adoption of the Belgic Confession by the Reformed church of the Netherlands as a mark of its uniform acceptance in the Dutch churches and certainly not as a mark of universal enthusiasm for its theology. In the late sixteenth and early seventeenth century, and particularly in the years of the Arminian controversy (1590–1620), considerable debate existed over the exact status of the confession in the church, the extent of its authority, and whether it should be binding on all ministers. In the context of the Arminian controversy, article 16, on election, was an especially contentious point. The debates surrounding the confession were not finally settled until the Synod of Dordrecht, which clearly affirmed the Belgic Confession, along with the Heidelberg Catechism and the Canons of Dordrecht, as the three forms of unity, or confessional standards, for the Reformed church of the Netherlands.

The Belgic Confession provides a Reformed (Calvinist) theological summary and parallels the French, or Gallic, Confession of 1559, which Calvin himself directly shaped. The thirty-seven articles of the Belgic Confession follow closely the order and topics of the Gallic Confession, but the Belgic Confession is more detailed than its earlier French counterpart. As with all the confessions of the Reformation, the Belgic Confession clearly distances itself from the theology of Rome; however, what distinguishes the Belgic Confession from many other Reformation confessions is its stress on distancing the Reformed position from Anabaptism.

After a brief statement on the nature of God, the Belgic Confession strongly confirms the authority and normative character of scripture (articles 2–7); it also strongly emphasizes the providence and sovereignty of God (article 13). In articles 22 and 23 the confession emphatically affirms the Reformation doctrine of justification by faith alone but goes on to place a typically Calvinist emphasis on sanctification (article 24). The Belgic Confession also strongly emphasizes church discipline and, in its only significant deviation from the Gallic Confession, declares that discipline—in addition to the true preaching of the word and the right administration of the sacraments—is one of the marks of the true church (article 29). It also affirms, if not in great detail, a presbyterian church order, or polity (articles 30–32), and a Calvinist position on the sacraments (articles 33–35), acknowledging the real, but spiritual, presence of Christ in the Eucharist. The confession's statement on the sacraments represents a clear rejection of Anabaptist theology, especially on baptism, and the confession's theology of the Incarnation (article 18) also rejects the Anabaptist position. Article 36, on the civil magistrate, clearly distinguishes the Reformed from the Anabaptist position on the state: the Belgic Confession affirms the positive role of the civil government as a source of order and justice in the world, emphasizes the importance of obedience to the government, rejects a "community of goods," and acknowledges the role of the godly magistrate, whose task it is to destroy false religion and to promote the true faith. The confession ends with a brief statement on the Last Judgment (article 37). After the Synod of Dordrecht, the Belgic Confession operated normatively in the Reformed church of the Netherlands and was also deeply influential in shaping the character of the Reformed churches that were established in North America.

BIBLIOGRAPHY

Bakhuizen van den Brink, J. N., ed. *De Nederlandse Belijdenisgeschriften in Authentieke Teksten met Inleiding en Tekstvergelijkingen.* 2d ed. Amsterdam, 1976. Contains the Dutch text of the Belgic Confession.

Bangs, Carl. *Arminius: A Study in the Dutch Reformation.* 2d ed. Reprint, Grand Rapids, Mich., 1985. Considers the debate over the status of the Belgic Confession in the context of the theological controversy between Arminius and Gomarus.

Cochrane, Arthur C., ed. *Reformed Confessions of the Sixteenth Century.* Philadelphia, 1966. Contains an English translation of the Belgic Confession.

Deursen, A. Th. van. *Bavianen en Slijkgeuzen: Kerk en Kerkvolk ten tijde van Maurits en Oldenbarnevelt.* Reprint, Franeker, 1991. Based on extensive archival research. Surveys the use and significance of the Belgic Confession for the Reformed church of the Netherlands in the period up to the Synod of Dordrecht.

Duke, Alastair. "The Ambivalent Face of Calvinism in the Netherlands, 1561–1618." In *Reformation and Revolt in the Low Countries,* pp. 269–293. London, 1990. This essay is also available in *International Calvinism, 1541–1715,* edited by Menna Prestwich, pp. 109–134, Oxford, 1985. The best brief survey on the rise of Calvinism in the Netherlands.

Hoenderdaal, G. J. "De Kerkorderlijke Kant van de Dortse Synode." *Nederlands Theologisch Tijdschrift* 23 (1968–1969), 349–363. Focuses on the debate over the status of the Belgic Confession and the Heidelberg Catechism in the decades preceding the Synod of Dordrecht.

Jong, Otto J. de. *Nederlandse Kerkgeschiedenis.* 3d ed. Nijkerk, 1985. See especially chapters 11 through 15 for the early history of the Belgic Confession in the Reformed church of the Netherlands.

Nobbs, Douglas. *Theocracy and Toleration: A Study of Disputes in Dutch Calvinism from 1600 to 1650.* Cambridge, 1938. A detailed source of information but not readily available.

Schaff, Philip. *The Creeds of Christendom.* 6th ed., rev. & enl. 3 vols. Grand Rapids, Mich., 1969. Volume 1 contains a brief history of the Belgic Confession, and volume 3 includes both the French text and an English translation.

Tex, Jan den. *Oldenbarnevelt.* 2 vols. Translated by R. B. Powell. Cambridge, 1973. Excellent on the political issues surrounding the adoption of the Belgic Confession by the Reformed church of the Netherlands.

MICHAEL A. HAKKENBERG

BELLARMINO, Roberto (Eng., Bellarmine; 1542–1621), Jesuit controversial theologian, spiritual writer, cardinal, archbishop of Capua, and Roman Catholic saint. He was born at Montepulciano in Tuscany of an impoverished noble family, but his maternal uncle was Pope Marcellus II. Although his father originally wanted him to be a doctor, he entered the Jesuit novitiate at Rome in 1560. His later Jesuit training was mainly at the Roman College, Padua, and at Louvain, where he was ordained a priest in 1570. He taught at the Jesuit college in Louvain from 1570 to 1576, a period during which the Low Countries were devastated by religious war. Bellarmino felt compelled to study Luther, Calvin, and the other leading Protestant theologians and devoted many of his lectures to their refutation. He also became involved in controversy with his fellow Louvain professor Michel de Bay over the issues of grace and free will. While at Louvain he published a concise Hebrew grammar, which long remained in print.

In 1576 Bellarmino was recalled to the Roman College to take the new chair in controversial theology. His lectures there formed the basis of his greatest work, the *Controversies* (*Disputationes de controversiis Christianae fidei adversus huius temporis haereticos*), whose three volumes appeared in 1586, 1588, and 1593. The work enjoyed twenty editions and was the greatest single Catholic refutation of Protestant theology of the Reformation era. It is clearly written, well organized, immensely learned, and by the standards of the time rather free of invective. Bellarmino put theology into a more historical and less philosophical context than did the other great Catholic theologians of what has been called the Second Scholasticism, such as Domingo Bañez and Francisco Suárez.

Bellarmino became involved in many specific theological and ecclesiastical disputes. He wrote against Henry IV's right to the French throne; defended his fellow Jesuit Leonard Lessius whose teaching on grace and predestination was condemned by the University of Louvain; supported the papal position in the controversy over the Venetian Interdict of 1606; and wrote against James I and Lancelot Andrewes on whether a Catholic could take the oath of loyalty demanded by the crown. Pope Sixtus V thought that Bellarmino's *Controversies* limited papal temporal jurisdiction too much; his plan to put the work on the Index of Forbidden Books was cut short by death. Years later Bellarmino returned to the problem in a controversy with William Barclay and Roger Widdrington; his *Tractatus de potestate summi pontificis in rebus temporalibus* (Rome, 1610) distinguished clearly between the spiritual power of the pope and his indirect temporal power.

Clement VIII put Bellarmino in charge of revising the official text of the Latin Vulgate; this was a nasty job since the headstrong Sixtus had taken a personal role in the work and had made many arbitrary revisions. Upon the death of Sixtus V Bellarmino warned Clement that the publication of the Vulgate as revised by Sixtus would stir up a major scandal. Bellarmino's revised version, known as the Sixto-Clementine Vulgate, became the official Catholic Latin Bible of the Catholic church and remained so until the twentieth century.

Bellarmino was named rector at the Roman College in

1592 and provincial of the Jesuit province of Naples in 1594. Returning to Rome as theological adviser to Clement VIII in 1597, he shortly thereafter published two catechisms that enjoyed enormous success with literally hundreds of editions until the mid-nineteenth century. The *Dottrina cristiana breve* (Rome, 1597) was designed for children, while the same material was developed more deeply for teachers in his *Dichiarazione più copiosa della dottrina cristiana* (Rome, 1598). The shorter catechism was translated into sixty-two languages.

Clement VIII appointed Bellarmino a cardinal against his wishes in 1599, declaring that "We elect this man because he has no equal for learning in God's Church." In a surprise move the same pope made Bellarmino archbishop of Capua in 1602. Bellarmino had long stressed the duty of bishops to reside in their dioceses and serve as chief pastor of their flocks. He immediately left the pomp of Rome and took up residence to begin reforming his small, rather backward archdiocese; he personally visited and preached in the rural parishes each year as often as possible. He also reformed religious communities and was noteworthy for his charity to the poor.

Bellarmino returned to Rome for the two papal elections of 1605; in both conclaves he worked against his reform-minded friends who wanted to make him pope. The new pope, Paul V, kept him in Rome, where his next decade was devoted to the paperwork of five congregations (papal administrative departments). The most important of these was the Holy Office or Inquisition. Bellarmino personally delivered the command of the Inquisition forbidding Galileo from teaching that the earth circled the sun.

The writings of Bellarmino's old age were largely devotional. He published a long, pious commentary on *Psalms* in 1611. In his last years he retired for a month to make the Spiritual Exercises of Ignatius Loyola at the Jesuit novitiate in Rome. From 1614 till 1619 during these retreats he wrote six short books of piety, but their contents are not very closely linked to Loyola's Exercises. All but one became extremely popular; *De Ascensione mentis in Deum* ("The Mind's Ascent to God." Antwerp, 1615), for instance, enjoyed more than sixty editions in fifteen languages. Almost equally popular was his contribution to a standard devotional genre, *De Arte bene moriendi* ("The Art of Dying Well," Antwerp, 1620).

Bellarmino's life illustrates many facets of the Catholic and Counter-Reformations. He was a popular preacher and writer of devotional works, a devout religious deeply committed to the development of his Jesuit order, a zealous and reforming archbishop, a strong but not uncritical supporter of the papacy; but he was also deeply involved in the work of the Inquisition and wrote the most comprehensive and learned Catholic answer of the era to the theological challenge of Protestantism. He was canonized in 1930 and named a Doctor of the Catholic church the next year.

BIBLIOGRAPHY

Primary Source

Donnelly, John P., and Roland J. Teske, eds. and trans. *Robert Bellarmine: Spiritual Writings.* New York, 1989. Bellarmino's *Mind's Ascent to God* and *The Art of Dying Well*, with a scholarly introduction.

Secondary Sources

Arnold, Franz Xaver. *Die Staatslehre des Kardinals Bellarmin: Ein Beitrag zur Rechts- und Staatsphilosophie des konfessionalen Zeitalters.* Munich, 1934. Detailed study.

Bellarmino e la Controriforma: Atti del Simposio internazionale di Studi. Sora, Italy, 1990. Two volumes of papers from a symposium at Sora in 1986.

Blackwell, Richard J. *Galileo, Bellarmine and the Bible.* Notre Dame, Ind., 1991. Scholarly reflection on the opening phases of the Galileo controversy and Bellarmino's involvement, with documents.

Brodrick, James. *Robert Bellarmino: Saint and Scholar.* Reprint, London, 1966. Updated and revised from the author's earlier two-volume biography (1928).

Cunningham, John. *The Concept of Ecclesiastical Jurisdiction in the Works of St. Robert Bellarmino.* Rome, 1964.

Galeota, Gustavo, ed. *Roberto Bellarmino: Archivescovo di Capua, teologo e pastore della riforma cattolica.* Capua, Italy, 1990. Two volumes of papers given at a conference at Capua in 1988, with detailed bibliography.

La Servière, Joseph de. *La théologie de Bellarmin.* Paris, 1909. This comprehensive work is still the best on Bellarmino's theology.

Le Bachelet, Xavier-Marie. *Bellarmin avant son Cardinalat, 1542–1598.* Paris, 1911. Scholarly biographical study.

Murray, John C. "St. Robert Bellarmino on the Indirect Power" *Theological Studies* 9 (1948), 491–535.

Ryan, Edward A. *The Historical Scholarship of Saint Bellarmine.* Louvain, 1938.

JOHN PATRICK DONNELLY

BELLAY, Guillaume and Jean du

BELLAY, Guillaume and Jean du (seigneur de Langey, 1491–1543; and 1498–1562, respectively), French diplomats. Born in Glatigny, France, they were the first and fourth sons of Louis and Marguerite de La Tour-Landry. After studying law at Angers and Paris, they became known for their shrewdness in the course of numerous diplomatic missions on behalf of Francis I to England, Germany, and Italy. Guillaume pursued a military career (attaining the rank of general), while Jean entered upon an ecclesiastical career (becoming a cardinal in 1535). They each played an important role in the history of the Reformation, particularly in the matter of Henry VIII's divorce and in the attempts at reconciliation between Catholics and Lutherans.

From 1528, the two brothers began to assist Cardinal Thomas Wolsey in resolving the marriage crisis. Guillaume was unsparing in using his influence, both privately and publicly, to promote Henry's interests among the theologians at the Sorbonne, particularly those who were least favorable, the syndic Noël Beda and the president, Pierre Lizet. Jean also took an active part in these negotiations, endeavoring to portray Francis I as being neutral and equally well disposed to both Henry VIII and Charles V. As a result of the decisive action of the du Bellay brothers, the Sorbonne finally declared Henry VIII's marriage with Catherine of Aragon illegal on 2 July 1530. On account of these services, Jean was promoted to the bishopric of Paris, and Guillaume received several benefices.

In 1534, with the general expectation of a council, Francis I tried unilaterally to achieve a religious agreement between Catholics and Lutherans in order to win the German princes over to his policy. For this reason Guillaume made contact with Oswald Myconius, Heinrich Bullinger, Martin Bucer, and Philipp Melanchthon, while Jean was sent to Rome with a *Mémoire pour le concile* (Memorandum for the Council; 24 June 1535). Despite the unfavorable mood of the Sorbonnistes and the Affaire des Placards, which threatened to jeopardize the religious negotiations, the du Bellay brothers continued to plead the case for concord by calling Melanchthon to France. After these attempts failed, Guillaume was again to render his services, this time in Piedmont as governor of Turin (19 November 1537). After falling ill, he died on 9 January 1543. As for Jean, he left his post as bishop of Paris upon the accession of Henry II and took up residence near Rome until his death. There he led the life of an ecclesiastical intellectual amid the splendor of the Renaissance.

BIBLIOGRAPHY

Primary Sources

Du Bellay, Guillaume. *Les Mémoires de Martin et de Guillaume Du Bellai-Langei.* Paris, 1753.
———. *Fragments de la première Ogdoade de Guillaume Du Bellay.* Paris, 1904.
Du Bellay, Jean. *Poëmata aliquot.* Paris, 1546.
———. *Ambassade en Angleterre, (1527–1529).* Paris, 1905.
Scheurer, Rémy, ed. *Correspondance du cardinal Jean Du Bellay.* 2 vols. Paris, 1969–1973.

Secondary Sources

Bourilly, V. L. *Guillaume Du Bellay, seigneur de Langey.* Paris, 1904.
———. *Le cardinal Du Bellay en Italie.* Paris, 1907.

MARIO TURCHETTI
Translated from French by Robert E. Shillenn

BELLERIVE, Antoine de. *See* Corro, Antonio del.

BENEDETTO DA MANTOVA (also Benedetto Fontanini; dates unknown), Cassinese Benedictine monk of the Congregation of Santa Giustina. The rare biographical notes on Benedetto da Mantova seem to divide his life into three periods, which parallel his ever more radical religious positions. The date of his birth is unknown (around the end of the 1400s at the latest). He made his religious profession in February 1511 in Mantua (Mantova), where he remained for about fifteen years. In 1534 he was among the deans of San Giorgio Maggiore in Venice. At this phase in his religious formation, he was influenced by notable proponents of an irenic approach, beginning with the abbot of San Giorgio Maggiore, the future cardinal Gregorio Cortese. Here, not by mere chance, he also met fellow members of his order who were destined for literary success but who were of doubtful orthodoxy, such as Teofilo and Giovambattista Folengo, as well as Francesco Negri, author of the famous *Tragedia del libero arbitrio* (Tragedy of Free Will) and soon to be exiled for his religious views.

From August 1537 up to 1541–1542 various accounting and administrative documents indicate that he was present in the monastery of San Nicolò l'Arena on the slopes of Mount Etna (Catania). It was in this monastery that his irenic religious formation encountered Waldensian and Protestant literature, which gave rise to the first edition of one of the most famous texts of the Reformation in Italy: the *Trattato utilissimo del beneficio di Giesu Christo crocifisso verso i christiani* (Useful Treatise on the Merits of Jesus Christ Crucified for Christians). The *Trattato*, hand written, was then reviewed in Viterbo in Cardinal Reginald Pole's circle by Marcantonio Flaminio, a friend of Benedetto's who, according to Pietro Carnesecchi's testimony, "sent him this book, asking him if he would be willing to polish and embellish it with his elegant style. . . and thus Flaminio, keeping the contents intact, revised it in the way he saw fit." (Still unknown are the ways in which the text was transmitted; it is hypothesized that it may have been carried by Bernardino Ochino.) The text, thus "polished" by Flaminio, was printed anonymously in Venice in 1543 by De' Bindonis, and from then on it is difficult to count the various editions and translations, not to mention the ecclesiastical condemnations. From that point the Roman Inquisition tried in vain to trace it back to its author. Only Carnesecchi's testimony in the trial of 1566–1567 pointed to its author, a "black monk of Saint Benedict, named don Benedetto da Mantova." The text, known only via Flaminio's revision, is presented as a "broad way" to salvation, utterly centered on the theme of God's great mercy (the forgiveness of sins obtained by Christ's sacrifice), and emphasizing justification by faith alone and predestination. Therein it united Waldensian mysticism and Calvinist doctrine; the conspicuous fragments from Juan de Valdés and John Calvin have been traced and are frequently repeated verbatim in the *Trattato*. Rather than being evocative of Pelagian themes, the *Beneficio di Cristo* (Benefice of Christ) appears to be more of a short work crafted by Cardinal Pole's "family" in view of the imminent debates at the Council of Trent and made part of a program of dissemination that soon after saw the edition, again in Venice, of other Waldensian tracts.

Shortly after the publication Benedetto da Mantova again headed north. In 1544 he was rector of the important abbey of Pomposa. Having thus advanced within the order—which led to his being mentioned in the conciliar *Diarii* of Angelo Massarelli, secretary of the Council of Trent—he suffered a serious setback in 1549, when he was detained in the Benedictine abbey of Padua. Although the causes of the arrest are unknown, they were presumably connected with the latest phase in his religious evolution—a radical spiritualistic evolution he had undergone along with other Benedictines, including Luciano degli Ottoni, Isidoro Chiari, and Antonio da Bozzolo. This had come about because of an encounter he had in his years in Catania (1537–1540) with his former brother in religion Giorgio Rioli, better known as Giorgio Siculo. Arrested in 1550, Siculo was condemned to death in Ferrara in 1551, implicating in his disgrace Benedetto da Mantova, who appeared to share his teachings and to be familiar with their more esoteric core (which is still unknown). Documents have, in fact, shown that in 1550 Benedetto da Mantova possessed most of Siculo's important books (some of which are lost) and circulated them through the Benedictine monasteries; for this reason he was again detained in Verona. Statements and memoranda to the Roman Inquisition in subsequent years (1568–1570) expressly refer to a "Georgian sect" that had spread through Ferrara, Mantua, and Bologna, at the head of which, after the death of Siculo, was none other than Benedetto da Mantova, who distinguished himself by translating the visionary's books from the "Sicilian language into good Italian" and by subsequently disseminating them secretly. It is still unknown how Benedetto da Mantova's involvement in the vicissitudes of the Inquisition turned out; even the data of his death is unknown.

BIBLIOGRAPHY

Primary Source

Caponetto, Salvatore, ed. *Il Beneficio di Cristo: Con le versioni del secolo XVI; Documenti e testimonianze.* Florence and Chicago, 1972.

Secondary Sources

Caponetto, Salvatore. "Benedetto da Mantova." In *Dizionario Biografico degli Italiani*, vol. 8. Rome, 1966.
Ginzburg, Carlo. "Due note sul protetismo cinquecentesco." *Rivista Storica Italiana* 78 (1966), 185–227.
Ginzburg, Carlo, and Adriano Prosperi. *Giochi di pazienza: Un seminario sul "Beneficio di Cristo."* Turin, 1975.

PAOLO SIMONCELLI
Translated from Italian by Robert E. Shillenn

BENEFICIO DI CRISTO is the most famous work associated with sixteenth-century reform thought in Italy. Despite extensive scholarly literature devoted to it, no agreement about the nature of its theology has been reached. Published anonymously in Venice in 1543 as *Trattato utilissimo del beneficio di Giesu Christo crocifisso verso i christiani*, the small book became immediately popular, although the statement of a contemporary, Pier Paolo Vergerio, that in six years forty thousand copies were sold is surely exaggerated. An elusive Benedictine monk, Benedetto da Mantova, is generally thought to have been its author, while the humanist and poet Marcantonio Flaminio is known to have revised and polished the text. The Dominican Ambrogio Catarino Politi's attack on the work as unorthodox appeared in 1544, followed by its prohibition by the Inquisition five years later. While translations into several languages assured it readers in other countries, in Italy the mere possession of the *Beneficio* came to be taken as evidence of the owner's heterodoxy. It was suppressed so successfully that no Italian copy came to light until the nineteenth century, when one was discovered in the library of Saint John's College, Cambridge. Since then, the work has taken its preeminent place in sixteenth-century Italian religious history.

Disagreements among scholars concern chiefly the indebtedness of the little book to the writings of Luther, Calvin, Melanchthon, and Juan de Valdés, paraphrases from all of which are present. For example, Tommaso Bozza has maintained that the *Beneficio* is little more than a summary of the 1539 edition of Calvin's *Institutes*. Others, like Salvatore Caponetto, editor of the splendid standard edition of the text, have argued for its affinity with the spirituality of Valdés. Still others have interpreted it as belonging to a specifically Benedictine theological tradition that came close to Pelagianism. But whatever its sources, the *Beneficio* can best be understood as a singular expression of Italian spirituality that did not exist in a theological vacuum. While it often echoes passages from the writings of major reformers, the work defies definition as a mere vehicle for the transmission of their thought to Italian readers. Its primary significance lies in showing that far from being untouched by the central issues of Reformation theology, Italians shared the deep yearning for a return to biblical Christianity and for personal, direct experience of God's grace and forgiveness that were common among European Christians in the sixteenth century.

The purpose of the *Beneficio* is spelled out clearly in its concluding section: "Our chief purpose has been to praise and exalt, in accordance with the little power we have, the magnificent benefit that the Christian has received from Jesus Christ crucified, and to show that faith by itself justifies, meaning that God accepts all those as righteous who truly believe that Jesus Christ has made full amends for their sins." The six chapters of the work explain these central ideas in detail. Of unequal length, they are written in a straightforward style employing nontechnical vocabulary that laypeople without schooling in theology could follow. Answers to their anxiety concerning personal salvation are given in simple and clear fashion. The more learned, however, were attracted by the work's many complex questions that they could ponder.

The main theme is repeated over and over: we are justified

by faith alone. The highest good humanity has received is the benefit of Christ's terrible death on the cross. Christians can respond to this supreme act of God's love by loving, trusting, and believing him in return. Reliance on works as a means of salvation is condemned, but the *Beneficio* stresses that genuinely good works cannot be separated from justifying faith any more than light can be separated from the flame that is its source. The familiar Pauline image of Christ as the groom is used repeatedly, as is that of the soul, his bride, who comes to him with a dowry of sin, which he annihilates through his cross.

Thus reform for a reader who assented to the main ideas of the *Beneficio* would mean establishing a personal relation with God. It was founded on the exercise of the will, made in response to grace, to turn away from sin. This decision was not seen as the result of fear but of faith, love, and gratitude, made with trust that one was predestined to share eternal life with God. Therefore dogmatic definitions, doctrine, and jurisdictional or administrative questions of the church became peripheral or irrelevant to the central religious concerns of the individual. This point the Inquisitors understood clearly when they proscribed the book.

[*See also* Benedetto da Mantova *and* Flaminio, Marcantonio.]

BIBLIOGRAPHY

Primary Source

Benedetto da Mantova. *Il Beneficio di Cristo con le versioni del secolo 16: Documenti e testimonianze.* Edited by Salvatore Caponetto. De Kalb, Ill., 1972. Standard edition by one of the foremost scholars of the history of Protestantism in Italy. Includes the Italian text together with sixteenth-century translations into English, French, and Croatian, as well as Ambrogio Catarino's attack on the *Beneficio*. Full bibliography.

Secondary Sources

Ossola, Carlo. "Nei labirinti del 'Beneficio di Cristo.'" In *Cultura e società nel Rinascimento tra riforme e manierismi,* edited by Vittore Branca and Carlo Ossola, pp. 385–425. Florence, 1984. Subtle and thoughtful discussion of the *Beneficio* as part of Italian culture.
Prelowski, Ruth, trans. "The Beneficio di Cristo." In *The Proceedings of the Unitarian Historical Society.* Italian Reformation Studies in Honor of Laelius Socinus (1562–1962), edited by John A. Tedeschi, vol. 14, pts. 1–2, pp. 21–102. Florence, 1965. Includes an extensive bibliography. Text is reprinted in *Reform Thought in Sixteenth-Century Italy,* edited by Elisabeth G. Gleason, pp. 106–161. Chico, Calif., 1981.
Simoncelli, Paolo. "Nuove ipotesi e studi sul 'Beneficio di Cristo.'" *Critica Storica* 12 (1975), 321–388. Important discussion of historiography, with full bibliography.
Welti, Manfred E. *Kleine Geschichte der italienischen Reformation.* Gütersloh, 1985. Recent discussion, interpreting the *Beneficio* as a product of Italian evangelism. Useful bibliography.

ELISABETH G. GLEASON

BERLICHINGEN, Götz von

(also Gottfried; c.1480–1562), Franconian knight "with the iron hand" (he had lost his right hand in a battle in 1504). A robber knight in the grand style, from which he profited considerably, Berlichingen is part of the history of the Reformation only insofar as he introduced it in his domain and was, for four weeks in 1525, the leader of the Odenwald peasants in the Peasants' War. Earlier he had been imprisoned by the Swabian League in Heilbronn for three years because of a serious violation of imperial law. There he heard sermons of Johann Lachmann and was converted to Lutheran ideas. Released toward the end of 1522, he appointed Lutheran clergy who introduced the Reformation in one of his domains in 1522 and in the others in 1533 and later. In the final phase of the Knights' Revolt against the archbishopric of Trier he sided with Franz von Sickingen; his motivation appears to have been more political than religious.

For Berlichingen the Peasants' War was initially an opportunity to settle old scores (on behalf of the imperial knights) with the Swabian League and the territorial rulers. He negotiated with the peasants, but, at the same time, he pursued a complex subterfuge to protect himself against all sides. Late in April 1525 he assumed the leadership of the Odenwald peasants (allegedly forced to do so by the peasants). He pursued the moderate approach of the Twelve Articles and the Declaration of Amorbach and wanted to avoid the use of force, but as peasant leader he felt compelled to adopt it. On 28 May, as the superior forces of the Swabian League approached, Berlichingen left the peasants and disappeared. In 1528 he was brought to trial, and in 1530, after one and a half years in prison, he swore to keep the peace; he remained under house arrest until the end of his life some 30 years later (23 July 1562). He had no deep inner relationship to religion; in his autobiography he did not even mention the Reformation.

BIBLIOGRAPHY

Ulmschneider, Helgard. *Götz von Berlichingen: Ein adeliges Leben der deutschen Renaissance.* Sigmaringen, 1974. Authoritative biography with good survey of sources.
Berlichingen, Götz von. *Mein Fehd und Handlungen.* Edited by Helgard Ulmschneider. Sigmaringen, 1981. Critical edition of his autobiography with a brief biographical sketch in the introduction.

ADOLF LAUBE
Translated from German by Hans J. Hillerbrand

BERN.

The greatest city-state north of the Alps and a member of the Swiss Confederation, Bern also included a number of territories belonging to monasteries and nobility over which it had only indirect jurisdiction. The Reformation subjected these territories to the city magistrate, who secularized the monasteries and integrated the nobility into the city's political system. The Reformation laid the ground for uniform territorial legislation in matters of religion, morality, poor relief, and education.

Two rebellions of the Bernese Oberland in support of "the old faith and the old liberties" were crushed by the city in 1528. Henceforth it was not possible "to convoke a communal assembly without the consent of the Bernese authorities." The city council developed an absolutist concept of government and vowed "not to acknowledge anyone except the Almighty as above us and to be accountable to no one"(1682).

The Bernese Reformation, however, did not begin as a magisterial Reformation. The preaching mandate of 1523 ordered all preachers to teach only what they could prove from scripture. The second religious mandate of 1524 and the third of 1525 combined this with a guarantee of all existing doctrines and practices. The preaching mandates, similar to those elsewhere (for example, the German imperial mandate of 1523), did not introduce the Reformation but prompted a religious cease-fire. Behind them lay a juridical and formalistic understanding of scripture, as manifested in the "Brunner-Handel." Georg Brunner was able to provide scriptural evidence for his claim that the ordinances and practices of the Roman church were not all based on the Bible. The Brunner-Handel was a lawsuit of defamation with the Bible as witness. The council—unlike Brunner or the reformers—did not accept it as a judge.

It opted instead for "Catholic reform." Following the Catholic "articles of Lucerne" in 1525, the council abolished letters of indulgence, customary dues to the clergy, the alienation of lands or rents in mortmain, and fiscal and legal privileges of the clergy. It also ordered priests to reside in their parishes. No one, the council decided, should be compelled to make offerings, pilgrimages, processions, or confessions. No one should be forced to believe in purgatory, and married clergymen were no longer exiled but simply deprived of their benefices. Only the magistracy had the right to appoint or dismiss the clergy.

The city council, however, did not want to go further. It mobilized the rural area (with its population of some seventy thousand) against the city (with its population of five thousand), which was not satisfied with a Catholic reform in the tradition of Gravamina and wanted a Christian biblicism. The consultation of rural districts (*Ämterbefragungen*) in 1524 favored what "is in use or practice." In February and March 1526 only one of nineteen rural territories supported the Reformation. At Whitsuntide that same year the Small Council, the inner circle of the political elite, secured the status quo by oath from both the city and the rural territories. The "peasant majority," in the words of the Bernese reformer Berchtold Haller, was meant as a *tregarium* ("laxative") for the Reformation.

When the council tried to expel Berchtold Haller in 1526 because of his refusal to celebrate the Mass, it provoked a small uprising. "A great number of honest men from within the community flocked together. . . to protect their true preacher," according to Valerius Anshelm. Haller was not expelled but appointed as town preacher. The most active enemies of the Reformation lost their seats on the council. The Great Council, the second most important political body (with 270 members), turned into an advocate of the community at large and especially of the guilds, of whose members it consisted. It became the court of appeal in all religious matters. In 1528 it obtained the prerogative to consider all religious matters first and—temporarily—the right to appoint the Small Council. The next elections brought a reform-minded majority to the Small Council.

The Great Council tipped the balance of political power toward the reformers' principle of scripture, and it began to interpret the mandate of 1523 in an increasingly "reformed" way. The guilds stood on its side and, in 1527, thirteen out of sixteen guilds abandoned their support of masses and benefices. The rural territories accepted a new mandate—maybe misunderstanding its intention—which gave only "provisional" support to the old practices of the church. The disputation of 6–26 January 1528 created the formal and legal basis for the Reformation mandate of 7 February 1528, which was carried out against the will of the Oberland. Scripture had become the arbiter of religion. The reversal of the Bernese position helped the Reformation to triumph in both Basel and Schaffhausen and strengthened Zurich's position in Switzerland.

The Reformation in Bern was supported especially by the burghers in the city. Nevertheless, in the long run it enhanced the power of the magistracy. However, the main result of the Reformation, the introduction of new religious and moral attitudes, required also the cooperation of the civic and rural communities, to which it transferred new duties concerning schools, poor relief, and marital and moral discipline. Even after the defeat of the Reformed forces of Zurich and Bern at Kappel in 1531, the rural communities stood by the Reformation that they had once opposed.

A morals court (*Chorgericht*), consisting of the pastor and members of the community, was established in every parish to deal with the moral demeanor of the people. The parishes, in turn, were combined into classes, with the Bernese *Oberchorgericht* (superior moral and marital court) at the top. The *Chorgericht* was an integral part of the general administrative system but had no right of excommunication. Bern's intervention against the siege of Geneva by Charles III, duke of Savoy, in 1536 secured the victory of the Reformation in Geneva. Nevertheless, although Bern officially accepted the Calvinist doctrine of predestination in 1588 and the Dordrecht Confession in 1618, the Bernese church and especially its moral jurisdiction was strongly marked by the system of the Zwinglian state-church in Zurich as defined by the synod in 1532. The council defended its state-church system also in the Vaud (which it had conquered in 1536 from the Savoyards and the bishop of Lausanne, Sebastian de Montfulçon) against the "Genevan" reform ideas of local preachers.

[*See also* Basel; Geneva; Haller, Berchtold; Switzerland; *and* Zurich.]

BIBLIOGRAPHY

Anshelm, Valerius. *Die Berner-Chronik des Valerius Anshelm.* 6 vols. Bern, 1884–1901.

Bierbrauer, Peter. *Freiheit und Gemeinde im Berner Oberland 1300–1700.* Archiv des Historischen Vereins Kantons Bern, vol. 74. Bern, 1991.

Feller, Richard. *Geschichte Berns.* 4 vols. Bern, 1946–1960.

Guggisberg, Kurt. *Bernische Kirchengeschichte.* Bern, 1958.

Holenstein, André. "Reformierte Konfessionalisierung und bernischer Territorialstaat." In *Territorialstaat und Calvinismus,* edited by Meinrad Schaab, pp. 5–33. Stuttgart, 1993.

Muralt, Leonhard von. "Stadtgemeinde und Reformation in der Schweiz." *Zeitschrift für schweizerische Geschichte* 10 (1930), 349–384. Interesting comparison of Basel, Zurich, and Bern.

Pfister, Willy. *Das Chorgericht des bernischen Aargaus im 17. Jahrhundert.* Aarau, Switzerland, 1939.

Rennefahrt, Hermann, ed. *Die Rechtsquellen des Kantons Bern.* Pt 1, *Stadtrechte vol. VI, 1 and 2: Staat und Kirche.* Aargau, Switzerland, 1960–1961.

Schmidt, Heinrich R. "Die Christianisierung des Sozialverhaltens als permanente Reformation: Aus der Praxis reformierter Sittengerichte in der Schweiz während der frühen Neuzeit." *Zeitschrift für historische Forschung* 9 (supp. 1989), 113–163.

———. "Stadtreformation in Bern und Nürnberg: Ein Vergleich." In *Nürnberg und Bern: Zwei Reichsstädte und ihre Landgebiete,* edited by Rudolf Endres, pp. 81–119. Erlangen, 1990.

———. *Dorf und Religion: Reformierte Sittenzucht in Berner Landgemeinden der frühen Neuzeit.* Stuttgart and New York, 1995. Long-term study of Bernese morals court, including English summary and data on diskette.

Steck, Rudolf, and Gustav Tobler, eds. *Aktensammlung zur Geschichte der Berner Reformation, 1521–1532.* Bern, 1918–1923.

Vuilleumier, Henri. *Histoire de l'église réformeé du pays de Vaud sous le régime bernois.* 4 vols. Lausanne, 1927.

Walder, Ernst. "Reformation und moderner Staat." *Archiv des Historischen Vereins des Kantons Bern* 64/65 (1980–1981), 445–583.

HEINRICH RICHARD SCHMIDT

BERNARDINO DE LOREDO

(1482–1540?), Spanish Franciscan lay brother and spiritual writer. Loredo was born in Seville of a lower noble family. He studied and practiced medicine before entering the Franciscans in 1510. As a lay brother he continued to practice medicine and published two medical books (1522 and 1527) that enjoyed enough success to be reprinted. He served briefly as physician to John III of Portugal and his wife Catherine. He is remembered, however, for two spiritual writings. The less important is his *Josephina* (1538), which encouraged devotion to Saint Joseph; Bernardino served as a pioneer of the growing cult of Joseph during the Counter-Reformation, which gradually replaced John the Baptist with Joseph as the most important saint after the Virgin Mary.

Bernardino's great work was *Subida del Monte Sion* (*The Ascent of Mount Sion*), which was first published anonymously at Seville in 1535; the third part was drastically revised in the second edition of 1538. The work enjoyed only limited popularity, with seven editions between 1535 and 1617. French and English translations appeared only in the twentieth century. The work contains many vivid images and homely examples to describe spiritual experiences but is often vague, rambling, and repetitious.

The Ascent has three parts, which take up in turn the classic spiritual stages of the purgative, illuminative, and unitive ways. The first part dwells on self-knowledge, renunciation, and how the soul can find God in all creatures. The second part takes up the Incarnation and the events of Christ's life. The third and most influential part deals with attaining the prayer of quiet; it provided Teresa of Avila with a confirmation of her own spiritual experiences. Here Bernardino prepared the way for the great flowering of Spanish mystical literature in the later sixteenth century.

BIBLIOGRAPHY

Bernardino de Loredo. *The Ascent of Mount Sion.* London, 1952. Translation of Book III and introduction by E. Allison Peers.

Gomis, Juan Bautista, ed. *Misticos Franciscanos Españoles.* Madrid, 1948. See vol. 2, pp. 15–442 for a modern text of *The Ascent of Mount Sion,* with introduction.

Peers, E. Allison. *Studies of the Spanish Mystics.* 2d rev. ed. London, 1951. Classic survey of Spanish mystical writers.

Ros, Fidèle de. *Un inspirateur de sainte Thérèse, le Frère Bernardin de Loredo.* Paris, 1948. The standard study.

JOHN PATRICK DONNELLY

BERNHARDI, Bartholomeus von Feldkirchen

(1487–1551), student of Martin Luther and first Lutheran provost in Kemberg. Originally from Schlins near Feldkirch in Vorarlberg (Austria), he began his studies at Erfurt in 1503 and continued in 1504 at Wittenberg, where he earned a master of arts degree in 1508, a *Baccalaureus biblicus* in 1512, a *Sententiarius* in 1516, and a *Formatus* in 1518. He was a close follower of Luther, who taught him about the reactions to his biblical exegesis and urged him to openly attack the Scholastics. On 25 September 1516, in a disputation chaired by Luther, Bernhardi defended the theses he had formulated on the basis of Luther's lectures on *Romans.* By making reference to the anti-Pelagian writings of Augustine, he attacked Gabriel Biel's high estimation of the free will. This disputation led to the breakthrough of Luther's theology (with its biblical foundation and its invocation of the church fathers) at the University of Wittenberg.

Bernhardi was rector of the University of Wittenberg during the winter term of 1518/19, but he became provost in Kemberg at the end of 1518 and quit his teaching post in the spring of 1519. The archdeaconate, which had been established in Pratau in 1196 to serve as a cathedral chapter, had been moved in 1298 some twelve kilometers south of Wittenberg to Kemberg. As one of the first priests who turned away from the Roman church, he married Gertrud Pannier in Kemberg. This circumstance probably served as grounds for his incarceration, from which he was able to procure his release by making a payment. His behavior triggered a heated discussion about the marriage of priests. With a preface dated 13 December 1521, Bernhardi's *Apologis*, in which he defended his marriage, was published by Andreas Bodenstein von Karlstadt. Between 1521 and 1523 this work was published in at least three Latin and six German editions, which made Bernhardi's marriage famous.

Upon the recommendation of Luther, who thereby granted a favor to Karlstadt, Elector Frederick III of Saxony allowed the latter to live in Kemberg under Bernhardi's supervision. Karlstadt remained there from 1526 until his departure in February of 1529.

BIBLIOGRAPHY

Verzeichnis der im deutschen Sprachbereich erschienenen Drucke des 16. Jahrhunderts. Stuttgart, 1984. Vol. 3, nos. 6100–6108.
Wagenmann, Julius August. "Bernhardi, Bartholomäus B." In *Allgemeine Deutsch Biographie*, vol. 2, pp. 459–460. Leipzig, 1875.

HELMAR JUNGHANS
Translated from German by Wolfgang Katenz

BERNHARDI, Johannes (also Velcurio; c.1490–1534), Wittenberg liberal arts professor and textbook author. Born near Feldkirch, a town in the Vorarlberg in Austria, Bernhardi was well known to generations of young students as Veltkirch and Velcurio, the toponyms under which his two popular textbooks were posthumously published. He attended Wittenberg University from 1512 to 1519. After receiving his master's degree he began teaching in 1520, lecturing on natural philosophy, history, and rhetoric. Bernhardi became an early adherent of Martin Luther, and in 1520 he published a brief defense of Luther against an attack by Augustin von Alfeld, a Franciscan from Leipzig. It was his only publication during his lifetime. Although Bernhardi was encouraged by students and colleagues to publish his lectures, he was unable to finish his work for publication; this inability was seemingly related to the severe melancholia from which he suffered. Indeed, Luther's remarkable pastoral visit at his deathbed, as recorded in the *Tischreden* (Table Talk), suggests that this disease of the soul was responsible for Bernhardi's death.

Concerning Bernhardi's textbooks, the first was a commentary on the *De copia* of Desiderius Erasmus. Philipp Melanchthon sent the manuscript to Peter Braubach, a printer in Hagenau, and it was published along with an edition of the *De copia* at the end of 1534, shortly after Bernhardi's death. The commentary was subsequently incorporated in some forty editions of Erasmus's work up to the end of the sixteenth century and became the standard edition of the *De copia* used in English schools. The commentary's only separate publication, a work of 154 pages in octavo, appeared in Paris in 1539 and was entitled *In Erasmi de duplici copia verborum ac rerum commentarius M. Veltkirchii.*

Bernhardi's second textbook, his lectures on Aristotle's natural philosophy, appeared under two separate titles. It was first published as *Epitomae physicae libri quatuor, autore Joanne Veltkirchio* (Erfurt, 1538), edited by his student Caspar Kanngiesser (c.1510–1576). The next year another student, Sebald Hawenreuter (1508–1589), brought out an edition entitled *Joannis Velcurionis commentarii in universam physicam Aristotelis libri quatuor* (Tübingen, 1539). The Hawenreuter edition, published from Lyon to London, went through at least twenty printings between 1539 and 1600. It was the most popular textbook of its kind and was still in use one hundred years after Bernhardi's death. Johannes Oporinus (1507–1568), a Basel printer and scholar, credited Bernhardi's enduring popularity to a Latin style that was "brief, easy and clear."

Because Bernhardi lived on only through his toponym, the bibliographic records have often become tangled, and his works have sometimes been incorrectly attributed to three other Wittenberg contemporaries: his older brother, Bartholomeus von Feldkirchen Bernhardi (1487–1551); Johannes Dölsch (c.1485–1523), also from Feldkirch; and Johannes Toltz (c.1495–1573), who is confused with Dölsch and thus with Bernhardi. This confusion, which has been pointed out since the eighteenth century, persists to the present day.

BIBLIOGRAPHY

Burmeister, Karl Heinz. "Ein Kommentar zur *Copia Verborunz* des Erasmus von Rotterdam von Johannes Bernhardi." *Monfort: Vierteljahresschrift für Geschichte und Gegenwartskunde Vorarlbergs*, 22 (1970), 272–282.
Fox, Wilhelm. *Drei vorarlberger Professoren zu Wittenberg*. Feldkirch, Austria, 1911.
Lohr, Charles H. "Velcurio (Veltkirchius), Johannes Bernhardi." *Renaissance Quarterly* 35 (1982), 212.
Luther, Martin. "Decumbente Magistro Veldkirchio sic consolabatur eum, doctor Martinus Cal. Feb. 34." In *Werke*, vol. 3, *Tischreden*, pp. 503–509. Weimar, 1914.

JAMES A. HINZ

BERQUIN, Louis de (c.1490–1529), French humanist, scholar, and reformer. Translator of numerous shorter writings by Erasmus, Berquin was among the first and most famous victims of the legal repression of Protestantism in France. He and others like him—people associated with Guillaume Briçonnet, bishop of Meaux, or Marguerite d'Angoulême, a sister of King Francis I—point to the mix of reform-minded humanists and distant readers of Martin Luther who formed the fragmented and individualistic "heresy" that constituted the early French reform.

Berquin initially benefited from the protection and patronage of King Francis I and his sister. When officials seized and examined his library at Paris in mid-1523, they found books by Luther, Philipp Melanchthon, and Andreas Bodenstein Karlstadt; Berquin's translations of these authors; and original manuscript works by Berquin himself. The Sorbonne theologians soon condemned the translations, as well as Berquin's own writings, and the Parlement of Paris imprisoned him. Only the king's direct intervention prevented a heresy trial by a special tribunal composed of judicial officers of the bishop of Paris and judges from the Parlement. Berquin agreed to renounce various religious opinions attributed to Luther and was freed, but his books and papers were publicly burned outside Nôtre-Dame.

This ordeal notwithstanding, Berquin continued much as before, and, in January 1526, the authorities arrested him again. This time a panel of religious and secular magistrates found Berquin guilty of heresy. Francis I, upon returning from Spanish captivity in April, again saved his protégé. Though the Parlement balked, royal officers secured Berquin's release from prison in November 1526. Yet the matter was not forgotten. Berquin's trial resumed in 1528 and, through a complex series of maneuvers, he appeared before the same stern judges who had condemned him two years earlier. The tribunal rendered a guilty verdict and, despite his subsequent appeal to the Parlement, Berquin was sentenced to death. On 17 April 1529 he was burned at the stake in the Place de Grève.

BIBLIOGRAPHY

Doucet, Roger. *Étude sur le gouvernement de François Ier dans ses rapports avec le Parlement de Paris.* 2 vols. Paris, 1921–1926. Places Berquin's trials within the general political context.
Knecht, R. J. *Francis I.* Cambridge, 1982. Examines Berquin in light of his great protector.
Mann, Margaret. *Erasme et les débuts de la réforme française 1517–1536.* Reprint, Geneva, 1978. Assesses Berquin's humanism.

RAYMOND A. MENTZER, JR.

BETHLEN, Gabriel (Hung., Gábor; 1580–1629), prince of Transylvania. Born into a noble family, Bethlen received his political training as a youth at the court in Gyulafehérvár. During the Fifteen Years' War he was an ally of Stephen (István) Bocskay. In 1613, with Turkish support, Bethlen was elected ruler of Transylvania but regarded the protection of the Ottoman Porte as a temporary expedient.

During the Thirty Years' War Bethlen was allied with Protestants abroad, but his military operations took place mainly in royal Hungary, where Habsburg kings had been ruling since 1526. Here Bethlen was greeted as "a prince of our own blood." During his first campaign he was supported by nearly all of the internal political factions. At the diet in November 1620, he was elected king of Hungary but was never crowned. His first campaign ended in December 1621, when, on the initiative of his former supporters, the Peace of Nikolsburg recognized the Habsburg rule of Hungary. The country thus avoided the fate of Bohemia after its defeat in the Battle of White Mountain in 1620. The peace was renewed in 1624 and in 1626, but these subsequent campaigns had decreasing domestic support.

In Transylvania the era of Bethlen was viewed as the golden age of the principality. With the strict regulation of every sphere of life, the prince created a peculiar, eastern-European type of absolutism. In the case of Transylvania, this meant prosperity and peace for the subjects and even political and religious toleration. Bethlen's most enduring achievements were in the realm of culture and education, and Reformed intellectuals were fervent supporters of his rule. The prince established an academy in Gyulafehérvár and hoped to make it into a university. This did not happen, however, and the school was transferred to Kolozsvár.

Bethlen had two marriages, one to Zsuzsanna Károlyi and the other to Katherine of Brandenburg. Neither produced descendants who survived to maturity.

BIBLIOGRAPHY

Primary Source

Szilágyi, Sándor, ed. *Bethlen Gábor fejedelem kiadatlan politikai levelei* (The Collected Letters of Prince Gabriel Bethlen). Budapest, 1879. Many letters in Latin.

Secondary Sources

Demény, Lajos. *Bethlen Gábor és kora* (Gabriel Bethlen and His Age). Bucharest, 1982.
Szekfü, Gyula. *Bethlen Gábor.* Budapest, 1920; reprint, 1990. The basic work on Bethlen.

KATALIN PÉTER

BETHLENFALVA, George Thurzo de. *See* Thurzo, George.

BÉTHUNE, Maximilien de (1560–1641), duke of Sully, early companion of Henry of Navarre (later Henry IV of France), and chief minister in France between about 1598 and 1610. Béthune was born near Mantes-la-Jolie, on the river Seine, into a family divided in its religious loyalties, as many French families were at this time. He was brought up as a Protestant and narrowly escaped death when as a schoolboy he was in Paris at the time of the Saint Bartholomew's Day Massacre (1572). Throwing in his lot with Henry of Navarre, the Protestant leader, he followed Henry during his campaigns of the late 1570s and 1580s, distinguishing himself at the battles of Arques (1589) and Ivry (1590).

He was increasingly employed in administrative and diplomatic tasks, and once Henry had come to the throne of France in 1589 and largely pacified the country by 1598, Béthune was a natural choice for high office. From about this time onward he was, in effect, chief minister, in charge of the finances, the roads and bridges, the buildings and forts, and even the artillery and navy. To all these posts he brought an exceptional degree of rigor and order, which may indeed have owed something to his Calvinist upbringing. He was in addition often used in negotiations with the disaffected French Protestants and with foreign Protestant rulers like James I of England; he knew well how to play the religious card while keeping his political objectives firmly in mind.

Although it would have been politically advantageous to have abjured his Protestantism, Béthune refused to do so. But he was no bigot and often seems to have entertained Catholic divines at his table in the Paris Arsenal, for he greatly enjoyed theological disputations. Moreover, he seems to have sympathized with Henry's attempts to reform the ancient church and on occasion would listen to Catholic preachers, afterward advising Henry about their quality and qualifications for preferment.

When Henry was assassinated in 1610, Béthune's position became untenable, and he soon fell from power, entering a prolonged and fractious retirement. During this time he wrote his memoirs, which offer a distinctive version of his role under Henry as well as an abundance of original documents concerning the reign. Béthune lived and died as a Protestant, but he was above all a Frenchman, concerned to restore and maintain the fragile national unity.

BIBLIOGRAPHY

Barbiche, Bernard. *Sully*. Paris, 1978.
Barbiche, Bernard and David Buisseret, eds. *Les Oeconomies Royales de Sully*. 2 vols. Paris, 1970-. This new edition of Sully's memoirs has reached the year 1599.
Buisseret, David. *Sully and the Growth of Centralized Government in France, 1598–1610*. London, 1968.

DAVID BUISSERET

BEUCKELSON, Jan. *See* John of Leiden.

BEURLIN, Jacob (1520–1561), German Lutheran professor of theology and chancellor of the University of Tübingen. Beurlin converted to Lutheranism in the 1540s. After a short pastorate at Derendingen, Württemberg, he received the Th.D. in 1551 and began teaching at Tübingen. Beurlin's abilities moved him from rector (1553–1554), to vice-chancelor (1557–1558), to chancelor (1561). His professorship at Tübingen (he lectured on the Bible and Melanchthon's *Loci*) and his efforts to forge and maintain a Lutheran theological consensus mark a transition from first- to second-generation German Lutheran reformers.

Duke Christoph of Württemberg regularly interrupted Beurlin's academic pursuits to press Beurlin into ecclesio-political service. In the first winter of Beurlin's Tübingen years (1551/52), he traversed the Alps four times under orders from his ruler to assist in the presentation and defense of Johannes Brenz's *Confessio Virtembergica* (Württemberg Confession; 1551) at the Council of Trent (1545–1563).

In 1554 Beurlin was sent to Königsberg, Prussia, in an unsuccessful attempt to mediate the Osiandrian controversy concerning the doctrine of justification. Beurlin was so impressive in this mission that Prince Albert of Prussia offered him a bishopric if he would stay in the north.

Upon his return to Tübingen, Beurlin's transitional role in the German Reformation became pointedly evident. When Jakob Andreae, the great negotiator and champion of confessional Lutheran consensus, joined the Tübingen faculty in 1561, Beurlin had already helped to identify the direction of Lutheran confessionalism that Andreae and others followed with such notable impact.

Beurlin's final commission from Duke Christoph was to attend the joint Roman Catholic–French Protestant Colloquy of Poissy, France, in 1561. When the meeting recessed abruptly, the Württembergers took up residence in Paris, so that they might be available if proceedings should resume. During this stay in Paris, Beurlin was infected with the plague and died.

BIBLIOGRAPHY

Primary Sources

Beurlin, Jacob. *Dispvtatio: De cavsis certitvdinis Doctrinae Ecclesiae Dei, desumpta ex Praefatione in Locos Communes D. Philippi Melanchthonis*. Tübingen, 1556.
———. *Oratio de ingenti incarnationis filii Dei miraculo*, Tübingen, 1556.
———. *Refutatio primae partis Sotici scripti*. Frankfurt a.M., 1561.

Secondary Sources

Bossert, G. "Beurlin, Jakob." In *Realencyklopädie für protestantische Theologie und Kirche*, edited by Albert Hauck, vol. 2, pp. 671–674. Leipzig, 1897. An abbreviated translation of this extensive article was published in *The New Schaff-Herzog Encyclopedia of Religious Knowledge*, edited by Samuel M. Jackson, vol. 2, p. 76, Grand Rapids, Mich., 1949.
Fausel, H. "Beurlin, Jakob." In *Die Religion in Geschichte und Gegenwart*, edited by Hans von Campenhausen et al., vol. 1, p. 963. Tübingen, 1957. Includes a helpful bibliography.
Tüchle, H. "Beurlin, Jakob." In *Lexikon für Theologie und Kirche*, edited by Josef Höfer and Karl Rahner, vol. 2, p. 323. Freiburg, 1958.

WILLIAM R. RUSSELL

BEYER, Absalon Pederssøn (1528–1575), Norwegian theological educator and humanist. Orphaned at age six, he was raised as the foster son of Bishop Geble Pederssøn, the first Lutheran bishop of Bergen. Beyer was educated in the bishop's home and sent to study for six years at the University of Copenhagen and three years at Wittenberg. In Copenhagen Beyer lived with Peder Palladius, bishop of Zealand (Sjælland) and a good friend of his foster father. At Wittenberg he was strongly attracted by Philipp Melanchthon's humanist training and theological outlook. In 1552 he returned to Bergen, where he became the theological lecturer at the cathedral (Latin) school and the royal chaplain in 1566. Both of these positions he held until his death, refusing calls elsewhere.

The Reformation in Norway was not the result of a grassroots evangelical awakening. Christian III's royal decree in 1536 proclaiming Norway to be Lutheran did not change the hearts and minds of the Norwegian people. It took a century-long process of education and indoctrination to make Norway Lutheran. Beyer is the leading example of Lutheran clergy who spent a lifetime educating and indoctrinating Norwegians into the Lutheran Reformation. Lutheran clergy in Norway during the sixteenth century were either trained overseas at various universities (most notably Copenhagen) or were ordained after studying at a diocesan cathedral school. Thus Beyer influenced many of the first generation of clergy who established Lutheranism in Norway.

From 1552 to 1572 he maintained a diary detailing the foibles and joys of each day, giving a unique and intimate picture of the Norwegian people, their church, and the process of Lutheran indoctrination. Beyer also wrote a history of the kingdom of Norway (*Om Norgis Rige*, 1567) revealing the ambivalence of Norwegian Lutherans toward the Reformation. Accepting the Reformation decree of the Danish king also meant the demise of Norwegian political independence, something that was not to be resurrected until 1814.

BIBLIOGRAPHY

Beyer, Absalon Pederssøn. *Absalon Pederssøn's Dagbok, 1552–1572.* Edited by Oluf Kolsrud and Kristen Valkner. Oslo, 1963.
———. "Om Norgis Rige." In *To norske historik-topografiske skrifter fra 1500-tallett*, edited by Gustav Storm. Oslo, 1968.

TRYGVE R. SKARSTEN

BÈZE, Théodore de (also Beza; 1516–1605), French Reformed scholar and theologian. Born 24 June 1516 in Vézelay, France, he was the son of Pierre de Bèze, king's bailiff and a member of the lesser nobility. When he was nine years old, Théodore was sent to Orléans to study with the humanist Melchior Wolmar, from whom he learned to write elegant Latin and Greek and to love poetry. Wolmar also introduced Bèze to the nascent reform. In 1530 Bèze accompanied Wolmar to Bourges, but five years later Pierre de Bèze ordered his son to return to Orléans to complete legal studies. Although Bèze obeyed, he spent most of his time with humanists and began to write poetry that eventually merited the favorable notice of Ronsard.

In 1539, with a degree in civil law, Bèze moved to Paris, where he pursued his humanist interests. He also continued to read Reformed literature, which gradually persuaded him

to give up his humanist friends and his inherited ecclesiastical benefices in the Roman Catholic church, and in 1548 he fled to Geneva. As a result, he was condemned by the Parlement of Paris and burned in effigy in the Place Maubert in 1550. Accompanying Bèze was Claudine Denosse, whom he had secretly married. When he found no openings in Geneva, Bèze responded to a call from Pierre Viret to teach Greek at the Lausanne academy, where he later served as rector. In 1557 Calvin called Bèze to Geneva to be the first rector of the new academy there. Bèze also joined the Genevan clergy and at Calvin's death in 1564 was elected moderator of the venerable Compagnie des Pasteurs ("company of pastors"), a post he held until 1580. After Calvin's death, Bèze became not only the leader of the Genevan church but chief counselor to the French Reformed churches, frequently traveling to France to participate in colloquies (Poissy, 1561; Saint-Germain, 1562), synods (La Rochelle, 1571; Nîmes, 1572), and as adviser to Gaspard II de Coligny after the Colloquy of Poissy at the beginning of the Wars of Religion.

In 1586 Bèze, with Swiss colleagues from Bern and Basel, met Jakob Andreae at Montbéliard in the duchy of Württemberg in response to a request from Frederick, count of Montbéliard, and the French refugees living there. The explicit purpose was for the two leading theologians of the Lutheran and Reformed camps to resolve their differences regarding the Lord's Supper. Since the Colloquy of Worms in 1557 and still more critically following the Maulbronn Colloquy of 1564, Lutherans and Reformed had become increasingly bitter toward one another. The focal point of their animosity was the interpretation of the Augsburg Confession's article 10 concerning the Lord's Supper. Did the Peace of Augsburg of 1555 intend only the 1530 *invariata* version, or did it include the more accommodating *variata* edition of 1541? For most German Lutherans, the matter was decided in 1577 by the Formula of Concord, whose principal authors were Martin Chemnitz and Jakob Andreae. During the 1580s these theological differences were also critical to the German Lutheran princes in deciding whether to continue to send troops to Henry III of France, and hence the Roman Catholic Guise faction, or to support Henry of Navarre, leader of the Huguenots, whom the Lutherans asked to sign the unaltered Augsburg Confession. The Colloquy of Montbéliard did nothing to heal the bitter division between the two main Protestant factions; indeed, some German Protestant princes supported the Catholic side in the Wars of Religion while others supported Henry of Navarre.

While Bèze's activities frequently took him from Geneva, he nevertheless firmly directed the academy and the Compagnie des Pastuers, especially in the continual tug of war between the Compagnie des Pasteurs and the magistrates of Geneva concerning the authority of each to punish immoral behavior. Bèze was determined that Geneva should not follow the pattern of Zurich and its Erastian government, and he managed to maintain a precarious balance between ecclesiastical and civic authorities, a balance signified by the council of Geneva, made up of magistrates, pastors, and elders.

Through his intense correspondence, Bèze maintained contact with Reformed churches throughout Europe and Britain. His most regular correspondent was Heinrich Bullinger of Zurich until the latter's death in 1575. Even so, Bèze's correspondence was not limited to fellow pastors; he dedicated his prayer book to Elizabeth I of England, and sent his precious *Codex Bezae* to the University of Cambridge. This codex is one of the earliest extant New Testament texts, found in a monastic library in Lyon when the Huguenots captured that city after the failed Colloquy of Poissy and the outbreak of the Wars of Religion in 1562. Bèze asked Elizabeth, "the Mother of the Churches," to help support refugees from the French Wars of Religion, especially in times of drought and plague when Geneva's supplies were inadequate to care for the influx of thousands of people arriving with little more than they could carry. From the time that Jeanne of Navarre asked Bèze for advice concerning the education of her son Henry, Bèze advised the Huguenot leaders of France. Even after Henry of Navarre's conversion to Catholicism in order to succeed to the throne of France as Henry IV, he and Bèze corresponded and even met on several occasions, the last time in 1600 while Henry was camped outside Geneva. The king summoned his aged counselor, whom he still called "Father." Bèze, then eighty-one years of age, mounted a horse to meet the king of France.

Besides his early poetry *(Juvenilia)*, and a play *(Abraham sacrifiant)*, Bèze completed Clément Marot's translation of *Psalms*. Bèze has a permanent place in the history of biblical studies through his translations, annotations, and Greek editions of the New Testament, for which his humanist studies and concern for correct grammar and language prepared him. Bèze's New Testament texts were incorporated into the English Geneva Bible of 1560. Later editions drew more heavily on Bèze's work. Bèze's theological agenda, however, prevented him from undertaking more biblical tasks and frequently influenced his interpretation of the excellent texts he had in his hands *(Cantabrigiensis* or *Codex Bezae* and *Claromontanus)*. For example, although Bèze possessed the *Codex Bezae* for nearly twenty years until he sent it to the University of Cambridge in 1581, he did not make much use of its variant readings, preferring established texts. Nevertheless, Bèze's corrections of previous texts made his Greek New Testament the best edition available at the time (1565). A committee of Genevan pastors led by Bèze and Corneille Bertram produced the influential Geneva Bible of 1588.

Another highly influential work of Bèze was published anonymously after the infamous Saint Bartholomew's Day Massacre. Out of his distress for his French compatriots,

Bèze wrote *Du droit des Magistrats sur leurs subjets* (1574), an important text in political history. Bèze's thesis was that all authority, including the authority of the French king, comes from God through election by the people. Kings remain responsible to the people, and if they abuse their authority by playing the tyrant, the people may rise up under the leadership of their elected magistrates. Calvin had counseled passive resistance; most political theory of the time required that a justified revolt must nevertheless be led by princes of the blood royal. Bèze removed both of those requirements for justified rebellion.

But the greatest body of writing left by Bèze is theological. His primary role throughout his long career in Geneva was as a professor at the academy that trained most of the French pastors as well as students from all the Reformed areas of Europe (e.g., England, Scotland, the Netherlands, Poland, Hungary, and the Palatinate). From his support of Calvin and Viret in Lausanne in the 1550s to his confrontation with Andreae in 1586 and beyond, Bèze professed Calvin's doctrine of double predestination. In addition, he never wavered from Calvin's doctrine of baptism and the Lord's Supper. Bèze was Calvin's epigone, but, as Calvin himself had argued regarding theology, while one would rather preach simply from the text, controversy requires extensive and precise commentary. Without wishing to be "original" doctrinally and certainly not with regard to scripture, Bèze nevertheless carried some of Calvin's teachings further than Calvin himself had done, though not beyond what Bèze considered to be Calvin's scripturally and christologically based doctrinal principles. A case in point was the debated issue of supralapsarian predestination (the decree of election is metaphysically prior as cause to all its consequences, e.g., creation and fall). Was this Bèze's doctrine or Bèze's polemical development of Calvin's doctrine (e.g., in the latter's commentary on *Jn.* 3:15)? Another case, although not a matter of such intense scholarly debate, was Bèze's refinement of Calvin's eucharistic doctrine. In this regard, Bèze developed Calvin's insight that the category upon which the doctrine relies is that of *relation*. One ought not to consider the bread and wine in their substance, that is, what they are by nature, but in their relation to the body and blood of Christ, that is, what they come to be as sacraments established by Christ's word and ordination.

These doctrines were also in harmony with Bèze's doctrine of justification and sanctification. Both are given simultaneously and inseparably, but they are distinct. Justification is the birth that entails growth in sanctification. Sanctification begins with the imputation of Christ's justice, but at the same time the justified one is given a new habit through grace, which is the instrument by which the Holy Spirit leads the true Christian. Under the tutelage of the Holy Spirit, the old Adam dies and the new Christian grows in Christ. But never may one call that sanctification one's own; one is always dependent on the imputation of the justice of Christ, without which nothing is holy. Justification and sanctification are therefore distinct but inseparable throughout the life of the Christian.

Scholars also debate Bèze's role in the development of the Reformed scholasticism of the seventeenth century. While Bèze wrote no systematic work beyond his relatively simple *Confession de foi chrétienne*, written for Pierre de Bèze in 1557, and his catechetically presented *Quaestionum et Responsionum Christianorum libellus* (part 1, 1570; part 2, 1576), he is still credited with (or accused of) being the father of Reformed scholasticism through his use of Aristotle, the later fathers of the church (e.g., John Damascene), and even some of the medieval scholastics. In this Bèze was more a man of his time than an innovator of a method. While Calvin did not use ecclesiastical authorities as heavily as did Bèze, nevertheless he did refer to them affirmatively as well as negatively, including Bernard of Clairvaux, Peter Lombard, and Thomas Aquinas. As theological dispute became more intense, the tendency was to use logic more and more as an arbiter in theological argument and to bolster that argument with patristic and even scholastic authorities. Bèze was a widely recognized biblical scholar, adroit in the use of logic and authority. The length of his life, his position in the Geneva academy, his activity on behalf of the Reformed cause wherever it struggled in Europe, his graceful style, and his prolific writings assured his profound influence on many theologians who would live well into the seventeenth century. His students proved capable of thinking for themselves, however, and included men as various as William Perkins, Lambert Daneau, and Jacobus Arminius.

Despite local variations and some real differences, the Reformed churches of Europe united to defend themselves against the attacks of Roman Catholics and Lutherans. The Lutheran Formula of Concord (1577) and *Book of Concord* (1580) were answered from Geneva by a gathering of the confessions of the Reformed churches that was published in 1581 as *Harmonia confessionum fidei* (the *Harmony of Confessions*). It was published anonymously, but its primary editor was Jean-François Salvart together with a team of theologians, among whom was Bèze. The ecumenical intent of the book failed, and Lutherans continued to anathematize Calvinists. Bèze's last major written effort to conciliate the Lutherans was a pacific treatise on the Lord's Supper, *De conciliatione*, published in 1593. Bèze continued to serve as professor of theology in the academy until 1599. He survived the Escalade of 1602, Geneva's valiant and successful resistance of the rapacious Savoyards. At the age of eighty-four, Bèze died peacefully in Geneva on 7 October 1605.

BIBLIOGRAPHY

Primary Source

Bèze, Théodore de. *Correspondance de Théodore de Bèze*. Geneva, 1960–. A volume of this beautifully edited series appears about every two years under the general supervision of Alain Dufour.

Secondary Sources

Gardy, Frédéric. *Bibliographie des oevres théologiques, littéraires, historiques et juridiques de Théodore de Bèze*. Geneva, 1960.
Geisendorf, Paul-F. *Théodore de Bèze*. Geneva, 1967.
Kickel, Walter. *Vemunft und Offenbarung bei Theodor Beza: Zum Problem des Verhältnisses von Theologie, Philosophie und Staat*. Neukirchen, 1967.
Kingdon, Robert M. *Geneva and the Consolidation of the French Protestant Movement, 1564–1572*. Madison, Wis., 1967.
Maruyama, Tadataka. *The Ecclesiology of Theodore Beza: The Reform of the True Church*. Geneva, 1978.
Raitt, Jill. *The Eucharistic Theology of Theodore Beza: Development of the Reformed Tradition*. AAR Studies in Religion, 4. Chambersburg, Pa., 1972, 1987.
———. "The Person of the Mediator: Calvin's Christology and Bèze's Fidelity." In *Occasional Papers of the American Society for Reformation Research* (December, 1977), 53–80.
———. "Probably They Are God's Children: Bèze's Doctrine of Baptism." In *Humanism and Reform: The Church in Europe, England and Scotland, 1400–1643*, pp. 51–170. Oxford, 1991.
———. *The Colloquy of Montbéliard, 1586: Politics and Religion in the Sixteenth Century*. New York, 1992.
Registres de la compagnie des pasteurs de Genève. Geneva, 1962–. The volumes in this series appear approximately every three years.

JILL RAITT

BIANDRATA, Giorgio (full name Giovanni Giorgio di Bernardino Biandrata; Lat., Georgius Blandrata; 1516–1588), Italian theologian and physician. Born in Saluzzo (Piedmont) in 1516, he studied medicine at Montrotier and subsequently obtained recognition of his studies from the universities of Pavia (1534) and Bologna (1538). His renowned medical and gynecological practice, as well as an edition of his volume on childbirth dedicated to the Polish queen Bona Sforza and her daughter Isabella, led to his being called to the court of Poland. He remained in Kraków until 1544 and then went to Alba Iulia to the court of Isabella. He returned in 1552 to Pavia, where he remained until 1556 and then settled in Geneva; here he became one of the most influential members of the Italian colony and obtained residence in 1557. He soon initiated debates, however, first with Celso Martinengo, pastor of the Italian community, and then directly with John Calvin on the divinity of Christ. As with Lelio Sozzini, these debates led to an abrupt break in relations, which resumed only when Biandrata was forced to accept Calvinist orthodoxy in May 1558. Yet the waters were not calmed, so much so that Biandrata judged it to be opportune to leave Geneva and settled in Zurich after brief stays in Farges and Bern. After he rejected Heinrich Bullinger's proposal for a reconciliation with Calvin, Biandrata was not able to stay in Zurich either, and so he headed east, returning to Poland and settling in Pinczow, where Francis Lismanino and Francis Stancarus were already active. The polemics continued as well as Calvin's accusations against him, and only the protests of Sigismund I of Poland and Prince Radziwill of Lithuania, along with yet another formal endorsement of trinitarian doctrine, saved Biandrata. At the Synod of Ksiaz in 1562, Biandrata attempted reconciliation with Calvin on condition that the previous accusations against him be withdrawn. Not without some confusion and debate, the synod accepted this condition.

After he moved to Transylvania in 1563 at the invitation of John Sigismund, king of Hungary, he was warmly welcomed at the court, which was now that of Isabella Jagiellon, and there he worked—in accord with the queen's long-standing wish—to avoid the doctrinal conflicts between Lutherans and Calvinists. For this reason at the synod of Nagyenyed (Aiud; 1564) he came to agreement with Calvinist pastor Francis Dávid, who was then won over to antitrinitarianism. Prepared by the activity of Stancarus and continually promoted by Biandrata, the antitrinitarian theses spread, thanks to Dávid's writings promoting them, until they encountered stiff Calvinist opposition, which became manifest at the Synod of Torda (Turda) in 1566. The doctrinal debates and the polemics that Biandrata carried out against the Calvinist pastor Pietro Melius were the source of the work *De vera et falsa unius Dei, Filii et Spiritus Sancti coanitione* (On True and False Knowledge of the One God, the Son and the Holy Spirit), written in collaboration with Dávid and published anonymously in Alba Iulia in 1568. In this work antitrinitarianism is advanced not as a new doctrine but as a discovery of the ancient and unconcealed doctrine of primitive Christianity, a discovery that had been made by Joachim of Fiore, and then by Desiderius Erasmus, Michael Servetus, Bernardino Ochino, and Valentino Gentile (which is reported in the volume *Brevis explicatio in primum Ionnis caput* [Short Commentary on the First Chapter of (the Gospel of) John]).

A few years later—in the midst of the polemics and heated disputes aroused by *De vera et falsa unius Dei, Filii et Spiritus Sancti cognitione* at the Diet of Maros Vásárhely (Tirgu-Mureș) in 1571—the Unitarian confession even obtained a recognition of equality with the other religious confessions. This recognition, however, was merely formal, as the immediate task taken up by John Sigismund's successor, Stephen Báthory, in that same year was to check the spread of Unitarianism. Yet Biandrata, thanks to the diplomatic moves he had made on behalf of Báthory's election, managed to keep his official posts as private physician and counselor, held since 1564, and was thus able to have Dávid recognized as superintendent of the Unitarians in 1576.

The last ten years of Biandrata's life were marked by the theological clash with Dávid, who had been his strongest ally up to that time. Dávid's radical development of the antitrinitarian theses (nonadorantism) had led to the accusation of Judaism and further threatened to split the Unitarian church. Thus, after seeing that the mediation he had requested by Fausto Sozzini was in vain, Biandrata accused Dávid of violating the resolutions imposed by the Catholic Christopher Báthory, namely that there was to be no doctrinal innovation

in the recognized churches. Biandrata obtained Dávid's condemnation to life in prison, but Dávid lived only a few months after the sentence.

Having remained as the only, though not undisputed, leader of the Unitarian church, Biandrata imposed abjuration on Dávid's followers and at the Synod of Koloszvár (Cluj-Napoca) reaffirmed that the "King of the Churches" is to be worshiped and adored. He then retired to private life, enjoying the benefits he had accumulated over the years in recognition for the political and diplomatic missions he had undertaken to the courts of Poland and Hungary. Rumors that Biandrata had returned to Catholicism—which were denied by the Jesuits called to Transylvania by Christopher Báthory, the king's brother—circulated a short time before his death in 1588.

BIBLIOGRAPHY

Caccamo, Domenico. *Eretici italiani in Moravia, Polonia, Transilvania, 1558–1611: Studi e documenti.* Florence, 1970.

Cantimori, Delio. *Eretici italiani del Cinquecento.* 3d rev. ed. Edited by Adriano Prosperi. Turin, 1992. Earlier edition available in English translation: *Italian Heretics of the Sixteenth Century,* Cambridge, Mass., 1979.

Heberle, W. "Aus dem Leben von G. Blandrata." *Tübinger Zeitschrift für Theologie.*

Rotondò, A. "Biandrata, Giovanni Giorgio." In *Dizionario Biografico degli Italiani,* vol. 10, pp. 257–264. Rome, 1968.

Trechsel, Fr. *Die protestantischen Antitrinitarier vor Faustus Socin.* Vol. 2, *Lelio Sozzini und die Antitrinitarier seiner Zeit,* Heidelberg, 1844.

Wilbur, Earl Morse. *A History of Unitarianism, Socinianism and its Antecedents.* Reprint, Boston, 1977.

Williams, George H. *The Radical Reformation.* 3d ed. Kirksville, Mo., 1992.

PAOLO SIMONCELLI
Translated from Italian by Robert E. Shillenn

BIBLE. [*To describe the history of biblical literature and its uses during the sixteenth century, this entry comprises four articles:*

Biblical Hermeneutics and Exegesis
Editions of the Bible
Translations of the Bible
Biblical Commentaries

The first surveys the history and development of biblical interpretation and exposition during the sixteenth century; the second and third discuss new editions and translations, respectively, of the Bible and their religious, social, and institutional significance for the Reformation; the fourth presents an overview of the explosion, both in quantity and variety, of works based on scripture during the Reformation.]

Biblical Hermeneutics and Exegesis

During the medieval period biblical exegesis followed a fourfold model of interpretation. Derived from classical antiquity, notably from Macrobius (*Saturnalia* vs. 1), who distinguished four types of discourse (eloquent, concise, insipid, bold) and associated each type respectively with Cicero, Sallust, Fronto, and Pliny the Younger, the fourfold theory of biblical interpretation went with the conviction that the Bible is too profound and complex for its meaning to be exhausted by one particular approach. The Christian "inventor" of the four senses method is considered by some to have been Clement of Alexandria, by others Augustine (*De utilitate credendi*). Both say or imply that scripture has a historical (literal), an allegorical (figurative), a moral/tropological, and an anagogical (pertaining to eschatology) sense. Origen in *Periarchon* 4.2 put forward a tripartite schema of biblical interpretation: physical (historical), moral, and spiritual (allegorical or anagogical), corresponding to his tripartite division of humans into body, soul, and spirit.

By the thirteenth century a tradition had developed linking each of the four senses to one of the principal doctors of the church. Thus Jerome normally represented the historical method, Origen the allegorical, Gregory the Great (and Chrysostom) the moral, and Augustine the anagogical. In fact, medieval biblical commentators often granted a more prominent place to one sense at the expense of the remaining three. Thus, for example, Nicholas of Lyra was notoriously literal, and the anagogical sense tended to play less of a role for most commentators in the later Middle Ages. One of the most illustrative examples of the full application of the four-senses method is the early twelfth-century *Expositio in Cantica canticorum* by Honorius Augustudinensis. According to Honorius, the *Song of Songs* is historically the story of a marriage. Allegorically it is the story of the union of two natures in Christ or the union between Christ and the church. Morally it is the story of the union between Christ and the soul through love or of the union between the (weaker, feminine) soul and the (stronger, masculine) spirit. Anagogically it is the story of the union between Christ and the church, or between Christ and the angels after the ascension. Few commentators were as extreme as Honorius. But the general schema of the four senses survived well into the sixteenth century, albeit in a variety of reduced and vastly modified forms.

Revival of Greek and Hebrew Studies. The revival of Greek and Hebrew studies influenced biblical scholarship long before the Reformation. Thus Lorenzo Valla's *Annotations* on the Vulgate (1444) and the work of Christian Hebraists and Cabbalists such as Giovanni Pico della Mirandola (whose *Heptaplus*, an allegorical exposition of the creation account, appeared in 1489) and Johannes Reuchlin (whose Hebrew grammar, *De rudimentis hebraicis*, 1506, provided a tool for commentators north of the Alps), paved the way for important changes in methods of scriptural interpretation. Although it would be presumptuous, given the present state of scholarship, to attempt a definitive synopsis,

a survey of some of the main developments and figures can be undertaken.

***Desiderius Erasmus,* Paraphrases *and* Annotations.** Erasmus's *Annotations* (1516) and *Paraphrases* (from 1517 onwards) of the New Testament constitute the most important landmark in the history of sixteenth-century New Testament exegesis. Although initially intended as textual glosses, the *Annotations* expanded between 1516 and 1535 into a theological commentary, with Erasmus sketching out his positions on issues as diverse as war, the oath, and the Eucharist. They also include remarks on the Greek text as well as offer a critical evaluation of patristic exegesis. The *Paraphrases*, not so innovative a work as the *Annotations*, were intended as a relatively unprejudiced explanation of the meaning of the New Testament. Moreover, while postulating the medieval four-senses theory of biblical exegesis (literal, moral, allegorical, and anagogical, or future-directed), Erasmus reformulated with great firmness the Augustinian principle of interpreting scripture by scripture, that is, clarifying obscure scriptural passages by those the meanings of which are more transparent. Erasmus was a first-rate Greek scholar but an extremely poor Hebraist. For that reason his Old Testament exegesis was limited to commentaries on isolated psalms.

Jacques Lefèvre d'Étaples. This is not true of Erasmus's contemporary Jacques Lefèvre d'Étaples, who, despite his poor knowledge of Hebrew, published in 1509 the *Quincuplex Psalterium* (parallel texts of the Old Latin, the Gallican, the Roman, and the Hebrew Psalters accompanied by the *Psalterium conciliatum* by Lefèvre himself and a commentary). While the practice of setting out Psalters in parallel columns was traditionally medieval, emendation of the translation and the commentary that Lefèvre published constituted an innovation. Far from distinguishing several senses, Lefèvre's method is characterized by a search for unity. The Old and New Testaments, Christ in his human and in his divine natures, philology and theology in scriptural exegesis—all are to him inseparable. Over the years, probably under the influence of Erasmus, Lefèvre became more critical in his approach to scripture and came to see it as the most important standard in determining faith. In *De Maria Magdalena* (1518) he tried to dispel the confusion, common in the Middle Ages, among the three Marys in the gospel narrative. By the time he published his *Commentarii initiatorii in quatour Evangelia* (1522) and especially *Commentarii in Epistolas catholicas* (1527), Lefèvre, although he never officially left the Roman Catholic church, was questioning many of its tenets, such as the doctrine of the real presence and the worship of saints.

Martin Luther and the Wittenberg school. From 1512 until the end of his life, Luther not only translated but also lectured and delivered sermons on various books of the Bible, notably *Psalms*, the prophets, the Pentateuch, and *Galatians*. Already in his first lectures on *Psalms* (*Dictata super*

Psalterium, 1513–1515) Luther replaced the anagogical meaning by the literal-prophetic sense. He also applied the text to the individual Christian (the moral sense) and to the church (the allegorical sense). The traditional medieval schema did not disappear. In his lectures on *Galatians* in 1519, Luther argued that the fourfold method was useful in so far as it helped one understand the text but could not support a doctrinal point in controversy. Luther's model for allegory was Paul's figure of Sarah and Hagar (found in *Galatians* 4:22–31).

Increasing preoccupation with the text in its historical setting led to further refinements. In his second *Psalms* course (*Operationes in Psalmos,* 1519–1521), Luther departs from the traditional emphasis on the christological meaning and discovers an independent edifying meaning in the Hebrew text. Luther called this procedure "a grammatical and theological exposition," that is, a theological analysis of Biblical terms (e.g., in *Ps.* 1:1, "ungodliness" having to do with an attitude of mind, not external behavior). The christological interpretation, however, was not done away with altogether and is present notably in his exposition of Psalm 3.

The combination of literal, historical, and christological elements is especially noticeable in Luther's treatment of the prophets. In the preface to the expanded second edition of his *Isaiah* lectures published in 1534, Luther extols the value of history for understanding the prophet's message and for teaching faith and charity. History here includes knowledge of Hebrew, yet Luther also affirms that the chief message of all the prophets is to prepare the faithful for the coming of Christ, and he does not hesitate to impose a christological interpretation on some biblical passages in a way that could only be called "allegorizing." In his lectures on *Genesis* (1544), the chief exegetical achievement of his old age, Luther also maintained something of the medieval schema, showing, for example, how *Genesis* 6:11–12 (the corruption of the earth) refers to God's anger at the Roman church but also instructs us on intrinsically corrupt human nature and on the Last Judgment. Like the *Dictata,* the commentary is future oriented without being anagogical.

It would be rash to underestimate the place occupied by polemics in Luther's exegesis. Like his followers, he was above all concerned with showing that Reformation doctrines were fully borne out by scripture, which was to replace the Roman church in dictating the norms of Christian life. Thus it is not surprising to find that the interpretation of ungodliness in *Psalm* 1:1 (already noted) was the very interpretation that the Roman church contested. But Luther's biblical exegesis, like that of the other reformers, is not independent of patristic, or for that matter, medieval commentators. Augustine, Gregory the Great, Hugh of Saint Cher, and Nicholas of Lyra all figure to a greater or lesser extent. Their testimony is used selectively; it is occasionally criticized but never ignored. At no point did Luther wish to be considered an innovator. On the contrary, he had a vested interest in showing that his biblical interpretations and therefore his theology corresponded to that of the early church.

With Philipp Melanchthon's appointment as professor of Greek in 1518 the Wittenberg school of biblical exegesis was to assume further shape. The series of commentaries on the New Testament, which appeared in Germany between 1522 and 1524, resulted from a concerted effort by Melanchthon, Luther, and their humanist colleague Georg Spalatin to spread the ideas of the Reformation. The New Testament books thus commented on included *Romans, 1* and *2 Corinthians, Matthew, John* (Melanchthon), *Galatians, 1* and *2 Peter, Jude* (Luther), *Luke* (François Lambert), *Ephesians* through *Hebrews* (Johannes Bugenhagen), *1 John* (Johannes Oecolampadius), and *Acts* (Justus Jonas). Was there a Wittenberg method of biblical exegesis common to all these works? Melanchthon's commentaries in particular have one important characteristic: they do not provide a step-by-step exposition of the text, be it philological or theological. What interests Melanchthon and the Wittenbergers is the attempt to divide the text into a number of theological themes (e.g., the relation of suffering to God's will in *Jn.* 8:12–25), which are then expounded. The number of themes within each biblical pericope naturally varies. The advantage of this method, known as the *loci communes* ("commonplaces") method, was that it greatly facilitated the consultation of commentaries by preachers preparing sermons. Philological issues, although by no means absent, did not play the role that they played in, for example, Erasmus's *Annotations.* Exegesis thus became the chief purveyor of the new doctrines. Among the later Lutheran commentators, Johannes Brenz, adversary of the Genevan church in the eucharistic quarrel, deserves special mention. Former pupil of the Basel reformer Oecolampadius (at Heidelberg), his commentaries, while expressing the orthodox Lutheran doctrine, follow the Strasbourg-Basel method and avoid the *loci communes* approach. This is particularly true of his commentaries on *John* (1528) and *Romans* (1564).

The Strasbourg-Basel school of exegesis. How far this school can be considered a synthesis of the Erasmian and Wittenberg schools is a matter of speculation. More oriented toward philology—it boasted the membership of some of the most distinguished Christian Hebraists of the age—it still maintained the training of clergy as its prime goal. Although some of the commentaries issuing from it (notably Martin Bucer's Gospel commentaries, 1527–1536) maintained a list of *loci communes,* these did not constitute the backbone of the Strasbourg-Basel exegetical method. Instead, the biblical text was divided up into pericopes, or sections, and each section was then commented on from diverse standpoints. If the section was difficult, it was first paraphrased. The philological issues (pertaining to Hebrew or Greek text, rhetorical figures, etc.) were discussed in the form of annotations on the Erasmian model, and theological issues such as Christology, the Trinity, and the real presence were treated by excursus. The commentaries (like most exegetical works of the time) were in Latin. The biblical text was cited in Latin with references to Hebrew and Greek; the translation used was sometimes the Vulgate, sometimes a contemporary Latin translation, sometimes the commentator's own version. Extremely learned, the commentaries of the Strasbourg-Basel school were characterized by extensive use of rabbinic and patristic literature, which contrasts strangely with the occasionally virulent polemics contained in the excursuses. The medieval exegetical tradition maintained a discrete but constant presence. Interest in the historical context of the Bible meant that allegory gave place to typology. As Martin Bucer explains in the third chapter of his commentary on *John*, not everything in the Bible points to Christ: it is quite legitimate to consider Isaac a foreshadowing of Christ, but nothing in the biblical text permits one to see the two women in *1 Kings* 3:16 as representative of the Jewish and Christian people.

Nearly all the commentators belonging to this school were Zwinglian. The main representatives were Sebastian Münster, whose edition of the Hebrew Bible with literal Latin translation and notes (1534–1535) and Hebrew grammars gave a new impetus to Old Testament exegesis; the Strasbourg reformers Martin Bucer and his associate Wolfgang Capito, who produced notable commentaries on *Hosea* (1528) and *Habakkuk* (1527); and the dissident spiritualist Martin Borrhaus, whose commentaries on the Pentateuch (1555), *Isaiah* (1561), and *Revelation* reveal his millenarist convictions: having been expounded in a shadowy way by Moses, Christ is revealed more clearly by the prophets until the full disclosure of *Revelation* and the realization of the future kingdom. Finally, one should not forget the Basel reformer Oecolampadius, chiefly known for his commentaries on *Isaiah* (1525) and *1 John* (1525).

The Zurich group. The aims and methods of the Zurich group did not differ fundamentally from those of the Strasbourg-Basel school. Huldrych Zwingli's *Exegetica*, which concern most of the books of the Old and New Testaments, have received little attention from scholars, although they represent a sizable percentage of his literary output. It is important to remember that the *Prophezei* meetings instituted in 1525 (which consisted in reading the scripture in Greek and Hebrew with Zwingli or his associate Leo Jud giving the Latin translation) provided a fertile soil for Zwingli's sermons and Biblical lectures. These cover the period 1525–1531 and are characterized—the lectures particularly—by their emphasis on linguistic matters. The word of God must be captured in the original and explained by the resources of grammar, rhetoric, and historical research before being applied to problems facing the church in Zwingli's time. Particularly interesting (and modern) was Zwingli's conviction that the Septuagint is a witness to a Hebrew text earlier than and not always identical to the Masoretic text, a point on which he disagreed with Bucer.

Konrad Pellikan, Zwingli's Hebraist colleague, commented on most of the Old Testament and the *Acts of the Apostles*. These commentaries appeared in six folio volumes in Zurich between 1532 and 1539. Like his Strasbourg contemporaries he drew heavily on rabbinic and patristic as well as medieval sources. More explicitly than Bucer, he saw the Old Testament covenants as direct foreshadowings of Christ's New Testament covenant and therefore an intrinsic part of God's salvation plan. But his approach does not differ fundamentally from Bucer's. Insisting on Old Testament events as types of New Testament events, he excluded allegory a priori.

Heinrich Bullinger, Zwingli's successor as head of the Zurich church, commented notably on *Revelation* in the form of sermons (1557), having begun in 1532 with commentaries on the Epistles (1537), commentary on *Acts* (1533), and the Gospel commentaries (1542–1546). His Old Testament commentaries include sermons on *Daniel* (1565). One of Bullinger's chief interests was the reassessment of the status of patristic tradition in Biblical exegesis. Although he refers overtly to commentaries by the Fathers more frequently than other reformers, in common with them he accepts tradition only insofar as it bears out his own doctrine. His basic exegetical method is a continuation of Zwingli's.

It is difficult to know in what category to place the commentaries of Peter Martyr Vermigli. Although the Italian adopted the Reformation notably under the influence of Bucer's commentaries on the Gospels and on *Psalms* and although his first appointment in exile was in Strasbourg (1542), Vermigli's commentaries rely more than Bucer's on the *loci communes* system. Thus his commentary on *1 Corinthians* (1551) contains *loci communes* on purgatory, free will, justification, excommunication, and so on. This ordering of subject matter is even more evident in his Old Testament commentaries.

Geneva: John Calvin and Théodore de Bèze. Between 1551 and 1564, Calvin commented on the Pentateuch, the prophets, and *Psalms*, having begun his exegetical works in 1540 with *In Pauli Epistolas . . . commentaria* (published in one volume in 1551). The *Comentarii in Epistolas canonicas* also appeared in 1551 and were followed by *In Evangelium secundum Johannem commentarius* (1553), *Commentaria in Acta Apostolorum* (1552–1554), and the *Harmonia ex Evangelistis composita* (1555–1556). Most of the works were published in Latin and in French. Perhaps as a result of his stay in Strasbourg (1538–1542), Calvin's exegetical method is not far removed from that of the Strasbourg-Basel school. Like Bucer and his colleagues he is interested in replacing biblical discourse in its context and thus considers, for example, the Sermon on the Mount a summary of Christ's doctrine assembled by Matthew and Luke. He finds it important to study the style of the diverse biblical books and rejects allegory, assimilating it to speculation. Scripture to him is first and foremost designed to instill doctrinal and ethical principles into its readers or listeners. Calvin thus often sacrifices historical accuracy to doctrinal considerations and relies on medieval compilations for his patristic references. His commentaries were not intended to rival the work of Erasmus or even Bucer. They do, however, provide a unique insight into the shaping of typically Reformed doctrines. Exegesis and systematic theology are uniquely interwoven in Calvin's work.

Calvin did not intend to replace Erasmus's work, but his successor, Théodore de Bèze (1519–1605), certainly did. In publishing his New Testament, editions of which appeared between 1565 and 1598 and which contained the (slightly) revised Greek text, the Vulgate, and his own Latin translation as well as linguistic and doctrinal annotations, Bèze gave the New Testament a new, Reformed identity. Erasmus's model was thus turned to the service of spreading Genevan doctrines; between 1557 and 1605 Bèze's Latin translation and notes appeared (sometimes together, sometimes separately) in fifty-three different editions of the Bible.

Bèze was also responsible for the typically Reformed phenomenon of "logical" analyses of the scripture, having stated in his unpublished "Ratio studii Theologici" (Grenoble, Bibl. mun. MS 1949) that a commentator must before all else strive to clarify the meaning of the section of text he is studying and the exact relationship between it and the sections preceding and following. Detailed studies of vocabulary, textual problems, and so on came later. This method found its full expression in the New Testament exegesis of the Herborn theologian Johannes Piscator, who limited himself to an analysis of the relationship among propositions in a given biblical book. Although Piscator includes under separate headings some philological *scholia* ("glosses") and some polemical observations, by and large rhetorical, polemical, linguistic-historical, and indeed ethical considerations play a subordinate role.

Works on Exegesis, Compilations, and Gospel Harmonies. The heterodox Lutheran Matthias Flacius Illyricus deserves special mention as the first author of a treatise on Biblical hermeneutics, *Clavis Scripturae sacrae* (1567). He considers Hebrew vowel points and indeed all of scripture to be divinely inspired: its *scopus* ("object") is Christ and every single proposition in it is true. The fundamental key to correct Biblical exposition is the law-gospel distinction. The *Clavis* is composed of a dictionary and seven treatises of rules for interpretation of scripture. Neither in the *Clavis* nor in his gloss on the New Testament (1570) does Flacius resort to the *loci communes* method. The gloss is comparable in scope and purpose (but not in theology) to Bèze's New Testament annotations.

Augustine Marlorat (c.1506–1562), a French Calvinist, is chiefly known for his *Novi Testamenti expositio ecclesiastica* (1570), an anthology of interpretations of the New Testament on the model of Thomas Aquinas's *Catena aurea in quatuor Evangelia*. As well as citing select church fathers and Roman Catholic authors (e.g., Santes Pagnini), Marlorat selects excerpts from the Wittenberg commentators, the Strasbourg-Basel and Zurich schools, as well as Genevan theologians (notably Calvin).

Among compilations of the latter half of the sixteenth century one can count the Gospel harmonies often emanating from Lutheran circles. The Nuremberger Andreas Osiander was a pioneer in the field with his 1537 Greco-Latin harmony, wherein he sets out to show (unlike authors such as Bucer) that every element in the Gospel narratives is the strictest historical truth. He thus establishes the period of Jesus' ministry as three years. The harmony was frequently republished in an adapted form. Osiander's method, with its multiplication of the number of events narrated, was explicitly rejected by the (orthodox) Lutheran Martin Chemnitz, whose harmony was expanded and published in 1593 by Polykarp Leyser, before being further expanded in 1626/27 by Johann Gerhard.

Roman Catholic Exegesis and Hermeneutics. Although the early Roman Catholic controversialists (e.g., Johann Eck) preferred to combat reformers by systematic treatises, with arguments drawn from the Bible and from tradition built around *loci communes* such as the church, the real presence, and so on, soon Roman Catholic biblical exegesis assumed new impetus. One of its earliest and most interesting representatives was Cajetan, author of commentaries on the entire Old and New Testaments with the exception of the *Songs of Songs* and *Revelation*. Independently of Erasmus he criticized the Vulgate as the received text and saw the necessity of restoring the Greek and Hebrew originals, despite knowing no Hebrew himself. His exegesis is strictly literal; he explicitly rejects a multiplicity of meanings and all forms of allegory. All that is necessary to our faith is found in the literal meaning of the Bible; there is no need to search any further. For his Old Testament commentaries he did not hesitate to consult Hebraists.

Methodologically interesting for different reasons is Jacopo Sadoleto's commentary on *Romans* in three books (1535), based on his own Latin translation (heavily dependent on that of Erasmus). The influential bishop of Carpentras conceived the commentary in the form of a dialogue between himself and his deceased brother Giulio. The chief theological problem discussed is naturally justification, notably in the context of *Romans* 8:29–31. Like Cajetan, Sadoleto considered knowledge of the Bible in its original languages a *sine qua non* of exegesis.

Santes Pagnini, the Luccan Dominican, was the first modern scholar to render the whole Bible from the original languages (1518). He did not subscribe to the new method of exegesis. In his treatise on the mystical senses of scripture (1536) he insists that knowledge of etymology and linguistic problems generally should help biblical commentators to "allegorize" all the better. This was also the opinion of another Dominican, Ambrogio Catarino Politi, who attacked the biblical commentaries of Cajetan in 1542 for their radical literalism.

After the Council of Trent, Sixtus of Siena, a Jew who first turned Franciscan then Dominican, published in 1566 his *Bibliotheca sancta*, in which he discusses the nature and purpose of biblical commentaries. He begins by discussing the commentators' working tools (dictionaries of Pagnini and Sebastian Münster, Bible summaries, anthologies, etc.), then distinguishes carefully between genres of exegesis: *commentatio* (notes on a text), *annotationes* (marginal remarks on specific points of difficulty), *enarratio* (lecture, sermon), *paraphrases*, and so on.

The most famous post-Tridentine Roman Catholic exegete is without doubt the Spanish Jesuit Juan Maldonado. Highly polemical in tone, his commentaries affirm that scripture, contrary to Protestant claims, is not clear. If it were, there would not be such a variety of interpretations. The final arbiter of the correctness (or incorrectness) of scriptural interpretation is the Roman church. Maldonado's Gospel commentaries were completed by the French Jesuit Fronton du Duc and published in 1596–1597. They are heavily marked by doctrinal questions, notably the doctrine of predestination.

Anabaptists and Other Dissidents. Although some religious dissidents (e.g., Borrhaus, already mentioned) did produce biblical commentaries of some standing, there was no school of "dissident" exegesis. The Anabaptists tended to find in scripture a direct and historical model, so that scriptural passages constitute an intrinsic part of their writings. The other extreme is provided by the Silesian Kaspar von Schwenckfeld, to whom faith was a spiritual matter and could not by definition be anchored to *any* written word. For Schwenckfeld and his followers, revelation was granted directly by the Holy Spirit without any reference to holy scripture.

Conclusion. A growth of interest in the text in its original setting and the need to provide clergy with new material for sermons were two decisive factors governing the development of sixteenth century exegesis. As allegory and the four-senses methods of interpretation slowly fell into disuse, attempts were made to place the biblical text in context, its structure and language were examined more carefully, and doctrine was extracted from it in the form of excursuses and *loci communes*. The biblical text (which all considered to be directly inspired, though few took the doctrine of inspiration as far as Flacius) was *read* more carefully. But reading in the sixteenth century was a process that was neither subjective nor spontaneous. One text was read with the aid of others, and that principle applied to the biblical text. Dictionaries, handbooks of rhetoric, works by classical authors, rabbinic literature, and, most importantly, earlier exegetical works, patristic, medieval, and contemporary, served as points of reference and guides in the interpretation of the Bible, although they were often not mentioned explicitly.

BIBLIOGRAPHY

Backus, Irena. *The Reformed Roots of the English New Testament: The Influence of Theodore Beza on the English New Testament.* Pittsburgh, 1980. Chapter 1 deals with Bèze's exegesis.

Backus, Irena, and Francis Higman, eds. *Théorie et pratique de l'exégèse: Actes du troisième colloque international sur l'histoire de l'exégèse biblique au XVIe siècle, Genève, 31 août-2 septembre 1988.* Geneva, 1990.

Backus Irena, et al. "Text, Translation and Exegesis of Hebrews 9, 1535–1599." *Journal of Medieval and Renaissance Studies* 14.1 (1984), 77–119. Articles on various methods of commenting.

Bedouelle, Guy. *Lefèvre d'Étaples et l'intelligence des écritures.* Travaux d'Humanisme et Renaissance, 152. Geneva, 1976. A standard work.

———. *Le "Quincuplex Psalterium" de Lefèvre d'Étaples: Un guide de lecture.* Travaux d'Humanisme et Renaissance, 171. Geneva, 1979.

Bedouelle, Guy, and Bernard Roussel, eds. *Bible de tous les temps.* Vol. 5, *Le temps des Réformes et la Bible.* Paris, 1989. Deals with all aspects of the Bible and its impact on the sixteenth century; does not always distinguish clearly between problems of translation and exegesis. Excellent bibliography.

Bucer, Martin. *Martini Buceri Enarratio in Evangelion Iohannis.* Edited by Irena Backus. Studies in Medieval and Reformation Thought, 40. Leiden, 1988. Critical edition of the commentary with an account of Bucer's exegetical method in the introduction.

Fatio, Olivier, and Pierre Fraenkel, eds. *Histoire de l'exégèse au 16e siècle: Textes du colloque international tenu à Genève en 1976.* Geneva, 1978. Papers on Cajetan and Osiander are particularly valuable.

Hagen, Kenneth. *Hebrews Commenting from Erasmus to Bèze, 1516–1598.* Tübingen, 1981. Deals mainly with the authorship problem.

Hendrix, S. H., et al. "Luther as Interpreter of Scripture." *Interpretation* 37 (1983). A collection of papers on the theme.

Lubac, Henri de. *Exégèse médiévale: Les quatre sens de l'écriture.* 4 vols. Paris, 1959–1964. A classic.

Montgomery, John W. "Sixtus of Siena and Roman Catholic Bible Scholarship in the Reformation Period." *Archiv für Reformationsgeschichte* 54 (1963), 214–234.

Parker, T. H. L. *Calvin's New Testament Commentaries.* 2d rev. ed. Louisville, Ky., 1993. Emphasizes Calvin's skills in Greek and Hebrew and his humanism.

———. *Calvin's Old Testament Commentaries.* Reprint, Louisville, Ky., 1993. Interesting account of Calvin's conception of Old Testament history as the expression of the will of God.

Pelikan, Jaroslav. *Luther the Expositor: Introduction to His Exegetical Writings.* Saint Louis, 1959.

Preus, James S. *From Shadow to Promise: Old Testament Interpretation from Augustine to the Young Luther.* Cambridge, Mass., 1969. A classic.

Rummel, Erika. *Erasmus' Annotations on the New Testament: From Philologist to Theologian.* Toronto, 1986. Helpful in showing the main theological issues discussed in the *Annotations*.

Steinmetz, David. "Hermeneutic and Old Testament Interpretation in Staupitz and the Young Martin Luther." *Archiv für Reformationsgeschichte* 70 (1979), 24–58. Particularly interesting on Luther and anagogy.

Steinmetz, David, ed. *The Bible in the Sixteenth Century.* Proceedings of Second International Colloquium on the History of Biblical Exegesis, Durham, N.C., 1982. Durham, N.C., 1990.

Walter, Peter. *Theologie aus dem Geist der Rhetorik: Zur Schriftauslegung des Erasmus von Rotterdam.* Tübinger Studien zur Theologie und Philosophie, vol. 1. Mainz, 1991.

Wengert, Timothy J. *Philip Melanchthon's "Annotationes in Johannem" in Relation to Its Predecessors and Contemporaries.* Travaux d'Humanisme et Renaissance, 220. Geneva, 1987. Particularly valuable chapters on Melanchthon and medieval exegesis, and on the Wittenberg School.

Wünsch, Dietrich. *Evangelienharmonien im Reformationszeitalter: Ein Beitrag zur Geschichte der Leben-Jesu-Darstellungen.* Berlin and New York, 1983.

IRENA BACKUS

Editions of the Bible

The importance of Codex Bezae for critical editions of the New Testament (Gospels and *Acts of the Apostles*) is well known. This fifth-century manuscript belonged to Calvin's successor, who had received it in 1562 after the looting of the Church of Saint-Irénée in Lyon. He in turn donated it to the University of Cambridge in 1581. This case has symbolic value in that it illustrates the relationship between the Protestant Reformation and the work of producing editions of the Bible. One could add the case of Codex Alexandrinus, which had belonged to the patriarch of Constantinople, Cyril Lucarius, whose Calvinist sympathies were well known. The patriarch presented this manuscript to King Charles I of England in 1627.

For the sake of clarity, this account of the printed editions of the Bible is divided along the lines of the three languages that sixteenth-century scholars considered to be the languages of the inspired text. Thus, in addition to Hebrew and Greek, the original languages, the editions of the Latin Vulgate are included, while the rather numerous Latin editions dating from the time of the Reformation are excluded. It was a commonplace of the time to refer to the three languages appearing on the inscription above the cross of Christ (*Jn.* 19:20). To the extent that they incorporate the original texts, reference will be made to the Polyglot editions. One can view the history of the editions of the Bible in the sixteenth century as occurring between two great undertakings of this kind: the Alcalá edition (*Complutensis;* 1514–1517), which had received its impetus from a man of politics at the time when he was head both of the church and the states in Spain, Cardinal Francisco Jiménez de Cisneros; and the Antwerp edition (1569–1571), produced by the publisher Christoffel Plantijn, who himself secretly belonged to an Anabaptist sect that was rejected by both Protestants and Catholics: the Familists (Family of Love), founded by Hendrik Niclaes.

Hebrew. Hebrew is the original language *par excellence,* the earlier historically, and through a combination of circumstances the Hebrew Bible was also the first to be printed. The first attempts at a complete edition of the Hebrew Bible were made in Italy, in the town of Soncino, near Mantua, which became a focal point for these early printed editions in Hebrew through the efforts of a family of Jewish printers who bore the name of that small town. After several excerpts were published, the *Psalms* came out in 1477, followed by the Pentateuch in 1482 on the presses of Bologna, then the Prophets in 1485 and 1486 (by Joshua Shelomo Soncino), and finally in 1488 the whole of what Christians call the Old Testament (Torah, Nebiim, and Ketubim—Hebrew for Law, Prophets, and Writings) was published with vowel pointing and accents. This *editio princeps* ("original edition") contained some minor errors that were corrected in the Naples edition from the years 1491–1493, a copy of which was acquired by Konrad Pellikan (1478–1556), who was the author of a Hebrew grammar and who joined the Reformation and played a major role in Zurich.

After the Soncino family printing house moved to Brescia, a new small-sized version was produced by Gershom Soncino in 1494. It was this text that Luther used for his translation of the Bible into German. The production of Hebrew Bibles, whether complete or partial, subsequently diminished, doubtlessly on account of the expulsion of the Jews from Spain and then from Portugal, since for the Jewish communities this expulsion created problems that were more pressing than producing painstaking editions of the sacred text. Nonetheless, some partial editions appeared in Lisbon as late as 1492.

As for the preparation of the Complutensian Polyglot, the task of editing the Hebrew text fell to Elio Antonio de Nebrija and especially to Alonso de Zamora, a convert from Judaism who had been teaching Hebrew at Alcalá from 1512. Cardinal Jiménez de Cisneros went to great expense to procure manuscripts and borrowed others from Venice and Rome. The sixth volume of the Alcalá Polyglot contained appendixes intended for a better understanding of the original text, including a Hebrew grammar, a glossary of biblical names, and the most complete Hebrew dictionary that had been published up to that time. The vocalization of the Hebrew text was modified, and the choice was made to omit all the accents except the main one.

In 1516–1517 the presses of Daniel Bomberg, a Flemish Catholic living in Venice, published a rabbinical Bible in four volumes accompanied by the Targums and commentaries. This edition was compiled by a Jew, the son of a rabbi, who had converted to Christianity and had become an Augustinian friar, Felice da Prato. The books of *Samuel* and *Kings* were separated as in Christian editions of the Bible. There are some indications that Luther had this version when he translated the Bible into German (Dominique Barthélemy, *Critique textuelle de l'Ancien Testament,* vol. 2, p. 18, Fribourg and Göttingen, 1986).

Since his potential readers were mainly Jewish, Bomberg proceeded to prepare a second edition to which both Masora were added in 1524–1525. This was more acceptable in that it was amply revised by Jacob ben Hayim ibn Adoniya, a refugee from Tunisia who converted to Christianity at the end of his life. He relied on the Masoretic text, which he discussed. It seems that Joseph Carvita, who was the financial backer, and also Bomberg facilitated his work by their generosity. It was on this occasion that Bomberg enlisted the services of the famous grammarian and Masorete Elijah Levita to correct the manuscript. In this connection one should note that in 1543, when it was time to name someone to the chair of Hebrew at Wittenberg, Levita's name was mentioned, but Luther would not hear of appointing a rabbi.

Sebastian Münster, the Hebrew scholar who became a Protestant, published a large Bible in Hebrew accompanied by his own Latin translation with the Bebel publishing house in Basel in 1534–1535, and then in 1546 with Petri and Isengrin. He did not use the far better text of Jacob ben Hayim, but rather that of Felice da Prato. Robert I Estienne made the opposite choice in the edition he published between 1539 and 1544. A letter from Pellikan to Calvin, dated March 1543, relates that he was seeking to obtain these volumes before they had even been published; they also contained David Kimhi's commentaries on the minor prophets edited by François Vatable. Another rabbinical Bible was printed in 1548 in Venice by Cornelius Adelkind.

As for Christoffel Plantijn, he had the first four volumes of his Antwerp Polyglot prepared by Benito Arias Montano according to the text of the Complutensian. Arias Montano, who was a Benedictine and had studied at Alcalá, was assisted by three professors from Louvain. Jean Emmanuel Tremellius had offered to collaborate on the project, but the complex evolution in his religious affiliation kept him from being accepted by Plantijn, who feared censure. Tremellius was a Jew who had become a Catholic in Padua under the influence of Cardinal Reginald Pole, but then became a Protestant in 1541.

Thus one can see that work done to obtain an accurate text of the Hebrew original of the Bible transcended factional boundaries and occasionally even the subsequent choices made by biblical scholars who later undertook this task. Here one should mention the important contribution made by the Dominican Sante Pagnini to the knowledge of the Hebrew text in the sixteenth century. He belonged to the priory of San Marco in Florence but had been residing in Lyon from 1523. Pagnini is especially known for his Latin translation of the Bible, which was quite accurate because of his solid knowledge of Hebrew. For this reason his translation served as a basis for various translations into vernacular languages. In his dedication of his 1528 translation to Clement VII, Pagnini notes the esteem that the Roman church should foster for the original languages of the Bible, and he cites the well-known words of encouragement given by the Council of Vienna in 1312 for the teaching of eastern languages. One should note that Pagnini held to the Hebrew canon and thus inserted the deuterocanonical books (the Apocrypha) between the two Testaments.

In the Reuchlin affair, in which the Christian use of Jewish sources was called into question, Luther had taken the side of the Cologne humanist in 1518. For his translation, Luther used various editions of the Hebrew text, but his mistrust not only of rabbinical exegesis but also of the Masoretic text grew over time. For him the meaning of the words and phrases came from the analogy of faith, not from grammar.

This was all the more so since he suspected the Jews of having corrupted the text, whether intentionally or not. Consequently he considered the vowel points to be a recent invention and subject to modification, especially if this could be done "in such a way that it agrees with the New Testament" ("Vom Schem Hamphoras," WA, volume 53, p. 646; see also Barthélemy, *Critique textuelle*, vol. 1, pp. 2–11).

In the early years of Protestantism there were few exceptions to this general mistrust. Wolfgang Capito in Strasbourg and Andreas Osiander combined their taste for the Hebrew of the Bible and the Talmud with genuine esteem for the Jews. Martin Bucer, an accomplished Hebrew scholar, sought to derive benefit from the rabbinical writings without conceding a single point of Christian exegesis. This is essentially the position that Sebastian Münster clearly affirmed: "Neither the text maintained by the rabbis, nor their commentaries will cause any harm, as long as you have learned to know Christ; what is more, you will derive benefit from them" (see Bernard Roussel, "Lire la Bible: Des auteurs," in *Le temps des Réformes et la Bible*, pp. 224–225).

Greek. The humanists considered the return to the study of the Greek sources a priority; they even considered the study of the Greek sources to be far more useful than resorting to the Hebrew. In a letter dated 13 March 1518 Erasmus exhorted Capito: "I could wish you were more inclined to Greek than to that Hebrew of yours, about which you are so uncritical" (*Opus Epistolarum Erasmi*, edited by P. S. Allen, vol. 3, letter 798, p. 253, Oxford, 1913). With respect to biblical studies, it was necessary to have available good editions of the Septuagint and the New Testament.

The Septuagint. The first printed edition of the Septuagint was the Alcalá Polyglot, but as was the case for the New Testament it was not the first to be published. (It was not available until 1522.) The printing house founded by Aldus Manutius (1449–1515) in Venice, which was being run at that time by Andreas Asolanus (Torresani), his father-in-law, published the Greek version of the Old Testament accompanied by the New Testament of Erasmus in February 1518. The basis for this "Aldine Bible" was the collection of manuscripts collated by Cardinal Bessarion (1403–1472) that could be consulted at San Marco in Venice.

This text was reprinted in 1526 at the Wolfgang Köpfel publishing house in Strasbourg by Joannes Lonicerus using Capito's work as a starting point. This edition was accompanied by a *Parasemeiosis*, a list of variants with respect to the Aldine edition based on other manuscripts. The listing of the biblical books is the same as in Luther's Bible. The deuterocanonical books, according to Catholic terminology, or the Apocrypha according to Protestants, were placed in an appendix.

In a 1545 printing in Basel (which accompanied the fifth edition of the New Testament of Erasmus, dating from 1535), Philipp Melanchthon judged the Septuagint to be "cruder" (*squalidiorem*) than the Hebrew and not very polished in its style. In this he was going along with the judgment voiced by Luther ("Enarratio in I. Cap. Genesis, IV, 7," WA, vol. 42, p. 142) whereby "the translators of the Septuagint had no idea of the scope of their undertaking." Still Melanchthon recommended the study of the Septuagint, since it was the version cited by Paul and the other authors of the New Testament. Melanchthon believed that a more careful examination could lead to the necessary purification of the church.

The Complutensian edition was based on manuscripts from the Vatican Library, those of Venice, and the collection of Cardinal Jiménez de Cisneros. However, the Vatican 1209 manuscript known as Codex B (Vaticanus) was not consulted; it would later enhance the value of the 1586 Sixtine edition of the Septuagint published in 1587 by Francesco Zanetti.

Indeed, at the Council of Trent, at the same time that there were calls for a more accurate edition of the Vulgate, certain council fathers, including Reginald Pole, insisted that an approved edition of the Septuagint be made available. This project was implemented by Cardinal Montanto, the future Sixtus V, who ordered it to be published at the beginning of his pontificate. It met with greater success than his own work on the Vulgate. The commission headed by Cardinal Antonio Carafa selected the manuscripts and understood the full significance of Codex B. The manuscripts were carefully checked and later served as a basis for the most important subsequent editions, that of Constantin von Tischendorf in 1850 and that of H. B. Swete in 1887. The Antwerp Polyglot, however, used the revised text of the Complutensian.

According to the hermeneutical principles of the Reformation, the harsh judgment expressed by Luther and Melanchthon on the Septuagint was relative to the interpretation that seemed most Christian to them. Even though the Septuagint deviates from the proper sense of the words (in Hebrew), it sometimes gives interpretations, according to Luther, "inspired by God" ("Operationes in Psalmos, II," *Archiv zur Weimarer Ausgabe der Werke Martin Luthers* 1 [1981], 130). This same position could be found in Calvin's writings: Calvin did not hesitate to level violent criticisms against the text of the Septuagint. In contrast Bucer viewed the Septuagint from the vantage point of a theology of the spread of the word of God and a prototype for future translations. But the most favorable judgment came from Huldrych Zwingli, who considered the Septuagint a witness to a Hebrew text that had not been corrupted by the "Tiberian rabbis" (i.e., with the vowel points of the Masoretes); Théodore de Bèze took up this same argument in 1598. The Parisian exegete Pierre Morin was the first to take an interest in the fragments of the Hexapla of Origen (i.e., the Greek versions of the Old Testament that came after the Septuagint), which he edited as an appendix to the Sixtine edition.

The New Testament. After his discovery of the *Adnotationes* of Lorenzo Valla led him to a clearer awareness of the divergences between the Vulgate and the Greek text of the New Testament, Erasmus embarked on a long project that culminated in the publication of the *Novum Instrumentum* in 1516. The daring innovations in its Latin translation, or more precisely his daring to supplant the Vulgate, led people to forget that the work was first and foremost the *editio princeps* of the Greek New Testament.

In 1508, during his stay with Aldus Manutius the Elder, a publisher in Venice, Erasmus developed his knowledge of Greek, as John Colet had recommended in 1499. There Erasmus read the Greek fathers, in particular Gregory of Nazianzus and Origen, who was greatly admired by Jean Vitrier, the Franciscan of Saint-Omer whom Erasmus had met in 1501. Erasmus finished his work of editing and translating at Cambridge in 1501. Recent historians believe that Erasmus and particularly the publisher Johann Froben wanted to get the edition out ahead of the publication of volume 5 of the competing Alcalá Polyglot, and they express a more favorable judgment on the accuracy of the text. It is true that some of Erasmus's expressions admit to some haste and that the first edition contained many typographical errors, which were detected by Johannes Oecolampadius, the future reformer of Basel, a proofreader for the printer Johann Froben.

This publishing house printed a first run of three thousand copies of the *Novum Instrumentum*, which sold quickly. The *Novum Instrumentum*, dedicated to Pope Leo X, consisted of an introduction, the Greek text, the new Latin translations, and notes. On the basis of the manuscripts he consulted, Erasmus omitted *1 John* 5:7, the *Comma Johanneum* ("Johannine Comma"), which he subsequently reinstated in his 1522 third complete edition. One of the harshest criticisms leveled against him was that he translated back into the Greek text six verses of *Revelation* 22:16–21 from the Vulgate that did not appear in the only manuscript of *Revelation* dating from the twelfth century that he had available to him. In like manner he replaced *Acts* 8:37 and 9:5–6. In his preface to Leo X, Erasmus states that he used ancient manuscripts of both languages in order to go back "ad grecae originis fidem" (to faithfulness to the Greek original), and this is also expressed by the title of the work. He used manuscripts preserved in the library of the Dominicans of Basel that they had inherited in 1443 from Johannes de Ragusio (Stojkovic), who had brought them back from Constantinople. Erasmus also took full advantage of his trip to England to consult early manuscripts.

Besides the numerous reprints, there were in all five editions of this work during Erasmus's lifetime (1516, 1519 [when he again uses the title *Novum Testamentum*], 1522, 1527, and 1535, all published by Froben). For the 1527 edition, Erasmus was able to take into account the Complutensian Polyglot, which had been finished in 1517, but which he was not able to consult until 1522. He used this text to replace the last verses of *Revelation*.

In Paris in 1534, Simon de Colines used both the 1522 version of Erasmus's text and the Alcalá text, while relying on other manuscripts that he did not identify. He also did not include the Johannine Comma. Specialists consider this edition reliable, but it was not followed by further editions.

The *textus receptus* (received or standard text) of the Greek New Testament would turn out to be the edition by Robert I Estienne, the royal publisher. After the first editions of 1546 and 1549, the folio edition of 1550, called the *editio regia*, composed in magnificent type by Claude Garamond, with the variants in the margin, was the one that won recognition. Estienne stated that the compilation was his own, based on the manuscripts of the Parisian libraries, done with the help of his son Henri II. (For a detailed study of the origin of the variants, see F. H. A. Scrivener, *A Plain Introduction to the Criticism of the New Testament*, vol. 2, pp. 180ff., London, 1894).

A fourth edition was published the following year, but this time in Geneva, since Robert I Estienne had gone to the city of Calvin in faithfulness to his Protestant convictions. It is often said that this small 1551 edition, which contains both the Vulgate and Erasmus's Latin translation, was the first to contain numbered verses. Robert I Estienne continued this numbering for the Old Testament in his 1555 Latin edition, which was imitated first by the Protestants and then by Catholics. But an almost identical numbering scheme for the verses of *Psalms* occurs in the *Quincuplex Psalterium* of Jacques Lefèvre d'Étaples, printed by Henri I Estienne in 1509 and in Pagnini's 1528 complete edition of the Bible, which in turn had been inspired by previous examples.

The editions proposed by Théodore de Bèze (four between 1565 and 1598, of which three were published by Henri II Estienne), follow the *textus receptus* almost exactly, although he did not make systematic use of the two great manuscripts that were in his possession, the one that bears his name and the Codex called the Claromontanus, which he had found in Clermont. In addition, he had available to him the papers and compilations of Henri II Estienne and also the Latin translation of the Syriac version of the New Testament that had been done by Emmanuel Tremellius. This text, called the Peshitta ("standard version"), had been published in Vienna in 1555 by Albert Widmanstetter, with the aid of Guillaume Postel, then in Geneva by Henri II Estienne in 1569, mainly for the use of the Jacobite church. Actually, Bèze followed the traditional version in the critical choices he made. In 1581, when the University of Cambridge acknowledged the receipt of Codex Bezae, it emphasized the extraordinary contribution to the study of the scriptures made by Calvin and by Bèze through their editions and commentaries.

The Antwerp Polyglot has the New Testament in two of the eight volumes. Volume 5 has four columns with the Greek text, which is close to Estienne's version, the Syriac (Peshitta) text, the Latin translation of the Syriac done by Guy Le Fèvre de la Boderie, and the Vulgate. Volume 7 also contains a Greek New Testament with modifications of fourteen passages, which points to the constant striving to improve the text.

Finally, a remarkable polyglot of the New Testament was produced in 1599, after that of the Old Testament, by Elias Hutter, who was professor of Hebrew for the elector of Saxony in 1579 and a publisher in Nuremberg. There he published a two-volume New Testament in twelve ancient and vernacular languages. His Syriac version was the one that Tremellius had established in 1569, but he added the missing passages by translating them from other texts. The third column carries the Greek text, but it does not offer a rigorously critical version. Indeed, Hutter had no qualms about including the apocryphal Epistle of Paul to the Laodiceans, which Lefèvre d'Étaples had held to be authentic and had even commented on, and he even adjusted the text to allow for a more strictly Lutheran interpretation.

Latin. It is appropriate to deal with the editions of the Latin Vulgate, inasmuch as it was considered at the beginning of the sixteenth century to be a text that we would call standard. It was used in the liturgy, by the magisterium, and by theologians; its authority came from its attribution to Jerome. The simple observations by Valla, echoed by Erasmus, in regard to the notable differences between the Greek of the New Testament and the common translation (this is what the word *vulgate* means) posed the problem of its authorship. Some humanists, such as Lefèvre d'Étaples, preferred to deny that Jerome was the author of the text, rather than to conceive that he might have deviated in his translation for any number of reasons. In the *Quincuplex Psalterium* through the synopsis method, however, he showed that the liturgical Psalter included in the Vulgate is only one of the versions attributed to Jerome. Over this version he preferred the last one, which he called *Psalterium hebraicum* because Jerome had translated it directly from the Hebrew, and he took his inspiration largely from this latter version to propose a *Psalterium conciliatum*. Thus, apart from new translations into Latin, one can see the direction that biblical scholars, both Catholic and Protestant, were taking: a correction of the Vulgate itself. This correction could take two forms, however, based either on texts in the original languages or on the study of the Latin manuscripts.

The first method was followed by Andreas Osiander in 1522 (Nuremberg, reprinted in 1527), Johannes Petreius (Nuremberg, 1527), Johannes Rudelius (Cologne, 1527), and by Luther himself in 1529 (*Deutsche Bibel*). Luther had devoted himself to translating the Bible into German and considered the problem of the accuracy of the original text to be secondary, as long as it did not touch the heart of the gospel message. This would also be Calvin's position. The suggestion of correcting the Vulgate according to the original texts or other translations was made by Cardinal Cajetan in his 1530 commentary on *Psalms*, and he made an attempt in this direction.

The other method consisted of scrutinizing the various extant Latin texts, both manuscripts and texts already published, and checking and comparing them. This was the method used in what could be called the first critical edition of the Vulgate, produced by Bernardino Gadolo, a Camaldolese monk, which was published in Venice in 1495. This method of compilation was also used for the Complutensian Polyglot. The Cologne Bible, published in 1530 by Gobelius Laridius with the publishers Eucherius Cervicornus, was based on the principle of modifying the text whenever a given variant of the ancient manuscripts coincided with both the Septuagint and the Hebrew. A similar but more critical attempt was made by Robert I Estienne, who, in his complete editions of the Bible of 1528 and 1532, gave priority among the various manuscripts of the Vulgate to the variant that best agreed with the original Greek. This choice of variant was accompanied by critical notes that alarmed the censors. Thus in 1540 Estienne limited himself to publishing the received text with a few of the variants along with an indication of their origin. He progressively moved away from simply producing an accurate text, however, and instead preferred to provide new translations.

It is easy to understand why the Council of Trent in its first meetings decided to clarify the status of the Vulgate. In its decree dated 8 April 1546, the council declared that the "ancient Vulgate edition," thus using "vulgate" as an adjective, is "authoritative in public lessons, discussions, preaching, and explanations." The council thus conferred on the Vulgate official recognition, but in no way did it issue a certification as to its accuracy. The same decree further stipulated that a new edition was to be printed "after correction that was to be as accurate as possible." This was tantamount to opting for the second method and calling for a critical edition based on existing recensions.

On the Catholic side, initiatives were about to be taken to carry out this task: in 1547 Johannes Hentenius, a member of the Hieronymite order who became a Dominican, published a version based on four published Bibles and thirty manuscripts (published by Barthélemy Gravius at Louvain). His text was reprinted in Antwerp by Plantijn publishers, as well as in Lyon and Venice. Luc de Bruges revised and corrected it in a version that appeared in Antwerp in 1547 and was accepted by the faculty of theology at the University of Louvain. To support the choices he had made, in 1583 he published *Notations*, dedicated to Cardinal Guiglielmo Sirleto, one of the great architects in the preparation of the Sixto-Clementine Vulgate.

When the Council of Trent finally ended in 1563, among the tasks it left for the papacy to complete was a new edition of the Vulgate. This was to be a long and delicate endeavor. Cardinal Sirleto, the Vatican librarian, had already undertaken a revision of the text, but since it could not be completed, Sixtus V, elected pope in 1585, decided to appoint a commission for this purpose. This commission did some serious work using the texts of Hentenius and Luc de Bruges, comparing them to manuscripts that had been loaned by various religious orders. But the pope, judging the modifications to be too numerous, thought it was possible for him to take on this task himself, despite his advanced age. He completed the task in May 1590. This "Sixtine" Vulgate immediately became the center of controversies in Catholic circles, since many feared derision from Protestant quarters, which inevitably surfaced: the *Bellum Papale* by Thomas James (1600) and the *Antibarbarus Biblicus* by Sixtinus Amama (1628) are examples of this criticism. Although at first reluctant to disavow his predecessor, Gregory XIV ordered a final but thorough revision on the basis of the Sixtine text after being advised by the Jesuit Roberto Bellarmino. It was Clement VIII who promulgated the new text on 9 November 1592. Hence this edition is known as the Sixto-Clementine version.

Thus in the sixteenth century many humanists, both Catholic and Protestant, devoted themselves to the difficult work of editing the Bible in the three languages recognized as having pride of place. Nonetheless, one must bear in mind that, even though they frequently differed over the proper place of scripture and over the interpretation of many passages, these scholars, having spent an enormous amount of time in establishing the best possible text, all agreed that this critical work was of only secondary importance.

For a person like Erasmus, an editor of and commentator on the Bible, although he demonstrates in the "Apologia" that precedes his edition of the New Testament how even a misplaced comma can lead to heresy or blasphemy, it is "Christian philosophy" that takes precedence. Christians should make the gospel message part of themselves, so as to make their own hearts the library of Christ, as the Methodus puts it (*D. Erasmus Roterodamus Ausgewählte Werke*, edited by Annemarie Holborn and Hajo Holborn, p. 160, lines 6–7, Munich, 1933). One must certainly drink from the wellsprings of revelation, but for the sake of "devotion more than for argumentation" (p. 162, line 21).

Luther also called for a return to scripture in a radical way: "Anyone who does not ceaselessly engage in the study of sacred scripture is doomed to perdition" (*An den christlichen Adel deutscher Nation von des christlichen Standes Besserung*, *WA*, vol. 6, p. 462). That is why it was a matter of urgency to deny the pope the monopoly of interpreting scripture. But for Luther it also came down to hearing the message of the word of God in the form of preaching that engenders faith (*Fides ex auditu*). "Letters are dead words, spoken utterances are living words" (*WA*, vol. 54, p. 74, line 17). Consequently, no matter how important a good edition of the Bible might be, for Luther the Bible was not primarily a text but rather a "loud shout" (*WA*, vol. 10, p. 305, line 2). Finally, looking beyond the controversies over *sola scriptura* and the reaffirmation of tradition and the need never to deviate from the "sense that our holy mother the Church has held and holds" (decree of 8 April 1546), the Council of Trent took pains always to refer to the "gospel" in the broad sense and to its purity, which the church must safeguard, for it is the gospel that is "the yardstick for all truth leading to salvation and for moral conduct" (decree of 22 March 1546).

The editions of the Bible in the sixteenth century bear the mark of a return to the sources that was in the end accepted by all, although they did not meet the critical demands that were to surface in the following century. For both Catholics and Protestants, the scriptures remained primarily an arsenal of arguments. Consequently, concern for the accuracy and authenticity of the biblical text never prevailed over the impassioned search for its life-giving and salutary meaning.

BIBLIOGRAPHY

Primary Sources

Bible. Texts and Translations of the Bible and the Apocrypha and their Books from the National Union Catalog, pre-1956 imprints. Washington and London, 1981.

Biblia. Catalogo di edizioni a stampa, 1501–1957. Istituto centrale per il catalogo unico delle Biblioteche italiane. Rome, 1983.

Biblia Polyglotta Complutensis, facsimile ed., 6 vols. Madrid, Valencia, and Rome, 1984.

Erasmus, Desiderius. *Novum Instrumentum* (1516). Facsimile ed. Introduction by H. Holeczek. Stuttgart, 1986.

Secondary Sources

Allgeier, A. "Haec vetus et vulgata editio." *Biblica* 29 (1948), 353–390.

Barthélemy, Dominique. *Critique textuelle de l'Ancien Testament.* Fribourg, 1986.

Bedouelle, Guy, and Bernard Roussel, eds. *Bible de tous les temps.* Vol. 5, *Le temps des Réformes et la Bible.* Paris, 1989.

Bentley, J. H. *Humanists and Holy Writ.* Princeton, 1983.

Büsser, F., ed. *Early Printed Bibles: Printed Bibles and Bible Translations in the Fifteenth and Sixteenth Centuries on Microfiche.* Leiden, 1988–. This collection that will ultimately contain 300 published Bibles and Bible translations from the fifteenth and sixteenth centuries is the first comprehensive collection of its kind, bearing unique testimony to the efforts of several generations of scholars, artists, publishers, and printers.

Centi, Timoteo M. "L'attività letteraria di Santi Pagnini nel campo delle scienze bibliche." *Archivum Fratrum Praedicatorum* 15 (1945), 5–51.

Greenslade, S. L., ed. *Cambridge History of the Bible.* Vol. 3, *The West from the Reformation to the Present.* Cambridge, 1963.

Oberman, Heiko A. "Discovery of Hebrew and Discrimination against the Jews: The *Veritas Hebraica* as Double-Edged Sword in Renaissance and Reformation." In *Germania Illustrata,* edited by Heiko A. Oberman. Kirksville, Mo., 1992.

Pani, Giancarlo. "Un centenaire á rappeler: L'édition Sixtine des Septante." In *Théorie et pratique de l'exégèse.* Geneva, 1990.

Rogerson, John W. "Bibelwissenschaft I: Reformation." In *Theologische Realenzyklopädie,* vol. 6, pp. 347–348. Berlin and New York, 1980.

Steinmetz, David C., ed. *The Bible in the Sixteenth Century.* Durham, N.C., 1990.

Wagenast, Klaus. "Bibel IV: Reformationszeit." In *Theologische Realenzyklopädie,* vol. 6, pp. 70–77. Berlin and New York, 1980.

GUY BEDOUELLE
Translated from French by Robert E. Shillenn

Translations of the Bible

At the advent of the Reformation era, the common Bible of the western church was a Latin text almost universally honored as the work of Jerome. With the exception of the *Psalms,* where two different Jerome versions (one translated from the Greek Septuagint, the other from the Hebrew) existed, this meant a single authoritative text for the church's liturgy, meditative life, and theology.

Numerous vernacular translations of the Bible were in circulation in manuscript throughout the late Middle Ages. With the advent of the printing press, a good number of these appeared in folio print editions—at least fourteen in German, for example—prior to the appearance of Martin Luther's New Testament in 1522. Late medieval movements of religious renewal emphasized a scripture-centered piety. This last was also a hallmark of heretical movements, such as the Waldensians and Hussites, a fact that encouraged in some regions constraints on vernacular scriptures. Thus, a 1408 Oxford statute directed against Lollardy required English episcopal approval for all vernacular translation, while in Spain Inquisitorial strictures apparently targeted the continuing desire of *Conversos* to read the scriptures of their former faith.

Beginning in the mid-fifteenth century, several new elements combined to make the Reformation era a major turning point in the history of the Bible in the West. Humanists were developing skills in Greek and Hebrew unknown among Christians for a millennium. To the humanists' philological preoccupations was added the conviction that the restoration of the biblical text could provide a religious center for their educational enterprise, as well as a foundation for a renewal of persons, the social order, and theology itself. Meanwhile, evangelical reformers—some of whom had strong roots in humanism—were building mass movements upon an ideology of the supremacy of scripture in the church, enhancing the market for biblical texts and translations and for the scripture-centered writings of various sorts they were producing. The printing press served admirably the ends of both groups.

Translations for the Learned Public. An obvious first concern was the establishment of a correct Latin text of the church's Bible, the so-called Vulgate, a problematic task given the deplorable state of text transmission.

Revisions of the Vulgate. Beginning about 1442 the Italian humanist Lorenzo Valla prepared proposals—discovered and published by Desiderius Erasmus in 1505—for correction of the New Testament by comparison with Greek manuscripts. Andreas Osiander of Nuremberg produced the first of a number of "corrected" text editions of the full Vulgate in 1522. The magnificent folios (from 1528 on) of Robert I Estienne, the French royal printer, are models of the genre, combining a quest for the most accurate manuscript readings of the Latin with marginal annotations referring to the readings of the Hebrew and Greek. Both Protestants and Catholics engaged in this task; Konrad Pellikan of Zurich did so from 1532–1539, as did the Italian Benedictine abbot Isidore Clarius in 1542, each producing a revised Vulgate rather than a new translation out of respect for the place of the former in the church's life.

The results of such revision, however, yielded a compromise unsatisfactory to both critics and traditionalists. Recognizing an undermining of authority in critics' dismissal, from Valla on, of the traditional attribution of the Vulgate New Testament to Jerome, the traditionalists redoubled their defense of the authenticity and integrity of the church's version; the Vatican librarian, Agostino Steuco, furnished extensive arguments in 1529 for the superiority of the Vulgate to both Hebrew and Greek texts. On similar grounds others opposed the edition and annotations of the Greek New Testament of Erasmus in 1516. Methodologically the opponents were on firmer footing when they insisted that the quest for the most authentic Vulgate readings not be confused by the introduction of new corrections; this was the position of Cardinal Francisco Jiménez de Cisneros in the Complutensian Polyglot (Alcalá de Henares, 1514–1520). It would also be the option sanctioned by the Council of Trent in 1546, leading eventually to the Sixto-Clementine text of the Vulgate completed in 1592. This last owed considerably to the collations of the Spanish Benedictine Benito Arias Montano in the magnificent Antwerp Polyglot of Christoffel Plantijn (1569–1572).

A new Latin Bible: base text. The obvious alternative was a new translation. This would provide an accurate base for renewal of the church and serve to confute heretics and unbelievers, the latter being a reference to Jewish polemical exposure of the errors of the Vulgate. Humanists and reformers alike were conscious, however, that certain fundamental questions had to be addressed at the outset of any such enterprise.

Fifteenth-century humanists had made the case for the superiority of Hebrew and Greek texts to the Latin; with papal encouragement the Florentine Gianozzo Manetti translated both the Psalter and the New Testament from their original tongues. These last two were still subject to some suspicion; in the printing of Complutensian Polyglot the preface noted that the page arrangement—Vulgate in the center, with Hebrew on the left, and Greek on the right— suggested Christ between the two thieves, apostate synagogue and schismatic Eastern church. It was certainly to anticipate such views that Hebraists regularly invoked the authority of Origen, Jerome, and the fourteenth-century Council of Vienne for their endeavors.

Accuracy of the base Greek text was a problem for the New Testament; the assaults upon Erasmus's edition, particularly those of Stunica, a collaborator on the rival Complutensian project, were often well founded. In fact, a sound Greek text would not be established until the nineteenth century. In contrast, the Hebrew text drew the praise of translators for its remarkable state of preservation, especially in the magnificent version, complete with Masoretic apparatus, prepared by Jacob ben Hayyim of Tunis for Daniel Bomberg's edition (Venice, 1524–1525). The old Christian cavil of Jewish polemical corruption of the text retained few scholarly adherents, although a fierce rear-guard action was fought, notably from Wittenberg, against medieval Jewish commentaries on the text. This bore directly upon translation questions since access to Hebrew and Greek originals required the creation in Latin of grammars and dictionaries of the ancient tongues, a task inconceivable without resort to individual Jewish and Green instructors, as well as their philological writings.

Questions of translation. A different issue was that of the appropriateness of translation itself. From the classical era the dictum was endlessly repeated that no language can adequately render the particularity of another. The emergence of trilingual colleges in Louvain and elsewhere and the introduction of Greek and Hebrew into the curriculum of evangelical schools clearly represented a recognition of the superiority of direct recourse to the original. In 1529 Martin Bucer of Strasbourg, contemplating a day when all Christians would speak the Hebrew tongue, viewed new translations as a passing necessity. But, meanwhile, this need had to be served, and the issue most pressing concerned the method of translation—that is, the practice of the "faithful translator."

Already in fifteenth-century Italy a lively humanist discussion turned around this ancient question, for Jerome had left to his successors an ambivalent heritage: in a well-known topos (*Epistle* 57) he had argued for translation according to sense, not word for word, while simultaneously exempting scriptures from the rule, owing to the divine mysteries contained in their very word order. Medieval biblical translation chose to hew to the latter standard, ignoring the considerable freedom Jerome demonstrated in his own work. Once humanists had reopened the debate over translation methods, however, each option found its adherents among sixteenth-century Bible translators.

That faithful translation requires a high degree of respect for the spatial characteristics (word order) of the original, as well as the rendering with exact lexical equivalences wherever possible, was the explicit assumption of the first new Latin Bible (Lyon, 1527–1528) from the Dominican Sante Pagnini. Pagnini's Old Testament work, which enjoyed papal patronage, was universally recognized as the product of impressive Hebrew scholarship; despite criticism for its literalism, it was reprinted and revised throughout the century.

Literal translation was given a pedagogical rationale as well. Humanists had revived the classical practice of teaching through such translation exercises, and at least one early Hebraist, Pellikan, taught himself the elements of Hebrew with the aid of an interlinear translation. In 1525 the Basel reformer Johannes Oecolampadius justified the solecisms of his *Isaiah* translation by his desire to aid students in the acquisition of Hebrew.

Such versions prompted an antiliteralist reaction from two upper Rhineland evangelicals, Huldrych Zwingli and Martin Bucer. Revisiting Jerome, they argued in 1529 prefaces to *Isaiah* and the *Psalms*, respectively, that overly scrupulous literalism was undermining the very authority it intended to serve; the versions so produced were in such barbarous Latin that the reader was frequently left to invent meanings where none were apparent. The truly faithful translator ought rather to employ the full range of philological tools—grammar, familiarity with the rhetoric of the author, and knowledge of his culture—to discern the sense of the source text. The author's meaning could then be rendered into comparable Latin expression.

These ideas were disseminated widely. At their best they are reflected in the Zurich Latin Bible of 1543, a text of considerable elegance, which was reprinted (without credit to its source) by Estienne in Paris in 1545 (parallel to his revised Vulgate) and then in 1584–1585 in Salamanca. The high-water mark of this method was reached in the Bible (Basel, 1551) of French refugee Sébastien Castellion, which gave graphic demonstration of the theories he had already articulated in his *Moses Latinus* of 1546: faithful translation requires that scripture speak with clarity, with an elegance comparable to that of the original. Castellion was fiercely attacked by Théodore de Bèze of Geneva and ridiculed in a number of quarters for his neologisms as well as his audacity (e.g., using "Jove" for the divine name). In 1575–1581 the last of the new Latin Bibles of the era—by a Jewish convert, Immanuel Tremellius, his son-in-law François Junon, and Bèze—marked a significant return to a style more consonant with that of Pagnini. A similar judgment probably lay behind Estienne's replacement of the Zurich Latin with that of Pagnini in his Genevan 1557 edition.

If the translation of a sacred text is to function in a role comparable to its original, its authority must be recognized by the community it serves. The decision of Trent confirmed for Catholics the traditional place of the Vulgate for another four centuries. Within Protestant circles a humanist respect for philology carried weight, but Wittenberg also proclaimed the accountability of the translator to sound theology. Despite Jerome's dictum that the translator is not a prophet, south German and Swiss evangelicals claimed the sanction of the Spirit for the interpreter having the knowledge of ancient languages (*I Corinthians* 14). Their peculiar institution for this was the Prophezei, and the collective translation projects of the 1530s and 1540s was a major con-

sequence. One must add that it was also their assumption that the Holy Spirit would lead others in the future to correct their work.

Other versions of the Bible were also translated for the learned public. The Complutensian Polyglot had a new interlinear rendering of the Septuagint; both that edition and the polyglot Psalter (Genoa, 1516) produced by the humanist bishop of Nebbio, Agostino Giustiniani, had some translation of the Aramaic Targums. The Tremellius Bible (1575–1579) was accompanied by a Latin translation of the Syriac New Testament.

Bibles in the Vernacular Tongues. It was in the Latin preface (the *Paraclesis*) to his Greek New Testament of 1516 that Erasmus issued his famous call for vernacular translations of scripture, a fact sometimes taken to symbolize the close link existing between the evolution of the two literatures, lay and learned. The same humanist and Reformation impulses were at work, *mutatis mutandis*, and a number of the issues discussed above recur here. To these must be added the assertion of Protestant reformers that all baptized Christians had the right and duty to explore and discern scriptural truth for themselves.

New translations. The other vernacular translations with their literalist fidelity to the Vulgate did not commend themselves for the new task. Nonetheless, some early Reformation translators persevered in the Vulgate tradition. Such was the case with Jacques Lefèvre d'Étaples, whose French New Testament (1523) was issued during his attempted reform of the diocese of Meaux. If this characteristic—which remained generally true of his full Bible (1530, 1534), despite some corrections drawn from the Greek—was in part the result of Lefèvre's age and linguistic limitations (he knew little Hebrew), it probably also reflected his respect for the weight of tradition. The rhythm of Lefèvre's work is also typical, in that Psalters and New Testaments generally preceded by several years the publication of complete Bibles.

Luther broke radical new ground with his High German New Testament (1522), the first element in a steady stream of translation and revision that continued throughout his lifetime. Possessing some competence in the biblical languages and assisted at the University of Wittenberg by a circle of gifted colleagues, Luther intended his Bible to render the original languages into a fresh, contemporary tongue, and in this he achieved extraordinary success. But while philology was an indispensable instrument, evangelical theology, not grammar, would be determinative for his translation according to sense. "Though the rabbis say thus, he would write, we know in Christ the meaning of these words, and so we translate instead."

Also based upon the Hebrew, though making full use of Jewish commentaries, was the German translation of the Old Testament prophets produced in Worms in 1527 by two emerging radical leaders, Hans Denck and Ludwig Hätzer.

Building on the work of both these projects, as well as on their own translations, the team of Zurich pastors led by Leo Jud completed their Swiss-German Bible (1531).

Similar preferences characterized the next French version (Neuchâtel, 1535), that of Pierre Robert Olivétan, financed by Piedmont Waldensians. But Olivétan, like most of the vernacular translators, was not a scholar of first rank, and although he did some independent work with the originals, he was indebted to other recent translations as well. This would be true of most vernacular versions of the Reformation period. New Latin texts, such as the Old Testament of Sebastian Münster of Basel (1534–1535), Erasmus's New Testament, Pagnini's Bible, and Luther's German New Testament, would make major contributions to various vernacular versions, the latter notably in Scandinavia. The Vulgate, however, also continued to be influential.

Some vernacular translators shared Luther's predilection for the translator's freedom. Others preferred to name their work paraphrase—for example, the Latin Psalms (1532) of the Louvain theologian Jan van Campen, which were put into Dutch, German, English, and French over the next decade. At the opposite extreme was the extremely literalist Spanish version of the Hebrew scriptures (Ferrara, 1553), demonstrably a Jewish edition intended for the use of the Sephardic diaspora.

Popular reception and official opposition. Popular enthusiasm for these editions is evidenced by the numerous references to them in bibliographies. That only a minority of even the urban public could read was an inconvenience, not a deterrent, while commitment to popular education became a hallmark of Protestant regimes. Examination of pamphlet literature even in the 1520s reveals a striking if sometimes naive biblical literacy. The German Catholic polemicist Johann Eck warned in his *Enchiridion* (1525) of the somber consequences of allowing "laymen and silly old women" to interpret scripture, and the issue was also present in the 1523–1524 conflict between Luther and Andreas Bodenstein von Karlstadt over the participation of laymen and laywomen in public biblical exposition. The appeal of Anabaptist movements must be understood in part in relation to lay reading of scripture.

Protestant liturgical use of the vernacular meant putting portions of scripture into poetic form for singing. From the first Wittenberg metrical psalms of 1524, the genre developed rapidly, with a Psalter available by late century in all regions that had a significant Reformed population. Here, too, styles varied, ranging from a strict attention to the letter of the Psalter to more free-flowing versions that frankly used the text to preach Protestant doctrine.

What had begun as a general evangelical reform concern was with difficulty soon dissociated from the taint of Protestant heresy. The Faculty of Theology of Paris censured the Catholic Lefèvre's translations in 1525, and vernacular versions regularly appeared on censors' lists everywhere. It is true that translation into languages with a not yet fixed theological vocabulary allowed for a considerable degree of interpretation. To this was frequently added the Reformation usage of borrowed prefaces, marginal notes, and indexes and even such issues as the placement of the Hagiographa or Apocryphal writings. In turn, the need to evade detection encouraged format decisions; small books were safer, as well as cheaper. Translators adopted pseudonyms, and publishers printed false title pages and colophons. Even as many Catholic authorities pursued suspect translations, Protestants demonstrated their awareness of the propaganda value of the medium. The career of Philbert Hamelin is instructive: upon conversion to the Reformed faith sometime between 1549 and his execution for heresy in 1557, this former priest divided his time between printing small format biblical texts in Geneva (often without indication of origin) and peddling them in his native Saintonge. In the face of the alarming spread of "Lutheranism," the reaction of France and Spain was to ban all vernacular editions, more effectively in the latter than the former. In other regions scripture versions of Catholic provenance continued to circulate freely—as, for example, the Dutch edition of Louvain (1548). This difference of opinion among Catholics surfaced in the debates of 1547 at the Council of Trent; in the end vernaculars would be tolerated if annotated appropriately and brought into line with the approved form of the Vulgate.

By the end of the century full Bibles existed in most western and central European languages, though Irish would have to wait until 1685. Versions carried an unmistakable confessional cachet: that of the German anti-Lutheran Johann Dietenberger was often reprinted despite his tacit dependence upon his rival's translation; two Emden Dutch editions of 1556 and 1558 from the same publisher were translated from different base texts for the Calvinist and Mennonite markets, respectively; and, likewise, the various Polish Bibles from 1563 to 1599 were intended for either a Calvinist, Socinian, or Roman Catholic audience. Also developing was a lay biblical piety (most markedly in Reformed and Anabaptist milieus) that privileged scripture reading in the home. The impact of these Bibles on the evolution of the vernacular tongue and its literature was enormous; similarly, the domestic and public use of confessionally sanctioned versions was a major contributor to the reinforcement of religious orthodoxies.

BIBLIOGRAPHY

Primary Sources

Erasmus, Desiderius. "Paraclesis." In *Christian Humanism and the Reformation. Selected Writings of Erasmus, with the Life of Erasmus by Beatus Rhenanus*, edited by John C. Olin, pp. 92–106. Rev. ed. New York, 1975. The preface to Erasmus' 1516 New Testament, which sets forth the humanist's vision of the reform of the Church through the reading of Scripture, and calls for access for the laity through vernacular translations.

Luther, Martin. "On Translating: An Open Letter; Defense of the Translation of the Psalms." Edited and translated by E. Theodore Bachman. In *Luther's Works*, edited by Halmut T. Lehman, vol. 35, pp. 203–232. Philadelphia, 1960. Luther's sparkling argument, with a number of illustrations, for the freedom and theologically directed character of his translations.

Secondary Sources

Backus, Irena Dorota, and Francis M. Higman. *Théorie et pratique de l'exégèse*. Etudes de Philologie et d'Histoire, vol. 43. Geneva, 1990. The papers of the Third International Colloquium on Sixteenth-Century Biblical Exegesis (Geneva 1988). Wide-ranging in themes, these conference papers (like those of the other colloquia) are a fundamental source for the study of the Bible in the sixteenth-century.

Bedouelle, Guy, and Bernard Roussel, eds. *Le temps des Réformes et la Bible*. Bible de Tous les Temps, vol. 5, Paris, 1989. A superbly documented and wide-ranging study of the Bible in the sixteenth-century; though its attention is more centered on the French-speaking world, it is indispensable for any serious study of the whole field. Splendid bibliographies.

Bentley, Jerry H. *Humanists and Holy Writ: New Testament Scholarship in the Renaissance*. Princeton, 1983. On the work of Lorenzo Valla, the New Testament of the Complutensian Polyglot and Erasmus, showing the significance of Renaissance humanism for the history of scholarship in New Testament studies.

Büsser, F., ed. *Early Printed Bibles: Printed Bibles and Bible Translations in the Fifteenth and Sixteenth Centuries on Microfiche*. Leiden, 1988–. This collection will ultimately contain 300 published Bibles and Bible translations from the fifteenth and sixteenth centuries.

Chrisman, Miriam Usher. *Lay Culture, Learned Culture: Books and Social Change in Strasbourg, 1480–1599*. New Haven, 1982. A study based upon an exhaustive analysis of Strasbourg publications for the period. Though there are some inaccuracies in the particular data due to earlier Strasbourg bibliographers, the work offers valuable insights into the world of readership both lay and clerical during the sixteenth century.

Fatio, Olivier, and Pierre Fraenkel. *Histoire de l'Exégèse au XVIe siècle*. Etudes de Philologie et d'Histoire, vol. 34. Geneva, 1978. Papers of the First International Colloquium on Sixteenth-Century Biblical Exegesis (Geneva, 1976), covering a wide range of scholars and works, giving particular emphasis to treatments of the Psalms, the Gospels, and Epistles.

Friedman, Jerome. *The Most Ancient Testimony: Sixteenth-Century Christian-Hebraica in the Age of Renaissance Nostalgia*. Athens, Ohio, 1983. An imaginative analysis of the world of Christian Hebraism in the first half of the sixteenth- century, with particular attention to works of Johannes Reuchlin, Michael Servetus, several exegetes of the Rhineland school (notably Sebastian Münster and Paul Fagius), and the conflict of the latter school with Wittenberg exegetes. The author does not bring into consideration Italian and French Hebraists.

Greenslade, S. L., ed. *The Cambridge History of the Bible. The West from the Reformation to the Present Day*. Reprint, Cambridge, 1987. Chaps. 1–6 offer a series of still standard and highly informative essays on the Bible in the Reformation. The bibliographies and numerous plates are valuable as well.

Higman, Francis M. *Censorship and the Sorbonne: A Bibliographical Study of Books in French Censured by the Faculty of Theology of the University of Paris, 1520–1551*. Travaux d'Humanisme et Renaissance, vol. 172. Geneva, 1979. Illustrates the relationship of the spread of evangelical activity to printed vernacular literature, with full censor's lists and bibliographical identification.

Hobbs, R. Gerald. "Zwingli and the Old Testament." In *Huldrych Zwingli, 1484–1531: A Legacy of Radical Reform*, edited by Edward J. Furcha, pp. 144–178. Montreal, 1985. An examination of the principal issues of Old Testament translation and commentary in the setting of the upper Rhineland school, as these are raised in particular in Zwingli's preface to his Isaiah commentary of 1529.

Lampe, G. W. H., ed. *The Cambridge History of the Bible*. Vol. 2, *The West from the Fathers to the Reformation*. Reprint, Cambridge, 1975. Valuable chapters on the history of the medieval "Vulgate" (chap. 5), medieval vernacular versions (chap. 9) and Erasmus in late medieval perspective (chap. 10).

Norton, Glyn P. *The Ideology and Language of Translation in Renaissance France and Their Humanist Antecedents*. Travaux d'Humanisme et Renaissance, vol. 201. Geneva, 1984. A seminal, at times highly technical exploration of the French Renaissance's understandings and debates on the nature of translation. Though predominantly dealing with secular literature, there is considerable of interest for the theoretical background to biblical translation as well.

Rice, Eugene F. *St. Jerome in the Renaissance*. Reprint, Baltimore, 1988. An elegant examination of the figure of the great translator in the Renaissance.

Russell, Paul A. *Lay Theology in the Reformation: Popular Pamphleteers in Southwest Germany, 1521–1525*. Cambridge and New York, 1986. Best study in English of the religious ideas of a selected group of German lay pamphleteers who contributed to the social turbulence of the early Reform years.

Schwarz, Werner. *Principles and Problems of Biblical Translation. Some Reformation Controversies and their Background*. London, 1955. An older study needing to be complemented by more recent work on humanist theory. Schwartz demonstrates that the roots of the sixteenth-century debate lie in the patristic discussion between Jerome and Augustine, and behind them, in the different versions concerning the origins of the Septuagint.

Steinmetz, David C., ed. *The Bible in the Sixteenth Century*. Durham, N.C., 1990. The papers of the Second International Colloquium on Sixteenth Century Biblical Exegesis (Durham, N.C., 1982); like the volumes from the first and third colloquia, an invaluable tool for detailed study of the field.

Strand, Kenneth Albert. *Reformation Bibles in the Crossfire: The Story of Jerome Emser, his Anti-Lutheran Critique and his Catholic Bible Version*. Ann Arbor, Mich., 1961. An account of the emergence of a Catholic translation in German to counter that of Luther.

Vogel, Paul Heinz. *Europäische Bibeldrucke des 15. und 16. Jahrhunderts in den Volkssprachen: Ein Beitrag zur Bibliographie des Bibeldrucks*. Bibliotheca Bibliographica Aureliana, vol. 5. Baden-Baden, 1962. A very extensive, though not exhaustive, survey of vernacular Bible editions by language, with good introductions for each language group; it concentrates upon New Testament and full Bible editions, passing notably over vernacular Psalters. The *British Museum General Catalogue of Printed Books*, vols. 17–19 (London, 1965) is a useful complement.

R. GERALD HOBBS

Biblical Commentaries

The links between biblical translation and commentary were close in the Reformation era. The more a translator was committed to rendering by sense with a certain freedom, the more he recognized the interpretive nature of his work; while commentators were faced with decisions similar to those confronting translators around the issue of base text and resources for its comprehension.

To begin, two methodological remarks. Biblical commentary in the sixteenth century took a range of forms and, particularly in the early decades, carried corresponding titles like *Annotationes, Enarratio[nes], Interpretatio, Expositio,* as well variants on *Commentarius.* With respect to the last term, Kenneth Hagen has shown ("What Did the Term 'Commentarius' Mean to Sixteenth-Century Theologians?" in *Théorie et pratique de l'exégèse,* Études de philologie et d'histoire, vol. 43, edited by Irena Backus and Francis Higman, Geneva, 1990) that no wider consensus attached to it than "a work on scripture"; and all of the former terms fit beneath this rubric. This discussion will then be similarly comprehensive in scope, while noting some discernable patterns within the genre. Second, the Reformation era saw a veritable explosion of biblical commentary. For example, the epistle to the Hebrews had at least forty-five commentators, while the perennially popular Psalter at least doubled that figure. There can be no question then even of identifying all commentators; what is attempted here is a synthetic overview. If the illustrations favor *Psalms* commentary, this is the terrain most familiar to the author as well as that most traveled by commentators.

Continuity and New Directions. Reformation commentary on the Bible exhibits both continuity and discontinuity with the late Middle Ages. The Renaissance concern for textual accuracy, the turning away from the common Latin text toward the Hebrew and Greek originals as base text with the frequently concomitant creation of new Latin as well as vernacular translations, the primary preoccupation with the philological, rhetorical, and historical questions raised by the text rather than with theological priorities, as well as an extraordinary interaction with market and readership made possible by the printing press: these represent a significant break with previous commentators, even before taking into account the impact of the new evangelical theologies upon a generation of scholars many of whom had embraced humanist presuppositions. The implantation of competing visions of the church would profoundly affect all dimensions of biblical study and publication, given the importance of the claim to scriptural authority in each.

Yet it would be an error to assume that none of these concerns appear in western Christendom before the Renaissance. The work of Beryl Smalley (*The Study of the Bible in the Middle Ages,* 2d ed., London, 1952) and others has demonstrated similar preoccupations among a number of medieval biblical scholars. It is unfortunate that fourteenth- and fifteenth-century exegetes have received relatively little attention in modern times. It is instructive to examine the work of Nicholas of Lyra (d. 1340), the great Franciscan master of Paris, whose postils were reprinted as one side of the magnificent carpet pages of the six-volume folio Latin Bible (Basel, 1498) edited by Sebastian Brant. Martin Luther's valuing of Lyra is well-known; the number of sixteenth-century re-editions show that he was not alone. With respect to the Old Testament Lyra makes regular use of medieval Jewish commentary in his quest for the literal sense, but his commentary betrays too the limitations of his understanding of his Jewish sources: he does not distinguish well between *peshat* (literal interpretation) and *derash* (the traditional homiletic application). Moreover, despite the use of these, his base text is the church's Latin, complemented (but only in the Psalter) by the *Hebraica veritas*—which is not the original, but Jerome's Latin translation of it. Finally, the lengthy prefaces to each book confirm Lyra's attachment to scholastic method, both in his handling of traditional topoi and his causal analysis and subdivisions of the text.

The foundation text for commentary. In the sixteenth century, base text remains a question for two reasons: lack of knowledge of the original languages or a prejudice in favor of the Latin. In the former category is a generation of older commentators like Erasmus, who abandoned the pursuit of Hebrew in favor of Greek studies, or his English friend John Colet, whose Oxford lectures on Paul disregarded Greek. In his Psalter commentary (Basel, 1524), Luther's colleague Johannes Bugenhagen compensated for this deficiency by noting differences between the Vulgate and the recent annotated Latin translation (Venice, 1515) of the Italian convert from Judaism, Felix of Prato. This was not characteristic of Wittenberg; in the sequence of Luther's own commentaries, his progress in Hebrew is evident. The humanist preference for the source was resisted stoutly, however, by commentators who underlined the orthodoxy, the universality, and dependability of the Vulgate. Frans Titelmans of Louvain, despite knowledge of both originals, entered the lists against Erasmus's *Annotations* and edition of the Greek New Testament text (1516) on these grounds. The preference could also be pragmatic. The evangelical Konrad Pellikan was a skilled Hebraist; but in his commentaries he preferred to work with the Vulgate on pastoral grounds. The Tridentine affirmation of the Vulgate's "authenticity" meant in practice that it would be the required base text for Catholic exegetes. Thus the Jesuit Roberto Bellarmino, in his popular 1611 Psalms, regularly commented upon differences between the Vulgate and the Hebrew but always managed to conclude in vindication of the former.

Philological exegesis. A second clear shift in direction was the humanist-inspired concern for philology. What precisely did the words of the text say? Fifteenth-century Italian humanists had made progress in the acquisition of Greek and Hebrew; by the early sixteenth century grammars and dictionaries were being written in Latin, such that universal access to these languages could now be envisaged. Not all commentators attained mastery; the Hebrew verb system, for example, was very imperfectly grasped by scholars accustomed to Indo-European tenses. But commentators sought to elucidate the text by a precise grasp of its grammatical constructions, its syntax, and by the usages of the source language within its historical context. Following the lead of Lorenzo Valla, Erasmus's New Testament *Annotations* hewed closely to this line; thus at *Matthew* 3:2 and 4:17 John the Baptist's (and Jesus') call for *metanoia* could not mean "poenitentiam agite"—despite the foundational importance of this text for the sacrament of penance—but "resipiscite," with its implications for moral renewal. In *Psalm* 1:1, the "man" upon whom blessedness is pronounced was said by some commentators, citing Saint Basil, not to exclude woman because man is her head; Luther in his 1519 *Operationes* drew upon classical Greek distinctions of "man" as "power" to find a place for woman; ten years later Martin Bucer of Strasbourg included her by demonstrating the use of the Hebrew *'ish* as a nongeneric distributive pronoun.

Philological exegesis also encountered resistance. In 1533 the Faculty of Theology of Paris accused François Vatable and the Royal Lecturers in Paris of commitment to the "dead letter" instead of the "life-giving spirit." The evangelical François Lambert, reflecting perhaps his Franciscan roots, spoke for a number of others in his 1525 treatise *De Prophetia* warning against the contempt for the Holy Spirit inherent in the insistence upon linguistic skills for interpretation; his argument may have been a personal defense, though he also voiced it in the name of biblical interpretation by uneducated laypersons, a concern he shared with Luther's former colleague Andreas Bodenstein von Karlstadt. Throughout his career Luther consistently defended the right of good theology to override the letter, as in his addition to Paul in *Romans* 3:28, "one is justified without doing the Law's work, by faith *alone*." This does not differ in kind from the accountability of post-Tridentine Catholic exegetes to the church's magisterium, or from Sébastien Castellion's exclusion from the Genevan pastoral corps owing to his conclusions on the *Song of Songs* and Christ's descent into hell.

In reality there were paths down which the commentator would follow the text at his peril. In 1528 Wolfgang Capito of Strasbourg learned that his Rhineland evangelical colleagues could not tolerate what he saw as the "plain sense" of the words of *Hosea* 2 regarding a future return of the Jews to Palestine; unconvinced by their arguments, he agreed to remain silent. In the case of the Spaniard Michael Servetus, his exegetical challenges to the orthodox trinitarian formulas would eventually cost him his life in Geneva. By late century the power of zealous Catholic censors made even orthodox commentators cautious in their findings.

The use of rabbinic resources. A third area in which new ground was effectively broken was the employment of Jewish resources for the understanding of the scriptures. Here there were precedents going back at least to Jerome; but the scale on which this developed, the breadth of familiarity with medieval rabbinic commentators, and the willingness to apply their insights in a philological exegesis that altered radically the traditional Christian reading of a text mean that one must effectively speak of change. By 1534-

1535 Sebastian Münster of Basel was repeating a commonplace when he stated that without the aid of the rabbis, in many instances he would never have understood the text. His Latin-Hebrew Bible, enlarged in 1546, was a compendium of rabbinic readings; its preface displays some awareness of the history of Jewish exegesis, an ability to discriminate between authors and exegetical methods.

This embrace of Jewish commentary, too, was variously received, reactions ranging from enthusiasm to refusal. In his *Quincuplex Psalterium* (Paris, 1508) Jacques Lefèvre d'Étaples denounced those who, by advancing rabbinic proposals for the historical context of a psalm's composition, destroyed Christian use of the Psalter, "making David a historian, not a prophet [of Christ]." Those who did so were accused of Judaizing, of insinuating the Jewish enemy into the Christian camp. The fear of such contamination was present in Wittenberg circles, where it would prompt one of the more curious projects of the century, Johannes Forster's production of a Hebrew dictionary (Basel, 1557) that studiously avoided all lexical information not only from rabbinic sources but also from their foolish Christian imitators (like Münster)! In reality, the most enthusiastic Christians read the rabbinic commentators with a good pinch of Christian salt. Johannes Reuchlin was one of a number who believed that through Cabbala and various mystical exegetical practices, the heart of Christian doctrine could be shown to exist in ancient Jewish texts, and that, for example, the name of Jesus could be derived from the tetragram, the ancient Hebrew name for God. Others like Bucer and Calvin, while rejecting such speculations, found the key to the use of Jewish sources in drawing upon their historical and philological insights, while noting their unfortunate inability to see in Jesus the promised Messiah. This suggests a dichotomy that could manifest itself, for example, in Cardinal Cajetan's early attempt to distinguish between what the words said and what they meant. In practice it frequently led to a typological exegesis in which a historical and philological approach elucidated the ancient Hebrew sense of a text, which was then taken as an anticipation of Christ and his reign.

Origins, Audiences, and Forms. Regarding the particular locus of commentary in the Reformation era, it should be kept in mind that renewal through the study of scripture was an objective of most, if not all, of the reform projects of the sixteenth century.

Origins. Commentary continued to serve as vehicle of meditation. Thus the *Psalms* commentary of Lefèvre d'Étaples originated in his effort to reawaken monastic contemplation at the abbey of Saint-Germain-des-Prés. A popular paraphrase (1535) on the same book by the Catholic physician Reyner Snoy of Gouda was clearly destined for devotional reading; and its numerous reprintings and translations attest to its success in meeting that objective. The same can be said for Erasmus's treatises on individual psalms; in an act evocative of his *Enchiridion*, he dedicated the last of these (1536) to a ferryman encountered on a journey down the Rhine.

One of the particularities of Reformation commentary was its frequent association with Bible translation. Of the supposed project of Pope Clement VII, a new translation of the Old Testament to be made by a learned commission of Christians and Jews, little concrete is known. But the several commentaries of Cajetan may belong within that context, as do perhaps the volumes of unpublished annotations to which Pagnini referred in the preface of his 1528 Bible. The Wittenberg translators and revisers issued a steady stream of commentary, while the impressive work of Calvin must be seen as being in dialogue with an ongoing Genevan perfecting of a French translation. From Trent onward, Catholic commentators worked to validate the church's preference for the revised Vulgate.

Within evangelical reform circles an exploration of scripture through lectures—whether to a restricted public of like-minded scholars, as in Cardinal Pole's household in Italy, a university audience as in Wittenberg or Basel, or a more general public, as in Strasbourg—was characteristic. Enthusiasm for the fruits of these labors led to printings pirated from student notes; Johannes Bugenhagen and Philipp Melanchthon of Wittenberg regularly lamented with some justice their victimization. Thus, far from being the studied products of the scholar's ivory tower, many early Reformation commentaries bore evident marks of the haste with which they were rushed to market. Zwingli's 1527 commentaries on *Genesis* and *Exodus* are nicely illustrative; to prevent the unauthorized appearance of notes by the Zurich *Prophezei*, his colleagues Leo Jud and Caspar Megander undertook to keep a written record of Zwingli's interventions in particular; these later appeared under the not-inappropriate title "A Farrago of Annotations."

Audiences. For whom were Reformation commentators writing? Certainly in some instances they wrote for fellow scholars. The New Testament *Annotations* that accompanied Erasmus's Greek text of 1516 would naturally have served the ends of the vernacular translators for whom he appealed. The notes culled from the *Midrash Tehillim* by Agostino Giustiniani in his eight-column Psalter of the same year are unlikely to have interested nonspecialists.

But the largest audience for the new commentary were the clergy and students in territories committed to reform. That there was a genuine public enthusiasm to hear and read the exposition of scripture cannot be doubted in the face of printers' avidity for the product. Practically, new priests-turned-evangelical-pastors, as well as their eventual successors, required resources from which to learn and preach the new faith; the furnishing of scripture exposition from an approved interpreter became an important instrument in the discipline of the new churches. Thus, for example, an ordinance of the city of Strasbourg in 1534 prescribed the library of commentaries to be in each parish, with a strong bias for local authors. Similarly, the requirement in the Jesuit *Constitutions* that biblical studies be vigorously pursued in Jesuit universities stimulated the production of a significant number of commentaries by members of the order. Nowhere is the linkage more apparent than in Zurich in the late 1520s, where an eighteen-month passage of various biblical books can be traced from *lectio continua* study in the *Prophezei*, through preaching in various city pulpits, to their appearance in print.

Commentary could also serve as propaganda. As their dedications and prefaces make clear, reformers early became conscious that the dissemination of the printed commentary had potential for attracting new adherents to the reform—although in this context Martin Bucer's adoption of a French pseudonym and persona for his 1529 *Psalms* commentary was seen by many as excessive. The book fairs, Frankfurt in particular, enabled printers to distribute on a continental scale; and the rhythm of Bucer's work—five commentaries in 1527–1529—was set by the Frankfurt calendar. Printers such as Christoph Froschauer of Zurich and Robert Estienne of Paris and later Geneva became identified with the biblical market.

Both these ends, preaching and propaganda, were served by vernacular commentary. In the early 1520s Lefèvre d'Étaples and Luther each produced vernacular works on the lectionary readings for the Mass; the latter's were subsequently translated into Latin and printed in Strasbourg for distribution in France and Italy. Similarly, in centers such as Basel and Antwerp publishers worked, often clandestinely, for these and the English market; while German centers served northern and eastern Europe. By mid-century a flood of French commentary issued from the presses of Geneva, most obviously destined for Calvin's homeland. Some was translation, but Calvin, like Luther, also wrote commentary directly in his native tongue.

The forms of commentary. As was observed at the outset, biblical commentary covered a wide range of forms. Erasmus popularized annotation as a vehicle for philological comment on the original text. But even the purest of grammatical notes were not without theological significance; these minutiae, as he and Pagnini pointed out, would enable sounder reflection upon the text. And Erasmus himself, as he revised his work, advanced ever deeper into the terrain of theological commentary. This would be even truer of Théodore de Bèze, in whose annotations philology and polemical theology were combined. From this form, in some instances excerpted directly, evolved the marginally annotated Bible. Evangelical assertions of the clarity and self-sufficiency of scripture notwithstanding, translators and editors were liberal in their assistance to the reader; cross-referencing was traditional, but now content summaries appeared, difficulties were explained, and the doctrinal import of key passages was underlined appropriately.

The genre of paraphrase was likewise popularized by

Erasmus. He himself was reticent about characterizing this narrative expansion of the text as commentary; conservative opponents had no doubt on this score, while the enormous number of small-format editions of his own and others' work, as well as such projects as the magnificent in-folio English translation of Erasmus for parish churches (1548), suggest that this form nonetheless served both private meditation and public preaching. Analogous to this form were postils and homilaries; reformers and their opponents both made extensive use of these instruments to influence local clergy and their parishioners.

All these stand alongside the more conventional form, the learned commentary. The shape of these varied considerably depending upon the exegete's methodological choices. Among the upper Rhineland school it became common practice to provide a new translation of the original as the starting point for commentary that would include lexical, rhetorical, and historical observations as well as a doctrinal exposition. The methods of this school were improved upon and refined by Calvin, who was probably the greatest commentator of the era. On the other hand, the Wittenberg school favored a loci method that privileged systematic presentation of theological issues suggested by the text. Some Protestants might bypass traditional authorities, but others, like Catholic commentators, routinely cited the Fathers. In the 1560s Augustin Marlorat revived the catena form, with a harmony of approved Reformed commentators. The first decade of Reformation commentary abetted the trend toward prolixity; in-quartos and -octavos gave way to lengthy folios, destined, one presumes, for the clergy and for school libraries.

A final observation: given the ecclesial context of all biblical commentary, church schism was bound to have an impact. At least until mid-century, however, divisions in matters biblical, while sharp, crossed the emerging confessional boundaries in a way that would no longer be true at the century's end.

BIBLIOGRAPHY

Anderson, Marvin Walter. *Peter Martyr: A Reformer in Exile, 1542–1562; A Chronology of Biblical Writings in England and Europe.* Nieuwkoop, 1975. Overview of the work of Vermigli, a later member of the Rhineland school.

Béné, Charles. "Introduction générale." In *Desiderii Erasmi Roterodami, Opera Omnia,* vol. 5/2, pp. 1–17. Amsterdam and New York, 1985. Introduction to the Erasmus *Psalms* commentaries.

Engammare, Max. *Qu'il me baise des baisiers de sa bouche: La cantique des cantiques à la Renaissance; etude et bibliographie.* Geneva, 1993. The disagreement between Calvin and Sébastien Castellion over the character of the *Song of Songs* is the starting point for an examination of sixteenth-century commentary on this book and the various issues it raised. Includes an exhaustive bibliography of sixteenth-century publications.

Fraenkel, Pierre, ed. *Pour retrouver François Lambert. Bio-bibliographie et études.* Bibliotheca Bibliographica Aureliana 108. Baden-Baden, 1987. Full bibliographical study and several articles on Lambert, an early French Lutheran and prolific commentator.

Hagen, Kenneth. *Hebrews Commenting from Erasmus to Bèze, 1516–1598.* Beiträge zur Geschichte der Biblischen Exegese, vol. 23. Tübingen, 1981. The author identifies forty-five Reformation *Hebrews* commentaries of varying size and importance, and gives a useful overview of their general approach to the epistle.

Hendrix, Scott H., et al. *Luther: Interpreter of Scripture. Interpretation* 37.3 (1983). Issue devoted to studies on various aspects of Luther's commentary on scripture.

Hobbs, R. Gerald "How Firm a Foundation: Martin Bucer's Historical Exegesis of the Psalms." *Church History* 53.4 (1984), 477–491. An examination of the style and character, in particular the use of Jewish sources, of the Old Testament commentary of one of the key figures in the Upper Rhine school.

Holfelder, Hans Hermann. *Tentatio et Consolatio: Studien zu Bugenhagens "Interpretatio in librum Psalmorum."* Arbeiten zur Kirchengeschichte, vol. 45. Berlin and New York, 1974. A study of the first evangelical commentary on the full Psalter (1524).

Parker, T. H. L. *Calvin's New Testament Commentaries.* Grand Rapids, Mich., 1971. This and the following study (the former deals with more technical questions, the latter with the character of Calvin's commentary on the Old Testament) provide an excellent introduction to the most important commentator of the era.

———. *Calvin's Old Testament Commentaries.* Edinburgh, 1986.

Pelikan, Jaroslav. *Luther the Expositor. Introduction to the Reformer's Exegetical Writings.* In *Luther's Works (American Edition),* companion volume. Saint Louis, 1959. From the editor of the thirty volumes of Luther commentary in the series, an examination of the principles that guided Luther's work and a series of illustrations from his commentaries.

Roussel, Bernard. "De Strasbourg à Bâle et Zurich: Une 'École rhénane' d'Exégèse c.1525-c.1540." *Revue d'histoire et de philosophie religieuses* 68.1, (1988) 19–39.

Roussel, Bernard, and Gerald Hobbs. "Strasbourg et 'l'école rhénane' d'exégèse, 1525–1540." *Bulletin de la Société de l'histoire du protestantisme français* 135.1 (1989), 36–53.

Rummel, Erika. *Erasmus' Annotations on the New Testament: From Philologist to Theologian.* Erasmus Studies. vol. 8. Toronto, 1986. The author, one of the translators of Erasmus for the Toronto project, traces the development of Erasmus as New Testament commentator through the several editions of the annotations, showing an increasing shift from philological notes to commentary.

R. GERALD HOBBS

BIBLIANDER, Theodor (Ger., Buchmann; 1504?–1564), linguist, theologian, and scholar. Born in Switzerland at Bischofszell in the Thurgau, Bibliander attended Latin school in Zurich, then the University of Basel, where he studied Hebrew with Konrad Pellikan and Johannes Oecolampadius. From 1527 to 1529 he taught school at Liegnitz (Silesia), then returned to Zurich. In 1531, he succeeded Zwingli as professor of Old Testament at the Zurich Academy.

Bibliander assisted in the publication of the letters of Zwingli and Oecolampadius in 1536, and actively opposed the Wittenberg Concord. He wrote polemical works against the Catholic church, the Council of Trent, and the pope. One of the great Hebraists in the early Reformed churches, he has been called the father of exegetical theology in Switzerland. In addition to writing numerous commentaries on the prophets, he published a Hebrew grammar for beginners in 1535, and, in 1542, a complete Hebrew grammar. He also published historical studies and produced studies on the New Testament. After Jud's death in 1542, Bibliander completed his translation of the Old Testament into Latin. In March 1542 Bibliander published a book warning Christians of the great threat of the Turks. However, the magistrates at Basel objected when he sought to publish a Latin edition of the Qur'an itself. The ensuing conflict was resolved only by a letter from Luther supporting its publication. The majority of Bibliander's writings remain in manuscript in Zurich.

Bibliander's teaching on predestination came under attack from Peter Martyr Vermigli, who had replaced Pellikan upon his death in the late 1550s. Bibliander has been called an Erasmian, a proto-Arminian, and a universalist. He believed that God predestined two classes of humans, believers and unbelievers. God wished to save all humans, and all were adopted as sons and daughters unless they forced God to reject them by refusing divine grace. No one was irrevocably lost. Vermigli, who held to a Calvinist view on predestination, emphasized absolute double predestination in his first lectures in Zurich. Bibliander responded by attacking Vermigli's point of view in his own lectures. In February 1560, Bibliander was forced to resign and was put on a pension. He died of the plague on 24 September 1564.

BIBLIOGRAPHY

Baker, J. Wayne. *Heinrich Bullinger and the Covenant: The Other Reformed Tradition.* Athens, Ohio, 1980. Describes Bibliander's point of view on predestination and places the controversy between him and Vermigli in its larger context.

Egli, Emil. *Analecta Reformatoria II. Biographien: Bibliander, Ceporin, Johannes Bullinger.* Zurich, 1901. A scholarly biographical sketch.

Pfister, Rudolf. "Das Türkenbüchlein Theodor Biblianders." *Theologische Zeitschrift* 9 (1953), 438–454. Brief scholarly treatment of Bibliander's little book about the Turks.

Staedtke, Joachim. "Der Zürcher Prädestinationsstreit von 1560." *Zwingliana* 9 (1953), 536–546. Deals with the controversy between Bibliander and Vermigli in Zurich over predestination.

J. WAYNE BAKER

BIEL, Gabriel (c.1410–1495), German theologian, called "the last scholastic" and *Doctor profundissimus.* Biel was the major representative of the scholastic tradition for reform theologians; he earned his designations both by his eminence during his lifetime and by his crucial, if indirect, impact upon Martin Luther.

Born at Speyer on the Rhine, Biel was already ordained a priest when he matriculated in arts at the University of Heidelberg (1432). He received the baccalaureate in arts in 1435 and in 1438 his master's degree in arts. He then taught at Heidelberg until 1442 or 1443, when he transferred to the University of Erfurt. There the thought of William of Ockham, although dominant, shared influence with that of John Duns Scotus and Thomas Aquinas. In 1451 Biel matriculated in theology at Erfurt; in 1453 he transferred to Cologne, where he encountered strong traditions of Albertus Magnus and Thomas. It seems that there he acquired his first text of Ockham. This orientation in the "ancient way" (*via antiqua*) of thirteenth century masters as well as in the "modern way" (*via moderna*) of Ockham is everywhere visible in Biel's writings.

Biel held the office of cathedral preacher and vicar at Mainz from 1462, and many printings of his sermon collections testify to his reputation as a pastor. Before 1468 Biel joined the Brothers of the Common Life with their "modern devotion" (*devotio moderna*) at Marienthal near Geisenheim; he became provost of the house of the brethren at Butzbach in 1470, helped to found houses in the Upper Rhine region in 1471, and served as provost at Urach in 1479 and as provost at Schönborn in Baden-Wüttemberg in 1479. On 22 November 1484 Biel became a regent master in theology at the University of Tübingen (founded in 1477 by the count of Württemberg, Biel collaborating) and twice served as rector (1485 and 1489). Near 1491 he retired to the house of the brethren at Einsiedel near Tübingen and died there in 1495.

On the verge of the Reformation and Counter-Reformation crystallizations of ecclesiology Biel produced (1462; printed 1499/1500) his *Defensorium obedientiae apostolicae* addressed to the church of Mainz, then under interdict, by which he strongly supported the papal office in church discipline. His interest in communal religious life inspired a *Tractatus magistri Gabrielis Byell de communi vitae clericorum* and a *Collatio de vita communi.* A *Tractatus de potestate et utilitate monetarum,* identical with a section of his major work on the *Sentences* of Peter Lombard, circulated separately and has been translated into English. An *Expositio sacri canonis missae* was printed many times under slightly different titles and was read by Luther before his own ordination in 1507. A number of short treatises on the liberal arts had minimal influence, and only *Tractatus artis grammaticae* and *Regula puerorum* (on Donatus) seem to have been printed (1486 and 1497 respectively). Biel's most influential theological writing, his *Collectio,* or *Epitome circa quattuor libros Sententiarum* (many times printed, including a modern critical edition), was known and unfavorably annotated by Martin Luther. Biel's allegiance to Ockham in this work was unqualified: "our project is to abbreviate the dogmas and writings of the Venerable Inceptor, the Englishman, William of Ockham. . . where he wrote little or nothing; other Doctors, not deviating from the principles of the aforesaid Doctor [are included]." Biel adduced a range of Scholastics: Duns Scotus, Thomas, Bonaventura, Albertus Magnus, and even Aristotle. This classical statement of the *via moderna* influenced the University of Salamanca in Spain and that at Coimbra in Portugal; the Council of Trent would cite Biel twice. Luther studied theology at Erfurt under a student of Biel's from Tübingen and was finally repelled by this eclectic version of Scholasticism with its heavily philosophical overtones. Luther's marginal notes in his copy of the *Collectorium* and his own *Lectures on Romans* give incontrovertible evidence of his conviction that in those works Biel had fallen into Pelagian or semi-Pelagian views on human freedom and divine grace. Roman Catholic theologians are less inclined to reject this claim today than were Luther's contemporaries Desiderius Erasmus and John Fisher.

Biel's efforts to reconcile theological and ecclesial factions in Western Christendom failed to meet the demands of reformers during the decades following his death. His exertions as "the last scholastic" retain historical value by their witness to the state of theology on the eve of the Reformation.

BIBLIOGRAPHY

Primary Sources

Biel, Gabriel. *Treatise on the Power and Utility of Moneys.* Translated by Robert B. Burke. Philadelphia and London, 1930.
———. *Gabrielis Biel Canonis missae expositio.* Edited by Heiko A. Oberman and William J. Courtenay. 4 vols. Wiesbaden, 1963–1967.
———. *Defensorium obedientiae apostolicae et alia documenta.* Edited and translated by Heiko A. Oberman, Daniel E. Zerfoss, and William J. Courtenay. Cambridge, Mass., 1968.
———. *Collectorium circa quattuor libros Sententiarum.* Edited by Wilfrid Werbeck and Udo Hofmann. 4 vols. Tübingen, 1973–1977.

Secondary Sources

Ernst, Wilhelm. *Gott und Mensch am Vorabend der Reformation: Eine Untersuchung zur Moralphilosophie und -theologie bei Gabriel Biel.* Leipzig, 1972.
McSorley, Harry J. *Luther: Right or Wrong? An Ecumenical-Theological Study of Luther's Major Work "The Bondage of the Will."* New York, 1969.
Oberman, Heiko A. *The Harvest of Medieval Theology; Gabriel Biel and Late Medieval Nominalism.* Cambridge, Mass., 1963.
Ozment, Steven E. *The Age of Reform, 1250–1550: An Intellectual and Religious History of Late Medieval and Reformation Europe.* New Haven, 1980.

EDWARD A. SYNAN

BILLICANUS, Theobald (c.1490–1554), Lutheran reformer who returned to Catholicism. Born Diepold Gerlacher, he took his surname from his birthplace, Billigheim (Rheinland-Pfalz). He studied at Heidelberg at the time of the 1519 Martin Luther–Johann Eck disputation. His first clerical appointment, in Weil der Stadt, ended quickly when city fathers suspected Lutheran tendencies in his sermons.

Billicanus became city pastor in the free imperial city of Nördlingen in October 1522. Reform in Nördlingen progressed rapidly thereafter. In February 1525 Billicanus published *Renovatio ecclesiae Nordlingiacensis,* outlining a worship service decidedly evangelical in its rejection of the Mass as sacrifice and in its emphasis upon scripture and justification by faith alone. Billicanus also initially took Luther's side in print in the Sacramentarian controversy.

In the course of this debate, Billicanus's Lutheran convictions began to waver. On two occasions, in 1529 and at the Diet of Augsburg in 1530, he publicly denounced the Lutheran "heresy." Meanwhile, however, he had married Barbara Schäufelin, a merchant's daughter. For the next five years Billicanus led a paradoxical life, presiding at Lutheran services, renewing his appointment as city pastor, and raising a family but maintaining his orthodoxy to Catholic thought.

Billicanus left Nördlingen in 1535 to study law at Heidelberg, receiving his licentiate in civil and canon law in 1542. Noteworthy among his writings from this period is his *Apology* of 1539, in which he claimed never to have been truly committed to the Lutheran cause: his statements of 1529 and 1530 were not actually recantations of Lutheranism but reaffirmations of his Catholicism.

Relieved of his teaching duties in 1544, Billicanus moved to Marburg, where he remained unemployed until 1548. His subsequent appointment as lecturer of rhetoric lasted only three years. Little is known of Billicanus's final years; he died in August 1554 and was buried in a Lutheran ceremony in Marburg.

BIBLIOGRAPHY

Benrath, Gustav A. "Theobald Billicanus." In *Pfälzer Lebensbilder,* edited by Kurt Baumann, vol. 3, pp. 31–63. Speyer, Germany, 1977. Among the few lengthy studies dedicated to Billicanus; details his life and writings.
Rublack, Hans-Christoph. *Eine bürgerliche Reformation: Nördlingen.* Gütersloh, 1982. Discusses briefly Billicanus's role in Nördlingen's conversion to Lutheranism.
Sehling, Emil. *Die evangelischen Kirchenordnungen des XVI. Jahrhunderts.* Vol. 12, pt. 2. Tübingen, 1963. Provides a useful synopsis of the Reformation in Nördlingen, as well as primary documents.

EILEEN T. DUGAN

BILNEY, Thomas (c.1495–1531), early English reformer. Bilney holds the unique distinction of having been denounced as a dangerous dissenter by both Sir Thomas More (*A Dialogue Concerning Heresies,* 1529 and *The Confutation of Tyndale's Answer,* 1532) and the poet John Skelton ("A Replication," 1528–1529). Yet he was far from a thorough-going radical in theology, leaving the martyrologist John Foxe to conclude that he was "a man of timorous conscience" who "touching the mass and the sacrament of the altar ... never differed from the most gross catholics" (*Acts and Monuments,* vol. 4, pp. 648–649). Doubt and controversy continue to obscure his true beliefs.

Bilney was twice tried for heresy. In 1527 he was accused of having preached against prayers to saints, pilgrimages, and devotion to images. But he resolutely denied these accusations, turning his trial into a *cause célèbre* in academic circles. His judges seem to have ultimately reached a compromise with him, allowing him to take an oath of abjuration that denounced the opinions alleged but fell short of a full acknowledgment of his own guilt.

Bilney seems subsequently to have regretted this temporizing, however, and resolved to preach again, a decision that led to his second trial and his execution for relapse in 1531. But controversy pursued Bilney to the last, as the authorities alleged that he recanted again at the stake, a claim his reformist allies denied.

It is perhaps safest to see Bilney's personal theology as combining orthodox doctrines with elements of both Lutheran thinking on justification and older Lollard traditions. But his historical importance is more personal than doctrinal. Through the example of pious living he offered his fellow students, his popular sermons, and the individual conversion of future reformers such as Hugh Latimer, Robert Barnes, and John Lambert, Bilney did much to inspire those who would go on to play important roles in the English Reformation.

BIBLIOGRAPHY

Davis, John. F. "The Trials of Thomas Bylney and the English Reformation." *Historical Journal* 24 (1981), 775–790.
————. *Heresy and Reformation in the South East of England, 1520–1559.* London, 1983. Sets Bilney in the wider context of the early Reformation in England.
Walker, Greg. "Saint or Schemer?: The 1527 Heresy Trial of Thomas Bilney Reconsidered." *Journal of Ecclesiastical History* 40 (1989), 219–238. Draws out the complexities of Bilney's defense at his first trial.

GREG WALKER

BISHOPS. *See* Episcopacy.

BISSCHOP, Simon Egbertszoon. *See* Episcopius, Simon.

BLACK RUBRIC. *See* Book of Common Prayer.

BLANDRATA, Georgius. *See* Biandrata, Giorgio.

BLARER, Ambrosius (also Blaurer; 1492–1564), south German Protestant reformer. Born on 4 April in the south German city of Constance, Blarer was raised in a respected patrician family, which contributed to the fact that while still a young man he had access to the leading authorities in the free imperial city. In 1505 Blarer began his studies at the University of Tübingen. About four years later he entered the Benedictine monastery of Alpirsbach, where he later also took on duties as a lecturer and prior. Because of his talents, he was promoted and continued his studies at the University of Tübingen, where he received the degree of master of arts in 1512. He became good friends with Philipp Melanchthon, who began to study in Tübingen in 1512. In the letters from Melanchthon to Blarer, one sees the common enthusiasm for the educational ideals of humanism and for the study of languages. The church father Jerome and the humanist Desiderius Erasmus of Rotterdam were for the young monk models in his striving for education (*eruditio*) and piety (*pietas*). This much is evident from Blarer's handwritten marginal notes and sketches in his books—the Jerome edition of Erasmus (Basel, 1516) and Erasmus's collection of sayings (*Adagia*, Basel, 1515), which can be found today in the Folger Shakespeare Library, Washington, D.C.

Blarer's humanist tendencies soon retreated in favor of his newly awakened interest in the ideas of Martin Luther, whom he read with enthusiasm. His turn to Luther was encouraged by his brother Thomas Blarer, who studied in Wittenberg and wrote enthusiastic letters to him from there. When Blarer began to interpret Luther's writings in the monastery, he was forbidden to preach or to teach. The conflict became acute, and on 5 July 1522 he left the monastery. In a pamphlet ("Wahrhaft Verantwortung Ambrosii Blaurer. . ."; 1523) he justified his departure from the monastery and publicly committed himself to Luther. The council of Constance supported Blarer, who at first did not speak out publicly but in 1525 began regular preaching.

As a preacher, inspirer, and adviser, Blarer essentially determined the implementation and formation of the Reformation in Constance. Religious and moral life were to be reformed according to the model of a "holy city." Blarer contributed to the introduction of a discipline order in 1531 (forbidding sexual offense, drinking, gaming, and cursing, among other things). In cooperation with other clergy, the council of Constance introduced a moral order that strictly controlled life in the city, reached deeply into all areas of life, and was in this way supposed to bring about the sanctification of the city. Blarer's zeal also contributed to the fact that the Constance order had a far-reaching effect on the south German Reformation. Recently discovered sermons of Blarer, which he delivered in 1539 in Augsburg, show how Blarer propagated his notion of moral and church discipline. In his opinion the city authorities should execute by means of proper mandates and by the establishment of a moral police force what the preachers were promoting through the preaching of the gospel. In addition to the moral police of the authorities, however, Blarer also advocated a voluntary discipline in which the community members would admonish each other in a "brotherly" fashion. From 1528 to 1533 Blarer was often in other cities of southern Germany (including Memmingen, Ulm, Esslingen, and Isny) to preach and to reorder churches according to the model of the Constance reformation.

In 1534 Blarer was called to the duchy of Württemberg as a reformer. Among his tasks were the reform of the University of Tübingen, inspection of the communities, and obtaining and installing new preachers. According to a draft order for monasteries, they were to be reformed and then reopened with the introduction of proper theologians as teachers. In the reordering of the liturgy and the removal of images, which Blarer pursued energetically, he came into conflict with Lutheran theologians, who had helped him introduce the Reformation in Württemberg. The constant disputes with the Lutherans caused the duke to dismiss Blarer abruptly in 1538. Cooperation between south German and Lutheran theologians proved impossible in the long run. In addition, Blarer refused to sign the Wittenberg Concord in 1536. Blarer had at first supported the efforts of Martin Bucer toward a concord, and he had represented a mediating point of view in the conflict over the understanding of the Eucharist, in which he rejected every dogmatization of speculative interpretations of the Eucharist and affirmed the simple use of the sacraments according to the words of institution. Thus, the Wittenberg Concord of 1536 contradicted his insistence on "simplicity" when it asserted that in the Eucharist "unworthy ones" also received the body and blood of Christ (*manducatio indignorum*). The rejection of the Wittenberg Concord brought the Constance church into an isolation that made Blarer's position in Württemberg more difficult and burdened his friendly relationship with Martin Bucer, which had up to then been untroubled.

After his dismissal from Württemberg (and a short stay in Augsburg in 1539), Blarer worked mainly in his hometown of Constance. During the time of the plague (1540–1542), for example, he worked intensively as the pastor of the Constance community. But the conquest of Constance by imperial troops in 1548 meant the end of the Reformation in this city. Blarer lived from then on in Switzerland, took over a parish in Biel (1551–1559), and died in Winterthur on 6 December 1564.

Blarer is an excellent representative of south German reform Protestantism. His theological convictions were formed in a constant dialogue with the leading reformers of south Germany and Switzerland. Huldrych Zwingli and Heinrich Bullinger in Zurich, Johannes Oecolampadius in Basel, and Bucer and Wolfgang Capito in Strasbourg were among his correspondents. His significance consists not of an individual contribution to Protestant theology but of the practical organization of the Reformation in the south German area. At times a real distaste for theological reflection and dogmatic fixation is noticeable in his work. Blarer dedicated himself completely to the *reformatio vitae*, which must follow a *reformatio doctrinae*.

Special attention is merited for Blarer's gift for language, which made of him a significant poet. Among his twenty-five songs and poems there are some religious songs that are still sung today in German Protestant communities. Some of his songs were included in the Constance hymnal that appeared in the sixteenth century in many editions and that molded church music in German-speaking Switzerland.

BIBLIOGRAPHY

Primary Source

Blaurer, Ambrosius, and Thomas Blaurer. *Briefwechsel der Brüder Ambrosius und Thomas Blaurer.* 3 vols. Edited by Traugott Schieß. Freiburg, 1908–1912.

Secondary Sources

Burkhardt, Martin, Wolfgang Dobras, and Wolfgang Zimmerman. "Konstanz zur Zeit der Reformation." In *Geschichte der Stadt Konstanz,* vol. 3, *Konstanz in der frühen Neuzeit: Reformation, Verlust der Reichsfreiheit, Österreichische Zeit,* pp. 11–146. Constance, 1991. Blarer's influence on the Reformation in Constance.

Dobras, Wolfgang. *Ratsregiment, Sittenpolizei und Kirchenzucht in der Reichsstadt Konstanz, 1531–1548: Ein Beitrag zur Geschichte der oberdeutsch-schweizerischen Reformation.* Quellen und Forschungen zur Reformationsgeschichte, 59. Gütersloh, 1993. On the cooperation of Blarer on a reform program that had the sanctification of the city society as its goal.

Hasse, Hans-Peter. "Ambrosius Blarer liest Hieronymus: Blarers handschriftliche Eintragungen in seinem Exemplar der Hieronymusausgabe des Erasmus von Rotterdam (Basel 1516)." In *Auctoritas Patrum: Zur Rezeption der Kirchenväter im 15. und 16. Jahrhundert,* edited by Leif Grane, Alfred Schindler, and Markus Wriedt, pp. 33–53. Veröffentlichungen des Instituts für Europäische Geschichte Mainz, supplement 31: Abteilung Religionsgeschichte. Mainz, 1993.

Moeller, Bernd. *Johannes Zwick und die Reformation in Konstanz.* Quellen und Forschungen zur Reformationsgeschichte 28. Gütersloh, 1961. Contains a bibliography of the reformation in Constance, 1523–1548/49.

———. "Blarer, Ambrosius, 1492–1564." In *Theologische Realenzyklopädie,* vol. 6, pp. 711–715. Berlin and New York, 1980. Best survey of sources and literature up to 1980.

———. "Bucer und die Geschwister Blarer." In *Martin Bucer and Sixteenth Century Europe: Actes du colloque de Strasbourg, 28–31 août 1991,* edited by Christian Krieger and Marc Lienhard, pp. 441–450. Studies in Medieval and Reformation Thought 52 and 53. Leiden and New York, 1993.

Moeller, Bernd, ed. *Der Konstanzer Reformator Ambrosius Blarer, 1492–1564.* Constance, 1964. Biographical essays; work as poet and preacher; relationships to Bucer, Bullinger, and Zwingli.

Oberman, Heiko. *Werden und Wertung der Reformation: Vom Wegestreit zum Glaubenskampf.* Late Scholasticism and Reformation 2. Tübingen, 1989. Blarer's relationship to the University of Tübingen (study, university reform).

Pressel, Theodor. *Ambrosius Blaurer's des schwäbischen Reformators Leben und Schriften.* Stuttgart, 1861. Most recent full-length biography; includes a list of original sources.

Rublack, Hans-Christoph. *Die Einführung der Reformation in Konstanz von den Anfängen bis zum Abschluß 1531.* Quellen und Forschungen zur Reformationsgeschichte 40. Gütersloh, 1971.

HANS-PETER HASSE

BLARER, Thomas (also Blaurer; 1492?–1567), German humanist, jurist, theological student (at Wittenberg), politician, and reformer of the imperial city of Constance. Brother of Ambrosius, he was born around 1492 in Constance (southern Germany) to a city councilman, Augustine Blarer, and his wife, Katherine Mässlin. Thomas pursued legal studies at Freiburg im Breisgau from 1514 to 1519 and then studied theology under Martin Luther at Wittenberg. From 1537 to 1547 he served as mayor of Constance. His correspondence regarding his exposure to Lutheran teachings contributed to his brother Ambrosius's conversion and eventual departure from the Benedictine monastery in Alpirsbach (southwest of Tübingen). In 1548 Thomas was forced to flee Constance. On 19 March 1567 he died in Gyrsburg, Thurgau (in northeastern Switzerland).

Few primary sources are available on Blarer. The key resource is the two-volume work *Briefwechsel der Brüder Ambrosius und Thomas Blaurer,* edited by Traugott Schiess (Freiburg im Breisgau, 1908–1912). From this correspondence various secondary sources have made mention of Thomas and his contribution to the Reformation.

In letters from 1520 to 1521 to his brother Ambrosius (1492–1564), Thomas, the theology student, praised Luther and his followers as true Christians rightly understanding and teaching the holy scriptures. He emphasized Luther's role as a pastor and preacher and early in 1521 used Luther as his confessor.

The Blarer brothers, both the lesser-known Thomas and the better-known Ambrosius, could very well provide access to the further understanding of certain particularities of the south German Reformation. In his *Imperial Cities and the Reformation* Bernd Moeller has noted that the imperial cities of south Germany appeared more receptive to Protestantism owing to the presence and participation of a lower class of artisans in their governments (Strasbourg and Memmingen becoming solely Protestant in 1529, with opposition led by a patrician magistracy). Constance, however, provided an exception, as the magistracy, led by a patrician class, including members of the Blarer family, initiated and sustained the Reformation in that city from 1528 to 1548.

Reasons justifying resistance to or acceptance of Protestantism in the imperial cities were similar. Two churches threatened unity and peace in the cities. The magistracy could maintain the status quo or risk the transition to a new faith. In Constance the Blarers lived through the change. Thomas's involvement remains a matter for further study.

In 1548 the Blarer family was not to survive another transition of faiths in Constance. In 1528 Austrian Habsburg pressure had allowed the Catholic bishop to remain in Protestant Constance. In 1548 Constance became one of twenty-eight cities to lose its imperial status under the Habsburg *Anschluss.* Catholicism dominated once more, and Ambrosius and Thomas were expelled from the city.

Besides the correspondence with his brother, Thomas is known to have written a defense of the 1529 execution of the south German Anabaptist Ludwig Hätzer (*Wie Ludwig Hetzer zu Constantz mit dem schwert gericht vsz disem zit abgeschaydem ist Constantz*). Samuel MacCauley Jackson made a case for a possible third work by Thomas Blarer in his 1912 English edition of Huldrych Zwingli's early works. In the early nineteenth century Melchior Schuler and Johannes Schultess, producing an edition of Zwingli's works, included two seemingly related short works entitled *Consilium homins ex animo satisfactum cupientis et Romanae sedis dignitati et Christiani orbis paci (Consilium cuiusdam ex animo cupientis esse consultum et pontificis dignitati et Christianae religionis tranquilliati)* and *Apologia Christi dni nostri pro Martino Luthero ad urban Rhoman.* They felt that both works reflected Zwingli's desire for a conciliatory spirit between Roman Catholicism and Protestantism. The fourth edition of Zwingli's works, however, produced by Georg Finsler and Emil Egli and included in the *Corpus Reformatorum,* noted certain of Zwingli's own allusions in his *Suggestio* and attributed the *Consilium* to Desiderius Erasmus and the *Apologia* to Thomas Blarer. Both were written in late 1520. Erasmus's *Consilium* is conciliatory in tone and seeks reform of scholastic theology, suggesting that Luther be read and thus instructed to the mutual benefit of the church and the reformer. Written in the first person singular, Blarer's *Apologia* is condemnatory, with Christ pronouncing judgment against Rome and its abuses. Blarer, then a student of Luther, would have written out of concern for faithfulness to the reformer's teachings.

Blarer's brother Ambrosius, a former Benedictine, is important for understanding the south German Reformation. But Thomas Blarer the politician—the son of a councilman and himself mayor of Constance during its last decade as a Protestant imperial city—also deserves further study. The scarcity of sources may well keep this reformer and politician little known.

BIBLIOGRAPHY

Brady, Thomas A., Jr. "In Search of the Godly City: The Domestication of Religion in the German Urban Reformation." In *The German People and the Reformation,* edited by R. Po-chia Hsia, pp. 14–31. Ithaca, N.Y., 1988.

Brecht, Martin. *Martin Luther: His Road to Reformation, 1483–1521.* Translated by James L. Schaaf. Philadelphia, 1985.

Hillerbrand, Hans J. *Anabaptist Bibliography, 1520–1630.* Saint Louis, 1991.

Jackson, Samuel Macauley, ed. *Ulrich Zwingli: Early Writings.* Durham, N.C., 1987.

Kellenbenz, Herman. "Les grands marchands de l'Allemagne du sud et la Réforme." In *Les Réformes: Enracinement socio-culturel,* edited by Bernard Chevalier and Robert Sauzet, pp. 161–167. Paris, 1985.

Moeller, Bernd. *Imperial Cities and the Reformation.* Edited and translated by H. C. Erik Midelfort and Mark U. Edwards, Jr. Durham, N.C., 1982.

Oberman, Heiko A. *Masters of the Reformation.* Cambridge, 1981.

Ozment, Steven E. *The Reformation in the Cities: The Appeal of Protestantism to Sixteenth-Century Germany and Switzerland.* New Haven, 1980.

PAUL DOUGLAS LESLIE

BLAUROCK, Georg

BLAUROCK, Georg (also Jörg Cajacob; c.1492–1529), Swiss Anabaptist founder and early leader, called "Strong George" and the "Second Paul" because of his decisive leadership. He came from Bonaduz, a village west of Chur in the Grisons (Graubünden). He studied at Leipzig in 1513, thereafter serving as pastor at Trins, near Chur, from 1516 to 1518. His marriage in 1523 signaled a break with the medieval Catholic church.

He appeared in Zurich in 1525, participating in the first baptismal debates in January, where he was called "Blaurock" because he wore a blue coat. He was the first to be baptized by Conrad Grebel as an adult believer during a gathering at the home of Felix Mantz on 21 January. He in turn baptized those present who requested it.

Blaurock was linked closely with Grebel and Mantz in the emergence of the nascent Anabaptist movement in the Zurich region. The depositions of the Anabaptists who were arrested often mention him. On two occasions in 1525 he created a public offense by interfering with the appointed pastors of Zollikon (Nicolaus Billeter, 29 January) and Hinwil (Hans Brennwald, 8 October) during Sunday worship. The first occasion likely precipitated the first general arrest of the radicals by the Zurich city council on 30 January.

Freed from prison on 18 February, he was reportedly preaching and baptizing in the Zollikon area in the days following. He was incarcerated at least three more times in Zurich before being beaten and driven out of town on the day of Felix Mantz's execution, 5 January 1527.

Blaurock never returned to Zurich but continued his Anabaptist mission work in the Bernese and Appenzeller regions of Switzerland. He appeared in the Tirol in 1529, where he frequently visited numerous radical congregations. Arrested in August 1529, Blaurock was burned at the stake in Clausen on 6 September 1529. The significance of Blaurock lies not only in his pioneering leadership of Swiss-Austrian Anabaptists but also in his effective activity among rural rather than urban radical congregations.

BIBLIOGRAPHY

Harder, Leland, ed. *The Sources of Swiss Anabaptism: The Grebel Letters and Related Documents.* Classics of the Radical Reformation, vol. 4. Scottdale, Pa., 1985. English translations of the most important writings of the early years of Swiss Anabaptism, providing access to numerous references to Blaurock especially as found in proceedings of the Zurich city council.

Moore, John Allen. *Der Starke Jörg: Die Geschichte Jörg Blaurocks, des Täufers und Missionars.* Kassel, 1955. General biographical treatment within the context of the Zurich reformation. Contains the text of two hymns from the 1583 Anabaptist hymnal (the *Ausbund*) that are attributed to Blaurock.

Neff, Christian. "Blaurock (Cajacob), Georg." In *The Mennonite Encyclopedia,* edited by Cornelius Krahn, vol. 1, pp. 354–359. Scottdale, Pa., 1955. Overview of the known biographical details of the life and works of Blaurock.

Vasella, Oskar. "Von den Anfängen der bündnerischen Täuferbewegung." *Zeitschrift für Schweizerische Geschichte* 19.2 (1939), 165–184. Places Blaurock within the context of the Anabaptist movement in the Grisons.

H. WAYNE PIPKIN

BOCKELSON, Jan.

BOCKELSON, Jan. *See* John of Leiden.

BOCSKAY, Stephen

BOCSKAY, Stephen (Hung., István; 1556–1606), first Calvinist prince of Transylvania. A large landowner in Hungary, Bocskay made a career as a successful general in the war against the Turks and as a prominent pro-Habsburg councilor in the client state of Transylvania during the 1590s. After 1600, however, he was alienated and driven into opposition by Emperor Rudolf II's brutal attack on the country's political and religious freedoms. Bocskay now assumed the leadership of an insurrection against imperial authority that quickly gained ground, helped by the freebooting ex-soldiers known as hajducks, who had served in the Habsburgs' Turkish campaigns and now demanded their reward. In 1605 he gained recognition as prince by both the Transylvanian and the Hungarian estates.

Although he was widely welcomed by Protestants, the vast majority of Hungary's population, as a liberator against Catholic tyranny, Bocskay's position remained insecure. His troops were impossible to control properly and were no match for imperial forces in open battle; while the political elite of Hungary, loath to depose the Habsburg dynasty altogether, fearful of losing power, and terrified by hajduck excesses, sought to use his insurrection as a bargaining chip, and to drive a wedge between Rudolf and his ambitious younger brother, Matthias. In 1606 negotiations with Matthias on these lines led to the Peace of Vienna, by which Bocskay was excluded from influence in Hungary but confirmed as hereditary prince of Transylvania. Bocskay accepted the settlement in August of that year but died suddenly on 29 December, amid unfounded suspicions of poisoning.

A tough and taciturn commander, imbued with a sense of religious mission that has earned him comparison to William of Orange and Oliver Cromwell, Bocskay's achievement in the history of the Reformation is to have established the international political significance of Hungarian Protestantism and to have secured its future. Although he ruled Transylvania only briefly and left no heir, Bocskay initiated a series of elected Calvinist rulers in the principality, among whom the most famous was Gabriel Bethlen (r. 1613–1629). Besides favoring their own church within Transylvania, they maintained toleration for Lutherans and Unitarians (as well as Catholics and Greek Orthodox) there; at the same time they were able to help defend Protestants in the rest of Hungary from the pressures of the Habsburg-led Counter-Reformation.

Among the most fervent and indomitable of Hungary's Calvinists were the descendants of Bocskay's hajducks, who at his personal insistence gained a privileged status and the grant of lands in the east of the country, around Debrecen. Bocskay's memory thus lived on as that of a patriotic warlord and religious leader with the common touch; as such he appears on the Reformation monument in Geneva.

BIBLIOGRAPHY

Benda, Kálmán. *A Bocskai-szabadságharc.* Budapest, 1955. Standard account, stressing the popular character of Bocskay's revolt.

———. "Hungary in Turmoil, 1580–1620." *European Studies Review* 8 (1978), 281–304. Accessible survey of the troubled conditions in which Bocskay flourished.

Makkai, László. "A bocskai-felkelés." In *Magyarország története, 1526–1686,* 2 vols., edited by Zsigmond Pál Pach and Agnes R. Várkonyi, pp. 709–773. Budapest, 1985. Latest survey, with full bibliography.

Molnár, Andrea. *Fürst Stefan Bocskay als Staatsmann und Persönlichkeit im Spiegel seiner Briefe, 1598–1606.* Munich, 1983. Outlines Bocskay's life and prints some of his letters.

R. J. W. EVANS

BODENSTEIN VON KARLSTADT, Andreas

(also Andreas Rudolff Bodenstein from Karlstadt; Carlstadt; 1486–1541), German theologian and radical reformer. Born at the Franconian territorial city of Karlstadt am Main, he studied at Erfurt (1499/1500–1503; bachelor of arts, 1502), Cologne (1502–1505), and Wittenberg (1505–1510; master of arts, 1505). As an instructor in the arts faculty of the University of Wittenberg, he represented the Thomistic scholastic tradition, but from the time of his first publications (*De intentionibus* and *Distinctiones Thomistarum,* 1507), he also sought to build bridges to Scotism. In 1510 Karlstadt concluded his theological studies with a doctorate. A year later he became archdeacon of All Saints collegiate church at Wittenberg, a position that also conferred a professorship of theology in the university. He broadened his education by studying jurisprudence, and during a stay in Rome (from about November 1515 to May 1516) the Curia Romana awarded him the degree of doctor in both civil and canon law. Karlstadt's efforts between 1514 and 1518 to bind theology and jurisprudence closely together stemmed from this program of studies.

Shaping Karlstadt's development in these years was a variety of intellectual and religious influences—above all, humanistic influences, including the study of Hebrew, the Cabbalistic works of Johannes Reuchlin, Martin Luther's new theology, Augustine and other church fathers, Bernard of Clairvaux, and the mysticism of Johannes Tauler. These influences flowed together in Karlstadt and effected a complete break with his own scholastic past. When Luther set forth his theology, oriented toward Paul and Augustine, in the disputation *De viribus et voluntate hominis sine gratia* in September 1516, Karlstadt at first opposed Luther; then he revised his judgment on the basis of works by Augustine. On 27 April 1517 Karlstadt supported Luther's position "against all the scholastics" with 152 theses (*De natura, lege et gratia*). For nearly the next two years Karlstadt lectured on Augustine's *De spiritu et littera,* which defined his temporary Augustinianism.

Karlstadt opened the conflict between the Wittenberg theologians and Johann Eck with the *Apologeticae conclusiones* of 9 May 1518. Here, as at the Leipzig Disputation of June and July 1519, Karlstadt defended his thesis about humankind's incapacity to will the good and its passivity in the reception of divine grace. After the Leipzig Disputation Karlstadt turned from the study of the church fathers to the Bible, and in August 1520 he published *De canonicis scripturis libellus,* an introduction to the Bible derived from Jerome and Augustine. Karlstadt's definition of the Old Testament canon according to the Hebraic Bible, as well as his complete acceptance of the traditional canon of the New Testament, generally prevailed in Protestantism. This work also made public for the first time Karlstadt's differences with Luther: Karlstadt defended himself against Luther's rejection of the canonical letter of James. In this context Karlstadt began to develop his abiding interest in the sanctification of the justified.

After the Diet of Worms (April–May 1521) Elector Frederick III of Saxony wanted Karlstadt to seek refuge at the Danish court while he protected Luther at Wartburg castle. Karlstadt, however, returned from Copenhagen after a stay of only about two weeks. In the following period he wrote against clerical celibacy and monastic vows. In the fall of 1521 the reformation of the city of Wittenberg began; one after another the reforms that had been demanded in the previous years were realized. Initially it was Philipp Melanchthon and the Augustinian monk Gabriel Zwilling who held positions of leadership, but beginning on Christmas 1521 Karlstadt stepped to the forefront of the "Wittenberg movement." At Christmas he celebrated the first public evangelical mass. On 19 January 1522 he, a priest, married Anna von Mochau, who was about fifteen years old. On 24 January he prevailed upon the city council to adopt the "New Order for the City of Wittenberg," in which religious and social reforms were tightly unified. Karlstadt's vision was of a "Christian city of Wittenberg" that would be configured according to biblical law. After the introduction of a mass modeled on Christ's example in the New Testament, the issue that commanded special attention was the abolition of cult images, a demand based on the Old Testament's prohibition of images. In his pamphlet *Vom Abtun der Bilder,* (On the Abolition of Images) Karlstadt pressed for the orderly removal of images, a task to be undertaken by the city council, but he unleashed an iconoclastic storm in the Wittenberg parish church. Frederick III, whose authority had been passed over in the promulgation of the city's reform legislation, now attempted—with only limited success—to curtail the reforms. In this context, Luther returned to Wittenberg. In his *Invocavit Sermons* (9–16 March 1522) Luther presented a justification of his claim to leadership on the basis of being the first-called among the reformers. Karlstadt was marginalized with the assistance of a university prohibition against his publishing anything. Theologically, Luther demanded that the weak, whom he thought should not be antagonized by the reforms, should be protected. Subsequently, in November 1524 at Basel, Karlstadt was able to publish his reply, *Ob man gemach fahren und des Ärgernisses der Schwachen verschonen soll in Sachen, so Gottes Willen angehen* (Whether One Should Proceed Slowly and Avoid Offending the Weak in Matters That Concern God's Will). According to Karlstadt, offense was always present when the status quo did not agree with scripture.

Karlstadt's public activities at Wittenberg were now restricted to teaching. In the fall of 1522, however, he preached at Jáchymov (Joachimsthal), and one of these sermons, *Ein Sermon von Stand der christgläubigen Seelen* (A Sermon on the Condition of the Souls that Believe in Christ), in which he challenged the existence of purgatory, was printed in Nuremberg at the end of 1522. Another tract on the same theme, published by Karlstadt in Nuremberg and opposed to the invocation of Mary's intervention for the dead, was *Eine Frage, ob auch jemand möge selig werden ohne die Fürbitte Marias* (A Question Whether Anyone May Be Saved Without the Intervention of Mary; July 1523, published 1524).

From 1523 Karlstadt temporarily rejected an academic career. This occurred in the context of a broad development of his mystical theology that he presented in two main writings: *Von Mannigfaltigkeit des einfältigen Willens Gottes* (On the Manifoldness of the Unity of God's Will; March 1523), and *Was gesagt ist: Sich gelassen* (On the Saying: Let Yourself Go; April 1523). A spiritualistic doctrine of revelation, which had long been implicit in Karlstadt's theology, is most explicitly expressed in the *Dialogus . . . von dem greulichen und abgöttischen Missbrauch des hochwürdigsten Sakraments Jesu Christi* (Dialogue . . . about the Horrible and Idolatrous Misuse of the Most Revered Sacrament of Jesus Christ; fall 1524). In the spring of 1523 Karlstadt received permission to minister personally to the Thuringian parish of Orlamünde, located on the river Saale, which was part of his archdeaconate. Here he was able, at least provisionally, to realize his model of a communal reformation: a democratic-synodical community constitution; an evangelical mass; the abolition of images, auricular confession, and fasting; an evangelical system of poor relief; and the curtailment of infant baptism. With the help of the Jena printer Michel Buchführer, Karlstadt was able to publish seven writings. When the university was about to call him back to Wittenberg in an effort to stem his influence, the congregation at Orlamünde elected him to be its pastor. On 22 July 1524 he re-

signed his archdeaconate. On 21 August 1524 a fruitless conversation between Luther and Karlstadt took place at Jena. In September Karlstadt was exiled from Saxony.

On a journey through southwestern Germany (Strasbourg, Basel, and Zurich), Karlstadt established contact with proto-Anabaptists. A *Dialogus* on infant baptism, whose printing Johannes Oecolampadius prevented in 1524 at Basel, was anonymously published at Speyer in 1527. Karlstadt rejected infant baptism without demanding a rebaptism. At Basel several additional tracts by Karlstadt on the doctrine of the Lord's Supper were published; in these works Karlstadt repudiated Luther's doctrine of the real presence of Christ's blood in the wine.

From December 1524 until the end of March 1525, Karlstadt gained influence with the reform movement in the Franconian city of Rothenburg ob der Tauber. During the Peasants' War he was caught between the fronts: Luther branded him as a rebel, but in fact he sought to dissuade the Franconian peasantry from using violence. He finally renounced further public activity, and in exchange Luther secretly gave him refuge (July 1525). Karlstadt's forced repudiation of his doctrine concerning the Lord's Supper was a condition that could not last in the long run. He was granted asylum, but his mobility was restricted to the immediate environs of Wittenberg, where he lived first as a peasant, and then as a petty merchant. His influence, however, had not been eradicated. At the start of 1529 he evaded arrest by fleeing electoral Saxony. Karlstadt was unable to participate in the Flensburg Disputation, where he planned to support Melchior Hoffman against Johannes Bugenhagen. He was expelled from Kiel in April 1529. Between August 1529 and January 1530 Karlstadt launched a reform program in the area around Oldersum, south of Emden, but Lutheran authorities suppressed these activities.

With the help of Huldrych Zwingli, Karlstadt found a position from 1530 to 1534 as a deacon at the Grossmünster in Zurich, a residency that was interrupted by a stay as a parish administrator at Altstätten in the Rhine valley. At Zurich he was active as both a preacher and teacher at the so-called *Prophezei*. In June 1534 he became professor of Old Testament at the University of Basel and pastor of Saint Peter's church. For his inaugural disputation he composed a brief systematic overview of his theology (*Axiomata disputationis*, January 1535). Karlstadt made the notion of humanity created in the image of God (*imago dei*)—which he identified with mysticism's divine spark of the soul—the central concept of his theology. The first justification is a regeneration of the image of God in the form of the image of Christ. The second justification—sanctification—is the subsequent unfolding, in a psychological condition of abandonment, of the divine will, which is written in the heart. In connection with his exegetical lectures, Karlstadt also taught Hebrew; he acquainted himself with literature and read on secular law and medical subjects. An alphabetically organized theological encyclopedia (*Loci communes sacrae scripturae*) remained incomplete when Karlstadt died on 24 December 1541.

It is a safe assumption that Karlstadt's activities as a publicist had a major impact; he produced about ninety published writings, which were printed in about 213 editions. Among evangelical authors during the years 1518–1525, Karlstadt, after Luther, published the largest number of works in German; and, after Luther's, his works had the second-largest number of editions. Karlstadt's battles against images and against Luther's doctrine of the Lord's Supper influenced the whole course of the Reformation in Germany. Although the strength of the movement among Karlstadt's followers reached its high point in 1523, for decades afterward Lutheran polemicists had to deal with his influence. Karlstadt's writings continued to be read secretly. Major spiritualists in later decades passed on Karlstadt's ideas in a variety of ways. Karlstadt's theology of regeneration and sanctification made him a precursor of Pietism. The mystic Valentin Weigel (1533–1588) and his followers were major mediators of Karlstadt's heritage between the Reformation and the age of pietism. At the start of the eighteenth century Karlstadt was rehabilitated by Gottfried Arnold (*Unparteiische Kirchen- und Ketzerhistorie* [Impartial History of the Church and Heresy]; 1699/1700) and by the Pietists at Halle.

BIBLIOGRAPHY

Primary Sources

Baylor, Michael G., ed. *The Radical Reformation.* Cambridge, 1991. See pp. 33–35, 49–73 for an English translation of two writings of Karlstadt of 1524.
Hertzsch, Erich, ed. *Karlstadt's Schriften aus den Jahren 1523–25.* 2 vols. Halle, 1956–57. The only modern edition of some of Karlstadt's German works is no longer available but remains important because of the absence of a complete edition of his writings.
Sider, Ronald J., ed. *Karlstadt's Battle with Luther: Documents in a Liberal-Radical Debate.* Philadelphia, 1978. Offers a selection of sources on the conflict between Luther and Karlstadt in the years 1522–1525.

Secondary Sources

Barge, Hermann. *Andreas Bodenstein von Karlstadt* (1905). 2 vols. Reprint, Nieuwkoop, 1968. The classic biography, which has not been superseded; takes a stand in favor of Karlstadt and against the Lutheran polemic. Incorrect in many of its dates.
Bubenheimer, Ulrich. *Consonantia theologiae et iurisprudentiae: Andreas Bodenstein von Karlstadt als Theologe und Jurist zwischen Scholastik und Reformation.* Tübingen, 1977. This work reveals the importance for Karlstadt's theology of his study of jurisprudence, which is partly situated in the larger context of the traditions to which he was heir. Source materials appear as an appendix.
Freys, Ernst, and Hermann Barge. *Verzeichnis der gedruckten Schriften des Andreas Bodenstein von Karlstadt* (1903). Reprint, Nieuwkoop, 1965. This bibliography remains the standard work, but it is incomplete.
Pater, Calvin Augustine. *Karlstadt as the Father of the Baptist Movements: The Emergence of Lay Protestantism* (1984). Reprint, Lewiston, N.Y., 1993. Pater examines Karlstadt's influence on the Anabaptists but exaggerates this topic in a speculative way. Numerous errors in the dates.
Preus, James S. *Carlstadt's "Ordinaciones" and Luther's Liberty: A Study of the Wittenberg Movement, 1521–22.* Cambridge, Mass., 1974. Traces the differences between Luther and Karlstadt in the years 1521–1522 to differing reform strategies rather than to theological differences. This approach corrects the one-sided view of the conflict as purely theological but also introduces a new one-sidedness.
Sider, Ronald J. *Andreas Bodenstein von Karlstadt: The Development of His Thought, 1517–1525.* Leiden, 1974. Emphasizes Karlstadt's "theology of regeneration" in the years 1523–1525. In comparison with the image of Karlstadt in Lutheran scholarship, the theological differences between Luther and Karlstadt are minimized. Current research is seeking to mediate between the two positions.
Zorzin, Alejandro. *Karlstadt als Flugschriftenautor.* Göttingen, 1990. Zorzin demonstrates through statistical analysis the enormous distribution of Karlstadt's German writings. Supplements the bibliography of Freys and Barge, which Zorzin also in part follows uncritically.

ULRICH BUBENHEIMER
Translated from German by Michael G. Baylor

BODIN, Jean (1529/30–1596), humanist and jurist. Bodin was one of the great humanist polyhistors of the later Renaissance. Despite an active career in public service, he was engaged throughout his life in an encyclopedic program of research and erudition that he had projected in his early years. Some sense of the scope of his interests can be gathered from his *Methodus ad facilem historiarum cognitionem* (1566). The vast corpus of his writings includes major contributions in almost every area of social thought, moral philosophy, cosmology, natural philosophy, and theology. His thought, no doubt, is sometimes credulous, for his Platonizing view of nature lent itself to a belief in numerology and astrology as well as to a fear of witchcraft (*De la demonomanie des sorciers*, 1580). But the originality and power of most of what he wrote is nonetheless impressive.

Bodin is celebrated most of all for his *Six livres de la république*, a massive treatise on comparative law and politics that appeared 1576. The theory of sovereignty, which provides its framework, is the first systematic exploration of that concept, and it served to establish the scientific study of public law in its modern form. Furthermore, in one of its aspects this exploration was of great ideological importance. Bodin believed, erroneously, that the prerogatives of sovereignty, or high powers of governance, could not be divided but had to be concentrated in a single individual or group. He thus arrived at an absolutist interpretation of the French kingship as well as the Spanish and the English, which provided a conservative reply to the constitutionalist and resistance doctrines engendered by the Wars of Religion. Although he held that the power of the king was limited, morally at least, by the law of nature and certain fundamental laws, Bodin's concept of absolute royal sovereignty seemed by contemporary notions to make all forcible resistance to a ruler illegitimate.

Bodin's religious thought was elaborate and is of extraordinary interest. Although outwardly a Catholic, his lifelong search for true religion led him far afield, and he was under suspicion of heresy at every phase of his career. Indeed, his dialogue on religion, the *Colloquium heptaplomeres de rerum sublimium arcanis abditis* (Colloquium of the Seven about Secrets of the Sublime), probably written in 1593, remained unpublished until the nineteenth century and achieved its notoriety among thinkers of the seventeenth and eighteenth centuries only through the circulation of manuscript copies.

Bodin's mature religious thought, as represented in the *Colloquium heptaplomeres*, is a kind of Judaizing Neoplatonism. Reason enables humans to recognize that God exists, that he intervenes in the cosmos by means of angels and demons, and that he reveals his purposes for history and nature to the prophets he inspires. This rational insight into God and the cosmos is latent in all humans and is the core of all the monotheistic religions. But the truest of these religions is Judaism in that its prophets and commentators confirm and elaborate the deepest truths about God's relation to the creation. Indeed, the last and longest book of the dialogue is mostly taken up by what amounts to a detailed critique of the theological claims of Christianity in that the three Christian interlocutors seem to be repeatedly bested by the others. But the ultimate message of the book is not the triumph of any one religion. None of the seven interlocutors—a skeptic, a natural philosopher, a Jew, a Muslim, a Lutheran, a Calvinist, and a Catholic—is driven to yield his position. All agree that the differences among them cannot be resolved, that sincere worship in any of the positive religions is pleasing to God, and that they will henceforth agree to disagree in the tolerant spirit of Venice, where the colloquium is laid.

Bodin's religious thought is of great interest for the development of religious universalism, natural theology, and the idea of toleration. His actual recommendations on religious policy, in the *Colloquium heptaplomeres* and in the *République*, although not especially generous and roughly *politique* in spirit, were cautiously liberal for their time. Bodin would outlaw public debate on religion under any circumstances, since it would undermine religious piety and political order by encouraging a habit of doubting authority. Where religious uniformity existed, it was to be preserved no matter what its character, since atheism was worse than superstition and a believer in the true religion could maintain his or her faith in private. Nonetheless, forced conversion is always to be shunned and where a religious minority is numerous, limited toleration is less demoralizing to piety and less dangerous to the state than forcible suppression.

BIBLIOGRAPHY

Primary Sources

Bodin, Jean. *Colloquium Heptaplomeres.* Princeton, 1975. An English translation.
———. *Les six livres de la Republique* (1576). Paris, 1986.

Secondary Sources

Chauviré, Roger. *Jean Bodin auteur de la "République"* (1914). Reprint, Geneva, 1969. Although now outdated in some aspects, still a useful treatment of Bodin's political thought as a whole.
Denzer, Horst, ed., *Verhandlungen der internationalen Bodin Tagung in München.* Munich, 1973. Comprehensive scholarly bibliography of Bodin's major works. Also contains a very extensive bibliography of secondary works as well as a number of important scholarly articles on divers aspects of Bodin's life and thought.
Franklin, Julian H. *Jean Bodin and the Rise of Absolutist Theory.* Cambridge, 1973. Critical analysis of the genesis, structure, and ideological impact of Bodin's theory of sovereignty.
Goyard-Fabre, Simone. *Jean Bodin et le droit de la republique.* Paris, 1989. Useful running commentary on the overall system of the *République.* Includes an extensive bibliography of secondary works.
Mesnard, Pierre. "La pensée religieuse de Bodin." *Revue du seizième siècle* 16 (1929), 77–121. Judicious treatment of Bodin's religious thought by the most eminent of Bodin's commentators. There is no book-length study by Mesnard, but for listings of his numerous articles on many aspects of Bodin's thought and biography, see the bibliographies in Denzer and Goyard-Fabre.
Rose, Paul Lawrence. *Bodin and the Great God of Nature: the Moral and Religious Universe of a Judaiser.* Geneva, 1980. Thorough study of Bodin's religious thought with special emphasis on its Judaizing component.

JULIAN H. FRANKLIN

BOEYENS, Adrian Florensz. *See* Adrian VI.

BOGERMANNUS, Johannes (1576–1637), Dutch Calvinist minister and theologian. This Frisian theologian made his *peregrinatio academica* to universities in Franeker, Heidelberg, Geneva, Zurich, Lausanne, and, unusually, Oxford and Cambridge. He was church minister in Sneek (Friesland) in 1599, Enkhuizen (Holland) in 1603 and Leeuwarden (Friesland) in 1604. He became professor in the academy of Franeker in 1636. He delivered an inaugural lecture, *Tractatus theologicus de salutari usu judiciorum Dei, orationibus aliquot absolutus*, in Franeker (1627).

As a theologian and minister Bogermannus played an important role in the history of the Reformed church in Friesland and in the Dutch Republic in general. While at Sneek he translated into Dutch Théodore de Bèze's *De haeretici a civili magi stratu puniendis* (1601). He was chairman of the synods of Friesland in 1605, 1610, and 1615. His role in the Synod of Dordrecht (1618–1619) is well known: the chairman with his long beard, who severely criticized the Contra-Remonstrants and sent them away from the synod. One of his most important works was his participation in the translation of the Old Testament into Dutch, the famous *Statenbijbel*, finished in 1637. He also had a good reputation as a Hebrew scholar.

He did not publish many theological works. One of his smaller books was a description of the death of Prince Maurice of Nassau, published in Dutch, *Het chrisatelijck over-*

lijden van den doorluchtichsten ende hooghgheboren prince, Mauritius van Nassau (1625). Bogermannus's importance lies in his defense of Calvinist orthodoxy and in particular the doctrine of predestination. His works contain few original observations.

BIBLIOGRAPHY

Kalma, J. J. *Johannes Bogerman, Voorzitter der Dordtse synode, 1618/19, en Bijbelvertaler: Bibliografie van de geschriften van en over hem.* Leeuwarden, 1977. Nearly complete bibliography.

Tuuk, H. Edema van der. *Johannes Bogerman.* Groningen, 1868. Contains an interpretation of all the primary and secondary sources. Still the most important biography.

WIEBE BERGSMA

BÖHEIM, Hans (also Behem; d. 1476), German lay preacher known as the "Piper of Niklashausen." He probably came from the village of Helmstadt, located between Würzburg and Wertheim. The year of his birth is not known. In 1476, when he appeared as a prophetic lay preacher, he was a young musician (drummer and piper) and herdsman in bondage.

From the spring of 1476 he preached in front of the pilgrimage church of Niklashausen in the Tauber Valley. The occasion was a miraculous appearance of an image of the Virgin Mary. He felt himself a prophet of the Mother of God. With reliance on her, he connected radical criticisms of the prevailing conditions in church and society with visions of a future world of universal equality, in which only God was lord. As far as the sources reveal, he rejected papal claims to power and called for a ruthless fight against the clergy, the implementation of the rule of poverty for priests, and their exclusion from secular affairs. He believed that all secular authorities, including emperors and princes, should be rejected; that interest, tithes, taxes, and duties, as well as all feudal services, should be done away with; and that forests, meadows, and waters, along with hunting and fishing, should be free. Specific theological demands focused on the rejection of excommunication, the prohibition of divorce, and the denial of purgatory.

It is telling evidence of the social and religious restlessness among the people that Böheim's sermons found great and widespread resonance. Pilgrims from Bavaria, Swabia, Hesse, the Rhineland and Alsace, and Thuringia and Saxony came to hear the young prophet. At the end of June 1476, as the situation became threatening for the authorities, they prohibited pilgrimages to Niklashausen and prevailed upon the bishop of Würzburg, Rudolf von Scherenberg, to arrest Böheim. This took place on 12 July. In front of the palace in Würzburg a crowd demanding his release was dispersed by the bishop's armed guards. Böheim was burned at the stake as a heretic in Würzburg on 19 July.

There is disagreement as to the extent that Böheim's program rested on the influences of Waldensians, Jan Hus, and reform programs such as the *Reformatio Sigismundi* and the extent to which he himself had appropriated these notions (or whether he was only the mouthpiece of other instigators). The sources do not permit a definite conclusion, but circumstances indicate that his was an independent treatment and reflection of widespread discord among the people, which later formed the sounding board for the Reformation.

BIBLIOGRAPHY

Arnold, Klaus. *Niklashausen 1476: Quellen und Untersuchunger zur sozialreligiösen Bewegung des Hans Behem und zur Agrarstruktur eines spätmittelalterlichen Dorfes.* Baden-Baden, 1980. Basic analysis with edition of the sources and discussion of the bibliogrpahy.

ADOLF LAUBE
Translated from German by Susan M. Sisler

BOHEMIA. The lands of the Crown of Bohemia embraced the kingdom of Bohemia proper, centered on Prague; the margravate of Moravia further east; and to the north the two Lusatias (Upper and Lower), and the miscellaneous duchies of Silesia. Bohemia possesses a peculiar importance in the history of the Reformation, since it witnessed the most significant expression in late medieval Europe of concerns that would subsequently be taken up by the Protestants. Resentment at the rapidly increasing power and corruption of the church became combined during the years after 1400 with ethnic grievances on the part of the majority Czech population over the dominance of Germans in both secular and ecclesiastical life. The outcome was the Hussite movement, which broke with Rome following the martyrdom of Jan Hus, reasserted the pristine purity and poverty of the clergy, placed the church under local lay control, and administered wine as well as bread to communicants.

After striking initial successes the Hussites came under severe international pressure, and the resulting wars divided, devastated, and isolated the country. By 1500 the majority faith among the Czechs was Utraquism, a watered-down version of the earlier creed mainly distinguished (as the name suggests) by the continued role of communion in both kinds (*sub utraque specie*). But the sect of the Bohemian Brethren perpetuated some of the more radical innovations of the Hussites, while Catholicism retained the allegiance of almost all the Germans, who formed the majority of the population in the Lusatias and Silesia, as well as of many Czechs in southern Bohemia and in Moravia. The advent of Martin Luther further complicated the picture, as did the accession to the Bohemian throne in 1526 of the staunchly Catholic dynasty of the Habsburgs.

Luther long remained ignorant of Hussite teachings; but when he became aware of their similarities with his own ideas, he firmly endorsed them. As Lutheranism spread like wildfire during the 1520s and 1530s among the Bohemian Germans, many of whom lived in close proximity to the Saxon border, the Utraquists found themselves in a paradoxical position: tempted by the new doctrine, yet restrained by old animosities as well as by fears that any further changes could jeopardize their hard-won constitutional guarantees. Meanwhile the Bohemian Brethren, likewise entrenched within their separate organization but lacking any firm legal safeguards, extended their membership and broadened their appeal, while extremer sectarians—Anabaptists, antitrinitarians, and others—profited from the high degree of religious toleration that obtained within the Bohemian lands.

This state of flux and license was profoundly disagreeable to the first Habsburg ruler of Bohemia, Archduke Ferdinand (later Emperor Ferdinand I); but for the first twenty years of his reign he could do little to control it, since the powers of the monarchy had been drastically attenuated by war and absentee rule. In 1546–1547, however, the repercussions in Bohemia of the Schmalkald War brought the situation to a head and gave him the opportunity to intervene. The country's Protestants sympathized with the rebellion in Germany, and the diet refused to vote military support for the campaign of imperial retribution undertaken by Ferdinand's brother, Charles V, but they were unable to prevent Habsburg victory, and Ferdinand now took steps to curb heterodoxy; he banned the Bohemian Brethren and renewed the formal prohibitions against all other non-Catholic religions except traditional Utraquism. A few years later he revived the defunct archbishopric of Prague and established the first Jesuit college in the city in order to promote the Counter-Reformation.

For the time being the practical effect of these steps was strictly limited. Protestantism continued to advance, and its leaders among the noble estates of the kingdom now increasingly identified their cause with that of political opposition to the Habsburgs. Although some of the Bohemian Brethren were forced into exile in Poland, where they set up a vigorous offshoot, their congregations weathered the storm at home, too, notably in Moravia. Their growing international contacts pointed them more and more in the direction of Calvinist rather than Lutheran theology. With the death of Ferdinand in 1564 and the accession of his open-minded and tolerant son Maximilian (Emperor Maximilian II), a new era opened for Protestants in public life. Mindful of previous experience, they sought constitutional assurances for the free exercise of their religion. At a protracted and dramatic meeting of the diet in 1575, the three main Protestant groups—the established "Old" Utraquists, now in steep decline; the quasi-Lutheran "New" Utraquists, a clear majority of the political nation; and the select but zealous community of the Bohemian Brethren—concerted their efforts to their efforts on the basis of a single *Confessio Bohemica*. Maximilian, who needed their support, gave them the required undertaking, but in the form of a verbal guarantee only, since he was under equal and opposite pressure from his Catholic family and advisers.

The acceptance of the *Confessio Bohemica*, like its immediate eastern European precedents, the Consensus Sendomiriensis in Poland and the Declaration of Torda in Transylvania, represents one of the landmarks of confessional coexistence in Reformation Europe. It did not, however, yield lasting stability in Bohemia. Whereas King Rudolf (Emperor Rudolf II, 1576–1612) held to the spirit of his father's concessions for most of his reign, the forces of international Counter-Reformation, directed by his blood relations in Spain and Bavaria, conspired to undermine them. The Jesuits built on their Prague bridgehead and founded a full-fledged Moravian university at Olomouc in 1579; other limbs of the Catholic body spiritual in Bohemia began to show signs of revival. Moreover, the various Protestant churches still went their separate ways, and those ways led them ever more inextricably into the great political contest of the late sixteenth century between estates and their rulers.

Tension mounted swiftly after 1600, when Rudolf tried to curb Protestant rights and to renew the prohibition of the Bohemian Brethren. Open disaffection broke out in Hungary under Stephen Bocskay and soon spread to the Bohemian lands. The emperor found himself outmaneuvered by his brother, Archduke Matthias, who—though firmly Catholic and guided by his advisor, Bishop (later Cardinal) Melchior Khlesl—saw the need for concessions and made a pact with the dissident estates. Forced back on his support within Bohemia proper, Rudolf in 1609 had to grant the celebrated Letter of Majesty, a full charter of religious freedoms. Lutheran groups and the Bohemian Brethren now began a process of clearer definition and organization, from a position of apparent strength.

Appearances were deceptive, for the Catholic camp retained a core of determined supporters in high places, who associated the promotion of their faith with the best interests of a more centralized and autocratic Habsburg state. After the compromised Matthias succeeded the broken Rudolf, these counter-reformers looked to the fervent, Jesuit-educated Archduke Ferdinand (later Emperor Ferdinand II), whom they managed to impose on the rest of the Bohemian estates as king-designate in 1617. As a new semiofficial campaign against Protestant positions gained momentum, the estates opposition swiftly realized its mistake, and resorted to violence the following year in the Defenestration of Prague. The resultant Bohemian Revolt was openly waged in defense of Protestant rights, and its leaders appealed to coreligionists elsewhere in central Europe (the estates of Austria and Hungary, the Calvinist prince of Transylvania, the Protestant Union in Germany) and beyond (the United

Provinces and the rulers of Great Britain, Denmark, and Sweden); by the same token they took tough measures against the local Catholic community—even though there were token Catholics on the side of insurrection—and expelled the Jesuits. With the deposition of Ferdinand in favor of the Elector Palatine, Frederick V, a prince convinced of his Calvinist calling, the die was cast for Bohemia's Reformation.

Disappointed by its purported foreign allies and weakened by divisions at home, especially between the more or less Lutheran orientation of most Bohemian Protestants and the open Calvinism of the new ruler, the revolt went down before the end of 1620 to a defeat that was sealed at the Battle of White Mountain. The victorious Ferdinand II now took his revenge in terms that were likewise strongly colored by confessional commitment. He banished from the country first Protestant ministers, then by 1628 all Protestant members of the estates unless they accepted conversion: hundreds of nobles emigrated, along with thousands of burghers. The peasantry had no choice but conversion, though many of them managed to find their way into exile, while some kept the faith alive in secret. Only in Silesia were Protestants able, thanks to pressure from abroad, to retain vestiges of toleration (while their coreligionists in Lusatia passed under the sovereignty of the Lutheran Elector of Saxony as the price for the latter's pro-Habsburg policy). Within a decade, one of the largest and in some ways the longest-established of Europe's Protestant communities had been destroyed.

The eclipse of Bohemian Protestantism followed inseparably from the role it came to play in the first phase of the Thirty Years' War. Yet other factors had already reduced its capacity to consolidate itself. Most important were two kinds of division that have already been noted. On the one hand, the Reformation had brought into being parallel and often rival religious groupings, which neither the *Confessio Bohemica* nor the campaign for the Letter of Majesty could draw into lasting harmony. Older and newer kinds of Utraquism were distinguished by the degree of their acceptance of Luther's doctrines and further fragmented by disharmonies between Czech and German believers. The Bohemian Brethren, who gradually shed their extremer aims and came to form a network of close-knit, highly disciplined communities embracing all social classes, were outflanked by miscellaneous sectarians of extremer persuasion. On the other hand, the several territories of the Bohemian crown exhibited no more cohesion on the spiritual front than on the political. Moravian church organization remained quite distinct from Bohemian, and the two sets of leaders held aloof from each other in the periods of constitutional struggle during 1546–1547 and 1606–1609, and even through the crucial first twelve months of the revolt in 1618. Silesia, whose German majority was orientated toward the Empire and whose Polish minority was orientated eastward, showed very little solidarity with developments in Prague until some of the duchies were dragged into the revolt; the Lusatias hardly figured with much consistency in anyone's calculations, except perhaps those of Saxony.

It was in good measure this lack of common purpose that determined Bohemian Protestantism's inadequate response to the increasingly grave situation in which it found itself. Yet disunity was often as much symptom as cause. The Reformation threw up few commanding religious personalities outside the ranks of the Bohemian Brethren—and the contributions of the latter tended to confirm a separate identity, not mold any broader one. Bohemian Lutheranism had its able literary propagators, notably the apostle of the German silver miners, Johannes Mathesius; but the genre looks pallid by comparison with the earlier great days of Hussite moralists and visionaries in the late fourteenth and early fifteenth centuries. Nor did mainstream Lutheranism display much organizational talent: only in the years immediately before 1618 did something like a clear church hierarchy emerge, along with a properly constituted parish structure.

This state of affairs needs to be understood in a squarely political context, for the growing confrontation between, on the one hand, a foreign dynasty that was staunchly Catholic and, on the other, local noble and urban power elites that were already steeped in Utraquism, proved both an opportunity and a tragedy for the Bohemian Protestant cause. It allowed religious dissent to spread, indeed to proliferate, in the interstices of authority; but it tied all larger manifestations of Protestantism ineluctably to the priorities of the political opposition. For decades it seemed as if spiritual reformers could play a waiting game: the Catholic church had, after all, been moribund over much of the country (though less so in Moravia) even before Luther preached his first inflammatory sermon. Yet they had little option, since the royal government remained strong enough to frustrate any general attempt at eliminating Catholic channels of command, especially after the events of 1546–1547. Only 1609 brought a change in this respect; but by that time the Counter-Reformation had begun to bite, and any encroachment on the privileges of the Church of Rome now encountered the fiercest resistance.

The Reformation century in Bohemia nevertheless yielded major achievements. The very plurality of religious experience and the atmosphere of comparative toleration left the country receptive to the cosmopolitan culture of the late Renaissance. Belatedly, humanist learning began to flourish in the area, much of it closely involved with Christian themes (the Bible of Kralice, published by the Bohemian Brethren, forms its greatest monument), and education made striking advances. Even though the historic Charles University of Prague, devastated by the Hussite wars, could not retain its European reputation, it served effectively as the seminary for a network of grammar school teachers in the numerous towns of Bohemia. Increasing numbers of students also went abroad, especially to the Protestant universities of Germany, and contacts were strengthened with coreligionists farther afield.

The culmination of these trends can be seen in the career of the famous philosopher, pedagogue, and theologian Jan Amos Comenius, who was born in Moravia in 1592 and grew up under the spell of international humanism as mediated by the community of the Bohemian Brethren. Forced into exile in the 1620s, Comenius carried with him the best traditions of the doomed Protestantism of his homeland, and his success abroad did something to compensate for its defeat in Bohemia. In the end, moreover, the values espoused by Comenius exacted their revenge against the Habsburg state and the Counter-Reformation that appeared to have engulfed them. The Czech national revival of the nineteenth century gained much of its initial impetus from the scholarly and political activity of a Protestant, Frantiek Palacký; and that national involvement eventually led to Czechoslovak independence under another Protestant, T. G. Masaryk.

[See also Bohemian Brethren and Hus, Jan.]

BIBLIOGRAPHY

Denis, Ernest. *Fin de l'indépendance bohême* (1889–1890). Reprint, New York, 1971. Classic account, and still one of the few available in a world language; very pro-Czech and critical of the tepidity of the "German" Reformation in Bohemia.

Eberhard, Winfried. *Konfessionsbildung und Stände in Böhmen, 1478–1530.* Munich, 1981. Dense but important study of the interrelation between religion and politics in the early sixteenth century.

———. *Monarchie und Widerstand: Zur ständischen Oppositionsbildung im Herrschaftssystem Ferdinands I. in Böhmen.* Munich, 1985. Major account of the first period of Habsburg-Protestant conflict.

Evans, R. J. W. *The Making of the Habsburg Monarchy, 1550–1700: An Interpretation.* Oxford, 1991. Includes a brief survey of the Bohemian Reformation and its decline.

Gindely, Anton. *Rudolf II. und seine Zeit.* 2 vols. Prague, 1862–1865. Still the best and most detailed treatment of the years 1600–1612.

———. *Geschichte des Dreißigjährigen Krieges.* 4 vols. Prague, 1869–1880. Classic account, not superseded, of the Bohemian Revolt and its aftermath. Despite the title, not to be confused with the general *History of the Thirty Years' War* (2 vols., London, 1885), which appeared under Gindely's name.

Heymann, Fredrick G. "The Impact of Martin Luther upon Bohemia." *Central European History* 1 (1968), 107–130.

Hrejsa, Ferdinand. *Česká konfese: její vznik, podstata a dějiny.* Prague, 1912. Still the fundamental account of the genesis of the *Confessio Bohemica* of 1575 and the most thorough analysis of the nature of Bohemian Protestantism in general.

Janáček, Josef. *České dějiny. Doba předbělohorská. Book I: 1526–1547.* 2 vols. Prague, 1968–84. Comprehensive account of the first stage of the contest between Bohemia's Reformation and its Habsburg rulers.

Winter, Zikmund. *Život církevní v Čechách: kulturně-historický obraz 15. a 16. století.* 2 vols. Prague, 1895–1896. Ecclesiastical history, still unsurpassed for its mass of illustrative detail.

Zeman, Jarold K. *The Hussite Movement and the Reformation in Bohemia, Moravia and Slovakia, 1350–1650: A Bibliographical Study Guide.* Ann Arbor, Mich., 1977.

R. J. W. EVANS

BOHEMIAN BRETHREN.

A sect that described itself formally as the Unity of Brethren (Lat., *Unitas Fratrum*; Czech, *Jednota bratrská*), the Bohemian Brethren are also known either as the Czech Brethren or, less accurately, as the Moravian Brethren. The denomination originated in the aftermath of the Hussite struggles of early fifteenth-century Bohemia as a radically nonconformist, fundamentalist, and chiliastic grouping. An early influence was the visionary anarchist thinker Petr Chelčický (c.1390–1460). The early brethren were largely uneducated people who rejected private property and all civil obligations, living on the margins of Bohemian society. Under Brother Luká of Prague (d. 1528), however, a majority of the sect forsook asceticism and pacifism and gradually opened up their community to selected converts from the higher orders of society. The dissenting minority swelled the ranks of the Anabaptists.

Although they never formed more than a small percentage of the total population, the brethren's stress on discipline and education and their closely ordered communal life lent them a distinctive profile in sixteenth-century Bohemia. By contrast, they set less store by doctrinal precision. For a time they inclined toward the Lutherans and were influenced especially by Melanchthon, who nurtured a succession of young men from the brethren as students at Wittenberg. Later they moved closer to Calvinist norms and tended to visit the Universities of Geneva, Basel, and Heidelberg. Their successive confessions of faith, in print from the 1530s, remained eclectic, and this diversity allowed them to play an important role in negotiating the compromise Bohemian Confession of 1575. Though the Brethren developed a clear hierarchy of church authority, with a bishop and elders at its head, each congregation retained considerable autonomy.

Unlike the Utraquists, the brethren enjoyed no legal protection and survived on sufferance from the authorities. After the advent of Habsburg rule in 1526, they made efforts to regularize their position but twenty years later found themselves the scapegoats for the campaign by local Protestants to keep Bohemia from taking the Catholic side in the Schmalkald War. King Ferdinand I imprisoned Bishop Jan Augusta and other leaders and banished the movement's rank and file from Bohemia proper. Most of the exiles settled in Great Poland (west of Warsaw). There they formed separate communities several thousand strong and maintained their own way of life; but they also contributed actively to the ecumenical movement among Polish Protestants, reaching a common platform with the Calvinists at Koźminek (1555) and cooperating in the broader-based Consensus Sendomiriensis (1570).

The damage suffered by the brethren at home proved, meanwhile, to be only temporary. Their increasingly numerous noble supporters protected them from further persecution over the next half century, especially in Moravia, and under the aegis of the cultivated bishop Jan Blahoslav the brethren underwent a spiritual and intellectual renaissance. A six-volume humanist translation of the Bible, published in the little country township of Kralice between 1579 and 1593, represents one aspect of their achievement. Another was a thorough and enlightened schooling system, centered on such places as Ivančice (Eibenschütz), Přerov (Prerau), and Fulnek. A third was the international recognition that the movement commanded, notably as a result of the travels of prominent brethren in Protestant Europe. Václav Budovec of Budov and Baron Karl Žerotín came to occupy particularly important places among the brethren in Bohemia and Moravia, respectively.

From 1600 the brethren were pitched into the denouement of the religious contest in Bohemia. Žerotín played an important part in forcing concessions from Archduke Matthias in the aftermath of the Peace of Vienna, as did Budovec in extracting the Letter of Majesty from Rudolf II. When the Bohemian Revolt broke out in 1618, leaders and ministers of the brethren supported it with enthusiasm. (Žerotín stood almost alone in his doubts about its legitimacy and wisdom.) They were correspondingly vulnerable when the revolt collapsed in defeat: Budovec was one of those executed. During the 1620s the congregations of the brethren were forced, along with other Protestants in the country, to choose between conversion to Rome and banishment.

The fate of the brethren was dramatically symbolized in the career of Jan Amos Komenský (Comenius), who left his native Moravia in 1628 as a rising minister and teacher. In exile Komenský became both the last bishop of his church and a celebrated scholar and pedagogue who sustained its best spiritual and intellectual traditions. With his death near Amsterdam in 1670 the brethren fell into institutional extinction. But remnants of the community survived in parts of Saxony and clandestinely in Moravia, and when Count Nikolaus Zinzendorf founded his model religious community at Herrnhut in 1725, many of them came to join him. Thence the new sect acquired its name of Moravian Brethren and regarded itself as heir to the legacy of the old Unity of Brethren.

[See also Bohemia; Hus, Jan; and Moravia.]

BIBLIOGRAPHY

Brock, Peter. The Political and Social Doctrines of the Unity of Czech Brethren in the Fifteenth and Sixteenth Centuries. The Hague, 1957. Surveys the gradual evolution of the brethren from exclusive sect to full participant in Bohemian society and politics.

Evans, R. J. W. "Calvinism in East-Central Europe: Hungary and Her Neighbours." In International Calvinism, 1541–1715, edited by Menna Prestwich. Oxford, 1985. Brief presentation of the brethren in a larger regional context.

Gindely, Anton. Geschichte der Böhmischen Brüder (1868). 2 vols. Reprint, Osnabrück, 1968. Pioneering account, still of value.

Hrubý, Frantiek. Etudiants tchèques aux écoles protestantes de l'Europe occidentale à la fin du 16e et au début du 17e siècle. Brno, 1970. Mainly correspondence from students among the brethren.

Řičan, Rudolf. Die Böhmischen Brüder. Berlin, 1961. Standard modern overview; abbreviated version of a Czech original (Prague, 1957).

Zeman, Jarold K. The Anabaptists and the Czech Brethren in Moravia, 1526–1628: A Study of Origins and Contacts. The Hague, 1969. Pursues the radical wing of the brethren.

———. "Responses to Calvin and Calvinism among the Czech Brethren, 1540–1605." Occasional Papers of the Society for Reformation Research 1 (1977), 41–52.

R. J. W. EVANS

BÖHME, Jakob (1575–1624), master shoemaker and lay theologian, author of philosophical-theosophical and mystical works. He was born in the Upper Lusatian village of Alt-Seidenberg. The manuscript of Böhme's Morgenröthe im Aufgang (1612), conceived as a memorial of the author's overwhelming spiritual illumination, was handed over by Karl Ender von Sercha to Schwenckfeldian circles in Upper Lusatia and Silesia and provoked the enmity of the orthodox Lutheran pastor Gregorius Richter in the city of Görlitz; consequently Richter prohibited any further literary production by Böhme. In the period of enforced silence Böhme was influenced by Paracelsian and alchemical ideas.

The writings produced in Böhme's new creative era beginning in 1618 excel in a successively clearer and improved articulation of his insights. In these works the author succeeded in expressing his lucid spiritual experience with great vigor and prophetic authority. His main works are Beschreibung der Drey Principien Göttliches Wesens (De Tribus Principiis; 1619), Von dem Dreyfachen Leben des Menschen (De Triplici Vita Hominis; 1619/20), Von der Menschwerdung Jesu Christi (De Incarnatione Verbi; 1620), Von der Geburt und Bezeichnung aller Wesen (De Signatura Rerum; 1621/22) and the two great works of his maturity, the tract Von der Gnaden-Wahl (De Electione Gratiae; 1623) and the extensive typological explanation of the biblical book of Genesis, Mysterium Magnum oder Erklärung über das Erste Buch Mosis (1622/23). In a series of apologetic tracts and letters Böhme rejected chiliasm (against Paul Kaym), predestinarianism (against Balthasar Tilke), and the deification of the world and humans (against Esaias Stiefel and Ezechiel Meth). The unique edition printed during Böhme's lifetime, entitled Der Weg zu Christo, containing the tracts "Von wahrer Buße," "Von wahrer Gelassenheit," and "Von dem übersinnlichen Leben," was published in 1624 by one of Böhme's followers, Johann Sigismund von Schweinichen.

Though Böhme's opponent Richter reiterated his reproaches and tried to turn the municipal council against the shoemaker (who was summoned and enjoined "to seek his fortune elsewhere"), Böhme's refutation (Schutz-Rede) and also his letters addressed to his friends (Sendbriefe) demonstrated his spiritual legitimacy. The eschatological forms of his mission as a prophet announcing the "era of the great reformation" deserves special attention: Böhme disclosed the destructive conditions of contemporary life before and after the beginning of the Thirty Years' War, but his message proclaimed a final benediction, rescue, and redemption, a "restitution of all that Adam lost"—universal integration and individual, social, and spiritual rebirth. Böhme died in Görlitz in 1624.

His view of the Lutheran Reformation was determined by spiritualistic patterns—confessional controversies, fruitless disputes, and dogmatic quarrels were all destroying faith: "Faith is not an outward thing." No externally imputed grace avails. Historical faith is sterile and must be followed by regeneration. Christ, the second Adam, restored the primal creation of humankind according to the image of God.

The Bible and Lutheran piety (Martin Moller served as chief pastor in Görlitz from 1600 to 1606) are the roots of Böhme's spiritual experience; both the growth of his thought and his terminology were influenced by medieval mystics (*Theologia Germanica*) and the traditions of spiritualism (Kaspar von Schwenckfeld, Valentin Weigel). The peculiarity of Böhme's theocentric and christocentric philosophy has been defined as post-Lutheran gnosticism, including theogony, cosmology, and redemption. In Böhme's system, Renaissance natural philosophy, spiritualism, and Christian mysticism were united with genuine Lutheran soteriology. Pansophic, alchemical, and Cabbalistic elements symbolized the archetypical process of spiritual transmutation of humanity. The central point of his all-encompassing dialectical philosophy was the testimony of God, the unity of all contradictions and the almighty creator: "Böhme tried to describe in metaphysical-psychological symbols the *living* God in whom the roots of every life must be sought" (Paul Tillich).

The influence of Böhme in cultural history is astounding. Schelling believed that Böhme was a "miracle in human history." Tillich, appreciating Böhme's philosophy as "one of the most profound and strangest systems of Western thought," remarked that Böhme's thoughts are "expressed in a language which mirrors speculative vision, mystical experience, psychological insight and alchemist tradition."

BIBLIOGRAPHY

Primary Sources

Böhme, Jakob. *Die Urschriften*. Edited by Werner Buddecke. 2 vols. Stuttgart and Bad Cannstatt, 1963–1966.
———. *Theosophia Revelata: Das ist; Alle Göttliche Schriften des Gottseligen u. Hocherleuchteten Deutschen Theosophi Jacob Böhmens* (1730). 14 vols. Reprint, Stuttgart, 1955–1961.
Law, William, ed. *The Works of Jacob Behmen, the Teutonic Philosopher*. 4 vols. London, 1764–1781.

Secondary Sources

Buddecke, Werner. *Die J. Böhme-Ausgaben*. Vol. 1, *Die Ausgaben in deutscher Sprache*. Göttingen, 1937.
———. *Die J. Böhme-Ausgaben*. Vol. 2, *Die Übersetzungen*. Göttingen, 1957. The English editions are listed on pp. 47–174.
Grunsky, Hans. *J. Böhme*. Stuttgart, 1957.
Koyré, Alexandre. *La philosophie de Jacob Boehme*. Paris, 1929.
Pältz, Eberhard H. "J. Böhme." In *Theologische Realenzyklopädie*, vol. 6, pp. 748–754. Berlin and New York, 1980. Contains a bibliography.
Schulitz, John. *J. Böhme und die Kabbalah*. Europäische Hochschulschriften, ser. 20, vol. 370. Frankfurt a.M. and New York, 1993.
Stoudt, John Joseph. *Sunrise to Eternity: A Study in J. Böhme's Life and Thought*. Philadelphia, 1957.
Wehr, Gerhard. *J. Böhme*. Reinbeck, 1971. Contains a bibliography.

EBERHARD H. PÄLTZ

BOLEYN, Anne (1507?–1536), second consort of Henry VIII. The daughter of Thomas Boleyn (earl of Wilshire and Ormond) and Elizabeth Howard, Anne was educated at Malines and Paris from about 1513 to 1520. Probably committed to Erasmian religious reform when she returned to England, she became a maid of honor to Catherine of Aragon in about 1527 when Henry VIII was challenging the validity of his marriage because of the death of his infant sons. Attracted to Anne, by July 1527 he decided to marry her. As Clement VII refused to grant the requested divorce from Catherine, Henry and Anne were secretly wed in January 1533; that spring, authorized by the Appeals Statute, Thomas Cranmer, archbishop of Canterbury, invalidated the first marriage, and in September Anne gave birth to her daughter Elizabeth. From 1534 to 1536 Thomas Cromwell oversaw the passage of statutes that recognized an autonomous church under the royal headship and limited the succession to the children of Anne. In January 1536 she miscarried a male fetus (probably a deformed one), and the following May, Henry had her and five men, including her brother, charged with illicit sexual behavior that was then associated with witchcraft. Two days after a special commission had declared her guilty of those charges, Archbishop Cranmer, without revealing his reasons, annulled her marriage.

The cause of her execution on 19 May is still debated, some scholars insisting that she was an innocent victim of factional politics rather than of the king's concerns about her miscarriage. For Reformation partisans she came to symbolize the schism from Rome, causing Catholics to depict her erroneously with monstrous features, including the compelling wen and sixth finger, and Protestants to compare her to Deborah the prophetess. During the reign of her child Elizabeth, Protestantism became firmly established in England.

BIBLIOGRAPHY

Ives, E. W. *Anne Boleyn*. Oxford, 1986. Sets out the standard view that, using the wiles of Jane Seymour, Thomas Cromwell manipulated the king into having an innocent Anne Boleyn executed for trumped-up charges of adultery and incest.

Warnicke, Retha M. *The Rise and Fall of Anne Boleyn: Family Politics at the Court of Henry VIII*. Cambridge, 1989. Provides a new interpretation that it was the king's concern about the succession after the nature of the miscarriage in January of 1536 that led him to have Anne charged with sexual acts then associated with witchcraft.

RETHA M. WARNICKE

BOLOGNA, CONCORDAT OF. An agreement made in 1516 by Francis I, king of France, and Pope Leo X, the Concordat of Bologna defined the relations between the French Crown, the papacy, and the church in France. Its most important provision was the annulment of the Pragmatic Sanction of Bourges (1438), which had severely curtailed papal authority in France, restoring capitular elections, abolishing annates, curbing judicial appeals to Rome, and asserting that a council of the church was superior in authority to the pope. By removing "this thorn driven into the eye of the church," the concordat satisfied a long-standing papal demand.

The king, who had just conquered the duchy of Milan, hoped the agreement would gain him papal support for his political designs in Italy. This it failed to secure in the long term, but the concordat served to strengthen royal authority in France. It destroyed the independence of the French church by depriving most chapters of their right of election in favor of a system of nomination by the king and institution by the pope. The king now had the right to appoint positions in 114 episcopal and archiepiscopal sees and 800 abbeys. The concordat was strongly resisted in France by the Parlement of Paris, which refused to register it until March 1518, and by the University of Paris, which feared that its graduates would suffer discrimination under the new system. In practice the recruitment of prelates in France was not substantially altered by the concordat; under Francis I they continued to be recruited mainly from the old nobility. In choosing candidates the king sometimes disregarded the canonical requirements of age and education, for he was more concerned about rewarding service to the Crown than promoting evangelization. The pope could object to a royal nominee but in practice rarely did. The advantages conferred on the king of France by the concordat removed some of the incentives other monarchs had to adhere to the Reformation.

[*See also* Francis I of France *and* Leo X.]

BIBLIOGRAPHY

Aubenas Roger, and Ricard, Robert. "L'Église et la Renaissance, 1449–1517." In *Histoire de l'Église*, edited by Augustin Fliche and Victor Martin, pp. 167–181. Paris, 1951.

Doucet, Roger. *Étude sur le gouvernement de Francois Ier dans ses rapports avec le Parlement de Paris*. Paris, 1921.

Edelstein, Marilyn M. "The Social Origins of the Episcopacy in the Reign of Francis I." *French Historical Studies* 8 (1974), 377–392.

Imbart de la Tour, Pierre. *Les origines de la réforme*. Melun, 1944.

Knecht, Robert Jean. "The Concordat of 1516: A Re-Assessment." *University of Birmingham Historical Journal* 9 (1963), 16–32.

Loirette, G. "La première application à Bordeaux du Concordat de 1516." *Annales du Midi* 68 (1956), 317–337.

Renaudet, A. *Préréforme et humanisme à Paris pendant les premières guerres d'Italie, 1494–1517*. 2d ed. Reprint, Geneva, 1981.

Thomas, Jules. *Le Concordat de 1516: Ses origines, son histoire au 16e siècle*. 3 vols. Paris, 1910.

ROBERT JEAN KNECHT

BOLSEC, Jérome (c.1524–1584), French physician and opponent of Calvin, born in Paris. A Carmelite monk, Bolsec left the Catholic church about 1545. Fleeing Paris because of doubts about his orthodoxy, he settled for a time at the court of Renée, duchess of Ferrara, where he married and studied medicine. About 1550 he became the personal physician of Jacques de Bourgogne, lord of Falais, a close friend of Calvin, at Veigny, Chablais, near Geneva, but in Bernese territory. By the time he arrived at Veigny Bolsec was a Reformed Protestant.

Bolsec was interested in theology, and he often attended the Friday Congregation, a weekly public discussion in Geneva about theological questions. Though he subscribed to Calvin's theology on almost every point, he disagreed on predestination. In October 1551, at a meeting of the congregation, he attacked Calvin's doctrine of double predestination, or more precisely his teaching about the cause of reprobation. He charged that Calvin's doctrine made God partial to some humans and the author of sin. Bolsec espoused a type of universalism: humans were of the elect because of their faith, and they were condemned because they refused the election common to all. He wished to view election within the realm of history and human responsibility instead of in terms of a pretemporal double decree.

Bolsec was imprisoned and put on trial for heresy. The Council of Geneva sent letters to the other Reformed churches asking their opinions on the matter. While the replies from Guillaume Farel at Neuchâtel and from Théodore de Bèze and Pierre Viret at Lausanne were predictably supportive of Calvin, the letters from the churches of Bern, Basel, and Zurich called for moderation and reconciliation. These churches were generally more favorable to Bolsec than to Calvin, and none of them was totally supportive of Calvin.

The Bolsec affair must be viewed within the context of the conflict over discipline that was reaching crisis proportions in Geneva in the early 1550s. Calvin had fought for his discipline for a decade against the recalcitrant, so-called libertines, and it has been suggested that these libertines were behind Bolsec's challenge of Calvin. Though this is unlikely, Calvin's position in Geneva was far from secure. His only post was that of interpreter of the Bible. If Bolsec was correct, Calvin was a false teacher. It is clear, then, that the magistrates had little choice but to deal with Bolsec in order to keep Calvin. They also wished to protect Geneva from any suspicion of heresy. Therefore, Bolsec was found guilty and exiled from Geneva for life on 23 December 1551.

It was, however, not clear to everyone that Bolsec's teaching was heretical. Falais supported Bolsec, writing on his behalf to the councils of Geneva and Bern. In Zurich, Bullinger was quite critical of Calvin's teaching. He agreed generally with Bolsec, though he did not specifically defend him. There were also many in Bern and Basel who did not agree with Calvin on predestination.

Leaving Geneva, Bolsec found temporary sanctuary at Thonon, in Bernese territory. Despite widespread disagreement in Bernese territory with Calvin's teaching on predestination, Bolsec was finally exiled from Bern in March 1555, apparently because he publicly disagreed with the Bernese recommendation on the fate of Servetus. Nothing is known of him until October 1561 when he again appeared in Bern and was allowed to stay. In April 1563 he was given permission to settle in Lausanne to practice medicine. Soon, however, it was determined that his theological views were at odds with the Confession of Bern, and as a result, in December 1563, he was again exiled from Bernese territory.

Bolsec then went to France, where he returned to Catholicism. In 1577 he published his *Histoire de la vie, moeurs, actes, doctrine, constance et mort de Jean Calvin,* and in 1582, his *Histoire de la vie, moeurs, doctrine et deportemonts de Théodore de Bèze,* in which he characterized the two men as heretics, liars, hypocrites, and sexual deviates. Bolsec died in 1584.

BIBLIOGRAPHY

Baker, J. Wayne. *Heinrich Bullinger and the Covenant: The Other Reformed Tradition.* Athens, Ohio, 1980. Places the Bolsec controversy within the context of Bullinger's thought and the discussions between Bullinger and Calvin on predestination.
Fazy, H. *Procès de Jérôme Bolsec.* Geneva, 1865.
Gautier, Jean-Antoine. *Histoire de Genève, des origines à l'année 1691.* Vol. 3. Geneva, 1898. Good, brief, and balanced description of the Bolsec controversy, based on the documents. See especially pp. 432–452.
Holtrop, Philip C. *The Bolsec Controversy on Predestination, from 1551–1555.* Lewiston, Idaho, and Lampeter, U.K., 1993. Exhaustive study of the controversy, including translations and summaries of the statements of Bolsec, Calvin, Bèze, Bullinger, and others.

J. WAYNE BAKER

BONCAMPAGNI, Ugo. *See* Gregory XIII.

BONNER, Edmund (1500?–1569), Catholic bishop of London. Educated at Oxford, he joined Thomas Wolsey's household and later entered royal service. He went on missions to Italy, Germany, and France and was rewarded in 1539 by appointment to the see of London.

Although Bonner appears to have supported the official religious changes during the reign of Henry VIII, including the break with Rome, he was unsympathetic to the more extensive reforms of Edward VI's minority. In the summer of 1549 he was criticized by the council for his tardiness in enforcing the use of the new *Book of Common Prayer.* Having failed to preach according to the instructions delivered to him by the council, Bonner was examined by a commission under the archbishop of Canterbury, Thomas Cranmer, and was deprived of his bishopric, which he regained only with the accession of Mary Tudor in 1553.

London had been the major center of English Protestantism, and the restoration of Catholicism in the diocese was a herculean task. Bonner acted with great vigor, visiting his diocese on his own initiative and ordering the restoration of processions and ceremonies. He used the printing press with more confidence than many contemporary Catholics, publishing thirteen "Homilies" for his clergy's use, a formulary of faith entitled *A Profitable and Necessarye Doctryne,* and a little catechism for children, *An Honeste, Godlye Instruction.* Bonner also persecuted Protestants with great energy; in four years about seventy-five Protestants were burned in his diocese (out of a national total of fewer than three hundred). For this, he earned the title "bloody butcher Bonner" among Protestants. It is clear, however, that he and his officials labored hard to persuade those accused of heresy to recant.

In 1559 Bonner refused to take the oath of supremacy as required by Elizabeth's government. He was once more deprived of his bishopric and spent the remainder of his life in the Marshalsea prison.

BIBLIOGRAPHY

Alexander, Gina. "Bonner and the Marian Persecutions." *History* 60 (1975), 374–391.
Brigden, Susan. *London and the Reformation.* Oxford, 1989.
Foxe, John. *Acts and Monuments.* 8 vols. London, 1837.
Slavin, Arthur J. "The Tudor Revolution and the Devil's Art: Bishop Bonner's Printed Forms." In *Tudor Rule and Revolution,* edited by DeLloyd J. Guth and John W. McKenna, pp. 3–23. Cambridge, 1982.

JENNIFER LOACH

BOOK OF COMMON PRAYER. The official order of worship of the Church of England and of the other churches of the Anglican Communion, *The Book of Common Prayer* was the result of efforts made from 1534 on to reform the medieval worship of the church in England. The reform began gradually in the reign of Henry VIII with the production of the Great Bible (1539), an English translation that was ordered by the Convocation of Clery in 1543 to be used in the public worship of the church. Thomas Cranmer, archbishop of Canterbury, was involved in this reform, writing a preface for the Great Bible. He was active also in the production of the book of homilies, or sermons, commissioned by convocation in 1542 but not published until 1547. He worked on a revision of the breviary, involving two schemes, one in 1538 influenced by the Lutherans who were negotiating with Henry VIII, and another produced during the conservative reaction between 1544 and 1546, influenced by the reforms of Francisco de Quiñones of Spain. The archbishop produced an English Litany in 1544, as requested by the king, and labored on further revisions of the medieval Processional. In addition, during Henry's reign revisions were made in the existing breviary to take into account the break with Rome, and in the primers as well. In all of this it is evident that Cranmer and those working with him were revising the medieval books of worship and were influenced in this work by Lutheran church orders, such as that of Nuremberg, the reformist activities of Quiñones of Spain, and the worship of the early church, especially the Eastern liturgies.

This reformist activity reached its culmination after the death of Henry VIII and the accession of Edward VI in 1547. It was then that the Protector Somerset, an admirer of the Lutherans, came to power and lifted restrictions upon reform maintained by Henry. Alarmed at the resulting threat of anarchy, the Parliament in December 1547 enacted a statute to control unlawful behavior and to promote orderly reform. A major element in the legislation was the order that from henceforth the Holy Communion should be administered in both kinds, wine as well as bread. To enable this the Order of Communion of 1548 in English was inserted into the Latin Mass following the priest's Communion, providing an exhortation, confession, absolution, comfortable words, prayer before Communion, words of administration, and a blessing. This communicants' service made use of the *Simplex et pia deliberatio* ("A simple and pious Consultation"), the Cologne church order, prepared for Archbishop Hermann von Wied by Martin Bucer and Philipp Melanchthon. The statute and the order placed emphasis upon the "Sacrament of the body and blood of our Saviour Jesus Christ," upon Communion and the partaking of the sacrament by all communicants, upon penitential preparation for the worthy receiving of the sacrament, and upon what was to be a major theme in the interpretation of the prayer book, mutual participation. This concept was clearly expressed in the Prayer of Humble Access in the desire that communicants may so eat the bread and wine, the flesh and blood of Christ, "that [they] may continuallye dwell in hym, and he in us, that [their] synfull bodyes may bee made clean by his body, and [their] soules washed through hys most precious blood." The Order of Communion was to be incorporated into *The Book of Common Prayer* and provided a tone and meaning amplified by future theologians (C. J. Cuming, *History of Anglican Liturgy*, London, 1969, pp. 364–366).

While work toward the Order of Communion was in progress, Cranmer was meeting with the Windsor Committee, composed of conservatives such as George Day, bishop of Chichester, and reformers such as Nicholas Ridley, then bishop of Rochester, and Richard Cox, almoner to the king. We know little about the work of this committee, but it seems that they were working with drafts prepared by Cranmer. Not all members of the committee were satisfied with the results. Thomas Thirlby, then bishop of Westminster, subscribed to the "book of agreements" but explained that he did so because he was under the impression that the book was the basis for further discussion and not final. In particular he objected to the way in which the proposed Mass seemed to run contrary to orthodox eucharistic doctrine. After debate in the House of Lords in December 1548, Parliament enacted a uniformity act, to which was appended *The Book of Common Prayer,* the statute requiring that it be in use in all places by Whitsunday 1549, at which time any use of the medieval liturgies should cease. The act (2 & 3 Edw. VI, ch. 1) explained that the "Archbishop of Canterbury, and certain other learned men of this realm," had been appointed to "draw and make one convenient and meet order, rite, and fashion of common and open prayer and administration of the sacraments," having in mind "the most sincere and pure Christian religion taught by Scripture" as well as "the usages of the primitive Church."

This book consisted of a preface derived from Cranmer's first breviary scheme, reflecting the influence of the breviary reform attributed to Cardinal Quiñones. There follow tables of psalms and lessons and a calendar providing for the orderly reading of scripture: the Psalter once each month, the Old Testament once a year, and the New Testament three times each year in the course of the daily offices. Taking into consideration the epistles and gospels appointed for use at the Mass, the book placed very heavy emphasis on the reading of scripture, which would have been done in English from the Great Bible, displacing "vain and superstitious fables" formerly found in the old services. The daily offices follow, Morning Prayer combining Matins, Lauds, and Prime in the breviary, and Evensong, based on Vespers and Compline. Terce, Sext, and None were ignored. Lutheran influences are apparent at this point. The Proper, Collect, Epistle, and Gospel follow, replacing the Temporale and the Sanctorale. The translation of the Latin collects is counted among Cranmer's finest literary achievements. Next is "The Supper of the Lord and the Holy Communion, Commonly Called the Mass," drawing on the *Sarum Missal,* the Cologne church order, and certain Lutheran church orders. The eucharistic prayer is unique among Reformation prayers of consecration in its close resemblance to the Roman *Canon Missae,* but it is clearly reformed in its emphasis on the death of Christ as "his one oblation offered," "a full perfect oblacion, and sattisfacyon, for the sinnes of the whole worlde," and the oblation of the people as "a reasonable, holy, and lively sacrifice" (*The First and Second Prayer Books of Edward VI,* E. C. Ratcliff, ed., London, 1910, pp.

222–223). Thus the medieval doctrine of the sacrifice of the altar was opposed. Holy Communion is followed by the Litany of 1544 somewhat altered, replacing the medieval Processional. Then replacing the manuale come the services of baptism, confirmation, matrimony, visitation of the sick, burial, and the churching of women. Finally there is the penitential service of commination, for use on Ash Wednesday, with its cursings and the *Miserere mei Deus* (Psalm 51). Between baptism and confirmation there is Cranmer's brief catechism, the basis of religious education, with instruction based on the Nicene Creed, the Ten Commandments, and the Lord's Prayer. The book concludes with the essay "Of Ceremonies, Why Some Be Abolished and Some Retayned," and with Cranmer's "Certain Notes for the Playne Explicacion and Descent Ministracion of Thinges, Conteined in Thys Booke." The first was derived from the Thirteen Articles of 1538, defending the use of ceremonies prescribed in the book for the sake of order and the proscription of some customary ceremonies now found to be superstitious and so numerous as to be a burden. In the next year, 1550, working out of the medieval pontifical, Cranmer produced an ordinal, with services for the ordination of deacons and priests and the consecration of bishops, a volume that was to become a part of *The Book of Common Prayer*. The prayer book contained all that was necessary in public worship, except for the musical settings for the singing of the services. It provided worship for every day of the year as well as Sunday by Sunday through the church year, and for all of life from birth to death. And it did so in one comparatively modest volume, printed in English.

This prayer book was not approved by all. From the moment of its publication it came under attack by conservatives who wanted the old Mass restored and by zealous reformers who believed that the reform had not gone far enough. Both Martin Bucer and Peter Martyr Vermigli wrote detailed critiques. Deeply disturbing to Cranmer was the claim made by the Henrician Catholic bishop of Winchester that the new Mass could be interpreted in the old ways. As a result Cranmer prepared a new prayer book. We know little about its production, but of some importance was the fact that the relatively moderate Protector Somerset was replaced by the more radical duke of Northumberland and a more Protestant settlement of religion encouraged. *The Second Book of Common Prayer* was attached to a new Act of Uniformity (5 & 6 Edw. VI, ch. 1) enacted on 14 April 1552 and was to be in use from All Saints' Day (1 November) of that year.

The new book was more pronouncedly reformed, adding penitential introductions to the daily offices and strengthening the penitential character of the Holy Communion (which was no longer called the Mass) with the addition of the Ten Commandments, combined with the Kyrie. Most dramatically, measures were taken to assure that the Holy Communion could not be interpreted in a medieval sense, either in terms of real presence or the sacrifice of the Mass.

But here Cranmer's genius was at work in a positive way. The eucharistic prayer was divided, the Communion of the people inserted after the narrative of the Last Supper and before the oblation of the people (or a thanksgiving prayer to the same effect). This reduced the possibility of adoration of the consecrated elements, they being consumed almost immediately; but the main thrust for Cranmer was in the emphasis on Communion as a part of the consecration, the bread and wine being consecrated in their use, as consumed by the faithful. The purpose of the sacrament, to change people, not things, involved the renewal of contrite communicants and their participation in Christ and he in them, which further involved their mutual participation to the benefit of the commonweal. This prayer book was in use for less than a year, King Edward VI having died on 6 July 1553. He was succeeded by his half-sister Mary, who rejected *The Book of Common Prayer* and reinstated the medieval liturgies in Latin.

The next prayer book was that of Queen Elizabeth I, who ascended the throne on 17 November 1558. The daughter of Henry VIII and Anne Boleyn, Elizabeth was raised a Protestant humanist and indicated at once that she favored the Reformation while opposing fanatics at both extremes. She was opposed both to Roman Catholics and Puritans and favored those of moderate tendencies who supported her claim to the throne. On 22 March 1559 a royal proclamation was issued concerning royal supremacy and ordering Communion in both kinds at the impending Easter masses, an order necessitating an order of communion such as that of 1548. Thus the beginning was made much as it was under Edward VI. We know little of the means by which the prayer book attached to the Uniformity Act of 1559 (1 Eliz. 1, ch. 1) was devised. We do know that it was based on the second book of Edward VI with certain alterations such as the elimination of the Black Rubric, forbidding kneeling at Communion, and removal from the Litany of the reference to the tyranny of the pope and all his "detestable enormities." A controversial Ornaments Rubric was added, as were a large number of saints' days. Most significantly the sentences of administration of both the 1549 and the 1552 books were conjoined, those of 1549 tending to support the medieval doctrine of real presence, those of 1552 the reformist, memorial understanding of the sacrament. Thus at the administration of the bread we read: "The body of our Lord Jesus Christ which was given for thee, preserve thy body and soul into everlasting life [1549]; and take and eat this in remembrance that Christ died for thee, and feed on him in thy heart by faith with thanksgiving [1552]" (*The Book of Common Prayer 1559: The Elizabethan Prayer Book*, J. Booty, ed., Charlottesville, Va., 1976, p. 264). The queen's own preferences were indicated by the retention of cross or crucifix and candles in her own chapel and her insistence that copes and surplices be worn by officiants at services. In 1561 more saints' days were added to the calendar while in 1560 a Latin version of the prayer book (*Liber precum publicarum*) had been prepared by Walter Haddon for use at the universities. This book professes to be an exact translation of the entire 1559 book, but it is not. Baptism and holy matrimony are omitted, and in the Communion of the sick, provision is made for reservation of the consecrated elements. The conservative tenor of this Latin book is further indicated by the note that Christ has given his own power of absolving penitents to his church (*Liturgies and Services of the Reign of Queen Elizabeth*, W. K. Clay, ed., Cambridge, 1847, p. 393). Such a statement is not found in the 1559 book.

The 1559 prayer book straddled the great divide, ultimately pleasing neither Roman Catholics nor Puritans. The Puritans protested that it was "an unperfect book, culled and picked out of that popish dungehill, the Mass book full of all abhominations" (W. H. Frere and C. E. Douglas, eds., *Puritan Manifestoes,* London, 1907, p. 21). In fact it was conservative in that it preserved the basic tenor of sacramental worship, but it was also reformed. E. C. Ratcliff, writing of the 1552 book, said, "The axiom [intended to control liturqical expression] is that of Scriptural sanction. What cannot plainly be seen to possess Scriptural sanction should not be found in a Prayer Book. The perfect Prayer Book should provide people and ministers with forms of worship which the Apostles and first believers could acknowledge and approve" (*Liturgical Studies*, A. H. Couratin and D. H. Tripp, eds., London, 1976, p. 196). Cranmer himself, answering the objections of the rebels in Devonshire in 1549, wrote that "in the English service appointed to be read there is nothing else but the eternal word of God" (*Works*, vol. 2, John Edmund Cox, ed., Cambridge, 1846, p. 180). Word and sacraments were conjoined in the Ordinal of 1550 (*Prayer Books of Edward VI*, Ratcliff, ed., p. 312), and the sacraments were viewed as "the visible words of God."

The focus of the sixteenth-century *Book of Common Prayer* was on the sequence of Morning Prayer, Litany, and the Holy Communion, with the Ministration of Baptism when required. A sermon was provided at the appointed place in Holy Communion and, according to surviving sermons, would have lasted an hour or more. In London it was expected that after the completion of Sunday corporate worship in the parish churches the people would assemble at Paul's Cross, the preaching station outside Saint Paul's Cathedral, to hear another sermon by some prominent cleric. In the afternoon there would be catechizing and Evening Prayer. In fact, as a general rule, Holy Communion was not celebrated in its entirety, but ended with the sermon and possibly a psalm. By some this service of Ante-Communion was derisively called the "dry Communion." The prayer book ordered that parishioners receive Communion "at least three times in the year, of which Easter shall be one" (*Book of Common Prayer 1559*, Booty, ed., p. 268), and thus

churches tended to limit celebrations to three a year. The reasons for this are various, including noncommunicating masses prior to the Reformation, the fear of communicating unworthily and thus incurring damnation, and the lack of understanding of the sacrament and the biblical and traditional doctrines constituting its meaning (J. Booty, "Preparation for the Lord's Supper in Elizabethan England," *Anglican Theological Review* 49.2, [1967], 131–148).

That ordinary folk as well as clergy seemed unable to grasp Cranmer's vision of corporate worship is apparent. One who did grasp the vision was Richard Hooker. The fifth book of his treatise *Of the Laws of Ecclesiastical Polity* (1597) was the first theological commentary on *The Book of Common Prayer*. In it (with further emphasis in Book VI), God's love and mercy are stressed, without which there can be no true contrition. And thus prayer book worship concentrated on praise to God and the establishment of a salvific rhythm of praise and contrition, whereby people become available to divine grace and are changed from death to life, from sin to righteousness, from brokenness to wholeness. Prayer book worship presents scripture doxologically. The public reading of scripture is something "we do to God, and not an exercise to spend the time" (Hooker, *Laws* V.19.5). That is to say, it is a form of prayer and praise offered in response to the God who forgives our sins and gives to us new life. In this worship the saving story of God's dealings with creation is rehearsed again and again, drawing the faithful into it so that the saving story becomes their story. In words spoken and in actions performed the liturgy becomes formative and reformative in the daily lives of the people. Such was the vision, in part.

The Book of Common Prayer, with this understanding, was at the center of the English Reformation. It, rather than a set of doctrines or a particular person, provided the basis for uniformity in religion. It was also the basis for doing theology in the Elizabethan church and after. In corporate worship the people heard the word in scripture read and preached, they affirmed their faith in the catholic creeds (Apostles' and Nicene), and they did so in the context of their praise toward God, with freedom to further understand and express their convictions in diverse ways.

Most importantly, all Englishmen lived out their lives going to church, participating in services of worship, however superficially, however reluctantly, and were affected by it. A. L. Rowse commented: "It is impossible to over-estimate the influence of the Church's routine of prayer and good works upon that [Elizabethan] society: the effect on imagination and conduct of the liturgy with its piercing and affecting phrases, repeated Sunday by Sunday" (*The England of Elizabeth*, New York, 1950, p. 433). Its influence is apparent in the plays of Shakespeare and the poetry of Donne and Herbert as well as in the development of the English language in the golden age of Elizabethan literature. Cranmer envisioned all of the people of a given community coming together to hear the word of God and gathering around a common table, partaking of the body and blood of Christ with penitent hearts, regarding one another physically present, one's best friends and one's worst enemies, both. He could hear them joining in their hearts and minds in the prayer after Communion, "We now most humbly beseche thee, O heavenly father, so to assist us with thy grace, that we may continue in that holy fellowship [the church / the commonweal], and do al such good workes as thou hast prepared for us to walk in: through Jesus Christ our Lord, to whom, with thee and the holy ghost, be all honor and glory" (*The First and Second Prayer Books of Edward VI*, Ratcliff, ed., p. 390). What was meant here was expressed by Cranmer in another place when, thinking of partaking of bread and wine at the one table, together, he said, "Surely, they have very hard and stony hearts, which with these things be not moved; and more cruel and unreasonable be they than brute beasts, that cannot be persuaded to be good to their christian brethren and neighbors, for whom Christ suffered death, when in this sacrament they be put in remembrance that the Son of God bestowed his life for his enemies" (*Works*, vol. 2, pp. 42–43).

[*See also* Acts of Uniformity; Anglicanism; *and* Liturgy, *article on* Protestant Liturgy.]

BIBLIOGRAPHY

Booty, John E. *The Godly Kingdom of Tudor England: Great Books of the English Reformation*. Wilton, Conn., 1981. Contains a substantial discussion of *The Book of Common Prayer* in historical context.

Brightman, F. E. *The English Rite*. 2 vols. Reprint, 2d rev. ed., Amersham, England, 1983–1984. Indispensable. The prayer book with its sources in parallel columns.

Davies, Horton. *Worship and Theology in England: From Cranmer to Hooker, 1534–1603*. Princeton, 1970. Serious presentation of worship and orders of worship in relation to theological developments.

Dugmore, C. W. *Eucharistic Doctrine in England from Hooker to Waterland*. London, 1942. Important for the theology of the prayer book and its interpreters.

———. *The Mass and the English Reformers*. London, 1958. A historical review from a particular point of view.

Ketley, Joseph, ed. *The Two Liturgies, A.D. 1549, and A.D. 1552: With Other Documents Set Forth by Authority in the Reign of King Edward VI*. Reprint, New York, 1968. Important primary materials.

Procter, Francis and Walter Howard Frere. *A New History of the Book of Common Prayer with a Rationale of Its Offices*. Reprint, London and New York, 1965. Still the standard history, but see *History of Anglican Liturgy*. by C. J. Cuming, London, 1969.

JOHN E. BOOTY

BOOK OF CONCORD. Officially published on 25 June 1580—the fiftieth anniversary of the Augsburg Confession—the *Book of Concord* has come to be the definitive compilation of the Lutheran confessions. It consists of seven Reformation documents recognized as authoritative by Lutherans throughout the world. Although the coalition supporting the Lutheran reform movement—the Schmalkald League—entered the 1540s with considerable political and military strength, it suffered a disastrous military defeat in 1547. In the aftermath, earlier subtle differences among Lutheran theologians turned them into warring factions.

One of the feuding groups, comprising Philipp Melanchthon and his close adherents, remained in Wittenberg, where they had the political support of the elector, the prince of a reuniting Saxony. With Melanchthon's strong support, they favored making ecclesiastical concessions demanded by Emperor Charles V, who had defeated them. The other party, a more diffuse group identified with Matthias Flacius Illyricus and Nikolaus von Amsdorf, were for a time associated with the city of Magdeburg. Flacius Illyricus, a Croatian, had been Melanchthon's secretary until the conflict; von Amsdorf was an old friend of Luther's who had become bishop in Magdeburg. They strongly supported resistance to the emperor.

The two parties, now identified as the Philippists and the Gnesio-Lutherans, fought a series of six pitched theological battles. The original controversy began when Flacius Illyricus published some of Melanchthon's correspondence, in which he privately deplored the concessions required by the emperor. It escalated with the publication of the Leipzig Interim, a provisional arrangement demanded by the emperor to which Melanchthon agreed while offering his own theological twist. Melanchthon's modifications and some offerings by others on related issues incited the polemics. The issues included the role of the will in conversion, the place of law in the Christian faith, the nature of the change that justification works in the person, the place of good works, the sacramental presence of Christ, and related questions.

Middling theologians from both parties, led by Martin Chemnitz from the Philippist side and Jakob Andreae, a Gnesio-Lutheran, began conciliatory negotiations in the late 1560s that eventually resulted in the Formula of Concord of 1577. Although the theologians consistently repudiated Melanchthon's later theological formulations in favor of earlier Lutheran views, they maintained Melanchthon's theological methods, setting the stage for the Lutheran orthodoxy that followed in the later sixteenth and seventeenth century.

Appealing to the earlier Lutheran consensus on the issues, the authors of the Formula of Concord assembled documents that had been previously recognized, legally or pragmatically, as authoritative. The Augsburg Confession, as originally set forth in 1530, had been formally subscribed by the Lutheran political leaders at the Diet of Augsburg; it was given priority along with Luther's Small Catechism (1529), which gained its authority informally but emphatically through its wide usage among Lutherans. Melanchthon's *Apology* of the Augsburg Confession (1531) and his later *Tractatus de Potestate et Primaty papal* (Treatise on the Power and Primacy of the Pope; 1537) were added, along with Luther's Large Catechism (1528–1529) and his Schmalkald Articles (1536). Holding varying degrees of status, these documents had gained authority in Lutheran communities primarily by use. The Formula of Concord in both its fuller statement, known as the *Solid Declaration,* and the condensed form made for the use of political leaders, the *Epitome,* complete the compilation. The formula was in effect a theologically defined treaty.

The *Augustana,* as the Augsburg Confession is also called, and Luther's Small Catechism have retained their formal priority among Lutherans, with pastors and teachers commonly being asked to subscribe to the statements. Lutherans have not always agreed about the other documents. When the settlement that resulted in the *Book of Concord* was circulated among the territories that had officially committed themselves to the Lutheran reform, which included portions of Germany and eastern Europe plus all of Scandinavia, Danish and Norwegian Lutherans confined their endorsement to the *Augustana* and the Small Catechism, while other Lutherans made no exception.

The *Book of Concord* modifies the use of the original Lutheran confessions. The early Lutherans, especially Luther but also Melanchthon, were apocalyptically driven. Expecting imminent cataclysm, they viewed confessions against their New Testament background, with overtones of martyrdom and witness. Consequently, they had little interest in church structures and permanent institutions. Confessing, they saw themselves in parallel to the prophets or Paul before the Roman emperor, setting forth the word, making provision for the moment.

While Luther maintained this apocalyptic sense of confession and regarded the confessions accordingly, Melanchthon saw an additional dimension, treating them as dogmatic standards. His students on both sides of the theological wars took the earlier confessions in this light, regarding them as authoritative theological tradition. The second- and third-generation Lutherans who complied the *Book of Concord* insisted that as tradition, the Lutheran documents had always to be tested against the norm of scripture. But the dogmatic function of the documents had by this time clearly taken ascendancy over the confessional function.

The three great schools of Lutheranism since the sixteenth century have each seen the significance of the *Book of Concord* in their own way. Lutheran orthodoxy viewed it as a dogmatic standard, the benchmark for sound theological formulation; though generally agreeing with the orthodox theologically, Lutheran pietists shifted the focus to the experience of faith underlying the formulations; rationalism, as a historical movement, has commonly resisted confessional authority as a dogmatic imposition, viewing the documents contextually as a starting point. In more recent use, Lutheran theologians have commonly emphasized the original confessional character of the documents, defining their

particular value in terms of the way the confessions of the *Book of Concord* support further confessing. Although the use has thus varied, with all but a few exceptions, Lutherans continue to make constitutional commitments to, the *Book of Concord* and to give it some priority in their theological reflection.

BIBLIOGRAPHY

Bente, Friedrich, and W. H. T. Dau, eds. and trans. *Concordia Triglotta: Die symbolischen Bücher der evangelisch-lutherischen Kirche, deutsch-lateinisch-englisch* (1921). Reprint, Milwaukee, 1988.
Die Bekenntnisschriften der evangelisch-lutherischen Kirche. Reprint, Göttingen, 1992.
Tappert, Theodore G., et. al. *The Book of Concord: The Confessions of the Evangelical Lutheran Church.* Philadelphia, 1959.

JAMES ARNE NESTINGEN

BOOK OF HOMILIES. Published in various editions, the *Book of Homilies* refers to the compilations of official sermons appointed by the monarch to be declared regularly at Church of England services between 1547 and 1689. The first *Book of Homilies* (1547) contains twelve sermons divided after 1559 into thirty-one particular lections. The second *Book of Homilies* (1563) contains twenty additional sermons in thirty-eight lections, and a separately published official sermon, *An Homilie agaynst Disobedience and Wilful Rebellion* (1570), contains six parts. Both *Books of Homilies* and the *Homilie agaynst Disobedience*—all together forming the canon of authorized Anglican sermons—were published in uniform editions in 1582, 1589, and 1595, in an authorized single edition in 1623; and in eight unauthorized unified editions between 1625 and 1687. The entire canon thus consists of thirty-three sermons in seventy-five particular lections, longer sermons being partitioned for simplicity. Between 1547 and 1687, the first *Book of Homilies* alone went through twenty-two editions, the second alone through sixteen; and the *Homilie agaynst Disobedience* alone, through two. The two books and the homily together appeared in twelve editions. The proper title of the *Book of Homilies* begins with the words *Certain Sermons or Homilies. . . .* Various wordings completed the title depending on the edition, but the most significant phrase was *for the Better Understanding of the Simple People,* added to the title after 1559.

The official homilists of the Church of England served two masters—not God and Mammon, but Caesar and God—hence the prominence of "An Exhortation to Obedience" (1547) and the *Homilie agaynst Disobedience* (1570). The compilation had two explicit religious purposes: to set for preaching in the Church of England a high standard and uniformity in sermon form and content and to instruct the simple people in the true Protestant faith. It also had one implicit but urgent political purpose: to inculcate good order and civil obedience into the English people. The plan for the *Book of Homilies* emerged during the late 1530s less as an Anglican *via media* than as a defense against the extremist perils of the Pilgrimage of Grace and the Anabaptist Kingdom of Münster.

The *Book of Homilies* has four principal doctrines: Erastianism, or state supremacy in religious matters; solifidianism, or Luther's doctrine of justification by faith alone; *sola scriptura*-ism, or the Protestant privileging of the Bible over church tradition; and, curiously, adiaphorism, or Philipp Melanchthon's counsel of latitude in things indifferent to salvation. While the *Book of Homilies* is decisively Protestant in its solifidianism and *sola scriptura*-ism, adiaphorism allowed a range of practices. It was so Erastian that it subsumed religious matters under obedience. Henry VIII had appointed Thomas Cranmer to chair the commission for the *Book of Homilies* in 1539. Although the homilies are anonymous, it is now known that Cranmer, Hugh Latimer, Thomas Becon, Edmund Bonner, and John Harpsfield wrote the sermons in the first book, and bishops Matthew Parker, Edmund Grindal, John Jewell, and perhaps others wrote the second and the *Homilie agaynst Disobedience.* Queen Elizabeth I herself supervised the revision of the homilies after her accession in 1558.

Of all the books published in early modern England—not excluding the Bible, *The Book of Common Prayer,* and John Foxe's *Acts and Monuments*—the *Book of Homilies* had the widest audience over the longest time and thus the greatest influence. Its sermons enjoyed continual iteration from every pulpit between 1547 and 1689, with interruptions briefly under Mary Tudor and during the English Civil War and Interregnum. Because it had a captive audience in all parishes of the realm, its sermons became overfamiliar. Before 1600 the word "homily" had acquired connotations of staleness and preachy moralizing. Shakespeare in "As You Like It" (1599) pokes fun at the tedious homily. The ecclesiastical court records are full of cases in which congregations disturbed homilies and walked out to the village alehouse to perform obscene parodies of them. In 1598 one obnoxious Cambridgeshire parishioner repeatedly interrupted the parson's homily with "the most loathesome farting, striking, and scoffing speeches." Catcalls, snoring, and low mockery were common interruptions.

Insofar as the *Book of Homilies* denounced untidiness, moreover, it seemed to endow messiness with allure, as, for example, when the poet Robert Herrick discloses much erotic *Delight in Disorder* (1648). Tedious continual iteration and official authority provoked such mockery and popular symbolic inversion rituals as alehouse sermon parodies, but this popular response acknowledged the moral authority of the book. The effect of the homilies on everyday behavior in early modern England is incalculable, probably great, but certainly not straightforward.

BIBLIOGRAPHY

Blench, J. W. *Preaching in England in the Late Fifteenth and Sixteenth Centuries: A Study of English Sermons, 1450–c.1600.* New York, 1964. Standard work on early modern English homiletics.

Bond, Ronald B., ed. *Certain Sermons or Homilies (1547) and An Homilie agaynst Disobedience and Wilful Rebellion: A Critical Edition.* Toronto, 1987. Important new scholarly edition, but lacking the second *Book of Homilies* (1563) and interpretation of the social and popular cultural significance of the sermons.

Griffiths, John, ed. *The Two Books of Homilies Appointed To Be Read in Churches.* Oxford, 1859. Monumental older scholarly edition of the whole *Book of Homilies.*

Maclure, Millar. *The Paul's Cross Sermons, 1534–1642.* Toronto, 1958. Preaching as propaganda from the premier pulpit of the realm.

Rickey, Mary Ellen, and Thomas B. Stroup, eds. *Certaine Sermons or Homilies Appointed to be Read in Churches in the Time of Queen Elizabeth I, 1547–1571: A Facsimile Reproduction of the Edition of 1623 with an Introduction.* Gainesville, Fla., 1968. Facsimile in black letter of the first authorized unified edition with a good, if summary, literary history of the *Book of Homilies.*

Thomas, Keith. *Religion and the Decline of Magic.* London, 1971. Vast study of systems of belief in Early Modern England that judiciously applies anthropology and social psychology to history. Indispensable work on sixteenth- and seventeenth-century English culture and society.

TERENCE R. MURPHY

BOOK OF RATISBON. *See* Colloquies.

BOOK OF REGENSBURG. *See* Colloquies.

BOOKS OF MARTYRS. On 1 July 1523, two Augustinian monks, Henri Voes and Jan van Esch, were burned as heretics in Brussels. Their supporters held them to be martyrs, not heretics. Four pamphlets, disseminated in over twenty editions, immediately proclaimed this perception. Martin Luther himself wrote a public letter of comfort to the Christians of the Low Countries. Voes and Esch were the first in a long series of people condemned to death because of their religious beliefs.

Reviving a tradition of the primitive church, all religious groups in the sixteenth century venerated their martyrs. After having first issued occasional publications, they put together more voluminous compendia, the "books of martyrs," which were not, however, all drafted according to the same formula. These testimonials, both in manuscript and in printed form, were widely circulated.

Throughout the century, jailed victims of religious repression managed to smuggle letters out of prison, proclaiming their faith, describing their trials, and comforting their loved ones. Some prisoners composed poems and hymns. Their followers bore witness to their courageous deaths and sometimes had access to the official proceedings of their trials.

Given that the title of martyr was limited to those included under the adage "martyrem non facit pœna, sed causa," each confession extolled only its own followers. Thus victims of opposing confessions were labeled as "martyrs of error and of falsehood" or even as "martyrs of the devil." The study of books of martyrs must thus take into account these confessional obstacles.

Reformed Churches. In 1554 three authors independently published Protestant martyrologies: in February the German Ludwig Rabus, in August the Frenchman Jean Crespin, and in September the Englishman John Foxe. Emanating from three different countries, their projects inevitably manifested substantial differences. Five years later, Adriann Corneliszoon van Haemstede inaugurated a different series of books of martyrs in the Netherlands.

Since all of these authors were second-generation Protestants, they narrated events that they had not necessarily witnessed themselves. Their publications grew out of the increasing Protestant awareness of the need for a new historiography that would reject papal primacy and clerical power.

Ludwig Rabus. Ludwig Rabus (1524–1592) was not so much a writer as a man of action. A faithful Lutheran, he was minister in Strasbourg from 1544 to 1556, then superintendent of the church of Ulm from 1556 to 1590. In 1553 he earned his doctorate and began giving courses on the holy scriptures.

The history of his book of martyrs falls into three stages. First, a "preoriginal" edition was entitled *Tomus I. De S. Dei confessoribus veterisque Ecclesiae martyribus* (Strasbourg, 1552). This *Märtyrerlexikon*, ordered alphabetically, covered the Old Testament and the first five centuries of the Christian era, with no mention of contemporary martyrs. Rabus translated it into German in 1552. Second, an eight-part German collection was published in Strasbourg from 1554 to 1558. The collection begins with the essay of 1552 and each section offers new documentation. During the publication of these first sections, Rabus left Strasbourg in 1556 but continued to compile new sections until 1558. Finally, from 1571 to 1572 Rabus divided his eight sections between two folio volumes, with no apparent attempt to renew his documentation. He accorded greater space to martyrs dating from before the sixteenth century.

The title of the sections dating from 1554 to 1558, *Historien der heyligen Ausserwöhlten Gottes Zeügen, Bekennern und Martyrern*, well expressed the contents of the collection. Rabus used the terms "confessors" and "martyrs" in the traditional sense. From the fourth part on, the "confessors" in general, and Martin Luther in particular, received a preponderant place. Rabus produced an enormous but disorganized compilation, prompting Catherine Schutz to characterize it as a "Krämerei und Tauscherei" ("mishmash and confusion").

After publishing a first version in Latin, Rabus shifted his focus to a popular audience and quickly adopted the use of German. While the first editions were intended for the lay community, the republication of 1571/72 aimed at helping preachers with their homilies.

Despite the fact that the book started with the Old Testament, Rabus did not emphasize the continuity of the Christian tradition into the era of the Reformation. Rather, he jumped from the early church to the fifteenth and sixteenth centuries. Furthermore, Rabus's emphasis on the first period of the Reformation (1517–1530) and its development in Germany revealed a choice both confessional and nationalist.

Rabus rarely invokes oral witness, preferring printed sources, which he cites scrupulously. The early period, for example, draws on German publications by Gaspard Hedion; the contemporary section is based mainly on documentation from the *Flugschriften* ("pamphlets"). He also uses the *Commentarii* of Johannes Sleidanus, and collections by John Bale, Foxe, and Crespin. When he draws on Crespin's *Acta martyrum*, his reservations about Calvinism led him to conceal his source. Rabus, an orthodox Lutheran, goes so far as to suppress both Calvin's name and any sacramentarian confession of faith.

The work received only a lukewarm welcome despite the apparent success of the years 1554–1558. At least two reasons explain this fact: first, Rabus's project lacked coherence—and his collection is full of disorder; second, the book of martyrs is a combative literary genre that feeds on militancy, yet the Lutheran churches had only limited experience of persecution.

Jean Crespin. Jean Crespin (1520–1572) was a lawyer from Arras who fled to Geneva in 1548 in order to avoid being persecuted for his faith. As a loyal disciple of Calvin, he founded a press to promote the Reformation. Crespin was, among other things, the pioneer of historical Protestant publications in French. The history of his *Livre des martyrs* is complex and involves three layers: the original work, amplifications by Simon Goulart, and, finally, German translations and extracts.

The development of Crespin's martyrology, always printed in Geneva, fell into several stages. In 1554 a period of trial and error occurred with changes in title and two different formats (8° and 16mo). From 1555 to 1563, Crespin published five successive sections; the first three were reprinted in 16mo format; he also tried Latin versions. Beginning in 1564, the martyrology became a folio volume that repeated and completed all the previously published documentation. Crespin published his last edition in 1570. Simon Goulart (1543–1628) continued to increase the scope of the *Histoire des martyrs* (Geneva, 1582, 1597, 1608, 1619). Christoph Rab completed an abridged German translation (Herborn, 1590); this *Märtyrbuch* was published ten times in German between 1590 and 1683 and once in Latin translation. Paul Crocius made a complete translation of the 1597

French edition (Hanau, 1608); this was republished three times between 1617 and 1722. Conradino Riola translated passages into Romansch (Strada, 1718). Extracts also appeared in German, French, and Dutch. Publication in Germany was done by David Chytraeus, Christophorus Pezel, and Rudolph Huber (1587, 1592, 1664), and in the Netherlands by Pierre Frémaut and Daniel DesMarets (1660, 1671, 1684).

The book was born of personal experience. In 1541 Crespin had witnessed a public burning in Paris, and he had personally had to flee arrest by officers of Charles V. In 1553, when Crespin observed that letters by contemporary martyrs were circulating in Geneva, he decided to give these letters greater distribution by means of the printing press. His first project consisted of publishing authentic documents, limited strictly to martyrs, but he soon increased the scope of his enterprise, adding expositions of general history. He also introduced polemical pieces denouncing subjects such as Nicodemism, Jean Morély's congregationalism, doctrinal deviations by the Anabaptists, and Lutheran theology on the Lord's Supper. Continuing along those lines, Goulart composed an index of theological themes developed in the work. The title of the collection fluctuated markedly, and Goulart finally imposed the definitive title of *Histoire des martyrs*.

Crespin never searched too far into the past, although he did take great care to illustrate the continuity of the Protestant churches with the ancient church. From the first edition on, he began with Jan Hus's witness. Crespin promised to delve further into the past, but this task was not accomplished until 1582 by Goulart. Crespin, who published his book in French, was not so much a historian as a journalist, his main preoccupation being current events. He gathered original and unpublished documents mainly concerning France and the Netherlands. As Crespin's book gained public attention, more information began to fall into his hands, and the publications of accounts of martyrs multiplied. Crespin exploited the martyrologies of Foxe and Haemstede, rarely citing his sources. Where Crespin did cite a reference, he had often merely copied it from the sources. He sometimes added unpublished elements to his documents but did not distort the evidence.

He mainly presented Calvinist martyrs, for whom he put forward long confessions of faith. The theme of the universality of the true faith in time and space counterbalances the narrowness of his confessional preoccupation. Crespin wished to demonstrate that Jesus' martyrs were everywhere, but he did not dwell on martyrs whose faith strayed from Calvinism.

The influence of Crespin's book of martyrs was far-reaching since it was regularly reprinted in French and also in German. It exerted an indirect influence through the Dutch book of martyrs, which was very close in conception and documentation.

John Foxe. John Foxe (1516–1587) was a humanist interested in ancient history; circumstances led him to draft a martyrology focused on contemporary events. A tutor for a wealthy family, he was forced into exile during the reign of Mary Tudor, but in 1559 he was able to return to London. From the time of his exile, history became his dominant passion; until his death, he was to dedicate himself to writing. Although he was ordained a priest in 1560, he really did not devote himself to this ministry.

His first project was to compose an ecclesiastical history of England and of Christianity, with particular emphasis on martyrs. In 1548 he began a chronicle of persecutions from the time of the Lollards until the reign of Henry VIII. The first part of this work appeared in Strasbourg in September 1554, but the persecutions during the reign of Mary Tudor dramatically disrupted Foxe's undertaking. Edmund Grindal suggested to Foxe that he publish the documentation resulting from the Marian persecutions. A Latin compendium, dealing only with Great Britain, appeared in Basel in 1559. This *Pars prima* was continued by Pantaleon. In collaboration with Genevan editors, the collection was translated and summarized by Crespin in 1561.

Once back in England, Foxe adopted the English language in order to reach the largest possible audience. He published his work henceforth in large folios, which continued to be printed with more or less significant additions. These appeared in 1563, 1570 (in two volumes), 1576, and 1583. After his death, these publications continued to appear (a ninth edition was issued in 1684). There was also an entire series of excerpts and summaries in English. The title of his collection varied from *Rerum in Ecclesia gestarum commentarii* to *Acts and Monuments of These Latter Dayes* to *Ecclesiasticall History Contaynyng the Actes and Monuments*; he eventually reverted to the original English title.

A staunch nationalist, Foxe gives a clear priority to events in England. He did, however, speak of other nations, putting Continental martyrologies to good use. From the first edition, Foxe places the phenomenon of martyrdom in a historical perspective; John Wycliffe provided the point of departure for his narrative. In 1563 Foxe went as far back as the year 1000, and in 1570 he began with the early church.

Foxe was the most scholarly of all the authors of martyrologies. This disciple of Bale was steeped in erudition; for example, he often provided references for his sources. From 1559 on, he systematically scrutinized source materials, in particular episcopal records, for both recent and earlier persecutions. His work constitutes a historical source of considerable merit, even if his judgments are those of his time. He did not always maintain the necessary distance from his sources, especially as concerned medieval history.

Foxe sought to nourish the piety of the faithful, to denounce the impiety of Catholics, and to exalt England, the elect nation. His work everywhere demonstrated his conviction that "God is an Englishman," as John Aylmer would have it. While Catholicism threatened the Anglican Church, the *Acts and Monuments* provided Anglicans with an arsenal of reasons to fuel their hatred of Rome. After James I came to the throne, the situation changed; the dissidents then used this martyrology to denounce the oppression of the true faithful by the established church.

Adriaan Corneliszoon van Haemstede. The Dutch book of martyrs was conceived five years after the preceding ones. Its first author, Adriaan Corneliszoon van Haemstede (1520–1562), graduated in civil and canon law from Louvain. In 1555 he served as a Reformed minister at Antwerp. Contested by his congregation, he left that city in 1559, heading to London, where his tolerance for the Anabaptists led to his excommunication. He died in Friesland.

The first edition of Haemstede's *De Gheschiedenisse ende den doodt der vromer Martelaren* was most likely printed in Emden, but the preface (and probably the entire volume) was composed in Antwerp during the height of the persecution. When Haemstede died shortly thereafter, others continued his book of martyrs. The identity of those responsible for the editions of 1565 and 1566 remains unknown. The 1566 edition assured the Calvinist orthodoxy of the collection; the editor deleted Haemstede's name as well as some passages deemed too favorable to the Anabaptists. The Synod of Dordrecht in 1578 made the book of martyrs an official work; eight editions followed from 1578 to 1616. In 1604 the work was illustrated with sixty-three engravings. Further revision led in 1633 to an abundantly illustrated folio edition of one thousand pages entitled *Historien der Vromer Martelaren*. The work continued to be augmented and reprinted on a regular basis. In 1657 Haemstede's name was reinstated at the end of the preface. All in all, some twenty editions appeared in the sixteenth and seventeenth centuries, and several others followed by the nineteenth century.

Haemstede's work was truly a book of martyrs. The author chose to evoke only those Christians put to death for their faith, avoiding all accounts foreign to that goal. This orientation was not modified in later editions. Haemstede presented the martyrs in a succinct fashion, summarizing narratives and confessions of faith. His work, published only in Dutch, was well adapted to a popular audience.

The Dutch book of martyrs deals with martyrs of all eras and all countries. From the first edition on, the work began with Saint Stephen. In the course of subsequent editions, the history of martyrs predating the Reformation was enriched, thus offering insight into all periods of Christianity.

For his 1559 edition, Haemstede used the three extant books of martyrs (Rabus, Crespin, and Foxe). Like Crespin, Haemstede wished to record recent martyrs; he thus took greater advantage of the Genevan book of martyrs. But for martyrs from Flanders and Antwerp, he also offered firsthand accounts that were sometimes based on archival sources. Subsequent additions present the same char-acteristics, such as systematic use of other historic works and original accounts, but Haemstede never detailed his sources.

The goal of Haemstede's book was clearly pastoral. It fell into the Calvinist line, without exaggerating dogmatic and confessional developments. The martyrs' faith was defined concisely. The reservations concerning Lutherans are less marked than in Crespin's work.

The Dutch book of martyrs was originally conceived for Calvinists who experienced the dangers of persecution, and it gained wide distribution for several hundred years. After 1579 it became an official work sponsored by the national synod. In this way, just like the English book of martyrs, it became an important instrument of propaganda, both in exalting the nation and in fighting the Catholics. In fact, its most notable period of success corresponds with the eighty-year-long war that forged the independence of the United Provinces from Spanish rule.

Heinrich Pantaleon. The Basel publishers of Foxe's 1559 Latin book of martyrs had presented the work as a *pars prima.* Wishing to give it a sequel, they asked the historian Heinrich Pantaleon (1522–1559) to compose a *pars secunda* dedicated to martyrs of France, Italy, and Germany. This work appeared in 1563.

Pantaleon seemed more concerned with history than with theology. He was familiar with the books of martyrs by Crespin and Rabus, and had access to some unpublished documents, particularly Italian.

The volume, almost entirely unsuccessful, shows by way of contrast what makes for a successful book of martyrs. In addition to being published in Latin, it was also a commissioned work put together with no great conviction. Thus the publishers never fulfilled their promise of a third volume. Furthermore, Pantaleon, a Protestant, was more concerned with exalting Germany than with spreading ideas of the Reformation. In his *Prosopographia heroum atque illustrium virorum totius Germaniae* (1565/66), he cited Protestant and Catholic theologians side by side, without even mentioning martyrs.

Cypryan Bazylik. In 1567 a printer in Brest Litovsk, Cypryan Bazylik (c.1535–1591), presented a survey of European martyrs from the time of Hus in *Historya o srogiem przesládowániu Kościoła bożego.* Conceptually, this book copied the model provided by Crespin's editions in Latin; the accounts and confessions of faith were shorter than in the French editions. Bazylik also used the Latin books of martyrs by Foxe and Pantaleon.

Anabaptists. The Anabaptist books of martyrs have a history different from that of the other Protestant collections. Begun rather modestly, they did not come to fruition until the seventeenth century. The Mennonites were the object of condemnation on the part of both Catholics and Protestants. Thus their martyrs were excluded from the books of martyrs cited above.

The Sacrifice of the Lord. The Anabaptist martyrologies began with a small volume, *Het Offer des Heeren* (The Sacrifice of the Lord; Emden, 1562), which presented twenty-two martyrs, almost all of them from the Netherlands. The collection included only documents about the martyrs: letters, testaments, and so on. In general the notes were dogmatic and spiritual in character, with a minimum of historical information. They were drawn in part from short, previously published works. In 1563 a small hymnal was added with twenty-five hymns evoking the martyrdom of Christ and of numerous Anabaptists. Recourse to song was typical of the Anabaptist tradition and appears in all of the following editions.

The double collection was reprinted regularly with few additions, the eleventh and last edition appearing in 1599. It numbered only 33 martyrs in its accounts, while the *Liedtboecxken* mentions 179. On the whole, the work concentrated on the history of the Netherlands.

Jakob Outerman, Joost Govertsz, Hans de Ries, and others. At the beginning of the seventeenth century, another *Historie der Martelaren* was published, this one more complete and more historical in focus that *Het Offer des Heeren.* A major investigation was undertaken by several authors at the suggestion of Jakob Outerman, the minister of Haarlem (c. 1547–1639) and Joost Govertsz. This collaboration transcended internal Anabaptist divisions and resulted in a publication to which Hans de Ries (1553–1638) wrote a preface. Here he invited Anabaptists to bury their differences and to defend the faith of their ancestors (Haarlem, 1615).

The collection presented only martyrs from after 1524, thus omitting the early and medieval periods, but it results from a far more extensive investigation than its smaller predecessor. The work was republished several times, first in Hoorn in 1617 and 1626, then in Haarlem in 1631/32. The Hoorn editions inveighed against the Haarlem edition because of some declarations about Christ's humanity.

Martyrs' Mirror. In 1660 Tieleman van Braght (1625–1664) finally created a first-rate book of martyrs, *Het Bloedigh Tooneel der Doops-gesinde* (Dordrecht, 1660). The re-edition of 1685, *Martelaersspiegel* (Martyrs' Mirror), is illustrated with beautiful copper plates by Jan Luyken. While Braght first intended simply to republish the 1631 book of martyrs, he quickly discovered the need for a broader scope.

This book of martyrs included a first volume presenting martyrs prior to the sixteenth century who rejected the baptism of children. The second part, devoted to more recent times, listed the names of 803 martyrs, of whom 613 were executed in the Netherlands of the time (today's Benelux). Braght considerably extended the documentation for this group, but he was working according to the criteria of his time; his goal was to edify his readers. The book was reprinted in Dutch (1685), in German (1748/49, 1780, 1814, 1870), and in English (1850/52, 1837).

Catholics. Since Catholics suffered less persecution, they did not compose martyrologies as large as those of the Protestants. Maurice Chauncy published the *Historia aliquot nostri saeculi martyrum* (Mainz, 1550), which treated several English martyrs. In 1573 in Munich, Erasmus Vendius published this work again, adding other accounts concerning Scotland and France. Then Richard Verstegan re-edited it as the *Theatrum crudelitatum haereticorum nostri temporis* (Antwerp, 1587). The work was republished several times, both in Latin and in French.

The Franciscans composed works exalting the martyrs of their order. Thomas Bourchier published a martyrology concerning those Franciscans executed between 1536 and 1582 (Paris, 1582; Ingolstadt, 1583; Paris, 1586). Florentinus Leydanus did the same for his confreres executed in the Low Countries (Ingolstadt, 1582). These two works were summarized in German by Valentinus Fricius (Ingolstadt, 1584 and 1585).

In addition, the Catholics criticized the Protestant martyrologies. In his *Dialogi sex* (Antwerp, 1566), Nicholas Harpsfield denounced the errors spread by Crespin and Foxe. Various polemical works contain violent attacks on Protestant martyrologies. But the pinnacle of this counter-propaganda came in the next century with Jacques Severt's *L'Anti-martyrologe* (Lyon, 1622). Arnoudt van Geluwe published a similar Dutch work at Antwerp in 1656.

Conclusion. The books of martyrs enjoyed great success in the vernacular language, while all attempts at Latin editions failed. Conceived during a time of persecution, these works presented in a relatively small format, were intended for individual reading; they subsequently were printed in folio editions and were used for communal reading in the established churches.

This literary genre was well received by readers who were experiencing religious intolerance firsthand. When the churches became better organized, these collections continued the anti-Catholic struggle by recalling the constant threat of persecution. They encouraged nationalistic feelings linked to the desire for religious and political independence.

The historian might ask two questions concerning these works. One might be interested in the martyrs themselves and seek to find out whether the collections are reliable sources. One might also choose to analyze the martyrologies themselves, in order to discern the authors' motivations and the influence of the literary genre. The two approaches can be complementary.

From a critical standpoint, considerable agreement exists among studies of the various books of martyrs. They deserve the historian's confidence, but, at the same time, they must be read with a critical eye. The authors of these books of martyrs are often content to reuse existing texts, more or less modifying them to their own needs. Generally speaking, they are faithful to their sources. But, in line with the standards of their time, they sometimes use unreliable sources, or they misinterpret their sources. Each entry must be scrutinized and verified, in order to determine the quality of the sources consulted. In addition, the various editions of a text need to be compared, for substantial modifications (intentional or accidental) often occur. When using modern editions that reproduce a relatively recent text, caution is in order. Examples include Crespin's *Histoire des martyrs*, published by Daniel Benoît (Toulouse, 1885–1889); and one of the four editions of the *Acts and Monuments* by S. R. Cattley and G. Townsend, and later by Josiah Pratt (between 1837 and 1877). The reprint of the 1570 *Het Offer des Heeren* by S. Cramer in Bibliotheca Reformatorica Neerlandica (The Hague, 1904) is more scholarly.

Moreover, most authors introduce themes other than that of the glorification of the martyrs. Studies of Foxe's work provide a model that can profitably be imitated in studying other martyrologies. For example, some have focused on Foxe's understanding of women's roles in society. The martyrologies speak of the continuity of the church since the time of Christ up to and including the present day, of the *successio martyrum* as guarantor of the faith of Luther's role in restoring the faith. They exalt one country or another as God's elect nation, warning of dangers within the Calvinist fold and taking a stand on theological questions such as the humanity of Christ and the meaning of the Eucharist.

The illustrations of the martyrologies also deserve study. These images offer a characteristic interpretation of martyrdom, stressing especially the serenity of the victims rather than their atrocious suffering and giving mocking caricatures of the executioners. No matter what perspective is adopted, the martyrologies of the sixteenth century constitute a rich source for the history of the Reformation.

BIBLIOGRAPHY

Alberda-van der Zijpp, T. "'Het Offer des Heeren': Geloof en getuigenis van de Martelaren." In *Wederdopers, Menisten, Doopsgezinden in Nederland 1530–1980*, edited by S. Groenveld, J. P. Jacobszoon, and Simon Leendert Verheus, pp. 46–61. Zutphen, 1981.

Brückner, Annemarie, and Wolfgang Brückner. "Zeugen des Glaubens und ihre Literatur: Altväterbeispiele, Kalenderheilige, protestantische Martyrer und evangelische Lebenszeugnisse." In *Volkserzählung und Reformation*, edited by W. Brückner, pp. 521–579. Berlin, 1974.

Dedeke, Gerhard. *Die protestantischen Märtyrerbücher von Ludwig Rabus, Jean Crespin und Adriaen van Haemstede und ihr gegenseitigen Verhältnis.* Unpublished thesis. Halle, 1924.

Gilmont, Jean-François. *Les martyrologes protestants du XVIe siècle: Essai de présentation générale.* Unpublished thesis. Louvain, 1966. A synthesis of the various martyrologies.

———. "La genèse du martyrologe d'Adrien van Haemstede (1559)." *Revue d'histoire ecclésiastique* 63 (1968), 379–414.

———. *Jean Crespin: Un éditeur réformé du XVIe siècle.* Travaux d'humanisme et Renaissance 186. Geneva, 1981. One chapter on his martyrology.

Halkin, Léon-Ernest. "Les martyrologes et la critique." In *Mélanges historiques offerts à Jean Meyhoffer, docteur en theologie*, pp. 52–75. Lausanne, 1952.

Haller, William. *Foxe's Book of Martyrs and the Elect Nation.* London, 1963. Study of nationalist ideology in Foxe's martyrology.

Jelsma, Auke Jan. *Adriaan van Haemstede en zijn Martelaarsboek.* The Hague, 1970.

Kolb, Robert. *For All the Saints: Changing Perceptions of Martyrdom and Sainthood in the Lutheran Reformation.* Macon, Ga., 1987. An extensive study of Rabus, with a biographical chapter and one on his martyrology.

Macek, Ellen A. "The Emergence of a FeminineSpirituality in 'The Book of Martyrs.'" *Sixteenth Century Journal* 19 (1988), 63–80.

Meylan, Henri. "Martyrs du diable." In *D'Érasme à Théodore de Bèze: Problèmes de l'Église et de l'école chez les réformés*, pp. 259–275. Geneva, 1976. On the intolerance shown toward the martyrs of other confessions.

Moreau, Gérard. "Contribution à l'histoire du Livre des martyrs." *Bulletin de la Société de l'histoire du protestantisme français* 103 (1957), 173–199.

Mozley, James Frederic. *John Foxe and His Book.* London, 1940.

Olsen, V. Norskov. *John Foxe and the Elizabethan Church.* Berkeley, 1973.

Piaget, Arthur, and Gabrielle Berthoud. *Notes sur le livre des martyrs de Jean Crespin.* Neuchâtel, 1930. A hypercritical study which minimizes the historical value of the martyrology.

Pijper, Fredrik. *Martelaarsboeken.* The Hague, 1924. On the martyrologies of Haemstede, Crespin, Rabus, and *Het Offer des Heeren.*

Pollard, Alfred W, and G. D. Redgrave. *A Short-Title Catalogue of Books Printed in England, Scotland and Ireland and of English Books Printed Abroad, 1475–1640.* 2d ed. London, 1986.

Smart, Stefan J. "John Foxe and 'The Story of Richard Hun, Martyr.'" *Journal of Ecclesiastical History* 37 (1986), 1–14.

Studer, Gerald C. "A History of the Martyrs' Mirror." *Mennonite Quarterly Review* 22 (1948), 163–179.

Vander Haeghen, Ferdinand, Th.-J.-I. Arnold, and R. Vanden Berghe. *Bibliographie des martyrologues protestants néerlandais.* Ghent, 1890. Good bibliographies of Continental martyrologies.

White, Helen Constance. *Tudor Books of Saints and Martyrs.* Madison, Wis., 1963. On Foxe, see pp. 132–195.

Yates, Frances A. "Foxe as Propagandist." *Encounter* 27 (1966), 78–86.

JEAN-FRANÇOIS GILMONT
Translated from French by Catharine Randall and Caroline Benforado

BOONEN, Jacob (1573–1655), sixth bishop of Ghent (1617–1621) and fourth archbishop of Mechelen (Malines) (1621–1655). The son of a member of the Council of Brabant, Boonen seemed destined to wear the robe. In Maastricht, Pont-à-Mousson, and Louvain he studied both civil and canon law, taking his "licentiaat" in 1595, then working as a lawyer in Brussels and The Hague.

Boonen's choice of vocation changed soon afterward, when during an emotional moment before a shrine in Mechelen he decided to enter the clergy. Though ordained only in 1611 at age thirty-seven, he had by then already served as canon of the cathedral chapter of Saint Rombouts in Mechelen (1604) and as judge of the ecclesiastical court of the archdiocese (1608). In these functions he became perhaps the closest collaborator of the reforming archbishop Mathias Hovius, whom he would eventually succeed. After ordination came a string of new positions: ecclesiastical councillor of the grand council of Mechelen (1611), dean of the chapter of Saint Rombouts (1612), and bishop of Ghent (1617). His episcopacy there proved to be a stepping-stone; for at the death of Hovius in 1620, Boonen was chosen as the new archbishop of Mechelen. He took possession of his see on 26 November 1621.

Boonen pursued a vigorous policy of Catholic reform. He regularly visited his diocese and arranged at least eight meetings with his suffragan bishops to discuss common pastoral concerns and policies. Boonen's particular vision of reform is reflected strongly in the records of these meetings and of those with the rural deans. He also made considerable efforts to reform lax monasteries and to encourage new, vigorous houses; the priests of the French *Oratoire*, for instance, settled in the archdiocese thanks to the support of Boonen, founding houses in Louvain (1626), Mechelen (1630), and Brussels (1632). Yet, relations with the abbey of Affligem, whose revenues largely financed the relatively new archdiocese, remained strained, as they had been under his predecessors.

Far more than his contemporary bishops in the Spanish Netherlands, Boonen played a major role on the political stage. Since as archbishop of Mechelen he was *ex officio* abbot of Affligem, he was entitled to a seat in the States of Brabant. From 1626 on he was a member of the council of state. Boonen also headed the delegation sent to the Dutch Republic in 1632 to negotiate peace. When the archduchess Isabella died in 1633, Boonen was given a seat on the council of regency.

Though his thirty-five years as archbishop were marked by a myriad of concerns and impressive accomplishments, Boonen is perhaps best remembered for the indulgent position he took toward Jansenism. It was not merely that he was a close friend of the first generation of Jansenist thinkers, including Cornelis Otto Jansen himself, Hendrik Calenus, and Libertus Froidmont, but also a question of temperament. His benevolent attitude toward Jansenism was in line with his own pursuit of sobriety and his struggle against what he considered the lax morality of the Jesuits. The good reputation he had built up in Rome over so many years was soon undone by his refusal to condemn the new theology. He permitted Jansenist writings to be published, and delayed publication of the papal bull *In eminenti* (1643), which condemned the *Augustinus* of Jansen. The antagonisms with Rome grew even worse during the late 1640s, when he refused to appear there as ordered, then peaked on 19 December 1652, when Innocent X suspended Boonen as well as Antoon Triest, bishop of Ghent. After several tense months, both submitted to the Holy See, though reluctantly. On 21 October 1653 Boonen was reinstated as archbishop of Mechelen; during the same year his friends Calenus and Froidmont died.

The last years of Boonen's life were marked by bitterness and a rapid decline in health. The anti-Jansenist party and especially the internuncio in Brussels kept a constant eye on the repentant archbishop. Plans were made to remove him from office and replace him with a bishop-coadjutor, but he died, on 30 November 1655, before they could be implemented.

The significance of Boonen's episcopacy has always been overshadowed by the events of 1652–1653 and the single but major issue of Jansenism. His obstinate opposition to *In eminenti* is condemned by some, praised by others, while his important pastoral policies and administration are relegated to the background. However one views him now, there is little doubt that his support of Jansenism in its early days permitted the movement to rise and flourish in the Low Countries, and that this movement influenced the religious history of the Spanish Netherlands in a radical way.

BIBLIOGRAPHY

Ceyssens, L. "Jacques Boonen face au laxisme pénitenciel." *Société des amis de Port-Royal* 9 (1958), 9–61. One of many publications by this expert on Jansenism and Boonen's role in it.

———. "Les dernières années de Boonen, archevêque de Mechelen." *Augustiniana* 11 (1961), 87–120, 320–335, 564–582. A sympathetic, detailed sketch of Boonen's disappointing last years.

Claessens, P. *Histoire des archevêques de Malines.* 2 vols. Mechelen, Belgium, 1881. Contains an adequate biographical sketch.

Marinus, M. J. "Jacob Boonen, 1617–1621." In *Het bisdom Gent, 1559–1991: Vier eeuwen geschiedenis,* edited by Michael Cloet, pp. 63–65. Ghent, 1991. Summary of activities as bishop of Ghent.

Ram, P. F. X. de, ed. *Nova et absoluta collectio synodorum . . . Synodicon Belgicum.* 2 vols. Mechelen, Belgium, 1828–1829. This collection of important ecclesiastical texts contains pastoral letters, minutes from the meetings of the bishops and rural deans, and so on, which reveal policies of the archbishops, including, of course, Boonen's.

CRAIG HARLINE AND EDDY F. PUT

BORGIA, Rodrigo. *See* Alexander VI.

BORNEMISZA, Péter (Lat., Abstemius; 1535–1585) Hungarian man of letters and Lutheran bishop. Born of a wealthy burgher family at Pest, Bornemisza lost his parents when the Turks captured the town in 1541. He was raised by noble relatives in Upper Hungary. After attending school in Kassa (Košice), Slovakia, Bornemisza visited for brief periods after 1557 several universities abroad. In Wittenberg he was a student of Philipp Melanchthon. Upon returning home Bornemisza started a secular career as a printer and then went as a clerk to the Vienna court. Sometime before 1564, after much inner turmoil, he turned to an ecclesiastical vocation. From then to nearly the end of his life, Bornemisza was court preacher for various magnates and intermittently served as parish preacher. In 1573 he was elected superintendent of a newly established Lutheran diocese in the northwestern part of the country. Around 1582 Bornemisza retired to his own estate near a small village, where he died in 1585.

Bornemisza started his literary activity already in 1558 while at the University of Vienna by rendering into Hungarian Sophocles' *Electra*. This was the first known work of the literary genre of tragedy in the Hungarian language. The most significant work of ecclesiastical interest is a five-volume collection of sermons for all the feast days of the year, called *Postilla*, which Bornemisza published in the 1570s. To produce the work he set up his own printing shop at Sempte (Šintava), Slovakia. The five-volume collection was a multi-faceted compostion; the sermons, far from being of the usual pattern, consisted of self-confession, true stories, anecdotes, and fables, all with a sharp edge of social and individual criticism. Bornemisza often named those he criticized. Part of this great work was the *Ördögi kisértetek* (Diabolical Temptations), a masterpiece of Hungarian prose that appeared in 1579 and then in several later editions, separate from the five-volume edition of sermons. Another voluminous collection of sermons, called *Foliopostilla*, appeared in 1584, with the same spiritual attitude. A hymnal, edited by Bornemisza in 1582, was also unusual. It contained more than three hundred hymns, most liturgical but also many didactic poems and biblical epic songs. This *Hymnal in Three Orders* contained the hymns most often sung in the period and was popular for many years.

Bornemisza had a difficult disposition, and he did not seek nor did he gain the appreciation of those around him. Instead, Bornemisza was often in conflict with ecclesiastical and secular authorities, with indidivuals, and with officials. His *ad personam* criticisms especially earned him many enemies. Bornemisza had three wives; the first and the second, together with five children and other relatives, died in the plague of 1576–1577. Bornemisza was the tutor of the greatest Hungarian Renaissance poet, Bálint Balassi (1554–1594), while officiating at the Zólyom (Zvolen), Slovakia, court of his father.

BIBLIOGRAPHY

Primary Sources

Bornemisza, Péter. *Négy kis könyvecske a keresztyéni hitnek tudományáról* (Four Little Books on the Science of Christian Faith). Sempte, 1572.
———. *Elsö része az evangéliumokból és az epistolákból való tanuságoknak, mellyeket a keresztyének gyülekezetibe szoktanak prédikálni minden ünnepnap* (First Part of the Lessons from the Gospels and the Epistles Which Are Usually Preached in the Congregations of Christians Each Holy Day). Sempte, 1573.
———. *Másik része. . . minden ünnepnap* (Other Part. . . Each Holy Day). Sempte, 1574.
———. *Harmadik része. . . minden ünnepnap* (Third Part. . . Each Holy Day). Sempte, 1575.
———. *Negyedik része. . . minden ünnepnap* (Fourth Part. . . Each Holy Day). Sempte, 1578.
———. *Ötödik és utolsó része. . . minden ünnepnap* (Fifth and Last Part. . . Each Holy Day). Sempte, 1579.
———. *Énekek három rendbe: Különb különb félék.* (Songs in Three Orders of Various Kinds; 1582). Edited by Sándor Ivan Kovács. Budapest, 1964. A facsimile edition.

Secondary Sources

Nemeskürty, István. *Bornemisza Péter az ember és az iró* (Péter Bornemisza The Man and the Writer). Budapest, 1959.
———. *Bornemisza Péter kisértései.* Budapest, 1984.
Schulek, Tibor. *Bornemisza Péter, 1535–1584.* Budapest, 1939.

KATALIN PÉTER

BORRHAUS, Martin (Lat., Cellarius; 1499–1564), German Reformed theologian. Born in Stuttgart, at thirteen he enrolled at the University of Tübingen, where he began to study philosophy and scholastic theology, but turned to mathematics and Aristotelian philosophy. He received his M.A. in 1515. In 1519, because of a war between the Swabian League and Württemberg, he transferred to the University of Ingolstadt to study under Johannes Reuchlin and Johann Eck. The arrival of the plague in 1521 forced him to flee Ingolstadt, and a quarrel with Eck turned his steps to Wittenberg. He arrived there while Luther was at Wartburg castle. For a time he stayed in the home of Philipp Melanchthon, taught mathematics to students preparing to enter the university, and had himself inscribed at the university on 7 April 1522. In the meantime, he joined the Reformation with the assertion that the Holy Spirit had illuminated his mind one day while reading Luther's pamphlet on the freedom of a Christian. When the Zwickau Prophets arrived in the city on 27 December 1521, Borrhaus was captivated by them, later defending Marcus Stübner and his views against the aspersions of Luther.

He left Wittenberg in the company of Stübner about the same time as Andreas Bodenstein von Karlstadt, returned to Stuttgart for a time, only to find his way to Zurich in October 1524, where he met Gerhard Westerburg—an advance man for Bodenstein—who had also been strongly influenced by the Zwickau Prophets and whom Borrhaus had come to know in Wittenberg. In Zurich Borrhaus contacted the group of radicals around Conrad Grebel, and apparently came to share their views on baptism. But before the January 1525 colloquy on baptism between Huldrych Zwingli and his former followers could take place, Borrhaus left the city, appearing in Königsburg some time before 11 June 1525. Suspected of harboring Müntzerian ideas by Paul Speratus, Borrhaus was incarcerated for a time and forced to put his views in writing. This done—it was published in Strasbourg (1527) as *De operibus Dei*—he was forced to return to Wittenberg for Luther's seal of approval. Though disagreements persisted between them, Luther nevertheless asked Borrhaus to remain in Wittenberg, but the latter thought it better to move on.

He went south once more, this time to Strasbourg, where

he was welcomed by both Martin Bucer and Wolfgang Capito. For a time the latter came under the influence of Borrhaus; but Bucer became more and more suspicious of him. Borrhaus encountered Michael Sattler and Hans Denck, getting into a debate with the latter over the freedom of the human will, Borrhaus being a strong predestinarian by now if he had ever been anything else. But attempts to reconcile with Zwingli failed, and the publication of his *De operibus Dei* did nothing to mollify the latter.

In 1527 Borrhaus married a wealthy widow (Uttenheim), upon her death in 1536 he moved to Basel. As he had earlier in Stuttgart, he again took up glass blowing to make ends meet. In 1538 he remarried. In December 1541 he was appointed professor of rhetoric at the university, and in 1546 he succeeded Bodenstein as professor of Old Testament. That year he was appointed rector of the university, again in 1553, and a last time in 1564.

His first book, *De operibus Dei*, was not only the first systematic Protestant treatise on predestination but also included some novel chiliastic notions in its concluding sections. His views may well lie at the foundation of Melchior Hoffman's and Bernhard Rothmann's speculation on the subject. If so, Borrhaus is of greater significance for the early years of the Reformation than he has heretofore been realized. His *De censura veri et falsa* of 1540 applied the rhetorical method to the study of Aristotle. He had preceded this in 1539 with a commentary on *Proverbs*; commentaries on the Pentateuch (1555), *Isaiah* (1561), and others, followed.

During his Basel years Borrhaus came to be highly regarded by his colleagues and revered by his students. But his interests continued to skirt the borders of heresy. His contact with Michael Servetus and Celio Secondo Curione aroused suspicion. Later he would recommend Kaspar von Schwenckfeld and Westerburg to Heinrich Bullinger. He even became a close friend of David Joris, who was living in Basel under an assumed name. (Did Borrhaus know his true identity?) When the latter died and his identity was revealed, Borrhaus and his theological colleagues were compelled to condemn his ideas posthumously. For the man who had defended Servetus's right to speak out and assisted many heterodox Italian refugees, this task must have been particularly distasteful. Though apparently rehabilitated, Borrhaus may have successfully camouflaged his earlier radicalism: he certainly never overtly renounced it.

BIBLIOGRAPHY

Friesen, Abraham. "Martin Borrhaus: On the Borders of Heresy." In *Profiles of Radical Reformers*, edited by Walter Klaassen, pp. 234–246. Scottdale, Pa., 1982.

Gerbert, Camille. *Geschichte der Strassburger Sektenbewegung zur Zeit der Reformation 1524 bis 1534.* Strasbourg, 1889.

Hulshof, Abraham. *Geschiedenis van de Doopsgezinde te Straatsburg van 1525–1557.* Amsterdam, 1905.

Riggenbach, B. "Martin Borrhaus." *Basler Jahrbuch* (1900), 47–84.

Seifert, Arno. "Reformation und Chiliasmus: Die Rolle des Martin Cellarius-Borrhaus." *Archiv für Reformationsgeschichte* 77 (1986), 226–264.

Williams, R. L. "Martin Cellarius and the Reformation in Strasburg." *Journal of Ecclesiastical History* 32.4 (October 1981), 477–497.

ABRAHAM FRIESEN

BORROMEO, Carlo (also Charles; 1538–1584), saint, cardinal, archbishop of Milan, and promoter of the Counter-Reformation. He was born at Rocca d'Arona (near Lago Maggiore), the fortress of his father, Count Giberto II. As a younger son, he was destined for an ecclesiastical career, and at the age of seven he was tonsured and given his first benefice. He studied canon and civil law at the University of Pavia and received the double doctorate in December 1559, just before his mother's brother, Cardinal Giovan Angelo dé Medici, was elected in the conclave. The new pope, Pius IV, called him to Rome, made him a cardinal, appointed him his secretary, and conferred many other dignities and emoluments on him, most notably the office of administrator of the archdiocese of Milan, even though such nepotism was contrary to the spirit of the Catholic reform movement.

As cardinal-nephew, Borromeo faithfully, diligently, and effectively directed the papal secretariat but did not make any important decisions on his own initiative; he dealt with the ambassadors and handled the correspondence with the nuncios and with the legates at Trent during the third period of the general council. After the death of his elder brother, Count Federico, he underwent a spiritual transformation; he adopted ascetic practices, curtailed the splendor of his style of life, associated with Jesuits and other religious men, and redirected the discussions of the Vatican Nights (the literary academy he had organized) from humanist to theological topics. In 1563 he was both ordained priest and consecrated bishop. Though he was convinced of a bishop's obligation to reside in his diocese, as the council had decreed, he was detained in Rome in 1564 by the business of the papal confirmation and the initial execution of the conciliar decrees; meanwhile, he appointed a reform-minded vicar-general, Niccolò Ormaneto, who held a diocesan synod at Milan. Soon, however, he obtained Pius's permission to leave Rome. He resigned all his curial offices except membership on the new Congregation of the Council and made his solemn entry into Milan as archbishop on 23 September 1565.

Taking up permanent residence in his see, he started the work of reform in conformity with the Tridentine norms. In October he convoked a provincial council, the first to be held in Milan since 1311. Subsequently he held five more councils at the three-year intervals prescribed by the Council of Trent. The decrees of these councils were approved in Rome, printed, and widely diffused and accepted elsewhere. He also held ten diocesan synods between 1568 and his death; their decrees regulated the deportment of the clergy, administration of the sacraments, liturgy, Lenten observances, funerals, the construction and furnishing of churches, the management of parochial property, and many other matters for the purpose of improving the care of souls. These decrees and the archbishop's pastoral letters were also published and disseminated far beyond the borders of his diocese.

Besides legislation, Borromeo undertook a systematic visitation of the parishes, monasteries, and institutions of the diocese, beginning with the cathedral in 1566. From then on he spent a considerable part of each year making pastoral visits, which often required long and arduous journeys in his extensive territory. Sometimes he encountered resistance from chapters, religious houses, hospitals, and lay confraternities—in one case an attempt was even made on his life—and he had to use the extraordinary powers and privileges that he had received from the Holy See. He was also appointed apostolic visitor for other dioceses and traveled to the German cantons of Switzerland on missions for the faith.

Further observing the Tridentine injunctions, he promptly opened a major seminary within his own diocese and then continually revised its statutes and increased its endowment. He also founded two smaller seminaries and several charitable, cultural, and social institutions. He reorganized the diocesan administration and employed trustworthy, earnest collaborators, some of whom came from and eventually became bishops of other dioceses. Furthermore, he made use of religious orders, especially the Jesuits, Barnabites, Theatines, and Capuchins, and founded a congregation of diocesan priests, the Oblates of Saint Ambrose, under his direction. For the religious instruction of youth, he greatly promoted the schools of Christian doctrine. He strove to protect his faithful from the contagion of Protestantism threatening from the north by controlling the printing and selling of books and by the vigilance of the archiepiscopal tribunal; he also worked to inhibit the spread of witchcraft, magic, and other superstitions in collaboration with the civil authority. In 1575 he secured papal authorization to restore or introduce the Ambrosian rite in all the churches and monasteries subject to his diocesan jurisdiction. He set an example of preaching for his clergy, enjoined the practice on them, and provided aids for their use. During the plague epidemic of the same year, he organized spiritual assistance for the sick and the dying and had food distributed; he even gave away the hangings of his palace and his own garments to clothe the poor or make covers for them. In these ways he became beloved of the people.

In his reforming zeal, however, he was opposed by some of the clergy and laity who benefited from the abuses he was intent on correcting or who accused him of excessive rigorism or of violating their vested rights. Moreover, he came into protracted conflict with both the successive Spanish governors and the senate of Milan, who were accustomed to interfering in religious matters and rejected his pretensions and efforts to expand his power. Believing that complete autonomy of ecclesiastical jurisdiction was necessary for the attainment of his pastoral goals, he wished to ensure the full application of the coercive powers invested in his office and thus to revive some practices of earlier centuries that had fallen into desuetude during the long absences of his predecessors. He based his claims not only on the common law of the church but especially on the particular customs of the see of Milan, but the civil authorities refused to recognize them. The main matters in dispute were the execution of sentences of the ecclesiastical court against laymen; the archbishop's right to maintain his own police force (*famiglia armata*); the right of clerics to hale laymen against their will before ecclesiastical courts, even in civil or profane cases; and the authority of civil magistrates over the clergy in certain respects. Borromeo even excommunicated the governor Requeséns for disregarding his prohibition of certain entertainments on religious holidays. The next governor, the marquess of Ayamonte, asked the pope to remove the archbishop from his see. These controversies were discussed in Rome in lengthy negotiations between representatives of Gregory XIII and those of Philip II, but they were settled only after Borromeo won the pope's unreserved support during a visit to Rome, after he issued a pastoral letter expressing his loyalty to the king, and after he sent to the Spanish court his own agent, Carlo Bascapè, who convinced the king of Borromeo's sincerity, of his lack of political designs or ambitions, and of his purely spiritual motives. In his last years, therefore, he enjoyed the full collaboration of the civil authorities, as well as the highest prestige in the duchy of Milan.

Essential features of his ecclesiology were not only the primacy of the Roman pontiff but also the authority of the diocesan bishop and of the metropolitan. He endeavored to reactivate the structure of the ecclesiastical province, headed by the metropolitan, as an intermediate institution between the diocese and the papacy.

He was canonized in 1610 and thereafter commemorated annually on 4 November. He came to be venerated and imitated by Catholics throughout Europe and the New World not only as an exemplar of heroic sanctity but also as the foremost model for bishops. As such he wielded enormous influence in the following centuries. He was the pioneer of the modern conception of pastoral ministry.

BIBLIOGRAPHY

Deroo, André. *Saint Charles Borromée: Cardinal réformateur, docteur de la pastorale, 1538–1584.* Paris, 1963. An extensive biography based on manuscript and published sources.

Headley, John M., and John B. Tomaro, eds. *San Carlo Borromeo: Catholic Reform and Ecclesiastical Politics in the Second Half of the Sixteenth Century.* Washington, D.C., and London, 1988. Comprises fifteen papers presented at an international conference for the fourth centenary of Borromeo's death.

Jedin, Hubert. *Carlo Borromeo*. Rome, 1971. This slender fascicle in the "Biblioteca Bibliografica" of the Istituto della Enciclopedia Italiana contains a good bibliography.

San Carlo e il suo tempo. Atti del Convegno Internazionale nel IV centenario della morte, Milan, 21–26 May 1984. 2 vols. Rome, 1986. Comprises numerous scholarly essays in which references to the earlier literature can be found.

Studia Borromaica: Saggi e documenti di storia religiosa e civile della prima età moderna. Published annually since 1987 by the Accademia di San Carlo in Milan.

ROBERT TRISCO

BOURBON, HOUSE OF. One of the greatest ruling dynasties of Europe, the House of Bourbon (Spanish, Borbón; Italian, Borbone) provided kings of France from 1589 to 1792, from 1814 to 1830, and, in an indirect line, from 1830 to 1848; after the Franco-Prussian War (1870–1871), a Bourbon was potentially king of France as Henry V, but France became a republic. Bourbons were Kings of Naples and Sicily from 1734 to 1808, of the Two Sicilies from 1816 to 1860, and of Etruria from 1801 to 1807; they have occupied the Spanish throne from 1700 to 1808, from 1814 to 1868, from 1874 to 1931, and from 1975 to the present.

The House of Bourbon is best known as the last dynasty that ruled France. It is a branch of the House of Capet. All the Bourbons are descended from King Louis IX (Saint Louis; 1214–1270) through his sixth son, Robert (1256–1317), count of Clermont, who married Beatrix of Bourbon of the future province of Bourbonnais, southeast of Paris in central France.

In 1328, the throne passed to the cousin of the last Capetian in the senior line, Philip VI (1293–1350) of the House of Valois, which had genealogical precedence over the Bourbons. In 1589, when the male line of the Valois died out, Henry IV (1553–1610) became the first Bourbon king. He was succeeded in 1610 by his son, Louis XIII (1601–1643) and grandson, Louis XIV (1638–1715). The line continued with Louis XIV's great grandson, Louis XV (1710–1774), whose grandson, Louis XVI (1754–1793), was guillotined during the French Revolution. His son (1785–1795?), who would have been Louis XVII, never became king of France. Louis XVI's brother ascended the French throne in 1814 as Louis XVIII (1755–1824). Another brother, Charles X (1757–1836), ruled from 1824 until deposed in 1830, when Louis-Philippe (1773–1850), of the House of Orléans, became king (1830–1848). He was a descendant of Louis XIV's brother, Philip, duke of Orléans (1640–1701). The Revolution of 1848 forced him out of office.

Thus, the Bourbons ruled when France led Europe. The sixteenth century was crucial to their rise to the throne. Early in that century a senior branch of the family, under Charles of Bourbon-Montpensier (1490–1527), was preeminent.

Then, Francis I (r. 1515–1547) recognized Charles (1489–1537), duke of Vendôme, of a junior branch of the family, as head of the House of Bourbon and first prince of the blood, in line to inherit the throne if the Valois line expired. In 1548 his son Antoine (1518–1562) married Jeanne d'Albret (1528–1572), daughter of Marguerite d'Angoulême (1492–1549), Francis I's sister, and of King Henry d'Albret of Navarre (1503–1555). From her father Jeanne inherited Navarre, which straddled the Pyrenees; she passed it and the Reformed religion on to her son Henry, king of Navarre (from 1572). Henry's claim to the throne of France was through his Bourbon father, Antoine.

The religious turbulence of the sixteenth century and the confessional allegiance of members of the House of Bourbon affected their rise to power. Before the outbreak of the Wars of Religion (1562), Antoine temporarily allied with the Reformed element, but he later switched sides and was mortally wounded in battle against them. Antoine's brother Louis (1530–1569), prince of Condé, was military leader of the Huguenots, though his licentious lifestyle offended them. He was killed in the Battle of Jarnac (1569). Henry, a teenager, became titular head of the Huguenot forces with his mother's help; Gaspard II de Coligny (1519–1572) was the real commander.

War ended in 1570, and to strengthen the peace, the queen mother, Catherine de Médicis (1519–1589), and Jeanne d'Albret negotiated a marriage between their children. Marguerite of Valois (1553–1615) and Henry wed six days before the Saint Bartholomew's Day Massacre, in the aftermath of which warfare was resumed. Charles IX (1550–1574) got Henry temporarily to abjure his Protestant faith and held him at court. Charles died, and his brother became King Henry III (1551–1589). Henry of Bourbon-Navarre escaped (1576) to lead the Protestants.

In 1584, upon the death of the king's brother Francis (1554–1584), duke of Anjou, Henry became next in line for the throne after the childless Henry III. The militant Catholic League, led by the Guise family, objected, and the "War of the Three Henries" ensued. With the assassination of Henry III, Henry of Bourbon-Navarre became King Henry IV; despite his subsequent abjuration of Protestantism (1593), opposition backed by Spain continued. Henry's sister, Catherine of Bourbon (1559–1604), remained Reformed. War was declared on Spain in 1595; with peace, Henry issued the Edict of Nantes (1598), granting limited tolerance to Protestant worship in France. In 1600, following the annulment of his first marriage by Pope Clement VIII, Henry married Marie de Médicis (1573–1642), who bore him, among other children, the future King Louis XIII (1601).

Henry IV's successors were Catholic, but the adherence of important members of the Bourbon family to Reformed Christianity in the latter half of the sixteenth century had an enormous impact on France. Bourbon backing sustained the

Huguenot cause and opened the possibility of toleration, but in the seventeenth century royal policy toward the Reformed church evolved in another direction. After the assassination of Henry IV in 1610, his heirs on the throne of France gradually eroded the provisions of the Edict of Nantes; finally, in 1685, it was revoked by Louis XIV, forcing Protestants into exile or hiding.

The Bourbons continued to rule France during an era of preeminence in Europe in the seventeenth and eighteenth centuries. The line spread to Spain, Naples, and Sicily in the eighteenth century. In 1814, after a republican era during the French Revolution and an empire under Napoleon, the Congress of Vienna called the Bourbon line back to the throne in France. They ruled until 1830, tolerating the minority of French Reformed Christians alongside the Catholic majority.

After 1830, the Bourbon family remained the lively hope of many monarchists. Having had little chance in the early sixteenth century of becoming monarchs, the Bourbons had risen to become one of the great ruling families of Europe.

[*See also* Antoine of Navarre; Henry IV of France; Lorraine-Guise, House of; Marguerite d'Angoulême; *and* Wars of Religion.]

BIBLIOGRAPHY

Avènement d'Henri IV quatrième centenaire. Vol. 1, *Quatrième centenaire de la bataille de Coutras*; vol. 2, *Provinces et pays du Midi au temps d'Henri de Navarre, 1555–1589*; vol. 3, *Henri IV, le roi et la reconstruction du royaume*; vol. 4, *Les lettres au temps de Henri IV.* Association Henri IV. Pau, France, 1988–1989. Papers related to the Bourbons, especially Henry IV, presented by foremost scholars.

Babelon, Jean-Pierre. *Henri IV.* Paris, 1982. Biography in French.

Buisseret, David. *Henry IV.* Reprint, London, 1992. Biography including plates, maps, chronological table.

Ritter, Raymond. *La sœur d'Henri IV, Catherine de Bourbon, 1559–1604.* 2 vols. Paris, 1985. Biography of Henry IV's sister, beautifully illustrated with plates suitable for classroom use depicting members of the House of Bourbon (and their spouses, in-laws, and mistresses), Gaspard II de Coligny, and others.

Roelker, Nancy. *Queen of Navarre: Jeanne d'Albret, 1528–1572.* Cambridge, 1968. The definitive biography of the mother of the first Bourbon king, Henry IV.

———. "The Role of Noblewomen in the French Reformation." *Archiv für Reformationsgeschichte* 63 (1972), 168–195. Highlights the leadership roles of Reformed women such as Jeanne of Navarre and Catherine of Bourbon in sixteenth-century politics.

Seward, Desmond. *The First Bourbon: Henri IV, King of France and Navarre.* Boston, 1971. Family trees, bibliography; no notes.

———. *The Bourbon Kings of France.* London, 1976. Chapters on each of the Bourbon kings of France plus the potential kings Louis XVII and Henri V. Family trees, bibliography; no notes; written in a popular style.

Sutherland, N. M. *The Huguenot Struggle for Recognition.* New Haven, 1980. Examines relations between Protestants, Catholics, and the Crown in sixteenth-century France, including the role of members of the House of Bourbon such as Antoine of Bourbon, the prince of Condé, and Henry of Bourbon-Navarre, King Henry IV of France.

Vaissière, Pierre de. *Henri IV.* Paris, 1928. A classic biography in French; cited by recent authors as the best biography.

JEANNINE E. OLSON

BOURG, Anne du (1520?–1559), counselor in the Parlement of Paris executed for heresy. Born into the provincial nobility of Auvergne and a nephew of Chancellor Antoine du Bourg, Anne du Bourg studied law at the University of Orléans, where he received his doctorate in 1550 and taught until 1557, when he assumed the position of counselor in the Parlement of Paris. Although it was doubtless at Orléans that du Bourg first became acquainted with Protestant ideas, he made his first active profession of the Reformed faith only at Easter 1559.

He was arrested for heresy following the famous *mercuriale*, or general assembly, of the Parlement of Paris held on 10 June 1559 to reconcile differences within the court over the punishment appropriate for convicted heretics. In the presence of King Henry II, du Bourg spoke out in favor of dealing leniently with religious dissenters. He criticized the papacy for its departures from scripture and warned the king not to ally himself with the "Antichrist." Henry II ordered him arrested on the spot. Protestant chroniclers reported that Henry II was so outraged by du Bourg's speech that he swore he would see him burn, and they interpreted Henry's death just a month later from an infection caused by a wound to his eye as divine retribution.

Four counselors were arrested with du Bourg, but they subsequently retracted their opinions and were released. Du Bourg tried legal maneuvers to escape but refused to moderate his views. Rather, he wrote a confession of faith that was later used against him. On 30 June, the bishop of Paris pronounced him a heretic and turned him over to the secular authorities for punishment. After a variety of further appeals, du Bourg was sentenced on 23 December to be hanged and burned in front of the Paris city hall. The sentence was carried out that same afternoon.

BIBLIOGRAPHY

Kelley, Donald R. *The Beginning of Ideology: Consciousness and Society in the French Reformation.* Cambridge, Mass., and London, 1981. See especially chapter 5, which, although inaccurate on some details of the *mercuriale*, sets the event into context.

Lelièvre, Matthieu. "Anne du Bourg, avant son incarcération à la Bastille." *Bulletin de la Société de l'histoire du protestantisme français* 36 (1887), 569–590. Particularly useful for its critical evaluation of primary sources on Anne du Bourg.

———. "Le procès et le supplice d'Anne du Bourg." *Bulletin de la Société de l'histoire du protestantisme français* 37 (1888), 281–295, 337–355, and 506–529. A continuation of the work cited above. Historically solid despite its obvious Protestant bias.

BARBARA B. DIEFENDORF

BRAHE, Tycho (1546–1601), Danish astronomer and astronomical observer. Tycho was the son of a noble Danish family and educated at the Lutheran University of Copenhagen; he pursued his interest in astronomy against his family's objections. By 1563, spurred by a conjunction between Saturn and Jupiter, he began making astronomical observations. In 1572 he observed a supernova and realized it was above the moon, by the constellation Cassiopeia; this observation helped to overturn the Aristotclian doctrine of the unchangeable heavens. In 1577 he observed a comet and realized that it, too, was supralunar, and this observation helped to overturn the popular notion of impenetrable crystalline spheres in the sky. From 1576 to 1597 the king of Denmark, Frederick II, set him up as lord of the island of Hven in the Danish sound. There he built a castle, which he called Uraniborg ("celestial city"), which was specially constructed as an observatory, and he also built superior instruments. Consequently, he was able to collect the most accurate observations possible without the use of a telescope. He also hoped that with the regular observations he made there, he would be able to draw the correct planetary paths. His data on Mars enabled Johannes Kepler to formulate his law of planetary motion.

Tycho was interested in the Copernican system as a mathematical model of the universe, but he rejected Copernicus's heliocentricism. His reasons were partly religious. He believed that the holy scripture taught that the Earth was immovable at the center, but he also believed that if Copernicus were correct, there would be an observable stellar parallax. Nevertheless, his observations taught him that the Ptolemaic universe was incorrect. He developed a compromise picture of the universe whereby the Earth was at the center and the Sun went around the earth, while the other planets orbited about the Sun. This theory, along with the rival Copernican theory, replaced Ptolemy's second-century ideas.

BIBLIOGRAPHY

Dreyer, J. L. E. *Tycho Brahe: A Picture of Scientific Life and Work in the Sixteenth Century* (1890). Reprint, Gloucester, Mass., 1977.
Hellman, C. Doris. "Brahe, Tycho." In *Dictionary of Scientific Biography*, vol. 2, pp. 401–416. New York, 1970.
Thoren, Victor E. *The Lord of Uraniborg: A Biography of Tycho Brahe.* Cambridge and New York, 1990.

SHEILA J. RABIN

BRANDENBURG. A margravate and electorate of the Holy Roman Empire, Brandenburg was bounded on the north by Mecklenburg and Pomerania, on the south by Magdeburg, Anhalt, Saxony, and Lusatia, on the east by Poland, and on the west by Braunschweig-Lüneburg and Braunschweig-Wolfenbüttel. In the sixteenth century it consisted of the Old Mark on the west bank of the river Elbe, the provinces Priegnitz and Ruppin east of the Elbe, the Uckermark in the north between the rivers Havel and Oder, the Middle Mark with the capital Berlin-Cölln in the south, and the New Mark beyond the river Oder; separated from these lands, to the south, lay the Lusatian enclave of Kottbus.

The region, whose first known inhabitants were the Teutonic Semnones, for centuries had been partly under Slavic, partly under German rule. The latter gradually prevailed as colonists from the west pushed eastward during the later Middle Ages. The state's true founder was Albert the Bear, originator of the very successful Ascanian dynasty, who in 1134 became margrave of Brandenburg, renewed the attack on the Slavs, extended Christianity, and brought in many settlers from the Rhineland. The region's growing geopolitical importance was recognized in the Golden Bull (1356), which named the ruler of Brandenburg as one of the empire's seven electors. In 1417 Emperor Sigismund awarded the margravate to Frederick of Hohenzollern, burgrave of Nuremberg, whose descendants would rule it, and later Prussia and Germany, until 1918. Primogeniture was introduced in 1473 (*Dispositio Achillea*) but not always observed in the sixteenth century.

The Reformation was slow in coming to Brandenburg. Under Elector Joachim I (r. 1499–1535) the principality remained a bulwark of Roman Catholicism against the rising tide of Lutheranism. Joachim was the brother of Albert, archbishop of Magdeburg and administrator of Halberstadt. His election to the archbishopric of Mainz in 1514, which gave the Hohenzollerns two seats in the empire's electoral college, set the stage for the famous indulgence controversy that marked the beginning of the Reformation. Joachim, one of the most adamant opponents of the new faith, took a strong stand against Martin Luther at the diet of 1521 and tried to enforce the Edict of Worms in his lands. He blamed the Wittenberg reformer personally for the outbreak of the Peasants' War in 1524 and, after the rebellion had been quashed, joined with his brother Albert and the dukes of Saxony and Brunswick in the anti-Lutheran League of Dessau (1525). He ordered his subjects to stop singing Lutheran hymns and demanded that they adhere to traditional religious observances. To assure that his heir, the future Joachim II, remain loyal to Rome, he had him betrothed to Magdalene, daughter of the staunchly anti-Lutheran Duke George of Saxony; when she died suddenly in 1534, he found him another Catholic wife—Hedwig, daughter of King Sigismund of Poland. And, to make doubly sure that at least one of his heirs remain loyal to the old faith, the elector ignored family tradition and divided his inheritance, leaving, in 1535, the New Mark to the younger John (of Küstrin) and the Old and Middle Marks, the core of his territories, to the older Joachim.

But Joachim I's efforts could not prevent the spread of Protestant doctrine among the people of the Mark. His own wife, Elizabeth, a sister of King Christian II of Denmark, became Lutheran in 1527 and, when threatened by her husband, sought refuge at the court of Luther's friend, John the Steadfast of Saxony. Upon the elector's death, the leaders of the Schmalkald League urged his heirs to join their camp. John of Küstrin went over to the side of the Lutherans in 1537; his brother, the new elector, hesitated, for, while sympathetic to the evangelical creed, he was determined to avoid any drastic action that might jeopardize his dynastic interests. Somewhat naively, and with encouragement from his Erasmian advisers, Joachim II initially hoped to bridge the widening chasm between the old and new faiths through a general church council. When it did not materialize—mostly because neither Catholics nor Protestants really wanted it—and his subjects became more clamorous for reform, Joachim, on the advice of his most trusted councillors (notably Bishop Matthew von Jagow of Brandenburg and Prince George III of Anhalt), decided to take matters into his own hands. On All Saints' Day, 1 November 1539, he received Communion in both kinds at Spandau's Saint Nicolai church (on the outskirts of Berlin), thereby officially signaling the introduction of the Reformation in his lands.

Joachim II, however, did not intend that this step should lead to a political rupture with the emperor or the Catholic princes. While stressing the centrality of the evangelical doctrine of justification by faith alone, the elector, a ceremonial traditionalist, sought to maintain continuity with the old church by preserving both its liturgical heritage and the episcopal form of church government: "Just as I do not wish to be tied to the Roman church, I do not want to be bound to Wittenberg. For I do not say: 'credo sanctam romanam' or 'wittenbergensem' but 'catholicam ecclesiam'; and my church here at Berlin and Cölln is as truly Christian as that of the Wittenbergers." With his "unique type of reformation," Franz Lau has argued, Joachim II aimed at "genuine re-catholization," not Lutheran innovation. He allowed his wife to remain Roman Catholic and did not join the Protestant Schmalkald League but continued to work for a compromise settlement. The ecclesiastical ordinance of 1540, which was greatly influenced by the moderate George III of Anhalt (r. 1507–1553), was quite conservative; in fact it has been called the most Catholic of all German Protestant church orders. It retained much of the old ritual and ceremony—including the elevation in the Mass, the preservation of the elements for shut-ins, exorcism and chrism in baptism, private confession and absolution, liturgical dramas at Easter and Pentecost, and a church calendar with Corpus Christi, Saint Catherine's Day, and several Marian festivals. He set up a consistory in 1543 to act as the highest ecclesiastical tribunal in the land. Among Germany's many ecclesiastical ordinances, Brandenburg's alone gained the seal of approval from both Luther and Charles V—a striking testimonial not only to Joachim's diplomatic skills but also to the very opaqueness of his reformation.

In the Schmalkald War (1546–1547) Joachim initially tried to remain neutral but then joined the imperial camp. While confessing the evangelical creed, he remained convinced that his political salvation lay with the emperor. Encouraged by Johann Agricola, his vituperative court preacher, he also supported the controversial Leipzig Interim after the war. In an at times blatantly cynical manner, he subordinated religion to dynastic interests as he sought to consolidate Hohenzollern control over the Mark's bishoprics (Brandenburg, Lebus, Havelberg) and in neighboring Magdeburg and Halberstadt.

The vehement reaction to the Interim, which most Brandenburgers viewed as a thinly veiled attempt to restore the old faith, the disputes over Melanchthon's teachings—notably the Majoristic controversy of the 1560s—and, of course, dynastic concerns led Joachim during the last years of his life to abandon his middle-of-the-road position and move further into the Protestant camp. This trend continued and even accelerated under his son and heir, Elector John George (r. 1571–1598). Meanwhile, when John of Küstrin died heirless, his lands passed into the hands of John George; thus the Markish provinces, separated since 1535, were reunited under one ruler.

A major issue that John George had to address almost immediately was the severe fiscal crisis he had inherited from his extravagant predecessor. To raise the money needed to pay off his debts he turned to the estates for help. The Junkers agreed to provide most of the funding but at a price: the elector had to confirm and extend their privileges. While gaining the financial assistance he so desperately needed, John George thus had to make concessions that strengthened the estates politically and also assured them a continued voice in ecclesiastical affairs.

With the knights' blessings and the guidance of Andreas Musculus, the Mark's superintendent-general, the Brandenburger church now was cast into the rigid mold of Gnesio-Lutheran confessionalism. A new church order (1572), which revised but did not abrogate the earlier 1540 ordinance, was accompanied by a "brief summary of the true, pure Lutheran doctrine," the Corpus Doctrinae Brandenburgicum. According to the "Visitation and Consistory Ordinance" of 1573, ministerial candidates had to demonstrate a solid understanding of the Augsburg Confession and Luther's teachings before ordination; by streamlining the church's organizational structure the ordinance provided the necessary administrative apparatus for enforcing religious uniformity and church discipline. The most dramatic expression of confessional consolidation, however, was the Formula of Concord, which two Brandenburgers—Andreas Musculus and Christoph Corner—helped draft. John George was one of the first to sign and enforce it in his lands (1577).

By the end of the century, therefore, the Markish church was firmly anchored in the camp of Concordianist Lutheranism. Most of the Joachimian ceremonial of the early Reformation had been retained. The difference was that Joachim II had used pomp and ritual to demonstrate continuity with the Roman church, whereas by now these elements had become a mark of genuine Lutheranism against the perceived onslaught of Calvinist and other heterodox dissenters. Doctrinal orthodoxy and ceremonial traditionalism thus had become the hallmarks of Lutheran confessionalism in late sixteenth-century Brandenburg.

[*See also* Albert of Brandenburg; Diet; Holy Roman Empire; Lutheranism; *and* Prussia.]

BIBLIOGRAPHY

Bainton, Roland H. "Elisabeth of Brandenburg, 1485–1545." In *Women of the Reformation in Germany and Italy*, pp. 111–124. Minneapolis, 1971. Sketches electress's role in the beginning of Brandenburg's Reformation.

Carsten, Francis L. *The Origins of Prussia*. Reprint, Westport, Conn., 1981. Focuses on the growth and decline of the Junkers and political institutions in early modern Brandenburg-Prussia.

Delius, Hans-Ulrich, ed. *"Dem Wort nicht entgegen . . ."* Aspekte der Reformation in der Mark Brandenburg. Berlin, 1988. Collection of essays on various religious and cultural aspects of Brandenburg's Reformation.

Delius, Walter. "Die Kirchenpolitik des Kurfürsten Joachim II. von Brandenburg in den Jahren 1535–1541." *Jahrbuch für brandenburgische Kirchengeschichte* 40 (1965), 86–123. Stresses Joachim's political and dynastic interests in supporting the Reformation.

Gericke, Wolfgang. *Glaubenszeugnisse und Konfessionspolitik der brandenburgischen Herrscher bis zur Preußischen Union, 1540–1815*. Bielefeld, 1977. Focuses on theological and ecclesiastical developments; includes a selection of documents.

Hahn, Peter-Michael. *Struktur und Funktion des brandenburgischen Adels im 16. Jahrhundert*. Berlin, 1979. Socioeconomic analysis of landed aristocracy's emergence as dominant political force.

Heidemann, Julius. *Die Reformation in der Mark Brandenburg*. Berlin, 1889. Indispensable, though somewhat one-sided (Lutheran), overview of the Reformation through the 1560s.

Heinrich, Gerd. "'Mit Harpffen, Paucken, Zimbeln und Schellen': Martin Luther, die Kirchenreform und Landeskirchen-Herrschaft in der Mark Brandenburg, den Herzogtümern Pommerns und in Preußen." In *"Gott Kumm mir zu hilff": Martin Luther in der Zeitenwende*, edited by Hans-Dietrich Loock, pp. 27–49. Berlin, 1984. Stresses Hohenzollerns' dynastic interests coalescing with religious developments of period.

Hintze, Otto. "Die Epochen des evangelischen Kirchenregiments in Preußen." *Historische Zeitschrift* 97 (1906), 67–118. Abbreviated version reprinted in *Moderne Preußische Geschichte 1648–1947*, edited by Otto Büsch and Wolfgang Neugebauer, vol. 3, pp. 1217–1242. Berlin, 1981. Surveys interaction of religion and politics in Brandenburg-Prussian state, claiming that Lutheranism had regressive and Calvinism progressive impact.

Lau, Franz. "Georg III. von Anhalt, 1507–1553, erster evangelischer 'Bischof' von Merseburg." *Wissenschaftliche Zeitschrift der Karl-Marx-Universität Leipzig* 3 (1953–1954), 139–152. Credits Anhalt's influence with Brandenburg's "unique type of reformation."

Lehmann, Ludwig. *Bilder aus der Reformationsgeschichte der Mark Brandenburg*. Berlin, 1921. General, popular account of religious changes in Brandenburg up to 1613; no critical apparatus.

Müller, Nikolaus. "Zur Geschichte des Interims." *Jahrbuch für Brandenburgische Kirchengeschichte* 5 (1908), 51–171. Still the most detailed treatment of the "Interreligion" in Brandenburg; very critical of Joachim II and Johann Agricola for promoting the Interim.

Nischan, Bodo. *Prince, People, and Confession: The Second Reformation in Brandenburg*. Philadelphia, 1994. Emphasizes Lutheran confessionalization resulting in Elector John Sigismund's abortive effort to achieve a Calvinist reform in the early seventeenth century.

Rudersdorf, Manfred, and Anton Schindling. "Kurbrandenburg." In *Die Territorien des Reichs im Zeitalter der Reformation und Konfessionalisierung: Land und Konfession, 1500–1650*. Vol. 2, *Der Nordosten*, edited by Anton Schindling and Walter Ziegler, pp. 34–66. Münster, 1990. Concise summary, with bibliography.

BODO NISCHAN

BRANT, Sebastian (1457–1521), German humanist and poet best known as the author of the satirical poem *The Ship of Fools*. In his life he participated in intellectual and literary movements that had a pronounced resonance in the cultural life of Germany and that contributed to the coming of the Reformation. The widespread popularity of his poem raised a motif that would be built upon during the Reformation by those who came to attack established authority. In this way he is a significant figure for understanding the origins of the Reformation, a movement in which he did not participate and of which he disapproved.

Brant's intellectual life was shaped by the incipient humanist movement in German-speaking Europe. As with many whose thought was shaped by humanism, Brant's work was marked by an intense moralism. Typical of many German humanists, Brant was patriotic and convinced that it was the destiny of the Holy Roman Empire to play a leading role in the world. His moralism was connected to his patriotism, as he feared that, should the German people fail to overcome their lack of wisdom, the German nation would lose its temporal leadership. One concrete consequence of this concern was his literary activity in the vernacular. He considered it of great importance to communicate with the German people by using the common tongue. All of these many concerns came together in his most famous work, *The Ship of Fools*. This work brings together representatives of a broad range of vices, and the consequences of their lack of wisdom are made manifest. Its message is that true wisdom comes from above, and the only way to correct one's folly is to replace human wisdom with that of heaven. The appeal of the poem to his age lay in part in this message, which caught the moralizing spirit soon to be aimed against the shortcomings of the church.

Brant himself died a loyal son of the Catholic church. Many of the ideas that he championed would soon be turned against the institution he honored above all others. In the career of Ulrich von Hutten, Brant's patriotism became one of the pretexts for a savage attack on Rome. While Brant kept loyalty to the pope the primary obligation, even above that to the emperor, at the outset of the Reformation the long tradition of grievances of the German nation against Rome prepared the way for rebellion against papal authority. The intense moralizing of the humanists was directed at the failings of the church and created a broad sense of discontent with its servants. The vernacular became a tool that facilitated the movement of German-speaking Europe away from Rome. Folly became one of its chief motifs for criticizing the church. The emphasis on human reason as a wayward guide to wisdom finally became a broad attack on all human agencies, such as the ecclesiastical hierarchy or the expostulations of the learned, who claimed to embody God's wisdom. Certainly Brant had not intended such implications to be drawn from his work, but one can see in his attitudes sources for the attack that would be made on the established church.

BIBLIOGRAPHY

Primary Source

Zeydel, E. H., trans. *The Ship of Fools by Sebastian Brant.* New York, 1962. This is the standard translation of Brant's most famous work.

Secondary Sources

Bernstein, Eckhard. *German Humanism.* Twayne's World Authors Series, vol. 690. Boston, 1983. An excellent short introduction to German humanism, which explains Brant's intellectual context.

Knape, Joachim, and Dieter Wuttke. *Sebastian-Brant-Bibliographie: Forschungsliteratur von 1800–1985.* Tübingen, 1990.

Könneker, Barbara. *Wesen und Wandlung der Narrenidee im Zeitalter des Humanismus.* Wiesbaden, 1966. This study sets Brant in his intellectual context by showing how the idea of folly developed into the period of the Reformation.

Verzeichnis der im deutschen Sprachbereich erschienenen Drucke des XVI. Jahrhunderts. Stuttgart, 1983–. Vol. 3, nos. 7044–7098.

Wilhelmi, Thomas. *Sebastian Brant Bibliographie.* Arbeiten zur mittleren Deutschen Literaturund Sprache, vol. 18. 3. Bern, 1990.

Zeydel, E. H. *Sebastian Brant.* Twayne's World Authors Series, vol. 13. New York, 1967. A compact introduction to Brant's life and work.

PATRICK HAYDEN-ROY

BRAUNSCHWEIG. The physical and political demarcations of the duchy of Braunschweig, which existed until 1918, can be traced back to the principality of Braunschweig-Wolfenbüttel, which was formed in the thirteenth century out of the division of the Welf territories. This division led in 1495 to the creation of four principalities: Braunschweig-Wolfenbüttel, Braunschweig-Lüneburg, Calenberg-Göttingen, and Braunschweig-Grubenhagen. From 1584 to 1634, Calenberg-Göttingen belonged to Braunschweig-Wolfenbüttel.

After Henry XII ("the Lion") was deposed in 1180, the city of Braunschweig lost its role as center of the Welf lands as a whole. It remained, however, the common property of all Welf lines. By virtue of its economic position in trade (as a member of the Hanseatic League), it was in fact independent well into the late seventeenth century. But Braunschweig was not a territorial unit; rather, it consisted of nine areas that differed in size and were in some instances distant from one another. This territorial disjointedness impeded its development.

The reform movement in the territory of Braunschweig emanated first from the cities. The conservative ruler Duke Henry (1514–1568) was expelled by the Schmalkald League in 1542. After his return in 1547, the territory returned to Catholicism, but the city remained Protestant. When the Protestant Duke Julius took office (1568–1589), Lutheran reforms were carried out in the territory. In the seventeenth century, strong currents of Pietism were supported by Duke Rudolf August (1666–1704). His coregent and successor, Duke Anton Ulrich (1685–1714), converted to Roman Catholicism in 1710. After 1704 Calvinist, and after 1705 Catholic, worship services were again allowed in the city and territory. After 1716 there was a synagogue.

The early phase of the Reformation in the city of Braunschweig was shaped by members of distinguished burgher families. Because of their level of education, these citizens were able to participate actively in theological discussions that had been taking place since the early 1520s. Attempts by the city council to impede the spread of the new teaching through prohibition of Lutheran books, and attempts to turn Catholic clergy who were eager for reform back on a course of preserving the existing structures, proved ineffective. An influential circle of Luther sympathizers, who had been recruited from a wide social spectrum, had been forming since the end of 1526 around the preachers Heinrich Lampe and his fellow clergyman Johan Oldendorp of the Sankt Magni church in the Altewiek district.

The pressures on the council from within the city from leading citizens and guild masters, that is, representatives of the commerce- and guild-oriented, economically strong groups of the community who sought participation in the city government, became so great by the beginning of 1528 that the council was forced to accept the appointment of a special citizens' committee. The council thereby dismissed the intervention by the conservative ruler of the city, Heinrich the Younger, who demanded that the traditional church be preserved. With approval of the citizens' committee, the Jena theologian Heinrich Winkel, a supporter of Luther and previously prior in Halberstadt, was appointed by the city council to lead the ordering of church reform. The demands that were formulated during negotiations between the council and the citizens' committee in the spring of 1528 included nonreligious isues as well. It is clear that in Braunschweig, as well as in other northern German Hanseatic cities, demand for church reform was closely tied to attempts by prominent citizens and guildsmen to participate in governance. That the city council quickly agreed to these demands shows that a majority among the councilmen agreed with the reformist-participatory program of the community.

Johannes Bugenhagen, a close colleague of Luther, was called from Wittenberg to Braunschweig in order to put an end to internal theological quarrels with adherents of Huldrych Zwingli and Anabaptists and to give a firm support to the rebuilding of the church. This happened again as a result of pressure from the citizen's committee. On 5 September 1528 the council, guild masters, and other leaders in the city accepted the church order that Bugenhagen had drafted in May. Detailed discussions among the participants concerning the acceptance of the new church order showed, on the one hand, a critical solidarity between the citizens of city districts and the council as the city's authority. On the other hand, the discussions confirmed that the reconstruction of the church was closely connected with patterns of political participation. The preservation of this right had been an important matter of concern for the citizens since late medieval struggles for constitutional reform, and it remained a concern into the eighteenth century.

The church order broke new ground in many areas; it became a model for further Reformation decrees. These changes became tangible in the creation of a church organization for the poor and a social welfare system (common chest), in the establishment of an independent marriage court, as well as in a marked increase of participation by the community in the selection of preachers. The duties of the preachers and schools were regulated, the oversight authority of a superintendent and his representative, or aide, was created, and this office was assigned to the city council. With these changes, the character of the pre-Reformation church was dismantled; prebends and benefices were distributed as income for service in the church. In 1529 a colloquium of preachers presented guidelines for the supervision of teaching by the superintendent. The first officeholder was Martin Görlitz (d. 1549), a scholar and theologian from Torgau, who served from 1528 until 1542.

While the city held to Reformation teachings despite disputes over doctrine, the surrounding territory remained Catholic with the exception of the years of occupation by the Schmalkald League (1542–1547). Only after the death of Duke Henry could his son, Duke Julius, finally establish the Reformation in Braunschweig-Wolfenbüttel. Even before he took office, Duke Julius had prepared himself for the tasks of reform. An undated report suggests that a visitation was planned with the intention of extensive reorganization of both church and schools. The political program of the duke after 1568 took form correspondingly. In a mandate of 1 August 1568, Julius first ordered the abolition of the Mass and the introduction of the Augsburg Confession. At the same time, he won the services of Jakob Andreae, theology professor from Tübingen, and Martin Chemnitz, the superintendent of the city of Braunschweig, to lead a general visitation of the church in his territory. The result of the

visitation, carried out in October and November of 1568, was less than favorable. The report revealed the low educational level of the clergy, the lack of spiritual care for the people, and a chaotic system of financial support for pastors. Despite these findings, few ministers were dismissed. The duke and his religious advisers hoped that clerical training would improve the situation.

This training was set up in a differentiated monastic school system that would, for the coming generation of theological and legal scholars, culminate in an educational system that led to the university. To the newly created leadership positions in the established territorial church, Duke Julius appointed principally foreign theologians who were already rooted in the evangelical faith. The educational system and hierarchy of ecclesiastical offices were central components of the church order in the duchy. The order was drawn up by Chemnitz and Andreae preceding the visitation and came into force on 1 January 1569. The church orders of Lüneburg (1564) and Württemberg (1559) were its models. In the preface to the *Corpus doctrinae*, which Chemnitz wrote alone but with the approval of Andreae, the rules and norms of faith were formulated for the now reformed territory. Beginning in 1569 the preface and *Corpus doctrinae* had to be signed by all ecclesiastical and secular officeholders as a visible sign of agreement with the common confession of the territory. At the beginning of 1569, the ordinances were sent to all parish offices so that the common fundamental principles of the doctrine were always on hand.

After organizational aspects of the church had been taken care of, theological matters followed. They included, among other things, a detailed order about worship and the performance of official duties by the parish priests. The filling of ecclesiastical positions and a regulation concerning examinations, which had to be taken by the candidates before the consistory, were included in a canonical portion of the order, which also regulated financial provisions for pastors and their widows. The concluding portion of the text consisted of orders concerning the educational system, to which the Pädagogium in Gandersheim belonged (its conversion to a university was planned), as well as orders concerning the common chest and a social welfare system to help regulate the care of the poor. The organizational structure of the church had four levels: parish priests, district superintendent, general superintendent, and consistory. The duke himself presided over the consistory. Besides the general superintendent, Chemnitz, the consistory was predominantly made up of officials schooled in law. These officials also advised the duke in political matters.

The reforms in the territory eventually ended the confessional antagonism between the city and territory of Braunschweig. The duke and the city (i.e., general superintendent Chemnitz) worked together for the confessional unification of Lutheranism. Even when the duke ended his support of concord (1578) because of sharp criticism by Chemnitz of his political decisions (the Catholic ordination of Prince Heinrich as bishop of Halberstadt), the territory remained affiliated with confessional Lutheranism. The city of Braunschweig accepted the Formula of Concord, while the territory regarded the *Corpus doctrinae* of Julius as the basis of its confession.

A comparison of the Reformation in the city with that in the territory of Braunschweig makes it clear that two different types of reform work went on. On the one hand, it can be attributed to the difference between city and territory; on the other hand, to chronological differences. The essential distinction between territory and city was that the early Reformation in the city derived its central impulse from the religiously motivated claims by the community to the right of participation. The late Reformation in the territory owed its success to the initiative and political will of the ruler. The duke received, however, substantial support from the nobility and the cities. Church reform and regional power politics complemented each other, in the case of the duchy, in an ideal way.

[*See also* Bugenhagen, Johannes; *and* Rhegius, Urbanus.]

BIBLIOGRAPHY

Mörke, Olaf. *Rat und Bürger in der Reformation: Soziale Gruppen und kirchlicher Wandel in den welfischen Hansestädten Lüneburg, Braunschweig und Göttingen.* Hildesheim, 1983.

LUISE SCHORN-SCHÜTTE
Translated from German by Susan M. Sisler

BREDERODE, Hendrik van (1531–1568), Netherlands nobleman, leader of the abortive Protestant revolt in 1566–1567. He was from an old noble family, which claimed descent from the counts of Holland. When keeping with this claim his father Reinoud in 1531 used the unbroken coat of arms of Holland, Charles V (then count of Holland) condemned him to death for treason but later pardoned him. Hendrik, who succeeded to his father's titles in 1556, had the same independent mind. A jovial, boisterous and quick-tempered character, he easily fraternized with the common people and resented clergy and government officials alike. He was one of the largest holders of land and manors in the county of Holland, and his free seigniory of Vianen was exempt from the jurisdiction of the central law court of Holland.

He probably became acquainted with the evangelical movement through his German wife, Amalia von Neuenahr. At first he maintained good relations with Antoine Perrenot de Granvelle, Philip II's chief minister in the Netherlands, but later joined the aristocratic league that caused Granvelle's (then cardinal) downfall in 1564. From that year on Brederode used the sovereign status of Vianen to issue printing licenses for illegal evangelical books and tracts. In 1566

the Vianen press produced an edition of the Augsburg Confession and the so-called Vianen Concordance, an attempt to reconcile Reformed Protestantism as it was preached in the Netherlands with the Lutheran Augsburg Confession, in line with William of Orange's policies at that time.

In December 1565 he was among the first to join the Compromise (or Confederation) of the Nobility, a pressure group for religious toleration. In April 1566 he was the compromise's spokesman when it offered a petition for the abolition of the antiheresy placards to Governess Margaret of Parma. At this occasion the nobles were for the first time called *Gueux* ("Beggars"), a term of abuse that Brederode's wit transformed into a tag of honor. He recruited members for the compromise and enlisted the support of the rich Calvinist merchants of Antwerp. During the iconoclastic riots of the late summer of 1566, he had the images removed from the parish churches in his manors, thus preparing them for Protestant service while avoiding disturbances.

When the central government regained strength and confidence, Brederode became the leader of the radical wing of the compromise, which favored armed resistance. He supported armed struggle at Antwerp and the island of Walcheren, recruited troops and fortified Vianen, while his lieutenant Anthonie van Bombergen took possession of the city of 's Hertogenbosch. Brederode tried to make a last stand at Amsterdam but failed to enlist the support of the city government. In April 1567 he fled to Germany, leaving his troops behind; Vianen was occupied by government troops. He went on rousing support for the revolt but died in exile, just before his condemnation by the Council of Troubles.

Brederode's significance for the history of the Reformation may be summarized as follows. He provided room for the only Protestant press to function within the Low Countries during the 1560's. He adopted the nickname "Beggars," by which the Dutch Calvinists continued to be designated during the revolt of the Netherlands. He greatly contributed to the popularity of the Compromise of the Nobility, which during the Wonder year of 1566 secured religious freedom. Finally, he was willing to take command of armed resistance a time when William of Orange was still trying to maintain good relations with the government.

BIBLIOGRAPHY

Duke, Alastair. *Reformation and Revolt in the Low Countries.* London, 1990. Provides important material on Brederode's role in Holland in 1566–1567.

Fontaine Verwey, H. de la. "Hendrik van Brederode en de drukkerijen van Vianen." *Het Boek: Nieuwe Reeks* 30 (1949–1950), 3–41. Important study of Hendrik van Brederode and the Protestant printing presses at Vianen.

———. "Le role de Henri de Brederode et la situation juridique de Vianen pendant l'insurrection des Pays-Bas." *Revue du Nord* 40 (1958), 297–302. Best concise introduction in the absence of a full, modern biography.

Nierop, Henk van. "A Beggars' Banquet: The Compromise of the Nobility and the Politics of Inversion." *European History Quarterly* 21

(1991), 419–443. On Brederode's role in shaping the nickname "Beggars".

Nierop, H. F. K. van. *The Nobility of Holland: From Knights to Regents, 1500–1650.* Translated by Maarten Ultee. Cambridge, 1993. Sets Brederode's role in the wider context of the history of the nobility.

HENK VAN NIEROP

BREMEN. Seat of the archbishopric of Bremen and a Hanseatic city, Bremen was oriented by trade to northern Europe and isolated from the Holy Roman emperor. It manifested hardly any pre-Reformation tendencies. The city, with its patrician constitution, was divided into four parishes, which were important for both religious and civic life. The lay influence on the church in Bremen was expressed through the institution of the *Bauherrn.* They were responsible for the maintenance of the church building, while at the same time they were community representatives who could voice religious and church demands to the canons. In Bremen there were the typical conflicts between the citizens and the clergy, but Lutheran influences cannot be demonstrated before 1522. Even the city's grievances, formulated in March 1522, caused no fundamental questioning of the traditional order of church doctrine and law. Thus, these grievances, addressed to the cathedral chapter, were considered irrelevant to the Lutheran controversy. Archbishop Christoph of Braunschweig-Wolfenbüttel did not publish the Edict of Worms of 1521 in Bremen—a further indication that Lutheran notions had not gained any noteworthy popularity up to then.

This ended abruptly with the appearance of the Augustinian hermit-prior Gerhart Zerbolt van Zutphen, who, coming from the Netherlands, chose to travel by way of Bremen to Wittenberg. At Saint Ansgarii on 9 November 1522, Zutphen, at the urging of the *Bauherrn,* preached for the first time in the city a Lutheran reform message. He soon acquired a wide and committed following among the citizens and the council. This early union of citizenry and city council under evangelical aegis is an exception to the usual pattern of urban reform. Only in a few communities did the transition to a Reformation church go so rapidly and so smoothly. In the spring of 1524 the development was solidified by the appointment of two additional evangelical preachers. One of these, Jacob Probst—an Augustinian friar from Ieper and a friend of Zutphen's—influenced the religious life of Bremen for decades.

From the end of 1522 the archbishop and the Catholic clergy opposed the introduction of the Reformation in Bremen. The common action of the city council and the citizenry to carry out the Reformation was related to the struggle of the council for complete independence from the archbishop. From 1528/30 onward the city consistently sought to obtain political autonomy at the imperial cameral court and the imperial regiment—the prerequisite for the

participation of Bremen in the negotiations of the Protestant estates for an alliance. Bremen was one of the founding members of the Schmalkald League of 1531.

Although the Reformation history of Bremen proceeded quietly and in a straightforward manner until 1530, the city was disturbed between 1530 and 1532 by the "Revolt of 104 Men." Even though one can discern in this revolt a connection with the Reformation, the agitation soon encompassed general problems of the city's constitution. Citizen committees of merchants and artisans made the claim for a voice in city government. In August 1532 the council was able to regain its power, manifested most importantly through the Bremen church order of 1534 in which the decentralization of the church was limited. As a rule the *Bauherrn* immediately became councillors, parish meetings could be convened only with the permission of the council, and the office of the superintendent was created. The superintendent, subordinate to the council, was to direct the church, but the most important ecclesiastical right—the appointment of the evangelical preachers—continued to be shared by the council and congregation.

Between 1540 and 1541 Bremen received important privileges. The remnants of the political dependence on the archbishop were removed by the empire, the jurisdictional authority of the council was strengthened, and the city was granted economic privileges. In the Schmalkald War of 1546/47, in which the city was besieged twice, Bremen was able to maintain an undiminished level of independence in ecclesiastical and political matters.

In the middle of the sixteenth century the course of the Lutheran Reformation had been completed. It brought for Bremen a change in general orientation, including an opening to the empire. Beginning with the controversy over the preacher Albert Rizaeus Hardenberg's understanding of Communion, the transition of Bremen to Calvinism was completed in the second half of the sixteenth century. The introduction of a Reformed confession according to the Nassau-Palatinate model was motivated not only by theological but political concerns as well. It was brought to completion by the council together with Christoph Pezel, who had been the superintendent of the church in Bremen from 1584. Through this Reformed confessionalization Bremen differed from the typical confessional-political development of most of the other imperial German cities.

BIBLIOGRAPHY

Barton, Peter F. "Der erwählte Bremer Superintendent Heshusius und die lutherische Spätreformation. *Hospitium Ecclesiae* 10 (1976), 21–36.

Bippen, Wilhelm von. *Geschichte der Stadt Bremen.* Halle, 1898. See vol. 2.

Heyne, Bodo. "Die Reformation in Bremen, 1522–1524: Am Vorabend, Der Beginn, Die Bahnbrecher." *Hospitium Ecclesiae* 8 (1973), 7–54.

Moeller, Bernd. "Die Reformation in Bremen." *Jahrbuch der Wittheit zu Bremen* 17 (1973), 51–73.

Moltmann, Jürgen. *Christoph Pezel, 1539–1604, und der Calvinismus in Bremen.* Bremen, 1958.

Rudloff, Ortwin. "Quod dictus assertus frater Henricus de Ambone publice praedicabet: Zu Heinrich von Zütphens Bremer Predigten im Januar und Februar 1523." *Hospitium Ecclesiae* 15 (1981), 77–116.

ILONKA EGERT
Translated from German by Walter D. Morris

BRENZ, Johannes (1499–1570), Lutheran reformer of the city of Schwäbisch-Hall (1522–1548) and subsequently (1551–1570) leading clergyman of the Lutheran church in the duchy of Württemberg. Arguably the most important Lutheran theologian of his time after Melanchthon, Brenz wrote numerous and highly regarded theological treatises, bible commentaries, and catechisms that made him one of the fathers of Lutheran orthodoxy and continued to be influential for about two centuries. Brenz was also an unusually gifted church organizer who played a crucial role in the establishment of the institutions of the Protestant territorial church in Germany. Among the Lutheran reformers, only Johannes Bugenhagen was of comparable importance in this regard.

In 1518, while still a student at the University of Heidelberg, Brenz was won for Luther's cause when he heard the Saxon reformer defend his theology at a meeting of the Augustinian order in Heidelberg. Although the influence of Luther was decisive in the formation of Brenz's theological views, the continuing influence of Christian humanism, the thought and alms of which Brenz had previously absorbed from his Heidelberg teacher, Johannes Oecolampadius, manifested itself in a number of ways, especially in his lifelong adherence to the Erasmian ideal of the Christian prince whose office includes that of instilling true religion and piety in his subjects.

In 1522 the city council of the little Franconian imperial city of Schwäbisch-Hall appointed Brenz to the office of city preacher (*Stadtprediger*) at Saint Michael's Church, the principal church of the city. Proceeding cautiously in a town hitherto unaffected by the Reformation, Brenz led in the gradual introduction of Lutheran doctrines and ceremonies. By the end of 1526, the main city churches were completely Lutheran in doctrine, ceremonies, and personnel, but the reformation of Hall's rural parishes, nearly all of which were controlled by patrons hostile to the Reformation, was undertaken only in 1540. In 1541 Hall's old rural chapter was transformed into a central organ of church government, and in 1543 the whole process was completed with the publication of a church order for the city and its territory.

Meanwhile, Brenz had begun to play a leading role in the Reformation beyond the narrow boundaries of Schwäbisch-Hall. In the summer of 1525 he published a pamphlet calling

on the victorious princes to show leniency toward the defeated peasants, whose rebellion, he said, would not have happened if the princes had provided their subjects with decent government and true preaching. Later that same year the publication of the so-called *Syngramma Suevicum,* a defense of Luther's view of the real presence against the Zwinglian view that Oecolampadius had urged pastors in Swabia and Franconia to adopt, established Brenz as the leading champion of Lutheran orthodoxy in southwestern Germany. By 1529, Brenz, while continuing in office in Schwäbisch-Hall, had established himself as the favorite adviser of Margrave George of Brandenburg-Ansbach on matters of theology and church order and as a man whose opinion was valued by the reformers in the city of Nuremberg. In 1530 he attended the Diet of Augsburg in the entourage of Margrave George, and in 1531–1532 he assisted with the preparation of the church order that Brandenburg-Ansbach and Nuremberg issued in common in 1533. In the meantime, he had helped persuade both governments to stay out of the Schmalkald League, insisting that to take up arms against the emperor was both unbiblical and unconstitutional and pointedly rejecting the arguments that had caused Luther and the other Wittenberg theologians to abandon their objections to armed resistance. Similarly, he had sided early on with Luther in advising both governments to refrain from imposing the death penalty on Anabaptists and other religious dissidents, and once again he adhered to his original position, even after Luther dropped his objections to the death penalty. The frequent republication of a treatise that Brenz wrote in 1528 condemning the death penalty (a work that Sébastien Castellion was to include in his *De Haereticis an sint persequendi* of 1554) served to strengthen the position of those reformers and governments in Protestant Germany who favored moderation in the treatment of Anabaptists.

In 1535, Duke Ulrich of Württemberg, having begun the process of introducing the Reformation into his duchy, turned for assistance to Brenz, who was now an established expert in matters of ecclesiastical organization with a reputation as an "admirable, learned, good-tempered man" (in the words of Margrave George of Brandenburg-Ansbach). In the summer of that year Brenz helped prepare a church order for the duchy (published in 1536) and then spent an entire year (1537–1538) leading the reorganization of the University of Tübingen, in both ways contributing to the establishment of Lutheran orthodoxy in an area where Zwinglian and Lutheran influences had been struggling for dominance.

Brenz's career in Schwäbisch-Hall came to an end in June 1548 when, faced with arrest and imprisonment because of his refusal to accept the Interim, he fled to Württemberg, where Duke Ulrich and Ulrich's successor (in 1550), Duke Christopher, offered him refuge and secretly took him into their service despite the forcible imposition of the Interim in their duchy. The abrogation of the Interim in Württemberg (June 1552) in the wake of Moritz of Saxony's successful uprising against Charles V made it possible for Brenz to assume public office once again (the provostship of the Stuttgart Collegiate Church, the highest ecclesiastical post in the duchy) and to proceed openly with the task of reorganizing the Württemberg church. This task, which had already begun in secret in 1551, was completed in 1559 with the publication of the so-called Great Church Order, put together under Brenz's supervision and incorporating all the major ecclesiastical legislation of the preceding decade.

The sections of the Great Church Order that have the broadest significance in the history of the Reformation are those that established the highly centralized ecclesiastical polity through which the duke exercised his responsibility for church government. The basic features of that polity had their origin in proposals that Brenz had made in the 1520s and 1530s (in Schwäbisch-Hall, Brandenburg-Ansbach, and Württemberg) but had only partially achieved in practice. Routine control of ecclesiastical matters (the appointment and dismissal of pastors and teachers, the enforcement of uniformity in doctrine and ceremonies, and the management and disbursement of church property and income) was concentrated in the hands of a *Kirchenrat* (consistory), that is, a committee of theologians and secular councillors in the ducal chancellery. The authority to make church law and to impose excommunication upon recalcitrant sinners was reserved to a body known as the *Synodus* (essentially just the *Kirchenrat* meeting under another name). Local control of the pastors and their congregations was entrusted to clergymen known as superintendents, the reports of whose regular parish visitations were the basis of the deliberations of the *Kirchenrat* and the *Synodus*. This system of ecclesiastical polity, which was widely copied in Protestant Germany (e.g., in the Rhineland-Palatinate, where it survived the introduction of Calvinism), lasted, with modifications, until 1918/19, which shows that Brenz's accomplishment as a church organizer was even more durable than his accomplishment as a theologian.

BIBLIOGRAPHY

Primary Source

Brenz, Johannes. *Werke: Eine Studienausgabe.* Edited by Martin Brecht, Gerhard Schäfer, et al. Tübingen, 1970–. This long-overdue modern critical edition progresses slowly (five volumes to date) and is still far from complete. For the older printed and unprinted sources that scholars must still consult, see the bibliographies in the works by Brecht and Estes. Virtually none of Brenz's works are available in English translation.

Secondary Sources

Brecht, Martin. *Die frühe Theologie des Johannes Brenz.* Tübingen, 1966. Ground-breaking work dealing with the period up to 1530. Brecht's article on Brenz in the *Theologische Realenzyklopädie*, vol. 7, 1981, pp. 170–181, offers a more balanced, though obviously much briefer, introduction to Brenz the theologian. Both works provide extensive bibliographies.

Estes, James Martin. *Christian Magistrate and State Church: The Reforming Career of Johannes Brenz.* Toronto, 1982. The only substantial work in English. Concentrates on Brenz's career as a church organizer; useful bibliography.

Maurer, Hans-Martin, and Kuno Ulshöfer. *Johannes Brenz und die Reformation in Württemberg.* Stuttgart and Aalen, n.d. Popular, well-informed, and lavishly illustrated account by two archivists.

JAMES M. ESTES

BRÈS, Guy de (d. 1567), Calvinist preacher in the French-speaking Netherlands and author (perhaps coauthor) of the Belgic Confession. A onetime glass painter from Mons, de Brès was converted to the Reformed faith in the 1540s and by the late 1550s was the most prominent organizer of Reformed congregations "under the cross" in and around Lille, Tournai, and Valenciennes. By 1559 he was pastor in Tournai, the mother church for the French-speaking congregations. To escape the watchful eye of the bishop of Tournai, de Brès took up residence in one of the three parishes on the right bank of the Schelde that were under the jurisdiction of the bishopric of Cambrai. He was either a co-author or (according to his biographer) the sole author of the Belgic Confession, a copy of which was tossed over the castle gate in Tournai (1561) as part of an effort to demonstrate to civil authorities that the Reformed were, unlike the Anabaptists, orthodox in doctrine and obedient subjects. De Brès had objected to the chanteries organized by the Reformed deacons of Tournai in which hundreds of the faithful proceeded through the streets singing from the Geneva Psalter.

In consequence of this disturbance and its aftermath, he fled to France, where he was court chaplain and preacher in Sedan (1563–1566), returning only intermittently to visit his flock in the Low Countries. Along with Geneva-trained Charles de Nielles, he was summoned in 1564 to a meeting with William of Orange, where he acceded to the prince's strategy of overlooking differences between Calvinists and Lutherans wherever possible for the sake of unity. He could not, however, endorse the Wittenberg Concord, and in this unwillingness to compromise Calvinist principles on the Eucharist, he was supported by Jean Taffin. In 1566, while in Antwerp to discuss with the Calvinist consistory the danger of Anabaptist inroads among the faithful of the French-speaking provinces, he received an appointment to Valenciennes, where he shared pastoral duties with Peregrine de la Grange. By celebrating a Reformed Communion service in public, he helped provoke the confrontation in which Valenciennes refused to open its gates to forces loyal to the regent (Margaret of Parma). The town was then placed under siege. De Brès's *Declaration sommaire du faict de ceux de la ville de Valencienne* (Brief Declaration of Fact by Those of the Town of Valenciennes; 1566) explained that the magistrates had chosen to safeguard the town in order to preserve its obedience to their sovereign lord, Philip II of Spain. During the siege he and the consistory blocked a proposal to appeal for help to Louis I Condé and his Huguenot army, choosing to remain loyal to the Habsburg government of the Netherlands. (In fact, if de Brès had had his way, the city would have surrendered at once to the besieging force.)

Imprisoned after the fall of Valenciennes, he was allowed to write letters to members of his family. From the scaffold (1567) he prayed for God's blessing on the government by whose laws he was sentenced to die. His most prominent writings include a defense of the new faith, *Baton de la Foi* (1555), and a lengthy denunciation of the falsehoods of the Anabaptists, *La Racine, source, et fondement des Anabaptistes ou Rebaptizes de Nostre Temps* (1565).

BIBLIOGRAPHY

Braekman, E. M. *Guy de Brès: Sa vie (premiere partie)*. Histoire du protestantisme en Belgique et au Congo Belge, vol. 6. Brussels, 1960.
———. "La pensée politique de Guy de Brès." *Bulletin de la Société pour l'histoire du protestantisme français* 111 (1969), 1–28.
Crew, Phyllis Mack. *Calvinist Preaching and Iconoclasm in the Netherlands, 1544–1569*. Cambridge, 1978.
Gelderen, Martin van. *The Political Thought of the Dutch Revolt, 1555–1590*. Cambridge, 1992.
Langeraad, L. A. van. *Guido de Bray: Zijn leven en werken*. Zierikzee, 1884.
Steen, Charlie R. *A Chronicle of Conflict: Tournai, 1559–1567*. Utrecht, 1985.

JAMES D. TRACY

BRIÇONNET, Guillaume (c. 1470–1534), bishop of Meaux from 1515 to 1534, abbot of Saint-Germain-des-Prés from 1507 to 1534, protector of humanists and reformers, and correspondent of Francis I's sister, Marguerite d'Angoulême. Briçonnet was the second of five surviving children of Cardinal Guillaume Briçonnet (d. 1514), whose ecclesiastical career had begun after his wife had died. The Briçonnets were a wealthy family from Tours engaged in finance and service to the kings of France. Guillaume received a humanist education and studied law. In Paris he studied at the Collège de Navarre and under Josse Clichtove, from whom he acquired appreciation for Jacques Lefèvre d'Étaples and Dionysius the Areopagite.

In 1489, while still a student, he became bishop of Lodève, east of Montpellier, a position he later passed on to his younger brother, Denis. He became the queen's chaplain in 1496; canon in Paris in 1503; abbot of Saint-Germain-des-Prés, succeeding his father; and bishop of Meaux and vassal to the king. He held other positions and benefices, with their revenues, concurrently.

Briçonnet served in the king's financial administration and in 1496 became president of the Chambre des Comptes, ceding the position to his older brother, Jean, in 1507. Louis XII sent Guillaume to Rome in 1507 to assure Pope Julius II of Louis's loyalty. Guillaume attended the Council of Pisa in 1511 and in 1516–1517 negotiated the Concordat of Bologna with Pope Leo X for Louis's successor, Francis I.

Guillaume attempted to reform his dioceses and the abbey of Saint-Germain-des-Prés. Patron of scholars, he offered lodging at Saint-Germain and a pension to Lefèvre d'Étaples from 1508. When Briçonnet took up residence in Meaux, he reformed the hospital and conducted diocesan visitations. Finding preaching neglected and priests absent, he divided the diocese into thirty-two preaching positions and encouraged exegetical preaching in French from the text of the Bible. In 1521–1522 Briçonnet welcomed Lefèvre d'Étaples and his humanist friends: the priests (Gérard Roussel, Martial Masurier, and Francois Vatable) received parishes, while the laymen (Guillaume Farel and possibly Jean Lecomte de la Croix) received preaching positions. Marguerite protected this "Meaux Group." Briçonnet's confidant, Michel d'Arande, served at the royal court after Marguerite began corresponding with Briçonnet in 1521.

Briçonnet favored reform of the parish clergy and preaching of the gospel, promoted the translation of the Bible into French by Lefèvre d'Étaples, permitted Bible studies, prohibited public dancing on Sundays and festival days, and envisioned reform of the church beyond his diocese. Luther's theology penetrated Meaux. Some of Briçonnet's preachers questioned veneration of saints, prayers for the dead, and purgatory, causing alarm among the Faculty of Theology of Paris. Briçonnet repressed this preaching in 1523, and Farel left. Conservative Franciscans challenged Briçonnet's position before the Parlement of Paris, and, although he exonerated himself, he withdrew his support from the "Meaux Group," which dispersed. Briçonnet himself continued good relations with the royal court.

Some scholars have interpreted Briconnet's stance after 1525 as cowardly, but Briçonnet wanted reform undertaken and controlled by bishops. As far as he was concerned, Luther was too egalitarian and too extreme in his theology. In a way, Briçonnet was leader of a uniquely French Reformation. Henry Heller considered him a politically expedient realist, unable to conceive of successful reform without the king's good will and unwilling to support changes that would fail or compromise him and his family.

BIBLIOGRAPHY

Primary Source

Briçonnet, Guillaume, and Marguerite d'Angoulême. *Correspondance, 1521–1524*. 2 vols. Edited by Christine Martineau and Michel Veissière. Geneva, 1975–1979. Annotated edition.

Secondary Sources

Febvre, Lucien. "Idée d'une recherche d'histoire comparée: Le cas Briçonnet." In *Au coeur religieux du XVIe siècle*, pp. 145–171. 2d ed.

Paris, 1983. Restores the image of Briçonnet as a reformer and leader of the Reformation in France. Febvre suggests Briçonnet may have been inspired by the Oratory of Divine Love in Italy.

Heller, Henry. "Marguerite of Navarre and the Reformers of Meaux." *Bibliothèque d'humanisme et Renaissance* 33.2 (1971), 271–310. Emphasizes the influence of Guillaume Briçonnet's letters on Marguerite's poetry and views; considers the impact of other reformers on her and her relationship to them.

———. "The Briçonnet Case Reconsidered." *Journal of Medieval and Renaissance Studies* 2.2 (Fall 1972), 223–258. Relates the French royal courts' toleration of reforming ideas in Meaux to periods of diplomatic alienation from the pope.

———. "Famine, Revolt, and Heresy at Meaux, 1521–1525." *Archiv für Reformationsgeschichte* 68 (1977), 133–157. Relates the spread of heresy in Meaux to times of physical and economic hardship.

———. "Popular Roots of the Reformation: 'Lutherans of Meaux,' 1525–1546." In *The Conquest of Poverty: The Calvinist Revolt in Sixteenth-Century France*, pp. 27–69. Leiden, 1986. Summary of historians' views of Briçonnet; describes his political, economic, and religious position in Meaux, as its bishop.

Rice, Eugene, Jr. "The Patrons of French Humanism, 1490–1520." In *Renaissance Studies in Honor of Hans Baron*, edited by Anthony Molho and John Tedeschi, pp. 687–702. Florence, 1971. Places the Briçonnet family in the context of the great patrons of humanism in the late fourteenth and early fifteenth centuries through a study of dedications of learned books such as those of Jacques Lefèvre d'Étaples.

Veissière, Michel. *L'evêque Guillaume Briçonnet, 1470–1534: Contribution à la connaissance de la Réforme catholique à la veille du Concile de Trente.* Provins, France, 1986. A scholarly biography, sympathetic to Briçonnet; covers his last years, which are often neglected.

JEANNINE E. OLSON

BRIESSMANN, Johann

BRIESSMANN, Johann (also Briesmann; 1488–1549), early supporter of the Reformation in Brandenburg and leading organizer of the Lutheran churches in Prussia and Livonia. He was born on 31 December 1488 at Kottbus, studied theology at Wittenberg and Frankfurt an der Oder, was ordained into the priesthood (1510), and joined the Franciscan order. He was awarded a doctorate of theology in 1522 and became a member of the Wittenberg faculty.

Briessmann first met Luther at the Leipzig Disputation (1519) and became an ardent, lifelong supporter of his cause. He spent most of 1522 in his native Kottbus, where his sermons at the Franciscan chapel attracted wide attention and made him a leading promoter of the burgeoning evangelical movement in the Brandenburg lands. On Luther's recommendation, he left Kottbus around Christmas 1522 to accept a call from Albert of Brandenburg-Ansbach, grand master of the Teutonic Order, to help introduce the Reformation into Prussia. He delivered the first evangelical sermon at the Königsberg cathedral in the fall of 1523. Through his close association with Albert and George von Polentz, bishop of Samland, Briessmann became the leading promoter of the Reformation in the duchy.

In 1527 he accepted a call from the people of Riga and spent the next few years in Livonia helping complete the reform movement there. His *Kurze Ordung des Kirchendienstes sammt einer Vorrede von Ceremonien* (1530) formed the basis for evangelical worship in Riga and Reval for many years to come. Briessmann returned to Königsberg in 1531 to assume the post of cathedral preacher. In that capacity he continued to exert a decisive influence in Prussia. He was prominently involved in the development of the duchy's evangelical school system and was one of the founders of the University of Königsberg (1544). On his recommendation George Sabinus, Philipp Melanchthon's son-in-law, was named rector of the university; Briessmann himself served on the school's board of trustees. His administrative skills led to his appointment as president of the Samland diocese when Bishop Polentz grew too ill to fulfill his responsibilities. In 1547 he made a tour of inspection to correct still-existing abuses in the diocese. He was an able and fervent opponent of Schwenckfeldian, Anabaptist, and Osiandrian notions. Briessmann died from the plague on 1 October 1549 and was buried in the Königsberg cathedral.

BIBLIOGRAPHY

Beeskow, Hans-Joachim. "Johannes Briesmann: Ein treuer Schüler und Mitstreiter von Martin Luther; Eine Studie zur Frühphase der Reformation in der Mark Brandenburg." In *"Dem Wort nicht entgegen . . .": Aspekte der Reformation in der Mark Brandenburg*, edited by Hans-Ulrich Delius et al., pp. 31–36. Berlin, 1988. Focuses on Briessmann's reformatory activities in Brandenburg; for a more detailed discussion of same, see Stupperich.

Erdmann, David. "Brießmann, Dr. Johannes." In *Realencyclopädie für protestantische Theologie und Kirche*, edited by Albert Hauck, vol. 3., pp. 398–405. 24 vols. 3d ed. Leipzig, 1896–1913. Dated yet solid study of Briessmann the reformer. A much shorter essay in English, by the same author, is found in *The New Schaff-Herzog Encyclopedia of Religious Knowledge*, edited by Samuel M. Jackson and L. A. Loetscher, vol. 2, pp. 269ff. 13 vols. Grand Rapids, Mich., 1950–1957.

Hubatsch, Walther. *Geschichte der Evangelischen Kirche Ostpreussens.* 3 vols. Göttingen, 1968. See especially vol. 1, pp. 1–86, on Briessmann's reforming activities in Prussia.

Stupperich, Robert. "Johann Briesmanns reformatorische Anfänge." *Jahrbuch für Berlin-Brandenburgische Kirchengeschichte* 34 (1939), 3–21. Discusses his education and early reforming activities at Kottbus.

BODO NISCHAN

BROTHERS AND SISTERS OF THE COMMON LIFE

BROTHERS AND SISTERS OF THE COMMON LIFE. Founded in the late fourteenth century, this religious community was the original element in a larger movement known as the Devotio Moderna. They were often treated by earlier church historians and Reformation scholars as "pre-reformers" who anticipated the teachings, pedagogy, and ecclesiastical concerns of sixteenth-century reformers, a position vividly argued early in the twentieth century by Albert Hyma. This view, still found in some textbooks and propounded by some nonmedieval scholars, was vigorously rebutted by R. R. Post, who, at the other extreme, interpreted the Devout (a useful contemporary name for the Brothers and Sisters) as wholly Catholic in their piety, ecclesiastical allegiance, and religious lifestyle.

Medieval scholars of all persuasions, reversing these Reformation approaches, have come to see the Brothers and Sisters of the Common Life as emblematic of a larger religious movement in the late Middle Ages (including, for instance, the observants) for which there is no single name. Its influence reached everywhere, and most sixteenth-century reformers took these late medieval developments for granted: they absorbed much of its spirituality into their own piety (especially its ascetic and Christocentric features), and they reacted theologically to its emphasis upon "works" and orientation toward the professed religious life. Few studies, following up on this medieval historiographic "reversal," have pursued the story into the sixteenth century. Desiderius Erasmus notoriously castigated the ascetic harshness and pedagogical sterility of the Brothers of the Common Life, though his own piety and learning almost certainly owed more than a little to the orientation he received in their circles as an adolescent. Martin Luther, by contrast, who knew as a young man the house at Magdeburg, praised the Brothers' lifestyle and piety as consonant with the gospel when one house (Herford) came under attack from reformers. Ignatius Loyola knew the devotional literature of the Devout at least secondhand, if not in some cases (*Imitation of Christ*) directly. But such isolated—and famous—cases do not adequately describe the larger fate of the movement in the sixteenth century, which becomes intelligible only after characterizing the fifteenth-century movement.

The Devout, in Elm's phrase, stood "between" the medieval world of religious orders and the Reformation world of lay congregations. The movement originated around 1375 in the conversion of Gerhard Groote, who, before his death in 1384, had converted his patrician's house into a hospice for sisters and gathered around him like-minded and "devout" priests and clerics (minor clerics and student clerics). The Sisters were the first and larger wing of the movement, with houses spreading outward from the IJssel River valley into northwest Germany. There were some thirty-four houses in the Netherlands (with that many again founded and transformed into, for instance, third-order Franciscans) and nearly twice that number in Germany, with the inhabitants in each house ranging from less than a dozen to more than a hundred. The peak period of expansion and membership came in the mid- to late fifteenth century; the numbers then remained steady or slowly declined. The key feature of Sisters' houses, distinguishing them from Beguines, was a strong commitment to the common life and to the keeping of common statutes. What distinguished them from convents was their refusal to take vows and their subordination to lay authorities, often town magistrates, with ad hoc arrangements for pastoral care, mostly by ordained Brothers or Windesheim canons.

The Brothers of the Common Life were less numerous, but they also expanded throughout the second half of the fifteenth century to reach a total of forty-one houses, the last expansion coming in the Upper Rhineland. The Brothers, too, took no vows, while committing themselves to the common life and a religious form of life described in local customaries. The canons and canonesses of the Windesheim congregation represented, by contrast, the regular part of the movement, religious professed under the rule of Saint Augustine, a union of three groups (with Groenendael and Neuss) subordinated to the customary and mother house of Windesheim. Here the male houses predominated (eighty-four houses to thirteen), with the later growth coming again in Germany. Their closest allies were consistently the observants, especially monks, and one of their members, Johannes Busch, wrote a long book describing his efforts to reform monasteries across northern Germany.

The Brothers and Sisters, more than the canons and canonesses, strove to maintain an "in-between" status, though they were looking more and more like a religious order. In large towns the Sisters offered a religious form of life without the alienation, permanent vows, and high entrance fees of cloisters. The Brothers appealed especially to "clerics"—their houses were often called the "clerks' house"—who were numerous, underemployed, and the object of much stringent criticism in towns. In the context of ever more embittered anticlericalism, the Brothers refused to take vows; remained attached initially to their local parishes; worked with town magistrates; lived in a "house"; earned their own incomes; maintained a mix of lay, clerical, and priestly members; and moved among the people as teachers and religious exemplars. While Sisters remained more dependent upon gifts and endowments, Brothers insisted upon supporting themselves, in part through their work as professional copyists. The Brothers also set up "interns" in which school-age boys were overseen in a kind of religious dormitory, sometimes taking on pedagogical responsibilities as well. Their piety was mostly nonmystical, strongly Christocentric, oriented to the personal and ascetic appropriation of the virtues, and reserved about many of the practices (e.g., pilgrimage, hiring mass priests, and visiting local shrines) that characterized late medieval piety. Open to learning in settings with school or university traditions (Deventer, Louvain, and Tübingen), Devout authors, with few exceptions (such as Gabriel Biel), wrote devotional rather than theological or literary works.

The fate of this movement in the sixteenth century, never studied in synthetic fashion, must be differentiated by region. In the southern Netherlands, where Catholic forces eventually prevailed, houses of canons persisted to the time of the French Revolution; subjects deserving further study include the quality of their religious life in early modern times, how indebted they were to the original impulses, and how influenced they were by later Tridentine and baroque pieties. The only houses of Brothers to flourish into the sixteenth century—those at Ghent and Brussels, both distinguished for their schools—were closed at the end of the 1560s, when printing destroyed income from copy work, religious upheaval apparently undermined vocations, and local authorities took over the schools.

In the northern Netherlands, home to the movement in all its four branches, Protestant regimes closed all the houses (the regulars along with the Brothers and Sisters) as religious institutions, and town authorities took over the pedagogical and hospice work. But this transpired comparatively late, mostly in the 1570s. Although houses of all four branches were still flourishing at the turn of the century, in some cases reaching their apogee in the first third of the sixteenth century, most were described as poor, poorly administered, or sparsely inhabited by midcentury—on the eve of their closing. This was in part the result of their noncorporate religious status and in part owing to the religious upheavals of the midcentury.

The German lands, with their patchwork of Catholic and Protestant regimes, present the most complicated picture and are worthy of additional study. Where Protestant regimes prevailed early, the houses were generally closed early (1520s or 1550s), as they were considered "Old Catholic." In Catholic areas, such as Emmerich and Cologne, the Brothers' houses survived to the French Revolution (with little study to date of their early modern activity or character). In Herford, where the Reformation movement gained considerable support from the Brothers, the house persisted uniquely as a Lutheran institution for preparing future or young pastors—not so dissimilar from the atmosphere of a "clerks' house." In Münster, by contrast, it seems to have survived in part as a Catholic priests' seminary. In Trier, also Catholic, the house, undermined by material decline, could not keep up its pedagogical functions in the face of the new Jesuit schools and was closed in 1570. Although there is some evidence of openness to the new evangelical preaching and reforms, particularly in Herford and in the Upper Rhineland (also possibly in the mother house at Deventer), the houses generally were regarded as "Catholic" and stood with the old order, even taking on pastoral care for the remnant Catholic community in Wesel. The "in-between" status of the Brothers and Sisters in particular (less so the canons) made them ill-suited for the controversies of the mid-sixteenth century, too "Catholic" to become the source of new Protestant congregations, and too indebted to a particular late medieval piety and order to fit easily into the post-Tridentine world led by Jesuits.

[See also Erasmus, Desiderius; Luther, Martin; and Piety.]

BIBLIOGRAPHY

Acquoy, J. G. R. *Het klooster te Windesheim en zijn invloed* (1875–1880). 3 vols. Reprint, Leeuwarden, 1984.

Brouette, Emile, and Reinhold Mokrosch. "Devotio Moderna." In *Theologische Realenzyklopädie*, vol. 8, pp. 605–616. Berlin, 1981. With extensive literature.

Elm, Kaspar. "Die Bruderschaft vom gemeinsamen Leben: Eine geistliche Lebensform zwischen Kloster und Welt, Mittelalter und Neuzeit." *Ons geestelijk erf* 59 (1985), 470–496. Reprinted in his *Mittelalterliches Ordensleben in Westfalen und am Niederrhein*, Paderborn, 1989; see pp. 214–230.

Hyma, Albert. *The Christian Renaissance*. Grand Rapids, Mich., 1924. Dated but interesting.

Kohl, Wilhelm, Ernest Persoons, and Anton G. Weiler, eds. *Monasticon Windeshemense*. 3 vols. Brussels, 1977–1980. Essential for access to the sources.

Leesch, Wolfgang, Ernest Persoons, and Anton G. Weiler, eds. *Monasticon Fratrum Vitae Communis*. 2 vols. Brussels, 1977–1979. Also essential for access to the sources. The volume for the Netherlands has yet to appear.

Lourdaux, Willem. *Moderne Devotie en christelijk humanisme*. Louvain, 1967.

————. "De Broeders van het Gemene Leven." *Bijdragen: Tijdschrift voor filosofie en theologie* 33 (1972), 372–416.

Lourdaux, Willem, and Ernest Persoons, eds. *Petri Trudonensis Catalogus Scriptorum Windeshemensium*. Louvain, 1968. For orientation regarding Netherlandish authors.

Moderne Devotie: Figuren en Facetten. Nijmegen, 1984. Exhibition catalog.

Ons geestelijk erf. Annual bibliography. Volume 59 (1985) was devoted entirely to Geert Grote.

Post, R. R. *The Modern Devotion: Confrontation with Reformation and Humanism*. Studies in Medieval and Reformation Thought 3. Leiden, 1968.

Rehm, Gerhard. *Die Schwestern vom gemeinsamen Leben im nordwestlichen Deutschland*. Berlin, 1985.

Staubach, Nikolaus. "Pragmatische Schriftlichkeit im Bereich der Devotio moderna." *Frühmittelalterliche Studien* 25 (1991), 418–461.

Van Engen, John. "A Brabantine Perspective on the Origins of the Modern Devotion." In *Serta Devota: In Memoriam Guillelmi Lourdaux, Pars Prior; Devotio Windeshemensis*, pp. 3–78. Louvain, 1992. Takes a new look at the question of origins. The volume includes other important contributions as well.

————. *Devotio Moderna: Basic Writings*. New York, 1988.

Wansem, C. van der. *Broederschaap van het Gemene Leven tot 1400*. Louvain, 1958.

JOHN VAN ENGEN

BRÜCK, Gregor (born Heinz Brück; Lat., Pontanus; c.1485–1557), jurist, councillor for the electorate of Saxony, and chancellor. He was probably born in 1485 in the city of Brück in Brandenburg, at that time part of the electorate of Saxony, where his father later became mayor. Brück studied in Wittenberg in 1502–1503, at the newly founded University of Frankfurt an der Oder in 1506 (fellow students included Georg Spalatin and Nikolaus von Amsdorf), and again in Wittenberg in 1508, where he obtained a baccalaureate in civil and church law; he did not receive his doctorate until 1521. In Wittenberg he attended lectures on law given by Hieronymus Schurf, who was later closely connected to the Reformation. Brück's career was decisively advanced by the "prince of legal learning," Henning Göde, who came to Wittenberg in 1508, and who had Brück observe legal hearings and deliver legal decisions and opinions to princely courts and cities.

Brück became councillor in Wittenberg in 1519 and that same year was appointed by Elector Frederick to succeed Degenhart Pfeffinger as "daily counselor." Shortly thereafter he was named chancellor, the highest administrative position in the electorate of Saxony, and one that involved him in both internal administration and external affairs. He served as chancellor until 1529; subsequently, as "extraordinary counselor," he lost none of his far-reaching influence over the policies of the electorate of Saxony. In 1547, in the aftermath of the Schmalkald War, he moved from Wittenberg to Weimar, and later to Jena, where he died on 15 February 1557.

Brück's influence was felt throughout the empire, for by 1529–1530 he had become the spokesman for the estates of the empire that embraced the Augsburg Confession. Sensible and deliberate action, restraint in decision making, and careful but clear pursuit of goals characterized the policies of the "Reformation chancellor." Over twelve hundred letters and expert opinions carry his signature. At the Diet of Worms in 1521 the imperial court attempted unsuccessfully to use Brück in order to turn the Saxon elector against Luther. In 1524 Brück carried on negotiations with Thomas Müntzer in Allstedt, and in 1529 he wrote the draft of the Protestation of Speyer. He devoted much energy to preparing the evangelicals for the Diet of Augsburg in 1530 and managed to have the Augsburg Confession read publicly in the German language. *Geschichte der Handlungen* . . . , his record of the events of this historic diet, may be read as a revision to the account of the adherents of the old faith. Johann Eck rightly called him the "mouthpiece of the Protestant estates."

Brück energetically supported the creation of the Schmalkald League. Although he disapproved of the election of Ferdinand as king, he took part in the negotiations for a settlement in the Bohemian town of Kaden in 1534. He strove to keep the door open for an understanding between the religious parties in the empire, as in Leipzig in 1534 and 1539, and he took the same approach regarding internal conflicts of the House of Wettin. In 1535 he participated in the talks with France and England; in 1541 he opened the way to reform in Halle. After 1547, despite his playing an active role in attempts at a settlement with the Albertines, he remained the trusted adviser of Elector John Frederick.

In 1526 Brück began to implement Luther's recommendations for a general visitation; he drafted the first *Instruction* in 1527, and he personally took part in the visitation of the Bitterfeld district. In 1537–1538 he lent his support to the establishment of the Wittenberg consistory. He looked after the University of Wittenberg and, beginning in 1548, the newly founded academy in Jena. In his relationship with Luther he found purpose and direction for his own work; mutual respect, recognition, and admiration characterized their

dealings with one another. The Reformation made Brück the most significant political adviser to the electors Frederick, John, and John Frederick.

BIBLIOGRAPHY

Brück, Ulrich von. *Im Dienste der Reformation: Ein Lebensbild des kursächsischen Kanzlers Gregor Brück.* Berlin, 1983.

Fabian, Ekkehart. *Dr. Georg Brück, 1557–1957: Lebensbild und Schriftwechselverzeichnis.* Tübingen, 1957.

———. "Brück (Brück genannt Pontanus), Gregor." In *Theologische Realenzyklopädie,* vol. 7, pp. 212–216. Berlin and New York, 1981. Contains bibliography.

Kolde, Theodor. "Der Kanzler Brück und seine Bedeutung für die Entwicklung der Reformation." *Zeitschrift für historische Theologie* 44 (1874), 343–408.

GÜNTHER WARTENBERG
Translated from German by Robert E. Shillenn

BRUEGEL, Pieter the Elder

BRUEGEL, Pieter the Elder (c.1527–1569), Flemish painter and designer of engravings. Accepted as a master in the Antwerp painters' guild in 1551, he traveled to Italy in 1552 and by the following year reached Rome, where he met the miniaturist Giulio Clovio. During the period 1554–1563 he designed prints for Hiëronymus Cock, whose Antwerp publishing house, "The Four Winds," became a center for humanists, artists, and craftsmen. Within this circle Bruegel was friends with the German immigrant merchant Hans Franckert and the Dutch poet and printmaker Dirk Volkerszoon Coornhert. Bruegel was also friends with the noted publisher Christoffel Plantijn and the geographer Abraham Ortelius, both of whom were associated with the sect known as the Family of Love. Bruegel's grisaille painting of *The Death of the Virgin* (Banbury) was created for Ortelius, and he in turn eulogized Bruegel in his *Album Amicorum.* The Antwerp baker Niclaes Jonghelinck acquired *Tower of Babel, Christ Carrying the Cross,* and *The Labors of the Months* from the painter, according to an inventory of 1566. After his marriage in 1563, Bruegel moved to Brussels, where his work was collected by Cardinal Antoine Perrenot de Granvelle, minister to Philip II. The cardinal owned *Flight into Egypt* and *Parable of the Blind* by the painter. In 1569 he was buried in Notre Dame de la Chapelle at Brussels. Thus, the painter was an associate of Protestant sympathizers and patronized by orthodox Catholics.

Bruegel's prints and paintings often focus on ethical or moralistic themes whose roots have been traced to the humanistic works of Desiderius Erasmus, as well as to theatrical traditions found in the Flemish chambers of rhetoric. These middle-class societies held dramatic competitions and presented allegorical or humorous plays at civic and religious festivals. Bruegel's friends Franckert and Cock were members of the Violieren (Gillyflower) chamber, which had merged with the Antwerp artists's guild in 1481. Bruegel's awareness of these traditions is evident from his

1560 drawing *Allegory of Temperance*, which shows a morality play in progress with a fool and a figure labeled Hope on stage. His early work, such as the series of drawings titled the *Seven Deadly Sins* and the *Seven Virtues*, reflects the influence of Hieronymus Bosch. Such paintings as the *Triumph of Death* (Prado), *The Battle Between Carnival and Lent* (Vienna), and *Dulle Griet* (Antwerp) have remained focal points of interpretation regarding the religious and political convictions of Bruegel and his humanist audiences.

BIBLIOGRAPHY

Gibson, Walter S. *Bruegel.* Reprint, London, 1988. Profusely illustrated with a good bibliography for Reformation studies on Bruegel.
Grossman, Fritz. *Pieter Bruegel: Complete Edition of the Paintings.* 3d rev. ed. London and New York, 1973. Includes criticism of Bruegel's major works.

CAROL JANSON

BRUNFELS, Otto (c.1488–1534), German botanist, evangelical, reformer, teacher, and physician. Born in Mainz, Brunfels entered the Carthusian monastery in Strasbourg in 1510. He studied natural science, joined a humanist circle, and made contact with the poet-knight Ulrich von Hutten and the future reformer Wolfgang Capito. An early convert to Luther's ideas, Brunfels fled his monastery in 1521. Between 1521 and 1524 he was on the move, pursuing his botanical interests and trying his hand as a pastor in the Breisgau town of Neuenberg. Late in 1523 he published a tract, *Von dem Evangelischen anstosz* ("On the Evangelical Scandal"), defending Luther against the Franciscan polemicist, Thomas Murner. Subsequently he returned to Strasbourg, where he opened a school. In 1524 he issued a response to Erasmus's attack on Hutten, his late protector, and *Von dem Pfaffen Zehenden* ("About the Tithe"), excoriating misappropriation of money paid to the church. His relations with the leading Strasbourg reformers, Wolfgang Capito and Martin Bucer, were uneasy because of his combination of loyalty to Luther, interest in the more radical theology of Andreas Bodenstein Karlstadt, and influence on local spiritualists, such as Clemens Ziegler, whom Bucer and eventually Capito regarded as opponents. Later in the decade Brunfels published guides to the Bible, identifying key passages for Lutheran interpretations of Christianity, and *Helden Büchlin* ("Little Book of Heroes"), containing biographies of biblical men and women. Brunfels argued that God granted salvation to very few and warned against belief in free will or reliance on human reason. His continuing concern for the spiritual needs of the laity led him to publish *Biblisch Bettbuchlin* ("A Little Biblical Prayerbook") in 1531. After 1525 he was increasingly engaged in creating the beautifully illustrated volumes that made him a leading Renaissance botanist. In 1532 he left for Switzerland, taking a med-

ical degree at Basel, then becoming city physician in Bern, where he died in 1534.

BIBLIOGRAPHY

Primary Sources

Brunfels, Otto. *Contrafayt Kreuterbuch nach rechter Vollkommener Art. . .* (1532). Munich, 1964.
———. *Biblisch Bettbuchlin.* Strasbourg, 1982.
Krebs, Manfred, and Hans Georg Rott, eds. *Elsass.* Pt. 1, *Stadt Strassburg, 1522–1532.* Quellen zur Geschichte der Täufer, vol. 7. Gütersloh, 1959. Annotated excerpts from Brunfels's religious writings.

Primary Sources

Chrisman, Miriam Usher. *Lay Culture, Learned Culture: Books and Social Change in Strasbourg.* New Haven, 1982. Discusses Brunfels and puts him in his religious and scientific milieu.
———. "Otto Brunfels." In *Contemporaries of Erasmus,* edited by Peter G. Bietenholz, vol. 1, pp. 206–207. Toronto, 1985. Gives more details of his life and a chronological list of his published work.
Weigel, Sylvia. *Otto Brunfels: Seine Wirksamkeit in der Frühbürgerlichen Revolution, unter besonderer Berücksichtigung seiner Flugschrift "Vom Pfaffenzehnten."* Stuttgart, 1986–.

LORNA JANE ABRAY

BRUNSWICK. *See* Braunschweig.

BUCER, Martin (also Butzer, Buczer, Boukeros, Bucerus, Bucaerus; pseudonyms, Aretius Felinus, Conrad Trew von Fridesleven, Waremund Luithold; 1491–1551), Reformed theologian and church organizer mainly in southern Germany, active in church politics in the empire as well as in Europe. Born in Schlettstadt (Sélestat) in Alsace on 11 November, Bucer came from a humble family background. Primarily for economic reasons, probably in 1507, he became a friar of the Dominican order in his hometown. Here he continued to be instructed, just as he had been at that town's famous Latin school, in the spirit of the older Alsatian humanism as well as the theology of Thomas Aquinas. When the superiors of the order sent him to Heidelberg in January 1517 to pursue studies and to acquire his doctorate, the gifted young man came under the influence of writings by Desiderius Erasmus of Rotterdam; he made through letters and personal acquaintances, and finally in the spring of 1518, at the disputation at Heidelberg he became profoundly and lastingly influenced by Luther. On the basis of these influences Bucer developed an independent theology to which, upon meeting with other influential people (Huldrych Zwingli, Johannes Oecolampadius, Philipp Melanchthon, and others), he may well have made adjustments but no fundamental changes. After his promotion to the status of secular priest (29 April 1521) and his tumultuous years in the circle of the knights Franz von Sickingen and Ulrich von Hutten, Bucer—meanwhile married—tried from November 1522 to bring the reform movement in the Alsatian town of Weißenburg to a successful conclusion. At the beginning of May 1523 he came to Strasbourg as an excommunicated refugee.

There Bucer immediately offered his services to the incipient reform movement, and in his first book, *Das ym selbs niemant sonder anderen leben soll,* he formulated his theological program. Using as a point of departure the divine order placed within creation according to which it lies in the nature of all beings to turn toward others with help and support, he presented the Fall as the destruction of that order, and the death of Christ on the cross essentially as the reinstatement of that order in such a way that the believer recognizes this reality and, at the same time, with the aid of the Holy Spirit, is enabled henceforth to live and to act in accordance with this original order of being. This view emphasizes once again the basic Reformation stances of *sola scriptura* as well as *solus Christus,* which is based on the first, along with *sola fide* from the doctrine of justification; however, special emphasis lies with sanctification and the new life of the Christian.

No less important and consequential was the "dialogical structure" of Bucer's theology, which was rooted in his ontology: in terms of cognition as well as actions and life everyone requires support as well as challenge from others in order to live, and to be fully well grounded; and everyone, in turn, acts according to those principles. This was the outline of what Bucer wanted to accomplish all his life: the establishment of active communities with various offices for the purpose of mutual edification as well as an ordered ecclesiastical discipline, the responsible participation of the authorities in implementing a Christian social order, and finally efforts toward an understanding within Protestantism as well as within the church on the basis of the recognition in principle of the Reformation doctrine of justification.

At first, however, dissent prevailed. In Strasbourg Bucer participated in the struggle against the Roman Catholics. Regarding questions of a new ecclesiastical order he also turned to Zwingli in Zurich, and at the beginning of the controversy over Communion he clearly sided with the Swiss. The Disputation of Bern (1528) marked the apex of his cooperation with Zwingli. But even then the two by no means completely agreed theologically. In this very period Bucer first published Latin translations of Johannes Bugenhagen's interpretations of *Psalms* as well as of Luther's sermons, followed by some of his own biblical commentaries (the synoptics and *Ephesians* in 1527, *John* and *Zephaniah* in 1528, *Psalms* in 1529). These had grown out of lectures to theologians and learned laymen in order both to educate the community as well as to edify them comprehensively in the spirit of true piety.

From 1529 onward Bucer's sphere of influence became larger. At the religious Colloquy of Marburg (1529) he was still a marginal figure. At the imperial Diet of Augsburg (1530) he witnessed the political and theological isolation of the south Germans, when the Strasbourg Confession (Tetrapolitan Confession) was signed only by Constance, Memmingen, and Lindau. Bucer strove for years to overcome this separation and to come to an agreement with Luther and the theologians from Wittenberg without having to give up his own views nor his connections with the Swiss; he traveled thousands of kilometers through southern Germany and Switzerland and ceaselessly drafted new formulas of concord. This effort was not driven by opportunism but by his belief in Christ's real presence in Communion, not removed from the elements of bread and wine but not incorporated within them either. Luther's notion of "sacramental union" (*unio sacramentalis*) seemed to Bucer to express this circumstance most fittingly: it was a mystery that to Bucer's mind was basically accepted by everyone within the Reformation camp. Therefore he could allow it to stand as such, and at the same time try to circumscribe it with words for those who expressed such a demand.

It was to this effect that in 1532 the theologians of Strasbourg thus agreed to the Augsburg Confession, that Melanchthon and Bucer agreed in Kassel (1534) on the understanding of Communion, and that finally in May 1536 the Wittenberg Concord was successfully concluded. This was a highlight in Bucer's life, for this was a matter of true concord, one which emphasized the common ground and nonetheless allowed room for diverging accentuations. Most southern German imperial cities endorsed the concord, but the Swiss towns did not, Bucer's efforts for years notwithstanding.

During the same period he acted as ecclesiastical adviser and organizer in many territories, especially in towns of southwestern Germany, such as Ulm (1531), Frankfurt am Main (1533), and Augsburg (1534–1537). He also wrote assessments for foreign countries, among others for the kings of England (1531) and France (1534–1535). He established particularly close ties with Philipp of Hesse. The Alsatian increasingly became Philipp's partner in conversation and confidant in theological and ecclesiastical matters. In 1538 Bucer reorganized ecclesiastical life in Hesse along with its ecclesiastical order, in which the rite of confirmation was included for the first time, and he won back to the church a considerable number of Anabaptists grouped around Peter Tesch. But he also played a considerable role in facilitating the bigamy of Philipp (1539–1540).

Finally, during these years he worked with dedication on the institution and organization of the church in Strasbourg. In 1533 a synod ratified its dogmatic and legal foundations. In 1534 its church order and a first catechism by Bucer were published, and at the same time with the aid of the city council the Anabaptists and spiritualists, among them Kaspar von Schwenckfeld, were expelled from the town. It was not possible, however, to establish a church independent of the authorities, much less an efficient church order. Nonetheless, Bucer kept up his hopes that through teaching, education, and edification he could come closer to the goal of a municipal community profoundly shaped by Christian principles. In 1536 his learned commentary on *Romans* was published; in 1538 the reorganization of the municipal Latin school was effected. Johann Sturm took over its lead. Other respected scholars, most of them renegades of Catholicism, also taught there, even for some time John Calvin, to whom Bucer was soon drawn in friendship. The great work *Von der waren Seelsorge* (Concerning True Pastoral Care; 1538) delineated once again his understanding of the church in the sense of a pastoral theology: the community as an association of faithful Christians who are willing to accept responsibility for one another—from which arose the need for both the church order and the institution of various offices within the community. This book marked his greatest effort in this field.

In the early 1540s Bucer came to be an eminent if not dominant figure of the Reformation. In this short time span, during which a majority in all religious factions subscribed to reconciliation and dialogue, all of his theological, political, and personal abilities and commitments came to bear formidably. Owing to the "dialogical structure" of his thought Bucer was able to maintain numerous connections and ties in high-ranking circles not only within the German empire but also in Europe—for example, in England, France, Italy, Denmark, Bohemia, Moravia, and Hungary. Among the reformers Bucer was the first truly European churchman and theologian in the sense that in all his pronouncements, publications, and decisions he was well aware of this European dimension. His political astuteness accrued from his keen sense of power and of what was viable. In addition, because of his background and his convictions he was a determined federalist and an opponent of absolutism; thus his view of the emperor was negative. At a personal level his industry and creativity, his knowledge, his eloquence, and certainly also his charm were impressive.

In light of the impending death of Duke George of Saxony and the question of church reforms in his territory, a colloquy was held in January 1539 in Leipzig between Bucer and Witzel, among others. Both Bucer and Witzel largely disregarded theological differences. Then the Alsatian advocated with great determination the convening of an independent national council. He wrote anonymous dialogues in order to garner support for this plan among the Roman Catholics; he prepared reports on the use of church property in order to win over the high-ranking clergy; finally, he urged leading politicians in letters—above all Philipp of Hesse—that they propose such a council to the estates of the empire.

Finally, when at the end of 1540 Melanchthon and Johann Eck negotiated at the religious Colloquy of Worms, Bucer and Johannes Gropper worked clandestinely at the order of the emperor on a text that was supposed to serve as the basis of a renewed, large-scale attempt at ecclesiastical unification. In the spring of 1541 in Regensburg an agreement was reached on the basis of this book regarding the doctrine of sin and finally even regarding the article on justification. But concerning the question of offices there was dissent, which became absolute when the issues of the Mass and Communion were at stake. Since Luther as well as the pope and finally the estates of the empire proceeded to dismiss the agreements reached thus far, the project of a German national council failed in the summer of 1541.

But Bucer was not discouraged; instead he tried through connections to the archbishop of Cologne, Hermann von Wied, to implement in Cologne a moderate program of church reform. Despite several months' work in Bonn in 1543, in which Melanchthon supported him temporarily, Bucer had to stop short of complete success. The military victory of the emperor over Baron William of Jülich-Cleve-Berg removed the basis of all far-reaching ecclesiastical and political plans. The dogmatic resolutions at the Council of Trent finally concluded the period of religious colloquies for theology as well.

In the course of reflection and repentance after the emperor's victory over the Schmalkald League (1546–1547), "Christian societies" were formed in some parishes of Strasbourg. Within these, people voluntarily accepted the responsibility to live a life in the spirit of charity and mutual church discipline. Bucer—from 1541 married again and since 1544 provost of the collegiate church of Saint Thomas—emphatically supported these circles even against the opposition by the authorities. But above all he fought against the introduction of the Interim in the city. The period of negotiations had ended for him as well since the opposing parties were no longer willing to discuss but were issuing orders.

Strasbourg was forced to bow to the rule of the emperor, and Bucer emigrated to England at the beginning of 1549. He never managed to feel at home in that foreign country, although he received a professorship in Cambridge, was given a doctorate in theology, and was solicited for advice several times. In the question of liturgical vestments he decided *de facto* against the rigorism of John Hooper, who was also influenced by Heinrich Bullinger, and in favor of the tradition represented by the archbishop of Canterbury, Thomas Cranmer. He criticized the first edition of *The Book of Common Prayer*. He resolutely warned against importing the dispute over Holy Communion to the British Isles. Bucer devoted his last energies to the writing of *De Regno Christi*, a great theological and sociopolitical reform text that he completed in October 1550. It dealt not only with church reform but with the reform of the entire British society. To implement it the king was supposed to issue fourteen laws that the people, represented by a national synod, would have had to approve along with numerous regulations regarding their enforcement. One may view this process as a kind of confirmation for the entire population, who thereby would vow to live a pious life, including church discipline. At this point Bucer once again demonstrated the goal that had determined his life: church and society were to be changed and improved by committed Christians in active communities in which the love of one's neighbor would reign over everyday life.

Bucer died during the night of 28 February 1551 and was laid to rest with all honors. In the course of the Counter-Reformation in England under Mary Tudor his remains and also his books were publicly burned by an executioner. Queen Elizabeth I ordered a ceremonial rehabilitation of Bucer in 1560.

BIBLIOGRAPHY

Primary Sources

Hubert, C., ed. *Martini Buceri Scripti Anglicana fere omnia.* Basel, 1577.

Lentz, Max, ed. *Briefwechsel Landgraf Philipp's des Großmüthigen von Hessen mit Bucer.* 3 vols. Reprint, Osnabrück, 1965.

Rott, Jean, ed. *Correspondance de Martin Bucer.* 2 vols. Leiden 1979–.

Stupperich, Robert, ed. *Martin Bucer's Deutsche Schriften.* 10 vols. Gütersloh 1960–.

Wendel, François, et al. eds. *Martini Buceri Opera Latina.* 5 vols. Paris and Leiden, 1954–.

Secondary Sources

Chrisman, Miriam U. *Strasbourg and the Reform. A Study in the Process of Change.* New Haven, 1976. Bucer's work in Strasbourg.

Eells, Hastings. *Martin Bucer* (1931). Reprint, New York, 1971. Comprehensive account in English, although somewhat dated.

Greschat, Martin. *Martin Bucer. Ein Reformator und seine Zeit.* Munich 1990. Most comprehensive account of Bucer's place within the context of the history of the Reformation.

Hopf, Constantin. *Martin Bucer and the English Reformation.* Oxford, 1946. Important text concerning Bucer's time in England.

Krieger, Christian, and Marc Lienhard, eds. *Martin Bucer and Sixteenth-Century Europe.* 2 vols. Leiden, 1993.

Pollet, J. V. *Martin Bucer. Etudes sur la Correspondance avec de nombreux textes inédits.* 2 vols. Paris 1958–1962. Significant because of the primary sources as well as the explanations regarding Bucer's work.

———. *Martin Bucer. Etudes sur les Relations de Bucer avec les Pays-Bas, l'Electorat de Cologne et l'Allemagne du Nord.* 2 vols. Leiden, 1985.

Rott, Jean. *Investigationes Historicae.* Edited by M. de Kroon and M. Lienhard. 2 vols. Strasbourg, 1986. Collection of groundbreaking essays on Alsace and on Bucer.

Stephens, W. P. *The Holy Spirit in the Theology of Martin Bucer.* Cambridge, 1970. Explicitly systematic treatment of the topic.

Stupperich R., ed. "Bibliographia Buceriana." *Schriften des Vereins für Reformationsgeschichte* 169 (1952), 37–96. Incomplete.

Wendel, François. *L'Eglise de Strasbourg. Sa constitution et son organisation, 1532–1535.* Paris, 1942. Fundamental account of the organization of the church in Strasbourg.

MARTIN GRESCHAT
Translated from German by Wolfgang Katenz

BUCHANAN, George (c.1506–1582), Scottish humanist. He is the intellectual embodiment of the "Auld Alliance" between France and Scotland. He was educated in Paris and spent much of his life in France as a noted academic and tutor. Only in 1561 did he return to Scotland, initially—and remarkably, in view of his later role as her most savage detractor—as a favored member of the court of Mary Stuart.

His career was spectacular. In an age of distinguished Scottish scholars, he was by far the most distinguished, one of the greatest European humanists of the late sixteenth century. In an age of the triumph of Calvinism in Scotland, Buchanan emerged as the leading propagandist; Elizabeth's hatred of its real apologist, John Knox, because of his *First Blast of the Trumpet against the Monstrous Regiment of Women*, brought Buchanan into the limelight when the deposition of the Catholic Mary had to be explained to an English queen who upheld both Protestantism and the divine right of monarchs. In an age of resistance theory, Buchanan ranks with the foremost Huguenot writers. And in an age of strenuous education of monarchs, Buchanan emerges as the most brutal opponent of the methods of Roger Ascham in his training of James VI, the pupil who banned Buchanan's works because of their attack on his mother and their advocacy of contractual kingship, had nightmares about him to the end of his life, and yet boasted with pride that he had been taught by this most prestigious of scholars.

Buchanan, this austere and formidable man, whose face lours out menacingly from his portrait, remains a mass of contradictions. Spokesman for the Calvinists, and yet—despite his dangerous encounter with the Portuguese Inquisition in 1551–1552—a man more concerned with secular than religious affairs, with the contract between king and people rather than king and God; "profane" poet and dramatist as well as scholar and psalmist; a man who inspired fear but also huge respect and even affection, terrifying his royal pupil and yet in old age gently teaching his servant to read. His learning was devastating, his personality outstanding; but perhaps he should be characterized as a man of the Renaissance rather than of the Reformation.

BIBLIOGRAPHY

Burns, J. H. "The Political Ideas of George Buchanan." *Scottish Historical Review* 30 (1951), 60–68. A splendidly vigorous and clear discussion. Essential.

Mason, Roger A. "*Rex Stoicus*: George Buchanan, James VI and the Scottish Polity." In *New Perspectives on the Politics and Culture of Early Modern Scotland*, edited by John Dwyer, Roger A. Mason, and Alexander Murdoch, pp. 9–32. Edinburgh, 1982. A detailed, carefully crafted analysis of the Scottish context of Buchanan's theory. Again, essential.

McFarlane, I. D. *Buchanan.* London, 1981. A brilliant and exceedingly comprehensive study of Buchanan's life and scholarship: a "must."

Salmon, J. H. M. "An Alternative Theory of Popular Resistance: Buchanan, Rossaeus and Locke." In *Renaissance and Revolt: Essays in the Intellectual and Social History of Early Modern France.* Cambridge,

1987. A subtle, fascinating, and thought-provoking essay, arguing that Buchanan cannot simply be labeled a "monarchomach" as if that explained everything, and linking his ideas on natural law to Locke's.

JENNY WORMALD

BUCHMANN, Theodor. *See* Bibliander, Theodor.

BUDÉ, Guillaume (also Budaeus; 1468–1540), prominent Parisian Hellenist and adviser to King Francis I of France. He was particularly instrumental in furthering the cause of humanism at the court of Francis I by urging the institution of royal lectureships—which became the Collège de France—and serving as "dean" of Greek studies in France. Coming from a family of royal officers, Budé studied law at Orléans and became the most famous French legal scholar (*Annotationes in Pandectas*, 1508) and student of ancient economics (*De asse et partibus eius*, 1515; this work also contains notable "digressions" on moral philosophy). His vernacular *Institution du Prince* is a landmark in French political theory.

Best known as a philologist and Hellenist (*De philologia* and *De studio literarum*, 1532; *Commentarii linguae graecae*, 1529), Budé corresponded in both Greek and Latin with Desiderius Erasmus, Thomas More, Juan Luis Vives, and others, mainly on philological matters. As the most prestigious French humanist of his generation, his views and support were sought by many, including the young François Rabelais. Budé translated works of Plutarch, Aristotle, and Demosthenes. He also developed a mystical religious philosophy, (found in his *De transitu hellenismi ad christianismum* of 1535).

Budé was a practicing Catholic all his life but shared with reform-minded Christian humanists a desire for a religious renaissance. As a royal officeholder, he supported the religious politics of Francis I, even after the heresy trials of the Erasmian Louis de Berquin. Following the Affaire des Placards of 1534, Budé denounced the excesses of followers of the reformers in *De transitu*. Because he ordered restraint in the ritualistic aspects of his funeral and because his wife and children moved to Geneva and became Calvinists after his death, Budé's position on religious matters has continued to attract the attention of scholars. His *Opera omnia* (4 volumes) of 1557 were reprinted in 1967.

BIBLIOGRAPHY

Primary Sources

Budé, Guillaume. *Omnia Opera Gulielmei Budaei.* Farnborough, 1966.
———. *De transitu hellenismi ad Christianismum.* Edited by M. Lebel. Sherbrooke, Que., 1973.

Secondary Sources

Bohatec, Josef. *Budé und Calvin: Studien zur Gedankenwelt des französischen Frühhumanismus.* Graz, Austria, 1950. Focuses on the milieu of French Christian humanism.
Delaruelle, Louis. *Études sur l'humanisme français: Guillaume Budé, les origines, les débuts, les idées maîtresses.* Paris, 1907. First part of uncompleted intellectual biography; out of print.
Garanderie, Marie Madeleine de la. *La Correspondance d'Erasme et de Guillaume Budé.* Paris, 1967.
———. *Christianisme et lettres profanes 1515–1535: Essai sur les mentalités des milieux intellectuels parisiens et sur la pensée de Guillaume Budé.* Paris, 1976. Emphasis on Budé's religious philosophy; analysis of *De transitu.*
McNeil, David O. *Guillaume Budé and Humanism in the Reign of Francis I.* Geneva, 1975. General biographical survey; attention to political and literary connections of Budé.

DAVID O. MCNEIL

BUDOVEC OF BUDOV, Václav (1551–1621), Czech nobleman, traveler, and writer, as well as the leading political figure in both the Unity of Brethren (Bohemian Brethren) and the evangelical anti-Habsburg estate movement. Born into an old Czech knighted family (raised to the estate of lords in 1607), Budovec was educated in the Unity of Brethren and at the foreign universities of Wittenberg and Geneva, where he was a pupil of Théodore de Bèze. From 1565 to 1577 Budovec traveled through Germany, Denmark, the Low Countries, England, France, and Italy and from 1577 to 1584 was a member of a Habsburg diplomatic mission to the Turkish sultan. He spoke several European languages, in addition to Turkish and Arabic, and had extensive contacts with European Protestants. Inspired by David Chytraeus, he also had a special interest in Christian-Islamic relations. He expressed his critical evaluation of Islam in the book *Antialkorán* (Prague, 1614).

After returning home Budovec served at the imperial court of Rudolf II. At the beginning of the seventeenth century, he decided to oppose the re-Catholization of Bohemia and, at the diet of 1603, strongly protested the persecution of the Unity of Brethren. He became a recognized leader of the whole non-Catholic Czech opposition. He was a central figure in the struggle for religious liberty, especially for the Letter of Majesty of 1609, in which the Bohemian Confession of 1575 and an autonomous Protestant church in Bohemia were legalized. In the course of the uprising of the Bohemian estates against the Habsburgs and their religious unification policy of 1618–1620, Budovec became one of the most influential members of the government of the estates. After the election of Frederick V of the Palatinate as king of Bohemia (1619), he was appointed president of the court of appeals in Prague. Following the defeat of the estates in the Battle of White Mountain (8 November 1620), he was sent to prison, sentenced to death, and, along with twenty-six other condemned men, executed in the Old Town Square of Prague (21 June 1621).

The political activities of Budovec were intimately connected with his theological ideas. He represented the Unity of Brethren in the period of its most profound Calvinization and threat to its existence. Budovec defended religious tolerance, however, and wanted a new Protestant church organization safeguarded by law and fully respected by Catholics. In the struggle for religious liberty, he was ready to apply the principle of *ius resistendi* against the ruler. Budovec wrote several theological, historical, and political treatises in Czech (e.g., *Antialkorán*) and two Latin publications: *Circulus horologii lunaris et solaris, hoc est brevissima synopsis historica* (Hanau, Germany, 1616) and *Gnomon apologeticus Circuli horologii historici* (Hanau, Germany, 1618).

BIBLIOGRAPHY

Budovec z Budova, Václav. *Antialkorán* (Anti-Koran). Edited by Noemi Rejchrtová. Prague, 1989. A critical edition of Budovec's most important literary work.

Glücklich, Julius. *O historických dílech Václava Budovce z Budova* (On the Historical Writings of V. Budovec of Budov). Prague, 1911. A useful, analytical monograph, comparing Budovec's conception of history with those of other Czech historians of the first half of the seventeenth century.

Glücklich, Julius, ed. *Václava Budovce z Budova korespondence z let 1579–1619* (The Correspondence of V. Budovec of Budov from 1579–1619). Prague, 1908.

———. *Nová korespondence Václava Budovce z Budova z let 1580–1616* (Newly Discovered Correspondence of V. Budovec of Budov from 1580–1616). Prague, 1912. Two very important collections of sources for the study of Budovec's political and religious thought.

Rejchrtová, Noemi. "La pensée eschatologique de Václav Budovec de Budov." *Communio viatorum* 18 (1975), 129–137. An interpretation of Budovec's theological thought.

———. *Václav Budovec z Budova*. Prague, 1984. The only available modern biography with extensive annotated bibliography.

JAROSLAV PÁNEK

BUGENHAGEN, Johannes (1485–1558), German Protestant reformer. Called Pomeranus after his native region of Pomerania, Bugenhagen was a municipal preacher at Wittenberg and a reformer alongside Martin Luther and Philipp Melanchthon. He was especially famous for his church orders for cities and territories in north Germany.

He became principal of the school in Treptow (Pomerania) in 1504, was ordained to the priesthood in 1509, and, in 1517, became lecturer at the Premonstratensian monastery at Belbuck. Between 1512 and 1515 he embraced, on his own, especially through the reading of Desiderius Erasmus, a humanist perspective of the Bible, which prompted him increasingly to work for reform of the church. Initially interested in scriptural exegesis and the practical aspects of an ethical reform of the Christian life, he moved toward the new evangelical teaching on justification in 1520 as a result

of his reflections on the meaning of the Eucharist and penance, together with his reading of several writings of Luther. His christological views also moved him in that direction. His lectures on the gospel of Matthew show his development in this regard. In order to deepen his theological competence, he traveled to the University of Wittenberg in the spring of 1521. Under Luther's influence he accepted the distinction between law and gospel, and he began to understand faith as trust in the divine promise of the forgiveness of the sinner. It must be emphasized that all in all he found his way to the Reformation independently. His critique of the institutions of the church thus received a new theological foundation with which he freed himself from the teachings of Erasmus.

In Wittenberg Bugenhagen initially studied with Melanchthon, who influenced him in various ways. In 1521 he resumed, at first privately, his exegetical teaching with a detailed and strongly philological interpretation of *Psalms*. This work was published in Basel in 1524 (with four reprints that same year, five others by 1544, and a German translation by Martin Bucer in 1526). It established Bugenhagen's reputation as an exegete. In it he further developed the new teaching on justification using the language of *Psalms*. He offered an interpretation of the situation of the sinner, who is under the law and is tempted but whom God accepts in view of the sufferings of Christ. Accordingly, Christ is the sole mediator of salvation, and by faith in him Christians are God's children who can perform through the Holy Spirit proper good works. These are the notions that Bugenhagen, concurrently with his *Psalms* commentary, developed in his lectures on Paul's minor epistles, which were published in 1525 (followed in 1527 by a commentary on *Romans*). Luther's initiative prompted in 1523 his appointment as rector in Wittenberg, which allowed him to demonstrate his practical and organizational gifts. Alongside his preaching and pastoral responsibilities, he continued to lecture in the theology faculty. He became a regular member of that faculty when he received the doctorate in 1533. Several of his sermons are extant, and quite a few of his publications are based on his homiletic activities.

In his open letter of 1525 to the city of Hamburg, entitled *Van dem Christen loven unde rechten guden wercken* (Of the Christian Life and Proper Good Works), he developed a comprehensive systematic delineation of justification. It was a programmatic summary of his position over against the adherents of the old faith (especially the reform-minded Augustin von Getelen), to which he added elements of a new evangelical church order. During that time (1525–1529) he defended reform with several writings about the Mass, the marriage of priests, confession, and monastic life. With a handbook of theological concepts for the scriptural texts for the church year (*Indices in Evangelia*, 1524), he paralleled Luther's church postil of 1521–1522. His most popular work, *Harmonie der Passions- und Auferstehungsberichte* (Harmony of the Accounts of the Passion and Resurrection), also grew out of his academic activities. He began this work as Latin lecturer in 1519 in the monastery at Belbuck, continued it in Wittenberg in 1522, and published it in modified form in 1524. This work attained its significance through a High and Low German translation in 1526 and 1530. As a private devotional book as well as a lectionary for the services of Holy Week, it was used frequently until the seventeenth century.

Even before 1521 Bugenhagen was interested in the improvement of ecclesiastical structures, which were to conform to the teachings of Christ. His experience with problems of church reform (as a minister in Wittenberg and in the visitation of electoral Saxony in 1527–1528) enabled him to design a general model of a new church order that combined the principles of the congregational ideal in the New Testament with the demands of practical life. His biblical studies between 1521 and 1525 were the basis for this work; hence, his organizational writings were "doctrine" (as he himself called them) and represented Reformation theology. The basic summary of his principles of church organization is found in his *Christlike ordeninge* for the city of Braunschweig in 1528: civic life was to be formed as Christian life, for which the word of God was the decisive norm. The community, as both a political and an ecclesiastical entity, was to be the carrier of the Reformation, which implied at least in part tendencies toward democratizing existing structures. One can find this in the Hamburg church order of 1529 and, more explicitly because of the specifics of the situation, in the Lübeck church order of 1531. At issue were the establishment of schools, the care of the poor by the community, and the reform of worship and of the clergy.

Bugenhagen was fundamentally responsible for the fact that the Reformation in its conservative Wittenberg form succeeded relatively quickly in northern Germany. Other reformers incorporated his principles for their church orders (for example, in East Frisia and the Hanseatic cities of Minden, Göttingen, Soest, Bremen, Herford, and Osnabrück). His personal efforts also led to the introduction of the Reformation according to his church orders in Pomerania in 1534–1535 and in Denmark in 1537–1539.

Bugenhagen tied his theological conviction and his biblical orientation to a realistic understanding of the political dimensions of the Reformation. This conviction found expression in the religious colloquies of 1536–1537, the new order of the duchy of Braunschweig-Wolfenbüttel after its forceful occupation by the Schmalkald League in 1542–1543, the turbulence of the Schmalkald War (1546–1547), and the controversies about the evangelical identity occurring between the Augsburg Interim (1548) and the Peace of Augsburg (1555). In his later years he devoted himself intensively to biblical lectures at the University of Wittenberg (printed commentaries on *Matthew* in 1543, *Jeremiah* in 1546, and *Jonah* in 1550). As a theologian he was heavily dependent on Luther, whose pastor and counselor he was, but he was also greatly indebted to Melanchthon. Still, he had his own identity. He showed his independence as an exegete and as an organizer of evangelical praxis of particular importance for north Germany, Scandinavia, and the Baltic territories.

BIBLIOGRAPHY

Geisenhof, Georg, ed. *Bibliotheca Bugenhagiana: Bibliographie der Druckschriften des Joh. Bugenhagen* (1908). Reprint, Nieuwkoop, 1963. Bibliography of printed works.

Hauschild, Wolf-Dieter. "Biblische Theologie und kirchliche Praxis: Die Kirchenordnungen 1528–1543 in Johannes Bugenhagens Gesamtwerk." In *Kirchenreform als Gottesdienst: Der Reformator Johannes Bugenhagen, 1485–1558*, edited by Karl-Heinz Stoll, pp. 44–91. Hannover, 1985.

Holfelder, Hans Hermann. "Bugenhagen, Johannes." In *Theologische Realenzyklopädie*, vol. 7, pp. 354–363. Berlin and New York, 1981.

Kötter, Ralf. *Johannes Bugenhagens Rechtfertigungslehre und der römische Katholizismus.* Göttingen, 1994.

Leder, Hans-Günter. "Bugenhagenliteratur." In *Johann Bugenhagen: Beiträge zu seinem 400. Todestag*, edited by Werner Rautenberg, pp. 123–137. Berlin, 1958. Historiographical summary.

———. "Zum Stand und zur Kritik der Bugenhagenforschung." *Herbergen der Christenheit* 11 (1977–1978), 65–100.

Vogt, Karl August Traugott. *Johannes Bugenhagen, Pomeranus: Leben und ausgewählte Schriften.* Elberfeld, 1867. A useful overview of life and work.

WOLF-DIETER HAUSCHILD
Translated from German by Hans J. Hillerbrand

BULLINGER, Heinrich

BULLINGER, Heinrich (1504–1575), Swiss reformer, *Antistes* at Zurich, and Reformed theologian. Born at Bremgarten (Aargau), the youngest of five sons of the parish priest there, Heinrich began Latin school and then joined his brother John at Emmerich in 1516. In 1519 he began his studies at the University of Cologne, earning a bachelor of arts in November 1520, and a master of arts early in 1522. The burning of Luther's books in 1522 and the ensuing controversy at the university aroused in him an interest in theology. First he read in the church fathers, then Luther's treatises of 1520 and Melanchthon's *Loci communes*, and finally the New Testament. He was an evangelical by the time he returned home in April 1522.

In January 1523 Bullinger accepted the position of head teacher at the Cistercian monastery at Kappel. There he wrote Latin commentaries on most of the books of the New Testament, while at the same time giving lectures on them in German to the monks. The fruition of his work was the reform of the monastery; the Mass was abolished in September 1525 and the Reformed Eucharist celebrated in March 1526. Bullinger first met Huldrych Zwingli in 1523. He then attended the first disputation with the Anabaptists in Zurich in January 1525 and acted as clerk at the second and third disputations in March and November. In January 1528 he accompanied Zwingli to the disputation at Bern, where he met other Swiss reformers.

Bullinger replaced his father as pastor at Bremgarten in May 1529, and by the end of June Bremgarten had become a Reformed town. He married Anna Adlischwyler in August. After the Zurich troops were defeated at Kappel in October 1531, Bullinger and his family were forced to flee from Bremgarten. They arrived in Zurich on 21 November. On 13 December he accepted the invitation to replace Zwingli as *Antistes* of the Zurich church.

During his tenure as *Antistes*, Bullinger had a full family life. He and Anna had eleven children, six sons and five daughters. Rudolf Gwalther, who joined the household in 1532 at the age of thirteen, was raised like a son. At times other students lived in the Bullinger house. Bullinger's parents lived with him, and he also cared for Zwingli's family. Anna and three of the Bullinger children died of the plague in 1564. In frail health during the last decade of his life, Bullinger finally died on 17 September 1575. His testament named Gwalther, who had married Zwingli's daughter Regula, as his successor.

Bullinger's first challenge as *antistes* was the crisis that resulted from Zurich's defeat at Kappel. Rumors circulated in the confederation that Zurich would again become Catholic, and there was some Catholic sentiment in Zurich itself. In response, Bullinger wrote the original draft of a mandate, issued by the council on 19 May 1532, that reaffirmed Zurich's adhesion to the Reformed faith and renewed all the morals legislation of prior years. Then Bullinger and Leo Jud wrote a mandate issued by the council on 22 October that reorganized and enlarged the scope of the synod. The synod dealt with the selection, the lives, and the teachings of the clergy. The pastors were required to swear a yearly oath of loyalty to Zurich and obedience to the council. Eight councilmen were members of the synod; one of the two presidents of the synod was a councilman.

The relationship between the church and the civil government in Zurich was thus firmly established. The council possessed all powers of coercion and the church none. The clergy was not subservient to the council but was under its ultimate control. Though the task of the clergy was simply to preach and to perform its pastoral duties, the office of pastor gained a special status in Zurich under Bullinger. As the spokesman of the clergy and the church, he had a means of speaking directly to the council. The *Fürtrag* ("oration") gave him regular access to the council, enabling him to instruct it on issues on which it disagreed with the leaders of the church, such as electing new pastors, education, censorship, the use of church wealth, the poor, and usury. The *Fürtrag*, plus his friendly relations with members of the council and mayors Diethelm Röist (1524–1544) and Rudolf Lavater (1545–1557), made possible the institutionalization of this cooperative arrangement, with the civil government as the senior partner.

Bullinger was a prolific preacher and writer. During his first decade of leadership in Zurich, he preached six to eight sermons a week. In 1542 his preaching activity was reduced to two sermons, on Friday and Sunday. He was director of the Zurich academy until 1537, after which he continued as professor of theology. In 1536 he was a principal author of the First Helvetic Confession. During his lifetime he published 119 separate works. His *Decades*, a collection of one hundred sermons that may originally have been lectures at the academy, summarizes his theology. He wrote commentaries on all the books of the New Testament except *Revelation*. He published collections of sermons on *Revelation, Daniel, Jeremiah,* and *Isaiah*. He wrote *De testamento seu foedere Dei unico et aeterno*, the first treatise on the covenant. His *Reformationsgeschichte*, a history of the Zwinglian Reformation up to 1532, is one of several historical works. His writings were translated into German, French, Dutch, and English.

One of Bullinger's crowning achievements was the Second Helvetic Confession (1566). A comprehensive affirmation of the Reformed faith, it was soon accepted by the Reformed churches in Switzerland, except for Basel, and by those in Germany, France, and eastern Europe. It was also influential in England, Scotland, and the Netherlands.

Bullinger had an influence throughout Europe because of his letters, his personal ministrations to exiles, and his voluminous publications. His extant correspondence numbers more than twelve thousand pieces. He corresponded with leading French Protestants and had French exiles in his home from time to time. In Germany his influence was mostly theological, although again he received exiles in midcentury when Reformed cities in southern Germany were re-Catholicized. In the 1550s, when Locarno was re-Catholicized, more than one hundred refugees poured into Zurich from Italy. He corresponded with Protestants in Poland and Hungary. His works were widely read in the Netherlands. His influence was especially strong in England, no doubt owing to his many contacts with the English, including John Hooper, who lived with the Bullingers from 1547 to 1549.

Bullinger's theology was, of course, influenced by Zwingli. He unavoidably built on the Zwinglian foundation, but he also went beyond Zwingli, adding his own genius and leaving a lasting legacy to the Reformed churches. His most distinctive doctrine was his theology of the covenant, which was closely connected with his view of the Christian community. In 1534 Bullinger published his *De testamento seu foedere Dei unico et aeterno*, which was reprinted as an appendix to five different editions of his New Testament commentary (1537, 1539, 1544, 1549, and 1558). The covenant doctrine, which Bullinger first developed late in 1525, is found throughout his works, although not in every one of them.

Bullinger taught that there was only one covenant in history, from Adam to the present. God formed his people by means of the covenant. In Old Testament times one became a member of the covenanted community through circumcision, and in New Testament times, through baptism. The covenant was bilateral and conditional. God promised to be all-sufficient for those who kept the conditions of the covenant. These conditions, faith in God and love of neighbor, had never changed in history. Therefore, even though all things became clearer with the advent of Christ, there was a unity of the people of the two eras as well as a unity of the Old and New Testaments, the New Testament being nothing but the interpretation of the Old. The pattern for the Christian community was thus found in the Old Testament: the pastor was the successor of the prophets, and the magistrate was the successor of the kings. Therefore, the magistrate alone, like the Old Testament kings, had the authority to establish religion and to discipline the Christian community. The covenant not only allowed Bullinger to defend infant baptism against the Anabaptists, but it also instructed his thought about divine grace, the importance of the law, the nature of the Christian community, and the process of history. Such a broad presentation went far beyond Zwingli's; though the two men had many similar ideas on the covenant and the Christian community, Bullinger developed these ideas independently and more fully.

Bullinger was clearly more than Zwingli's disciple. His independence is even evident in the development of his doctrine of the Eucharist. Before consulting with Zwingli, in the mid-1520s, Bullinger came to a new understanding of the Eucharist that was close to, but not identical with, Zwingli's doctrine. He agreed with Zwingli in rejecting the real presence, but he also closely connected the Eucharist with the covenant. He viewed it as a sacrament of the covenant, a symbol of God's promise of redemption to those who were in the covenant by virtue of baptism. Even though his view of the Eucharist was not identical with Zwingli's, he readily defended Zwingli's viewpoint against both the Catholics and Luther as early as 1532. Then, in 1536, Bullinger opposed the Wittenberg Concord, the result of Martin Bucer's labors to find a compromise between the Swiss and the Lutherans. Bullinger and Luther again disagreed in print in the 1540s.

By the 1540s Bullinger faced conflicts with Calvin in Geneva over three issues. The issues were the Eucharist, predestination, and the Christian community. First, while Bullinger viewed the Eucharist as a testimony of God's grace, Calvin saw it as an instrument of divine grace. After extensive correspondence and a personal encounter in Zurich, they agreed to the Consensus Tigurinus in 1549, which omitted Calvin's instrumentalism.

Second, Bullinger disagreed with Calvin on predestination. Though Bullinger was careful to guard the Protestant principle of *sola gratia, sola fides*, he also developed a carefully stated doctrine of single predestination and never accepted Calvin's concept of a double decree. He wished to affirm God's freedom and free grace, but he also was concerned with protecting God's goodness and human responsibility. His predestinarian thought is thus permeated with a universalist tone; the Dutch Arminians therefore appealed to him later in the century. Though some scholars see him as accepting double predestination in the 1550s and 1560s, Bullinger's thought evidences no developed doctrine of reprobation.

The third area in which Bullinger disagreed with Calvin was the nature of the Christian community. Bullinger taught that the Christian community was rightfully under the rule of the Christian magistracy. This doctrine of the single sphere, which he had used against the Anabaptists since the early 1530s, contrasted sharply with Calvin's view of two spheres, the civil and the ecclesiastical, with the church having control over Christian discipline. The two men never agreed on the issues of discipline and the relationship between the civil and ecclesiastical authorities.

They did agree, however, on how to deal with heretics. Bullinger made his position clear in 1535 when he wrote a document giving his opinion to the council that the civil magistrate should punish and even execute intransigent Anabaptists and other false teachers. The attitude expressed in this document and in Bullinger's letters and publications about the Anabaptists goes far in explaining his later support for the execution of Michael Servetus, his sanction of the exile of Bernardino Ochino from Zurich, and his approval of the opinions of Calvin and Théodore de Bèze in their writings against Sébastien Castellion.

BIBLIOGRAPHY

Primary Sources

Bullinger, Heinrich. *Heinrich Bullingers Diarium der Jahre 1504–1574*. Basel, 1904.
———. *Werke*. Zurich, 1972–1992.
Gäbler, Ulrich, et al., eds. *Heinrich Bullinger Werke*. Pt. 2, *Briefwechsel*. 5 vols. Zurich, 1973–. A critical edition of Bullinger's correspondence.
Staedtke, Joachim, ed. *Heinrich Bullinger Werke*. Pt. 1, *Bibliographie*. Vol. 1, *Beschreibendes Verzeichnis der Gedruckten Werke von Heinrich Bullinger*. Zurich, 1972. A complete bibliography of Bullinger's published writings.

Secondary Sources

Bächtold, Hans Ulrich. *Heinrich Bullinger vor dem Rat: Zur Gestaltung und Verwaltung des Zürcher Staatswesens in den Jahren 1531 bis 1575*. Zürcher Beiträge zur Reformationsgeschichte, 12. Bern, 1982. Study of Bullinger's use of the *Fürtrag* as he spoke before the council.
Baker, J. Wayne. *Heinrich Bullinger and the Covenant: The Other Reformed Tradition*. Athens, Ohio, 1980. Study of Bullinger's concept of the covenant, how it flavored the rest of his thought, and how it differentiated his theology from that of Calvin.
Biel, Pamela. *Doorkeepers at the House of Righteousness: Heinrich Bullinger and the Zurich Clergy, 1535–1575*. Zürcher Beiträge zur Reformationsgeschichte, 15. Bern, 1991. Study of how Bullinger's concept of the relationship between church and state became normative in

Zurich as he elevated the office of the minister above other governmental offices and thus gave the ministry a special status.

Blanke, Fritz, and Immanuel Leuschner. *Heinrich Bullinger: Vater der reformierten Kirche.* Zurich, 1990. The first half of this volume is a reprint of Blanke's *Der junge Bullinger, 1504–1531,* Zurich, 1942, a concise, reliable biography covering the first twenty-seven years of Bullinger's life, and the only biography that is not part hagiography. The second half consists of twenty-six short vignettes by Leuschner on a variety of topics covering the rest of his life.

Bouvier, André. *Henri Bullinger, réformateur et conseiller oecuménique, le successeur de Zwingli d'apres sa correspondance avec les réformés et les humanistes de langue française.* Reprint, Geneva, 1979. Study of Bullinger's relations with French Protestants.

Dowey, Edward A. "Heinrich Bullinger's Theology: Thematic, Comprehensive, Schematic." In *Calvin Studies V,* edited by John Leith, pp. 41–60. Presented at a colloquium on Calvin studies at Davidson College and Davidson Presbyterian Church, Davidson, N.C., 19–20 January 1990. Presents Bullinger's theology under several themes. He denies that Bullinger was a systematic theologian and specifically rejects the centrality of the covenant in his thought.

Fast, Heinold. *Heinrich Bullinger und die Täufer: Ein Beitrag zur Historiographie und Theologie im 16. Jahrhundert.* Weierhof (Pfalz), Germany, 1959. A study of Bullinger's writings against the Anabaptists.

Gäbler, Ulrich, et al., eds. *Heinrich Bullinger Werke.* Pt. 2, *Briefwechsel.* 5 vols. Zurich, 1973–. A critical edition of Bullinger's correspondence.

Herkenrath, Erland, ed. *Heinrich Bullinger Werke.* Pt. 1, *Bibliographie.* Vol. 2, *Beschreibendes Verzeichnis der Literatur über Heinrich Bullinger.* Zurich, 1977. A bibliography of writings about Bullinger and writings that relate to Bullinger up to 1976.

Hollweg, Walter. *Heinrich Bullingers Hausbuch: Eine Untersuchung über die Anfänge der reformierten Predigtliteratur.* Neukirchen-Vluyn, Germany, 1956. A study of the *Decades* and its impact in Europe.

Koch, Ernst. *Die Theologie der Confessio Helvetica Posterior.* Neukirchen-Vluyn, Germany, 1968. Argues that the covenant is the underlying structure of the Second Helvetic Confession.

McCoy, Charles S., and J. Wayne Baker. *Fountainhead of Federalism: Heinrich Bullinger and the Covenantal Tradition; With a Translation of De testamento seu foedere Dei unico et aeterno 1534 and a Bibliography on Federal Theology and Political Philosophy.* Louisville, Ky., 1991. Argues that Bullinger's covenant thought was seminal for the further development of covenant or federal theology and for the creation of federal political philosophy in the sixteenth and seventeenth centuries.

Pestalozzi, Carl. *Heinrich Bullinger.* Elberfeld, Germany, 1858. The standard biography.

Rorem, Paul. *Calvin and Bullinger on the Lord's Supper.* Bramcote, England, 1989. Study of the differences between Bullinger and Calvin on the Eucharist, their negotiations, and their eventual agreement in the Consensus Tigurinus.

Staedtke, Joachim. *Die Theologie des jungen Bullinger.* Zürich, 1962. A thorough, systematic study of the young Bullinger's theology through 1528.

Walser, Peter. *Die Prädestination bei Heinrich Bullinger im Zusammenhang mit seiner Gotteslehre.* Zurich, 1957. Argues that Bullinger came to a double predestinarian formula by the 1550s, but he can find no developed concept of reprobation.

J. WAYNE BAKER

BÜNDERLIN, Johann (also Johannes; Hans Wunder; Hans Fischer; c.1498–1533), Anabaptist preacher and spiritualist. Born in Linz, Bünderlin studied from 1515 until 1519 in Vienna, where he became acquainted with the ideas of Erasmian humanism. His acquaintance with Conrad Grebel, subsequently the Anabaptist leader in Zurich, dates from this period. After his studies Bünderlin became a preacher in Upper Austria in the domain of Bartholomäus von Starhemberg, a Lutheran who did not tolerate Bünderlin's Anabaptist leanings after 1524. In 1528, during his subsequent stay in Augsburg, he probably received adult baptism and by this publicly declared himself part of the Anabaptist congregation. In 1527 he became a preacher in Nikolsburg (Mikulov, Moravia) in the territory of Leonhard of Liechtenstein, who was receptive to Anabaptist ideas. In the same year, Bünderlin took part in the so-called Augsburg Anabaptist synod and became acquainted with Hans Denck, whose ideas he henceforth embraced in his writings. But his activities in Nikolsburg were not of long duration. As early as 1528 he appeared in Strasbourg, where he probably remained until 1529. He was seen as the leading figure of the Anabaptists until Pilgram Marpeck disputed his right to this role.

Until 1530 Bünderlin's writings were printed and published in Strasbourg. His four most important writings are *Aus was Ursach sich Gott in die nyder gelassen und in Christo vermenscht ist* (1529), *Eine gemeine Berechnung über die heyligen schrifft inhalt* (1529), *Eine gemayne einlaytung in den aygentlichen verstand Mosi* (1529), and *Erklerung durch vergleichung der Biblischen geschrifft, das der wassertauf samt andern eüsserlichen gebreuchen in der Apostolischen kirchen gebeut on Gottes befelch und zeugnis* (1530). These writings are characterized by notions of spiritualism that bear the stamp of humanism, ideas that align him with Denck and Sebastian Franck. Of the spiritual authorities, he placed the medieval mystic Johannes Tauler and Desiderius Erasmus above Martin Luther. According to sources, a lecture by Bünderlin about his views was delivered in March 1529 to an Anabaptist gathering in the house of Claus Bruch, a citizen of Strasbourg.

In those years Strasbourg served as a place of refuge for persecuted Anabaptists and other radicals. They were continually confronted by the leading reformers of the city—Martin Bucer, Wolfgang Capito, and Caspar Hedio—and were for the most part sooner or later expelled by the city council. In addition to the Anabaptists of Strasbourg, Bünderlin also became acquainted with Michael Sattler, Melchior Hoffman, and, later, Marpeck. The antagonism between Marpeck and Bünderlin became known from the years of the Anabaptist polemic. In a 1531 tract (*Ein clarer fast nützlich Unterricht . . .*) Marpeck opposed Bünderlin's interpretation of the church. In 1529 the Constance reformer Johannes Zwick invited Bünderlin to visit Constance, disregarding Johannes Oecolampadius's previous admonition from Basel. In a letter to Johannes Campanus dated

1531, Franck praised Bünderlin's piety, and the letter on the whole shows the similarity of interpretation between Franck and Bünderlin.

What is probably Bünderlin's last writing (*Clare Verantwortung etlicher Artikel*) also dates from 1531. A possible connection with Kaspar von Schwenckfeld, formed in Strasbourg between 1529 and 1531, might explain Bünderlin's 1532 stay in Prussia, where he engaged in discussions on reform and spiritualist views in Prussia and Silesia. The last information about Bünderlin comes from a letter of 9 May 1533 from Julius Pflug to Erasmus; Bünderlin was probably executed in May 1533.

BIBLIOGRAPHY

Foster, Claude R., Jr. "Johannes Bünderlin: Radical Reformer of the Sixteenth Century." Ph.D. diss., University of Pennsylvania, 1963. The most comprehensive work on Bünderlin.

Nicoladoni, Alexander. *Johannes Bünderlin von Linz und die oberösterreichischen Täufergemeinden in den Jahren 1525–1531*. Berlin, 1893. Outdated, to be sure, but still valuable because of its thorough use of primary sources.

SIGRID LOOß
Translated from German by Susan M. Sisler

BURCKHARDT FROM SPALT, George. *See* Spalatin, Georg.

BURGHLEY, Lord. *See* Cecil, William.

BYRD, William (1543–1623), English composer. The most distinguished English musician of the sixteenth century, Byrd was born in 1543, very likely in Lincoln, but was probably brought up in London, where he was a pupil of Thomas Tallis. Little is known about his early years. In 1563 he was appointed organist and master of the choristers at Lincoln cathedral. Seven years later he was named a gentleman of the Chapel Royal. For some time he continued to receive a stipend from Lincoln on condition that he send "church songs and services" to the cathedral. He finally left Lincoln in 1572.

As director of music for Elizabeth I's chapel, Byrd became acquainted with a number of leading courtiers and aristocrats. In 1575 he and Tallis were granted a monopolistic patent for the printing and sale of music. Although this did not prove lucrative, it did give Byrd the impetus to publish a number of important religious compositions, including the *Cantiones sacrae* (1575) and the *Gradualia* (1605).

Despite his court connections and his compositions written for the Anglican liturgy, Byrd remained a committed Catholic. Some members of his family were fined for recusancy, but Byrd himself escaped, perhaps because of the queen's respect for his musical abilities. During the last years of his life, he left his position in London and moved to Stondon Massey, Essex, close to the home of his patrons, the Petres of Ingatestone Hall. Edward Somerset, earl of Worcester, and Robert Cecil, earl of Salisbury, were also among his friends. He died in 1623.

Byrd's compositions include both settings of the English liturgy and Latin motets and masses. The late Latin motets and the masses for three, four, and five voices are often considered to be his most eloquent works. Although the Latin Mass was illegal in England, Byrd's music was performed privately in the homes of his aristocratic Catholic patrons. It is possible that the queen allowed the performance of some Latin motets in her private chapel, although they could not have been sung publicly in Anglican churches or cathedrals. The *Great Service* is perhaps Byrd's finest setting of canticle texts from *The Book of Common Prayer*. He wrote more than sixty English anthems, mainly settings for full choir but also some of the newer verse anthems with sections for solo voices. Byrd also left more than fifty short dances for keyboard performance, as well as a number of secular works for viols, one hundred English part-songs, and more than fifty secular songs for solo voice. He experimented with a wide range of styles and forms, including rich imitative polyphony and more concise chordal writing. His verse anthems were influential in developing the style of such later composers as Orlando Gibbons and Henry Purcell.

BIBLIOGRAPHY

Fellowes, Edmund H. *William Byrd*. London, 1936. The standard older study.

Kerman, Joseph. "William Byrd." In *The New Grove High Renaissance Masters*. London, 1984. A recent account of Byrd's life and work, based on Kerman's article in the *New Grove Dictionary of Music and Musicians*.

Le Huray, Peter. *Music and the Reformation in England, 1549–1660*. London, 1967. The best general account of church music in England during this period.

Wulstan, David. *Tudor Music*. London, 1985. Includes some discussion of performance practices and problems.

STANFORD E. LEHMBERG

C

CABBALA, CHRISTIAN. The use of medieval Jewish mystical sources among Christian scholars, known as Christian Cabbalism, flourished during the fifteenth and sixteenth centuries. Devotees of the ancient theology such as Pico della Mirandola, Johannes Reuchlin, Cornelius Agrippa, and Guillaume Postel believed that the constellation of neo-gnostic, neo-Pythagorean ideas that developed in the late medieval Spanish and Provençal Jewish communities represented a secret and divine oral tradition that originated in the garden of Eden. Moreover, Cabbala constituted a conceptual bridge between Hermetic notions of "the celestial ministrant," the Neoplatonic concept of Jesus Christ as the Logos in the gospel of John, and numerological methods developed by Pythagorean thinkers. Through use of Cabbalistic method Christian scholars transposed the original Hebrew scriptural text into an equivalent mathematical code predicated upon the numerological equivalents of Hebrew letters. This, in turn, permitted the discovery of hidden Christian ideas in the Old Testament that might be interpreted to deliver a stridently Johannine concept of Christ.

The most significant Christian Cabbalists were *Conversos*, Spanish Jewish converts to Catholicism, such as Flavius Mithridates, for whom "Christian" Cabbalistic mysticism provided a bridge from Judaism to Christianity. Mithridates was also Pico's translator and his most important source of Jewish mystical ideas. It was these sources, in turn, that Reuchlin popularized, Postel systematized, and that subsequently circulated in Christian circles for the next two centuries.

Protestant reformers were less enthusiastic about Christian use of Cabbalistic ideas since this numerological method departed from "the plain sense of scripture" even more than did the traditional medieval Catholic fourfold method of interpretation. Even more, Luther and other reformers correctly appreciated the danger of Judaizing inherent in the use of a Jewish mystical system never intended for Christian purposes.

[*See also* Böhme, Jakob; *and* Jews.]

BIBLIOGRAPHY

Blau, Joseph L. *The Christian Interpretation of the Cabala in the Renaissance.* Reprint, Port Washington, N.Y., 1965. This is the standard introduction to the subject in English.

Secret, François. *Les kabbalistes chrétiens de la renaissance.* Enl. ed. Neuilly-sur-Seine, 1985. The best one-volume discussion of the subject by its foremost authority.

Wirszubski, Chaim. *Pico della Mirandola's Encounter with Jewish Mysticism.* Cambridge, Mass., 1989. An excellent textual analysis demonstrating Mithradates' importance to Pico and to subsequent generations of Christian Cabbalists.

JEROME FRIEDMAN

CAJACOB, Jörg. *See* Blaurock, Georg.

CAJETAN (Ital., Tommaso or Giacomo Gaetano de Vio; Lat., Caietanus or Cajetanus; 1469–1534), Dominican theologian, exponent of Thomism, and critic of early Reformation doctrines. Born in Gaeta in the kingdom of Naples as Giacomo de Vio, he took the name Tommaso upon entering the Dominican order in 1484. During studies at Naples, Bologna, and Padua he began to be known as *Caietanus* from the Latin name of his city of birth.

Cajetan attained his academic degrees between 1491 and 1494 while at Padua, where he began teaching metaphysics in 1494, working out Thomistic philosophical positions against theses of John Duns Scotus and the naturalistic and deterministic worldview of Paduan Aristotelians such as Nicoletto Vernia. Cajetan's early philosophical treatises on being and essence, analogical predication, and the causal influence of divine providence were accompanied by a series of commentaries on works of Aristotle, including an exposition of *De anima* (1509) that questions the philosophical argument for the human soul's immortality, while holding to it as given by revelation.

While teaching in Pavia and Milan (1497–1501), Cajetan wrote on issues of social and economic morality, taking account of the changing world of business and finance. In Pavia he began his commentary on the *Summa theologiae* of Thomas Aquinas, a work published in four parts (1508–1523), to which thinkers in the scholastic tradition down to the twentieth century have referred (modern edition in vols. 4–12 of the Leonine *Summa*, Rome, 1888–1906). In 1506 Cajetan published a collection of his shorter works on ethical and theological topics. This grew in subsequent editions to the ample proportions of his *Opuscula omnia* (frequently reprinted between 1530 and 1612).

In 1501 Cajetan was called to Rome to serve as the official Dominican liaison with the Curia Romana. From 1508 to 1518 he was master general of the order and promoted a renewed dedication to studies and the use of more stringent norms in the approval of friars as teachers and confessors. He sent Dominican missionaries to the New World and from their reports formulated a critique of the Spanish conquest. In 1511 Cajetan mobilized Dominican opposition to the dissident council of Pisa and in two treatises set forth the case for papal superiority over general councils. During the Fifth Lateran Council (1512–1517) he worked successfully to defend the relative independence of religious orders from local episcopal control but gained no backing for his position on the autonomy of philosophy in treating matters connected with doctrines of faith.

Named cardinal in 1517, Cajetan went as papal legate to the imperial Diet of Augsburg in mid-1518. His commission was to gain financial support from the emperor and estates for a papally sponsored crusade against the Turks in the Balkans and the eastern Mediterranean. Once in Augsburg, Cajetan was also mandated to examine Martin Luther as part of the canonical procedure resting on the accusation of error and heresy. Cajetan diligently examined Luther's available writings and arrived at a differentiated judgment. In three encounters, 12, 13, and 14 October 1518, Cajetan called for Luther to recant positions taken on indulgences and on faith in the sacramental word, but Luther held fast to what he had written. Luther's appeals to the pope and a general council (22 October and 18 November 1518) led to his teaching being judged in Rome in 1520 and to the bull *Exsurge Domine*.

Cajetan followed the development of the Reformation and responded with carefully argued counterpositions on the Roman primacy (1521), the eucharistic presence of Christ's body and blood (1525), sacrifice of the Mass (1531), and justifying faith and good works (1532). Cajetan's controversial works never descend to personal attack but reflect his own sobriety and rigor. In 1530 he recommended that Pope Clement VII seek to heal the confessional division by conceding to the Lutherans communion under both forms, the chalice, and clerical marriage.

During a second legation, to Hungary in 1523–1524, Cajetan completed a handbook for confessors, the *Summula peccatorum* (1526), which marks the transition from medieval casuistry dominated by canon law to pastoral practice on a theological basis. The major effort of Cajetan's last decade was the composition of strictly literal commentaries on scripture, beginning with *Psalms* and then treating the New Testament (except *Revelation*) and the Old Testament historical and wisdom books (except the *Song of Songs*). A five-volume edition of his commentaries came out in Lyon in 1639.

Cajetan's works shaped the development of early modern Catholic thought in logic and metaphysics, philosophical anthropology, and social ethics. He gave Thomism a new viability that was subsequently exploited at Salamanca beginning with Francisco de Vitoria. Cajetan's biblical exegesis, however, was censured by the Sorbonne for denigrating received traditions. In his responses to Reformation doctrines, Cajetan was an able theological craftsman, ever attentive to texts and arguments, discriminating in his assessment, and gradually moving toward profound statements on issues such as eucharistic sacrifice and the meritorious value of good works done in and by the grace of Christ.

BIBLIOGRAPHY

Congar, Yves M.-J. "Bio-Bibliographie de Cajétan." *Revue thomiste* 17 (1934), 3–49. Complete chronological list of the works.

Fabisch, Peter, and Erwin Iserloh, eds. *Dokumente zur Causa Lutheri, 1517–1521.* 2 vols. Münster, 1988–1991. Vol. 2, pp. 37–240, provides in the original Latin the principal texts connected with Cajetan's meeting with Luther in 1518, with ample commentary.

Hallensleben, Barbara. *Communicatio, Anthropologie und Gnadenlehre bei Thomas de Vio Cajetan.* Münster, 1985. Comprehensive monograph on Cajetan's theology of human nature and grace, redemption, and justification.

Morerod, Charles. *Cajetan et Luther en 1518: Edition, traduction et commentaire des opuscules d'Augsbourg de Cajetan.* Fribourg, 1994. Latin-French edition, detailed study of Cajetan's treatises of September-October 1518 assessing Luther's doctrine.

Stöve, Eckehart. "De Vio, Tommaso." In *Dizionario biografico degli Italiani,* vol. 39, pp. 567–578. Rome, 1991. Dense presentation, attentive to Cajetan's efforts to reform his order. Good bibliography of works and studies.

Wicks, Jared. *Cajetan Responds: A Reader in Reformation Controversy.* Washington, D.C., 1978. Texts, in English, from Cajetan's controversial works against Protestant positions.

———. *Cajetan und die Anfänge der Reformation.* Münster, 1983. On Cajetan's work to 1521, especially his meetings with Luther.

JARED WICKS

CALENDARS. *See* Festivals; Liturgical Calendar; Time.

CALVIN, John (Fr., Jean Cauvin; Lat., Johannes Calvinus; 1509–1564), French reformer in Geneva. He was born on 10 July 1509 in Noyon, a town in the Picardy region of France. His father, who had raised himself from simple circumstances to a burgher's position, was a trustee for the cathedral chapter in Noyon. His mother, who died during his youth, was much given to popular piety. John and his older brother received church benefices to provide for their study of theology. From 1523 Calvin studied first with Mathurin Cordier at the Collège de la Marche in Paris; he then devoted himself to the liberal arts at the Collège Montaigu. After a break with the cathedral chapter, his father urged him to give up his study of theology. From then on he was to devote himself to the study of law in Orléans. In this way he escaped a Scholasticism tinged with speculative one-sidedness and could ground his faith, unmediated, upon the Bible and church fathers. Calvin was spurred on in these studies by a succession of educators who either were adherents to a Christocentric spirituality called the *devotio moderna,* such as Cordier, or were scholars already influenced by Martin Luther, such as Melchior Wolmar, scholar of the New Testament in the original Greek.

After the death of his father, Calvin went to Paris in order to deepen his knowledge of the biblical languages and classical and Christian antiquity at the newly founded Collège Royal. This college was intellectually influenced by Desiderius Erasmus and Faber Stapulensis and formed an intellectual polar opposite to the archconservative Faculty of Theology of Paris (Sorbonne), which at that time was also involved with the Inquisition. It was during this period that the twenty-three-year-old Calvin published his first work—a commentary on the Stoic philosopher Seneca's tractate *De clementia* (Concerning Clemency) in order to exhort King Francis I in a disguised manner to more religious toleration. With the coming of Luther's Reformation, Calvin made acquaintance with the French "Circle of Reformers" (*Reformisten*) who gathered around Bishop Guillaume Briçonnet of Meaux. The members of this group read both Luther and Erasmus and found the former to be in no way a heretic, despite this judgment by the Sorbonne in 1521. A medical doctor from Basel, Nicolas Cop, who was Calvin's friend and whom Calvin had given theological counsel, was surprisingly named rector of the University of Paris on 1 November 1533. When Cop gave his inaugural address on the beatitudes of Jesus and justification by faith "without the works of the Law," the Inquisition stepped in (A. Ganoczy, 1987, pp. 80–83).

Because of his association with Cop, who was suspected of Lutheranism, Calvin had to leave Paris, fleeing to Basel. There he probably completed his final turn toward the reforming faith. It remains controversial whether Calvin really experienced a "sudden conversion to being instructed" through the gospel, as Calvin wrote a quarter century later in 1557. The contemporary documents are less indicative of a sudden "conversion" and more supportive of a gradual spiritual development, which bore fruit in a theological work, *Christianae Religionis Institutio* (Basel, 1536). For this compendium of evangelical faith, the young autodidact worked mainly from Luther's two catechisms, the *Freiheit eines Christenmenschen* and the *Babylonische Gefangenschaft.* Accordingly, the succession of chapters are "Law," "Confession of Faith," "Prayer," "The Sacraments," "The False Sacraments," and "Christian Freedom." The young author drew on the works of Martin Bucer, Philipp Melanchthon, and Huldrych Zwingli only to clarify individual questions.

The epistle Calvin wrote to open his book is dedicated to Francis I and is revelatory of Calvin's attitude toward the church at the time. The "pious" (meaning those who are maligned as "Lutherans" by their enemies) are neither religious zealots, nor schismatics, nor sectarians, nor anarchists who seek to attack the church and royal authority. They belong to the "true" church of Christ, as opposed to the "Church under the papacy," which in visible form (meaning power, wealth, and the use of legal power) raises its claim above consciences. In contrast, the "true" church possesses as marks, in the sense of the Augsburg Confession, only the pure preaching of the word and the right administration of the sacraments (CR 1, 21; compare *Bekenntnisschriften der evangelisch-lutherischen Kirche* [hereafter cited as *BSLK*], Göttingen, 1967, p. 61). Written in the pleasing Latin of the humanists, the *Institutio* represented a palatable systematic synopsis of Reformation doctrine. Its success spurred on the twenty-seven-year-old lay theologian to further self-guided study. For that reason he wanted to settle in evangelical Strasbourg, but an undesired layover in Geneva radically altered his plans. Guillaume Farel—who had already preached the evangelical faith in this free imperial city for four years without being able to give fitting structure to the church—made Calvin swear to become his fellow worker. Calvin conceded and took the title of "lecturer in holy scripture." In 1537 he created a church ordinance with his *Articles concernant l'organisation de l'Eglise.* This provided for the celebration of the Lord's Supper at least once a month, with exclusion of the unworthy. Calvin wrote a catechism and a confession of faith that "all citizens must be obliged by oath to follow and to keep" (CR 22,85). As "servants of God," the civil magistrates were bound to promote "pure religion."

Nevertheless, the Geneva city council turned against Calvin and the party of the pastors. On 23 April 1538 the council expelled Calvin and Farel. Disappointed, Calvin wanted to withdraw to Basel, but he gave in to the pressing invitation of Bucer and in Strasbourg took over the leadership of the French-speaking parish congregation. He remained there three years, creating an order for worship according to the local practice and publishing an expanded version of the *Institutio* in Latin (1539) and French. He took part in religious dialogues in Frankfurt, Hagenau, Worms, and Regensburg, where he met Philipp Melanchthon. The relative openness of his theology manifested itself when he consented to a compromise over the doctrine of justification in Regensburg, which, however, proved to be futile.

In the meantime the church in Geneva was admonished by letter to return to Catholic unity by Cardinal Jacopo Sadoleto, the bishop of Carpentras. The adherents of the expelled reformers asked Calvin to answer the cardinal. Calvin did so without hesitation and used the occasion to lay out again his conception of the true church. The church rests not on the centuries-long consensus of human tradition but rather solely on God's word (CR 5, 392); with this the Holy Spirit is most closely connected and protects the church through the repeated sending of prophets (CR 5, 393f). After the church had reached a nearly ideal form in the first centuries, it was now in need of reform, to which Calvin and his followers knew they were called, without the least intention of introducing schism or spreading new doctrines (CR 5, 393). The "Answer to Sadoleto" made a great impression upon its readers, and in 1541 Calvin was recalled to Geneva, where without delay he wrote a new church ordinance and order of worship, as well as a new catechism, all of which were approved by the city council. He also undertook to put into effect the schema of a doctrine of four offices, which he had first conceived in Strasbourg and was based on the pattern there. The first office—that of "pastors," who were ordained by the laying on of hands—was charged to arrange the service of the word through preaching and the sacraments. Pastors were also to form together a group (*a collegium*), known as the *Compagnie des Pasteurs* ("Company of Pastors"), and to gather regularly for Bible study, pastoral counsel, censuring conduct, and drawing in new members. (Calvin himself was probably never ordained; possibly it sufficed for him to be aware that he was following a prophetic calling.)

The second of the four offices—that of "teacher," to the extent that teaching was not exhausted by the pastors—was dedicated to the religious instruction of school pupils, catechumens, and theology students. The third office, that of "elders," fulfilled the assignment of overseeing how members of the congregations conducted their lives. The elders formed with the pastors the "consistory," in which both secular and ecclesiastical needs were administered. (In Geneva the city council members selected the elders.) Because their service amounted to a practical proclamation of the word, the deacons took their place during the Lord's Supper next to the pastors, with whom they distributed the bread and wine.

In his new catechism, Calvin departed from Luther's understanding of the law. The divine law was intended not only to reveal the sinfulness of humanity but also to function as an order for the covenant and to spur on moral progress. The law serves a lively faith: whoever obeys it performs an act of faith. In this context one may evaluate the disciplinary proceedings on doctrine in Geneva, during the course of which Calvin also made use of Inquisitorial methods. Thus, in 1544 Sébastien Castellion was forced to leave Geneva. He was a rector of the Geneva Latin school who had rejected the place of the *Song of Songs* in the canon and had criticized the symbolic interpretation of Christ's descent into hell as portrayed by Calvin. Castellion went to Basel, where he wrote his famous tract on toleration *De haereticis, an sint persequendi* (Whether Heretics Should Be Persecuted). Jérome Bolsec met a similar fate in 1551 after rejecting Calvin's doctrine of predestination. Doctrinal proceedings were carried out against the Spanish physician and humanist Michael Servetus; this episode remains the most enduring blot upon Calvin's reputation. Servetus held the opinion that the doctrine of the trinity meant not the unity of three persons

but rather the three manners of working of the one God; he accused the reformer, as well as Rome, of falsifying Christianity. Calvin went so far in his reaction that he even relied on the support of the archiepiscopal Inquisition of Lyon concerning the heresy of Servetus. When Servetus later came to Geneva, Calvin allowed him to be condemned to death after several unsuccessful attempts at conversion. On 27 October 1553 the Spaniard was burned at the stake. The Reformed congregations of Basel, Bern, Schaffhausen, and Zurich and later Melanchthon himself gave their approval.

Calvin showed greater patience in conflicts with other reforming theologians from Switzerland and Germany. After clarifying the doctrine of the Lord's Supper, Calvin gave his signature in 1541 to the version of the Augsburg Confession, written by Melanchthon, according to which the body and blood of Christ are really and truly offered "with the bread and the wine" to the communicant (BSLK 65, 45f). In 1549 Calvin contributed greatly to the effort that produced the Consensus Tigurinus (Zurich Consensus), a synthesis of his own theology of the Eucharist with that of Heinrich Bullinger, the disciple of Zwingli.

In the city of Geneva itself the reformer never fully succeeded in winning a complete following for his strict church ordinance. The Geneva patriots, for a period of time under the leadership of syndicus Ami Perrin, offered bitter resistance until their defeat in the elections of 1555. They especially resented the regulation of private life through a consistory set up by "foreigners." From the outside world, however, Geneva won a growing regard; it was already becoming one of the most important centers of the reforming fellowship. Calvin carried on a brisk correspondence with many people, especially those persecuted in France, as well as with rulers, for example, in England and Poland. Contributing to this dissemination was the Geneva academy, founded in 1559 on the model of Lausanne. It had two divisions: the *schola privata* was for elementary instruction, and the *schola publica* offered more advanced studies, including a curriculum in the liberal arts, biblical languages, and theology. Students came from all over the world—Francy, Germany, the Netherlands, Scotland, and eastern Europe. Many became pastors and professors who would spread the Reformed faith, such as Kaspar Olevianus, the later professor at Heidelberg; Philip Marnix van Saint Aldegonde, an early figure in the Dutch Reformed churches; and John Knox, the Scottish reformer. The students in the academy were obliged to subscribe to the Geneva Confession of Faith. On the other hand, they had access to a philosophy and theology library, which probably even in Calvin's time included such authorities as the Catholic Scholastics Thomas Aquinas, Cajetan, Catharinus, and Pighius, as well as the humanists Erasmus, Faber Stapulensis, Vatable, Guillaume Budé, Pietro Bembo, and Sadoleto. In addition, the newest editions of the church fathers were available there. Finally, the dissemination of Genevan ideas was facilitated by a series of publishers, such as Henri II Estienne and Robert I Estienne, Jean Crespin, Conrad Badius, and Jean Rivery.

Calvin's health could not long keep pace with the enormous burden of work pressing on him. After a final, painful illness, he died on 27 May 1564, at the age of 55. His wish was to be buried at an unknown place without witnesses or ceremony in the belief that the glory of God should not be overshadowed by honoring people.

As a theologian, Calvin exerted a universal and lasting influence, not only in the ecclesiastical arena but also in social and cultural realms. The intellectual stream that sprang from "Calvinist" theology (the reformer himself rejected the name Calvinism; CR 20, 76f) "transmitted through means of a doctrinal, structural, confessional and missionary dynamic a world view grounded in religion and led to specific forms of secular structures in state and public affairs, economics and careers" (E. W. Zeeden, "Calvinismus," in *Staatslexikon: Recht, Wirtschaft, und Beruf*, Freiburg im Breisgau, 1958, pp. 339–347) His theology can be regarded as an imposing synthesis of wisdom and knowledge that addresses the entire person—mind and heart, individually and collectively—from God's initiative toward the goal of salvation. From an intellectual perspective Calvin's synthesis employs the advances made in biblical and classical studies by humanism, together with logic and dialectic, as instruments for formulating the truth of faith. The actual "systematic" (which Karl Barth called "dogmatics") is found in the *Institutio*, to which Calvin continually added and expanded after its first publication in 1536. That which is formalized in the context of the *Institutio*, however, rests on fundamental and comprehensive exegetical work, which presupposes studying the scriptures in their original Hebrew and Greek. There is no impulse whatsoever to neglect the Old Testament in favor of the New Testament. Calvin strove to explicate scientifically all of canonical scripture, including the letter of James, which Luther had wanted to reject. Calvin equally endeavored in his sermons to explain the scriptures with a view to the life of faith. His works printed in *Corpus Reformatorum* fill fifty-nine volumes. Characteristic of Calvin's hermeneutical approach is the first sentence of the *Institutio*, "The sum of our wisdom . . ." consists of two parts: the knowledge of God and of ourselves. It is no less unthinkable to speak about people in a meaningful manner apart from their relationship with God than to speak of God apart from the divine relationship with people. Anthropology is turned theocentrically, and the doctrine of God answers the question, how does God's lordship over people and the world come about? At one time the first human was fully related to God and bore the image of God "in his spirit and in his heart"; also his body was illuminated by the image of God. The first human possessed "free will" until "his spirit fell into corruption" and became "guilty of the divine judgment." Nevertheless, Calvin maintained with Augustine that

reason "was not completely destroyed" but rather made susceptible to error. The Holy Spirit overcomes this misery through the holy scripture and the grace of illumination. Wherever a person is justified thanks to Christ, Christ's Spirit effects the renovation of the lost image of God. God is the one God and so the triune God. Even in turning graciously toward sinners, God manifests himself in the fellowship of the Father, the Son, and the Holy Spirit in love (see A. Ganoczy, 1989).

The characteristics of God are not understood statically but rather as "virtues," as effective manifestations of power through which God works in history. God does this through creation and through revelation, the means by which he confronts reason and leads it into the way of truth. The glory of God is simply unapproachable for people. The ability to comprehend the knowledge of salvation is fulfilled only where Christ as the "image of the Invisible" (*Col.* 1:15) is appropriated. This concept of the self-communication of the transcendent is essential in comprehending correctly Calvin's much-discussed doctrines of divine omnipotence and providence. Nothing happens without the "hidden will" of the creator. As such, God predetermines everything. Neither our election nor our damnation may be attributed to pure accident or chance. "Divine predestination" cannot be seen apart from Jesus Christ. In him, who is the salvation of all humanity, the decision of God for people is completed, and the miracle happens that out of evil good comes forth. Jesus Christ comes to us as the condescension of divine majesty, to which we are incapable of ascending. "The merciful God Himself has therefore made Himself our redeemer in the figure of the Only-begotten."

Calvin shows a preference for Johannine Christology, which proceeds from the Logos, the eternal Word become flesh. Therein also lies the last reason that Calvin's doctrine is truly reformist: the content of the Word in the divine-human relationship is present on all levels—eternal and incarnate Logos, or Christ as the Word simply and completely, and the scripture, gospel, sermon, and sacramental deeds of the Word of the mediator in his church. Closely related to the working Spirit of God, the Word must be heard, believed, and followed by all. The Word has "chosen for himself the womb of the Virgin as a temple"—that is, a truly human existence. The Son of God has lowered himself to become "like us in all things except for sin," "our brother." "Although he governed all things, he manifested himself as a man, who prayed, and not just in appearance did he do this, but he has shown his true love to us" (CR 73, 441). "In our flesh and in our nature justification must be accomplished for us" (CR 74, 225). As Jesus suffered and took the cross upon himself, the omnipotence of God remained "equally hidden." Thus, the cry of the crucified one—"My God, my God, why have you forsaken me?"—becomes comprehensible. From such depths sprang the resurrection and the exaltation of the true man: "He ascended, that he might fill all things [*Eph.* 4:10]. . . he went away from us, in order that he might be present in a much more useful manner than during his earthly life." "Christ has ascended into heaven; there he intercedes for us"; therefore, he remains eternally the mediator of our salvation, the royal and priestly intercessor. The exalted one effectively connects himself with believers through the working of his Spirit, who continually bridges the "distance" between heaven and earth. Thanks to the connecting Spirit of God, the justification earned by Christ for sinners flows into progressive sanctification.

Both of these "moments" of the one grace are "two connected things," inseparable as the "light from the sun," which "cannot be separated from its fire." Without the spirit of rebirth there is no justification. "We cannot be justified by faith alone as a gift, if we do not also live a holy life." Like Luther, Calvin professes the "imputation" of Christ's righteousness to the sinner, but he also emphasizes the role of conduct in the practical sanctification process stemming from justification. In visible ways people should be renewed images and children of God, truly a "second creation." "This renewal does not come to completion in a minute"; people are directed toward continual renewal, rebirth, purification, and sanctification. It is necessary that "the Lord guide, lead and direct our heart through his Spirit" and that his grace continually precede us so that his grace may "effect in us the willing and the completing." The "outward helps" of this progressive transmission of sanctification are the church and the two sacraments. In the "true" church, Calvin sees the "mother of all the pious." Agreeing with Cyprian, he says, "Whoever has God as father must also have the Church as mother." Outside of "her bosom there is no hope for forgiveness of sins and salvation."

Horrified by the practice of certain Anabaptists of his time, Calvin ascribed especially an important role, both of protecting and instructing, to the teaching office of the ecclesiastical community. No one should read the scripture "alone, for himself," thus neglecting exegetical preaching and the tradition of the Fathers. For God himself has joined his Spirit to preaching in order to preserve the unity of believers in the truth revealed through preaching, even though it consist of the pitiful words of humans. The church "is the faithful watchwoman" so that "God's truth should never disappear from the world."

In truth God does not care only for pure doctrine but also for the fulfilling of the lives of his adoptive children. Therefore, God instituted the sacraments. How can they enrich life? They do so in that both baptism and the Lord's Supper transmit the reality of Christ himself: he is "the substance of all sacraments; for in him they have all their firmness, and they do not promise anything apart from him." Hence, their task is shown to be identical to that of the Word. Baptism is "the sign of consecration, through which we are received into the fellowship of the Church, in order to be planted into Christ and counted among the children of God." In the Lord's Supper Christ is "truly given to us through the signs of bread. . . and wine . . . , so that we may grow together with him into one body . . . and also experience his power." Calvin anticipates some of the modern theory of the symbolic, in that he sees in the cultic actions, as it were, the accomplishment of a communication in which God "tempers himself" in his self-communication, thereby allowing his "spiritual goods" to be experienced through physical means. The sacraments, however, do not represent merely cognitive symbols; they are, to quote Augustine, much more "a visible form of an invisible grace."

Concerning the real presence of Christ in the Lord's Supper, Calvin's sentence is important: the visible elements, signed by God's Word, become something "which they were not before." This means that here an event occurs without analogy: "we say, that Christ condescends to us both in the outward symbol as well as in his Spirit, in order truly to make our souls alive with the substance of his flesh and blood." As matter that mediates between people and God, the sacraments must be preached and received in faith. They possess, therefore, a fundamentally dialogic structure, not the character of "one-way speaking." Should someone merely receive the Sacrament without active participation and without faith—that is, as a pure formality—the Sacrament would remain fruitless for that person, as, for example, a seed thrown into a fire. Calvin understands the Sacrament not only as a mirror but also as a seed, which should bring forth fruit.

In order to understand what Calvin thought ecclesiastical office required, one should take into account his doctrine of the "four offices," which Calvin strove to translate into practice in Geneva, together with his fundamental theological judgment of the apostolate, the responsibility of leading the congregation. He could not imagine a church without leadership, although leadership admittedly implied something other than "lordship." The term he uses is *diakonia*, a concept that holds for "all offerings of service in the Church." Calvin's conception was drawn from the apostle Paul, a "minister of the gospel" (*minister evangelii*). Apostles "serve God and Christ" in order to promote the honor of God and Christ. They "serve the Church for salvation." As those sent out, they "represent the person of the One whose place they take." They do this as interconnected colleagues, as equals and peers (*collegae et socii*), under the one Lord. Only thus do they become, together with others, bearers of charisma, "fellow workers of God" and organs of the Holy Spirit. Unlike Luther, Calvin did not make a common "priesthood of all believers" the foundation of his doctrine of offices. Calvin explained his view first as an attack against Roman Catholic clericalism and second as a pronouncement concerning the fundamental equality and freedom of all Christians. Next to the unique, extraordinary services of the apostles, prophets, and evangelists (*Eph.* 4:11), the reformer ascribed to pastors and teachers an enduring ordained commission. With historical acuity he recognized the function of the presbyter and the bishop in the ancient church as a structure of pastoral service justified by scripture. They were "charged to individual congregations." The difference between presbyters and bishops (*episkopen*) was only one of degree. The name of "bishop" was applied to the elected president over the presbyterium. "Archbishops" and "patriarchs" had as their essential function the convoking of synods and general councils, and this only in correspondence with the Christian principal of the common search for pure doctrine and familial unanimity. According to the model of the ancient church, Calvin always ascribed to deacons a meaningful role in social care. At the election of official servants in the ancient church, the "consent of all the people" was sought in order to avoid demagoguery. Ordination, with the laying on of hands (which Calvin, with reservation, accepted as a biblically sanctioned "third sacrament"), was to take place under the "direction" of the bishop through the "college of presbyters."

On the question of papal primacy over the church universal, Calvin's utterances reveal great complexity of thought. He recognized the functional primacy of Peter within the college of apostles on the basis of his exemplary confession of the Messiah, the propriety of the preeminence of the Roman patriarchate because of its apostolic founding and antiquity, and the recognized authority of the patriarchate for arbitration. There is, however, a strict rejection of the papal claim to be monarchical head of the entire church, bishop over all bishops, vicar of Christ, and *pontifex maximus*. The possibility remained open that the ministry of Peter, once renewed according to its original purpose, could take over a legitimate ministry to the worldwide *communio ecclesiarum*. The ministry of Peter and arrogation of control over the gospel were contradictory; ministry to true doctrine was necessary on all levels. From that position the reformer's optative statement on the "succession of Peter" should be understood: "If God wanted that this succession, with which they falsely pride themselves, should reach up to the present day, we would gladly give the deserved honor. The pope would be certainly the successor of Peter, if he only adopted the task of the Apostle. But wherein consists the succession, if not in the continuity of doctrine?" A primacy contrary to the gospel deserved to be called Antichrist, a name introduced by Luther.

Calvin's theology distinguishes itself through its strong relationship to society. It contributed to the formation of the modern state and to the development of awareness among the bourgeoisie of their place in the economy. His faith that God's word possesses the character of action led him to a high estimation of work and vocation. The law of God also fulfills the role of leading to a disciplined use of freedom in social coexistence. The church itself must be free, especially in its relationship with the state. This belongs together with

his *politica administratio*, to the *media salutis*. Secular society and the state are derived from God's will in creation and redemption. Consequently, they must also protect against anarchy and tyranny. Secular legislation may not ignore the double commandment of love. The Christian is obliged to obedience to secular authority, even when that authority conducts itself against the law. Nevertheless, the Christian must offer resistance when the secular authority demands that which is contrary to God. For his time Calvin held that the best possible form of social organization would be an oligarchy tempered by democracy.

BIBLIOGRAPHY

Primary Sources

Calvin, John. *Opera quae supersunt omnia.* 59 vols. Edited by Guilielmus Baum, Eduardus Cunitz, and Edwardaus Reuss. Corpus Reformatorum, vols. 29–87. Braunschweig, 1863–1900.

———. *Opera selecta.* 5 vols. Edited by Petrus Barth and Guilielmus Niesel. Munich, 1926–1952.

———. *Theological Treatises.* Translated with introduction and notes by John K. S. Reid. Philadelphia, 1954.

———. *Tracts and Treatises.* 3 vols. Translated by Henry Beveridge. Grand Rapids, Mich., 1958.

———. *Institutes of the Christian Religion.* Edited by John T. McNeill. Translated and indexed by Ford Lewis Battles. The Library of Christian Classics 21–22. Philadelphia, 1960.

Wevers, Richard F. *A Concordance to Calvin's Institutio 1559.* 6 vols. Grand Rapids, Mich., 1992.

Secondary Sources

Balke, Willem. *Calvin and the Anabaptist Radicals.* Grand Rapids, Mich., 1981.

Bieler, Andre. *L'homme et la femme dans la morale calviniste.* Geneva, 1963.

———. *La pensée économique et sociale de Calvin.* Publications de la Faculté des sciences économiques et sociales de l'Université de Génève 13. Geneva, 1959.

Bouwsma, William. *John Calvin: A Sixteenth-Century Portrait.* New York, 1987.

Breen, Quirinus. *John Calvin: A Study in French Humanism.* Hamden, 1968.

Conditt, Marion W. *More Acceptable than Sacrifice: Ethics and Election as Obedience to God's Will in the Theology of Calvin.* Theologische Dissertationen 10. Basel, 1973.

Cunningham, William. *The Reformers and the Theology of the Reformation.* Edited by James Buchanan and James Bannerman. London, 1979.

Dankbaar, Willem F. *Calvijn: Zijn weg en werk.* Reprint, Nijkerk, 1982.

De Klerk, Peter. "Calvin Bibliography 1972." *Calvin Theological Journal* 7 (1972), 221–250. Henceforth published annually in the November issues.

Doumergue, Emile. *Jean Calvin, les hommes et les choses de son temps.* 7 vols. Lausanne, 1899–1927.

Dowey, Edward A., Jr. *The Knowledge of God in Calvin's Theology.* New York, 1952.

Erichson, Alfred. *Bibliographia Calvinia.* Nieuwkoop, 1960.

Forstman, H. Jackson. *Word and Spirit: Calvin's Doctrine of Biblical Authority.* Stanford, 1962.

Gamble, Richard C., ed. *Articles on Calvin and Calvinism: A Fourteen-Volume Anthology of Scholarly Articles.* New York, 1992.

Ganoczy, Alexandre. *Ecclesia Ministrans: Dienende Kirche und kirchlicher Dienst bei Calvin*. Translated by Hans Sayer. Freiburg, 1968.

———. *The Young Calvin*. Translated by David Foxgrover and Wade Provo. Philadelphia, 1987.

Greef, Wulfert de. *The Writings of John Calvin: An Introductory Guide*. Translated by Lyle D. Bierma. Grand Rapids, Mich., 1993.

Hancock, Ralph C. *Calvin and the Foundations of Modern Politics*. Ithaca, N.Y., 1989.

Hesselink, I. John, Jr. *Calvin's Concept of the Law*. Princeton Theological Monograph Series, vol. 30. Allison Park, Pa., 1992.

Hopfl, Harro. *The Christian Polity of John Calvin*. Cambridge, 1982.

Jansen, John F. *Calvin's Doctrine of the Work of Christ*. London, 1956.

Kempff, Dionysius. *A Bibliography of Calviniana, 1959–1974*. Medieval and Reformation Thought 15. Leiden, 1975.

Kendall, Robert T. *Calvin and English Calvinism to 1649*. New York, 1979.

Krusche, Werner. *Das Wirken des heiligen Geistes nach Calvin*. Göttingen, 1957.

Linde, Simone van der. *De leer van den heiligen Geest bij Calvin*. Wageningen, Netherlands, 1943.

McGrath, Alister E. *A Life of John Calvin: A Study in the Shaping of Western Culture*. Oxford, 1990.

McKee, Elsie Anne. *John Calvin on the Diaconate and Liturgical Almsgiving*. Travaux d'Humanisme et Renaissance 197. Geneva, 1984.

McNeill, John T. *The History and Character of Calvinism*. New York, 1954.

Monter, E. William. *Calvin's Geneva*. New York, 1967.

Mueller, William A. *Church and State in Luther and Calvin: A Comparative Study*. Garden City, N.J., 1965.

Niesel, Wilhelm. *Calvin Bibliographie, 1901–1959*. Munich, 1961.

———. *The Theology of Calvin*. Translated by Harold Knight. Philadelphia, 1958.

Olson, Jeannine E. F. *Calvin and Social Welfare: Deacons and the Bourse Française*. London, 1989.

Parker, Thomas H. L. *John Calvin*. Berkhamsted, England, 1977.

———. *Calvin's Preaching*. Edinburgh, 1992.

Partee, Charles B. *Calvin and Classical Philosophy*. Studies in the History of Christian Thought 14. Leiden, 1977.

Peter, Rodolphe, and Jean-François Gilmont. *Bibliotheca Calviniana*. 2 vols. Geneva, 1991–.

Plomp, Johannes. *De kerkelijke tuche bij Calvijn*. Kampen, 1969.

Richard, Lucien J. *The Spirituality of John Calvin*. Atlanta, 1974.

Sprenger, Paul. *Das Ratsel um die Bekehrung Calvins*. Beitrage zur Geschichte und Lehre der reformierten Kirche 11. Neukirchen-Vluyn, Germany, 1960.

Stauffer, Richard. *Dieu, la création et la Providence dans la prédication de Calvin*. Bern, 1978.

Torrance, Thomas F. *Calvin's Doctrine of Man*. Westport, Conn., 1957.

Wallace, Ronald S. *Calvin's Doctrine of the Christian Life*. Tyler, Tex., 1982.

———. *Calvin's Doctrine of the Word and Sacrament*. Tyler, Tex., 1982.

———. *Calvin, Geneva, and the Reformation*. Edinburgh, 1988.

Wendel, François. *Calvin: Origins and Developments of His Religious Thought*. Translated by Philip Mairet. Reprint, Durham, N.C., 1987.

Willis, E. David. *Calvin's Catholic Christology*. Leiden, 1966.

ALEXANDRE GANOCZY
Translated from German by Jeff Bach

CALVINISM. Despite what the term *Calvinism* seems to imply, the spread of what are more correctly called "Reformed" churches in Europe in the second half of the six- teenth century was not inspired solely by Calvin and the Genevan Reformation. The Reformed movement began with Huldrych Zwingli's preaching in Zurich from 1518 onwards; it had spread to other important centers, such as Bern, Constance, Basel, and Strasbourg years before it reached Geneva; Calvin himself owed much to Heinrich Bullinger, Zwingli's successor in Zurich (whose influence in some other parts of Europe in their lifetimes was as great as Calvin's) and to Martin Bucer. Several of the key ingredients in the "Calvinist" ethos were already in place before Calvin unwillingly embarked in 1538 on his career as a Genevan reformer. For example, the insistence on the second commandment and a prohibition of idolatry; the tendency toward a highly didactic reconstruction of forms of worship; the emphasis on an ethics of obedience, responsibility, and modesty (sometimes described as "this-worldly asceticism"); the high value placed on education; and the suspicion that the Lutheran Reformation had stuck half-way, most clearly reflected in the series of eucharistic conflicts that began in the 1520s and flared up more than once later.

Why, then, "Calvinism"? The answer lies in part in the sheer energy and ability of Calvin and the astonishing range of his activities, particularly his writing. In terms of education, erudition, clarity of style, and coherence of theological vision, he very early emerged as the most penetrating thinker, exegete, author, and organizer in the Reformed movement. Then there was the geographical position of Geneva: a relative latecomer to the Reformation, but as a French-speaking city on the borders of France and Savoy ideally placed to be the base for a fresh wave of reforming mission in France, up through western Germany and the Low Countries, and as far as England and Scotland. (In the Reformed territories of East Frisia in north Germany Bullinger's influence was greater than Calvin's, while Zacharias Ursinus, the main author of the classic Heidelberg Catechism [1563] owed as much to Melanchthon as to Calvin. "Purer Calvinism" was stronger west and east of the German empire than in Germany itself, where Zurich maintained a certain predominance, at least up to Bullinger's death; Bullinger's Second Helvetic Confession [1566] came to rank alongside the Heidelberg Catechism as a normative confessional document.) Finally, the model of church polity developed by Calvin in Geneva, based on the four offices of pastor, teacher, elder, and deacon and governed by a consistory of pastors and elders secured for the Genevan church a greater measure of freedom from control by the city council than was the case in most Swiss Reformed cities. It also supplied a pattern that proved durable and effective when, as in France and the Low Countries, the Reformed churches found themselves confronted by an openly hostile government. Together, these aspects help to explain in retrospect why it is Calvin and Geneva that dominate our view of the Reformed movement in the middle of the sixteenth century.

Calvinist (and Reformed) teachings were in most respects

close to those of Luther, as Calvin himself repeatedly emphasized in his attempts to promote Protestant unity. The authority of the Bible; justification by grace through faith; the centrality of preaching, word, and sacrament as the marks of the visible church; rejection of papal claims and teaching on indulgences, mediation of saints, relics, the sacrifice of the Mass, and the like—all this was common ground. Even before Calvin's time, however, differences of emphasis had become manifest. Unlike Luther, Zwingli and the Swiss reformers enacted radical changes in worship, making the pre-Reformation preaching service (the "pronaus") their model rather than the traditional Roman Mass. They also insisted on removing images, crucifixes, and painted depictions from church buildings—a step Luther refused to endorse, just as he also held to the medieval renumbering of the Ten Commandments, which eliminated the second and divided the tenth into two. Related to this, though not easy to define precisely, was a concern on the part of the Reformed to value the Old Testament, and in particular the perennially valid elements of Old Testament law, more highly than was the case in Lutheranism. Not that Luther was an antinomian—see his Catechism—but he did tend to read the whole of scripture in the light of the Pauline dichotomy of law and gospel. The law had for him two main functions: to convict us of sin (*usus elenchticus*) and to supply norms for civil society (*usus civilis*). The Reformed did not deny or downplay any of this but went a step further, identifying a "third use for the law" (*usus in renatis*) as the guide to life lived in gratitude for the grace of redemption. According to Calvin, this (and not the *usus elenchticus*) was the most important use of the law for Christian believers. So, for example, the Heidelberg Catechism devoted its third and final section to the Lord's Prayer and the Ten Commandments under the single title "Of Gratitude." There can be no doubt that this comes closer to the authentic Jewish understanding than an exclusive insistence simply on the opposition between law and gospel; it may also have contributed to the fact that antisemitism generally did not flourish on Reformed soil. In this connection it is worth noting another liturgical point that was to make history: while Zwingli (though himself highly musical) had banned organ music and singing from his services, Calvin introduced the singing of metrical psalms set to simple, singable tunes, many of them still in use today throughout the world.

Related to this was an inclination, present in Calvin and explicitly stated in other Reformed sources of the time, to make "ecclesiastical discipline"—in the twofold sense of church polity and superintendence of behavior—a mark of the visible church. In retrospect, it is easy to caricature this aspect and to overlook the genuine pastoral concern behind it. Arguably, this stress on good administration and responsible living was one of the great strengths and main attractions of the Genevan model in a world full of turmoil and of the exercise of arbitrary power. The strong lay involvement in governing congregations through the consistories was to become one of the hallmarks of the Reformed churches, as was the development of synodal structures with parity among pastors and among congregations.

It would, however, be wrong to describe this ecclesiology as "democratic" in the modern sense: it was in reality oligarchic. The church was generally governed by a social elite of pastors together with prosperous tradesmen and senior craftsmen. Apart from its appeal to a limited number of German princes and some sections of the French nobility (though less so in France after the Saint Bartholomew's Day Massacre in 1572), Calvinism proved particularly popular with the urban "middle clases"—lawyers, physicians, merchants, and skilled artisans. While simplistic theses about the alleged contribution of Calvinist teaching to the rise of bourgeois capitalism should be treated with caution, there is clearly *some* connection, if only via the Calvinist insistence on developing new forms of social responsibility.

It is a commonplace that Calvinism also came to develop a much more revolutionary understanding of political responsibility than the Lutheran wing of the Reformation. This was, however, only indirectly due to Calvin. He in fact subscribed to a version of the "Two Kingdoms" doctrine that was virtually indistinguishable from Luther's: tyrannous rulers must be endured as divine punishment, and the people have no right to rise against them, though the intermediate nobility might (e.g., the German princes against the emperor). Passive disobedience was the only other option. However, the experience of persecution and religious wars in France led Calvin's successors to a different understanding of the right and even duty of armed resistance, opposition to absolutist monarchy, and support for republicanism (e.g., Théodore de Bèze, François Hotman, Philippe Duplessis-Mornay, George Buchanan). It is not going too far to say that Calvinism was one of the forces that shaped the modern world.

One factor in the process was undoubtedly an increasing emphasis in Calvinism through the latter part of the sixteenth century on the biblical leitmotif of the "covenant," which was devloped not only theologically but politically, leading to later notions of a "social contract" (Rousseau) as the foundation of civilization. The theme of the covenant did not play a major role in Calvin's theology; it was first systematically unfolded by Bullinger, who used it to oppose Anabaptist individualism and rejection of infant baptism. Under the influence of the Heidelberg school and then of Scottish and Irish theologians (Andrew Melville, James Ussher) it generated a framework for understanding the history of salvation in the light of the contrast and tension between a (legal) "covenant of works" given in Creation and an (evangelical) "covenant of grace" adumbrated in *Genesis* 3 and unfolded in God's dealings with Israel on the way to its final establishment in Jesus Christ. In this way, the Lutheran tension between law and gospel was taken up afresh into Reformed theology; its full flowering was, however, only reached in the middle of the seventeenth century with the Westminster Confession and the theology of Cocceius at the Dutch University of Franeker.

Another aspect deserving mention is the intellectual and scientific interest generated by Reformed, in particular Calvinist, teaching and education. The radical break with subservience to received tradition characteristic of Renaissance humanism led in the first generations of the Reformed movement to a new concern for accuracy in the study of ancient texts, to a fresh historical sensitivity, and to an interest in distinguishing critically and incisively between the authentic sense and import of biblical and other documents and the accretions of institutionalized interpretation. The new mentality thereby encouraged—an attitude prepared to search empirically for truth as yet undiscovered instead of seeking merely to reaffirm given views—was to contribute significantly to the rise of natural and experimental science in the seventeenth century. It would be an exaggeration to claim that this was the intent of Calvin and other Reformed leaders in the sixteenth century, but it was an indirect fruit of their contribution to education, rigorous thought and disciplined investigation guided by the search for reality rather than the reinforcement of received ideas. Francis Bacon's *Novum Organon*, written in the second and third decades of the seventeenth century, is a striking witness of the fruitfulness of these impulses.

By comparison with these historical perspectives, the main point of dissension between Lutherans and Reformed in the sixteenth century—the presence of Jesus Christ in the Lord's Supper—may appear rather obscure. It was in fact an issue over which Lutherans did most of the attacking; and the violence of their attacks—whether by Luther on Zwingli or later by Westphal on Calvin and the Consensus Tigurinus of 1549—did less than justice to the real concerns of the Reformed. This applies particularly to Calvin, whose understanding of the meaning of the Lord's Supper was certainly not Zwinglian and represented at the same time a necessary correction of Luther and (even more) the Gnesio-Lutherans.

It is a curious part of this same controversy that Lutheranism came to identify another element as peculiarly Calvinist: the doctrine of "double predestination," although, apart from Calvin's systematizing of the matter, there was actually little difference here between Calvin and Luther. Both stood firmly in the Augustinian tradition of Western theology, according to which the great mass of humanity is enmired in the corruption of original sin, out of which only God's elect are saved by grace alone. (So, for that matter, did such great medieval theologians as Thomas Aquinas.) However, controversy on the issue led Calvin to put particular emphasis on the doctrine, especially on the divine decree of reprobation, though he never made it the cornerstone of his theological system. That step was taken by Bèze in Geneva and William Perkins in England; this led in turn to the Arminian Controversy in the Netherlands and the formulation of "classical Calvinism" in the Decrees of Dordrecht (1619) with their "five points"—total depravity, unconditional election, limited atonement, irresistible grace, and perseverance of the saints. But although all of these points can in one way or another be traced back to Calvin, the total shape of the resulting system represents more a fossilization than a genuine continuation of his theology, a fossilization that has repeatedly caused turmoil and upheaval in the Reformed tradition up to the present time.

For a time it seemed as if Calvin might be able to achieve a reconciliation between the Lutherans and the Reformed. In 1540 Melanchthon revised the Augsburg Confession, modifying the article on the Lord's Supper to make it acceptable to Calvin. This became known as the Confessio Augustana Variata, and for some years was the most widely circulated version. Later, however, Melanchthon's willingness to compromise not only with the Reformed but also with Rome led to his being marginalized in the Lutheran camp. With the Peace of Augsburg in 1555, which recognized only the Roman and Augsburg confessions, Lutheran insistence on holding to the original text (the Confessio Augustana Invariata) effectively excluded the Reformed from toleration with the Holy Roman Empire (at least in theory), a position that was not corrected until the Peace of Westphalia in 1648.

The Reformed exodus from northern Italy, the southern Netherlands, and to a lesser degree France during the second half of the sixteenth century was primarily brought about by the aggressive Counter-Reformation policies initiated by the governments of these countries, even if economic considerations, especially among the merchant elite, may have played a considerable part in the timing of the emigration. This development, however, would have been reinforced by Calvin's attack on Nicodemism, first put forward in the 1540s. Calvin argued that true Christians—that is, Calvinists—if not able to profess their faith openly, must "depart out of Babylon." Similarly, the growing feeling among the Reformed of being under God's special providence and part of the New Covenant can only have served to enhance the willingness to emigrate.

Initially, a considerable number of the refugees from France and Italy settled in Geneva. At the time of Calvin's death in 1564 more than ten percent of the city's population consisted of immigrants. The presence of Calvin, Guillaume Farel, and later Bèze helped to give the city a special aura among the Reformed, who came to see it as the New Jerusalem. At first, this image of Geneva was not shared by the city's original inhabitants, who felt antagonized by the zealous religious refugees, who not only dominated their congregations—not a single pastor in the sixteenth century was a native Genevan (a few were Italian, the rest French)—but also used Geneva as a base from which to evangelize their homelands.

The identification of Geneva with the New Jerusalem among the Reformed faded rapidly after the death of Calvin. Genevan influence over the Reformed churches, especially among the French-speaking communities, reached its zenith under the leadership of Bèze in the early 1570s. From then on other centers such as Heidelberg, Herborn, and Leiden gradually assumed prominence. Lambert Daneau, who had been one of Calvin's colleagues in Geneva during the 1540s and who later served the Huguenot churches in France and the Walloon communities in the Netherlands, had originally compared the Dutch cities, whose governments were outside direct influence of the Reformed churches, unfavorably with the godly regime in Geneva. When he returned from France in the aftermath of the Saint Bartholomew's Day Massacre, he found Geneva a place sadly changed since the days of Calvin. Geneva was still able to exploit the image of the New Jerusalem when it was seriously threatened and besieged by the dukes of Savoy in 1589, 1590, and 1602—using it to promote collections and loans from Germany, the United Provinces, England, Scotland, Poland, Bohemia, and the Swiss cantons—but it had fallen from prominence long before the death of Bèze in 1605. The Reformed faith, meanwhile, although not yet in retreat, had stopped making further significant gains in Europe.

Reformed emigration from France, northern Italy, and the southern Netherlands was gathering speed during the 1560s. The outbreak of the Revolt of the Netherlands caused a flood of refugees, primarily originating from Flanders, Liège, Tournai, and Valenciennes, but after the Saint Bartholomew's Day Massacre considerable numbers also fled France. It has been estimated that some 100,000 people from the southern Netherlands became part of the Reformed diaspora between 1567 and 1590. They settled primarily in Germany, where they sought refuge in most of the important trading centers such as Frankfurt, Nuremberg, Cologne, Hamburg/Stade, Aachen, Wesel, and Frankenthal; in England, where they showed a clear preference for London and other towns and cities of southeast England, such as Colchester and Norwich, where they constituted between a fifth and a third of the population around 1600; and, of course, in the United Provinces, where the towns and cities of Holland and Zeeland were their preferred destinations.

It should be emphasized that this diaspora was made up of a series of emigrations and hardly ever constituted a simple migration from one place to another. It was complex and would often continue for several generations, not coming to an end until the first decades of the seventeenth century. For example, some of the leading and closely connected merchant/banking families who left Lucca in Italy in the 1560s initially found a new home in Lyon, then moved to Paris, where they remained until the Saint Bartholomew's Day Massacre, when they left for Sedan. By 1575 members of these families had sought refuge in Geneva, Hamburg/Stade, Frankfurt, and Nuremberg, eventually seeing some of their relations settled in Amsterdam and London toward the end of the century. The social experience of upheaval and emigration undoubtedly served to reinforce their Reformed faith. As these refugees settled in the major cities in Germany, Switzerland, England, and the United Provinces, they came to form a Calvinist "International," bound together not only by their conviction of being God's chosen people and their shared sense of displacement and minority status, but also by their natural tendency to intermarry and do business with each other. The exile churches they established in these places more often than not became model communities that inspired the local population to follow suit.

This international dimension of the Second Reformation was further enhanced by the foundation of the academy in Geneva (1559). Intended to provide a center for the education of Reformed ministers, Calvin's academy proved a resounding success, attracting more than three hundred students from all over Europe in 1560, among whom were some of the Calvinist leaders of the next generation, such as Philip Marnix van Saint Aldegonde, adviser to William of Orange, and Kaspar Olevianus, who was instrumental in introducing Calvinism into the German Palatinate in 1562. Under Bèze's supervision, the academy published the Geneva Bible (English version, 1560; French version, 1588), which provided "Calvinism" with a common textual foundation. It was of particular importance given the Reformed emphasis on the Bible as the primary source of knowledge and authority. The Geneva version was a product of decades of collective Reformed scholarship and provided the new communities with a highly useful tool, for it was packed with summaries and marginal cross-references.

It is no coincidence that the decline of Genevan influence within the Reformed world corresponds with the decline of the academy during the 1570s. By the 1580s Geneva was no longer the only, nor necessarily the best, place for candidates for the Reformed ministry to study. It had been supplanted by the University of Heidelberg and a number of newly founded academies (Ghent, 1578–1583, and Herborn, 1584); there were new Dutch universities as well, of which Leiden (1575) became the most famous, and later, at the turn of the century, the French Reformed academies such as Sedan and Saumur. These new centers of Reformed learning continued the Genevan tradition of attracting large numbers of students from abroad, thus reinforcing the international dimension of Calvinism. Furthermore, the Reformed academies and universities became centers of humanist learning, often promoting a more liberal, irenical, and latitudinarian aspect of the Reformed faith than the "Genevan model." Consequently, the seeds were sown for a serious confrontation with the less tolerant Reformed theology developed by Bèze in particular. Eventually, this conflict reached its climax in the next century, at the Synod of Dordrecht (1618–1619).

Apart from its dominance of the northern city-states of Switzerland, such as Geneva, Lausanne, Bern, Basel, Zurich, St. Gall, and Schaffhausen, the Second Reformation took permanent hold in France, the Netherlands, Scotland, and Hungary; in Germany it took temporary hold of the Palatinate, Hesse, Anhalt, Nassau-Dillenburg, and Jülich, Berg, and Cleves; in central and eastern Europe, it established itself temporarily in Poland, Silesia, Moravia, and Bohemia; and it influenced the doctrine of the Church of England and inspired a significant Calvinist opposition within the Elizabethan church.

In practice, but in opposition to ecclesiastical principle, the Calvinist communities in France and the Netherlands began their existence as gathered churches of believers. Geneva and Calvin proved particularly important for the diffusion of the Second Reformation in France. Together with those in Basel and Strasbourg, the thirty-four printing houses in Geneva guaranteed that the accelerating demand for Reformed pamphlets in France could be met.

From the mid-1550s the French exile community in Geneva witnessed an apostolic age. Eighty-eight refugee ministers returned to France between 1555 and 1562, while Calvinism in France witnessed an explosive growth. From the foundation of the Reformed church in Paris (1555) to the start of the Wars of Religion (1562), more than 1,750 churches came into existence. The spread of Reformed ideas in France, however, was uneven. It appears to have followed the trade route from Toulouse to Bordeaux and to have spread further along the rivers that connected Dauphiné, Languedoc, and Provence. By 1562 Calvinism had traced a crescent across the map of France, with Lyon and La Rochelle at its tips; there were a community in Paris and a cluster of churches in Normandy as well.

From the start, French Calvinism was distinctly aristocratic in character. "Baronial Calvinism" probably reached its apex when Louis, prince of Condé, was elected protector-general of the Huguenot churches shortly before the outbreak of the Wars of Religion. Until the Saint Bartholomew's Day Massacre the Huguenots, as the French Calvinists were known, recruited most of their leaders from within the French aristocracy, such as Gaspard II de Coligny, François de La Noue, Henri de Rohan, Louis, prince of Condé, and Henry of Navarre, later King Henry IV. Together with Coligny, more than two hundred Huguenot nobles were murdered in Paris during the Saint Bartholomew's Day Massacre, while it has been estimated that more than thirty thousand Huguenots were killed nationwide. Subsequently, French Calvinism became more bourgeois in character. This is not to say that Calvinism in France had not from the outset been particularly attractive to merchants, the

professional classes of doctors, lawyers, and schoolmasters, and skilled craftsmen, but only that these groups of town dwellers came to dominate the movement to a much larger extent after 1572. The Saint Bartholomew's Day Massacre also affected the development of the Reformed churches in France in other ways. One casualty was the locally inspired move toward creating a more democratic church structure, which had been in evidence at the first national synod of the French Reformed churches in 1559. It had originally been promoted by Jean Morély (*Traité de la discipline et police chrestienne*, 1562), but most of its supporters, including the philosopher Petrus Ramus, did not survive the massacres in 1572. Consequently, the Genevan aristocratic and oligarchic consistory model became the norm. Even if the momentum of conversion to Calvinism had slowed by 1570, the dramatic events of 1572 proved extremely harmful to further Reformed expansion in France. Massive abjurations followed in northern France, especially in Paris and Normandy, and the existing frontier between a Catholic north and a Calvinist south became even more pronounced.

In 1562 the Edict of Toleration granted the Huguenots limited rights of assembly and worship at a time when they constituted around ten percent of the population. But Huguenot optimism was quickly dashed when the edict precipitated the Wars of Religion; the Huguenots were defeated, and the privileges that had been offered only a year earlier were curtailed by the Peace of Amboise of 1563. Faced with defeat, the French Reformed churches demonstrated a true Calvinist ability for social organization. They adopted a paramilitary structure and issued a detailed directive covering such matters as enforcement of discipline, salaries of ministers, charity for the poor and war victims, loans to be raised from wealthy citizens and nobility, and the payment of troops. This structure was further elaborated during the 1570s, in the wake of the Saint Bartholomew's Day Massacre. A high point of Huguenot privilege was reached with the Edict of Beaulieu (1576), which granted complete freedom of worship except in Paris and some royal towns. Eventually, after nearly half a century of civil war, Huguenots were granted full political and religious privileges with the Edict of Nantes (1598), but by then Calvinism in France had already started to wane, constituting no more than 7 percent of the population.

As in France, the first Reformed church in the Netherlands was established in 1555; but, unlike Paris, the church in Antwerp remained short of sister churches for the next seven years. By 1561 only twelve churches had been formed, of which only two were in the French-speaking Walloon areas of Tournai and Valenciennes. A few years later more than three hundred churches "under the cross" (i.e., in hiding) had come into existence. This rapid growth in the early 1560s was undoubtedly helped, especially in the Walloon areas, by Huguenot immigrants who were fleeing the Wars of Religion. At the same time, the Reformed communities in Antwerp proceeded to establish a synodal system along French lines. Ecclesiastical discipline remained high on the agenda among the first Reformed churches in the Netherlands, not least because of the strength of the Anabaptists in these areas. It is exactly this preoccupation with Anabaptism which sets the Belgic Confession (1561) apart from the Gallic Confession (1559) and the Scottish Confession (1560) from the same years. Calvin's and Geneva's influence on the Reformed churches in the Netherlands was initially surpassed by that of other reformers such as Bucer, Bullinger, Maarten Micron, and Jan Łaski. Even among the thirty-six Netherlanders who studied at the academy in Geneva from 1559 to 1568, Genevan Calvinism appears to have had a limited impact. Thus, Jacobus Arminius and several of the theologians who supported his more "liberal," antipredestinarian theology were educated under the supervision of Bèze. For the Reformed churches in the Netherlands, the University of Heidelberg and the training offered by the refugee churches in Emden, London, and Germany proved far more significant.

It was the Revolt of the Netherlands against Spain (1566) that proved decisive for Calvinism in the Netherlands. Until the rebellion, the Reformed communities had been centered in the south around Antwerp, in Flanders, in Tournai, and in Valenciennes; now they not only grew locally but also expanded into the northern provinces. By the summer of 1566 Calvinist preachers and their supporters, often recently returned from exile abroad, gained the initiative among the rebels. Their "hedge-preaching" (outdoor-preaching), taking place in the context of economic decline and agricultural crisis, brought about the popular iconoclasms of August 1566. It began in the south, where it was conducted by professional image-breakers, often hired among the refugee communities abroad, then gradually spread to the north, where it was perpetrated by locals.

The arrival of Fernando Álvarez de Toledo, duke of Alba, and his Spanish troops in 1567 temporarily halted the revolt. The accelerating economic hardship caused by the war and the accompanying religious persecution by the duke of Alba's Council of Troubles caused more than sixty thousand, most of them Reformed, to flee the south for the northern provinces, Germany, and England. The importance of the Reformed churches to the struggle against Spain was quickly recognized by William of Orange, the leader of the revolt. He was personally represented by his Genevan-educated adviser, Philip Marnix van Saint Aledgonde, at the first national synod of the Dutch Reformed churches, which met in Emden in 1571. The significance of the Reformed diaspora for the Dutch Reformed churches is evident in the ecclesiastical organization adopted in Emden. Three separate provinces were established for Germany, England, and the Netherlands. Furthermore, the wish to retain close contacts with the powerful Huguenot churches in France was demonstrated by the synod's decision to subscribe to both the Belgic and Gallic confessions of faith.

By 1572 the momentum of the revolt and, to some extent, Dutch Calvinism had swung to the north, especially to the provinces of Holland and Zeeland. Calvinists began to take control of buildings and property belonging to the Catholic church; the large refugee churches in Emden and London were asked to provide ministers. In accordance with the Synod of Emden, the new churches established themselves in classes and provincial synods—in Holland biannual synods were in existence by 1574, while Zeeland had to wait another five years owing to the disruptions of war.

The new Reformed churches' relations with town councils and provincial authorities often turned out to be tenuous. The tolerant and Erastian outlook among civic leaders in the north clashed with the rigorous Calvinism dominant within the Reformed communities. Lay authorities generally held the upper hand and remained in control, aided by the financial hold they exercised over the new churches, providing salaries for ministers and money for the general maintenance of church buildings.

Furthermore, the preference within Dutch Calvinism for a narrow church, restricted to those who unquestioningly accepted its discipline, meant that a sharp distinction was drawn between the minority, *lidmaten* ("members"), who received Communion, and the majority, *liefhebbers* ("sympathizers"), who would come to the sermons. This proved an obstacle to growth and guaranteed that the new churches found it difficult to attract members of the civic elite until the Union of Utrecht (1579), which put the revolt on a more secure footing and created the United Provinces. Even after the Act of Abjuration (1581) the Reformed churches witnessed only slow growth. In 1587, when Calvinism had been extirpated by the Spaniards in its original strongholds in the south, the civil authorities in the north took the opportunity to remind leading ministers that fewer than 10 percent of the population belonged to the Reformed faith. Even when it became the official church of the Dutch Republic, the Dutch Reformed church remained a minority church; its influence on Dutch politics and society in the sixteenth and seventeenth centuries, however, was often far greater than its limited membership would suggest.

In Germany, Calvinism was temporarily entrenched along the Lower Rhine, in areas adjacent to the Reformed communities in the United Provinces, Switzerland, and France, such as the Lower Palatinate, Jülich, Berg, and Cleves, and Nassau-Dillenburg, but during the same period it also took hold in Anhalt, Lower Hesse, and the Upper Palatinate. The Second Reformation in Germany was characterized by the dominant part played by princely and territorial rulers. Accordingly, the traditional association between Calvinism and republicanism was of no consequence here.

The Palatinate became of paramount importance to German Calvinism in the sixteenth century, being the only German principality to embrace the Reformed faith. Elector Frederick III (r. 1559–1576) introduced Calvinism in 1561, probably as a result of deep disappointment with the ability of Lutheranism to bring about an effective reformation of his country's churches. Not only did the Palatinate quickly become a center for the Reformed faith in Germany, it also evolved as a center of European Calvinism, providing both theological guidance through the University of Heidelberg and political inspiration. In Germany it attracted a considerable number of Reformed exiles from the imperial cities, such as Strasbourg, who felt exposed after the Interim (1548) and the Peace of Augsburg (1555). Apart from the brief reign of Louis VI (1576–1583), who brought back Lutheranism, the Palatinate played a major role in European Calvinism until the outbreak of the Thirty Years' War (1618). The ruling Wittelsbach family's dynastic alliances with other Calvinist rulers and its religious/political ambitions were restrained only by the country's limited economic resources.

Undoubtedly, most German rulers attracted to Calvinism saw it as a means of achieving greater religious uniformity among their subjects, and as especially well suited to preventing the spread of Anabaptism. In the Palatinate it was instrumental in creating a more absolutist type of government. Thus in the Upper Palatinate, Lutheran nobles who had reacted against forcible Calvinization were bought off, while Lutheran imperial knights in the Lower Palatinate were removed from the administration.

Apart from the churches in Jülich, Berg, and Cleves which, inspired by the presence of Dutch and Walloon exiled churches, were organized along traditional consistorial-synodal lines, the Calvinist churches in Germany developed a hybrid ecclesiastical structure, combining Lutheran and Reformed elements. They took over the centralized Lutheran ecclesiastical councils and the superintendents, later given the Reformed title of inspectors. Only gradually did consistories come into existence in Nassau-Dillenberg, Zweibrücken, and the Palatinate, and then in a diluted form.

England and Scotland were the only kingdoms to adopt a reformed faith as their official doctrine in the sixteenth century. In both countries this led to decades of controversy about how thoroughly reformed the kingdoms were to be. In Scotland a Calvinist church was established, while the Church of England retained most of its liturgy, services, and ecclesiastical structure, allowing changes only in doctrine.

Reformed congregations, so-called "privy-kirks," were established in Scotland during the later 1550s (Edinburgh, Saint Andrews, Dundee, and Perth). Developments accelerated after John Knox's return to Perth from exile in Geneva in May 1559, setting off popular iconoclasm. A considerable percentage of the Scottish nobility supported the Reformed cause for both religious and political reasons. The Scottish Reformation Parliament abolished Catholicism and adopted the Scottish Confession and the *First Scottish Book of Discipline*, the latter heavily influenced by Knox, in 1560. By the early 1560s Scotland found itself in the paradoxical situation of having a Catholic monarch, Mary Stuart, presiding over a Reformed church. Even after Mary Stuart's deposition in 1567, the ecclesiastical structure in Scotland remained in flux for a couple of decades. Bishops remained in place and the government kept filling vacant bishoprics. A heated controversy took place from the late 1570s about parity of ministers and the relationship between church and state. A former Genevan exile, Andrew Melville, became the leading spokesman for a presbyterian system and an autonomous church. An attempt (the *Second Scottish Book of Discipline*) to introduce a more Calvinist church structure failed to pass the Scottish Parliament in 1578. The Crown and its supporters wanted to retain the episcopal system as a guarantee of some form of Erastian control over the church. Gradually, however, presbyteries (classes) were established during the 1580s, finally eclipsing the influence of the bishops in 1592. In the seventeenth century, under James VI, who favored an Erastian church, this development was reversed.

In England Reformed theology started to make an impact shortly after the accession of Edward VI (1547). At the invitation of Archbishop Thomas Cranmer a number of leading Continental reformers, such as Peter Martyr Vermigli, Bernardino Ochino, Martin Bucer, Paul Fagius, and Jan Łaski, settled in England between 1547 and 1550. During Edward's short reign (1547–1553) appeared the first signs of conflict between those who were satisfied with a limited reform of the Church of England and those who, like John Hooper and some of the recently arrived foreign Reformed theologians, wanted to turn the Anglican church into a fully Reformed church. *The Second Book of Common Prayer* (1552) of Edward VI went some way in meeting the criticism by the Reformed wing of *The First Book of Common Prayer* (1549). The 1552 version, purged of some of its more strident anti-Catholic rhetoric, was reintroduced by Elizabeth when she succeeded Mary (1559) and reversed what had been a brief Catholic interlude in the English Reformation.

The dissatisfaction with *The Second Book of Common Prayer* and its liturgy, especially the use of the surplice, which had already surfaced in the reign of Edward VI, reappeared more forcefully under Elizabeth, especially during the 1570s, as evidenced by the Vestiarian Controversy. An influential minority within the Elizabethan church, most of whom had spent the Marian years in exile in Switzerland and Germany, made repeated efforts during the last three decades of the sixteenth century to introduce Reformed changes in liturgy, ecclesiastical structure, and doctrinal instruction. This group of "experimental predestinarians," who wanted to place predestination, election, and assurance at the center of practical divinity, eventually led their supporters down the road toward separatism. However, sectarianism remained rare in sixteenth-century England. Apart from a few instances in the late 1560s and early 1590s which were dealt with by the Anglican bishops, who were mainly moderate, "credal predestinarians," separatism did not really take root in England until the early seventeenth century.

In central and eastern Europe broadly Reformed churches established themselves in Bohemia and Greater Poland during the 1540s, and in Hungary in the following decade. Initially the prospects for Calvinism seemed better in Bohemia and Poland than in Hungary, where it eventually took permanent hold. In Bohemia it grafted itself onto the Bohemian Brethren, the radical survivors of the Hussite movement. The Bohemian Brethren developed close contacts with Geneva, Basel, and Strasbourg in the 1540s. Bohemia's disastrous involvement in the Schmalkald War, however, sent thousands of brethren into exile in Greater Poland, where their arrival coincided with the accession of the tolerant and humanist King Sigismund II. In the 1550s Calvinism gained further ground in Poland, especially around Kraków in the south and in Lithuania, often inspired through close contacts with Geneva.

In Hungary the Reformed faith was introduced through contacts with Zurich and Heinrich Bullinger beginning in 1549, but the establishment of Reformed churches in the 1550s owed much to fears of the Counter-Reformation and pressures from the Ottoman empire. During the next two decades the Reformed movement in central and eastern Europe split into orthodox Calvinist churches and groups of antitrinitarians and freethinkers.

[*See also* Bèze, Théodore de; Calvin, John; Consensus Tigurinus; Duplessis-Mornay, Philippe; Erastianism; France; Gallic Confession; Geneva; Geneva Academy; Hungary; Knox, John; Palatinate; Poland; Saint Bartholomew's Day Massacre; Scotland; *and* Wars of Religion.]

BIBLIOGRAPHY

Clasen, Claus-Peter. *The Palatinate in European History, 1559–1660.* Rev. ed. Oxford, 1966. A concise overview and the best work in English on the German Palatinate in this period.
Collinson, Patrick. *The Elizabethan Puritan Movement.* London, 1967. A seminal study of the hard-line Calvinist minority within the Church of England.
———. *The Religion of Protestants: The Church in English Society, 1559–1625.* Oxford, 1982. Portrays the Anglican church under Elizabeth and James I as a broadly based and heterogeneous Calvinist institution.
Cowan, Ian B. *The Scottish Reformation: Church and Society in Sixteenth-Century Scotland.* London, 1982. A comprehensive study that underlines the spiritual impact of Calvinism on Scottish society.
Crew, Phyllis Mack. *Calvinist Preaching and Iconoclasm in the Netherlands, 1544–1569.* Cambridge, 1978. Points out that mid-sixteenth-century Calvinism was far from being a homogeneous movement nor the only form of Protestantism in the region.
Deursen, A. Th. van. *Plain Lives in a Golden Age: Popular Culture, Religion and Society in Seventeenth-Century Holland.* Cambridge, 1991. Published in Dutch in 1978, it offers a fascinating study of popular culture and religion in Holland from the middle of the sixteenth century.
Duke, Alastair. *Reformation and Revolt in the Low Countries.* London and Ronceverte, W.Va., 1990. A collection of essays about the Reformation in the Netherlands both before and after the revolt. The last three chapters deal specifically with Calvinism.
Kendall, R. T. *Calvin and English Calvinism to 1649.* Reprint, Oxford, 1981. A detailed study of the development of Reformed theology in England.
Kingdon, Robert M. *Geneva and the Coming of the Wars of Religion in France, 1553–63.* Geneva, 1956.
———. *Geneva and the Consolidation of the French Protestant Movement, 1564–1572.* Geneva, 1967. Two seminal studies of the Genevan influence on French Calvinism.
Pettegree, Andrew, Alaistair Duke, and Gillian Lewis, eds. *Calvinism in Europe, 1540–1620.* Cambridge, 1994.
Prestwich, Menna, ed. *International Calvinism, 1541–1715.* Oxford, 1985. Extremely useful and comprehensive collections of essays dealing with Geneva, France, the United Provinces, Germany, central and eastern Europe, Scotland, and England.
Salmon, J. H. M. *Society in Crisis: France in the Sixteenth Century.* London, 1975. Comprehensive study with a strong socio-religious emphasis.
Sutherland, Nicola M. *The Huguenot Struggle for Recognition.* New Haven and London, 1980. A comprehensive treatment of the Huguenot struggle for religious and political recognition from 1521 to 1598.
Wormald, Jenny. *Court, Kirk, and Community: Scotland, 1470–1625.* Reprint, Edinburgh, 1991. Concise survey with a useful annotated bibliography.

OLE PETER GRELL AND A. I. C. HERON

CAMBRIDGE, UNIVERSITY OF. Of the English institutions of higher learning—Oxford, Cambridge, and the London Inns of Court—Cambridge contributed most to the Reformation and gained most. Ironically, Oxford's Wycliffite reputation provoked investment in Cambridge by the Crown, from Henry VI (King's College, 1441) to Henry VIII (Trinity College, 1546). Henry VII's mother, Lady Margaret Beaufort, directed by John Fisher (Cambridge University chancellor from 1504), founded Christ's College (1505), Saint John's (1511) and the Lady Margaret Professorship of Divinity, held by Erasmus during his three years at Cambridge (1511 to 1514). In all, seven Colleges were founded in Tudor Cambridge, and all university members came to be resident in colleges.

It has been argued that conservative Erasmianism could have made Cambridge by the 1530s the center of a reformed Catholic England. The facts were to be otherwise. Official Cambridge could certainly not countenance Tyndale's New Testament, circulating underground in 1527, when Thomas Bilney of Trinity Hall and the Cambridge Augustinian friar Robert Barnes had been condemned as heretics for attacks on traditional spirituality, and Luther and Johannes Oecolampadius had been specifically banned by John Fisher. Evidence about Cambridge reformers in the 1520s is exceptionally sparse. They were a minority, possibly minute, and they cannot precisely be labeled "Protestant." But Cambridge, an inland port, was susceptible to winds of change blowing across the North Sea. Over sixty later adherents of the Reformation resided in Cambridge as undergraduates or senior members during the 1520s: many were from East Anglia.

Bilney was burned in 1531. But the future lay with radical, not conservative, Erasmians. By 1535 Thomas Cranmer of Jesus College was archbishop of Canterbury, Hugh Latimer of Clare College a bishop, and Thomas Cromwell, Henry VIII's chief minister, successor to Fisher as university chancellor. In the late 1530s monks and friars, once one-fifth of the university population, departed. Cromwell's regulations stressed Greek and Hebrew, biblical (not scholastic) divinity, abolition of courses in canon law (too popish), and establishment of new university professorships. Under Edward VI three of these professorships were held by four Lutherans associated with Strasbourg. The Spaniard Francisco de Enzinas taught Greek; Paul Fagius, succeeded by Immanuel Tremellius, Hebrew; and Martin Bucer, who died in Cambridge in 1551, divinity. Cromwell's Edwardian successors as chancellor were the two chief men of state: Edward Seymour, duke of Somerset, followed by John Dudley, duke of Northumberland.

Cambridge was at the center of Reformation politics, but not at the center of Reformation hopes. Bucer thought Cambridge insufficiently devoted to his version of "the pure doctrine of Christ" and negligent in producing adequately prepared clergy. Similar criticisms by advocates of "purity" continued, eventually to inspire purges of university and colleges in the 1640s and 1650s. Although about seventy percent of the students became clergymen, most of these graduated in arts without going on to divinity. The two English universities were never theological seminaries. Training was for service to the commonwealth as well as the church. Sixteenth-century Cambridge undergraduate numbers rose from about 500 to about 1,650—nearly half being members of the gentry: another cause of concern. Under Mary Tudor forty-four fellows or former fellows fled to purer centers of reform in Germany and Switzerland. Some returned later to Cambridge. In the early 1560s seventeen percent of Saint John's fellows were sometime exiles—a clue to the "Puritan" tradition there from 1565.

But all tensions in Elizabethan Cambridge must be placed in the context of Anglican supervision: the control as chancellor (1559–1598) of William Cecil (Lord Burghley), Elizabeth's first minister, and, as archbishops of Canterbury, of Matthew Parker, Edmund Grindal, and John Whitgift. All four were Cambridge men. The lay and clerical organizers of the Elizabethan Settlement of 1559 have been grouped under the description "the Cambridge connection." But, Cambridge contacts with European Protestantism continued. Zwingli's grandson came to England in 1571 to study at Cambridge; he died before arriving there. In 1581 Théodore de Bèze sent from Geneva to Cambridge University Library a fifth-century Greek and Latin manuscript

of the Gospels, now a star attraction (*Codex Bezae*). Thomas Cartwright withdrew to Geneva in 1571 after advocating, as Lady Margaret Professor, a presbyterian church platform. The presbyterian ("classis") movement in 1580s England had Cambridge supporters, though the role of the university here can be exaggerated. Cambridge University Press (established in 1584) published an English version of a "harmony" of Reformed confessions (Geneva, 1581)—to the chagrin of Archbishop Whitgift, former master of Trinity and adversary of Cartwright. Cambridge University Press authors in the 1590s included Zacharias Ursinus of Calvinist Heidelberg and the "high Calvinists" Bèze and Girolamo Zanchi, in addition to Cambridge followers of Bèze—preeminently William Perkins of Christ's College.

Cambridge "high Calvinism," which developed in the late 1580s, was challenged by, among others, the Frenchman Peter Baro, Lady Margaret Professor from 1574, and was never "official," albeit influential until the 1640s. Works by Perkins appeared in Latin, German, Dutch, Spanish, Czech, Hungarian, Welsh, and Irish. Arminius replied to his 1598 treatise on predestination. Congregationalism attracted other Cambridge authors: Robert Browne, John Greenwood, and John Robinson of Corpus Christi; Henry Barrow of Clare; Henry Ainsworth of Caius; and William Ames of Christ's. Among the ninety-six Cambridge men who migrated to New England between 1620 and 1645, attracted by the congregational way, thirty-five were members of Emmanuel College, including John Cotton, Thomas Hooker, and John Harvard. Emmanuel was founded in 1584 by Elizabeth's chancellor of the exchequer, Sir Walter Mildmay, a Christ's graduate. The Emmanuel statutes (1585) repeated the imperatives of the statutes of Christ's (1506): the worship (*cultus*) of God, the purity of morals, the increase of the faith (*fides*). But *cultus* and *fides* had changed. Fisher and Margaret Beaufort would not have felt completely at home—nor would they have been completely out of place. There were changes and similarities in concepts of piety and good letters, continuities and discontinuities within developing Christian traditions, in Tudor Cambridge as elsewhere.

[*See also* Oxford, University of.]

BIBLIOGRAPHY

Curtis, Mark H. *Oxford and Cambridge in Transition, 1558–1642.* Oxford, 1959. Study of the changing relations between the English universities and English society. Includes two chapters on religion.

Hudson, Winthrop S. *The Cambridge Connection and the Elizabethan Settlement of 1559.* Durham, N.C., 1980. Discusses the importance of Cambridge training for the first Elizabethan politicians and ecclesiastics.

Lake, Peter. *Moderate Puritans and the Elizabethan Church.* Cambridge, 1982. Concerned with issues and authors in Elizabethan Cambridge; especially good on Laurence Chaderton, Master of Emmanuel.

Leader, Damian R. *A History of the University of Cambridge.* Cambridge. 1988. First in a projected series of four volumes, by various authors, covers the university history up to 1546.

Morison, Samuel E. *The Founding of Harvard College.* Cambridge, Mass., 1935. Includes seventy pages on the Cambridge background.

Mullinger, J. Bass. *The University of Cambridge.* Vol. 1, *From the Earliest Times to the Royal Injunctions of 1535.* Vol. 2, *From the Royal Injunctions of 1535 to the Accession of Charles the First.* Cambridge, 1873–1884. Dated but stylish and essential.

Porter, Harry C. *Reformation and Reaction in Tudor Cambridge.* Cambridge, 1958. From Fisher to the mid-seventeenth-century Cambridge Platonists.

Roach, John P. C., ed. *A History of the County of Cambridge and the Isle of Ely.* Vol. 3., London, 1959. Comprehensive essay on the history of the university by Roach; college histories by various authors.

Stubbings, Frank. *The Statutes of Sir Walter Mildmay for Emmanuel College.* Cambridge, 1983. Latin text (1585) and new translation, with essay on the historical background.

Thomson, Douglas F. S., and Harry C. Porter. *Erasmus and Cambridge.* Toronto, 1963. Translation by Thomson of Erasmus's letters from and about Cambridge; introduction and notes by Porter.

HARRY C. PORTER

CAMERARIUS, Joachim

CAMERARIUS, Joachim (Ger., Kammermeister; 1500–1574), Protestant scholar, educator, and humanist. Camerarius was born in Bamberg, in Franconia, the son of a noble councilor and episcopal official. He studied at the universities in Leipzig and Erfurt and became widely known as a classical scholar, particularly for his thorough knowledge of Greek. He became a lifelong friend of Philipp Melanchthon after moving to the University of Wittenberg in 1521, and, like Melanchthon, was one of the network of younger humanists whose support of Luther in the early 1520s was vital to the success of Protestantism.

Camerarius pursued a successful academic career, moving from rector of the new gymnasium in Nuremberg (1526–1535), to professor at the University of Tübingen (1535–1541), to rector and dean at the University of Leipzig (1541–1574). He was an accomplished administrator and played a major role in the promotion of classical studies in German universities and in the development of Tübingen and Leipzig as leading Protestant universities. Considered one of the greatest polymaths of the century, Camerarius was a prolific classical scholar, historian, and poet, publishing over 150 works, mostly editions and translations of Greek works. Indeed, contemporaries regarded Camerarius the successor of Desiderius Erasmus as the greatest German philologist. Camerarius's most influential works were his biography of Eobanus Hessus and especially his valuable (if perhaps over-admiring) life of Melanchthon.

Like many humanists of his generation, Camerarius hoped Protestantism would lead to a moral and spiritual renewal of Germany. He understood his role in rebuilding important universities as part of this process, which was reflected in his inaugural address at Leipzig in 1541. Perhaps fighting old battles, he defended the value of a classical ed-

ucation for training good Christians and good servants of church and state. Thus, his religious writings, such as a life of Jesus for young readers, broke no new ground but were instead part of this humanist pedagogical program.

His humanist inclinations and close association with Melanchthon make him an important representative of those German intellectuals who sought religious compromise in the period between 1530 and 1555. In this effort, he served as Melanchthon's adviser at the Diet of Augsburg (1530), helped write the Augsburg Confession, took part in the peace negotiations at Augsburg in 1555, and participated in discussions between Catholic and Protestant theologians at Vienna in 1568. In all cases he supported Melanchthon's view that flexibility in doctrine and willingness to compromise on "matters indifferent" (adiaphora) might bring religious peace.

Camerarius outlived Melanchthon by fourteen years and, despite the academic success of his five sons and his continued prominence at the University of Leipzig, his influence faded. In his last years, in a manner that nineteenth-century German scholars loved to quote, he openly bemoaned the factionalism, intransigence, and contentiousness of the theologians, which he linked to the political disintegration and moral decline of Germany.

BIBLIOGRAPHY

Baron, Frank, ed. *Joachim Camerarius, 1500–1574: Beiträge zur Geschichte des Humanismus im Zeitalter der Reformation.* Munich, 1978. Articles focusing on Camerarius's literary activities and significance.

MARC R. FORSTER

CAMPANUS, Johannes

CAMPANUS, Johannes (c.1500–after 1574), Belgian antitrinitarian theologian. Born in Maaseik (province of Limburg), Campanus studied in Cologne and in 1526 at the latest joined the Wittenberg movement. (See his satirical poem against Tymann Kemener.) After a probable stopover in the duchy of Jülich in 1529, he traveled with Georg Witzel to the Colloquy of Marburg. Here, given his notions on the Lord's Supper, he sought to mediate between Martin Luther and Huldrych Zwingli, but to his dismay he was not allowed to participate in the debate. Early in 1530 he was arrested in Wittenberg, primarily for antitrinitarian views. As soon as he was free again, he delivered to Philipp Melanchthon a "horribilem disputationem." With letters of recommendation from the Jülich nobility, he appeared at the end of March 1530 in the Saxon electoral residence city of Torgau, delivered his "dogmata" to the electoral advisers, and demanded a debate, which was, however, again denied him.

Hurt by this lack of attention, he left Saxony and, by way of Strasbourg, went to the lower Rhine to visit friends (possibly to the Wassenberg district). In the fall of 1531 he stayed for a short while in Braunschweig. During this time Campanus wrote the tract *Contra totum post apostolos mundum,* which has since been lost. Melanchthon had several times warned him against writing it because he feared that the ideas might cause a disturbance and discredit the Wittenberg cause of reform.

In 1532 he published his tract *Göttlicher vnd heiliger Schrifft vor vilen jaren verdunckelt vnd durch vnheylsame leer vn Lerer (auß Gottes zulassung) verfinstert Restitution vnd besserung durch den hochgelerten Johannem Campanum* (The Restitution and Improvement of the Divine and Holy Scriptures) which was probably based on three earlier, originally Latin treatises. Although he put the whole development of the Christian church in question, his primary attack was against the old church dogmas and the reformers' teaching of the Sacrament.

From the end of 1532 his area of effectiveness was greatly curtailed: Duke John III of Jülich-Cleve-Berg ordered him arrested. Nevertheless, he was allowed to remain two more decades in Jülich because the church situation there was undecided and because two nobles (Werner von Pallant and Heinrich von Olmissen) granted him protection. He became active again in connection with the reform attempt of the Cologne archbishop Hermann von Wied. He strongly advised von Wied not to join the Schmalkaldens, and he supported the opposition under the leadership of Johannes Gropper. Between 1555 and 1557 he was jailed by Duke Wilhelm von Cleve on the charge of heretical and apocalyptic teaching. Attempts to convert him by the ducal adviser Georg Cassander and later by the Roermonder bishop Wilhelmus Lindanus, who corresponded with him about his writing *De Eucharistia vera expeditio,* were unsuccessful. It is not known whether he regained his freedom before his death. The only complete remaining writing of Campanus is his "Restitution." This work—as well as several writings of his opponents, in which there are citations from his other writings—clearly express his teaching.

Rejecting the dogma of the Trinity, Campanus propounded a ditheism influenced by Desiderius Erasmus. Although God and Christ were one being (*Jn.* 10:30), they had to be differentiated. Just as man and wife are two persons but one being (*Gn.* 1:26–27), God and Christ are two persons but one being. To be sure, the two are not completely equal; God is superior. God has priority in existence, as Christ himself admits (*Jn.* 5:26). Christ must be considered eternal since he was born before creation—that is, before time. In this timelessness, however, there was a phase in which only God existed. Also, God has more power than Christ (*Jn.* 14:28). Christ, as the natural son of God, has all the qualities of God, but he is subordinated to God. As an illustration, Campanus pointed to the relationship between father and son, as well as to the relationship between man and wife in marriage (*Cor.* 11:3). He denied that the Holy Ghost had personhood and understood it to be the power or the effect of God and Christ. According to Campanus,

salvation cannot be achieved without holy scripture and the sacraments, which are not to be understood as merely symbolic. Faith is accorded a basic significance. Through baptism the human being is bathed in Christ and receives a new quality that cannot be lost, comparable to a white cloth that has been dipped into a purple color that can never be washed out again (Restitution, chapter 6). Although the believer falls into sin again and again, he cannot lose his relationship to God: "If I am now in the House, and he [God] is my father, he can punish me, but he cannot dismiss me" (Restitution, folio no. 4, reverse side).

Campanus considered himself to be the true restorer of the Roman Catholic and the Protestant church; he was even convinced that his teaching could make the unity of Christians and Muslims possible. He did have a certain significance for the radical Reformation, for the mystical spiritualists (such as Sebastian Franck), and for some Anabaptists. No close contacts with the early antitrinitarians of western Europe can be demonstrated.

BIBLIOGRAPHY

MacCormick, Chalmers. "The Restitution göttlicher Schrifft of John Campanus: An Interpretation and the Text." Ph.D. diss., Harvard University, 1959.
Rembert, Karl. *Die "Wiedertäufer" im Herzogtum Jülich: Studien zur Geschichte der Reformation, besonders am Niederrhein.* Berlin, 1899.
Weigelt, Horst. "Campanus, Johannes (c.1500–nach 1574)." In *Theologische Realenzyklopädie,* edited by Gerhard Krause and Gerhard Müller, vol. 7, pp. 601–604. Berlin and New York, 1981.

HORST WEIGELT

Translated from German by Walter D. Morris

CAMPEGGIO, Lorenzo (also Campeggi; 1474–1539), eminent Italian jurist, papal diplomat, and cardinal. Born into a distinguished family of Bolognese jurists at Milan, he studied law at Padua and Bologna, where he received his *doctor utriusque juris* in 1500. He taught law at Padua with his father in 1493, at Venice (1496–1499), and at Bologna (1500–1511). Following the death of his wife in 1509, he entered upon an ecclesiastical career.

Pope Julius II quickly utilized his talents. By early 1511 he was one of the twelve auditors of the Rota, and within several months the pope sent him on a mission to Emperor Maximilian I to dissuade him from sending representatives to the schismatic Council of Pisa. With the help of Mattheus Lang, an imperial councillor and bishop of Gurk, and of Margaret of Austria, the emperor's daughter, he succeeded in convincing Maximilian to send Lang instead to the rival papal Fifth Lateran Council. On his return Campeggio was rewarded with the bishopric of Feltre. From November 1512 to August 1513 he represented the popes in Milan, where he persuaded Duke Massimiliano Sforza not to support the

Pisan Council or the Bolognese rebels and to restore to the papacy Parma and Piacenza, over which Pope Leo X then appointed Lorenzo Campeggio and his brother Tommaso as governors.

Under Leo X Campeggio also served on two other missions. From 1513 to 1517 he returned to Germany as nuncio in order to work for a reconciliation of the empire and Venice as part of a general peace among Christians, who would then unite in a crusade against the Turks. While in Germany Leo X named him a cardinal (1517), but he was invested with this office later in Bologna on his return, and at the requests of Maximilian I and Charles V he served as cardinal-protector of the empire. From 1518 to 1519 he was papal legate in England. While unsuccessful in promoting Leo's peace plan, Campeggio established good personal relations with Cardinal Thomas Wolsey and King Henry VIII, who promised him nomination to the see of Salisbury when it next became vacant and granted him the palace in Rome of the recently deprived cardinal and former promoter of English interests at the papal court, Adriano Castellesi. On his return to Rome, Leo X appointed him in 1520 to the Signature of Justice.

Campeggio was also on good terms with Pope Adrian VI. He supported his election in the conclave and wrote for him a memorial, *De depravato statu ecclesiae* (1522), that urged the defense of Christendom and a reform of the Church. Adrian confirmed him in his posts and allowed him alone of all the cardinals to live in the papal palace as his close adviser.

Pope Clement VII entrusted Campeggio with important missions. Appointed legate to Germany in 1524, he attended the third Nuremberg Reichstag in March and April but could secure only a weakened agreement to try to enforce the Edict of Worms against Luther and his followers. The diet was also reluctant to support a crusade and urged a German national council. As an alternative, Campeggio obtained permission from Rome to assemble a conference of Catholic lay and ecclesiastical leaders in June and July at Regensburg where he worked out an agreement on the payment of the crusade tax, and enacted thirty-eight decrees that regulated bishops' relations with their clergy and ordered reforms in the areas of preaching, clerical attire, entertainments, fees, celibacy, qualification for ordination, blasphemy, simony, and superstitious practices. Campeggio hoped these decrees could bring about a reform of the church in Germany, and they were often published as his legatine legislation. In addition to signaling the beginnings of the Catholic Reformation, the Colloquy of Regensburg resulted in the formation of a Catholic league to implement seriously the Edict of Worms. After working in Vienna (1524) on the Hussite question and then in Budapest (1525) on promoting a crusade, he returned to Rome, where Clement's anti-imperial foreign policy led to the revolt of Pompeo Colonna (1526) and the Sack of Rome (1527). When Clement withdrew from the city for safety, he left Campeggio in charge as legate.

From September 1528 to October 1529, Campeggio was in England as legate to hear the case on the juridical validity of Henry VIII's marriage to Catherine of Aragon. Having failed to find other solutions, Campeggio, together with Wolsey, presided over a trial. Refusing all offers of gifts and after hearing the evidence, Campeggio was prepared to declare the marriage's validity but was under instructions from Clement to avoid a decision. After he had prorogued the trial for a summer's recess on 23 July, word came that the pope had revoked the case to Rome seven days earlier. In the Roman consistory that finally decided the case on 23 March 1534, Campeggio backed the unanimous decision in favor of the marriage's validity. The king's displeasure was registered in the Parliamentary act (1534) depriving the cardinal of his administration of Salisbury and the loss of the customary fees attached to the protectorship of England, both of which positions he had held since 1524.

Campeggio's last important legation was to Germany (1530–1532). Having assisted at Charles V's coronation in Bologna, he accompanied the emperor to the Diet of Augsburg. While initially urging the emperor to make no theological concessions to the Lutherans, Campeggio entered into negotiations with Philipp Melanchthon to restore church unity. He came to regard Lutheran theological views as compatible with traditional Catholicism and supported their requests for Communion under both kinds, an end to obligatory celibacy for diocesan clergy, and modifications in the canon of the Mass, but he opposed calling a general council. Given the opposition of Martin Luther to this plan, Campeggio subsequently backed away from concessions, broke off negotiations, and approved the *Confutatio* of the German Catholic theologians, who saw the Lutheran and Tetrapolitan confessions as heretical and urged the use of force to suppress heresy. After the diet Campeggio followed Charles V to the Low Countries, where Girolamo Aleandro joined him in urging the emperor to delay a military showdown with the Protestants until the Turkish threat had been eliminated. Campeggio and Aleandro, therefore, did not oppose the Peace of Nuremberg of July 1532, which they saw as a judicial and political compromise—allowing toleration of Lutherans until a council was called in return for support against the Turks.

Under Pope Paul III, Campeggio tried unsuccessfully to reconcile Henry VIII with Rome, sat on a reform commission, and helped to plan for the upcoming council. In 1538 he was named president of the council to meet in Vicenza. After waiting in vain for the delegates to arrive, he returned to Rome, where he died on 25 July 1539 of dysentery. He had suffered for the last fifteen or so years from bouts of acute gout and double tertian fever.

The most important papal diplomat of his generation, Campeggio used his legal skills to protect the church's interests. These frequently merged with his own: he held numerous sees, at times resigning them to members of his family. He was not considered an ardent proponent of reform.

BIBLIOGRAPHY

Primary Sources

Campeggio, Lorenzo. *Constitutio ad removendos abusus et ordinatio ad cleri vitam reformandam.* In *Acta Reformationis Catholicae Ecclesiam Germanicae concernentia saeculi XVI: Die Reformverhandlungen des deutschen Episkopats von 1520 bis 1570,* edited by Georg Pfeilschifter, vol 1, pp. 334–344. Regensburg, 1959–. These 38 decrees were issued by Campeggio on 7 July 1524 at the Colloquy of Regensburg to reform the German church.

————. *De depravato statu ecclesiae.* In *Concilium Tridentinum: Diariorum, actorum, epistolarum, tractatuum nova collectio,* edited by Görres-Gesellschaft, vol. 12, pp. 5–17. Freiburg, 1930. Campeggio's memorial (1522) to Adrian VI urged a reform of the church, the suppression of Lutheranism, and the defense of Hungary.

————. *Legation Lorenzo Campeggios 1530–1531 und Nuntiatur Girolamo Aleandros 1531.* In *Nuntiaturberichte aus Deutschland nebst ergänzenden Aktenstücken,* erste Abteilung 1533–1559, I Ergänzungsband 1530–1531, edited by Gerhard Müller. Tübingen, 1963. This includes his reports from the Diet of Augsburg (1530).

————. *Römische Dokumente zur Geschichte der Ehescheidung Heinrichs VIII. von England 1527–1534.* Quellen und Forschungen aus dem Gebiete der Geschichte, vol. 2. Edited by Stephan Ehses. Paderborn, 1893.

Secondary Sources

Cardinal, Edward V. *Cardinal Lorenzo Campeggio: Legate to the Courts of Henry VIII and Charles V.* Boston, 1935. Although dated, a still valuable work.

D'Amico, John F. "Lorenzo Campeggi of Bologna, 1474–25 July 1539." In *Contemporaries of Erasmus: A Biographical Register of the Renaissance and Reformation,* edited by Peter Bietenholz, vol. 1, pp. 253–255. Toronto, 1985.

Müller, Gerhard. "Die Korrespondenten: Lorenzo Campeggio." In *Nuntiaturberichte aus Deutschland,* erste Abteilung 1533–1559, I Ergänzungsband 1530–1531, pp. XLVII–LXXIII. Tübingen, 1963. Müller provides the basic survey of Campeggio's life up to 1530.

Skalweit, S. "Campeggi, Lorenzo." In *Dizionario biografico degli Italiani,* vol. 17, pp. 454–462. Rome, 1974. This is an excellent overview of Campeggio's life with ample bibliography.

Wilkie, William E. *The Cardinal Protectors of England: Rome and the Tudors before the Reformation.* Cambridge, 1974.

NELSON H. MINNICH

CAMPION, Edmund (1540–1581), English Jesuit missionary and Roman Catholic martyr. A London native, Campion abandoned a promising career at the University of Oxford when his study of theology increased his doubts about the Elizabethan Settlement (1570). He was reconciled to the Roman Catholic church at the English Douai College in 1571, and he joined the Society of Jesus in 1573. Along with Robert Parsons and a lay brother, Ralph Emerson, he was chosen to initiate the Jesuit mission to England (June 1580).

Campion's work in England, although brief, was influential. The premature release of a personal statement (commonly known as "Campion's Brag"), drafted to counteract possible false confessions disseminated by the government, brought unexpected publicity to its author. Although its open invitation to a debate caused the rapid publication of two rejoinders, no one accepted the public challenge. Campion developed his "Brag" into his best known work, *Rationes decem* (the intended title was *De haeresi desperata*). Addressing the academic world, Campion repeated his challenge and offered ten arguments in favor of Roman Catholicism. On 17 July 1581 Campion was captured at Lyford Grange (Berkshire). Because of the notoriety of the "Brag," the government staged four separate disputations between Campion and leading Anglican controversialists (e.g., Alexander Nowell and William Whitacre). Throughout Campion was given no warning, permitted only a Bible for consultation, and allowed to respond only to objections raised by his opponents. Tried on 20 November on the charge of high treason, he was found guilty and sentenced to death. He was executed at Tyburn on 1 December. In the subsequent martyrologies published by the English Catholics to justify their cause and to embarrass the Elizabethan government, Campion was consistently given a place of honor and held as an example of the type of person who professed Catholicism. He was beatified in 1886 and canonized by Paul VI on 25 October 1970.

BIBLIOGRAPHY

Primary Sources

Allison, A. F., and D. M. Rogers. *The Contemporary Printed Literature of the English Counter-Reformation between 1558–1640.* Vol. 1, *Languages other than English;* vol. 2, *English.* London, 1989, 1994. Contains full bibliographic details regarding the works of Campion.

Campion, Edmund. *The great bragge and challenge of M. Champion a Iesuite, commonly called Edmunde Campion, lately arrived in Englande, contayning nyne articles here severallye laide down, directed by him to the Lordes of the Counsial, confuted & aunswered by Meredith Hanmer, M. of Art, and Student in Divinitie.* STC 12745. London, 1581. Although this was a rejoinder to Campion's statement, in it the "Brag" was published for the first time.

————. *Rationes decem, quibus fretus, certamen adversariis obtulit in causa fidei Edmundus Campianus.* 1581. John H. Pollen translated it as *Campion's Ten Reasons,* London, 1914; also reprinted as *Rationes decem,* Menston, 1971.

————. *Two Bokes of the Histories of Ireland.* Dublin, 1633. Alphonsus Franciscus Vossen has published a newly edited version. Assen, 1963.

————. *Ambrosia: A Neo-Latin Drama.* Edited by Joseph Simons. Assen, Netherlands, 1970.

Secondary Sources

Allen, William. *A Brief Historie of the Glorious Martyrdom of XII Reverend Priests.* N.p. [Reims], 1582. Most recent edition was done by John H. Pollen, London, 1908. This work illustrates Campion's significance to English martyrology.

McCoog, Thomas M., ed. *Monumenta Angliae.* Rome, 1992. Contains full bibliography on Campion; see especially vol. 2, pp. 255.

Reynolds, E.E. *Campion and Parsons.* London, 1980. Most recent study of the early Jesuit mission, in which the author avoids most of the complex historical, theological, and historiographical issues.

Simpson, Richard. *Edmund Campion.* Corr. ed. London, 1896. Historiographically dated, this is still the best biography of Campion available.

Waugh, Evelyn. *Edmund Campion.* Reprint, Oxford, 1980. Most famous and best written biography, highlights the faith and literary ability of the author. A number of errors and the absence of a historical context reduce its value for historians.

THOMAS M. McCOOG, S.J.

CAMPO, Francisco del. *See* Sonnius, Franciscus.

CANISIUS, Peter (Dutch, Kanijs; 1521–1597), Jesuit preacher, theologian, and administrator. Born at Nijmegen in the Netherlands, the eldest son of a cultural businessman who repeatedly served as Nijmegen's mayor, Canisius received a solid grounding in Latin before being sent to the University of Cologne. When his best friend, Lawrence Surius, later a famous hagiographer, entered the Carthusian monastery of Saint Barbara at Cologne, Canisius considered following him. In 1539 his father tried to persuade him to marry and to study law, but Peter decided to become a priest. At Cologne he received a traditional training in scholastic theology, although his own interest centered on Greek, Hebrew, scripture, and the church fathers. In 1541 he made the *Spiritual Exercises* under the direction of the Jesuit Pierre Favre; six months later he became the first Jesuit in Germany. He was ordained in 1546 and published the fruit of his patristic studies, editions of Cyril of Alexandria and Leo the Great, the first books published by a Jesuit. While at Cologne he opposed the efforts of Archbishop Hermann von Wied to introduce Lutheranism.

In 1547 Canisius attended the Council of Trent as theological adviser to Cardinal Georg Truchsess von Waldburg; after the council was transferred to Bologna and then prorogued, Ignatius Loyola sent Canisius to Messina to teach at the first Jesuit college. He returned to Germany in 1549 to teach theology at the University of Ingolstadt. Canisius was in Germany during a period of very rapid Jesuit expansion (1549–1580). From 1550 to 1567 he served as provincial superior, often stationed in Augsburg, where his preaching revived a nearly moribund Catholic community. His sermons were plain, direct, and carefully prepared. Five volumes have been published from the twelve thousand pages of his surviving sermon notes.

Supported by Catholic leaders such as Emperor Ferdinand I and the dukes of Bavaria, Canisius played an important role in founding Jesuit colleges at Augsburg, Dillingen, Fribourg, Halle, Ingolstadt, Innsbruck, Mainz, Prague, Regensburg, Speyer, Vienna, and Würzburg. These colleges produced the leaders of the Catholic revival in the late sixteenth century. Canisius enjoyed the respect of Ferdinand

and encouraged him to foster Catholicism to the full extent allowed by the Peace of Augsburg of 1555. In 1557 Ferdinand made Canisius one of the Catholic theologians at the Colloquy of Worms, one of the last attempts to reach a doctrinal compromise in Germany. Canisius, who thought that such efforts had no hope of success because there were no common criteria of doctrine, argued that scripture was insufficient since Protestants could not agree on its interpretation. He successfully drove a wedge between moderate Lutherans such as Melanchthon and the followers of Matthias Flacius Illyricus. The ensuing split in the Lutheran ranks ended the colloquy. At the urging of Ferdinand, Canisius began writing the first effective Catholic catechism to counter that of Luther. Eventually he wrote three catechisms, parallel in structure but adapted to various levels of maturity. The first was the large catechism published in 1555; it was designed for priests and educated adults. Subsequent editions published more and more marginal references to back up its statements; these eventually numbered two thousand citations to scripture and twelve hundred to the church fathers and put an arsenal in the hands of Catholics to answer Protestant charges. In 1556 Canisius published a short catechism for children, then a midsize one for adolescents, which often came with lavish engravings. The Canisius catechisms remained in use for four centuries and appeared in many hundreds of editions and in many languages. In addition to the traditional sections on the Apostles' Creed, the Ten Commandments, the Lord's Prayer, and the sacraments, the Canisius catechisms added long sections on devout Christian living. His catechisms do not explicitly attack Protestant teaching, but their stress on a Catholic understanding of controverted issues such as justification, sacraments, the role of ritual and of the visible church, and practical piety were designed to counter Protestant teaching.

Canisius wrote several polemical works against Protestantism. His greatest contribution here was his attempt to refute the first part of the *Magdeburg Centuries* in his lives of John the Baptist (Diligen, 1571) and the Virgin Mary (Ingolstadt, 1577). In 1580 Canisius was sent to found a Jesuit college at Fribourg, the most important Catholic stronghold in Switzerland. He remained there in gradually failing health until his death in 1597. His last years were devoted to writing books of piety. He was canonized and declared a doctor of the Catholic church in 1925.

BIBLIOGRAPHY

Primary Sources

Braunsberger, Otto, ed. *Beati Petri Canisii Societatis Iesu epistulae et acta.* 8 vols. Freiburg, 1896–1921. Massive collection of Canisius's correspondence.

Streicher, Fridericus. *S. Petri Canisii Doctoris Ecclesiae Catechismi latini et germanici.* 2 vols. Rome, 1933 and 1936. Critical edition of the Canisius catechisms.

———. *S. Petri Canisii Doctoris Ecclesiae Meditationes seu notae in evangelicas lectiones.* 3 vols. Freiburg and Munich, 1939–1961. Critical edition of Canisius's sermon notes.

Secondary Sources

Brodrick, James. *St. Peter Canisius, S.J.* Reprint, Baltimore, 1950. The standard large biography.
Buxbaum, Engelbert M. *Petrus Canisius und die kirchliche Erneuerung des Herzogtum Bayern. 1549–1556.* Rome, 1973. Detailed, scholarly study.
Donnelly, John Patrick. "Peter Canisius, 1512–1597." In *Shapers of Religious Traditions in Germany, Switzerland and Poland. 1560–1600,* edited by Jill Raitt, pp. 141–156. New Haven, 1981. A short biographical sketch.

JOHN PATRICK DONNELLY

CANISIUS'S CATECHISM. The late medieval church did not take advantage of the newly invented printing press by developing effective catechisms to teach Christian doctrine. The enormous success of Martin Luther's large and small catechisms after 1529 presented a challenge to which Catholics responded only slowly. By 1550 a number of Catholic catechisms were available in Germany, notably those of Johannes Gropper, Georg Witzel, and Michael Helding; but Ferdinand I, king of the Romans, who governed Austria during the frequent absence of his brother Charles V, was dissatisfied with them and applied pressure to the Jesuit Claude Lejay to write a substitute. Lejay gathered notes but despaired of the project and turned his notes over to his fellow Jesuit Peter Canisius, (1521–1597), who began preparing a catechism in 1552. The first edition of his *Summa doctrinae christianae* (Compendium of Christian Doctrine) was printed anonymously in Vienna in 1555. Ferdinand was so pleased that he made it the exclusive catechism for Austria; it had twenty printings during its first four years.

The *Summa* was written for priests and teachers and employed the question-and-answer format. Canisius soon added marginal references to the Bible, the church fathers, and councils to support its statements. These passages were later printed *in extenso* (some 2,500 pages) in the *Opus Catechisticum* prepared by the Jesuit Peter Buys with Canisius's help. The original length of the *Summa* was modest, with sixty-nine folio pages and 213 questions; but after the Council of Trent, Canisius (who served briefly as a theologian at the council) added nine new questions, far more marginal citations to scripture and the church fathers, and reprinted most of Trent's decrees on original sin and justification. The editions after Trent run about 50 percent longer than the 1555 edition.

Canisius divided his catechism into two major parts, devoted to wisdom and justice. The arrangement of the wisdom section was traditional: sections explain the Apostles' Creed, the Lord's Prayer, the Hail Mary, the Ten Com-

mandments, the precepts of the church, and the seven Catholic sacraments. The justice section was more innovative in its format but not in its content. It aimed less at teaching doctrine than at encouraging Christians to flee sin and do good. This section takes up four categories of sin, the works of mercy, the cardinal virtues, the gifts of the Holy Spirit, the evangelical counsels, and the four last things (death, judgment, heaven, and hell). Here Canisius strove to encourage a practical, Catholic, sacramental piety among his readers and to turn them from habits of sin.

Canisius's catechism rarely attacked Protestant teaching openly, as did many other Catholic catechisms, notably that by his fellow Jesuit Edmond Auger. But several previous Catholic catechisms in Germany, such as those of George Witzel and Johannes Gropper, owed much to Erasmianism and had softened differences with Protestantism. Canisius's catechism represents post-Tridentine Catholicism and is less given to compromise on disputed doctrine. The second section of his catechism, with its emphasis on good works and traditional patterns of piety, can be seen as a reaction to the Lutheran doctrine of justification by faith. Canisius devoted disproportionate attention to the five sacraments generally rejected by Protestants. He gave as much space to defending the distribution of Communion under one species as to his whole treatment of baptism. He was careful to stress the role and authority of the visible church and of the popes.

To help younger Catholics, Canisius prepared simpler and shorter versions of his *Summa.* For children there was the *Catechismus minimus* (Ingolstadt, 1556), about twenty small pages, whose later editions often added prayers, hymns, and instructions on Communion and confession. The most popular of all was his *Parvus Catechismus catholicorum* (Cologne, 1559), aimed at adolescents. Many later editions contained extensive engravings, a calendar of the liturgical year, and scripture quotations selected to buttress Catholic teaching and tradition and to assert the church's authority to teach. The *minimus* and the *Parvus* versions soon appeared in German. All three versions used the same basic arrangement of material and vocabulary so that students could easily progress from one to another while they were gaining a more sophisticated knowledge of their faith. The catechisms avoided scholastic terminology and built their arguments on scriptural and patristic authority.

In Germany Canisius's catechisms remained popular into the nineteenth century. They also had considerable vogue in France during the sixteenth century, where they largely replaced Auger's catechism. By 1615 Canisius's catechisms had been translated into twelve languages.

[*See also* Canisius, Peter; *and* Charles V.]

BIBLIOGRAPHY

Brodrick, James. *Saint Peter Canisius, S.J., 1521–1591.* Reprint, Chicago, 1962. Standard biography. See especially pp. 173–179 and 221–252.

Dhotel, Jean-Claude. *Les origines du catéchisme moderne.* Paris, 1967. Centered on France, but much background on the Canisius catechisms, pp. 15–98.

Donnelly, John Patrick. "Peter Canisius, 1521–1597." In *Shapers of Religious Traditions in Germany, Switzerland and Poland, 1560–1600,* edited by Jill Raitt. New Haven, 1981.

Kötter, Franz Josef. *Die Eucharistielehre in den katholischen Katechismen des 16. Jahrhunderts bis zum Erscheinen des Catechismus Romanus (1566).* Münster, 1969. Discusses the Eucharist in Canisius's catechism on pp. 85–95 and 239–261.

Streicher, Friedrich. *S. Petri Canisii doctoris ecclesiae Catechismi latini et germanici.* 2 vols. Munich, 1933 and 1936. Volume 1 gives a critical edition of the Latin catechisms with an extensive introduction. Volume 2 does the same for the German translations.

JOHN PATRICK DONNELLY

CANO, Melchior (1509–1560), Spanish Dominican theologian, courtier to Charles V and Philip II, and eminent representative of the School of Salamanca. As complex as he was pugnacious, Cano is remembered for his role at the Council of Trent, his involvement in a variety of controversies, and his contribution to the development of Catholic theological method. He studied at the University of Salamanca (1527–1531) and became the favorite disciple of the noted theologian Francisco de Vitoria (1483/86–1546). Cano taught at the Dominican college of Saint Gregory in Valladolid (1533–1542), held the principal chair of theology at the University of Alcalá (1542–1546), and succeeded his mentor Vitoria at the University of Salamanca (1546–1552). At Trent, he led the council away from compromise with Protestantism and toward its reaffirmation of the real presence of Christ in the Eucharist, transubstantiation, the sacrificial dimension of the Mass, and private auricular confession. Cano's conservatism also led him to distrust the new order founded by Ignatius Loyola (1491–1556), the Society of Jesus, which he maligned as a sectarian movement with heretical leanings. The vehemence of his attacks became legendary: Cano once compared the Jesuits to the *Alumbrados,* Lutherans, and Calvinists and identified them as precursors of the Antichrist.

Ever faithful to his mentor, Vitoria—who was one of the principal defenders of the rights of the American Indians against their Spanish conquerors—Cano became a formidable opponent of those who considered the Indians inferior beings and "natural" slaves. Cano's chief opponent in this controversy was Juan Ginés de Sepúlveda, chaplain and official chronicler to Emperor Charles V. When Sepúlveda defended the right of Charles to wage war upon and enslave the Indians in *Democrates secundus sive de justis causis belli apud Indos* (1544), Cano ensured the book's condemnation by the faculties of Salamanca and Alcalá. Moreover, Sepúlveda's defeat at the hands of Cano and other Dominicans in a debate held in Valladolid in 1550 led to the enactment of laws protecting the rights of native peoples in the New World.

Awarded the bishopric of the Canary Islands in 1552, he resigned from teaching at Salamanca. Nonetheless, Cano's close involvement with the royal court prevented him from taking up residence there; unwilling to serve as an absentee bishop, he resigned this post in 1554. His final years were filled with controversy. In 1556 King Philip II went to war against Pope Paul IV—who had allied himself with France—and Cano defended Philip's right to contend against the pope as a temporal ruler. At Rome, Cano was accused of challenging pontifical authority, and though he was twice elected provincial of Castile by his fellow Dominicans, Pope Paul IV refused to confirm him. Cano was also instrumental in the downfall of his old rival Bartolomé Carranza (c. 1503–1576), archbishop of Toledo and primate of Spain, who was accused of heresy and imprisoned by the Inquisition for seventeen years (1559–1576). In his own lifetime Cano came to be regarded as the embodiment of Catholic orthodoxy: when the first Protestants discovered at Valladolid were executed in an auto-da-fe (1559), Cano was selected to preach the opening sermon.

Cano's most enduring legacy is his contribution to theological methodology. Cano and other representatives of the School of Salamanca sought to enlarge the scope of theology by turning away from the abstract dialectics of Scholasticism and by placing a greater emphasis on ethical concerns. Like all Thomists, Cano defended the capacity of humans to understand or even intuit the truths revealed by God, and he engaged in an exegesis of the *ius naturae,* or law of nature. Cano's *De Locis Theologicis* (published posthumously in 1563) owes much to Rudolph Agricola's *De Inventione Dialectica* (1548), as interpreted by Francisco de Vitoria. This opus outlines ten sources, or loci, of theology. Aimed squarely against the paradigm of *sola scriptura,* Cano's theological method sought religious truth in a variety of sources, which included not just the Bible but also oral tradition; the pronouncements of councils, bishops, and popes; the writings of the Fathers; and even the teachings of pagan philosophers and the testimony of human history as interpreted by natural reason. Cano's method was enthusiastically embraced by post-Tridentine theologians, and, ironically, was taken to greater heights by some of his Jesuit followers in the School of Salamanca; four centuries later such influential thinkers as Joseph Maréchal (1878–1944) and Karl Rahner (1904–1984) continued to build on its foundations. The spirit of this positive or fundamental theology, as it came to be known, was neatly summarized by Cano in his *De Locis:* "Whoever constructs a theology unlinked to reason, and measures dogmas through Scripture alone, does nothing for theology, or for the faith, or for humanity."

BIBLIOGRAPHY

Primary Source

Cano, Melchior. *Tratados Espirituales.* Edited by Beltrán de Heredia. Madrid, 1962.

Secondary Sources

Andrés Martin, Melquiades. *La teología española en el siglo XVI*. 2 vols. Madrid, 1976. See vol. 2, pp. 386–429.

Belda Plans, Juan. *Los lugares de Melchor Cano en los comentarios de la Suma*. Pamplona, 1982.

Caballero, F. A. *Conquenses Ilustres*. Vol. 2 *Melchor Cano*. Madrid, n.d.

Klinger, Elmar. *Ekklesiologie der Neuzeit: Grundlegung bei Melchior Cano und Entwicklung bis zum Vatikan Konzil*. Freiburg, 1978.

Lang, A. *Die "Loci Theologicis" Melchior Cano und die Methode des dogmatischen Beweises* (1925). Reprint, Hildesheim, 1974.

Marcotte, E. *La nature de la théologie d'après Melchor Cano*. Ottawa, 1949.

Marín-Sola. F. "Melchor Cano et la conclusion théologique." *Revue thomiste* 25 (1920), 1–13, 101–115.

Martinez, Luis. *Fuentes para la historia del método teológico en la escuela de Salamanca*. 2 vols. Granada, 1952–1973.

Pagden, Anthony. *The Fall of Natural Man, The American Indian and the Origins of Comparative Ethnography*. Reprint, Cambridge, 1987. Chaps. 4 and 5 deal with the School of Salamanca, and particularly with Cano's contribution to the Indian debate.

Sanz y Sanz, José. *Melchior Cano: Cuestiones fundamentales de crítica histórica sobre su vida y escritos*. Santa Rita, 1959.

Tapia, Joaquín. *Iglesia y teología en Melchor Cano, 1509–1560: Un protagonista de la restauración eclesial y teológica en la España del siglo XVI*. Rome, 1989.

CARLOS M. N. EIRE

CANON LAW. *See* Law, *article on* Canon Law.

CAPITALISM. Most scholars agree that modern capitalism was born in the "long sixteenth century" (1450–1640). Karl Marx first noted this in his *Das Kapital*, starting a debate about the nature and causes of capitalism that focuses on varying eras and geography but that gives the late Middle Ages a special place. Undoubtedly by the early seventeenth century the religious and economic life of Europeans had undergone important changes that were both a response to and a cause of the dramatic spiritual, intellectual, social, demographic, and political changes of the Reformation era.

One trigger for the changes was the "crisis of feudalism" identified by Frantisek Graus (*Das Spätmittelalter als Krisenzeit*, Prague, 1969) and Rodney Hilton ("A Crisis of Feudalism," *Past and Present* 80 [1978], 3–19). Sparked by the demographic crisis of the fourteenth century, it was marked by a stagnation of productivity in the later Middle Ages caused by the inability of the feudal economy to generate investment for technical improvements. The habits of the landed nobility, supported by methods of production based in households, could no longer be supported, setting off a "crisis of the aristocracy." In response landlords, including the upper stratum of the peasantry, turned to producing raw materials for manufacturing. The textile industry predominated, leading the way toward new forms of industrial organization and weakening the traditional social structure.

This change undermined the traditional forms of political control, strengthening the states and the merchants while weakening the aristocrats whose incomes were tied to fixed rents. They responded with attempts to change labor rents into cash rents and to modify feudal relationships, but the peasants frequently ran away or resisted by asserting their traditional rights. It caused tensions that were manifested in revolts, such as the German Peasants' War of 1525, in which the peasants linked their claim for justice to the liberty of the gospel. One outcome of the crisis was the successful refeudalization of eastern Europe, where the agricultural labor supply was guaranteed by draconian laws. In England it manifested itself as the enclosure movement, in which feudal lords and yeoman farmers converted arable land into sheep pastures, displacing their tenants. In order to protect themselves against their declining fortunes, the aristocracies relied more heavily on their rulers, ceding power to the state in return for help against the peasants. In urban areas of Italy, previously the economic heart of Europe, the sixteenth century saw a slow decline. The French invasion of Italy in 1494 heralded its decay. The tug-of-war between France and Spain over Italy and the warfare in the Mediterranean against an expansionist Ottoman empire disrupted and drained the Italian economy, though the Venetians enjoyed a burst of prosperity in the sixteenth century.

The military revolution spawned by the endemic wars of the era stimulated the further consolidation of state power, prompted by the need for much higher taxes. Of course, purchasing military supplies spurred demand and made the developing states important consumers. The Reformation itself—which gave the Protestant states greater power by allowing them to take over many of the medieval church's governmental functions—was a product of, as well as a stimulus for, this growth. As central power increased, it commanded more of the economy and was better able to manage and aid the economy it controlled.

An important impetus for change was the international expansion begun by Spanish and Portuguese mariners, who opened direct trade with the markets of India and Africa and added the Americas to Europe's maps in the late fifteenth century. The wealth they derived from their colonies stimulated others to emulate them. Ironically, while this wealth fed Spain's war machine, it undermined the country's domestic economy. Spain went bankrupt several times in the sixteenth century.

By the early seventeenth century the Netherlands and England were emerging as the masters of a new economic system based on a world economy. In the Netherlands in particular, the government was using its power in the service of its merchants. The Dutch and English joint-stock trading companies had found a way to broaden their investor base and brought more and more people into the competition for world markets, encouraging their rulers to adopt a policy, sometimes called "mercantilism," that blurred the lines between economy and polity and encouraged export trade in order to enrich the nation and guarantee its strength. Monopolies and patents became tools of the new mercantilist states and were used to encourage the international expansion of markets. England's East India, Levant, Muscovy, and Merchant Adventurers companies, as well as the Dutch East India Company and other nationally licensed trading monopolies were founded in the second half of the sixteenth century, illustrating the way export trade was being embraced.

Another stimulant to economic change was the "price crisis," or inflation, that dogged the century. Its appearance has been ascribed to the introduction of massive amounts of American bullion into the European monetary system, but it was more likely the product of demographic crisis. Having recovered from the setback it sustained in the Black Death, the population exploded in the early sixteenth century. This caused increasing demand for goods, which led to higher prices and lower real wages, creating widespread misery and forcing people to innovate in their businesses, which in turn caused ethical dilemmas. As the communal and guild outlook on economic relations was undermined by inflation, by networks of trade and production that spread beyond their immediate hinterlands, and by new sources and forms of labor, people sought new ways to understand and justify behavior that broke so uncomfortably with tradition.

An economic change that was a direct consequence of the Reformation was the great divestiture of church property formerly held by the Catholic church in Protestant lands. As monasteries, chantries, and dioceses were dissolved, their lands and incomes passed into secular hands. This transfer of property both enriched individuals and redistributed incomes. In England the policy of Henry VIII and his successors created the greatest real estate boom in English history. In Prussia the Teutonic Knights secularized themselves and turned the vast lands of the order into private estates. Arising from theological roots, this transfer of land urged people to think in new ways about their relationship to the state and the economy. The economic advantage of a strong ruler became apparent as the Reformation dissolutions fed the agrarian revolution already underway.

The traditional moral theology on economics had matched the traditional economy and stressed communal solidarity, defined as Christian love. As economic changes occurred, however, there appeared within the traditional, controlled, local market economies various private, invisible, and unregulated forms of economic relations. This created great tension, forcing reconsideration of the way the economy ought to work. Nominalist theologians—and most Protestants followed them on economics—had stressed intent over effect as the proper moral yardstick. For instance, Johann Eck, Martin Luther's foe, and Charles du Moulin, a French Protestant, concluded that well-intentioned, friendly

loans at moderate interest were licit ways to acquire capital. In Spain Martín de Azpilcueta took a different tack but reached a similar conclusion about the moral acceptability of investment, since money could be invested for good purposes. By the late sixteenth century intellectuals, stressing the sovereignty of conscience, had created legitimate ways of rationalizing economic activity that made living with the new economic realities comfortable.

Taken together, the vast changes in the European economy, the stronger states, and the new theology produced by the end of the sixteenth century an attitude and an experience that encouraged people to pursue the accumulation of wealth for its own sake within the European world economy. The philosophical and theological skepticism that was spreading in the later sixteenth century had its economic equivalent in a capitalist mind-set that allowed the individual to choose his or her own economic ethics.

By the early seventeenth century the European religious, economic, and political worlds had been transformed, but did this transformation amount to "capitalism"? Part of the answer to this question is in how one defines capitalism. An alien concept to sixteenth-century people, it was identified by Marx as a "mode of production." Since he believed the mode of production determined the institutions and culture of a society, he saw the change from feudal to capitalist society as the evolution from a primarily agrarian society of petty producers and unfree tenants ruled by landlords to a society producing commodities for exchange on the market using wage labor dominated by capital-owning entrepreneurs. He found that this began to occur in the late Middle Ages as society progressed from a feudal mode of production to a capitalist one.

In 1902 Werner Sombart popularized the concept of capitalism, and scholars subsequently began hunting for the reasons for the development of a capitalist mode of production, though their definitions of capitalism varied. Maurice Dobb (*Studies in the Development of Capitalism,* London, 1946) noted that capitalism may be defined as (1) a mentality or spirit of a civilization; (2) the organization of production for a distant rather than local market; or (3) a mode of production under which labor is a commodity bought and sold in a market controlled by a minority, which therefore controls the labor of the majority.

Economic historians in the late twentieth century have blended the second and third definitions to achieve a fourth, arguing that capitalism appeared in Europe during the "long sixteenth century" (1450–1640) because of a series of conjunctures. Immanuel Wallerstein (*The Capitalist World Economy,* Cambridge, 1979) represents this school, defining capitalism as a system of production for sale at a maximum profit in a world market. According to Wallerstein, who is in part supported by the arguments of Fernand Braudel (*Civilization and Capitalism, 15th-18th Century,* New York, 1973–1984), capitalism was midwifed by the culmination of the "crisis of feudalism," which grew out of the "agrarian crisis" of the fourteenth and fifteenth centuries, the demographic expansion of Europe in the sixteenth century, climate changes, and, most importantly, the colonial expansion of Europe that altered the labor supply. Geographical expansion of European power allowed changes in labor methods, notably the "new" serfdom of eastern Europe and slavery in the New World, and increased stabilization and centralization of government. Wallerstein and Braudel part company, however, on the location of the driving force behind capitalist development. Braudel sees it stimulated primarily by internal forces, while Wallerstein argues that it was provoked by the development of a colonial periphery, which absorbed manufactures and supplied raw materials for the developing capitalist core.

Some characterize the capitalism that emerged during the era as "commercial capitalism," recognizing that it was built on long-distance trade rather than industrialized production. This, however, is contrary to the Marxist emphasis on the means of production. Scholars who are attracted to the theory of "proto-industrialization" advanced by Franklin Mendel hold that the economic change in the early modern period was marked by the development of regional networks of rural industry involving peasants in handicraft production for markets outside the region. This production was tied to both commercial agriculture and urban merchants, creating a transition from traditional rural economies to industrial economies. Some, notably Robert Brenner ("The Agrarian Roots of European Capitalism," *Past and Present* 97 [1982], pp. 16–113), believe this connection is so important that the era should be characterized as "agrarian capitalism" because the surplus wealth generated by agricultural production was the mainspring that drove capitalism's development.

These economic models of capitalist growth in early modern Europe downplay cultural change as a factor, preferring exoteric forces to changes in human priorities. The followers of Max Weber reverse the poles of the argument and insist that the ability to choose capitalist modes of behavior was dependent on a cultural change, creating an ethic that justified economic self-aggrandizement. Weber (*The Protestant Ethic and the Spirit of Capitalism*, 1905, many editions) defined the capitalist ethic as the free accumulation of wealth without the inhibitions of traditional communal ethical norms. This attitude toward wealth arose, he believed, from the internalization of Christian asceticism and the concept of worldly vocation found in Protestant theology, especially the "ascetic Protestantism" of Calvinism. The devout Protestant lived a life of disciplined self-denial and hard work, counting God's approval in growing personal wealth. In turn, this created a new cultural norm for economic activity, the "capitalist spirit."

Writing without the benefit of Weber's insight, R. H. Tawney produced a powerful argument linking the Refor-

mation and economic change in his 1925 *Religion and the Rise of Capitalism*. Though inspired by Marx, he nonetheless believed that changing ethics were part of what made capitalism happen. In his study of the sixteenth-century English economy, he concluded that religious change followed and explained economic change to contemporaries. The real mystery, he insisted, was how economics ceased to be a branch of moral theology and became a separate, self-justifying form of knowledge by the early seventeenth century. Somehow the Reformation produced "a dualism which regards the secular and the religious aspects of life. . . as parallel and independent provinces."

Sociologists enjoyed the explanatory power of the Weber Thesis and have defended it. Cultural and economic historians, however, have been less eager to embrace these "spirit" theories because they are hard to prove empirically. They have been especially disturbed by the willingness of sociologists to generalize from scattered evidence and have criticized their work by pointing out the terribly complex realities of economic and religious activity. To them Weber's theory can only be demonstrated through contextualization.

Investigations of usury law in sixteenth-century England have shown that both Tawney and Weber were correct in some ways (Norman Jones, *God and the Moneylenders: Usury and Law in Early Modern England*, Oxford, 1989). The economic change in the sixteenth century demanded explanatory models different from the traditional moral theology that Europeans had used to direct their economic choices. Among Protestants in England it has been shown that the emerging Protestant theology—with its stress on salvation by faith alone and the concomitant necessity of freedom to follow one's conscience—permitted economic self-aggrandizement. It allowed people to escape the constraints of a communal, guild economy that put the group before the individual. In a Weberian way, then, fulfillment of one's vocation required freedom to maximize wealth. This came at a time when the external economic pressures were intense, and people used a religious explanatory system to free themselves in conscience to behave as the new economic system demanded. This change in their religious thought allowed them to see new opportunities and make different decisions, leading to further economic change.

Certainly the "long sixteenth century" saw parts of Europe moving toward modern capitalism in both spirit and action, but there is not yet a consensus on what capitalism was, where and when it occurred, who initiated it, or why it emerged. As Braudel remarked, the term is "ambiguous, hardly scientific, and usually indiscriminately applied . . . above all . . . a word that cannot be used of the ages before the industrial period without being accused of anachronism." Nonetheless, it is a concept that has forced us to look closely at how the economy worked and how it was rationalized in the era of the Reformation.

[*See also* Church Finances; Nobility; Peasants; Usury; *and* Weber Thesis.]

BIBLIOGRAPHY

Brenner, Robert. "Agrarian Class Structure and Economic Development in Pre-Industrial Europe." *Past and Present* 97 (1982), 16–113. A response to the debate sparked by his 1976 article.

Coleman, D. C. "Proto-Industrialization: A Concept Too Many." *Economic History Review*, 2d ser., 36 (1983), 435–448. A critical bibliographic review.

Hilton, Rodney. *Class Conflict and the Crisis of Feudalism: Essays in Medieval Social History.* 2d ed., rev. London and New York, 1990. A collection of his articles that contains several applicable to the debate over the feudal crisis and the emergence of capitalism.

Landes, David S., ed. *The Rise of Capitalism.* New York, 1966. A reader, but it contains a valuable introduction by Landes reviewing the debate.

Marshall, Gordon. *In Search of the Spirit of Capitalism: An Essay on Max Weber's Protestant Ethic Thesis.* New York, 1982. An excellent introduction to both the Weber Thesis and the debates around it.

———. *Presbyteries and Profits: Calvinism and the Development of Capitalism in Scotland, 1560–1707.* Reprint, Edinburgh, 1992. Partially redefines the Weber Thesis and then tests it using Scotland as a case study.

McNally, David. *Political Economy and the Rise of Capitalism: A Reinterpretation.* Berkeley, 1988. Argues that agrarian developments were much more important than commercial developments in the rise of capitalism. Critiques the assumptions of liberal political economists.

Nelson, Benjamin N. *The Idea of Usury: From Universal Brotherhood to Universal Otherhood.* Chicago, 1973. An attempt by a Weberian sociologist to demonstrate, using usury as a case, how changing religious ideas stimulated social change.

Riemersma, Jelle C. *Religious Factors in Early Dutch Capitalism, 1550–1650.* The Hague, 1967. Considers the Weber Thesis in the Dutch context.

Stone, Lawrence. *The Crisis of the Aristocracy, 1558–1641.* Corr. ed. Oxford, 1979. Studies the way the English aristocracy responded to the "crisis of feudalism" and the new economic system.

Sweezy, Paul, ed. *The Transition from Feudalism to Capitalism.* Introduction by Rodney Hilton. Atlantic Highlands, N.J., 1976. A collection of important contributions to the debate.

Wright, William John. *Capitalism, the State, and the Lutheran Reformation: Sixteenth Century Hesse.* Athens, Ohio, 1988. Influenced by Wallerstein, Wright examines the ways Lutheranism, commercial capitalism, the feudal crisis, and population trends combined to change the Hessian state and economy.

NORMAN JONES

CAPITO, Wolfgang (also Wolfgang Fabricius Capito; born Wolfgang Köpfel; 1478?–1541), German humanist, scholar of Hebrew, reformer, and theologian. Born in the free imperial city of Hagenau, just to the north of Strasbourg, Capito was educated at the Latin school of Pforzheim and the universities of Freiburg in Breisgau and Basel, where he received doctorates in theology and in both canon and civil law. He took a leave from Freiburg to serve as preacher for the Benedictine foundation in Bruchsal, where, in 1512 and at the recommendation of Konrad Pellikan, he began to study Hebrew with Matthew Adrianus, a converted Jew from Spain. At that time he also began to adhere to John Wycliffe's spiritualist understanding of the elements in the Eucharist.

Capito came to prominence after he accepted a call to Basel in 1515 as professor and cathedral preacher and received his doctorate in theology from Freiburg. While in Basel, he published his first two Hebrew grammars, became an intimate of Desiderius Erasmus, and corresponded with fellow humanist scholars throughout south and central Europe. Like so many of the younger generation of humanists, he rallied early to Martin Luther's cause, even though his own lectures on Romans, which he began one year after Luther's famous series, followed Erasmus rather than Luther. Capito nonetheless translated Luther's early German works into Latin for the printer Johann Froben, who was delighted to sell the first three thousand copies in Paris within two weeks.

Erasmus forced Froben to stop printing Luther's works, and in 1521 Capito, still an Erasmian, moved to Mainz and the court of Archbishop Albert, where he became, first, cathedral preacher and, then, the archbishop's confessor and most trusted adviser in ecclesiastical affairs. From these posts he both blocked the suppression of Luther and his followers and criticized Luther (as he had earlier) for being too harsh. While Luther was still at the Wartburg castle, Capito visited Wittenberg and suggested to Philipp Melanchthon that Luther might be in error with respect to the clarity of the scriptures and the freedom of the will—the same two issues Erasmus later raised in *De libero arbitrio*.

When Luther returned to Wittenberg, Capito chose to visit again, this time in March 1522 for their first of two face-to-face conversations. A letter to Heinrich Cornelius Agrippa after this meeting demonstrates that Capito underwent a twofold change of mind. He became convinced, first, that the truth of the matter could be known and, then, that Luther was right, at least in general. He then returned to Mainz, secured his position as provost of the collegiate church of Saint Thomas in Strasbourg, moved there in 1523, decided in midyear to cast his lot openly with the reform movement, admonished Erasmus to do so, and a year later criticized Erasmus's very same sentiments as expressed in *De libero arbitrio*.

In becoming a reformer, Capito thus illustrates the relationship between humanism and the Reformation. His career as a reformer also sheds light on how Luther's views were implemented and received. Capito began his active work by holding a series of theological lectures for both Strasbourg's clergy and the city's leading laymen, in which, with the assistance of Martin Bucer, Caspar Hedio, and Matthias Zell, he converted most of them to the Reformation. His reform program consisted not just of altered liturgical practices, church life, and teachings but also of educational changes, public welfare, and public governance of marriage and morals. After a brief flirtation with the Anabaptists (a period that remains under debate among scholars), he joined Bucer in the synods of 1533–1534 and the writing and defense of the church order of 1534. He thus became a reformer in the active sense of the term.

Nonetheless, Capito's past by no means disappeared. He continued to be a scholar, one who wrote a full edition of his Hebrew grammar (1525) and commentaries on *Habakkuk, Hosea,* and *Genesis,* all of them in Latin, as well as polemical works, two catechisms, several hymns, and a formal defense of the city's religious settlement. He also remained something of a spiritualist on the subject of the Lord's Supper. In all likelihood he composed the article on the Lord's Supper in the Tetrapolitan Confession, which Strasbourg, Memmingen, Lindau, and Constance submitted as an alternative non-Roman statement of faith at the Diet of Augsburg in 1530.

Above all he retained a certain irenic spirit from his Erasmian past. He accompanied his colleague Bucer to the meetings in 1536 that produced the Wittenberg Concord, which he signed and by which these very cities subscribed to the Augsburg Confession. He then devoted much of his energies until his death to efforts to persuade the theologians of Zurich and Basel to subscribe as well. With respect to Zurich he was unsuccessful, but Basel remained at least semi-Lutheran until the late sixteenth century. His basic attitude was that there were indeed issues on which one must take a stand and for which one must be willing even to die, if necessary. But not every detail of Christian doctrine and practice required such tenacity. Hence, Capito's life reveals both the relationship between humanism and the Reformation and what it meant to have been a humanist who became a reformer.

BIBLIOGRAPHY

Kittelson, James M. *Wolfgang Capito: From Humanist to Reformer.* Leiden, 1975. The only complete biography. Contains a full listing of his published works, many manuscripts, and their locations.

Millet, Olivier. *Correspondance de Wolfgang Capiton, 1478–1541: Analyse et index.* Publications de la bibliothèque Nationale et Universitaire de Strasbourg, no. 8. Strasbourg, 1982. The most complete list of his correspondence; available only in research libraries.

Stierle, Beate. *Capito als Humanist.* Quellen und Forschungen zur Reformationsgeschichte, no. 42. Gütersloh, 1974. Thorough on his Basel years and the *Romans* lectures.

JAMES M. KITTELSON

CAPUCHINS. Founded in 1528, the Capuchins were one of the new orders of the Counter-Reformation, rivaled in importance only by the Jesuits. In 1525 Matteo da Bascio, an observant Franciscan friar from Montefalcone in the Marches, resolved to observe the rule of Saint Francis literally and devote himself to a life of prayer and preaching. In his habit with a pointed hood (*cappuccio,* from which the popular name of the order is derived) and with his long beard he intended to emulate the first Franciscans. He was joined by the brothers Ludovico and Raffaele Tenaglia da Fossombrone. While Matteo provided inspiration, the founder of the order in the juridical sense was the more practical Ludovico, who gained the support of Caterina Cibo, duchess of Camerino. Her second cousin, Pope Clément VII, issued the bull *Religionis zelus* on 3 July 1528, permitting the formation of the "Friars Minor of the Eremitical Life," the first name of the Capuchins. Pope Paul III confirmed this bull in 1536, but placed them under the jurisdiction of conventual Franciscans. The Capuchins were granted full independence by Pope Paul V in 1619.

The order grew rapidly despite internal disputes, the obstinacy of Ludovico Tenaglia (which led to his expulsion), and the defection to Protestantism of the vicar-general Bernardino Ochino in 1542. In 1574 Pope Gregory XIII allowed the Capuchins to expand outside Italy, and they established their first branches in France, 1574; Spain, 1577/78; Switzerland, 1581; Bohemia, 1599; and Bavaria, 1600. At the close of their first century of existence they had 16,967 members in 1,260 houses in 42 provinces.

The constitution of the Capuchins, issued in 1536, has remained the basic document spelling out their spirit and organization despite emendations and additions of 1552, 1575, 1608, 1643, and changes in the twentieth century. The friars had two models: Christ and Saint Francis, whose rule without glosses or interpretations was their basic charter. A fruitful tension between action and contemplation was to shape each friar's existence and had to be resolved on an individual basis.

The mission of the order was the spreading of the gospel. In their golden age of the sixteenth and seventeenth centuries, the Capuchins devoted themselves to preaching to the mass of the Catholic population in town and country, especially to the poor and neglected. Their aim was to strengthen Catholics in their faith, convert Protestants where possible, and teach pagans. They ministered to soldiers, whom they accompanied to the battlefield, and to sailors, whose chaplains they were on board ship. After 1600 they embarked on missionary work in Africa, Asia, and the Americas.

The Capuchins produced a remarkable number of spiritual writers. Giovanni da Fano's *The Art of Union [with God]* (1536) was the beginning of a long series of treatises on prayer, meditation, and the nature of Christian life, like *The Ministry of Prayer* (1564) by Bernardino da Balbano and *The Way in which the Spiritual Person Should Pray* (1574) by Silvestro da Rossano. *The Compendium of One Hundred Meditations* (1592) by Cristoforo da Verrucchio is especially suffused by Franciscan piety. Two works had a profound impact on French Catholicism: Benet of Canfield's *Rule of Perfection,* and Laurent de Paris's *The Palace of Divine Love.* While the Capuchins upheld an ancient form of piety and devotion, their success in early modern Europe was due to their adaptability to new ways of preaching and pastoral care, their identification with the common people, and their embodiment of the Franciscan ideal.

[*See also* Religious Orders.]

BIBLIOGRAPHY

Primary Sources

Cargnoni, Costanzo, ed. *I frati cappuccini: Documenti e testimonianze del primo secolo.* 5 vols. in 6. Perugia, 1988–1993. These massive volumes of over 10,000 pages are now an indispensable collection of source material for any further work on the early history of the Capuchins.

Olin, John C., ed. *The Catholic Reformation: Savonarola to Ignatius Loyola; Reform in the Church 1495–1540.* New York, 1969. Contains an English translation of the Constitution of 1536.

Secondary Sources

Cuthbert, Father. *The Capuchins: A Contribution to the History of the Counterreformation.* 2 vols. Reprint, Port Washington, N.Y., 1971. Remains a solid and attractively written first book to read.

Isidoro de Villapadierna. "The Capuchins—Hermits and Preachers." *Greyfriars Review* 2 (1988), 93–113. Best up-to-date bibliographical orientation for early history of the Capuchins.

Melchior da Pobladura. *Historia generalis Ordinis Fratrum Minorum Capuccinorum.* 3 parts in 4 vols. Rome, 1947–1951. General history of the order by an expert. Each section is preceded by good bibliography.

———. "Cappuccini." In *Dizionario degli Istituti di Perfezione*, vol. 2, pp. 203–252. Rome, 1975. Very useful summary with good bibliography.

ELISABETH G. GLEASON

CARAFA, Gian Pietro. *See* Paul IV.

CARIONI, Battista

(c.1460–1534), Italian devotional writer and inspiration to the founders of three Catholic Reformation religious orders. His works articulated a spirituality that combined a fifteenth-century Italian humanist emphasis on man's potentiality with a commitment to religious reform in the world.

Born in the northern Italian town of Crema, Carioni was the son of a goldsmith and jeweler. Battista, a shortened form of Giovanni Battista, was the name he assumed upon entering the strict observant branch of the Dominican order in Lombardy at an unknown date. After ordination and profession of final vows in 1494, Carioni lived in, and sometimes served as superior of, several Dominican convents in northern Italy. At Vicenza in 1519 he was spiritual director of Gaetano da Thiene (1480–1547), cofounder of the Theatine order of male religious who worked for clerical reform.

Carioni's greatest influence began in 1528 or 1529, when he became personal confessor to Countess Lodovica Torelli (1500–1569), a wealthy noble widow and ruler of a small state. Under the spiritual guidance of Carioni and the lay leadership of Torelli, a group of men and women gathered at Torelli's court to work for personal sanctity and religious reform. In 1530 Torelli founded a new order of uncloistered nuns, the Congregation of the Angelic Sisters of Saint Paul the Converted. Approved by the papacy in 1535, the Angelic Sisters worked to reform female convents, to educate girls, and to assist poor women. Another of Carioni's spiritual protégés was Antonio Maria Zaccaria (1502–1539), a well-born layman from Cremona. In 1530 Zaccaria and two laymen from Milan founded the Clerics Regular of Saint Paul the Beheaded, usually called the Barnabites. After receiving papal approval in 1533 and 1535, the Barnabites engaged in catechetical, devotional, pastoral, and preaching activities; education of boys was added to their mission in the seventeenth century. The Angelic Sisters and Barnabites worked as a team in the first twenty years of their existence. Carioni was the spiritual leader of the two orders, and his works continued to be essential reading for Angelic Sisters and Barnabites after his death in 1534.

Carioni's *Via di aperta verità* was a collection of devotional treatises first published in 1523, with three to five additional printings. Next came *Opera utilissima de la cognitione & vittoria di se stesso* of 1531, followed by two more Italian printings plus two Spanish translations in four printings. *Filosofia divina di quello solo vero Maestro Iesu Christo Crucifixo* also appeared in 1531, followed by two or three more printings. *Specchio interiore* was published in 1540, with three or four additional printings. Finally, *Detti notabili* appeared in 1583 under the name of Antonio Maria Zaccaria, but scholars believe that Carioni was the author of this collection of sayings, which enjoyed more than twenty printings. Carioni wrote all his devotional treatises in Italian.

Carioni emphasized man's greatness and free will, a conception close to the views of the fifteenth-century humanists Giovanni Pico della Mirandola and Marsilio Ficino. Carioni saw man as poised between higher and lower things—that is, between divine and animal nature. If he followed his better nature, man could become "almost a God" or "similar to God." Having made a decision to follow Christ, man proved himself by doing good works of charity, a constant theme in Carioni's writings. Carioni scorned "ceremonial Christians," those who said that they loved Christ but did not act on their love by doing good deeds. Carioni especially appealed to well-educated, upperclass men and women who desired personal renewal and were committed to secular good works.

But critics saw Carioni as a semi-Pelagian, the heretical view that original sin had not completely extinguished good in man's nature or his ability to make tentative efforts to do good on his own initiative. Semi-Pelagianism did not sufficiently emphasize God's grace, which enabled man to reach toward God. Complaints about the activities of the Angelic Sisters and Barnabites in Venice also focused attention on Carioni's books. A papal investigation of his books after his death concluded that Carioni placed too much confidence in man's unaided efforts to achieve salvation. The papacy condemned Carioni's books in 1552, although the Council of Trent eased the condemnation to emendation. Nevertheless, they were no longer printed under his own name in sixteenth-century Italy. The papacy also ordered the Barnabites and Angelic Sisters to separate and subjected both orders to stricter discipline. Despite the condemnation, Carioni's influence lived on in the Angelic Sisters and Barnabites. His emphasis on a humanist conception of man and an interior spirituality that manifested itself through good works was a major theme of the Italian Catholic Reformation.

BIBLIOGRAPHY

Bogliolo, Luigi. *Battista da Crema: Nuovi studi sopra la sua vita, i suoi scritti, la sua dottrina.* Turin, 1952. Study of his works with bibliography of editions.

———. "Crema, Battista Carioni da." In *Dizionario degli istituti di perfezione*, vol. 3, cols. 258–259. Rome, 1976.

Grendler, Paul F. "Man Is Almost a God: Fra Battista Carioni between Renaissance and Catholic Reformation." In *Humanity and Divinity in Renaissance and Reformation: Essays in Honor of Charles Trinkaus*, edited by John W. O'Malley, Thomas M. Izbicki, and Gerald Christianson, pp. 227–249. Leiden and New York, 1993. Only study in English. Emphasizes similarity to humanist conceptions of man's greatness and influence on Catholic Reformation.

Pezzella, S. "Carioni, Battista (Battista da Crema)." In *Dizionario biografico degli italiani*, vol. 20, pp. 115–118. Rome, 1977. Best short life of Carioni; contains full bibliography.

Premoli, Orazio. *Fra' Battista da Crema secondo documenti inediti: Contributo alla storia religiosa del secolo XVI.* Rome, 1910. Pioneering study with documents.

———. *Storia dei Barnabiti nel Cinquecento.* Rome, 1913. Basic study on Barnabites with information on Carioni as well.

PAUL F. GRENDLER

CARLOS I OF SPAIN. *See* Charles V.

CARLSTADT, Andreas. *See* Bodenstein von Karlstadt, Andreas.

CARMELITES.
The Order of Our Lady of Mount Carmel, known as the Carmelites, was founded after the Holy Land had been reopened to Christians at the time of the Crusades. By 1209 the Latin patriarch of Jerusalem, Albert of Vercelli, gave a rule to the former Crusaders and pilgrims, both clerics and laymen, who had settled on Mount Carmel in Palestine to follow the eremitic spirit of the prophet Elijah. This rule was officially confirmed in 1224 by Pope Honorius III. By 1238 Carmelites began to move to rural areas of western Europe, and after the fall of Acre in 1291, they disappeared from Mount Carmel. In 1247 they had received a rule from Pope Innocent IV, adapted to their new European circumstances, which classified them among the mendicant orders. They gradually moved from the rural areas toward the cities.

In 1451 Pope Nicholas V gave permission for the Carmelite friars to organize a second order for women. This second order enjoyed growth in Spain, where many Carmelite convents of women were originally Beaterios, or communities of Beguines. Often, however, the change to Carmelite status meant little change in lifestyle.

One community of Beguines in the city of Ávila (in Old Castile), founded in 1478 and dedicated to Saint Mary of the Incarnation, sought admission into the Carmelite second order in 1513. By the year 1550 the Carmelite convent of the Incarnation had 180 nuns. It was into this convent that twenty-one-year-old Teresa de Ahumada y Cepeda, Teresa of Ávila, was admitted in 1535.

In her first reform convent of Saint Joseph in Ávila, established in 1562 to foster strict observance of the rule among the Carmelites in Spain, Teresa's mystical quality and literary writing began to flourish. Her disciple, the much younger Juan Álvarez (John of the Cross; 1542–1591), fostered Teresa's reforms among the first order Carmelite friars. He accented the eremitic and prophetic origin of the Carmelites, and his teaching described in poetic rhythm the search for God, which often involved the "dark night" of the soul. Out of the mutual efforts of this woman and man, the reformed Discalced Carmelite friars were established in 1593 as an independent religious order. By 1600 there were forty-seven convents of Discalced Carmelite nuns.

In other parts of Europe the sixteenth-century Carmelite reform took a different direction. John Bale (1495–1563), an English Carmelite hagiographer and antiquarian, wrote his famous *Anglorum Heliades* in 1536. In showing the development of corruption within the Carmelite order, he began to see that this same disillusionment applied to the Roman Catholic church. He left the order in 1536 and embraced Protestantism. In his commentary on *Revelation*, titled *Image of Bothe Churches* (1545), he explained the stages of decay of the Catholic church. Subsequently he created a Protestant hagiography with the theme "few faithful" in every age.

In Germany at Wittenberg, Carmelite Johann Frosch "de Bamberga" (Bamberg) was examined in 1516 by Martin Luther for the licentiate in theology. In 1523 he accepted Luther's understanding of scripture and, as an effective teacher of the new learning, he became known as one of the twelve apostles of Lutheranism. In Denmark the sixteenth-century Carmelites were exceptionally learned, particularly those who came from the convents of Helsingør and Århus. Important figures, Catholic and Protestant, of the Danish Reformation came from the Carmelites: Paul Helgesen (c.1480–c.1539), who remained Catholic; Frans Vormordsen (1491–1551), who became the first Lutheran superintendent in Lund; and Peder Laurentsen (1485/90–1552), who became a Lutheran teacher of theology in Malmö.

At the end of the sixteenth century another scholar important for the expansion of Catholicism to the New World, the Spanish Carmelite Thomas of Jesus, produced a compendium of mission theology, *Stimulus Missionum* (1610), containing writing of the previous decades. When the Congregation for the Propagation of the Faith was later established (1622), copies of his expanded version, *De Procuranda Fidei*, were ordered to be distributed.

[*See also* John of the Cross; Religious Orders; *and* Teresa of Ávila.]

BIBLIOGRAPHY

Rohrbach, Peter T. *Journey to Carith: The Story of the Carmelite Order.* Garden City, N.Y., 1966.
Smet, Joachim. *The Carmelites: A History of the Brothers of Our Lady of Mount Carmel.* 3 vols. Rome, 1975.

J. A. WAYNE HELLMANN

CARNESECCHI, Pietro (1508–1567), Italian humanist. Born in Florence the son of Andrea and Ginevra Tani, both families with a Medici political tradition, Pietro was soon sent to Rome and guided into a career in the Curia Romana. He seemed destined for great success with the election of the new Medici pope, Clement VII, in 1523. In fact, he soon received benefices, revenues, and prestigious offices. In September 1533 he attained the position of pontifical secretary, and in this office he followed the policies of the nuncios Girolamo Aleandro and Pier Paolo Vergerio from Venice and the empire. Leaving Rome after the pope's death, he returned to Florence and then wandered through Tuscany, where he consolidated his relations with the Medici court of the new duke, Cosimo I, who is said to have become one of his great admirers and protectors from that time on.

Toward the end of 1539 he decided to go to Naples to join Juan de Valdés, whom he had previously met in Rome. It was in Naples in 1540–1541 that he began to deviate from Roman Catholic orthodoxy. Even more decisive for his doctrinal maturation was his brief stay in Florence in 1541. Here he read Calvin's *Institutio christianae religionis*. Thus, while in Viterbo at the end of 1541, he accepted the invitation to join the "family" of Cardinal Reginald Pole, who had been appointed legate of the Patrimony of Saint Peter. It was during this stay in Viterbo that Carnesecchi defined his own doctrinal options, reading and studying not only the works of Valdés, but also those of Martin Luther, John Calvin, and Martin Bucer. He also took part in the common discussions that led to Marcantonio Flaminio's reworking of the *Beneficio di Cristo* (The Benefice of Christ). After returning to Florence for his father's death, he went to Venice, where he lived until 1545 and where he became friends not only with the nuncio Giovanni della Casa but also with the vast array of heterodox thinkers who protected him and afforded him

economic aid. (The only extant doctrinal writing of Carnesecchi's dates from this period; it is a long letter to Flaminio refuting Huldrych Zwingli's views on the Eucharist and favoring those of Bucer.) Because of such activities he was summoned to Rome to appear before the Inquisition. Still strong on account of the favor he enjoyed with important political and religious figures, he succeeded in blocking the course of the trial, which therefore had no judicial follow-up. He left in 1547 for France and was welcomed to the court of Catherine de Médicis, where he remained until 1552. These were the years of his Calvinist "madness," as he himself later put it to the inquisitors. These convictions, however, did not lead him to the logical consequence of moving to Geneva. Instead, he returned to Padua, where he resumed following the fortunes of his friends and where he was caught unawares by the election to the papacy of the great inquisitor of the Carafa family, Paul IV, who quickly initiated well-publicized proceedings against all the advocates of the old Waldensian and Protestant circles in Italy. The most prominent of these trials was that of Cardinal Giovanni Morone, to whom Carnesecchi was very close and whose doctrinal leanings he knew well and shared. This was quickly followed by a summons for Carnesecchi to appear again before the tribunal of the Holy Office. This time Carnesecchi refused to obey and held out in Venice, but the trial against him continued all the same and ended with his being condemned to death in absentia (1559). He was saved by the pope's death and by the election to the papacy of Pius IV, who was close to Cosimo I and hostile to the rigorist Inquisitorial policies that had marked the previous Carafa pontificate. In May 1561 Carnesecchi was promptly pardoned and his ecclesiastical benefices were restored to him. After wandering about Italy, he again established residence in Venice, corresponding regularly with Giulia Gonzaga (commenting harshly and sometimes caustically on the vicissitudes of the Curia) and with those exiled in Geneva and Lyon for religious reasons. Thereafter he moved to Florence.

His personal fortunes took a turn for the worse in 1566 with the election of Pius V to the papacy. Pius V had fought Carnesecchi's pardon in 1561 in every possible way, and now he reopened the case. Carnesecchi's position was made even more precarious by Gonzaga's death (1566) and the confiscation of her letters, among which were letters from Carnesecchi that were compromising and damaging. Pius V ordered the trial against him to be reopened. Cosimo I turned him over to the Roman Inquisition, perhaps because he was convinced he could still save him.

The judges, as they sifted through the successive events of Carnesecchi's personal life, also reviewed the recent history of religious dissent that had troubled the life of the Roman church. The questions focused on the leaders and proponents of those circles of Protestants and followers of Juan de Valdés, even though some had died decades earlier, as had Valdés himself, Pole, and even Gasparo Contarini (who was considered guilty of having attempted doctrinal reunification with the Protestants at the 1541 imperial Colloquy of Regensburg). The only proponent still alive was Cardinal Morone, over whom the threat of a trial reopening hung, even after the pardon granted after the death of Paul IV. For this reason the proceedings against Carnesecchi were to implicate relentlessly Cardinal Morone. The real significance of Carnesecchi's trial was therefore to uncover further evidence against Morone, and Carnesecchi was well aware of this. Although he knew he might barter with this knowledge for his own life, Carnesecchi stood firm in refusing to provide the inquisitors with the testimony they were looking for. The death sentence was read on 21 September 1567 in the church of the Minerva in Rome before an impressive array of ecclesiastics, among whom Morone was conspicuous by his absence, but the sentence was not executed until nine days later, as the inquisitors, it seemed, hoped he would still implicate Cardinal Morone.

In the end, it was not so much Carnesecchi on trial as the recent past of the Roman church—with its political uncertainties and doctrinal wavering—as well as an entire generation of leaders with a Renaissance outlook who had failed to confront the historic tasks that challenged them. All this is what the inquisitors were attempting to remedy. Thus, in the eyes of the inquisitors, Carnesecchi was a symbol of those weaknesses, the laxism and the religious ambiguities of the 1530's and 1540's—that had threatened to wreck the ship of Peter in the midst of the Protestant storm.

BIBLIOGRAPHY

Firpo, Massimo, and Dario Marcatto. *Il processo inquisitoriale del cardinal Giovanni Morone*. 5 vols. Rome, 1981–1989.

Manzoni, G., ed. *Estreatto del processo di Pietro Carnesecchi*. Miscellanea di Storia italiana, vol. 10. Turin, 1870.

Rotondò, A. "Carnesecchi, Pietro." In *Dizionario Biografico degli Italiani*, vol. 20, pp. 466–476. Rome, 1977.

Schelhorn, Johann G. *Amoenitates historiae ecclesiasticae et litterariae.* Frankfurt a.M., 1738. See vol. 2, pp. 155–179.

Simoncelli, Paolo. "Inquisizione romana e Riforma in Italia." *Rivista Storica Italiana* 100 (1988), 5–125.

PAOLO SIMONCELLI
Translated from Italian by Robert E. Shillenn

CARNIVAL was one of the major festivals of sixteenth-century Europe, especially in the Mediterranean world. (In colder areas, spring and summer festivals were more important and took similar forms.) The carnival season, which began in late December but generally reached its climax in the week culminating on Shrove Tuesday, was an officially tolerated time of license. The most popular activities included eating meat and drinking alcohol on the grandest possible scale, wearing masks (or complete fancy dress),

pursuing members of the opposite sex; engaging in various rituals of aggression, such as throwing eggs, oranges, fireworks, or water; tormenting animals, exchanging insulting words and gestures, singing songs with double meanings, and enacting various kinds of combat, from ball games to mock tournaments and mock jousts (like the one unforgettably portrayed in Pieter the Elder Bruegel's *Combat of Carnival and Lent*, 1559). In some cities, notably Florence and Nuremberg, a procession or parade of decorated floats was a central part of the festival. In Rome there were races in which Jews and old men were forced to take part, in Venice a bull and twelve pigs were beheaded by the public executioner, in Nuremberg the butchers danced in the marketplace, and in Königsberg in 1583 ninety butchers carried a gigantic sausage through the streets. Women were also able to participate in the proceedings to some extent, notably by launching missiles from their balconies. But young adult males, organized in guilds or festive societies like the French "Abbeys of Misrule," usually played the leading roles in the proceedings, frequently sponsored by town councils.

Historians and folklorists disagree over the meaning of this festival. For some, Carnival is a fundamentally Christian ritual. As John Bossy argues, "The object of the feast was . . . to bring the corpus of sin to light, in order that it might be got rid of in time for Lent" (*Christianity in the West, 1400–1700*, Oxford, 1985, p. 43). Bossy supports his argument with the observation that proceedings often terminated with the trial and execution of Carnival in the form of an image of a fat man. According to this view, the emphasis on meat, drink, and sexual activity during the time of Carnival is to be explained by the need to abstain from them in the period that followed. The German and Dutch names for the festival (*Fastnacht*, *Vastenavond*, respectively, meaning the night before the fast) suggest that the meaning of Carnival derives from its juxtaposition and opposition to Lent.

Other scholars interpret Carnival as an enactment of the "world turned upside down," in which what is normally forbidden is permissible, indeed compulsory. They note that the festival was associated not only with food, drink, and sex but also with speaking one's mind and criticizing one's neighbor, the authorities, or society in general. Indeed, to judge from the texts of Carnival plays, this element of social criticism seems to have been gaining in importance in the sixteenth century. The feast was thus a safety valve permitting society to function in a more or less orderly manner for the rest of the year—though the valve did not always function, and Carnival violence sometimes turned into riot. Violent deaths were not uncommon at this season.

A third group of scholars regard Carnival as essentially an agrarian fertility rite dating from pagan times; they point to phallic symbols such as long noses and sausages and to the recurrent figure of the hairy "wild man." It was, appropriate for a spring festival, a ritual of rejuvenation, in which young people played a prominent role and the Fountain of Youth was a recurrent symbol (as in Nuremberg in 1510). The folklorist Claude Gaignebet goes so far as to describe Carnival as itself a religion, going back to pre-Christian times, in which the cult of the moon plays an important role (*Le carnaval*, Paris, 1974, ch. 1).

A fourth possibility complements rather than contradicts the others. One could interpret the festival—despite the opportunities for female participation—as essentially an affirmation of the values of masculinity as sixteenth-century men saw them.

All these views had their equivalents in the sixteenth century itself. How ordinary people viewed the festival it is impossible to say, but the reformers (for example, the Bavarian Lutheran Thomas Kirchmeyer), asserted frequently that Carnival was a survival of the pagan Saturnalia and Bacchanalia. Defenders of Carnival, like Folly in Erasmus's *Moriae Encomium* (1516), argued that human beings need to laugh. (Curiously, Erasmus himself was not amused when he encountered a carnival on his visit to Italy.) In the 1520s some German Lutherans used Carnival as a way of mocking the Catholic church and thus of spreading the ideas of the Reformation. But both Catholic and Protestant churchmen waged war on the festival because they interpreted it as an occasion of sin or an excuse for disorder.

In Nuremberg, for example, the Lutheran pastor Andreas Osiander, of the parish of Saint Lorenz, preached against the Carnival on the grounds that it was a relic of paganism and popery. Thanks to Osiander's influence, the town council suspended the so-called *Schembartlauf* or "masked run". Carnival returned to Nuremberg in 1539, complete with a figure in a black gown representing Osiander afloat in a ship of fools, only to be suspended once more, this time until the nineteenth century. On the Catholic side, a similar role to Osiander's was played by Carlo Borromeo, archbishop of Milan, who did his best to drive Carnival from the city in the 1570s, provoking the same kind of resistance. In Counter-Reformation Rome, the popes tried to modify if not to abolish the Carnival, and it is possible to detect a withdrawal of the upper classes, who increasingly preferred to celebrate by themselves within their palaces rather than rejoice in the streets with everyone else. Changes in the festival reflect not only what the sociologist Norbert Elias has called the "process of civilization" (i.e., increasing self-control) but also the increasing social and cultural distance between the elite and the people.

BIBLIOGRAPHY

Bakhtin, Mikhail M. *Rabelais and His World.* Reprint, Bloomington, Ind., 1984. A classic if dated study by a major literary theorist of the relation of Rabelais to the "culture of folk humour" of his time, written in Russian in the 1940s but not allowed to be published until 1965.

Burke, Peter. *Popular Culture in Early Modern Europe.* New York, 1978.

Cattaneo, E. "Carnevale e Quaresima nell'età di San Carlo Borromeo." *Ambrosius* 34(1958), 51–66.

Grinberg, Martine. "Carnaval et société urbaine à la fin du 15e siècle." In *Les Fêtes de la Renaissance,* edited by Jean Jacquot, pp. 547–554. Paris, 1975.

Kinser, Samuel. "Presentation and Representation: Carnival at Nuremberg, 1450–1550." *Representations* 13(1986), 1–41.

Scribner, Robert W. "Reformation, Carnival, and the World Turned Upside-Down." *Social History* 3 (1977), 303–329.

Sumberg, Samuel L. *The Nuremberg Schembart Carnival.* New York, 1941. Descriptive.

PETER BURKE

CAROLI, Pierre (d.1550?), Parisian doctor of theology and maverick reformer. From conventional beginnings as a theologian (he took his doctorate in 1520 and taught in the colleges of Burgundy and the Sorbonne), Caroli followed Jacques Lefèvre d'Étaples in the evangelization of the diocese of Meaux in the years 1521–1525. Accused of preaching various evangelical "heresies," he recanted in 1523 but resumed his evangelical preaching. He was excluded from the Faculty of Theology of Paris in 1524, and his arrest was ordered in October 1525. But he was protected by Marguerite d'Angoulême, duchess of Alençon and sister of the French king; she made him parish priest of Alençon in western France from 1526 to 1533. He is believed to have been responsible for the revision of Lefèvre's translation of *Psalms* (adding Luther's preface and Martin Bucer's "arguments") printed by Simon Du Bois in Alençon in 1532.

After the Affaire des Placards (1534) Caroli's name was first on a list of wanted persons, and he thus fled to Geneva (which was not yet Reformed). He participated in the Dispute of Rive in Geneva in June 1535 and in that of Lausanne in October 1536, which led to the establishment of the Reformation in the two cities. He became first pastor of Lausanne and married the daughter of a local pastor. The following year he accused Guillaume Farel and John Calvin of denying the divinity of Christ; the Bernese authorities cleared Farel and Calvin of the charge and deposed Caroli. He abandoned his wife and fled to Lyon, where he obtained a papal pardon and restitution of his doctoral status but no job. He was again banished in December 1537 for preaching justification by faith and disappeared for eighteen months. In July 1539 he met the Neuchâtel pastors, claiming to be reconverted, and was reconciled with them; this was followed by a reconciliation with Bucer and Johannes Sturm in Strasbourg. (Calvin maintained his hostility.) Having failed to hold down a post as chaplain to Jean de la Marck, duke of Bouillon, Caroli moved to Metz in 1540 and once again turned against the reformers. After writing a hostile letter to Farel (1543) and *Refutatio blasphemiae Farellistarum . . .* (1545), he once again disappeared; it is believed that he died in Italy around 1550.

BIBLIOGRAPHY

Douen, Orentin. "L'Imprimeur Simon Du Bois et la Réformateur Pierre Caroli, 1529–1534." *Bulletin de la Société de l'histoire du protestantisme français* 45 (1896), 200–212.

Farge, James K. *Biographical Register of Paris Doctors of Theology, 1500–1536.* Toronto, 1980. Contains the most up-to-date and thorough study of Caroli.

FRANCIS HIGMAN

CARPI, Pio da. *See* Pio, Rodolfo.

CARRANZA, Bartolomé (also Bartolomé de Miranda; c.1503–1576), Spanish theologian. Born in Miranda de Arga in the kingdom of Navarre, he studied in Alcalá and then as a Dominican at San Gregorio de Valladolid, where he was also to be a professor and later regent. He became a master in Rome (1539); he was also a preacher, a consultor of the Holy Office, prior at Palencia, and provincial of the province of Castile. He took part in the Council of Trent as the emperor's theologian (1546–1547 and 1551–1552). He was taken to England (1554–1557) by King Philip II and was his adviser, and he also advised Queen Mary Tudor and Cardinal Reginald Pole and played a part in the Catholic restoration. The Synod of London, for which he wrote the official minutes, charged him with editing a catechism for pastors. He published it in Antwerp in 1558—by which time he had already been appointed archbishop of Toledo and primate of Spain (1557)—and began the work of translating it into English.

After carrying on remarkable pastoral activity for a few months in Toledo, he was arrested by the Inquisition under suspicion of being the head of the Protestant groups that had been recently uncovered in Castile and that were quickly suppressed (1559). The excessive delay of the trial—initiated with the authorization of the pope and the king and the recusal of the inquisitor general as judge—caused Pope Pius V to bring the trial, along with the accused, to Rome (1567). Since Pius V died just as he was considering absolving Carranza, Gregory XIII (1576) brought the trial to completion, and he found him *vehementer suspectus de haeresi* ("greatly suspected of heresy") on 14 April 1576. Carranza was released after making his abjuration; he died in Rome on 2 May and was buried at Santa Maria sopra Minerva, where his tomb carries a laudatory epitaph composed by Gregory XIII himself. In 1993 the body was moved and solemnly interred in the cathedral of Toledo.

During his lifetime he published *Controversia de necessaria residentia praelatorum*, which had a deeply reformist tone, as well as four other polemical works (in relation to Protestantism) and the *Summa Conciliorum,* which was published many times in the sixteenth and seventeenth centuries. In London (1555) he published the small work *Del modo de oír misa* (On the Way to Hear Mass), and in Antwerp he published *Los Comentarios sobre el Catecismo Christiano* (1558). He left a large part of his works unpublished (such as a discussion of commentaries on Saint Thomas Aquinas, biblical commentaries, and sermons).

For his conciliar works he read, as did other Spanish theologians, works by Martin Luther, Philipp Melanchthon, and François Lambert; earlier he had read some of the work of Johannes Oecolampadius, Martin Bucer, and Johannes Brenz. The notes he took from these works, as well as a minute examination of his catechism, led to his being considered a Lutheran, a position that is no longer tenable today. Nonetheless, he was willing to acknowledge the great mastery the Protestants had of the Bible; he admired the moral courage of the victims of Mary Tudor's repression, in which he himself took part; he posed problems regarding the vernacular with respect to the original biblical text; and he showed an affinity with certain themes characteristic of Melanchthon, such as *De spiritu et littera, De lege et evangelio,* and *De libertate christiana.*

BIBLIOGRAPHY

Primary Sources

———. Carranza, Bartolomé de. *Summa Conciliorum . . . Ouattuor controversiae.* Venice, 1546.

———. *De necessaria residentia episcoporum* (Venice, 1547). Critical ed. Madrid, 1994.

———. *Comentarios sobre el Cathechismo Christiano* (1558). 2 vols. Edited by J. I. Tellechea Idígoras. Madrid, 1972. Contains a long introduction and bibliography.

Secondary Sources

Tellechea Idígoras, J. I. *El Arzobispo Carranza y su tiempo.* 2 vols. Madrid, 1968.

———. *Fray Bartolomé Carranza y el Cardenal Pole.* Pamplona, 1977.

———. *Melanchton y Carranza. Préstamos y afinidades.* Salamanca, 1979.

———. *Bartolomé Carranza. Mis treinta años de investigación.* Salamanca, 1984.

———. *El proceso romano de Carranza: Las audiencias en Sant'Angelo.* Rome, 1988.

J. IGNACIO TELLECHEA IDÍGORAS
Translated from Spanish by Robert E. Shillenn

CARTHUSIANS. The first Carthusian monastery, the Grande Chartreuse, was established at a remote mountain site above Grenoble in the late eleventh century. Rapid expansion first came to the extremely austere and semieremitic Carthusian order with the founding of about one hundred houses during the fourteenth century. Although the majority of foundations between 1350 and 1500 were still rural, significant expansion into the environs of German, Flemish, Italian, and French cities occurred, beginning with Paris in 1257. These suburban and urban houses were founded by bishops, the higher nobility, territorial lords, and royalty and occasionally also by urban patricians. Intellectuals, particularly humanists in the Rhineland cities and in Nuremberg, maintained contact with leading Carthusians and their rich libraries. Some charterhouses, especially in Italy, became artistic and architectural tourist attractions. On the eve of the Protestant Reformation, the order numbered nearly two hundred houses.

Carthusian Losses during the Protestant Reformation. Thirty-eight charterhouses disappeared during the sixteenth century as a result of the Protestant Reformation (two more during the seventeenth century); six succumbed to instability in the Habsburg border regions (Lower Styria and Hungary) and in the Netherlands during the sixteenth century. Approximately fifty monks and lay brothers died for their faith. The major areas of loss were England (100 percent), the northern Netherlands, and north-central Germany. Although two-thirds of the sixty-four charterhouses in French-speaking areas were sacked, all survived (except for three in French Switzerland and Savoy, which came under Swiss Protestant control). During the iconoclastic riots of 1566 and military campaigns between 1578 and 1585, all the charterhouses in the northern Netherlands, except one, were eliminated. (The charterhouse at Roermond survived a savage attack by William of Orange's troops—eight of sixteen choir monks and three of eight lay brothers were killed, several after extended torture—only because the town was reoccupied by Spanish soldiers.) The Belgian Carthusian communities survived largely by relocating inside the walls of nearby cities. Only a handful of defections to Protestantism in the Low Countries are known. Of the urban-suburban houses in major German cities, those in Protestant cities (Nuremberg, Basel, Strasbourg) were lost, while those in Catholic cities (Mainz, Cologne, Freiburg, Würzburg) survived. Some rural German houses managed to survive even though their noble patrons became Protestants. The pattern is clear: only the more politically consolidated Protestant territories and towns of Germany, Switzerland, England, and the Netherlands had no room for Carthusians.

In French-speaking regions two waves of Protestant attacks between the 1530s and 1600 struck hard against the Carthusian provinces of Picardy and Aquitaine (100 percent of houses attacked) but only lightly in (imperial) Burgundy (10 percent). Among the other areas affected were Provence (85 percent), Chartreuse (Dauphiné and Savoy, 36 percent), Loire (70 percent), and Seine (70 percent). The Grande Chartreuse itself was sacked. Apostasy, however, was rare: the French historian Gérald Chaix lists just three priors (at Castres, Villaneuve-les-Avignon, and Bonpas) who defected during the sixteenth century.

In southern Germany the entire Nuremberg Carthusian community turned Protestant (1524–1525), a unique instance within the order. Conversely, the Carthusian community in Basel is striking for its adherence to faith: apart from two early apostasies, it stood its ground under seven years of harassment (1525–1532) and several years of virtual house arrest, in the end forcing the city to await the death of the last monk (1564). Notorious instances of defection included Otto Brunfels, a Carthusian of Freiburg who became a Reformation pamphleteer, and Georg Koberer, prior at Würzburg, who led the Nuremberg Carthusians into the Protestant camp. Scattered defections occurred elsewhere.

Northern Germany, where most charterhouses were located in urban-suburban settings, lost nearly all its charterhouses, including Frankfurt an der Oder; Crimmitschau, near Zwickau (owned by Martin Luther's father-in-law, Johann von Bora, from 1548 to 1560); Hildesheim, in Lower Saxony; Schivelbein, in west Pomerania; and Rostock. Carthusians at Hildesheim and Rostock put up particularly stubborn resistance.

In Lower Austria, although the nobility largely became Protestant, relatively few monks defected. Despite the severe financial and personnel pressures created by Turkish invasions, the Carthusians took a number of measures designed to counteract the growth of Protestantism.

The resistance of the London Carthusians to Henry VIII brought public executions by drawing and quartering for some and for others slow death by starvation while immobilized in shackles for months. Some English Carthusians did, however, submit to the new ecclesiastical regime. The Stuart foundation at Perth in Scotland did not survive Mary Stuart's abdication in 1567.

Some of the violence against the Carthusians was motivated by a desire for material plunder. The Carthusians' obstinately silent resistance, however, as well as the air of mystery that traditionally surrounded the world-withdrawn Carthusians, may have added to the intensity of ritual violence against them. At Castres near Toulouse the wives of the Huguenot leaders relieved themselves inside the monastery church. Repeatedly monks were forcibly stripped of their cowls. Several were castrated (in one instance after refusing to eat meat). At Roermond many of the eleven monks and brothers killed were murdered inside the church.

Italian charterhouses were little affected by Protestantism, but especially those built just outside city walls did suffer under the military campaigns that ravaged the peninsula (e.g., Siena and Pavia). On the Iberian peninsula no houses were lost, and four new foundations were made. Three new urban foundations were made in France.

Carthusians and the Catholic Reformation. Carthusians played a central role in the Catholic Reformation in Germany, with Cologne and, secondarily, Buxheim (near Memmingen) as rallying points. After 1543, from his base at Buxheim, Dirk Loher (c.1495–1554) sought to save a number of German houses, lobbying Emperor Charles V for support at Augsburg (1547–1548).

Two outstanding priors, Peter Blommeveen (1507–1536) and Gerhard Kalkbrenner (1536–1566), led the Cologne house. Heinrich Bullinger, as a student in Cologne, for a time considered becoming a Carthusian. Blommeveen translated the German contemplative writings of the Franciscan Hendrik Herp (d. 1477) into Latin, wrote a number of works of edification directed at lay and clerical circles outside the monastery, and defended Catholic teaching against Lutherans and the Münster Anabaptists (*Candela evangelica*, 1526–1527; *Assertio purgatorii*, 1534). Under Blommeveen, Johann Justus of Landsberg (Lanspergius; 1489–1539) wrote devotional works (*Alloquia Jesus Christi ad fidelem animam*, 1532) and, together with Loher and Kalkbrenner, edited the writings of the contemporary Dutch Beguine Maria van Hout and the thirteenth-century Cistercian mystic Gertrude of Helfta.

The Cologne Carthusians also published a massive edition of the collected writings of Denis the Carthusian (d. 1471), beginning with his commentaries on the penitential Psalms and on Paul's letter to the Romans (1530), intended as a response to Lutherans. Another Cologne Carthusian, Laurentius Surius (1523–1578), made Johannes Tauler's writings available in Latin; he based his translation on a German edition by his protégé, Peter Canisius (1521–1597), the future German Jesuit leader. In addition to the Tauler edition, the writings of two fourteenth-century mystics (Jan van Ruusbroec and Heinrich Suso) and two contemporary Rhineland mystics (Nicholas Eschius and the Carthusian Florentius of Haarlem) appeared under Carthusian auspices (1548–1553). These Latin editions made German spiritual writings available to the rest of Europe. Surius also published Latin translations of German writings by Johann Fabri, Johannes Gropper, and other contemporary Catholic controversialists (1557–1563) before turning his attention to history and hagiography. The Cologne Carthusian publishing apostolate continued well into the seventeenth century.

In France the handful of new foundations made by the Catholic elites before 1650 were intended to raise the level of piety. Nothing like the Cologne charterhouse, however, developed in France or Spain.

Ludolf the Carthusian's fourteenth-century *Vita Christi* meditations, in a translation made by Spanish Carthusians in 1502, helped convert Ignatius of Loyola, who considered joining the spiritually thriving charterhouse at Seville (where Christopher Columbus is buried). While studying at Paris Loyola had frequent contact with the Paris Carthusians, and he drew on Denis the Carthusian and other Carthusian writers in his spirituality. Francisco de Osuna (1492–1541?), a Franciscan writer and early Catholic reformer in Spain, drew on Ludolf the Carthusian, Denis the Carthusian, and Hendrik Herp, as well as some of the German mystics edited by the Cologne Carthusians, for his widely read *Tercer Abcedario espiritual* ("Third Spiritual Alphabet," 1527).

The English Carthusian John Batmanson (d. 1531) and Pierre Cousturier (Petrus Sutor; 1480–1510) of the Paris charterhouse took umbrage at Desiderius Erasmus's Bible translations. They also took pen in hand to attack Luther.

Protestant perceptions of the Carthusians may be seen in a pamphlet by Hans Hergot (d. 1527), *Von der neuen Wandlung eines christlichen Lebens*, which envisioned a society purged of all leisured elites and where the common people all owned their houses and lived together "in the Carthusian manner." Luther referred to the Carthusians repeatedly as quintessential representatives of monasticism. This constitutes something of a backhanded compliment, despite his sweeping denunciation of supposed monastic faith in "works righteousness." As far as the Carthusians are concerned, the question of monastic Pelagianism can be perhaps laid to rest by considering the remarkably evangelical confession made in 1456 by Martin Ströulin of the Basel charterhouse (*Basler Chroniken*, vol. 1, pp. 514–515).

Despite recent challenges, the slogan "Cartusia nunquam reformata quoniam nunquam deformata" ("The Chartreuse was never reformed because never deformed") does apply to the sixteenth-century Carthusians. They could not help but bow to external political pressure in areas that became Protestant, but they seldom bowed without stubborn, occasionally heroic, resistance.

[*See also* Denis the Carthusian.]

BIBLIOGRAPHY

Primary Sources

Hogg, James, ed. *The Evolution of the Carthusian Statutes from the Consuetudines Guigonis to the Tertia Compilatio, Documents.* Vols. 1–4, Analecta Cartusiana 99. Salzburg, 1989. Contains successive legislation for the order from the early twelfth century onward, as well as a list of houses at the outset of the sixteenth century.

Laube, Adolf, and Hans Werner Seiffert, eds. *Flugschriften der Bauernkriegszeit.* 2d rev. ed. Berlin, 1978. See pp. 158–177 on Brunfels and pp. 447–457 on Hergot.

Vischer, Wilhelm, and Alfred Stern, eds. *Basler Chroniken.* Vol. 1. Leipzig, 1872. Half of this volume is made up of remarkable chronicles kept by Carthusians.

Secondary Sources

Auriol, Abbé. "La destruction de la chartreuse de Castres par les huguenots en 1567." *Bulletin de la Société archéologique du Midi de la France* 11 (1898), 132–141.

Beyer, Jean. "Saint Ignace de Loyola chartreux." *Nouvelle revue théologique* 78 (1956), 937–951.

Chaix, Gérald. *Réforme et Contre-Réforme Catholiques: Recherches sur la Chartreuse de Cologne au XVIe siecle.* 3 vols. Analecta Cartusiana 80. Salzburg, 1981. The best overview of Carthusian involvement in the Catholic Reformation; supersedes the 1935 monograph on the same topic by Joseph Greven.

———. "Laurentius Surius, 1523–1578." *Rheinische Lebensbilder* 2 (1988), pp. 77–100.

Gómez, Ildefonso M. *La Cartuja en España.* Analecta Cartusiana 114. Salzburg, 1984.

Gruys, Albert, comp. *Cartusiana: Un instrument heuristique.* 3 vols. Paris, 1976–1978. Entries for each house and each Carthusian writer, with extensive bibliographies of manuscript and published primary and secondary sources; marred by errors and phantom items, but still the indispensable starting point for prosopographic and statistical studies. Note especially the index of entries pertaining to Protestantism, vol. 2, pp. 418–419. German and Flemish entries were updated and corrected in *Die Kartäuser: Der Orden der Schweigenden Mönche,* edited by Marijan Zadniker and Adam Wienand. Cologne, 1983.

Hogg, James. "Die Ausbreitung der Kartäuser." In *Die Ausbreitung der Kartäuser / La Chartreuse de Lugny, 1182–1798,* edited by James Hogg and Leon Landel, pp. 5–26. Analecta Cartusiana 89. Salzburg, 1987. Surveys the growth of the order with references to recent literature in the Analecta Cartusiana series.

Hogg, James, ed. *Die Kartäuser und die Reformation.* Analecta Cartusiana 108.1. Salzburg, 1984. The best concentrated overview of the Reformation era, with surveys of French, Austrian, and Flemish charterhouses by Gérald Chaix, Jan de Grauwe, and Gerhard Jaritz, as well as specialized studies of German houses; lacks articles on Italy or Spain.

Knowles, David. *The Religious Orders in England.* Vol. 3, *The Tudor Age.* Reprint, Cambridge, 1979. See especially pp. 230–36, on the London martyrs.

Leoncini, Giovanni. *Le Certose della "Provincia Tusciae".* 2 vols. Analecta Cartusiana 60. Salzburg, 1989. An illustrated study of one region of the Italian Carthusian architectural flowering.

Martin, Dennis D. *Fifteenth-Century Carthusian Reform: The World of Nicholas Kempf.* Leiden, 1992. Not limited to the fifteenth century, studies Carthusian and monastic theology as a medieval Catholic paradigm for understanding Reformation theology.

———. "Carthusians during the Reformation Era." *Catholic Historical Review* 81 (1995). Contains full documentation and expanded detail for the present entry.

Martin, T. H. "Los misticos alemanes en la España del 16 y 17." *Revista de Espiritualidad* 48 (1989), pp. 111–23.

Scholtens, H. J. J. "Het Roermondsche Kartuizerconvent in de zestiende eeuw." *Publications de la Société historique et archéologique dans le Limbourg* 76 (1940), 91–121.

Scribner, Robert U. "Civic Unity and the Reformation in Erfurt," *Past and Present* 66 (1975), 29–60. Sheds light on one of the more complicated German urban settings for the Carthusians.

Spaapen, B. "Kartuizer-Vroomheid en Ignatiaanse Spiritualiteit." *Ons geestelijk Erf* 30 (1956), 337–366; 31 (1957), 129–149.

Wendehorst, Alfred. "Der Kartäuser Georg Koberer: Ein Beitrag zur Geschichte der Reformation in Würzburg und Nürnberg." In *Ecclesia Militans: Studien zur Konzilien- und Reformationsgeschichte,* edited by Walter Brandmüller, vol. 2, pp. 395–406. Paderborn, 1988.

DENNIS D. MARTIN

CARTWRIGHT, Thomas

CARTWRIGHT, Thomas (1535–1603), the leading ideologue of the Elizabethan presbyterian movement. He started out as a university divine, was elected a scholar of Saint John's College, Cambridge, in 1550, and had to leave the university three years later on Mary Tudor's succession. A fellow of Trinity College, Cambridge, he became Lady Margaret professor of divinity in 1570 and immediately caused controversy with his lectures on the *Acts of the Apostles,* in which he broached pseudo-presbyterian opinions. Removed from his chair in 1569 and his fellowship in 1571, he went into exile in Geneva. His return in 1572 and his sympathies for the *Admonition to the Parliament* caused him

to be embroiled in a major controversy over church government with John Whitgift. Renewed exile followed, first at Heidelberg and Basel and then at Antwerp and Middelburg, where he served as minister to the (presbyterian) church of the English merchants. Francis Walsingham tried to protect him from the queen's continuing displeasure, but it was ultimately Robert Dudley, earl of Leicester, who engineered his return, interceding on Cartwright's behalf with Archbishop Whitgift and granting him the mastership of his hospital in Warwick in 1585. There he remained until Whitgift's final crackdown against the presbyterian movement in 1589/90. Cartwright was imprisoned in the Fleet and was tried before the High Commission and Star Chamber. Released in 1592, he spent the years 1595 to 1601 in the congenially presbyterian context of the Channel Islands before returning to Warwick, where he died in 1603.

Although he ceased publishing on the controversial points after his return from exile, throughout the late 1580s Cartwright had been discreetly involved in the classis movement, a clandestine attempt both to establish an underground presbyterian church and to agitate for the formal adoption of the discipline by the authorities. Always a presbyterian, he came gradually to moderate his position. In 1576 he had conceded that ministers should not give up the ministry for the sake of ceremonies they considered popish and offensive. Though the ceremonies were indifferent, the duty to preach the word was not. In exile he had been brought face to face with Separatism. The Separatists used many of the same arguments as did the presbyterians, and in answering them Cartwright had to concede that, although deeply disfigured, the Church of England was still a true church, citing the spiritual experiences of its more godly members to prove it. In the 1580s, probably to mollify an increasingly hostile authority, he turned to antipapal polemic, writing a massive *Confutation of the Rheimists Translation,* in which he largely avoided the Puritan and presbyterian consequences of his antipapal arguments and equated his own uncompromising Calvinism with the doctrinal position of the Church of England.

Cartwright was an ambiguous figure. Driven out of the academic establishment by his early notoriety as the leading proponent of the discipline, he became an unwilling exile. The failure of the presbyterian platform and the dual threats of separation and popery forced him to try to reconcile his commitment to further reformation with his commitment to the Elizabethan regime. His silence on the issue of the discipline, his polemicizing against popery, and his clandestine involvement in the classis movement were all designed to do this. But his high profile as the symbol of the presbyterian cause and the death of his lay patrons rendered what had always been a difficult position untenable after 1590. His legacy was as ambiguous as his life; a variety of edificational works (a catechism, a letter to a divinity student, and a commentary on *Colossians*, among them) survived him. These were entirely typical of the pietism and gradualism of his more moderate contemporaries and heirs. But his literary executor was William Bradshaw, one of the founding fathers of Independency and the New England Way.

[*See also* Puritans, Separatists, *and* Presbyterianism.]

BIBLIOGRAPHY

Collinson, Patrick. *The Elizabethan Puritan Movement*. Reprint, Oxford, 1990.

Lake, Peter. *Moderate Puritans and the Elizabethan Church*. Cambridge, 1982.

———. *Anglicans and Puritans? Presbyterianism and English Conformist Thought from Whitgift to Hooker*. London, 1988.

Pearson, A. F. Scott. *Thomas Cartwright and Elizabethan Puritanism*. Cambridge, 1925.

Peel, A., and L. H. Carlson, eds. *Cartwrightiana*. Elizabethan Nonconformist Texts 1. 1951.

Porter, Harry C. *Reformation and Reaction in Tudor Cambridge*. Cambridge, 1982.

PETER LAKE

CASAUBON, Isaac (1559–1614), Swiss Protestant classics scholar. The son of a Calvinist pastor, Casaubon grew up in poverty and obscurity in Geneva but became the greatest Hellenist in Europe and one of the dominant figures in Protestant scholarship. He spent much of his early life teaching the classics in Geneva and Montpellier, producing a steady stream of editions of and commentaries on classical texts, from Diogenes Laertius's *Vitae philosophorum* ("Lives of the Philosophers") and Theophrastus's *Characteres*, on both of which he wrote important commentaries, to the works of Aristotle, which he edited. In 1600 he moved to Paris, where he worked under the supervision of Jacques-Auguste de Thou in the Royal Library. Here he did exhaustive research in the magnificent manuscript collections, not only on his own behalf but on that of Joseph Justus Scaliger, with whom he maintained an extensive correspondence.

He also found himself drawn into religious controversy, after serving (along with Canaye de Fresne) as one of the Protestant commissioners called on to judge the theological scholarship of Philippe Duplessis-Mornay at the Fontainebleau conference of 1600. Casaubon's religious position evolved gradually. He had long disliked what he regarded as the illiberal Calvinism of his Genevan youth (and felt that the Genevan authorities had wronged him in many ways during his early career). Now the ablest Catholic polemicists of the time, Fronto le Duc and Davy du Perron, pressed him to convert. Casaubon became more and more convinced that Calvinist theology represented a wrong turning, a departure from the traditions of the early church, which

he studied exhaustively. Rumors of his impending move to Rome circulated widely among both Calvinists and Catholics, and the Jesuit pamphleteer Carolus Scribani, who skewered such leading Calvinist lights as Scaliger, did not abuse Casaubon in the *Amphitheatrum honoris* of 1605. In the end, however, Casaubon remained within the Protestant tradition.

An invitation from the archbishop of Canterbury, Richard Bancroft, who provided him with a prebend, took him to England. Here he discovered a monarch, James I, who, unlike Henry IV, appreciated his learning and conversed with him volubly in French and Latin; a church that combined a Protestant commitment to scripture with a theology and ritual that drew heavily on the fathers of the church; and a few men of real learning, like Lancelot Andrewes and John Overall, whose company he enjoyed. He loved the great English libraries; "*hodie vixi*" ("today I lived"), he wrote, after spending a day in Thomas Bodley's great foundation at Oxford. He did exactly the sort of work that Bodley had hoped to promote.

Casaubon dedicated his last years to producing a systematic critique of the enormous *Annales ecclesiastici* of Cesare Baronio, the vast polemical Catholic history of the church that had begun to appear in 1588 and that had apparently buried the Protestant church history of the *Magdeburg Centuries* under its weight of learning. Casaubon's superior knowledge of Greek and of the history of the early church enabled him to show that Baronio had frequently relied on apocryphal sources and misinterpreted important texts. He exposed the lateness of the works of Dionysius the Areopagite and Hermes Trismegistus, producing little gems of historical criticism that he embedded in his *Exercitationes* against Baronio (1614). He also provided the work with a methodological introduction that would set the terms of debate about how to study and write ecclesiastical history for at least two centuries to come.

Casaubon's later years were not altogether peaceful. Both Continental Calvinists and Jesuits savaged him, and he ended up writing polemical pamphlets instead of the monumental scholarly works he preferred. Even independent thinkers like Paolo Sarpi deplored what they saw as Casaubon's weak-minded inclination to listen to Catholics who sought to beguile him. But the work against Baronio stands as one of the most independent and penetrating pieces of systematic historical criticism brought into being by the Reformation, and Casaubon emerges as one of those Calvinists who managed to preserve something of the independent Christian humanist enterprise of Erasmus in an age of theological orthodoxies.

BIBLIOGRAPHY

Birrell, T. A. "The Reconstruction of the Library of Isaac Casaubon," In *Hellinga Festschrift*, edited by A. R. A. Croiset van Uchelen, pp. 59–68. London, 1980.

Burke, Peter. *The Renaissance Sense of the Past.* New York, 1969.

Cozzi, Gaetano. *Paolo Sarpi tra Venezia e l'Europa.* Turin, 1979.

Glucker, J. "Casaubon's Aristotle." *Classica et Medievalia* 25 (1964), 274–296.

Grafton, A. *Defenders of the Text.* Cambridge, Mass., 1991.

Momigliano, Arnaldo. "Un appunto di I. Casaubon dalle 'Variae' di Cassiodoro." In *Tra Latino e Volgare: Per Carlo Dionisotti,* edited by G. Bernardoni Trezzini et al. vol. 2, pp. 615–617. Padua, 1974.

Pattison, Mark. *Isaac Casaubon, 1559–1614,* 2d ed. Reprint, Geneva, 1970.

Vivanti, Corrado. *Lotta politica e pace religiosa in Francia fra Cinque e Seicento.* Reprint, Turin, 1974.

Yates, Frances A. *Giordano Bruno and the Hermetic Tradition.* Reprint, Chicago, 1991.

ANTHONY GRAFTON

CASSANDER, Joris (also George; 1513–1566), Flemish humanist and irenicist theologian. After studies at the Collegium Trilingue at Louvain, he directed a Latin school at Ghent from 1540 to 1541. Afterward he became an instructor in ancient languages at the Cuba Foundation, a respected humanist school in Brugge. Dissatisfied with the repressive climate in the Netherlands, he undertook a journey in 1543–1544 to the great European centers of the *bonae litterae.*

In 1544 he settled at Cologne to dedicate himself to learning, where his faithful colleague was his former patron Cornelis Wouters, canon of Saint Donatian at Brugge. While on a trip through the Rhineland, they discovered in the abbey of Werden on the Ruhr River the famous *Codex Argenteus* (now in the university library of Uppsala), with a portion of the Gothic Language Bible. Leading a reclusive life, Cassander immersed himself in the study of the church fathers of the first six centuries and thoroughly acquainted himself with the views of the Protestant reformers. He did not regard them all as heretics; rather, he hoped to establish unity among the parties founded on the church of the first centuries, thus placing less value on the councils and pronouncements of the church of more recent times. The basis for his theology was the fifth-century principle that the essential articles of faith are those that have been accepted everywhere and at all times.

He was well regarded as an erudite theologian, and adherents of both parties turned to him to request his judgment. Emperors Ferdinand I and Maximilian II, as well as the French court, consulted with him about drawing the Catholics and Protestants closer together. He set forth his views primarily in two works that became famous: *De Officio pii ac publicae tranquillitatis vere amantis Viri in hoc Religionis Dissidio* (1561) and *De Articulis Religionis inter Catholicos et Protestantes controversis Consultatio* (published posthumously in 1577 by Wouters). The first work was written with an eye on the religious Colloquy of Poissy in 1562, organized at the initiative of Catherine de Médicis. Cassander recognized the right of the civil authorities to combat heresy but urged that punishment be meted out with the utmost caution; in particular, the death penalty should be used only in extreme cases. Duke William V of Cleves invited him to Duisburg in an effort to reconcile Anabaptists to the church. At Brugge, Cornelis van Baersdorp, formerly physician to Charles V, defended Cassander's position of proceeding mildly against heretics and of restricting the church's intervention in city affairs; this landed him in an irreconcilable conflict with conservative theologians.

The life and teaching of Cassander were full of contradiction. P. Polman (*L'Element historique dans la controverse religieuse du XVIe siecle,* Louvain, 1932, p. 383) calls him one of the most noble yet tragic figures among the irenic theologians. Although Cassander himself remained Catholic, his dogmatic concessions and his plan for reform, based on the common elements from the first centuries of Christianity, were considered to be in conflict with Catholic views. Cassander later recanted an early treatise urging Communion in both kinds for the laity. The Council of Trent judged differently on his positions. His works were condemned by Rome.

BIBLIOGRAPHY

Dolan, John Patrick. *The Influence of Erasmus, Witzel, and Cassander in the Church Ordinances and Reform Proposals of the United Duchies of Cleve during the Middle Decades of the Sixteenth Century.* Münster, 1957.

Kantzenbach, F. W. *Das Ringen um die Einheit der Kirche im Jahrhundert der Reformation.* Stuttgart, 1957. See pp. 203–229.

Schrevel, A. C. de. *Histoire du séminaire de Brugge.* Brugge, 1895. See vol. 1, pp. 450–474, 590, 802–833. Deals with his influence at Brugge and in the Netherlands and gives a strong judgment on his theological views.

JOHAN DECAVELE
Translated from Dutch by Jeff Bach

CASTELLION, Sébastien (Lat., Sebastianus Castalio or Castellio; Fr., Châtillon or Châteillon; 1515–1563), humanist scholar and advocate of religious toleration. Castellion was a peasant's son from the northwestern part of the duchy of Savoy. He was born in Saint-Martin-du-Fresne. As a student in Lyon he embraced the Reformation. In 1540 he moved to Strasbourg, where he gained Calvin's confidence and was appointed principal of the local Latin school. As a text for the combined teaching of biblical knowledge and classical Latin, he wrote the *Dialogi sacri* (1542, widely used and often reprinted in Protestant Europe to the end of the eighteenth century). But Castellion soon came into conflict with Calvin regarding doctrine and Calvin's unwillingness to admit Castellion to the ministry.

In 1545 he settled in Basel as an editor and corrector in

Johannes Oporinus's printing firm. With his growing family he lived in great poverty. In addition to his editorial work he completed two Bible translations, one into humanist Latin (1551 and many later editions), the other into popular French (1555). In the preface to the Latin Bible (dedicated to King Edward VI of England) Castellion for the first time set forth his plea for toleration.

In 1553 he was appointed professor of Greek at the University of Basel. On 27 October of that year, the Spanish antitrinitarian Michael Servetus was burned at the stake in Geneva, prompting a vehement reaction from Castellion. In March 1554 he published *De haereticis an sint persequendi,* an anthology of statements by early Christian and sixteenth-century authors unanimously denouncing the killing of human beings for religious reasons. In several contributions Castellion stated his own views, notably in the preface addressed to Duke Christoph of Württemberg that he wrote under the pseudonym of Martinus Bellius. The book caused great irritation in Geneva. It gave rise to an increasingly bitter debate that lasted until Castellion's death. In the midst of this debate the Savoyard humanist wrote a number of tracts in defense of toleration that were circulated only as manuscripts during his lifetime (e.g., *Dialogi quatuor*). Théodore de Bèze and Calvin also expressed their views in writing and never missed an opportunity to condemn their one-time associate as a traitor to the Reformation. The debate also touched on Castellion's Bible translations, both of which were criticized as desecrations of the word of God. Another issue was the doctrine of predestination which Castellion rejected.

Castellion's concept of toleration was firmly rooted in scripture. Like Erasmus he believed that the renunciation of theological speculation and the practice of an exemplary *imitatio Christi* would eventually bring the heretics back to the evangelical truth and to religious consensus. Unlike the Dutch humanist, however, the Savoyard scholar emphasized human reason whenever he reflected on the basic biblical doctrines and on how to deal with those who were drifting away from them. He stated repeatedly that putting alleged heretics to death was against God's will because it anticipated the Last Judgment.

Not directly related to the debate with the Geneva reformers was Castellion's *Conseil à la France désolée* (1562), in which he admonished both the Protestants and Catholics of France to abstain from persecuting each other. His last work, *De arte dubitandi,* is a kind of summa of his theological, philosophical, and moral views. It contains distinctive allusions to religious skepticism and rationalism. It was begun in 1563 and remained unfinished.

Castellion's last years in Basel were difficult. Although tolerated and even appreciated as a teacher by many students, he had to suffer mistrust, suspicion, and intrigues. For a while he contemplated emigration to Poland, but he died before making a final decision.

BIBLIOGRAPHY

Primary Sources

Castellion, Sébastien. *De haereticis an sint persequendi.* Edited by S. van der Woude, Geneva, 1954.
———. *Concerning Heretics.* Edited and translated by Roland H. Bainton. Reprint, New York, 1965.
———. *De l'impunité des hérétics / De haereticis non puniendis.* Edited by Bruno Becker and Marius F. Valkhoff. Geneva, 1971.
———. *Conseil à la France désolée.* Edited by Marius F. Valkhoff. Geneva, 1967.
———. *De arte dubitandi et confidendi, ignorandi et sciendi.* Edited by Elizabeth Feist Hirsch. Leiden, 1981.
———. *Dialogi quatuor.* In *Sebastiano Castellion, il riformato umanista contro il riformatore Calvino,* edited and translated by Carla Gallicet Calvetti. Milan, 1989.

Secondary Sources

Buisson, Ferdinand. *Sébastien Castellion, sa vie et son oeuvre, 1515–1563.* 2 vols. Paris, 1892. Work of fundamental importance, rather old, but not outdated.
Guggisberg, H. R. "Castellio, Sebastian." In *Theologische Realenzyklopädie,* vol. 7, pp. 663–665. 1981.
———. "Sebastian Castellio and His Family." In *The Process of Change in Early Modern Europe,* essays in honor of Miriam Usher Chrisman, edited by Phillip N. Bebb and Sherrin Marshall, pp. 97–115. Athens, Ohio, 1988.
———. "Castellio auf dem Index, 1551–1596." *Archive for Reformation History* 83 (1992).
———. "Sebastian Castellio and the German Revolution." In *Archive for Reformation History* 84 (1993), 325–343.
———. *Sebastian Castellio, a Biography.* Forthcoming.

HANS RUDOLF GUGGISBERG

CASUISTRY. From *casus* "having happened," the past participle of the Latin verb *cado,* casuistry is the method of moral reasoning that incorporates the particularity of a situation and its attendant circumstances through a short narrative depiction. In continental Europe, the method enjoyed considerable popularity among Roman Catholics from the early sixteenth to the mid-seventeenth century. In Britain the reformers used it for instructing their members on the formation of a right conscience.

Sixteenth-century casuistry developed because of the inability of existing moral principles to address new, urgent moral concerns of two kinds. First, explorations of the New World and extensive trading with the East prompted new questions about property, financing, governance, and evangelization that long-standing principles never anticipated and were unable to answer. Often groups of financiers and tradespeople petitioned different university faculties to determine whether in light of new circumstances a particular way of proceeding was still considered morally prohibited. The resourcefulness of principles collapsed eventually under the weight of the needs of a European population bent on expansionism. As a result, academicians sought new methods of moral reasoning to replace principles as standards for determining right conduct.

At the same time, scholastic philosophy was dramatically influenced by nominalism, which denied the existence of common essences. This led to a rejection of universals: without essences, there were no underlying or overarching common natures. Nominalists insisted, then, on the priority of the individual and on the radical singularity of each existent. In determining standards for right ways of acting, they referred not to some objective, essential norm, but rather to a particular, recognizable depiction or case of right acting. In lieu of a rule that governed actions having the same essential object, they sought proper analogous cases of action to serve as suitable standards against which new cases could be resolved by comparison and contrast. They used a particular case of action if it enjoyed a certitude of its own, that is, if its solution was cogent. The case that enjoyed internal certitude eventually replaced the inadequate principle or rule. Thus the method was not a deductive moral logic like the early, syllogistic, principle-based one that it replaced; rather it was an inductive comparison of congruencies between a case already solved with internal certitude and an unsolved case with a similar set of circumstances.

This method took on a life of its own in the universities. At the University of Paris, the popular Scottish nominalist logician John Mair (1467–1550) responded to inquiries as disparate as merchants asking questions about maritime insurance and Catherine of Aragon wanting to know about her rights. But as Mair and other academicians developed a new method to answer new questions, they also began to revisit old issues, like pleasure in marriage. In the Age of Discovery, as it considered itself, even old terrain was reexamined.

Members of the newly emerging Society of Jesus, having studied at Paris with Mair and others, opened their own schools throughout Europe and appropriated the method. Since many members were also missionaries, they continued to feed their schools with new cases from the West and the East, such that all moral analysis at these schools was completely case dependent. In fact, their schools became the first to offer moral theology as a separate academic discipline. Finally, these casuists, familiar with the rhetorical devices that they learned from Paris professors, also employed some of the imaginative flourishes found in their own members' sermons. Cases became rhetorically rich and imaginatively captivating.

Along with the Dominicans, the Jesuits found a second use for Continental casuistry. Confession, prior to the foundation of the Society of Jesus (1540), was strongly influenced by confessional manuals that appeared in the late fifteenth and early sixteenth century. These manuals, especially the *Summa Angelica* (1486) by the Franciscan Angelus de Clavasio and the *Summa summarum, que Sylvestrina dicitur* (1514) by the Dominican Sylvester Mazzolini Pri-

erias, used circumstances in order to establish more definitively the specific application of a principal to a sin. The presumption that one's soul could be judged by writers who anticipated the law's application even in its most minute detail led Luther to burn the *Angelica* and Erasmus to decry the presumptuous belief that a manualist could describe definitively the nature of another's personal sin.

As confessors, the Jesuits assumed the traditional double task of judge (about sin's gravity and its suitable penalty) and physician (assigning the proper penitential remedies to cure the sinner). But their ministries of preaching, teaching, and directing made them known as ministers of consolation; this eventually became the central one of the now three duties of the confessor. To mitigate harsh judgment, casuists helped their brother confessors by considering one circumstance after another that they appended to the law's interpretation so as to give it a more human context.

The Jesuit casuists transformed these manuals by introducing circumstances in order to highlight the uniqueness of the subject's situation. Rather than being tools for applying the law, the casuists' circumstances were used to understand the penitent. This appreciation of the singularity of the individual's situation later influenced the singularity of the casuist's own opinion. The external certitude that accompanied the casuist became a matter of choice: one confessor could choose among casuists' opinions. This was the birth of probabilism, first articulated by the Spanish Dominican Bartolomeo de Medina, in his *Expositio in Summa Theologiae Partem I–II* (1577), "if an opinion is probable (namely, if it is asserted by wise men and confirmed by good arguments) it is licit to follow it, even if the opposite is more probable." This freedom to choose from diverging opinions made the casuist more adviser than judge, more consoler than arbiter. Spanish Jesuits like Juan Azor (1535–1603), Anthony Escobar y Mendoza (1589–1669), John de Lugo (1583–1660), Luis de Molina (1535–1600), Thomas Sanchez (1550–1610), Francisco Suárez (1548–1617), and Gabriel Vasquez (1549–1604) appropriated and perfected probabilism. As Albert Jonsen and Stephen Toulmin note (*The Abuse of Casuistry*, Berkeley, 1988), Suárez developed principles to deal with matters of doubt, while Vasquez differentiated internal and external certitude, the latter being when a case's solution is approved by a specific probabilist. The probabilists were eventually attacked by Blaise Pascal, who in his *Provincial Letters* (1656) cited and ridiculed Escobar in particular, but the whole probabilist position in general, as nothing more than moral laxism.

Though the Redemptorist casuist Alphonsus Liquori (1696–1787) later defended a more modified form of probabilism, by the end of the seventeenth century the case method lost significant popularity, in part due to the reputed charge of laxity. But also the case method achieved its purpose: finding new, reliable guidelines. Thus the congruencies among so many cases were ultimately formulated into new rules and principles, and Jesuits and others began applying the newly minted rules and principles to cases, thus inverting the process and returning to a deductive form of moral logic similar to the confessional manuals.

Though Lutheran casuistry was negligible, Calvinist casuistry appeared vigorously in the British Reformation beginning with the writings of the Cambridge Anglican and Puritan divine William Perkins (1558–1602), whose forty-six works set a standard for his successors: William Ames (1576–1633), Richard Baxter (1615–1691), Joseph Hall (1574–1656), Robert Sanderson (1587–1663), and Jeremy Taylor (1613–1667).

With the loss of the confessional practice, Perkins noted a void in the moral instruction that the church provided. In its absence, Perkins used the pulpit to apply practically the scriptures to ordinary life and eventually put to print, in the form of pamphlets, the moral instruction that both preachers and congregation members could use. Moreover, disturbed that the only moral manuals to be found at English universities were Jesuit manuals of casuistry, Perkins set out to write his own manual, *The Whole Treatise of Cases of Conscience* (1606).

Perkins's casuistry grew out of his Puritan, expository preaching. First, attentive to detail while unfolding the exact meaning of a text, Perkins brought to his moral instruction the same appreciation of circumstances that the Jesuits and Dominicans did. Second, unlike them, Perkins extensively appealed to narratives from the scriptures for his analogies instead of the constructed paradigm cases that the Continental casuists developed. Third, Perkins's exegesis was fairly spartan and his cases were as well; they have none of the imagination that marked Continental writings.

But Perkins's casuistry is vintage Reformation writing: he begins his casuistry by asking how the reader can know that he or she has faith. This turn to the reader's own experience in conscience gives British Reformed casuistry a distinctiveness all its own. Unlike the Roman Catholic, Continental casuistry, Perkins and his successors wrote not for confessors but for ordinary people and often in the vernacular. This hundred-year period, from the late sixteenth to the late seventeenth century, marks probably the first time that moralists wrote for congregation members. Moreover, by turning away from the confessional and the confessor, their casuistry was concerned not as much with sin as with right living in following the way of the Lord.

Nonetheless, for all its divergences, Puritan and Anglican casuistry is marked by two similarities with Catholic Continental casuistry. First, it is consoling. Perkins knew that his people suffered from doubts and were troubled by whether they had sufficient faith. Moreover, he knew that the severest of all judges is often oneself. Second, when faced with the moral dilemmas particular to the British concerns at the time (e.g., oath taking, lying to protect others, keeping secrets), the British reformers recommended the same courses of action, if not even more lenient ones, as their Roman Catholic casuists whom they held in deep suspicion.

Perkins's casuistry inspired many in the American colonies and helped Puritan communities there to become self-governing. After studying with Perkins, Ames went to and taught successfully in Holland. Despite these influences, this casuistry remained for the most part among the British. It too faded away at the end of the seventeenth century, largely because later writers like Taylor were so extraordinarily attentive to detail that it could hardly be applied to ordinary people's experiences.

[*See also* Law, *article on* Theological Understanding of Law.]

BIBLIOGRAPHY

Keenan, James F., and Thomas Shannon, eds. *The Context of Casuistry.* Washington, D.C., 1995. A collection of essays on casuists, including Mair, Perkins, and Taylor.

Kelly, Kevin. *Conscience: Dictator or Guide?; A Study in Seventeenth-Century English Protestant Moral Theology.* London, 1967.

Kirk, Kenneth. *Conscience and Its Problems: An Introduction to Casuistry.* New York, 1948.

Leites, Edmund, ed. *Conscience and Casuistry in Early Modern Europe.* Cambridge, 1988.

Mahoney, John. *The Making of Moral Theology: A Study of the Roman Catholic Tradition.* Oxford, 1987. Two important chapters on probabilism and nominalism.

McAdoo, Henry. *The Structure of Caroline Moral Theology.* Reprint, Cleveland, Ohio, 1969. The first contemporary study of British Reformed casuistry.

Noonan, John T. *The Scholastic Analysis of Usury.* Cambridge, Mass., 1957. The most important extensive study of a particular problematic as it developed through the period of high casuistry.

Tentler, Thomas. *Sin and Confession on the Eve of the Reformation.* Princeton, 1977.

Vereecke, Louis. *De Guillaume D'Ockham à Saint Alphonse de Liguori: Études d'histoire de la théologie morale moderne, 1300–1787.* Rome, 1986. A collection of essays on some of the most important casuists.

Wood, Thomas. *English Casuistical Divinity during the Seventeenth Century.* London, 1952.

JAMES F. KEENAN, S.J.

CATEAU-CAMBRÉSIS, TREATY OF.

Late in the winter of 1558–1559 international negotiations were undertaken in the run-down Castle Cateau-Cambrésis, belonging to the bishop of Cambrai, technically neutral territory in the much-contested borderlands between northern France and the Spanish Netherlands. The most significant result of the settlement was to end over six decades of war between the French monarchy and Spain and the Habsburgs of the Holy Roman Empire, fought mostly in Italy from the mid-1490s. Some sort of peace was predictable and necessary, as both monarchies had effectively declared bankruptcy two years earlier, but the details were complicated. Pressures arose from Turkish conflicts with the Habsburgs in the Danube valley and on the Mediterranean and rising religious conflicts in France.

Foremost among the agreements reached early in April was the exclusion of France from any position of power in Italy, an ambition that ran back to the fifteenth century, and the effective cession to French control of "the three bishoprics" on France's northeastern frontier—the imperial cities of Metz, Toul, and Verdun. An associated agreement also effectively confirmed French possession of Calais, on the channel coast, to the disgruntlement of England. The usual dynastic marriages sealed the pacts. Contemporaries generally thought the settlement a defeat for France, even a humiliation, though this reaction was offset by pleasure that the two great western Roman Catholic kingdoms were again at peace.

Probably the most significant result of the Treaty of Cateau-Cambrésis was that in July, during the celebrations of the peace in Paris, King Henry II was killed in a jousting accident, opening the age of Catherine de Médicis—three decades of civil and religious wars during which Catherine tried to preserve the crown for her family, a struggle ended only by the accession of Henry IV of France and the temporary institution of religious toleration in France.

BIBLIOGRAPHY

Elliott, J. H. *Europe Divided, 1559–1598*. Glasgow, 1968. The best modern study of the context and conditions surrounding the Treaty of Cateau-Cambrésis; uses the treaty as a sort of launching pad.
Wernham, R. B., ed. *The New Cambridge Modern History*. Vol. 3. Cambridge, 1968.

GEORGE A. ROTHROCK

CATECHISMS. The word *catechism* derives from the Greek *Katéchein*, meaning to instruct orally. In early Christianity the term was used in various ways: it could refer to the pedagogical process itself or to the content of that instruction. By the fifteenth and sixteenth centuries the word could also designate the small books used for such instruction. Though the earlier usages persisted, this last meaning came to dominate. In what follows, therefore, "catechisms" means books of instruction in the basics of the faith written for the laity. This new literary genre was born in the fifteenth century and came to full flower in the various reforms of the sixteenth century.

The Catechetical Tradition. Instructing the faithful in the fundamental truths of the Christian religion was from the beginning a matter of great concern to church leaders. In the first three centuries, when baptism was administered primarily to adults, such instruction was a pre-baptismal preparation for full membership in the Christian community. In various places these candidates for admission were organized into a "catechumenate." With the ascendancy of infant baptism in the fourth century, postbaptismal instruction for adolescents and adults replaced the earlier arrangement. The content of instruction was at least to some extent gradually standardized. Even before Augustine wrote his catechetical *Enchiridion ad Laurentium* (423), the Lord's Prayer and the Apostles' Creed seem to have been required elements. Augustine himself was probably the first to recommend that the Decalogue be taught to all the faithful (in *De catechizandis rudibus*; 399/400), a suggestion rarely followed until the thirteenth century.

Historians have frequently described the Middle Ages as a catechetical vacuum, filled at length by the burgeoning catechetical literature of the early modern period. This view is becoming increasingly difficult to sustain as more medieval texts are brought to light and as more attention focuses on the interaction between elite culture and popular culture. The catechetical literature of this period, although written mainly for priests and religious, time and again exhorts priests, parents, and godparents faithfully to instruct the young, upon pain of eternal damnation. In all likelihood, the bulk of such instruction took place in catechetical sermons that, bishops expected, parish priests would regularly offer. Although the bishops' hopes may have been disappointed at times, and although the effectiveness of such sermons is open to doubt, the church clearly did not utterly ignore the instruction of the laity.

The more immediate background of the Reformation catechism was a new type of catechetical literature in the fifteenth century. The reasons for its emergence are complex. First, writing in the vernacular was becoming an increasingly popular and even respectable enterprise among ecclesiastics. A growing literacy rate among the laity meant that there was a new market for such writings. The invention of printing at midcentury ensured that the demand for new books could now be met as never before. The religious needs of the laity in the fifteenth century may also have helped to create a demand for such literature. Many historians have characterized the time as an age of anxiety evidenced by a notable preoccupation with death and suffering, an increase in bizarre and almost frantic public manifestations of piety, new religious fads, grotesque attempts to accumulate indulgences or to endow requiem masses, and so on. Above all, many seem to have taken to heart the clergy's insistence on making a perfect confession (i.e., contrite, complete, etc.) on the understanding that if they failed, eternal damnation awaited them. In this matter especially, the laity felt the need for instruction; accordingly, much of the century's catechetical literature focuses directly on the sacrament of penance.

The abundance and variety of fifteenth century catechetical literature makes it difficult to give a general description. Focusing on a few examples will, therefore, be preferable. First, the catechetical writings of Jean de Gerson (1363–1429) are of signal importance because of their widespread influence. Having himself taught Christian basics to youths in Paris, Gerson was convinced that religious instruction of young people should be the first step in church reform, and he defended this view in his *Tractatus de parvulis trahendis ad Christum*. Gerson also composed a vernacular tract to be read by or to the laity: *L'ABC des simples gens, de très grande utilitié et proufit*. Finally, he also wrote an *Opus tripartitum de praeceptis decalogi, de confessione et de arte moriendi*, presumably to assist catechetical instructors. This work included brief expositions of the Apostles' Creed, the Decalogue, sins to be confessed, and a meditation on the "art of dying"—a common theme in the religious world of the late Middle Ages. All of Gerson's catechetical writings exercised an enormous influence throughout the fifteenth and sixteenth centuries.

A second example of fifteenth century catechetical literature, typical of many such books, was the anonymous *Spiegel des Sünders* (Mirror of Sinners) printed in Augsburg in 1470. Like a long list of titles from this period, this one employs the mirror concept because the book was intended as an aid to self-inspection, the examination of conscience that was the crucial and indispensable preparation for the sacrament of penance. In his preface the author states that this material "was not made in my own brain and head" (col. 49) but rather is a compilation drawn from Thomas Aquinas, Henry of Langenstein, Anthony of Florence, and Jean de Gerson. Chapters 1–4 deal with confession and especially the conditions necessary for a "good" confession. Chapters 5–26 then deal with the various types of sins, their seriousness, and so on. Finally, the longest section, chapters 27–37, focuses on the Decalogue and lists the dozens of ways in which each commandment can be broken. A major element in the late medieval catechetical enterprise was clearly the pedagogy of guilt.

This preoccupation with human sinfulness also characterizes the *Christenspiegel* (Mirror of a Christian) of Dietrich Kolde (1435–1515). Nineteen printings before 1500 and at least twenty-eight editions thereafter make this one of the most popular of late medieval catechisms. Kolde begins with a short explanation of the Apostles' Creed, and then follows with a long section on the Decalogue, the laws of the church, the seven deadly sins, the six sins against the Holy Spirit, sins of the tongue, and so on—a massive enumeration amounting to several hundred sins. He ends with instruction on confession, various prayers including the Lord's Prayer and the Hail Mary, and practical advice on finding grace and forgiveness. In the last analysis, however, Kolde admits that even he cannot be sure of his eternal destiny.

These representative forerunners of the sixteenth-century catechism already call into question the traditional view of Reformation catechisms as a dramatically new departure in the history of Christian indoctrination. A wider sampling than is possible here would reinforce this conclusion. The relationship between late medieval and Reformation catechisms is one of continuity and development—not a radically new literary form springing *ex nihilo* out of the supposed "catechetical vacuum" of the late Middle Ages.

Lutheran Catechisms. The earliest reformers placed a new emphasis on the importance of instructing the young and the laity in general. Such teaching was surely one of the most significant factors in quickly transforming Luther's academic protest into a mass movement. From the outset, Luther's followers produced pamphlets, books, posters, and so forth geared to such instruction. Ferdinand Cohrs lists thirty-nine such works that appeared before Luther's catechisms. Though these attempts generally included the Decalogue, the Apostles' Creed, and the Lord's Prayer, they differed widely in other respects. While Luther himself had called for such works from his followers, he was deeply dissatisfied with at least some of them.

Luther's own forays into the area of catechesis began as early as 1516/17. From that time on he preached with some regularity on the commandments, the Apostles' Creed, the Lord's Prayer, and the sacraments. Brief writings such as his 1520 "Eine kurze Form des zehn Gebote, des Glaubens, und des Vaterunsers" (WA 7, pp. 204–229) were explicitly didactic in their intent. His many devotional writings in the vernacular were also to some extent catechetical in nature. He directed all of this material first and foremost to the heads of households, who, he held, had the primary responsibility for "impressing" or "imprinting" (*einbilden*) these basic Christian truths on the minds of the young through memorization and frequent repetition. By the mid-1520s, however, Luther's emphasis shifted: now he increasingly began to stress the catechetical responsibility of government-run schools. The need for standardizing such instruction now became obvious.

Luther's catechisms were the direct result of a 1528–1529 visitation to the churches in Saxony. His questioning of numerous pastors and laypeople had left an overwhelming impression: almost all were appallingly ignorant of basic Christian doctrine and many were obviously disinterested. Catechesis, he decided, was now to be made obligatory, and he set about writing his two catechisms.

The first appeared in April 1529, entitled *Deudsch Catechismus*, known henceforth as the Greater or Large Catechism (WA 30.1, pp. 125–238). Written primarily for pastors, the book began with a preface denouncing the negligent who "would make better swineherds or dogkeepers than spiritual guides and pastors"; these deserve "to be chased out by dogs and pelted with dung." Lay people who refuse to learn should not be admitted to the Sacrament, and fathers must insist that children learn to recite these basics. Drawing then on several series of sermons he had preached the year before, Luther continued with a long explanation of the Ten Commandments and two shorter expositions of the Apostles' Creed and the Lord's Prayer. Following these "three chief parts" are two substantial sections on the meaning of baptism and the sacrament of the altar. Finally, Luther added "A Brief Exhortation to Confession" to his first revision already in 1529. On the whole, the explanations offered here, though they tend toward verbosity, are simple and accessible. Despite his unrestrained polemic against Roman Catholics and "sectarians," Luther formulated his basic theological insights here in unusually moderate language. Thus, for instance, his explanation of the Decalogue has hardly a hint of his radical doctrine of Christian freedom from the law. So too, Luther's doctrine of the Christian as *simul iustus et peccator* is almost submerged in his discussion of sanctification (the third article of the Apostles' Creed). It was in this balanced form that Luther wished to transmit his theology to pastors, and through them to the laity.

Luther's second catechism appeared in May of the same year under the title *Der kleine Catechismus für die gemeine Pfarherr and Prediger* (The Small Catechism for the Simple Pastor and Preacher), known usually as the Small Catechism (WA 30.1, pp. 243–425). Though this one too was written for the use of pastors, the difference between it and the first is striking. Here an elegant simplicity and a single-minded focus on the essentials replace the rambling and polemical style of Luther's earlier effort. The following subjects are treated: the Ten Commandments, the Apostles' Creed, the Lord's Prayer, baptism, confession, the sacrament of the altar, morning and evening prayers, grace at table, and a "Table of Duties." Throughout the work one senses the great care and attention that Luther lavished on it. Indeed, to the end of his life Luther regarded it as one of his most profound and worthwhile writings.

In some respects this work stands within the late medieval catechetical tradition while in other respects it supersedes that tradition. For instance, the basic components are the same: Decalogue (code), Creed, and Lord's Prayer (cult). The traditional order, however, of "creed, cult, code" is altered here to "code, creed, cult," reflecting Luther's understanding of the law (code) as that which shows humans their sinfulness and drives them to Christ. The remedy, faith in Christ, is the central message of the creed. Finally, this remedy can be appropriated through prayer and the sacraments (cult). As Luther had already put it in 1520, there are "three things a man must need to know to be saved. . . . The law shows man his disease . . . the Creed tells him where to find his medicine . . . the Lord's Prayer teaches him how to seek it and to appropriate it" (WA 7, pp. 195f). Thus Luther's distinctive theological approach is reflected in his rearrangement of the traditional catechetical elements. Furthermore, Luther dispenses with the customary elaborate listing of sins. In its place one finds not a downplaying of human sinfulness but an insistence that it is definitively overcome in Christ. Finally, to mention only one more way in which Luther stands within and yet develops the late medieval tradition: he upholds confession and absolution, while he decisively abandons the insistence on a *perfect* confession. All that is required for forgiveness is the recognition that we as humans cannot extricate ourselves from our own sinfulness.

In these and many other ways Luther's catechisms build on and yet transcend the medieval tradition.

The Small Catechism was an immediate success in terms of circulation. Evangelical pastors preached from it; city councils adopted it as the basic school textbook; schoolmasters drilled it; parents instructed out of it; and at least some children learned it by heart. Religious leaders, even some who detested Luther, admired it and allowed it to influence their own attempts at writing catechisms.

At the same time new catechisms proliferated enormously among Luther's followers. Luther had said that pastors should choose the kind of catechism that they like and then use it continually. Here was a virtual invitation to each pastor to compose his own. Many in fact did, though their efforts were often little more than expansions of, or commentaries on, Luther's. Thus, for example, more than fifty different catechisms circulated in Hamburg alone.

This exuberant flowering of catechisms was reined in during the 1570s and 1580s. Since many of them served the interests of theological factions within Lutheranism, there were now calls for a return to the Small Catechism alone. New laws in Saxony in 1580 required that only this catechism could be used and that it was to be read every Sunday in church "in a loud voice and distinctly." Governments promoted its use, perhaps because of its deep conservatism in the area of social ethics. Lutheran theologians exalted it as the layperson's Bible. Indeed, a 1573 commentary held that "the words in Luther's Shorter Catechism are not the words of a man, but of the Holy Spirit." Though this was perhaps untypically extravagant, it indicates the high regard in which Luther's followers held his catechism. The inclusion of both his catechisms in the *Book of Concord* in 1580 was another measure of the esteem church leaders had for it.

Finally a word must be said about the controverted issue of "success." If one defines the success of the Reformation in terms of territorial rulers and city councils going over to the evangelical side, then one can say that these catechisms surely contributed to this success. They did indeed help to spread and to consolidate the Reformation. Some historians, however, define success in terms of a widespread deepening of religious knowledge and piety among the laity. Foremost among these historians is Gerald Strauss, who has argued that if this was the purpose of these catechisms, they were a failure. Based on visitation records from the later half of the sixteenth century, Strauss found no improvement in religious knowledge and no great concern for religious matters among the laity in Lutheran territories. In this sense, he contends, these catechisms were failures.

Anabaptist Catechisms. In the Anabaptist movement catechetical instruction reverted in a sense to its ancient, prebaptismal format. It seems unlikely, however, that such instruction was formal or standardized in the sixteenth century. While the production of devotional literature flourished, few genuine catechisms were written.

The one important exception to this was Balthasar Hubmaier's book of 1527, *Ein Christennliche Leertafel, die ein yedlicher mensch, ee und er im wasser getaufft wirdt, vor wissenn solle* (A Christian Catechism that Every Person Should Know before He Is Baptized in Water). The work is marked by a somewhat rancorous polemic, featuring a lengthy treatment of baptism and a substantial foray into the Luther-Erasmus debate on grace and free will. This last, highly technical theological issue is ultimately resolved by the simple assertion that those who have fulfilled the works of mercy to their neighbor are the ones who will inherit eternal life. This catechism's most significant innovation, however, is in its external structure. Abandoning the traditional tripartite division (creed, code, cult), Hubmaier divides his catechism into two parts: the first part centers on the ordinance of baptism, which is understood as a symbol of the human relationship to God (i.e., faith); the second part focuses on the ordinance of the Lord's Supper symbolizing the human relationship to the neighbor (i.e., love). The rectification of these relationships is, for Hubmaier, the sum and substance of Christian teaching, the central core from which all else follows.

It is doubtful that Hubmaier's catechism was widely used among Anabaptists, perhaps because it lacked the simplicity and brevity that make catechisms usable. Moreover, Hubmaier was not in full agreement with other early Anabaptist leaders on theological anthropology and the Christian's use of the sword. This factor too limited its usefulness in the Anabaptist Reformation.

Reformed Catechisms. Huldrych Zwingli's 1523 booklet, *Ein kurtze christenliche inleitung* is sometimes taken to be the first catechism in the Reformed tradition. One can maintain this view only if "catechism" is loosely defined, for this booklet was directed to Zurich clerics who were now required by the city council to preach "God's word." More typical were the catechisms of early leaders such as Leo Jud (1482–1542) in Zurich, and Wolfgang Capito (1478–1541) and Martin Bucer (1491–1551) in Strasbourg.

All of these early Reformed catechisms were eclipsed when John Calvin's *Instruction et confession de Foy, dont on use en L'église de Genève* appeared in 1537. In response to the Geneva ordinances of that year, Calvin wrote this "brief and simple summary of the Christian faith, to be taught to all children." While the thematic structure of the work is somewhat murky, the content of the thirty-three individual chapters is crystal clear. After an opening section on the purpose of human life, human nature and free will, Calvin continues with an exposition of the law and includes here his views on predestination. This exposition is followed by a section on faith and an explanation of the Apostles' Creed. A final section takes up prayer (the Lord's Prayer in particular) and the sacraments. Though the work touches on all

the typical Calvinist themes, one can scarcely imagine that it would have been accessible to the ordinary child. Calvin clearly intended that this *Instruction* was to be mediated to children by pastors.

His own dissatisfaction with the work led Calvin to write a much more polished and usable catechism in 1542. It bore the title *Le catechisme de l'Église de Genève: C'este à dire Le Formulaire d'instruire les enfans en la Chrestienté* (The Catechism of the Church of Geneva, that is, a Plan for Instructing Children in the Doctrine of Christ), appearing first in French (1542) and then in Latin (1545). Unlike his first catechism, Calvin adopts the question-and-answer format in this one, though it is not so much an interrogation as a dialogue between minister and child. The pedagogical intent is kept in clear focus throughout, and material is ordered with much greater clarity. Calvin begins with the assertion that the purpose of human life is to honor and to worship God. The question then is how one is to do this. Calvin teaches that one does this, first, by trusting God (this is section one on faith and the Apostles' Creed). One honors God, second, by doing his will (section two on the law). Third, invocation (the Lord's Prayer) is another way of worshiping and honoring God. Finally one does this also by praise and thanksgiving (Calvin's last section on the sacraments). Though predestination is only mentioned, Calvin's theological program had never been articulated with greater clarity and simplicity. Other Reformed catechisms, including his own earlier effort, now largely fell into disuse. Though other Reformed leaders such as Heinrich Bullinger (1504–1575) later tried their hand at catechism writing, Calvin's was the dominant one until 1563.

In that year Elector Frederick III of the Palatinate commissioned two Reformed theologians at the University of Heidelberg to compose a manual for instructing the youths and uniting the regional churches in his territory. As a result, Kaspar Olevianus and Zacharius Ursinus wrote the Heidelberg Catechism. Its one hundred and twenty-nine questions are grouped into fifty-two sections to facilitate catechetical preaching throughout the year. More important, all Christian teaching is treated under three rubrics. First, a section on "Human Misery" sets forth the fundamentally problematic nature of human existence. We are, in short, "altogether unable to do good and prone to evil." The second section, on "Human Redemption," outlines the Christian answer to this human predicament: faith, the Apostles' Creed and the sacraments. A final section treats the Christian response to redemption: gratitude. Here the Decalogue and the Lord's Prayer are explained, for all worship and all moral actions are motivated by thankfulness. The catechism articulates a moderate Calvinism (no predestination) in an elegant simplicity and a warm personal style. It quickly became the most widely used Reformed catechism of the sixteenth century, and it has functioned ever since as the standard of German Calvinism. Just as Luther's catechisms had been put into the

Book of Concord, so now the Heidelberg Catechism was elevated to the level of a confessional statement by the Synod of Dordrecht (1618).

English Catechisms. Already during the reign of Henry VIII, royal injunctions were issued (1536 and 1538) requiring parish priests to teach children the Ten Commandments, the Apostles' Creed, and the Lord's Prayer. With Edward VI's accession to the throne, steps were taken to regularize such instruction and to ensure that it reflected the views of those now in charge. Thus in 1548 Thomas Cranmer translated the continental reformer Justus Jonas's catechism into English. The first "Anglican catechism" appeared in *The Book of Common Prayer* (1549). Though its authorship is uncertain, Cranmer doubtless had a hand in it.

The most advanced catechism written during Edward's reign was John Ponet's *A Short Catechisme*, which appeared in 1553. It was written for use not in the home or church, but in the grammar schools, and it treated the law, Apostles' Creed, sacraments, and Lord's Prayer from a moderate Reformed theological standpoint. Ponet succumbed, however, to a common hazard of catechism writing: he allowed a pet interest to upset an otherwise orderly and balanced exposition. Thus the ascension of Christ receives more attention than any other subject in his catechism.

Protestant catechisms such as this one were not widely used, because Mary Tudor came to the throne in 1553. When Elizabeth I succeeded her in 1558, Anglican divines tended to write new catechisms rather than revive the older ones. Thus the 1559 *Book of Common Prayer* included a new section entitled "Confirmation, Wherein Is Contained a Catechism for Children." Based on Cranmer's previous catechetical writings and compiled perhaps by Alexander Nowell, this effort did little more than set forth the Apostles' Creed, Decalogue, and Lord's Prayer with minimal explanations. It warned, however, that "none hereafter shall be confirmed, but such as can say in their mother tongue the articles of faith, the Lord's Prayer, and the Ten Commandments, and can also answer to such questions of this short catechism as the bishop . . . appose them in." Here was a summary so brief that it could be required of all. This official catechism of the Church of England was soon supplemented by longer explanatory catechisms such as Alexander Nowell's 1570 work, *A Catechisme, or first Instruction and Learning of Christian Religion*.

Roman Catholic Catechisms. Though the Protestant challenge focused and stimulated Roman Catholic catechetical efforts, the reform of Christian education was already of some concern before 1517. This was especially the case in humanist circles, evidenced for example by Jakob Wimpfeling's essay on Christian education, *De adolescentia* (1500). In Desiderius Erasmus one can already see a program for such educational reform, beginning with his *Christiani hominis institutum* of 1514. In 1522 Erasmus proposed

a rejuvenation of the ancient church's catechumenate, now for baptized youths. His 1533 catechism, *Dilucida et pia explanatio symboli . . . decalogi praeceptorum, et dominicae praecationis*, failed to rise above the Reformation polemic in which he was engaged. For the most part, such humanist catechisms had a limited influence, perhaps because of suspicions of heterodoxy, and perhaps because they aimed more at creating an educated elite than at instructing the ignorant masses.

Nonetheless, large numbers of Catholic catechisms of unquestioned orthodoxy were produced between 1530 and 1600, all in some measure in response to Protestant catechetical attempts. A typical example is the *Catechismus* written by the Dominican Johann Dietenberger in 1537, a work that went through many editions and translations. Though he shuns the question-and-answer format, Dietenberger gives lucid and simple explanations of the Apostles' Creed (including a section on merit), the Decalogue (the traditional listing of sins is continued here), the Lord's Prayer and Hail Mary, and finally the seven sacraments.

Georg Witzel's 1542 *Instruction puerorum Ecclesiae* represents a more innovative approach. Writing expressly for children, Witzel utilized a salvation-history model, telling the Christian story from creation to the coming of the Messiah, his life, death and resurrection, the church, and so on. Almost as an appendix to this main section, Witzel added brief explanations of the Apostles' Creed, the Lord's Prayer and Hail Mary, and the Decalogue (in that order). Not only is there a heavy use of biblical references throughout, but the catechism ends with a series of quotations from scripture on the church, the Bible, and the sacraments.

As Catholic reform efforts gathered momentum at midcentury, church leaders stressed the need for improved pedagogy in response to the Protestant challenge. Perhaps the most influential works written to meet this demand were the catechisms of the Jesuit Peter Canisius. He wrote three: a massive *Summa doctrinae christianae* in 1554, a short *Catechismus minimus* in 1556, and a mid-size *Parvus catechismus catholicorum* in 1558. All employed the question-and-answer format, all were written initially in Latin, and all were subsequently translated into various vernaculars and reissued in multiple editions. Canisius's warm personal style and clarity helped to make his *Parvus catechismus* probably the most widely used Catholic catechism in German-speaking territories for at least a century. Setting aside long-held conventions, Canisius returned to Augustine's ordering of Christian instruction: faith (the Apostles' Creed), hope (the Lord's Prayer and Hail Mary), charity (the Decalogue and laws of the church), the sacraments, and a final chapter on Christian righteousness (vices and virtues).

Meanwhile the Council of Trent itself had commissioned a catechism. Written by three obscure Dominicans, this huge work appeared in 1566. It was divided into four major sections on faith and the Apostles' Creed, the sacraments, the Decalogue and other laws, and prayer. Though it quickly became known as the Roman Catechism, it was in effect a doctrinal manual for parish priests. Approved and recommended by popes from Pius V on, it was regarded as authoritative, appearing in multiple translations and editions. Though many paid lip service to its excellence, it seems in fact to have been little used.

Catholic authors continued to write new catechisms through the remainder of the century. One of the most widely used was the Jesuit Roberto Bellarmino's 1597 work *Dottrina christiana breve da imparsi a mente* (A Brief Christian Doctrine to Be Learned by Heart). This was one of the shortest and most basic of the sixteenth-century Catholic catechisms, intended for memorization. After an opening section on the sign of the cross, it dealt with the Apostles' Creed, prayer, the commandments, sacraments, virtue, vices, the last things, and the rosary. By being clear, simple, and succinct, Bellarmino assured the popularity of his work among catechists.

Conclusion. All of the sixteenth-century catechisms surveyed here were instruments of indoctrination, designed first to imprint different versions of "basic Christian teaching" on the minds of the young, the simple, the illiterate, and so on. Later, as confessional lines hardened, the catechisms were intended to shore up these people's loyalty to a particular church. They were in the last analysis attempts to inculcate a piety and moral behavior in the laity, attempts by the clergy (i.e., elite culture) to impose their values on the masses (i.e., popular culture). How successful were these catechisms as instruments of social control? This question is still an open one, though in the case of Lutheranism, at least, historians have recently made a good beginning. What already seems clear, however, is that in general, most attempts at Christian indoctrination of the masses were met with substantial indifference, boredom, and even resistance. Catechesis had to be made mandatory: some form of coercion was necessary. Moreover, the simplest and shortest catechisms were the most successful: most of the faithful were unwilling to learn more than the bare essentials. Clergy of all confessions complained bitterly about the ignorant, immoral, and uncaring laity. By and large, the masses were not buying what the elite had to sell. To their great disappointment, sixteenth-century religious leaders had to relearn what seems to be a perennial truth—that in any age only a small minority of human beings are willing to make godliness of any kind the central preoccupation of their lives.

[*See also* Luther's Catechisms.]

BIBLIOGRAPHY

Barth, Karl. *The Faith of the Church: A Commentary on the Apostles' Creed According to Calvin's Catechism.* Reprint, New York, 1965. Lectures on Calvin's 1542 "Catechism of the Church of Geneva."

Bradley, Robert I. *The Roman Catechism in the Catechetical Tradition of the Church.* Lanham, Md., 1990.

Geffcken, Johannes. *Der Bildercatechismus des fünfzehnten Jahrhunderts und die catechetischen Hauptstücke in dieser zeit bis auf Luther.* See cols. 47–80. Leipzig, 1855.

Hollweg, Walter. *Neue Untersuchungen zur Geschichte und Lehre des Heidelberger Catechismus.* Neukirchen-Vluyn, 1968.

Lentner, Leopold. *Die Religiöse Unterweisung in der Reformationszeit.* Innsbruck, 1958. Chapters 4 and 5 deal with sixteenth-century catechisms.

Nieto, José C., ed. *Valdés' Two Catechisms: The 'Dialogue on Christian Doctrine' and the 'Christian Instruction for Children.'* Lawrence, Kans., 1981. Works by the Spanish evangelical reformer Juan de Valdés (c.1509–1541).

Padberg, Rudolf. *Erasmus als Katechet: Der literarische Beitrag des Erasmus von Rotterdam zum katholischen Katechese des 16. Jahrhunderts: Eine Untersuchung zur Geschichte der Katechese.* Freiburg, 1956.

Reu, Johann Michael. *Quellen zur Geschichtedes kirchlichen Unterrichts in der evangelischen Kirche Deutschlands zwischen 1530 und 1600.* Vol. 1, *Quellen zur Geschichte des Katechismus-Unterrichts.* Gütersloh, 1911.

Scaer, David P., and Robert D. Preus, eds. *Luther's Catechisms: 450 Years.* Fort Wayne, Ind., 1979. Contains some important historical essays.

Torrance, Thomas F., ed. *The School of Faith: The Catechisms of the Reformed Church.* London, 1959. Several sixteenth-century Reformed catechisms together with Torrance's insightful interpretation.

Visser, Derk, ed. *Controversy and Conciliation: The Reformation and the Palatinate, 1559–1583.* Allison Park, Pa., 1986. Essays on Ursinus, the Heidelberg Catechism, and the dispute over its authorship.

Weidenhiller, Egino. *Untersuchungen zur deutschsprachigen katechetischen Literatur des späten Mittelalters.* Munich, 1965.

DENIS R. JANZ

CATHARINUS, Ambrosius. *See* Politi, Ambrogio Catarino.

CATHEDRALS. [*To survey the fate of the cathedral both as building and institution during the sixteenth century, this entry comprises two articles. The first considers the particular impact of the Henrician Reformation on cathedrals in the British Isles; the second covers its fate on the Continent. For a general discussion of the effects of the Reformation on building in Europe, see* Architecture.]

British Isles

The organization of cathedrals in England was significantly altered as a result of the Reformation. At the beginning of the sixteenth century there were nineteen cathedral churches in England. All owed their status to the fact that they were the seat of a bishop and thus the mother church of a diocese. Nine of the English cathedrals—Salisbury, Lincoln, York, Exeter, Hereford, Lichfield, Chichester, Wells, and Saint Paul's in London—were secular cathedrals, served by a dean, chapter, and inferior clergy who were in holy orders but not monks. The remaining ten cathedrals were monastic. Canterbury, Winchester, Worcester, Rochester, Durham, Ely, Norwich, Coventry, and Bath were Benedictine priories, while the cathedral at Carlisle was staffed by Augustinian canons.

As part of the dissolution of the monasteries (1536–1540), most of the monastic cathedrals were converted to institutions staffed by secular clergy. Often referred to as cathedrals of the new foundation, they were given royal charters that allocated revenues and fixed the number of canons or prebendaries in the cathedral chapters. Two of the cathedral priories, Coventry and Bath, were dissolved. In both cases they served dioceses that had two cathedrals; the bishop of Lichfield and Coventry retained a seat at Lichfield, and the bishop of Bath and Wells continued to reside at Wells.

Six new cathedrals were established in 1539, primarily in order to provide new functions for some large monastic churches that might otherwise have been demolished. Westminster Abbey was converted into a cathedral, and for a short time there was a bishop of Westminster. The Benedictine churches at Gloucester and Peterborough became cathedrals, as did the Augustinian houses at Bristol and at Osney outside Oxford. In 1546 the cathedral at Oxford was transferred to its present site within the college of Christ Church, utilizing the former monastic building of Saint Frideswide's. Westminster Abbey was once again given monastic status by Mary Tudor as part of her restoration of Catholic faith and practice, but the monks were turned out under Elizabeth, and the abbey assumed its present unique status as a "royal peculiar" closely associated with the monarchy.

There were four cathedrals in Wales (Saint David's, Llandaff, Saint Asaph, and Bangor). All of them were secular and were much smaller than similar establishments in England. After the Reformation these were administratively part of the Church of England. Scotland had more than a dozen cathedrals and Ireland more than forty, but few of these were major buildings.

The English cathedrals suffered severely from the iconoclastic movements of the sixteenth and seventeenth centuries. Shrines and images were denounced by an injunction of 1538. Nearly all of the cathedrals had shrines, the most famous being those dedicated to Saint Thomas Becket at Canterbury, Saint Cuthbert at Durham, Saint Swithun at Winchester, and Saint Hugh at Lincoln. Large quantities of gold and jewels were confiscated when these shrines were dismantled, as were crosses, chalices, and embroidered vestments. Statuary was demolished or defaced. Rood lofts were removed. Additional images were pulled down or mutilated under Edward VI, and some stained glass windows were smashed because they included depictions that were thought to be idolatrous. The dissolution of the chantries in 1547 affected the fabric as well as the finance of cathedrals; even the chantry at Worcester memorializing Henry VII's son Prince Arthur was defaced.

Music played an important part in the life of the English cathedrals, all of which had choirs of men and boys, schools for choristers, and accomplished organists who were often distinguished composers. Thomas Tallis and William Byrd were among the musicians who served the sixteenth-century cathedrals, while Orlando Gibbons and Henry Purcell wrote extensively for the chapel royal and the cathedrals in the Stuart period. The introduction of the English-language *Book of Common Prayer* in 1549 made it illegal to sing settings of the Latin Mass and canticles or anthems with Latin texts, thus creating an urgent need for new music and stimulating the creativity of the Elizabethan church.

During the seventeenth century cathedrals became a focus for Puritan attacks on the established church. Elaborate music, ritual, vestments, and architecture were denounced as popish and superstitious, or at best things that diverted the mind from the pure worship of God. Several of the cathedrals were fought over during the English Civil War, with Lichfield and Carlisle suffering the greatest damage. Organs and windows were smashed almost everywhere. At Durham, Scottish prisoners housed in the cathedral burned choir stalls and other wooden objects for heat. Choirs were disbanded and Anglican services suspended during the Interregnum (1649–1660), and the endowments of deans and chapters were confiscated. The restoration of the monarchy in 1660 was accompanied by the restoration of the church. Cathedral properties were returned, clergy and musicians were reinstalled, buildings were repaired, and new organs were erected.

Despite the attacks of their critics, the cathedrals continued to play an important role in English society following the Reformation. The great buildings attracted visitors, perhaps more like modern tourists than medieval pilgrims. Cathedral acted as models of liturgical and musical excellence. Schools were maintained in association with most of the cathedrals. Preaching assumed a greater significance than it had in the Middle Ages. Cathedrals were able to offer well-paid, attractive employment to a number of the most able clergy of the sixteenth and seventeenth centuries. Many of these men achieved distinction as scholars and writers: at least eight hundred books were published by cathedral clergy during the sixteenth century, with the number rising to more than four thousand during the following hundred years. Cathedrals played an important role in civic pageantry and in the economy of the cities in which they were located. Tombs and monuments attest to the relationship between prominent laymen and the cathedrals in which they were memorialized. By the end of the seventeenth century, however, cathedral communities became more and more inbred, and interaction with the whole fabric of society appears to have declined.

The cathedrals in Wales were affected by the Reformation and subsequent religious changes just as the English cathedrals were. So, at least in theory, were the cathedrals in Ireland. The situation in Scotland was different, though there were similarities: Saint Andrew's cathedral was allowed to fall into ruin, but Saint Guiles's kirk in Edinburgh was promoted to cathedral status in the seventeenth century.

[See also Chantries and Monasteries, article on British Isles.]

BIBLIOGRAPHY

Aston, Margaret. *England's Iconoclasts: Laws against Images*. Oxford, 1988. Sympathetic discussion of the scriptural and theological grounds for iconoclasm.

Edwards, Kathleen. *The English Secular Cathedrals in the Middle Ages*. Manchester, 1949. Sound account of the period before the Reformation.

Lehmberg, Stanford. *The Reformation of Cathedrals: Cathedrals in English Society, 1485–1603*. Princeton, 1988. Only general study of English cathedrals during the age of the Reformation, largely based on local archives.

———. "Writings of English Cathedral Clergy, 1600–1700." *Anglican Theological Review*, 75 (1993), 63–82, 199–217.

STANFORD E. LEHMBERG

The Continent

Throughout the Reformation, cathedrals served as focal points for civic and religious activities, providing settings for the expression of religious sentiments and opinions. While their fate varied widely, dependent upon the political and religious conditions of the city in which they were located, cathedrals proved durable and adaptable to religious change.

The role of the cathedral in civic life went beyond the religious services provided within the walls. Spiritual leadership, judicial jurisdiction, and property rights overlapped inside and outside the walls of the early modern city. Bishops, cathedral chapters, and town councils both cooperated and fought over their respective roles in the leadership of the city. The bishop and the cathedral chapter were often at loggerheads with each other, as well as with city officials. In addition, the physical space of the cathedral played multiple roles. It was the site of religious services, confraternity activities, royal processions, mystery plays, and public announcements, both in front of the cathedral and from the pulpit. Its outer walls supported merchants' stalls, while its porches were the time-honored haunt of beggars. The late medieval cathedral provided merchant and noble families with opportunities to display their wealth and patronage through gifts of paintings and sculpture and the dedication of side chapels. Cathedral canons were often drawn from the families of local notables. In short, the cathedral played an integral role in civic life.

Cathedral as Public Space. The Reformation expanded the uses of the public space of the cathedral. Cathedral pulpits became the site for both Reformation and Counter-Reformation preachers to exhort the urban population. The cathedral and the square in front of the cathedral were favorite sites for the burning of heretical books, the recantation of heretics, opinions, and the humiliation of penitent heretics. Such activities served to highlight and publicize the fate of the heretic, as well as to begin the process of the purification of the city. In 1534 the prohibited books of a condemned cathedral canon from Amiens, Jean Morand, were burned publicly in front of the cathedral. A procession to the cathedral culminated in a sermon by the noted Dominican preacher Thomas de Laurent, designed to explain and eradicate the dangerous ideas. A few years later heretics throughout France condemned by the *Chambre ardente* were forced to recant publicly and assist at a mass in their local cathedral. Their penitence was underscored by their appearance in white gowns, feet and head bare, carrying a lighted wax torch.

Processions utilizing the relics of the cathedral or the Host were common in late medieval towns. These processions involved the entire town and concluded with the return of the sacred objects to the cathedral. Processions occurred on special feast days, but could also be used to celebrate special events and to ward off unusual dangers. With the onset of the Reformation, processions became increasingly used to rally the faithful and to fight the infection of heresy. Francis I's reaction to the Affaire des Placards in 1534 was to order an elaborate procession in Paris culminating in a high mass at Notre-Dame Cathedral, followed by the execution of convicted heretics. The focal point of the procession was the consecrated Host. While a huge number of relics accompanied the procession, the Eucharist took pride of place, underscoring the doctrine of the real presence that the placards had attacked.

One of Henry II's first acts as king was to order a similar procession in 1549. Diefendorf has argued that while these processions were designed to educate the population about the dangers of heresy, they could also ignite an already volatile crown into eruptions of violence. Sermons preached at Notre-Dame often led to violence against Huguenots. The cardinal of Lorraine, Charles de Guise, helped cement his family's popularity in Paris by preaching inflammatory sermons at Notre-Dame. Simon Vigor, a popular Parisian preacher, gave sermons stressing the dangers of heresy to the body politic, arguing that if the king failed to root out the heretics, the Huguenots would destroy the city. Such activities were not confined to Paris. Incendiary sermons by both Protestant and Catholic preachers throughout Europe led to riots and iconoclasm. The setting for the sermon, the procession, or the iconoclasm was often the cathedral.

Attendance at and participation in civic events centered around the cathedral became tools for identifying both the faithful and the suspect. In 1562 Amiens produced a list of nonparticipants in the annual Corpus Christi procession as a guide for ferreting out potential heretics. Behavior of citizens during processions to the cathedrals in Paris and Lyons appeared in heresy accusations and trials.

Cathedral Personnel: Preachers, Canons, and Bishops. Cathedrals also affected the Reformation through the personnel they supported and trained. Men who would later be identified with the Reformation often got their start as preachers in cathedrals, while controversial sermons in cathedrals, or by cathedral canons, sparked active discussion, dissent, and occasional violence in cities throughout Europe. Soon banned from cathedrals in Catholic cities and countries, these same preachers helped mold the new divine service of the Reformation, with its emphasis on the sermon.

Bishops often provided the leadership for both early Protestants and Catholic reaction. Many were infected with the Lutheran "disease" and were forced to choose between their vocation and their faith. The archbishop of Toledo, Bartolomé de Carranza, was indicted for heresy in 1559 and persecuted for Lutheranism until his death in 1576. Antonio Caracciolo, bishop of Troyes, attempted to maintain his position as bishop while seeking an appointment as a minister to the Protestants. His sermons attracted attention, criticism, and reaction from Protestants and Catholics alike. Others maintained their allegiance to the Catholic church on religious issues but found themselves in ambiguous positions regarding their more secular responsibilities. Wilhelm von Hohnstein, bishop of Strasbourg during the early years of the Reformation, was a staunch opponent of the reformers while continuing to interact with the city council on judicial and economic matters. His support of the cathedral canons in their legal battles with the council resulted in retention of their separate legal status and many of their possessions, even though they no longer fulfilled any civic religious functions.

The Catholic Reformation called for renewed vigor in the role of the bishop. The Council of Trent demanded a reform of the episcopacy, condemned pluralism, and mandated the residency of bishops in their dioceses. Bishops were to preach regularly and to insure that good preaching occurred throughout their jurisdictions. A new group of resident bishops established new preaching programs and encouraged the building of new chapels and the redecoration of old foundations. New and revitalized confraternities often centered their devotional activities in the cathedral. In practice these changes were implemented slowly, particularly in countries, such as France, that resisted the council's decrees. Pluralism, nepotism, and nonresidency continued to plague the Counter-Reformation church. Where the residency decrees were enforced, however, renewed interest in the cathedral followed.

Cathedral as Liturgical Space. The fabric of the cathedral also underwent change during the Reformation. Late medieval cathedrals were filled with devotional images of the Virgin and the saints. Whether violently or legally conducted, the removal of images left its mark on many cathedrals, particularly in northern Europe. While Reformed leaders condemned illegal and violent iconoclasm, they often applauded the resulting "purification." Empty niches and chapels were refilled or restored if the cathedral remained under Catholic control, providing opportunities for new artistic and devotional styles. The old images and altars were sometimes destroyed by violence, but where the magistrates oversaw the removal, as was the case in Nuremberg and Zurich, many works of art were returned to the families that had donated them. Occasionally the population did not feel that the magistrates were sufficiently fast or thorough. In Strasbourg the magistrates removed popular devotional images from the cathedral in 1524, but these actions were followed by popular iconoclasm throughout the city. Even the most exhaustive cleansing of images from cathedrals left traces behind. The upper reaches of the building were usually untouched, as were those images most closely integrated into the structure of the building.

In cities where the Reformation prevailed, cathedrals were adapted architecturally to highlight the new central function of the sermon. The medieval cathedral had been designed as a setting for its principal liturgical function, the Mass. The arrangement of the choir and altar served to increase the separation between lay and clerical participation in the Mass, with the choir screen often obscuring much of the proceedings from lay view. In Reformation cathedrals, this separation and obscurity were rejected. Choir screens were removed and altars brought forward, so that the minister faced the congregation during the Eucharist. The lectern or pulpit from which the scripture was read and the sermon preached became the central focus of both the liturgy and the architecture. Huldrych Zwingli even called for the removal of organs from the churches and cathedral of Zurich.

Churches built after the sixteenth century in Reformation cities reflect these design changes. Most European cities, however, already had an existing cathedral that they attempted to adapt to the new usages. While preaching was no stranger to cathedrals, having been a growing feature of late medieval religious life, the centrality of the sermon in the divine service called for new architectural responses. A 1650 painting of the Basel Münster illustrates one solution. Instead of facing the eastern end of the nave, where the altar is placed, the pews of the congregation are centered on the pulpit, which was constructed in the second half of the fifteenth century about halfway down the nave on one of the southern piers. The choir and side chapels have been opened up to allow for additional seating, all facing the pulpit. While the altar has been moved in front of the choir screen, the focus of all the action has been shifted to the pulpit, where the scripture would be read and the sermon preached.

A different solution was found in Zurich. In June 1524 the churches of Zurich, including the Grossmünster, were systematically stripped of religious images and architectural elements, such as the choir screen and choir stalls, which related to the old order of worship. Gutscher and Senn have argued that some of the building materials from the choir were used to construct a new "pulpit screen" that housed the chair from which Zwingli preached. By locating the pulpit on the site of the old choir screen the natural architectural focus of the cathedral was retained, while the liturgical focus was shifted to the sermon.

The new emphasis on the sermon affected Catholic and Counter-Reformation architecture as well. Some late sixteenth- and early seventeenth-century Catholic churches adopted this placement of the pulpit at the front of the church. This innovation was slow to affect cathedrals, however, as few new cathedrals were built during this period.

Even when no major architectural changes were made in the cathedral, the Reformed liturgy reflected a change in the use of space. In Strasbourg the stone altar was replaced with a movable wooden table that was placed at the eastern end of the nave, in front of the choir screen. This allowed the pastor to perform liturgical functions facing west toward the nave, while standing either behind or in front of the table. The celebration of the Lord's Supper, as well as baptisms and weddings took place at this table. The separate baptismal font fell out of use, as did the side chapels of the cathedral. For scripture readings and the sermon, the pastor moved to the pulpit, which was elevated and located more centrally in the nave. While this use of the pulpit was not new, the movement of the pastor and all of his activities now took place in full view of the congregation.

Whether modified or not, in both Protestant and Catholic lands cathedrals maintained a central place in the religious life of their cities. The financial and spiritual resources of the church were concentrated in the bishop and cathedral chapters and dispensed from there in an attempt to retain, capture, or recapture the souls of the faithful.

[See also Monasteries, article on The Continent.]

BIBLIOGRAPHY

Bornert, René. *La réforme protestante du culte à Strasbourg au XVIe siècle, 1523–1598.* Studies in Medieval and Reformation Thought, vol. 28. Leiden, 1981.

Chrisman, Miriam Usher. *Strasbourg and the Reform: A Study in the Process of Change.* Reprint, New Haven, 1983.

Christensen, Carl C. "Iconoclasm and the Preservation of Ecclesiastical Art in Reformation Nuremberg." *Archiv für Reformationgeschichte* 61 (1970), 205–221.

Delumeau, Jean. *Catholicism between Luther and Voltaire: A New View of the Counter-Reformation.* Philadelphia, 1977.

Diefendorf, Barbara B. *Beneath the Cross: Catholics and Huguenots in Sixteenth-Century Paris.* New York, 1991.

Galpern, A. N. *The Religions of the People in Sixteenth-Century Champagne.* Cambridge, Mass., 1976.

Garside, Charles. *Zwingli and the Arts.* Reprint, New York, 1981.

Gutscher, Daniel, and Matthias Senn. "Zwinglis Kanzel im Zürcher Grossmünster: Reformation und künstlerischer Neubeginn." *Unsere Kunstdenkmäler Nos monuments d'art et d'histoire* 35.3 (1984), 310–318.

Rotach, Peter. "Das Münster als Reformiertes Gotteshaus." In *Das Basler Münster,* pp. 16–31. Basel, 1982.

Smith, Jeffrey Chipps. *German Sculpture of the Later Renaissance c.1520–1580: Art in an Age of Uncertainty.* Princeton, 1994.

MARY JANE CHASE

CATHERINE DE MÉDICIS (1519–1589), daughter of Lorenzo de Médicis, who was a nephew of Pope Leo X. Catherine was married to Henry of Orléans, second son of Francis I. Her husband, ruling France as Henry II (r. 1547–1559), increased the repression of the Protestants. After the Treaty of Cateau-Cambrésis (1559) with Spain and England, the accidental death of the king brought his son Francis II to the throne. The young king, married to Mary Stuart, came under the influence of her uncles, the ultra-Catholic Duke Francis of Guise and his brother Charles, cardinal of Lorraine. The Queen mother was therefore unable to avoid the hardening of the persecution of Protestants until the death of Francis II resulted in Catherine becoming regent for her young son, Charles IX in December 1560. She attempted then a religious conciliation with the help of Chancellor Michel de l'Hôpital: in September 1561, at Poissy, she convoked a colloquy between leaders of the Roman Catholics and French Calvinists, but without success. After the massacre of Protestants at Wassy by the duke of Guise on 1 March 1562, the first civil and religious war began. At the Peace of Amboise (19 March 1563), a degree of religious toleration was decreed and French Catholics and Protestants were united in expelling English soldiers from French soil. Catherine tried to consolidate the pacification by accompanying Charles IX, now declared old enough to rule, on a tour of the realm from 1564 to 1566.

In Bayonne, Catherine met her daughter Elizabeth, wife of Philip II, king of Spain, and Fernando Álvarez de Toledo, duke of Alba, both of whom urged her to punish Protestants as rebels. Meanwhile the allies of the king of Spain, especially the Guise family, formed the Catholic League. The victory of Duke Henry of Anjou, second son of Catherine, over the Huguenot prince of Condé at Jarnac (13 March 1569), and Catholic victories against Admiral Gaspard de Coligny, the new chief of the Huguenots, at Moncontour on 3 October 1569, led to the Peace of Saint-Germain (1570), which gave the Protestants some secure towns and permitted some Calvinists the free exercise of their faith.

Admiral Coligny then became a conspicuous political figure at the court of Charles IX, and Catherine feared Coligny's influence over Charles. Whether Catherine was in collusion with the young Duke Henry of Guise is a matter of scholarly dispute. In any case, at the time of the wedding feast of Princess Marguerite, Charles IX's youngest sister, to the Calvinist Henry of Navarre (Henry IV), the Catholic League struck. A deliberate attempt to murder Coligny on 22 August 1572 was successful the next day when troops led by the duke of Guise attacked and killed the wounded Coligny. This act precipitated the general massacre of Protestants in Paris, on Saint Bartholomew's Day, 24 August 1572, and in areas beyond Paris in the following weeks.

In 1573 Catherine helped her son, the duke of Anjou, to become elected king of Poland, and in France she tried to reestablish peace. Meanwhile, Protestants and *politiques* set up a confederation in the south of France, and the Catholics resumed the struggle when, after the death of Charles IX on 30 May 1574, his brother became Henry III. But Catherine's youngest son, Duke Francis of Alençon, escaped from the court on 15 September 1575, to become a leader of the Huguenots, and through him his mother earnestly tried to negotiate a truce. The Peace of Monsieur (2 May 1576) involved both limited toleration of the Protestant religion and political reform. The king granted to the Huguenots public exercise of the Calvinist religion throughout France, except near the court and Paris. He established mixed Parlements, half Catholic, half Protestant. Eight security towns were given to the Huguenots. The memories of Admiral Coligny and of the victims of Saint Bartholomew's Day were rehabilitated. But the Huguenots, led by King Henry IV, engaged in long and acrimonious debate over these articles.

In 1576 the Catholic League attempted to use the ambition of the Guise family to increase Spanish power. Politics thus became dominant in the succeeding Wars of Religion. During the years marked by two sessions of the Estates-General at Blois, Catherine tried to negotiate for her son Henry III an accommodation with the opposing factions of Duke Henry of Guise and of Henry of Navarre, each contending to be heir to the French crown after the death of the duke of Alençon-Anjou. The war of the three Henrys marked her failure to reconcile her son with the powerful leaders of the Catholic League in France and of the Huguenots. Henry III took matters into his own hands and ordered the murder of the duke and the cardinal of Guise. Catherine died in Blois a few days later. Henry III was assassinated in 1589, and thus ended the house of Valois and the reign of the sons of Catherine de Médicis.

Catherine was truly concerned to bring about civil and religious peace and to keep control of the government of France in the hands of her children. She seems to have been without a clear position in the matter of religion, and her actions against the Huguenots were dictated primarily by political considerations.

BIBLIOGRAPHY

Cloulas, Ivan. *Catherine de Medicis.* New ed. Paris, 1987. Contains important bibliography.

Constant, Jean-Marie. *Les Guise.* Paris, 1984.

Erlanger, Philippe. *Saint Bartholomew's Night: The Massacre of Saint Bartholomew.* Translated by Patrick O'Brian. Westport, Conn., 1975.

Shimizu, J. *Conflict of Loyalties: Politics and Religion in the Career of Gaspard de Coligny, Admiral of France, 1519–1572.* Geneva, 1970.

Stephan, Raoul. *Histoire du protestantisme français.* Paris, 1961.

Sutherland, N. M. *The French Secretaries of State in the Age of Catherine de Medici.* Reprint, Westport, Conn., 1976. Presents the story of the wheels of French government.

Thompson, James Westfall. *The Wars of Religion in France, 1559–1576: The Huguenots, Catherine de Medici, Philip II.* New ed. New York, 1957/58.

IVAN CLOULAS

CATHERINE OF ARAGON (1485–1536), first consort of Henry VIII.

The daughter of Ferdinand of Aragon and Isabella of Castile, she was given a learned education, having been taught to read Christian works in Latin. In 1501, at the age of sixteen, she sailed to England, where she married fifteen-year-old Arthur, prince of Wales, who died some five months later. After his succession in 1509, Arthur's younger brother Henry, on the authority of a papal dispensation, wed Catherine, and they were crowned queen and king together. In 1516 their only surviving child, Mary, was born, for whom they provided a humanist education. By 1527, because he was greatly concerned about the deaths of his male infants, Henry had begun to question the validity of his union with Catherine. Charging that their marriage violated the Levitical text that a man may not take his brother's wife, he ordered Thomas, Cardinal Wolsey, to institute divorce proceedings. At a legatine hearing at Blackfriars that Wolsey and Cardinal Lorenzo Campeggio convened in 1529, Catherine denied that she had known Arthur carnally, attempting thereby to negate the authority of the Levitical text. The proceedings were subsequently transferred to Rome, where Pope Clément VII ultimately decided in her favor. In 1531 she was expelled from court and prevented from seeing her daughter.

In 1533, after the king had secretly wed Anne Boleyn, his chief minister Thomas Cromwell began to supervise the passage of statutes that resulted in the English Reformation. These authorized Thomas Cranmer, archbishop of Canterbury, to annul her marriage, to favor the children of the new queen in the succession, and to set up an autonomous church. Catherine died on 7 January 1536, leaving the Reformation as her legacy, for when she refused to accept the divorce and retire to a nunnery, the king decided to adopt this drastic solution to his succession crisis.

BIBLIOGRAPHY

Mattingly, Garrett. *Catherine of Aragon.* Boston, 1941. Standard, extremely sympathetic biography of this queen.

Warnicke, Retha M. *Women of the English Renaissance and Reformation.* Westport, Conn., 1983. Contains useful information about the classical training of women, including Catherine.

RETHA M. WARNICKE

CATHOLIC CHURCH. See Roman Catholicism.

CATHOLIC LEAGUE. In response to what many French Catholics regarded as the laxity of the monarchy in eradicating heresy in France, political-religious organizations (or leagues) of Catholics appeared as early as 1561 to confront the Huguenots on the local level. The first kingdomwide league appeared in 1576 in response to the Peace of Monsieur in which Henry III had given the Huguenots important political and religious concessions. This agreement imposed a Protestant governor on the strongly Catholic province of Picardy and granted the Huguenots the stronghold of Péronne as a place of security. A group of Catholic nobles led by the commander of Péronne, Jacques d'Humières, issued a call for the Catholics of Picardy to resist the Protestant takeover. Having organized Picardy, d'Humières took his call for a Catholic league to the entire realm. Henry, duke of Guise, head of a family long active in the Catholic cause, became the head of this league. Henry III, however, quickly recognized the threat to his power posed by the league, with its oath of "full prompt obedience and service to the chief." The king rescinded some of the concessions he had given to the Protestants and proclaimed himself the head of the league, costing the league much of its appeal to the Catholic nobility. It declined rapidly, and historians do not agree on whether it continued to exist over the next eight years.

Suddenly in June 1584 the French Catholics had a powerful new reason to reorganize the league. The death of Henry III's younger brother placed the king of Navarre, Henry of Bourbon, next in line for the throne, if the customary law of succession, the Salic Law, were followed. Henry of Navarre was not only a Huguenot but also had commanded the Protestant forces for the previous several years in the civil war then raging. The revitalized league had a vastly broader base of support than in 1576. Catholic nobles in much larger numbers joined it, and more significantly, the urban Catholics, especially in Paris, also became involved. The league of the nobility and that of the cities were really two separate organizations tied together by their common cause and the leadership of Henry of Guise.

The first important move of the new league was the secret Treaty of Joinville in December 1584 between Guise and Philip II of Spain. Philip saw the league and the Guises as the means by which any French aid for the Dutch rebellion might be forestalled. He agreed to recognize Cardinal Charles of Bourbon, Henry's uncle, as the rightful successor to the French throne and to provide a large subsidy to the league in exchange for a pledge to help defeat the rebellion against Philip in the Low Countries. In Paris and other strongly Catholic cities, the league organized opposition to the succession of Navarre and to Henry III, who was disliked both because he seemed too accepting of Navarre and for his extravagant and immoral lifestyle.

In Paris the league was organized according to the sixteen wards of the city, hence the name "Sixteen" for the radical urban element of the league. The social background of the Sixteen has been the subject of a great deal of historical scholarship. The current consensus is that they drew their greatest strength from the petit bourgeoisie—the lesser merchants and minor government officials. The league's control of most of the Parisian presses allowed it to engage in a large propaganda campaign against Henry III, Navarre, the *politiques* (those who believed that Protestantism had to be tolerated for the good of the state), and the Huguenots. Perhaps more importantly most of the Parisian preachers were also adherents. Fiery curés such as Jean Boucher thundered league propaganda at their congregations. The urban league combined a populist political agenda with rigorous opposition to Protestantism and those regarded as too sympathetic to heresy.

At the national level the Catholic League issued the Declaration of Péronne (1585), proclaiming its goals as the reform of the state and the protection of the Catholic church. It declared that a fundamental law of Catholicity required the king to be Catholic, thereby excluding Henry of Navarre from the succession. The league organized an army under the duke of Guise, who defeated a Protestant force at Auneau (1587). A royal force in the area prevented Guise from pursuing and destroying the Protestant army. The Parisian leaguers were outraged by this act, and antagonism toward Henry III increased rapidly. They were eager for Guise to come to Paris in order to proclaim him king. Determined not to let it happen, Henry III forbade Guise to enter Paris and ordered Swiss troops into the city. When the duke did nevertheless enter Paris, popular enthusiasm for him combined with anger at the presence of the foreign troops to precipitate a popular uprising known as the Day of the Barricades (12 May 1588). At day's end Henry III had fled, and the league was in control of Paris. The Sixteen purged the city government of royalists and installed their own men in the positions of authority. Paris became the center of a broad confederation, the Sainte Union, of league-controlled towns across France.

Henry III hoped to gain time for a counterstroke by agreeing to the league's demand for a meeting of the Estates-General. When it met in July 1588, the league presented a broad program of reform that included triennial meetings of the Estates-General to approve any new taxes. It also required the king to accept the law of Catholicity and to recognize the cardinal of Bourbon as his successor. Henry's acquiescence was only feigned. He revenged himself on the Guises by ordering the assassination of the duke and his brother, the cardinal of Guise (December 1588), and slapped the cardinal of Bourbon and several league leaders into prison.

The rage of the Sixteen spilled over in a great number of pamphlets and sermons that proclaimed the right of the people to control the monarchy, take arms against an evil king, and impose the punishment due tyrants—tyrannicide. A young Dominican friar took them at their word. Pretending to be a royalist, he gained an audience with Henry and stabbed him to death (August 1589). Henry III's death left the succession to the throne in doubt. Most French Catholics refused to accept Navarre as king because of his religion, but his uncle, Charles, remained in prison so the league could not crown him king. But enough of the royalist Catholic nobles joined forces with Navarre that he was able to place Paris under siege during the summer of 1590. Philip II sent the army of Flanders to relieve the city, stalemating the military situation. The political situation became equally stalemated when Charles, cardinal of Bourbon, died.

The Sixteen's control over Paris began to waver, especially after the murder of Barnabé Brisson, a respected magistrate, and two other magistrates (1591) for communicating with Navarre. The league tried to break the stalemate and reassert its control by convoking the Estates-General for Paris to elect a Catholic king (1593). Factionalism in the league prevented the league estates from agreeing on a candidate, but the possibility that they might be able to come up with a king prompted Henry of Navarre to announce his intention to convert to Catholicism. Despite strong skepticism on the part of many leaguers about his sincerity, Henry's attendance at mass in July 1593 began a steady wave of defections from the league. His coronation at Chartres (February 1594) was shortly followed by his triumphal entry into Paris. While some of the Sixteen, such as Jean Boucher, never accepted Henry as king and some league nobles continued to fight in alliance with Spain, Henry IV's securing of Paris, the heart of the league, marked the effective end of the Catholic League.

The ten years of the Catholic League marked the worst period of the over thirty years of civil war and instability. When it was over, the French people found that they agreed with the *politiques* that a strong monarchy was necessary to prevent any recurrence of the troubles, paving the way for the acceptance of royal absolutism, and that toleration of the Huguenots was a necessary evil, allowing Henry IV to issue the Edict of Nantes (1598) without a great deal of opposition.

[*See also* Henry III of France; Huguenots; Lorraine-Guise, House of; Navarre, House of; Paris; Philip II of Spain; Politiques; *and* Wars of Religion.]

BIBLIOGRAPHY

Ascoli, Peter, ed. *Dialogue d'entre le maheustre et le manant.* Geneva, 1977. Modern edition of the most informative source on the Paris league.

Barnavi, Elie. *Le parti de Dieu: Étude sociale et politique des chefs de la Ligue parisienne, 1585–1594.* Louvain, 1982. Sees the league as a prototype of more modern political parties.

Barnavi, Elie, and Robert Descimon. *La Sainte Ligue, le juge et la potence.* Paris, 1985. Interesting collaboration of two historians with strongly contradictory views on the league.

Baumgartner, Frederic J. *Radical Reactionaries: The Political Thought of the French Catholic League.* Geneva, 1976. A thorough analysis of leaguer thought.

Benedict, Philip. *Rouen during the Wars of Religion.* Cambridge, 1981. Valuable account of the league outside of Paris.

Buisseret, David. *Henry IV.* London, 1984. The best recent biography of that king.

Crouzet, Denis. *Les guerriers de Dieu: La violence au temps des troubles de religion.* 2 vols. Paris, 1990. Provocative study of the Wars of Religion that ties the league to an outburst of eschatological anxiety and argues strongly for the primacy of religious motivation in its creation.

Descimon, Robert. *Qui etaient les Seize? Mythes et réalités de la Ligue parisienne.* Paris, 1983. Finds that the league was a continuation of medieval urban movements.

Greengrass, Mark. *France in the Age of Henry IV: The Struggle for Stability.* New York, 1985. Does a fine job of placing the league in its political context.

Jensen, DeLamar. *Diplomacy and Dogmatism: Berardino de Mendoza and the French Catholic League.* Cambridge, Mass., 1964. Emphasizes the role of the Spanish in the league's activities.

Salmon, J. H. M. *Society in Crisis: France in the Sixteenth Century.* New York, 1975. Essential work on France in the era of the league.

FREDERIC J. BAUMGARTNER

CATHOLIC REFORMATION. The program of the *reformatio Ecclesiae* had been officially placed on the agenda of Christian society from the time of the Great Schism (1309–1417). The Council of Constance opened on 6 November 1414 with a document from the antipope John XXIII (1370–1419) that called for working "*ad pacem, exaltationem et reformationem ecclesiae, ac tranquillitatem populi christiani*" ("for the peace, exaltation and reformation of the Church and the tranquility of the Christian people"). From that time on, among those who held responsibility for governing the church and society, there was continual discussion and debate of *reformatio* as an urgent problem, but when the work of Martin Luther, Huldrych Zwingli, John Calvin, and the other reformers in conflict with the papacy took center stage in Europe, the term began to be suspect in the Catholic world. The Lombard priest Castellino da Castello, who had founded a "Company for Christian Reformation" in 1536, had to change its name. Anyone who maintained that the church had need of reform had to make the term more specific by adding the adjective "Catholic" if he wanted to distinguish himself from the Reformation led by Luther, Calvin, and others. According to Johannes Gropper, a canon of Cologne, a "*pia et catholica Reformatio*" was what good Christians longed for (1541). Thus, as early as the sixteenth century, people were consciously using the term *Catholic Reformation* to designate a movement that sought the reform of the church but that distanced itself from the path chosen by Luther, Zwingli, Calvin, and the other leaders of the Protestant Reformation. Even so, although some promoters of a Catholic Reformation took pains to delineate their differences with respect to the Protestant Reformation, the climate of spiritual warfare that became dominant from the mid-1500s caused a suspicion of heresy to hang over any kind of criticism regarding the clergy and particularly the papacy. Yet it was precisely the need to silence the criticisms coming from the Protestant world that made it possible to carry out a series of reform measures that had been blocked up to that point by the Curia Romana.

The Council of Trent represented the historic opportunity offered to the currents of reform within the church. It was precisely by studying the history of the church between the reform councils of the 1400s and the Council of Trent that nineteenth-century Protestant historians, such as Leopold von Ranke and Wilhelm Maurenbrecher, discovered the existence of reform currents within the Catholic world. These currents had fed a revival in Catholicism, which, in turn, made possible a renewal of the church of Rome. The term *Catholic Reformation* was then taken up by Catholic historians in the twentieth century, thanks to the work of Hubert Jedin. This term, by the common consensus of historians, has come to be used to designate all those attempts, plans, and initiatives beginning in the 1400s that aimed at a renewal of Christian society and a moral and disciplinary reform of the church *in capite et in membris* ("in its head and members"). The main lines of these movements will be outlined here briefly. It is important to note first, however, that the *renovatio* ("renewal") of the church, which many of these movements aimed at (for example, in Girolamo Savonarola's movement), was something different from *reformatio* in the sense of a return to the ancient "form." The political and legal life of medieval society had experienced "reform" in the sense of a periodic elimination of irregularities and deformations that had become attached to the trunk of the ancient norm. Even at the end of the 1500s, the idea of reform was portrayed in Cesare Ripa's treatise as the operation of cutting away from the trunk of a plant those branches that have been growing in a haphazard way. It was in this sense that Dante acclaimed the Emperor Justinian as the lawgiver who had removed "excess and vanity" from the laws. In contrast, the expectation of an overall renewal of religious life and society, nourished by astrological and millenarian calculations and by apocalyptic and prophetic messages, gave rise between 1400 and 1500 to movements to create new forms of living in society. These movements ranged from Savonarola's movement in Florence to various forms of millenarianism inspired by Joachim da Fiore.

The preaching of Savonarola offers a good example of how the ideas of reform and renewal could meet and overlap while remaining distinct. During the first part of his life, Savonarola was a penitential preacher not unlike others, except on account of his fame and his effect on so many who were active in the priories of the time and who had been won over to a return to the strict observance of the rule. In contrast, beginning in 1494 and up to his death, Savonarola's preaching became visionary and prophetic; from themes of reform he shifted to themes of a general renewal of Christian society. Until the Council of Trent the two trends, that of reform and that of renewal, fed on one another, yet without merging. They were like two distinct streams that continually intertwined, sometimes hindering each other and sometimes joining together. The moral condemnation of the ecclesiastical world and especially of the Curia Romana constituted their common premise, but after Luther's emergence and with the deepening of the rift between Catholics and Protestants, any form of critique and polemics directed against the clergy and against Rome now appeared suspect. After the council any expectation of a general renewal of Christian society was condemned as heretical.

The agenda of reforming the church *in capite et in membris*, which the councils of Constance and Basel had intended to carry out, did not succeed. The papacy regained the initiative, thanks to the alliance between the popes and national monarchies, through the policy of concordats. Even so, the idea that the council could resolve the problems of the church retained its full strength: it was to the council that Savonarola appealed against Alexander VI, and later Luther followed that same path. These appeals were worrisome for the popes, who feared a resurgence of conciliarism (the idea that the authority of ecumenical councils is higher than that of the pope). This is why the Council of Trent had such a long prehistory beset by obstacles. There was the possibility that the council would become a weapon in the hands of a hostile political power; that is precisely what happened with the convocation of the Gallican council of Pisa-Milan in 1511, which the French faction sought in order to attack Julius II. The Fifth Lateran Council, convened by Julius II in response and which Leo X continued, was the papal reply to the conciliarist idea: a council under the direct control of the pope and ready to accede to his wishes.

The Fifth Lateran Council may be considered as the last possible opportunity available to the Catholic Reformation. In his opening address the general of the Augustinians declared that the reform of the church was the council's task. The council, interrupted by the death of Julius II, was resumed by the new pope, the very youthful Leo X. On account of his youth and his reputation for having many good qualities, Leo X was hailed as the "angelic pope" that many had hoped for. Among the many proposals for reform that reached him when the council resumed, there was one of great breadth: the *Libellus* of the Camaldolese monks Peter (alias Vincenzo Querini) and Paul (alias Tommaso Giustiniani). For these two monks the inner "restoration" of the church was the necessary prerequisite for taking on tasks of a worldwide scope. It was a question of unifying the known world under the one Christian church by obliterating—by force, if necessary—the resistance of other religions (beginning with the Jewish religion and then by defeating the Muslims militarily), by unifying all Christians under obedience to Rome, and finally by conquering for Christianity the peoples who had been recently discovered. For these monks the vast horizons of a world that had recently become wider and the urgency of religious conquest made the inner reform of the church necessary. This "reformation" had to embrace all the members of the hierarchy, from the head in Rome (the Curia and the papal court) down to the religious orders, the bishops, the secular clergy, and the Christian people. The great number of religious orders was to be eliminated, with the greater part of those remaining brought under the rule of Saint Benedict, while the conventual branches of the mendicant orders were to be condemned to extinction. To remedy the ignorance and superstition rampant among the clergy and people, the two Camaldolese monks proposed drastic measures: theological studies and rigorous examinations for the clergy; translation of the Bible into the various modern languages to offer all the people the possibility of reading sacred scripture; strict laws and even the use of the stake against witches and sorcerers; and reform of the liturgy to abolish all aspects that smacked of magic. It was a long and detailed list that left untouched no aspect of the ecclesiastical structure, from the worldly lifestyle of the cardinals' courts—which, as Paolo Cortesi's contemporary work *De Cardinalatu* illustrates, were like the courts of lay princes—to the problem of nonresidence of bishops in their dioceses and the violent clashes among preachers of the various orders. As for the more cultural aspects, the two monks denounced the renaissance of pagan culture and proposed for the clergy a religious formation founded not on Scholasticism but on the church fathers. The Fifth Lateran Council appeared to take into account these demands: Leo X set up a commission for reform (25 April 1513) that was to deal with the dicasteries of the Curia in particular, which were under attack for their excessive Inquisitorial methods. The outcomes, however, were disappointing. The reform bull approved by the council on 5 May 1514, for example, regulated the matter of conferring benefices, forbidding the conferral of more than four benefices on a single person; however, it exempted cardinals from even this rather weak measure. As for the religious orders, the decree on preaching (approved on 19 December 1516) imposed a certain measure of control over their activity, but it did so mainly to rein in prophetic and apocalyptic preaching of the kind Savonarola practiced. The Florentine provincial council, summoned in 1517 by Cardinal Giulio de' Medici (later Pope Clement VII), adopted and reinforced these measures. Meanwhile, the concordat of Leo X with France (1516) showed how even the supporters of the council preferred to come to an agreement with the papacy, relinquishing any attempt to impose the *reformatio capitis*, or "reform of the head" (i.e., the pope).

The path of the "reform of the members" was followed by many, both laity and clergy, as well as individuals and entire religious congregations. In the religious orders there was a movement toward the observance of the rule, which had begun as early as the end of the fourteenth century.

What was intended was a return to the rigid observance of the rule while striving to realize the model of perfection in the religious life. This meant a return to the vow of poverty, with renunciation of personal property; the respect of the cloister; and much more severe inner discipline. Thus were born within the Benedictine order the congregations of Santa Giustina, Valladolid, and Chézal-Benoît and the unions of Melk and Bursfeld. In the five mendicant orders (the Franciscans, Dominicans, Norbertines, Augustinians, and Trinitarians) the observantist movement overtook one priory after another. At the Council of Constance the observants of Burgundy, France, and Lorraine obtained the right to be under their own vicars, with a jurisdiction separate from that of the conventuals, even though they remained subordinate to them at least formally. In Italy the protection accorded to the observants by Pope Martin V and the extraordinary success of the preaching of Bernardino of Siena caused their number to increase significantly: at Bernardino's death (1444) there were more than four thousand members. Among the Dominicans the observance of the rule was a matter of overriding concern: the major concern of Savonarola was for the Florentine priory of San Marco and his attempt to set up a Tuscan congregation of reformed Dominican priories. The fundamental problem for the religious orders was to prevent the Roman benefice system from bringing priories to the brink of economic and moral ruin through the system of temporary transfers of ecclesiastical benefices. By becoming affiliated with congregations, such as that of Santa Giustina, rich Benedictine abbeys could evade the temporary benefice system that allowed lay and ecclesiastical princes to exploit the abbey's revenues.

From the observantist movement there emerged a number of famous preachers, such as Bernardino of Siena and John of Capistrano. In addition, throughout the fifteenth century many bishops came from religious orders and brought a new sense of commitment to the pastoral leadership of their dioceses. Among these were the Carthusian monk Nicolo Albergati, bishop of Bologna; Giovanni Tavelli of Tossignano from the order of Saint Jerome, who was bishop of Ferrara; and the Dominican Antonino Pierozzi, the archbishop of Florence. Thanks to the work of the Franciscan Francisco Jiménez de Cisneros, there was a profound renewal of the entire Spanish episcopate, the results of which were apparent at the Council of Trent. Manifestations of renewal, however, and of the "reform of the members" had spread even beyond the religious orders. The model of religious life offered by Gerhard Groote (1340–1384) gave birth to the congregation of Augustinian canons at Windesheim and the Brothers and Sisters of the Common Life, a lay movement that was active over a large area of Europe. The most famous text that reflects the religiosity of this movement is *De Imitatione Christi* (Imitation of Christ) by Thomas à Kempis. Small circles that had considerable influence at the grass roots also formed around some great women who had significant mystical experiences—for example, Catherine of Genoa and Catherine of Bologna. It was one of the followers of Catherine of Genoa, the Genovese lawyer Ettore Vernazza, who founded the Oratory of Divine Love. The brothers of the oratory practiced forms of charity and aid that were traditional in confraternities, such as caring for the sick in hospitals (in particular the "incurable" victims of syphilis) and ministering to those condemned to death, but they did so to attain a kind of moral perfection that consisted in "planting charity in hearts" and the imitation of Christ. In these movements the religious problem of justification and the desire to escape the punishments of purgatory went hand in hand with the desire to attain Christian perfection in secular life. The Oratory of Divine Love spread from Genoa to other cities. Its presence was particularly significant in the Rome of Leo X, where some important members of the Curia became members. The outcome of these lay movements was varied: some members remained lay, and their religious concern led them to heretical outcomes, as in the case of Marcantonio Flaminio; others translated their desire to ascend toward perfection into a religious rule. In this manner some members of the Roman oratory founded the Congregation of Clerics Regular, also called the Theatines or "Chietini," the latter derived from the name of the diocese of one of the founders, Gian Pietro Carafa, bishop of Chieti (later Paul IV).

Thus, along with the reform of the traditional orders, new orders were founded. Besides the Theatines, founded by Cajetan and Carafa, there were the Barnabites (founded by Antonio Maria Zaccaria, Antonio Morigia, and Bartolomeo Ferrari), the Somaschi (founded by Jerome Emiliani), and the Jesuits. In contrast to the medieval mendicant orders, these were congregations of clerics regular. They arose from the need to offer the laity high-quality ecclesiastical ministry and a model of a priest equipped with solid preparation and good morals, in contrast to the majority of secular clergy of the time. Alongside the men's branches, there often arose corresponding congregations of women: the Angelicans, founded by Luigia Torella, countess of Guastalla, were linked to the Barnabites, on whom they exerted a profound influence through the "divine mother" Paola Antonia Negri. The specific problems of women, however, led to innovative solutions without parallel in the men's orders; related to this was the work of Angela Merici of Brescia, who founded the Ursulines, an innovative attempt to accommodate the condition of unmarried women who did not wish to subject themselves to the restrictions of the cloister connected with conventual life.

In these religious congregations and foundations of the first part of the 1500s, there was still remarkable freedom of initiative and a search for new formulas for spiritual perfection. That freedom subsequently decreased in the climate of conflict and suspicion that marked the middle of the century. It was a different matter in Spain, where the activity of the Inquisition led to conflict with the tendencies of the *Alumbrados* and to suspicion of any experiment that was even remotely similar. This explains, for example, why the young Basque nobleman Ignatius Loyola (1491?-1556) was more than once the object of suspicion and scrutiny on the part of church authorities. The same was to occur later with Luis de León and Teresa of Ávila. In Italy there were few condemnations issued by the Inquisition, and those were mainly against preaching on the model of Savonarola or against the philosophical teaching of Pietro Pomponazzi. One condemnation in 1510 was issued against the popular preacher Pietro Bernardini da Lucca for his teaching on Christ's conception.

Many new orders sprouted on the trunks of older orders and were motivated by the desire to create an institutional setting more conducive to the observance of the rule. The most fertile ground in this sense was the Franciscan order. There were the Minims, founded in 1435 by Saint Francis of Paola, as well as the Capuchins, founded in 1526 by Matteo da Bascio. In all these cases the initiative was undertaken by friars dissatisfied with the lifestyle in religious houses that had been won over by the observantist movement and who desired a stricter religious life. Indeed, the observant communities, owing to their success, had become numerous. In 1517 Leo X officially recognized their supremacy within the Franciscan order, thus reversing the traditional subjection of the observants to the conventuals. Francisco de Quiñones, who enjoyed the trust of Charles V, was chosen as general of the order. (In 1523, when Hernán Cortés requested that religious be sent to preach the gospel in Mexico, Quiñones chose a group of observants of the ascetic "Guard of the Holy Gospel" of Estremadura.) Their growing success, however, also had its drawbacks: the religious houses of the observants became ever larger, richer, and more comfortable; their libraries were well stocked; and their preaching became elaborate. All these things were a source of disillusionment for men who thirsted for penance and gospel simplicity. Thus, they opted for an eremitic lifestyle, with coarse religious dress that bespoke poverty and with the closest possible similarity to the habits worn by the first nucleus of Franciscans. Matteo da Bascio, for example, chose a capuche, or hood, that was not round but rectangular and connected to the tunic, which, according to the oral and pictoral descriptions, more closely resembled the habit worn by Francis himself. The preaching of these men was deliberately sparse and harsh: Matteo da Bascio's preaching was often pared down to the cry "All sinners to hell!" which he shouted as he ran into the public squares. This made an enormous impression that was enhanced by his appearance. His was not an isolated case: in the Italy of the late 1400s and early 1500s the preaching of penance found its most popular expression in the so-called hermits—men who would come down from remote refuges in forests and on mountains brandishing large crosses and announcing terrible scourges from God in punishment for sin. The wars in Italy and all over Europe, along with pillaging, epidemics, the pressing menace of the Turks, and finally the news about Luther, appeared to be the fulfillment of these penitential prophecies. Among the causes for periodic waves of fear and expectation of extraordinary events was the renewed pagan belief in astral conjunctions. Thus, Christian prophecy and pagan divination had a combined effect. For 1524 a conjunction under the zodiac sign of Pisces gave rise to predictions of such natural disasters as, for example, another Great Flood, but the astrological prediction often took on a penitential tone: God wished to punish the sins of his church, which was not reforming itself. The spread of the Lutheran movement and the fire storm of the Peasants' War began to raise concerns even in Rome, where at first there had been a tendency to minimize the prophecies.

Nevertheless, in 1524 a somewhat reformist agenda was implemented in Rome: a jubilee was declared for the following year, and in preparation for the jubilee clerics were ordered to return to the observance of canonical norms in their manner of dress and were prohibited from wearing long beards. Clement VII tried to organize a meeting in Rome of a group of prelates from various parts of Christendom to listen to their advice on reform measures. The wars in Italy then diverted the pope's attention, but with the Sack of Rome the question of reform was raised with renewed urgency, while individual religious crises led various churchmen to perform their duties in a more rigorous manner. Of particular significance was the turn taken by Gian Matteo Giberti, the powerful datary of Clement VII, who left Rome for the diocese of Verona, where he became an exemplary bishop. In addition, Jacopo Sadoleto, bishop of Carpentras; Gian Pietro Carafa, who had given up the two bishoprics to which he held title for reasons of conscience; Onofrio Bartolini, bishop of Pisa; and Ercole Gonzaga, from a powerful family in Mantua, began, along with Giberti, to represent a new awareness of episcopal duties. Meanwhile, the call for a reform *in capite* was becoming stronger. On the political side the victory of Charles V was hastening the convocation of a council. The Erasmian faction, represented in the chancellery of the emperor by Alfonso de Valdés, undertook a campaign to promote a reform of the church that would be entrusted to the emperor; however, Clement VII's resolute hostility to the proposal of a council, as well as the vicissitudes of European politics, made the possibility of a council more remote.

With Pope Paul III (Alessandro Farnese) things changed. As a shrewd and able politician, the new pope, inasmuch as he was personally a perfect representative of the world of the Curia and its customs, gave an important sign of an about-face. By convening a council at Mantua and by sending the nuncio Pier Paolo Vergerio to Germany, where he even met with Luther, Paul III showed his willingness to change policy. Nonetheless, the plan for a council failed.

Still, the naming of the Venetian patrician Gasparo Contarini (1535) as a cardinal—along with the naming of Carafa, Reginald Pole, and Sadoleto in 1536; Juan Álvarez de Toledo, Marcello Cervini, and Federico Fregoso in 1539; and Giovanni Morone, Gregorio Cortesi, and Tommaso Badia in 1542—profoundly renewed the composition of the college of cardinals and turned it in the direction of reform. Moreover, in 1536 Paul III appointed a commission in Rome composed of the prelates most favorable to Catholic reform (Giberti, Contarini, Carafa, Pole, Sadoleto, Fregoso, Cortesi, and Badia) that drafted the *Consilium de emendanda Ecclesia* (A Plan for Reforming the Church; 1537). The proposal of the commission addressed especially the issue of ecclesiastical benefices and curial practice, as well as the problems connected with preaching and the discipline of members of religious orders. The distinction between the benefice and the office connected to it—as well as the official doctrine of the Curia, which intended the pope to be *dominus beneficiorum* ("master of benefices")—had led to the widespread abuse whereby ecclesiastics often did not reside in the dioceses or parishes to which they held title. It was therefore necessary to reform the praxis of the Curia, requiring that benefices be conferred only after examination of the candidates; that the obligation of residence for benefices connected with the care of souls be enforced; that bishops be granted the powers necessary to govern their dioceses; and that permissions no longer be granted to religious to live outside their own orders upon payment of a fee. The document aroused violent opposition in the Curia, while the Lutherans published it as proof that their accusations against the Curia were well founded. What stood under indictment was the very structure that had secured the financial and political power of the papacy. The reforms required a profound restructuring of the operation of the Roman dicasteries, including the datary, the penitentiary, and the chancery. Paul III charged various commissions to undertake studies of the modifications needed, but nothing concrete was accomplished.

At the same time, the reform-minded group moved ahead with an attempt at reaching an accord with the Protestants. The religious debate broadened, and in Roman circles favorable to reform the writings of Philipp Melanchthon, Zwingli, and Martin Bucer were being read in a search for points of contact and agreement. In the circle that gathered around Juan de Valdés in Naples, the freedom of theological inquiry was already exceeding the limits of Roman orthodoxy. Meanwhile, the hope for an agreement between Catholics and Protestants was also fading fast. Contarini led the Roman delegation to the Colloquy of Regensburg (1541); the agreement reached on the question of justification generated great enthusiasm, but the colloquy foundered on the questions of the sacraments and papal authority. Furthermore, Contarini had to face accusations and suspicions that his position on justification had aroused among conservatives. After falling into disgrace, he was sent away from Rome to be cardinal legate in Bologna, where he fell sick and died in 1542. In the same year the adjournment of the council and the institution of the Sacred Congregation of the Holy Office signaled the new direction of papal policy: this marked the victory of the Counter-Reformation, or, in the words of Cardinal Carafa, the "spiritual war" against the Protestants. A wave of suspicion and trials swept over the circles that had shown any interest or openness to the idea of church reform. The famous preacher Bernardino Ochino, general of the Capuchins, when summoned to appear before the Holy Office, fled to Switzerland, asserting that it was no longer the time to preach Christ "with a mask" (i.e., to reduce the importance of doctrinal conflicts and to give more emphasis to gospel morality and the imitation of Christ). Thus, certain currents of the Catholic reform were eliminated as suspect or even heretical. The problem of correct ecclesiastical discipline, along with how to make the care of souls more rigorous and effective, remained alive. This was the problem that faced the Council of Trent (1545–1563).

Paolo Sarpi, in his *Istoria del concilio tridentino*, described the council as the "Iliad of our time" on account of its long and dramatic history. It was interrupted and resumed several times, and it functioned as a seismograph of the delicate European political situation. Sarpi also remarked that the papacy, which had so feared the council and sought to prevent it, ended up deriving great benefit from it. The objectives of the council, set forth in the bull *Laetare Jerusalem* (Rejoice, Jerusalem; 1544), were to eliminate religious discord and to reform the Christian people. The pro-empire party sought to postpone the examination of controversial doctrines to avoid the possibility of reinforcing the fracture in the unity of the church and proposed instead that the questions of moral and disciplinary reform be dealt with. Compromise was reached with the decision to deal with both problems simultaneously. The questions that immediately appeared on the agenda were the two most important: justification on the doctrinal plane and residence on the disciplinary plane. The way in which the decree on justification was defined, after a long and tortuous drafting process, was unacceptable to the cardinal legate Reginald Pole. On a pretext he withdrew from Trent to avoid being part of the approval of the text. The condemnation of the doctrines of the Protestant Reformation closed the door on the accord that had seemed possible at the Colloquy of Regensburg. Pole's behavior shows how intense the dissensions were within the college of cardinals. Later Carafa, his adversary, initiated Inquisitorial proceedings against him and his friends.

As for the questions of reform, issues were dealt with concerning the privileges of the regular clergy, which exempted them from the authority of the bishops. This was crucial in the matter of preaching. The privileges of the regular clergy were not abolished, but the bishops were granted limited power of governing as delegates of the pope, and they were thus armed with special power. Other heated debates were touched off around the question of whether the obligation of a bishop to reside in his own diocese was a matter of divine law. The proposal to declare it divine law, which was strongly supported by the Spanish episcopate, aimed at cutting off at the root any possibility of having recourse to Rome to obtain dispensations in the matter. It was during the last phase of the council that the battle over this problem was touched off, thanks to the massive support of the Spanish episcopate, which was less tied to the will of Rome than was the Italian episcopate. Only the skill of the legate Giovanni Morone and the contribution of the theologians of the newly founded Jesuits made it possible to break the impasse with a compromise.

The reform decrees approved by the council substantially modified ecclesiastical organization. The structure of territorial governance entrusted to the secular clergy, bishops, and pastors was reinforced. To the clergy that exercised the care of souls, a higher standard was proposed, with the requirement of a cultural preparation and a level of moral conduct (the obligation of celibacy), which were to be checked periodically through a system of examinations, periodic visits, synods, and reports. As for the people, it was the pastor's duty to ensure that they were well informed on the doctrines of the faith through teaching imparted in sermons and through parochial schools. A set of parish records was to allow for periodic checks of the fulfillment of sacramental obligations, particularly the duty to confess and receive Communion during the Easter season. The reform approved at Trent thus had a strong pastoral component. It remained in the planning and proposal stage, however, and did not modify the mechanisms of the Curia or the papal powers, which had been mainly responsible for the decline in morals and the problem of the residence of the clergy. The question of papal authority was proposed in the final session of the council, when an attempt was made to decide whether the decrees had to be submitted to the pope for approval. The negative vote cast by the unshakable leader of the Spanish episcopate, Pedro Guerrero, was the only sign of episcopal opposition to placing the entire work of the council into the hands of the pope.

Pope Pius IV gave oral approval to the conciliar decrees on 26 January 1564; the bull of approbation was not issued until July. During these months the last battle was fought between those who wanted immediate implementation of the Tridentine decrees and those who were opposed for fear the Curia would be damaged by them. The pope's decision was a compromise between the reformers and the conservatives: the work of the council was approved in its entirety, but its interpretation and implementation were assumed by the papacy. Indeed, the bull stipulated, under the pretext of avoiding confusion and errors, that it was forbidden for anyone to publish, without papal authorization, any type of commentary or annotated interpretation of the council. On 2 August 1564 a commission of cardinals was charged with monitoring and promoting the resolutions of the council. From that moment the implementation of the reform was under direct papal control: the numerous and significant guidelines that the council had provided for modifying the functioning of the ecclesiastical structure and its relationship to the laity were filtered through the Roman authorities. The Congregation for the Council was the channel through which the revision of the entire code of canon law passed so it could be adjusted to the new norms. Also with respect to direct control of diocesan institutions, and following the initiative of Gregory XIII, the papacy made provisions for apostolic visitations. The apostolic representative, exercising authority granted him directly by the pope, could intervene in matters under dispute concerning those who were exempt from the authority of the bishop—religious orders (women's convents in particular) and canonical chapters.

Understandably, the pope was the only power really interested in implementing the decrees of Trent. The German Protestants had already refused to recognize the council in 1562; England under Elizabeth I had broken off relations with Rome; the representative of the king of Spain refused to ratify the decrees; and in France Catherine de Médicis appointed a commission of legal experts, who advised her against formally ratifying the decrees of the council. The papacy, therefore, strove to implement at least some of the reform decrees. This was done through the Congregation for the Council and apostolic visitations or by supplementing the work of the council on certain points. Thus, the so-called catechism of the council was drawn up and published in 1566; the *professio fidei tridentinae* (1564) was drafted; and the revised edition of the Bible, known by the name *Vulgata Clementina* (1593), was published. The decisive thrust for reform, however, came from other quarters. On the one hand, there was the example of some bishops who returned to their dioceses to implement the pastoral model of the Tridentine reform: among these the example of Carlo Borromeo stands out. He was the young nephew of Pius IV who abandoned a brilliant career in Rome to lead the archdiocese of Milan. His synodal decrees represented the most significant model of a vigorous reform thrust that existed in the church of that time. On the other hand, a no less significant thrust came with the missionary expansion outside Europe. The work of orders, both new and old, was decisive in this respect. Under the urgency of millenarian expectations, the Franciscans in the Americas had begun to preach the gospel like "new Apostles" to the native populations. They were followed with renewed energy by members of the Society of Jesus, whose special missionary vocation had already been sanctioned by the first constitutions approved by Paul III (1540). Their work was also directed to the populations of the European countryside, considered to be the other Indies

(*otras Indias*). The fight against outdated and incorrect forms of religion (superstitions, magic, and witchcraft) was a fundamental aspect of the profound transformations introduced by the Catholic reform into the church of the modern age. The proposal of models of conduct imbued with a strict criterion of uniformity and of submission to authority has led some to speak of this era in terms of a vast program of "social regimentation."

[*See also* Erasmus, Desiderius; Humanism; *and* Renaissance.]

BIBLIOGRAPHY

Bossy, John. *Christianity in the West, 1400–1700.* Oxford, 1985.
Delumeau, Jean. *Catholicism between Luther and Voltaire: A New View of the Counter-Reformation.* London and Philadelphia, 1977.
Evennett, Henry Outram. *The Spirit of the Counter-Reformation: The Birkbeck Lectures in Ecclesiastical History, May 1951.* Edited with a postscript by John Bossy. Cambridge, 1968.
Headley, John M., and John B. Tomaro, ed. *San Carlo Borromeo: Catholic Reform and Ecclesiastical Politics in the Second Half of the Sixteenth Century.* Washington, D.C., 1988.
Jedin, Hubert. *Katholische Reformation oder Gegenreformation?* Lucerne, 1946.
———. *Papal Legate at the Council of Trent: Cardinal Seripando.* London, 1947.
O'Donohoe, James A. *Tridentine Seminary Legislation: Its Sources and Its Formation.* Louvain, 1957.
Olin, John C., ed. *The Catholic Reformation: Savonarola to Ignatius Loyola.* Reprint, New York, 1992.
O'Malley, John W. *Catholicism in Early Modern History: A Guide to Research.* Saint Louis, 1988.
———. "Was Ignatius Loyola a Church Reformer? How to Look at Early Modern Catholicism." *Catholic Historical Review* 77 (1991), 177–193.
———. *The First Jesuits.* Cambridge, Mass., 1993.
Taveneaux, R. *Le catholicisme dans la France classique.* Paris, 1980.
Tellechea, Idigoras. *El arzobispo Carranza y su tiempo.* 2 vols. Madrid, 1968.
Wright, A. D. *The Counter-Reformation: Catholic Europe and the Non-Christian World.* London, 1982.

ADRIANO PROSPERI
Translated from Italian by Robert E. Shillenn

CATS, Jacob (1577–1660), Dutch poet and statesman, the most widely read author of Holland's Golden Age. Born in Brouwershaven (Zeeland) and educated in Zierikzee, Leiden, and Orléans. His long political career culminated in positions as grand pensionary of Holland and West Friesland and as keeper of the seal (1645–1651). He was an envoy to England in 1626 and 1651–1652. His literary works appeared in collected editions (*Alle de Wercken*) in Amsterdam in 1655, 1658, and 1665.

Cats was influenced by Joseph Hall and by such Nonconformist thinkers as William Perkins during a visit to England (1603?) and subsequently by Willem Teellinck and Stampert van der Wiele. Under their influence he became the literary defender of the Dutch Reformed church, then a symbol of Dutch independence and national pride. Today he is known chiefly as an emblem writer (*Proteus ofte Minne-beelden*, 1627), but he was above all the author of lengthy didactic works written chiefly in fluent, if monotonous, alexandrines. Cats combined apparent classical learning, Calvinist morality, and familiar everyday images so successfully that his works were often the only books (except the Bible) found in Dutch homes. Numerous fine illustrations by Adrian van de Venne and others undoubtedly contributed to the popularity of these works.

Cats's principal themes were Protestant home and family life and above all Christian marriage. These themes are treated most extensively in *Houwelijck* (1625), *Spiegel van den Ouden en Nieuwen Tijdt* (1630), and especially *Trouringh* (1637) and *Selbst-Strijt* (1620). *Selbst-Strijt*, written in the form of a dialogue, is an excessively moralizing version of the story of Joseph and Potiphar's wife, while *Trouringh* is a collection of edifying tales of love and marriage. Cats used stories from the scriptures, starting with Adam and Eve, as well as from classical history and medieval legend, and managed to combine erotic situations with ethically and theologically sound conclusions.

Although he was at best a moderately gifted poet, Cats both reflected and helped form the conscience of his countrymen. He formulated and helped establish the values of Dutch Calvinism at a time when a more secular culture was already challenging its values.

Outside the Netherlands Cats was influential, chiefly in Nonconformist and Calvinistic circles, in England and Germany. His version of the Adam and Eve story may well have influenced John Milton's *Paradise Lost*. Thomas Heywood (1637) and John Quarles (1684) translated selections from his works into English. Two notable German writers—Hans Jacob Christoph von Grimmelshausen and Philipp von Zesen—wrote versions of the Joseph story that owe at least some debt to Cats's *Selbst-Strijt*, and his verse novellas were greeted in Germany as a new, or at least revived, genre. *Minne-beelden* successfully adapted the emblem to Calvinist thought and influenced both Dutch and English emblematists. Cats's greatest contribution to European civilization, however, was certainly his pervasive influence on the development of German Pietism.

BIBLIOGRAPHY

Berge, Domien ten (usually D. J. M. ten). *De hooggeleerde en zoetvloeiende dichter Jacob Cats*. Leiden, 1979. The standard modern study of Cats.

Bullough, Geoffrey. "Milton and Cats." In *Essays in English Literature from the Renaissance to the Victorian Age Presented to E. S. P. Woodhouse*, edited by Millar Maclure, pp. 103–124. Toronto, 1964. Introductory treatment of a complicated and unresolved problem.

Es, Gustaaf Amandus van, and Gerrit Siebe Overdiep. *De letterkunde van Renaissance en Barok in den zeventiende eeuw*. Geschiedenis van de letterkunde der nederlanden, edited by Franz Bauer, vol. 4. s'Hertogenbosch, Netherlands, 1949. Contains best concise and objective account available.

Kalff, Gerrit. *Geschiedenis der nederlandsche letterkunde*, vol. 4, pp. 341–362. Groningen, Netherlands, 1909.

Maatje, Chr. J. H., Jr. *Jacob Cats*. Rijswijk, Netherlands, 1938.

Postmus, Johannes. "Jacob Cats." In *Calvinistische vertoogen: Studiën en schetsen*, pp. 162–275. Zwolle, Netherlands, 1906.

Schroeter, Sophie. *Jacob Cats' Beziehungen zur deutschen Literatur. 1. Teil: Die deutschen Übertragungen seiner Werke*. Ph.D. diss. Heidelberg University, 1905. Helpful introduction to Cats's influence in German-speaking areas.

W. GORDON MARIGOLD

CAXTON, William (1420/24–1491/92), first English printer and publisher. Many details about Caxton's life are either sketchy or unknown. From 1438 to 1446 he was apprenticed to the mercers' trade, first in London and then in Brugge. While self-employed in the trade, Caxton served for a year (1462–1463) in Brugge as governor of the English Nation of Merchant Adventurers and represented Edward IV's government in the negotiation of commercial treaties in the late 1460s. In 1471 Caxton became part of the household of Margaret, duchess of Burgundy, in Ghent and perhaps at her urging began translating from French into English the popular History of Troy. Desiring to learn the printing trade, Caxton went to Cologne and studied under Johannes Veldener from 1471 to 1472 before returning to Brugge and publishing, probably in 1473, his translation of the *History of Troy*, the first book printed in the English language. From 1476 until his death Caxton printed over one hundred editions, many his own translations, at his shop near Westminster Abbey. These books include Geoffrey Chaucer's *Canterbury Tales* (1478?), *Reynard the Fox* (1481), and *Golden Legend* (1484); Thomas Malory's *Morte Darthur* (1485); and writings by John Lydgate, John Gower, and Marcus Tullius Cicero, as well as numerous other romances and tales of chivalry.

Caxton scholarship has begun to focus on his talents as a publisher and bookseller rather than as a printer. The supposedly uninspired selection of works he chose to publish led many earlier critics to relegate his importance to the introduction of printing into England. But this view has been changing with the revival in fifteenth-century literary studies and a renewed emphasis on the printer's business acumen. Caxton knew his readers and spent most of his later life collecting books and manuscripts that would find a market once they were translated and printed. A legacy of England's didactic and moralistic literary tastes, to which Caxton contributed, can be found in the popularity for printed Protestant works that developed once the Church of England was established in the 1530s.

BIBLIOGRAPHY

Blake, N. F. *William Caxton and English Literary Culture*. London, 1991. This series of essays by today's preeminent Caxton scholar is the most up-to-date assessment of his life and career.

Deacon, Richard. *A Biography of William Caxton, the First English Editor, Merchant and Translator.* London, 1976. Popular biography that provides a good context for the introduction of printing into England. Debunks several myths.

Painter, George D. *William Caxton: A Biography.* New York, 1976. Groundbreaking study that integrates publishing choices with Caxton's life experiences; may be a bit too ambitious in its conclusions (see Blake, chap. 4). Includes chronological list of Caxton's editions.

BEN LOWE

CECIL, William (1520–1598), English statesman, chief minister of Queen Elizabeth I, and committed Protestant. Cecil was born into a middling gentry family in Lincolnshire and educated first at grammar schools at Grantham and Stamford before going up, at the age of fourteen, to Saint John's College, Cambridge, where he was a notable student. The connections he made at Cambridge, where he was confirmed in the strong Protestantism that he retained throughout his life, stood him in good stead on the accession of the boy-king, Edward VI, in 1547, and he soon became a prominent figure in court and political circles, first as private secretary to Edward Seymour (Protector Somerset) and then, from 1550, as secretary of state under Seymour's supplanter as the chief power in the state, John Dudley, duke of Northumberland. The accession of the Catholic Mary Tudor in 1553 sent his career into temporary eclipse, but he found his destiny after Elizabeth I's accession in November 1558, when he was made secretary of state once more. At the same time the queen indicated that he was to be her chief adviser, thus initiating a partnership that lasted for forty years, during which Cecil, created Lord Burghley in 1571, was successively elevated to the mastership of the Court of Wards in 1561 and then, in 1572, after he had given up the secretaryship, to the high office of lord treasurer. He wielded great influence in the distribution of royal patronage—an unmistakable sign of the queen's favor—and after the crisis years 1568 and 1572, when his power was threatened by conservative noblemen, he emerged as the linchpin of the Elizabethan regime, clearly the most important person in England after the queen herself. He died in 1598, full of years and honors, mourned by Elizabeth and widely recognized, abroad as well as at home, as one of the great men of sixteenth-century Europe.

His retirement into private life during Mary's reign was a sign that he was not prepared to lend public support to a Catholic regime whose religious tenets he firmly believed to be against God's word, but on his return to power under Elizabeth he helped the queen to establish the ecclesiastical settlement that was enshrined in the acts of Supremacy and Uniformity of 1559 and that made the queen "supreme governor" of a church that retained episcopal government and some ceremonial but was founded on a Protestant theology expressed in the Thirty-nine Articles of 1563. That settlement, which endured in England in its essentials right up to the twentieth century, faced attacks in Elizabeth's reign from both Puritans and Catholics. Precise definition of Puritans has caused much dispute among historians, but one can sensibly describe them as those "hotter" Protestants who wanted to purge the Church of England of remaining popish abuses. No one has suggested that Cecil had any sympathy with those more extreme Puritans who counted bishops among the popish abuses and who wished to convert the church to Presbyterianism, but he has been seen as the patron of the more moderate Puritanism that was influential throughout his Elizabethan career and that, while accepting episcopal government of the church, stressed predestinarian theology, preaching, and a learned ministry. He certainly employed men with Puritan views in his household—his secretaries Vincent Skinner and Michael Hickes are examples—but his will has no trace of Puritan ideas, and one of its overseers was that hammer of the Puritans, Archbishop John Whitgift.

In general, Cecil believed that the clergy should be kept in their places—he was a committed supporter of the Erastianism that was strong in Elizabethan England—and his horror of excessive clerical claims found clear expression in his most important literary work, *The Execution of Justice in England* (1583), a defense of the treatment of Catholic missionaries in England. The 180 Catholics, 120 of them priests, who were executed for treason between 1581 and 1603 were in his eyes traitors to their country, men who in the last resort were prepared to support the right of a foreign ruler, the pope, to depose England's reigning sovereign. As such they were a fundamental threat to the English nation-state, created by Henry VIII and Thomas Cromwell during the 1530s, rejected by Mary Tudor in the early 1550s, and recreated by Elizabeth and himself in the late 1550s and early 1560s. In his eyes they deserved no mercy, and by the time of his own death he had the satisfaction of knowing that the Catholic threat had been contained and the Church of England firmly established as an institution. That achievement he valued very highly.

BIBLIOGRAPHY

Beckingsale, B. W. *Burghley: Tudor Statesman, 1520–1598.* London, 1967. Attempts an analytical treatment of some aspects of William Cecil's career.

MacCaffrey, Wallace T. *The Shaping of the Elizabethan Regime, 1558–1572.* Princeton, 1968. Contains important discussions of Cecil's role in both the domestic and foreign politics of the time.

———. *Queen Elizabeth and the Making of Policy, 1572–1588.* Princeton, 1981. Contains important discussions of Cecil's role in both the domestic and foreign politics of the time.

Read, Conyers. *Lord Burghley and Queen Elizabeth.* London, 1960.

———. *Mr Secretary Cecil and Queen Elizabeth.* Reprint, London, 1965. Taken together these two works by Read form the standard life, a massive quarry, almost entirely narrative in approach.

Smith, Alan G. R. *William Cecil, Lord Burghley: Minister of Elizabeth I.* Bangor, Wales, 1991. A short study.

ALAN G. R. SMITH

CELIBACY AND VIRGINITY.

CELIBACY AND VIRGINITY. In both Jewish and Roman society at the time of Christ, some groups rejected marriage and advocated celibacy and abstinence from sexual activity for their members. The early Christians built on these ideas, with many writers interpreting the Gospels and Epistles, especially *1 Corinthians* 7, as teaching that voluntary celibacy and virginity were preferable in the eyes of God to marriage. Monks and nuns in both the Eastern Orthodox and Western Catholic churches were prohibited from marrying, though in the Eastern church ordinary parish clergy who were married were not prohibited from being ordained. These clergy could not remarry, nor could married clergy assume the office of bishop in the Eastern church. Antipathy toward clerical marriage was never strong in the East.

In the West, despite official disapproval of clerical marriage, the practice was common throughout the early Middle Ages, with priests' and bishops' sons often inheriting their fathers' positions and livings. Those clerics who were not married often lived in long-term relationships of concubinage, receiving special dispensations from their clerical superiors to have their children legitimated. This practice began to change in the twelfth century, when at the Lateran councils the church declared all clerical marriages invalid and prohibited clerical concubinage. Many lesser clergy responded by rioting and demonstrating, but gradually celibacy became the norm, especially among the higher clergy, and women from honorable families no longer entered into relationships with priests, knowing that these could never be declared valid marriages. The prohibition of concubinage and other types of nonmarital sexual activity among the clergy was much harder to enforce, however, and by the fourteenth century church officials instead simply advocated discretion.

Though unbiased estimates are hard to calculate, it is clear that on the eve of the Reformation many male clergy and at least some females were not paying much attention to the church's proscriptions of sexual activity. All of the major Protestant Continental reformers saw the church's inability to enforce celibacy as proof that the policy was against God's will. They rejected the notion that virginity was a higher spiritual state than marriage, declared that monastic vows should no longer be binding, and advocated clerical marriage.

These ideas were not completely new; arguments against clerical celibacy had been made from within the Church by canon lawyers and officials since the twelfth century. Many of the Christian humanists who remained loyal to Catholicism, including Erasmus, also advocated clerical marriage as a way to rid the church of scandal. What was new was the number of priests who put this idea into practice; during the early 1520s priests in many areas of Germany began to marry openly, and in 1525 Luther also married, choosing a former nun, Katharina von Bora. Secular governments often supported these moves, particularly in areas where they were closing monasteries anyway, though even Luther realized that marriage was not a realistic possibility for many former nuns and monks. In a 1543 letter to Georg Spalatin, he suggested that older nuns who had no chance of finding husbands should be allowed to remain in their convents. Popular opinion on the Continent varied widely; in some cases married clergy and their families were accepted as honorable members of the community without any difficulties, though in other areas pastors' wives, at least in the first decades after the Reformation, were derided as "priests' whores."

Clerical celibacy was also a highly contentious issue in sixteenth-century England. Though clerical marriage had been supported in books and pamphlets published in the 1520s, and though some high church officials had secretly married, Henry VIII refused to allow priests to marry, and the Six Articles promulgated in 1539 supported vows of chastity and clerical celibacy. This situation was particularly difficult for English monks and nuns, for by this time Henry VIII had dissolved the monasteries; by one estimate over ten thousand nuns had no place to live but were nevertheless not allowed to marry. With Edward VI's accession clergy began to marry openly, and the Forty-Two Articles passed in 1552 formally allowed priests and bishops to do so. There is evidence of stronger popular opposition to clerical marriage in England than on the Continent, with people refusing to take Communion from married priests and midwives refusing to treat priests' wives, so that the Crown felt it necessary in 1552 to pass a bill declaring that clerical marriages were not simply valid as a necessary evil but actually preferable to clerical celibacy.

At her accession in 1553, Mary Tudor prohibited married priests from officiating, and it is estimated that one English priest out of every five was thus deprived of his living. She wanted to carry the prohibition further, requiring even priests who were willing to give up their offices also to give up their wives, but her reign was too brief to carry out all of her measures. Elizabeth I took no formal action initially, refusing to allow clerical marriage officially but also making no moves against married clergy, which included many of her advisers. Those in favor of clerical marriage won out gradually in public law, but Elizabeth continued to disapprove, expressing open hostility especially to bishops' wives. English bishops were members of the House of Lords, and archbishops took precedence in processions and other state occasions over all secular lords, though their wives had no rank at all and were often excluded from official celebrations.

Clerical celibacy became an important issue for secular authorities on the Continent during the mid-sixteenth century, with Charles V standing as a firm supporter and advocate of stronger measures against clerical concubinage. Many Catholic rulers, however, including Albrecht V, duke of Bavaria, and Emperor Ferdinand I, appealed to the pope to allow clerical marriage as a solution to problems of clerical immorality. The issue was taken up at the last session of the Council of Trent, with the council reaffirming the policies of mandatory celibacy and the prohibition of concubinage; celibacy was again declared a more meritorious state than marriage. The council also called for the establishment of seminaries for the training of priests, which turned out to be the most effective tool in the church's long campaign for the enforcement of clerical celibacy and chastity. By instilling the values of sexual continence and weeding out those unable to follow a celibate lifestyle, seminaries were more effective at enforcing clerical celibacy than any church courts or secular authorities had been.

While one can trace attitudes toward and the actual practice of clerical celibacy through public laws and marriage records, it is more difficult to discern changes in ideas about virginity itself, as these are often tied to notions of the body and its relationship to the mind and to ideas about female and male sexuality. For example, the ceremonies celebrating women's becoming professed nuns—and thus devoted to a life of virginity—took much of their symbolism, such as the veil and ring, from traditional marriage ceremonies; church authorities viewed these virgin spouses of Christ as visible signs of the union of Christ and the church. The women themselves appear to have had a view of their unusual status—simultaneously virgin and wife—that was both more physical and more mystical. The complexity in ideas about women's virginity may also be seen in a shift in the definition of virginity in the later Middle Ages from a purely physical one to a more spiritual one, so that individuals, particularly women, who were not physically virgins could still achieve a status of spiritual virginity through a life of purity and holiness. Some of these "spiritual virgins" even became saints, for their status as widows, mothers, or former wives did not prevent their achievement of this highest honor. This situation appears to have changed after the Council of Trent, when most female saints again were those who were physically virgins.

Protestant areas also had some change in ideas about virginity once the initial attacks on clerical celibacy were over. By the late sixteenth century, Protestant pastors frequently wrote prayer books directed at unmarried women, consoling them with comments that virginity was also a state blessed by God. Given that many women did not marry until their late twenties, and some not at all, such books had a wide audience; there are no similar books for unmarried men, however, despite the fact that in theory Protestants advocated premarital chastity for both sexes. A few Protestant women wrote more vigorous defenses of virginity, linking themselves with heroic virgins of the early church and refusing to accept the more widely held Protestant notion that marriage was a woman's only true calling.

[See also Family; Marriage; and Women.]

BIBLIOGRAPHY

Atkinson, Clarissa. " 'Precious Balsam in a Fragile Glass': The Ideology of Virginity in the Later Middle Ages." *Journal of Family History* 8 (1983), 131–143.

Brundage, James A. *Law, Sex and Christian Society in Medieval Europe.* Chicago, 1987. Magisterial and comprehensive survey of legal doctrines in all areas of sexuality from the early Middle Ages through the Catholic Reformation, with good coverage of the debates over clerical celibacy.

Denzler, Georg. *Das Papsttum und der Amtszölibat.* Päpste und Papsttum, vol. 5, pts. 1 and 2. Stuttgart, 1976. Discussion of the official position of the papacy toward clerical celibacy from the early church through Vatican II, and of its actual practice among secular and regular clergy.

Lea, Henry Charles. *History of Sacerdotal Celibacy in the Christian Church.* New York, 1966. First published in 1867, and with a strong Protestant bias, this remains the fullest discussion of the issue, though it lacks a critical apparatus.

Prior, Mary. "Reviled and Crucified Marriages: The Position of Tudor Bishops' Wives." In *Women in English Society, 1500–1800*, edited by Mary Prior, pp. 118–148. London, 1985.

Yost, John K. "The Reformation Defense of Clerical Marriage in the Reigns of Henry VIII and Edward VI." *Church History* 50 (1981), 152–165.

MERRY E. WIESNER-HANKS

CELLINI, Benvenuto (1500–1571), Italian artist. Born in Florence, Cellini was first trained in the art of music by his father. In 1513 he began practicing goldsmithery. As much because of his art as his violent character, he had to leave Florence and each of the many cities in which he lived. After his first stay in Rome in 1519–1520, he returned there in 1523 and stayed until 1528. During this time he worked for Pope Clement VII and participated in the defense of the Castel Sant'Angelo during the siege of 1527. In his autobiography he claims that at that time he was responsible for shooting Charles of Bourbon, for wounding the Prince of Orange, and for preventing the Castel Sant'Angelo from capitulating. He was again in Rome in 1529–1534 and in 1537–1539 and was thrown into the dungeons of the Castel Sant'Angelo after being accused of stealing papal jewelry. After a successful escape and another imprisonment, he was finally released by Pope Paul III upon the intercession of Cardinal Ippolito from Este. He claims that, during the cruelest moment of his imprisonment, he had a celestial vision, after which a halo (*uno isplendore*) surrounded his head. He traveled to France (1540–1545), where he worked for Francis I, for whom he made the famous gold saltcellar. Enmities and accusations convinced him to return to Florence, where Cosimo I de' Medici commissioned the *Perseus* (1549). He took the minor ecclesiastical orders in 1558, but he later received dispensation in order to marry. From 1558 until 1566 he partly wrote and partly dictated his autobiography, which includes events of his life up to November 1562. He died on 13 February 1571; on the 15th, he was buried in the Church of the Annunziata in Florence.

Although Cellini was not a writer by profession, he has become famous especially for his autobiography, which he left incomplete and which remained unpublished until 1728. Cellini witnessed some of the most tragic political events of the sixteenth century. The *Vita* offers no specific record, however, of Europe's religious upheavals. From the perspective of religious awareness, although Cellini claims to have experienced a spiritual conversion and a mystical experience during his imprisonment in the Castel Sant'Angelo, the *Vita* reveals that he belongs less to the City of God than to the city of man.

BIBLIOGRAPHY

Cellini, Benvenuto. *Autobiography.* Translated and introduced by George Bull. Harmondsworth, 1956.
————. *Opere: Vita, trattati, rime, lettere.* Edited by Bruno Maier. Milan, 1968.
————. *La Vita.* Edited by Guido Davico Bonino. Turin, 1973.
Cervigni, Dino S. *The Vita of Benvenuto Cellini: Literary Tradition and Genre.* Ravenna, 1979.

DINO S. CERVIGNI

CELSI, Mino (1514–1575), Italian politician and administrator. Born in Siena, Celsi was the son of Giovanni and Vittoria Tancredo. As long as the independence of the Republic of Siena lasted, Celsi took active part in the political life of the state. Indeed he was several times a member of the consistory and of the governing council up to 1555. With the sudden advent of Medici rule, the Celsi family (like other Siena families with republican sentiments) had to accommodate themselves to the new political situation, and Mino obtained political and administrative posts under the new Medici regime. He was again a member of the governing council between 1557 and 1561, as well as *podestà* (municipal official in charge of law enforcement and head of the army in times of emergency) and captain of lands of the surrounding countryside—San Quirico, Massa Marittima, Casole d'Elsa, and Montalcino.

His life, which seemed to be consumed in high-level political and administrative routine, took a drastic turn in 1569 with his sensational flight from Siena and his initial refuge in the Grigons. Nothing—with the exception of his friendship with some individuals of doubtful orthodoxy who were members of the city Academy of the Intronati, in whose cultural life Celsi took part—would have given any hint of such an intention. Still, it is certain that the well-known trial of Aonio Paleario (who had stayed in Siena and Colle Valdelsa) by the Roman Inquisition at about that time drove Celsi to flee. After his stay in Piur he moved on to Basel, where he enrolled at the university (1571) and began to work with Pietro Perna's printing company. In the hope of finding a better economic situation, he moved in 1573 to Vienna and from there to Frankfurt (where he was for a short time

a bill collector for Dietz). In the autumn of 1547, however, he arrived penniless in Basel, where he was aided by Giovanni Bernardino Bonifacio. There is no precise documentation concerning Celsi's death, which, according to some indications, occurred in 1575.

Two years later there appeared in Basel a posthumous work, *De haereticis coercendis quatenus progredi liceat Mini Celsi Senensis disputatio* (Debate on Curbing Heretics and to What Extent Mino Celsi of Siena Should Be Allowed to Go Forward; a second edition with additions and modifications became available seven years later). This work was long in preparation (a first Italian edition is known) and pertained to the continuing debate over toleration that had been stirred up, particularly in the Italian exile colony, by the death sentence imposed on the Spanish antitrinitarian Michael Servetus in Geneva in 1553. On that occasion, against the rigorist tendencies and the justifications of John Calvin and Théodore de Bèze concerning the legitimacy of condemning heretics to death, Sébastien Castellion had already published *De haereticis an sint persequendi* (Heretics—Should They Be Persecuted?). Celsi was clearly appealing to this work when he condemned recourse to capital punishment while recognizing the power of the authorities of the state to intervene in these matters.

BIBLIOGRAPHY

Primary Source

Celsi, Mino. *In haereticis cöercendis quatenus progredi liceat, Poems, Correspondence.* Edited by Peter G. Bietenholz. Naples and Chicago, 1982.

Secondary Sources

Bietenholz, P. G. "Celsi, Mino, Gregorio, Romolo," In *Dizionario Biografico degli Italiani,* vol. 23, pp. 478–482. Rome, 1980.
Cantimori, Delio. *Eretici italiani del Cinquecento.* 3d rev. ed. Edited by Adriano Prosperi. Turin, 1992. Earlier edition available in English translation: *Italian Heretics of the Sixteenth Century,* Cambridge, Mass., 1979.

PAOLO SIMONCELLI
Translated from Italian by Robert E. Shillenn

CELTIS, Conradus (Ger., Conrad Pickel; 1459–1508), the best lyric poet among the German humanists. Known as *Der Erzhumanist* ("The Archhumanist"), Celtis was a peasant's son born in a village near Würzburg in central Germany. He ran away to school and studied at Cologne, Heidelberg, Rostock, and Leipzig. He was the first major humanist to get his basic humanist, or classical, education in the north before his Italian journey. At Heidelberg he encountered Rudolf Agricola, the "father of German humanism," and Celtis, in turn, became the teacher of reformers such as Joachim Vadian and Huldrych Zwingli. He lived on the eve of the Reformation and as yet was personally untouched by the new religious power of the evangelical movement. Celtis then began ten years of wandering, crossing the Alps for a quick tour of Italy, where he visited Venice, Padua, Bologna, Florence, and Rome. He hurried back to the north to the University of Kraków and from there moved on to Nuremberg and Ingolstadt, where he delivered his famous inaugural address calling on the Germans to rival the Italians in learning and letters.

In 1487 at the citadel in Nuremberg, Emperor Frederick III crowned the twenty-eight-year-old Celtis with laurel as the first German poet laureate of the empire. His ambition was to be remembered as the German Horace. His three major poetic works were the *Amores*, the *Odes*, and the *Epigrams*, though he wrote a number of lesser pieces and plays, and he planned to do a complete *Germania illustrata*, a combination of history and topography analogous to Flavio Biondo's *Italia illustrata*. In 1501 he published a manuscript of Roswitha, the tenth century nun of Gandersheim, and later the *Ligurina*, another early medieval discovery. In many urban centers he organized the Rhenish and Danubian sodalities of young humanists, who, during the course of the first twenty years of the Reformation movement, made the acceptance and the spread of the Reformation possible. In Vienna at the invitation of Emperor Maximilian I, he founded the College of Poets and Mathematicians, and he lies buried beneath the bell tower of Saint Stephen's Cathedral, where his gravestone reads *Vivo/Vivo*, ("I live"). He represented the two major tendencies in German humanism—the mounting tide of romantic cultural nationalism and the interest in religious enlightenment.

BIBLIOGRAPHY

Forster, Leonard. *Selections from Conrad Celtis, 1459–1508*. Cambridge, 1948.
Rupprich, Hans, ed. *Der Briefwechsel des Konrad Celtis*. Munich, 1934.
Spitz, Lewis W. *Conrad Celtis, the German Arch-Humanist*. Cambridge, Mass., 1957.
———. *The Religious Renaissance of the German Humanists*. Cambridge, Mass., 1963. See pp. 81–109, 312–316.

LEWIS W. SPITZ

ČERVENKA, Matthias (also Erythraeus; Erythacus; 1521–1569), Czech theologian and bishop of the Bohemian Brethren (Unity of Brethren or Unitas Fratrum). Born 21 February 1521 in Čelákovice, near Prague, he studied at the brethren school in Mladá Boleslav and at the University of Wittenberg with Martin Luther and Philipp Melanchthon. He subsequently worked as the *scholarius* of Jan Augusta in Litomyl. Augusta tried to establish contacts between the Bohemian Brethren and reform movements in other European countries, especially with those in Germany. He sent Červenka on an embassy abroad in 1540 with information concerning the theology of the brethren to Johann Hess in Wrocław (Breslau), Martin Bucer in Strasbourg, and John Calvin. He was to discuss differences, as well as areas of possible cooperation, within the Reformation movement as a whole. Červenka also corresponded regularly with Melanchthon.

After the Czech Utraquist nobility failed in their struggle to gain recognition from the emperor and king of Bohemia, Ferdinand I, Červenka, as a member of the brethren, had to flee to Königsberg, Prussia, where he stayed until 1553. Upon his return to Přerov, he became the bishop (senior) of the brethren in Moravia. As an author, he spearheaded the theological and scholarly members of the brethren, and he was recognized as an important leader of the reform movement among the Czechs. He wrote several influential tracts and treatises, including a report of his travels to Wrocław and Strasbourg (1540), *Obrana Jednoty braterské* (The Defence of the Unity of Brethren; 1558), *Krátká zpráva o počátcich Jednoty bratrské* (A Short Report on the Origin of the Unity of the Brethren; 1561), a psalterium (1562), and a *summa theologiae*, which, however, he never completed. Červenka died on 21 December 1569 in Přerov.

BIBLIOGRAPHY

Primary Sources

Červenka, Matthias. "Zpráva o cestě do Vratislavě" (The Report of Travel to Wrocław and Strasbourg). In *Cesty Českých bratří M. Červenky a Jana Blahoslava*, edited by Timotheus C. Zelenka, pp. 57–65, 67–90. Prague, 1942.
Červenka, Matthias, and Jan Blahoslav. *Česká přislovi* (Czech Proverbs). Edited by J. Spilka. Prague, 1970.

Secondary Sources

Bock, P. *The Political and Social Doctrines of the Unity of Czech Brethren in the Fifteenth and Early Sixteenth Centuries*. Haag, Germany, 1957.
Jireček, J. *Rukovět k dějinám literatury české I* (Handbook of the History of Czech Literature). Prague, 1875.
Kaňák, M. *Čeští bratři a Martin Bucer* (The Czech Brethren and Martin Bucer). Prague, 1972.
———. *Význačné postavy staré Jednoty Bratrské* (Important Persons of the Old Unity of Brethren). Prague, 1982.
Molnár, A. "Bratr Červenka o svobodné vůli" (Brother Červenka on Free Will). *Theologická příloha Křesťanské revue* 19 (1952), 52–57.
———. "Theologická suma Bratra Matěje Červenky." *Křesťanská revue* 19 (1952), 80–88.
———. *Pohyb teologického myšlení* (The Movement of Theological Ideas). Prague, 1982.
Říčan, R. *Die Böhmischen Brüder*. Berlin, 1961.

MILOSLAV POLÍVKA

CERVINI, Marcello. *See* Marcellus II.

CHADERTON, Laurence (d. 1640), English scholar and administrator. The son of Lancashire papists, he was converted to Protestantism at the University of Cambridge, where he became first a fellow of Christ's and then, in 1584, master of Emmanuel, a Puritan foundation set up by Walter Mildmay to train godly preaching ministers. Chaderton remained master until 1622, when he resigned in order to allow a managed succession to the suitably Puritan John Preston. He continued to live in the college until his death in 1640.

Chaderton published little, and his main significance was as an eminence grise at Cambridge, a crucial conduit for those evangelical assumptions and doctrinal shibboleths that constituted the English Puritan tradition. He was also a crucial link between Puritan families (at court and in the country) and the world of the university. Chaderton was involved in the classis movement and published an overtly presbyterian sermon as part of the Puritan propaganda campaign of 1584. At the Hampton Court Conference he was a proponent of change so moderate that he angered other more radical Puritans, but here he was at least being consistent. He had always argued that since the ceremonies at issue were inherently indifferent, ministers should try to avoid suspension over conformity in order to fulfill their overriding duty to preach the word.

In matters of doctrine he was an uncompromising Calvinist. In collaboration with Walter Travers and other London presbyterian ministers, the French church in London, and the university authorities, he led a campaign in 1583 against what he took to be the heterodox opinions of Peter Baro. He was also at the forefront of the later attack on Baro and William Barrett in 1595/96 that produced the Lambeth Articles. In his striking combination of Calvinist rigor, presbyterian theory, and Nonconformist practice (the surplice was not seen in Emmanuel until 1604, the chapel was unconsecrated, and Communion was received sitting), along with a formally moderate attitude toward the issue of conformity, Chaderton typifies the complex accommodations whereby Puritans could achieve and maintain positions of considerable power at the heart of the Elizabethan clerical and intellectual establishments.

BIBLIOGRAPHY

Lake, Peter. *Moderate Puritans and the Elizabethan Church.* Cambridge, 1982.
Stubbings, Frank. *The Statutes of Sir Walter Mildmay for Emmanuel College.* Cambridge, 1983.

PETER LAKE

CHAMBRE ARDENTE. Shortly after his accession in 1547, King Henry II created a second criminal chamber, or *Tournelle,* in the Parlement of Paris to deal exclusively with the growing problem of heresy. Dubbed by the Protestants the *Chambre ardente* ("chamber for burning") because of the zeal with which its judges exercised their functions, the court was abolished in 1550, presumably in response to complaints from other judges in Parlement and from the clergy, who resented the power it wielded. Staffed by fourteen judges drawn from Parlement's regular chambers, the court had two presidents, one of whom, Pierre Lizet, was notorious for his hostility to any deviation from Catholic orthodoxy. In addition to trying cases passed on from lower courts, the tribunal's magistrates sent out their own agents to investigate reported cases of heresy in towns subject to the Parlement of Paris. Religious houses appear to have been a special object of these investigations.

Records have survived from the court for the period May 1548 to March 1550, with one six-month gap. Of approximately three hundred cases that came before the court during this period, 215 received a final disposition. Analyzing these decisions, Frederic Baumgartner (*Henry II: King of France 1547–1559,* Durham and London, 1988, pp. 128–129 and 264–266) has calculated that death sentences were handed down in 17 percent of the cases, for a total of thirty-seven executions. Thirty-nine persons were acquitted. The rest received punishments that ranged from reprimand and public display of penitence to public whipping, the confiscation of property, and banishment. Thirty-six persons were ordered tortured in the hope that they would not only confess their guilt but also name their associates in heresy and their secret meeting places. The court records specify an occupation for 160 of the persons indicted. Of these, fifty-five, or more than one third, were clerics. The rest came from all walks of life, except for the peasantry. Only twenty-nine of those indicted were women, of whom five were executed.

[*See also* Henry II of France *and* Wars of Religion.]

BIBLIOGRAPHY

Salmon, John H. M. *Society in Crisis: France in the Sixteenth Century.* New York, 1975. Analyzes the occupations of the accused.
Sutherland, N. M. *The Huguenot Struggle for Recognition.* New Haven and London, 1980. Sets the court in the context of jurisdictional quarrels and changing laws on heresy.
Weiss, Nathanael. *La chambre ardente* (1889). Reprint, Geneva, 1970. Includes a transcription of the court's registers as well as a study of its functions.

BARBARA B. DIEFENDORF

CHANDIEU, Antoine de la Roche (1534–1591), French noble and Reformed theologian. After losing his father at the age of four, Chandieu was sent to Paris, where he developed Protestant sympathies from his teacher. These views were strengthened during the course of his studies of law at Toulouse, after which he traveled to Geneva to study theology. Returning to Paris (1555), he was quickly pressed into service as copastor of the underground Reformed church in the city at only twenty years of age. After a Protestant meeting was attacked and 140 people arrested, he wrote the *Remonstrance au Roi* and the *Apologie des bons*

Chrétiens contre les ennemis de l'église catholique. He was himself arrested in 1558 but subsequently released at the request of Antoine of Bourbon, king of Navarre.

Chandieu was a key figure in the calling of the first national synod of the French Reformed churches (Paris, 1559) and seems to have been involved in drafting both the Gallic Confession and the *Discipline ecclésiastique* issued by that synod. He was elected moderator of the third national synod (Orléans, 1562), which first addressed Jean Morély's challenge to the polity of the Reformed churches of France, after which Chandieu wrote what would become the churches' semiofficial defense of their polity, *La confirmation de la discipline ecclésiastique observée en églises réformées de France* (1566).

After the Saint Bartholomew's Day Massacre (1572), Chandieu fled to Geneva. He worked for a time in Lausanne as an unofficial teacher of theology before joining the pastoral corps in Geneva (1584). During this time, the French Reformed churches continued to seek his advice and leadership; both the ninth national synod (Sainte-Foy, 1578) and the twelfth national synod (Vitré, 1583) requested his involvement in discussions of church union proposed (but never actually carried out) by Johann Casimir. Chandieu was appointed field chaplain to Henry of Navarre in 1585, but his ill-health forced him to return to Geneva. He resumed his position as pastor in the city and taught Hebrew in the Geneva academy until his death.

Chandieu was by all accounts a remarkable orator as well as a prolific writer, publishing under the pseudonyms of Zamariel, Theopsaltes, La Croix, and Sadeel. In addition to the works already cited, significant works include *Histoire des persécutions et martyrs de l'église de Paris depuis l'an 1557 jusqu'au temps de Charles IX* (1563), *Meditationes in Psalmum xxxii* (1578; English translation by W. Watkinson, 1578), *De verbo Dei scripto* (1580), *De unico Christi sacerdotio* (1581), *De veritate naturae humanae Christi* (1585), *De spirituali manducatione corporis Christi* (1589; English translation, 1859); and *De sacramentali manducatione corporis Christi* (1589).

As a theologian, Chandieu moved away from the essentially humanist orientation of French Reformed theology toward a more scholastic approach and thus can be considered one of the pioneers of Protestant Scholasticism. Of equal importance, however, was his role in the development of Reformed ecclesiology, as demonstrated by his involvement in the events leading up to the first national synod, his work on the Gallic Confession and *Discipline,* and his defense of the polity of the French Reformed churches in his *Confirmation de la discipline.*

BIBLIOGRAPHY

Bernus, A. "Le ministre Antoine de Chandieu d'après son journal autographe inédit, 1534–1591." *Bulletin historique et littéraire de la Société de l'Histoire du Protestantisme français* 37 (1888), 2–13, 57–69, 124–136, 169–191, 393–415, 449–462, 561–577, 617–635.

Haag, Eugène, and Émile Haag. *La France Protestante, ou vies des protestants français.* Revised by Henri Bordier. 2d ed. Paris, 1877–1888.

Sinnema, Donald. "Antoine de Chandieu's Call for a Scholastic Reformed Theology (1580)." In *Later Calvinism: International Perspectives,* edited by W. Fred Graham. Kirksville, Mo., 1993.

GLENN S. SUNSHINE

CHANTRIES. An important part of the late medieval church in England, chantries were endowments, generally in the form of lands, given to parish churches or cathedrals for the purpose of providing prayers for the souls of the dead. The belief that intercessions offered by the living could aid the departed was intimately linked with the medieval doctrine of purgatory. Benefactions for chantries were especially common in the fourteenth century as a response to the Black Death, but they continued into the 1540s. Many parish churches employed a chantry priest in addition to the rector or vicar. Chantries were especially significant in London, where there were more than two hundred chantries in the parish churches and more chantry priests than ordinary parish clergy. Many churches and cathedrals had special chantry chapels and altars where "masses satisfactory" were offered. Some of these, such as Prince Arthur's chantry at Worcester, were exceptional examples of perpendicular Gothic architecture and contained fine sculpture. Large chantry endowments might provide for the daily singing of a mass satisfactory; smaller sums could assure periodic remembrance (a "month's mind" or "year's mind").

The belief in purgatory and the chantries associated with it came under attack during the early phases of the English Reformation, largely through the influence of Martin Luther's teachings. According to the Lutheran doctrine of justification by faith alone, salvation depended on the faith of the individual, not the prayers of priests or survivors. While these doubts about the efficacy of chantries were arising, Henry VIII's government was solving financial problems by confiscating church properties. The dissolution of the monasteries (1536–1540) brought vast amounts of monastic wealth into the hands of the king, but these revenues were dissipated rapidly. Chantries were equally vulnerable.

In 1545 Parliament passed an act for the dissolution of all chantries, colleges of priests, hospitals, and religious fraternities or guilds. It did not invoke theology but justified suppression on the grounds of the king's "inestimable charges" for foreign wars. Since the provisions of the act expired with the death of Henry VIII early in 1547, new legislation was required under Edward VI. The second chantries act (1547) did begin with a theological preamble, which attributed "a great part of superstition and errors in Christian religion" to "vain opinions of Purgatory and masses satisfactory to be done for them which be departed." Under this statute 2,374 chantries were dissolved.

The Court of Augmentations, a financial bureau that had handled the dissolution of the monasteries, was given responsibility for administering chantry properties as well. Two special commissioners, Sir Walter Mildmay and Robert Keilway, were instructed to make a complete survey of endowments and recommend cases where funds should still be allocated for such purposes as the maintenance of schoolmasters and vicarages, poor relief, and the maintenance of seawalls and bridges.

The impact of the dissolution of chantries was felt most keenly in the area of elementary education, since many chantry priests also acted as schoolmasters. At one time it was common for historians to lament the demise of the chantry schools, but more recent scholarship suggests that the chantry priests were poorly prepared to teach and that their schools were not of high quality. In some areas the commissioners allocated funds for the continuation of educational institutions, while in others the closing of a chantry school motivated local leaders to found new grammar schools. A number of towns—for instance, Stratford-upon-Avon and Chelmsford—still have grammar schools named for Edward VI that were erected under these conditions. Although some chantry chapels were demolished and others suffered from iconoclastic movements in the sixteenth and seventeenth centuries, most English cathedrals and a number of parish churches retain chapels originally built as chantries.

BIBLIOGRAPHY

Cook, G. H. *Medieval Chantries and Chantry Chapels.* London, 1963. Includes illustrations and a description of cathedrals and churches with chantry chapels.

Kreider, Alan. *English Chantries: The Road to Dissolution.* Cambridge, Mass., 1979. The standard monograph on the dissolution.

Richardson, Walter C. *History of the Court of Augmentations, 1536–1554.* Baton Rouge, La., 1961. Describes the process of dissolution.

Simon, Joan. *Education of Society in Tudor England.* Cambridge, 1966. The best discussion of the impact of the dissolution on the schools.

Wood-Legh, K. L. *Perpetual Chantries in Britain.* Cambridge, 1965. Especially good on the medieval period.

STANFORD E. LEHMBERG

solution of the monasteries, Henry created eight new secular chapters to replace the lost monastic ones. Moreover, he established six new sees, each with its own cathedral and chapter. Thereafter the cathedral canons proved tenacious survivors in the upheavals of the Reformation, despite the grave reservations about their utility expressed by zealous Protestants, who saw them as "dens. . . of. . . loitering lubbers." Archbishop Thomas Cranmer hoped to transform them by making the cathedral the focus of reformed preaching, and some chapters, notably that of Durham in the first years of Elizabeth's reign, did provide spiritual leadership to their dioceses. Too often, however, they became merely valuable sources of patronage for the Crown and bishops and comfortable niches for clergy who enjoyed the proper connections. Yet they did offer a major element in a flexible career structure that helped to attract able men to the church in the difficult years after the Reformation, and they protected one element in ecclesiastical endowments from direct depredation by the laity.

The most obvious comparison with the Anglican chapters are those of the post-Tridentine Catholic church. The decrees of the Council of Trent gave the bishops greatly enhanced powers to enforce residence and discipline, and chapters were expected to provide intellectual leadership within their dioceses. The results were mixed: old habits of resistance to episcopal authority died hard, as the efforts to enforce the Counter-Reformation in the southern Netherlands in the 1560s showed, and chapters, even when purged of the worst abuses, remained a focus of privilege and of the struggle for ecclesiastical patronage.

BIBLIOGRAPHY

Chrisman, Miriam Usher. *Strasbourg and the Reform: A Study in the Process of Changes.* New Haven, 1967.

Janelle, Pierre. *The Catholic Reformation.* Milwaukee, 1963.

Lehmberg, Stanford E. *The Reformation of Cathedrals: Cathedrals in English Society, 1485–1603.* Princeton, 1988.

Marcombe, David, and C. S. Knighton, eds. *Close Encounters: English Cathedrals and Society since 1540.* Nottingham, 1991.

FELICITY HEAL

CHAPTERS. The Reformation threatened the existence of cathedral chapters in most territories where it triumphed. In the Calvinist lands they were swept aside; elsewhere they were allowed to atrophy after the loss of their property, as in Sweden, or left as islands of irrelevant privilege in a Reformed polity, as at Strasbourg. The Danes managed to transmute their chapters into moderate supporters of the reformed bishops.

Continuity with the Catholic past was most visible in England, where their role was affirmed after Henry VIII's breach with Rome. The nine cathedrals served by secular canons were left relatively undisturbed and, after the dis-

CHARITY. In its comprehensive sense, charity is for the medieval church the principle of Christian spirituality. The concept of charity includes the concepts of *amor* ("love") and *dilectio* ("preferential love"). Charity signifies loving and desiring intentionality that is rightly ordered. The various kinds of love of God, love of neighbor, and love of self are rightly ordered when they are related to one another in a descending rank corresponding to the order of all goods. According to Augustine (*De doctrina christiana* 1. 22–33), all people must will appropriately four goods worthy of love: first, God, who is the highest good and stands at the pinnacle of all goods; second, the good that each person represents as a spiritual being in relationship with God; third, the good of others, who are equally valuable spiritual beings; fourth, goods subordinate to humans as spiritual beings but part of the physical nature they share. Augustine used the Neoplatonic order of goods in order to clarify the Christian virtue of charity. Although only the love of God and neighbor were commanded (*Mt.* 22:37–40; *Mk.* 12:29–31; *Lk.* 10:27) and not love of self and earthly goods, Augustine offered the explanation that fallen humanity was inextricably motivated by love of self and of the lower goods. These two kinds of love, namely, of self and of lower goods, are not forbidden by the scriptural commandment but must be brought into the right order. For next to God, men and women in desiring their salvation should love themselves, and thereby distinguish the salvation of their souls from their physical wellbeing. Also one's neighbors should be loved primarily as spiritual beings in view of eternal life. The Augustinian doctrine of the order of charity became a firm component of scholastic doctrine through the efforts of Peter Lombard in his *Sententiarum* (compare Thomas Aquinas, *Summa theologiae*).

Independently of the scholastic discussion, the notion of the order of goods is, with the corresponding kinds of charity, a basic element of medieval piety. In ecclesiastical and cultural life the primacy according to God's revelation of salvation is the love of God and the longing for the salvation of one's own soul and that of one's neighbor. As the comprehensive virtue, charity gives to the human will the right ordering of the various goods. Charity is the steering, formative principle of all human virtues. Consequently, it is also the principle of all works, with which the faithful may merit eternal life. To live with the virtue of charity is made possible only through the church's grace, which is basically given in baptism. Charity, in turn, calls on humans to realize the love of God through the acknowledgment of the sacraments of the church and through obedience to the precepts of the church and to the Decalogue. Serious sins, the so-called mortal sins, destroy the habitus of charity. The sacrament of penance renews the habitus of charity. Otherwise, one will suffer eternal damnation. In his catechism of 1512/1513 (*Christiani Hominis Institutum*), Desiderius Erasmus of Rotterdam offered an exemplary model of how charity, in its three forms of love of God, of self, and of neighbor, was connected to the acknowledgment of the ecclesiastical doctrine of faith and the sacraments.

What Christianity says about the love of God for men and women and about the revelation of this love of God in Jesus Christ did not become a factor of discussion in the Reformation. Nevertheless, the Reformation broke with the traditional doctrine of charity as the principle of Christian religiosity. Faith, now understood differently, became in the Reformation the principle of Christian religiosity, which was the result of the doctrine of justification by faith alone. As Luther developed his theology with increasing clarity in the

context of his biblical exegesis in the first decade of his teaching at Wittenberg (1512–1521), he gave up the traditional system of Christian virtues. He did more than shift the emphasis from charity to faith. Luther, and the other Protestant theologians following him, no longer related humanity to a hierarchical ordering of goods. Men and women had to orient themselves, on the one hand, to God's demanding will, as it was manifest in the law of God, and, on the other hand, to appropriate in faith the message of God's salvation, the gospel message of Christ. The double commandment of love now meant that men and women in their relationship with God should trust the message of the gospel. If love and hope, or fear, of God appear next to faith, then they are to be understood as connotations of the concept of faith. In other words, love of God is a trusting commitment. It is decisive for the human relationship with God that humans acknowledge themselves as sinners and surrender themselves to the good news of God's forgiving love. Out of this faith grows love of neighbor, which according to the gospel also entails the love of one's enemy. Faith and love of neighbor became a formula of Reformation theology in the place of the traditional complex concept of charity. If the Reformation related both the tables of the Decalogue to the double commandment of love (i.e., for God and for neighbor), the commandment to worship God was functionally related to faith and its connotations, for example, the fear of God. These connotations received stronger weight with Calvin than with Luther.

Faith bears its fruits in the form of love of neighbor and the self-discipline necessary for this purpose. Reformation theologians interpreted *Galatians* 5:6 in this way. Therefore, this passage had supported the belief that the virtue of charity had to be added to faith as the effective principle of the Christian life. Analogously, the new interpretation of scriptural passages such as *Romans* 13:10 and *I Timothy* 1:5 changed. For in the love of neighbor, which faith brought forth as its fruit, the law of God found its fulfillment. Love of neighbor no longer encompassed one's neighbors according to an order of goods, which lay at the base of an order of charity. Perhaps the Reformation's interest in a new ordering of aid to the poor can be explained from this esteem for love of neighbor. The orders for poor relief (*Kastenordnungen*) document this lively interest. Ecclesiastical foundations fulfilled their purposes if they took care of the indispensable external (personal and material) requirements for congregational worship and enabled instruction in schools. The remaining funds of the foundations and other offerings should aid the poor as an expression of love of neighbor. Luther wrote "There is no greater service of God than Christian love which helps and serves the needy." The concept of love also attained the meaning of communal consciousness or responsibility. The neighbor becomes a member of the community, and the nature of the community is taken into consideration for the sake of its members.

In the defense of traditional doctrine, Roman Catholic theologians of the Reformation era seldom explicitly expressed their interest in charity as the principle of religiosity (for example, Nicolaus Herborn, *Locorum communium adversus huius temporis haereses enchiridion*). The controversy mainly revolved around whether works were necessary for justification and eternal life. It was taken as self-evident, chiefly by recourse to *Galatians* 5:6, that charity as the virtue of rightly ordered love of God and others brought forth required good works. By the same token, the reformers did not always adequately clarify that the doctrine of justification by faith alone represented a new understanding of faith and that the concepts of law and gospel required coordinates for the experience of God other than those that had previously been important for the order of charity.

BIBLIOGRAPHY

Haikola, Lauri. *Usus legis.* Helsinki, 1981.
Kuhn, Helmut. *Liebe; Geschichte eines Begriffs.* Munich, 1975.
Rousselot, Pierre. *Pour l'histoire du problème de l'amour au Moyen Âge.* Paris, 1933.
Singer, Irving. *The Nature of Love.* Vol. 1, *Plato to Luther.* Chicago, 1984.

REINHARD SCHWARZ
Translated from German by Jeff Bach

CHARLES V (Span., Carlos; 1500–1558), Holy Roman Emperor (1519–1556) and, as Charles I, king of Spain (1516–1556). He is arguably the most significant political figure of the age of the Reformation. His proclaimed goals were to uphold the Roman Catholic faith, oppose the spread of Protestantism, and defend the borders of Western Christendom against the expansion of the Ottoman Empire. Whatever side of national or religious issues historians take, they tend to find him an attractive personality.

Charles was born in Ghent on 24 February 1500. He was the son of Philip I the Handsome, duke of Burgundy and sovereign of the Netherlands and of Joan, eventual heiress of Ferdinand I of Aragon and Isabella of Castile. Philip was heir to the Austrian Habsburg possessions of his father, Holy Roman Emperor Maximilian I.

Charles's inheritance was the most extraordinary in European history and excited the awe and envy of contemporaries. When his father died in 1506, he succeeded to the Netherlands (Brabant, Flanders, Holland, Zeeland, and a dozen other provinces), Luxembourg, and Franche Comté. On the death of Ferdinand I in 1516, he was proclaimed king of Castile and its Indies, Aragon, Navarre, Sicily, Sardinia, and Naples, even though his mother, judged mentally incompetent, lived until 1555. Maximilian I died in 1519, leaving Charles the domains of the House of Austria. These Charles ceded in 1521 to his younger brother, Ferdinand, whom he made regent of all German Habsburg possessions in 1522. Maximilian also prepared the way for the election of Charles as Holy Roman Emperor. To defend his possessions and keep them in his family became for Charles an obsession.

Education and Family. Charles scarcely knew his parents, who journeyed to Spain in 1501–1503 and again in 1504, when they claimed the inheritance of Queen Isabella. When he next saw his mother in 1517, she had become mentally deranged. His sisters Eleanor (1498–1558), Isabella (1501–1525), and Mary (1505–1558) stayed with him in Brussels. In 1556 Eleanor and Mary would retire with him to Spain. His brother Ferdinand (1503–1564) and sister Catalina (1507–1578) were born in Spain.

Charles's early education fell to his intelligent aunt, Margaret of Austria (1480–1530), widow both of Joan's brother and Duke Philibert of Savoy. The pious humanist, Adrian, dean of Utrecht (later Pope Adrian VI), supervised Charles's studies. In boyhood and adolescence, however, Charles found hunting and the rites of chivalry more to his liking. Indulged in these pastimes by his chamberlain, Guillaume de Croy, Sieur de Chièvres (1458–1521), and his cronies of the Court of Brussels, Charles acquired the habits of eating and drinking too much, which contributed to later ailments and gout.

Charles was proclaimed of age in 1515 as duke of Burgundy, though he appeared but a gangling blond boy who had not yet shaved. He had the protruding Habsburg jaw that sometimes hung agape and made him look foolish. In the 1520s he grew a beard that gave his face the stronger look depicted in the famous Titian portraits.

In 1526 he married Princess Isabella of Portugal (1503–1539). They honeymooned in Granada, and she gave birth the following May to his heir, the future Philip II of Spain (1527–1598). Two other children survived—Maria (1529–1603), who married future Emperor Maximilian II (1527–1576), and Juana (1535–1573), who married Prince John of Portugal. Charles loved and respected Isabella, whom he left regent of Castile on three occasions. He felt strongly about his obligations as a father and took an active interest in the education of his children, especially of his heir, Philip. Before and after his married years, Charles sired two illegitimate children—Margaret (1522–1586), duchess of Parma, and John of Austria (1547–1578).

In religion he was devout and found consolation in prayer and contemplation. On Empress Isabella's death in 1539, he withdrew to a monastery for over a month, and many years later, after abdicating his crowns, he would retire to a monastery.

Statecraft and Government. Charles left several remarkable treatises on statecraft and a memoir of his life to 1551. Not yet twenty when elected emperor and by then already sovereign of many kingdoms and states, Charles learned statecraft through hard experience. Chièvres and his

"Flemings" nearly cost Charles control of Spain through their appetite for offices and privilege. From their arrival in Castile in 1517 until their departure for the imperial coronation in 1520, they successively alienated the representative *cortes* ("parlaiment") of Castile, Aragon, and Catalonia. In Castile and Valencia rebellions ensued, and only the power of the Spanish nobility—threatened by the radical urban interests of the Castilian *Comuneros* and Valencian *Germanías* and wooed in desperation by Charles's government—saved his throne. Chastened, Charles spent the years 1522–1529 in Spain to consolidate his regime.

With Chièvres dead, he turned to others, most importantly Mercurino Arborio di Gattinara (1465–1530), his grand chancellor. He sought advice, however, from various persons of experience, dealt with them increasingly through secretaries, and reached his own decisions. He did not appoint another grand chancellor after Gattinara died and later warned his son to guard his counsel and never let one person dominate him.

A number of prominent persons, many of them prelates, administered the government. For Castile Francisco de los Cobos proved most important and assisted Charles in refining its governing councils. For Charles's growing American empire, a new Council of the Indies was established. Debates about the legitimacy of the American conquests and the rights of native peoples stirred Spain and prompted him to promulgate in 1542 the relatively humane *Leyes nuevas: ordenanzas para la gobernación de las Indias y buen tratamiento y conservación de los indios* (New Laws: Ordinances for the Government of the Indies and Good Treatment and Preservation of the Indians), though their enforcement proved a different matter. Viceroys oversaw the government across the Atlantic, in Mexico and Peru, as they did in the European realms of the Crown of Aragon.

Charles regarded the maintenance of religion as his principal obligation. In Spain the church had been purged of its worst abuses, and the Reformation made little headway. Even Erasmian ideas, favored by the youthful Charles, were suppressed. The Spanish Inquisition was thorough and widely supported, and Charles urged his heirs to uphold its power for the preservation of their state. He strengthened the Inquisition in Sicily, but his efforts to introduce it into Naples were blocked by popular protest. In the Netherlands he arranged for an Inquisition that answered to Rome, which proved both unpopular and ineffective.

Government in the Netherlands, ruled through its own institutions, continued under Margaret of Austria until 1530 and under Charles's sister Mary, the widowed queen of Hungary, from 1530 to 1555. The Austrian domains became the business of Ferdinand, who served as Charles's deputy in the empire and was elected in 1531 king of the Romans.

To finance his increasingly costly wars, Charles badgered the *cortes* of Castile and the Estates-General of the Netherlands for subsidies. He occasionally confiscated American treasure, which reached impressive sums only after 1545, borrowed heavily, and left a bankrupt treasury.

Foreign Relations, War, and the Spread of the Reformation. The patterns of foreign relations and war in Europe had been set before Charles was born. The rivalry he inherited with France—centered around dynastic claims and the dominion of Italy—provoked the Habsburg-Valois Wars (1521–1559). During the same years, the advance of the Ottoman Empire in the Balkans and Mediterranean reached its high-water mark under Sultan Süleyman I the Magnificent (r. 1520–1566). The Reformation added a new dimension to affairs, and the twin menace of France and the Turks, often in alliance, would repeatedly frustrate Charles's efforts to restore Catholicism in the Holy Roman Empire.

Charles in his memoirs blamed the machinations of Francis I of France for compelling him to leave Germany in 1521 before he could settle the matter of Martin Luther. When Charles returned to Germany in 1530 to deal with the spread of Lutheranism, he claimed that he had to temporize with the Protestant princes because he needed their support against the threat to Christendom of the Turks, who in 1529 had besieged Vienna.

The papacy, caught between its Italian interests and the need to confront the Reformation, proved another problem. Charles found the Sack of Rome (1527) by his troops an embarrassment yet fit punishment for Clement VII's conduct.

In Charles's statecraft, touches of chivalry occasionally appeared: challenges to personal combat with Francis I over Burgundy and Milan, resplendent state visits to Francis and Henry VIII, and his imperial coronation at Bologna (1530), the last ever by a pope. For the Reformation his most significant chivalric gesture came at Worms, where he honored his safe-conduct to Luther rather than seize him as urged by advisers, who reminded him that Emperor Sigismund (1410–1437) had not honored his word to the heretic Jan Hus. He came later to regret the gesture, and in his mature statecraft proved tough-minded and learned to dissemble when he felt it necessary.

Gattinara, a Savoyard, convinced Charles that Savoy and Milan were strategically central to the defense of the four European components of his inheritance. In 1535 Charles acquired Milan through escheat; he kept Savoy in alliance, though the French occupied the duchy in 1536, and it was not recovered for its duke until 1559 by Philip II. During the occupation of Savoy, Geneva broke free and became Calvinist.

An appreciation of Gattinara's concepts persisted in Charles's later advisers—Nicholas Perrenot de Granvelle (1486–1550), his son Cardinal Antoine Perrenot de Granvelle (1517–1586), and Fernando Álvarez de Toledo, duke of Alba (1507–1582). On occasion, however, Charles was willing to concede Milan on hard terms to France to buy the peace he needed to deal with Protestantism and the Turks.

French policy under Francis I (r. 1515–1547) and Henry II (r. 1547–1559) included claims on Milan, Savoy, Naples, and Charles's possessions bordering France. Charles's naive effort to recover Burgundy, after Francis I became his prisoner at Pavia (1525), confirmed French fears of a "Habsburg encirclement." Against France Charles's natural ally was Henry VIII of England (r. 1509–1547). Their alliance unraveled during Henry's divorce of Charles's aunt, Catherine of Aragon, but was briefly restored after her death (1536).

Defying the sentiments of Christendom, France made alliances with the Turks, who waged war in Hungary and the Mediterranean during the greater part of Charles's reign. Charles personally took the field against them in 1532, when he checked a threat to Vienna (though he failed to recover Hungary, which the Turks annexed in 1541); in 1535, when he captured Tunis; and in 1541, when he failed to take Algiers.

The French kings also sought alliances with German princes, playing on their common fear of Habsburg power and Protestants' concern for the Reformation. Charles made his own religious position clear at the Diet of Worms on 19 April 1521, the day after Luther had taken his stand. He stated that he would uphold the faith of his fathers, for which he was prepared to risk everything, and that Luther, a single monk, erred to go contrary to the opinion of Christendom.

He issued the Edict of Worms against Luther and then left for Spain, not yet knowing that the *Comuneros* were defeated. By the time he returned to Germany in 1530, the upheavals of the Knights' Revolt and Peasants' War had passed, formal recesses had weakened the edict and called for debate, and, at Speyer in 1529, "Protestant" princes had rallied in defense of their religion. The Augsburg Confession of 1530, presented to Charles, clarified Lutheran beliefs and, despite efforts at compromise prompted by the Turkish menace, differences between Protestants and Catholics hardened.

Though Charles rejected advice that he simply ignore the differences, he dared not use force because he wanted Protestant support for the election of Ferdinand as king of the Romans and for his planned campaign against the Turks. He continued to seek a German solution to the Lutheran problem through imperial diets and intensified his demands, made in person to Clement VII in 1530 and Paul III in 1536, for a general council of the church.

To protect the Reformation and their interests, German Protestant princes in 1531 formed the Schmalkald League, which quickly received emissaries from Francis I and Henry VIII. War and diplomacy kept Charles from Germany from the end of 1532 until 1541, when at the Diet of Regensburg he took part in fruitless colloquies with Philipp Melanchthon and Cardinal Gasparo Contarini. When he left to attack Algiers, he felt constrained to accede once more to interims

that protected Protestant gains, though by secret codicils he insisted on the rights of the Catholic church.

He won support sufficient enough that in 1544 he was able to invade France from Lorraine and force Francis again to peace. Peace permitted the opening in 1545 of the Council of Trent, in which Charles now put his hope for a solution to the religious division of the empire. Peace also permitted Charles to take up arms in 1546 against the Schmalkald League for reasons he insisted were political. He gained as ally the Lutheran Duke Moritz of Saxony, and imperial forces, a third of them Spaniards, triumphed at the Battle of Mühlberg (24 April 1547). The leaders of the league, Elector John Frederick of Saxony and Landgrave Philipp of Hesse, were soon his prisoners, and Charles rewarded Moritz with John Frederick's electorship.

Differences between Charles and Paul III dashed Charles's hope that the empire's religious problems might be solved following his apparent political triumph. Paul, over Charles's objection, removed the Council of Trent to Bologna, but worse, he accused Charles of complicity in the assassination in 1547 of Pier Luigi Farnese, duke of Parma, Paul's son and father-in-law of Charles's natural daughter Margaret. Parma had been meddling in the affairs of Genoa and Milan.

Thus, after Mühlberg, Charles found no solutions and could only renew conciliatory interims that left neither Catholics nor Protestants satisfied. He kept the two Schmalkald leaders prisoner while Spanish garrisons maintained peace. To the irritation of the Germans, he separated the Habsburg Netherlands (enlarged in 1543 by the conquest of Gelderland) from the empire, and gained through his sister Mary of Hungary and Bohemia the reluctant assent of Ferdinand, designated to succeed him as emperor, that Philip II would succeed Ferdinand and that Ferdinand's son Maximilian would only succeed Philip.

When a Turkish offensive in the Mediterranean forced Charles to send his Spanish garrisons south in 1551, Moritz of Saxony formed a new league of Protestant princes and allied with Henry II of France. Early in 1552 Moritz chased Charles from Innsbruck across the Alps, while Henry seized the imperial bishoprics of Metz, Verdun, and Toul. The Council of Trent, which had reconvened in 1551, scattered, not to reassemble until 1562.

Charles besieged Metz in vain, as Ferdinand and Maximilian negotiated with Moritz the Truce of Passau (1552), which established the principle of *cujus regio, ejus religio* ("whose region, his religion") for the empire and led to the Peace of Augsburg. Refusing to accept terms that recognized religious division, Charles yielded his imperial responsibilities to Ferdinand, who in 1558 was crowned emperor. Humiliated and embittered by his failure to maintain the Roman Catholic religion in the empire, he blamed others for it. The Saxon electors were traitors, the German princes were self-seeking, and the German bishops unwilling to reform abuses. Francis I and Henry II put dynastic gain ahead of religion. Henry VIII was a victim of lust. Pope Clement VII feared a church council, and Pope Paul III put it off, though again Francis I could be blamed. Even Ferdinand had let him down for the sake of Maximilian, who curried the favor of his enemies and heretics. Finally, there was his continual shortage of money, since his expenses far outpaced his revenues.

Charles's failures were alleviated by the renewal of the English alliance, which led to Philip II's marriage in 1554 to Mary Tudor, queen of England (r. 1553–1558), and seemingly secured the Netherlands. Suffering poor health, Charles believed the time was right to abdicate his remaining responsibilities to Philip. In October 1555, in a tearful ceremony in Brussels, he recounted his travels and campaigns for God and his subjects and abdicated the Netherlands. In 1556 he abdicated Castile and Aragon with all their possessions. He retired to a remote Hieronymite monastery at Yuste in Spain, though he continued to follow the world, overeat, and find time for fishing, as well as for devotion. He died of malarial fevers on 21 September 1558.

BIBLIOGRAPHY

Bataillon, Marcel. *Erasme et l'Espagne.* New ed., 3 vols. Geneva, 1991.

Brandi, Karl. *The Emperor Charles V.* Translated by C. V. Wedgwood. Reprint, London, 1980. This is the first volume of Brandi's two-volume *Kaiser Karl V,* Munich, 1937–1941, and remains the standard work. The second volume contains sources and commentary.

Carande, Ramón. *Carlos V y sus banqueros.* 3 vols. Reprint, Barcelona, 1990. Details the financial problems.

Durme, Maurice van. *El Cardenal Granvela.* Barcelona, 1957. Originally published in Flemish in 1953.

Fernández Álvarez, Manuel. *Política Mundial de Carlos V y Felipe II.* Madrid, 1966. The best treatment of Charles's thoughts on statecraft.

———. *Charles V.* London, 1975. A Spanish perspective.

Fernández Álvarez, Manuel, ed. *Corpus Documental de Carlos V.* 5 vols. Salamanca, 1973–1981. Includes Charles's memoirs.

Gutiérrez Nieto, Juan Ignacio. *Las Comunidades como movimiento antiseñorial.* Barcelona, 1973.

Headley, John M. *The Emperor and His Chancellor: A Study of the Imperial Chancellery under Gattinara.* Cambridge, 1983.

Keniston, Hayward. *Francisco de los Cobos, Secretary of the Emperor Charles V.* Pittsburgh, 1960.

Lutz, Heinrich. *Christianitas Afflicta.* Göttingen, 1964.

Maltby, William S. *Alba.* Berkeley, 1983.

Merriman, Roger B. *The Rise of the Spanish Empire in the Old World and the New.* Vol. 3, *The Emperor.* Reprint, New York, 1962. A solid study with extensive bibliographies.

Rodríguez Salgado, M. J. *The Changing Face of Empire: Charles V, Philip II and Habsburg Authority, 1551–1559.* Cambridge, 1988. An important revisionist look at the shift in power.

PETER O'M. PIERSON

CHARLES IX OF FRANCE (1550–1574), second son of Henry II and Catherine de Médicis. Charles IX became king of France on the death of his brother Francis II (5 December 1560). As he was only ten years old, his mother Catherine was put in charge of the government, with the first prince of the blood, Antoine of Navarre, lieutenant general of the realm. Against the will of the Catholic triumvirate of Saint-André, Montmorency, and Guise, Catherine promulgated edicts of toleration on the advice of Chancellor Michel de l'Hôpital. In 1561, Catherine called for a colloquy in Poissy in an unsuccessful attempt to reconcile the Catholic church and the French Calvinists. On 1 March 1562, the duke of Guise murdered Protestant worshipers at Wassy and the Wars of Religion began.

At Catherine's insistence, the young Charles IX formally solicited military assistance from Catholic foreign princes, especially the pope and the king of Spain. The Catholic triumvirate thus formed placed Antoine of Navarre in charge of the royal army. Louis I de Condé, Gaspard II de Coligny, and François d'Andelot were at the head of the Huguenot forces and requested help from Elizabeth of England, promising her Le Havre and Dieppe.

After the Battle of Dreux (19 December 1562), a disaster for the Huguenots, and numerous sieges of towns in the Loire valley and in Normandy, the Peace of Amboise was concluded 19 March 1563. Religious toleration, of a sort, was decreed and the prince of Condé appointed as lieutenant general of the realm. Then Catholics and Protestants joined together to drive English soldiers out of Normandy. Thus the first civil war in Charles IX's reign seemed to result in a national and religious reconciliation. The young king was proclaimed of age after his thirteenth birthday on 17 August 1563. To strengthen his prestige, Catherine took Charles on a tour of France from 1564 to 1566. In Bayonne they met the queen of Spain, Elizabeth, sister of Charles, and Fernando Álvarez de Toledo, duke of Alba, both of whom, in the name of Philip II of Spain, urged France to strike out against the Protestants. Hostilities began again (second and third Wars of Religion, 1567–1570), with victories for the Duke of Anjou at Jarnac and Moncontour. The Peace of Saint-Germain in August 1570 permitted Calvinist worship in all places in the possession of the Huguenots. Surety towns were designated, and Protestant nobles enjoyed free exercise of their faith.

Charles and his mother wished to strengthen France against Spanish domination, which had been increased by the repression of the Revolt of the Netherlands and victory over the Moriscos and Turks at the Battle of Lepanto in October 1571. A double marriage arrangement was made. The first was the marriage of the duke of Anjou, brother of the king and hero of the third civil war, to Queen Elizabeth of England; the second was the marriage of Marguerite, sister of Charles IX, to the Protestant Prince Henry of Navarre (Henry IV). The latter was managed by Admiral Gaspard II de Coligny, who exercised great influence at the royal court and tried to obtain from the king men and money for a Flanders expedition against Spain.

One version of the events of August 1572 is that Catherine was jealous of Admiral Coligny. When numerous Protestants crowded Paris for the nuptials of Prince Henry and the king's sister, Catherine decided to have the admiral murdered to maintain her influence over her son and to avoid a disastrous war with Spain. In this version, after a failed attempt on Coligny's life, Catherine, to avoid a reprisal of the Huguenots then concentrated in Paris, drew from King Charles a resolution to instigate a general massacre on Saint Bartholomew's Day, 24 August 1572.

This massacre precipitated the fourth War of Religion, marked by numerous assaults by the royal army against the Protestant city of La Rochelle. In the first week of July 1573, Charles IX allowed La Rochelle, Montauban, Sancerre, and Nîmes free exercise of religion. But the southern part of the realm resisted and formed a Huguenot confederation. The Crown wanted to end the conflict to permit the brother of the king, Henry, duke of Anjou, to obtain the throne of Poland. In the summer of 1573, a deputation of Polish nobles went to France to notify the duke of his royal election. But the Huguenots persevered in their resistance, joined by new opponents of royal policy, the *politiques*, headed by the duke of Damville. A plot was discovered against the king and the queen mother.

Meanwhile, Charles, increasingly melancholy since the Saint Bartholomew's Day Massacre, died of tuberculosis on 30 May 1574. Charles left no son from his consort, Elizabeth of Austria, but he had one son, Charles, later duke of Angoulême, from his Protestant mistress, Marie Touchet. Although emotionally disturbed, Charles IX was a cultivated man, educated by the humanist Jacques Amyot. He wrote poetry and a book on hunting, and he was a protector of the famous literary group the Pléiade.

BIBLIOGRAPHY

Bourassin, Emmanuel. *Charles IX*. Paris, 1986.
Cloulas, Ivan. *Catherine de Médicis*. New ed. Paris, 1987.
———. *Philippe II*. Paris, 1992.
Erlanger, Philippe. *Saint Bartholomew's Night: The Massacre of Saint Bartholomew*. Translated by Patrick O'Brian. Westport, Conn., 1975.
Thompson, James Westfall. *The Wars of Religion in France, 1559–1576: The Huguenots, Catherine de Medici, Philippe II*. New ed. New York, 1957.

IVAN CLOULAS

CHARLES IX OF SWEDEN (Swed., Karl; 1550–1611), regent and subsequently king of Sweden (r. 1599–1611). His importance in the prolonged and often convoluted history of the Reformation in Sweden lies in three areas: his resistance to the Catholic tendencies of his brother, John III, and his nephew, Sigismund I; his roles in the Uppsala Meeting (25 February–20 March 1593), which defined the liturgical forms and confessional position of the church

in Sweden; and his battles with the clergy over a variety of issues following the success of the revolution against Sigismund in 1598/99, which left Charles first regent and subsequently king of Sweden.

Although his personal religious position has been a matter of debate (Lutheran, Calvinist, scripturalist, etc.), he consistently supported the Protestant cause in Sweden. As duke of a large portion of central Sweden during the reigns of John III and Sigismund I, Charles repeatedly resisted attempts to recatholicize Sweden. He insisted on his right to appoint bishops in his duchy and to influence the beliefs and practices of the church there. Following John's death in 1592, Charles headed the move to call a national assembly of church leaders at Uppsala to establish the Protestant bases of religion in Sweden in response to the threat posed by the succession of Sigismund, a Catholic. The final document of the Diet of Uppsala affirmed the church in Sweden as Lutheran, on the basis of the Augsburg Confession and Lars Petri's Church Ordinance of 1571. The assembly also chose Abraham Angermannus to be the new archbishop. Following Sigismund's deposition, Charles entered into a series of prolonged struggles with the church over its independence and governance, the power to appoint bishops, the handbook, Mass, and catechism, his own "orthodoxy," the quality of the clergy, the religious content of his Coronation Charter, and toleration. Few of these were resolved during his reign, and the church found a more enthusiastic and less contentious supporter in his son and successor, Gustavus II Adolph.

BIBLIOGRAPHY

Cornell, Jan, Sten Carlsson, and Jerker Rosén, eds. *Den svenska historien*. Vol. 3. Stockholm, 1967–1968. Includes an overview of the period and brief pieces on key individuals and events. Superbly illustrated.
Roberts, Michael. *The Early Vasas: A History of Sweden. 1523–1611*. Cambridge, 1968. Best work in English on sixteenth-century Sweden. Excellent annotated bibliography.
Scott, Franklin D. *Sweden: The Nation's History*. Rev. & enl. ed., Carbondale, Ill., 1988. Excellent treatment of subject. Includes notes and bibliography.

BYRON J. NORDSTROM

CHATEAUBRIAND, EDICT OF. Issued in June of 1551, this edict marked a turning point in the policy of the French crown toward religious dissent. Though self-styled "King of the Renaissance," Francis I (d. 1547) had undertaken some restrained persecution of what he considered excessive religious tumult; but basically he was a patron of scholars and did not mind seeing conservative theologians made uncomfortable. His son, Henry II, had neither Francis's intelligence nor toleration and appears to have held rather inflexibly to the French equation of "one king, one law, one faith." Religious conflict—largely drawn from the

Rhineland evangelicals and the teachings of Jacques Lefèvre d'Étaples at the University of Paris—had been intensifying since the 1520s; but Francis I had generally moderated his response unless confronted with something that he found dearly offensive, such as the *Affaire des Placards* in October 1534, when vicious attacks on the church were posted widely (including on the door of the king's chambers). The result was that some publications were censored, some people were incarcerated, and others (including Calvin) fled the kingdom. But bloody persecutions appear to have owed more to the fanaticism of the Parlement of Paris (the high court) and the Faculty of Theology of Paris.

Henry II was determined to increase the pressure, and the Edict of Chateaubriand marked the inauguration of a new policy, away from what one author has called "negative opposition" to "positive and persuasive persecution" (Sutherland, *Huguenot Struggle*, p. 44). The edict addressed publication, distribution of literature, education, regular attendance at Mass, careful verification of the orthodoxy of officials, and various other matters largely unenforceable. The edict produced little change, but it is significant as an indicator of the much harsher policy that Henry II was to follow until his death in 1559.

[*See also* Calvin, John; Francis I of France; Henry II of France; *and* Huguenots.]

BIBLIOGRAPHY

Rothrock, George A. *The Huguenots: A Biography of a Minority.* Chicago, 1979.

Salmon, J. H. M. *Society in Crisis: France in the Sixteenth Century.* London, 1975.

Sutherland, N. M., *The Huguenot Struggle for Recognition.* New Haven and London, 1980. Indisputably the best source for the edicts, instruments of pacification, treaties, and other documents generated during the Wars of Religion in France, with many printed or summarized in a useful appendix.

GEORGE A. ROTHROCK

CHÂTEILLON, Sébastien. *See* Castellion, Sébastien.

CHEMNITZ, Martin

(1522–1586), German Lutheran theologian and co-drafter of the Formula of Concord. Born on 9 November 1522 in Treuenbrietzen, near Wittenberg, Chemnitz, the son of a clothmaker, struggled in poverty to gain an education at Wittenberg and Magdeburg before attending the universities of Frankfurt an der Oder and Wittenberg (1543–1545 and 1545–1547). He combined both formal and private study of theology with service, first as a schoolteacher and then as the librarian and astrological consultant of Duke Albrecht of Prussia in Königsberg (1547–1553). He read especially Peter Lombard's "Sentences" and Luther's postils (prepared sermons). In Königsberg, under the tutelage of his friend Joachim Mörlin, he learned the art of polemic in engagements with the Roman Catholic Friedrich Staphylus and Lutheran Andreas Osiander, whose deviations from Luther's understanding of justification seriously divided the Prussian church. This dispute caused Chemnitz to return to Wittenberg for further theological study. There he was drawn into Philipp Melanchthon's inner circle and began to lecture on his *Loci communes* while serving on the arts faculty and pursuing patristic studies. Mörlin arranged his call to Braunschweig, where Mörlin himself was ecclesiastical superintendent. Chemnitz served as his coadjutor in the city, continuing his lectures on Melanchthon's *Loci communes* for the education of the local ministerium. He also joined Mörlin in efforts to secure the proper interpretation of Luther's teaching throughout Lower Saxony and Germany. Mörlin represented a Gnesio-Lutheran position, and although Chemnitz is seldom closely identified with that party because of his continuing loyalty to Melanchthon, his views closely matched Mörlin's. Together they attempted to reconcile Melanchthon to Matthias Flacius Illyricus and his Gnesio-Lutheran comrades in the Coswig-Wittenberg negotiations of 1557. In 1561 Chemnitz joined other Lower Saxon theologians in rejecting the sacramentarian position of Albert Hardenberg of Bremen; Chemnitz had opposed "Zwinglian" elements among the common people in Braunschweig as well. He supported the *Lüneburg Articles* of 1561, composed by Mörlin, which put forth Gnesio-Lutheran views on a number of issues.

In 1562 Chemnitz first criticized Roman Catholicism in print with his *Theologiae Jesuitarum praecipua capita,* an analysis of Jesuit teaching, particularly of the catechism of Johannes Monheim (1560). Replies, particularly from the Spanish theologian Diego Payva d'Andrada, a leader at the Council of Trent, elicited Chemnitz's four-volume critique of Trent, *Examen Concilii Tridentini* (1565–1573).

In 1567, when Mörlin returned to Königsberg to reorganize the Prussian church, Chemnitz assumed the office of superintendent of the Braunschweig churches. Chemnitz assisted Mörlin in drafting the Prussian *Corpus doctrinae* in that year. The following year Duke Julius of Braunschweig-Wolfenbüttel enlisted Chemnitz, along with Nicholas Selnecker and Jakob Andreae, to introduce the Reformation to his lands. Over the next decade Chemnitz and Julius worked closely together in the restructuring of the church in Julius's lands and in ecclesiastical politics across the empire. In 1568 and 1569 Chemnitz formulated *corpora doctrinae* for both Julius (published in revised form as the *Corpus Julianum,* 1576) and Duke Wilhelm of Braunschweig-Lüneburg (*Corpus Wilhelminum*). He also assisted Julius in establishing the University of Helmstedt.

With Selnecker, Andreae, and others, Chemnitz, recognized as one of the leading theological minds of the time, was drawn into the process of formulating a doctrinal agreement to end Lutheran disputes in the early 1570s. He and

David Chytraeus revised Andreae's Swabian Concord into the Swabian-Saxon Concord (1574–1575), the document that served as the chief basis for the Formula of Concord. Elector August of Saxony engaged these four theologians—who were joined by two representatives of Brandenburg, Andreas Musculus and Christoph Körner—in drafting and revising the Formula of Concord (1575–1577). Chemnitz provided the most vital theological leadership for shaping the text. His earlier writing and negotiating had prepared him well for the task. His *Repetitio sanae doctrinae de vera praesentia corporis et sanguinis Domini in coena* (1561) had set forth Luther's view against sacramentarian divergences, a position repeated in other works on the Lord's Supper, and his *De duabus naturis in Christo* (1570, rev. ed., 1578) presented a Christology that mediated between the Swabian view of Johannes Brenz and Andreae (which held that Christ's human nature is, through the communication of attributes, omnipresent) and Philippist rejections of this view. Chemnitz taught that through the communication of attributes Christ's human body and blood could be present wherever, whenever, and in whatever form he willed ("multivolipresence"). Chemnitz had also studied other controverted issues in detail—justification through faith (in the Osiandrian controversy), original sin (against Flacius), and election—and he shaped the way in which Andreae's original suggestions on solving disputes in these areas were finally formulated.

Chemnitz continued to assist in the propagation of the theology of the Formula of Concord, participating in the composition of the *Apologia. . . deß. . . Concordienbuchs* (Apology of the Formula of Concord) with Selnecker and Timotheus Kirchner (1583) and in the Colloquy at Quedlinburg, which failed to win support for the Formula from the theologians of Braunschweig-Wolfenbüttel. This colloquy was in part necessary because Duke Julius had withdrawn from the Concordianist effort, largely because of differences with Chemnitz. In order to win territory, the duke had two sons tonsured according to Roman Catholic rite and named to ecclesiastical offices carrying secular lordship; Chemnitz had steadfastly worked to maintain the integrity of the church in relationship to secular political authority in the city of Braunschweig, and he had no reservations about criticizing what he viewed as Julius's capitulation to the "Roman Antichrist" for temporal gain. Julius broke completely with his favorite ecclesiastical counselor over this issue, and this incident probably hastened Chemnitz's death, which occurred on 8 April 1586.

In addition to the Formula of Concord and the previously mentioned works on Trent and on the Lord's Supper and Christology, several of Chemnitz's works continued to shape the thought of Lutheran orthodoxy. Chemnitz's sons and his successor in Braunschweig, Polycarp Leyser, completed unpublished works for the press, most importantly his commentary on Melanchthon's *Loci communes,* his postil, and his harmony of the Gospels. Chemnitz accommodated Luther's theology to his Melanchthonian rhetorical-dialectical training, perhaps not always recognizing where method intruded on message. Ever faithful to the memory of both preceptors, he tended to favor the Gnesio-Lutheran interpretation of the Wittenberg heritage over the Philippist. It hardly overestimates the significance of this "second Martin" for Lutheran orthodoxy to repeat the dictum of that age: "If Martin [Chemnitz] had not been, Martin [Luther] could hardly have remained."

BIBLIOGRAPHY

Primary Sources

Chemnitz, Martin. *The Two Natures in Christ.* Translated by J. A. O. Preus. Saint Louis, 1971.
———. *Examination of the Council of Trent.* 4 vols. Translated by Fred Kramer. Saint Louis, 1971–1986.
———. *The Lord's Supper.* Translated by J. A. O. Preus. Saint Louis, 1979.
———. *Ministry, Word, and Sanraments: An Enrichiridion.* Translated by Luther Poellot. Saint Louis, 1981.
———. *Loci Theologici.* Translated by J. A. O. Preus. 2 vols. Saint Louis, 1989.

Secondary Sources

Jungkuntz, Theodore R. "Martin Chemnitz: The Confessor?" In *Formulators of the Formula of Concord: Four Architects of Lutheran Unity,* pp. 46–68. Saint Louis, 1977. A brief biographical overview based on extant published sources and analyses.
Jünke, W. A., ed. *Der zweite Martin der Lutherischen Kirche: Festschrift zum 400. Todestag von Martin Chemnitz.* Braunschweig, 1986. Essays by European and American scholars on Chemnitz's theology and significance.
Klug, E. F. *From Luther to Chemnitz on Scripture and the Word.* Grand Rapids, Mich., 1971. Chemnitz is put to use in twentieth-century dogmatic dispute.
Kramer, Fred. "Martin Chemnitz, 1522–1586." In *Shapers of Religious Traditions in Germany, Switzerland, and Poland, 1560–1600,* edited by Jill Raitt, pp. 39–51. New Haven, 1981. A brief overview of Chemnitz's career and significance.
Mahlmann, Theodor. *Das neue Dogma der lutherischen Christologie.* Gütersloh, 1969. Helpful analysis of Chemnitz's Christology.
Teigen, Bjarne Wollan. *The Lord's Supper in the Theology of Martin Chemnitz.* Brewster, Mass., 1986. Argues for a "consecrationist" interpretation of Chemnitz's doctrine of the real presence.

ROBERT KOLB

CHRISTIAN II (1481–1559), king of Denmark and Norway (1513–1523) and of Sweden (1520–1523). After the death of his father, King John, Christian took over the Danish-Norwegian throne (1513), and following the conquest of Sweden he was also crowned king of Sweden (1520). In 1515 he married Elisabeth (Isabella), sister of the later Emperor Charles V.

His domestic policy was marked throughout by attacks on

the privileges of the nobles and high clergy, while at the same time favoring the middle class and farmers, a policy that was meant to serve the king's own interests. He never succeeded in eliminating the Swedish revolutionary movement, which chose Gustavus Vasa in 1521 as its national leader. A year later war broke out with the Hanseatic cities under the leadership of Lübeck and Gdańsk (Danzig). A short time later a revolt began in northern Denmark, and Christian II chose to go into exile with his wife, children, and a few loyal advisers (1523). He settled near Antwerp and hoped for support from the imperial family but was treated coolly by the queen's family. His attempt to reconquer Denmark and Norway ended with his capture, and he spent twenty-seven years in prison before dying in 1559.

Several circumstances in the king's aggressive policy toward the high clergy and nobility became conditions for the subsequent breakthrough of the Reformation in Denmark and Norway. He stepped in dictatorially again and again in the appointment of bishops. Worst of all were the scandals surrounding the archbishop's seat. Here, partially in cooperation with the Curia Romana, he appointed and dismissed five men in two years. This caused respect for the Roman church to decline, and some high clergy members were included in the barbaric execution of about eighty men after the conquest of Sweden (the Stockholm Bloodbath, 1520). Moreover, he forcefully began (1521–1522) an extensive complex of legislation against church jurisdiction and finances and against the bishops' discharge of their offices and the monastic system. He tried to establish a national appellate court and intended to reform the University of Copenhagen in a humanist direction. For this purpose he called in a few learned men from Wittenberg, including Andreas Bodenstein von Karlstadt (1521), who, however, fled after a few weeks.

These measures were an expression of reform Catholicism, but in exile he and the queen became convinced Lutherans. He lived for several months in Wittenberg and began a personal acquaintance with Martin Luther, who supported the king politically and condemned the Danish subjects for betraying their God-chosen lay authority (*Ob Kriegsleute auch in seligem Stande sein können* [Whether Soldiers Too Can Be Saved], 1526, WA 19). In addition to conducting an extensive correspondence with Luther and other men in Wittenberg, the king had the New Testament translated into Danish (1524) and had books smuggled into still Catholic Denmark that were laden with political propaganda for himself.

Politically, the conversion of the royal pair to Lutheranism was a blunder. Emperor Charles V turned his back on Christian, and only after Christian had renounced heresy did the emperor help him in his attempt at reconquest (1531). The king's correspondence from the years of exile and scattered sources from the years of imprisonment make it probable, however, that in his heart he remained a convinced Lutheran. Even though Denmark officially introduced Lutheranism (1536) under his cousin, Christian III, foreign and domestic policy considerations prevented his release from prison.

BIBLIOGRAPHY

Allen, C. F. *De tre nordiske rigers historie* (The History of the Three Scandinavian Kingdoms). 5 vols. Copenhagen, 1864–1872.

Lausten, Martin Schwarz. *Reformationen i Danmark* (The Reformation in Denmark). 2d ed. Copenhagen, 1992.

Lindhardt, P. G. "Reformationens forberedelse. . . 1513–1523" (Precursors of the Reformation. . . 1513–1523). In *Den Danske Kirkes Historie*, edited by Hal Koch and Bj. Kornerup, vol. 2, pp. 109–272. Copenhagen, 1965.

Venge, Mikael. *Christian 2.s Fald* (Christian II's Fall). Odense, 1972.

———. "Christian II." In *Dansk Biografisk Leksikon*, 3d ed., vol. 3, pp. 293–297. Copenhagen, 1979.

MARTIN SCHWARZ LAUSTEN

CHRISTIAN III (1503–1559), king of Denmark and Norway from 1534 to 1559. He was educated by the Saxon Wolfgang von Utenhof and the Holstein nobleman Johan Rantzau, and both were important for his early conversion to the Lutheran faith. When this happened is not known, though the experience of seeing Martin Luther at the Diet of Worms in 1521 may have played a large part. After Christian was married in 1525 to Dorothea, daughter of the Lutheran Duke Magnus of Sachsen-Lauenburg and his wife Catherine, he carried out the Lutheran Reformation (1526) in the area he had been given around the city of Haderslev in the duchy of Schleswig. With the help of Eberhard Weidensee of Hildesheim and Johann Wenth of Goslar, both educated in theology, law, and administration, he established a typical Lutheran principality, the first in Scandinavia, which had an evangelical Wittenberg church system for the approximately fifty clergy, as well as visitations, a seminar for ministers, and the requirement that the ministers swear loyalty to the duke.

During the chaotic conditions and the civil war (the Counts' War) occurring after the death (1533) of Christian's father, Frederick I, the predominantly Catholic national council in Denmark felt compelled to offer Christian the throne, despite their previous reluctance. At a meeting of the council of nobles (October 1536) in Copenhagen, Christian was able, as the victor in the civil war, to reorganize the Danish state and church. He had all the Catholic bishops taken prisoner and unjustly made them solely responsible for the war. They were dismissed permanently, and all church property was confiscated by the Crown. In the future the national council was to become completely secular, and the Lutheran religion was to be the only one allowed. With this Christian solved his economic, legal, and confessional problems after the war. An appointed commission worked out a proposal for a church ordinance, which was sent to Wittenberg for approval, and from there Johannes Bugenhagen was sent to Copenhagen (1537–1539) to lead the establishment of the Lutheran church.

Ceremonies in August and September 1537 marked the change to the new national administration and the new confession. First, the royal couple was crowned and anointed according to the medieval church ritual, which was adapted to reflect evangelical concepts. Second, the king signed the Latin church ordinance. Third, seven new Lutheran bishops (superintendents) were ordained by Bugenhagen. Because Bugenhagen was not himself an ordained bishop, Denmark had thus consciously relinquished the apostolic succession. Finally, the university at Copenhagen was reopened, using the University of Wittenberg as a model.

Texts preserved from the coronation ceremony, as well as the royal introductory letter to the church ordinance, show that Christian followed Philipp Melanchthon's humanist reform concept of the prince's relationship to the church, emphasizing his responsibility for religion and his role as defender of the faith and prinicpal member of the church, with the right and duty to lead the church. This was substantiated by the following year's legislation and by his demand for an oath from the clergy, his selection policy, the church's legal procedure, and his intervention in theological disputes. It is also seen in his cooperation with the church's bishops, particularly Peder Palladius, on social and moral questions, on the observation of holy days, and on his censorship and control of the clergy. In addition to the confessional change and the reforms that followed in the church, in the educational system, and in the care of the poor, Christian's reign also saw a reform of the army and an extensive reform of entailed estates to the benefit of the leading landed nobility and of the market towns but to the detriment of the lesser nobility and the farmers.

Personally, Christian was a deeply religious man, completely convinced of the truth of Lutheran Christianity. He led an intensely pious life, was interested in theological subjects, and exchanged letters all his life with Luther, Melanchthon, Bugenhagen, and other learned men, whom he also supported economically. His views on the territorial prince's religious and dynastic responsibilities were similar to those of his friends Landgrave Philipp of Hesse and Duke Albert of Prussia. His significance in the introduction and establishment of Lutheranism in the kingdom cannot be overestimated.

In foreign policy he bound himself closely to Emperor Charles V (Speyer Agreement, 1544). This meant that time and again he deserted his Lutheran comrades in Germany, as he did, for example, in the Schmalkald War (1546–1547). On the other hand, the agreement with the emperor ensured that the peace would be kept so that the Lutheran confession could be consolidated in the kingdom.

BIBLIOGRAPHY

Lausten, Martin Schwarz. *Religion og politik: Studier i Christian IIIs forhold til det tyske rige i tiden, 1544–1559* (Religion and Politics: Studies on Christian III's Relations with the German Empire, 1544–1559). Copenhagen, 1977. Contains a summary in German.
———. *Christian d.3 og kirken, 1537–1559* (Christian III and the Church, 1537–1559). Copenhagen, 1987. Contains a summary in German.
———. *Reformationen i Danmark* (The Reformation in Denmark). 2d ed. Copenhagen, 1992.
Slottved, Ejvind. "Christian III." In *Dansk Biografisk Leksikon*, 3d ed., vol. 3, pp. 197–302. Copenhagen, 1979.

MARTIN SCHWARZ LAUSTEN

CHRISTIAN CABBALA. *See* Cabbala, Christian.

CHRISTIAN HEBRAICA is the study of Hebrew, Aramaic, and medieval rabbinic sources for Christian religious purposes. During the Renaissance and Reformation, Christian Hebraica contributed to such diverse pursuits as mystical Cabbalistic studies, Catholic Old Testament textualism, Protestant exegetical concerns, and the reconstruction of New Testament apostolic Christianity.

Cabbalistic sources provided devotees of the ancient theology with a Mosaic component that complemented Hermetic, Pythagorean, and Orphic sources of wisdom. Pico della Mirandola, Johannes Reuchlin, and other early Christian Cabbalists believed that the essence of the Cabbalistic tradition entailed deciphering secret numerological permutations of Hebrew (Old Testament) names of God, the discovery of which could release into the world God's own creative powers. This power had been given to Adam in order to name the animals and plants in Eden and thereby to realize the potential of creation. On Mount Sinai, God again imparted this wisdom to Moses as a secret oral tradition with which to interpret the Old Testament. This same wisdom enabled Christ to perform miracles, and Reuchlin believed that by discovering the "wonderworking word" the contemporary magus might also transmute physical existence. Hence the early Christian Cabbala was a conceptual bridge uniting the *prisce theologia* ("ancient theology") with contemporary concepts of alchemy and magic. Later in the sixteenth century Guillaume Postel used the more significant Cabbalistic philosophical ideas from the *Book of Splendor* to create an encompassing mystical system. Seventeenth-century Cabbalistic emanationist theory provided an important conceptual backdrop for the cosmological views of the Cambridge Platonists.

Hebraica scriptural studies were far different. Printing made the Bible more available, but Renaissance linguistic erudition found Jerome's translation of the Old Testament increasingly inadequate. Catholic Hebraists at the University of Alcalá, primarily devoted to producing accurate Hebrew texts, published the Complutensian Bible (1517), which was closely followed by the Pagninus Bible (1528) and yet other accurate presentations of the Old Testament text. These efforts emphasized the importance of interpreting the biblical text from within the contemporary author's historical and cultural milieu. Both the Alcalá and Pagninus Bibles also stressed ancient traditions of grammatical interpretation and consequently included the rabbinic Targum (Aramaic translations) and other apparatus that explained the intellectual and conceptual Pharisaic background of the early Christian era. Despite avid Catholic scholarly interest in the new Bible study, the Vulgate remained the official and working text for determining Catholic doctrine; as a result, Catholic interest in textual Hebraica was short-lived.

Among Protestant scholars, however, interest was high. The Protestant rejection of the traditional fourfold method of scriptural exposition amplified contemporary scholarly desire for a more historical and literal translation of the Old Testament. To retrieve the simple meaning of the text, Protestant exegetes turned to David Kimhi, Abraham Ibn Ezra, and other medieval Jewish scholars who had advanced the notion of a historical rather than a mystical or spiritual interpretation of the biblical text. Not all Protestants were satisfied with the results. Luther's dichotomy of law and gospel dampened enthusiasm for rabbinic materials, and Johannes Forster and other Lutheran Hebraists distinguished clearly between Jewish and Christian grammatical traditions. Calvinist theologians emphasized the continuity of the old and new covenants, however, and some Reformed Hebraists attempted to locate Christian ideas within Pharisaic culture or, alternately, to reinterpret Pharisaic Judaism along Christian lines. Sebastian Münster, professor of theology at Basel and the foremost Christian Hebraist of the sixteenth century, translated the gospel of Matthew into Hebrew (1537) and added an ethnographic gloss to provide the reader with an appreciation of how Jesus' Pharisaic contemporaries might have understood *Matthew*. Paul Fagius, Wolfgang Capito's successor in Strasbourg, translated the moralistic apocryphal work *Ben Sira*, (1542) and the minor Talmudic treatise *Pirké Avot* (The Ethics of the Fathers; 1541) from Aramaic into Latin, providing a textual gloss demonstrating parallels between central Christian and Jewish teachings. Even more, Fagius's detailed description and analysis of the Jewish long grace in *Hebrew Blessings* (1542) provided readers with a Pharisaic religious framework to understand the proper meaning of the Lord's Supper.

Radical and restitutionist theologians made even more extensive use of rabbinic opinion to recapture the lost spirit of apostolic Christianity. Even Luther wrote of "Hebraisms" permeating the New Testament text and reminded Christians that Jesus was, after all, Jewish. Michael Servetus believed that at the time of Constantine the erroneous doctrine of the Trinity was accepted by Greek Christians who were unfamiliar with the Old Testament Hebrew idiom and Jesus'

contemporary culture. To return to "what the first Christians believed," Servetus used rabbinic nomenclature to introduce Old Testament monotheism into New Testament theology and to reconstruct apostolic Christianity along rabbinic lines. Similar restitutionist efforts in Italy led "Ebionite" and "Josephite" Christians to reject Jesus' divinity and to create an ethical/rational religious system predicated upon moral and religious values common to both Judaism and Christianity. The Transylvanian Unitarian bishop Francis Dávid and the Lithuanian theologian Jacob Paloelogus also attempted to restore Christianity to its allegedly Jewish roots. Benito Arias Montano, Matthew Vehe-Glirius, and Jean Bodin represented other heavily Judaized positions predicated on the use of yet other rabbinic sources.

Sixteenth-century Christian Hebraica eventually led to the development of modern Semitic studies and modern higher biblical criticism. It had less fortunate immediate results. Erasmus, Luther, Bucer, Calvin, and many other major scholars feared that extensive restitutionist use of Jewish materials to rephrase the New Testament would lead to the Judaization of Christianity. Despite the fact that no Judaized religious positions proved acceptable to orthodox denominations, the mere accusation of Judaization became a bogyman providing contending denominations with an easy condemnation of their opponents. Catholic authorities condemned Protestants for being pro-Jewish, while Lutherans and Calvinists accused each other, as well as Catholicism and Anabaptism, of undue Judaization. Even in liberal eastern European Unitarian circles, accusations of Judaization soon stifled debate of central doctrinal questions. Indeed, the fear of Jewish contamination was so great that Münster, Fagius, and other prominent orthodox Hebraists were forced to write anti-Semitic tracts to demonstrate their Christian loyalties.

[See also Antisemitism; Cabbala, Christian; Jews; *and* Judaizers.]

BIBLIOGRAPHY

Blau, Joseph L. *The Christian Interpretation of the Cabala in the Renaissance.* New York, 1944; reprint, Port Washington, N.Y., 1965. The best and shortest introduction to the subject in English.

Friedman, Jerome. *The Most Ancient Testimony: Sixteenth-Century Christian Hebraica in the Age of Renaissance Nostalgia.* Athens, Ohio, 1983. This is the most complete new assessment of sixteenth-century Christian Hebraica available.

Geiger, Ludwig. *Das Studium der Hebräische Sprachen in Deutschland vom Ende des 15 bis zur Mitte des 16. Jahrhunderts.* Wroclaw, 1870. A classic and fundamental study of Christian Hebraica. This and Perles are starting points.

Gorny, Léon. *La Kabbale: Kabbale juive et Cabale chrétiennes.* Paris, 1977. A sophisticated interpretation of the important difference between traditional Jewish mystical studies and the use Christians made of these same ideas.

Perles, J. *Beiträge zur Geschichte der Hebräischen und Aramäischen Studien.* Munich, 1884. This is a classic study of Christian Hebraica from the vantage of the development of medieval semitic studies.

Secret, François. *Les Kabbalistes Chrétiens de la Renaissance.* Rev. ed.

Neuilly, 1985. The best work on the subject of Christian Cabbala by its most competent and accomplished author.

Sweitlicki, Catherine. *Spanish Christian Cabala: The Works of Luis de León, Santa Teresa de Jesús and Juan de la Cruz.* Columbia, Mo., 1986. An excellent discussion of the literary importance of Cabbalistic images in the works of major Spanish mystics.

Wirszubski, Chaim. *Pico della Mirandola's Encounter with Jewish Mysticism.* Cambridge, Mass., 1989. An excellent demonstration of the importance of Spanish Jewish converts to the creation of the Christian Cabbala.

JEROME FRIEDMAN

CHRISTIAN PHILOSOPHY. *See* Philosophy of Christ.

CHRISTOLOGY refers to the study of the person of Christ, particularly the issue of Christ's divine and human natures. At the Council of Nicaea (325) it was determined that Christ was of one substance with God. However, this neglected Christ's human nature. The first Council of Constantinople (381) reaffirmed Christ's humanity, but then left undefined its relationship with Christ's divinity. Nestorius (d. 451?), archibishop of Constantinople, who denied the unity of Christ's divinity and humanity, preferring rather a coexistence, prompted the Council of Chalcedon (451) to declare emphatically that there is "one . . . Christ . . . in two natures, without confusion, without change, without division, without separation." In the Reformation the christological debate readdressed these considerations concerning the precise relationship of the unity of Christ's divinity and humanity.

Luther. Until 1520, the young Martin Luther's Christology was kerygmatic, interpreting the salvific work of Christ in soteriological terms. In his marginal notes on Augustine (1509) and on Peter Lombard (1510), he still essentially follows the christological tradition that stretched from Augustine to late scholasticism. However, beginning with his first lectures on *Psalms* (1513–1515), he increasingly abandoned the scholastic framework and developed his Christology exegetically. This became particularly apparent in the hermeneutical foundations of his first *Psalms* lectures. Here, in terms of the four senses of Scripture, Luther related the *sensus literalis propheticus* ("literal sense"), which pointed to Christ, to the *sensus tropologicus* ("figurative sense") of faith. Thus the basic theme of his early Christology becomes apparent, namely that God's work in Jesus Christ is aimed at faith. Nevertheless, it cannot be claimed that Luther's early Christology is merely a description of God's work acting in faith, rather Luther takes care to make his Christology coincide with the christological dogma defined at the Council of Chalcedon. Yet it is also clear that he is more intent on seeking to explain justification by Christ's salvific work than on explaining the doctrine of the person of Christ in this time. In his first *Psalms* lectures, Luther relates christological knowledge to the incarnation. The purpose of this knowledge is to come to know the God hidden in Christ's humanity, as this is made possible through the word of God, which is effected in faith through the Holy Spirit. The Godhead dwells in Christ *corporaliter et hypostatice* ("in a physical and hypostatic manner"). In accordance with Luther's early theology of the Crucifixion, both God's judgment on sin and God's righteousness is revealed in the Crucifixion to anyone who humbly accepts God's judgment in faith in Jesus Christ and acknowledges himself as a sinner before God.

After 1515 Luther's exegesis of Paul increasingly places the reconciling work of Jesus Christ at the center of his christological reflections. Christ reconciles God and humans and redeems them from sin, death and the devil. He is a *satisfactio sufficientissima* ("most sufficient satisfaction"), the very righteousness of God that makes us righteous. Following Paul, Luther locates God's salvific work in Jesus Christ ever more clearly as being *extra nos* ("outside of us"). In contrast to scholastic theology, he points out with ever greater clarity that, on account of Christ, the original sin remaining in us is covered and is not imputed to us as guilt. Christ accomplishes this work of salvation by virtue of his divine person. "For . . . Christ was at the same time mortal and immortal, and while in his humanity he was subjected to death, it is true that his whole person could not be killed." Through the power of his divine person, Christ frees us from sin, from death, and from the devil, and as high priest he removes our sin. In 1517, on the basis of these christological insights, Luther attacked the institution of indulgences, since indulgences run the risk of reducing the significance of the Crucifixion in the believer and of limiting its soteriological significance. Christ is the church's only treasure. The church cannot dispose of this treasure in a jurisdictional manner; it can only bear witness to it through the power of the keys and the preaching of the gospel.

In the framework of his understanding of the church, Luther also clarifies the meaning of Christ. Christ is the sole head of the church, and he rules spiritually in the faithful through word and sacrament. Accordingly, the church is spiritually the body of Christ and the communion of saints. Inasmuch as Luther centers his Christology in the Crucifixion, he can sum up his theology in the statement "Crux sola est nostra Theologia" (The cross alone is our theology). On the cross Christ suffered in his own person and not in the person of the church, and in solidarity with the tormented conscience of the sinner he effected our redemption from sin, death, and the devil. From 1520 on, Luther begins to ground Christ's work of salvation ever more explicitly in the early church's teaching on the two natures of Christ. Conversely, he reinterprets this ancient teaching from the standpoint of his own teaching on justification grounded in the salvific work of Christ. Just as a happy exchange occurs between the riches of Christ and the shortcomings of the sinful soul through the imputing of Christ's work of salvation to the believer, so Christ's riches have power to overcome sin, death, and the devil in the divine-human person of Jesus Christ.

> For since Christ is both God and man, and is also that person who did not sin, does not die and is not condemned, but also the one who cannot sin, die or be condemned; His righteousness, life and salvation is unconquerable, eternal and all-powerful. I emphasize that since such a person takes on the sins, the death and the hell of his spouse as common property through the ring of faith, and even makes them his very own; and in terms of these things he considers himself in no other way than as though they were his own and as though he himself had sinned, he therefore suffers, dies and descends into hell to overcome them all; and since sin, death and hell cannot absorb him, they are necessarily absorbed by him in an awesome duel. (WA 7:55)

In this happy exchange Christ simultaneously fulfills his office as king and high priest for the believer, and he does so in such a way that he makes them spiritually kings and priests. Subsequently Luther continued to demonstrate that the soteriological proclamation he had discovered in scripture was in harmony with the teaching of the ancient church. This occurs in the years following 1521, particularly in his sermons on the church in a series of Advent and Christmas postills, in postills from the year 1522, and in the Lenten sermons of 1525. In the dogma of the early church Luther found the proper interpretation of the Holy Scriptures and focused his considerations on the Incarnation as the recognition of the God of faith. God wants to be found through the human nature of Christ. In the incarnate Christ God has revealed himself in history in a contingent manner. Here the insights of the nominalist-Ockhamist tradition continue to influence Luther. In contrast to direct mystical devotion to Christ, Luther turns unequivocally to the incarnate Christ as the place where God encounters man. Whoever wants to come to God must take God's own path "from below."

Against the hubris of human reason, which continually strives to uncover the hidden God with its own powers, Luther repeatedly and emphatically referred to *Deus incarnatus* ("the incarnate God") and thereby to God's self-definition in the gospel. In accordance with this significance of the incarnate God, Luther emphasized the hypostatic union of the two natures in the divine person of Christ. "Although the two natures are distinct, yet there is one person; all that Christ does or suffers, God has certainly done and suffered, even though only one of Christ's natures is affected." Through the hypostatic union, the earthly Christ partakes in the attributes of divine nature, but in accord with *Philippians* 2:5–11, he renounces their use. Christ served us as a servant, which he freely accepted, and in this form he bears witness to God's love for us. Luther described Christ's work that is grounded in this love as the reconciliation of humans

with God; as liberation and redemption from sin, death, and the devil and from the law as an instrument of God's wrath directed against sin, or, in short, as satisfaction for our sins. Luther did not interpret this satisfaction legalistically as does Anselm of Canterbury.

Luther's Christology, with its emphasis on the incarnation, also shaped his line of argument against Erasmus in 1525 and the distinction he made between *Deus absconditus* ("God as hidden") and *Deus revelatus* ("God as revealed"). With this distinction, Luther made clear that the hidden God has made himself so definitively manifest in the revealed God that everything that must be known for the sake of salvation is revealed in him. Even if God's majesty is in the end unfathomable for us, this does not apply to the salvific will of God revealed in the incarnate God, which aims at the justification of the sinner. Therefore, we must cling to God's self-definition in Jesus Christ, which makes it possible to distinguish life from death and gives reason for the consolation and assurance of believers.

This incarnation-oriented Christology was also decisive in the controversy over the Lord's Supper with Huldrych Zwingli and Johannes Oecolampadius. In the controversy over Christ's real presence in the Eucharist, Luther appealed to the words of institution, as well as the *communicatio idiomatum* ("communication of attributes") derived from the hypostatic union of the two natures of Christ. By virtue of this communication, through Christ's divine person, his human nature partakes in the attributes of divine nature, ubiquity in particular, and therefore can be really present in the Eucharist. "For Christ is a human being who is one person with God in a supernatural manner, and apart from this man there is no God, so it must follow that he is and can be everywhere where God is; and everything is thoroughly filled with Christ even according to his humanity, not according to the first physically understandable manner, but rather according to the supernatural divine manner." Accordingly, Luther interpreted the biblical phrase of the right hand of God—to where the human person of Jesus was raised—in a manner that differed from tradition (Augustine) and from Zwingli (i.e., not in the sense of a determined place in heaven). Thus "Christ's body is everywhere . . . because he is at to the right hand of God which is everywhere, although we do not know how this occurs." For Luther, ubiquity so understood is the basis for the real presence of the body of Christ in the Eucharist. In contrast to Luther, Zwingli denied the notion that the majestic attributes of divine nature are shared with the human nature of Christ. Instead he spoke of a simple *communio naturarum* ("communion of natures") and made a strict distinction between the two natures. Thus he came to the conclusion that the glorified human nature of Christ is located in a limited way in a certain particular place in heaven and that Christ can only be present in his divine nature among those celebrating the Lord's Supper. Zwingli understood the *communicatio idiomatum* only as a perichoresis of the two natures that was to be interpreted linguistically. Predication of mutual attributes is merely a *predicatio verbalis* ("a predication that is valid only on the verbal level"). In contrast, Luther affirmed the assumption of the human nature by the divine logos—i.e., the human nature became one with the divine person of Christ—and he held the real community of the two natures. Correspondingly Luther rejected the notion of the *logos asarkos* ("fleshless word")—that is, considering the logos (Word), apart from the Incarnation—which occurred in Zwingli's thought. While Zwingli opted for a Christology with a Nestorian hue, which is concerned with maintaining a clear distinction between the two natures of Christ, Luther stressed the close communion of the two natures of Christ and the real communication of attributes that stems from it. Luther does so both in the interest of theological insight and for the sake of the real presence.

In the 1530s Luther, in the context of the eucharistic controversy, continued to permeate the doctrine of the two natures of Christ with his theology of justification, while continuing to interpret his Christology soteriologically. Thus, in the second article of the 1529 *Kleinen Katechismus* (Small Catechism) he wrote: "I believe that Jesus Christ, true God born of the Father in eternity and also true man born of the virgin Mary, is my Lord, who has released, acquired and won me, a lost and condemned human being, and freed me from all sins, from death, and from the power of the devil." He supported this soteriological interpretation of his Christology through his exegetical lectures, particularly his 1531 lecture on Paul's letters to the Galatians. It is in this soteriological interpretation of Christology that Luther saw the real conflict with Roman Catholicism.

Yet by the same token he was of the opinion that the dogma of the early church was not in dispute. Accordingly, in the Schmalkald Articles in 1537, after Pope Paul III had invited him to the council in Mantua, Luther argued that the "high" articles of the "divine majesty" were "neither in conflict nor in dispute," but that in the "articles that deal with the office and work of Christ or our redemption" there could be "neither deviation nor concession." The council, which had been planned for 1537 and was then postponed, led Luther to deal with the history of the ancient councils in greater detail in his 1539 tract *Von den Konziliis und Kirchen* (Concerning Councils and the Churches) against the background of *Concilia omnia, tam generalia quam particularia . . .* by Peter Krabbe in 1538. Luther agreed with the ancient dogma both critically and constructively, and conceded that it had the function of defending threatened truth of faith on the basis of scripture. The growing need for the theological education of pastors for the new evangelical congregations in the 1530s led to reintroduction of theological disputations in Wittenberg starting in 1533. This included disputations on Christology, which, besides dealing with its interpretation

within Protestantism, delineated it from traditional scholastic Christology.

In contrast to scholastic Christology, Luther concluded that the logic of syllogisms was unsuited to providing a dogmatic description of the mystery of the Incarnation. "However it is certain that all words take on a new significance in Christ in the very matter they signify." Faith in Jesus Christ demands its own logic in the explanation of Christology. Consequently, even the understanding of human nature changes, when it is considered theologically from the vantage of the hypostatic union, rather than philosophically as existing in and of itself. Luther also discussed christological-trinitarian issues in his 1534 work *Von den letzten Worten Davids* (Concerning the Last Words of David) and dealt with questions concerning Christ's salvific work in his 1544 lectures on *Isaiah*.

Zwingli. Like Luther, Huldrych Zwingli also presupposed the witness to Christ in scripture and accepted the traditional doctrine of the two natures of Christ more or less without reflection. What is in keeping with the witness to Christ in the scriptures is not *fides historica* ("historical faith"), but rather *fides iustificans* ("faith that justifies"). Zwingli comes to a more precise interpretation of the christological dogma as a result of the controversy over the Lord's Supper with Luther. "While Luther places his emphasis on the wonder of God becoming man, Zwingli emphasizes the divinity of the God-man. . . . It is this approach that results in the 'Nestorian' coloring of the relationship of the two natures in Christ, in other words the two natures remain clearly distinct . . . , joined together only through the 'person' of Christ; and the person of Christ is, in a trinitarian perspective, identical with his divinity" (Locher, 1979, p. 206). Since Zwingli distinguishes the two natures in Christ from one another, he admits to the *communicatio idiomatum* ("communication of attributes") only as a *communicatio naturarum* ("communication of natures"). Accordingly, the attributes of the two natures of Christ are ascribed to one another not in a real manner, but only verbally through the rhetorical figure of transposition (*per alloiosim*), attributing the actions of a part to the whole. It is only "[in speaking] about the *person* of the God-man that it is possible to speak of the attributes of the two natures 'per aloiosim'; thus, for example, we say 'Christ is eternal God', and at the same time 'Christ died for us' " (Lockers, 1979, p. 207).

Since he made a strict distinction between the two natures of Christ, Zwingli held that Christ's human nature is limited in space and time even when one speaks of the glorified Christ and, therefore, is located in some determined place in heaven. Consequently, in his debate with Luther, he argued against the ubiquity of the body of Christ and its real presence in the Eucharist. The human nature of the glorified Christ retains the attributes proper to it, including its limitations, and these attributes must be clearly distinguished.

Something that is limited cannot become unlimited. "What has been created is not infinite, nor is it ever made to be infinite." Since Zwingli made a real distinction between the two natures of Christ, he also noted that Christ was born *in* Mary and not *of* Mary and disputed attributing the term "God-bearer" (i.e., Mother of God) to Mary. As to Christ's earthly existence, Zwingli's *Commentarius* ascribed Jesus' healings and the authority of his teaching to his divinity. Christ's suffering should be attributed to Jesus' human nature only. Christ's suffering in his humanity serves the purpose of satisfaction in Christ's work of salvation. Since Zwingli ascribed the suffering only to the human nature of Christ, he avoided Luther's notion of the "tempted" Christ. Zwingli maintained that, in terms of Christ's work of salvation, Christ is both redeemer and exemplar. "For Christ in every instance impresses on us these two realities, namely redemption in itself, and that we who have been redeemed by him now ought to live according to his example." "Let each one look to his captain Christ Jesus . . . he will not lead us astray." Zwingli interpreted the reconciliation and redemption that have their foundation in Christ's work of salvation using Anselm's concepts of the justice and mercy of God (*iustitiaet misericordia Dei*) and he understood Christ as the mediator between God and humankind and as the "advocate and peacemaker between God and us."

Calvin. John Calvin likewise derived his Christology from the witness to Christ contained in scripture. However, from the outset, he gave careful consideration to the function of the dogma of the early church in clarifying theologically the biblical witness to Christ. What was still indistinctly presented in the scriptures is stated clearly in the dogma of the early church. Even though the dogma uses new concepts different from those of scripture, "such new expressions are absolutely necessary, whenever the truth must be asserted against its enemies." Thus the witness to Christ in the scriptures finds its classical interpretation in the Council of Chalcedon. "It was absolutely necessary that he, who was to be our mediator, should be really true God and true man." The divine-human mediator Jesus Christ was needed to restore the disrupted relationship between God and sinners.

The salvific work of Christ, as it is described by Anselm's notion of satisfaction, presupposed the unity of the divine and human nature in the divine person of Jesus Christ. Like Zwingli, Calvin emphasized the distinction of the two natures in Christ, and he did so in order to avoid jeopardizing the specificity of the divine nature. Any change in the divine nature "would necessarily amount to lessening it. Here we see an important, perhaps even the most original facet of Calvin's theology" (Wendel, 191). Already in his *Institutio* of 1536, Calvin explained that just as the body and soul of humans each retain their own characteristics, the same holds true for the two natures in the person of Jesus Christ. In his 1537 *Confession de la Trinité* Calvin stressed the integrity of each of the two natures in Christ and concluded in his *Institutio* of 1539 that the "Son of God did not become son of man through a mixing of substances, rather through the unity of his person: in other words, he [Christ] joined and united his divinity with the human nature he assumed in such a way that each of the two natures retained their specific characteristics; and yet Jesus Christ does not consist of two different persons, but only of one." Although Calvin thus distinguished the natures in Christ, he did not interpret the *communicatio idiomatum* merely figuratively or rhetorically as did Zwingli. Thus the *Institutio* of 1536 held to a *communicatio idiomatum* properly understood. Scripture ascribes to Jesus Christ "some characteristics that can be attributed only to his humanity, other characteristics that especially belong to this divinity, and finally characteristics that are proper to both natures through their being joined to one another, but not to either nature individually. Finally through the *communicatio idiomatum* scripture attributes to the divinity what belongs to the humanity and to humanity what pertains to divinity."

Calvin changed his understanding of the *communicatio idiomatum* beginning with the *Institutio* of 1543. There he warned against drawing conclusions from the communication of attributes—which serves to describe the mystery of the person of Jesus Christ and his office of mediator—that might call into question the integrity of the natures of Christ. Thus Calvin also denied that the human nature of Christ partakes in the ubiquity of his divine nature. However, concerning the ubiquity of the divine nature he asserted that it fills all things. While this divine nature has dwelled in Christ's humanity since the Incarnation, it is not bound to Christ's humanity. "Though he has united his eternal being with our nature, yet his being is not enclosed or entrapped by it; for he came down from heaven in wondrous fashion, and yet still remained there; and he entered into the womb of the virgin in wondrous fashion, and he dwelt on earth and was crucified, yet in such a manner that was in keeping with his divinity he continued to fill the world just as he had in the beginning."

This christological thesis of Calvin's, which was later described as the *Extracalvinisticum* and is also found in Augustine, Peter Lombard, and Thomas Aquinas, had consequences for Calvin's understanding of the Lord's Supper, in that Calvin denied ubiquity to Christ's human nature. Like Zwingli, Calvin was of the opinion that Christ's human body is located in some determined place in heaven. In contrast to Zwingli, Calvin does recognize a presence of Christ in the Eucharist through word and element, but this presence is a spiritual presence effected by the Holy Spirit, in which believers are united with the heavenly Christ through their partaking in the Eucharist.

A further characteristic of Calvin's Christology, which he most likely developed under Martin Bucer's influence and which appears beginning in 1539, was his doctrine of the *triplex munus Christi* (i.e., Christ's threefold office as prophet, king, and high priest). In his prophetic office Christ gives us the insight that "in his proclamation all wisdom is contained in its perfection." In his kingly office (his spiritual lordship) Christ strengthens believers in their misery, cares for them, and leads them to eternal life. In his priestly office Christ, through his holiness, gains for us God's favor and makes us pleasing before God. The *triplex munus Christi* is founded in the eternal decree of God and leads to the rescue of humans who have fallen into sin.

Melanchthon. Following Erasmus and his *Ratio verae theologiae* (1519), Philipp Melanchthon in his early stage avoided a systematic theological investigation of the dogma of the early church. Instead he echoed Erasmus in his opinion that the knowledge of Christ ought to be oriented to knowing Christ's work of salvation and honoring him. "This is to know Christ: to know his benefits; not what those people teach, i.e., to admire his natures or the manners of his incarnation." This doxological reception of early church dogma would prefer to avoid investigating it in a speculative and scholastic manner. Accordingly, following Paul, Melanchthon in his *Loci communes* of 1521 presented the salvific work of Christ as a bestowed blessing, and he dispensed with any full treatment of the Trinity or the person of Christ.

This did not contradict the acceptance of the early church dogma, as Melanchthon emphasized in the Augsburg Confession, where he acknowledged the early church doctrine of the Trinity and the doctrine of the two natures of Christ as defined at the Council of Chalcedon. Both the eucharistic controversy and the necessity for theological teaching in the education of pastors led Melanchthon to deal with the doctrine of the Trinity in lectures he presented in 1523. He placed the doctrine of the Trinity at the beginning of his second and completely revised edition of the *Loci communes*. Even there Melanchthon did not develop his teaching on the Trinity in a speculative way, rather he posed the question of the various terminological and logical possibilities of expressing it and of its biblical and exegetical foundation. In his *De ecclesia et autoritate verbi Dei* of 1539 Melanchthon concluded that the church, in interpreting the word of God to which the scriptures attest, made correct decisions in formulating the dogma of the early church. Melanchthon subsequently elaborated these reflections on the Trinity in the third edition of the *Loci theologici* of 1543, which was the basis for the *Loci praecipui theologici* of 1559.

As he had done in his theological treatment of the doctrine of the Trinity, Melanchthon in these years turned to the systematic study of the doctrine of the two natures of Christ and defended it in his *Enarratio Symboli Niceni*. In the revised edition of 1557 Melanchthon refuted christological errors, as they occurred in the works of Francis Stancarus, Andreas Osiander, Kaspar von Schwenckfeld, and others.

Melanchthon elaborated on this defense of the ancient dogma in his tracts *Antwort auff das Buch Herrn Andreae Osiandri* (1552), *Responsio Philippi Melanthonis de controversiis Stancari* (1553), *Responsiones Scriptae a Philippo Melanthone ad impios articulos Bavaricae inquistionis* (1558), and finally *Examen ordinandorum* (1559). In this systematic theological examination Melanchthon endeavored to explain the proper sense of the *communicatio idiomatum*. "And the communication of attributes should not be understood as a physical fusing together of natures, but careful thought should be given to what is meant by person." Melanchthon made it clear that the characteristics of the two natures of Christ are not attributed to one another abstractly, but rather concretely to the divine person of Jesus Christ, which logically represents the subject to which the doctrine of the two natures is applied. "However there is a communication of attributes, a predication, in which a property that is proper to one nature, is attributed to the person in the concrete sense, because these two natures, the logos and the assumed nature, are one in hypostatis union." The statements concerning the *communicatio idiomatum* are valid only in the concrete sense in terms of the person of Jesus Christ, but not in the abstract sense in terms of each of the natures. "The abstract terms signify nature as considered in and of itself, such as divinity or divine nature, and humanity or human nature." Thus the communication of attributes has the meaning "of making logically possible the predication of God to man and man to God that has been made in christological statements—on the material basis of the biblical witness" (Mahlmann, 1955, p. 70).

What Melanchthon thus developed concerning the communication of attributes, he also applied to an interpretation of the doctrine of ubiquity understood in a personal sense. "Christ is everywhere, thus (antiquity) declares: Christ is everywhere in a personal manner." However, this is not valid for the statement relating in a merely abstract manner to the human person: "The body of Christ is everywhere." It is in the abstract sense—that is, only in view of the human nature of Christ alone and as related to it—that Melanchthon can subscribe to the Augustinian statement "Corpus Christi est in certo loco" ("The body of Christ is in a certain place"). However, in view of the hypostatic union (i.e., related to the concrete reality of the divine person), he concluded, "However, Augustine's statement, 'the body of Christ is in a certain place' and others like it do not contradict such statements as 'Christ is at the right hand of the Father,' 'Christ is everywhere,' because his mysterious exaltation in kingship and priesthood is not physical locality in the sense that Augustine speaks of physical place." This personal interpretation of the doctrine of ubiquity allowed Melanchthon to hold to the ubiquity and real presence of Christ in the Eucharist understood in personal terms.

As to the connection between Christology and justification, he brought to bear his understanding of the communication of attributes in opposition to Osiander. Osiander does not understand the communication of attributes properly when he maintains that Christ "is our righteousness according to his divine nature *and not* according to his human nature" (Mahlmann, 1979, p. 97) and that it is the *iustitia essentialis* ("righteousness in essence") springing from the divine nature of Christ that justifies us and that this righteousness is also the basis for the imputation of Christ's righteousness to the believer. In contrast to this position Melanchthon pointed out that "the whole Christ is intermediary and redeemer." This is because Christ has gained our righteousness before God according to both the natures united in his person. Melanchthon also used this argument against Stancarus, who maintained, in contrast to Osiander, that Christ is our righteousness not according to his divine nature but according to his human nature.

Brenz and Chemnitz. In the context of the eucharistic controversy, the Württemberg Reformer Johannes Brenz, in his 1526 *Syngramma Suevicum*, affirmed the real presence against Zwingli and Oecolampadius by emphasizing that it is a presence that occurs through word and element. The real presence of Christ is in keeping with the divine promise contained in the institution of the Lord's Supper. In his commentary on John (1527), Brenz based the ubiquity and real presence of Christ on the communication of attributes that resulted from the incarnation. "For the human nature of Christ possesses 'from the beginning of the Incarnation the same goods [i.e., 'attributes' or 'positive qualities'] as the divine nature, not through a confusion of substance but through the unity of the person' " (Brecht, *Die frühe Theologie*, 211). Already from the moment of the Incarnation the human nature of Christ partook in the ubiquity of God. But, this occurred in a hidden way and was manifest only after Christ's ascension.

Under the influence of Luther's writings on the Eucharist in 1527/28, Brenz began to develop his Christology independently. Above all, he emphasized the teaching on the unity of Christ's person, indeed he stressed this in the foreword of his tract on the Eucharist, where he refuted in his apology of the Württemberg Confession the attacks of the Dominican Pedro de Soto. The real presence of Christ in the Eucharist, like the ubiquity of Christ's human nature, has its foundation in the unity of the person of Jesus Christ. "Therefore, since the Son of God has assumed man into the unity of his person and has transported him up to the same sublimity and majesty with which he himself is endowed, it obviously follows that wherever the Son of God (who is himself true and eternal) is, there too is man who has been assumed by God into the unity of his person and transcends both all times and all places." Appealing to a statement of Luther's "Where God is, there too is the human being" Jesus, Brenz placed the unity of the two natures of Christ in

his person at the center of his Christology. However, while Luther held to the contingent foundation of this unity of person in the incarnation, Brenz made it the object of theological-logical inferences. In the face of the Christ kerygma of scripture, christological reflection begins to become speculatively independent. In this reflection Brenz, like the Lutheran theologian J. Botker, placed particular value on the interpretation of the communication of attributes as a *communicatio idiomatum realis.*

In 1559 differences arose between Brenz and Melanchthon, who especially reflected on the declarative logic of the communication of attributes. In particular, in his *Bekanntnus und Bericht der Theologen und Kirchen-Diener im Fürstenthum Württemberg . . . ,* Brenz opposed the thesis of the localized presence of the body of Christ in heaven that Melanchthon presented in his *Enarratio epistolae Pauli ad Colossenses* in 1559. In 1561/62 Brenz deepened his christological positions in his *De personali unione duarum naturarum in Christo et ascensu Christi, Sententia de libello D. Henrici Bullingeri* and *De maiestate Domini nostri Iesu Christi.*

In contrast to certain speculative tendencies in the Christology of Brenz, Martin Chemnitz once again gave greater emphasis to the words of institution in the Lord's Supper as the authority for the real presence of Christ in the Eucharist. He does this in his writings of 1561 *Repetitio sanae doctrinae de vera praesentia corporis et sanguinis Domini in coena* and in his *Anatome propositionum Alberti Hardenbergii de coena Domini.* In the latter he wrote: "Let us not subject the body of Christ to our debates, whether concerning ubiquity, or locality; rather let us hold, believe and speak of him, as he said." Chemnitz also pursued this reflection on the material foundation of Christology in his *Über die persönliche Einigung der beiden Naturen in Christus* of 1566 and in his *Propositiones de persona et beneficiis filii Dei* of 1568, which was his doctoral thesis. In 1570 he expanded his *Repetitio* of 1561 with his writings *Fundamenta sanae doctrinae de vera et substantiali praesentia, exhibitione et sumptione corporis et sanguinis Domini in coena* (The Foundations of the Healthy Doctrine of the True and Substantial Presence, Exhibition and Reception of the Body and Blood of the Lord in the Lord's Supper) and *De duabus naturis in Christo: De hypostatica earum unione; De communicatione idiomatum* (The Two Natures in Christ: Their Hypostatic Union; The Communication of Attributes). In this latter writing he understands the *communicatio idiomatum* as being *vera et realis* ("true and real"). In particular Chemnitz interpreted the communication of attributes in terms of energy (i.e., the divine dwells in Christ not as a substance but rather as energy). The divine properties that are shared with the human nature in the communication of attributes cannot be thought of as being natural, essential, or inherent; rather they point to God's acting in human nature. For the real presence in the Eucharist this means that God is present in the Eucharist through his own effective will. "The Son of God with his assumed [human] nature by reason of the hypostatic union can be present wherever, whenever and however he wills; that is, where he promised and assured by his certain word that he wanted to be present with that [human nature]."

The idea of the real presence in Chemnitz thereby received a particular interpretation in terms of a presence that is willed for many reasons. Chemnitz began to expand on this interpretation of the real presence and the communication of attributes in his *Repetitio* of 1561, but then developed the doctrine of the three *genera* ("classifications") of *communicatio idiomatum* in 1570. The first classification emphasizes that the attributes of both natures are to be ascribed in concrete terms to the divine person of Jesus Christ. The second classification establishes the effective unity of the divine person of Christ in both natures, while the third classification stresses that the divine characteristics of majesty are shared with the human nature of Christ in a real and not merely verbal manner. However, these characteristics are not inherent in the human nature of Christ in an essential manner, rather they are active in and through his human nature in a dynamic manner. In this way Chemnitz further developed Lutheran theology and established the prerequisites for the Lutheran Christology in the Formula of Concord of 1577.

The Formula of Concord. In 1577 the Formula of Concord summed the basic intentions of Lutheran Christology and thus became the basis for Lutheran orthodoxy. Thus article 7 insisted on the Lutheran concept of the real presence of the body and blood of Christ in the Lord's Supper. It appealed to Luther's writing *Vom Abendmahl Christi: Bekenntnis* (1528) and explained that Christ's suffering is present in the Eucharist in a divine or heavenly manner, "since he is one person with God."

In article 8 the Formula of Concord interpreted the unity of person of the divine nature as a *communicatio idiomatum realis* and rejected a Nestorian-tinged concept of a merely verbal community of the two natures of Christ occurring in name only. Specifically, Zwingli's view of the merely rhetorical *alloiosis* in terms of the mutual sharing of the properties of the two natures is rejected by the Formula of Concord. In contrast, the Formula of Concord defines the *unio personalis* ("unity of person") to the effect that "the divine and human nature are united in Christ in a personal manner, in other words, there is not a twofold Christ, one the Son of God and the other the son of man, rather there is a single [Christ], Son of God and son of man." The *unio personalis* thus should not be interpreted as a mere coupling (*copulatio*) or joining (*combinatio*), but rather as a communion in the highest sense (*summa communio*). This reflected tradition, which described this communion with the metaphor of glowing iron or the analogy of the unity of body and soul.

Still, following the teaching of Chalcedon on the two natures of Christ, it is strictly a matter of a *unio personalis* of the two natures, not of any mixing or transformation of the two natures. Following Chemnitz, the Formula of Concord developed the concept of the three *genera* that were only later designated as such in a terminological sense, and designated the first classification as *genus idiomaticum*. This means that the properties of both natures are to be predicated to the concrete entity of the divine person of Christ. The second classification is the so-called *genus apotelesmaticum*. This refers to the work or the office of Christ and means that the person of the God-man effects his salvific work or office "not in, with, through or according to one nature alone, but rather in, according to, with and through both natures." "Thus Christ is our mediator, redeemer, king, high priest, head, shepherd, etc. not according to one nature alone." As to the third classification, the Formula of Concord speaks of the *genus maiestaticum*, a teaching that was rejected by Reformed theology. This classification asserted that the divine attributes of majesty are shared with the human nature of Christ in a real manner on the basis of the *unio personalis*. Conversely, the divine nature does not take on the characteristics of human nature.

In view of the life of the earthly Christ the Formula of Concord goes on to explain that the partaking by the human nature in the divine attributes of majesty "at the time of the 'lowering' was hidden and held back." In his earthly existence Christ divested himself of his divine attributes or else possessed them only in a hidden manner. This understanding of the *unio personalis* or *communicatio idiomatum* as a real community of the two natures in Christ was expressly defended against the Calvinists' objection that human nature was not capable of assuming divine nature.

Finally, in article 9 the Formula of Concord deals with the teaching of Christ's descent into hell as a particular theme of Lutheran Christology. Although Lutherans had fluctuated between an existential interpretation of hell, following Luther, and an interpretation of the torments of hell in a localized sense, in 1544 Johannes Aepin of Hamburg again presented a vivid conception of hell in his commentary on *Psalms*. He cited one of Luther's sermons in Torgau in 1533, in which Luther adhered to the traditional conception of hell.

In contrast, the Formula of Concord itself, citing Luther, advised against needless arguing over this subject, but rather advocated simply believing in Christ's victory over hell. "For it is enough that we know that Christ descended into hell, destroyed hell for all believers, and rescued them from the power of death, the devil, and the eternal condemnation of the vengeance of hell." Following the medieval vivid conceptions, it was then added that "the whole person, God and man, descended into hell after the burial" and overcame the devil.

Schwenckfeld, Hoffman, and Simons. Article 12 of the Formula of Concord rejected the monophysite interpretation of the *unio personalis*, as it surfaced in a doctrine of the heavenly flesh of Christ during the time of the Reformation. The Formula of Concord especially targeted Kaspar von Schwenckfeld as a representative of this kind of monophysite Christology. Schwenckfeld held to the monophysite concept that the flesh of Jesus Christ was from the very beginning divine flesh, which became manifest only in the exalted and glorified humanity of Jesus. Believers come to partake in this divine flesh in their justification and are divinized through this divine flesh. This understanding of the heavenly flesh of Christ amounted to diminishing the true humanity of Christ, no matter how much Schwenckfeld endeavored to maintain Christ's humanity. This monophysite Christology was taken over by the Anabaptist Melchior Hoffman, who had come in contact with Schwenckfeld in Strasbourg in 1529. Hoffman proceeded to radicalize Schwenckfeld's ideas in 1533 by asserting that in the Incarnation the eternal word did not assume flesh from the Virgin Mary. Rather the word became flesh in a new act of creation *in* and not *from* Mary, so that "there exists only *one* nature, but a heavenly flesh" (Schoeps, p. 46).

Later the Anabaptist leader Menno Simons, along with Hoffman, held to the idea that Christ was not born of Mary the virgin (*natus ex Maria virgine*), but rather became human in the Virgin Mary (*factus in Maria virgine*). Menno Simons held for this monophysite Christology of the heavenly flesh of Christ, because it was not permissible for the redeemer to have any part in the sinful substance of the creature. In Strasbourg in 1555 and in the Palatinate in 1571 the Anabaptists of Upper Germany distanced themselves from Menno's monophysite Christology. Thereafter, subsequent groups of Anabaptists no longer consistently held to this type of Christology.

[*See also* Philosophy of Christ.]

BIBLIOGRAPHY

Primary Sources

Brenz, Johannes. *Werke: Eine Studienausgabe.* Edited by Martin Brecht and Gerhard Schäfer. Tübingen, 1970–.
Calvin, John. *Opera quae supersunt omnia.* Edited by G. Baum, et al. Corpus Reformatorum 29–87. Braunschweig, 1864–1900.
———. *Opera selecta.* 5 vols. Edited by Peter Barth and Wilhelm Niesel. Munich, 1926–1936.
———. *The Institutes of the Christian Religion.* Edited by John T. McNeill. Philadelphia, 1960.
Chemnitz, Martin. *De duabus naturis in Christo.* Translated by J. A. O. Preus. Saint Louis, 1971.
———. *Decoena Domini.* Translated by J. A. O. Preus. Saint Louis, 1971.
Die Bekenntnisschriften der Evangelisch-Lutherischen Kirche. Göttingen, 1963.
Luther, Martin. *Werke. Kritische Gesamtausgabe.* Weimar, 1883–.
Melanchthon, Philipp. *Opera quae supersunt omnia.* Corpus Reformatorum 1–28. Halle, 1834–1860.
Stupperich, Robert, ed. *Melanchthons Werke in Auswahl.* Gütersloh, 1951–1975.
———. *Corpus Schwenckfeldianorum.* Leipzig and Pennsburg, 1907–1961.
Zwingli, Huldrych. *Selected Works.* Reprint, Philadelphia, 1972.

Secondary Sources

Adam, Alfred. *Lehrbuch der Dogmengeschichte.* Vol. 2. Gütersloh, 1981.
Althaus, Paul. *The Theology of Martin Luther.* Philadelphia, 1970.
Andresen, Carl, ed. *Handbuch der Dogmen- und Theologiegeschichte.* Göttingen, 1980.
Bornhäuser, Christoph. *Leben und Lehre Menno Simons.* Neukirchen-Vluyn, 1973.
Brecht, Martin. *Die frühe Theologie des Johannes Brenz.* Beiträge zur historischen Theologie, 36. Tübingen, 1966.
Burkhart, J. E. "Menno Simons on the Incarnation," *Mennonite Quarterly Review* 4 (1930), 113–129, 178–207; 6 (1932), 122–123.
Domini, Max. *L'humanité de Jésus d'après Calvin.* Paris, 1933.
Ebeling, Gerhard. "Luther II: Theologie." *Religion in Geschichte and Gegenwart* 4 (1960), 495–520.
Emmen, Egbert. *De Christologie van Calvijn.* Amsterdam, 1935.
Gäbler, Ulrich. *Huldrych Zwingli: His Life and Work.* Edinburgh, 1986.
Gennrich, Paul. *Die Christologie Luthers im Abendmahlsstreit, 1524–1529.* Königsberg, 1929.
Grass, Hans and Werner Georg Kümmel, eds. *Jesus Christus. Das Christusverständnis im Wandel der Zeiten, eine Ringvorlesung.* Marburg, 1963.
Harnack, Theodosius. *Luthers Theologie mit besonderer Beziehung auf seine Versöhnungs- und Erlösungslehre (1862–1886).* 2 vols. Reprint, Amsterdam, 1969.
Hoogland, Marvin P. *Calvin's Perspective on the Exaltation of Christ in Comparison with the Post-Reformation Doctrine of the Two States.* Kampen, 1966.
Jansen, John Frederick. *Calvin's Doctrine of the Work of Christ.* London, 1956.
Klempa, William J. "The Obedience of Christ in the Theology of John Calvin." Diss., University of Edinburgh, 1962.
Koopmans, Jan. *Das altkirchliche Dogma in der Reformation.* Munich, 1955.
Lienhard, Marc. "Notes sur un texte christologique du jeune Luther." *Revue d'histoire et de philosophie religeuses* 49 (1969), 331–340.
———. *Luther, Witness to Jesus Christ: Stages and Themes of the Reformer's Christology.* Minneapolis, 1982.
Locher, Gottfried W. *Die Theologie Huldrych Zwinglis im Lichte seiner Christologie.* Zürich, 1952.
———. "Zwingli II: Theologie." *Religion in Geschichte und Gegenwart* 6 (1961), 1960–1969.
———. *Die Zwinglische Reformation im Rahmen der europäischen Kirchengeschichte.* Göttingen, 1979.
Lohse, Bernhard, et al. *Die Lehrentwicklung im Rahmen der Konfessionalität.* Handbuch der Dogmen- und Theologiegeschichte, vol. 1. Göttingen, 1980.
Mahlmann, Theodor. *Das neue Dogma in der Reformation.* Munich, 1955.
———. "Chemnitz, Martin." *Theologische Realenzyklopädie*, vol. 7, pp. 714–721. Berlin and New York, 1981.
Maier, Paul L. *Caspar Schwenckfeld on the Person and the Work of Christ.* Assen, 1959.
Maurer, Wilhelm. *Der junge Melanchthon zwischen Humanismus und Reformation.* 2 vols. Göttingen, 1967–1969.
Müller, Gerhard. "Luthers Christusverständnis." In *Jesus Christus. Das Christusverständnis im Wandel der Zeiten*, edited by Hans Grass and Werner Georg Kümmel, pp. 41–57. Marburg, 1964.
Nijenhuis, Willem. "Calvin, Johannes." In *Theologische Realenzyklopädie*, vol. 7, pp. 568–592. Berlin and New York, 1981.
Peters, Albrecht. *Realpräsenz: Luthers Zeugnis von Christi Gegenwart im Abendmahl.* Berlin, 1960.
Ratschow, Carl-Heinz. "Christologie und Rechtfertigung: Luthers

Christologie nach seinen Disputationen." In *Iustificatio impii*, edited by J. Talasniemi, pp. 204–226. Helsinki, 1977.

Schoeps, Hans Joachim. *Vom himmlischen Fleisch Christi. Eine dogmengeschichtliche Untersuchung.* Tübingen, 1957.

Schroten, Hendrik. *Christus, de Middelaar, bij Calvin.* Utrecht, 1948.

Schwarz, Reinhard. "Gott ist Mensch: Zur Lehre von der Person Christi bei den Ockhamisten und bei Luther." *Zeitschrift für Theologie und Kirche* 63 (1966), 289–351.

Spitz, Lewis W. and Wenzel Lohff, eds. *Discord, Dialogue and Concord: Studies in the Lutheran Reformation's Formula of Concord.* Philadelphia, 1977.

Torrance, James Bruce. "The Vicarious Humanity and Priesthood of Christ in the Theology of John Calvin." In *Calvinus Ecclesiae Doctor*, edited by W. Neuser. Kampen, 1980.

Tschackert, Paul. *Die Entstehung der lutherischen und der reformierten Kirchenlehre samt ihren innerprotestantischen Gegensätzen* (1910). Reprint, Göttingen, 1979.

Vogelsang, Erich. *Die Anfänge von Luthers Christologie nach der ersten Psalmenvorlesung, insbesondere in ihren exegetischen und systematischen Zusammenhängen mit Augustin und der Scholastik dargestellt.* Arbeiten zur Kirchengeschichte, vol. 15. Berlin, 1929.

Vorländer, Dorothea. *Deus incarnatus: Die Zweinaturenchristologie Luthers bis 1521.* Untersuchungen zur Kirchengeschichte, vol. 9. Witten, 1974.

Wendel, François. *Calvin: The Origins and Development of His Religious Thought.* New York, 1950.

Willis, Edward David. *Calvin's Catholic Christology: The Function of the So-called Extra-Calvinisticum in Calvin's Theology.* Leiden, 1960.

KARL-HEINZ ZUR MÜHLEN
Translated from German by Robert E. Shillenn

CHRISTOPH OF WÜRTTEMBERG

CHRISTOPH OF WÜRTTEMBERG (1515–1568), Protestant ruler who established a model centralized Lutheran territorial church. Christoph was the son of Duke Ulrich of Württemberg and Sabine of Bavaria. Born on the eve of the Reformation, he belongs rather to the consolidators than the initiators of Lutheranism in Germany. A less colorful figure than his father, Christoph was widely admired as a conscientious ruler of broad-ranging interests and capacities, a man of peace and a dedicated Christian. He built a solid and durable state church on foundations laid by his father between 1535 and 1550.

Christoph appears to have grown up relatively unscathed by the troubled circumstances of his early life. Shortly after his birth, his mother fled her husband's unbearable rages and returned to her homeland, leaving her infant son behind. In 1520, after Duke Ulrich was dispossessed by the Swabian League and Württemberg came under Habsburg dominion, Christoph became a ward of Emperor Charles V. His life was long overshadowed by conflicting loyalties to men with claims to his allegiance who were at political or religious odds, or both, particularly his father, his Bavarian relations, and his liege lord and guardian, Charles V.

In 1530 Christoph joined the entourage of the emperor, who was making his way through Europe in search of a religious consensus and support for his anti-Turkish crusade.

He balked, however, at the prospect of accompanying the imperial retinue to Spain, taking refuge in 1532 with his uncle, Duke William of Bavaria. The wily duke, hoping to strike a blow for the Catholic as well as anti-Habsburg cause, sought to have Christoph recognized as rightful ruler of Württemberg in place of his (now Protestant) father. Small wonder that, after regaining his territory with the aid of the Schmalkald League in 1534, Ulrich distrusted the son who was still a Catholic and an apparent competitor for his lands and title.

To keep Christoph at a distance, Ulrich placed him in service to his political ally and inveterate Habsburg foe, Francis I of France. The young prince distinguished himself at the French court not only as a master of knightly sport but also as a military commander and diplomatic aide. He was appointed to various foreign missions, attracting notice on one occasion for refusing to kiss the feet of Pope Paul III—a gesture signaling the independence of mind he was to demonstrate once free of his strictly Catholic surroundings.

By 1542 Ulrich was prepared for a reconciliation with his estranged son and assured his succession on the condition that Christoph commit himself and his heirs to upholding the Protestant faith in Württemberg (Treaty of Reicheneier). Ulrich also made Christoph governor of Montebéliard, a small domain attached to the House of Württemberg. Here Christoph studied the various arguments and positions of both Catholic and Protestant theologians before his final conversion to the Augburg Confession. A sign of his new religious commitment was Christoph's marriage in 1544 to Anna Maria, daughter of the staunchly Lutheran Margrave George of Brandenburg-Ansbach.

On the death of Ulrich in 1550, Christoph assumed his Württemberg inheritance during troubled times for his religion and his territory. Charles V had placed Württemberg under the constrictions of the Interim he imposed on the Lutheran princes after defeating them in the Schmalkald War. Catholic worship had been restored, church property, particularly the great abbeys had reverted to their former occupants, and Protestant services were forbidden. In order not to lose his evangelical pastors, Ulrich had arranged for them to be employed as schoolmasters and religious instructors. Charles's attempt to re-Catholicize Württemberg met with widespread passive resistance, and Christoph was assured of popular support for his restoration of exclusively Protestant worship with the lifting of the Interim in 1552. From this time on he earned his reputation as a peacemaker and mediator for his ceaseless efforts on behalf of Christian concord and unity. He attended or arranged to send delegates to every assembly, council, and diet that addressed these issues, including the Council of Trent. His bid to present the "Württemberg Confession" at Trent was ignored, along with similar initiatives prepared by other supporters of Protestantism.

Christoph's theological statements were mostly formulated by the eminent reformer and religious counselor to Ulrich, Johannes Brenz. In the ongoing conflicts between Charles V and the German estates Christoph took a leading position in the neutral Heidelberg League (1553), holding firmly to his Lutheranism without taking up arms against the emperor. He was a strong voice in the negotiations leading to parity for the evangelical and Catholic religions in the Peace of Augsburg (1555).

Christoph was also an active mediator in the theological controversies over justification and the Lord's Supper that plagued the Protestant camp after the death of Martin Luther in 1546. He supported the moderates at the Diet of Naumberg (1561), which produced a deceptive show of unity against the Catholics by adopting a compromise version of the Augsburg Confession. Christoph was no friend of Calvinism, however, and forbade any deviation from Luther's teaching on the real presence and the ubiquity of Christ. Nonetheless, he interceded, though without success, on behalf of Calvin's followers with the Catholic party in France, while opposing any kind of military aid for the Huguenots. Closer to Christoph's heart were efforts to nurture Lutheranism in eastern Europe, particularly the Balkans, where he sponsored an evangelical biblical academy and the printing of the first Slovenian Bible brought out by Pier Paolo Vergerio.

Christoph's major contribution to the consolidation of Lutheranism was, of course, in the German lands, especially his own duchy of Württemberg. He applied himself with equal vigor and deliberation in both church and realm, creating the well-ordered polity he deemed essential to the maintenance and good order of the church. Convinced that the primary responsibility of his God-given office was to see that in his territory of Württemberg the word of God be known, believed, obeyed, and lived, Christoph left little to chance in his grand design for a well-ordered church.

Württemberg's Great Church Order, adopted in 1559, reflected Christoph's overriding concern with ecclesiastical discipline and his insistence that the church be guaranteed an income sufficient to meet its administrative, educational, and pastoral obligations. He established a highly centralized system of ecclesiastical supervision based on regular visitations by church officials, who reported on the condition of the church and its members to a central synod of clergy and laymen. The central body also examined and appointed pastors, leaving the local congregations only the right of refusal. To meet the expense of his well-organized church, Christoph showed unusual restraint in reserving to it most of the income from formerly Catholic church lands and properties. Of particular importance was the conversion of the great monasteries into theological seminaries and the establishment of a system of primary education, exemplary for the time.

BIBLIOGRAPHY

Brecht, Martin. *Kirchenordnung und Kirchenzucht in Württemberg vom 16. bis zum 18. Jahrhundert.* Stuttgart, 1967.

Ernst, Viktor, ed. *Briefwechsel des Herzogs Christoph von Wirtemberg.* Stuttgart, 1899–1907.

Estes, James Martin. *Christian Magistrate and State Church: The Reforming Career of Johannes Brenz.* Toronto, 1982.

Kugler, Bernhard. *Christoph, Herzog zu Wirtemberg.* 2 vols. Stuttgart, 1868–1872.

Maurer, Hans Martin, and Kuno Ulshöfer. *Johannes Brenz und die Reformation in Württemberg.* Stuttgart, 1974.

Uhland, Robert, ed. *900 Jahre Haus Württemberg.* Stuttgart, 1984. Contains a short biography of Christoph (pp. 136–162).

KARIN BRINKMANN BROWN

CHURCH. In many ways, sixteenth-century theology can be viewed as a debate not only about justification but also about the question "ubi ecclesia" ("Where is the church"). The divisions within Western Christendom between Catholicism and various forms of Protestantism made the question of ecclesiology a complex and crucial one. Issues in the ecclesiological debates included the interrelated questions about the nature of authority, the "marks" of the church, the proper administration of the sacraments, the correct interpretation of scripture, the role of tradition, and the dialectic between visibility and invisibility.

The urgency of the ecclesiological question did not originate in the sixteenth century. The late Middle Ages was a period preoccupied with the search for the *vera ecclesia* ("true church"). There have been serious disagreements among historians regarding the nature of ecclesiastical life on the eve of the Reformation. The later Middle Ages were certainly a "time of troubles." Overpopulation, famine, the plague, economic insecurity, the war between France and England, and the Great Schism (1378–1417) all contributed to the appraisal of this era as a time of crisis. The church in the late Middle Ages has been portrayed as one of decadence, religious decline, and theological confusion. The French humiliation of Boniface VIII in 1303 and the removal of the papacy from Rome to Avignon has been interpreted as the critical turning point that led eventually to the schism and later to the conciliar era. Moreover, contemporaries constantly criticized the church for several abuses: financial burdens, traffic in ecclesiastical benefits, and the intellectual and pastoral unresponsiveness to the laity. Did this complex of events and complaints bring about an inevitable collapse of ecclesiastical governance within medieval Catholicism?

In recent decades scholars have revised this portrayal of decadence and have concluded that the image of the church in a state of total decay has little historical basis. The revised understanding of the "Babylonian Captivity"—the time when the papacy was located in France—has shown that the Avignonese papacy was less subservient to the French monarchy than was first assumed. Even the moral character of the popes (except for Clement VI) has been more positively reassessed. The alleged fiscalism of the Avignonese church is now more likely to be relegated to the later years of the fourteenth century. Even the stereotype of the "stupid priest" is contradicted by the evidence that clerical learning before the Reformation appears to have been improving.

Nonetheless, late medieval thinkers were preoccupied with the crisis over the identity and authority of the church (see Hendrix, 1976). The quest for the true church combined the traditional ideal of the primitive apostolic church with a variety of ecclesiastical theories. As early as the later thirteenth century, the Spiritual Franciscans (as did the earlier Waldensians) made the primary issue the nature of the church and the authority to interpret scripture. Like the Waldensians, the Spiritual Franciscans came to believe that they constituted the true spiritual church because they upheld the rule of apostolic poverty. The ideal of the primitive church was eventually combined with the notion of a remnant church characterized by persecution.

The controversy between Boniface VIII and Philip IV (the Fair) gave rise to debates about the authority of the papacy. Curialists such as Giles of Rome upheld radical claims to papal sovereignty. When the conflict shifted to antagonism between the papacy and the emperor, the curialists used the Donation of Constantine to support the sovereignty of the pope. They also argued for the idea that membership in the true church required obedience to papal rulings. In opposition to the curialists, thinkers such as Marsilius of Padua and William of Ockham attacked the inordinate authority attributed to the pope. For Marsilius only scripture was certain and only a general council representing all the faithful could claim the true revelation of the Spirit. Ockham placed authority in the faithful who adhered to Catholic truth without ever dissenting. Both men opposed excessive papal power but on different bases. Marsilius transferred the right to interpret scripture from pope to council while Ockham shifted this responsibility to right understanding.

The Great Schism and the Hussite crisis furthered passionate inquiry into the nature of the true church. Conciliar theory, which had its basis in canonist thought, held (according to Jean Gerson) that a general council could exercise the power of authority to reform the church when the pope proved incapable of governing the church. More radical conciliarists argued for an absolute conciliar supremacy, a view most commonly associated with the Council of Basel.

The Council of Basel also dealt with the Hussite crisis. This controversy was not about conciliar supremacy; Jan Hus's direct appeal to the authority of Christ had meant a bypassing of both pope and council. The later Hussite ecclesiology held that only the predestined were members of the true church. Although Hus himself did not require secession from the Catholic church, his execution at Constance was justified by Gerson because of the denial of authority inherent in his view of the church as determined only by the elect, who are unknown in this life.

The sixteenth-century debates about the church were a continuation of the debate of the late Middle Ages over the identity and authority of the church. When Luther triggered the indulgences controversy, he had no intention of splitting with the Catholic church. By the time of the Leipzig debate in 1519 Luther defended his famous "proposition 13," which denied the claims of papal rule by *divine* right. The excommunication of Luther in 1521 by Leo X drove Luther from the church and also caused him to denounce the papacy as the seat of the Antichrist. With the formal break with the Roman church, the sixteenth century was plunged even deeper into the question, Where is the church that cannot err? Since soteriology was closely linked to ecclesiology, the question had deep spiritual and existential implications in the course of the Reformation. As in the era that preceded Luther, the sixteenth century offered a broad spectrum of ecclesiological options.

In Luther's ecclesiological formulations, several distinctive characteristics emerge. After 1521 Luther, of course, insisted that the church could exist apart from the Roman hierarchy. *John* 6:45 and *1 Corinthians* 12:15 served as key texts upon which Luther developed his concept of the priesthood of all believers. He argued that a spiritual priesthood of all Christians replaces the hierarchical clerical priesthood of the Roman church.

Luther also stressed the invisibility of the true church. Faith does not depend on any particular institutional form or structure. Moreover, because faith is invisible the true church is an invisible fellowship. The church cannot be fixed to one place or person but is spiritual and is built invisibly in the Spirit of Christ. But Luther's affirmation of the invisibility of the church sparked criticism from opponents such as Ambrogio Catarino Politi; a purely spiritual church lacked any visible and tangible embodiment by which people could safely locate the church (see Hendrix, 1981). We see here reminiscences of the Hussite implication of anarchy and denial of authority detected by Gerson. This problem would recur with the debate between Huldrych Zwingli and Johann Eck.

Luther was not insensitive to this criticism. He argued that the church was, indeed, known through visible marks, especially baptism, the Eucharist, and the preaching of the word of God. In his 1539 treatise, *Von den Conciliis und Kirchen,* Luther listed seven visible marks of the church: the sermon, baptism, Communion, absolution, ordination, worship, and persecution. As Heiko A. Oberman has shown, Luther's church was the church of confessors (see Oberman, 1989). In the apostolic age the devil had attacked the church from the outside. In his own time Luther perceived that the diabolical persecutions came from inside. However, the suffering of the church was not surprising since Christ crucified constituted his church and determined the life of all Christians. Throughout his writings, especially the commentaries on the Old Testament, Luther joined the theme of suffering to a remnant ecclesiology. Hence the suffering communion of Christians throughout history. For Luther, then, the church was invisible in faith and in election but visible in suffering and in ceremonies. Above all else, the most important mark of the church was the preaching of the word of God.

Calvin was equally (if not more) concerned with the visible church. Following Augustine, he distinguished between the invisible predestined church, which stands in the presence of God, and the visible earthly church. The name "church" also designates the visible church that is necessary as a "mother" and "school" to beget and increase faith. Like Luther, Calvin identified the visible marks of the church as "the word of God purely preached and heard and the sacraments administered according to Christ's institution" (*Institutes of Christian Religion* 4.1.9). Calvin argued that where there is the preaching of the gospel and the correct administration of the sacraments, "there no ambiguous form of the church is seen" (*Inst.* 4.1.10).

In his definition of the church, Calvin attacked primarily three groups: the Catholics, the "fanatics" or Libertines, and the Anabaptists. Against both the Libertines and the Catholics, Calvin insisted on the inseparability of the word and the Spirit. The "fanatics" he argued, exalted the Spirit but despised the reading of scripture. Against such "giddiness," Calvin emphasized the immutability of the Spirit, who does not invent new revelations and teachings. Instead, Calvin maintained, "by a kind of mutual bond the Lord has joined together the certainty of his word and of his Spirit so that the perfect religion of the word may abide in our minds when the Spirit . . . shines; and that in turn we may embrace the Spirit with no fear of being deceived when we recognize him in his own image" (*Inst.* 1.9.3). Calvin detected the same error among the Catholics, who, like Jacopo Sadoleto, referred to the church and the Spirit but neglected the word by which the church is governed. Calvin refused to accept Sadoleto's use of the Vicentian Canon that Catholic truth is taught everywhere (*ubique*), always (*semper*), and by all (*ab omnibus*). Calvin did adopt the Vicentian Canon but further refined it by anchoring the church in the word. The church, according to Calvin, "is a society of all the saints, a society which, spread over the whole world, and existing in all ages, and bound together by the one doctrine and the one Spirit of Christ, cultivates and observes the unity of faith and brotherly concord" (Steinmetz, pp. 85–98).

In opposition to the Anabaptists Calvin warned against seeing holiness as a prerequisite for membership in the church or as a visible sign of the church (*Inst.* 4.1.23). In Calvin's view, demands for perfection undercut the certainty of faith and of the church. Therefore he asserted that the church's holiness was not yet complete. The church is the Augustinian "mixed body" and was only daily advancing toward holiness (*Inst.* 4.1.13). More important than some illusory perfection was that Christians were daily pardoned within the church. Labeled as the "Evangelical Anabaptists" by George Williams, this group included figures such as Michael Sattler (formulator of the 1527 Schleitheim Articles) as well as Ulrich Stadler, Dirk Philips, and Menno Simons. Several traits characterized their teachings and, in particular, their ecclesiologies.

Foremost was their belief in the connection between the true church and believer's baptism. The Anabaptists believed that the church was a *voluntary* organization. They attributed great importance to adult decision and the ability to make a deliberate choice. The church was made up of believers who had voluntarily entered it by responding to the word in adult baptism. Moreover, for the Anabaptists, the New Testament alone was normative for doctrine, polity, and ethics. (The Old Testament was not rejected but was interpreted allegorically or typologically.) The Anabaptists strove to pattern their life after the New Testament church. In accordance with the New Testament, most Anabaptists (with the exception of Balthasar Hubmaier) rejected the use of the sword. Some groups, notably the Hutterites, believed that the commandment of love required a disciplined life of communism.

The Anabaptists placed great emphasis on the *visible* church. This visibility included the preaching of right doctrine and the scriptural use of sacramental signs. The visibility of the church was also evident by the life of discipline or obedience undertaken by all members. Discipline, indeed, was a basis for church unity. Dirk Philips defined the church of God as a "church of holy beings, namely, of the angels in heaven and the believing reborn men on earth who have been renewed in the image of God." This meant increasingly a heavy reliance on the ban and excommunication. This is the church "without spot or wrinkle," visible in the life of obedience and discipleship.

Two other features of Anabaptist ecclesiology should be noted. The principle of separation from "the world" was fundamental. The most characteristic trait of all the radical Reformers was a rejection of the Constantinian synthesis, a common resistance to the joining together of church and state. According to Cornelius Dyck, there developed in Anabaptist thought a "cosmic dualism" that portrayed history as a battle between divine and satanic orders. As did Luther and many other contemporaries, the Anabaptists believed they were living in the last days, during which the devil was desperate. The church was the power of light and obedience in the midst of a world that was increasingly in the hands of the evil one or the forces of darkness.

Inseparable from this emphasis on separation from the world was the emphasis on suffering. In fact, Menno Simons listed "oppression and tribulation for the sake of the Lord's Word" as the sixth sign of the true church (see *Reply to Gellius Faber*). The suffering church was the persecuted church of martyrs. (Typical of the Anabaptists was their martyrology, *Het Offer des Heeren*, 1562, which begins with the martyrdom of Stephen in *Acts* 6–7 and jumps to the death of Michael Sattler in 1527 and then to the death of twenty-one martyrs from the Low Countries.) For the Anabaptists, the suffering of persecution was both an imitation of and a participation in Christ. Suffering was a testing and purifying of the faith, the narrow way to salvation, and an indispensable mark of the true church separated from the world.

The Catholic controversialists who were Luther's earliest opponents saw that the central issue of the controversy was not justification but authority. Who was to be the supreme arbiter and infallible judge in questions about the interpretation of scripture and authority in the church? Exemplary of this emphasis on authority was Eck, who explicitly attacked Zwingli's conception of the church in 1530. Zwingli had replied in 1524 to Hieronymus Emser that the church that cannot err is the elect illumined by God and "known only to God." This link between authority and invisibility infuriated Eck, who insisted on the priority and authority of the visible church, which is a mixed body represented plainly by the councils, bishops, cardinals, and the pope. In his *Enchiridion*, Eck attacked the reformers for being unable to agree on the scriptural interpretation of the Eucharist. He argued that the alleged clarity of scripture could not act as a sole authority in the church since agreement on interpretation of scripture could not be reached: "Who among them will judge? Scripture or the church? Apart from these no other judge can be provided" (*Enchiridion* 4.44).

Eck was one of the most formidable opponents of the Reformation. He ably represented the core of ideas that made up the Catholic refutation of Reformation ecclesiologies. In particular, he exposed the weakness of biblicism as the sole authority for the church. The writings of Eck and his fellow controversialists are the strongest attacks against what David C. Steinmetz has called the "exegetical optimism" of the early Protestants (Steinmetz, p. 96). The attempt to base authority primarily on the clarity of scripture floundered under the impact of the controversies over the Eucharist and baptism. In opposition to this reliance on scripture alone, Eck asserted that the church took priority and granted scripture its authority (a position Calvin rejected explicitly).

Eck also directly attacked another assertion central to the ecclesiology of the reformers, namely, the possession of the Holy Spirit. Luther, Zwingli, Calvin, and a wide variety of Radical Reformers claimed the authority to interpret scripture in opposition to Catholicism because of their illumination by the Spirit. In the sixteenth century the Spirit was the agent or giver of certainty and provided the foundation for the authority to interpret scripture and to dissent. Like Sadoleto, Eck insisted that the Spirit would not desert the church. Therefore the church that does not err was the vis-

ible, hierarchical Catholic church to whom the Spirit was promised throughout its history.

Ecclesiology, with the attendant issue of authority, played a crucial part in the failure of attempts at reconciliation between Protestantism and Catholicism. This role of ecclesiology is illustrated by the failure of the Protestant and Catholic representatives at the Colloquy of Regensburg (1541) to agree on the nature of the church and its authority. Even after reaching a consensus on justification, the question of authority of the church remained unsolved.

The Council of Trent did not promulgate any dogmatic decree on the nature of the church. Nonetheless, Trent did address many individual issues that contributed to debates about ecclesiology. In its final decree, Trent upheld the two sources of church authority: scripture and tradition. Authority thus included the rulings of popes and councils. While calling for an end to abuses, Trent reaffirmed purgatory, indulgences, the veneration of relics, and the worship of the saints. The council also reaffirmed the seven sacraments. Chief among its reform measures was the restoration of the power of bishops. Trent passed measures restricting absenteeism, encouraging regular preaching, annual visitations, the holding of annual synods, and the attending of triennial provincial synods. Along with these important administrative reforms were the support for new seminaries and the necessity to ordain only highly educated and thoroughly examined priests.

The sixteenth century was, indeed, a debate over the nature of the true church. The belief that one's salvation depended on the correct location and membership in the true church made the question a crucial one for the religious life of this age. These various ecclesiologies were not pluralistic options: they offered the stark alternative between life and death. The sixteenth century did not solve the ecclesiological question with any one uniform answer. Nonetheless, by focusing on the problem of ecclesiology, the historian gains insight into the heart of sixteenth-century religious concerns and debates.

[*See also* Church Discipline; Church Offices; *and* Law, *article on* Theological Understanding of Law.]

BIBLIOGRAPHY

Bagchi, David V. N. *Luther's Earliest Opponents: Catholic Controversialists, 1518–1525.* Minneapolis, 1991.

Duggan, Lawrence G. "The Unresponsiveness of the Late Medieval Church: A Reconsideration." *Sixteenth Century Journal* 9.1 (1978), 3–26.

Dyck, Cornelius. "The Suffering Church in Anabaptism." *Mennonite Quarterly Review* 59 (1985), 5–23.

Evans, G. R. *Problems of Authority in the Reformation Debates.* Cambridge, 1992.

Hendrix, Scott H. *Ecclesia in Via: Ecclesiological Developments in the Medieval Psalms Exegesis and the Dictata super Psalterium, 1513–1515, of Martin Luther.* Leiden, 1974.

———. "In Quest of the Vera Ecclesia: The Crisis of Late Medieval Ecclesiology." *Viator* 7 (1976), 347–378.

———. *Luther and the Papacy: Stages in a Reformation Conflict.* Philadelphia, 1981.

Klaasen, Walter. "The Anabaptist Understanding of the Separation of the Church." *Church History* 46 (1977), 421–436.

Klug, Eugene F. "Luther on the Church." *Concordia Theological Quarterly* 47 (1983), 193–207.

Littel, Franklin H. *The Anabaptist View of the Church.* New York, 1952.

Oakley, Francis. *The Western Church in the Later Middle Ages.* Reprint, Ithaca, N.Y., 1985.

Oberman, Heiko A. *Forerunners of the Reformation.* Philadelphia, 1981. See pp. 205–241.

———. *The Dawn of the Reformation.* Edinburgh, 1986.

———. *Luther, Man between God and the Devil.* New Haven and London, 1989.

Steinmetz, David C. *Luther in Context.* Bloomington, Ind., 1986. See pp. 85–97.

Vajta, Vilmos. "Die Kirche als geistlich-sakramentale communio mit Christus und seinen Heiligen bei Luther." *Lutherjahrbuch* 51 (1984), 10–62.

Williams, George H. *The Radical Reformation.* 3d ed. Kirksville, Mo., 1992.

SUSAN E. SCHREINER

CHURCH AND STATE. [*This brief review is designed to provide access to the numerous articles in the encyclopedia that deal with the complex of church-state relations in the sixteenth century.*] Persistent conflict over the proper spheres of civil and ecclesiastical authority is arguably a distinctive feature of the Latin Christian religious tradition, especially since the time of the Investiture Controversy (1076–1122), in the course of which the more extravagant claims of both the Roman pontiff and the Holy Roman Emperor were severely tested [*see* Law, *article on* Theological Understanding of Law]. The development of university law faculties over the next few centuries presented both the lords spiritual and the lords temporal with more refined intellectual arsenals [*see* Law, *articles on* Canon Law *and* Roman Law]. But in the late Middle Ages secular rulers gradually assumed a stronger position vis à vis the church, partly because of the growing moral authority of national monarchs, territorial rulers, and urban magistrates and partly because a more educated laity grew increasingly distrustful of powerful priests [*see* Anticlericalism].

Against this background the Protestant Reformation, with its radical critique of the theological foundations of sacerdotal authority, could not fail to invest the secular office with a new spiritual dignity [*see* Secular Magistrate, Office of]. In most newly Protestant territories, the affairs of the new churches came to be supervised by the secular power or its representatives, even if leading Protestant divines often regarded this turn of events with considerable misgivings. Only churches that looked for guidance to John Calvin's Geneva were able, in some cases, to create an autonomous ecclesiastical polity with extensive authority over the lives of believers, sufficiently so that Protestant critics more friendly to secular authorities often accused Calvinists of aspiring to

"a new popery" [*see* Magistracy, *articles on* England, France, *and* Germany and the Low Countries]. To fill the gap left by the abolition of Catholic Europe's separate system of ecclesiastical courts (which had dealt with, among other things, marriage law), new tribunals had to be created, more often having a civil rather than an ecclesiastical character [*see* Courts, *articles on* Church Courts *and* Marriage Courts]. Moreover, preachers of all persuasions, Catholic as well as Protestant, were eager to prove the truth of their doctrines by achieving a genuine reformation of morals; to this end the power of the state had to be mobilized to persuade the reluctant, and temporal rulers, often devout themselves, were not loath to see their authority enhanced by the high purposes now entrusted to them [*see* Social Discipline].

Common opinion also expected a Christian government to prevent false doctrine from gaining a hold on the populace, although the fresh memory of persecution by Catholic authorities prevented Protestant states from adopting a similar harshness [*see* Persecution]. The advance of state power into new religious and moral terrain was not universally approved, but it was in this period exceedingly difficult to resist. Radical sectarian movements that challenged the legitimacy of the coercive state served only to enhance the widespread fear of anarchy, which was, in an age of turmoil, a strong psychological support for the emergent early modern state [*see* Anabaptists, Community of Goods, Münster, *and* Radical Reformation].

JAMES D. TRACY

CHURCH COURTS. See Courts, *article on* Church Courts.

CHURCH DISCIPLINE. In the 1960s and 1970s, scholars became interested in the notion of "discipline" as a means of social control and cultural formation. By far the most influential was Michel Foucault, whose work *Discipline and Punish* (*Surveiller et punir: Naissance de la prison,* Paris, 1975) brought a Nietzschean attention to power and domination to Marxist views of discipline as a means by which one class dominated, and incorporated into its formulation of "discipline," medicine and science, "discourses on the body." This scholarship has colored subsequent understandings of discipline, relating connotations of control, coercion, and a kind of self-conscious extension of authority to the practice of "discipline."

Recognizing that influence is particularly important for any effort to understand church discipline during the Reformation. In the last two decades, Reformation scholars have increasingly come to place church discipline within larger narratives of the history of the incipient absolutist state, making church discipline the central mode by which states extended control and authority over the lives of those who lived within their borders—church discipline becomes both a tool of "social control" and the means by which states seized moral authority. Most have severed church discipline from the different theologies that called for it.

The use of "discipline," *disciplina*, on the members of the Christian community had its origins in the gospel of Matthew (18:15–21). As early as the first century, the Christian church claimed the right to discipline its members, that is, to use punishments ranging from exclusion from communion to excommunication (complete exclusion from the Christian community and all its benefits). Early on it also assumed the right to define and determine those actions, patterns of behavior, and personal conduct that would be subject to discipline. For the laity and uncloistered clergy, the mechanism for the enforcement of church discipline in the Middle Ages was the episcopal hierarchy, whose immediate agent was the parish priest and whose final authority was the papal court. The monastic tradition enriched and complicated that understanding of *disciplina*: monks and nuns lived under *regula* ("rule"); in their lives discipline became both an inward exercise and an externally imposed order.

Echoing the medieval monastic tradition, sixteenth-century Protestant reformers linked inner discipline and that external discipline the church imposed upon its members. They differed as to the relation between the two. For Martin Luther, one's inner life was primarily an issue of education, the primary medium of which was preaching. Church discipline, on the other hand, was an issue of order, restraint, and regulation, not education. Luther retained much of the episcopal structure, while repudiating papal authority: church discipline followed much the same course as medieval practice, with the local pastor representing the bishop. Luther also instituted visitations, which were intended to monitor and regulate the morals, as well as the Christian practices, of men and women.

For the Reformed tradition, Huldrych Zwingli in Zurich, Martin Bucer in Strasbourg, and John Calvin in Geneva, inner discipline was inseparable from church discipline—"discipline" was inseparable from salvation. This Reformed tradition gave a new prominence to church discipline in its ecclesiology, developed new institutions of church discipline, and specified most fully what sorts of behavior and actions were subject to that discipline. For them, mechanisms of church discipline served essential functions, both in the life of the individual Christian, supporting and enforcing the realization of the true Christian life, and in the life of the church, reinforcing patterns of behavior, dress, and marital conduct that would signal the presence of the Holy Spirit among the community of Christians. In Zurich, Zwingli with the city council instituted a marriage court, whose jurisdiction extended from the conduct of marriage,

encompassing such matters as sexual fidelity, financial responsibility, and sexual deviancy, to individual issues of moral infraction, which included not only gambling but also flamboyance in dress or manner and excesses of eating or drinking. By far the most important and lasting of the mechanisms developed within the Reformed tradition, however, was the consistory established by Calvin in Geneva, which then was instituted in Calvinist communities throughout Europe, more or less along the lines of the Genevan model. Its functions included supervision, investigation of such lapses and forms of misconduct as had been stipulated in Zurich—gambling, prostitution, flamboyance of dress or manner, extravagance, marital misconduct of various kinds, as well as false worship, including blasphemy and idolatry—and the enforcement of the moral life of each member of the community through a range of punishments, from public proclamation of wrongdoing, through exclusion from communion, to excommunication. The consistory received its authority within Calvin's theology as that means by which both the saved were strengthened in their process of sanctification and the damned were restrained from damaging the larger community.

Like the Calvinist-Reformed tradition, the Anabaptists were strong in their affirmation of church discipline. They insisted that the church, composed of true believers joined by voluntary baptism, must be "without spots and wrinkles." Discipline was the means to maintain that purity. Church discipline was a crucial aspect of Anabaptist thought; internal discussions, particularly in the second half of the sixteenth century, largely dealt with discipline, the ban, excommunication, and shunning. The Anabaptist use of church discipline differed from other Protestant traditions in one important way. Since they nowhere enjoyed governmental support, the means to enforce discipline were purely ecclesial: excommunication from the church, together with "shunning" (the discontinuation of any and all social contact).

The practice of discipline within different communities was shaped not only by different ecclesiologies but also by each church's relation to its political community. If the government supported the church, then church discipline acquired access to corporal or capital punishment. Calvinism was particularly adept politically. Governments frequently served the local consistory in its pursuit of moral discipline; magistrates often served on consistories, blending in their persons two different jurisdictions that became thereby complementary, and consistories often benefited from having representation on the town councils. For those states that confronted Calvinist minorities—Spain and the Low Countries, England and Scotland, the Huguenots in France, and principalities throughout the Holy Roman Empire—the consistory, in ensuring the uniform practice of Calvinist morals, served to reinforce the boundaries of the Calvinist community against political pressure. It served, in other words, to enforce certain kinds of civil disobedience; in the case of the Low Countries, it abetted rebellion.

For each of the Protestant reformers, discipline was bound up with an Augustinian understanding of the human will and its need to be restrained, as well as with humanist concerns about education and moral action—with questions of moral choice and conduct. In the Reformed tradition, the purpose of church discipline was not subjection as such, but salvation. That purpose defined the parameters and applications of church discipline and gave it its authority. Insofar as the state served the church, church discipline served the state, but, as Philip II of Spain learned, if the state did not serve salvation, church discipline served that state's opposition.

[See also Mysticism; Saints, article on Sainthood; and Sanctifiation.]

BIBLIOGRAPHY

Hsia, Ronnie Po-chia. *Social Discipline in the Reformation: Central Europe, 1550–1750*. Reprint, London and New York, 1992. The only summary in English of the scholarship on confessionalization in the German Reformation.

Kingdon, Robert M. "The Control of Morals in Calvin's Geneva." In *The Social History of the Reformation*, edited by Lawrence P. Buck and Jonathan Zophy, pp. 3–16. Columbus, Ohio, 1972. Reprinted in *Church and Society in Reformation Europe*, London, 1985. The best treatment of the consistory in Geneva.

Köhler, Walther. *Zürcher Ehegericht und Genfer Konsistorium* (1932). Reprint, Leipzig, 1992. Still the best study of the Zurich marriage court and its relation to the Geneva consistory.

Schilling, Heinz. *Konfessionskonflikt und Staatsbildung: Eine Fallstudie über das Verhältnis von religiösem und sozialem Wandel in der Frühneuzeit am Beispiel der Grafschaft Lippe*. Gütersloh, 1981. One of the most influential studies of confessionalization, social control, and state formation.

———. "Between the Territorial State and Urban Liberty: Lutheranism and Calvinism in the County of Lippe." In *The German People and the Reformation*, edited by R. Po-chia Hsia, pp. 263–283. Ithaca, N.Y., 1988. A brief summary of the position argued in *Konfessionskonflikt*.

Schnabel-Schüle, Helga. "Der große Unterschied und seine kleine Folgen: Zum Problem der Kirchenzucht als Unterschiedungskriterium zwischen lutherischer und reformierter Konfession." In *Krisenbewußtsein und Krisenbewältigung in der Frühen Neuzeit/Crisis in Early Modern Europe*, edited by Monika Hagenmaier and Sabine Holtz, pp. 197–214. Frankfurt a.M. and New York, 1992. An important comparison of Lutheran and Calvinist forms of church discipline in the later sixteenth century.

LEE PALMER WANDEL

CHURCH FINANCES.

The income of the late medieval Catholic church was derived from three distinct sources: tithe, land, and spiritual dues. The papacy drew on the most complex range of revenues: the various benefice taxes, such as annates, payable for spiritual promotions; clerical taxation; the sale of indulgences and the profits of jubilees; and, increasingly, territorial profits from the Papal States. Cardinals, archbishops, and bishops also benefited from both spiritual and temporal sources of income, the latter usually proving the most significant element in their income and wealth. The regular clergy depended even more exclusively upon land and retained their hold on as much as a quarter to a third of territory in some areas of Europe. At the parochial level, on the other hand, tithe still provided the main source of income in most parts of Western Christendom, supplemented by payments for spiritual services, the latter often particularly important in urban contexts. Few of these sources of revenue were wholly immune from lay intervention: monarchs rarely permitted full clerical taxation to be paid to the papacy, revenues were diverted to fund national projects, and laymen disputed the detail, if not the principle, of tithe collection. Moreover, the nobles in many European states were deeply enmeshed in the property interests of the church as monastic founders with vested rights, as leaseholders, and as patrons. The independence of the church's control over its own wealth was thus in some measure an illusion. In Henry VII's England, for example, it has been estimated that less than £5,000 per annum was transmitted to Rome, while in a "normal" year, beset by no war crises, the Crown could hope to derive about £12,000 from the clergy.

Nevertheless, the Protestant Reformation marked a sharp break in the pattern of ecclesiastical finance wherever it took root. Monarchs, princes, and cities were no longer constrained by anxieties about sacrilege in their attacks upon church wealth; indeed the reformers lent much legitimation to their assaults. Luther's direct challenge to Rome, and its initial focus in the indulgences controversy, justified withdrawal of payments to the papacy; his later attack on monasticism released one of the most profitable sectors of the church from clerical control. These were particularly dramatic developments in Germany, where fragmented political structures had often made it difficult for rulers to impose their will on the church. Luther's first intention was that the profits derived from dissolution and confiscation should be paid into "common chests" and dispensed for charitable purposes and the support of the clergy. By the end of 1525, however, he was assuring the elector of Saxony that the revenues of the church belonged to the state, and that after proper payments to clergy, schools, and charity, the surplus could be employed by the prince. Huldrych Zwingli and Martin Bucer, on the other hand, held that church property belonged to the religious community and that the secular ruler merely administered it.

Princes who established powerful political control over their churches obviously inclined toward Luther's view. A ruler like Duke Ulrich of Württemberg showed little sensitivity to the needs of reform when in 1534 he confiscated all monastic property and expropriated almost all the proceeds for state and military purposes. Philipp of Hesse was more cautious: he claimed that he employed his church revenues to fund the University of Marburg, to support other institutions of learning, to supplement ministerial stipends, and only then used the remainder for the military support of Protestantism. Close study of the Hessian evidence suggests, however, that far more wealth passed into Philipp's hands than was returned to the church. The parochial clergy, in particular, benefited little from Philipp's largess: they were still funded mainly from inadequate tithes and dues, supplemented in some cases by the local common chest revenue from former mass endowments and minor benefactions.

It was the imperial free cities that often conformed most closely to Bucer's expectations. Political caution, the presence of independent ecclesiastical institutions, and the need to maintain internal political harmony disposed cities like Nuremberg, Strasbourg, and Augsburg to use available ecclesiastical revenues to promote education and to fund the new order. Common chests were established to serve the needs of the community; the clergy were fully integrated into the body politic as citizens and were paid for their services, the residue providing for social needs.

Princes and cities could consider the best ways to employ the considerable wealth of the higher clergy, but for most ordinary parishioners it was the issue of the tithe that dominated debates on church finance. For the peasantry the tithe was identified as one of those fiscal burdens that made rural existence intolerable, and during the German Peasants' War (1525) there were demands for the abolition of all but the great tithe on grain (in the Twelve Articles) or its limitation to the basic needs of the incumbent (the Forty-six Frankfurt Articles). Swiss radicals went further, denying the scriptural basis of the tithe and rejecting any compulsory payments to the clergy, forcing from Zwingli a determined defense of the legitimacy of this means of ministerial support. After 1525 agitation for tithe abolition in Switzerland and Germany was inevitably muted, but acceptance of voluntarism as the proper means of funding the church and deep hostility to the tithe remained major tenets of radical belief. Moreover, the religious conflicts of the 1520s encouraged people to withhold payments to the church: in Thuringia, for example, it was only in the late 1530s that Lutheran clergy were able to collect dues at levels similar to those of their Catholic predecessors.

In the Scandinavian lands monarchs seized the excuse of reform to increase their wealth and power. The Danish monarchy was already allowing the alienation of church to the nobility in the early 1520s, well before the beginnings of official reform. By the end of the 1530s episcopal property had been appropriated to the Crown, and the monasteries were being slowly secularized: only the revenue needed to maintain the new superintendents and their modest house-

holds was returned by the monarchy. But it was in Sweden that Gustavus Vasa pursued material ambitions to their logical extreme. Between the Recess of Västerås in 1527 and the end of the 1540s, the monarchy slowly eroded the independence of the old church, appropriated most of its wealth, and ensured that the new Lutheran hierarchy abandoned any pretensions to novel power. In the first decade the wealth of the monasteries and of the bishoprics was assailed; thereafter it was the turn of the parishes, which between 1545 and 1548 lost most of their independent endowments. The Crown took a share of the tithe in return for a promise of adequate stipend to the clergy, a promise that was very imperfectly discharged. The magnitude of the transfer can be gauged by the counting of estates: at the beginning of his reign Gustavus held 3,754, the church 14,340; by the end of the reign the Crown held 18,936, the church none. The consequence was the impoverishment of the Lutheran church, from which it took at least a century to recover.

The parallels between England and Sweden are striking. In both realms governments expropriated church property and movable valuables; in both the profits were overwhelmingly consumed by the lay authorities, with little restitution to the new establishment. In both, finally, much of the structure of the old ecclesiastical order survived within the new. The English Crown seized much of the parish plate between 1549 and 1553, and in 1547 the chantries were dissolved for its benefit. However, the key parochial change was the transfer of many appropriated benefices, ones in which a monastery had held the rectory, from the regular clergy to the Crown at the dissolution of the monasteries, and thence by sale or grant to laymen. This placed a significant part of the tithe income of parishes in lay hands and became a major source of dispute between laity and clergy. The monasteries were dissolved, yielding to the Crown an approximate profit of £1.3 million between 1536 and Henry VIII's death a decade later. However, the long-term beneficiaries were again the laity who purchased monastic property. The English bishops survived with a part of their possessions and authority intact, and the funding of the Anglican church appeared by Elizabeth's reign to be in many ways more conservative than that of most European Protestant states. The clergy remained vulnerable to the financial demands of the laity throughout the Tudor period: the prelates had lost about a third of their most profitable manors, and many of the rest were in long and unprofitable lease to Crown and gentry. The deans and chapters had also surrendered many of their most valuable lands. Complaints about clerical poverty met with little sympathy either from Elizabeth or her influential subjects.

The Calvinist church was more fully separated from past modes of finance than its Lutheran and Anglican counterparts. Geneva itself followed the model of other Reformed cities in expelling all the regular clergy and divorcing itself from episcopal jurisdiction in 1536. The profits of dissolution were appropriated by the municipality, which henceforth paid the pastors of the new church. Elsewhere, Calvinism was often a minority faith and had to depend on the voluntary support of its members. When, as in Scotland or the United Provinces, it became the established church, it was not necessarily easy to replicate the working arrangements of Geneva. The Dutch Reformed church was funded by the magistracy after several false starts in the 1570s, but not at a particularly generous level. In Scotland the settlement was bedeviled from the outset by the failure of the Calvinists to gain access to the revenues of the old church. The nobility had acquired powerful interests in these revenues in the decades before the Reformation through the "feu" system. This in turn made it impossible to rationalize the episcopate or to improve the stipends of parish ministers for a generation after 1560. The lay elite were determined to block schemes that would have diminished their profits from the parishes. The provisional solution was to permit the Reformed church access to a third of the fruits of each benefice. Only after the end of civil war in 1573 did attempts to give the Reformed church control over the old parochial structure begin in earnest.

The Catholic church after the Council of Trent remained firmly based on traditional principles of finance. Papal revenues proceeded further along the evolutionary path already marked out during the Renaissance. Taxation in the Papal States continued to provide the principal source of revenue: income from this source quadrupled during the sixteenth century, while prices approximately doubled. Spiritual revenues also increased, but only to twice their former amount. The striking feature here is that the Protestant Reformation made little difference to these yields, since they were derived predominantly from Italy. Papal fiscal stability is indicated by the ability of successive pontiffs to borrow capital and to repay short-term loans, even during periods of economic difficulty. Much of this revenue was used to finance the reconstructions of the Eternal City, most famously that undertaken by Urban VIII in the early seventeenth century. Papal funds were used as well to subsidize princes fighting for the defense of Catholicism: these payments were especially significant in the early stages of the Thirty Years' War. More explicitly spiritual causes, such as the provision of seminaries and the funding of missions, accounted for only one percent of all papal expenditure in the late sixteenth century.

Some of the more unscrupulous princes seized on the Protestant threat to extract wealth from the Catholic church. An extreme example is that of the dukes of Bavaria, who threatened concessions to Protestants in order to wring more revenue from their clergy. The Austrian Habsburgs, even after they became active exponents of Catholic reform, were slow to return lands lost to the church during periods of Protestant ascendancy in the disputed German lands. Even

after the Thirty Years' War, restitution was limited: in Bohemian territory, for example, nobles retained their church estates in return for an excise on salt payable to the clergy. The fiscal security of the clergy was uncomfortably dependent, in Catholic as in Protestant Europe, on the goodwill of the laity. But the Catholic hierarchy could appeal, with some confidence, to the separate status to be accorded to a sacramental priesthood. Protestants ministers had to prove constantly to princes, magistrates, and congregations that they were "worthy their hire."

[*See also* Capitalism; Church and State; *and* Church Ordinances.]

BIBLIOGRAPHY

Cohn, Henry J. "Church Property in the German Protestant Principalities." In *Politics and Society in Reformation Europe*, edited by E. I. Kouri and T. Scott, pp.158–87. London, 1987.

Donaldson, Gordon. *The Scottish Reformation*. Cambridge, 1960.

Dunkley, E. H. *The Reformation in Denmark*. London, 1948.

Evans, R. J. W. *The Making of the Habsburg Monarchy, 1550-1700*. Oxford, 1979.

Heal, Felicity. *Of Prelates and Princes: A Study of the Economic and Social Position of the Tudor Episcopate*. Cambridge, 1980.

Karant-Nunn, Susan C. "The Economic Position of Pastors in Ernestine Thuringia, 1521–55." *Archiv für Reformationsgeschichte* 63 (1972), 94–113.

O'Day, Rosemary, and Felicity Heal, eds. *Princes and Paupers in the English Church, 1500–1800*. Leicester, 1981.

Partner, Peter. "Papal Financial Policy in the Renaissance and Counter-Reformation." *Past and Present* 88 (1980), 17–62.

Potter, G. R. *Zwingli*. Reprint, Cambridge, 1984.

Prestwich, Menna, ed. *International Calvinism, 1541–1715*. Oxford, 1985.

Roberts, Michael. *The Early Vasas: A History of Sweden, 1523–1611*. Reprint, Cambridge, 1986.

Scarisbrick, J. J. "Clerical Taxation in England, 1485–1547." *Journal of Ecclesiastical History* 11 (1960), 41–45.

Strauss, Gerald. *Nuremberg in the Sixteenth Century*. Rev. ed. Bloomington, Ind., 1976.

FELICITY HEAL

CHURCHING. Little research has been published on the ritual purification of women after childbirth, a practice known as churching. Deriving from Levitical prescriptions (*Lv.* 12:1–8) and the Gospel account (*Lk.* 2:22–39) of Mary's conformity to them as she presented herself and her infant to the priest Simeon, Justinian set the date of Christian commemoration of Mary's purification at 2 February (Candlemas), forty days after Christmas. Popular conviction that parturient women were impure reinforced observance of this feast day, as well as of various lustral rites for individual mothers after a period of isolation (usually eight to forty-two days) from public life and sexual abstinence. Official church opinion that menstruating women and new mothers were not impure seems not to have persuaded the laity. Parish priests usually agreed with their congregations.

According to liturgical handbooks on the eve of the Reformation, a woman to be churched came to the sanctuary door with a midwife, other birthing-room attendants, and often her infant, who had previously been baptized. Her face was veiled. The priest or his assistant sprinkled her with holy water, giving her the left-hand end of his stole or his left hand to hold as he led her to the altar. The woman bore lighted candles. Intoned were various prayers, psalms, and other biblical passages, which often referred to women's vulnerability to the devil during pregnancy and delivery and begged for God's mercy. The priest recited the *Genesis* account of Eve's punishments for sin: subordination to her husband and bearing children in pain. Sometimes mass was said. The new mother made an offering, for the priest's use, of money, yarn, or cloth; she was blessed and aspersed again and then dismissed. Afterward she provided her attendants with cake or other food. The ceremony has been interpreted as one that concluded an interlude of feminine independence, during which women were "on top," and that reintegrated them into the society of (superior) men; it has also been seen as a rite of transition from a semisacred and separate condition back into secular normalcy.

Martin Luther and, later, English Puritans regarded the Catholic ritual as intolerably superstitious. There appears to have been wide variation in its reformed fate, though this needs further study. Some women were content to dispense with it, while, according to parish visitation records, many others wished to retain it. In much of Lutheran Germany a modified rite of churching was imposed upon all new mothers. Aspersion and the leading-in were eliminated, and pastors told congregations that parturient women were not impure; nonetheless, they retold the story of Eve's subjugation and pain because of her disobedience, and they emphasized women's weaker moral and intellectual condition. They thanked God for the mother's safe delivery. Reformed women continued to make an offering and, following their benediction, to entertain the women of the birthing chamber. Adulteresses were not to be churched.

In England, beginning with *The Second Book of Common Prayer* of 1552, "purification of women" gave way to "the thanksgiving of women after child birth." In popular opinion, however, "green" (unchurched) women should be sequestered, and to die unchurched meant almost certain damnation. Pastors debated the rectitude of churching during the second half of the sixteenth century, but women continued to undergo it and to indulge themselves generously in the customary repast that followed. In the seventeenth century, veiling became an issue; women were often forced to wear veils at their churching. Puritans rejected the entire ceremony as "Jewish" and "popish."

In Catholic lands the Jesuits evidently objected to churching. The ritual has nevertheless persisted into the twentieth century.

BIBLIOGRAPHY

Coster, William. "Purity, Profanity, and Puritanism: The Churching of Women, 1500–1700." In *Women in the Church*, edited by W. J. Sheils and Diana Wood, pp. 377–387. Studies in Church History, 27. Oxford, 1990. On English churching.
Cressy, David. "Purification, Thanksgiving, and the Churching of Women in Post-Reformation England." *Past and Present* 141 (November 1993), 106–146. Excellent on veiling controversy; valuable on changes during sixteenth and seventeenth centuries. Does not accept anthropological interpretations.
Davis, Natalie Zemon. "Women on Top." In *Society and Culture in Early Modern France*, pp. 124–151. Stanford, Calif., 1975.
Karant-Nunn, Susan C. "Churching, a Women's Rite: Ritual Modification in Reformation Germany." Forthcoming in a volume on applications of anthropology to religious history, edited by R. W. Scribner and R. Po-chia Hsia. Says that women, laymen, and clergy may have had different views of churching.
Rushton, Peter. "Purification or Social Control? Ideologies of Reproduction and the Churching of Women after Childbirth." In *The Public and the Private*, edited by Eva Gamarnikow, pp. 118–131. London, 1983.
Shorr, Dorothy C. "The Iconographic Development of the Presentation in the Temple." *Art Bulletin* 28 (1946), 17–32.
Wilson, Adrian. "The Ceremony of Childbirth and Its Interpretation." In *Women as Mothers in Pre-industrial England: Essays in Memory of Dorothy McLaren*, edited by Valerie Fildes, pp. 68–107. London and New York, 1990.

SUSAN C. KARANT-NUNN

CHURCH OFFICES. [*This entry comprises four articles focusing on the development and evolution of ecclesiastical authority in the four main confessional groupings of Reformation Europe: Lutheran, Calvinist, Anglican, and Roman Catholic.*]

Lutheran Offices

The fact that Lutheranism has no theory of office can be traced back to Luther's own inconclusive theology of office. This has stimulated extensive research, which has established that Luther's utterances about ecclesiastical office may be understood only within the framework of the often-polemical settings of his argumentation. Two major considerations were determinative: the first was to differentiate the Lutheran from the Catholic conception of office; the second emerged after the mid-1520s, when it became necessary to differentiate the Lutheran from the radical wing of the Reformation. Arising from the first was Luther's conception of the "priesthood of all believers." According to Luther, the jurisdictional authority for absolution from sins (*potestas jurisdictionis*, "power of the keys") lay with the church, meaning the communion of all believers, and not with the pope or those holding office within the church (WA 6, 566, 26–28). The doctrine of the priesthood of all believers did away with the difference between priests and laity. Accordingly, Luther rejected the Catholic concept of the sacramental character of ordination to the priesthood, and the *character indelebilis* connected with it. However, although the concept of a "special office of the church" is found in all of his writings, his formulations generally remained ambiguous. Luther designated this special office as "ministry of the word" or as "ministry of the gospel" (WA 6, 566, 32f). Thus the office was to be understood as a ministering activity, with the officeholder exercising no power over fellow Christians. From a spiritual perspective, all were equal (*communio sanctorum*). A minister held special authority solely because he served the word.

By viewing the ministerial office as conveying the word (in contrast to the Catholic view of office, where the priest was conveyer of salvation), Luther advanced a "functional concept" of office. Wherever the "word functions"—that is, wherever it is proclaimed—there is also the office. For Luther, however, the office was available only to those especially called. This was made clearer and more explicit during his conflict with the spiritualist forces of the radical Reformation after 1525. The calling should be the result of election by the congregation or the authorities and confirmed the right to preach and to exercise other public functions in the congregation. The proclamation of the word thereby received its legitimate character. According to Luther one might receive a calling in either of two ways: an unmediated calling was made by the Holy Spirit; and a mediated calling was accomplished through the congregation or secular authorities (WA 17/1, 360, 1519). Luther attached strict conditions to the legality of an unmediated calling; his endorsement of it at all must be seen as a concession to the radical wing of the Reformation.

The specific tasks of a minister of the word were preaching and administering the sacraments. Luther did not create a hierarchy among ministerial tasks nor establish a ministerial hierarchy on that basis; in the preface to Melanchthon's *Unterricht der Visitatoren* of 1528, however, Luther emphasized the necessity of a higher ecclesiastical office. The task of this "supervisor or visitor" was to provide spiritual support for pastors and to instill unity among them. Luther did not view this as an instrument for control.

Melanchthon, Bugenhagen, and the First Church Ordinances. After Luther's death, the concept of office would be refined by Melanchthon and others. Already during Luther's lifetime Melanchthon had sharpened the definition of office in the official confessional documents of emerging Lutheranism (Augsburg Confession, 1530, and its Apologia, 1531, and *De potestate et primatu papae tractatus*, 1537). For Melanchthon, it was imperative that the Lutheran conception of office be distinguished from that of the radical Reformation. This may be seen in article 5 of the Augsburg Confession, which is devoted to preaching. Its foundation was scripture, and the office was considered as instituted by God (*iure divino*). Melanchthon also considered the *ministerium* as a special office that should be exercised by persons especially called to it. The function of the

office, namely, proclamation of the word, remained separate from the person who held the office (Apologia 13, 12). The priesthood of all believers was confined to the right to perform emergency baptism and the right to choose a pastor. Likewise in article 5 of the Augsburg Confession, in clear contrast to the Roman Catholic understanding of the "office of sacrifice," the content of the ministerial office was defined as *ministerium docendi evangelii et porrigendi sacramenta*. Elsewhere Melanchthon restated Luther's earlier opinion that there were no "differences between bishops and pastors" (*De Potestate* 27), although the office of bishop was thereby expressly legitimated as a higher spiritual office. Both Luther and Melanchthon affirmed an undivided preaching office. In contrast to Reformed teaching, emerging Lutheranism did not recognize a division of New Testament offices.

Johannes Bugenhagen's significance to the development of a Lutheran understanding of office, meanwhile, lay in his practical-theological activity as organizer of the renewal of the church in northern Germany. Bugenhagen's theology of office followed that of Luther and Melanchthon. Bugenhagen subscribed to the notion of a special office as instituted by God. More clearly than Melanchthon, he affirmed the right of the congregation to choose a pastor as an expression of the priesthood of all believers. This was manifest in his emphasizing the convergence of "sending" and "electing" by the congregation, both of which must operate for there to be spiritual office ("Von dem christlichen Glauben und rechten guten Werken," Wittenberg, 1526, pp. 330–331). This doctrine of office was expressed in a number of church ordinances written by Bugenhagen, (including, among others, those for Braunschweig (1528), Hamburg (1529), Lübeck (1532), Stralsund (1535); Braunschweig-Wolfenbüttel (1543), and the Duchy of Pomerania (1535). In these ordinances the special spiritual office was recognized as one of the central institutions of the new church structure, although it was tied to specific forms for electing pastors. The practical requirements of church renewal, however, necessitated a hierarchy of spiritual offices. In the church ordinances of Bugenhagen one finds, on the one hand, independent ecclesiastical bodies (*Wahlgremien*) comprising laity, which may be designated as church offices, and, on the other, a hierarchical differentiation among spiritual offices. The unity of the office of pastor was not preserved in practice.

The offices for the laity included treasurers (*Schatzkastenherren* or *Gotteskastenherren*) in Hamburg, Braunschweig, and Lübeck and deacons, or "church fathers" (*Kirchenväter*), in Hamburg, and Lübeck. Although there were substantial internal differentiations of offices, differences among lay church offices disappeared by the end of the sixteenth century. For example, the church ordinance for Braunschweig-Wolfenbüttel, which went into effect in 1569 and which borrowed from the Württemberg church ordinance of 1559, restricted the participation of the congregation in pastoral elections to the small number of congregations that possessed the right of patronage. Similar conditions obtained in other territories.

Already in Bugenhagen's first church ordinance, a leadership position over the city pastors was introduced in the form of the superintendent, who had a so-called coadjutor as deputy. Bugenhagen justified this solution by pointing to the necessity, in view of Anabaptist activities, of anchoring within the new structure of the city church a spiritual authority who would know how to resolve theological controversy. Here was the theological legitimation of a superior spiritual office in the ecclesiastical organization. A few months later, similar steps were taken in electoral Saxony. Building on Melanchthon's *Unterricht der Visitatoren* (which was published in March 1528), the electoral Saxon visitors after autumn 1528 ordered that in the larger cities of the territory so-called superintendants be appointed who in place of the visitors would see to the preservation of pure doctrine. In electoral Saxony as in the city of Braunschweig, this did not entail the traditional conveying of prebendary lands. As a rule, the new officeholders in Braunschweig were appointed and paid by the city council. In electoral Saxony they were appointed by the ruler and paid from a special fund for this specific purpose.

Thus the connection between the material benefice and the spiritual office that was typical of the old faith was broken for the new positions of leadership. The superintendent was invested in an "office" for which specific qualifications were required. While Bugenhagen and Melanchthon were concerned that the superior office be dedicated to spiritual oversight, the official instruction of electoral Saxony outlined a thoroughly formal supervisory obligation for the superintendents.

Beginning with these positions, emerging Lutheranism became increasingly hierarchical in subsequent decades. Doctrinal oversight was combined with the regulatory function. Corresponding hierarchies of office were formed first in electoral Saxony and served as a model for other church ordinances such as those Bugenhagen drafted in 1543 for the territory of Braunschweig-Wolfenbüttel. Ideas emanating from Württemberg carried developments further. Württemberg's church ordinance of 1559 was vastly influential in the second half of the sixteenth century, for example in the principality of Braunschweig-Wolfenbüttel, which committed to the Reformation in 1569. Four levels of order were established: in ascending order, these were the parish pastor, the special superintendent, general superintendent, and then finally the consistory, which was responsible for leadership of the entire church and which advised the prince in spiritual matters. In the church ordinances of the second half of the sixteenth century, spiritual office had been differentiated in ways that went beyond the concept of legitimate vocation as Luther and Melanchthon had conceived it.

In the church orders for Hamburg and Lübeck Bugenhagen had formalized ordination during worship service as confirmation of the vocation of pastor. The emphasis in these orders on a spiritual "mission" led to a strengthening of the character of office in the specific historical situation of the late 1520s. Contrary to Luther's notion of centralized ordinations in Wittenberg, Bugenhagen left ordination to the local congregation and thereby emphasized the "relatedness of the preaching office to the congregation" (*Gemeindebezogenheit des Predigtamtes*). Developments continued along these lines in the following decades. The regulations of the territorial and urban church orders by the end of the sixteenth century might be summarized as taking a twofold approach to ministerial calling. As a first step, the formal qualifications for the calling and the conferring of benefices would be ascertained; second, the spiritual component included the three steps of ordination, presentation, and installation into office in the setting of a congregational worship service.

Synodal structures played no decisive role in developing Lutheranism. Luther himself attributed to the synods of the old faith only a judicial function, one that could be fulfilled by consistories or judicatories (*Kammergerichten*). This was intended to secure the participation of the laity. In accordance with this understanding, in some territories synodal structures developed that lasted until the end of the sixteenth century. This was true, among others, of the principality of Braunschweig-Wolfenbüttel, which followed the example of Württemberg, for in Braunschweig-Wolfenbüttel a so-called general consistory was active for almost fifty years (1572–1624). Headed by a chancellor, it consisted of representatives of the clergy, the nobility, and the cities, whose purpose was to advise and decide on matters of church organization and of marriage. Meanwhile, there were synods of clergy in almost all territories inclined toward Lutheranism (that is, meetings of all pastors of a given ecclesiastical governance level, usually superintendencies). However, their significance continually declined until the beginning of the seventeenth century. The landgravate of Hesse occupies a special place, because it officially adopted reform only at the beginning of the seventeenth century (as Hesse-Cassel). In the Reformation ordinances of the sixteenth century, the general synods (1531–1610) of the clergy were the central decision-making bodies in questions of ecclesiastical policy.

Early Orthodoxy. The second half of the sixteenth century accordingly witnessed the complete institutionalization of the spiritual office in Lutheranism, which did not, however, lose the congregational dimension in the process. Characteristic was the symmetry of office and congregation, whereby the special worth of the office of preaching was underscored. The difference in the estates of clergy and laity as displayed by Roman Catholicism was eliminated. The spiritual office in Protestantism was transformed into a vocational status. "Vocation" and "office," as a spiritual calling and activity relating to the world in the economic and political realm, were symmetrical and influenced the self-understanding of the new social group.

From this also arose the claim for a special social status, the *status ecclesiasticus* as distinct from the congregation, which was composed of the *status politicus* and the *status oeconomicus*. Echoing the doctrine of the three estates, such arguments upholding the special status of the spiritual office played an important role in Lutheranism in the second half of the sixteenth century. In various drafts of church constitutions, for example those drawn up by Tilemann Hesshus, Martin Chemnitz, and Basilius Sattler, the doctrine of the three estates was held to be the central organizing principle for both the *ecclesia interna* and for the *ecclesia externa*. This was the attitude of emerging orthodoxy. The spiritual office would safeguard against the encroachment of the *status politicus*. At issue was the boundary between secular and ecclesiastical authority, between the secular and spiritual office. Thus the question of who would judge vocational competence became the core issue. The position of the secular authority, as a member of the church, was one of subservience: the ordering principle of the doctrine of the three estates attained a practical-political importance. "Therefore *vocatio* does not belong to the clergy alone, neither to the secular authority alone, and therefore also not to the common people alone, because one without the other cannot be the whole church. Rather, *vocatio* is and should remain in the whole church" (Chemnitz, *Die fürnemsten Heuptstück der christlichenn Lehre*, Wolfenbüttel, 1569).

The many theological-political conflicts that arose from the notion of the spiritual office as counterbalance to secular authority have long been underestimated as the "bickering of theologians." The Magdeburg Confession of 1550, in which Matthias Flacius Illyricus and Nicolas des Gallars had a hand, was the first to express the right to challenge secular authority and prepared the ground for the formulation of a right of resistance against un-Christian authority. Differences in the corpus of the ministers were challenged no more than were those between preachers and auditors. But none of the estates alone was the church; together they constituted the whole.

All the controversies of the following decades were linked to these positions. The appeal to the threefold composition of the church (i.e., the three estates) relativized the power of secular authority as well as that of spiritual office. It therefore would be wrong to say that Lutheran orthodoxy of the late sixteenth century showed an exclusive interest in the ministerial office while simultaneously devaluing the congregation. Representative of the period was Martin Chemnitz (1522–1586), superintendent of the city of Braunschweig. Understandably, he emphasized the unique quality of the spiritual office: "We may well be all spiritual priests, but we are not all ministers" (Magdeburg Confession). Chemnitz thus underscored the necessity of a special calling

by the church or the congregation. At the same time, however, he pointed out that "the ministers are not the entire church, but rather only a part thereof; the rulers are also not the church, but rather its servants and overseers" (Magdeburg Confession).

The early seventeenth century witnessed a noteworthy shift in interest among the orthodox. One of the leading figures here was the Jena professor Johann Gerhard (1582–1637), whose emphasis lay first of all on the spiritual office. The congregation was greatly reduced in importance and became the personal sphere of the individual Christian. The notion of the three estates constituting the church was central for Gerhard; however, its importance was confined to the realm of the church. Here began the separation of *ecclesia interna* from *ecclesia externa*, in which different principles obtained. Thus Gerhard relativized the significance of the spiritual office as safeguard against abuse by the secular authority. Within the church, however, the spiritual office maintained a limited authority. A special calling to such office was therefore indispensable.

[*See also* Lutheranism.]

BIBLIOGRAPHY

Primary Sources

Bugenhagen, Johannes. *Von dem christlichen Glauben und rechten guten Werken*. Wittenberg, 1526.

Chemnitz, Martin. *Die fürnemsten Heuptstück der christlichen Lehre*. Wolfenbüttel, 1569.

Melanchthon, Philip. *De potestate et primatu papae tractatus*. N.p., 1537.

Secondary Sources

Reller, Horst. *Vorreformatorische und Reformatorische Kirchenverfassung im Fürstentum Braunschweig-Wolfenbüttel*. Göttingen, 1959. See pp. 68ff.

Schorn-Schütte, L. "Popocaesarismus der Theologen?" in *Archiv für Reformationsgeschichte* 79 (1988), 230–261.

LUISE SCHORN-SCHÜTTE
Translated from German by Jeff Bach

Calvinist Offices

To understand the teaching and practice of Calvinist church offices, this branch of the Reformed tradition must be set in context. Chronologically, Calvinists are the second major stream in the Reformed tradition, the first being the Zwinglian. The two were officially joined in 1549 with the Consensus Tigurinus (Zurich Consensus), which established intercommunion in the Lord's Supper, but even after the sacramental agreement there continued to be varied nuances within the Reformed tradition.

One key area of dissimilarity between Zwinglians and Calvinists was ecclesiology, in particular the teaching on church offices. This divergence on ecclesiastical structure and autonomy began in the first generation of the Protestant Reformation in disagreements between Huldrych Zwingli of

Zurich and Johann Oecolampadius of Basel on questions of church discipline. Martin Bucer of Strasbourg developed further some of Oecolampadius's ideas and his own, though Bucer's teaching on church offices remained somewhat fluid, and circumstances limited full practice of the teaching.

Full development of Calvinist church office theory and practice is found in the Genevan work of John Calvin, who gave classical form to the theory. Calvinists generally followed Calvin, though teaching and especially practice varied somewhat in different contexts. The structure of Calvin's practice is seen in the *Les ordonnances ecclesiastiques* written for Geneva in 1541, but the teaching is most fully developed in the *Institutio Christianae Religionis* (book 4, chapter 3, in 1559, though the doctrine is completed in the third edition of 1543). This classical Calvinist doctrine can be best understood by comparison with that of the medieval Latin church and Calvin's Protestant predecessors, while nuances within the Calvinist teaching are made evident by comparing Calvin's own doctrine with that of some of his Calvinist successors.

For Calvinists, church order is not a matter of indifference. While not insisting that a particular form is necessary for salvation, Calvinists did insist that the Bible teaches what the right ordering of the church should be, and to ignore this is to disregard God's will. Normally Calvinists reasoned from function to office, beginning with the functions necessary for the church to be the church and then proceeding to the offices necessary to carry out these tasks.

Following New Testament lists of church leaders in *Ephesians* 4:11, *1 Corinthians* 12:28, and *Romans* 12:6–8, Calvinists wrote of a variety of ministers responsible for various offices, some temporary, some permanent. Temporary, or "extraordinary," offices are those raised up for specific situations (e.g., the original founding of the church); apostles, prophets, evangelists (*Eph.* 4:11), and gifts of healing and tongues (*1 Cor.* 12:28) were among the extraordinary. Calvin recognized that some extraordinary means are needed at particular times in history, such as his own; he considered Martin Luther an evangelist, raised up to reform the church. However, in the normal, rightly ordered situation of the church, only "ordinary" offices are necessary, and Calvinists identified four of these.

The Ministry of Word and Sacraments. The first office in importance is the ministry of word and sacraments. These ministers are often called "pastors" or "presbyters," terms Protestants considered interchangeable with "bishop" in the New Testament. (Calvin accepted the title "bishop" for one who moderates an assembly of presbyters but insisted strongly on a collegial understanding of the presbyterate and of ministries generally.)

Like most Protestants, Calvinists reshaped the understanding of the pastoral office in conjunction with the teaching on the priesthood of believers. Ministers of word and sacraments are not priests who offer sacrifice but men charged with proclaiming the gospel of Jesus Christ through words and visible signs. Calvinists emphasized the equality of all believers before God, but they gave great honor to the ministry of word and sacraments because the pure preaching of the word and the right administration of the sacraments are the two (or two of the three) marks of the church.

The ministry of word and sacraments has also a third major function, usually summarized under the heading "discipline." For many Calvinists—including Martin Bucer, the Scots, and English Puritans, though not Calvin himself—discipline became a third mark of the church. (For Calvin, discipline is a means used by "charitable judgment" to regulate membership in the earthly church.) The exercise of discipline is fundamentally a kind of pastoral ministry or training, which is shared by pastors with elected lay Christians in the office of elder.

Pastors should be properly trained, called, examined, and ordained. Calvinists demanded a fairly rigorous education, both humanist and theological. A person's inner sense of call is important but not decisive. No one enters a regular church office without the proper public call of the corporate church; ordinary ministries are ordered, not charismatic. When a pastor has been called to a church, examined by colleagues, and approved by the people, he should be ordained by other pastors with prayer and laying on of hands. (The latter ceremony is not essential, though desirable.)

Recognizing that ministers are human and sinful, Calvinists nevertheless insisted that Christians are not to separate from the church's ministry as long as the latter is proclaiming the gospel purely and rightly. Ministers' knowledge and behavior are important, but the critical issue is the true gospel, and intellectual or moral perfection cannot be required. Although God is not bound to use only this human ministry, the church is bound to it because God has chosen to work through it.

The Ministry of Teachers. The second regular Calvinist office of the word—doctors or teachers—is the most fluid of the Calvinist offices; Calvin himself sometimes grouped pastors and teachers together, though normally he distinguished these two kinds of presbyters. Teachers do not exhort (apply scripture), administer the sacraments, or discipline, but they share the pastor's teaching function, though in a fuller and nonliturgical fashion. One major task of teachers is to keep the interpretation of scripture pure and to teach religious doctrine, though professors of other disciplines (e.g., philosophy) might also be counted doctors and share the status of pastors (and be subject to the same discipline). Those charged with education more generally were also regarded as teachers; *Les ordonnances ecclesiastiques* includes the Genevan school system under the office of teachers. (Teachers had certain similarities with elders and deacons as "lay ecclesiastical ministers.")

The definition and practice of the office of doctor in the wider Calvinist tradition was afflicted with more ambiguity than in Geneva. Later sixteenth-century French, Dutch, and Scottish Calvinists often accepted professors, who were not pastors, as ministers of the church by virtue of their doctoral office, though sometimes the definition of the office was extremely vague. English Puritans rejected an academic arena for doctors but often made teachers necessary officers of each congregation, which contributed to a confusion of teacher and pastor. By the seventeenth century few Calvinists recognized the doctorate as a distinct office; theological professors had ministerial status when they were ordained pastors, but not simply by their educational calling, and non-theological education was no longer clearly related to the church's ministry.

Lay Ecclesiastical Ministries: Elders and Deacons. The Calvinist church offices of elders and deacons must be understood in the broader spectrum of Western Christianity, especially Protestantism. Protestant revision of traditional ideas of the locus of the holy, expressed in justification by faith and the doctrine of the priesthood of believers, had important consequences for the ministries of *diakonia* (care for the afflicted) and discipline.

According to Roman Catholic tradition, a religious vocation was essentially equated with an ecclesiastical office, which must have a spiritual function as its primary purpose. Spiritual offices might in addition have temporal duties, but one normally was not ordained to care for temporal business. Protestants, however, insisted that by God's grace, all callings that served God and the neighbor were religious vocations. Especially the Christian duty of giving material care to the needy was a religious, spiritual calling.

On the other hand, for Roman Catholics, government in the church was clearly the prerogative of those ordained to holy orders. Protestants regarded lay people as fit to rule in the church and indeed thought that laity must be involved in church discipline. Most Protestants considered Christian princes particularly called to exercise leading offices in the church. Lutherans, Zwinglians, and most of the Church of England generally assigned the ministries of poor relief, church government, and education to the Christian ruler, who was the chief lay leader of the church.

Calvinists were Protestants, but Protestants with a Roman Catholic side. Like all Protestants, Calvinists were convinced that temporal business, such as *diakonia*, was a religious vocation. Like Lutherans, Zwinglians, and Church of England, Calvinists also approved of Christian rulers having a role in religious affairs. (Anabaptists were the only sixteenth-century reformers who objected to civil or worldly rulers' involvement in ecclesiastical matters.) Calvinists differed from most Protestants, however, in their views of the relationship between Christian church and Christian society. For Calvinists, church and society were necessarily distinct though not necessarily separate. Each society (church or state) must have the means—offices—to fulfill its necessary functions. Among the functions for a rightly ordered church, besides the ministry of the word and sacraments, were *diakonia*, government, and education, and these must be exercised by the church with or without state support. In claiming these ministries for the church as distinct from the Christian prince, Calvinists were following a more Catholic view than most Protestants.

The Calvinist office of elders. The ministry of elders was the lay ecclesiastical office established to share with pastors in the government of the church in a council usually called the consistory. Church government was always a corporate act, never the prerogative of one individual or the clergy alone. As with other ministries, Calvinists believed the eldership to be based on biblical texts: *Romans* 12:8, *1 Corinthians* 12:28, and *1 Timothy* 5:17, with *Matthew* 18:15–18 (the key text for discipline) in the background. Elders, like pastors and teachers, were considered presbyters.

The common name for the elders' work was discipline, otherwise expressed as pastoral oversight, combining guidance and education, rebuke and reconciliation, and counseling and correction. (The work done by Robert M. Kingdon and others in editing the *Registres* of the Genevan consistory has provided much new insight and the correction of some common negative legends.)

The primary controversy over the Calvinist office of elders concerned whether ecclesiastical or civil authorities held the power of discipline. Ecclesiastical autonomy vis-à-vis civil powers was first clearly demanded by Oecolampadius, later taken up by Bucer, and finally achieved by Calvin in Geneva. Revisions of the *Les ordonnances ecclesiastiques* in 1561 indicate that the city council essentially accepted Calvin's position (e.g., noncitizens could be elected elders, and magistrates functioning as elders laid aside the symbol of their civil office).

Calvinist insistence on ecclesiastical autonomy for discipline met with theological, as well as political, resistance. The most vigorous opponents of Calvinist ideas were Zwinglians and their followers, especially among the English. Théodore de Bèze, Heinrich Bullinger, the English Admonitioners, and others developed the argument: "presbyterian" government by autonomous elders versus "Erastian" discipline exercised by civil rulers. Calvinists outside state churches experienced different difficulties: not competition with civil authorities, but the challenge of a congregationalist system. In 1562 the French pastor Jean Morély published a treatise entitled *Traité de la discipline & police Chrestienne*, which proposed that discipline be exercised by all church members—though by church members Morély meant adult men, not women and children.

The Calvinist office of deacons. The Calvinist diaconate was the lay church office established to care in the name of the church for the needy, poor, and sick. The key Biblical bases for this office are *Acts of the Apostles* 6:1–6 and *1 Timothy* 3:8–13. Protestants put the greater weight on *Acts*, the story of the apostles "ordaining" (laying their hands on) seven men "to serve tables" (care for the poor). Calvinists agreed, on the basis of patristic evidence, that deacons should have a part in the liturgy, especially collecting the alms and offering the cup in the Lord's Supper, though their primary diaconal business was caring for the afflicted.

Calvinists developed a double diaconate of men and women, sketched for the first time in Calvin's 1540 *Commentarii in Epistolam Pauli ad Romanos*, and complete in the 1543 edition of the *Institutio Christianae Religionis*. Men were ordained to administer the business of the poor (*Acts* 6, *1 Tim.* 3); women were accorded a subordinate, nonordained diaconal task of nursing the sick and giving personal care to the poor (*Rom.* 12:8, 16:1–2, *1 Tim.* 5:3–10). Some scholars see this development as a way of explaining biblical texts on women (e.g., Phoebe the deacon, *Rom.* 16); others believe Calvin was copying the secular social welfare pattern.

Calvinist deacons might or might not be state supported. Geneva had both a state diaconate (for citizens) and several voluntary diaconates for refugees. The first and most important of the latter, the *Bourse française*, became involved in not only caring for poor refugees but also supporting ministers for the beleaguered French Calvinists.

The theory of the diaconate did not always correspond to the actual practice. Calvinists continued to cite the double diaconate theory with Calvin's supporting texts (even non-Calvinists sometimes adopted the exegesis), but normally men did both diaconal tasks. Only rarely did any church attempt the unconventional notion of instituting women deacons. Geneva had none, though Calvin regretted this; some churches in the Rhineland and a few later English Calvinists experimented with women deacons. Nuances of Calvin's theory were also altered in some Reformed churches (e.g., French deacons shared with elders and pastors in the rule of the church through the consistory).

The Significance in Church History and the Reformation. The space here devoted to the various Calvinist offices is not proportional to the importance accorded to each ministry but to the significance of the ministry for history. Calvinists, like others, counted the ministry of word and sacraments as the central and most important office.

In terms of distinctive historical influence, however, the most significant feature of the Calvinist church offices is the development of a clear theory of a plurality of ministries, both "clerical" and "lay," especially including ministries having primarily "secular" functions. It is essentially the establishment of offices of elders and deacons as "lay ecclesiastical offices" of the church that is distinctively Calvinist. According to Calvinist ecclesiology, there are some functions or ministries that are biblically necessary for the church to be the church; the church, no matter what its civil status, must be able to carry out these responsibilities and thus must have its own officers for all necessary ministries, including "temporal" ones. The church is, however, eager for cooperation with Christian society where that is possible without compromising its integrity. The development of this constitution was an important factor in the survival of Calvinist churches under persecution and played a significant role later when church and state were separated.

Calvinist theory is also important for the roles of leadership assigned to lay people. Lay ecclesiastical offices expressed the priesthood of believers in a concrete structural way by formally associating "secular" activities with ordained ministry and by ordaining lay people. Though its view of women is clearly culture-bound, the Calvinist office theory is also innovative here, since Calvinists were the only Protestants (except some Anabaptists) to accord women a place among the regular (noncharismatic) ecclesiastical ministries.

[*See also* Calvinism.]

BIBLIOGRAPHY

Calvin, John. "Draft *Ecclesiastical Ordinances* (1541)." In *Calvin: Theological Treatises*, edited by J. K. S. Reid. Library of Christian Classics, vol. 22. Philadelphia, 1954. The church order Calvin wrote for Geneva, including the four ministerial offices and double diaconate. It gives very limited theological material, and received modifications from the civil government.

———. *Institutes of the Christian Religion.* Edited by John T. McNeill and translated by Ford Lewis Battles. Library of Christian Classics, vols. 20 and 21. Philadelphia, 1960. Classic development of ecclesiology in book 4, chapters 1–19; chapter 3 especially important for church office theory.

Ganoczy, Alexandre. *Calvin: Théologien de l'église et du ministère.* Paris, 1964. Best one-volume treatment of the whole area of Calvin's ecclesiology and church offices. Judicious work by an excellent Roman Catholic Calvin scholar, this gives most attention to the ministry of word and sacraments, including Calvin's discussion of episcopacy.

Henderson, Robert W. *The Teaching Office in the Reformed Tradition: A History of the Doctoral Ministry.* Philadelphia, 1962. Only substantial work in English giving both teaching and practice for the sixteenth and seventeenth centuries.

Kingdon, Robert M. "The Deacons of the Reformed Church in Calvin's Geneva." In *Mélanges d'histoire du 16e siècle offerts à Henri Meylan*, pp. 81–90. Geneva, 1970. Describes the functioning of the institution of the state diaconate in Geneva.

———. "Calvin's Ideas About the Diaconate: Social or Theological in Origin?" In *Piety, Politics, and Ethics: Reformation Studies in Honor of George Wolfgang Forell*, edited by Carter Lindberg, pp. 167–180. Kirksville, Mo., 1984. Argues that the basis of Calvin's double diaconate is the social welfare system.

———. "Calvin and the Establishment of Consistory Discipline in Geneva: The Institution and the Men Who Directed It." *Nederlandsch Archief voor Kerkgeschiedenis* (1990), 158–172. Discusses the organization and development of the Consistory in Geneva, using new sources that Kingdon and colleagues are editing.

Köhler, Walther. *Zürcher Ehegericht und Genfer Konsistorium.* 3 vols. Leipzig, 1932 and 1942. Major work on development of practice of discipline in Switzerland and southern Germany. Selective sources used for Geneva now lead generally to out-dated conclusions, but overall study is still essential.

McKee, Elsie Anne. *John Calvin on the Diaconate and Liturgical Almsgiving.* Geneva, 1984. Discusses Calvinist teaching on the diaconate and relationship of diaconate to worship, in the context of exegetical history, with some attention to social history.

———. "Calvin's Exegesis of Romans 12.8: Social, Accidental, or Theological?" *Calvin Theological Journal* 23 (1988), 6–18. Argues that Calvin's development of the double diaconate is primarily influenced by theological problems posed by having to integrate biblical passages about women into wider picture of biblical evidence.

———. *Elders and the Plural Ministry: The Role of Exegetical History in Illuminating John Calvin's Theology.* Geneva, 1988. Discusses Calvinist teaching on the office of elders and the theory of plural ministries, setting them in historical theological context.

Olson, Jeannine E. *Calvin and Social Welfare: Deacons and the Bourse Française.* Selinsgrove, Pa., 1989. Describes the functioning of the French refugee diaconate in Geneva.

Thompson, John Lee. *John Calvin and the Daughters of Sarah: Women in Regular and Exceptional Roles in the Exegesis of Calvin, His Predecessors, and His Contemporaries.* Geneva, 1992. Full study, including many more aspects than women as deacons.

ELSIE ANNE MCKEE

Anglican Offices

The Tudor Church of England developed theologically in close communion with its Reformed Continental neighbors. What set it apart from all other Reformed polities was its retention of an essentially Catholic form of ecclesiastical organization. Under the monarch as supreme head, or governor, the church adhered to the ancient orders of bishops, archdeacons, deans, prebends, and parish clergy. The last were still appointed through customary patronage arrangements and approved by the prelates: no formal idea of congregational nomination existed. The political explanation for this structural conservatism was that no Tudor ruler was willing to subvert traditional hierarchies or to challenge the proprietary rights that leading laymen held in the church. Although it was James I who explicitly defended bishops as a necessary part of the structure of church and state, he merely articulated the assumptions of Henry VIII and Elizabeth I. The ideological defense of tradition, from Thomas Cranmer to Richard Hooker, emphasized continuity with the early church and congruity with the teaching of the Fathers. But for much of the century clerical adherents of the existing order argued for the legitimacy of the supreme head's choice—the godly prince's ability to "edify" the church by defining its structural arrangements—rather than for the doctrinal necessity of the old offices. Meanwhile, many fundamental changes occurred within these fixed boundaries, changes that ensured that by 1600 there was only limited resemblance between the Protestant clergy and their Catholic predecessors.

The Bishops. The nature of the Henrician Reformation—first cautiously reformist, then reactively Catholic, but never explicitly Protestant—ensured that the bishops would remain the chief agents of spiritual discipline. The construction of six new dioceses after 1540 is one sign that Henry VIII remained committed to the old order. The status and influence of the episcopate were challenged in the 1530s by the appointment of Thomas Cromwell as vicegerent in spirituals, exercising royal authority in matters of jurisdiction, but the office was not renewed after this fall. Cromwell believed that the episcopate should be clearly defined as servants of the Crown in matters of religion. The Act in Restraint of Annates (1534) introduced a system of episcopal nomination that compelled cathedral chapters to accept the Crown's candidate, while accompanying the letters missive with a license to elect, or *congé d'élire*, that offered some faint sense of due process. In 1547 Edward VI's regime swept away the *congé d'élire* and made the appointment of prelates dependent entirely on the king's will, articulated through letters patent. It is also characteristic of the tortuous history of the English Reformation that the Elizabethan Settlement of 1559 deliberately restored the formality of capitular election, thereby once again differentiating the Crown's ecclesiastical servants from its secular ones.

Thomas Cranmer supported episcopacy as a valuable bulwark of order accepted from the primitive church onwards, but like Cromwell he perceived it as dependent on the will of the supreme head. Authority was not exercised by the bishops *iure divino*. By 1550 this impulse to deny the distinctiveness of the episcopal estate led the government, and on occasion the bishops themselves, to appropriate Lutheran language and refer to prelates as superintendents. John Dudley, duke of Northumberland, seems to have thought of the bishops as salaried officials in need of adequate but not generous remuneration. Yet in these same years the leaders of the church were alerted to the dangers of this change. John Hooper, nominated as bishop of Gloucester, refused to be consecrated using the Oath of Supremacy and wearing the "popish" remnants of vestments. Behind these apparently minor issues lay Hooper's denial of separated status to the hierarchy. Cranmer and Nicholas Ridley, bishop of London, reacted by asserting that hierarchy under the supreme head was necessary to discipline and order. The dispute was compromised by the Privy Council, and Hooper consecrated: a radical moment when the nature of Anglican orders might have been altered passed.

Under Elizabeth the Cranmerian compromise largely prevailed. The bishops made no claim to *iure divino* powers before the 1590s but defended their role within the church on grounds of the royal will and of order and tradition. In response to the Presbyterian challenge, they denied that there was one ecclesiastical structure legitimated by scripture. Church government was *adiaphora*, a thing indifferent, to be regulated by the godly prince. In the last years of the reign, however, the persistence of Puritan attacks led some of the younger generation of bishops, notably Richard Bancroft, to a more vigorous defense of episcopal power, which was now claimed to be divinely ordained, a reflection of natural hierarchy sanctioned by biblical precedent and Christian history.

These transmutations in the defense of episcopacy were more than matched by changes in the exercise of the office.

After 1532 the jurisdictional autonomy of the Catholic prelates was subverted. First the king, and then through him his vicegerent in spirituals, assumed a control over the ecclesiastical courts that cast in doubt the whole structure of church discipline. Since the Reformation had been initiated through Parliament, it was Parliament that assumed many of the powers previously held by the church, a process aided by the hostility that parliamentary common lawyers displayed to ecclesiastical law. Even after the 1530s the disciplinary control that the bishops had previously exercised was inevitably weakened. A key manifestation of this weakness was the failure to ratify a new version of church law for the new Protestant settlement. Cranmer's *Reformatio Legum,* prepared at the very end of Edward VI's reign, was never enacted. Under Elizabeth it was the Puritans who tried to revive this systematic document; the bishops preferred to deflect lay hostility by piecemeal legislation when absolutely necessary. It was also symptomatic of the prelates' new dependence on the Crown that, for the enforcement of conformity, they turned to the Ecclesiastical Commission, a court held under direct royal commission with stronger penalties than those available to the ordinary ecclesiastical courts.

Nowhere did the practical change in the power of prelates show so clearly as in the loss of material wealth. All the antipapal Tudor regimes were happy to appropriate episcopal property and use the revenues of the church for the reward of royal servants. Most of the English sees lost manors and other revenues, usually in unequal exchanges for increased income from spiritualities—but sometimes simply by expropriation. Edward's reign saw the most dramatic losses: the revenues of the bishopric of Winchester, for example, were reduced by more than half, and a plan to divide Durham into two sees, each with vastly curtailed income, was partially implemented. Under Elizabeth the process of alienation largely ceased, but bishops were compelled to make long leases to the Crown. These assaults would have been tolerable if the obligations of the bishops had been correspondingly reduced. Both Crown and laity, however, continued to expect them to act as temporal lords, exercising political influence in their dioceses and dispensing hospitality. Clerical marriage imposed additional strains in expenditure, though here the dynastic ambitions of some Elizabethan bishops, such as Edwin Sandys and John Aylmer, brought the whole order into disrepute.

Although the circumstances of the English Reformation made it difficult for bishops to transform themselves into model Protestant pastors, there were significant changes in behavior. The Crown expected them to reside in their dioceses, where they were more likely to discharge the basic episcopal functions, such as ordination and visitation in person. The shortage of clergy, especially under Elizabeth, forced many bishops to close supervision of those who remained. Their record as preachers was patchy, but from Bishop Hugh Latimer onward, there was always a minority of vigorous preachers on the episcopal bench. Tobie Matthew, who died in 1622 after a long episcopal career, notes in his diary the extraordinary total of 1,992 sermons he had preached. John Whitgift preached every Sunday in his diocese, even after his elevation as archbishop of Canterbury. The Elizabethan bishops strove to reconcile their traditional authority and their Protestant pastoral role, and the relative stability of the episcopate in the Jacobean church would suggest that they were largely successful.

Lesser Offices. Below the episcopate lay the traditional offices of archdeacon, the deans and chapters of the cathedral churches, and a hierarchy of diocesan administrators. All appeared in some measure anomalous in the world of Protestantism, but most played a necessary part in the maintenance of discipline. The archdeacons maintained their jurisdictional authority over parts of each diocese; their courts, for their extensive control over sexual misdemeanor, became known popularly as the "bawdy courts." The degree to which archdeacons themselves, rather than their court officials, played an active role in the dioceses seems to have depended on individual circumstance and capacity. Thomas Bentham, bishop of Coventry and Lichfield, employed the Puritan Thomas Lever as a very active archdeacon of Coventry in the 1560s; indeed, it was Lever who led the Reformation in the diocese. This could have provided a model for the management of reform within the subunits of a diocese, but traditional patronage considerations often prevailed. Promotion to an archdeaconry was often the reward for aspiring pluralist clerics attached to a bishop or courtier. It rarely passed to those whose primary service was pastoral.

Deans and chapters were more debated during the Reformation. Henry VIII had no apparent reservations about transmuting the former monastic chapters into secular ones or adding to their number at the time of the creation of the six new sees in 1541. Yet the reformers were acutely aware that deans and chapters needed new functions to justify their continued existence. For Cranmer these were to be found in the provision of education "for poor men's children" and above all in leadership of the Reformed movement through preaching and teaching. There are notable examples of chapters that provided this leadership: Durham under Dean William Whittingham in the 1560s and York under Dean Matthew Hutton in the next decade. Yet conservatism and apathy were also commonplace throughout the sixteenth century. Bishops had imperfect control over discipline, and prebendal seats continued to be seen primarily as items of patronage to reward the upwardly mobile. The office of dean attracted many men of ability and was regarded as the senior diocesan office beneath the bishop, but incumbents were not always resident, nor was the traditional image of the office as one of routine disciplinarian to an enclosed corporation fully altered.

The reform of the dioceses was difficult without adequate

clerical leadership at a local level. Hence, some of the bishops attempted to revive or sustain the office of rural dean. A dean supervised a cluster of parishes, usually focused around one marketing center. In York, Norwich, Ely, Gloucester, and Coventry and Lichfield deans were employed to provide another tier to the disciplinary administration, and there were projects for a fuller revival of the office into that of a supervising minister teaching and guiding the ordinary clergy. This may have happened informally in some dioceses when enthusiasm for reform was at its height in the 1560s and 1570s.

Parish Clergy. The beneficed parish clergy provided of key element a continuity throughout the upheavals of the Reformation. Having received ordination after examination at the hands of the bishop, a cleric needed to seek patronage to gain a benefice. After the dissolution of the monasteries, the overwhelming majority of livings were in lay hands, with the gentry as the dominant social group in control. Bishops, chapters, and the colleges of Oxford and Cambridge also held livings, as did the Crown, which exercised most of its patronage through the lord chancellor. Once offered promotion, a cleric again had to submit to episcopal examination before institution.

Within the parish continuity with Catholicism was maintained both in the modes of financing the minister and in many of the duties he was required to perform. The tithe system—with the great tithe on grain apportioned to the rector and the lesser tithe on other agricultural products to the vicar—was an inheritance from the Middle Ages. As for duties, apart from the maintenance of divine worship, the minister was obliged to instruct the laity, to present to the bishop or archdeacon faults not delated by the churchwardens, to provide some form of care for the poor, and to secure the proper upkeep of the chancel, as well as of the rectory or vicarage. Since the violent oscillations or royal religious policy afforded no certainty or stability in the mid-Tudor years, it is understandable that many clerics focused their minds upon these parochial continuities and managed to survive in their benefices as conforming "vicars of Bray."

In so doing they must have disguised from their parishioners, and perhaps from themselves, the fundamental changes that had occurred in the nature of their office. The abolition of the Mass under Edward VI destroyed not only the heart of the Catholic liturgy but also the role of the sacrificing priest. The *raison d'être* of the Catholic priesthood was swept away, and with it many of the customary assumptions about the role of the local incumbent. The justification for the separate estate of the clergy had lain largely in their unique ability to reenact Christ's sacrifice on the cross; now their identity had to be remolded under the new Protestant order. Since Protestantism was above all a religion of the word, the priesthood had to learn to place preaching and instruction at the heart of their parochial duty. This in turn intensified the need for a learned clergy

and for an increased number of university-trained ordinands, men who would not be "dumb dogs," to use the language of the Puritans.

There were various obstacles to the construction of such a learned body of parochial clergy. Although bishops might stress the need for learning, neither lay patrons nor ordinary parishioners always saw the need for change. The slow acceptance of a full Reformation in many parts of the realm inhibited demand from below for a preaching ministry. The second obstacle was the traditional structure of patronage and wealth: many lay patrons saw their benefices as an opportunity to reward relatives and dependents, and it was largely coincidental if the criteria of godly ministry were met. The funding of the parishes was even more crucial. Where a vicarage was ordained and the great tithe was paid to an impropriator (often a layman), the situation of the minister was likely to be difficult. Moreover, since many tithes had been commuted for fixed money sums, in an inflationary century a parish could yield a mere pittance.

But the main problem in constructing a new clerical order was the experience of the Reformation itself. Clerical recruitment had been sufficiently high in the 1520s to staff the more than nine thousand livings in England and Wales and also to ensure that curates and chantry priests supplemented incumbents. Despite the dissolution of the monasteries, which released more clerical manpower onto the market, vacancies began to appear in many parishes by the mid-sixteenth century, and the number of ordinands diminished to almost nothing. By the time of the Elizabethan Settlement between 10 and 15 percent of benefices were vacant, and in such areas as the archdeaconry of London the figure rose to 33 percent. The bishops stressed financial uncertainty as the explanation for the crisis—as late as the 1580s Archbishop Whitgift believed that only six hundred livings could support a learned, married minister. But where there was no religious certainty, the Elizabethan church was unlikely to attract an adequate body of clergy. By the end of the sixteenth century, when the universities had provided several generations of clerical recruits, the parishes were once more supplied, and the bishops were able to insist that ordination should usually be restricted to graduates. Moreover, these graduates were expected to be preachers, ministers of the word. Gradually, therefore, patrons and parishioners were presented with a more educated cleric able to defend Protestant settlement.

Yet the change should not be exaggerated. Patrons appear to have recruited the same type of priest in 1600 as half a century earlier. Graduate education did not necessarily equip a man for full pastoral care, and it was difficult for the bishops to remedy this in the absence of a seminary system. Belief in a preaching ministry was also in tension with concerns for conformity, especially under Archbishop Whitgift, who moved to control Puritan preaching. The parochial clergy may have been more educated in Christian belief at the end of the century than at the break with Rome, but they were part of a structure only "halfly reformed," a structure permanently separated from the ideals of the Continental Reformed churches.

[*See also* Anglicanism.]

BIBLIOGRAPHY

Collinson, Patrick. *The Religion of Protestants: The Church in English Society, 1559–1625.* Oxford, 1982. Important study of the state of the clergy under Elizabeth I and James I.

Dickens, A. G. *The English Reformation.* 2d ed. London, 1989. Includes valuable chapter on the structure of offices in the early Reformation.

Heal, Felicity. *Of Prelates and Princes: A Study of the Economic and Social Position of the Tudor Episcopate.* Cambridge, 1980.

Houlbrooke, Ralph. "The Protestant Episcopate, 1547–1603: The Pastoral Contribution." In *Church and Society in England: Henry VIII to James I*, edited by Felicity Heal and Rosemary O'Day, pp. 78–98. London, 1977.

Lehmberg, Stanford E. *The Reformation of Cathedrals.* Princeton, 1988. Includes an important chapter on the careers of canons, prebendaries, and deans.

Loades, D. M. *The Oxford Martyrs.* London, 1970. Valuable analysis of episcopal attitudes to office and authority under Edward VI.

MacCulloch, Diarmaid. *The Later Reformation in England, 1547–1603.* New York, 1990. Discusses the differences on orders between Cranmer and Hooper.

Marcombe, David, and C. S. Knighton, eds. *Close Encounters: English Cathedrals and Society since 1540.* Nottingham, 1991.

O'Day, Rosemary. *The English Clergy: The Emergence and Consolidation of a Profession, 1558–1642.* Leicester, 1979.

O'Day, Rosemary, and Felicity Heal, eds. *Continuity and Change: Personnel and Administration of the Church in England, 1500–1642.* Leicester, 1976.

FELICITY HEAL

Roman Catholic Offices

Porter, lector, exorcist, acolyte (minor orders), subdeacon, deacon, and priest (major orders) are the seven orders or levels of ordination of what is essentially one sacramental church office (*sacramentum ordinis*) that theologians in the sixteenth century generally designated according to medieval tradition. The criterion for differentiation is their relation to the sacrifice of the Mass and thus to the power to consecrate and to sacrifice (*potestas ordinis* or *potestas conficiendi*). By contrast, the canonists also count tonsure as the entrance step into the clerical state and ordination to the episcopacy (bishop) as the highest level of orders, and therefore designate nine orders. Since the canonists are oriented to the power of jurisdiction (*potestas jurisdictionis*), they see the end point and center of the orders in the office of bishop. In church offices as they exist concretely, the hierarchy of orders and the hierarchy of jurisdiction are interwoven, always to be distinguished but never fully separate. All offices outside that of bishop itself (e.g., archbishop, metropolitan, primate, patriarch, cardinal, or even pope) do not have any higher power of orders than any bishop. Other offices (*dignitates*), such as prior, dean, provost, provincial, general,

minister, master, and most of the offices in the Curia Romana, are functional and purely jurisdictional, mainly on the basis of priesthood, in abbeys, foundations, chapters and religious houses.

Each of the nine offices conferred a right to the reception of the benefice corresponding to it, with which was attached a precisely defined *officium*; for priests, for example, it was the duty of celebrating masses, optionally also the care of souls (*cura animarum, beneficia curata*) or a definite jurisdictional power (*praelatio, iurisdictio*). To fulfill this office, the holder of the benefice could engage another cleric with a lower compensation and thus enjoy the benefice as a simple source of income, without any further concern about it. This was a source of serious abuse and one cause of the decline in church life. Because all offices were organized and financed through benefices, any effective reform of church offices had to be a reform of the system of benefices, with the purpose of ensuring the fulfillment of the office by the original holder and of giving a benefice to such clerics who had the capacity and the willingness personally to fulfill the office in the proper manner.

Church Offices before the Council of Trent. The point of departure for a historical survey of Roman Catholic church offices in the sixteenth century is 1517, when the Fifth Lateran Council came to a close and the Reformation began with Luther's publication of his theses in Wittenberg on the eve of All Saints' Day. The two major conflicts dealt with at the council were symptomatic: bishops against the Curia Romana and bishops against the regular clergy. In short, the bishops wanted to regain control and direction of the care of souls in their dioceses.

Luther's three polemical writings in 1520—*An den christlichen Adel deutscher Nation von des christlichen Standes Besserung* (To the Christian Nobility of the German Nation on the Improvement of the State of Christianity), *De captivitate Babylonica ecclesiae praeludium* (Introduction on the Babylonian Captivity of the Church), and *Von der Freiheit eines Christenmenschen* (On the Freedom of the Christian Person)—made a frontal attack on the church hierarchy. Luther blamed the hierarchy for the destruction of Christian brotherhood through the mere existence and conduct of the clerical estate and denied any theological foundation for orders. According to Luther there was only the common priesthood of all the baptized.

Against Luther's understanding of orders, which reduced the office to the functions of proclamation and the administration of the sacraments, many Catholic theologians defended the sacramentality of ordination and stressed the care of souls as the integrating finality of priestly ministry, with the celebration of the Mass as the center, and of ecclesiastical offices. There were many local reform initiatives, but they were unable to assert themselves against the Reformation. The expectations placed on a priest at the beginning of the sixteenth century were at first slight: he had to administer the sacraments in accordance with scripture, he had to be the legal holder of a benefice, and occasionally he had to explain the Apostles' Creed and the Lord's Prayer. Many only went through a short apprenticeship with an older priest. There were no universal requirements or uniformly enforced regulations on the training of the clergy or admission to orders until the Tridentine Decree on Seminaries of 1563.

Principal Trends and Decisions at the Council of Trent (1545–1563). In an express rejection of Reformation theology regarding church offices, the Catholic church at the Council of Trent dogmatically reasserted its hierarchy of offices as sacramentally grounded and both sacramentally and jurisdictionally differentiated in the Decree on Orders of session 23 on 15 July 1563. The perspective and praxis concerning church offices that the council intended can be gathered from the canons on reform, which translate the concerns and goals of the reform into canonical norms or enforceable laws and regulations. All church offices are placed at the service of the care of souls.

Ecclesiastical offices were discussed at all three sessions of the council (1545–1547, 1551/52, 1562/63) both in terms of dogma and with a view to the reform of these offices. In 1547 the issue of the priesthood as one of the seven sacraments stood in the foreground; in 1551/52 the main issue was the priesthood (*sacerdotium*) in its relation to the sacrament of penance, the sacrament of the Eucharist, and the relation of the priesthod to the sacrifice of the Mass. The debates of 1562/63 show that to hold the basis and foundation of the sacramental office as being only a sacrifice and the priesthood necessary for it are not false, but insufficient, because this line of argument neglects the position and significance of the bishop within the sacramental hierarchy of orders. In contrast many bishops saw their office as successors of the apostles as not primarily grounded in the power to offer (*potestas offerendi*). Thus the bishop is not just a priest (*sacerdos*) with greater jurisdiction but is rather the normative model for all church orders founded on the model of the apostles. Therefore, it follows that the basic apostolic duties of the bishop are proclamation and the care of souls. This apostolic understanding of the office of bishop did not manage to prevail in the Decree on Orders, because it seemed to many bishops to be irreconcilable with the rights claimed by the pope while it also aroused their fear of a renewal of conciliarism that they had so struggled to overcome. This is clearly set forth in chapter 4:

> Wherefore, the holy council declares that, beside the other ecclesiastical grades, the bishops, who have succeeded the apostles, *principally* (*praecipue*) belong to this hierarchical order, and have been placed, as the same Apostle says, by the Holy Ghost to rule the Church of God; that they are superior to priests, administer the sacrament of confirmation, ordain ministers of the Church, and can perform many other functions over which those of an inferior order have no power.

The consensus on the level of the priesthood without jurisdiction was undisputed. As a result the Canons on Orders emphasize the sacramentality of the New Testament priesthood as well as its power of forgiveness, of consecrating and offering sacrifice, without disputing its duty of proclamation. On the basis of sacramental ordination, which confers the Holy Spirit and imprints an (indelible) character, a priest cannot become a layman again. The ordained office comprises besides priesthood other ranks of orders and according to divine ordering (*ordinatione divina*) is hierarchically structured into bishops, presbyters, and ministers (*ministris*, i.e., deacons). The precedence of bishops over priests holds true sacramentally and is visible in the authority to confirm and ordain, and also includes a *potestas pascendi* (power to feed the flock), while no statement is made on *iurisdictio contentiosa* (*coercitiva, cohibitiva*; these canonical expressions refer to a bishop's authority to pass judgment and impose sanctions and penalties). This sacrament is grounded on its institution by Christ without any more detailed specification and is not limited to the function of offering sacrifice.

The bishops expressly belong to the sacramental hierarchy and form its summit. Thus the bishop moves up to being the key figure of the sacrament of orders, and the reality of that sacrament is to be understood with the bishop as its starting point. The priesthood manifests itself as a differentiated hierarchy of orders (*hierarchia ordinis*). The sacrament of orders establishes and structures the priesthood, rather than an asserted priesthood establishing the sacrament of orders and structuring its offices. This in essence overcomes the opposition between a one-sided canonical or a one-sided theological understanding of the offices. An understanding of orders that was heretofore shaped by priesthood is transformed into an episcopal and ecclesial understanding that is sacramentally differentiated into bishops, presbyters, and ministers (deacons); in the reform canons the minor orders become merely transitional steps to the priesthood.

Thus the reform decrees free the ecclesiastical offices from the alternative of either being treated in purely canonical terms (a dispensable as opposed to an indispensable obligation to the personal fulfillment of the office connected to the benefice) on the one hand, or being considered in purely theological terms as offering Mass and prayer on the other hand. Instead, the decrees place all offices under the divine precept of the charge to be shepherds of the flock and to care for the souls of believers:

> Since by divine precept it is enjoined on all to whom is entrusted the *cura animarum* to know their own sheep, to offer sacrifice for them, and to feed them by preaching of the divine word, the administration of sacraments, and the example of all good works, to exercise a fatherly care in behalf of the poor and other distressed persons and to apply themselves to all other pastoral duties, all of which cannot be rendered and fulfilled by those who do not watch over and are not with their flock, but desert it after

the manner of hirelings, the holy council admonishes and exhorts them that, mindful of the divine precepts and made a pattern of the flock, they in judgment and in truth be shepherds and leaders (session 23, reform canon 1).

The care of souls thus becomes the motif and both the shaping and the driving principle of the whole Catholic reform on every level. The care of souls is no longer forced into a canonical straitjacket, but rather church law is subordinated to the care of souls and placed at its service. Concretely, the reform of the benefice systems binds priests to the service of caring for souls and to their bishop. The (developing) capacity for catechesis, proclamation, and pastoral care becomes the criterion for admitting all future priests to the individual stages of orders—the minimum age for subdeacons being twenty-two, for deacons twenty-three, and for priests twenty-five years. For admission to orders the bishop alone is responsible. The criterion for the selection of bishops—minimum age being thirty years, a licentiate or doctorate in theology or canon law as a prerequisite—is the pastoral quality of the candidate and his usefulness for the diocese (*digniores et ecclesiae magis utiles*; "more worth and more useful to the church"). The observance of these criteria is spiritually sanctioned for all those responsible. The bishop as shepherd also ends up being the key figure of the reform, and not just as a standard for the theological understanding of the church offices.

Developments after the Council of Trent. Pius IV approved and promulgated the decrees of the Council of Trent without modification in 1564. In the same year the Tridentine Index of Prohibited Books appeared. As a basis for proclamation, prayer, and liturgy the *Catechismus Concilii Tridentini* (*Catechismus Romanus* or *Catechismus ad parochos*) followed in 1566, the Tridentine *Breviary* in 1568, the *Missale Romanum* in 1570, the *Pontificale Romanum* in 1596, and the *Rituale Romanum* in 1615. The revision of the Latin text of the Bible comes to a conclusion in 1592 (*Vulgata Clementina*).

The new role of bishops. The reform ideal of a bishop, inspired by the Pauline pastoral epistles and the great bishops of the ancient church, which found its classical expression in *Stimulus pastorum*, written for the cardinal-nephew Carlo Borromeo (1538–1584), was realized and embodied by this same Borromeo as archbishop of Milan after 1568. His example had greater weight than all the decrees of the Council of Trent, wrote a Venetian ambassador. Borromeo borrowed much from the example of Gian Matteo Giberti (1495–1543), who was bishop of Verona beginning in 1528. Giberti had begun to give continuing formation to his clergy in the form of regular lectures and pastoral conferences; he was planning catechesis for children and had introduced adult catechesis after Sunday Vespers and had the pastors keep a register of baptisms and a *liber animarum* ("book of souls"). Giberti had organized the laity engaged in social assistance into a *Societas caritatis* ("society of charity"). In

short, he had initiated a modern, organized form of pastoral care. As prescribed by Trent, Borromeo made visitations of his diocese, held diocesan and provincial synods, and energetically enforced their decisions. These synodal decisions were adopted all over Europe. He put the Tridentine Decree on Seminaries into effect by founding various seminaries for priests and entrusted their administration to the Oblates of Saint Ambrose that he himself had founded. Borromeo himself preached, the principal duty of bishops according to Trent, and personally took care of the sick during the plague in Milan.

The new role of priests. Just as for the bishop, the new guiding image for the priest is the good shepherd, who cares for the sheep entrusted to him in direct personal pastoral care, rather than simply celebrating Mass and praying as the mere holder of a church income. Proclamation, catechesis, hearing confessions, and administering the sacraments fill his everyday life. In the newly opened seminaries he receives the needed theological formation and spiritual discipline.

The new role of the religious orders. As an eremitic reform movement of Franciscans living in strict poverty, the branch known as the Capuchins emerged as an independent order before the mid-sixteenth century. In a short time the Capuchins developed into an effective order devoted to pastoral care and brought the Tridentine reform and the Counter-Reformation to the uneducated segments of the population, in particular.

Officially recognized in 1540, the Jesuits represented an order of an entirely new type. For the sake of the apostolate, the Jesuits gave up common choral office, a particular religious habit, and living in cloister. Moreover, they bound themselves to the pope in a fourth vow of apostolic obedience in order to be available for duty anytime, anywhere, and under any circumstances. The general of the order, elected for life, can transfer them anywhere in the world. *Iuvare animas* (to help souls), the driving theme of their basic model, Ignatius Loyola (1491–1556), is the hallmark of their order. Their manner of action is derived from the *Exercitia spiritualia*, which aim at personal conversion through the "discernment of spirits" and a life lived according to the call that the will of God has issued to each person making the exercises. Concern for the education and formation of youth found its most effective instrument in the secondary schools, which soon spread throughout Europe. From the beginning they complemented preaching with individual pastoral care in the formal spiritual direction, particularly in confession, and social assistance.

The new role of the papal curia. Although the consistory of cardinals was still considered to be the highest organ, the popes in the postconciliar period set up congregations as permanent commissions for particular tasks, for example the Congregation for Council in 1546, the Congregation on the Index in 1571, and the Congregation on Bishops in 1572.

In 1588 Sixtus V enacted a thorough reform of the Curia by making it into a governing body structured into congregations, each with a given area of responsibility. The Congregation for the Inquisition remained in the first position. It was later called the Holy Office and had been founded in 1542 as the Roman Inquisition. New bodies included the Congregation for Religious, the Congregation for Rites (also in charge of canonization proceedings), as well as Congregations for the Vatican Printing Press, the Consistory, and the Apostolic Signature; six congregations administered the papal states. In 1622 Gregory XV founded the Congregation for the Propagation of the Faith in order to regain control of the missions, especially in the Spanish and Portuguese colonial regions. The position of (secret) papal secretary developed as the central organ through which all diplomatic correspondence passed and from which the secretary of state emerged.

Sixtus V raised the number of cardinals to a maximum of seventy. In 1585 he obliged bishops to make regular *ad limina* visits to Rome—Italian bishops every three years, bishops from the other side of the Alps every four years, bishops from farther away every five years, and bishops from overseas every ten years. During this visit they were to submit a status report on their diocese according to preset questions.

The new role of the nunciatures. The nuncios developed out of purely political representatives of the pope during the sixteenth century because of the more frequent appointment of legates and apostolic vicars or visitators as instruments of the Catholic Reform and Counter-Reformation. In Cologne and Graz purely reform nunciatures emerged. To this day the nunciatures conduct the inquiry process that is required for every appointment of a bishop, and its significance is illustrated by Jedin's assessment: "the principal question remains here again the renewal of the episcopate."

What was decisive for the offices in the Catholic church were the main aspirations of the Council of Trent: first, to maintain the sacramental foundation of church offices in the office of bishop and priest; and second, to focus all offices on the service of caring for souls. "Priesthood" becomes "ordained ministry."

[*See also* Catholic Reformation; Curia Romana; Papacy; *and* Roman Catholicism.]

BIBLIOGRAPHY

Alberigo, Giuseppe. "Borromeo, Carlo, 1538–1584." In *Theologische Realenzyklopädie*, vol. 7, pp. 83–87. Berlin and New York, 1981. Biography, works, current research; includes a bibliography.

———. "Giberti, Gian Matteo, 1495–1543." In *Theologische Realenzyklopädie*, vol. 13, pp. 257–261. Berlin and New York, 1984. Biography, works; includes a bibliography.

Becker, Karl Josef, *Der priesterliche Dienst II. Wesen und Vollmachten des Priestertums nach dem Lehramt.* Quaestiones Disputatae 47. Freiburg, 1970. See pp. 60–126 for the sacerdotal orientation.

Delumeau, Jean. *Catholicism between Luther and Voltaire: A New View of the Counter Reformation*. Philadelphia, 1977. His thesis of the Christianization of the common people as first occurring through the Reformation and the Catholic Reform has been both disputed and refined.

Freitag, Josef. *Sacramentum Ordinis auf dem Konzil von Trient: Ausgeblendeter Dissens und erreichter Konsens.* Innsbruck, 1991. Exhaustive, detailed, historically systematic presentation of the genesis, results, and significance of the definitions of sacramental offices at Trent; includes bibliography.

———. "Schwierigkeiten und Erfahrungen mit dem 'sacramentum ordinis' in Trient." *Zeitschrift für Katholische Theologie* 113 (1991), 39–51.

Jedin, Hubert. *Geschichte des Konzils von Trient*. 4 vols. Freiburg, 1951–1975. Best account of the council by the recognized dean of research on the Council of Trent; includes bibliography. Also available in English translation.

———. *Kirche des Glaubens, Kirche der Geschichte: Ausgewählte Aufsätze und Vorträge* Freiburg, 1966. See particularly "Die Reform des bischöflichen Informativprozesses auf dem Konzil von Trient," pp. 441–459, and "Das Bischofsideal der katholischen Reformation," pp. 75–117.

———. "Nuntiaturberichte und Durchführung des Konzils von Trient: Hinweise und Fragen." *Quellen und Forschungen aus italienischen Archiven und Bibliotheken* 53 (1973), 180–213.

Massaut, J.-P. *Josse Clichtove: L'humanisme et la réforme du clergé.* 2 vols. Paris, 1968. Fundamental and complete study covering the influence of the Sorbonne up to 1520.

Meier, Johannes. *Der priesterliche Dienst nach Johannes Gropper, 1503–1559: Der Beitrag eines deutschen Theologen zur Erneuerung des Priesterbildes im Rahmen eines vortridentinischen Reformkonzeptes für die kirchliche Praxis.* Reformationsgeschichtliche Studien und Texte 113. Münster, 1977. Outstanding for its analysis of the theological conception and description of the duties of church offices before Trent. Gropper stands among the great theologians and forerunners of Catholic reform in Germany.

O'Malley, John W. "Priesthood, Ministry, and Religious Life: Some Historiographical Considerations." *Theological Studies* 49 (1988), 223–257. Significance of Jesuit activities. Important reflection on the meanings of priesthood, ministry, and office.

O'Malley, John W., ed. *San Carlo Borromeo: Catholic Reform and Ecclesiastical Politics in the Second Half of the Sixteenth Century.* Washington, D.C., 1988.

Ott, Ludwig. *Das Weihsakrament.* Freiburg, 1969. The history of dogma on the sacrament of orders.

Venard, Marc, ed. *Histoire du Christianisme*. Vol. 8, *Les Temps des Confessions, 1530–1620/30.* Paris, 1992. The most informative presentation of the role, duties, situation, position, social background, and formation of the clergies of all the churches; includes bibliography.

JOSEF FREITAG
Translated from German by Robert E. Shillenn

CHURCH ORDINANCES.

One of the most tangible aspects of the theological and ecclesiastical innovations associated with the Protestant Reformation are the church ordinances. Rooted in the Pauline admonition, "Let everything be done decently and in order" (*1 Cor.* 14:40) the church orders concentrated initially on reforms in worship but touched on diverse aspects of early modern social and religious experience. These documents, referred to variously as church orders (Ger., *Kirchenordnungen*, Lat., *kirke ordi-*

nans), ecclesiastical ordinances (Fr., *ordonannces ecclésiastiques*), agendas, and books of discipline, were multifaceted religious constitutions that permitted both the reformers and their constituencies to address a wide range of institutional considerations. The term *church ordinance* could be employed in a variety of settings. The church orders consistently featured the following elements: doctrinal statements, catechisms, sacramental prescriptions, liturgical formulations and aids to worship, descriptions of ecclesiastical offices and hierarchies, disciplinary proceedings, regulations for schools and universities, and instructions for pastoral care and poor relief. No single church order incorporated all of these elements, even though most sought to be as comprehensive as possible, especially during the latter half of the sixteenth century.

Church ordinances were written for nearly every Protestant region of Europe but were particularly abundant in the cities and territories of the Holy Roman Empire. That these orders were usually formal statements of religious policy has meant that they have been associated almost exclusively with the magisterial Reformation. Despite the apprehensions of early reformers like Martin Luther and Huldrych Zwingli, both of whom despised the prescriptions of canon law, church ordinances increasingly assumed the stature of Protestant ecclesiastical legislation.

Pattern and Origins. The diverse nature of the church ordinances and the factors that contributed to these ecclesiastical regulations are evident in the constitutional patterns upon which they were founded. Three recognized approaches to addressing the institutional affairs of the church served as the basis for the church orders: city constitutions (*Stadtverfassungen*), diocesan or provincial synodal statutes (*statuta synodalia*), and territorial legislation (*Landesordnungen, Policeiordnungen*).

City constitutions. Throughout the period of the late Middle Ages city magistrates battled with bishops and princes for authority to control the religious affairs of their communities. The introduction of the evangelical message prompted numerous city councils to assume an even more active posture in regulating public worship, either to support the evangelical movement or to prohibit tendencies in this direction. Andreas Bodenstein von Karlstadt's proposed *Ordnung* for Wittenberg (1522) was the first that directly associated worship innovations with familiar civic terminology. Subsequent regulations regarding the establishment of community chests in Nuremberg (1522), Leisnig (1523), and Magdeburg (1524) featured explicitly doctrinal affirmations of the movement of reform and thereby emerged as a type of church order.

Johann Aepinus's order for the Hanseatic city of Stralsund (1525) should be regarded as the first Lutheran church order. Its fifty-one articles incorporated a greater range of issues than the community chest orders, including an initial emphasis on teaching and the pastoral office, educational reforms, and details of church administration. Numerous German territorial and imperial free cities followed the example of Stralsund and adopted an evangelical church order into their constitutional structure, notably Braunschweig, Hamburg, Lübeck, Nuremberg, Bremen, Strasbourg, Hannover, and Augsburg. City councils relied on theologians and jurists (e.g., Johannes Oldendorp in Rostock and Auctor Sander in Braunschweig) to frame documents, then issued these ordinances as statements of civic policy.

The cities associated with the Reformed movement in Switzerland pursued a similar approach regarding church orders. Following the success of the 1523 disputations, Zwingli and the Zurich council introduced a series of orders related to the sacraments and marriage (1525). These proposals were revised (1529) and formalized as the Zurich church order (1532). Basel adopted its Reformed order (*Reformationsordnung*) almost simultaneously (1529), while Bern had established a church order the previous year.

Synodal statutes. The institutional agenda of the Protestant reformers combined occasionally with a traditional Catholic mechanism of reform: the decrees and statutes of diocesan synods. The jurisdictional authority of the bishop (*iudex ordinarius*) to initiate regional church reforms (*ius reformandi*) had been recognized since the Fourth Lateran Council (1215) and recalled on several occasions (at Basel, 1433, and the Fifth Lateran Council, 1512). The hostility between Protestant reformers and Catholic hierarchy usually inhibited the use of this authority as a means to legitimate institutional changes. Nevertheless, both directly and indirectly the notion of synodal authority could be adapted to suit Protestant aspirations.

The earliest use of the synodal model of reform to introduce a Protestant church order occurred in the newly established duchy of Prussia, outside the boundaries of the empire. With the support of Duke Albert, bishops George Polentz (Samland) and Erhard of Queiß (Pomesania) issued reform mandates (1524/25) in the traditional style of a synodal statute. Their names were attached to these revisions in ecclesiastical legislation and to a subsequent territorial order, adopted by the Prussian estates in 1525. Following apparent concessions granted at the Diet of Regensburg (1541), a similar adaptation of the synodal reform model was employed by the bishop of Osnabrück/Münster (Franz Waldeck) and by the archbishop of Cologne (Hermann von Wied). Waldeck managed to gain support for his Osnabrück order (1543), while von Wied's reforms for Cologne (1543) encountered overwhelming clerical resistance. Somewhat later, Laurentius Petri, first Lutheran bishop of Uppsala, relied on synodal support to establish the Swedish church order (1571).

Protestant reformers could also appeal to the authority inherent in the synodal model without the direct support of a bishop. This was the case in Hesse, when Philipp, counseled by François Lambert, convened the Synod of Homberg (1526) and assumed the role of the bishop. Philipp failed in this initial attempt to expand the boundaries of territorial church rule, and he was forced to moderate the position outlined in the Hessian church order (*Reformatio Ecclesiarum Hassiae*).

Protestant communities that lacked the support of bishop or prince, especially those in officially Catholic territories, drew heavily on the intrinsic and almost autonomous authority of the synod. The Reformed churches of France gathered around a series of national and provincial synods beginning in Paris (1559) and distributed the documents that resulted from these meetings as their church ordinances. The Protestant churches in the Netherlands (the "churches under the cross") relied on synodal legislation first adopted in exile communities (e.g., London, 1550, 1554; Wesel, 1568; and Emden, 1571).

Territorial legislation. Although the beginning of territorial church government (*landesherrliche Kirchenregiment*) preceded the Reformation, the impetus of the Reformation movement allowed many princes to formalize the religious constitutions of their territories. These statements of religious policy were published and distributed as the church orders.

Within the empire initial attempts to enact evangelical concerns at a territorial level followed the recess of the Diet of Speyer (1526). Philipp of Hesse acted almost immediately by convening the Synod of Homberg and commissioning his theological advisers to draft a territorial church order. Duke Ernest ("the Confessor") of Braunschweig-Lüneburg proceeded in a similar fashion yet framed a more moderate constitution (*Artikelbuch*, 1527).

The first church order for Ernestine Saxony, the *Unterricht der Visitatoren* (Instructions for Visitors of the Parish Clergy), served as a particularly important model for German territories. This document grew out of a more comprehensive program of ecclesiastical reorganization that included preliminary instructions, initial reports of the visitors, and a summary territorial order (the *Unterricht*). Variations of this procedure were replicated in numerous other German territories, for example, Württemberg (1536), Albertine Saxony (1539), electoral Brandenburg (1540), and the Braunschweig duchies of Calenberg-Göttingen (1542) and Wolfenbüttel (1543). The realignment of several Lutheran territories with Calvinism was also expressed formally in territorial church ordinances, notably in Palatine-Neuburg (1554), the Electoral Palatinate (1563), Hesse (1566), and Nassau-Dillenberg (1586).

The model of territorial reform legislation translated easily to a national level in both Lutheran and Reformed regions. Lutheran church orders were adopted in Denmark (1537) and Sweden (1571; Synod of Uppsala, 1591). Scotland (*Books of Discipline*, 1560 and 1578) and the Netherlands (the Synodal Acts, 1572; Dordrecht, 1618/19) adopted Reformed church ordinances that were essentially national in scope. Even the aborted *Reformatio legum ecclesiasticorum* (1552) was an attempt to provide the nation with something closer to a typical Protestant church order.

Interrelationships: Lutheran and Evangelical Church Orders. Although Luther and even Lutheranism as a whole has been characterized as institutionally passive, the energy invested in creating church orders reveals a different picture. An overwhelming number of Lutheran ordinances were composed for cities, territories, and ecclesiastical jurisdictions of the empire. The fragmented constitutional configuration of Germany and a series of events hindered a more coordinated effort. The inception of the process in the 1520s was clearly influenced by reactions to the Peasants' War (1525), although the apparent legal concessions granted at Speyer (1526) had more immediate implications for those most interested in promoting and establishing church orders. The decades of the 1530s and 1540s witnessed a remarkable expansion of this endeavor, partially in response to the perceived threat of Sacramentarians and Anabaptists, especially after the disaster at Münster (1534/35). The Schmalkald War (1546-1552) completely disrupted the process of enacting church orders, but the provisions of the Peace of Augsburg (1555) reinforced especially the territorial orientation of religious constitutions (*cuius regio, eius religio*).

Luther rejected Landgrave Philipp's Hessian church order (1526) for being too much like canon law, and warned the citizens of Göttingen against exaggerated expectations from their church order (1531). Nevertheless, Luther constantly received church ordinances for review (e.g., Göttingen; Brandenburg-Nuremberg, 1533; Bremen, 1533; Albertine Saxony, 1539; Cologne, 1543) and was quick to praise what he felt were commendable efforts. Luther also contributed directly to the task by composing the German Mass (1526), writing a wedding and baptismal book (1526), and collaborating with Philipp Melanchthon on the various Saxon ordinances.

Luther, however, was but one of a group of reformers who assumed primary responsibility in the task of composing the evangelical church orders. Although some have attempted to note what has been referred to as families of church orders (clustered under the names of Johannes Bugenhagen, Johannes Brenz, Martin Bucer, Melanchthon, and Andreas Osiander), the interrelationships of the various territories, reformers, and the ordinances themselves are far more complex.

Several individuals played a prominent role in the early expansion of the Lutheran church orders and shared their organizational expertise as they crisscrossed political boundaries. Wittenberg served as an obvious center for much of this effort, and church orders composed by Nikolaus von Amsdorf (Magdeburg, 1524; Goslar, 1531; Einbeck, 1543) and Justus Jonas (Anhalt, 1538; Albertine Saxony, 1539;

Halle, 1543; Regensburg, 1553) attest to this influence. Wittenberg superintendent, Bugenhagen demonstrated an exceptional ability in organizing religious affairs, and his extended travels resulted in orders for the cities of Braunschweig (1528), Hamburg (1529), and Lübeck (1531); for the territories of Pomerania (1535), Schleswig-Holstein (1542), and Braunschweig-Wolfenbüttel (1543); and even for the kingdom of Denmark (1537).

Bugenhagen's sphere of influence extended to a number of other authors of church orders. He received his doctoral promotion at Wittenberg with Johann Aepinus, author of the Stralsund order (1525) and of subsequent orders for Hamburg (1539, 1556) and Buxtehude (1552). Bugenhagen collaborated with Antonius Corvinus on the Hildesheim order (1544). Corvinus composed additional church orders for Northeim (1539) and the duchy of Braunschweig-Calenberg, and along with Urbanus Rhegius (author of orders for Lüneburg, 1531, and Hannover, 1536) was the leading reformer of Lower Saxony. Although Corvinus labored with Bugenhagen, his ideas about church order had been shaped by Bucer, author of church orders for Strasbourg (1534), Hesse (the Ziegenhain Discipline order, 1539), and Cologne (1543).

While Bugenhagen and others provided church orders for northern Germany, Bucer, Brenz, and Osiander assumed a leading role in the south. Brenz wrote church orders for Schwäbisch Hall (1526) and Württemberg (1536, 1553, 1559), while Osiander wrote an order for Palatine-Neuburg (1544). Brenz and Osiander worked together on the influential Brandenburg-Nuremberg order, which along with the Saxon *Unterricht* served as a basis for the electoral Brandenburg and Mecklenburg orders (1540).

Nearly all of these reformers completed their organizational contributions within the first half of the sixteenth century. In most instances the task at hand shifted during the second half of the sixteenth century from establishing the church to institutional refinements. The earlier pastoral thrust of the Lutheran church orders, most of which were published as pamphlets, yielded to more precise and comprehensive policy statements, circulated in imposing folio volumes. In contrast to the prewar years, few cities adopted church orders; the direction was clearly territorial.

Leadership shifted to a new generation of reformers, all of whom, with the exception of Jakob Andreae, had Wittenberg connections. Andreae, Brenz's successor in Württemberg, was also exceptional in the range of his activities, as he composed church orders for Rothenburg ob der Tauber (1559), Braunschweig-Wolfenbüttel (1569), Brandenburg-Ansbach (1578), and Saxony (the order of Elector August, 1580). Andreae assisted Nicholas Selnecker in composing the Oldenburg church order (1573) and collaborated with Martin Chemnitz on the Braunschweig-Wolfenbüttel order. Chemnitz had succeeded Joachim Mörlin, author of the

Peine-Steurwolt order (1561), as city superintendent in Braunschweig immediately after the two of them completed major revisions to the Prussian church order (1568). Both Chemnitz and Mörlin had spent early years at Wittenberg, as had the Swedish archbishop Laurentius Petri (Swedish order, 1571) and the Mecklenburg reformer David Chytraeus, who contributed a consistorial order for Mecklenburg (1570) and, at the invitation of Emperor Maximilian II, composed an agenda for his Austrian territories.

The interpersonal network that held the early evangelical movement together eroded steadily during the latter half of the sixteenth century. The Formula of Concord forged a reinvigorated confessional allegiance, but structural deficiencies escalated. By the end of the century, the contributions of theologian-reformers who maintained their transterritorial network disappeared as territorial sovereigns turned increasingly toward their own bureaucracies to serve the needs of church order.

Interrelationships: Reformed Church Orders. The Reformed church's emphasis on discipline (*nervus ecclesiae*) clearly predominated in its church orders to a greater degree than in the Lutheran orders. But additional considerations such as liturgical forms and catechisms also played a significant role in Reformed orders.

The Swiss cities of Zurich, Bern, and Basel pioneered the Reformed church ordinances. Zwingli's liturgical reforms (1525) and the subsequent Zurich order (1532) established an early pattern of reform. The magistrate played a critical role in Zwingli's constitution, particularly in the "marriage court" (*Ehegericht*). Other cities adapted these innovations, especially as they spread through German-speaking Switzerland and southwest Germany.

Compared to the more elaborate Lutheran documents of the early 1540s, the proposals contained in Calvin's *Ordonnances ecclésiastiques* (1541) appear modest. His outline of the four ecclesiastical offices, pastors, doctors, elders, and deacons, had no precise parallels, but his understanding of the role of discipline in the religious community had been influenced by Bucer during his stay in Strasbourg. Discipline emerged as a primary concern in the formation of the consistory and in the detailed discussion given to the office of elder.

The Genevan model of reform exercised enormous influence within the Reformed community, even though adjustments were made to fit local considerations. The first French ecclesiastical ordinance, which appeared initially with the French Gallic Confession at the Synod of Paris (1559), had roots in Geneva, although the actual contributions of Calvin are uncertain. Subsequent national synods continued to debate the French discipline until a form of consensus was achieved at La Rochelle (1571; formally adopted at Nîmes, 1572). The French ordinance, in turn, had an immediate impact on the Scottish *Book of Discipline*, assembled by John

Knox and his collaborators. The question of oversight and mechanisms for clerical support remained unsettled in Scotland until the appearance of the *Second Book of Discipline* (1578).

For churches in the Netherlands, Reformed ordinances were initially adopted in exile communities. The church order of the London exile community (1550–1554), composed by Jan Łaski and Maarten Micron, and the subsequent Synod of Emden (1571), framed the constitutional structure that would be followed during the *nadere reformatie* ("further reformation") of the Dutch estates. The series of synodal acts, which culminated at Dordrecht, evidenced the continuing process of reform that characterized the church in the Netherlands. The Reformed church in the Spanish Netherlands (later Belgium) lacked the organizational structures of its neighbor, but congealed around the Belgic Confession (1561). The basic Genevan pattern pervaded all of these expressions of Reformed polity.

Contents and Issues. Placing the church ordinances within the larger context of early modern society has resulted in diverse interpretations. The gains and losses associated with these documents have been variously linked with the triumphs of urban elites (Thomas Brady), or with the entrenchment of traditional patriarchies (Lyndal Roper). An appreciation for the accomplishments of the church orders must, therefore, be tempered by recognizing the limitations these ordinances introduced into the religious and social environment of the Reformation.

From an internal perspective, however, three elements were generally considered as essential to the creation of a sound church order: attention to issues of belief and doctrine (*credenda*), reforms associated with worship (*agenda*), and various structural and organizational concerns (*administranda*). The church orders were perhaps the most significant element of the confessional literature of the Reformation, and adopting a church order represented a critical aspect of confession building, or confessionalization.

Doctrinal matters (Credenda). Sound teaching took priority in most church ordinances, especially for Lutherans. Overall, the distinction between divine law (*ius divinum*) and human prerogatives (*ius humanum*) made the church orders subordinate to strictly confessional statements. In order to clarify and affirm this relationship, sections on doctrine and teaching usually appeared first in the church orders.

The precise confessional nature of the church orders changed during the course of the sixteenth century. On the one hand, several early church orders, such as Bugenhagen's order for Braunschweig (1528), contained elaborate doctrinal statements, and it would be difficult to separate these documents from a confession of faith properly so called. Melanchthon and Luther's "Instructions," on the other hand, presented something closer to doctrinal outlines. Later Lutheran orders did not reproduce confessions specifically but recognized confessional statements (*corpora doctrinae*) in an attempt to articulate particular allegiances. The advent of the Lutheran *Book of Concord* (1580) supplanted this necessity.

From the outset, Reformed church orders tended to distinguish organizational expressions from explicit doctrinal statements. This segregation is evident in the differences between the Gallic Confession and the companion *Discipline ecclésiastique*, or between the Scottish Confession of Faith and the *Book of Discipline*.

One way to ensure sound teaching was to regulate carefully the requirements for pastoral office holding. In addition to describing procedures for electing, calling, and installing clergy, several church orders outlined detailed examinations for ordination, for example, Melanchthon's Examen Ordinanden contained in the Mecklenburg order (1552). A different approach, with essentially the same purpose in view, involved the specification of sanctions against ministers who served in a clandestine fashion, one of the primary concerns of the French and Scottish disciplines.

The recognition of the role of catechisms was an additional aspect of the doctrinal element of the church orders. No document was appealed to more often in the Lutheran orders than Luther's Small Catechism (1529). In Reformed circles, no catechism was more highly regarded than the Heidelberg Catechism composed by Kaspar Olevianus and Zacharius Ursinus, which appeared first in the Palatine order (1563).

Liturgical matters (Agenda). Several church orders circulated under the title of *Agenda*, and many viewed the concept of a church ordinance and a book or order of worship as essentially synonymous. This was not the case in Scotland, where *The Book of Discipline* (1560) was clearly distinct from *The Book of Common Order* (1564).

Changes in the primary liturgy of the Mass in many instances served as the earliest church ordinances. This was true for Luther (Deutsche messe) and for Zwingli, and even for radical reformers such as Andreas Bodenstein von Karlstadt (the Wittenberg order) and Thomas Müntzer (the Allstedt order, 1523). Several later church orders, such as Veit Dietrich's *Agendbüchlein* for Nuremberg, included musical notations to accompany worship. Thomas Cranmer's liturgical reforms for England (*The Second Book of Common Prayer*, 1552), influenced by Martin Bucer and Jan Łaski, reflect a similar concern and in this context could also be considered a church order.

In addition to general designs for worship and the sacraments, most church orders contained collections of prayers. In a few cases the church order was essentially a book of collects (e.g., the Regensburg order, 1553), but typically the order would contain a section dedicated to prescribed prayers.

Related to the assignment of specific prayers for liturgical seasons were general regulations surrounding the observance of religious holidays. The church orders customarily discussed which Christian festivals and holy days would be observed in a given territory or city. Neither Lutheran nor Reformed orders developed any universal set of days for religious observance, yet the number of holy days was drastically reduced from typical observances of the later Middle Ages.

Administrative concerns (Administranda). A host of ecclesiastical regulations and several aspects of social reform clustered under the general notion of administration. Details of church organization became interrelated with other dimensions of civil order, especially changes in educational policy and poor relief. The boundaries between the three dimensions of church order never existed as entirely discrete issues, and administrative issues frequently intersected with matters of doctrine and worship.

Ecclesiastical structures were obviously a fundamental consideration. Definitions of clerical office and support structures often merited first consideration, as was the case with Calvin's Genevan order. The French *Discipline* and the Scottish *Book of Discipline* followed this pattern, with even greater attention given to pastors and deacons. In addition to pastors and deacons, Lutheran orders included a more elaborate set of officials: sacristans, trustees, wardens of the community chest, and, above all, superintendents.

For Lutherans, the office of superintendent was introduced in the Stralsund order, then developed in the Saxon "Instructions" and in the orders of Bugenhagen. Andreae's orders for the territories of Braunschweig-Wolfenbüttel and Saxony presented a developed scheme of regional superintendents under the jurisdiction of a territorial superintendent. The office of superintendent also appeared in the revision of the Scottish *Book of Discipline.*

The activity most often associated with the office of superintendent was visitation. Customarily, visitation instructions preceded the church order proper, but many Lutheran orders included these statements. Visitations were primarily implemented to guarantee the adequacy and competence of ministers, but they often did so by assessing the religious understanding and behaviors of church members. Although the intent was pastoral, the vocabulary of many visitation instructions bordered on the rigors of an inquisition.

In Reformed regions, visitations were generally replaced by ecclesiastical synods, and the church orders frequently concentrated on discussing the fundamental characteristics of a synod. Synodal arrangements tended to be more fluid than the rigid structures of the Lutherans. The French synodal model as well as the *Acta* of the Dutch synods (1572–1619) reveal this evolutionary thrust.

Both synods and visitations gave considerable attention to the question of discipline, ecclesiastical and civil. Traditional distinctions between lax Lutheran and rigorous Calvinist approaches to discipline disappear in the church ordinances.

The 1528 Saxon "Instructions," and most subsequent Lutheran orders, retained the use of ecclesiastical discipline, or the "small ban" (*excommunicatio minor*), which carried no civil sanctions. But church discipline at any level was supposed to proceed in cooperation with the secular authorities. Even the strongest advocates of church discipline (e.g., Brenz and Bucer) found it nearly impossible to protect a primarily religious procedure from secular interference. Reformed church ordinances had greater success in establishing procedures for discipline either by placing greater responsibility in the hands of the magistrates (Zurich) or by guaranteeing autonomous church discipline (Geneva).

The concern for discipline demanded that serious attention be given to procedural matters. Both Lutheran and Reformed church ordinances encountered the need to find a replacement for the old system of episcopal courts. Within the Reformed community, Zwingli's model of the marriage court eventually yielded to Calvin's consistory. Although Lutherans used the same terminology, their notion of the consistory involved a more official blending of lay and clerical representation that was directly accountable to the prince. The general concern for marriage regulations received additional attention in detailed degrees of consanguinity that accompanied most of the territorial orders (e.g., Württemberg, Strasbourg).

From the outset, Protestant church ordinances also included sections on poor relief. Early ordinances (Nuremberg, Leisnig, and Magdeburg) established community chest regulations. Bugenhagen advocated the same approach in his orders for the towns of northern Germany (e.g., Braunschweig, Hamburg, and Lübeck), and separated funds for general church responsibilities (*Schatzkasten*) from those reserved for care of widows and the infirm (*Armenkasten*). Calvin's order placed similar responsibilities in the office of the deacon, with an interest in both financial support and medical care. The experiences of religious exiles, both in Geneva and in the Netherlands community of London, intensified concerns for those living in destitute situations and expanded the general duties of the diaconate.

Reforms linked with education and the establishment of schools were a final component of most church ordinances. Some of these documents were entitled school orders (*Schulordnungen*), while others featured significant sections dedicated to education. School personnel, financial support, and determinations of curriculum were all addressed in the church orders. Vernacular primary education for children received the largest amount of attention in the church orders. Latin schools, which blended the writings of classical authors with the teachings of the reformers, also resulted from many of the orders.

Higher levels of education were likewise included in several church orders. Regulations of studies, student life, and administrative responsibilities were outlined in the orders. Several Protestant universities were either formally inaugurated in the church order, or had their earliest roots in these documents, notably Marburg and Jena in Germany, Leiden in the Netherlands, and the academies at Strasbourg, Hamburg, and Geneva.

The message of the reformers could never have survived without the attention to forms found in the church orders. Clearly these efforts could only prove partially successful in their sweeping attempts to reform not only the church but society at large. Nevertheless, the remarkable variety of these documents enables one to see the more concrete aspects of the Protestant movement.

[*See also* Church Finances; Diaconate; *and* Social Discipline.]

BIBLIOGRAPHY

Primary Sources

Cameron, James K., ed. *The First Book of Discipline.* Edinburgh, 1972. Scotland's first church ordinance.

Luther, Martin. *Luther's Works.* Saint Louis, 1958. See vol. 40, pp. 263–320. Contains the Saxon "Instructions for the Visitors of the Parish Pastors" (*Unterricht der Visitatoren*).

Niesel, Wilhelm. *Bekenntnisschriften und Kirchenordnungender nach Gottes Wort Reformierten Kirche.* Reprint, Zurich, 1985. Reformed church orders, especially the Palatine order.

Reid, J. K. S., ed. *Calvin: Theological Treatises.* Library of Christian Classics, vol. 22. Philadelphia, 1954. Calvin's *Ecclesiastical Ordinances.*

Richter, Aemilius Ludwig, ed. *Die evangelische Kirchenordnungen des sechzehnten Jahrhunderts: Urkunden und Regesten zur Geschichte des Rechts und der Verfassung der evangelischen Kirche in Deutschland* (1846). 2 vols. Reprint, Nieuwkoop, 1967. Selections of Lutheran and a few Reformed orders. Good sampling, but many incomplete texts.

Sehling, Emil, et al., eds. *Die evangelischen Kirchenordnung des XVI. Jahrhunderts.* Vols. 1–5. Leipzig, 1902–1913. Vols 6–. Tübingen, 1955–. A comprehensive, critical edition of Lutheran church orders.

Sunshine, Glenn. "French Protestantism on the Eve of St. Bartholomew: The Ecclesiastical Discipline of the French Reformed Churches, 1571–1572." *French History* 4 (1990), 340–377. The French church ordinance approved at La Rochelle and Nîmes.

Secondary Sources

Blickle, Peter. *Communal Reformation: The Quest for Salvation in Sixteenth Century Germany.* Translated by Thomas Dunlap. Atlantic Highlands, N.J., 1992. Church ordinances in opposition to communal reformations.

Brecht, Martin. *Kirchenordnung und Kirchenzucht in Württemberg vom 16. bis 18. Jahrhundert.* Stuttgart, 1967. The ecclesiastical systems of Johannes Brenz and Jacob Andreae.

Burnett, Amy. *The Yoke of Christ: Martin Bucer and Christian Discipline.* Sixteenth Century Studies and Essays, vol. 26. Kirksville, Mo., 1994. Discusses the church orders of Bucer.

Dolan, John Patrick. *The Influence of Erasmus, Witzel, and Cassander in the Church Ordinances and Reform Proposals of the United Duchees of Cleve during the Middle Decades of the Sixteenth Century.* Münster, 1957. Church orders that seek to implement an Erasmian spirit of reform.

Estes, James Martin. *Christian Magistrate and State Church: The Reforming Career of Johannes Brenz.* Toronto, 1982.

Graham, W. Fred. *Later Calvinism: International Perspectives.* Sixteenth Century Studies and Essays, vol. 22. Kirksville, Mo., 1994. Church orders discussed in essays on France, Scotland, the Palatinate, and the Netherlands.

Heckel, Johannes. *Lex Charitatis: Eine juristische Untersuchung über das Recht in der Theologie Martin Luthers.* Cologne, 1973. Luther's contributions to church order according to an expert in canon law.

Jaynes, Jeffrey P. "Ordo et libertas": Church Discipline and the Makers of Church Order in Sixteenth-Century North Germany." Ph.D. diss., Ohio State University, 1993. Constructs a narrative surrounding the numerous North German church orders.

Kittelson, James. "The Confessional Age: The Late Reformation in Germany." In *Reformation Europe: A Guide to Research,* edited by Steven E. Ozment. Saint Louis, 1982. Best short article on the place of church orders.

Köhler, Walter. *Zürcher Ehegericht und Genfer Konsistorium.* 2 vols. Quellen und Abhandlungen zur Schweizerischen Reformationsgeschichte. Leipzig, 1938. Classic study on models of Swiss reform and church order.

Münch, Paul. *Zucht und Ordnung: Reformierte Kirchenverfassungen im 16. und 17. Jahrhunderts; Nassau-Dillenberg, Kurpfalz und Hessen-Kassel.* Stuttgart, 1978. The role of church orders in German territories associated with a "second Reformation."

Ozment, Steven. *The Reformation in the Cities: The Appeal of Protestantism to Sixteenth Century Germany and Switzerland.* Reprint, New Haven, 1980. Helpful description of church orders in an urban context.

Pettegree, Andrew. *Emden and the Dutch Revolt: Exile and Development of Reformed Protestantism.* Oxford, 1992. Includes the development and influence of the Emden church order.

Preus, James S. *Carlstadt's Ordinaciones and Luther's Liberty: A Study of the Wittenberg Movement 1521–1522.* Cambridge, Mass., 1974.

Schilling, Heinz. *Religion, Political Culture, and the Emergence of Early Modern Society: Essays in German and Dutch History.* Studies in Medieval and Reformation Thought 50. Leiden, 1992. Accessible introduction to Schilling's notions of confessionalization and his understanding of church orders.

Schwarz, Reinhard, ed. *Die Augsburger Kirchenordnung von 1537 und ihr Umfeld.* Schriften des Vereins für Reformationsgeschichte, 196. Gütersloh, 1988. Collection of essays on the influential Augsburg order.

Strauss, Gerald. *Law, Resistance, and the State: The Opposition to Roman Law in Reformation Germany.* Princeton, 1986. Places church orders in the context of early modern legal struggles.

Wartenberg, Günther. *Landesherrschaft und Reformation. Moritz von Sachsen und die albertinische Kirchenpolitik bis 1546.* Gütersloh, 1988. Church orders in the policies of Maurice of Saxony.

JEFFREY P. JAYNES

CHYTRAEUS, Nathan (Ger., Kochhafe; 1543–1598), German humanist, scholar, and Neo-Latin poet. Chytraeus came from the family of a south German pastor and received a good humanist education both in Strasbourg and in the Hanseatic city of Rostock, located in Mecklenburg. His older brother, David Chytraeus, was already a professor at that university. In 1564 Nathan became professor of Latin language and grammar at Rostock, where he spent the longest and most important time of his life. In 1568 Chytraeus married Gertrud Prenger of Rostock; together they had seven children. After 1579 he additionally served as organizer and first director of the municipal school. In 1593 he requested from Duke Ulrich of Mecklenburg to be released from his duties for theological reasons. Nathan then became rector of the Latin school at Bremen, where he died on 25 February 1598.

Important for Chytraeus's education were his travels, which took him after April 1565 through western and southern Europe (Netherlands, France, Italy, Switzerland, England, and southern Germany) for more than a year. Later he traveled to Denmark, Frankfurt an der Oder, and in 1590 to Danzig. As he acknowledged, during these trips he was especially interested in academia and its history, an interest that according to his own opinion differentiated him from his traveling companions.

One fruit of these travels was the publication of travel accounts in Latin verse (*Hodoeporica sive itineraria*, 1575). With this publication he followed the example of Georgius Agricola, the rector of the saxon princes' school in Meissen. Up to the present these publications remain an important source because of the inscriptions that Chytraeus collected. He had gathered these in cities of Italy, Austria, southern Germany, France, and England, and later in Silesia, Poland, and Denmark (for example in *Variorum in Europa itinerum deliciae*, 3d ed., 1606). Chytraeus liked to use the poetry in school instruction and to practice Latin style with his students. They were also published in *Poematum praeter sacra omnium libri septendecim* (1579), an important volume of collected works that included much of Chytraeus's Latin poetry (panegyrics to princes, elegies, poetry for weddings and for funerals, eclogues, rhymed invitations to masters' promotions, and songs). This large number of Latin poems confirmed his title of poet laureate, which he had already garnered before 1575, and made him one of the most important Neo-Latin poets in the second half of the sixteenth century.

Along with his own poetry, Chytraeus also edited new editions of texts already used in school instruction, including *Disticha moralia* (the so-called *Cato*) with explanations and actual amplifications, the *Orpheus* of Gaius Cassius (1585), and the metrical *Psalms* of George Buchanan (*Psalmorum Davidis Paraphrasis poetica Georgii Buchanani Scoti. . .*, 1595), to which he added his own explanatory notes. After his death, this work was published again in 1610 with tune settings for four voices for use in school.

Equally suited for use in school was his Latin grammar (*Grammatica latina*; 1st ed. is unknown, but there were reprints, for example, in 1621, 1633, and many more). Also useful was his new edition of the Greek grammar of Johannes Caselius, who was a colleague from Rostock (*Graecae Grammaticae Progymnasmata*, 1581). A collection of Latin conversations, together with a collection of Latin idioms and their translation in Low German (*Colloquiorum et rebus et verbis puerilium duo . . .*, 1588), document the efforts spent on the beginning didactic problems of Latin instruction. It is remarkable with what intensity Chytraeus, who came from the area of south German-Swabian language, labored

with the didactic problems of Latin elementary instruction in the area of Low German. That labor may be seen also in a comprehensive Latin–Low German dictionary, *Nomenclator latino-saxonicus*, which appeared in nineteen editions between 1582 and 1659.

Equally intended for use in school was a High German translation of Giovanni della Casa's *Galateus*. Chytraeus's translation of this text, which had served the Counter-Reformation instruction of the Jesuits, transformed it into an introduction to bourgeois good conduct, that is, Chytraeus humanistically revised the text.

The spiritual poetry of Chytraeus represents an original Neo-Latin form of poetry. A series of poems for the festival of the nativity of Christ belonged to this form. They appeared annually between 1577 and 1598, with the exception of 1580, 1591, 1592, and 1593, under the title *Natalis Domini nostri Jesu Christi* (or similar titles). From 1573 on, Chytraeus published a further series of spiritual poems that were brought together and printed in one volume in 1578 and later in 1594. They imitated the *Fasti* of the Roman poet Ovid and transformed the nonreligious calendar of Ovid into a calendar of Christian festivals. The poems had as their subjects the Christian commemoration days in the individual months of the year. Besides the traditional saints' days of the Roman Church, Chytraeus included in his poetic calendar the birth and death days of Martin Luther, Philipp Melanchthon, and significant humanists such as Desiderius Erasmus of Rotterdam, Eobanus Hessus, and Conradus Celtis.

Along with his literary activity for the educational system in Rostock and Bremen, Chytraeus occupied himself with editing and translating devotional literature. Prefaced with a foreword dated 1594, the *Viaticum itineris extremi* appeared in 1602 in the Hessian town of Herborn (the location of an important Protestant postsecondary school). This volume collected texts of the church fathers, of Luther, and of Philippist and Reformed authors of the sixteenth century, along with texts of prayers. Chytraeus recommended to his readers that they prepare themselves for eternal life through acknowledging sins, proclaiming liberation from sin, thanking God for this liberation, observing the hindrances on the way, and contemplating the goal of the journey. An appendix offered his *Carmen protrepticon, summam doctrinae Christianae et confessionis fidei suae complectens*, dated 8 November 1582 and presented to five of his children as his confession of faith. A High German translation of *Preces et soliloquia* by Christoph Pezel, the former Wittenberg professor of theology lately come to Bremen, appeared for the first time in Herborn in 1592. The book contained a partial translation of John Calvin's sermons on the Old Testament book of Job, and prayers and texts from *Histoire des Martyrs persecutez et mis à mort* by Jean Crespin.

The place of publication and content of *Preces et soliloquia* call attention to the change in his religious attitudes, which was so consequential for him. This change led him from a position strongly oriented toward Melanchthon to a leaning toward Calvinism. He belonged to a group of philologists, medical doctors, and theologians who from about 1570 had taken a similar path, and among whom were some of his friends. The common thread connecting these scholars was a late humanism that conceived controversies in theological doctrine as disturbing and harmful to the humanist ideal of unity.

The religious change of Chytraeus proceeded gradually. As early as 1590 the school rector's utterances criticizing the Lutheran doctrines and practices of baptism and the Eucharist and the wording of the Ten Commandments in Luther's catechism (which did not forbid images) had drawn the attention of the city pastors in Rostock. When Chytraeus did not change his position, he was no longer admitted to Communion. He presented his objections cautiously but clearly in a comprehensive defense written in High German.

Since there was no chance that those in Rostock would accept him, he requested on 27 July 1593 that the duke of Mecklenburg release him from his duties, after he had received an offer from Bremen to take over the rectorate of the school there. The Hanseatic city of Bremen at this time was already on the way to becoming a city bearing the stamp of Calvinism. Christoph Pezel, together with his colleagues in Bremen, saw the difficulties that Chytraeus experienced in Rostock as a welcome occasion to call to their city this pedagogue and philosopher, who stood so near to the developments in Bremen. It had become necessary to find a good successor for Joachim Meister, who had died young.

Little concrete is known about Chytraeus's time in Bremen, where he worked for four and a half more years until his death. Presumably his activities were similar to those in Rostock: along with directing the school, he gave instruction in ancient languages and philosophy to the uppermost classes.

The influence of the work of Chytraeus was notable in the literary realm. Subsequent editions of his works continued to appear into the second half of the seventeenth century. Thereby the influence of humanistic pedagogy was extended up to the threshold of the eighteenth century.

BIBLIOGRAPHY

Primary Sources

Chytraeus, Nathan. *Nathan Chytraeus: Nomenclator latinosaxonicus.* Foreword by Gilbert de Smet. Reprint, New York, 1974. Contains bibliography of Chytraeus's works.

Timm, Gustav, ed. "Ludi literarii ab amplissimo Senatu Rostochiensi in ciuium suorum utilitatem nuper aperti Sciographia Nathanis Chytraei primi rectoris: Rostochi, 1580." In *Programm des Gymnasii und der Realschule im Rostock*, pp. 1–38. Rostock, 1882. A bibliography of Chytraeus and of the first school ordinance for the Latin school in Rostock.

Secondary Sources

Casa, Giovanni della. *Galateus: Das Büchlein von erbarn höflichen und holdseligen Sitten, verdeutscht von Nathan Chytraeus 1579.* Edited by Klaus Ley. Tübingen, 1984. Contains an interpretation of the revision of the work by Chytraeus and bibliography with references to locations.

Elsmann, Thomas. "Reformierte Stadt und humanistische Schule: Nathan Chytraeus in Bremen, 1593–1598." In *Nathan Chytraeus, 1543–1598: Ein Humanist in Rostock und Bremen; Quellen und Studien*, edited by Thomas Elsmann, Hanno Lietz, and Sabine Pettke, pp. 71–93. Bremen, 1991. Portrays the history of the schools of Bremen in the sixteenth century and Chytraeus's place in it.

Fuchs, Thomas. "David and Nathan Chytraeus: Eine biographische Annäherung." In *David and Nathan Chytraeus: Humanismus im konfessionellen Zeitalter*, edited by Karl-Heinz Glaser, Hanno Lietz, and Stephan Rhein, pp. 33–46, 183–187. Ubstadt-Weiher, 1993. Biographical sketch.

———. "Das Entlassungsgesuch des Nathan Chytraeus an den Bürgermeister und Rat der Stadt Rostock." In *David and Nathan Chytraeus: Humanismus im konfessionellen Zeitalter*, edited by Karl-Heinz Glaser, Hanno Lietz, and Stephan Rhein, pp. 171–174, 230. Ubstadt-Weiher, 1993. Annotated publication of the texts.

Händel, Astrid, and Hanno Lietz. "Bibliographie bis 1600." In *Nathan Chytraeus, 1543–1598: Ein Humanist in Rostock und Bremen; Quellen und Studien*, edited by Thomas Elsmann, Hanno Lietz, and Sabine Pettke, pp. 107–136. Bremen, 1991.

Index Aurelianus I. Vol. 7. Baden-Baden, 1982. See pp. 560–568 for a bibliography of Chytraeus's works.

Kaufmann, Thomas. "Die Brüder David und Nathan Chytraeus." In *David and Nathan Chytraeus: Humanismus im konfessionellen Zeitalter*, edited by Karl-Heinz Glaser, Hanno Lietz, and Stephan Rhein, pp. 103–116, 202–212. Ubstadt-Weiher, 1993. Brief account of the activities and significance of both brothers at the University of Rostock.

Koch, Ernst. "Der Weg von Nathan Chytraeus von Rostock nach Bremen auf dem Hintergrund der kirchlichen und theologischen Bewegungen der Zeit." In *Nathan Chytraeus, 1543–1598: Ein Humanist in Rostock und Bremen; Quellen und Studien*, edited by Thomas Elsmann, Hanno Lietz, and Sabine Pettke, pp. 53–59. Bremen, 1991. Sketches the contexts of Chytraeus's religious change.

Lehsten, Lupold von. "Zur Genealogie der Familie des David Chytraeus." In *David and Nathan Chytraeus: Humanismus im konfessionellen Zeitalter*, edited by Karl-Heinz Glaser, Hanno Lietz, and Stephan Rhein, pp. 147–159, 224–226. Ubstadt-Weiher, 1993. A family history.

Peters, Robert. *Nathan Chytraeus' Nomenclator latinosaxonicus, Rostock 1582: Ein Beitrag zur Erforschung der Lexikographie des 16. Jahrhunderts.* Münster, 1976. Investigation of the originality of and influences on the work of Chytraeus.

Pettke, Sabine. "Die Entlassung des Nathan Chytraeus aus Rostock: Zeitweise verschollene Akten des geistlichen Ministeriums." In *David and Nathan Chytraeus: Humanismus im konfessionellen Zeitalter*, edited by Karl-Heinz Glaser, Hanno Lietz, and Stephan Rhein, pp. 165–170, 230. Ubstadt-Weiher, 1993. Overview of Chytraeus's rediscovered work.

Schnurr, Harry C. *Lateinische Gedichte deutscher Humanisten.* 2d ed. Stuttgart, 1966. Chytraeus in the context of German humanists of the sixteenth century.

Timm, Gustav. *Die Gründung der Grossen Stadtschule zu Rostock und ihr erster Rector M. Nathan Chytraeus: Festrede, gehalten für Feier ihres 300-jährigen Jubiläums am 1. Februar 1880.* Rostock, 1880. Biography and portrayal of his activity in Rostock.

Wiegand, Hermann. *Hodoeporica: Studien zur neulateinischen Reisedichtung des deutschen Kulturraums im 16. Jahrhundert.* Baden-Baden,

1984. Places the travel poetry of Chytraeus within the history of this genre in the sixteenth century.

———. "Nathan Chytraeus als neulateinischer Dichter." In *Nathan Chytraeus, 1543–1598: Ein Humanist in Rostock und Bremen; Quellen und Studien,* edited by Thomas Elsmann, Hanno Lietz, and Sabine Pettke, pp. 41–47. Bremen, 1991. Evaluation of Chytraeus's activity as a poet.

———. "Aber der Heimatboden ist mir doch viel lieber . . . Heimatbeziehungen im poetischen Werk von Nathan Chytraeus." In *David and Nathan Chytraeus: Humanismus im konfessionellen Zeitalter,* edited by Karl-Heinz Glaser, Hanno Lietz, and Stephan Rhein, pp. 63–82, 193–195. Ubstadt-Weiher, 1993. Traces influences of Kraichgau and the von Mentzingen family on the poetry of Nathan Chytraeus, includes a Latin poem on death by Peter von Mentzingen with a German translation.

ERNST KOCH
Translated from German by Jeff Bach

CISNEROS, Francisco Jiménez de. *See* Jiménez de Cisneros, Francisco.

CITIES. The association of the Reformation with cities reflects both the historical conditions of sixteenth-century Europe and the interests of modern historians. For the early evangelical reformers, Europe's walled towns provided a concentrated audience quickly accessible to both preaching and pamphlets. Civic evangelical parties, in turn, directly influenced their political leaders, who could effect religious reforms and were not distant lords but fellow citizens. In the 1520s the reform movement spread quickly in the German-speaking towns. Over the next two centuries European cities, as political, economic, and cultural centers, would be critical for the propagation of diverse Protestant beliefs and reformed Catholicism.

Modern historians, however, have sought to isolate something in the nature of civic culture and society that helped shape the nature of the Reformation. This objective made sense because traditional scholarship treated both cities and the Reformation as reified historical constructs—that is, as coherent historical phenomena with definable characteristics. Historians, since the work of Karl Marx, Max Weber, and Ernst Troeltsch, have claimed that both played critical roles in the evolution from medieval to modern Europe, and theoretical issues have continued to inform the scholarship. Since 1962 Bernd Moeller's essay *Reichsstadt und Reformation* has stimulated much research and critical debate. By 1974 A. G. Dickens could make the oft-quoted pronouncement that the Reformation was an "urban event" (*The German Nation and Martin Luther,* New York, 1974, p. 182), and historians still echo that claim.

Moeller argued that the Reformation penetrated into the sixty-five free imperial cities, those towns that normally attended imperial diets as autonomous members, earlier and more deeply than elsewhere in the German-speaking world.

During their medieval struggles for independence, Moeller contends that civic communities envisioned themselves as constituting "collective individuals," embodied by the sinews of law and mutual duties. At the essential spiritual level the civic community formed a "sacral community," and late medieval cities employed this model when dealing with neighboring princes and the church. According to Moeller, early reformers in the south German imperial cities, led by Martin Bucer (1491–1551) and Huldrych Zwingli (1484–1531), reaffirmed the sacral bonds between individuals and the communal character of Christian faith, mutually reinforcing the goals of the Reformation and civic liberty. There was a congeniality between south German cities, very much characterized by their guild systems, and their Zwinglian leanings, while Lutheran leanings of the Franconian cities (Nuremberg) is prefigured in their conciliar constitutions. Furthermore, this urban Reformation movement sharply contrasted with Luther's Reformation, which isolated individuals before God and in its religious imagery presaged the relationship between the individual and the modern state. For Germans the Christian society promised by the urban Reformation was ultimately undone by the Protestant defeat in the Schmalkald War in 1548, when many imperial cities lost their medieval constitutions and accepted Lutheranism. Moeller concludes that John Calvin (1509–1564) carried the urban Reformation's social and religious values to Geneva and from there into modern culture.

Historians have reacted to Moeller's thesis on four fronts. First, Thomas Brady argued that Moeller's static conceptualization of urban "sacral communities" fails to appreciate both the degree and function of conflict in implementing the civic reformations, and numerous case studies have borne out Brady's critique. Second, Peter Blickle asserted that Moeller's communal values were as strong in the countryside as in the imperial cities and that the reformers' image of a sacral society triggered a revolution of the "common man." Blickle's critics, however, find his rural communities just as structurally static as Moeller's urban ones. Third, Heinz Schilling uncovered communally oriented urban reformations in north German territorial towns undermining Moeller's criteria that limited the movement to the imperial cities of the south. At Lemgo in the north German county of Lippe, Schilling has isolated a Lutheran city defending its corporate rights against a Calvinist territorial prince, which denies Moeller's association of particular confessions with particular political ideologies. Finally, Richard Schmidt demonstrated, on the basis of the minutes of the *Städtetage* ("meetings of the cities"), that in all imperial cities the support of the Reformation initially came from the "common man" and was theologically influenced far more by Zwingli and Bucer than by Luther (even in Nuremberg). Methodologically, the study, by using the minutes of the *Städtetage* meetings, by all odds has sources as objective as possible, since discussions took place unhampered by popular sentiment at home or concern about the emperor and territorial rulers. These critiques and others have sharpened the understanding of the civic reformations and their place in the history of the Reformation. This article discusses the towns' role in sixteenth-century society, then surveys various civic reformations in the empire, and finally examines briefly their relationship to Calvin and his legacy.

Medieval Cities. Modern culture is urban culture, centered in great cities, and scholars seeking the political, economic, and institutional origins of modern culture—the origins of liberalism, capitalism, and the state—have pursued them in medieval European towns. In their quest historians assumed that medieval cities were somehow separated from the society that encompassed them. In the countryside the peasants were unfree laborers, bound to their lords as serfs, with their lives constrained by limited technology and clouded by ignorance. Walls separated medieval towns from this feudal world and sheltered a free and politically active populace engaged in manufacturing and trade.

Research, however, has shown that this dichotomy between town and country simply distorts historical conditions. Medieval towns emerged primarily to accumulate and distribute agricultural surpluses. Gradually these "peasant markets" erected walls and became permanent centers of both trade and handicraft production in household workshops. Most central markets exchanged food and manufactures in limited regional networks. Cities, such as Florence and Augsburg, however, sheltered thousands of workers devoted to cloth production, a merchant elite with contacts in distant cities, and customers that included kings, but even these cities never lost their ties to the regional agricultural economy. Town walls never circumscribed zones of economic activity, for as many as one-fifth of urban residents engaged part-time in agriculture work, while rural craft production probably contributed as much to the volume of manufactured goods as urban workshops.

By 1500 town and country were integrated into a single economic system in which towns as market centers concentrated wealth and attracted the powerful, whether clerical or noble. Church spires dominated civic skylines, and universities were urban institutions that filled towns with a privileged and educated elite. Towns also housed the fiscal and judicial officials of seignorial and monarchical governance. Urban merchants furnished the noble and clerical residents with exotic goods transported via the intercity trading network. In the shadow of the churches, workshops employed families of crafts folk. Towns attracted the young, who came as servants or to learn a trade; the old, who came for medical care; and the poor, who came to beg. Urban societies were complex, highly stratified, and profoundly feudal.

Most medieval towns possessed charters that granted the politically active community (the citizenry) certain collective rights and privileges in their dealings with neighboring nobles and with the city's suzerain lord, whether bishop, ter-

ritorial prince, or king. By law no city was free of overlordship, but civic leaders exercised some autonomy, particularly during periods of external political disorder. Under these circumstances the citizens assumed responsibility for communal peace, and towns allied in leagues for collective self-defense. In Italy and Germany, where the central authorities had the most difficulty maintaining order, the towns became significant political players. Where royal power remained more consistently strong, as in England, the towns had fewer rights.

Medieval cities also nourished a participatory political culture grounded in elections and the ethos of public service. Municipal officials usually came from the city's wealthiest merchant or noble families, who served for life in the civic regime (*Regierung*). Though oligarchical, civic governments were not inherently oppressive; rather, intramural politics were conservative and grounded on the consensus that normal politics safeguarded peace, concord, and commonweal. It was also normal politics for the regime's opponents to protest and even riot when official behavior betrayed these communal norms. Citizens engaged in civic life not as individuals but as members of smaller corporate units, such as family, parish, neighborhood, or guild (craft association), through which they expressed and understood their membership in the civic community. The webbing of corporate memberships integrated and situated nearly everyone within the walls. Medieval corporations were metaphorically bodies with two possible structures: hierarchical or egalitarian. In hierarchical bodies members served preassigned roles and were governed by their "better parts," while in egalitarian corporations members shared equally. Most civic corporations were hierarchical, with members distinguished by gender, age, wealth, and other factors; moreover, given the medieval blending of spiritual and physical space, nearly all corporations clothed themselves in sacral language. In summary, medieval cities were integral parts of the political, economic, and religious fabric of feudal society, a society in crisis on the eve of the Reformation.

The Late Medieval Crisis. Late medieval towns faced economic and political pressures that were extremely disruptive to civic peace. In 1348–1349 the Black Death, a virulent form of bubonic plague, killed one-fourth to two-thirds of the population, depending on the locality, and the demographic impact shocked the European economic system. In 1348 the plague struck everywhere, but afterward it became essentially an urban disease. Rapid depopulation strained relations of production, accumulation, and distribution and concentrated the plague's economic impact on the towns. People died, but liquid wealth or available resources were unaffected, and soon institutional structures, inheritance patterns, systems of trade, and even the lord's ability to control the peasantry came under stress because their social foundations assumed a large population and limited resources. Meanwhile, the redistribution of wealth among the survivors benefited peasants and skilled artisans, whose labor was in demand. When feudal authorities reinforced traditional economic regulations, the commoners rebelled. In many cities the wealthier guildsmen gained a larger voice in civic government, and the decades immediately following the Black Death were perhaps a "golden age" for commoners, who had more disposable income, available land, and political leverage than in previous centuries.

As the fifteenth century progressed, however, conditions for peasants and artisans began to deteriorate. In many European cities artisan householders lost their economic cushion and became essentially working poor. Simultaneously, the civic elites distanced themselves from their poorer neighbors as the descendants of the fourteenth-century guild rebels intermarried with older elite families. Civic governance again became the prerogative of a small circle of oligarchs who, with the revival of Roman law, saw themselves as patricians maintaining order among their subjects.

Order was at a premium all over Europe in the fifteenth century. Chronic civil war ravaged England and France, while in Italy this was the age of despots and mercenaries. In the German-speaking lands, dynastic struggles over the imperial throne combined with the expansionist policies of the dukes of Burgundy in the Rhine Valley to disrupt peace and trade. In response, imperial cities formed defensive leagues, but larger armies and improved firearms made medieval civic fortifications obsolete. Other imperial princes also endeavored to integrate the imperial cities into their budding dynastic states. Adding to the political disorder, the church suffered decades of schism when two, then three, rival popes claimed spiritual authority over all Christendom. The expense of sustaining multiple courts and, after 1415, papal involvement in volatile Italian politics stimulated the church's fiscal appetite at a time when lay princes were undertaking the expensive first steps of state building. The princes found in the church a wealthy and privileged estate in need of closer lay supervision, while clergy and lay individuals with a stake in the old church resisted reform to protect vested interests. Earlier the plague had prompted increased pious donations and religious exercises among surviving commoners, but, as the economy soured, their poorer descendants grew frustrated with the cost of salvation and the real or imagined unholiness of its purveyors, the clergy. It was into this volatile mix of anticlericalism, social division, and shifting political power that the Reformation preachers brought their message.

The Early Evangelical Movement. In hindsight the division of medieval Christendom into several Christian churches appears to be the inevitable outcome of Martin Luther's dispute with Rome, but for the early reformers, their audiences, and their opponents, the impact of their actions was far from clear. Initially reformers attacked the old church along a broad, diffuse front and set against its practices their faith in the power of scripture alone to clarify proper Christian living. As printing presses disseminated biblical texts and preachers read and interpreted those texts to various audiences, the evangelical message inspired many with the faith that God granted salvation directly to them without privileged clerical intermediaries. The political and social potential of scripture's unassailable authority became clear when thousands of peasants and artisans rose in rebellion in 1524. Their defeat ended the first and radical phase of the evangelical movement, and in the wake of the Peasants' War some magistrates and princes defined themselves as Protestants and assumed greater control over reforming ecclesiastical institutions and practices.

Between 1517 and 1521 Martin Luther found his personal resolution of faith transformed into a debate over the future of the church. Luther was never a self-conscious urban reformer nor did his writings demonstrate sensitivity to urban political culture, but by 1522 he was actively engaged in instituting religious changes at the Saxon university town of Wittenberg, for which he wrote on Christian life under a new religious order built on scripture. His growing reputation ensured that these works were widely disseminated in print, while other reformers, inspired by Luther and emboldened by the church's slow response, carried the evangelical message to various urban pulpits. By 1523 more than a dozen Saxon towns had taken the first steps toward reform, and preachers and pamphlets had reached Nuremberg and Augsburg, from where the message quickly spread throughout the urban trading network along the river valleys of southern Germany and northward to the Baltic coast.

In city after city pamphlets brought the cry of "scripture alone" to the literate, and humanists were among the movement's earliest supporters. Meanwhile, preachers openly criticized ecclesiastical authorities before civic congregations, and pamphlets and broadsides desecrated the papacy and other traditional institutions. Most cities had endowed preacherships, and though some established preachers, such as Huldrych Zwingli, adopted the evangelical platform, more often reformers, such as Thomas Müntzer (d.1525), wandered about in search of a sympathetic following. Large city churches and open squares ensured a crowd, so towns attracted ambitious preachers, whose slogans juxtaposed the Christian community of faith against the "faithless" church. The preachers called on people from all walks of life to examine their faith. Townspeople became informed, converted, and then spoke out in self-righteousness, but in 1523–1524 there was a cacophony of inspired voices.

The evangelical message undermined the entire medieval ecclesiastical structure, and soon reformers attacked the civic clergy as a corrupt and privileged corporation. In Constance and Basel the reformers eventually drove out the resident bishops, but everywhere the demand that the clergy submit to civic law appealed to municipal officials, who were frustrated with the clergy's legal immunities. The reformers also called for churchmen to marry and join a guild. The duties of household and guild life would "domesticate" the clergy and integrate them into traditional urban community. Reformers and their guild supporters also hoped to bring undomesticated women, such as nuns, clerical concubines, and prostitutes, under the new moral order.

The evangelical reformers posited the authority of scripture alone against which all human constructions should be judged. Scripture proved an all-purpose yardstick and was soon invoked for various social and political grievances. Popular preachers eventually provoked confrontations, first with ecclesiastical officials but eventually with municipal authorities. Some cities expelled the preachers, while others tolerated the rival evangelists, who argued with one another, as well as with the established church. In many communities women openly preached and actively defended preachers, but women's public involvement demonstrated to male officials the disorder implicit in unregulated preaching.

Ultimately civic regimes had to resolve the religious controversy. Though patricians may have felt secure in the social foundation of their authority, their effective governance depended to some degree on popular assent. Municipal officials had not created the situation, but to preserve public peace they needed somehow to satisfy the evangelical faction (or risk internal unrest) and at the same time avoid external interference from neighboring powers committed to the old church. Meanwhile, they, too, wrestled with their own consciences. The short-term solution was to buy time with "scriptural mandates," which required all preachers to confine themselves to scripture. No party found these objectionable, but eventually regimes had to define appropriate scriptural preaching. If the evangelical party gained sufficient communal support, civic officials often stage-managed public disputations that "resolved" the issue in favor of reform, but the underlying mix of faith and social animosity remained unresolved.

The evangelical movement unleashed deep-seated resentment among citizens against patrician policies. In the northern German towns of Rostock and Lübeck, evangelized citizens organized special committees that inspected the regimes' fiscal records and correspondence, expelled patrician incumbents, and elected new officials from among the guildsmen. In the northeastern town of Hannover the entire oligarchy was expelled, and a new constitution formalized the coup. In southern Germany civic elections in the early 1520s became volatile affairs with new men entering formerly restricted branches of government, but constitutional changes were limited. Simultaneously in Swabia, the Upper Rhine Valley, Franconia, and Thuringia, the evangelical message had also reached the peasants, converted many, and aroused their anger against the social inequities ingrained in the hierarchical, privileged, and unholy clerical order. As in the late fourteenth century, urban and rural protest moved in concert, and the "Gospel of social unrest," which envisioned an egalitarian Christian corporate community, exploded in rebellion in the spring of 1524. The peasants found allies among the urban "peasants" and artisans, who opened their cities to rebel bands. The Peasants' War of 1524–1526 directly threatened the nobility in a way that urban disorder could not. Territorial lords gathered armies and bloodily crushed the peasants, whose defeat took the social steam out of the evangelical movement. The year 1525 was a critical juncture for many civic reformations. At Schwäbisch Gmünd and Wangen it ended budding evangelical movements, in other towns it delayed implementation, and nearly everywhere the threat of further unrest strengthened the hand of municipal authorities.

German Civic Reformations after 1525. Popular pressure had done much to drive the early reform movement, but the crushing defeat of the peasants drove the surviving radical evangelical leaders underground. After 1525 civic regimes regulated the pace and direction of the civic reformations, and their strategies must be understood as a reaction to the evangelical movement's unruly first phase. In Luther's writings civic leaders found an emphasis on human sinfulness and the need to submit to God's authority. By assuming control over the civic church, a regime sequestered divine authority in the name of civic law, and Nuremberg and many northern German cities turned to Luther early. Luther, however, offered no model for an orderly Christian civic community. Martin Bucer at Strasbourg and Zwingli at Zurich had such prototypes and sought to build them in their respective communities. Like most evangelicals, both had initially been inspired by Luther, but, unlike Luther, both were essentially urban reformers. As they set up their new order, they employed the vocabulary of corporate urban culture—the civic norms of peace, unity, and commonweal. In the wake of 1525, however, the image of the city as a sacral society or a gathered church had again become hierarchical, which comforted the civic elite.

Municipal authorities had begun haphazardly to abolish the medieval ecclesiastical order before 1525, but in the following decade they approached the process carefully and systematically. Both Luther and Zwingli spoke out in favor of caution, and old forms of worship faded slowly. Civic officials moved more aggressively against the privileged religious houses, though some effectively resisted dissolution. For example, the nuns of Saint Clara's convent at Nuremberg, who were members of wealthy Nuremberg families, were allowed to die out rather than disband, and at Ulm several houses survived because of the patronage of local patricians and nobles. Civic regimes confiscated and in some cases demolished church properties. These acts of iconoclasm desecrated paintings, statues, religious vessels, altars, and organs—everything that detracted from direct contact with scripture. Medieval Christianity focused heavily on the local spiritual power of objects and places, so iconoclasm cut at the core of the old faith. In the heady days before 1525, public image breaking often entailed disturbance of the peace, but in the 1530s riotous iconoclasm was rare in the German-speaking towns.

Having expelled the representatives of the old order, civic reformers and officials began to build a meaningful and politically viable new order. By 1530 the German evangelicals were called Protestants, but their common name masked divisive internal feuds, represented in the formulas of belief, or "confessions," compiled by the rival camp. Luther's supporters signed the Augsburg Confession, while Bucer rallied the south German towns of Strasbourg, Constance, Lindau, and Memmingen under the banner of the Tetrapolitan Confession and Swiss Protestant cities followed Zwingli's leadership. By requiring reformed ministers and public officials to swear adherence to these documents, civic regimes maintained the appearance of consensus, but securing public peace required tolerance and patience. The reformers now preached in defense of their confessional program and compiled catechisms to nurture the young in the official doctrines. Historians still debate over how many citizens believed or even understood the tenets of their civic church, but evidence from Strasbourg suggests both a significant degree of general knowledge and an underlying deviance down to the end of the sixteenth century.

In addition to defining proper faith, officials introduced "reformed" rituals to replace the medieval Mass with daily preaching services and occasional gatherings for the Lord's Supper. Except for isolated radicals, nearly all Protestants preserved some ritual reenactment of Jesus's last meal with his disciples. These Communion services brought the citizens together as a sacral community, and disputes between "Lutherans" and "Zwinglians" over the nature of Communion forced civic officials to choose confessional sides. Official control further included supervision over the Protestant ministers and the institution of civil replacements for the former ecclesiastical bodies of moral and social oversight, in particular the marriage court and the schools. Regimes took over the charitable functions of the medieval religious communities, including hospital care, the supervision of orphans, and poor relief. Gradually civic Protestant leaders constructed their new sacral society, one marked by hierarchy, respect for authority, and social discipline, which by century's end were the same social objectives pursued by their Catholic neighbors.

The Schmalkald War and the Interim. The expansion of Protestantism and Emperor Charles V's opposition to it threatened imperial peace, and soon imperial estates, both Catholic and Protestant, formed leagues for mutual self-defense. Beginning in 1531 Protestant cities rallied under the Protestant princes in the Schmalkald League. The cities' decision to join their traditional enemies, the princes, against their legal protector, the Catholic emperor, proved an insecure foundation for peace. The emperor and the princes eventually came to war, and the Schmalkald League was soundly defeated.

In 1548 the victorious emperor issued the Interim (The Imperial Clarification of Religion), which restored some Catholic religious houses in the Protestant cities, led to the exile of Bucer and other leading Protestant reformers, and rewrote several civic constitutions to secure offices for Catholic minorities and to undermine the guilds' electoral role. Charles V went so far as to forcibly re-Catholicize Constance and absorb it into Austria. Ultimately the emperor could not force re-Catholicization on all imperial estates, and in 1555 the Peace of Augsburg, signed by all imperial parties, legalized the Lutheran Augsburg Confession and granted territorial rulers, though not explicitly civic authorities, the right to determine the religion of their subjects. Their defeat in the Schmalkald War signaled the end of the cities as an independent force in imperial politics, and the Interim permanently altered their communal political base. In the 1520s the evangelical message had fit neatly into the religious and political aspirations of citizens, rich and poor. By midcentury political defeat was the legacy of civic religious change, and in many ways the urban Reformation was over.

Civic Reformations after 1555. After 1555 the Peace of Augsburg placed civic religious order under imperial law, which recognized only Lutheran and Catholic worship. The religious parties had drawn up clear confessional statements, and nearly all Protestant imperial cities signed Lutheran formulas. Given urban dependence on immigrants and the empire's mottled confessional landscape, nearly every community sheltered confessional minorities. In the south German "parity cities"—Dinkelsbühl, Biberach, Ravensburg, and mighty Augsburg, where both Lutherans and Catholics were legally recognized—imperial law safeguarded the rights of the two "sacral societies," which demonstrated the municipal regimes' inability effectively to secure peace. Though several regimes introduced Protestant worship after 1555 by claiming their "right" as rulers to reform their churches, none felt strong enough to expel the Catholic clergy, and confessional divisions plagued these late civic reformations. By the seventeenth century most cities sheltered officially recognized, or at least unofficially tolerated, religious minorities comprised of individuals or households either powerful enough to discourage meddling or powerless enough not to threaten the peace.

In the early seventeenth century confessional disputes continued to endanger the imperial peace and would eventually help trigger the Thirty Years' War, but in these instances cities such as Dinkelsbühl were victims of external confessional pressure. Civic economic ties to a hinterland, which often honored a different faith, required a degree of tolerance. The image of the sacral community might be confirmed every Sunday as civic householders gathered together to worship, but it only lightly covered social antagonisms, guild rivalries, personal animosity, and the distinct experiences of gender. Ultimately, given the circumstance of early modern demography and economics, no civic community could survive as an isolated sacral society.

The Urban Reformation and the Swiss Cities. Moeller suggested that the social and religious values fostered in the imperial urban Reformation passed through the early Swiss reformations to Calvin, who molded them into a dynamic, modern form of Protestantism and ensured their historical legacy. In the 1520s the Swiss Confederation was technically part of the empire, but its rural and urban communes had ousted their lords centuries before. The Swiss cities seldom participated in imperial assemblies, and their regimes had a freer hand in implementing religious change. Whereas scriptural preaching occurred in Basel, Bern, and Zurich by 1523, only Zurich broke with the old church before 1525. After 1525 Basel, Bern, Schaffhausen, and St. Gall gradually reformed, but Lucerne and other cities expelled the evangelicals and remained Catholic. By 1529 Catholic and Protestant camps developed, and the military confrontation that followed cost Zwingli his life. In 1531 the adversaries agreed to peace at Kappel. In Switzerland it was peasants and burghers and not the emperor and princes who stopped the spread of Protestantism.

After the Peace of Kappel Bern sent evangelical missionaries, such as Guillaume Farel (1489–1565), into its French-speaking rural territories. Their preaching brought the Protestant message to western Switzerland, where the episcopal city of Geneva became the hub of Protestant activity. Unlike other Swiss cities, Geneva still recognized political overlords, both its own bishop and the dukes of Savoy, and so, like many earlier civic reformations, religious reform and political autonomy were interwoven goals. To defend its fragile independence, Geneva became a Bernese protectorate in 1536 and accepted Bern's offer to send Farel to supervise religious reform. Farel brought in Calvin as a companion. The two reformers soon irritated Geneva's political leaders, and Calvin left for Strasbourg. His experience as a religious refugee, first from his native France and then from Geneva, molded Calvin's ecclesiology. Calvin developed a model for a community of worship that was self-sufficient and could survive under persecution or where it came to power, could remold political institutions in its interest. Calvin's dynamic sense of sacral society transcended the political and sacral space of any civic reformation. When he returned to Geneva in September 1541, his efforts to reform the city again met local resistance, and only in 1555 was his authority in Geneva unchallenged. This victory, however, was personally unimportant, for by that time he was waging a religious struggle in France, in other parts of Europe, and beyond. As Heiko Oberman has suggested, it is this international struggle over belief, not his civic reformation, that is Calvin's legacy to modern culture.

Conclusion. Early modern cities served as centers of economic production and exchange, as hubs of governance and administration, and as shelters for the propertied lords of the surrounding countryside. These complex communities offered the earliest and fullest opportunity for a broad-based and active response to the religious, social, and political challenges of the Reformation. Nevertheless, efforts to compile individual histories into a collective biography of the urban Reformation distort the historical events. Cities served as stages where the various conflicts associated with the Reformation took place, but urban society was so intimately integrated within the overall political, social, religious, and economic systems that it seems misplaced on an interpretive level to separate the urban Reformation experiences from the course of the overall historical experience. From the 1520s through 1555 the original evangelical message triggered religious reforms, civil war between social groups, and eventually a power struggle within the imperial estates. Cities played a part in each of those dramas but never a defining role. In the late sixteenth century and afterward, the narrow, crowded streets of walled towns remained centers for religious conflict, pressure points for religious indoctrination and social discipline, and seedbeds for nurturing modern Catholic, Lutheran, Calvinist, nonconformist, and secularist religious sentiments. In this sense the history of the Reformation in the cities continued into the eighteenth century as the Reformation's cultural and political steam gradually played out in ancien régime Europe. Nevertheless, throughout the early modern era, the histories of the civic reformations were only local examples of Europe's overall experiences.

BIBLIOGRAPHY

Abray, Lorna Jane. *The People's Reformation: Magistrates, Clergy, and Commons in Strasbourg, 1500–1598.* Ithaca, N.Y., 1985. Examines changing relations among citizens, civic regime, and Protestant ministers over century. Useful in considering reception of Reformation values by lay public.

Blickle, Peter. *The Communal Reformation.* Atlantic Highlands, N.J., 1992. Originally published in German as *Gemeindereformation,* Munich, 1985.

Brady, Thomas A. *Ruling Class, Regime, and Reformation at Strasbourg, 1520–1555.* Leiden, 1978. Critical study on the role of social conflict and class antagonism in a civic Reformation.

———. *Turning Swiss: Cities and Empire, 1450–1550.* Cambridge, 1985. Analysis of political context of the Reformation for the south German cities.

Cameron, Euan. *The European Reformation.* New York, 1991. Valuable and readable survey. Chapter 15 discusses cities.

De Vries, Jan. *European Urbanization, 1500–1800.* Cambridge, Mass., 1984. Explores economic interrelationships of cities. Written for a scholarly audience.

Greyerz, Kaspar von. *The Late City Reformation in Germany: The Case of Colmar, 1522–1628.* Wiesbaden, 1980.

Hohenberg, Paul M., and Lynn Hollen Lees. *The Making of Urban Europe, 1000–1950.* Cambridge, Mass., 1985. Helpful and accessible introduction.

Hsia, R. Po-Chia. *Society and Religion in Münster, 1535–1618.* New Haven and London, 1984.

———. *Social Discipline in the Reformation: Central Europe, 1550–1750.*

London and New York, 1989. Surveys literature on the long-term impact of the Reformation. Chapter 5 covers cities.

Hsia, R. Po-Chi, ed. *The German People and the Reformation.* Ithaca, N.Y., 1988. A valuable collection of essays by various authors concerned with the Reformation's social history.

Isenmann, Eberhard. *Die deutsche Stadt im Spätmittelalter, 1250–1500: Stadtgestalt, Recht, Stadtregiment, Kirche, Gesellschaft, Wirtschaft.* Stuttgart, 1988.

Langton, John, and Göran Höppe. *Town and Country in the Development of Early Modern Western Europe.* Norwich, England, 1983. Emphasizes urban and rural economic integration.

Moeller, Bernd. *Imperial Cities and the Reformation: Three Essays.* Translated and edited by H. C. Erik Midelfort and Mark Edwards, Jr. Philadelphia, 1972. Includes English translation of *Reichsstadt und Reformation*, Göttingen, 1962.

Oberman, Heiko A. "*Europa Afflicta*: The Reformation of the Refugees." *Archiv für Reformationsgeschichte* 83 (1992), 91–111. An excellent summary of his thesis.

Ozment, Steven E. *The Reformation in the Cities: The Appeal of Protestantism to Sixteenth-Century Germany and Switzerland.* Reprint, New Haven and London, 1980. Seeks to explain why the cities turned to the Reformation.

Roper, Lyndal. *The Holy Household: Women and Morals in Reformation Augsburg.* Oxford, 1989. Considers how gender variegated the urban reform experience.

Rublack, Hans Christoph. "Political and Social Norms in Urban Communities in the Holy Roman Empire." In *Religion, Politics and Social Protest: Three Studies on Early Modern Germany*, edited by Kaspar von Greyerz, pp. 24–60. London, 1984. A rich introduction into premodern urban values.

———. "Martin Luther and the Urban Social Experience." *Sixteenth Century Journal* 16 (Spring 1985), 15–32.

Schilling, Heinz. *Civic Calvinism in Northwestern Germany and the Netherlands: Sixteenth to Nineteenth Centuries.* Kirksville, Mo., 1991. A collection of essays.

Schmidt, Heinrich Richard. *Reichsstädte, Reich und Reformation: Korporative Religionspolitik, 1521–1529/30.* Stuttgart, 1986.

Scott, Tom. *Freiburg and the Breisgau: Town-Country Relations in the Age of Reformation and Peasants' War.* Oxford, 1986.

PETER G. WALLACE

CLARENBACH, Adolph (d. 1529), teacher and Protestant martyr. Born toward the end of the fifteenth century on the farm "Zum Busche" (in the parish of Lüttringhausen, near Lennep, duchy of Berg), Clarenbach was one of many children of a peasant family. Although academic training was not customary for his family, parents and friends made it possible for the alert youngster to receive a sound education. He first attended elementary school in Lennep. Until 1514 he studied in Münster, where he was influenced by the ideals of the Brothers of the Common Life and by humanist teachers. He then studied for three years as a member of the *Laurentianerburse* in Cologne under Johannes Reuchlin's bitter enemy, Arnold von Tongen, who would later become Clarenbach's judge. In 1517 Clarenbach earned the master of arts degree. Around 1520 he became a teacher at one of the three Latin grammar schools in Münster, where he was made assistant headmaster in 1523.

During these years he devoted himself to the Reformation, which he propagandized to the best of his ability, although he never was a cleric. Therefore, he was forced to leave Münster and in 1524 received a position as assistant headmaster at the municipal school in Wesel. Here, too, and in the neighboring town of Büderich, where the Lutheran-minded minister Hermann Boest held office, he conducted meetings in the spirit of the reform movement at which the former Franciscan monk Heinrich Verken and the Büderich vicar Johannes Klopreis were his assistants.

Permanent intrigues of the Franciscan monks of Wesel forced Clarenbach to leave this town. He moved to Osnabrück with a large number of students in 1526. In a private home belonging to a wealthy widow, he taught Latin, conducted Bible interpretations (especially of the books of the New Testament), and pleaded for a true life according to the gospels. These reformist discussions caused his expulsion by the powerful cathedral chapter of Osnabrück. He rejected a call to Meldorf (Dithmarschen). Shortly before Easter 1527 he moved with his students to Lennep. But even here, in his hometown, he had to face hostilities of the Catholics. In an open letter to the mayor of Lennep (1527), he defended his reformist conviction, attacked the major teachings of the Catholic church, and conveyed to the city council that the study of ancient languages was the key to understanding the Bible. Here, too, he was soon driven away, and he fled to his friend Klopreis in Büderich. When the latter was summoned before the ecclesiastical court in Cologne, Clarenbach accompanied him and took over his defense. This led to his arrest in April 1528.

While Klopreis was able to escape on New Year's Eve of 1529, Clarenbach was unable to do so. The Cologne Inquisition instituted a heresy trial against both him and Peter Fliesteden, also an adherent of the Reformation. This trial lasted eight months and ended on 4 March 1529 with the conviction of both. The sentence was not carried out immediately, however, since the authorities feared unrest among the people. The outbreak of an epidemic was taken as an occasion to stir up public opinion against both, and on 28 September 1529 he was burned at the stake in Melaten, near Cologne. Clarenbach, who no doubt saw himself as a Lutheran, had expressed common reform ideas that cannot be assigned to a distinct movement.

BIBLIOGRAPHY

Bluhm, A., ed. *Allein Gottes Wort: Vorträge, Aussprachen, Besinnungen anläßlich des 450. Todestages der Märtyrer Adolf Clarenbach und Peter Fliesteden.* Schriftenreihe des Vereins für Rheinische Kirchengeschichte 62. Cologne, 1981. Summary of scholarship. Lists old and new literature on Clarenbach, including numerous articles in reference works.

Kraft, C. *Die Geschichte der beiden Märtyrer der evangelischen Kirche*

Adolf Clarenbach und Peter Fliesteden. Elberfeld, 1886. Still the most comprehensive monograph.

SIGRID LOOß
Translated from German by Susan M. Sisler

CLASSIS refers to an assembly of neighbor churches in the Reformed church, held at regular intervals. The term, the plural of which is *classes*, is a direct loan word from classical latin, meaning "assembly"; it was not used in ecclesiastical Latin before 1537. It then occurred for the first time, in Switzerland, when the Synod of Lausanne decided to divide the churches in the Pays de Vaud, which were newly conquered by Bern, into six classes. These classes were assemblies of the ministers of the churches in a given region, held for maintaining and promoting unity and concord among the churches. In the French Reformed church such assemblies, which were called *colloques*, were held at least from 1558. In the next decade the *colloques* gradually developed into a part of the presbyterial-synodal church system. In 1572 this development was completed. The local churches were governed by the consistory, comprising ministers and lay elders. These consistories sent one minister and one elder to the *colloque*, the assembly of neighbor churches of a region. The *colloques* sent their representatives to the provincial synods, and the provincial synod to the general synod. In all these bodies ministers and elders together represented the churches. In the meantime the Dutch refugee churches in England and Germany had adopted the French model; here, however, the name *classis* was introduced, and this term was taken over in all other Reformed churches.

In France and in the Dutch Republic the classes played an important role in building the Reformed church. In France the Reformed church was always a minority in an essentially Catholic country. In the Dutch Republic the Reformed church was the officially recognized church, but nevertheless the old church and the Mennonites were formidable competitors. However, the main obstacle to the rapid growth of the Reformed church was the unwillingness of a large part of the population to commit itself to a church that required a solemn profession of faith. People were afraid of a "new Inquisition" and were unwilling to join the church. In both countries one of the church's weapons in the struggle for public favor was the building up of a strong organization; classes in France sought to defend the church's position, while those in the Dutch Republic sought to set the church's stamp on public life. In this respect the classis was the most important means of strengthening the church's influence in the countryside. In the Netherlands the classis influenced the civil authorities to promote church work and to provide village churches with necessary means.

Usually the region of a classis consisted of one or several important towns with their surrounding villages. In the Dutch Republic the Classis Dordrecht, with its fifty towns and villages and its thirty ministers, was the largest and, together with the Classis Amsterdam, the most influential. The classis met for three or four ordinary sessions of two or three days; extraordinary sessions of one or two days were rather frequent. The president and the other members of the governing board were either elected for a single meeting or appointed in rotation. In practice the ministers of the towns were the leaders of the church, and in the classis itself they dominated the governing board.

Among the main tasks of the classis were the organization of visitations of the churches and the discussion of visitation reports that could end in recommendations or measures to correct abuses. The visitation involved the doctrine and life of the ministers, elders, and deacons and all aspects of church work. The discussion of the reports in the meeting of the classis contributed to the unification of ecclesiastical life in all parishes. The classis also had the obligation to examine prospective ministers, who either had received their training at the universities or academies or had already worked as parish priests in the old church or as schoolmasters. The acts of the classes make it sufficiently clear that the classes had strict standards for admission to the ministry.

The weak side of the classical organization was the lack of a permanent body to handle business between meetings. In the Dutch Republic this problem was mitigated by the *deputati classis*, a committee whose members were elected by the classis to serve during the period between two classis meetings. The task and the authority of this committee were rather restricted: it had to carry out previous decisions of the classis, and in its handling of new issues it was to defer important questions to the next classis meeting. In actual fact the ministers of the main towns were members of the committee or were present at its meetings as advisers. Moreover the *deputati classis* were inclined to dispose of all new problems arising between two classis meetings. In spite of frequent protests by the classis against *deputati* exceeding their authority, this committee actually provided necessary continuity.

BIBLIOGRAPHY

Deursen, A. Th. van. *Bavianen en Slijkgeuzen. Kerk en kerkvolk ten tijde van Maurits en Oldebarnevelt.* Van Gorcum's Historische Bibliotheek 92. Assen, Netherlands, 1974. On the strong position of the classis in the republic.

Dooren, J. P. van, ed. *Classicale Acta 1573–1620.* Vol. 1. Rijks Geschiedkundige Publicatiën, Kleine Serie 49. The Hague, 1980.

Duke, Alastair, Gillian Lewis, and Andrew Petegree, eds. *Calvinism in Europe, 1540–1610: A Collection of Documents.* Manchester and New York, 1992. Important for the history of the Reformed church in the Netherlands and for the position of the classes.

Hoffmann, Hermann Edler von. *Das Kirchenverfassungsrecht der niederländischen Reformierten bis zum Beginne der Dordrechter National-*

synode von 1618/19. Leipzig, 1902. Important for its information on France.

Richard, Willy. *Untersuchungen zur Genesis der reformierten Kirchenterminologie der Westschweiz und Frankreichs mit besonderer Berücksichtigung der Namengebung.* Romanica Helvetica 57. Bern, 1959. On the origin and history of the terms *classis* and *colloque.*

Roelevink, J., ed. *Classicale Acta, 1573–1620.* Vol. 2. Rijks Geschiedkundige Publicatiën, Kleine Serie 68. The Hague, 1991.

Tukker, C. A. *De classis Dordrecht van 1573 tot 1609.* Leidse Historische Reeks 10. Leiden, 1965. On the history of the most important Dutch classis.

CORNELIS AUGUSTIJN

CLEMENT VII (born Giulio de' Medici; 1478–1534), pope from 1523 to 1534. The illegitimate son of Giuliano de' Medici and Antonia del Cittadino, Giulio traveled throughout Europe during his family's exile from Florence (1494–1512) and received appointment as archbishop of Florence from his cousin Giovanni (then Pope Leo X) in 1513. He was legitimized and made cardinal in the same year and exercised substantial governmental authority in the Papal States throughout Leo's reign (1513–1521) because of the latter's penchant for recreation rather than administration.

Giulio secured papal election in a six-week conclave noted for the obstinacy with which he defended his own candidacy. When he ascended the papal throne at the age of forty-five, it was amid the delight of the Roman people, who anticipated a long pontificate renewing the happiness and extravagance of the reign of Leo X. While parsimonious and indefatigable in work, his reputation as miserly is deserved only in comparison with Leo, as Clement gave considerable alms and patronized both artists (notably Raphael and Michelangelo) and large building projects in Rome.

During his nearly eleven-year pontificate, Clement focused attention on the familial, political concerns that interested him most, but with disastrous results. He procrastinated in decision making and wavered in self-doubt on decisions already made. How such a characteristic failed to manifest itself in his earlier administrative activity remains unexplained. The problem was nowhere more apparent than in his choice of political advisers, as the two upon whom he relied the most represented rival, contradictory positions in the Habsburg-Valois dispute over territories in Italy and elsewhere (Gian Matteo Giberti for the French position and Nicolas von Schönburg for the imperial). Clement entered an alliance with France in January 1525 out of fear of Holy Roman Emperor Charles V (r. 1519–1555), and that action, plus his participation in the so-called Holy League of Cognac (1526), set into motion the sequence of events (not to mention Charles's determination to take vengeance) that ultimately resulted in the Sack of Rome (1527). After the now infamous ransoms, tortures, murders, desecrations and pillaging that took place in those weeks that

followed 6 May 1527, Clement spent seven months in captivity at the hands of imperial forces in Castel Sant'Angelo. In 1529 the relationship between Clement and Charles was patched up, in part because of Clement's hope that through the emperor's help Florence might once again be ruled by his family. On 24 February 1530 Clement crowned Charles in the Bolognese cathedral of San Petronio.

Clement resumed administration of the papacy from locations in Orvieto and Viterbo before returning to a decimated, plague-ridden Rome in October 1528. There emaciated, sorrowful, and wearing the long beard he had grown in captivity, he exhorted curial cardinals to lead a more praiseworthy life as a chastisement for their sins. This admonishment—recommending the action as a punishment, not as a good in itself—reflects Clement's lack of action and direction in the matter of ecclesiastical reform. Many have argued that he was hindered from any such action by political necessity, but his own character affected this as well, for he was not an exemplary prelate, even in sixteenth-century terms—he said Mass only on principal feast days. Hopeful initiatives on reform took place during his reign, but he had little to do with them directly, despite his aversion to simony and his approbation of both the new Theatine order and the Capuchin reform movement. Protestant initiatives, about which he was notoriously ill-informed, gained strength throughout his pontificate. Some historians have lauded his apparent preference, against the opposition of the Curia Romana, for peaceful means in handling the growth of heresy. As late as September 1530 he was allegedly willing to grant Communion under both kinds and clerical marriage if Protestants would consent to give in on the other disputed issues. Still, he consistently objected to the convocation of a general council. On 11 July 1533 he issued the sentence of excommunication against Henry VIII after his divorce from Catherine of Aragon and remarriage to Anne Boleyn.

He became ill in the summer of 1534, as family problems, notably his nephew Ippolito de' Medici's desire to throw Alessandro de' Medici out of Florence, and the Turkish threat, exemplified by Khayr ad-Dīn's (Barbarossa) sack of Fondi, heated up. He died on 25 September. Although shaken like so many others by the sack, he failed to grasp its importance. He returned rapidly to the tangle of Medicean and Habsburg-Valois politics, and real ecclesiastical reform took place only under his successors.

BIBLIOGRAPHY

Caravale, Mario, and Alberto Caracciolo. *Lo Stato pontificio da Martino V a Pio IX.* Storia d'Italia, no. 14. Turin, 1978.

Chastel, André. *The Sack of Rome, 1527.* Translated by Beth Archer. Princeton, 1983. A reliable account of the most famous event in Clement's pontificate, originally delivered as the Mellon Lectures at the National Gallery, Washington, D.C., in 1977.

Müller, Gerhard. *Die römische Kurie und die Reformation 1523-1534.* Gütersloh, 1969. On Clement, the Curia, and the international and religious politics of the time. Includes a useful, brief appendix of documents.

Pastor, Ludwig. *The History of the Popes from the Close of the Middle Ages*. 3d ed., 40 vols. Saint Louis, 1938–1953. The second half of vol. 9 and all of vol. 10 remain the best extended study of Clement VII, and the only one in English. The work was originally published as *Geschichte der Päpste seit dem Ausgang des Mittelalters*, 21 vols., Freiburg, 1866–1938.

Reeves, Marjorie, ed. *Prophetic Rome in the High Renaissance Period*. Oxford, 1992. Several of the essays published here, especially those of Angus MacKay, Roberto Rusconi, and Marjorie Reeves, examine the context of Rome during Clement's rule.

Stinger, Charles L. *The Renaissance in Rome*. Bloomington, Ind., 1985.

WILLIAM V. HUDON

CLERGY. The Reformation was in its theology and practice largely a reform and redefinition of the clergy. By the early sixteenth century the Catholic clergy faced a caesura like those that had remade the clerical order repeatedly, most recently in the Gregorian reform and in the thirteenth century. Trapped in the procrustean bed of a ramshackled and venal structure that stifled the universally acknowledged need for reform, deeply divided within itself, confronting rising lay hostility, and facing the necessity of completely reevaluating the nature of Christian piety and their role within it, the Catholic clergy on the eve of the Reformation was poised for deep-reaching change. The theology of the Protestant reformers would remove many of the obstacles to reform, but it would also introduce remarkable new elements and would produce radical solutions that went beyond anything that the late medieval trajectory would have forecast. Nonetheless, the results of the Protestant and Catholic reformations with regard to the clergy show underlying similarities.

Late Middle Ages. The medieval Catholic clergy was defined narrowly by sacramental function and broadly by legal privilege. The inner core was constituted by the ordained clergy, all men, who had received one of the seven (according to the theologians) or nine (according to the canon lawyers) orders. These orders impressed an indelible character that marked the cleric into eternity and imparted to him certain specified sacramental powers. In the case of the essential order, that of the priesthood, the character enabled the priest to consecrate the Eucharist and to forgive sins in the sacrament of penance regardless of his own personal worthiness or sanctity. This official and objective sacrality also separated and elevated the cleric above the laity, creating a division that both enhanced the status of the clergy and made it the target of lay dissatisfaction. The gulf was further widened by the requirement that all in major orders (subdeacon, deacon, presbyter, and bishop) remain celibate. The clergy was also hedged about by their special legal status. They claimed immunity from secular taxation, exemption from military service and other civic duties, and the *privilegium fori,* the right to be tried in special clerical courts for criminal and some civil offenses. This "benefit of clergy" actually extended to groups beyond the ordained and produced the broader definition of the clergy. Included in this more amorphous categorization were monks, nuns (and other female religious), and simple tonsured clerics (one of the nine canon law orders excluded by the theologians). In England, since a simple literacy test established clerical status, anyone who could read might claim the "benefit." Leaving aside this last incalculable group, the clergy broadly defined probably formed 1.5 percent of the total population, though in some cities, such as Toulouse, it might have reached 15 percent. For Europe as a whole that meant approximately three-quarters of a million clerics.

Their numbers, combined with the wealth and political power that was the product of centuries of lay generosity, made the clergy a formidable legal and political estate. But it was a polity badly divided within itself. Alongside the secular clergy who staffed the parishes and cathedrals, there had developed the regular clergy, monks in holy orders who lived under a monastic rule (*regula*) and who were normally barred from holding pastoral office since it was viewed as incompatible with the separation from the world expected of the religious. But the new monks of the thirteenth century, the mendicant friars (Franciscans, Dominicans, Carmelites, and Augustinian Hermits), were co-opted by the papacy as an instrument of pastoral reform and given privileges to preach and dispense sacraments. This produced a running battle between the secular clergy and the friars for the souls and the financial support of the laity in the parishes. But even the traditional cloistered monks were viewed with hostility by the seculars. Monasteries were increasingly given permission to incorporate or impropriate parishes in the late Middle Ages. The monastery became the legal "pastor" of the parish, appropriated its revenues, and provided services through "hireling" priests, who received a modest stipend. In Scotland four-fifths of the parishes were incorporated. In Europe as a whole it may have been between a quarter and a third.

The monks, however, were not the only burden on the parish clergy. The benefice system that permitted monasteries to "own" parishes and that viewed the church office as property produced a veritable market in ecclesiastical positions. Nobles and middle-class clerics (many not even in major orders) invested heavily in church offices, accumulating numbers of incompatible posts that they proceeded to fill with ill-paid substitutes. This pluralism brought in its wake absenteeism. Approximately 25 percent of all parishes in England may have been held by absentees. One of the results was that, despite the wealth of the church as a whole, the distribution of the wealth within the clergy was very uneven. There were wealthy bishops and canons, a middle rank, and a clerical proletariat leading a hand-to-mouth existence. This reinforced a growing tension between the upper reaches of the hierarchy and the mass of parochial clergy. Episcopal taxation and episcopal disciplinary courts (which were often used as revenue devices) were particularly oppressive and resented by the lower and middle ranks of the clergy. The financial pressure from above reinforced the parish clergy's insistence upon the payment of tithes, fees, and traditional free-will offerings from their subjects. The resulting anticlericalism confronted a clerical solidarity that was badly eroded.

Perhaps the most fateful division was developing within the clerical identity itself, the product of a slow drift in the definition and function of the clergy. Although the causes are complex and reflect the virtual transformation that all of Christianity had experienced in the high and late Middle Ages, the new vision of the clergy was clearly a product of the universities. The late medieval clergy was the most educated that the church had ever seen. In England, which was precocious in this regard, 20 percent of parish clergy had attended university in the early fourteenth century. Germany reached an average of 40 percent in the decades preceding the Reformation. Complaints about clerical ignorance, often coming from university-trained clerics, were in many ways a product of the higher expectations of the age. The impact of scholastic theology and canon law, which was conveyed to the mass of the clerical population through numberless printed manuals, was to lower the threshold of sacrality surrounding the priesthood. In these late medieval manuals the cultic specialist of the early Middle Ages developed into a pastor, a preacher, and a professional counselor of souls. There was, in fact, an often explicit tension between the sacrament and the sermon, with the latter having the advantage. In reality, few eras have seen more preaching than the late Middle Ages. Signs of an incipient desacralization can also be seen in attitudes toward clerical celibacy. The hierarchy's insistence upon celibacy had found only imperfect and uneven acceptance in the late Middle Ages. Although clerical incontinence seems to have been statistically insignificant in Lincoln in the early sixteenth century, earlier visitations in the archdiocese of Prague (1379–1382) had produced charges of sexual misconduct against 42 percent of all parish priests. It is estimated that in Spain and Scandinavia 10 to 15 percent of all clerics were the illegitimate sons of priests. There were many in Holland and Switzerland, such as Desiderius Erasmus and Heinrich Bullinger, who were the offspring of enduring clerical marriages. Priests colluded in each others failings, and the hierarchy often turned a blind eye or, as happened in some German dioceses, exploited the situation by imposing an annual fine or tax on concubinous priests. Perhaps more importantly, some reformers had begun to question the theological and religious rationale underlying celibacy, as well as its practicality. Pope Pius II (r. 1458–1464) is reported to have favored the reinstitution of clerical marriage. These growing fissures within hierarchical structure and within the clerical soul itself made certain that some sort of reform would take place and help explain why so many Catholic priests either led or embraced the Protestant Reformation.

Luther. Martin Luther, with his customary boldness, laid an ax to the roots of the entire Catholic hierarchy. His doctrine of the "priesthood of all believers" effectively erased the sacral distinction of the clergy. All Christians are made priests through baptism; pastors or ministers (the single order, or office, that Luther recognized) are merely those individuals who for the sake of order in the church are chosen to exercise the common right to preach and dispense the sacraments. Ordination, which was retained by the Protestant churches, is the public conferring of those offices upon individuals; no indelible character or special sacramental potencies are conveyed. Luther also rejected clerical celibacy. Few if any Christian thinkers have waxed so eloquent about the joys of married life as did Luther, the adoring husband and loving father of a large family. Perhaps at least in part as a reaction to the Catholic practice, most Protestant churches so emphasized the right of clergy to marry that they made it a veritable duty. Unmarried clergy were viewed with grave suspicion by both church officials and congregations. Though women were not permitted to become pastors in Protestant churches until the twentieth century, the role of the pastor's wife unofficially assumed the status of a second church office of immense importance. In fact, the example of the pastor's family as a whole provided the model for Christian family life for Protestants.

Luther also redefined the function of the clergy. He eventually acknowledged only two of the seven Catholic sacraments, baptism and the Lord's Supper. Rejecting the Catholic teaching that the latter was a sacrifice offered by the priest to God for the congregation, Luther also refused the function and distinctive title of priest to the minister. For Luther the sacraments were the visible word, concrete parts of the proclamation of the gospel. It is in the preaching office that the Protestant tradition has seen the true locus of the ministry. These changes in the essence and function of the clergy were given expression in the physical appearance of the Protestant ministry. Late medieval Catholic priests had been tonsured and had been required to wear distinctive clothing at all times, as well as to don consecrated vestments during the liturgy. Luther and Huldrych Zwingli set the new pattern by adopting sober bourgeois attire both during services and in daily life and by rejecting the tonsure as superstitious.

Luther and the Protestant tradition leveled the sacral boundaries circumscribing the clergy. The new ministry that ruled the church from the eminence of the pulpit was a preaching clergy, and that meant a learned one. After the initial years of the Reformation, when a shortage of Protestant clerics opened the way for less-educated applicants, ministers of the main Protestant churches were almost invariably university trained. From being a sacred order and clerical estate, the ministry had become one of the learned professions. Their higher levels of education, however, did occasion some mutual incomprehension between pastors and congregations in rural parishes. There was also some grumbling about the cost of paying for an educated clergy and their families, but as a result of a new alliance of the clergy with the secular authorities, such support was legally enforced.

The Protestant critique of the Catholic hierarchy had effectively undermined the traditional governing structure of the church. Luther and other reformers had looked to the secular rulers as "emergency bishops" (*Notbischöfe*) to provide for order and the material support of the church. The result, in Lutheran lands, was the formation of territorial state churches (*Landeskirche*). The local ruler became the head of the church and was advised by a consistory of clerics and other princely servitors. Local overseers—superintendents—replaced the Catholic bishops. The church became a branch of government, and the clergy were absorbed into civil service and civil society. Clerical exemptions, immunities, and the benefit of clergy were abolished. Though the clergy still occupied a privileged position in an inegalitarian society, their legal status now approximated that of lay professional groups.

Other Protestants. Though Luther's theology formed the basis for all subsequent Protestant ministries, there were distinctive elements in other traditions. While the spiritualists tended to downplay the ministry altogether, the Anabaptists eventually established an unremunerated threefold ministry (bishop, preacher, and deacon) chosen from and by the male members of the congregation and ordained by laying on of hands. In the *Ordonnances ecclésiastique* (1541) Calvin established four offices—pastor, presbyter, teacher, and deacon—of which only the first was clearly clerical. In general the Reformed tradition carried the desacralizing thrust of the Protestant message much further than Luther. The diminished sacramental weight of the clergy, however, did not lead to a correspondingly diminished power and authority, since the Reformed ministry assumed greater responsibility in the area of discipline, one of the marks of the true church for the Reformed tradition. The Genevan consistory, composed of pastors and presbyters, became the model for control of religious, moral, and even civic behavior in Reformed communities throughout Europe. The alliance of church and state that was required was often an uneasy one since the Reformed tradition usually maintained a much higher sense of the autonomy of the church than did the Lutheran.

Though greatly influenced by the Reformed tradition, the Church of England remained much closer to the medieval Catholic vision of the clergy. The clergy were allowed to marry, though many (including Elizabeth I) found it distasteful, and a tradition of voluntary clerical celibacy remained among those who were high church. An ambiguous Protestant theology denied the sacrificial nature of the Eucharist, but Anglican ministers remained priests, however unclearly defined. The Anglican liturgy retained much that was Catholic, including some clerical vestments. This provoked controversy with the Puritan wing of the church, who rejected all vestiges of "popishness." But it was the episcopacy that drew the most sustained criticism of the Puritans. The English royalty had converted the Catholic church in England into an English national church with the monarch as its head but had retained its episcopal structure along with many of the courts, canon law, and legal privileges. Even the medieval benefice system was retained. All of this was anathema to the more thoroughgoing reformers, and especially after the conservative liturgical reforms put in place by Archbishop William Laud (1573–1645), the result was a certain schizophrenia in the nature of the clergy. High church ecclesiastics were in many ways quite similar to the Roman Catholic clergy in outlook and function and claimed to belong to the unbroken apostolic tradition of episcopal descent. Low church ministers, on the other hand, looked much like Calvinist pastors.

With the elimination in Protestant lands of the regular clergy, of the nonpastoral sinecures, of Mass priests who said only anniversary masses for the dead, and of minor orders (including the simple cleric), the number of clergy in those lands dropped by three-quarters or more. In the cities the effects were even more startling. In Lutheran Kitzingen, for example, the secular clergy alone shrunk from twelve to four. Geneva, which had hundreds of Catholic clerics in the early sixteenth century, had only nine Calvinist ministers in 1542 (it would rise to nineteen by 1564). The numerical decline of the Protestant clergy, combined with their diminished visibility, contributed greatly to the pace of secularization in succeeding centuries.

Counter-Reformation. The cataclysm that rocked the church in the sixteenth century did not leave the Catholic clergy unchanged. Although the Council of Trent reaffirmed the Catholic understanding of holy orders, the sacraments, and the hierarchy, it also recognized a significant shift concerning the function of the clergy. For the first time it enjoined regular preaching on Sundays and holy days for all parish clergy. The council also ordered the establishment of seminaries in every diocese, though it was not until the late seventeenth century that such seminaries became prevalent. In the interval the new religious orders of the Catholic Counter-Reformation—the Jesuits, Capuchins, and Theatines, among others—provided models of clerical training and effectiveness. Their emphasis on teaching, preaching, and spiritual direction embodied an aggressive outreach in which the clergy, still hedged about by a reemphasis upon celibacy, reestablished its preeminence in doctrine, the sacramental life of the church, and discipline. With their powers enhanced by Trent, a new breed of reform-minded model bishops, such as Carlo Borromeo of Milan, began the process of reforming the secular clergy along similar lines. As a result, the clergy retained its hegemony within the Roman Catholic church.

[*See also* Anticlericalism *and* Clerical Vestments.]

BIBLIOGRAPHY

Bowker, Margaret. *The Secular Clergy in the Diocese of Lincoln, 1495–1520.* Cambridge, 1968. A detailed look based upon diocesan archives.

Congar, Y. M. J. "Aspects ecclésiologiques de la querelle entre mendiants et séculiers dans la seconde moité du XIIe siècle et au début du XIVe." *Archives d'histoire doctrinale et littéraire du moyen âge* 28 (1961–1962), 35–158. Magisterial treatment of the medieval battle between the secular clergy and the mendicants; contains extensive bibliography.

Cowan, Ian B. "Vicarages and the Cure of Souls in Medieval Scotland." *Scottish Church History Society Records* 16 (1967), 111–127. An examination of the problem of impropriation or incorporation of parishes.

Delumeau, Jean. *Catholicism between Luther and Voltaire: A New View of the Counter-Reformation.* London, 1977. Translation of *Le catholicisme entre Luther et Voltaire*, Paris, 1971. Very rich bibliography and interesting chapters on the clergy.

Denzler, Georg. "Grundlinien der Zölibatsgeschichte vom Constanciense bis zum Tridentinum, 1414–1545." In *Von Konstanz nach Trient: Beiträge zur Geschichte der Kirche von den Reformkonzilien bis zum Tridentinum: Festgabe für August Fransen,* edited by Remigius Bäumer, pp. 343–362. Munich, 1972. A good review of the arguments for and against clerical celibacy in the years leading up to the Reformation.

Dickens, A. G. *The English Reformation.* 2d ed. University Park, Pa., 1991. A treasure trove of information about the pre-Reformation and early Reformaton clergy.

Evennett, H. Outram. *The Spirit of the Counter-Reformation.* Reprint, Notre Dame, Ind., 1975. A very useful overview of the changes ushered in by the Counter-Reformation.

Gabel, Leona C. *Benefit of Clergy in England in the Later Middle Ages.* Reprint, New York 1969. The best treatment in English of the *privilegium fori.*

Karant-Nunn, Susan. *Luther's Pastors: The Reformation in Ernestine Saxony.* Philadelphia, 1979. An invaluable look at sixteenth-century Lutheran clergy.

Kingdon, Robert M. "Was the Protestant Reformation a Revolution? The Case of Geneva." *Transition and Revolution: Problems and Issues of European Renaissance and Reformation History,* edited by Robert M. Kingdon, pp. 53–107. Minneapolis, 1974. An examination of the revolutionary impact of the Reformation on the clergy and the clerical state in Geneva.

McLaughlin, R. Emmet. "Universities, Scholasticism, and the Origins of the German Reformation." *History of Universities* 9 (1990), 1–43.

O'Day, Rosemary. *The English Clergy: The Emergence and Consolidation of a Profession, 1558–1642.* Leicester, 1979.

O'Day, Rosemary, and Felicity Heal, eds. *Continuity and Change: Personnel and Administration of the Church of England, 1500–1642.* Leicester, 1976. Valuable collection of articles on the status of the clergy.

Rapp, François. *Réformes et Réformation à Strasbourg: Église et sociéte dans le diocèse de Strasbourg, 1450–1525.* Paris, 1974. A remarkably detailed analysis of the clergy in the diocese of Strasbourg on the eve of the Reformation.

Schimmelpfennig, Bernhard. "Zölibat und der Lage der Priestersöhne vom 11. bis 14. Jahrhundert." *Historische Zeitschrift* 227 (1978), 1–44. Uses records of dispensations for illegitimacy to quantify success of church laws on clerical celibacy.

Stein, Wolfgang. *Die kirchliche Amt bei Luther.* Wiesbaden, 1974. A thorough examination of Luther's teaching on the clerical office.

Weyrauch, Erdmann. "Informationen zum Sozialprofil der evangelischen Geistlichkeit Kitzingens im 16. Jahrhundert." In *Die bürgerliche Elite der Stadt Kitzingen: Studien zur Sozial-und Wirtschaftsgeschichte einer landesherrlichen Stadt im 16. Jahrhundert,* edited by Ingrid Bátori and Ermann Weyrauch, pp. 291–312. Stuttgart, 1982. A statistical analysis of the Protestant clergy in Kitzingen.

Wisniowski, Eugeniusz. "Das Problem des Zölibats der Geistlichen in der Diözese Prag im XIV. Jahrhundert." In *Pascua Mediaevalia: Studien voor Prof. Dr. J. M. de Smet,* edited by Robrecht Lievens, Erik van Mingroot, and Werner Verbeke, pp. 172–180. Louvain, 1983.

Zijpp, N. van der. "Ministry." In *Mennonite Encyclopedia,* vol. 3, pp. 699–701. Hillsboro, Kans., 1957.

R. EMMET MCLAUGHLIN

CLERICAL VESTMENTS. In their efforts to restructure the liturgy the reformers dealt with the issue of traditional liturgical dress, and they established new criteria both in terms of theology and in practice. In order to put these changes into historical perspective, a brief glance back into the history of liturgical dress is necessary.

Liturgical vestments that distinguished the priest from the community are attested only from the fourth century onward. There are no guidelines or regulations given in the New Testament. Moreover, the early Christian communities did not place themselves in the tradition of the Old Testament priesthood and its cultic dress. The hierarchical structuring of the community was in the fact that the priest as presbyter took the first place in the liturgical assembly. All the participants in the liturgical celebration wore festive clothing.

As the customary everyday dress changed, the clergy held on to the old style of dress. This older form of dress was seen as fitting for the liturgy and served to distinguish the clergy from the other members of the community. The clergy thus came to be seen as a class. The priest was no longer seen as presiding over the celebration, but increasingly as a "cultic priest." In Rome as early as the sixth century it seems that there existed blessings for liturgical vestments. From the ninth century onward prayers were said as the vestments were put on.

Long before the Reformation criticism had been voiced concerning liturgical vestments. John Chrysostom (344/354–407), for example, rejected the use of luxurious vestments at the expense of caring for the poor. He asked how one could honor Christ in the liturgy in silk vestments while ignoring him on the street where he was perishing from the cold (*Commentary on Matthew,* Homily 50).

Liturgical vestments were given ever new allegorical interpretations reflecting salvation history (Rabanus Maurus [780–856] and Amalar of Metz [775–850]). These writers made connections between the individual vestments the virtues that were necessary for the priest, the role of the priest in the Eucharist as the representative of Christ, and the representation of the sufferings of Christ. Vestments were also interpreted from the standpoint of the Old Testament and the dress of the high priest.

Of the liturgical vestments that were in use in the fifteenth century, the following are of particular significance. The liturgical vestments worn underneath the others were the amice (a rectangular shoulder cloth that was tied into place with two bands and in the Roman rite was worn under the alb), the alb (a white liturgical vestment in the shape of a tunic that was worn by clerics of all levels of orders), the cincture (a belt to hold the alb in place), the rochette (an article of liturgical clothing used as choir dress; otherwise an article of extraliturgical clerical dress; a vestment with narrow sleeves that could be worn only by bishops and prelates and those who had special privileges), and the surplice (a short choir robe with wide sleeves that was worn for the administration of sacraments and public blessings).

The outer liturgical vestments included the chasuble (the outer vestment of the priest that varied in shape and design at different times in history and from one region to another), the dalmatic (originally a white outer vestment made of linen or wool with red trim on the sleeves and two stripes on the front and the back; the outer liturgical vestment of the deacon and part of the pontifical vestments of the bishop), the tunicle (a vestment related to the dalmatic that was narrower in cut and worn by the subdeacon), and the cope (an open choir cape, worn by bishops at synods and solemn processions, by priests on feast days when incensing the altar during Matins or at the magnificat during Vespers and when giving blessings, and by cantors when they sang at office).

As insignia, or signs of office, there were several items: the maniple (a decorated strip of cloth worn over the middle of the left forearm by subdeacons on up), the stole (a band of material worn by bishops and priests under the chasuble around the back of the neck and draped over the shoulders and hanging in the front, and worn by deacons as a sash draped over the left shoulder and joined at the right side), the pallium (worn by the pope, metropolitans, and archbishops; a ring-shaped wool stole with bands of material that draped in the front and the back, decorated with black crosses), and the rational (the corresponding emblem of bishops, worn over the chasuble and covering both shoulders).

The reformers dealt with the traditional vestments in very different ways. In the adiaphorist controversy Zwingli, Calvin, the Anabaptists, and Matthias Flacius Illyricus and his followers among other things called for doing away with liturgical vestments. As early as the first Zurich Disputation of 1523 Zwingli rejected liturgical vestments; he allowed for them in his work *De canone missae epicheiresis*, which appeared that same year; finally, toward the end of the year, presumably under external pressure, he adopted a stance against vestments. In the Zurich ecclesiastical regulations of 1535 he disapproved of external adornments such as silk, gold, and silver in the churches on the grounds that the early church not only did not possess these things, but even rejected them. The Swiss ecclesiastical regulations of 1566 also rejected any excess in vestments in religious services as a matter of confessing Reformed faith and based this on the idea that discipline, modesty, and fear were the proper attitudes before God (*Confessio et expositio simplex orthodoxae fidei*, 1566).

Martin Luther and his followers took an entirely different approach. Luther regarded vestments as being among the so-called "intermediate things," that is, those church customs that did not directly affect doctrine itself. In the *Formula Missae et Communionis pro Ecclesia Vuittembergensi* of 1523 he posed the question of the significance of liturgical vestments in the Mass. He permitted them to be used freely but preferred that excess and useless expense be avoided. Luther emphasized that the vestments, being externals, did not touch the essence of the Mass. The priest who wears liturgical vestments does not please God any more than one who does not. Accordingly, Luther rejected any blessings or consecrations of vestments that would create the impression that the vestments are sanctified objects (*Formula Missae*). Luther's tolerant attitude can also be seen in the *Deudsche Messe und ordnung gottis diensts* of 1526. Mass vestments could be used until they were worn out or until changes had been adopted. If someone wished to proceed otherwise, this was to be allowed (*Deudsche Messe*). In his *Brief an Georg Buchholzer*, dated 4 (5?) December 1539, Luther permitted complete freedom regarding the use of liturgical vestments as long as it did not become an abuse. Vestments neither add to nor subtract from the gospel. However, vestments may not be considered a necessity for salvation nor an obligation binding in conscience. Here there is no theological foundation either for or against liturgical vestments. Luther again stressed freedom of conscience and rejected any legislation on the matter.

Other reformers held similar positions, as shown by a letter of 27 September 1530 from Johannes Bugenhagen to M. Görlitz. Bugenhagen explains that chasubles may be worn without this being an irritation to those who hear the gospel. The assertion that the use of such vestments is forbidden is to him a "lie of the devil."

Between rejection and tolerance of vestments several other positions can be distinguished. In a number of places, although Mass vestments were rigorously rejected, people wanted to retain the alb as a liturgical vestment. In other places, in contrast, there was an attempt to retain as many of the vestments as possible. Often, as Gerhard Jüngst has shown, financial difficulties may have forced the young Protestant communities to dispose of some of their vestments. However, in such communities the vestments were then generally not considered to be superfluous. The role of the ecclesiastical hierarchy in the abolition and retention of liturgical vestments has still been insufficiently studied.

That Reformation doctrine also affected practice can be documented in many ways. Whereas in some areas the traditional vestments were quickly scaled down, in other areas vestments that were destroyed during the Thirty Years' War (1618–1648) along with other church property were later replaced. (As to the regional variations, see the examples given by Arthur Carl Piepkorn and by Jüngst, who discovered that retention of vestments was more common in areas that were far from ecclesiastical centers in Saxony and Württemberg.)

The alb and the chasuble continued to be used among Lutherans. In contrast, the stole was only seldom worn (there are examples from Sweden, Hungary, and Slovakia during the second half of the sixteenth century and the first half of the seventeenth century). There is evidence of only occasional use of the maniple (from Hungary and Slovakia). Evidently the liturgical outer vestments were retained in some places long after the Reformation, while the insignia were soon abolished.

Alongside the traditional vestments the mantle came into use. The mantle was a long black cloak that hung in folds and was often adorned with a fur piece. Luther is said to have preached in this garment for the first time on 9 October 1524. The mantle was actually an article of secular clothing that belonged to the wardrobe of scholars from the second half of the sixteenth century onward. The mantle was often combined with other vestments; thus the alb was often worn over it. With the mantle a ruff (a ruffled collar) was worn, which was in turn reduced to the Geneva band (two white linen strips that rested on the upper chest). A *barett* ("biretta") served as a head covering.

The emergence of the mantle in the liturgical realm has been variously interpreted. Some see it in terms of striving to enhance the solemnity of religious worship and interpret the use of middle-class clothing as an attempt to follow the tradition of the early church (see Merkel); others discern here an attempt to present the preacher as a scholar without wanting to express a distinction in rank with respect to other members of the community (see Bringemeier).

The attitude toward liturgical vestments in the Reformation developed in a multitude of directions and cannot be grasped in simple terms of either "decline" or "continuity." If it is possible to speak of any "continuity" at all, this only applies to the Lutherans, and even here regional differences can be observed. On the other hand, in the case of the Reformed churches, there was a break with tradition. In terms of the history of the liturgy it undoubtedly marks a significant breakthrough that the unquestionable status of liturgical vestments no longer prevailed. From then on vestments were considered as to their usefulness or their misuse. Moreover, the emergence of the mantle, a middle-class article of clothing, shows that liturgical vestments were no longer un-

derstood as clothing that marked the clergy as a separate class, but more as a kind of "work uniform."

[*See also* Clergy *and* Vestiarian Controversy.]

BIBLIOGRAPHY

Berger, Rupert. "Liturgische Gewänder und Insignien." In *Gestalt des Gottesdienstes*, pp. 309–346. Gottesdienst der Kirche 3. 2d ed. Regensburg, 1991. A history of liturgical vestments and the individual vestments; contemporary Roman Catholic practice.

Bringemeier, Martha. "Priester- und Gelehrtenkleidung: Ein Beitrag zur geistesgeschichtlichen Kostümforschung." *Rheinisch-Westfälische Zeitschrift für Volkskünde* 45 (1974), 197.

Braun, Joseph. *Die liturgische Gewandung im Occident und Orient: Nach Ursprung und Entwicklung. Verwendung und Symbolik* (1907). Reprint, Darmstadt, 1964. Standard work on the history of the liturgical vestments; numerous illustrations.

Cope, Gilbert. "Vestments." In *A Dictionary of Liturgy and Worship*, edited by J. G. Davies, pp. 365–383. London, 1972.

Graff, Paul. *Geschichte der Auflösung der alten gottesdienstlichen Formen in der evangelischen Kirche Deutschlands*. Göttingen, 1937. See vol. 1, pp. 106–109.

Hofhansl, Ernst. "Gewänder, Liturgische." In *Theologische Realenzyklopädie*, vol. 13, pp. 159–167. Berlin and New York, 1984. An overview of the development of liturgical vestments which deals in great detail with the Reformation. Bibliography.

Jüngst, Gerhard. "'Nimm hin das weiße Kleid . . .': Zur Frage des liturgischen Gewandes." *Jahrbuch für Liturgik und Hymnologie* 33 (1990–1991), 151–158. This work critically pursues earlier studies on the liturgical vestments in the Reformation.

Kranemann, Benedikt, "Kleidung, liturgische." In *Lexikon des Mittelalters*, vol. 5, pp. 1201–1203. On the history of liturgical vestments up to 1500.

Laurance, John D. "Vestments, Liturgical." In *The New Dictionary of Sacramental Worship*, edited by Peter E. Fink, pp. 1305–1314. Collegeville, Minn., 1990.

Lotz, Walter. *Das hochzeitliche Kleid: Zur Frage den liturgischen Gewänder im evangelischen Gottesdienst*. Kassel, 1949. A brief description of the attitude of the German Reformation to liturgical vestments.

Merkel, Friedemann. "Schwarz oder Heler? Zur Amtstracht evangelischer Pfarrer." In *Sagen, Hören, Loben: Studien zu Gottesdienst und Predigt*, pp. 205–217. Göttingen, 1992.

Norris, Herbert. *Church Vestments: Their Origin and Development*. London, 1949; New York, 1950. A thorough description of liturgical vestments; many illustrations.

Piepkorn, Arthur Carl. *Survival of the Historic Vestments in the Lutheran Church after 1555*. 2d ed. Saint Louis, 1958. Standard work on the liturgical vestments in the Lutheran church; also gives an insight into regional differences. Available in German translation.

Rietschel, Georg. *Lehrbuch der Liturgik* (1900). Edited by Paul Graff. Reprint, Göttingen, 1951. See vol. 1, pp. 121–127.

BENEDIKT KRANEMANN
Translated from German by Robert E. Shillenn

CLEVE. *See* Jülich-Cleve.

CLICHTOVE, Josse van (1472/73–1543), Flemish priest, humanist, and Catholic theologian. Born at Nieuwpoort, Flanders, he spent nearly all his life in France, where after 1488 he mingled with pious humanists in Paris and where he was first the disciple and then the principal collaborator of Jacques Lefèvre d'Étaples. Receiving a doctorate in theology in 1506, he recommended a return to the church fathers and to the authors who preceded scholasticism, many of whose works he edited and annotated. Through his sermons and publications, he encouraged the reform of religious orders. In *De laude monasticae religionis* (1513) he challenged Desiderius Erasmus, though he did not mention him by name. On intimate terms with reforming bishops (Georges d'Amboise; Guillaume Briçonnet; Étienne Poncher, bishop of Paris; Louis Guillard, bishop of Tournai and then of Chartres), he devoted his efforts to campaigning for the reform of the secular clergy. He participated actively in diocesan synods (Paris, 1515; Tournai, 1520; and Chartres, 1526), and he explained the liturgy in *Elucidatorium ecclesiasticum* (Paris, 1516; 2d ed. Basel, 1517). His *De vita et moribus sacerdotum* (1519) called for the acceptance of a new ideal for the priesthood, which later would inspire members of the Council of Trent. He defined the call to priesthood first in terms of the priest's role in the Eucharist and then in terms of his pastoral functions. By the eminent dignity of his position, the priest was a separated man, dedicated to the sacred and obliged to live like a monk. The reform of the whole church depended on the consideration of the priesthood and on the principle of "as the priests, so the faithful."

Up to 1521 Clichtove defended himself and Lefèvre d'Étaples against charges leveled by Parisian theologians; then he gave way. Luther had created a new situation. In Tournai at the beginning of 1520, Clichtove was amazed to discover how widely Luther's writings had been diffused. He immediately set himself to fight the "innovators," but he did so with judgment and moderation that distinguished him from his colleagues in the Faculty of Theology of Paris. He was the first prominent author in France to oppose Luther. In *Antilutherus* (1524) and *Propugnaculum Ecclesiae* (1526), he defended the hierarchical constitution of the church, its legislative and coercive powers, the sacrifice of the Mass, ecclesiastical celibacy, fasting, abstinence, and monastic vows. A scrupulous controversialist, he always quoted accurately and at length those parts of Luther's books that he intended to refute.

In 1527 he published *De sacramento Eucharistiae contra Oecolampadium* and in 1528 took a prominent part in the provincial council of Sens, held at Paris, the decrees of which he published with his own explanations. The last fifteen years of his life were spent at Chartres as a theological canon.

BIBLIOGRAPHY

Fabisch, Peter. "Judocus Clichtoveus, 1472–1543." In *Katholische Theologen der Reformationszeit*, edited by Erwin Iserloh, vol. 2, p. 82–91. Münster, 1985.

Farge, James K. *Biographical Register of Paris Doctors of Theology, 1500–1536*. Toronto, 1980.

————. *Orthodoxy and Reform in Early Reformation France: The Faculty of Theology of Paris, 1500–1543*. Studies in Medieval and Reformation Thought, vol. 22. Leiden, 1980.

Massaut, Jean-Pierre. *Josse Clichtove: L'humanisme et la réforme du clergé*. 2 vols. Bibliothèque de la Faculté de Philosophie et Lettres de l'Université de Liège, no. 183. Paris, 1968. Clichtove in his historical and spiritual context, especially before 1520.

————. "Josse Clichtove." In *Contemporaries of Erasmus: Biographical Register of the Renaissance and Reformation*, edited by Peter G. Bietenholz, vol. I, pp. 317–320. Toronto, 1985. Detailed bibliography.

————. "Thèmes ecclésiologiques dans les controverses antiluthériennes de Josse Clichtove: Ordre, pouvoir, hiérarchie." In *Les réformes: Enracinement socio-culturel*, edited by Bernard Chevalier and Robert Sauzet, pp. 327–335. Paris, 1985.

JEAN-PIERRE MASSAUT

COCHLAEUS, Johannes (Ger., Johann Dobneck; 1479–1552), German polemical theologian and the first Catholic biographer of Luther. Born in Wendelstein and educated under the auspices of his uncle, Cochlaeus (a toponymic) studied in Cologne (master of theology, 1507) and taught at the Latin school in Nuremberg, where he became a member of the humanistic circle of Willibald Pirckheimer. Accompanying Pirckheimer to Italy, Cochlaeus spent two years in Bologna studying law and moved to Ferrara to continue his theological studies; he received a doctorate in theology at Ferrara in 1517. There followed another two years in Rome, where he became a protegé of the Catholic reform movement and was ordained as a secular priest. He returned to Germany in 1519, having already heard about Luther. Although his initial attitude toward Luther was positive, by 1520 his view had changed, and in 1521 he was adviser to the Roman legate, Girolamo Aleander, at the Diet of Worms.

Although he was motivated by a purpose that never diminished in importance in his mind, Cochlaeus continued to live an itinerant life. In addition to participating in all the important German diets and colloquies, he lived in Frankfurt, Rome, Cologne, Dresden, Saint Victor (near Mainz), and Meissen, where he was court chaplain to George, duke of Saxony, and cathedral canon until the conversion of the territory in 1539. He spent the last thirteen years of his life in Vratislava (Breslau; Wrocław), where he is buried. Increasing bitterness about what he saw as his secondary place in the Catholic opposition to Luther may account for the increasing vehemence of his works over time. Little is known about his work as a pastor or his personality, and thus we cannot know why his career took the path that it did. His surviving letters show a man concerned about his status who zealously curried favor with the powerful. Despite such efforts, Cochlaeus's inability to participate in the Council of Trent, as well as his failure to have his works printed in a collected edition, led him to feel slighted by his contemporaries. Nevertheless, he was regarded as one of the leading members of the movement in Germany, his works were widely read, and some of his writings made a lasting impact on the Catholic view of the Reformation.

The judgment of scholars that Cochlaeus was among the most conservative of the opponents of the Reformation is indisputable. On the causes of such a reaction, however, there is less agreement. Depending upon which texts of Cochlaeus one reads, he is defending either the papacy, the integrity of the dogmatic system held by the church, the Catholic church in Germany, or the German people. The first three of these had come under attack from the reformers and thus were open questions to be defended by a Catholic theologian. The fourth is a theme in Cochlaeus's work related to the idea that heresy is seditious by nature, a concept he put to work in his appeals to secular nobility to eradicate Protestantism for the sake of the people.

For Cochlaeus the Reformation was primarily the work of Luther. Although he wrote against other reformers, a central theme in all of his controversial writings is that the origins of the new religious movement were to be found in the flawed thought of Luther, the principal flaw of which, according to Cochlaeus, was inconsistency. Cochlaeus attacked Luther's developing thought synchronically in order to accuse him, on account of differences in wording, of being in contradiction with himself. Cochlaeus felt that such a lack of systematic coherence in Luther invalidated the principles on which the Reformation was based. By contrast, Cochlaeus's works continually emphasized the unity and coherence of Catholic teaching, and lists of his contemporaries are no less numerous than are the lists of traditional authorities.

His works against other Protestants also focus on the difference between uniformity and diversity. Where discrepancies within the works of a single author are found, Cochlaeus exploits them for the sake of discrediting the integrity of his opponent's thought. Where the opponent seems to be disagreeing with Luther, then that disagreement is used to demonstrate the confusion of the Reformation as a whole. Cochlaeus holds firmly to the idea that inconsistency is a defining characteristic of heresy. Finally, in all his works of controversy Cochlaeus points out disagreements with traditional church teaching, arguing that the development of the tradition and even the personal sanctity of authoritative figures in the Catholic church attest to the validity of Catholic doctrine. Protestants, by contrast, are few in number, hark back mistakenly to apostolic and patristic authorities that only seem to corroborate their doctrines, and are led by married former clergy.

These points of emphasis make it clear that Cochlaeus's polemical strategy is a combination of historical, theological, and even personal arguments. Of the personal side little need be said: whether one finds in Cochlaeus's comments about married former priests puritanical shrillness or justifiable indignation at the breaking of vows is largely a matter

of the reader's own beliefs and sympathies. Theologically, the connection of heresy with novelty, as well as his insistence that he was defending what was unanimously held by all the faithful, prevented Cochlaeus from being an original thinker. What is distinctive about Cochlaeus's work, therefore, is the historical aspect of his argumentation: the emphasis that he places upon the continuity of the Catholic church and its tradition. What Cochlaeus defends and the way in which he defends it are closely linked.

Although Cochlaeus may have wished for more prominence in his own day, his influence was considerable both then and since. As A. Herte demonstrated, Cochlaeus was responsible for discrediting Luther and for creating the impression, still found among some Catholics, that Luther was too inconsistent, even evil, to have accomplished anything beneficial for the church. Even if his work lacked the originality that would have assured him a place in the history of Christian thought, Cochlaeus was prolific enough to give substantial weight to the anti-Protestant response in Germany, and his importance for that reason cannot be denied.

BIBLIOGRAPHY

Primary Sources

Cochlaeus, Johannes. *Adversus cucullatum Wittenbergensem: De sacramentorum gratia iterurm, 1523.* Edited by Joseph Schweizer. Münster, 1920. Valuable as an example of Cochlaeus's methods.

——. *Brevis Germaniae descriptio, 1512.* 3d ed. Edited by Karl Langosch. Darmstadt, 1976. Geographical work from Cochlaeus's humanistic period.

Friedensburg, Walter. "Beiträge zum Briefwechsel der katholischen Gelehrten Deutschlands im Reformationszeitalter." *Zeitschrift für Kirchengeschichte* 18 (1898), 106–131, 233–297, 420–463, 596–636. Greatest volume of Cochlaeus's surviving correspondence, most of it with Italian churchmen.

Keen, Ralph, ed. and trans. *Responsio ad Johannem Bugenhagium Pomeranum.* Nieuwkoop, 1988.

Secondary Sources

Bagchi, David V. N. *Luther's Earliest Opponents: Catholic Controversialists, 1518–1525.* Minneapolis, 1991. Cochlaeus and other theologians on the question of authority, very thoroughly investigated.

Bäumer, Remigius. *Johannes Cochlaeus, 1479–1522: Leben und Werk im Dienst der katholischen Reform.* Münster, 1980. Updating of Spahn's biography, and a positive appraisal of Cochlaeus's work.

Herte, Adolf. *Die Lutherkommentare des Johannes Cochläus.* Münster, 1935. Thorough analysis of Cochlaeus's sources and methods in the 1549 *Commentary on the Life of Luther.*

Jedin, Hubert. *Des Johannes Cochlaeus Streitschrift de libero arbitrio hominis, 1535: Ein Beitrag zur Geschichte der vortridentinischen katholischen Theologie.* Breslau, 1927.

Keen, Ralph. "The Arguments and Audiences of Cochlaeus's *Philippica VII.*" *Catholic Historical Review* 78 (1992), 371–394.

Pfnür, Vinzenz. *Einig in der Rechtfertigungslehre?* Wiesbaden, 1970. Analysis of theological differences between Catholics and Protestants, based in part on Cochlaeus's refutation of the Augsburg Confession.

Samuel-Scheyder, Monique. *Johannes Cochlaeus: Humaniste et adversaire de Luther.* Nancy, France, 1993. Comprehensive analysis of Cochlaeus's thought.

Spahn, Martin. *Johannes Cochläus: Ein Lebensbild aus der Zeit der Kirchenspaltung* (1898). Reprint, Nieuwkoop, 1964. Bibliography, pp. 341–372, is especially valuable.

RALPH KEEN

COINS.

The impact of the Reformation on various types of visual media (woodcuts, paintings, altarpieces, and medals) was enormous. In turn the role played by these media in the dissemination of doctrine and propaganda was not only profound but is also an area of Reformation studies that has attracted much attention since the 1980s. On only a few occasions, however, has medallic art, defined as medals and coins produced and issued privately and publicly, been employed as a source. This represents no failure on the part of medallic art, however, to qualify as a form of image. The motifs and symbols were, in effect, images, as were the medals and coins themselves. The political and religious imagery depicted on the medallic art pieces conveyed symbolic messages universally recognized by the Christian community, Catholic and Protestant.

The Reformation period witnessed the issuance of a great variety and number of coins and medals, particularly in Lutheran states in Germany. By contrast, their production and use in other Protestant areas (non-Lutheran Germany, Switzerland, Sweden, England, and the Netherlands) by Lutherans, Calvinists, Zwinglians, Anabaptists, and Anglicans was markedly less. And the Catholic Reformation apparently made little use of medals and coins, either to combat Protestant propaganda or to clarify and restate its position.

Lutherans used medallic pieces for sundry reasons: commemorative, instructional, and propagandistic. For example, the death of Luther and the centenary of the Reformation in 1617, the Ausgburg Confession in 1630, and the conversion of Regensburg to Lutheranism in 1642 were all celebrated with coins (ducats and talers) and medals. In addition to Luther, Philipp Melanchthon, Frederick III of Saxony, John George, duke of Saxony, and Gustavus Adolphus were depicted often on medallic art pieces. Lutherans also produced a number of medals for instruction in doctrine. Most notable are a 1528 *pesstaler* depicting the brazen serpent on the obverse and some 1617 medals and *reichstalers* showing the removal of the bushel measure, with a lighted candle on the obverse. Luther interpreted these two symbolic devices to signify that justification by faith is a free gift revealed in the word of God. These examples clearly demonstrate the retention by Protestants, through adoption and adaptation, of pre-Reformation images and symbols. While instructional and commemorative medallic pieces represented a form of propaganda, there were satirical medals in which the inversion motif (pope/devil, cardinal/fool) was used effectively for propaganda purposes.

It is worth noting that nearly all such coins and medals had inscriptions that often verbalized Reformation polemics or doctrine. The short slogans clarified, reaffirmed, and highlighted the pictorial representations. That medallic art was affected by the religious upheaval of the period is attested by the large number of coins and medals produced and their continued use well beyond the Reformation era, especially by the Lutheran church.

BIBLIOGRAPHY

Barnard, Francis Pierrepont. *Satirical and Controversial Medals of the Reformation: The Biceps or Double-Headed Series.* Oxford, 1927. Most comprehensive work on satirical medals of the Reformation; interpretive and well illustrated.

Habich, Georg. *Die Deutschen Schaumünzen des XVI. Jahrhunderts.* 5 vols. Munich, 1929–1934. Excellent illustrations and superb commentary on sixteenth-century medalists and portraiture medals, a good number of which are Reformation related.

Juncker, Christian. *Das Guldene und Silberne Ehren-Gedächtniss des Theuren Gottes-Lehrers D. Martini Lutheri.* Frankfurt a.M., 1706. Reprinted with an introduction by Herbert Rittmann under the title *Die Geschichte der Reformation in Münzen und Medaillen bis zum Jahre 1706,* Karlsruhe, 1982. Most comprehensive compilation and study of Reformation medals, particularly strong on Luther and the Reformation in Germany. Well illustrated. Work is not definitive, however; needs to be supplemented with other sources.

Kreussler, Heinrich Gottlieb. *D. Martin Luthers Andenken in Münzen (Iubel-Münzen) nebst Lebensbeschreibungen merkwürdiger Zeitgenossen desselben.* Leipzig, 1818. Illustrated with plates of engravings of medallic pieces through the tercentenary of the Reformation. Some narrative but not nearly as informative as Juncker.

Schnell, Hugo. *Martin Luther und die Reformation auf Münzen und Medaillen.* Munich, 1983. Comprehensive display and description of photographs of Reformation coins and medals by subject, event, and historical period, from the early Reformation through 1983. Weak on interpretation but has thorough bibliography.

Tentzel, Wilhelm Ernst. *Saxonia Numismatics oder Medaillen-Cabinet von Gedächtnismünzen und Schaupfennigen welche die Chur- und Fürsten der Albertinischen Linie und Ernestinischen Linie haben prägen und verfertigen lassen.* 6 vols. 1705, 1713, 1714; reprint, Berlin, 1981. Strong on Saxon coins and medals of the Reformation. Illustrated engraved plates. Good historical background of medallic pieces in both German and Latin.

THURMAN L. SMITH

COLET, John

(1467–1519), dean of Saint Paul's; founder of Saint Paul's School, London; and writer on biblical and related subjects. Oldest of twenty-two children, Colet survived all his siblings and inherited his father's large estate in 1505. He studied divinity and ecclesiastical law in Italy (1496–1499) and returned to complete a doctorate in divinity at Oxford in 1504 or 1505. Thanks to his family's connections with Henry VII he was promptly made dean of Saint Paul's, London (June 1505). There the wealthy young dean soon made himself known as a forceful preacher who denounced the vices of the age.

Colet soon concluded that preaching to adults was of limited use. Real moral reform would have to begin with the rising generation of as yet unspoiled children. He decided to put the greater part of his fortune into refounding the existing but insignificant Saint Paul's School as a major foundation whose purpose was "the instruction of boys in the faith of Christ" and "in good literature." Its curriculum was conservative, with emphasis on Christian writers. Little or no room was found for Greek in the curriculum until Desiderius Erasmus's Greek New Testament of 1516 showed that Greek was indispensable for interpretation of the Bible. Colet himself never learned Greek.

The real novelties in Colet's school were administrative and practical. The headmaster was exceptionally well paid, for this was the only way to attract and keep good men. Colet also commissioned new textbooks, including Erasmus's highly successful *De duplici copia verborum ac rerum,* whose twin goals were to enlarge the pupils' means of expressing their ideas and to increase the number of ideas they had to express. Colet's own contributions were a brief introduction to the eight parts of speech, called *Aeditio,* and a five-page catechism in English.

Educational writings apart, Colet published during his lifetime only one work, a convocation sermon delivered in Latin in January 1510 (not 1512, as used to be thought). It contains a fiery catalog of existing abuses that has made the sermon famous, but those who heard it were not offended.

His other writings, all in decidedly non-classical Latin, remained in manuscript until mid-Victorian times. These include highly individual scriptural commentaries, especially on *Romans* and *1 Corinthians;* his personal reading of the *Hierarchies* of Pseudo-Dionysius the Areopagite (which Colet thought genuine); and Colet's only longer work that is not a commentary, a treatise, *On the Sacraments.* Victorian scholars contended that in his scriptural commentaries Colet showed himself the first Englishman to interpret scriptural writings against their historical setting, but this view now has to be abandoned. The commentaries themselves, when read attentively, make clear that Colet thought successful exegesis depended on one's being "spiritual," not on one's scholarship. Illuminated by prayer, the exegete "digs out" eternal spiritual principles from the text.

His method is illustrated by a letter written while he was giving his well-attended lectures on Paul's epistles at Oxford (from 1496 to at least 1499, perhaps as late as 1504). The letter was not made available in English until 1989, but it shows how Colet's "spiritual" method worked. The other extant document from the period of the Oxford lectures is a *Disputatiuncula* with Erasmus, then visiting Oxford, concerning the reasons for Christ's dread of his passion. Colet gives the problem an inflexibly spiritual answer that ignores counter-evidence, but Erasmus uses his patristic learning and skill in rhetorical analysis to undercut Colet's case. Erasmus published the whole debate (1503).

The treatise *On the Sacraments,* strongly influenced by Pseudo-Dionysius, describes angelic spirits who seek to bring humans to God through the three Dionysian steps of purging, illumining, and finally perfecting them in the spirit. Equally pronounced is the Franciscan tradition in which the felt presence of God in the soul is the dynamic source for the attainment of truth. Colet shows how the sacraments strengthen the spiritual element in humans' dual nature and thereby bring them back to their true home. The central sacrament is matrimony, which Colet identifies with the sacrament of orders, and Christ is the bridegroom who fecundates humankind, his wife, with "righteousness."

In Colet's later years he was increasingly drawn into ecclesiastical politics and the royal service. He became a member of the Royal Council, sat in judgment on Lollard heretics, and furthered the policies of Cardinal Thomas Wolsey. Colet's life was described in a long letter (published 1521) by his old friend Erasmus, who showed himself a judicious admirer of the zealous dean.

BIBLIOGRAPHY

Primary Source

Colet, John. *Opera.* 4 vols. Ridgewood, N.J., 1965.

Secondary Sources

Gleason, John B. *John Colet.* Berkeley, 1989. The standard treatment. Includes bibliography of Colet's writings and extensive listing of secondary literature.

Knight, Samuel. *The Life of Dr. John Colet, Dean of St. Paul's.* New ed. Oxford, 1823. Contains a useful appendix of documents bearing on Colet's life.

Lupton, Joseph H. *A Life of John Colet, D.D.* (2d ed., 1909). Reprint, Hamden, Conn., 1961. Contains a useful appendix of documents relating to Saint Paul's School.

JOHN B. GLEASON

COLIGNY, Gaspard II de (1519–1572), admiral of France, the Huguenot leader whose attempted assassination was instrumental in touching off the Saint Bartholomew's Day Massacre. The second son of Gaspard I de Coligny, marshal of France, and Louise de Montmorency, Gaspard II de Coligny benefited from his family's powerful connections at the French court. Along with his brothers Odet (1517–1571) and François d'Andelot (1521–1569), he enjoyed the special protection of his uncle Anne de Montmorency, constable of France, after his father's death in 1522. He took up the military career expected of a nobleman of his lineage and fought in the Italian Wars. Knighted at Cérisoles in 1547, he received the office of colonel general of the infantry from King Henry II that same year. He subsequently took part in the campaign to retake Boulogne from the English and was active in the French theater of the Habsburg-Valois wars. In November 1552 he was named admiral of France, an honorific position that, in the sixteenth century, did not entail the command of maritime forces.

Made governor of Picardy in 1555, Coligny served as chief of the French delegation for the Treaty of Vaucelles

(February 1556). When war broke out again in 1557, Constable Montmorency sent him in with eight hundred men to defend the key outpost of Saint-Quentin. The duke of Savoy turned his whole army against Saint-Quentin, and the French army was dealt a disastrous defeat (10 August 1557). Although Coligny's personal role in these events was a valiant one, he suffered both the privations of imprisonment and the humiliation of being accused, along with his uncle, of incompetence and even betrayal for his failure to defend the northern frontier.

Little is known about Coligny's conversion to Protestantism. He is thought to have become amenable to conversion during the two years he spent as a prisoner after Saint-Quentin. His brother d'Andelot sent evangelical books, and a letter written by Calvin in September 1558 suggests that Coligny was receptive to the reform but not yet a believer. The English ambassador noted Coligny's failure to attend Mass in May 1559, but his first overt adherence to the Reformed church came in January 1561, when he had his son baptized by a Calvinist minister. Already in August 1560, at the Assembly of Fontainebleau, however, he had presented the king a petition on behalf of the Protestants of Normandy, and he gradually moved closer to the Huguenot leadership, while using his good relations at court to try to mediate an increasingly tense situation.

He left court after the Massacre of Wassy (March 1562) and, after some final hesitations, joined the Huguenot army assembling at Orléans. Named lieutenant general under Louis, prince of Condé, he took a leading part in the Huguenots' military campaigns, while continuing in Huguenot councils to urge moderation and negotiation. Accused of complicity in the assassination of François, duke of Guise (March 1563), he formally protested his innocence, but antagonism with the Guises remained acute. After Condé's death at Jarnac (March 1569), Coligny assumed command of the Huguenot army.

Following the Peace of Saint-Germain (August 1570), Coligny responded to King Charles IX's overtures by returning briefly to court, and he used the king's apparent goodwill to urge strict enforcement of the peace and to try to gain support for a war against Spain in the Netherlands. This issue caused tensions with Catherine de Médicis and the Guises, and Coligny retired to his estates, returning to court only in the summer of 1572. Historians disagree about how committed Coligny was to the Netherlands war, how much support Charles IX gave the plan, and what precise role this project played in events that followed. They generally agree, however, in identifying Coligny's advocacy of the project as a key reason that agents of one of his enemies (identified variously as Catherine de Médicis, the Guises, or King Philip II of Spain) wounded him in an assassination attempt on 22 August 1572. The angry response of Huguenot leaders, gathered in Paris for the marriage of Henry of Navarre (Henry IV) to Marguerite of France, raised tensions in the capital to the boiling point and pushed King Charles to the desperate order to assassinate the Huguenot leadership that touched off the Saint Bartholomew's Day Massacre on 24 August 1572. The first to die in the massacre was Coligny, killed by a party of soldiers led by the duke of Guise.

BIBLIOGRAPHY

Crété, Liliane. *Coligny*. Paris, 1985. The most recent French biography; too much dependence on old hagiography and too little new research.

Delaborde, Jules. *Gaspard de Coligny*. 3 vols. Paris, 1879. Still the standard biography; reproduces many documents, but gives little analysis of Coligny's beliefs and motives.

Haag, Eugène, and Emile Haag. *La France protestante*. 2d ed., vol. 4, cols. 152–159, edited by Henri Bordier. Paris, 1884. Incorporates much of the hagiography produced by early biographers, but solid on the basic events and dates.

Kingdon, Robert M. *Myths about the Saint Bartholomew's Day Massacres, 1572–1576*. Cambridge, Mass., and London, 1988. Chapter 2, "The Hero," contains a good analysis of the hagiographical literature on Coligny.

Roelker, Nancy Lyman, "Family, Faith, and *Fortuna*: The Châtillon Brothers in the French Reformation." In *Leaders of the Reformation*, edited by Richard L. DeMolen, pp. 247–277. London and Toronto, 1984. A good summary of recent research on Coligny and his brothers.

Shimizu, J. *Conflict of Loyalties: Politics and Religion in the Career of Gaspard de Coligny, Admiral of France, 1519–1572*. Geneva, 1970. The best recent work in English; good analysis of Coligny's political motives. Prone to underrate the importance of religion, but a good corrective to Protestant hagiography.

Sutherland, N. M. *The Massacre of St. Bartholomew and the European Conflict, 1559–1572*. New York, 1973. A convincing revision of the role of Catherine de Médicis with respect to the Saint Bartholomew's Day Massacre; also good on the international situation and its meaning for the Huguenots.

———. *The Huguenot Struggle for Recognition*. New Haven, 1980. A study of shifting royal policy with regard to the Huguenots; provides important context for understanding Coligny's role in the religious conflicts.

BARBARA B. DIEFENDORF

COLIGNY, Odet de (1517–1571), cardinal of Châtillon, often called "the Protestant Cardinal." Born into one of France's most powerful noble families, he was the eldest son of Gaspard I de Coligny and Louise de Montmorency. Protected by his powerful uncle, Anne de Montmorency, constable of France, after his father's death in 1522, Odet profited from the favor his uncle enjoyed with King Francis I. At the age of sixteen, he was one of four French cardinals named as part of the marriage alliance formed in 1533 between the king's second son, Henry, and the pope's niece, Catherine de Médicis. He was made archbishop of Toulouse in 1534 and count-bishop of Beauvais in 1535, a position which made him a peer of the realm. In addition, he was prior or commendatory abbot of sixteen abbeys. Yet he never advanced in religious orders beyond the diaconate, which he received in 1534 with dispensation for age.

Odet left his personal religious opinions shrouded in ambiguity. Drawing wealth from multiple benefices that he never served, in many respects he represents precisely the abuses the reformers wished to end. In other respects, however, he appears to have been an open-minded and liberal churchman. Through his mother, as well as through his humanist tutor Nicholas Béraud, he was early exposed to the ideas of the evangelical reformers who frequented the humanist circle of Marguerite d'Angoulême. His youngest brother, François d'Andelot (1521–1569), quietly converted to Protestantism while a prisoner of war in 1556 and began overtly to assist in Calvinist proselytization in 1558, when he provided armed escort for two ministers on a preaching tour of Brittany. Odet's middle brother, Gaspard II de Coligny, may also have been attracted to the reform at this time, but he kept his opinions to himself. Odet did the same. The profits he drew from an unreformed Catholic church (estimated at over 100,000 livres a year) discouraged adherence to the Protestant faith; indeed, in 1557 he was one of three French cardinals named by King Henry II as "grand inquisitors" in an attempt to purge the country of the Protestant heretics. Opposed by the Parlement of Paris, the act creating a French Inquisition remained a dead letter and was voided in 1558, so that Odet's willingness to cooperate in this venture was never put to the test.

For as long as he could, he walked a narrow line, appearing to favor the Protestants without taking any action that might cost him his Catholic benefices. He provoked consternation in 1561 when he began to appear publicly with a Protestant noblewoman, Elisabeth de Hauteville, whom he introduced as his wife (they were finally married in the Reformed church in 1564), and riots broke out among the populace of Beauvais at Easter that year when the cardinal-bishop offered the laity Communion in both kinds. At the Colloquy of Poissy (September–October 1561), Odet found his place among the group of liberal Catholic bishops who unsuccessfully attempted to promote ecumenical harmony. He continued to work with Catherine de Médicis for internal reform of the church after the failure of Poissy, but his proposals were ignored in Rome, which was preparing for a new session of the Council of Trent and insisted that this was the proper setting for any discussion of church reform.

When the first religious war broke out in the spring of 1562, Odet remained neutral and tried to work for compromise. By the end of summer neutrality was impossible, and he took up arms for the Huguenot cause. In November 1562, the curia cited him for heresy, along with seven other prominent French churchmen, and in March 1563 the pope declared him excommunicated and stripped of his titles and benefices, a decision Odet ignored as contrary to the liberties of the Gallican church. An assembly of French bishops convened by the cardinal of Lorraine in December 1564 urged

the king to depose Odet. The king temporized, but eventually a compromise was worked out whereby Odet resigned his benefices in favor of a friend.

Odet helped to negotiate the Peace of Longjumeau that ended the second War of Religion in March 1568. When war broke out again in September of that year, he fled to England, where he spent the remaining three years of his life as one of the principal spokesmen for the Huguenot cause at the court of Elizabeth I. He died in March 1571 as he was preparing to return to France after the Peace of Saint-Germain (August 1570).

BIBLIOGRAPHY

Baumgartner, Frederic J. *Change and Continuity in the French Episcopate: The Bishops and the Wars of Religion, 1547–1610.* Durham, 1986. Relatively little on Odet personally, but essential for placing his ambiguous situation into context.

Christol, Marguerite. "Odet de Coligny, cardinal de Châtillon." *Bulletin de la Société de l'histoire du protestantisme français* 107 (1961), 1–12. Better on his patronage of the arts than on his career or beliefs.

Haag, Eugène, and Émile Haag. *La France protestante.* 2d ed., vol. 4, cols. 152–159, edited by Henri Bordier. Paris, 1884. Solid biographical data.

Roelker, Nancy Lyman. "Family, Faith, and *Fortuna:* The Châtillon Brothers in the French Reformation." In *Leaders of the Reformation,* edited by Richard L. DeMolen, pp. 247–277. London and Toronto, 1984. The best summary of recent research; the sections on Odet de Coligny draw upon the unpublished Ph.D. dissertation of Lawrence S. Metzger, "The Protestant Cardinal, Odet de Coligny, 1517–1571," Boston University, 1979.

Shimizu, J. *Conflict of Loyalties: Politics and Religion in the Career of Gaspard de Coligny, Admiral of France, 1519–1572.* Geneva, 1970. Discussion of Odet de Coligny is scattered and occurs largely in the context of, and in contrast to, his brother the admiral.

BARBARA B. DIEFENDORF

COLLÈGE DE FRANCE

COLLÈGE DE FRANCE is the modern name applied to the *lecteurs royaux,* or regius professors, dating from 1530, appointed to introduce philological studies in Paris. Because of the hostility of Paris scholastic masters toward humanist methodology, and after their condemnation of Johannes Reuchlin in 1514, Guillaume Budé and other Parisian humanists urged King Francis I to endow chairs for humanist professors in Paris similar to those newly founded in Louvain and Alcalá. In 1530 provision was made for two professors of Greek (Pierre Danès and Jacques Toussaint), two in Hebrew (François Vatable and Agathias Guidacerio), and, later, for chairs in mathematics and Latin philology and a third chair in Hebrew. In the early seventeenth century, their successors assumed the name "College royal de France" and, after the French Revolution, "Collège de France."

Traditional historiography attributes the foundation to Francis I, presumes its lay character independent from and opposed to the clerical university, and imputes radical theological positions to its first professors. Much of this view calls for revision. The foundation, which was more the work of Budé and other humanists than of Francis I, never received a charter, royal or otherwise. A proposal in 1539 for royal endowment and a separate building came to pass on a much-reduced scale eighty years later under Louis XIII. Salaries promised by the king were often paid years late or assured by humanist bishops. The professors were commonly reputed to be members of the University of Paris, and were subject like other university regents to the jurisdiction of the Parlement of Paris. Most of them were priests or clerics. None of the early professors was ever accused of heresy.

The most notable challenge to the Collège de France occurred in 1534 after three professors advertised public lectures on the Bible. Noël Beda, syndic of the Faculty of Theology, cited them before the Parlement, arguing that public teaching of the Bible was the exclusive domain of professional theologians; that the philological training of the humanist professors was no substitute for the long studies required in the Faculty of Theology; and that tampering with the authorized Vulgate Bible was dangerous for doctrine. The Parlement concurred, but the humanist bishop Jean du Bellay rallied the Privy Council to remove the case from the Parlement's jurisdiction. The regius professors remained suspect in some quarters. For example, Ignatius Loyola warned one of his associates away from their lectures and told another that "those who dabbled in Greek turned to Luther."

None of the early professors of the Collège de France joined the Reformation, although several of their auditors—notably John Calvin—did. Petrus Ramus, appointed in 1551, embraced the Reformation about ten years later. Robert I Estienne used François Vatable's commentaries in annotating his Bibles, which were censured in 1548, but he had employed several other commentators as well. In succeeding decades the Collège de France appointed illustrious humanist scholars, but traditional scholastic studies continued to dominate the arts and theology curricula in Paris.

[See also Budé, Guillaume; Faculty of Theology of Paris; and Francis I of France.]

BIBLIOGRAPHY

Farge, James K. "La Faculté de théologie de Paris et les débuts du Collège de France." In Le parti conservateur au XVIe siècle: Université et Parlement de Paris à l'époque de la Renaissance et de la Réforme. Documents et inédits du Collège de France, pp. 29–46. Paris, 1992. Establishes a contextual understanding of Paris institutions at the time of the founding of the Collège de France. See also Document 7, pp. 117–131, "Les lecteurs royaux et la Bible: Requêtes et Plaidoiries au Parlement de Paris." Critical edition of court proceedings in 1534.

Goujet, Claude-P. Mémoire historique et littéraire sur le Collège royal de France (1758). Reprint, Geneva, 1971. Contains much information on the early history and on the professors of the College.

Lefranc, Abel. Histoire du Collège de France depuis ses origines jusqu'à la fin du premier Empire. Paris, 1893. Standard work, but flawed by its

antipathy toward the prevailing traditionalist mentality in sixteenth-century France.

JAMES K. FARGE, C.S.B.

COLLOQUIES. In the sixteenth century colloquies were formal conversations about the contested religious issues of the Reformation. "Through God's grace I have broken their courage that they do not dare to enter into a disputation but only a friendly conversation just as in Augsburg, Worms, and Regensburg" (Johann Eck, Replica 46.v). In accord with this sixteenth-century usage, namely, to differentiate between "disputations" and "colloquies" as cordial conversation, this article discusses the colloquies held in the empire: Augsburg 1530, Hagenau/Worms 1540/41, Regensburg 1541, Regensburg 1546 (Interim 1548), and Worms 1557.

Augsburg, 1530. The following attempts were made to overcome the religious division that endangered tranquility and the uniform administration of law in the empire and in the individual territories. First, there was an attempt to gain a clearcut victory over the reformers in a disputation. Shortly before the arrival of the Saxon delegation in Augsburg, Johann Eck published 404 articles that he had culled from Reformation writings and labeled "disputation theses" of the Catholic opponents. He offered to repudiate them in a great disputation with the emperor as referee. The format of a disputation confronted the reformers with either having to defend these extremist positions or to distance themselves from them, thereby acknowledging themselves as having been defeated. Philipp Melanchthon's counterstrategy against this "altogether devilish" attempt was to delineate what was being taught in the churches.

Second, the work preparatory to the Confutatio attempted to label the reformers as heretics by listing their earlier extreme statements. In the Confutatio itself, however, the Augsburg Confession is taken seriously as a formulation of Lutheran theology and is only tentatively rejected (that is, if articles 2 and 7 of the confession are interpreted in a certain way). This opened the way to serious dialogue as an alternative to a victory in a disputation and the condemnation of heretics.

Third, a religious colloquy as a friendly, unbiased conversation was attempted with the goal of conciliation. For the negotiations after the public reading of the Confutatio, fourteen individuals were appointed by the emperor to explore if "conciliation might be possible." The dialogue was to be conducted without quarrel or disputation in collegial discussion between the two sides with each delegation being evenly represented. On this premise the 14–21 August negotiations in the committee of fourteen (consisting of Elector John Frederick of Saxony, Margrave George of Brandenburg-Ansbach, Christoph of Stadion, Duke Henry of Braunschweig, Gregor Brück, Sebastian Heller, Bernhard

Hagen, and Hieronymus Vehus, Philipp Melanchthon, Johannes Brenz, Erhard Schnepf, Johann Eck, Johannes Cochlaeus, and Konrad Wimpina) led to the following results regarding the first twenty-one articles of the Augsburg Confession: as had already been done in the *Confutatio*, eight articles (1, 3, 9, 13, 16, 17, 18, 19) were judged not to be controversial. This understanding resulted from a willingness to take the Augsburg Confession seriously as a basis for conversation and to refuse to pin the opponents to earlier extremist and unclear statements. Concerning seven additional articles (2, 4, 5, 6, 7, 8, 10) agreement was reached after the evangelical side had explained its understanding.

Regarding article 2 (Original Sin), the Lutherans stated with reference to the German version of the Augsburg Confession that they did not understand Original Sin as actual sin but as a basic lack. As regards sin remaining after baptism, Thomas Aquinas provided the stimulus for agreement. The material part of sin, the concupiscence related to Original Sin, remains (this entailed a correction of the nominalist understanding of sin); the formal part, namely, the guilt of sin, is removed.

Regarding articles 4–6 (justification), the Lutherans gave up the term *sola*, ("alone") after Eck reminded them of the misunderstanding of the common people. The two sides declared that forgiveness of sins takes place formally (*formaliter*) through the grace that makes humans acceptable before God (*gratia gratum faciens*) and through faith, effectively (*instrumentaliter*) through word and sacrament. This agreement was based on the mutual willingness to translate one theological language into another: the Reformation language of justification by faith corresponding to the Catholic language of justification by grace. Regarding articles 7 and 8 agreement was reached with the acknowledgment that to speak about the church as the "communion of saints" does not preclude the inclusion of sinners.

As regards article 12 there was agreement that "there are three parts of repentance, namely (1) contrition, which refers to the terror of conscience after the recognition of sin; (2) confession, which looks at absolution and believes it, for sin is not forgiven if one does not believe that it is forgiven for the sake of the merits of the suffering of Christ; (3) satisfaction, namely, appropriate fruits of repentance. No agreement prevailed with respect to article 20, namely whether works resulting from faith and grace are to be considered meritorious. As regards article 21, agreement prevailed that the saints in heaven intercede with God and that the celebration of the memory of saints is Christian. There was no agreement about the invocation of saints. As regards the remaining differences concerning these three articles, Eck saw a disagreement in vocabulary rather than in substance.

In the negotiations about the seven articles of the second part of the Augsburg Confession there was agreement concerning episcopal jurisdiction, especially over preachers and ministers. Agreement also existed concerning holy days, including All Saints, and confession. The main difficulties arose concerning the following points: Was Communion under one kind contrary to the institution and instruction of Christ? Should (apart from the toleration of married priests until a general council had made a decision) priests and members of religious orders be allowed to marry? What was to be done with the property of monasteries that had been dissolved? What about the sacrifice of the Mass? These four articles provoked the most disagreement, and it was not possible to reach an accord. Even a committee of six (Brück, Heller, Melanchthon, Hagen, Vehus, Eck) meeting between 24 and 29 August could not reach agreement.

Alongside substantive disagreement on theological issues, Eck was aware that his own position regarding the sacrifice of the Mass, which emphasized its *ex opere operato* character, had yet to be decided by a council. Nontheological issues surfaced increasingly: for example, the question of the validity of endowments for masses and especially the question of the restitution of monastic property and the recognition of episcopal jurisdiction, which was opposed by Philipp of Hesse and the imperial free cities. Eventually conciliation failed, as did the notion of tolerating religious changes that had already been made. The draft for the recess of 22 November explicitly listed the four controversial points. The actual recess of 19 November 1530 concluded that a conciliation in all articles had not been possible.

The decision about the controversial religious issues was tabled by the recess of the diet until a general council, which was to be convened by the pope within six months after the adjournment of the diet and to meet within a year, could be assembled. Until that time all further religious reforms were prohibited; the old legal order was to be restored (no toleration of married priests, restitution of church and monastic property, and restitution of dismissed incumbents of ecclesiastical positions).

The measures identified in the recess of the Diet of Augsburg could not be implemented. The council was not convened until 2 June 1536 by the new pope, Paul III, but was immediately suspended. By the same token, the religious division endangered a uniform legal order in the empire, suggested an alliance of Protestants with Francis I of France, and precluded a common defense against the Turks (defeat at Essag, 9 October 1538). Accordingly, in the Peace of Frankfurt of 19 April 1539 the emperor returned to the notion of a friendly Christian conversation, which in the meantime had received various new theological impulses: Erasmus, *De sarcienda Ecclesiae concordia* (1534); Julius Pflug, *De concordia ecclesiae*; the Saxon colloquy of 29 April–3 May 1534 with Michael Vehe, Christoph Türk, Melanchthon, and Brück; Melanchthon, *Consilium Gallis scriptum* (1534); Luther's negotiations with English emissaries leading to the *Wittenberger Artikel der Christlichen Lehre* (1536); the Wittenberg Concord (1536); *Consilium de emendanda Ecclesia*

(1537); Georg Witzel, *Typus ecclesiae prioris* (1538); and the Colloquy of Leipzig (1539), with Martin Bucer and Georg Witzel.

Hagenau, 1540. In his missive of 18 April 1540 Charles V issued an invitation for a colloquy to be held at Speyer on 6 June 1540, but the plague forced the colloquy to be transferred to Hagenau. The main issue was procedural. Johann Fabri, bishop of Vienna and adviser to King Ferdinand, sought in several briefs to convince the king that (1) even after the Wittenberg Concord the Zwinglians in Strasbourg and other places were not to be included among those adhering to the Augsburg Confession and related to the same religion; and (2) that the Augsburg Confession was not to be the sole item of discussion and that Catholic theologians should not be prevented, as had been the case in Augsburg, from enumerating the heresies, blasphemies, and errors of their antagonists. However, the recess of Hagenau (28 July 1540) and the emperor's letter of 15 August 1540 announcing a colloquy to be held at Worms 28 October 1540 stipulated that the Augsburg Confession and its Apology were to be the basis of the negotiations. The Protestants, in turn, rejected using the results of the discussion in Augsburg as a point of departure.

Worms, 1540/41. The determination that each side should have eleven representatives meant particular difficulties for the Catholics since three of the secular territories (Brandenburg, Palatinate, and Jülich-Cleve) were friendly to the Reformation. The evangelical representatives (which included Strasbourg) began on 4 November in preliminary conversations to prepare their argumentation against the Catholics by ascertaining their internal unity. On 8 November the theologians, including Calvin, agreed to the Variata version of the Augsburg Confession. Concerning article 1, Melanchthon admonished his colleagues not to defend any of his earlier statements that might be presented by the opponents because mishaps were easy in these difficult questions. Concerning article 2 he did not expect problems. Justification, the sacrifice of the Mass, monastic vows, and papal primacy were also discussed.

The first meeting of the two parties took place on 20 November. On 25 November Antoine Perrenot de Granvelle gave the opening speech, and on the following day the parties were asked to name eleven voting representatives (including up to three counselors). The Catholic participants complained about the changes and expansions of the Variata that had been submitted by the evangelicals but could not agree on their own uniform position. After extensive negotiations concerning voting (Bavaria and Mainz vetoed voting by individual participants) and the future agenda, agreement was reached on 5 January 1541 to have a single spokesman for each side—Eck and Melanchthon.

In conversations between 14 and 18 January 1541 concerning articles 1 and 2 of the Augsburg Confession, full agreement was reached after lengthy discussions concerning Original Sin. This agreement was based on the discussions at Augsburg in 1530, again in the setting of a "friendly conversation" and the willingness not to pin down the opponents with extremist positions, to concede mistakes and weaknesses in one's own views, and to accept views contrary to one's own but viable in the context of the Christian tradition. (For example, Eck accepted Melanchthon's interpretation of *Romans* 7 and the designation of concupiscence after baptism as sin.) "We agree that as descendants of Adam we are born according to a common disposition with original sin and therefore under the wrath of God. Original sin consists in the absence of an original righteousness connected with concupiscence. We also agree that in baptism the guilt of original sin together with all sins is forgiven through the merits of Christ. Instructed not only by apostolic writings but also through direct experience we hold that concupiscence, perversion of nature, weakness and sickness remain" (Eck, *Apologia*). Despite this success Granvelle ordered the adjournment of the negotiations and announced their transfer to Regensburg. There the colloquy was to continue, on the basis not of the Augsburg Confession but of a draft document prepared by theologians of both sides.

The Book of Regensburg. In accord with this plan, Martin Bucer and Johannes Gropper, supported by Wolfgang Capito and the imperial secretary, Gerhard Veltwyck, drafted in secret negotiations (December 1540), on the basis of a prior draft of Gropper, the so-called Book of Regensburg. On 10 January 1541, Bucer transmitted a copy to Landgrave Philipp of Hesse, who sent it without knowing its background via Joachim II of Brandenburg to Luther. Luther refrained from comments and suggestions while Melanchthon appraised it as fictional. He noted on the first page: *politia platonis*.

Regensburg, 1541. The Diet at Regensburg opened on 4 April 1541. The emperor himself had reserved the right to name the participants for the colloquy. They were announced on 21 April: Pflug, Eck, and Gropper, together with Melanchthon, Bucer, and Johannes Pistorius. Their task was not to defend certain theses in controversial manner, but rather to explore which doctrinal statements might be reconciled. The presiding officers were the Palatinate Count Friedrich and Granvelle. In preliminary consultations with Pflug, the papal legate Gasparo Contarini, the Master of the Sacred Palace Badia, and Eck, who were introduced to the book as the publication of certain learned theologians from Flanders who had died two years earlier, Gropper and Granvelle agreed to some twenty textual changes proposed mainly by Contarini. In this modified form, it became, despite the opposition of Eck and Melanchthon, the basis of the colloquy that began on 27 April.

The first four articles (concerning the creation of humans and the integrity of their nature before the Fall; free will; the cause of sin; and Original Sin) were considered uncontested and were accepted unchanged despite some critical remarks by Eck about Gropper's theology. Neither Eck nor Melanchthon was pleased with the statement on justification that was discussed on 28 April. Their insistence caused the draft to be abandoned and replaced by an open discussion of the topic. After new drafts by Eck and Melanchthon had been submitted, as well as further consultation of the Protestants, agreement was reached on the basis of a draft that resulted from Gropper's cutting half of the first draft and reworking it with significant help from Contarini. This led to a third draft, which was accepted on 2 May. The basic notion is expressed in the following sentence: "It is secure and wholesome teaching that the sinner is justified by a living and effectual faith, for through such faith we will be acceptable to God and accepted for the sake of Christ." This key sentence appropriated notions from both the Reformation and Scholasticism as is evident by the further explication: "A living faith therefore both appropriates the mercy in Christ and believes that the righteousness which is in Christ will be freely reckoned for nothing and also receives the promise of the Holy Spirit." This meant the repudiation of a misunderstanding of *sola fides*. Love is given and poured out by God (*Rom.* 5:1)—not as human effort out of one's own power—and it becomes part of justifying faith incorporated into justification. At the same time, it is clearly stated that we are justified, that is, accepted and reconciled, by faith when faith appropriates the mercy and righteousness that for the sake of Christ and his merits are imputed to us, but not because of the meritoriousness and perfection of the righteousness transferred to us in Christ. Even though in contrast to the first draft the explicit phrase "double righteousness," a "first righteousness" of the godless and a "second righteousness" through the works of faith, is eliminated, a distinction is made between Christ's righteousness freely imputed to us and inherent righteousness, according to which we are called righteous (*1 Jn.* 3:7) because we do what is righteous. The reward promised for good works has its ground not in those works themselves but in the fact "that they are done in faith and are from the Holy Spirit who dwells in us, while the free will parallels as a participant." "Therefore, the blessedness of those will be greater who do more and greater good works."

Contrary to Eck's and Melanchthon's expectations, the negotiations after 3 May were based again on the Book of Regensburg, whose sixth chapter anticipated the subsequent eighteen chapters: the Word (chaps. 7–9), the Sacraments (chaps. 10–17), and the bond of love (chaps. 18–23) as signs of the church and its authority. Article 6 (concerning the church and its signs as well as its authority), article 7 (concerning the sign of the Word), and article 8 (concerning repentance after the Fall), were accepted in principle. For Chapter 9 (concerning the authority of the church in discerning and interpreting scripture), however, the Protestants proposed a draft of their own. They recognized a threefold authority of the true church: (1) to testify to apostolic writings and distinguish them from those that are only attributed to the apostles; (2) to understand and interpret scripture rightly, for which the unanimous testimonies of scripture and the consensus of the early church apostolic traditions are the criteria; and (3) to make judgments concerning doctrine. The authority of the true church is restricted only to the pious as living members of the church and is not dependent on a majority or certain persons or places; accordingly, even councils can be in error.

This disagreement was tabled, and the discussion of the sacraments began on 4 May. Article 10 (concerning the sacraments), article 11 (concerning the sacrament of ordination), and article 12 (concerning the sacrament of baptism) did not present problems. Article 13 (concerning the sacrament of confirmation) was also accepted, even though Melanchthon was displeased that both confirmation and last unction as sacraments were taken to be "signs of infallible grace." Serious disagreement erupted about article 14 (concerning the sacrament of the Eucharist). The Worms draft, which read "after consecration the true body and the true blood of the Lord are truly and substantially [*substantialiter*] present and received by the faithful under the form of bread and wine," was supplemented at Contarini's urging by the addition, "after these, namely, bread and wine, have been changed and transubstantiated into the body and blood of the Lord." The disagreement focused less on the question of transubstantiation (Fourth Lateran Council) than on the consequences derived from that premise: procession and veneration of the Host. Alongside the communication difficulties because of the changing concept of substance in late Scholasticism there was also the issue of Protestant unity. In the Wittenberg Concord it was tied to the repudiation of the teaching of transubstantiation and the rejection of processions. Against a background of reported destructions of sanctuaries and attacks on priests on the way to giving Communion to the sick, Contarini interpreted the repudiation of transubstantiation as a questioning of the real presence because of the Wittenberg Concord between Lutheranism and Zwinglianism. Since no agreement was reached after nine days, the article was set aside on 13 May until the remaining articles had been discussed. The position of the Protestants was expressed in a separate draft article.

In article 15 (concerning the sacrament of penance or absolution) agreement prevailed concerning the continuation of private confession, but there was disagreement whether in confession the specific listing of sins was necessary for forgiveness. On this topic, as on the topic of satisfaction, the Protestants drafted a separate article.

On 19 May article 16 (concerning the sacrament of marriage) and article 17 (the sacrament of unction) were accepted as "sacred symbols to support and heal human weakness not necessary but very profitable and salvatory," article

17 containing the notation "the Protestants do not reject the rite once abuses have been removed."

The last articles are introduced by article 18 (concerning the bond of love that is the third sign of the church). Article 19 (concerning church order and the authority for ordering ecclesiastical affairs) began with the concept of the church as mystical body in which when "one member suffers others suffer as well." This bestowed on the bishops, with reference to the early church (Cyprian, Tertullian, Irenaeus, and Augustine), a special responsibility for the retention of unity. In Melanchthon's view the article presented the church as an administrative structure of the pope and condemned those not keeping the traditions as apostates from the church. And that meant nothing other than the condemnation of the Protestants. The counterarticle submitted by the Protestants basically recognized the traditional episcopal structure as a useful institution for the retention of the unity of the church (to convene synods, make authorized judgments, remove existing abuses, punish causes of evil through excommunication), but to "popes and bishops who are enemies of pious teaching we cannot attribute such authority."

Article 20 identified individual "points of doctrine that are explained and confirmed by the power of the church," for example, the Apostles' Creed, the consubstantiality of the Trinity, concerning the two natures and the unity of the person of Christ, Original Sin, infant baptism, and similar topics. Disagreement focused on the veneration of saints and the sacrifice of the Mass. Both Gropper and Bucer agreed that "it has been received through common consensus in the church that God may be piously petitioned that he would grant, through the merits and petitions of the saints, that we be strengthened in everything through the aid of his protectors, of course not through their merits themselves, but through Christ, our Lord." Also, it is not to be condemned that in personal prayer we appeal directly to the saints, "but in such a fashion that the entire trust is put solely on Jesus Christ, the origin of all good things," just as we would entreat the living for support of our petitions before God. Despite such safeguards against abuses the Protestant draft article rejected the notion that "we are helped because of the merits of the saints and that the saints are to be directly and personally approached." In distinction to the thesis of late Scholasticism and Eck concerning the *ex opere operato* value of the Mass, the Book of Regensburg held that "this sacrifice is not less effective today for those who in respectful faith present it before God than it was on the day when blood and water flowed from the side." Since the dead also belong to the body of Christ, they are included in the celebration of the sacrifice of the Mass. Properly understood, the canon of the Mass contains nothing inappropriate. However, the notion that the power of the sacrifice of the Mass flows to those who have no living faith because of the external work performed by the priest was condemned as superstition. The counterarticle of the Protestants rejected the Mass as a sacrifice benefiting, or offering forgiveness of sins to, anyone other than those who are faithfully present.

Article 21 (concerning the use and administration of the sacraments and several particular ceremonies) summarized the differing positions of both sides (*sunt ex una parte, sunt ex altera*): attendance at Mass includes receiving Communion by those present versus the possibility of a purely spiritual Communion in the co-celebration with the priest; Communion under both kinds versus Communion under only one kind; the liturgy in the language understood by the people versus the liturgy in Latin. The outcome was the recommendation of temporary mutual toleration with the goal of reform in the spirit of the early church. The counterarticle of the Protestants repudiated private masses and the usefulness of the Mass for both the living and the dead. Concerning the question of Communion under both kinds, the Protestants stated that the church did not have authority to alter Christ's institution.

Article 22 (concerning ecclesiastical discipline) referred to the historical development of celibacy. The Protestant draft article saw this as an indirect vote for the practice in the early church and declared the obligation of celibacy an unjust law.

Article 23 (concerning popular discipline) advocated public penance as in the early church. The regulation of fast days and of food and holy days was to be turned over to pious and learned men.

On 22 May the first reading of the Book of Regensburg was concluded. On 24 and 25 May the participants—with the exception of Eck, who was ill and had not in fact participated in the discussions after article 15—met for final editorial work on the document. On 31 May they submitted the book, together with the Protestant counterarticles, to the emperor, who in turn transmitted the results to the estates on 8 June. In the recess of the diet of 29 July, the assessment of the efforts of the participants was turned over to a general council, or, if a council would not convene, to a national council, or, at least within eighteen months, a future diet. Until that time the Peace of Nuremberg was to be observed and the current litigation before the imperial cameral court was to be suspended.

In the conviction of the participants of the colloquy, the agreement concerning the doctrine of justification was not based on a formula that obscured the existing differences but on a mutual willingness to subordinate different theological language to a commonly confessed matter. Luther and Johannes Bugenhagen were "fully one" with the statements of article 5 but considered them dubious as long as the opponents had not publicly repudiated specific nominalistic positions noted by Luther. The Saxon elector John Frederick rejected the agreement because it could be used by the opponents to put the Augsburg Confession in a bad light, as if previously there had been no right teaching. Rome rejected the agreement because it lent itself to different interpretations. As regards ecclesiology and church order the agreement between Bucer, Gropper, and Pflug was based on recourse to the early church. Eck's repudiation of the book did not pertain to the agreement on justification, the sacraments, and the church, but was based on his personal animosity toward Gropper and a different theological position concerning the sacrifice of the Mass, Communion under both kinds, Latin liturgy, and celibacy. Accordingly, the Catholic majority of the college of territorial rulers rejected the Book of Regensburg: several articles (for example, the first four) were deemed superfluous since they were not controversial. Concerning Original Sin, agreement had already been reached in Worms. In a new colloquy the articles had to be theologically reworked and cast into a new linguistic form. The agreement related to articles that "are not very controversial among the scholars and not even among the common people." However, the most important articles concerning the Eucharist, the Mass, the marriage of priests, Communion under both kinds, and so on not only were not reconciled, but the Catholic participants had been too agreeable during the discussion. The book could cause the emperor and all Christian estates damage and embarrassment.

Regensburg, 1546. Since the council was not convened and the primary issue at the next several diets was to marshal support against the Turks, it was not until the recess of the Diet of Speyer of 10 June 1544 that a new diet was announced to resolve the controversial religious issues. The diet was to meet in the fall or winter and eventually opened on 24 March 1544. The Protestants refused to let the controversial questions be decided at the council announced on 19 November 1544 and convened on 15 March 1545 in Trent. Accordingly, the recess of 4 August 1545 stipulated the procedures for a new colloquy to take place at the next diet (6 January 1546). There were to be two presiding officers, four actual participants, and four auditors. Gropper could not be persuaded to participate in the colloquy. Since Pflug and Michael Helding refused to participate as well, the emperor named Cochlaeus, Eberhard Billick, Johannes Hoffmeister, and Pedro Malvenda, while Elector John Frederick and Philipp of Hesse named Melanchthon (whose place was taken by Georg Major), Bucer, Schnepf, and Brenz. The emperor appointed Moritz von Hutten, the Bishop of Eichstätt, and Count Frederick of Fürstenberg as presiding officers. The opening session took place on 27 January. The Augsburg Confession was to be the basis for the colloquy, with the first three articles of the confession considered resolved. In a letter of 3 February 1546 Charles V appointed Pflug as copresiding officer.

After the issue of how to record the discussions had been tentatively resolved, the colloquy was opened on 5 February by Malvenda with a discussion of the Catholic notion of justification. Bucer responded on 9–11 February, and on 13 and 14 February Malvenda and Billick responded in turn. Bucer replied on 17 February and then again on 23 February. The proceedings were tedious since with the exception of 20–22 February Malvenda and Billick dictated their statements to the notaries, largely followed by Bucer. This was done in order to refer to the minutes if distorted reports of the positions of the opponents were to arise. Bucer was of the opinion that nothing could be expected of the other side, which was unwilling to accept the agreement concerning justification reached in Regensburg in 1541. The content of the colloquy, which approached the format of a disputation, was the concept of faith, including such questions as whether faith and deadly sin could coexist, and hence whether it were possible to talk of justification solely by faith. On 24 February the presiding officers received the emperor's instruction to have only the results, agreements, and disagreements (not the speeches) recorded by notaries to be appointed by the presiding officers. At the same time the participants were to be sworn to secrecy concerning the deliberations. The Protestants rejected the latter stipulation and the colloquy was suspended on 10 March. When Charles V arrived in Regensburg on 10 April the Protestant estates had already left the city so that the second Colloquy of Regensburg, already burdened by anticipation of the Schmalkald War, ended without result.

After the military victory over the Protestants, the emperor's theological advisers made their point that the religious question was not to be resolved simply by the implementation of the Edict of Worms or, for that matter, by the restitution of the old state of affairs or submission to the council in session in Bologna. Rather, the solution of the religious controversy was to be effected by reform and a tentative acknowledgment of the Lutheran ecclesiastical changes, especially the marriage of priests and the cup for the laity in the context of a far-reaching agreement concerning faith.

Worms, 1557. The Peace of Augsburg of 1555 stipulated that at the next diet a "conciliation of matters of faith and religion was to be sought through appropriate and decent ways." Rejecting the alternatives of a general council or a national council, the Diet of Regensburg (5 July 1556–16 March 1557) agreed in lengthy negotiations with unwilling estates on the modalities of the religious colloquy desired by King Ferdinand. It eventually opened on 11 September 1557. Its direction rested with the two presiding officers, Pflug and Georg Sigmund Seld, and two assistants, Jacob von Eltz and Bartholomäus von der Leyen, as well as Bartholomäus Latomus and Martin Herkules Rettinger on the Catholic side; and Count Ludwig of Eberstein and Neugarten supported by Heinrich, count of Einsiedel, Georg Cracov, and Balthasar von Gültingen (who was replaced in mid-November by Count Heinrich von Castell), on the Protestant side.

The six Catholic participants were Michael Helding, Johannes Dephius, Jodokus Ravesteyn, Maarten van Riethoven, Peter Canisius, and Friedrich Staphylus. (Gropper could not be persuaded to participate.) Adjunct Catholic participants were Franciscus Sonnius, Georg Witzel, Nikolaas Florisz Goudanus, Johannes Gressenicus, Matthias Sittardus, and Johannes Sylvanus. The evangelicals named as participants Melanchthon, Schnepf, Brenz, Pistorius, Georg Karg, and Jakob Runge. Adjunct Protestant participants were Heinrich Stoll, Johannes Marbach, Erasmus Sarcerius, Joachim Mörlin, Viktorin Strigel, and Johannes Stössel. The notaries were Johannes à Via and Nikolaus Driel for the Catholics and Jakob Anderae and Paul Eber for the evangelicals. In addition, both sides also had representatives of the estates as auditors.

All participants were enjoined to respect the confidentiality of the negotiations. The basis of the colloquy was to be the Augsburg Confession. In the Protestants' preparatory meeting on 4 September the Gnesio-Lutherans demanded, along the lines of Matthias Flacius Illyricus, the specific condemnation of all deviations from the pure teaching of Luther and the unchanged Augsburg Confession. After intense disagreements, on 9 September the two Lutheran factions agreed on a common platform. On 11 September in the first session Melanchthon presented it. "We reject all errors and those sects, old as well as new ones, which are contrary to this confession, particularly the godless decisions of the so-called Senate of Trent, the book with the title 'Interim,' and all other actions that are contrary to our Confession."

After the participants had been sworn to secrecy and procedural matters had been resolved (public reading of written briefs that were to be shared with the opposing party), Helding formally opened the colloquy in the third session on 14 September. He saw no better route to unity than to place at the center of the deliberations the teaching that forty years before was agreed upon unanimously, which all faithful had always maintained, and which from the beginning of the church had been delivered from generation to generation. At the same time he demanded from the opponents an affirmation of the Augsburg Confession as it had been presented in 1530. Finally, he handed Melanchthon a summary of the controversial points in twenty-three items drafted by Canisius (Original Sin, free will, justification, good works, sacraments, baptism, confirmation, Eucharist, Communion under both kinds, sacrifice of the Mass, penance, extreme unction, orders, marriage, celibacy, religious vows, the church and its head, worldly and spiritual government, human traditions, veneration of saints, images, ceremonies, purgatory, and intercession for the dead).

Melanchthon's response was presented by Karp in the fourth session. According to Melanchthon, the superstition of the last generation could not constitute the norm for adjudicating controversial questions. Proofs of deviation from apostolic origins were the prohibition of marriage for priests, private masses, the invocation of the dead, the veneration of the Host, indulgences, and the theory of the two swords. Helding referred to the necessity of principles for the distinction of truth and error: (1) the recognition of the complete canon of holy scripture; and (2) the recognition of the genuine and proper meaning of scripture that is expressed in the consensus of the early Fathers. Melanchthon referred to the clarity of scripture and the creeds of the early church and to the disagreements among the Fathers. The true church was not tied to popes or godless rulers. With reference to the first controverted point, namely, original sin, to which Helding had referred in the fourth session, Karp justified the accusation of Pelagianism since the scholastic theologians had affirmed the integrity of natural prowess after the fall. Canisius's question of how the insistence on the clarity of scripture could be maintained in light of the great differences in the interpretation of the words of institution (Zwingli, Calvin), justification (Osiander), the necessity of good works (Flacius, Gallus, Major), and the bondage of the will (Flacius) became the key issue of the colloquy.

In the next session the Gnesio-Lutherans promptly demanded to present their prepared anathemas against the deviations from the Augsburg Confession. After extensive negotiations the two Lutheran assistants threatened Schnepf and his followers with exclusion. They saw in this a violation of the agenda and submitted an official complaint to Pflug, who did not want to decide the matter on his own and presented it to all the assistants. When they met the two Lutheran assistants insisted, despite concerns voiced by Pflug, on the exclusion. The Gnesio-Lutherans departed on 2 October after they had deposited with the Catholic auditors three statements, which were read in the session of 6 October. That in turn led to the departure of most of Melanchthon's followers. The following day Melanchthon emphasized once again his agreement with the Augsburg Confession and denied the propriety of discussing intra-Lutheran differences at the colloquy.

In the final common session of 12 October the Catholics insisted that deviations had to be rejected since the colloquy could be conducted only with unwaning followers of the Augsburg Confession. Pflug's compromise, to repudiate explicitly only Zwinglianism, was rejected by both sides. Helding referred to Calvin, who in his tract against Joachim Westphal had claimed Melanchthon's agreement. In the face of an increasing polemic Pflug interrupted the negotiations of 27 October and requested further instructions from King Ferdinand. Both sides interpreted these instructions differently. The Catholics insisted on re-admitting the Gnesio-Lutherans while the Lutheran side rejected this. Pflug no longer saw any possibilities for agreement and allowed the participants to return home on 29 November.

After 1557 religious colloquies were held regionally (Baden and Emmendingen 1589/90, Regensburg 1601, Neuburg 1615, and Leipzig 1631); by Lutherans and Reformed (Maulbronn 1564, Mömpelgard 1586, Kassel 1661, Berlin

1662/63); between Lutherans (Weimar 1560 and Altenburg 1568/69); and by non-Germans (Poissy 1561, Sandomir 1570, and Thorn 1546).

Significance and Assessment. The colloquies emphatically demonstrate the multi-layered dimensions of the conflict known as the Reformation. Conditions for a truly friendly conversation existed only rarely. A mixture of theological and nontheological factors prevailed. For example, concern for the maintenance of the old faith but also fear of a powerful imperial neighbor were the motivation for the rejection of the colloquies by the Bavarian dukes; the issues of the sacrifice of the Mass, monastic vows, and the episcopal office were connected with questions of ecclesiastical endowments and monastic property, and their relationship to secular power; there were personal animosities among the theologians, even those on the same side, such as Eck and Gropper in Regensburg or between Melanchthon and Schnepf in Worms in 1557. There also was the burden of negative experiences (iconoclasm and destruction of monasteries; physical violence against Catholic priests; the martyrdom of followers of Luther, such as Leonhard Kaiser and Adolph Clarenbach) and a deep mistrust that characterized the opposition as marginal and extreme. The fronts had become rigid, which made slogans such as *sola fides* or certain church practices into non-negotiable or offensive items.

No colloquy succeeded in a definitive clarification of the religious division. Yet, thanks to the colloquies, adherents to the Augsburg Confession were not simply declared heretics but accepted as partners in dialogue, despite the bull of excummunication against Luther and the Edict of Worms. This was an important precondition for the Peace of Augsburg (1555). Moreover, the partial agreements at the colloquies at Augsburg (1530), Worms (1540/41), and Regensburg (1541) demonstrated despite differing terminology a far-reaching commonality in substance regarding central questions such as trinitarian and christological creeds, Original Sin, justification, sacraments, and church.

[*See also* Hagenau, Colloquy of; Marburg, Colloquy of; Maulbronn, Colloquy of; Montbéliard, Colloquy of; Poissy, Colloquy of; *and* Saint-Germain, Colloquy of.]

BIBLIOGRAPHY

Augustijn, Cornelis. "De gesprekken tussen Bucer en Gropper tijdens het godsdienstgesprek te Worms in december 1540." *Nederlands archief voor kerkgeschiedenis*, n.s. 47 (1965–1966), 208–231.
——. *De godsdienstgesprekken tussen rooms-katholieken en protestanten van 1538 tot 1541.* Haarlem, 1967.
Barth, Hans-Martin, ed. *Das Regensburger Religionsgespräch im Jahre 1541: Rückblick und aktuelle ökumenische Perpektiven.* Regensburg, 1992.
Bäumer, Remigius. "Vermittlungsbemühungen auf dem Augsburger Reichstag." *Theologie und Glaube* 70 (1980), 304–330.
Braunisch, Reinhard. "Die 'Artikell' der 'Warhafftigen Antwort' (1545) des Johannes Gropper: Zur Verfasserfrage des Worms-Regensbur-
ger Buches, (1540/41)." In *Von Konstanz nach Trient. Beiträge zur Geschichte der Kirche von den Reformkonzilien bis zum Tridentinum; Festgabe für August Franzen,* edited by Remigius Bäumer, pp. 519–545. Munich, 1972.
Bundschuh, Benno von. *Das Wormser Religionsgespräch von 1557 unter besonderer Berücksichtigung der kaiserlichen Religionspolitik.* Münster, 1988.
Cardauns, Ludwig. *Berichte Tommaso Campegios vom Wormser Kolloquium, 1540/41.* Nuntiaturberichte aus Deutschland I, 6. Berlin, 1910.
——. *Zur Geschichte der kirchlichen Unions- und Reformsbestrebungen 1538–42.* Rome, 1910.
Decot, Rolf, ed. *Vermittlungsversuche auf dem Augsburger Reichstag 1530: Melanchthon, Brenz, Vehus.* Stuttgart, 1989.
Förstemann, Karl Eduard, ed. *Urkundenbuch zu der Geschichte des Reichstages zu Augsburg im Jahre 1530* (1833–1835). Reprint, Osnabrück, 1966.
Fraenkel, Pierre. *Einigungsbestrebungen in der Reformationszeit. Zwei Wege, zwei Motive.* Wiesbaden, 1965.
Grundmann, Herbert, ed. *Valentin von Tetleben: Protokoll des Augsburger Reichstages, 1530.* Göttingen, 1958.
Hollerbach, Marion. *Das Religionsgespräch als Mittel der konfessionellen und politischen Auseinandersetzung im Deutschland des 16. Jahrhunderts.* Frankfurt a.M., 1982.
Honée, Eugène. "Die theologische Diskussion über den Laienkelch auf dem Augsburger Reichstag 1530: Versuch einer historischen Rekonstruktion." *Nederlands Archief voor Kerkgeschiedenis* n.s. 52/53 (1973), 1–97.
——. " 'Pax politica' oder Wiedervereinigung im Glauben: Die Vorüberlegung der katholischen Mehrheit auf dem Reichstag von Augsburg über den recessus imperii vom 22. September 1530." In *Reformatio Ecclesiae. Beiträge zu kirchlichen Reformbemühungen von der Alten Kirche bis zur Neuzeit: Festgabe für Erwin Iserloh,* edited by Remigius Bäumer, pp. 441–466. Paderborn, 1980.
——. *Über das Vorhaben und Scheitern eines Religionsgesprächs: Ein Verfahrensstreit auf dem Konvent von Hagenau, 1540. Archiv für Reformationsgeschichte* 76 (1985), 195–216.
Immenkötter, Herbert. *Um die Einheit im Glauben: Die Unionsverhandlungen des Augsburger Reichstages im August und September 1530.* Münster, 1974.
Iserloh, Erwin, and Barbara Hallensleben, ed. *Confessio Augustana und Confutatio: Der Augsburger Reichstag 1530 und die Einheit der Kirche.* Proceedings of an international conference, Augsburg, Germany, 3–7 September 1979. Münster, 1980.
Jedin, Hubert. "An welchen Gegensätzen sind die vortridentinischen Religionsgespräche zwischen Katholiken und Protestanten gescheitert?" In *Kirche des Glaubens und Kirche der Geschichte,* vol. 1, pp. 361–366. Freiburg, 1966.
Kretschmar, Georg. "The Imperial Diet of Regensburg and the 1541 Variata of the Augsburg Confession." In *Piety, Politics, and Ethics: Reformation Studies in Honor of George W. Forell,* edited by Carter Lindberg, pp. 85–102. Kirksville, Mo., 1984.
Krieger, Christian, and Marc Lienhard, eds. *Bucer and Sixteenth Century Europe.* Proceedings of an international conference, Strasbourg, France, 28–31 August 1991. Leiden, 1993. See esp. the essays by Karl-Heinz zur Mühlen (vol. 2, pp. 659–670) and Cornelis Augustijn (vol. 2, pp. 671–680).
Luttenberger, Albrecht P. *Konfessionelle Parteilichkeit und Reichspolitik: Zur Verhandlungsführung des Kaisers und der Stände in Regensburg 1541.* Göttingen, 1988.
Mackensen, Heinz. "The Debate between Eck and Melanchthon on Original Sin at the Colloquy of Worms." *Lutheran Quarterly* 11 (1959), 42–56.
——. "Contarini's Theological Role at Ratisbon in 1541." *Archiv für Reformationsgeschichte* 51 (1960), 36–57.

Matheson, Peter. *Cardinal Contarini at Regensburg.* Oxford, 1972.

Mehlhausen, Joachim. "Die Abendmahlslehre des Regensburger Buches." In *Studien zur Geschichte und Theologie der Reformation: Festschrift für Ernst Bizer,* edited by Luise Abramowski and J. F. Gerhard Goeters, pp. 198–211. Neukirchen-Vluyn, Germany 1969.

Moses, Reinhold. *Die Religionsverhandlungen zu Hagenau und Worms 1540 und 1541.* Leipzig, 1889.

Müller, Gerhard. "Johann Eck und die Confessio Augustana." *Quellen und Forschungen aus italienischen Archiven* 38 (1958), 205–242.

———. *Die römische Kurie und die Reformation 1523–1534: Kirche und Politik während des Pontifikates Clemens' VII.* Gütersloh, 1969.

Müller, Gerhard, ed. *Die Religionsgespräche der Reformationszeit.* Gütersloh, 1980.

Nebelsieck, Heinrich. "Elf Briefe und Aktenstücke über das Religionsgespräch in Regensburg von 1546." *Archiv für Reformationsgeschichte* 32 (1935), 127–136, 253–283.

Neuhaus, Helmut. "Der Augsburger Reichstag des Jahres 1530: Ein Forschungsbericht." *Zeitschrift für Historische Forschung* 9 (1982), 167–211.

Neuser, Wilhelm H. "Calvins Beitrag zu den Religionsgesprächen von Hagenau, Worms und Regensburg, 1540/41." In *Studien zur Geschichte und Theologie der Reformation: Festschrift für Ernst Bizer,* edited by Luise Abramowski and J. F. Gerhard Goeters, pp. 213–237. Neukirchen-Vluyn, Germany, 1969.

Neuser, Wilhelm H., ed. *Die Vorbereitung der Religionsgespräche von Worms und Regensburg 1540/41.* Neukirchen-Vluyn, Germany, 1974.

Pastor, Ludwig von. *Die kirchlichen Reunionsbestrebungen während der Regierung Karls V.* Freiburg, 1879.

Pfnür, Vinzenz. *Einig in der Rechtfertigungslehre? Die Rechtfertigungslehre der Confessio Augustana (1530) und die Stellungnahme der katholischen Kontroverstheologie zwischen 1530 und 1535.* Wiesbaden, 1970.

———. "Die Einigung bei den Religionsgesprächen von Worms und Regensburg 1540/41 eine Täuschung?" In *Die Religionsgespräche der Reformationszeit,* edited by Gerhard Müller, pp. 55–88. Gütersloh, 1980.

———. "Johannes Ecks Verständnis der Religionsgespräche, sein theologischer Beitrag in ihnen und seine Sicht der Konfessionsgegensätze." In *Johannes Eck (1483–1543) im Streit der Jahrhunderte,* edited by Erwin Iserloh, pp. 223–249. Münster, 1988.

Roth, Friedrich. "Der offizielle Bericht der von den Evangelischen zum Regensburger Gespräch Verordneten an ihre Fürsten und Obern. 27. Januar bis 10. März 1546." *Archiv für Reformationsgeschichte* 5 (1908), 1–30, 375–397.

Scheible, Heinz. "Melanchthon und Luther während des Augsburger Reichstags 1530." In *Martin Luther, "Reformator und Vater im Glauben,"* edited by Peter Manns, pp. 38–60. Stuttgart, 1985.

Schirrmacher, Friedrich Wilhelm, ed. *Briefe und Acten zu der Geschichte des Religionsgespräches zu Marburg 1529 und des Reichstages zu Augsburg 1530* (1876). Reprint, Amsterdam 1968.

Stupperich, Robert. *Der Humanismus und die Wiedervereinigung der konfessionen.* Leipzig, 1936.

———. "Der Ursprung des 'Regensburger Buches' von 1541 und seine Rechtfertigungslehre." *Archiv für Reformationsgeschichte* 36 (1939), 88–116.

Vetter, Paul. *Die Religionsverhandlungen auf dem Reichstag zu Regensburg 1541.* Jena, 1889.

Ziegler, Donald J., ed. *Great Debates of the Reformation.* New York, 1969.

zur Mühlen, Karl-Heinz. "Die Edition der Akten und Berichte der Religionsgespräche von Hagenau und Worms 1540/41." In *Standfester Glaube: Festgaben zum 65. Geburtstag von Johann Friedrich Gerhard Goeters,* edited by Heiner Faulenbach, pp. 47–62. Cologne, 1991.

———. "Die Einigung über den Rechtfertigungsartikel auf dem Re-

gensburger Religionsgespräch von 1541: Eine verpaßte Chance?" *Zeitschrift für Theologie und Kirche* 76 (1979), 331–359.

VINZENZ PFNÜR
Translated from German by Hans J. Hillerbrand

COLOQUY OF ———. *See under latter part of name.*

COLOGNE. The largest city in Germany at the beginning of the sixteenth century, with a population of 40,000, Cologne was also one of its greatest economic and ecclesiastical centers. Its wealth was founded on the production of textiles, metalwares, and leather goods drawn from its extensive hinterland, as well as on Rhineland and international trade. It dominated the regional economy of the lower Rhine and formed the natural economic capital of northwestern Germany. An unnamed Italian cardinal in 1515 compared it with Florence, but it certainly surpassed the Tuscan city in the wealth of its ecclesiastical and educational institutions. Besides its powerful cathedral chapter, it could boast of a dozen collegial foundations and almost ninety churches, chapels, and religious houses. In addition, there were perhaps 150 Beguine houses and 35 hospitals, hostels, and leprosariums, while 15 other abbeys from the region maintained branchhouses there. Not surprisingly, the city was universally known in Germany as "holy Cologne."

Cologne was the only imperial city with a university, founded in 1388 and the oldest of the three civic universities (alongside Erfurt and Basel) in the Holy Roman Empire. Its economic and cultural vitality predestined it to be one of Germany's major printing centers. Its first press dated from 1465, and the number of printers had grown by the sixteenth century to more than a hundred. Cologne was also proud of its imperial status, gained in a long struggle against its archbishop and formally confirmed by Frederick III in 1475. The town council kept the archbishop at arm's length and frustrated all his attempts to gain influence through the back door by intriguing with discontented groups of burghers. The election of each archbishop provided a fresh occasion for Cologne to assert its independence and for the archbishop to attempt to reestablish his overlordship, the main conflict revolving around the oath of recognition taken on his entry into the city. That this issue had lost none of its intensity was shown by the fact that Hermann von Wied, who became archbishop in 1515, was unable to make his formal entry until 1522.

Despite the archbishop's limited influence, Cologne was an important center of religious orthodoxy, ensured by the close relationship between its leading religious institutions and the university: since 1374 a canonry had been reserved for a university professor in each of the city's collegiate foundations. The theology faculty enjoyed such high standing that its opinion was regularly sought on disputed doctrinal issues, as occurred in 1509 in the Johannes Reuchlin controversy over the banning of Jewish books. This intervention served to identify the university as hostile to humanist learning, helped by the highly polemical *Epistolae obscurorum virorum* (Epistles of Obscure Men; 1515), which stigmatized leading Cologne theologians as narrow-minded obscurantists. Cologne, however, was as permeated by the new spirit of humanism as any other major urban center of Germany, even if its humanists had a lower profile than those elsewhere. It also stood in the forefront of new movements of piety and devotion. In Cologne in 1475 the Dominican prior Jacob Sprenger founded the confraternity of the Rosary, a movement that encompassed one hundred thousand members by the 1480s and that attained its full development in the Counter-Reformation. The *Devotio moderna* was also a powerful force for religious renewal in the city's religious houses and educational institutions.

It is scarcely surprising that Cologne theologians played a leading part in opposing Martin Luther's ideas when the controversy over indulgences flared up in 1518–1519. The university openly condemned Luther on 30 October 1519, and Cologne was the only major city of Germany formally to publish the papal bull branding him a heretic. Luther's books were burned there at the end of 1520. In consequence of this early opposition, the evangelical movements agitating other German towns never gained any significant toehold in Cologne. A few Cologne printers dared to publish Luther's works in the early 1520s, but a formal prohibition of printing or distributing Lutheran works issued by the town council on 17 August 1524 cut off this possibility for dissemination of the new ideas. There was no public proclamation of the Lutheran message, despite some support among Cologne's Augustinians, and certainly no significant public preaching, given the tight grip of the advocates of strict orthodoxy on Cologne's religious institutions. The professor of Greek and Hebrew Theodore Fabricius expressed mild evangelical sentiments in his lectures, but the few heterodox views abroad in the 1520s were confined to a tiny circle of adherents. Anticlericalism was unable to provide impetus for the reception of Lutheran ideas as it did elsewhere. The town council had long since asserted control over the clergy resident within its walls (who accounted for only five percent of the population before 1530), and in May 1525 it removed the clergy's economic privileges and subjected them to civic taxation. This shrewd preemptive strike prevented anticlericalism from developing any effective popular voice. A civic disturbance of June 1525 demanded, alongside numerous other grievances, the free preaching of the word of God, but its impact was feeble and short-lived. The great urban revolt of 1515 seems to have exhausted significant civic dissent, and Cologne was thus deprived of the vehicle on which the evangelical movement rode to prominence in many other German towns.

The increasingly educated Cologne elites seemed uninterested in the new ideas, and the town council successfully asserted Catholic uniformity, on 18 September 1526 warning all officials and guilds against accepting as citizens anyone of unacceptable religious views. Evangelical ideas were not entirely silenced and in 1527 the evangelical printer Arnd von Eich even dared to publish a *Handbuch des evangelischen Bürgers* (Handbook for the Evangelical Burgher). In 1528, however, the town council showed its resoluteness by arresting two Lutherans, Adolph Clarenbach and the chaplain Johann Klopreiss, who were turned over to the Inquisition. Klopreiss was exiled, but Clarenbach was burned alongside student Peter Fliedesten. In the wake of the events in Münster in 1534, the town council was presented with forty names of suspected Anabaptist sympathizers, one of whom, Richard von Richrath, was burned. The town council's religious policy was heavily influenced by economic and political considerations. It was wary of ceding any advantage to the archbishop by offending the emperor on religious matters, since any condemnation of the city under the terms of the Edict of Worms would have played into the archbishop's hands. Moreover, Cologne's economic interests were so firmly rooted in the lower Rhine region, its wine and grain trade so dependent on free transit through imperial territory, that it would have been suicidal to provoke the emperor. The town council kept a wary eye on all potential manifestations of heterodoxy, even encouraging spies and informers. It rarely stooped to open persecution but probably had no need to do so. A clandestine Protestant community did grow up in the more tolerant atmosphere of the second half of the century and may have accounted for as many as ten percent of the population at its height. The first traceable Protestant community, in 1565, belonged to the Reformed church, while a Lutheran community appeared only in 1575. Throughout the sixteenth century there were certainly sympathizers with evangelical reform, and there was a surge of Protestant influence in the 1570s, fostered by immigrants fleeing religious persecution in the lower Rhine area. The town council was aware of the danger and in 1576 insisted that all new citizens be tested on their religious orthodoxy, as well as providing testimonials on their place of origin. In 1579 the town council refused to recognize a Protestant councillor elected by one of the craft guilds, thus establishing the principle that all city magistrates must henceforth be Catholic. Protestant, especially Dutch, refugees were eventually tolerated on economic grounds, and at the beginning of the seventeenth century Cologne Protestants may have numbered as many as a thousand in a population of 37,000, but they were denied any political influence or opportunity to propagate their faith.

The town council also supported the cathedral chapter in its stubborn resistance to two attempts to Protestantize the archdiocese. In 1542 Archbishop Wied sought to introduce an evangelical reformation, calling Martin Bucer to Bonn to assist in drafting the key doctrinal document. Wied's printer was the son-in-law of Arnd von Aich, Laurenz von der Mülen, who in 1544 published a new edition of the *Handbuch des evangelischen Bürgers* . Wied was successfully deposed by the cathedral chapter, and it was undoubtedly in consequence of the affair that Johannes Oldendorp, an eminent Cologne jurist known for evangelical sympathies, was sacked from his university post in 1543. A second attempt was made to reform the archdiocese in 1582 by Gebhard von Truchsess, who was elected archbishop in 1579 and who wished to marry his pregnant mistress, the nun Agnes von Mansfeld. Gebhard had previously alarmed the Cologne town council in 1582 by addressing a letter directly to the city's craft guilds, an old ploy to gain political influence behind the council's back. In December 1582 Gebhard declared his intention to turn Protestant and to allow his subjects a free choice of religious allegiance. The cathedral chapter aroused the estates to opposition and declared him deposed. The subsequent armed conflict unsettled the archdiocese until Gebhard gave up his claims in 1588. Throughout the affair, the city of Cologne never wavered in its support of religious orthodoxy.

Cologne thus remained an important bastion of Catholicism throughout the sixteenth century, contributing significantly to the emergence of the German Counter-Reformation. As the only major printing center not to go over to the Reformation, Cologne provided the spearhead for a significant program of printed works, ably led by the workshop of Peter Quentell countering those of the Reformers. An early vernacular Bible had been published in Cologne in 1478/79 under the influence of the *Devotio moderna*, and it was wholly appropriate that the German Bible that was to provide the main Catholic competitor to Luther's translation was produced in Cologne in 1534. The city was also an important printing center for religious orders, especially the Carthusians and the Jesuits. In common with most Catholic counterpropaganda, however, the popular impact of its output was blunted by appearing largely in Latin. Yet the Cologne Counter-Reformation was not confined merely to repression or counterpolemic. The Cologne Carthusians and (from 1544) the Jesuits successfully engaged in popular catechizing. The Jesuits founded a college there in 1556, although it was not officially recognized by the town council until 1582. "Holy Cologne" thus remained resolutely Catholic, a banner it carried proudly into the modern period.

BIBLIOGRAPHY

Berglar, Peter, ed. *Der Bischof in seiner Zeit.* Cologne, 1986.
Bosbach, Franz. *Die katholische Reform in der Stadt Köln, 1550–1662.* Cologne, 1988.
Chaix, Gérald. "Humanisme et élites urbaines à Cologne au XVIe siècle." In *Humanismus und höfisch-städtische Eliten im 16. Jahrhundert,* edited by Klaus Malettke and Jürgen Voss, pp. 195–210. Bonn, 1989.
Ennen, Leonard. *Geschichte der Stadt Köln.* Vols. 4 and 5. Cologne, 1875; Düsseldorf, 1880. Still the best general history.
Fuchs, Peter, ed. *Chronik zur Geschichte der Stadt Köln.* Vol. 2. Cologne, 1991.
Gechter, Marianne. *Kirche und Klerus in der stadtkölnische Wirtschaft im Spätmittelalter.* Wiesbaden, 1983.
Goerters, J. F. G. "Die Stadt Köln und die Prozesse und Hinrichtung von Peter Fliedesten und Adolf Clarenbach." In *Bekenner und Zeugen,* edited by J. F. G. Goeters, pp. 11–27. Düsseldorf, 1979.
Herborn, W. "Verfassungsideal und Verfassungswirklichkeit in Köln während der ersten zwei Jahrhunderte nach Inkrafttreten des Verbundbriefs von 1396." In *Städtische Führungsgruppen und Gemeinde in der werdenden Frühneuzeit,* edited by Wilfried Ehbrecht, pp. 25–52. Cologne, 1980.
———. "Die Protestanten in Schilderung und Urteil des Kölner Chronisten Hermann von Weinsberg." In *Niederland und Nordwestdeutschland,* edited by Wilfried Ehbrecht and Heinz Schilling, pp. 136–155. Cologne, 1983.
Irsigler, Franz. *Die wirtschaftliche Stellung der Stadt Köln im 14. und 15. Jahrhundert.* Wiesbaden, 1979.
Schäfke, Werner, ed. *Der Name der Freiheit: Aspekte Kölner Geschichte, 1288–1988.* Cologne, 1988.
Scribner, Robert W. "Why Was There No Reformation in Cologne?" In *Popular Culture and Popular Movements in Reformation Germany,* pp. 217–241. London and Ronceverte, W.Va., 1987.
Zimmermann, Albert, ed. *Die Kölner Universität im Mittelalter.* Berlin, 1989.

ROBERT W. SCRIBNER

COLONNA, Vittoria

COLONNA, Vittoria (1490–1547), Italian poet and reformer. Born into the highest rank of the Roman nobility, she was married to the Neapolitan soldier Ferdinando d'Avalos, marquis of Pescara. The governorship of the papal city of Benevento, which she exercised first for her absent husband and later in her own right, brought her into contact with the councillors of Clement VII, particularly Gian Matteo Giberti, and from 1520 to 1526 she frequented literary circles in Rome and Naples. Widowed by Pescara's death in 1525, she devoted herself to celebrating his glory in verse (*Rime profane*) and to ascetic religious devotions. On moving from Ischia to Rome in 1532, she became caught up in the struggle to preserve the autonomy of the Capuchins, whom she saw as a vehicle of reform, interceding with Clement VII and again with Paul III in 1536. A visit to Ferrara in 1537–1538 enabled her to converse with Renée of France and to fall more completely under the spell of Bernardino Ochino, whom she followed on a preaching tour of Tuscany.

In 1541 her brother Ascanio's rebellion against Paul III caused her to retire to the convent of San Caterina at Viterbo, where she joined the group gathered about Cardinal Reginald Pole, including Marcantonio Flaminio and Pietro Carnesecchi. She credited Pole with moderating the severity of her penitential discipline. It was probably through Ochino and Pole's circle that she encountered the ideas of Juan de Valdés. She was interested enough in the issue of justification that Cardinal Gasparo Contarini had her sent a copy of his 1541 letter "De iustificatione" (a defense of article 5, the compromise on justification, of the *Book of Regensburg*), but the extent to which she may have accepted justification *ex sola fide* has been a matter of debate hinging principally on interpretations of her religious poetry and on Carnesecchi's testimony that Pole had advised her to believe as if salvation depended on faith and to live as if it depended on works. Evidence uncovered from the trial of Cardinal Giovanni Morone and from the archives of the Inquisition gives greater reason to believe that under Pole's guidance she may have developed a spirituality based on the primacy of faith. Her religious sonnets (*Rime spirituali*) and her *Pianto sulla passione di Cristo* (Lament for the Passion of Christ Crucified; 1556) breathed an evangelical mysticism centered on the crucified Christ. Along with Pole, she became increasingly suspect of heresy after Ochino's widely circulated letter to her justifying his flight (1542). Her years after 1544, spent in the convent of Santa Anna at Rome, were clouded by ill health and by suspicion, despite the friendship and support of Paul III. She died on 25 February 1547, leaving Pole her heir.

Universally admired by the poets and writers of her age, many of whom enjoyed platonic friendships with her, she embodied the aristocratic manners and dignified culture celebrated in *Il cortegiano* (The Courtier, an etiquette manual written by Baldassare Castiglione), enhanced by the transcendent aura of lofty morals and ardent faith. Her most famous literary friendships were with Castiglione, Ludovico Ariosto, and Pietro Bembo. Michelangelo felt her spiritual influence deeply and dedicated to her a number of his poems and a series of Crucifixion drawings.

BIBLIOGRAPHY

Primary Sources

Colonna, Vittoria. *Carteggio.* Edited by Ermanno Ferrero and Giuseppe Müller. 2d ed., with a supplement edited by Domenico Tordi. Turin, 1892.
——. *Rime.* Edited by Alan Bullock. Bari, 1982.

Secondary Sources

Firpo, Massimo. *Inquisizione romana e controriforma.* Bologna, 1992. See chap. 2, "Vittoria Colonna, Giovanni Morone e gli 'spirituali.'" Up-to-date and authoritative.
Jerrold, Maude F. *Vittoria Colonna.* London, 1906. Old and outdated but the most recent biography in English.
Jung, Eva-Marie. "Vittoria Colonna between Reformation and Counter Reformation." *Review of Religion* 15 (1951), 144–159. An assessment of her significance. Outdated.
Pagano, Sergio M., and Concetta Ranieri, eds. *Nuovi documenti su Vittoria Colonna e Reginald Pole.* Collectanea Archivi Vaticani, 24. Vatican City, 1989. Important for her religious views.
Patrizi, Giorqio. "Vittoria Colonna." In *Dizionario biografico degli italiani*, vol. 27, pp. 448–457. Rome, 1982. Outdated; contains some errors.
Thérault, Suzanne. *Un cénacle humaniste de la Renaissance autour de Vittoria Colonna.* Paris, 1968. For her early life.

T. C. PRICE ZIMMERMANN

COMMON MAN. "The common man is the peasant, the burgher of the country town, the townsman barred from imperial city offices, the miner." This definition may be gleaned from sources of the time in which the word was in wide use, the time of the Reformation. The term *common man* had its basis in something general, as in the "common" Christendom, the "common" good, or the "common" penny, which was collected from all inhabitants of the empire. It is therefore etymologically and semantically incorrect to equate "common man" with "community man" (*Gemeindemann*) (Lutz, p. 62). This confusion of terms is rooted in the fact that in a community, no matter whether it was an urban city or a rural community, only those peasants and burghers who had political rights were designated as the "common man." In the country, priests, magistrates, Jews, and gypsies were not the "common man," though artisans were; in the city the same groups, and the patricians as well, were not considered the "common man." In the city, at least in an imperial city with a guild constitution, access to the governing city council was in principle wide open. In practice, however, guild masters did not have the time to sit on the city council, so the concept of the "common man" took on a double sense: on the one hand the "common man" referred to the townspeople as subjects and recipients of council policy, while on the other hand it referred to the group potentially eligible to serve on the city council by virtue of membership in a guild. Therefore the concept had a broad and a narrow significance. The broad definition of the "common man" was the same as the later, often-used term *subject*, while the narrow definition referred to burghers and peasants with a house in the city or in the village and was therefore much the same as "head of household." In depersonalizing the concept of the head of a household, women were also integrated into the concept; this appears, though rarely, in the expression "common man of both sexes." "Common woman" was never used as the female equivalent of "common man," as "common woman" meant prostitute. "Common man" was not actually a legal concept, but one of official correspondence, of grievance documents, and of pamphlets. As such it was not altogether unsusceptible to emotionalism and could be given a positive or a negative meaning.

It was often negatively accentuated when the demarcation between "common man" and "common trash" (*gemeiner Pofel*) or "common people" (*gemeines Volk*) was not maintained. "Trash, rabble," in the language of the time, were those who did not have houses in cities and villages; "rabble" were travelers, beggars, and vagrants, the dishonest professions, the soldiers, and possibly domestic servants.

Even today little is known of the etymology of the term *common man.* Special studies of the history of the term beyond the narrow confines of the time of the Reformation are lacking. Nevertheless, one can assume that it replaced the *laboratores* of the medieval system of orders, so that it was a synonym for the "third estate." In this sense the concept is not foreign to the French and English languages ("alle the comyns of Inglond," 1450). *Laboratores* referred first of all to manual labor, but it did not distinguish between farm work and craft work. Similarly, "common man" included both peasants and burghers. But the frequent synonymous use of "common" man and "poor" man may be considered a German version of the medieval concepts *potens-pauper*. Potens means capable of ruling and therefore designates nobility and (high) ecclesiastical dignitaries. Pauper means not capable of ruling.

Martin Luther implied this connection and identified the common man with the third estate. "Therefore it has come about," he writes in his *An den christlichen Adel deutscher Nation* (Open Letter to the Christian Nobility) of 1520, "that one says to the pope and his adherents, 'Tu ora' [You shall pray]. To the emperor and to his retinue, 'Tu protege' [You shall protect]. To the common man, 'Tu labora' [You shall work]." In these variations it becomes clear that exclusion from traditional rule was normative in the definition of the "common man." The concept was used in German from the fifteenth to the eighteenth century, but it underwent changes, limitations, and modifications during that time. The earliest references to the "common man" come from the fourteenth century and signify the judge who made the decision in courts of arbitration. The courts of arbitration, which normally had four judges, brought in a fifth "common man" when the vote was split. The common man thus replaced the king as the judge of final appeal and represented a nonauthoritative element.

How "common man" came to be a collective name for peasant and burgher is still not clear. The first documented evidence of this meaning comes from the time after 1400.

From the end of the sixteenth century, "common man" was increasingly replaced by the term *subject*. The political authorities were clearly interested in employing the label of "subject" and eliminating "common man." Historical word studies, which have been carried out only with sources from Württemberg, show that after 1600 the burgher was no longer designated as "common man," and that the word, with such variants as "common man in the country" and "common hard-working peasant," finally referred solely to the peasants.

The term was used frequently during the Reformation and the Peasants' War of 1525. Its malleability permitted it to be used in an ideal sense as "the Lutheran peasant of the Reformation," and as the embodiment of the "Protestant man" with its best-known expression being "plowman" (*Karsthans*) (Wohlfeil, p. 284). Pamphlets are full of positive connotations in which the true Christians, the followers of the gospel and of "Lutheran teaching," are referred to collectively as the "common man." The peasant and the simple artisan became the protagonists of the Reformation. Norms and values were ascribed to the common man focusing on

the concepts of "common weal" and "Christian, brotherly love." It is also undeniable that the common man, at least in south Germany, became the bearer of the Reformation. "The common man is the patron of the Reformation" (Schmidt, p. 332) was said in reference to the cities, and this was also true for the rural areas.

Both the rebels themselves and the political authorities defined the Peasants' War as one of the common man. In the Tirol the protest was voiced in 1525 that "the common man must with heavy cost bring the nobleman and the clergy to the courts." In Franconia the peasants demanded that "the clergy and the laity, noble and not noble, must from now on have only the same rights as the ordinary burgher and peasant and be nothing more than a common man." An important pamphlet for political theory, "An die versammlung gemayner Pawerschaft," rebukes the arbitrariness "of the nobility and other authorities" for "treating the common man constantly and mercilessly contrary to all justice with un-Christian, tyrannical violence."

The authorities also use the term in the same way. The Innsbruck government of 1525 spoke of an "uprising of the common man," and Margrave Ernst von Baden noted an "assembly of the common man." A particularly revealing interpretation of the term is found in the words of the elector Frederick III of Saxony, who commented as follows on the events of 1525: "If God so desires, then it will come about that the common man will rule." This and many other examples are the reason why the Peasants' War has been called the "revolution of the common man."

The peasant grievances, contemporary utopias, and theoretical programs fostered a social and political order organized by the common man and adjusted to his norms and values. It was an order in which the clergy was eliminated as the bearer of political functions, the nobility was weakened, if not completely eliminated, and the traditional territorial authorities were removed or at least subjected to a type of parliamentary control by peasants and burghers in so far as their functions were concerned. Theoretically and conceptually "the state of the common man" made its appearance (Ganseuer). The identification of the social basis of the Reformation and the Peasants' War by means of the concept of the "common man" has been strongly echoed in scholarship since the 1970s and has become partially accepted as a countertheory to the Marxist model of the "early bourgeois revolution" (Brady).

[*See also* Peasants *and* Peasants' War.]

BIBLIOGRAPHY

Blickle, Peter. *Landschaften im Alten Reich: Die staatliche Funktion des gemeinen Mannes in Oberdeutschland.* Munich, 1973.
———. *The Revolution of 1525.* Translated by Thomas A. Brady, Jr., and H. C. Erik Midelfort. Baltimore and London, 1981.
———. "Untertanen in der Frühneuzeit." *Vierteljahrschrift für Sozial- und Wirtschaftsgeschichte* 70 (1983), 483–522.
Brady, Thomas A., Jr. "From the Sacral Community to the Common

Man: Reflections on German Reformation Studies." *Central European History* 20 (1987), 229–245.

Ganseuer, Frank. *Der Staat des "gemeinen Mannes": Gattungstypologie und Programmatik des politischen Schrifttums von Reformation und Bauenkrieg.* Frankfurt a.M., 1985.

Lutz, Robert H. *Wer war der gemeine Mann? Der dritte Stand in der Krise des Spätmittelalters.* Munich, 1979.

Roper, Lyndal. " 'The common man', 'the common good,' 'common women': Gender and Meaning in the German Reformation commune." *Social History* 12 (1987), 1–21.

Schmidt, Heinrich R. *Reichsstädte, Reich und Reformation: Korporative Religionspolitik, 1521–1529/30.* Stuttgart, 1986.

Wohlfeil, Rainer. "Der 'Gemeine Mann' im 'Bauernkrieg'." In *Die Bauernkriege und Michael Gaismaier,* edited by Friedolin Dörrer, pp. 283–289. Innsbruck, 1982.

PETER BLICKLE
Translated from German by Walter D. Morris

COMMUNALISM. German historians in the 1980s used the term *communalism* to designate attempts to achieve autonomous self-government in town and country during the Reformation period. The notion emphasizes the importance of the commune (*Gemeinde*) for the political, administrative, social, and religious life of urban and rural communities, drawing on an older tradition of German history that stressed an inherent dualism at all levels of constitutional development between a corporate principle and one based on domination (*Herrschaft*). The corporate principle was founded on the equality of all members sharing common rights and obligations in a form of collective association. In late medieval Germany the basic form of association in both town and country was the commune, which possessed or sought to possess autochthonous rights to regulate its own affairs. This included the administration of justice, maintenance of peace within the community, economic functions such as distribution of common land or grazing, administration of church finances and church fabric, and in some places communal appointment of pastors. All these communal functions were justified by appeal to the ideal of the "common good" (*gemein nutz*), to which all individual self-interest (*eigen nutz*) was to be strictly subordinate.

The historian most associated with these ideas has been Peter Blickle, who has sought to elevate these undeniable aspects of urban and rural communal life into a broader interpretation not only of the Reformation but of German history as a whole (increasingly with reference to Switzerland as a prototypical model). The demand for communal autonomy was the precondition for positive resistance by the rural classes to attempts at domination by feudal-aristocratic classes, thus providing the basis for a Swiss-German tradition of populist, antifeudal politics. The existence in some parts of Germany of forms of communal representation in territorial or regional assemblies (*Landschaften*) provided an alternative to princely rule supported by estates comprised largely of social elites. Thus, Blickle argues, German history has not been one of continuous subjection of subordinate classes but one with an alternative parliamentarian tradition. The desire expressed in both urban and rural communities to take control of the church and the means of salvation Blickle sees as an important precondition for the Reformation in Germany and Switzerland, a process somewhat misleadingly labeled "christianization." The Reformation in its popular form was a "communal Reformation," opposed by a "prince's Reformation" that emerged as the ultimate victor in the religious upheavals. This strengthened a trend toward authoritarian rule, which nonetheless could not completely overcome the communal impulse. Communalism remained a continual influence in Swiss and German history.

There have been numerous criticisms of this interpretation, although to some extent they were directed against a moving target as Blickle developed and enlarged his conceptions in a sequence of publications extending from 1965 to 1991. Initially he focused largely on the German southwest, supplemented by work on Switzerland, leading him to posit a north-south distinction similar to Bernd Moeller's interpretation of a south German-Swiss Zwinglian and a north-central German Lutheran Reformation. However, as evidence emerged of the existence and vigor of both rural and urban communal forms in all parts of the Holy Roman Empire, especially through the work of Heinz Schilling, Blickle began to elevate communalism into a phenomenon applicable to ancien régime Europe as a whole and to present it as a preliminary stage to a process of "democratization." This was no unique insight, since Jerome Blum and David Sabean in the 1970s saw the existence of strong communal forms as the precondition for active peasant resistance. In Blickle's version, however, the communalism thesis resembles a neo-whig interpretation of German history, scarcely weakened by its most recent qualification as a "heuristic strategy."

The most incisive criticisms of the thesis relate to the very nature of the commune, which by no means represented the entire urban or rural community. Only those legally recognized as members shared in its rights: in the countryside usually male heads of households or full tenants; in the towns, male citizens. The majority of the population, especially women, were thus excluded, and it is difficult to present this essentially elite body as a preliminary stage to democracy. The commune was also far from intrinsically hostile to lordship, and in many places was easily integrated into structures of hierarchical domination, sometimes even seeking that integration. Lordship helped to preserve the dominance of communal elites against other sections of the community who may have demanded more rights, while the communal constitution was a highly efficient means of maintaining law and order in the name of the lordship by shifting both costs and responsibility onto the local community. Ideologically, the "commune" represented no consistent ideal, but one whose content was often regarded pragmatically and which was a site of conflict within the community, especially in towns. In the countryside, the commune was often regarded as representing the interests of village elites, as was the regional assembly. The "communal Reformation" also scarcely seems to correspond to the actual complexity of either Reformation movements or the outcomes of strivings for religious reform.

That "communalism" provides an overarching model of the Reformation or German history in general now seems questionable, although it has been invaluable in directing attention to the importance of communal forms throughout Germany and Switzerland, while emphasizing the independence of rural social and political action. The paradigm of the "communal Reformation" may prove to have limited regional validity, perhaps only for the south German-Swiss area, but it has helped creatively to refocus thinking away from traditional elites and to call attention to neglected aspects of rural society.

BIBLIOGRAPHY

Blickle, Peter. *Landschaften im Alten Reich: Die staatliche Funktion des Gemeinen Mannes in Oberdeutschland.* Stuttgart, 1973.
————. *Die Revolution von 1525.* Munich, 1975. Available in English as *The Revolution of 1525: The German Peasants' War from a New Perspective,* Baltimore, 1981.
————. *Deutsche Untertanen. Ein Widerspruch.* Munich, 1981.
————. "Der Kommunalismus als Gestaltungsprinzig zwischen Mittelalter und Moderne." In *Gesellschaft und Gesellschaften. Festschrift zum 65. Geburtstag von Ulrich im Hof,* edited by Nicolai Bernard and Quirinius Reichen, pp. 95–113. Bern, 1982.
————. *Die Reformation im Reich.* Stuttgart, 1982.
————. *Gemeindereformation: Die Menschen des 16. Jahrhunderts auf dem Weg zum Heil.* Munich, 1985. Available in English as *Communal Reformation. The Quest for Salvation in Sixteenth Century Germany,* Atlantic Highlands, N.J., 1992.
————. "Kommunalismus, Parliamentarismus, Republikanismus." *Historische Zeitschrift* 242 (1986), 529–556.
————. "Communal Reformation and Peasant Piety: The Peasant Reformation and Its Late Medieval Origins." *Central European History* 20 (1987), 216–228.
Blickle, Peter, ed. *Landgemeinde und Stadtgemeinde in Mitteleuropa.* Munich, 1991. The essays represent the most searching assessment of the concept through specific examples.
Blickle, Peter, and Johannes Kunisch, eds. *Kommunalisierung und Christianisierung: Voraussetzungen und Folgen der Reformation, 1400–1600.* Berlin, 1989.
Blum, Jerome. "The Internal Structure and Politics of the European Village Community." *Journal of Modern History* 43 (1971), 541–576.
Brady, Thomas A. "From the Sacral Community to the Common Man: Reflections on German Reformation Studies." *Central European History* 20 (1987), 219–245.
Press, Volker. "Kommunalismus oder Territorialismus? Bemerkung zur Ausbildung des frühmodernen Staates in Mitteleuropa." In *Die Bildung des frühmodernen Staates: Stände und Konfessionen,* edited by Heiner Timmermann, pp. 109–135. Saarbrücken, 1989.
Sabean, David. "The Communal Basis of pre-1800 Risings in Western Europe." *Comparative Politics* 8 (1976), 355–364.
————. *Power in the Blood: Popular Culture and Village Discourse in Early Modern Germany.* Cambridge, 1984.
Schilling, Heinz. "The Communal Reformation in Germany: An Upper German, Zwinglian Phenomenon before the 'Turning Point of the Reformation' in 1525?" In *Religion, Political Culture and the Emergence of Early Modern Society,* pp. 189–201. Leiden, 1992. (Also available in original German in *Zeitschrift für historische Forschung* 14 [1987], 325–333.)
Scribner, Robert W. "Communalism: Universal Category or Ideological Construct?" *Historical Journal* 37 (1994), 199–207.
————. "Communities and the Nature of Power." In *Germany: A New Social and Economic History,* edited by Robert W. Scribner, vol. 1. London, 1995. Most recent discussion of concepts of community in late medieval and early modern Germany.

ROBERT W. SCRIBNER

COMMUNITY OF GOODS is the ideal of Christian sharing based on the model of *Acts* 2 and 4, generally practiced by early Anabaptist groups, most effectively and continuously by the Hutterites. The message of *Acts* 2 and 4 was, of course, not lost to medieval Christianity. Together with descriptions in the Gospels of Christ saying that he had nowhere to lay his head and telling the rich young man to sell his goods and give to the poor, the practice of the post-Pentecostal apostles in Jerusalem became part of the basis of monastic counsels of perfection, the higher way of the Christian ethical elite. The mendicant orders of the thirteenth century and afterward, with their debates about the character of apostolic poverty and the relative merits of endowed clergy and begging friars, continued to treat *Acts* 2 and 4 as a description of Christian life that applied only to the clergy. Not the least important sign of the Christian humanists' advocacy of lay self-assertion was their application of *Acts* 2 and 4 to the laity. Thomas More in *Utopia* wrote of an imaginary community in which everyone practiced community of goods with beneficial effects. Like More, Erasmus and Zwingli believed that community of goods was a proper ideal for all Christians. As late as 1522 Zwingli wrote that among true Christians "no one calls any possession his own; all things are held in common."

Given the broad affirmation of *Acts* 2 and 4 by the biblical humanists who ushered in the Reformation, Thomas Müntzer's statement that his Allstedt league held the principle that *omnia sunt communia* ("everything belongs to everyone") and that "goods should be distributed to everyone according to need," contains no surprise. But appeals to the model of *Acts* 2 and 4 were relatively rare in the Peasants' War. The vastly influential Twelve Articles were primarily concerned to apply divine law to reject property in persons (serfdom) and to protect the traditional common property of village communes. The bitter aftermath of the Peasants' War produced appeals for radical equality such as Michael Gaismaier's Tirolean *Landesordnung* of 1526, and in 1527 a vision of community of goods in the *Von der neuen Wandlung eines christlichen Lebens* (New Transformation of a Christian Life) published by Hans Hergot. But the reaction against the commoner's uprising of 1525 ended the flirtation of the powerful and the educated with community of goods. *Utopia* was celebrated in humanist circles in the years of its first publication (1516–1518), but ten years later it cost Hergot his head to look forward to an age of the Holy Spirit in which people would say no longer, "That is mine."

Just as the suppression of the Peasants' War marked the end of humanist dalliance with community of goods as a high ideal, perhaps realizable only in utopia (nowhere), attempts to put *Acts* 2 and 4 into practice by direct, popular action began in 1525 in the wake of the rebellion. In Switzerland and the Upper Rhine Anabaptist leaders often were either themselves entangled in the commoners' resistance or directed their appeal to people who had lost their confidence in the established Reformed pastors because they had abandoned the cause of the commoners. In Thuringia, Hesse, and Franconia Anabaptist leaders were often persons who had earlier fought in or supported the uprising. Although most of these Anabaptists accepted the defeat of the Peasants' War as a negative judgment of God, they did not abandon the 1525 goal of realizing the "divine law." For them the lesson of 1525 was that ordinary people would have to reestablish the church of the apostles described in the Reformation's vernacular Bibles in the face of the betrayal of university-trained theologians and rulers.

The various Anabaptist groups had different approaches to community of goods as described in *Acts* 2 and 4, but almost all early Anabaptists accepted the communism of the early church as a desirable norm. The Swiss Anabaptists aimed above all at the recovery of the practice of the New Testament church. For instance, believers' baptism was in their eyes a New Testament ceremony to be restored. The St. Gall chronicler Johann Kessler, like Zwingli, describes the first Swiss Anabaptist congregation in Zollikon as practicing community of goods on the model of *Acts*. Felix Mantz wrote in early 1525 that whenever he baptized people he "taught them further about love and unity and community of all things, as in *Acts* 2." Johannes Brötli, the Anabaptist preacher in Zollikon, directed the congregation to Jesus' telling the rich young man to sell his possessions and give them to the poor. Wealthy members of the Zollikon congregation were pressed to sell land from which they received income and to live strictly from their work. An early Swiss Anabaptist congregational ordinance (c.1527) stated the characteristic application of *Acts* 2 and 4: "Of all the brothers and sisters of this congregation none shall have anything of his own, . . . as the Christians in the time of the apostles held all in common, and especially stored up a common fund, from which aid can be given to the poor."

The early Swiss Anabaptists tried to restore the order of *Acts* 2 and 4 by creating congregations of working people, without idle *rentiers*, and with aid to the poor from a common chest. In the disputations with Reformed pastors in Bern in the 1530s, they insisted on a strict definition of the sin of usury as any profit from loans, while the pastors said that usury was only excessive profit from loans. Under the attack of the governments and the established church that connected community of goods with political subversion and sexual irregularities, however, the Swiss Anabaptists clarified repeatedly that it had nothing to do with unwillingness to pay tithes, debts, or rents, and was certainly not meant as a claim on the property of others. Moreover, some Swiss Anabaptists began quite early to retreat from the ideal of the early church. For instance, the statement of Hans Hausmann in Bern, 1527: "I don't reject property. In the beginning of Christianity everything was common; but it is no command."

The Anabaptists of south and central Germany had a different sort of spirituality from the Swiss. Leaders like Hans Hut, Melchior Rinck, Hans Denck, and Hans Römer all had a close association with Thomas Müntzer and had been involved in the Thuringian peasant rebellion of 1525. In his tracts against Luther in 1524 Müntzer articulated a mystical piety in which he called on Christians, rich and poor, to renounce creaturely attachments to pleasure, power, and property so that the Holy Spirit could purge their souls. He was impressed by a version of Eusebius's church history that he interpreted to mean that the great age of the church ended in the second century, when community of goods was abandoned and the inspiration of the Holy Spirit was smothered by empty ceremonies.

Müntzer's message, that true Christians must renounce ceremonialism and materialism and cultivate mystical receptivity (*Gelassenheit*) to God's Spirit, was replicated in diverse ways by the Anabaptists whose lives he touched. For some of them, such as Hut and his visionary disciple Augustin Bader, community of goods was associated with God's action at the end of the world. For others, such as Leonhard Schiemer, antimaterialist *Gelassenheit* was connected with the acceptance of persecution, a piety of martyrdom. In the interim before Christ's return these south German Anabaptists pledged to "help the poor better than others." The overarching theme was that "everything should be in common" because they wanted to "remove their hearts from everything external." The heightened eschatological expectancy of Hut's type of Anabaptism and the fierce persecution that it suffered in 1527–1529 interfered with the establishment of fixed congregations and common chests. Wolfgang Brandhuber, who worked for Hut's Anabaptism in Austria and the Tirol, maintained that community of goods could be practiced even in isolated households: ". . .each father of a household should work together in a common purse with those who share his faith, whether they be lord, servant, wife, or maid." In Switzerland community of goods was a rule of imitation of post-Pentecostal apostolic practice; in south Germany it was a piety of renunciation of the material; in both regions, whether congregational life was weak or strong, it was practiced by persons living in individual family households, the characteristic economic units of early modern European life.

The rupture of community of goods from the economy of the traditional family household, which occurred in the two most striking cases of Anabaptist community of goods (Moravia and Münster), was in both cases the result of a large number of socially uprooted refugees. A combination of attempts to enforce religious conformity with the belief that Anabaptists continued the commoners' resistance of the Peasants' War led to rigorous persecution of Anabaptists throughout Switzerland and south and central Germany. The executions of Anabaptists reached a peak in 1528 and 1529.

Meanwhile, beginning in 1526 at the south Moravian German community at Nikolsburg, the Anabaptist theologian Balthasar Hubmaier won the support of the local clergy and the ruling Liechtenstein family for an Anabaptist Reformation. Frequently using the Danube, thousands of Anabaptists fled to Moravia, where the Hussite wars had led to legal guarantees of religious diversity and had drastically weakened Catholicism. They came from many regions, but particularly from the Tirol, which contributed its most prominent leader, Jacob Hutter, and from Swabia. In 1527 a series of controversies broke out that undermined Hubmaier's attempt at an established Anabaptist church. A major issue was that a group of *Gemainschaffter* ("community people") insisted on the religious duty of sharing their homes and property with the destitute refugees. These *Gemainschaffter* were adjudged to be schismatic and expelled from Nikolsburg in March 1528. According to the Hutterite Chronicle, which regarded this event as the beginning of its religious tradition, the leaders of the banished *Gemainschaffter* "spread out a cloak in front of the people, and each one laid his possessions on it with a willing heart—without being forced—so that the needy might be supported in accordance with the teaching of the prophets and apostles, *Isa.* 23; *Acts* 2, 4 and 5."

Moravian Anabaptist history was dominated by immigrants from the Holy Roman Empire, German speaking but living in areas where the indigenous population was mainly Czech. After the initial immigration owing to persecution, subsequent recruits were attracted to Moravia (and neighboring Hungary) by systematic missionary activity that presented Moravia as the wilderness that God had provided for his church pending the second coming of Christ. But the Hutterites, who became the leading Moravian Anabaptist group after two decades of bitter internal schisms and fierce Habsburg persecutions, also based their missionary appeal on the economic and social success of their system. From the first separation of *Gemainschaffter* in 1528 to the seventy Hutterite settlements of 1600 the number of people practicing their form of community of goods had increased from about two hundred to perhaps thirty-five thousand.

The Hutterites lived in *Haushaben* ("settlements") of four to six hundred persons, consisting of up to forty large houses, almost seventy feet long and three stories high. Each settlement was an autonomous community managed by its own preachers ("servants of the word") and economic officers ("servants of temporal needs"). Family ties were systematically weakened, in that children were removed from their parents after weaning and placed in community schools until age twelve, when they began to learn a trade. Marriages were arranged by community elders with little apparent attention to affectional ties or family preferences. The communities were tightly integrated places of work and worship, run with paternalistic authority by male elders. Their economic focus was on craft production, with as many as thirty-four distinct forms of handicraft taught to their members. Grain and vineyards were also cultivated, but the profits of craft production were used to purchase foodstuffs, in which the communities were not self-sufficient. All but one of the presiding elders of the Hutterite sect were craftsmen (the exception was a peasant), from the time of Jacob Hutter to their expulsion from Moravia in 1622 in the Thirty Years' War.

In their time of self-confident prosperity after 1555 the Hutterite *Haushaben* greatly profited the Moravian nobility, from whom they leased their land, and they received tacit toleration from the Habsburg monarchs. They regarded themselves as the only properly ordered Christian church in the world and directed their missions not only to non-Anabaptists but to Anabaptists who continued to live in single-family households. In defense against Hutterite missions, Swiss Brethren and followers of Marpeck affirmed private property and deemphasized community of goods as an Anabaptist ideal.

Nevertheless, the Hutterite writings justifying community of goods compiled and integrated the religious themes of earlier Swiss–south German Anabaptism. Particularly in the Great Articlebook of Hutterite presiding elder Peter Walpot, it was argued that members of the New Testament church from Pentecost onward had lived in Hutterite *Haushaben*, not only in Jerusalem but in Antioch, Thessalonika, and Alexandria. For Walpot the *Gelassenheit* of Müntzer and Hut was transmuted from a general renunciation of creaturely attachments into a specific rejection of property. The Hutterites joined an emphasis on restoring New Testament practice with an antimaterialistic spirituality. Economically they had created what Robert Scribner calls a "sacral welfare state" aiming to produce a modest sufficiency for their members. Here echo themes of the *Neue Wandlung* ("new transformation") and of the commoners' resistance of 1525—in Hutterite Moravia ordinary people organized their lives with a high degree of effectiveness without priestly, noble, or merchant estates. Of course, Hutterite communism was at the mercy of its Moravian and Hungarian political hosts, and the Thirty Years' War and the Counter-Reformation nearly destroyed it in the seventeenth and eighteenth centuries before its reflorescence in nineteenth- and twentieth-century Canada and the United States.

Münster Anabaptism's experiment with community of goods was also in part the result of displacement of populations, in that about twenty-five hundred Anabaptists emigrated to Münster, while about two thousand non-Anabaptist Münster residents either fled or were expelled in connection with the Anabaptists' taking power in February 1534. Thus there were refugees to accommodate and support as well as émigré property to be confiscated. Above all, Münster was different from Anabaptist Moravia in that communism was not exclusively the economy of a refugee community but was imposed on a population two-thirds of whom were residents of the town. Moreover, Münster communism accompanied a siege that continued throughout the sixteen months of Anabaptist rule.

Undoubtedly the leading Münster preacher, Bernhard Rothmann, and the baptizing prophet, John Matthijs, upheld community of goods. Rothmann was influenced by the writings of Sebastian Franck, a non-Anabaptist who was nevertheless a moderately sympathetic observer of south German Anabaptism. Émigré property as well as all money and precious metals were confiscated, records of debts and financial account books were destroyed, and a barter economy put into practice. The death of Matthijs in April 1534, however, marked the crest of Münster communism. His successor, John of Leiden, lacked Matthijs's authority and had to compromise with the Münster notables who had helped the Anabaptists to power. The immovable property of Münster residents, their houses and lands, as well as their right to bequeath it to heirs, remained inviolable. Although personal possessions were inventoried, they, too, were not confiscated. Rations were provided by deacons in the last stages of the siege, but they were pitifully inadequate, and much of the confiscated wealth was squandered in display in a lavish court after John of Leiden was proclaimed king in September 1534. Writing his *Restitution* to Anabaptists in the Netherlands, Rothmann declared that Münster Anabaptism had ended human exploitation: "the eating and drinking of the sweat of the poor, that is, to use our servants and our neighbors, so that they must work so that we may feast." That was rhetoric; the reality was closer to that described by the hostile eyewitness, Heinrich Gresbeck: "Whoever was poor stayed poor. The person who had something was able to draw on it at the end, despite the fact that goods were supposed to be common. So hunger first afflicted the poor people, who suffered great misery."

Lacking the background of the Peasants' War, Münster Anabaptism had a different social composition in which urban notables were prominent. Their influence and the constant military emergency seriously warped the communist objectives of Rothmann and John Matthijs. In later north German–Dutch Anabaptism, the episode at Münster helped discredit community of goods like everything else associated with it. Menno Simons stated that he had never taught or practiced community of goods and that it had been discontinued by the early church, perhaps with good reason.

[*See also* Anabaptists; Hutterites; *and* Münster.]

BIBLIOGRAPHY

Clasen, Claus-Peter. *Anabaptism: A Social History, 1525–1618; Switzerland, Austria, Moravia, South and Central Germany.* Ithaca, N.Y., 1972. Includes an excellent chapter on the Hutterites, who are said to have "achieved the most radical and successful social revolution in sixteenth-century Germany."

Durnbaugh, Donald F., ed. *Every Need Supplied: Mutual Aid and Christian Community in the Free Churches, 1525–1675.* Vol. 1, *Documents in Free Church History.* Philadelphia, 1974. Contains substantial source translations from various sixteenth-century Anabaptist groups.

Goertz, Hans-Jürgen. "Eigentum." In *Theologische Realenzyklopädie*, vol. 9, pp. 417–428. Berlin, 1984. A survey of the institutions, the practice, and the theory of property in the medieval and Reformation periods.

Klaassen, Walter, ed. *Anabaptism in Outline.* Scottdale, Pa., 1981. Vol. 3, *Classics of the Radical Reformation*, contains a short chapter of various Anabaptist statements on economic ethics and practice, including selections from the Hutterites and from Münster.

Klassen, Peter James. *The Economics of Anabaptism, 1525–1560.* The Hague, 1964. Argues for the preponderance of mutual aid over community of goods among Anabaptists, which is described as the practice of a "small minority."

Plümper, Hans-Dieter. *Die Gütergemeinschaft bei den Täufern des 16. Jahrhunderts.* Göppingen, 1972. Focuses on Münster and, particularly, Moravia; describes Hutterite communism as essentially democratic and guided by a protectionist guild-craftsman's mentality of *Nahrung*, defined as "provision of the necessities of life without striving for luxury."

Scribner, Robert W. "Konkrete Utopien: Die Täufer und der vormoderne Kommunismus." *Mennonitische Geschichtsblätter* 50 (1993), 7–46. An essay that surveys all Anabaptist communist initiatives but emphasizes the Hutterites, whose system is described as resembling an urban mercantilist economy.

Stayer, James M. *The German Peasants' War and Anabaptist Community of Goods.* Montreal, 1991. Argues that the Peasants' War and southern, non-Melchiorite Anabaptism were largely geographically congruent, had a considerable overlap of membership (although Anabaptism was much the smaller movement), and had the same social composition and the same social goals.

JAMES M. STAYER

COMPAGNIE DES PASTEURS.

In creating the Compagnie des Pasteurs ("Company of Pastors"), the Protestants of Geneva broke emphatically with the monarchical model of church government to which their community and most of Europe had been accustomed. They replaced a church governed by a single person, the bishop, with a church governed by a group of equals. This move toward collective leadership proved to be of decisive importance for the whole future development of ecclesiology among Reformed (as distinguished from Lutheran and Anglican) Protestants. The Geneva company was informally created by William Farel and others as the Reformation began in the 1530s. It was described in writing within the ecclesiastical ordinances drafted by John Calvin in 1541 and 1561 and it assumed more formal shape as it functioned. In its mature form the company met every week and included all the pastors assigned both to city parishes and to the villages dependent on Geneva. The ordinances drafted by Calvin announced as the purpose of these meetings the maintenance of pure doctrine by regular discussion of holy scripture, and these meetings clearly did involve regular discussion of theology and biblical exegesis. The ordinances also provide that once every three months a session was to be devoted to mutual criticism.

The company's records make it clear that its meetings were also used to make personnel decisions and to exercise powers equivalent to ordination. Whenever the government authorized the appointment of another minister, candidates for the position were closely examined by the company on doctrine and on speaking skills. If found satisfactory, a candidate was then presented to the city council. If the council approved, the candidate was finally presented for approval to the parish to which he had been assigned. Of these decisions, the crucial one was that made within the company. Ministers were thus chosen, in fact, by co-optation.

Increasingly the company also examined candidates for service outside of Geneva, particularly in France. Many of these candidates had come to Geneva from the localities in which they hoped to serve in order to gain not only a final stage of training but also formal certification by Calvin and his associates of their fitness to serve as Reformed ministers. In these circumstances the company was acting as a kind of placement service, organizing the staffing for an international missionary campaign to advance the Reformed cause.

Meetings of the company were also used to prepare positions for negotiation with the city government. The company had under its control none of the financial and physical resources possessed by any Roman Catholic ecclesiastical entity of the period. It depended completely on the civil government for all of its expenses, including the maintenance of its buildings, and the salaries of its individual members. Each minister served at the government's pleasure and could be dismissed without notice if he irritated the government through imprudent preaching or unseemly behavior. The company, thus, often found itself obliged to negotiate with the city for support of the most mundane kind.

All decisions of the company were taken by the group as a whole—as a collective. Great efforts were taken to avoid any appearance of one-man rule or any remnant of episcopalianism. Important decisions if written were usually signed by every single member in attendance at a given session.

The company had two officers. One was a secretary who kept written registers of its deliberations. These registers were preserved and are now being published in a critical edition. The other officer was a moderator who called the meetings, presided over them, announced decisions, and negotiated on behalf of the company with external authorities, most commonly the governing council of Geneva. Calvin served as moderator until his death in 1564. This was his only position of preeminence, but he constantly deprecated it, always claiming to speak for the company as a whole and indignantly denying accusations that he was behaving like a new bishop. After Calvin died, Théodore de Bèze was elected as moderator for a year and then reelected every year until 1580. He then refused to continue in office, and the company began electing a new moderator every week. This constant rotation irritated the city government, but the company insisted on maintaining rotation. In later times the terms were extended, sometimes even to periods of several years. It became an established principle, however, that the office would never become permanent and that any minister was believed capable of handling it. The Compagnie des Pasteurs was the first of many institutions that represented in concrete form the commitment of the Reformed movement to collective rather than individual leadership within the church and to centralized control rather than to grassroots autonomy.

This commitment to collective leadership spread to other institutions created to govern the Reformed churches inspired by Calvin. It characterized representative bodies designed to control churches in limited areas, called colloquies in France, classes in the Netherlands and England, and presbyteries in Scotland. It characterized provincial and national synods, or assemblies, in every area in which the Reformed branch of Protestantism spread. Collective leadership presented an evident alternative to other forms of church organization and most obviously to the monarchical or episcopalian forms favored by Catholics and Anglicans, as well as many Lutherans. But it was also an alternative to the more decentralized forms of church government featuring congregational autonomy, which were favored by many religious radicals of the period. Leadership by elite groups became one of the most important defining characteristics of the entire Reformed movement.

[See also Bèze, Théodore de; Calvin, John; Church Offices, *article on* Calvinist Offices; *and* Geneva.]

BIBLIOGRAPHY

Hughes, Philip Edgcumbe, trans. *The Register of the Company of Pastors of Geneva in the Time of Calvin.* Grand Rapids, Mich., 1966. Translation of volumes one and two of *Registres de la Compagnie des Pasteurs. . . in a single volume.*

Labarthe, Olivier. "En marge de l'édition des Registres de la Compagnie des pasteurs de Genève: Le changement du mode de présidence de la Compagnie, 1578–1580." *Revue d'histoire ecclésiastique suisse* 67 (1972), 160–186. By one of these register editors (who later served a term himself as moderator of the Geneva Company of Pastors); explains in detail the institution of moderator and how it evolved.

Kingdon, Robert M. "Calvin and 'Presbytery': The Geneva Company of Pastors." *Pacific Theological Review* 18 (1985), 43–55. Provides a useful overview of this institution.

Registres de la Compagnie des Pasteurs de Genève au temps de Calvin. Geneva, 1962–. A critical edition of the registers of the Geneva Company of Pastors, underway since 1962, had by 1993 resulted in eleven volumes.

ROBERT M. KINGDON

COMPLUTENSIAN POLYGLOT. *See* Bible, *article on* Translations of the Bible.

CONCILIARISM. This term denotes a strand in late-medieval ecclesiological thinking concerning the nature of the church's unity and the location of supreme authority within it. It provided a theological basis for the efforts of the general councils of Pisa (1409) and Constance (1414–1418) to put an end to the Great Schism by deposing the rival claimants to the papacy, as well as for the attempt of the councils of Pavia-Siena (1423–1424) and Basel-Ferrara-Florence (1431–1449) to promote a thoroughgoing reform of the church in "head and members." Traditionalist in many of its dimensions, conciliarism was firmly grounded in the corporate history and conciliar practice of the early church and also in the canonistic legal tradition of the high Middle Ages. It survived the dissolution of the Council of Basel to remain a viable ecclesiological option in the church at large well into the Reformation era. As one of the fundamental presuppositions of Gallican theology, conciliarism enjoyed widespread currency in France into the nineteenth century, when the First Vatican Council's solemn definitions of papal primacy and infallibility (1870) banished it from Roman Catholic circles into the outer darkness of heterodoxy. It did so in apparently definitive fashion, but, with the convocation of the Second Vatican Council (1962–1965) and the publication of Hans Küng's *Strukturen der Kirche* (1962), it found its way back into the arena of Catholic theological discussion, where it has since maintained a diffidently marginal presence.

A growing recognition of the complex variations and shifting combinations in the ideas of the leading conciliarists has evoked words of caution about the willingness of historians like August Franzen and Remigius Bäumer to categorize them into several different "schools" (Alberigo, 1981, p. 345), and there has even been nervous skepticism about the viability of such terms as "conciliar theory" and "conciliarism" (Fasolt, 1991, pp. 318–319). Given the differing contexts in which the leading conciliarists were writing and the several callings that had helped shape their thinking, the complex of ideas they advanced betrayed too many variations to permit its characterization by the simple formulation of the superiority of council to pope. All would agree, however, that the conciliar thinkers—moved by the scriptural vision of the Christian community as forming a single body with Christ, by the conciliar practice of the early church in which that vision had found expression, and by the belief that the papal headship of the church was nonetheless of divine foundation—were engaged in an attempt to harmonize those several convictions. All would agree, too, that they were led in that attempt to argue that it was necessary, without detracting from the institution of papal monarchy, to give more prominent and regular institutional expression to the corporate dimension of the universal church—most notably by the assembly of general councils representing the entire community of the faithful. Moreover, prescinding still from individual differences, it is possible to discern in the writings of those typically called conciliar theorists the presence of three broad strands, distinct in both their origins and subsequent fate but interwoven during the conciliar epoch into a complex of ideas that may properly be called conciliarist.

Demand for reform of the church "in head and members," together with the insistence that this could best be effected through the periodic convocation of general councils, constitutes the first, the most prominent, and the most enduring of these three strands. Rooted in the defensive reaction of the provincial churches of Europe in the thirteenth century to the encroachment on their authority by the remorseless progress of papal centralization, it had taken on a tone of greater hostility in the demand for churchwide reform and the call for the regular assembly of general councils elicited by the convocation of the Council of Vienne (1311–1312). A comparable advocacy of conciliar leadership in the work of reform can be found in the thinking of most of the leading conciliarists at both Constance and Basel—from Jean Gerson, Pierre d'Ailly, and Francesco Zabarella to Andrew of Escobar, John of Segovia, Nicholas of Cusa, and Panormitanus (Nicholas de Tudeschis). The decree *Frequens*, promulgated in 1417 at the Council of Constance and legislating the assembly of future councils at stated and regular intervals, gave it official conciliar ratification. Although in the minds of its framers it was closely associated with the council's superiority decree, *Haec sancta synodus/Sacrosancta* (1415), it is important to note that in itself it did not necessarily involve the assertion of the superiority of council to pope that lies at the heart of "the strict conciliar theory."

This assertion of superiority was also not inherent in the second strand in conciliarism, which was, moreover, less prominent than the first. Present in the thinking of Gerson, Nicholas of Cusa, and Denis the Carthusian but most clearly expressed at Constance in the *Tractatus de potestate ecclesiastica* of d'Ailly and the *Tractatus de schismate* of Zabarella, it envisaged the institutional expression of the church's unity in quasi-oligarchic terms, with the Curia Romana being the normal agency of government and the cardinals limiting the pope's exercise of power. This vision of the church's constitution was grounded both in the *de facto* share in the government of the universal church that the college of cardinals had come to enjoy in the twelfth and thirteenth centuries and in the complex theories that some of the canonists, drawing on corporation law, had developed to legitimate that role.

In 1378 the dissident cardinals were moved by this point of view when they rejected the demand for a general council and took it upon themselves to pass judgment on the validity of Urban VI's election, thereby precipitating the Great Schism. Only after the immediate circumstances of the original dispute had receded into history did it become possible for such conciliarists as Gerson, d'Ailly, and Zabarella (the last two themselves cardinals and all three writing in the early years of the fifteenth century) to envisage a constitutional role in the church's governance for the college of cardinals, as well as for the general council. If d'Ailly's formulation of this position was in subsequent years the more influential, it was Zabarella who gave it the more coherent and legally precise expression.

If Zabarella saw the pope and cardinals as together forming in the apostolic see (or local Roman church) a single corporate body of which the pope was the head and the cardinals the members (with the latter possessing under certain circumstances the right to exercise the full corporate power), he also saw that apostolic see as, in turn, the head of the universal church, a greater corporate body the well-being of which it existed to promote and the source from which it derived whatever authority it possessed. Hence came Zabarella's further endorsement of the third and most fundamental strand in "the strict conciliar theory."

While it once was common to assume that the roots of this strict conciliar theory were engaged in heterodox (or quasi-heterodox) soil—in the teachings of such radical thinkers as William of Ockham (d. 1349) or Marsiglio of Padua (d. 1342)—scholars have since come to realize that Ockham was in fact something other than a conciliarist and that Marsiglio (with his insistence that the great hierarchical structure of bishops, archbishops, and pope was nothing more than a human contrivance) was something a good deal more radical than that. Instead, the conciliar theory has come to be widely seen as having had much older and less questionably orthodox origins, not least of all in the commentaries of some of the canon lawyers themselves. On this issue and despite some recent expressions of skepticism (Sieben, 1984, p. 255), the field is still dominated by Brian Tierney's magisterial argument (Tierney, *Foundations of Conciliar Theory*, 1968) that the origins of the strict conciliar theory are to be sought in the combination of a twelfth- and thirteenth-century canonistic teaching concerning the case of the heretical pope with the later canonistic application of the Roman law of corporations to the universal church itself.

Of course, even if one limits oneself to those writing during the conciliar epoch itself (1378–1449), the strict conciliar theory will be found to have taken a variety of forms. Those forms reflected, however, a shared pattern of belief. In common with their papalist opponents, the conciliarists assumed the divine institution of all ecclesiastical power. That power they divided, again like the papalists, into a sacramental power or power of order (*potestas ordinis*) and a power of ecclesiastical jurisdiction (*potestas jurisdictionis*). About the former they had little to say, for the pope did not base his claim to preeminence in the church on his possession of orders. His claims to invulnerability rested instead upon the nature of his jurisdictional power and, more precisely, upon his power of jurisdiction in the public sphere (*potestas jurisdictionis in foro exteriori*). It is this coercive, governmental power alone that the conciliarists of Constance and Basel had in mind when they asserted the superiority of council to pope, and it is upon the analysis of that jurisdictional or governmental power and of the precise manner in which it was distributed through the ranks of the faithful that they bent their efforts.

Against the claims of the high papalists, they denied that Christ had given the power of jurisdiction to Peter alone and not to all the apostles and that the jurisdiction of inferior prelates must therefore be derived from the pope and not immediately from God. Against those claims, accordingly, they also insisted that the plenitude of jurisdictional power could not reside in the pope alone. They did not wish thereby to deny the divine origin of the papal primacy, but if the office itself was of divine institution, its bestowal upon a particular individual was the work of men. Moreover, when the cardinals elect a pope, they do so not in their own right but as representatives of the community of the faithful. For the final authority in the universal church, as in other more particular congregations, resides in the whole body of its corporate membership, and that final corporate authority is by no means exhausted by the mere act of electing a head. Even after a papal election the fullness of power still resides in some sense in the church, as well as in the pope. If it may be ascribed to the latter by virtue of his normal exercise of it and his superiority to any other single ecclesiastic, he is not superior to the universal church or the general council representing it, and he must exercise the power entrusted to him for the good of the whole church. As a result, like any other corporation in relation to its head, the council has the right to set limits to the pope's exercise of his power in order to prevent his abusing it to the destruction of the church.

That right is conceived of as being in some fashion exercised on a continuing basis but more clearly so under emergency conditions. If the pope lapses, for example, into heresy, or, by being the occasion of schism, endangers the faith of the whole church, that church—which unlike the pope possesses the gift of doctrinal inerrancy—possesses also the power to prevent its own ruin. It can exercise that power via its representatives assembled in general council, who can judge, chastise, and even depose a pope.

This was the point of view—articulated with great clarity at Constance by Gerson, d'Ailly, and Zabarella and widely shared by the council fathers—that found historic expression after John XXIII's flight to Schaffhausen had threatened the council's very existence. Under those circumstances and at its fifth general session, the council formally promulgated the decree *Haec sancta synodus*, the crucial section of which reads:

> This sacred synod of Constance. . . declares, in the first place, that it forms a general council, legitimately assembled in the Holy Spirit and representing the Catholic Church Militant, that it has its power immediately from Christ, and that all men, of every rank and position, including even the pope himself, are bound to obey it in those matters that pertain to the faith, the extirpation of the said schism, and to the reformation of the said Church in head and members. It declares also that anyone, of any rank, condition or office—even the papal—who shall contumaciously refuse to obey its mandates, statutes, decrees or instructions made by this holy synod or by any other lawfully assembled council on the matters aforesaid or on things pertaining to them, shall, unless he recovers his senses, be subjected to fitting penance and punished as is appropriate.
>
> (Alberigo et al., 1962, p. 385).

Among Roman Catholic theologians *Haec sancta* has continued to be controversial. It is clear, however, that the activity of the councils of Pisa and Constance in deposing the rival claimants to the papacy, in electing Martin V (the first pope in forty years to command a universal allegiance), and, thereby, in ending the schism was grounded in the conciliarist ecclesiology to which the decree gave expression. Despite papal wishes to the contrary, it proved impossible at the subsequent councils of Pavia-Siena and Basel-Ferrara-Florence to lose sight of that ecclesiology. Without its continuing vitality, the later convocation by the cardinals of the opposition of the dissident assembly, which has gone down in history as the *conciliabulum* of Pisa (1511–1512), would have been utterly inconceivable.

The abandonment, then, of the Council of Basel by some of the most prominent conciliarists of the day, as well as the papacy's subsequent triumph over its conciliarist opponents, did not mark the end of conciliarism as a potent force in the life of the church. It is true that the three strands woven together in the conciliarist views of the leading figures at Constance came now to be teased apart. Thus, the oligarchic strand disappeared from the arguments of most later conciliarists and came, instead, to find a home in the thinking of their curialist opponents. There was a comparable unraveling of the threads that had stitched together in a common fabric the strict conciliar theory and the more generalized advocacy of a periodic assembly of general councils to promote the achievement of churchwide reform.

Thus, in the works of the leading Parisian conciliarists of the early sixteenth century, Jacques Almain (d. 1515) and John Mair (d. 1550), reform is barely mentioned. At the same time, many of those who in the half century and more after the end of the Council of Basel had still looked to the assembly of general councils as the best hope for achieving reform in head and members seem increasingly to have found it impossible to endorse the strict conciliar theory—for example, Torquemada in his highly influential *Summa de Ecclesia* (c.1450), Cajetan in his *De comparatione auctoritatis papae et concilii* (1511), and Tomasso Giustiniani and Vincenzo Querini in the great reform program, *Libellus ad Leonem X*, which they submitted to the pope during the Fifth Lateran Council (1512–1517).

If the complex conciliarism characteristic of the conciliar epoch unraveled after Basel, the work of Hubert Jedin, Olivier de la Brosse, Josef Klotzner, Remigius Bäumer, and others has made it quite clear that the strict conciliar theory itself retained a good deal of vitality into the age of the Reformation, surviving both the partisan strictures of *Execrabilis* (Pius II's bull of 1460 condemning as "erroneous and abominable" appeals from papal policies to the judgment of a future general council) and the ambivalent indirection of *Pastor aeternus* (the decree promulgated in 1516 at the Fifth Lateran Council and stating that popes, having authority over all councils, had the right to convoke, transfer, and dissolve them). Over the centuries historians (especially those of ultramontane sympathies) have vastly overestimated the importance of *Execrabilis*. In 1460 and for centuries thereafter, it was widely disregarded, being viewed less as a binding dogmatic judgment than as the understandable reaction of one particular faction. Similarly, as Bishop Jacques-Bénigne Bossuet suggested long ago, *Pastor aeternus* touches upon the question of conciliarism in only indirect fashion and, contrary to the claims so often made, involves no condemnation either of *Haec sancta* or of the superiority decrees of Basel.

Had it done so, of course, it would be hard to imagine the Faculty of Theology of Paris taking the step it did in March 1518 by way of protest against the Franco-papal concordat of 1516—namely, that of appealing from the judgment of the pope to that of a future general council and doing so in language on which Martin Luther could subsequently draw in the first of his own two appeals to a general council. Similarly, without the continuing vitality of conciliarist views in much of western and central Europe, it would be hard to explain the reluctance of successive popes to assemble a reforming general council in response to the Protestant challenge or, indeed, when such a council finally met, the failure of the fathers assembled at Trent to promulgate any dogmatic decree on the nature of the Christian church. It would similarly have been pointless in the 1530s for English supporters of Henry VIII's break with Rome to bolster their attacks on papal jurisdiction by evoking the superiority decrees of Constance and Basel, as it would have been later on in Scotland and France (as well as in England) for such Protestant advocates of a right of resistance against persecuting or tyrannous rulers as John Ponet, Théodore de Bèze, the anonymous author of the *Vindiciae contra tyrannos*,

George Buchanan, William Bridge, and William Prynne to evoke by way of analogy the bold action of the fifteenth-century councils in disposing of papal monarchs. And, it would certainly have been pointless, when in most of the Catholic world an essentially ultramontane historiography had succeeded finally in dimming the memory of the conciliarist experience, for the Gallican theologians of the Sorbonne (Edmond Richer in the seventeenth century, and Louis-Ellies Dupin in the eighteenth) to have insisted on keeping that experience alive by reprinting the works of the Parisian conciliarists from Gerson and d'Ailly to Major and Almain. But, about that insistence there was nothing at all odd. For the University of Paris, as Dupin noted in 1707, had always held "as a fundamental point of its ecclesiastical discipline" that the council was above the pope.

BIBLIOGRAPHY

Alberigo, Giuseppe. *Chiesa conciliare: Identità e significato del conciliarismo.* Brescia, Italy, 1981.

Alberigo, Giuseppe, et al., eds. *Conciliorum oecumenicorum decreta.* Basel and Rome, 1962. See pp. 309–631 for a useful selection from the decrees of the general councils from Vienne to Lateran V.

Bäumer, Remigius. *Nachwirkungen des konziliaren Gedankens in der Theologie und Kanonistik des frühen 16. Jahrhunderts.* Münster, 1971. Covers the continuity of conciliarism into the Reformation era.

Beck, Hans-Georg, et al., eds. *From the High Middle Ages to the Eve of the Reformation.* Translated by Anselm Biggs. Montreal, 1970; reprint, New York, 1986. See especially the essay by Karl August Fink, who gives a good narrative account of the Great Schism and the efforts of the fifteenth-century councils; good bibliographic data.

Black, Antony J. *Council and Commune: The Conciliar Movement and the Fifteenth-Century Heritage.* London, 1979.

Crowder, C. M. D., ed. *Unity, Heresy and Reform, 1378–1460: The Conciliar Response to the Great Schism.* New York, 1977; reprint, Kingston, Ont., 1986. Contains English translations of extracts from pertinent conciliar documents and conciliarist tracts; good bibliographic data.

Fasolt, Constantin. *Council and Hierarchy: The Political Thought of William Durant the Younger.* New York, 1991.

Krämer, Werner. *Konsens und Rezeption: Verfassungsprinzipien der Kirche im Basler Konziliarismus.* Münster, 1980.

Küng, Hans. *Structures of the Church.* Translated by Salvatore Attanasio. Reprint, New York, 1982. A fundamental work on the origins and doctrinal status of conciliar theory.

Mayer, Thomas F. "Thomas Starkey: An Unknown Conciliarist at the Court of Henry VIII." *Journal of the History of Ideas* 49.2 (1988), 207–227. Covers the continuity of conciliarism into the Reformation era.

Oakley, Francis. *Council over Pope? Towards a Provisional Ecclesiology.* New York, 1969. Summarizes and comments on the extensive literature focused on the Constance decree *Haec sancta synodus* and its subsequent career.

———. *Natural Law, Conciliarism and Consent in the Late Middle Ages: Studies in Ecclesiastical and Intellectual History.* London, 1984. Covers the continuity of conciliarism into the Reformation era.

Schneider, Hans. *Der Konziliarismus als Problem der neueren Katholischen Theologie.* Berlin, 1976. Summarizes and comments on the extensive literature focused on the Constance decree *Haec sancta synodus* and its subsequent career.

Sieben, Hermann Josef. *Die Konsilsidee des lateinischen Mittelalters, 847–1378.* Paderborn, 1984.

Stieber, Joachim W. *Pope Eugenius IV, the Council of Basel, and the Secular and Ecclesiastical Authorities in the Empire.* Leiden, 1978.

Tanner, Norman P., ed. *Decrees of the Ecumenical Councils.* London and Washington, D. C., 1990. Reproduces texts of the *Conciliorum oecumenicorum decreta,* with English translations.

Tierney, Brian. *Foundations of the Conciliar Theory.* Reprint, London, 1968. A fundamental work on the origins and doctrinal status of conciliar theory.

Vooght, Paul de. "Les controverses sur les pouvoirs du concile et l'autorité du pape au concile de Constance." *Revue théologique de Louvain* 1.1 (1970), 45–75. Comments on the extensive literature focused on the Constance decree *Haec sancta synodus* and its subsequent career.

FRANCIS OAKLEY

CONCORD, FORMULA OF. *See* Formula of Concord.

CONCORDAT OF BOLOGNA. *See* Bologna, Concordat of.

CONCORD OF WITTENBERG. *See* Wittenberg Concord.

CONCUBINAGE. The state in which men and women lived together as a couple without being married, concubinage was practiced in the sixteenth and seventeenth centuries by both clergy and laypeople, as it had been throughout the Middle Ages. During the Reformation it was one of a series of misdemeanors of which the clergy were accused. Priests were criticized for betraying their vows of celibacy by having sexual relations with women, usually their maids or housekeepers. Their concubines were often compared to prostitutes. Contemporary woodcuts portrayed monks traveling in the company of nuns and girls being sold to priests as "servants." Critics also emphasized the hypocrisy of a church that promoted priestly celibacy while enjoying an income from fines (known in Germany as the *Milchzins*) on clergy who were permitted to continue living with their concubines.

In addition to attacking the clergy for immorality, early German reformers argued that the widespread priestly custom of living with female partners demonstrated the weakness of the principle of priestly celibacy, and they called for all priests to marry henceforth. The case was put with great force in 1523 in a pamphlet by Katharina Zell, the wife of the Strasbourg reformer Matthias Zell, and in the influential *Wolfaria Statutes* of 1521, which stated that the clergy must either have legitimate wives or live alone, a practice later adopted universally by Lutherans.

Clerical concubinage is no longer seen as a major factor in the decline in confidence in the priesthood on the eve of the Reformation, which brings into question the extent to which criticisms of this practice reflected general societal attitudes. Much of the evidence for this revised interpretation has come from medieval sources and from areas of Europe that remained predominantly Catholic after the Reformation. Though images of the promiscuous monk and the concubinous priest were commonplace in medieval literature, the low incidence of fines for concubinage in the fiscal records of the bishops of Strasbourg throughout the later Middle Ages suggests that few cases were actually being brought to the notice of the authorities by scandalized laymen or pursued by the church. Edicts passed by the Council of Trent in 1563 to prohibit clerical concubinage and to end the practice by which clergy renounced benefices in favor of their illegitimate sons were only limited in effect. Twelve of the twenty-two priests who were subject to a visitation in the German bishopric of Speyer in 1583 were living with concubines. While this level of concubinage was unusually high, it does not appear to have troubled the laity, who expressed no criticism of clergy with concubines and spoke with approval of the way in which they carried out their paternal responsibilities. By adopting a pattern that conformed most closely to the practices of their parishioners, these priests enjoyed a high level of social acceptance.

Criticisms of the minority of priests who had abandoned their long-term concubines for younger women were based on secular rather than religious morals. In France clerical concubinage persisted well into the seventeenth century. The new bishop of Autun, Louis Doni D'Attichi, noted with disapproval in 1652 that priestly concubinage in his diocese was so widespread and had been the subject of so little official concern that the laity were under the impression that the clergy were allowed to have concubines. They approved of the way in which the clergy ran orderly households and conformed to social norms by giving dowries to their daughters. The ambiguity of clerical concubinage was highlighted by the behavior of members of the cathedral chapters. At the turn of the sixteenth century the practice was widespread in Münster, where occasional attempts by the church to end long-term partnerships were frustrated both by the reluctance of members of the chapter to end the relationships and by the difficulty of enforcing Tridentine policy on men of noble status, who frequently had not taken holy orders.

The Council of Trent also acted to end concubinage among the laity. Those who lived together without marriage were in a state of damnation and had committed a most grave sin in contempt of the sacrament of marriage. Lay concubinage occurred at all social levels. Its incidence is difficult to establish. While the Tridentine decree on marriage led to a sharp increase in prosecutions for *stuprum voluntarium* ("sexual relations between unmarried men and women"), these figures exclude many cases that did not reach the attention of the courts, as lay concubinage was easily concealed and aroused little suspicion when the social behavior of a man and his concubine conformed to that of a married couple. As one late sixteenth-century Venetian witness stated, the subject's concubine sat at the head of the table, commanded his servants, shared his bed, and was addressed by him as his wife. How could he have thought that they were not man and wife?

Despite great variations in their social status, all those who chose to live together without being married were united by some form of social marginality. In some cases living in concubinage was no more than the adherence to an older tradition of marriage, prohibited by Trent, by which an exchange of promises between the couple before witnesses sufficed, and for many couples even an exchange of promises without witnesses was enough. The persistence of the "hand-clasp marriage" in isolated rural areas is an indication of the failure of the new Catholic and Protestant orthodoxies to reach down beyond a certain level of society. Recent immigrants to large urban centers found partners in an environment in which the customary restraints on intercourse without marriage were much weaker than in more settled communities. There was even an element of marginality among the Venetian noblemen who chose to take concubines. Men who wished to have households of their own but were unable to do so because custom limited marriages to one male per generation were obliged to live in concubinage with partners of their choice.

Little is known about how women who became clerical or lay concubines were considered by their contemporaries. Prosecutions for concubinage focused on male partners. Responses to ecclesiastical visitations were given by men, and their expressions of approval or disapproval embraced the entire household, without specific reference to female concubines. Their presentation in Protestant literature as "priest's whores" should therefore be treated with circumspection. According to secular investigations in Venice, concubines of noblemen were deemed to be socially acceptable if they conformed to the behavior of gentlewomen.

[*See also* Anticlericalism; Celibacy and Virginity; *and* Marriage.]

BIBLIOGRAPHY

Forster, Marc. "The Counter Reformation and the Traditional Church in the Villages of Speyer." *Fides et Historia* 2 (1989), 30–37. Reviews reports of a visitation to the bishopric of Speyer that found that ecclesiastical concubinage was widely accepted by Catholic laymen.

Kohl, Wilhelm. "Die Durchsetzung der tridentischen Reformen im Domkapital zu Münster." In *Reformatio Ecclesiae*, edited by R. Bäumer, pp. 729–747. Paderborn, 1980. Argues that Tridentine reforms of concubinage were largely ineffective among the Münster cathedral chapter.

Martini, Gabriele. "La Donna Veneziana del '600 tra sessualità legittima ed illegittima: Alcune riflessioni sul concubinato." *Atti dell'Istituto Veneto di Scienze, Lettere ed Arti* 145 (1986–1987), 301–339. The most detailed review available of lay concubinage in seventeenth-century Venice.

Ozment, Steven. *The Reformation in the Cities: The Appeal of Protes-*

tantism in Sixteenth-century Germany and Switzerland. New Haven, 1975. Considers ecclesiastical concubinage in the diocese of Constance and early Protestant thinking on the subject.

Rapp, Francis. *Réformés et Réformation à Strasbourg: Église et société dans le diocèse de Strasbourg, 1450–1529.* Paris, 1974. Reviews the evidence for the incidence of clerical concubinage in the diocese of Strasbourg in the fifteenth and sixteenth centuries.

Schroeder, H. J. *Canons and Decrees of the Council of Trent.* Rockford, Ill., 1978. See pp. 147–148 for an English translation of the decree that forbade all clergy to keep concubines.

ALEXANDER COWAN

CONDÉ, Henri I (1552–1588), Huguenot prince of the blood, one of the leaders of the Protestant rebellion against the French Crown during the French Wars of Religion of the sixteenth century. At the age of sixteen, Henri I de Condé became titular head of the Protestant armies, along with his cousin Henry of Navarre (later Henry IV), after the death of his father, Louis I de Bourbon, first prince of Condé, in 1569. Both young princes, however, remained subordinate to Gaspard II de Coligny as political leader and military commander until after the admiral's death in the Saint Bartholomew's Day Massacre in 1572.

Henri and his cousin were inevitably closely associated until Condé's death. The association was markedly strained. Henry of Navarre adopted an inclusive political and religious stance, befitting the heir presumptive to the throne. His political acumen enabled him to maintain his association with both Huguenots and more strictly political malcontents. In contrast, Condé was austere and intractable where Navarre was affable and capable of compromise. Condé was narrowly devoted to the Huguenot cause but, though admired and trusted by many Protestants, he had neither the political skills nor the military skills adequate for the leadership of the cause—the role that was thrust on him at his father's death.

A prisoner at court after the Saint Bartholomew's Day Massacre, Condé revealed his strength of character by initially resisting forceful conversion to Catholicism. In 1573 the king named him governor of Picardy, as his father had been, as a way of detaching him from Henry of Navarre, who was seen as a more tractable adversary. In 1574, when war broke out again, Condé fled to Strasbourg, where he immediately and publicly returned to Huguenot worship.

Although proclaimed "governor and protector of the church" by the Huguenot assembly at Millau (July 1574), Condé nevertheless began to demonstrate his weaknesses as a leader at this time. He spent months negotiating for support from Protestants abroad with slim results. When he finally managed to enter France with a small force in 1576, it achieved almost nothing, owing to his inexperience as a military commander.

After the Peace of Monsieur ended this phase of fighting in 1576, Condé was confirmed in his governorship of Pi-

cardy. He was denied entrance to the town of Peronne there, however, even though it had been granted to him as a surety town in the treaty. Local Catholic nobles, who constituted themselves as the Catholic League, opposed both his religion and his potential local influence.

From this point forward, Condé was forced to seek a territorial base close to Huguenot strength in western France. He was still more trusted than Navarre by Huguenot townspeople in the west, though his seizures of strongholds, in typical aristocratic fashion for his own purposes, alarmed them. Once again, the limits of his political and military skills were evident in that, unlike his father, he was never able to raise an adequate army in Saintonge and Poitou, despite his seizures of territory there. Rather than fielding an army when war broke out again in 1577, he took refuge in La Rochelle.

Tensions with both Henry of Navarre and the Crown led Condé to an abortive seizure of the town of La Fère in Picardy in 1579. La Fère was one of the principal Bourbon seigneuries in the region, but Condé could not extend his control beyond it to the rest of Picardy. He was forced to abandon La Fère in 1580 when confronted by royal armies fielded in response to new aggression by Henry of Navarre. He fled abroad, travelling to the Low Countries, Germany, and England, once again seeking help from any potential Protestant ally. Meanwhile, the successful siege of Cahors by Navarre's troops in May 1580 made clear that, of the two men, Navarre was the only reliable military leader.

Condé now was forced to associate more closely with his talented cousin. Ironically, his stature became more significant at this point. Navarre could not disregard his cousin's support among Huguenots and make peace with Henry III on terms favorable to himself alone. Henry III was driven to look for allies among the extreme Catholics, and the wars continued. Condé had minor successes fighting in the west in 1585, but then failed in an ill-advised attempt to seize Angers. The wars continued after a brief armistice in 1586, again, in part, because of Condé's unwillingness to compromise on religious matters. But Navarre kept him in close check in his own army where Condé participated in the Protestant victory at Coutras late in 1587. The prince died in March 1588 from illness, perhaps as a result of having been poisoned.

BIBLIOGRAPHY

Aumale, Henri d'Orléans. *Histoire des princes de Condé pendant les XVIe et XVIIe siècles.* 7 vols. Paris, 1863–1896. Despite its age, a reliable source of data on Condé, Navarre, and their associates.

Salmon, J. H. M. *Society in Crisis: France in the Sixteenth Century.* New York, 1975. A survey of conditions and events in France that sets Condé's career in context.

Sutherland, N. M. *The Huguenot Struggle for Recognition.* New Haven and London, 1980. A detailed survey of the political and military struggle of the Huguenots in the second half of the sixteenth century.

KRISTEN B. NEUSCHEL

CONDÉ, Louis I (1530–1569), French Protestant nobleman and commander of Protestant armies in civil wars against the French Crown, 1562–1569. The twelfth of thirteen children of Charles de Bourbon, duke of Vendôme (d.1538) and Françoise d'Alençon, Louis became influential at the French court only after the deaths of older brothers and of Henry II (r. 1547–1559), when his stature as prince of the blood gained importance. He owed much of his wealth, in lands in Picardy and Brie, to his 1551 marriage to Eléonore de Roye. She preceded Louis in conversion to Protestantism and undoubtedly influenced his conversion (c.1555). Condé's ties to the Protestant leader Gaspard II de Coligny, Eléonore's uncle, were encouraged by the marriage.

Condé first emerged as a Protestant leader in 1560, following the Conspiracy of Amboise, a plot by disgruntled noblemen to wrest control of the young king, Francis II (r. 1559–60), from members of the Guise family. Condé had advance knowledge of the plot and was tried and convicted of lèse-majesté. He made his first public declaration of adherence to the Reformed faith while in prison awaiting execution. His courageous demeanor when faced with execution impressed many at court and contributed to his stature as Huguenot leader.

Condé's personal and political fortunes were reversed by the death of Francis II. Saved from execution, he became influential at the court of the minor king, Charles IX (r. 1560–1574). He sponsored Protestant gatherings at court and used his stature as prince of the blood to press the queen mother, Catherine de Médicis, for official toleration of the Reformed faith. He became definitive political and military leader of the Huguenot movement as his older brother, Antoine de Bourbon, rejected the reform, and as his own religious and political rivalries with other courtiers (notably the Guises) spilled over into war in 1562. The first of the Wars of Religion began when Condé retreated from a confrontation with the duke of Guise in Paris and gathered an army at Orléans in the spring of that year.

The Edict of Amboise, which ended the war in 1563, reflected Condé's personal interests in its generous provisions for freedom of worship by noble families; Condé was criticized for not securing similar guarantees for townspeople. He was also criticized by fellow Huguenots in subsequent years for his personal morality—particularly liaisons with other women while the much-respected Eléonore (d. 1564) was still alive. Although at the height of his political fortunes after the war, he was assured of power at court only through threat of further rebellion. He led an attempt to seize the person of the king in September 1567 that triggered the second civil war (1567–1568). The third civil war began later in 1568 when Condé, as well as Coligny and other leading nobles, fled to western France to avoid arrest by the Crown, now determined to end their influence. He was killed in battle at Jarnac, near Angoulême, in March 1569.

Condé was a typical nobleman of the era in his personal ambition and assumption of the right to violence. His notable courage and his stature as prince of the blood proved useful to the Huguenot cause, especially in rebellion. He lacked the political and religious vision of his contemporary and ally, Gaspard II de Coligny—qualities that might have better served the Huguenot cause in the long run.

BIBLIOGRAPHY

Aumale, Henri d'Orléans. *Histoire des princes de Condé pendant les XVIe et XVIIe siècles.* 7 vols. Paris, 1863–1896. Despite its age, a reliable source of data on Condé and his family.

Neuschel, Kristen B. *Word of Honor: Interpreting Noble Culture in Sixteenth-Century France.* Ithaca, N.Y., 1989. A study of nobles' political culture that focuses on Louis de Bourbon, prince of Condé, and his clients in Picardy.

Salmon, J. H. M. *Society in Crisis: France in the Sixteenth Century.* New York, 1975. A survey of events and conditions in France that sets Condé's career in context.

KRISTEN B. NEUSCHEL

CONDUCT BOOKS. An important literary genre of early modern Europe, the conduct book adapted the perennial handbook of manners to the court of the Renaissance age of absolutism. Easy accommodation with despotism distinguishes the conduct book from both the medieval book of courtesy and the modern etiquette book. Its premise that manners can be learned, however, made the conduct book an agent of social mobility and the civilizing process. Its many forms include court dialogue, parental advice, and treatise of civility. The early modern conduct book stands out from other handbooks of manners in regarding deportment as an art form, stressing ingratiating outward manners over inward virtue and avoiding the knotty problem of counseling the new prince.

Il libro del cortegiano (1528) by Baldassare Castiglione is the prototype of the conduct book, its finest exemplar, and the only work in the genre to become a classic. *Il cortegiano* complemented Niccolò Machiavelli's *Il Principe* (1532) since the courtier's role is to ingratiate himself with his prince, not to check or contest his power. Along with the *Cortegiano*, the *Galateo* (1558) by Giovanni della Casa and *La civil conversatione* (1574) by Stefano Guazzo constituted the standard trinity of advanced conduct books. The standard elementary educational treatise of civility was *De civilitate morum puerillium libellus* (1530) by Desiderius Erasmus of Rotterdam. These books were translated into all major European languages, imitated by many other conduct books, and summarized in such comprehensive works as the *Compleat Gentleman* (1622) by Henry Peacham the Younger and the *Noveau Traité de la civilité* (1671) by Antoine de Coutin. The body of conduct book literature soon grew to be enormous.

Ingratiating manners and especially the courtier's ideal of

a studied casualness and nonchalance, or *sprezzatura*, informed this literature with fundamental insincerity and more subtly the courtly posture with irony of indirection, understatement, and deception. Popular proverbs identified courtliness with craftiness and the Italianate Englishman (or other nationality) with a devil incarnate. Lorenzo Ducci in *Arte aulica* (1601) stripped off the mannerly veneer to expose the courtier's amoral struggle for survival and self-promotion at court. In *King Lear* Shakespeare plays with courtliness by contrasting despicable "good" courtier Oswald with admirable counselor Kent, who is so unmannerly that he addresses Lear as "thou."

The conduct book nevertheless supplied the text for the civilizing process. The courtier reined in aggressive and sexual urges, sublimated them into courtliness, and polished away coarse behaviors. A lower threshold of repugnance paradoxically represented both a new individualism and privacy and a new conformism and sense of social discipline. Good manners emphasized mode of satisfaction over instinctual source, aim, and object. The conduct book made the early modern court the cocoon in which ravening medieval baronial caterpillars were transformed into the beautiful noble court butterflies of the old regime. Perhaps, as Edmund Burke contended, vice lost half its evil by losing all its grossness, though Samuel Johnson's stern disapproval of Lord Chesterfield's *Letters to His Son* (1774) for teaching the morals of a whore and manners of a dancing-master is not amiss for the whole genre.

BIBLIOGRAPHY

Ariès, Philippe, and Georges Duby, eds. *A History of Private Life.* 5 vols. Translated by Arthur Goldhammer. Reprint, Cambridge, Mass., 1987–1991. See especially vol. 3, *Passions of the Renaissance*, edited by Roger Chartier, which covers 1500–1800. An ambitious project of the new social history from the French perspective, containing the provocative interpretation "The Uses of Civility," by Jacques Revel, vol. 3, pp. 167–205. Vol. 2 is also pertinent as well as the other volumes for definitions and methods.

Becker, Marvin B. *Civility and Society in Western Europe, 1300–1600.* Bloomington, Ind., 1988. Perceptive study of shifting cultural forms and values in Renaissance Tuscany and England, especially "the tilt toward civility."

Castiglione, Baldassare. *The Book of the Courtier* (1528, in Italian). Translated by Charles S. Singleton. New York, 1959. First translated by Sir Thomas Hoby as *The Boke of the Courtyer*, London, 1561. Finest conduct book and most authoritative on *sprezzatura*.

Elias, Norbert. *The Civilizing Process.* 2 vols. Translated by Edmund Jephcott. Reprint, New York, 1978–1982. Seminal work on social control in early modern Europe. Vol. 1, *The History of Manners*, contains many excerpts from conduct books with illuminating commentary, interpretation, and theory, but Vol. 2, *Power and Civility*, is very general and mostly tangential.

TERENCE R. MURPHY

CONFESSIO AUGUSTANA. *See* Augsburg Confession.

CONFESSIO BOHEMICA. *See* Confessions in Eastern Europe.

CONFESSIO GALLICANA. *See* Gallic Confession.

CONFESSIO HELVETICA. *See* Helvetic Confessions.

CONFESSION. In Roman Catholicism since the Middle Ages, private or auricular confession of sins had been made to a priest, whose ordination granted him power to absolve from guilt (*culpa*) and to fix penances for the satisfaction of punishment (*poena*). Public penance persisted in the early modern period, but it was punishment in the "public forum," where sins are treated like crimes, not the "inner forum," where conscience and the moral law intersect in the confessional. Thus, public shaming and publicized acts of restitution might be decreed for various public sinners (such as usurers, notorious offenders of the peace, practitioners of "white" magic, single pregnant women, lovers caught in the act, and priests' concubines) as part of the expiation of their sins, but, by an understanding long antedating the Reformation, priests were to keep private confession private and not assign a public penance that might reveal the nature of the confessed sin.

The Medieval Framework. Medieval theologians asserted that private confession to priests was commanded in the New Testament (the most common places are *Mt.* 16:18f, 18:15ff.; *Jn.* 20:21; *Jas.* 5:6; and *Lk.* 17:14) even though in no text does Christ explicitly command confession. The decree *Omnis utriusque sexus* in 1215 made yearly confession obligatory by ecclesiastical law for all males and females who had attained the age of reason. That legislation helped confirm what Thomas Aquinas was to label the "virtual necessity" of the sacrament of penance, a necessity inferred from a set of assumptions almost universally held at least since the central Middle Ages: that human beings inevitably sin after baptism; that anyone conscious of sin needs to confess; that one must confess before Communion; and that a happy death includes a final confession. In short, to be assured of forgiveness, one had better confess and be absolved. The nature of that assurance was a subject of theological speculation and became central in the Reformation debate over confession.

The Practice of Confession. Europeans had been confessing sins to priests for centuries before scholastic theologians constructed theories about what penance was, how it worked, and where it came from. The Reformation broke that continuity and eventually turned the presence or absence of confession into a defining denominational attribute. Although Protestant churches—especially Lutheranism and high-church Anglicanism—tried to preserve some features of the medieval practice, sixteenth-century religious reform led ultimately to the modern rule: "Catholics confess, Protestants do not." Indeed, to be considered a practicing Catholic by some secular political authorities at the beginning of the seventeenth century, one had to give written evidence of having confessed, a requirement that might extend to subjects living in or returning from foreign territories. Observance of yearly confession seems to have been general in Europe even before the Reformation.

Manuals of confession usually direct the penitent to kneel in front of a seated confessor in an open place in the church. The priest is to encourage a full and honest confession and promise forgiveness, listen patiently, not betray surprise or shock, refrain from staring (especially at women and children), and interrogate diligently but prudently. A priest might be directed to ascertain the diocese and parish of a penitent he does not know, as well as such central details as social and marital status. Other possible preliminary questions concern the time of the last confession, whether the penances have been completed, and the state of the penitent's religious knowledge (e.g., the Ten Commandments, the Apostles' Creed, the Lord's Prayer, and the Hail Mary). The penitent is commanded to tell all remembered mortal sins and all details relevant to a judgment about their gravity: when, with whom, how, how often, and especially why the sins were committed. They are, however, forbidden to name companions in sin. A common order has the penitent begin with the sign of the cross; recite the *confiteor*, breaking off at the *mea culpa* to tell the sins one by one and in detail; complete recitation of the *confiteor*; answer questions by the priest; receive instruction and a penance; and be absolved. Evidence from the manuals, as well as from visual representations, indicates that, in the absence of a confessional box, there was an attempt to preserve privacy. The same evidence suggests that it was common for the priest to place his hand on the penitent's head while he recited the absolution. A voluntary payment seems to have been widely practiced. After absolution penitents were to perform the penances assigned as satisfaction for sin.

It is impossible to generalize about the length and detail of confessions. Some authorities clearly envisage long and meticulous encounters, but evidence of the contrary—revealed when moralists complain about rushed confessors and penitents who seek out easy confessors—confirms the commonsense suspicion that variety in practice favored brevity. It is equally impossible to generalize about the practice of assigning penances. Authorities continued to pay lip service to severe norms, but the universal agreement that "penances are arbitrary"—and that good confessors never give a penance that a penitent is unwilling to accept—probably means that lengthy penances were seldom if ever imposed. Two popular summas for confessors advise priests to give no more than one or two prayers as the official pen-

ance so that it could be completed before the penitent left the church and committed a sin that would render completion of the penance ineffective.

The decree of 1215 demanded complete secrecy of confession and stipulated lifelong incarceration in a monastery for those who violated the seal of the confessional. Mitigations of the rule of secrecy were minimal, and the institution seems to have maintained a reputation for guaranteeing privacy. (Voltaire admired the response of Pierre Coton, Henry IV's Jesuit confessor, who told the king he would not unmask a penitent planning an assassination but would interpose himself between the king and the assassin [*Philosophical Dictionary*, "Confession"]). That secrecy also means that historians have virtually no direct evidence about what went on in confession.

The Dissolution of Consensus. Reservations about the divine foundation and necessity of private auricular confession predate the Reformation. When Duns Scotus argued that the apostles would not have introduced so burdensome a custom on their own authority, he was admitting that he found no absolutely clear reference to its institution by Christ in the words of scripture. Yet the divine institution of confession was sufficiently entrenched that Pedro Martinez de Osma was forced to retract propositions (formally condemned in 1479) denying its necessity and divine institution (Denzinger, 724–733). The Lollards rejected the traditional scriptural supports for auricular confession; repudiated compulsory confession and priestly absolution on historical, theological, and moral grounds; and, like the Waldensians, preferred confession to laymen.

Late medieval arguments against the scriptural foundation and antiquity of private confession anticipated the more devastating humanist historical critique. Desiderius Erasmus's *Annotations* systematically undermined the traditional interpretation of passages alleged to support its institution by Christ or the apostles. He also argued against the continuity of the practice between the ancient and medieval church and thereby heightened the sense among the learned that the institutions of forgiveness were not divinely fixed but historically contingent. That historical sense was a powerful ally of Protestant critics.

All mainline Protestant reformers rejected compulsory confession, the doctrine of free will, human cooperation in forgiveness of and satisfaction for sin, and the requirements of a worthy sorrow and a complete confession, all of which they judged to be novel and oppressive violations of Christian liberty inspired by scholastic Pelagianism. Although Martin Luther denounced papal compulsion to confess and denied the possibility of even knowing, much less confessing, all one's sins, he nevertheless continued to insist that confession (before a pastor, as well as God and one's neighbor) was essential to consolation and therefore to forgiveness itself primarily because personal absolution confirmed what might otherwise be doubtful to the penitent. The

Augsburg Confession, Philipp Melanchthon's *Loci Communes,* and Luther's Small Catechism preserve that solution. Moreover, in 1523 Luther, to ensure devout reception of the sacrament, instituted the *Verhör,* the pastor's examination and instruction in faith of individual communicants, and linked the *Verhör* with individual confession of sin. Fifty Lutheran church ordinances between 1525 and 1591 decreed individual confession with the *Verhör* as a precondition of admission to the Lord's Supper: no Lutheran polities failed to adopt it, and many forbade general absolution of the congregation. The tendency in Lutheran orthodoxy was to confine absolution to ministers of the word and support their judicial function of binding and loosing from sin (Laurentius Klein, 1961; see pp. 75–80, 89–87, and 173–184). On the other hand, when Luther proclaimed "Christian liberty," denied that ordination conferred on priests an inherent power to absolve, affirmed that all believers had the right to pronounce forgiveness, discouraged detailed inquiry into sins (especially secret sins), and rejected the possibility of a complete confession, he prepared the way for the decline and eventual demise of confession, even though religious and secular authorities in Lutheran Germany tried to maintain it.

The Reformed tradition was more hostile. John Calvin called auricular confession "butchery of conscience" and, in an apparently autobiographical passage of his *Responsio ad Sadoleti epistolam,* spoke of psychological torments like Luther's. Yet his concern for safeguarding the sanctity of the Lord's Supper made him reluctant to abandon it without an evangelical substitute that would allow oversight of communicants (Calvini opera, vol. 9, p. 41), and that function of the medieval institution was preserved in other forms of Calvinism. Even more systematic in their opposition were Huldrych Zwingli, who found little use for anything but brotherly counsel, and Martin Bucer, who insisted that individual confession was a matter of conscience and only justifiable when a minister was wise enough to provide instruction or consolation to a believer who needed it. In England's Henrician Reformation, both the Ten Articles (1536) and the Six Articles (1539) endorsed auricular confession, but the later Anglican prayer books, influenced by Calvinism, merely allow it.

Justification, Confession, and the Causes of the Reformation. In explaining why the Reformation happened, Steven E. Ozment (1980) has made confession central to his portrait of a burdensome religion that Luther and his followers wanted to overthrow. That medieval penance was as tormenting as the reformers claimed has found some support in the work of Jean Delumeau (1990), although he contradicts Ozment's corollary argument that the evangelical theology of forgiveness consoled. Lawrence Duggan (1984), meanwhile, has systematically challenged every element in this argument, especially the major premise that late medieval and sixteenth-century believers were overwhelmed by the burdens of confession (see Larissa Taylor, *Soldiers of Christ,* New York and Oxford, 1992, pp. 232–233). Moreover, Euan Cameron (*The European Reformation,* Oxford, 1991, pp. 305–307) retains justification and penance as the central religious issue in the Reformation but rejects the burdensome-religion argument. These critics are more impressed by Protestant revulsion at hypocrisy and immorality than by tormented Protestant consciences. Both sides have a point (see Tentler, pp. 345–370). The testimony of the major reformers, whose polemics assumed that the anxieties they had experienced were widespread, seems to provide irrefutable support for the burdensome-religion thesis. Other evidence at the popular level is consistent with this interpretation. On the other hand, the vast edifice of Counter-Reformation practice, which saw most of Europe retain confession and resolutely defend it as morally, spiritually, and psychologically beneficent, is equally irrefutable evidence against the thesis. The history of the Society of Jesus repeatedly confirms Catholic Europe's commitment to this element in the cure of souls. Additional confirmation might be found in the determination of Lutheran churches to preserve or restore an evangelical form of confession at the end of the sixteenth century. Even Zwingli could allude to a "relaxation" and "a great joy and refreshing" as if it were common knowledge that penitents ordinarily found at least a temporary psychological release through confession (Zwingli, "Of Baptism," in *Zwingli and Bullinger,* translated and edited by G. W. Bromiley, Philadelphia, 1963, pp. 156–157).

The discordant judgments of historians echo the dissensions of centuries. Rogier van der Weyden's representation of confession is nothing like Hans Holbein the Younger's parody. What for Luther and Calvin was a source of anxiety could inspire comedy in both Giovanni Boccaccio and Erasmus (whose comic treatments of confession in the *Decameron* and the *Colloquia familiaria* [Familiar Colloquies], respectively, are themselves radically different). Francis Bacon called confession an *arcanum imperii*—a secret of domination—superior to that of ancient Rome. Among those in the twentieth century impressed, like Bacon, with confession's disciplinary function were the Protestant theologian Dietrich Bonhoeffer, who admired it as insurance against "cheap grace," and the philosopher Michel Foucault, who was appalled by Western Christianity's creation of a "confessing beast." Nor do those who find confession psychologically comforting agree. Max Weber considered it key to the Middle Ages' lenient Christianity, which was incapable of producing an anxiety adequate to the needs of a capitalistic ethic, whereas Carl Jung celebrated its psychotherapeutic power. At the end of the twentieth century a beleaguered John Paul II struggles to maintain in existence a practice that until recently was integral to a Roman Catholic identity, while most Roman Catholic laity seems determined to forget that tradition and reenact the history of its decline in Protestant Europe. Historicism, or the sociology of knowledge, seems best suited to account for such contradictory judgments of confession and to subdue the temptation to assign a single meaning to a complex historical phenomenon.

BIBLIOGRAPHY

Bossy, John. "The Social History of Confession in the Age of the Reformation." *Transactions of the Royal Historical Society* 5th ser. 25 (1975), 21–38. A spirited, speculative exposition of the thesis that the medieval conception of sin, practice of confession, and understanding of reconciliation were primarily social, and that the sixteenth century initiated a more individualistic discipline and sense of sin.

Delumeau, Jean. *L'aveu et le pardon: Les difficultés de la confession, XIIIe-XVIIIe siècle.* Paris, 1990. Thoughtful, balanced, brief examination of the psychological issues, in fairly simple French.

Duffy, Eamon. *The Stripping of the Altars: Traditional Religion in England, 1400–1580.* New Haven and London, 1992. An affectionate appreciation of late medieval religion and a less-than-affectionate judgment on its reform in England. The author sees close connections between "elite" and "popular" religion. For confession, see especially pp. 53–87, 310–327.

Duggan, Lawrence. "Fear and Confession on the Eve of the Reformation." *Archiv für Reformationsgeschichte* 75 (1984), 153–175. Succinct but comprehensive rejection of the burdensome-religion thesis.

Klein, Laurentius. *Evangelisch-Lutherische Beichte.* Konfessionskunde und kontroverstheologische Studien, 5. Paderborn, 1961. Confession in Lutheranism from Luther to the present in clear, jargon-free German.

Lea, Henry C. *A History of Auricular Confession and Indulgences in the Latin Church* (1896). 3 vols. Reprint, New York, 1968. Old, informed by a rationalist's distaste for his subject, Lea's massive survey is still indispensable. He had a command of the stages of confessions' historical development and an eye for the salient and entertaining detail.

Nichols, Ann Eljenholm. "The Etiquette of Pre-Reformation Confession in East Anglia." *Sixteenth Century Journal* 17.2 (Summer 1986), 145–163. Detailed and imaginative description of confession as depicted in English baptismal fonts sculpted between 1463 and 1544.

Ozment, Steven E. *The Reformation in the Cities: The Appeal of Protestantism to Sixteenth-Century Germany and Switzerland.* Reprint, New Haven, 1980. Readable, powerful statement of Lutheranism's appeal to overburdened believers.

Rublack, Hans-Christoph. "Lutherische Beichte und Sozialdisziplinierung." *Archiv für Reformationsgeschichte/Archive for Reformation History* 84 (1993), 127–155. Argues that Lutheran confession persisted in the seventeenth century, but became a social ritual, not a foundation for individual piety and the rationalization of moral life required in a Weberian model of modernization.

Tentler, Thomas. *Sin and Confession on the Eve of the Reformation.* Princeton, 1977. For a more extensive treatment of the main points in this article.

THOMAS TENTLER

CONFESSIONS IN EASTERN EUROPE.

Throughout eastern Europe during the sixteenth century, numerous confessions of faith were prepared by individuals and by reform communities in cities, regions, and territories to define and defend their particular theological stance. Their confessions responded to external and internal challenges, to the threats of persecution or expulsion made by political and ecclesiastical authorities, and to alternate doctrinal positions. Following the pattern established at Augsburg in 1530, the authors of corporate confessions sought to establish the legitimacy or orthodoxy of their doctrine and frequently presented confessions to ecclesiastical or secular officials in attempts to obtain formal toleration and legal recognition for their faith. While some confessions, such as the Confessio Bohemica (1575), the Consensus Sendomiriensis (1570), and the Confessio Polonica (1575), attempted to formulate a single doctrinal statement that several groups could accept as they sought toleration, most of the confessions produced in eastern Europe during the second half of the sixteenth century were exclusive rather than inclusive. They delineated specific doctrinal formulations as normative for individual ecclesiastical communities as well as those views that they deemed unacceptable, thereby more clearly establishing the identity and integrity of individual churches.

During the first half century of the Reformation in eastern Europe, especially in the lands of the Austrian Habsburgs, the confessions that were prepared presented doctrinal formulations generally compatible with those of the Augsburg Confession—the Confessio Bohemica (1575) of the Bohemian Brethren (Unitas Fratrum), for which Luther prepared an introduction, and the brief confessions of the Lutherans of the cities of Upper Hungary, the Confessio Pentapolitana (1549) and Confessio Montana (1558).

After 1560, however, the majority of confessions tended to define doctrine more precisely as distinct ecclesiastical and theological communities emerged. The Confessio Carinthica and Confessio Austrica, both prepared in 1560, represented an anti-Philippist Gnesio-Lutheran position, while the Brief Confession concerning the Lord's Supper of the Saxon Church (1561) and the Pious Formula of Agreement among the Pastors of the Saxon Church (1572) in Siebenburgen, or Transylvania, were more Philippist in spirit. In Heidersdorf (Gosciejowice) Lutherans of the Silesian principality of Brieg (Brzeg) accepted the Formula Concordia Heidersdorfensis (1574) to dissociate themselves from the views of Kaspar von Schwenckfeld, Zwingli, Calvin, Bèze, and Matthias Flacius Illyricus. Helvetic theological positions, especially those of the Second Helvetic Confession (1562), were enunciated by the two confessions of Debrecen (1567), the Confessio Czengerini (1570), and the Szikszó Confession (1568). Similarly, the Hutterites presented Peter Riedemann's *Rechenschaft* (1545) to the lords of Moravia as a statement of their faith, the Anabaptists of Moravia prepared the so-called Nikolsburg Articles (1527), and the Czech neo-Utraquists reiterated their allegiance to the Prague Articles in their confession of faith of 1562.

BIBLIOGRAPHY

Barton, Peter F., and László Makkai. *Ostmitteleuropas Bekenntnisschriften der Evangelischen Kirchen A. und H. B. des Reformationszeitalters.* Budapest, 1987.

Binder, Ludwig. *Die Kirche der Siebenbürger Sachsen.* Erlangen, 1982.

Bucsay, Míhaly. *Der Protestantismus in Ungarn, 1521–1978.* Vienna, 1977.

Reingrabner, Gustav. *Aus der Kraft des Evangeliums, Geschehnisse und Personen aus der Geschichte des österreichischen Protestantismus.* Erlangen, 1986.

Řičan, Rudolf. *Das Reich Gottes in den Böhmischen Ländern, Geschichte des tschechischen Protestantismus.* Stuttgart, 1957.

DAVID P. DANIEL

CONFESSIO SCOTICA. *See* Scottish Confession.

CONFESSIO TETRAPOLITANA. *See* Tetrapolitan Confession.

CONFIRMATION. By the eve of the Reformation the Western Christian understanding of the sacrament of confirmation had evolved to a point of relative stability, clarity, and consensus. In 1439 the Council of Florence declared in its Decree for the Armenians:

> The second sacrament is confirmation. Its matter is chrism blessed by a bishop and made from oil, which signifies the lustre of conscience, and balsam, which signifies the odor of good reputation. The form is: 'I sign you with the sign of the cross and confirm you with the chrism of salvation, in the name of the Father, and the Son, and the Holy Spirit.' The ordinary minister is the bishop. . . because we are informed that the apostles alone, whose office the bishops hold, were imparting the Holy Spirit through the imposition of hands. . . . In place of that imposition of hands confirmation is given in the church. . . . The effect of this sacrament is that in it the Holy Spirit is given for strength, as he was given to the apostles on the day of Pentecost, so that the Christian might courageously confess the name of Christ.
>
> (Denzinger-Schönmetzer, *Enchiridion Symbolorum Definitionem et Declarationem De Rebus Fidei et Morum* Rome, 1976; nos. 1317–1319).

Dissenting voices from the past, such as the Waldensians, the Cathari, Wycliffe, and Hus, were thus relegated to the periphery. Within the mainstream the only matters still in dispute were whether the sacrament was absolutely necessary for salvation and whether it was instituted by Christ or the apostles.

Luther inherited this late medieval consensus and showed no discomfort with it for some time. In 1517 he mentioned confirmation as one of the unrepeatable sacraments, and in 1520 it still appeared in his listing of the sacraments. But already a process of development in his theology of the sacraments was well under way, and in 1520 he sketched out for the first time its implications for confirmation. In his *De Captivitate Babylonica* (Babylonian Captivity) of that year he argued that the gifts conferred by the laying on of hands in *Acts* 9 and 18 were only temporary. Confirmation then is not to be found in scripture, there is no divine promise attached to it, and it does not work salvation. It is therefore not a sacrament but an ecclesiastical rite. In the following years Luther repeated this argument while at the same time allowing that confirmation could be administered, provided no one regard it as a sacrament. By 1523 Luther came to associate the rite with the final examination after a course of catechetical instruction. Melanchthon largely concurred, though later sixteenth-century Lutheran church orders are marked by controversy and diversity on the details.

Luther was not the first to think of confirmation in this way. The Bohemian Brethren already used the imposition of hands as the ritual consummation of a catechetical process and saw this as a necessary completion of baptism. Perhaps under their influence, Erasmus suggested in 1522 that pubescent children be instructed and examined on the fundamentals of the faith. Huldrych Zwingli in fact began such a practice in 1523, essentially replacing the sacrament of confirmation with catechesis. Others such as Kaspar von Schwenckfeld saw it as an instrument of church discipline and required it for admission to the Lord's Supper.

These and other elements coalesced in the teaching of Martin Bucer, who is sometimes seen as the father of Protestant confirmation. To counter the Anabaptist protest, Bucer held that infant baptism needs completion; its deficiency is supplied by confirmation. Together baptism and confirmation incorporate individuals into the church. Confirmation is the crowning act of the catechetical process, a rite of admission to the Lord's Supper, and an implicit submission to church discipline on the part of the recipient. Whether intentional or not, the wording of Bucer's rite echoes that of the Council of Florence and suggests that, in the last analysis, he regarded confirmation as sacramental.

In England, where Bucer's influence was strongly felt, the discussion over whether confirmation was a sacrament began in 1537 and continued throughout the century. Cranmer's *Book of Common Prayer* (1549) included a rite of confirmation which excluded the chrism but retained much of the traditional wording and functioned as the culmination of the catechetical examination.

John Calvin's understanding of confirmation had already achieved great clarity when he published the 1536 edition of his *Institutes;* the final edition of 1559 merely expanded on this foundation. Confirmation, Calvin argued, is not to be found in scripture, and therefore it is not a true sacrament. The apostles did indeed impose hands and confer the Holy Spirit, but this was a temporary gift that quickly ended. In the early church, Calvin believed, confirmation was first and foremost an examination on the basics of the faith, and this is what it should be now. Its corruption at the hands of the

Roman church was regrettable, particularly because this tradition attributed some of the effects of baptism to confirmation and thus diminished baptism. It was Calvin's teaching above all that prevailed in the Reformed tradition.

On the Roman Catholic side, a long list of controversialists beginning with Henry VIII attacked these Protestant views. At midcentury the Council of Trent finally added its authoritative voice to this chorus of denunciations. At its seventh session in 1547 it anathematized those who denied the sacrament's institution by Christ and its indelible character. Furthermore, the council insisted, it is a true sacrament and not merely a ceremony in which those approaching adolescence give an account of their faith to the church. One can legitimately ascribe power to the chrism in confirmation, and its ordinary minister is the bishop alone. In these declarations the council issued a full reaffirmation of traditional Catholic theology and practice.

Perhaps the most articulate defense of this position was that of Roberto Bellarmino (1542–1621) in his 1586 work *Disputationes de controversiis Christianae fidei adversus huius temporis haereticos*. Adopting the reformers' criteria for a sacrament, Bellarmino argued that there was indeed a divine promise of grace attached to this act, namely Christ's promise to send the Holy Spirit. Furthermore, there was a sign and word attached to it, namely the imposition of hands for conferring the Holy Spirit (*Acts* 8 and 19). Finally, Bellarmino insisted, the divine command to do this can be assumed, since otherwise the apostles would not have done it. This line of argument subsequently became the foundation for all Roman Catholic defenses of confirmation as a sacrament.

[*See also* Education.]

BIBLIOGRAPHY

Dienst, Karl. "Konfirmation." In *Theologische Realenzyklopädie*, edited by G. Krause and G. Müller, vol. 19, p. 437–445. Berlin, 1977–.

Fisher, J. D. C., ed. *Christian Initiation—The Reformation Period: Some Early Reformed Rites of Baptism and Confirmation and Other Contemporary Documents*. London, 1970. A collection of primary texts especially useful for the English Reformation.

Frör, Kurt, ed. *Confirmatio: Forschungen zur Geschichte and Praxis der Konfirmation*. Munich, 1959. Several important historical essays bearing on Reformation developments.

Hareide, Bjarne. *Die Konfirmation in der Reformationszeit: Eine Untersuchung der lutherischen Konfirmation in Deutschland, 1520–1585*. Göttingen, 1966. Particularly helpful in detailing the various sixteenth-century church orders and the early intra-Lutheran controversies.

Kretschmar, Georg. "Firmung." In *Theologische Realenzyklopädie*, vol. 11, pp. 192–204. Berlin, 1977–.

Turner, Paul. *The Meaning and Practice of Confirmation: Perspectives from a Sixteenth-Century Controversy*. New York, 1987. Detailed analyses of the argumentation in Calvin, Martin Chemnitz, and Bellarmino.

Vischer, Lukas. *Die Geschichte der Konfirmation: Ein Beitrag zur Diskussion über das Konfirmationsproblem*. Zollikon, Switzerland, 1958. A useful summary chapter on the Reformation period.

DENIS R. JANZ

CONFRATERNITIES. Lay confraternities were associations of people who came together to promote their religious life in common, according to agreed-upon rules. Such associations were also called fraternities, brotherhoods, religious guilds, companies, sodalities, and so on (with many variations in different languages). Confraternities still exist in small numbers, but they played their main role in religious-social life from the late thirteenth to the eighteenth century. Protestant reformers curtailed them, but their numbers and roles expanded considerably in Catholic lands, notably in Italy and Iberia from the sixteenth century, and in France and parts of Germany from the seventeenth. Though often primarily concerned with preparing for the afterlife and praying for souls, the confraternities could be fully involved in the social, political, charitable, and cultural life of communities. They were predominantly for laymen, but they could also involve clergy, women, and children—as members or as recipients of philanthropy.

Background. Lay confraternities are documented from the early Christian centuries, in both the Eastern and Western churches; but the major expansion came from the thirteenth century under the impact of new Marian cults, flagellant movements, hospital expansion, and the diversification of some trade guilds. On the eve of the Reformation confraternities were certainly widespread through Italian, Iberian, French, and Rhineland cities as well as many villages. Their roles were and remain controversial in the context of the Protestant Reformation. Reformers like Luther and Bucer attacked the German brotherhoods for their drunkenness and lack of concern for the poor; Nuremberg brotherhoods were condemned locally as drinking clubs. More positively, some fraternities fostered the new successful evangelicals (in Strasbourg) and less successful Italian heretics (in Siena). In England fraternities are now seen as having been vital centers for popular lay Christianity and charity, right up to their curtailment by the Chantries Act (1547). If for no other reason, the Protestant attack on purgatory and prayer for souls therein removed the most significant target of the fraternities' devotions and so led to their demise where Protestantism prevailed.

Confraternities and Catholic Reform. Confraternities, at least in Italy, were at the forefront of early Catholic reform in promoting more outward-looking philanthropy, new Marian cults, more respectful adoration of the Host, and more frequent Communion for the laity. Medieval fraternities had offered some welfare to members of the fraternity and close relatives, but from the late fifteenth century some embraced poorer members of society outside the fraternity. Following precedents from fraternities in Brescia and Ferrara, the Companies of Divine Love (initiated by Ettore Vernazza in Genoa in 1497) best spread new charitable and devotional ideas. The effects were felt both within the confraternity movements and in the new religious orders like the Oratorians and Theatines. The promotion of the rosary by the Dominicans led to the growth of confraternities dedicated to it, initially in Germany (Colmar, c.1484), then France and Italy (Venice's San Domenico in Castello, in particular). The rosary confraternities were especially important throughout the Counter-Reformation period for the spiritual lives and social roles of women.

The reforming Catholic hierarchy's attitudes to confraternities were ambivalent; while Bishop Gian Matteo Giberti of Verona early on valued new Corpus Christi fraternities for the veneration of the Host, other authorities were suspicious of lay confraternities because they were dominated by laymen and allowed laymen to preach or to discuss the Bible and doctrine, because they were often very secretive, and because they had unseemly feasts. Spanish fears led to the debate on confraternities at the Council of Trent and the ultimate ruling (1563) that confraternities, hospitals, and similar pious places should be subject to episcopal control, especially through the scrutiny of their statutes and accounts. Fraternities did subsequently come under fuller clerical supervision or control, though not without notable protests from some lay leaders.

Following the lead of Archbishop Carlo Borromeo of Milan, reforming bishops tended to encourage rosary, Sacrament, and Christian doctrine confraternities based on the parish church and under the priest's supervision, and to discourage societies that existed independently in their own oratories. The expansion of clerically dominated fraternities was greatly encouraged by the new and reformed orders, especially the Capuchins and Jesuits, as part of their missionary efforts in city slums or rural fastnesses. The Jesuits spawned the greatest variety of devotional and philanthropic fraternities. Scholars have recently emphasized the Jesuit networks of clerical congregations and lay fraternities dedicated to the Marian cult, which aimed to curb heretics and worldly immorality. Led by Fathers Antonio Possevino (from Rome) or François Coster (from Cologne), such fraternities and congregations fostered the Catholic recovery not only in Italy but also (from the 1570s) in Cologne, Munich, Swiss Fribourg, and Prague, culminating in French seventeenth-century examples.

By about 1600 fraternities in Catholic lands had a considerable variety of devotional and philanthropic preoccupations. Those linked to Marian devotions, especially the rosary, and to the protection and adoration of the Sacrament probably predominated. Some societies (at first mainly in Spain, then in Italy and France) specialized in praying for the anonymous mass of souls in purgatory. There was some revival in the serious practice of flagellation (the "discipline"), particularly under Capuchin and Jesuit influence.

While some fraternities were highly secretive, others flourished publicly in great religious processions on feast days, as in Venice, Naples, Toledo, and Lyon. The welfare roles of confraternities were quite varied, though much was undertaken first for the salvation of the soul of the donor, then for the spiritual, and lastly for the physical, well-being of the recipients. Many fraternities provided dowries for poor girls to marry honestly or to enter a nunnery. Others provided alms for the "deserving" poor—preferably elderly and female. Some specialized in comforting condemned prisoners until execution, releasing debtors from prison, or even running prisons (as in the papal state). They might ensure decent burial for abandoned corpses or (in Bavaria) suicides. Fraternity members visited the sick; they provided almshouses and hospices for travelers, the sick, and the aged; confraternities ran great hospitals (as in Rome, Naples, Toledo); they coped with foundlings and abandoned children; they provided conservatories for vulnerable girls, repentant prostitutes, and battered wives. Confraternities of Christian doctrine (as across north-central Italy and in Valladolid and Zamora) improved knowledge of Christian doctrine—and sometimes literacy.

Much of these devotional and philanthropic activities can be seen as buttressing the Catholic cause and saving the faithful, behind the confrontational lines. A more militant contribution is notable in France. During the Wars of Religion from the 1560s to 1590s, confraternities were variously mobilized against the Calvinist Huguenots; the Holy Ghost fraternities of Limoges and Mâcon (1567–1568) were major militant groups, while the Penitents across a wider area combined aggressive Catholic politics (to prevent moderates from compromising with the Huguenots) with penitential exercises and charity. But French confraternity activities were often divisive, mutually conflicting, and distrusted by leaders of the league in the 1590s, by local notables, or by the hierarchy. New kinds of confraternities, under the parish priests or Orders, were to assist in the French Catholic Reformation of the seventeenth century.

Later sixteenth-century confraternities varied considerably in type, composition, and distribution. Membership ranged from a handful to many thousands. (The Dei Bianchi in Naples had 6,000 in 1563, the Holy Sacrament in Lyon, 1,300 in 1561.) A city might have over a hundred confraternities. (Toledo had 143 in 1576; Venice, 120 in the early sixteenth century, 387 in the eighteenth). Some were exclusively male or, occasionally, female (often dedicated to the rosary or to Saint Anne); others were sexually mixed, though men dominated the offices. Some were socially exclusive—for nobles, students, or particular craftsmen; others deliberately mixed social ranks, rich and poor, in the interests of social harmony or to group the most religiously committed of a parish. Activity might be occasional and limited or very full: regular Communion, singing lauds and offices of the Virgin, flagellation, public processions, annual general meetings, business meetings of officials to allocate alms and dowries, and helping equip and decorate the parish church. Some fraternities had no fixed location; most were based on an altar or chapel in a parish church. Others had modest oratories or rooms of their own, while a few had spectacular premises, especially the top Venetian group of discipline fraternities, the *Scuole Grandi*, which made significant contributions to religious art and music. The contribution of confraternities to lay Catholic devotion, philanthropy, and culture was considerable.

[*See also* Piety *and articles on individual religious orders.*]

BIBLIOGRAPHY

Black, Christopher F. *Italian Confraternities in the Sixteenth Century.* Cambridge, 1989. The most comprehensive study, indicating the range and diversity of confraternity activity and devotion. Some non-Italian comparisons; extensive bibliography.

Chambers, David, Brian Pullan, and Jennifer Fletcher, eds. *Venice: A Documentary History, 1450–1630.* Oxford and Cambridge, Mass., 1992. Makes available in English some interesting documentation on Venetian confraternities (*scuole*), and poor relief.

Châtellier, Louis. *The Europe of the Devout: The Catholic Reformation and the Formation of a New Society.* Translated by Jean Birrell. Cambridge, 1989. For the European-wide Jesuit network.

Flynn, Maureen. *Sacred Charity: Confraternities and Social Spain, 1400–1700.* Basingstoke and Ithica, N.Y., 1989. Primarily a study of confraternities in Zamora, with some valuable comparisons elsewhere in Spain.

Gutton, Jean-Pierre. "Confraternities, *Curés* and Communities in Rural Areas of the Diocese of Lyons under the Ancien Régime." In *Religion and Society in Early Modern Europe, 1500–1800,* edited by Kaspar von Greyerz, pp. 202–211. London, 1984. A valuable local French study.

Harding, Robert R. "The Mobilization of Confraternities against the Reformation in France." *Sixteenth Century Journal* 11.2 (1980), 85–107. For the variety of confraternity activities during the Wars of Religion.

Hoffman, Philip T. *Church and Community in the Diocese of Lyon.* New Haven and London, 1984. Includes significant work on confraternities in the changing French parochial context.

Martz, Linda. *Poverty and Welfare in Habsburg Spain: The Example of Toledo.* Cambridge, 1983. Most important for the Santa Caridad fraternity-hospital; useful on other confraternities, as well as non-fraternity welfare, in Toledo and further afield.

Paglia, Vincenzo, ed. *Confraternite e Meridione nell'età moderna.* Rome, 1990. Valuable work on southern Italy, appearing since Black, 1989, cited above.

Pullan, Brian. *Rich and Poor in Renaissance Venice: The Social Institutions of a Catholic State, to 1620.* Oxford, 1971. A pioneering work, including the primary study of Venice's top group of confraternities, the *Scuole Grandi.*

Russell-Wood, A. J. R. *Fidalgos and Philanthropists: The Santa Casa da Misericordia of Bahia, 1550–1755.* London and Berkeley, 1968. For an example of fraternity welfare extended outside Europe.

Scarisbrick, J. J. *The Reformation and the English People.* Oxford, 1984. Stresses the vitality of English fraternities on the eve of the Reformation.

Terpstra, Nicholas. "Apprenticeship in Social Welfare: From Confraternal Charity to Municipal Poor Relief in Early Modern Italy." *Sixteenth Century Journal* 16.1 (1994), 101–120. Important study of Bologna illustrating the evolution of institutions and ideas.

Weissman, Ronald F. E. *Ritual Brotherhood in Renaissance Florence.*

New York and London, 1982. Valuable for understanding the nature of confraternities and changes between the Renaissance and Catholic Reformation periods.

CHRISTOPHER F. BLACK

CONFUTATION. At the Diet of Augsburg, 3 August 1530, an answer to the Augsburg Confession was read in the name of Emperor Charles V. After the delivery of the Augsburg Confession (25 June 1530), the "orthodox" estates decided on the following move: since they had not departed from the doctrine of the church, they were not a religious party. Accordingly, they did not want to present any confession of their own. Instead, they preferred that the emperor present a response to those articles of the Augsburg Confession that dealt with faith, "to several learned, honest, good, and peace-loving theologians, who have not pursued matters with envy." The papal legate was also to give his judgment. The articles of the second part of the Augsburg Confession should be given to legal experts and to other practitioners (Tetleben's report).

The first result of the work of the theologians, the *Responsio theologorum* to articles 1–4, transmitted by Johannes Cochlaeus, was too discursive. Therefore on 2 July Johann Eck assumed all the editing of the work of refutation, in which some twenty-six theologians took part. On 12 July Johann Fabri presented the *Catholica et quasi extemporalis responsio* to the papal legate, who approved it and had it delivered, together with nine additional writings, to the emperor. But the emperor and the majority of the diet rejected this response. The Confutation (*Confutatio*) was the result of the rework begun on 16 July, which was done in German and Latin. It was read publicly in German on 3 August 1530 as the emperor's response to the Augsburg Confession, but was not given out in written form.

The Confutation occupies a middle position between its predecessor, the *Catholica responsio*, and the negotiations of mid-August. The tendency of the argumentation of the Catholica responsio becomes clear in the titles of the writings delivered with it: *Antilogiarum, hoc est contradictionum M. Lutheri Babylonia; Haereses et errores ex diversis Martini Lutheri libris in unum collecti; Haereses in sacris conciliis antea damnatae per Lutheranos iterum ab inferis reductae; Haereses et errores Martini Lutheri per Leonem Pontificem ante decennium condemnati; Haereses et errores Martini Lutheri ante septennium per Universitatem Parisiensem condemnati; Condemnatio facultatis theologiae Lovaniensis; Epitome aliquot haeresium et errorum Martini Lutheri; Monstra sectarum ex Luthero et Lutheranis enata;* and *Lutherani Evangelii abominabiles nimiumque perniciosi damnatissimi fructus.* It is not so much a matter of a response to the Augsburg Confession itself as a reckoning of the theological position of the Lutheran "preachers" (*concionatores*). That position is self-contradictory, is heretical, and was condemned long ago in holy synods, by the pope, and by the university theologians. It creates discord and tumult and is the source of the various sects of the Carphanites, Anabaptists, and fanatics. The determination of Lutheran teaching was based on exaggerated formulations from the early 1520s. For example, the *responsio* says "the Lutherans deny that the children are granted grace by baptism." The clear statement in article 9 that grace is granted by baptism is taken as confession of the "princes," while "Luther and Melanchthon teach: 'Baptism justifies no one, nor does it benefit anyone.'" Rejected statements in the Augsburg Confession are attributed to the preachers, who falsely assigned them to the princes.

In contrast, the Confutation lacks "that hateful reminder of everything that was written or that happened ten years ago." The "emperor ordered that hateful catalogue of heresies, errors, and slander, etc., to be removed, as well as everything that did not serve to answer our confession." With this, an important reorientation took place. The picture of the enemy (still effective in the present) that regarded the Lutheran Reformation negatively (violent assaults, plundering of monasteries, iconoclasms, and exaggerated formulations mainly from 1520–1522) taken out of context and from fringe groups of the Reformation, was given up; the Augsburg Confession was taken seriously in its own theological context and as a basis for discussion (the tension between princes and preachers is revised; there was even the tendency to remove such words as "princes" [*principes*], and "preachers" [*concionatores*] in the final phase of editing). On this basis the Confutation reaches a theological communality concerning the doctrine of the Trinity, the evaluation of the Council of Nicea, Christology, the condemnation of the Pelagians, the gifts of the Holy Spirit in word and sacrament, baptism, the presence of Christ in the Eucharist, absolution, civil authority, condemnation of the Anabaptists, Christ's return to judgment, freedom of the will, cause of sins, and so on. The sentences cited in the *Catholica responsio* in opposition to the Augsburg Confession, if read in the context of their intent, lose their heretical appearance, or have been since then revised, as for example the statements of Luther and Melanchthon of 1520 that "everything happens according to absolute necessity," or that God is the cause of sin.

The controversy over the definition of original sin, particularly the designation of concupiscence as a sin, remain—in contrast to the negotations in mid-August—unresolved in the Confutation; but even though the *Catholica responsio* sees in Luther and his "pupil" Eberhard Weidensee a denial of the effectiveness of baptism, the way to a possible agreement is noted through the reference to the language of Augustine. The understanding of the church as a *congregatio sanctorum,* as an assembly of saints (article 7), was seen by the *Catholica responsio* as a long-condemned Hussite error.

Other controversial points are justification by faith alone (*sola fides*), satisfaction, the merit of good works, invocation of the saints, (with reference to the second part of the Augsburg Confession) the notion of Communion under one kind as abuse, celibacy, completeness of confession of sin, Mass in German, private masses, the Mass as sacrifice, church rules, monastic vows, legal immunity of the churches and clerics (prosecution by secular courts), rules of fasting and abstinence, canonical hours, Easter confession, and episcopal jurisdiction. With respect to doctrine, Melanchthon noted that even if some rotten slander had been attached, "our articles are in themselves all conceded in the Confutation," so that the path for further discussions remained open. Accordingly, the Confutation did not appear as an edict but rather as the emperor's admonition, and the reference to the Edict of Worms was removed in the final version.

[*See also* Augsburg *and* Augsburg Confession.]

BIBLIOGRAPHY

Primary Sources

Ficker, Johannes, ed. *Die Konfutation des Augsburgischen Bekenntnisses: Ihre erste Gestalt und ihre Geschichte.* Leipzig, 1891. Critical edition of the *Catholica responsio.*

Förstemann, Karl Eduard, ed. *Urkundenbuch zu der Geschichte des Reichstages zu Augsburg im Jahre 1530* (1833–1835). Reprint, Osnabrück, 1966.

Grundmann, Herbert, ed. *Valentin von Tetleben: Protokoll des Augsburger Reichstages 1530.* Series of the Historical Commission of the Bavarian Academy of Sciences, vol. 4. Göttingen, 1958.

Immenkötter, Herbert, ed. *Die Confutatio der Confessio Augustana vom 3. August 1530.* Rev. ed. Münster, 1981. Extensive introduction, first critical text edition.

Schirrmacher, Friedrich Wilhelm, ed. *Briefe und Acten zu der Geschichte des Religionsgespräches zu Marburg 1529 und des Reichstags zu Augsburg* (1876). Reprint, Chicago and Amsterdam, 1969.

Secondary Sources

Dittrich, Bernhard. *Das Traditionsverständnis in der Confessio Augustana und in der Confutatio.* Leipzig, 1983.

Immenkötter, Herbert. "Confutatio." In *Lexikon für Theologie und Kirche,* 3d ed., vol. 1, p. 1229. Freiburg, 1993.

Iserloh, Erwin, ed. *Confessio Augustana und Confutatio.* Internationales Symposion der Gesellschaft zur Herausgabe des Corpus Catholicorum, Augsburg, 3–7 September 1979. Münster, 1980.

Müller, Gerhard. *Causa Reformationis: Beiträge zur Reformationsgeschichte und zur Theologie Martin Luthers.* Gütersloh, 1989. See pp. 131–236 regarding the positions of L. Compeggio and of the Curia Roman.

Pfnür, Vinzenz. *Einig in der Rechtfertigungslehre? Die Rechtfertigunslehre der Confessio Augustana (1530) und die Stellungnahme der katholischen Kontroverstheologie zwischen 1530 and 1535.* Wiesbaden, 1970. See especially pp. 222–250 regarding articles 2, 4, 5, 6, 12, and 20 and the Confutation.

———. "Review of Klaus Rischar's *Johann Eck auf dem Reichstag za Augsburg 1530.*" *Theologische Revue* (1971), 63–66. See regarding the question of Eck's participation.

Wicks, Jared. *Luther's Reform: Studies on Conversion and the Church.*

Mainz, 1992. See especially pp. 223–316 regarding articles 22–28 and religious practice.

VINZENZ PFNÜR
Translated from German by Walter D. Morris

CONGREGATIONALISM. Although an anachronism for the age of the Reformation, the term *congregationalism* can be usefully applied to forms of ecclesiastical polity in England and France that accorded a significant degree of autonomy to individual congregations. In this period the term did not, however, refer to a religious denomination; not until the 1640s and 1650s did the phrase "the Congregational way" come to be used for adherents of the Independent movement in England such as William Bridge, Jeremiah Burroughs, Thomas Goodwin, Philip Nye, and Sidrach Simpson, all of whom signed the *Apologeticall Narration* (1643) as "Dissenting Brethren" in the largely Presbyterian Westminster Assembly.

Principles of congregational polity were espoused in Elizabethan England by various radical Puritans and Separatists who embraced the notion of a "gathered" church of visible saints. A church so constituted could be governed in either a presbyterian manner, with power ascending in synods and provincial and national assemblies, or a congregational fashion, with fundamental power residing in local congregations. While Elizabethan Separatists were proponents of the right of each congregation to be free from the control of any other ecclesiastical institution, they recognized the value of synods for mutual support and guidance. The Separatists valued catholicity and unity, but not at the expense of congregational autonomy. In part, of course, this was due to the historical context of state persecution in which they operated, which effectively ruled out synodical experiments.

The Separatists disagreed among themselves as to the role synods might play. Robert Browne, the earliest major Separatist leader, advocated synods to resolve particularly controversial issues; just as the authority of a congregation was greater than that of an individual member, so the power of a synod exceeded that of a single church. Henry Barrow cited the biblical example of the Council of Jerusalem (*Acts* 15) as proof of the value of synods to settle doubts and controversies. Such synods, he thought, would include not only duly chosen elders from each congregation but also any church member who opted to participate, with all those in attendance having the right to speak freely on the issues under consideration so long as they were not disruptive or disrespectful to the elders. Unlike a presbyterian synod, the congregational assembly proposed by Barrow would have no authority to impose its decisions on individual churches; rather, its power depended on its ability to persuade, not decree. The position of Francis Johnson was much the same as Barrow's, for he too recognized the value of synods to

resolve difficult religious issues while insisting that they not usurp the jurisdiction of local congregations.

In practice, the presbyterian and congregational polities could be virtually congruent. Members of the presbyterian Dedham Classis (synod) in the 1580s demonstrated a striking willingness to defy synodical decisions when they went against the interests of their individual congregations. This was possible in the absence of strong synodical sanctions, so that the discipline that the classis attempted to impose on its members was voluntary. The seeds of a congregational outlook were thus present at the pragmatic level even among members of a presbyterian organization.

In France the case for a congregational polity was most strongly put by Jean Morély in his *Traicté de la discipline & police chrestienne* (Treatise on Christian Discipline and Polity), published at Lyon in 1562. Above all, Morély was interested in the maintenance of ecclesiastical discipline, which he thought could be done most effectively by the church as a whole rather than by bishops, the clergy, or secular authorities. Using the apostolic church as his model, he propounded the case for popular government in the church, with discipline administered by members of each congregation aged fifteen and above. Each local church, he argued, should have the authority to administer ecclesiastical punishment, including excommunication. Ministers should be chosen by the members of the congregations they would serve, unlike the Calvinist system, which first required nomination by the Compagnie des Pasteurs and the approval of a magistrate. Morély did, however, modify his democratic system to the extent that a church in a university town could select pastors for neighboring congregations and have the right to depose its minister for just cause.

Like some of the radical Puritans and Separatists in England, Morély favored the establishment of synodical bodies. The hierarchy of councils he designed corresponded more closely to the system of synods and assemblies favored by the radical Puritans than to the single-tier synod suggested by the Separatists. He proposed to group a small number of local congregations into a *bailliage*, the governing body of which would consist of ministers and elected laymen. Above the *bailliages* would come provincial synods, responsible for preserving correct doctrine, administering the churches, and monitoring magistrates. National or universal councils could meet on rare occasions, but only for general instruction and admonition and to present remonstrances to the national government; they could not legislate.

Morély's proposals sparked a controversy in the French Reformed church that lasted for more than a decade. The fight against Morély was led by Théodore de Bèze, Calvin's successor as spiritual leader of Reformed Protestantism. Morély's book had hardly appeared before the Synod of Orléans condemned it in the spring of 1562 on the grounds that it contained wicked doctrine and caused confusion in the church. Morély was not, however, without his defenders, notably Petrus Ramus, a leading French humanist. Ramus entered the fray in the aftermath of the Synod of La Rochelle (1571), over which Bèze had presided as moderator. Although this synod had not denounced Morély by name, it had effectively repudiated his proposed polity and further angered Morély's supporters. So intense did the controversy become that the Synod of Nîmes was convened in May 1572 primarily to deal with it. Nîmes constituted a major triumph for Bèze's faction, for the synod ruled categorically that the proposals for the reform of polity had no foundation in the Bible and endangered the church. Ramus perished in the Saint Bartholomew's Day Massacre, and henceforth the dispute over congregational polity ceased to be a serious cause of disruption in the French Reformed church.

[*See also* Baptists; La Rochelle, Synod of; Nîmes, Synod of; Nonconformity; Puritans; *and* Separatists.]

BIBLIOGRAPHY

Brachlow, Stephen. *The Communion of Saints: Radical Puritan and Separatist Ecclesiology, 1570–1625*. Oxford, 1988. Contains an excellent analysis of the ecclesial views of radical Puritans and Separatists.

Collinson, Patrick. *Godly People: Essays on English Protestantism and Puritanism*. London, 1983. Chapter 20 discusses the historiographical treatment of congregationalism.

Kingdon, Robert M. *Geneva and the Consolidation of the French Protestant Movement, 1564–1572*. Madison, Wis., 1967. Definitive account of the Morély-Bèze dispute.

Nuttall, Geoffrey F. *Visible Saints: The Congregational Way 1640–1660*. Oxford, 1957. Substantive historical introduction traces the development of congregational principles.

Tolmie, Murray. *The Triumph of the Saints: The Separate Churches of London, 1616–1649*. Cambridge, 1977. Superb account of the early Baptist, Separatist, and Independent congregations, including their polity.

White, B. R. *The English Separatist Tradition: From the Marian Martyrs to the Pilgrim Fathers*. London, 1971. Provides the historical context for the emergence of congregational polity in England.

RICHARD L. GREAVES

CONGREGATION OF SAN BENITO OF VALLADOLID.

Observant congregations in the late Middle Ages sought to correct abuses within the various religious orders much as had earlier been done by Cluny (909) and Citeaux (1098) through a more rigorous observance of the order's rules. In addition, Benedictines in the fifteenth century attempted to circumscribe the autonomy of individual monasteries through the creation of regional congregations. In these congregations, several monasteries would form a federation in which the abbot of one monastery was owed obedience by all others.

In 1417 the Benedictine monastery of San Benito el Real of Valladolid began to form such a congregation, gradually expanding its influence over other Castilian monasteries. Its efforts were backed by the monarchy, which had founded it in 1390 with reform in mind. Strict cloistering was one of the most significant traits of this reform—and the one most strenuously resisted, for the Spanish Benedictines enjoyed considerable freedom of movement. By the mid-fifteenth century, San Benito el Real had imposed its strict observance of the Rule of Saint Benedict on over a dozen other monasteries and had formulated a congregational structure that gave its prior ultimate authority. In the late fifteenth and early sixteenth century, first under the leadership of the Catholic monarchs, Isabella of Castile and Ferdinand of Aragon, and later under Emperor Charles V, the Congregation of San Benito would further expand its influence and enter a golden age of reform. Prompted by Ferdinand and Isabella, Pope Alexander VI formally constituted the congregation in 1497, elevating San Benito el Real from a priory to an abbacy and granting it more control over its subordinate monasteries. Ferdinand and Isabella also encouraged the civil powers throughout their realms to expedite these reforms, and in some cases, such as in Galicia in 1498, recalcitrant Benedictines were reformed by brute force.

Two dynamic abbots reorganized and further enlarged the congregation in the early sixteenth century, gaining control of the oldest and most powerful abbacies of Castile and Aragon. Pedro de Najera, twice abbot of San Benito el Real (1499–1507 and 1513–1517), added twelve male and ten female monasteries, built a new chapel at Valladolid, improved the education of the monks, strengthened their devotional life, and embarked upon a publishing program. Najera was aided by García Jiménez de Cisneros, abbot of Montserrat (1494–1510) and cousin of Cardinal Francisco Jiménez de Cisneros. From his abbacy at Montserrat, one of the holiest places in all of Spain, García Jiménez de Cisneros accomplished a similar expansion of the congregation in Aragon and Catalonia. He also disseminated Benedictine spirituality through his two treatises, *Directorio de las horas canónicas* and *Exercitatorio de la vida espiritual* (published posthumously, in 1550). This latter handbook would later make a pronounced impression on Ignatius Loyola during his stay at Montserrat and Manresa, inspiring him to draw up his own *Spiritual Exercises*. Reforms such as those initiated by the Congregation of San Benito of Valladolid set the tone for the Council of Trent and also ensured the regular Spanish clergy a dominant role in the Catholic Reformation.

[*See also* Jiménez de Cisneros, García.]

BIBLIOGRAPHY

Beltrán de Heredia, V. *Historia de la reforma de la Provincia de España*. Rome, 1939.

Besse, J. M. "La congrégation espagnole de S. Benoît de Valladolid." *Revue bénédictine* 19 (1902), 257–267.

Colombás, G. M. *Corrientes espirituales entre los benedictinos observantes españoles del siglo xvi*. Barcelona, 1963. See especially pages 136–159.

Garcia Oro, José. *La reforma de los religiosos españoles en tiempo de los Reyes Católicos*. Valladolid, 1969.

Peers, E. Allison. *Studies of the Spanish Mystics.* 2d ed. London, 1951. Contains a synopsis of the work of García Jiménez de Cisneros (vol. 2, pp. 1–38).

Pérez de Urbel, Justo. *Historia de la orden benedictina.* Madrid, 1941.

Rodríguez Martínez, Luis. *Historia del monasterio de San Benito el Real de Valladolid.* Valladolid, 1981.

Zaragoza Pascual, Ernesto. *Los generales de la congregación de San Benito de Valladolid.* 3 vols. Silos, Spain, 1973–1980.

CARLOS M. N. EIRE

CONGREGATION OF SANTA GIUSTINA OF PADUA.

The abbey of Santa Giustina, Padua, reformed in 1409 by Ludovico Barbo, became the hub of a congregation of abbeys based upon the centralized authority of a chapter-general that appointed abbots on limited tenure and moved monks from one house to another according to the needs of piety and scholarship. The congregation grew rapidly after 1500, attracting many able young men. When joined by the ancient monastery of Monte Cassino in 1505, it became known as the Cassinese Congregation.

The congregation's piety was influenced partly by the *devotio moderna* and Franciscan ideas but more strongly by biblical studies based upon humanist scholarship. After 1480 the order expanded its libraries, intensified its studies, and published biblical commentaries, translations, and devotional works. Studies concentrated upon Paul and the Greek fathers—particularly Chrysostom and the school of Antioch—and emphasized the mortality and alienation of fallen humanity, the pathological nature of sin, the inadequacy of the law, the mercy of God in the "benefit of Christ," the necessity of "living faith," and the restoration of freedom, wholeness, and the *imago dei* to human nature.

During the 1520s the theology of the congregation made it sympathetic to but also critical toward Reformation doctrines of justification and faith. Gregorio Bornato and Isidoro Chiari used their order's traditional piety to argue that fallen mankind was saved by grace alone but that salvation involved restoration to wholeness rather than justification of the guilty; thus, good works were therapeutically necessary for the "convalescence" of sanctification and the healing of free will. In 1538 Luciano degli Ottoni published his Latin translation of Chrysostom's commentary on *Romans*, adding his own explanation of the way Reformation debates could be resolved by Greek patristic theology, "which preserved liberty yet in no way diminished grace." The congregation's pre-Augustinian theology was intended to cut through the Latin presuppositions common to Protestants and Catholics, but in practice it was suspected of heresy, and paradoxically, of being Pelagian and Protestant.

After 1538 the congregation attempted to avert the deepening divisions of Western Christendom, expressing its theology in translations and revisions of the Bible, as well as in tracts on piety, social issues, and the priesthood. The first draft of Benedetto da Mantova's popular *Beneficio di Cristo* (1543) was traditional in its Cassinese piety, probably intended as a reconciling tract, but later revisions were inspired by Juan de Valdés and John Calvin. Despite increasing intolerance, the congregation made one last attempt at the Council of Trent to reconcile the antagonistic ideologies of Western Christendom and to heal the Western schism with Greek theology. They failed, for when Ottoni expounded his order's Antiochene theology during the session on justification in November 1546, there was an uproar at what was taken for Lutheranism.

Following its failure at Trent, the congregation fell under ill-defined suspicions of heresy: some monks adopted exaggerated affective piety, others were led by Giorgio Siculo into legalistic doctrines of works and perfection, and several emphasized doctrines of the Holy Spirit. Its distinctive Antiochene theology waned, but the congregation continued to produce distinguished works of biblical scholarship and strengthened its traditions of vigorous piety and learning until it was dispersed during the Napoleonic wars.

BIBLIOGRAPHY

Collett, Barry. *Italian Benedictine Scholars and the Reformation.* Oxford, 1985. The major work in English on the congregation's theology, its Greek patristic origins, and its significance for Reformation controversies and Italian reform movements.

Penco, Gregorio. "La Congregazione Cassinese all'epoca di Teofilo Folengo." *Benedictina* 39.1 (1992), 37–71. A concise overview of the debate on the congregation and its relation to contemporary events.

BARRY COLLETT

CONSANGUINITY. *See* Marriage.

CONSENSUS GENEVENSIS.

In defense of his doctrine of predestination John Calvin wrote an elaborate theological treatise, the Consensus Genevensis. It was published in Geneva in 1552 in the name of the Compagnie des Pasteurs of that city. It bore the full title "Concerning the eternal predestination of God by which he has chosen some to salvation and left others to their own destruction and concerning the providence of God by which he governs all human affairs."

Calvin was prompted to write this treatise in response to a series of predestinarian controversies that had troubled the church at Geneva for several years. A decade earlier, in 1543, he had answered an attack by Albertus Pighius of Kampen, a Catholic controversialist, who had impugned the Reformation doctrines of total depravity and absolute predestination. Calvin's treatise of 1543 dealt only with Pighius's attack on free will. Before he could draft a reply to Pighius's challenge to predestination, he received news of the demise of his opponent. At that time Calvin decided to drop the issue "in order not to insult the dead dog."

In the meantime, a more virulent controversy arose in Geneva itself. At the heart of this dispute was Jérome Bolsec, a former Carmelite monk, who had professed the Reformed faith and come to Geneva in 1551 to serve as a doctor of medicine. On 16 October of that year Bolsec was imprisoned following his public and vehement repudiation of the Genevan position on predestination. After a lengthy examination by the ministers of the city, Bolsec was tried for blasphemy and expelled from Geneva on 22 December. Bolsec found temporary refuge at Bern but afterward retired to Paris, where he was reunited with the Roman church. In 1577 he published a stringent attack on the character of Calvin.

The Bolsec affair and Calvin's response to it showed up the tenuous nature of the Reformed consensus on predestination. The ministers of Geneva received a mixed response to their appeal for support from the other Reformed churches of Switzerland in their action against Bolsec. While Neuchâtel and Basel sided with Calvin, Bern and Zurich warned against taking such a harsh view of the matter and called for a more moderate statement of predestination.

The Consensus Genevensis, or *De aeterna Praedestinatione Dei*, as it is often called, is itself a rather uneven treatise in that it was intended to be a definitive summary and refutation of several attacks on the doctrine of election. Calvin never mentions Bolsec by name but merely refers to him as "this impure and worthless fellow." His primary targets are Pighius, or more precisely the latter half of his 1542 work that Calvin had left unanswered, and the writings of a certain Benedictine monk whom he calls Georgius the Sicilian. In chapters 1–2 Calvin characterizes his opponents and their views. Chapters 3–5 present a catena of texts from holy scripture and from Augustine delineating traditional support for Calvin's views. Chapters 6–8 take up the main points of Pighius's arguments, while chapter 9 is devoted to those of Georgius. The concluding chapter concerns the providence of God and the related issues of causation, necessity, and theodicy. Bolsec's primary thrust against Calvin was to claim that his doctrine made God the author of evil. Calvin responds to this charge in his closing comments.

The Consensus Genevensis remains one of the most important official statements on the doctrine of election in Reformation theology, comparable in its passion and magnitude to Luther's *De servo arbitrio* (Bondage of the Will; 1525). The conflicts stimulated by its publication and reception contributed to the definitive victory of Calvin's partisans within Geneva as evidenced by the trial and execution of Michael Servetus in 1553 and the political downfall of Calvin's opponents in the Genevan elections of 1555. The controversy surrounding the Consensus Genevensis also had an important effect on Théodore de Bèze, then a professor at Lausanne, who published his own influential exposition of the doctrine of election in 1555. For his part, Calvin reshaped his doctrine of predestination and incorporated the insights gained from controversy in his definitive treatment of the issue in the 1559 edition of his *Institutes*.

[*See also* Bolsec, Jérome; Calvin, John; *and* Predestination.]

BIBLIOGRAPHY

Calvin, John. *Concerning the Eternal Predestination of God*. Translated by J. K. S. Reid. Greenwood, S.C., 1961.

Holtrop, Philip Cornelius. *The Bolsec Controversy on Predestination, 1551–1555*. Lewiston, N.Y., 1993.

Niemeyer, H. A. *Collectio Confessionum*. Leipzig, 1840. See pp. 218–310.

Schaff, Philip. *Creeds of Christendom* (1877). Reprint, Grand Rapids, Mich., 1977. See vol. 1, pp. 474–477.

TIMOTHY GEORGE

CONSENSUS SENDOMIRIENSIS.

Lutheranism (1518), the confession of the Bohemian Brethren (1548), and Calvinism (after 1550) appeared one after the other in Poland, but the people who embraced the new religions represented a minority. In 1559 the menace of Francis Stancarus's heresy loomed, about 1562 the movement of the Polish Brethren developed, and from 1564 the Catholic Counter-Reformation increased.

The evangelical churches wanted to ward off these tendencies by developing a united front. The Minor Poland Calvinists and the Bohemian Brethren in Great Poland already closely cooperated in the first half of the 1550s (the union in Koźminek in 1555), but this was interrupted by the activity of Jan Łaski. In 1565 attempts to unite all the Polish Protestants on the basis of the Augsburg Confession began. In 1567 the synod in Poznań attempted to establish closer relations between the Lutherans and the Bohemian Brethren.

During the late 1560s the main leaders of the unification movement were the Calvinist magnates of Minor Poland: the Krakow *voivode*, Stanislas Myszkowski; the Sandomierz *voivode*, Peter Zborowski; and the *starost* of this area, Andrew Firlej. A forceful Bohemian Brother, Simon Theophilus Turnowski, also proclaimed himself in favor of the union, whereas the superintendent of the Lutherans, Erasmus Gliczner, remained hesitant.

The general synod of the three churches commenced in Sandomierz, in mid-Poland, on 10 April 1570. The resistance of the Lutherans was overcome, the attempt to include the antitrinitarians was rejected, and the rest of Stancarus's followers were joined to the Calvinist community. On 14 April the confession and the consensus, in which the three churches mutually acknowledged one another as orthodox, were accepted and the convention was over. The leading author of the acts of the Sandomierz synod was a Calvinist teacher of noble descent from Minor Poland, Christopher Trecy.

Following the Polish example the Czech Protestants attempted to unite in 1575. The Consensus Sendomiriensis was a basis for the Polish Protestants' resistance to the Counter-Reformation until the general synod in Thorn in 1595, after which it was terminated by the Lutherans. The Calvinists and the Bohemian Brethren merged in the Polish-Lithuanian Commonwealth in the seventeenth century, and in the eighteenth century the Consensus Sendomiriensis was revived in the ecumenical activity of Daniel Ernest Jabłoński.

[See also Confessions in Eastern Europe and Poland.]

BIBLIOGRAPHY

Halecki, Oskar. Zgoda sandomierska 1570 r. Warsaw, 1915.
Jabłoński, Daniel Ernest. Historia Consensus Sandomiriensis. Berlin, 1731.
Jordt-Jørgensen, Kai Eduard. Ökumenische Bestrebungen unter den polnischen Protestanten bis zum Jahre 1645. Copenhagen, 1942.
Lehmann, Jerzy. Konfesja sandomierska. Warsaw, 1937.

WACŁAW URBAN

CONSENSUS TIGURINUS. The accord on the doctrine of the sacraments concluded by Zurich and Geneva reformers Heinrich Bullinger and John Calvin in 1549 in the names of their respective churches is known as the Consensus Tigurinus (Zurich Agreement). This agreement united the two leading Reformed churches in a durable way and formed the basis for the Reformed doctrine of the sacraments.

Zurich reformer Huldrych Zwingli modified the tone and the terminology of his "symbolic" eucharistic theology in treatises penned after his encounter with Luther at the 1529 Marburg Colloquy. After Zwingli's premature death in 1531, it fell to his successor, Bullinger, to manage Zwingli's doctrinal legacy. Bullinger's own eucharistic theology was strongly influenced in the 1530s by Strasbourg reformer Martin Bucer. This influence led Bullinger to retain his predecessor's later eucharistic doctrine as normative for Zurich. Bullinger's writings in the 1530s thus manifest a Zwinglian eucharistic doctrine still in the process of definition.

In addition to this evolution within Zwinglianism, the politico-religious events of the 1530s and 1540s brought great pressure toward doctrinal unity among the various currents of Swiss Protestantism. But the Swiss Zwinglians' refusal of the Wittenberg Concord (1536) and maintenance of their own (First) Helvetic Confession (1536) brought about harsh, anti-Zwinglian invectives from Luther.

Bullinger sought the support of his friend Calvin in this affair. Although Calvin clearly preferred Luther's theology to Zwingli's, the Genevan reformer's own personal, doctrinal, and political situation necessitated doctrinal concord with Zurich and significant contact with the Zurich Antistes ("chief pastor"). In 1546 Bullinger sent his Genevan colleague an unpublished, revised copy of his reply to Luther,

the De Sacramentis. Calvin replied in February 1547 with a detailed critique of Bullinger's treatise. The ensuing exchange of correspondence gradually evolved into theological negotiation, noticeable especially from Bullinger's letter to Calvin in November 1548, detailing twenty-four propositions. This document became the object of further correspondence up to May 1549. In that month Calvin decided suddenly to return to Zurich in order to conclude these laborious negotiations, without forewarning either the Genevan authorities or the Zurichers. Using the previously mentioned documents as well as Calvin's Genevan Confession (1549) as a basis, the Consensus was drafted with the Zurich ministers very quickly ("within two hours," according to Calvin). Three Calvinian articles contained in the Genevan Confession were set aside, and an introduction in five articles was added, as well as two other articles desired by Zurich. The final document contained twenty-six articles. The original prologue and an epilogue were subsequently replaced by two dedicatory epistles. The relative secrecy of the negotiations and their sudden conclusion embarrassed Calvin, who had to explain to other Swiss churches why they were not consulted during the negotiations. The text, set in summer 1549, was finally printed, at Calvin's insistence, in March 1551.

The agreement is a compromise document. It does not say everything that Bullinger and Calvin would have affirmed individually but brings to the fore their minimal points of agreement. The arduous task of the two reformers was to represent, in a biblically and theologically correct fashion, the link between the faithful on earth and God in heaven, the object of their faith. The fundamental question they faced was: What, if anything, uniquely takes place during the celebration of the sacraments? The correct answer had to be presented using Latin terminology acceptable to the cadre of Reformed theologians. The length and detail of the discussions reveal the difficulty of the enterprise, the invention of a Reformed sacramental doctrine.

The following elements summarize the salient points of the agreement: (1) The Sacrament is defined as a sign or seal in Zwinglian fashion but also as an instrument of divine grace for communicating spiritual gifts to the believer. (2) The relationship between the sacramental sign and its corresponding spiritual reality allows for no causal link between the sacrament and eternal salvation. These separate terrestrial and celestial realities are nonetheless linked and made efficient through the ministry of the Holy Spirit. (3) Sacramental grace is limited to the elect and is therefore sanctifying grace, sovereignly given by God to the believer, which not only confirms, but also increases the believer's faith. (4) The sacraments bring nothing to nonbelievers other than condemnation, but seal the believer's faith through the work of the Spirit. (5) Clearly rejecting Catholic and Lutheran conceptions of the presence of Christ, the consensus adopts Honius's exegesis of the words of institution: since heaven is a place (*locus*), the risen Christ cannot be corporally present in the Supper, although present by the omnipresent Spirit (*praesens est per spiritum*).

As a compromise document, the consensus presents the basic issues and forges acceptable "Reformed" terminology to describe a "Reformed" doctrine of the sacraments and of the Eucharist in particular. Some issues do remain unresolved, however. At the express wish of the Zurichers, the agreement set aside articles using terms such as *substantia* for describing Christ's presence in the sacrament. This unresolved vocabulary issue became a subject of considerable controversy between Geneva and Zurich in the years following the consensus, both in Switzerland and in France. Although it undeniably contributed toward the deepening of relations between Zurich and Geneva, bringing both Calvin and Geneva into the circle of Swiss Reformed churches, the consensus also significantly widened the rift between Lutherans and Reformed in the mid-sixteenth century.

Historians have often been guilty of attributing the merit of the consensus to Calvin alone. The negotiation process itself, the concessions made on both sides and the efforts by both parties to respect the consensus, both in Switzerland and in France, show that the agreement was truly a doctrinal reference point. It was the contribution of Calvin and Bullinger, of Geneva and Zurich.

[*See also* Bullinger, Heinrich; Calvin, John; Eucharist; *and* Helvetic Confessions.]

BIBLIOGRAPHY

Bunting, Ian D. "The Consensus Tigurinus." *Journal of Presbyterian History* 44 (1966), 45–61. Good basic introduction to the text with English translation.

Bouvier, André. *Henri Bullinger, réformateur et conseiller oecuménique, le successeur de Zwingli, d'après sa correspondance avec les réformés et les humanistes de lanque française....* Reprint, Geneva, 1979. See pp. 110–149 for a detailed description of events surrounding the consensus.

Gäbler, Ulrich. "Das Zustandekommen des Consensus Tigurinus im Jahre 1549." *Theologische Literatur-Zeitung* 104 (1979), 321–332. Good background on the political and ecclesiastical dimensions of the consensus.

———. "Consensus Tigurinus." In *Theologische Realenzyklopädie*, vol. 8, pp. 189–192. Berlin and New York, 1977–. Fundamental introduction to the consensus with indispensable bibliography.

Kolfhaus, Wilhelm. "Der Verkehr Calvins mit Bullinger." In *Calvin-studien: Festschrift zum 400. Geburtstag Johann Calvins*, edited by Josef Bonatec, pp. 27–125. Leipzig, 1909. Uses the correspondence between Calvin and Bullinger to reconstruct their personal and theological relations, including events leading up to and following the consensus.

McLelland, J. C. "Meta-Zwingli or Anti-Zwingli? Bullinger and Calvin in Eucharistic Concord." In *Huldrych Zwingli, 1484–1531: A Legacy of Radical Reform*, edited by E. J. Furcha, pp. 179–195. Montreal, 1985. Salient analysis of the place of the consensus in the framework of historic Reformed theology.

Sanders, Paul. "Henri Bullinger et l'invention (1546–1551) avec Jean Calvin d'une théologie réformée de la Cène: la gestion de l'héritage zwinglien lors de l'élaboration du 'Consensus Tigurinus' (1549) et de la rédaction des 'Décades' (1551)." Ph.D. diss., University of Paris IV-Sorbonne, 1990. Detailed analysis and synthesis of eucharistic texts of Zwingli, Bullinger, and Calvin between 1519 and 1551.

Usteri, Martin. "Vertiefung der Zwinglischen Sakraments- und Tauflehre bei Bullinger." *Theologische Studien und Kritiken* 56 (1883), 730–758. Dated but useful treatment of Bullinger's management of Zwingli's sacramental heritage.

PAUL ROBERT SANDERS

CONSILIUM DE EMENDANDA ECCLESIA.

The report of 1537 bears the full title of "Proposal of a Select Commission of Cardinals and Other Prelates Concerning the Reform of the Church, Written and Presented by the Order of His Holiness Pope Paul III." Unlike his indecisive predecessor Clément VII, Pope Paul III realized the necessity of summoning a general council to deal with the challenge of Protestantism to the Catholic church. In preparation for the council, which was to meet in Mantua in 1537, the pope appointed a committee to make recommendations for dealing with pressing issues facing the church. This committee of nine included advocates of reform; its members were cardinals Gasparo Contarini, Gian Pietro Carafa (later, Paul IV), Jacopo Sadoleto, and Reginald Pole; the archbishops Federico Fregoso and Girolamo Aleander, bishop Gian Matteo Giberti; abbot Gregorio Cortese; and Tommaso Badia, master of the sacred palace.

Beginning their meetings in November 1536, these prelates presented their recommendations in a consistory on 9 March 1537. Since no information about their deliberations has come to light, it is not possible to identify the author or authors of the final report, which was outspoken in its criticism of conditions in the church. It stated bluntly that all abuses were the result of exaggerated claims made by curial jurists about the absolute nature of papal power, and singled out for special blame their teaching that the pope was free to do as he pleased with the material and spiritual goods of the church. The report stressed that "from this source, just as from the Trojan horse, very many abuses and grave ills have invaded the church of God." Rome was held responsible for the lack of discipline and order and for abuses throughout the church.

Although the consilium became famous, its significance has frequently been overstated. It was not the beginning of a fresh approach by Rome to matters of church reform. The college of cardinals was sharply divided about it, and Pope Paul III did not put its recommendations into practice. The text was leaked to a Roman printer in 1537, and a German translation appeared in 1538 accompanied by caustic comments from Luther. Unwilling to concede that the prelates on the commission were sincere men of goodwill, Luther portrayed them as hypocrites bent on misleading Christians even further.

Despite a number of specific proposals made in it, the

report was a striking example of an old-fashioned view of reform even at the time. It presupposed that by purifying Rome the world would be cleansed, in keeping with the old adage *purga Romam, purgatur mundus* ("clean up Rome and the [whole] world will be purified"). While stressing that members of the entire church hierarchy, beginning with the pope, must become true Christian shepherds serving their flock, the report did not mention ways of dealing with the thorny doctrinal issues raised by Protestants or the complex problems of the relation between central, intermediate, and local authority in the church. In essence, it offered palliative rather than substantive remedies. Its framers were admirable men and advocates of reform, but they failed to realize that by 1537 much more drastic changes were necessary in the Catholic church.

[*See also* Contarini, Gasparo.]

BIBLIOGRAPHY

Primary Source

"Consilium delectorum cardinalium et aliorum praelatorum de emendanda ecclesia S.D.N. Paulo III iubente conscriptum et exhibitum." In *Concilium Tridentinum: Diariorum Actorum Epistularum Tractatuum nova collectio.* Edited by Societas Goerresiana, vol. 12, pp. 131–145. Freiburg, 1929. Best edition of the text. English translation in *Reform Thought in Sixteenth-Century Italy*, edited by Elisabeth G. Gleason, pp. 85–100. Chico, Calif., 1981.

Secondary Sources

Douglas, Richard. *Jacopo Sadoleto, 1477–1547.* Cambridge, Mass., 1959. Good sketch of the report, with the focus on Sadoleto.
Jedin, Hubert. *History of the Council of Trent.* Vol. 1, Saint Louis, 1957. Excellent brief discussion on pp. 423–433 of the report in a masterful volume dealing with the complexities and difficulties that preceded the first meeting of the Council of Trent.
Luther's Works. Vol. 34, *Career of the Reformer.* Philadelphia, 1960.

ELISABETH G. GLEASON

CONSISTORY. Established by John Calvin, the consistory was an institution in Geneva for controlling as closely as possible Christian behavior, as distinct from Christian belief. It served as a model for similar disciplinary institutions in most early Reformed communities. Calvin insisted on the consistory's creation before he agreed to return to Geneva in 1541, and he personally drafted the legislation that created it. He participated actively in its deliberations and fought for its sole right to excommunicate people who would not accept its discipline.

In legal form the consistory was a standing committee of the local government. It was made up of lay elders elected annually, all the ordained pastors, *ex officio*, and one of the four municipal syndics (or ruling magistrates), who served as its presiding officer. It also hired a secretary to keep a full record of its weekly meetings and retained a hired officer to serve primarily as a summoner. The consistory met once a week to examine members of the community referred to it on suspicion of misbehavior. Accusations included charges of religious misbehavior, such as "idolatry" (Catholic practices), "superstition," or witchcraft, or heretical activity; marital and sexual problems; disorderly conduct; and evidence of disrespect for church and state authorities. It could provide counseling or refer the charges to city courts. It also claimed the right to excommunicate, but it had to fight for that right, which it won in a dramatic showdown, provoked by a faction led by the prominent local patrician Ami Perrin, in 1555. That showdown led to a complete victory of the party that supported the consistory. From then on excommunication was used frequently and effectively, forcing people either to submit to the demands of the consistory or leave the community.

In its early years the consistory spent much of its time trying to educate Genevan laymen in the meaning for them of the Reformation. It frequently summoned ordinary people—in majority women, often illiterate—to make sure that they had put behind them the rituals of Catholicism and were adopting those of Protestantism. It questioned them on their prayers, their knowledge of the creed, their attitude toward the Virgin Mary and the saints, and such practices as the purchase of votive candles, the use of the rosary, and fasting. It generally required people judged insufficiently informed about Protestant practice to attend sermons more frequently. It required some to join the weekly catechism classes that had been established to teach children but that were now expanded to instruct uninformed adults in the basic doctrines of Reformed Christianity. It suggested to others that they seek private instruction. In its later years the consistory also tried to control those who deviated from official Calvinist positions on theological matters. When the ex-Carmelite friar Jérome Bolsec was convicted and expelled from the city for challenging the Calvinist doctrine of predestination, for example, a number of his sympathizers were questioned and disciplined by the consistory. Its registers, thus, reveal much of popular impressions of the nature of religious change in the early years of the Protestant Reformation.

From the beginning the consistory also devoted much of its attention to marital problems. In this it inherited the functions of the pre-Reformation bishop's court. It frequently heard suits alleging breach of promise, in which one party claimed and the other denied that they had agreed on marriage in a form that constituted a valid contract. It occasionally heard suits for divorce with permission to remarry, something that had not been possible under Roman Catholic canon law but now became possible in Protestant courts. Divorce suits, however, remained rare. In contrast, the consistory frequently explored allegations of threats to marriage posed by fornication, adultery, or spouse abuse and tried to punish them in exemplary ways. It probably became best known for these attempts to control morals.

An even larger and growing portion of the consistory's time was devoted to the regulation of quarrels—between spouses, between neighbors, and between parents and children. It spent much of its time trying to arrange reconciliations between people who had had violent disagreements, and it was frequently successful.

Much of the consistory's time was also devoted to defending the reputation of the authorities, including elected leaders of the government and hired leaders of the church. A number of memorable cases were devoted to harshly disciplining local people who had complained too openly about the growing role of Calvin within the community, about the other ministers, and in general about the substantial number of French refugees who had settled in Geneva during these years. Several of the more celebrated early cases in the city fell into this category, including those involving Mme. Perrin, her father, her brother, and other leaders of the local opposition to the consistory.

At the height of its activity, shortly after Calvin's death, the consistory summoned to its sessions a significant percentage of the entire population of Geneva, perhaps as much as one-fifteenth in a single year. It had a great impact on the behavior of Genevans, which helps to account for the austere style of life that evolved in the community. That life-style was something that attracted many people to Calvinism throughout Europe and even in North America. In England and its colonies this style of life came to be labeled "Puritan." In many countries, institutions similar to the consistory were established to promote this life-style, but they were not always called consistories. In some areas, notably in France, consistories took over both general administrative and disciplinary functions. In almost all of these areas, however, some ecclesiastical institution took responsibility for controlling human behavior. This "consistorial" concern became characteristic of Reformed Christianity.

[See also Calvin, John; Calvinism; Church Offices, article on Calvinist Offices; Compagnie des Pasteurs; Geneva; and Luther, Martin.]

BIBLIOGRAPHY

Kingdon, Robert M. "Calvin and the Establishment of Consistory Discipline in Geneva: The Institution and the Men who Directed It." *Nederlands Archief voor Kerkegeschiedenis* 70 (1990), 158–172. Describes a projected study of the consistory to be based on the first full transcription of all its registers for the period of Calvin's ministry.

Köhler, Walther. *Zürcher Ehegericht und Genfer Konsistorium*. Leipzig, 1942. See vol. 2, pp. 505–652. Most detailed study available, setting the consistory in a useful context of similar institutions in other Reformed communities. It is flawed, however, by its failure to use the original registers, depending instead on an inadequate set of a relatively few samples from the originals.

Monter, E. William. "The Consistory of Geneva, 1559–1569." *Bibliothèque d'Humanisme et Renaissance* 38, (1976), 467–484. Excellent overview of one decade of the consistory's operations, based on fresh archival research.

ROBERT M. KINGDON

CONSPIRACY OF AMBOISE. *See* Amboise, Conspiracy of.

CONSTANCE. Martin Luther's writings were known in the free imperial city of Constance by 1518/19. The Reformation was preached as early as 1519 by the local preachers Jacob Windner, Johannes Wanner, and Bartholomäus Metzler. Catholic countermeasures began in 1522, when Bishop Hugo tried to take steps against Wanner. In 1523 Hugo accused Metzler of heresy. The city council protected both Wanner and Metzler and, on the day set for Metzler's trial, informed the bishop and his court they had no authority in matters of faith.

Thus the city council took the lead in Constance's reform movement. In 1524 the council issued an "Instruction" whereby the clergy were to preach the gospel without the addition of human traditions having no scriptural basis. The council defended the marriage of the clergy with appeals to scripture in 1525. In 1525 and 1526 the council forced all clergy, with the exception of the bishop and the cathedral chapter, to swear an oath of allegiance to the city and to assume the normal obligations of citizenship. During the years 1527–1529 the city council began the reform or abolition of the monasteries, implemented a new system for the care of the poor, issued a new marriage ordinance, subjected the clergy to taxation, confiscated church property for civic purposes, ended the celebration of the Mass, and ordered the removal of images from churches. In 1526 Bishop Hugo left the city, and in 1527 most other Catholic clergy left the city in obedience to him. The council's activities in support of the Reformation dovetailed with its pre-Reformation wishes for closer ties to the Swiss Confederation rather than to Austria, as well as with its desire to limit the power of the bishop and the privileges of the clergy.

Ambrosius Blarer and Johannes Zwick, Constance's two most influential Protestant reformers, began preaching in the city in 1525. They were not paid by the city until 1538, a fact that gave them a certain independence. They maintained contact with other Upper German reformers, such as Huldrych Zwingli and Martin Bucer. In the 1529 controversy over the Lord's Supper, Constance tended toward the Zwinglian position but did not define the exact nature of Christ's presence; at the Diet of Augsburg of 1530 Constance signed the Tetrapolitan Confession rather than the Augsburg Confession. Constance became a member of the Schmalkald League in 1531.

More important than theological positions were Constance's attempts to build a church and community modeled on obedience to God. With the issuance of the *Zuchtordnung* in 1531, the Reformation in Constance entered a new phase. Both clergy and civil authority supported efforts to carry the Reformation into daily life through the regulation of morals and thus to sanctify both church and society. Scholars differ as to whether the Constance reformation ended because the *Zuchtordnung* diminished the support for reform ideals among influential circles in the city or because the reform elite and most of the community continued to support it when political considerations should have dictated otherwise. In any case, the defeat of the Protestants in the Schmalkald War led to the conquest of Constance in 1548 by Austrian troops and its re-Catholicization.

BIBLIOGRAPHY

Brady, Thomas A. *Turning Swiss: Cities and Empire, 1450–1550*. Cambridge, 1985. Brady's consideration of the social and political aspects of the reformation in upper German imperial cities includes Constance.

Dobras, Wolfgang. *Ratsregiment, Sittenpolizei und Kirchenzucht in der Reichsstadt Konstanz. 1531–1548*. Quellen und Forschungen zur Reformationsgeschichte, vol. 59. Gütersloh, 1993. An exhaustive description of the latter phase of the reformation in Constance.

Moeller, Bernd. *Johannes Zwick und die Reformation in Konstanz*. Quellen und Forschungen zur Reformationsgeschichte, vol. 28. Heidelberg, 1961. The last three sections are devoted to Zwick's time in Constance, 1526–1542. An appendix contains a useful bibliography which lists 63 works which originated in the Constance reformation or which were directed against it.

Moeller, Bernd, ed. *Der Konstanzer Reformator Ambrosius Blarer 1492–1564: Gedenkschrift zu seinem 400. Todestag*. Konstanz, 1964. This work contains articles on different aspects of Blarer's work, e.g., as reformer, preacher, and poet, and on Constance in the early sixteenth century.

Ozment, Steven E. *The Reformation in the Cities: The Appeal of Protestantism to Sixteenth-Century Germany and Switzerland*. New Haven, 1975. The reformation in Constance is described in several places. There is an extensive description of Jörg Vögeli's defense of Metzler in reply to the heresy accusations of the bishop.

Rublack, Hans-Christoph. *Die Einführung der Reformation in Konstanz von den Anfängen bis zum Abschluß 1531*. Gütersloh, 1971. The definitive description of the early years of the reformation in Constance.

MARY JANE HAEMIG

CONSUBSTANTIATION.

A theory of the eucharistic presence of Christ, consubstantiation was developed by scholastic theologians of the Middle Ages. In contrast to the more commonly held doctrine of transubstantiation, which affirms a supernatural change of the substance of the bread and wine into the body and blood of Christ, consubstantiation holds that the body of Christ is uniquely and locally present in the eucharistic celebration by virtue of the omnipotence of God. In its medieval form consubstantiation was held to be a possible explanation of the sacramental presence of Christ by John Duns Scotus, John of Jandun, and William of Ockham.

During the Reformation Martin Luther and all of the Protestant reformers rejected the doctrine of transubstantiation, which, in turn, was reaffirmed by the Council of Trent. Luther, however, retained a strong doctrine of the real presence of Christ in the sacrament of the altar. In defense of his view, Luther appealed to what he took to be the clear literal meaning of the words of institution, "This is my body." He also appealed to the patristic doctrine of the *communicatio idiomatum*, by which the properties of Christ's divinity are transferable to his humanity. On this basis Luther taught the ubiquity of Christ's glorified body. This led him to affirm the real bodily presence of Christ "in, with, and under" the bread and wine of the Eucharist (Large Catechism, 1527).

In the acrimonious debates between Lutheran and Reformed theologians over the nature of the Eucharist in the later sixteenth century, the term consubstantiation reappeared as a Reformed characterization of the Lutheran understanding of the real presence. Huldrych Zwingli, John Calvin, and other Reformed thinkers attacked the Lutheran doctrine because it seemed to imply a "physical, Capernaitish" (i.e., cannibalistic) eating of Christ's body along with the denial of the reality of his ascended status at the right hand of the Father. Luther himself never used the word consubstantiation to describe his doctrine of the real presence, and Lutheran theologians protested that their Reformed opponents misunderstood their true teaching. Thus Johann Gerhard (1582–1637) wrote, "On account of the calumnies of our adversaries, we would note that we do not believe in impanation nor in consubstantiation, nor in any physical or local presence."

The Formula of Concord (1577) set forth a consensus Lutheran view of the Eucharist, distinguishing it from both Roman Catholic and Calvinist interpretations. The formula affirms the Lutheran doctrine of real presence while denying that it implies a conversion of elements or a mingling of the body and blood with the bread and wine.

A. G. Voigt provides a helpful summary of the sacramental presence of Christ in the Eucharist from a Lutheran perspective: "In the Lord's Supper there is an earthly material, bread and wine, and a celestial material, the body and blood of Christ. The doctrine of transubstantiation identifies these. That of consubstantiation, or impanation, confuses and mingles them. The symbolic doctrine [Calvinism] separates them. The Lutheran doctrine of the real presence unites them. The Lutheran church holds to a sacramental union, unique in its nature, of the terrestrial and the celestial, but only in the sacramental act of eating and drinking" (*Biblical Dogmatics*, Columbia, S.C., 1917, pp. 214–215). Most Lutherans reject consubstantiation and consider it an inappropriate description of their eucharistic theology because of its controverted meaning and polemical history.

[*See also* Eucharist *and* Transubstantiation.]

BIBLIOGRAPHY

"Consubstantiation." In *The New Schaff-Herzog Encyclopedia of Religious Knowledge*, edited by Samuel M. Jackson. Grand Rapids, Mich., 1949.

Mueller, J. T. "The Issues Involved in the Lutheran Rejection of Consubstantiation." *Concordia Theological Seminary* 21 (August 1950), 602–605.

Muller, R. "Consubstantiation." In *Dictionary of Latin and Greek Theological Terms*, pp. 80–81. Grand Rapids, Mich., 1985.

TIMOTHY GEORGE

CONTARINI, Gasparo (1483–1542), Italian diplomat, statesman, cardinal, and papal legate to the colloquy between Catholic and Protestant theologians at Regensburg in 1541. Member of a venerable Venetian patrician family, he received his early education in Venice and enrolled in the University of Padua in 1501. While the specific courses he followed cannot be ascertained, he acquired a thorough formation in philosophy, studying under the famous Aristotelian Pietro Pomponazzi. Other subjects he studied included Greek, natural philosophy, mathematics, and theology. He left the university without a degree in 1509, when the War of the League of Cambrai caused its closure.

Contarini formed a number of close friendships with likeminded patricians, among whom Tommaso Giustiniani and Vincenzo Querini stand out. He was deeply shaken by their decision to leave Venice for the hermitage of Camaldoli, and his letters to the two monks, written between 1510 and 1523 but found only in 1956, are a unique testimony to his search for an ethic to support his own choice of a Christian vocation in the world rather than in the cloister. On Holy Saturday, 1511, he came to the realization that the Christian, whatever his way of life, is justified by faith in the benefits of Christ's suffering and death rather than through works. While seemingly similar to Luther's *Turmerlebnis*, or experience in the tower, Contarini's insight had a different thrust. He never drew the reformer's conclusions from it, but accepted the sacramental theology of the Catholic church, which he repeatedly tried to reconcile with his unwavering personal belief in justifying faith.

Contarini revealed himself best in his letters, but his considerable literary output remains more famous. It began in 1517 with a reply to Pomponazzi's *De immortalitate animae* and a treatise on the office of the bishop, *De officio viri probi ac boni episcopi*. The latter showed his deep concern even as a layman with church reform both as a personal and institutional endeavor.

Contarini entered Venetian public life in October 1518 at the age of thirty-five, following a period of ill health and possibly even depression. His ascent to ever more important offices proceeded smoothly. From 1521 to 1525 he was ambassador to Emperor Charles V, and between 1528 and 1530 to Pope Clement VII. After his return he became a member of the inner circle of the Venetian ruling elite, holding many high posts, among which that of head of the Council of Ten was most conspicuous. Keenly aware of the political realities of Europe, he counseled a moderate and cautious foreign policy while generally taking a conservative position in the internal affairs of his state.

The decade from 1525 to 1535 was one of extensive literary activity. His writings included *De magistratibus et republica Venetorum*, which later spread the so-called "myth of Venice" throughout Europe by exalting the republic as a model state, and *Primae philosophiae compendium*, a purely philosophical work. More significant to Reformation history is the *Confutatio articulorum seu quaestionum Lutheranorum* of the early 1530s, which shows Contarini's familiarity with the Augsburg Confession and considerable sympathy with Lutheran doctrines, but also his naive view that Lutherans could be won back by kindness and good example. A briefer work had more immediate consequences for him. His defense of papal power, *De potestate pontificis*, probably played a role in the decision of Pope Paul III to appoint him a cardinal on 21 May 1535. Although the appointment was not as unexpected as Contarini's secretary and biographer Ludovico Beccadelli would have readers believe, the reasons for it are not easily determined, since they presuppose a better insight into the mind of Paul III than available evidence makes possible.

Unlike many cardinals at the time, Contarini became a priest and celebrated his first mass in June 1537. In Rome he was among the so-called "poor" cardinals with an income barely sufficient for a modest lifestyle. His chairmanship of the commission that in March 1537 produced the memorial "Consilium de emendanda Ecclesia," a frank report of abuses to the pope and a plea for church reform, made him the acknowledged leader of the *spirituali*, a group of reform-minded and irenic prelates. During the next three years Contarini was a member of several commissions that made fruitless proposals for curial reform, above all of the papal Dataria. To this period belong his outspoken tracts *De potestate pontificis in compositionibus epistola* and *De usu potestatis clavium*, both sharply critical of the misuse of papal power, and his support for the foundation of the Jesuit order.

At the request of Charles V, intent on healing the schism in Germany, Contarini was appointed papal legate to the Colloquy of Regensburg, which opened on 27 April 1541. The Protestant theologians Philipp Melanchthon, Martin Bucer, and Johannes Pistorius faced the Catholics Johannes Gropper, Julius Pflug, and Johann Eck. When they arrived at a common formulation of the doctrine of justification and agreed on article 5 of the document that was the basis for their deliberations, the so-called Book of Regensburg, hopes for concord seemed justified. Contarini was overjoyed since he considered the article sound Catholic teaching. But soon bitter divisions between the two sides surfaced, as shown in their inability to agree on the doctrine of the eucharist. Neither Luther nor the pope accepted article 5, which Contarini had defended in an *Epistola de iustificatione*. The colloquy ended unsuccessfully on 22 May 1541.

Contarini died on 24 August 1542 as papal legate in Bologna. Some historians have interpreted his last post as exile from Rome or evidence that he was discredited at the papal court. However, the pope continued to trust him even after Regensburg. But his policy of seeking conciliation had not worked, and Paul III now turned with greater confidence to the curial hard-liners who favored repression of dissent by means such as the Inquisition and the Index of Prohibited Books. The search for concord with Protestants that was consistently championed by Contarini and his friends was abandoned in the sharpening confessional conflicts of the Counter-Reformation.

BIBLIOGRAPHY

Primary Source

Dittrich, Franz, ed. *Regesten und Briefe des Cardinals Gasparo Contarini, 1483–1542*. Braunsberg, 1881. Calendar of letters from and to Contarini. Despite inadequacies and omissions it remains indispensable.

Secondary Sources

Dittrich, Franz. *Gasparo Contarini, 1483–1542: Eine Monographie* (1885). Reprint, Nieuwkoop, 1972. Standard older biography.

Fragnito, Gigliola. *Gasparo Contarini: Un magistrato veneziano al servizio della Cristianità*. Florence, 1988. Five important essays by the foremost Italian scholar on Contarini.

Gleason, Elisabeth G. *Gasparo Contarini: Venice, Rome, and Reform*. Berkeley and London, 1993. Study of Contarini's thought, emphasizing his ideas on reform.

Romanelli, Francesca Cavazzana, ed. *Gaspare Contarini e il suo tempo: Atti convegno di studio*. Venice, 1988. Papers of international congress commemorating the five hundredth anniversary of Contarini's birth. Full bibliography.

ELISABETH G. GLEASON

CONTROVERSIAL THEOLOGIANS. A collective label for some four hundred writers of the sixteenth and early seventeenth century, controversial theologians defended Catholic doctrines and church practices contested by the Protestant Reformation. Some prolific early opponents of Martin Luther were of the diocesan clergy, such as Johann Eck (1486–1543), Hieronymus Emser (1478–1527), and Johannes Cochlaeus (1479–1552). Dominicans who entered the fray were Sylvester Mazzolini Prierias (1456–1523), Cardinal Cajetan (1469–1534), and Johann Dietenberger (c.1475–1537). The Franciscan opponents of the early Reformation included Germans Thomas Murner (1475–1537), Kaspar Schatzgeyer (1463–1527), and Nicholas Herborn (c.1480–1535), along with the Spaniard Alfonso de Castro (1492–1558), whose *Adversus omnes haereses* (1534) was widely consulted.

A formidable opposition to the Reformation developed in the theology faculty of Louvain in the works of Jacob Latomus (c.1475–1544), Johann Dreido (c.1480–1535), Albertus Pighius (c.1490–1542), and Ruard Tapper (1487–1559). In France the Flemish theologian Josse van Clichtove (1472/73–1543) wrote energetically against Luther. The English martyrs of conscience, John Fisher (1469–1535) and Thomas More (1477/78–1535), published rebuttals of Reformation claims, with Fisher's 1523 *Confutatio* of Luther being widely used as a compendium of Lutheran errors and Catholic refutations.

The Catholic controversialist writers are at times helpful in understanding the positions taken by the reformers themselves. Desiderius Erasmus saw Luther's daring views on the papacy, first voiced at the Leipzig Disputation (1519), as understandable reactions, though admittedly extreme, to the excessive claims of Dominicans such as Prierias for the papal plenitude of authority. Luther espoused scripture as the overriding norm of doctrine and practice as an alternative to Prierias's claim that the Roman church was more authoritative than the biblical word. Erasmus's own arguments for human freedom set the stage for many startling passages in Luther's *De servo arbitrio* (The Bondage of the Will; 1525). Eck's *Articuli 404* (404 Articles; 1530), listing all the alleged Protestant errors, pressed Philipp Melanchthon to emphasize traditional beliefs in the Augsburg Confession.

The debate that began in 1518 over Luther's penitential spirituality soon shifted focus to the forgiveness of sins and to the main structures of the church itself. Luther's first theses framed convictions about personal conversion, lifelong penance, and trust in God's forgiving word, but when he related these issues of personal religiosity to the church institution of indulgences, Luther had to confront the papal documents authorizing indulgences, and this led quickly to his ecclesiological debates with Prierias and Eck.

The early works of Prierias against Luther stand at the point of intersection between the Dominican tradition of anti-conciliarist ecclesiology, which had undergone new development around 1510, and Luther's views on the ecclesial structures of mediation and teaching. Prierias saw Luther as one more exponent of conciliarism, and this resulted in Luther being hit with huge broadsides drawn from the armory already built up and recently restocked by the apologists of the papal supremacy over councils.

Eck, theology professor in Ingolstadt for thirty-three years, stands out among the German Catholic literary opponents of the early Reformation. Emblematic is the Leipzig Disputation of 1519, where Eck amassed arguments for a cooperating role for *liberum arbitrium* (against Andreas Bodenstein Karlstadt's version of justification by grace alone) and for the divine institution of the Roman primacy (against Luther's denial). Eck was the superior disputant against the Wittenberg opponents, but the debate shows as well the weakness of technical correctness when confronting profound personal witness, as Joseph Lortz once noted.

The earliest literary opponents of Luther practiced methods rooted in the medieval academic disputation, and this inhibited the impact of their responses, as it required a full statement of the opponent's view and a line-by-line refutation. The early controversialists evinced a broad knowledge of scripture but lagged behind Luther in the ability to construct moving arguments from the Gospels and the apostle Paul. They often charged the reformers with reviving heresies long ago condemned by the church. This tactic, however, obscured for many the fundamental differences over the understanding of faith, salvation, and the mediation of God's saving grace by the sacraments.

Eck's *Enchiridion locorum communium* (1525) went through 116 reprints in a half century and thus merits close attention. Eck defended thirty-eight *loci*, or particular points of doctrine and practice, and on each he gave first Catholic theses, with supporting biblical texts, and then Protestant objections, to which Eck gives concise rebuttals that show the faulty argumentation of the opponents.

Eck, in fact, practiced a new methodology forged some years before, especially in his own *De primatu Petri*, written in the aftermath of the Leipzig Disputation. With the aim of securing a traditional understanding of New Testament texts central to the Reformation debate, Eck argues that the true sense of the Gospel passages concerning Peter emerges in a long chain of texts culled from patristic and early conciliar writers on the authority of Peter and his successors. The Lutheran position is wrong because it diverges from the consensus. For Eck, early teachers show the latent sense of biblical passages, and they contribute to a historical proof for a perennial Catholic understanding. The reformers are innovators who follow their own heads and end by diverging from positions that go back to the early postapostolic era. Eck's method contributed to the broader conviction that those in communion with Rome maintained a consistent and universal tradition from which the Protestants had departed.

Eck's treatment of the theological sources exemplifies a momentous early modern shift to "positive" theology. This reorientation received its codification in a work of the Spanish Dominican Melchior Cano, *De locis theologicis* (1563), the premier methodological treatise on the probative use of the theological sources.

A further generation of controversialists, working after the Council of Trent (1545–1563), saw the Protestants as established in their heresies and sought mainly to marshal all possible evidence for the doctrines laid down as normative by Trent. Gradually Calvinism became the main opponent, and members of the Jesuit order came to the forefront of Catholic apologetics. Little known still are some prolific later controversialist writers, such as Lawrence Faunt (1554–1591), Peter Michael Brillmacher (1542–1595), Gregory of Valencia (1549–1603), Jean Gontery (1527–1616), François de Coster (1532–1619), Martin Becanus (1563–1624), Pierre Coton (1564–1626), Adam Tanner (1571–1632), and Francois Véron (1575–1638).

The two figures looming largest in post-Tridentine controversialist theology are Thomas Stapleton and Roberto Bellarmino. Stapleton, an English diocesan priest living and writing in exile in the Spanish Netherlands from 1559 to his death in 1598, lucidly codified the divisive ecclesial and soteriological issues in *Principiorum fidei demonstratio* (1578) and *De universa justificationis doctrina* (1582). Bellarmino created the comprehensive work of Catholic controversial theology, which was the fruit of his twelve years of lecturing at the Jesuits' Roman College (1576–1588). His *Disputationes de controversiis Christianae fidei adversus huius temporis haereticos* cover the whole span of Reformation argument in seventeen parts, filling three hefty volumes: on the word of God and the church (1586), on the sacraments (1588), and on grace and justification (1593). Bellarmino culled his adversaries' views from a notable span of Protestant works, especially by Calvin, Luther, Martin Chemnitz, Matthias Flacius Illyricus, Peter Martyr Vermigli, Johannes Brenz, Melanchthon, and Théodore de Bèze. Against these he showed, with massive collections of citations, that Trent had taught perennial and well-grounded doctrine.

The emphases of the controversialists, both early and late, were of long-term influence in defining the doctrinal identity of Catholicism. The beliefs and positions they singled out for defense against the errors of their Protestant opponents were fundamental tenets of Catholicism from Trent to Vatican II. The energy they devoted to culling arguments and mounting their case led to a cluster of characteristic emphases in modern Catholic instruction, preaching, and piety.

On justification the controversialists held fast to free choice in human beings to accept or reject God's grace, with acceptance entailing cooperation with God's interior movements of the heart. In persons thus justified, they maintained that good works merit from God both an increase in holiness and the final reward of eternal life. On sacraments the Catholic apologists argued that Christ instituted seven; not just the two sacraments of baptism and the Lord's Supper, as admitted by the reformers. In the Mass Christ's body and blood are really present by a change of the elements of bread and wine. The Mass further entails a true sacrificial offering of Christ. On penance the controversialists advanced proofs that for sins to be forgiven confession, contrition, and satisfaction are required and that after absolution church-authorized indulgences are valid aids to reduce the required satisfaction. The controversialists made the case that it is good to venerate and invoke the aid of the saints and very good to take religious and monastic vows and to live a celibate life.

The church for these writers is a visible society bound to unwritten apostolic traditions in addition to scripture. Supreme authority is lodged in the pope, who has authority to judge and resolve controversies and whose laws and constitutions (e.g., on Holy Communion under only one form) bind Christian consciences. Church structures are sharply defined and serve effectively to overcome any doubt or unclarity about God's word and law. The student of these theologians must often overlook the mediocrity of their rhetoric and theology. Only occasionally do they rise to the challenge posed by the Reformation and compose works of artistry and insight. Three such examples can be noted.

The Bavarian Schatzgeyer wrote with penetration in the mid-1520s on the sacrificial character of the Mass. His leitmotiv is that the Mass is not a new or distinct offering of Christ to God by the priest or the church but a latter-day *representatio* or *Gegenwärtigung* of the offering Christ once made of himself for the world. Christ instituted the Eucharist to provide the church a vivid memorial of his loving offering of himself for humankind. To present this memorial before God is an authentic work of faith in which the church expresses its oneness with Christ, the high priest before God.

Another effective presentation of Catholic conviction was by Dietenberger, who published treatises in the wake of the Diet of Augsburg of 1530. Against the Protestant principle of *sola scriptura*, Dietenberger urged the amplitude of the Holy Spirit's modes of instruction of the church—as, for example, through the unwritten traditions, general councils, and the Fathers—which all serve to unpack the virtualities of meaning lodged in the original apostolic message. Scripture cannot suffice by itself to give full clarity regarding faith and the obligations of a Christian life, but the Holy Spirit poured out at Pentecost continues to dwell in the church and is present to guide the church when it expresses normative teachings.

In countering the Reformation principle of *sola fide*, Cajetan's *De fide et operibus* (1532) first states that Christ's merits and satisfaction are, in fact, completely and utterly sufficient for human salvation. This does not, however, render the merits of believers superfluous or make them derogate from Christ's sufficiency. Divine sufficiency means that Christ works in his members, sharing with them what he is and what he does. Believers do not receive Christ's gifts in mere passivity but are conformed to the values of his own action as they become active participants in good that benefits themselves and others.

The controversialists prepared cases for the doctrines that Trent taught authoritatively, and they later supplied lengthy apologias. Some few attained depths not realized by Trent.

BIBLIOGRAPHY

Backer, Augustin de, and Carl Sommervogel, eds. *Bibliographie de la Compagnie de Jesus.* 2d ed. 11 vols. Brussels, 1890–1932. Lists the works of the Jesuit controversialists.

Bagchi, David V. N. *Luther's Earliest Opponents: Catholic Controversialists, 1518–1525.* Minneapolis, 1991.

Desgraves, Louis. *Répertoire des ouvrages de controverse entre catholiques et protestants en France, 1598–1685.* 2 vols. Geneva and Paris, 1984–1985. Listing of 7,171 works of controversy, especially between Catholics and Calvinists, with complete titles at first entry and ample index.

Fabisch, Peter, and Erwin Iserloh, eds. *Dokumente zur Causa Lutheri, 1517–1521.* Corpus Catholicorum, vol. 41. 2 vols. Münster, 1988–1991. Includes works of Prierias, Eck, Cajetan.

Iserloh, Erwin, ed. *Katholische Theologen der Reformationszeit.* 5 vols. Münster, 1984–1988. Capsule studies, by various authors, of forty-five controversialists, mostly pre-Tridentine, with bibliographies of their works and of modern studies.

Klaiber, Wilibrigis. *Katholische Kontroverstheologen und Reformer des 16. Jahrhunderts: Ein Werkverzeichnis.* Münster, 1978. A first attempt at listing controversialist works, giving 3,456 entries from 355 authors. Omits important authors already covered elsewhere, such as Eck and Cochlaeus.

Lortz, Joseph. "Wert und Grenzen der katholischen Kontroverstheologie in der ersten Hälfte des 16. Jahrhunderts." In *Um Reform und Reformation,* edited by August Franzen, pp. 9–32. 2d ed. Münster, 1983.

O'Connell, Marvin R. *Thomas Stapleton and the Counter Reformation.* New Haven and London, 1964. On an author not included in Iserloh, *Katholische Theologen.*

Polman, Pontien. *L'élément historique dans la controverse religieuse du XVIème siècle.* Gembloux, 1932. Older study, still not superseded, on the argument from history in the controversialists.

JARED WICKS

CONVENTS. *See* Monasteries.

CONVERSOS. *See* New Christians; Spain.

CONVOCATIONS. Before the Reformation the convocations of the two English provinces of Canterbury and York combined the functions of tax-granting to the Crown and legislation for the church. Like their lay counterpart, the two convocations had an upper and lower house, the former consisting of the bishops, abbots, and priors; the latter of deans, archdeacons, and representatives of the monasteries, secular cathedrals, and parochial clergy. Proctors spoke for the cathedral and parochial clergy, the latter group having only two representatives per diocese. Unfortunately, a full study of the activities of the Convocation of Canterbury during and after the Reformation is impossible, since the original records of its proceedings were lost in the 1666 Great Fire of London.

The 1532 session of the Convocation of Canterbury proved a watershed in the history of the institution. When, in May, the clergy offered their submission to Henry VIII, their legislative autonomy was broken, and they were inhibited from assembly without the express permission of the Crown. Since the Tudors constantly needed money from their clerical subjects, this permission was unlikely to be withheld at the time of parliamentary meetings, and the summoning of convocations continued as it had done before the Reformation. However, the loss of legislative autonomy was a grave blow, scarcely compensated for by the retention of the right of petitioning. Although Henry as head of the church sought the advice of the clergy in matters of doctrine, he felt free to employ parliamentary legislation, or his own fiat, when it proved more convenient to do so. A pessimistic view of convocations between the 1530s and the Civil War concludes that they "consisted merely of aids and subsidies constantly increasing in amount" (Cardwell, 1842, vol. 1, p. xi). The Convocation of York certainly conforms to this image: on the rare occasions for which information survives, the northern province apparently followed the southern in a *pro forma* manner. The unwillingness of monarchs to grant any significant independence to convocations meant that their utility also declined for the leaders of the church. The bishops of the upper house could normally be confident of dominating the whole assembly, particularly after the dissolution of the monasteries, yet they often found other instruments of government more effective. This was especially true after Elizabeth's accession, when the ecclesiastical commission was employed extensively. Moreover, while convocation was notionally supreme under the monarch in matters of doctrine, the superior coercive power of statute made it necessary to implement major changes through Parliament.

Yet the fact that the bishops bypassed them should not automatically be read as evidence that convocations were powerless. There was strong opposition to reform throughout the early Reformation from a lower house dominated by clerical traditionalists, who accepted the royal supremacy but not its doctrinal consequences. In 1547 the lower house petitioned the bishops that ecclesiastical law be clearly defined, and that they be associated with the House of Commons in the passage of any legislation on matters of religion. Their clear intention was to halt or delay change. Neither of the Edwardian *Book of Common Prayer* were validated by convocation, and even the Forty-two Articles of 1552 were never presented to it, despite the claim of the Privy Council to the contrary. In 1559 the Crown avoided convocation because it gave yet another forum to conservatives opposed to the Elizabethan settlement.

By the time of the 1563 session, the most interesting of the post-Reformation period, there was greater harmony between Crown, bishops, and lower house. This session saw the passage of the Thirty-nine Articles, but also intense debate on various reform proposals from the lower house, supported by some of the bishops, designed to accommodate "Puritan" anxieties about vestments, preaching, and ministerial calling. Although most of this came to nothing, convocation had revealed a capacity for serious debate that surprised observers. Yet even when the assembly showed itself vigorous and effective, the limitations of its power were obvious. The queen wished it to pronounce on doctrinal matters, but only in conformity to her own will. The Thirty-nine Articles were not given their necessary parliamentary sanction until 1571, when it was politically convenient for the Crown to adopt a strong Protestant formulary, and then only after strong pressure from Archbishop Matthew Parker. Convocation might propose, but Elizabeth and her ministers unquestionably disposed. In the later years of the century the Convocation of Canterbury passed useful legislation promoting clerical education and protecting the interests of the church, but some sessions did little more than process royal subsidies. Yet under Elizabeth's successor, when royal authority was temporarily less burdensome, there was a moment of renewal when the two convocations of 1604 finally passed the canons that gave an adequate body of law to the English church.

BIBLIOGRAPHY

Cardwell, Edward. *Synodalia* (1842). 2 vols. Reprint, Farnborough, England, 1968.
Collinson, Patrick. *The Religion of Protestants*. Reprint, Oxford, 1984.
Dickens, A. G. *The English Reformation*. 2d ed. London, 1989.
Haugaard, William P. *Elizabeth I and the English Reformation*. London, 1968. This provides an important examination of the 1563 convocation.
Lehmberg, Stanford E. *The Reformation Parliament, 1529–1536*. Cambridge, 1970.
———. *The Later Parliaments of Henry VIII, 1536–1547*. Cambridge, 1977.
Wilkins, David. *Concilia Magnae Brittaniae et Hiberniae* (1737). Reprint, Brussels, 1964.

FELICITY HEAL

COOLHAES, Caspar

COOLHAES, Caspar (1534–1615), Reformed minister and Libertine opponent of Calvinist confessionalism in the Netherlands. Born in Cologne, Coolhaes studied at the University of Cologne and the Düsseldorf high school. In 1554 he joined the Carthusian order. In 1560 he embraced the Reformation and left his monastery; soon after he married. Between 1563 and 1566 Coolhaes held various ministerial posts in the county of Nassau. Then from September 1566 to May 1567 he served the Reformed congregation in the Dutch city of Deventer. Upon the arrival of Fernando Álvarez de Toledo, duke of Alba, in the Netherlands, Coolhaes returned to Germany, where he found a post in the city of Essen. The Essen magistracy dismissed him, however, in 1571 after deciding to enforce Lutheran orthodoxy. Coolhaes then served for two years in the Palatinate. In 1573 he returned to the Netherlands and in 1574 was called to Leiden. He gave the inaugural oration at the opening of the University of Leiden (February 1575) and for a brief time lectured on theology there.

In Leiden Coolhaes soon came into conflict with his fellow minister Pieter Corneliszoon and the Leiden consistory. It was this dispute that propelled him to fame and made him a central figure in the early history of the Dutch Reformed church. The most important part of this conflict began in 1578. It concerned the involvement of secular magistrates in the selection of church officers. Coolhaes held Erastian views on church-state relations, and in 1579 he assisted the Leiden magistrates when they replaced by fiat the city's elders and deacons. When Corneliszoon refused to recognize this new consistory, the magistrates summarily dismissed him. A panel of mediators managed to resolve the dispute in 1580. In 1581, however, a national synod demanded that Coolhaes disavow certain statements that he had made in two published pamphlets. Coolhaes refused. A provincial synod consequently deposed him from the ministry and ordered his excommunication in 1582. Excluded from the ministry, Coolhaes learned the art of distillery and supported his family by it for the rest of his life, first in Leiden and after 1587 in Amsterdam. Coolhaes continued to write pamphlets, however, thus keeping public attention focused on his religious views. By the time of his death his publications numbered at least twenty-eight.

In his day Coolhaes was the best known of a group of Dutch ministers who considered themselves Reformed and yet rejected certain distinctly Calvinist doctrines and practices. This group of so-called Libertines denied that confessions of faith and synodal decisions had any binding authority. Coolhaes accused the church of building a "new papacy" and destroying Christian freedom by making new human additions to scripture. A champion of tolerance, he called for the moderation of ecclesiastical discipline so that people of varying beliefs could belong to the church. Coolhaes's writings also reveal spiritualist influence; one of them was a Dutch translation of Sebastian Franck's *Apologia*. Coolhaes played down the importance of religious ceremonies and insisted that parts of scripture had to be understood not literally but "according to the sense of the Holy Spirit." Because of his Erastianism and his views on predestination, Coolhaes came later to be considered a forerunner of the Remonstrants.

BIBLIOGRAPHY

Bangs, Carl. *Arminius: A Study in the Dutch Reformation.* 2d ed. Grand Rapids, Mich., 1985. See pp. 52–55 for a brief treatment of the Coolhaes affair as background to the Remonstrant controversy.

Bie, J. P. de, and J. Loosjes, eds. *Biographisch woordenboek van Protestantsche godgeleerden in Nederland.* 6 vols. The Hague, 1919–1949. See vol. 5, pp. 172–205 for a detailed biographic article.

Kamphuis, J. *Kerkelijke besluitvaardigheid.* Groningen, 1970. Shows the relation between Coolhaes' Erastianism and his spiritualism.

Rogge, H. C. *Caspar Janszoon Coolhaes, de voorloper van Arminius en der Remonstranten.* 2 vols. Amsterdam, 1865. Still essential reading; includes long excerpts from Coolhaes's writings.

BENJAMIN KAPLAN

COOLTUYN, Cornelis (d. 1567), evangelical pastor in north Holland and later a Reformed minister. He came from Alkmaar, in north Holland, but little is known about his youth and education. After becoming a priest in Alkmaar, he combined the performance of Catholic ritual with Protestant preaching. He continued this after moving in 1556 to Enkhuizen (also in north Holland), where he served as pastor of the Saint Pancraskerk. Cooltuyn's preaching made him popular among the Enkhuizen laity but made him some enemies as well, especially among the clergy. Fortunately for him, his supporters had influence with the inquisitor Ruard Tapper, himself from Enkhuizen. At their urging, Tapper protected Cooltuyn. Twice summoned to The Hague, Cooltuyn avoided punishment only as a result of Tapper's intervention.

For a while Cooltuyn had to stop preaching and content himself with caring for the sick and the poor. After his second summons in 1557 to The Hague, however, he faced a choice: either leave Enkhuizen or perform his pastoral duties there in a proper Catholic manner. (By this time Cooltuyn had ceased to perform the Mass and other rituals.) Against the wishes of some supporters, Cooltuyn refused the latter path and returned to Alkmaar, where he soon received a new pastorate. Once again denounced, Cooltuyn this time had to flee the Netherlands altogether in order to escape arrest. He went to Emden, in East Friesland, and there in 1559 he was ordained as a Reformed minister. In that capacity he served Emden's Reformed church until his death.

Cooltuyn is sometimes called the father of the Reformation in Holland. He exercised considerable influence there as a teacher and preacher, as a leader of the Emden Reformed church, and as a writer. Several men who later were to play prominent roles as reformers in Holland studied with Cooltuyn. One was Jan Arendszoon, who in the summer of 1566 began the so-called hedge-preaching (illegal Protestant preaching outside the gates of cities) in Holland; Arendszoon also served briefly as Amsterdam's first Reformed minister. Another was Pieter Corneliszoon, a Reformed minister in Alkmaar for fifty years. In Emden, although outside the Netherlands, Cooltuyn was actually at the center of developments in Dutch Reformed Protestantism; Emden's church served during his years there as "mother church" to the Reformed churches "under the cross" in the Netherlands. As one of the leaders of the Emden church, Cooltuyn coordinated the 1566 hedge-preaching in the Netherlands, sending preachers where they were needed.

Cooltuyn also exercised influence through his widely read book, *Dat Evangeli der armen* (Alkmaar, 1559). The book begins with a letter of apology, defending Cooltuyn's decision (apparently criticized) to flee abroad rather than face martyrdom at home. Most of the book takes the form of a dialogue between a reformer and a sick Catholic woman. It is meant to offer instruction and consolation to Protestants living under the threat of persecution. The work is clearly Reformed without in any way being specifically Calvinist; for all its stress on justification by faith alone, it does not even mention the doctrine of election.

In nineteenth- and early twentieth-century historiography, Cooltuyn was commonly considered a representative of a distinctly Dutch "national-Reformed" movement. Though most historians have since denied the existence of such a movement, they do see Cooltuyn's life and beliefs as representative of a common pattern among supporters of the Reformation in the northern Netherlands.

BIBLIOGRAPHY

Primary Source

Cooltuyn, Cornelis. *Dat Evangeli der Armen.* Alkmaar, Netherlands, 1559. Newer edition in *Bibliotheca reformatoria neerlandica*, edited by F. Pijper, Vol IX, The Hague, 1912, pp. 187–480.

Secondary Sources

Nauta, D., et al., eds. *Biografisch Lexicon voor de geschiedenis van het Nederlandse protestantisme.* 3 vols. Kampen, 1978–. See especially vol. 2, pp. 138–140.
Voets, B. "De hervorming in West-Friesland." Part 2, "De ontwikkeling der hervorming, Hoofdstuk IV: Cornelius Cooltuyn en zijn tijd, 1555–1566." *Nederlandsch Archief voor Kerkgeschiedenis* 36 (1948), 24–29.

BENJAMIN KAPLAN

COORNHERT, Dirck Volkertszoon

COORNHERT, Dirck Volkertszoon (1522–1590), radical Dutch protagonist of religious tolerance and autodidact humanist scholar. Throughout his life Coornhert found himself bound up with the conflicts that accompanied the birth of the Dutch Republic and the introduction of the Reformed church. He was born to a family of well-to-do Amsterdam cloth merchants. He did not receive a classical education because he was probably destined for a commercial career. In 1539 he married Cornelia Symonsdochter, who was twelve years his elder and sister to the mistress of Reinoud III van Brederode. Brederode was first among the lesser nobility of the Netherlands, a convinced Protestant, and a leader of the Revolt of the Netherlands when it broke out in 1568. Coornhert's parents were opposed to this marriage and disinherited him. The couple settled in Haarlem, a neighboring town renowned for its breweries and the hometown of a circle of painters strongly influenced by the Italian Renaissance.

Coornhert began a career as an etcher and engraver, for which he showed considerable talent. This artistic career was interrupted by a two-year stewardship to Reinoud van Brederode (1541–1543). For twelve years he worked closely with Maerten van Heemskerck, a leading figure in the Haarlem school of painters and member of the town's reigning patriciate. The often enigmatic prints Coornhert made while with van Heemskerck (and later also with other artists) closely interweave Christian tradition, humanist moralism, and Renaissance imagery. Thus they illustrate Coornhert's mental background and are an important complement to his writings.

Around 1560 Coornhert's contacts with the Haarlem pa-

triciate intensified. In 1561 he was registered as notary, and in 1562 he became town clerk. In the years preceding the outbreak of the revolt he sided with the faction in the Haarlem magistery that supported William of Orange. During the years of repression under Fernando Álvarez de Toledo, duke of Alba (1568–1572), Coornhert was forced into exile in the Rhineland, just over the border of the German empire. There he helped to raise funds for a counteroffensive by Orange. On Orange's return to Holland in 1572 he became secretary to the states of Holland, which had assumed power in opposition to the king of Spain's (Philip II) government in the Netherlands. In this capacity Coornhert strongly criticized the cruelties perpetrated by William van der Mark, lord of Lumey, one of Orange's lieutenants. Probably because of threats from Lumey he went back to the Rhineland in 1573, returning for good in 1576. Coornhert resumed his office as notary in Haarlem.

Most important in this period were his writings. A prolific author in prose, poetry, and drama, all his works are highly moralistic. He was convinced that one should conquer passions in order to attain virtue. Following one's passions he considered as sin and described as the product of faulty understanding. For him human passion is evidently at the root of all misfortune. With determined effort one can learn virtue and even reach perfection. Here Coornhert shows influence from classical philosophy as received by contemporary humanism. His perfectionism seems partly derived from Hendrik Niclaes, a self-styled prophet and founder of the sect called the Family of Love. Coornhert befriended Niclaes in the 1550s but later fiercely criticized his doctrines.

The most influential aspect of Coornhert's work was his rejection of the Calvinist doctrine of predestination, which was diametrically opposed to his own perfectionism. He denied that this doctrine had any scriptural foundation. For Coornhert Christianity was simply living according to evangelical precepts. A truly evangelical church should do away with all human institutions, especially with all interpretations of the Bible and with the doctrinal systems all the churches in the sixteenth century were so diligently building. For a short period he thought he would find allies in Mennonite circles, but they proved less radical than he had imagined.

His often vehement assertions that all dogmatism, and especially Calvinist dogmatism, must eventually lead to persecution of heretics led to divergent evaluations of his views, both in his day and in the present. His extreme use of invective irritated even his sympathizers. Church leaders denounced him in often equally fierce polemics and feared his influence, which is said to have been considerable, although it remains difficult to trace. In more libertine circles his tireless defense of liberty of conscience met—and still meets—with admiration and acclaim.

After his wife, William of Orange, and a powerful patron in Haarlem all died in 1584, Coornhert seems to have no longer felt happy in Haarlem. In 1590 he died in Gouda, reputedly the most libertine town in Holland.

BIBLIOGRAPHY

Primary Source

Coornhert, Dirk Volkertszoon. *Wercken*. 3 vols. Amsterdam, 1633. Collected works in Dutch. Coornhert wrote in the vernacular from nationalistic pride and to reach a wide audience.

Secondary Sources

Becker, Bruno. *Bronnen tot de kennis van het leven en de werken van D. V. Coornhert*. Rijks Geschiedkundige Publicatiën, Kleine serie 25. The Hague, 1928. Important source material on Coornhert and his works.

Bonger, H. *Leven en werk van D. V. Coornhert*. Amsterdam 1978. Authoritative biography.

Bonger, H., et al., eds. *Dirck Volkertszoon Coornhert: Dwars maar recht*. Zutphen, Netherlands, 1989. Contains a number of essays on various aspects of Coornherts's work that add a critical touch often absent in the biography.

JOKE SPAANS

COP, Nicolas

COP, Nicolas (c.1501–1540), Parisian-born humanist and physician of evangelical leanings who unintentionally provoked a persecution of reformers in 1533, with lasting detrimental consequences for the French Reformation. The third son of Guillaume Cop, physician to King Francis I, Nicolas was hired in 1530 by Andrés de Gouveia to teach philosophy at the Collège Sainte-Barbe. On 10 October 1533 he was elected rector of the University of Paris for the three-month fall term. His inquiry into the censure of Marguerite of Navarre's book *Miroir de l'âme pécheresse* exonerated the university from blame. His university sermon, delivered on All Saints' Day (1 November) on the theme of the Beatitudes, offended traditionalist Catholics by advocating the doctrine of justification by faith alone. On 19 November Cop denied most of the charges brought against him by the Franciscan friars, his principal accusers. The case was referred to the Parlement of Paris and reached the ears of King Francis I, who, showing unexpected outrage at Cop's sermon, ordered his arrest; but Cop fled to Basel. The king instructed the Parlement to investigate and to suppress the "Lutheran sect infesting Paris," thereby laying a foundation for the more serious persecutions that followed the *Affaire des Placards*.

Théodore de Bèze believed that Calvin wrote Cop's sermon, part of which exists today in Calvin's hand, but this opinion is no longer current. Cop returned to Paris in 1536, probably under the amnesty granted by the Edict of Coucy on the condition of living peacefully in the Catholic faith. After receiving the license in medicine, he lectured in Paris. Early in 1537 he went to Scotland to attend to Francis I's daughter Madeleine, newly wed queen of King James V, who was seriously ill. When she died, perhaps before his arrival, Cop returned to Paris, where he died in the spring of 1540.

BIBLIOGRAPHY

Concasty, Marie-Louise, ed. *Commentaires de la Faculté de médecine de l'Université de Paris, 1516–1560*. Paris, 1964. Basic archival source for Cop's university career.

Droz, Eugénie. *Chemins de l'hérésie*. 3 vols. Geneva, 1970. Vol. 1, pp. 93–96, gives a short treatment of John Calvin's association with Cop.

DuBoulay, César-Égasse. *Historia Universitatis Parisiensis*. 6 vols. Paris, 1673. Vol. 6, pp. 238–239, original sources about Cop, some of which are no longer extant.

Herminjard, A.-L. *Correspondance des réformateurs dans les pays de langue française*. 10 vols. Geneva and Paris, 1870. Vol. 3 contains several letters of reformers about the events of 1533 and 1534 in Paris.

JAMES K. FARGE, C.S.B.

COPENHAGEN, CONFESSION OF.

COPENHAGEN, CONFESSION OF. From 1526, King Frederick I of Denmark had pursued a reformist church policy, and in 1529, when he summoned a diet to be held on 2 July 1530, he ordered reformers ("preachers") from a number of Danish towns to appear and to be prepared for a disputation with the bishops. Both parties were to be ready to present their cases so that a Christian reformation might be made and unity obtained in doctrine. Twenty-one of the reformers appeared, and the bishops enlisted the help of Paul Helie and two German theologians.

As this was the first occasion in which reformers from all of Denmark could meet, they took the opportunity to draw up a confession in forty-three articles, which they expounded afterwards in numerous sermons all over town. When the bishops delivered a complaint in twenty-seven articles to the king, he forwarded it to the reformers, and a debate in writing ensued. However, no public disputation was held; during the first half of 1530, the risk of an attack from the exiled Christian II had increased so much that the king was no longer interested in a religious confrontation. Consequently, no definite settlement was obtained, and the diet issued only a general license of evangelical preaching. Neither the bishops nor the reformers were quite satisfied by this outcome.

The Confession of Copenhagen (Confessio Hafniensis) provided both the doctrine and the reformation program of the Danish reformers. Initially it establishes the Bible as the only and absolute rule for a Christian life. This is significant. The confession is characterized by a humanistic interest in the Bible, which tends to consider it as law rather than gospel. Consequently, the answers given to individual questions are all supposed to be founded on scripture as distinct from the teachings of the Catholic church. Compared with the views of Luther, the formal authority of scripture is stressed so much that the dialectics between the principles of *sola scriptura* and *sola fide* vanishes. The confession represents an anti-Catholic radicalization of the biblical humanism supported by Helie, and, in fact, former disciples of Helie were prominent among the reformers. It was probably framed by Peder Laurentsen.

As an interpretation of the doctrine of the pre-Reformation movement in Denmark, the confession is important, but from a historical point of view its significance is limited. Frederick I did not see another chance to carry through with the Reformation, and when reform was actually instituted by Christian III after the Counts' War, it assumed the shape of a Lutheran Reformation under the aegis of the king. The reformers of Wittenberg had a decisive influence, and the confession was subsequently put aside. This does not imply, however, any hostility between the king and the reformers. Several of them became bishops, and, in fact, the theology of the confession, which was simpler and less sophisticated than that of Luther, may very well have set the pace for much of the preaching in Danish churches after the Reformation.

BIBLIOGRAPHY

Andersen, Niels Knud. *Confessio Hafniensis*. Copenhagen, 1954.
Andersen, Niels Knud, and P. G. Lindhardt. *Den Danske Kirkes Historie*. Vol. 3. Copenhagen, 1965.

THORKILD C. LYBY

COPENHAGEN, DIETS OF. The Diets of Copenhagen in 1530, 1533, and 1536 were instrumental in shaping the course of the Reformation in Denmark. The first two (1530 and 1533) collectively weakened the power of the Catholic church and gave cohesion to the Lutheran movement within Denmark; the Diet of 1536 signaled the official reception of the Lutheran faith and the demise of the Catholic state church in Denmark.

The Diet of 1530. As the Lutheran faith grew in popularity within the Oldenburg state, King Frederick I (r. 1523–1533) was slow in giving a clear indication of his confessional stance. Despite a clause in his coronation charter obliging him to protect the Roman church and to halt the practice of the Lutheran "heresy," King Frederick openly tolerated and even protected such leading lights of Danish Lutheranism as Hans Tausen in Viborg and Claus Mortensen in Malmö. At the *Herredage* ("assemblies") at Odense (1526–1527), Frederick cut off all episcopal and financial ties with Rome, thereby establishing a Danish national church. Nevertheless, the constant threat of invasion from the recently deposed King Christian II (r. 1513–1523), Frederick's Lutheran nephew and predecessor, precluded any official recognition of the Lutheran faith.

Frederick I's extraordinary tolerance may have been politically expedient, but it satisfied neither the growing Lutheran movement nor the thoroughly frightened Catholic state church. Escalating friction between the two, in addition to a number of lesser issues, compelled King Frederick to summon a *Herredag* at Copenhagen, to commence on 2 July 1530. The first concerns at the *Herredag* were the necessary preparations to fend off a possible invasion attempt by the ousted Christian II, but the imminent showdown between Catholic and Lutheran theologians attracted the most attention. In addition to the Danish council of state and representatives of the nobility, twenty-one evangelical preachers attended the meeting, including Tausen, Mortensen, and Peter Laurentsen of Malmö. The size of the Catholic contingent is more difficult to ascertain, but it included such luminaries as Paul Helgesen and Hans Nielsen, as well as a handful of German theologians.

Shortly after the diet commenced on 2 July 1530, the Catholic prelates reminded King Frederick that his toleration of Lutheran preachers violated the terms of his coronation charter. Luther's theology had already been condemned elsewhere, the bishops argued, and the king's laxity in condemning it within his realm only encouraged open attacks on the papacy and the clergy. The bishops, in short, hoped to settle the issue by appealing solely to the king's obligation to fulfill his coronation oath, obviating the open debate for which the evangelical preachers hoped.

Over the first eight days of the diet, the Lutheran preachers met quietly to prepare a common statement of faith, later known as the Confession of Copenhagen (*Confessio hafniensis*). The confession, likely composed by the Malmö reformer Peter Laurentsen, was far more direct and inflammatory in its overall tone than that presented by Lutheran territories at the Diet of Augsburg at the same time. Its forty-three articles chastised the Roman church for not recognizing the primacy of the scriptures; it attacked celibacy as a "teaching of the devil"; it questioned the intellectual qualities and moral character of the priesthood.

The Lutheran preachers submitted the confession to Frederick I around 10 July 1530. As the king pondered its contents, its authors took the somewhat presumptuous action of preaching collectively on each of its forty-three articles every weekday at the Church of the Holy Spirit (*Helligåndskirken*) in Copenhagen. The initial protest of the Catholic prelates—that the king had been led astray from the solemn promise embodied in his coronation charter—compelled Frederick I to reconsider his stance of toleration, and to prohibit the Lutherans from preaching on the confession. But Frederick, with characteristic vacillation, revoked the ban two days later, and the Lutheran preachers could now be heard lecturing on the confession four times daily and twelve times each Sunday.

So far the Lutheran party had been unable to reach their goal—an open debate with their Catholic opponents—nor were the Catholic prelates able to limit the issue to a simple dispute over the king's coronation charter. The constant agitation of the Lutheran preachers, however, turned much of

Copenhagen's populace against the bishops. Even regarding the secular issues addressed at the diet, the Catholic church proved powerless. Defense preparations against Christian II required the financial assistance of the larger towns, which they willingly granted in return for the virtual assurance of complete religious freedom.

Faced with mounting popular opposition and unsupported by their king, the Catholic prelates pursued another course of action. In a list of twenty-seven grievances presented to Frederick I during the third week of the diet, the prelates asked that the Lutheran preachers draw up a more cogent statement of their faith, as well as an explanation of their dispute with "us and the Christian church in general." The Catholics would draw up a similar statement; an indeterminate number of "impartial" scholars would examine the two statements and proclaim one the winner. A number of lesser disputes, however, precluded the possibility of such a resolution. The Lutheran preachers demanded that the bishops who had composed the grievances affix their signatures to the unsigned document, and they hoped for an open debate adjudicated by the king and the council of state; the bishops refused to sign, demanding in their turn that the preachers respond to the grievances both in Danish and in Latin, rather than in the vernacular alone. At the king's request, the preachers responded to the Catholic clergy's grievances in Danish only, correcting its misrepresentations of Lutheran theology and seeking to force the Catholics into a debate before the king and the council through an additional set of twelve grievances. The grievances portrayed ordinary parish priests as unlettered and indolent, preaching "fables and the mendacious fabrications of man."

The disputes over the missing Catholic signatures and the use of Danish and Latin in written documents, in which Frederick I refused to intervene, brought the diet to a standstill well before its dismissal on 2 August 1530. The stubbornness of both parties on this issue prevented the diet from addressing Denmark's religious rift. But since the Catholic prelates, who though in the right, were unable to persuade the king to follow the oath he had sworn at his coronation, the diet was a major victory for the Lutheran faith in Denmark.

The Diet of 1533. Since Denmark was an elective monarchy, the issue of the succession to the throne after Frederick engendered a heated debate within the council of state even before Frederick's death on 10 April 1533. Frederick's eldest son, Duke Christian of Holstein, was the logical choice by birth, but his German upbringing and his open attachment to the Lutheran faith severely compromised his candidacy; the king's next son, Hans, had been raised in Denmark from the age of nine and was firmly Catholic. In order to settle this matter, as well as a number of diplomatic issues, Frederick I summoned a joint Danish-Norwegian *Herredag* to meet at Nyborg, Sjælland, on 8 June 1533. The king's death in the meantime hastened the urgency of the

situation, but unfortunately deprived the diet of his tactful and persuasive guidance. Members of the council changed only the date and location of the diet, now slated to meet at Copenhagen on 1 June. Other issues pushed the succession dispute into the background. Jurgen Wullenwewer, Lübeck's aggressive burgomaster, appeared at the diet to demand war with the Netherlands and the emperor, and possibly to offer his support to Duke Christian. The young duke rejected Wullenwewer's diplomatic advances, instead orchestrating a military alliance between Denmark and the duchies of Schleswig and Holstein, as well as a peaceful settlement of commercial disputes with the Netherlands. The likelihood of war with Lübeck compelled the council of state to postpone the selection of a new king for one year.

This formally imposed interregnum presented the Catholic clergy with a perfect opportunity to regain the losses they had suffered under Frederick I. Of the thirty-eight members of the council of state present at the diet, a sizable majority were either Catholic clerics or committed Catholic lay members; consequently, the council made an attempt to reiterate the Odense Recess of 1527 and thereby strengthen the position of the Catholic episcopacy. This was embodied in a new church ordinance, approved by the council of state on 3 July 1533. The ordinance stipulated that only a bishop would have the power to ordain priests within his see, and that individuals preaching without the bishop's permission would be tried and severely punished. Nonetheless, the council promised that individual priests who proved to be "unwilling" and "unsuitable" would be replaced if their disaffected parishioners petitioned the bishop. It promised to return all ecclesiastical lands confiscated during the reign of Frederick I.

The church ordinance of 1533, while it did remove the protection that Frederick I had extended to the Lutheran lay preachers, nevertheless did not fulfill the expectations of the Catholic clergy; many had expected a much sharper attack on the Lutheran "heresy." Yet it was harsh enough to alarm a significant minority on the council. Fifteen of the thirty-eight members present refused to sign the ordinance, and many of these left the diet in protest. The remaining councilors, all decidedly pro-Catholic, summoned the renowned Lutheran preacher and theologian Hans Tausen to appear before the council. Tausen met with the council on 14 July 1533. The line of questioning was simple and straightforward, concerning Tausen's slanderous remarks on the Catholic clergy and his views on the Eucharist. (Several councilors labeled Tausen a "Zwinglian.") Though the meeting itself was undramatic, and neither condemned Tausen nor forced him to recant his remarks, this was due in part to the hostile public reaction to his interrogation: fearing for the popular preacher's life, the burghers of Copenhagen asked Wullenwewer for military assistance in securing Tausen's release. The diet adjourned several days later, having accomplished nothing beyond the cryptic church ordinance.

The Diet of 1536. When the Lutheran Duke Christian of Holstein, having been elected king of Denmark as Christian III by the Danish nobility in 1534, rode in triumph into Copenhagen at the conclusion of the Counts' War (1534–1536), he launched almost immediately into a confessional and constitutional restructuring of Denmark and Norway. On 12 August 1536 Christian III summoned the lay members of the council of state to a secret meeting. Here he informed the councilors of his intentions to revoke the temporal authority of the Catholic episcopacy, to subsume the church hierarchy completely under the state, and to confiscate all ecclesiastical lands. The lay councilors agreed, and the bishops were arrested and incarcerated that evening. Nevertheless, Christian III decided to summon a national diet, to meet in Copenhagen in October 1536. This was not of the same limited scope as the *Herredag* of 1530 and 1533, to which only nobles and clergy were invited; this was to be a *Stændermøde*, or meeting of the estates, to which representatives of all orders—including the burghers and the peasants—were to be invited. This was a rare occurrence in Danish politics.

The diet, with approximately twelve hundred in attendance, convened in Copenhagen during the last half of October. The meeting opened with a list of grievances against the Catholic bishops, including the claim that they had been responsible for precipitating the Counts' War. The actual course of the debates is unknown, but the results of the meeting are well documented. On 30 October 1536 the diet promulgated a new ecclesiastical law—the Recess of 1536—which declared the abolition of the bishops, the removal of their temporal and spiritual authority, and their replacement by a new series of "bishops and superintendents" appointed by the state. The "Crown of Denmark" confiscated all ecclesiastical properties for the "common good of the realm." The diet also composed a coronation charter for Christian III, but one that altered the constitutional constraints that had always limited the powers of Danish kings; for example, Christian III's charter was the first in Danish history to omit any mention of the right of popular resistance (*folkelige modstandsret*) if the king should violate the terms of his charter. Although Denmark would continue to be an elective monarchy, Christian's two-year-old son, Frederick (later King Frederick II), received the title of prince-elect. Moreover, the diet declared that Norway was no longer an affiliated kingdom, but a subject province of the kingdom of Denmark. The Diet of 1536 not only consolidated the popular gains of the Lutheran Reformation in Denmark but also ushered in a new era in the constitutional structure of the Oldenburg monarchy.

BIBLIOGRAPHY

Andersen, J. O. "Er 1527 i retslig Henseende Epokeaaret i dansk Reformationshistorie?" In *Festskrift til Erslev*, pp. 227–270. Copenhagen, 1927. Although concerned predominantly with the Odense diets of 1526 and 1527, Andersen views the Diet of 1530 as setting a precedent for toleration based on the primacy of scripture.

Andersen, Niels Knud. *Confessio Hafniensis: Den københavnske Bekendelse af 1530.* Copenhagen, 1954. Primarily a study of the Copenhagen Confession, its origins, authorship, and theological implications; Andersen's treatment of the Diet of 1530 remains the most thorough.

Göbell, Walter. "Das Vordringen der Reformation in Dänemark und in den Herzogtümern unter der Regierung Friedrichs I, 1523–1533." In *Schleswig-Holsteinische Kirchengeschichte*, edited by Verein für Schleswig-Holsteinische Kirchengeschichte, vol. 3 pp. 35–113. Neumünster, 1982. A solid overview of the Copenhagen diets of 1530 and 1533.

Helveg, Ludvig N. *Den Danske Kirkes Historie til Reformationen.* Vol. 2. Copenhagen, 1870. Though quite dated, still the most detailed accounts of the Copenhagen diets. Coverage of the Diet of 1533 is clearly the most thorough and readable in print.

Lindhardt, P. G. *Nederlagets Mænd: Det katolske bispevældes sidste dage i Danmark.* Copenhagen, 1968. A collective biography of three Catholic bishops. Lindhardt's biography of Joakim Rønnow, who played a major role in the interrogation of Hans Tausen in 1533, is especially important.

Petersen, E. Ladewig. "Omkring Herredagsmødet i København 1533." *Kirkehistoriske samlinger* (1972), 24ff.

Petersen, E. Ladewig, and Knud J. V. Jespersen. "Two Revolutions in Early Modern Denmark." In *Politics and Society in Reformation Europe: Essays for Sir Geoffrey Elton on his Sixty-fifth Birthday*, edited by E. I. Kouri and Tom Scott, pp. 473–501. London, 1987. Petersen's half of the article ("The Revolution of 1536 and Its Aftermath, the Domain State," pp. 475–486), while dealing only briefly with the Diet of 1536, gives a terse explanation of the constitutional implications of the diet.

Schäfer, Dietrich. *Geschichte von Dänemark.* Vol. 4. Gotha, 1893. Like Helveg, Schäfer's work is somewhat outdated, but nonetheless its discussion of the political background of the diets—particularly of that of 1533—is still without equal.

Scharling, Suno William. "Frederick I.s kirkepolitik." *Kirkehistoriske samlinger* (1974), 40–88. The most balanced treatment of the religious policies of the enigmatic Frederick I.

PAUL DOUGLAS LOCKHART

COPERNICUS, Nicolaus (also Nicholas; 1473–1543), Polish astronomer and proponent of the heliocentric universe. A canon in Frombork (Frauenburg), he performed his ecclesiastical duties and pursued his interest in astronomy there. He first suggested that the Earth is a planet revolving around a stationary Sun in his *Commentariolus*, which he wrote sometime before 1514. He circulated this booklet privately. Although some criticized it because it contradicted generally accepted authorities and appeared to contradict holy scripture, he was encouraged to publish more especially because the calendar needed to be reformed. He did not, howover, produce a new work at that time. His reputation as a mathematician and astronomer continued to grow. In 1539 a mathematician from the University of Wittenberg, Georg Joachim Rheticus (1514–1576), joined him in Frombork to learn more about his theories. Rheticus wrote the first piece for publication, *Narratio Prima* (First Report), and it began to circulate in 1540. He also persuaded

Copernicus to publish his magnum opus, *De revolutionibus* (On the Revolutions), the manuscript of which was completed by 1541. Rheticus started supervising publication of the work in Nuremberg, but in 1542 he took a new position in Leipzig, and the task was left to Andreas Osiander (1496–1552), a Lutheran preacher from Nuremberg who had become interested in the work of Copernicus.

Osiander added an unsigned "Address to the Reader" as a preface to *De revolutionibus,* and in it he asserted that the work was merely a hypothesis for astronomical calculation, a claim that contradicted the body of the text. Copernicus saw the finished book on his deathbed, but Rheticus protested the inclusion of this preface. Nevertheless, Osiander's preface gave Philipp Melanchthon a reason to accept the work (although Martin Luther called its author a fool), and Wittenberg became a center for its study. Copernicus's own preface was addressed to Pope Paul III (r. 1534–1549), but at this time the Holy See issued no response, possibly because it was too absorbed with the Council of Trent.

BIBLIOGRAPHY

Primary Source

Copernicus, Nicholas. *On the Revolutions. Minor Works.* 2 vols. Translated by Edward Rosen. Reprint, Baltimore and London, 1992.

Secondary Sources

Kuhn, Thomas S. *The Copernican Revolution.* Reprint, Cambridge, Mass., 1985.
Rosen, Edward. "Copernicus." In *Dictionary of Scientific Biography,* vol. 3, pp. 401–11. New York, 1971.
———. *Copernicus and the Scientific Revolution.* Malabar, Fla., 1984.
Westman, Robert S., ed. *The Copernican Achievement.* Berkeley, 1975.

SHEILA J. RABIN

CORDATUS, Conrad (Ger., Conrad Hertz; c.1480–1546), humanist, Lutheran theologian, and recorder of Martin Luther's *Tischreden.* Born between 1480 and 1483 at Leonbach, southeast of Wels, Austria, Cordatus came from a peasant family with Hussite sympathies. After studying in Vienna with German arch-humanist and poet laureate Conradus Celtis, Cordatus entered the priesthood in 1505. He took his doctorate in theology from Ferrara, Italy, and returned to Ofen, Austria, in 1510. When Cordatus began supporting the Reformation, he was jailed. In 1524 he fled to Wittenberg, staying a year as a poverty-stricken refugee. His return to Habsburg lands led to his arrest in Hungary and more than nine months in prison until a sympathetic guard left his cell unlocked, allowing his escape to Wittenberg.

In July 1526 Philipp Melanchthon suggested that Cordatus help Nuremberg's new gymnasium, but by fall he was off to Silesia, where Duke Frederick II hoped to start a university at Legnica. The venture failed, and in April 1527

Cordatus returned to Hungary but found no permanent post. Now married, Cordatus reappeared in Wittenberg. Luther tried to find him suitable positions such as a spring 1529 call to Saint Mary's parish in Zwickau. Strife with Zwickau's city council in July 1531 prompted Cordatus's temporary return to Wittenberg before Luther arranged a pastorate at nearby Neimeck. Cordatus's zeal for orthodoxy sparked harsh criticism from Caspar Cruciger and Melanchthon in 1537, as Cordatus argued against good works having any place in explaining justification. Luther intervened and encouraged Cordatus to accept a call to Eisleben. By 1540 he was again on the move, now to Brandenburg, where he helped promote the Reformation as superintendent in Stendal. Cordatus died 6 April 1546.

Cordatus was known for his staunch defense of doctrine and firm commitment to the Reformation. Despite their clash. Melanchthon penned a generous preface for Cordatus's postils, published posthumously in Nuremberg in 1554. During his 1532–1533 Wittenberg stay, he recorded Luther's *Tischreden* (Table Talk), but his devotion to Luther led him to make favorable editorial revisions, which are apparent when compared to Veit Dietrich's more immediate version.

BIBLIOGRAPHY

Primary Source

Cordatus, Conrad. *Tagebuch über Dr. Martin Luther.* Edited by H. Wrampelmeyer. Halle, Germany, 1885. Cordatus's 1537 publication of Luther's *Tischreden* redone just over a hundred years ago together with the editor's look (pp. 9–26) at Cordatus's relationship with Luther.

Secondary Sources

Hammann, Gustav. "Conradus Cordatus Leombachensis: Sein Leben in Österreich." *Jahrbuch des Oberösterreichischen Musealvereins* 109 (1964), 250–278. Deals with Cordatus's activities in his home region.
Wiczián, Deszö. "Beiträge zu Leben und Tätigkeit des Conrad Cordatus." *Archiv für Reformationsgeschichte* 55 (1964), 219–222. Explains family's Hussite roots and why Weißkirch and Leonbach are both given as the Cordatus home, the latter being the actual village included in the larger parish.

ROBERT ROSIN

CORNELISZOON, Arend (also Arent; Arnoldus Cornelisz; Crusius; 1547–1605), influential Calvinist minister and church organizer during the Dutch Reformation. The son of a Protestant burgomaster in Delft, Corneliszoon received his formal theological training at the seminary of the University of Heidelberg (1565–1568) and at the academy in Geneva (1568–1570). After leaving Geneva, Corneliszoon served as a minister to the Dutch refugee church at Frankenthal in the Palatinate from 1571 until 1573. He returned to his home in 1573 shortly after Delft had joined the side of William of Orange in the war against Philip II of

Spain. He subsequently accepted the call of the Reformed congregation in Delft to serve as a pastor and he labored in that capacity until his death.

Called by his critics "the pope of Delft," Corneliszoon was the driving force behind the Delft church from 1573 to 1605, a period of significant growth. Motivated by his vision of the church as a pure community of "true Christians," Corneliszoon's primary concern in Delft was pastoral care over a congregation without interference from political authorities. To that end he implemented the Reformed conception of a tripartite ministry, which consisted of pastors for preaching and administering the sacraments, elders for disciplining members, and deacons for administering poor relief. Helped by his family's connections within regent circles, he successfully fought to guard these ministries from encroachment by city magistrates.

Outside Delft, Corneliszoon was one of the most notable ministers in Holland. He played an important role in early attempts to set forth a precise protocol for the Dutch Reformed church. He served as secretary to the provincial synod at Dordrecht (1574) and the national Synod of Dordrecht (1578), president of the national synod at Middelburg (1581), and *assessor* of the national synod at The Hague (1586).

Along with Reynier Donteclock, his colleague at Delft, Corneliszoon championed a strict adherence to the Belgic Confession and Heidelberg Catechism, opposing the more latitudinarian ministers known as Libertines. Beginning in 1577 Corneliszoon participated in a long polemical campaign against the semi-Pelagian views of the noted humanist Dirck Volkertszoon Coornhert. Against Coornhert's criticisms, Corneliszoon defended the strict Calvinist position on such issues as original sin and capital punishment for heretics. On the troublesome matter of predestination, Corneliszoon and Donteclock in 1589 attempted to refute Coornhert by softening Théodore de Bèze's stringent supralapsarian position with a sublapsarian interpretation. This effort attracted the ire of Martinus Lydius, a professor at the new academy in Franeker, who, in a choice that would later seem ironic, called upon Jacobus Arminius to defend Bèze. Corneliszoon's efforts to moderate one of the most thorny doctrinal issues failed to gain a broad consensus. Nevertheless, until his death, Corneliszoon continued to exercise a leadership role in the Dutch Reformed church during a period of increasing doctrinal and political tension in the northern Netherlands. Although Corneliszoon makes cameo appearances in most monographs on the Dutch Reformation, his life and theological writings call for more singular attention.

BIBLIOGRAPHY

Bangs, Carl. *Arminius: A Study in the Dutch Reformation.* Nashville, 1971. An excellent study of the theological controversies surrounding Jacob Arminius, which also treats Corneliszoon's involvement.

Jaanus, Hendrik Johan. *Hervormd Delft ten tijde van Arent Cornelisz, 1573–1605.* Amsterdam, 1950. Despite its date, it remains the only modern biography of Corneliszoon. A very sympathetic account of Corneliszoon's activity as a pastor and theologian; contains an overview of the Reformed church at Delft.

CHARLES H. PARKER

CORNPUT, Hendrik van den. *See* Corput, Hendrik van den.

CORPUS CATHOLICORUM. The name of an ongoing project begun in 1919, the *Corpus Catholicorum* (abbreviated *CCath*) has had as its objective the publication of the writings of Catholic authors of the age of the Reformation. The project was, in a real sense, a Catholic response to the formidable Protestant editing of the writings of the major reformers, which had begun early in the nineteenth century with the *Corpus Reformatorum* and had, in the quadricentennial of Luther's birth (1883), found an impressive expression in a new scholarly edition of Martin Luther's works (the so-called Weimar Edition, named after its place of publication).

The concerns of the *CCath* project were the leading Catholic theologians of the Reformation, such as Johann Eck, Hieronymus Emser, and Johannes Cochlaeus, whose writings were not available in modern editions. This lack of modern editions meant that an authentic understanding of Catholic polemics and theology in the sixteenth century, particularly as it pertained to the Catholic reaction to the Protestant polemic, was not easy to come by. More than forty-three volumes of the *CCath* have been published, among them scholarly editions of the writings of Augustin Alveldt, Johannes Cochlaeus, Thomas Murner, Johannes Faber, Aigistamis Dietenberger, and even Henry VIII (his *Assertio septem sacramentorum*). The sponsor of the project is the Gesellschaft zur Herausgabe des Corpus Catholicorum, which has its seat in Münster, Germany. The publishing program of this society has also included a monograph series (Reformationsgeschichtliche Studien und Texte) with some 132 titles and a series of semipopular writings on topics pertaining to the age of the Reformation.

HANS J. HILLERBRAND

CORPUS DOCTRINAE. This term, meaning "body of doctrine," is used for a collection of writings that was meant to summarize authentic apostolic teaching and doctrine. A number of such collections were compiled in Germany in the second half of the sixteenth century. Their content included diverse types of writings—early Christian creeds, sixteenth-century Lutheran church orders, and writings of individual sixteenth-century (Lutheran) theologians. The concept emerged in the context of the doctrinal controversies in German Lutheranism after Martin Luther's death, when it was thought necessary to have a normative compilation of theological writings. The term itself was coined by Philipp Melanchthon and was expressive of his formal understanding of doctrine and the church. The intra-Lutheran controversies precipitated the emergence of several regional collections that expressed the understanding of the apostolic faith regnant in a particular town or territory. In general, these collections included, in addition to the Apostles' and Nicene creeds, a heavy dose of writings from the pen of either Melanchthon or Luther. About a dozen regional collections can be identified—for example, those at Württemberg (1559), Hamburg (1560), Lübeck (1560), Pomerania (1564), Thuringia (1570), and Brandenburg (1572).

After the Formula of Concord and its literary embodiment, the *Book of Concord* (1580), had resolved the internal theological disputes within German Lutheranism, the notion of regional collections gave way—in large measure because of the cohesiveness of the *Book of Concord*—to the notion of a single, generally accepted *corpus doctrinae*. Those Lutheran territories, such as Hesse, that did not sign the Formula of Concord retained their individual collections.

In neither the Calvinist nor the Anglican tradition did the notion of a *corpus doctrinae* become prominent. The theological authenticity of these traditions was assured by emphasizing single creedal statements from the sixteenth century.

Hans J. Hillerbrand

CORPUS REFORMATORUM.

CORPUS REFORMATORUM. Abbreviated *CR*, the *Corpus Reformatorum* is the name of a scholarly publication project that began in the middle of the nineteenth century, intended to publish the writings of all major reformers active before the Peace of Augsburg (1555). Obviously this program would have entailed the inclusion of an edition of the writings of Martin Luther, but since an effort was already under way to publish a new scholarly edition of Luther's works (the so-called Erlangen Edition), the decision was made not to include Luther's writings but rather to begin with the second most prominent Lutheran theologian, Philipp Melanchthon. Twenty-eight volumes of Melanchthon's writings were published between 1834 and 1860. The editors were K. G. Bretschneider and H. E. Bindseil. Unfortunately this edition is not characterized by the highest scholarly or editorial standards. For example, Melanchthon's correspondence is not nearly complete. Accordingly, a host of scholarly corrections have been necessary.

A second section of the *CR—Calvini Opera,* or *CO* (volumes 29–78)—contains the writings of John Calvin. Published between 1863 and 1900, these volumes were edited by several scholars with vastly improved editorial skills and competence. The final section of the *CR—Zwingli's Werke,* or *ZW* (volumes 88–101)—contains the writings of Huldrych Zwingli and was begun in 1905. Scholarly citations either employ the volume number of the entire project (e.g., *CR* XX) or the volume number of the section of Melanchthon's, Calvin's, or Zwingli's writings (e.g., *CO* XX). Other Protestant reformers, such as Martin Bucer and Johannes Brenz, as well as radical reformers, such as Thomas Müntzer and Bernhard Rothmann, have received their own freestanding editions.

Hans J. Hillerbrand

CORPUT, Hendrik van den (also Cornput; 1536–1601), Dutch Reformed minister. He was born in Breda the son of a jurist who was clerk of the court and town secretary, and later burgomaster of Breda. Van den Corput studied law in Louvain, and became a lawyer in Breda, but he had to leave the Netherlands with his elders and family in 1567 because of the persecutions that took place after the events of the Wonderyear. He then studied theology at Heidelberg; in 1578, after a short period of ministry in the Palatinate (1574–1576?), he was appointed minister at Dordrecht (1578), a post he held until his death.

By birth and training van den Corput belonged to the leading intelligentsia in the first three decades of the existence of the Dutch Republic, and to the minority of this group that preferred a post in the church to public service. From the beginning he was part of a small group of leading theologians who had the ability to govern the church, to mediate problems of a theological and personal nature, and to uphold the rights of the church vis-à-vis the state.

The church of Dordrecht, with its two to four ministers and six to ten elders, numbered among the influential churches that, in spite of internal difficulties, provided an example to the surrounding village churches. The internal difficulties, in Dordrecht as well as in the republic in general, were mainly due to the influence of a vaguely religious, nonchurch committed mentality which was referred to derogatorily by its Reformed opponents as "spiritualism." A large part of van den Corput's efforts were therefore devoted to strengthening the stability of the church and to opposing spiritualist trends.

Van den Corput's organizational talent revealed itself in his role in the meetings of the consistory, the Classis Dordrecht, the provincial synods (nine times), the national synod of Middelburg of 1581, and in his work as *deputatus synodi* (to handle the necessary affairs between two provincial synods) and *deputatus classis*. At almost every provincial synod van den Corput was appointed member of a committee to mediate a particular problem somewhere in the province.

The most serious difficulties arose as a result of the careful but persistent efforts of the leading churchmen to emphasize the Calvinist character of the church. In a painful process several ministers who opposed this development were removed. Often this happened against the wishes of their flocks, who appreciated their sermons because they fitted in with spiritual trends. This is the framework in which van den Corput's efforts in the proceedings against Hermannus Herbertszoon in Dordrecht and Caspar Coolhaes in Leiden can best be understood.

Van den Corput was among the ministers who were decidedly Calvinist, if still moderate. His attitude in several committees appointed by the States of Holland, which tried to draw up a church order acceptable both to the church and the state, shows that he was amenable to a considerable measure of state influence in internal church affairs.

He translated the first explanation of the Heidelberg Catechism, written by his Dordrecht colleague Jeremias Bastingius, into Dutch in 1591. This rather free translation brought the work a wide readership among ministers, who used it for their weekly sermons on the catechism, as well as among the laity.

BIBLIOGRAPHY

Itterzon, Gerrit P. van. "Corput, Hendrik van den." In *Biografisch lexicon voor de geschiedenis van het Nederlandse protestantisme*, vol. 3, pp. 83–85. Kampen, Netherlands, 1988. Excellent biographical dictionary with full bibliography.
Tukker, C. A. *De Classis Dordrecht van 1573 tot 1609.* Leiden, 1965.

CORNELIS AUGUSTIJN

CORRO, Antonio del

CORRO, Antonio del (Lat., Corranus; Fr., Antoine de Bellerive; 1527–1591), converted Spanish monk and priest, moderate Calvinist minister. Corro, the nephew of an Inquisitor, was born in 1527, probably in Seville in southern Spain. He was presumably educated at the University of Seville, was ordained, and entered the Observant Hieronymite monastery of San Isidro, into which he introduced evangelical literature. When the Inquisition became aware of Protestants in the city, he fled to Geneva with a dozen monastic companions and received a scholarship from the rulers of Bern to study theology in Lausanne under Théodore de Bèze. He served rather erratically as a pastor in Béarn and Navarre in southwestern France. For a time he was a tutor to the future king Henry IV of France. After trying to attract his friend Casiodoro de Reina from England, he went to Orléans to accompany him to Bergerac. Forbidden as foreigners to remain in the area, in 1565 both were taken by Renée of France to Montargis near Paris, where Corro became her domestic chaplain with Juan Pérez de Pineda. Called in 1566 to a pastorate in Antwerp, he arrived just before foreigners were forbidden to minister there. He had time to publish *Epistre aux pasteurs de l'église flamengue d'Anvers de la Confession d'Augsbourg* (1567), which although ostensibly irenic in intention, succeeded in embittering relations between Lutherans and Calvinists in the city and jeopardized William of Orange's policies; and *Lettre envoyée à la Majesté du roy des Espaignes* (1567), pleading for religious tolerance and denouncing Roman Catholic practices. It can also be argued that he wrote the pseudonymous *Sanctae Inquistionis Hispanicae artes detectae* (1567), by Reginaldus Gonsalvius Montanus, which, with Corro's Antwerp publications, was a major instrument in the creation of the Black Legend.

Arriving in London in 1567, he attempted to revive the pastorless Spanish Protestant congregation; he was unsuccessful, however, largely because his liberal, irenic views caused continual conflict with the pastors of the strangers's churches, increasingly so after his *Tableau de l'oeuvre de Dieu* (1569), which, they said, attacked the doctrines of election and reprobation and undermined orthodox Christology by denying the humanity of Christ. His basically undogmatic Christianity is summed up in a statement attributed to him: if you are a Jew, a Turk, or a Christian, do good and you will be saved. He exacerbated his relations with the strangers's churches by publishing his *Letter to the Antwerp Pastors* and two revised, expanded editions of the *Tableau*. In 1571, after arbitration, Corro signed a repudiation of the views of the Anabaptists and papists, as well as of Michael Servetus, Andreas Osiander, Kaspar von Schwenckfeld, and others. This was a prelude to his entry into the Church of England, although he never quite lost his opposition to predestination, nor his doubts about christological doctrines.

In 1571, sponsored by William Cecil and Robert Dudley, earl of Leicester, Corro was appointed reader in divinity with the task of extirpating "popery" from the Inner and Middle Temples (London law schools). There his learning and eloquence were admired, and he published his lectures on *Romans* (Latin, 1574; English, 1575). Bèze named Corro in the 1575 edition of his letters, and accusations of Arianism increased. In 1577 his *Letter to Philip II* appeared in English, as did a second edition of his *Letter to the Antwerp Pastors*.

In 1577 he began teaching theology at Christ Church, Oxford, and in other colleges. He published a *Sapientissimi Regis Salomonis Concio* (Latin, 1579; "Commentary on Ecclesiastes," English, 1586), which was highly regarded and used for over a century. He frequently visited the Frenchman Peter Baro, Cambridge professor of divinity. He influenced Jean Hotman's views on interconfessional reconciliation. He received prebends in Saint Paul's Cathedral, London

(1581), and in Lichfield Cathedral (1585). He retired from Oxford in 1587, dying in London in 1591. His work was taken up and used by the Dutch Remonstrants.

BIBLIOGRAPHY

Boehmer, E. "Antonio del Corro," In *Bibliotheca Wiffeniana: Spanish Reformers of Two Centuries,* vol. 3, pp. 3–146. London, 1904.
Kinder, A. Gordon. "Antonio del Corro." In *Bibliotheca Dissidentium,* edited by André Séguenny, vol. 7, pp. 70–176. Baden-Baden, 1986.
McFadden, W. "Life and Works of Antonio del Corro, 1527–1591." Ph.D. diss., Queen's University, Belfast, 1953. Indispensable.

A. GORDON KINDER

CORVINUS, Antonius (1501–1553), north German theologian and church administrator. Although educated in the humanist tradition (at Leipzig), Corvinus was expelled from the Cistercian abbey at Riddagshausen for alleged "Lutheran" sympathies. He assisted the reform movement in Goslar and served as its delegate to Wittenberg (1529). This first encounter with Martin Luther and Philipp Melanchthon prompted Corvinus to withdraw from the humanist circle of Desiderius Erasmus. He attacked Erasmus's conciliatory posture toward Rome and subsequently vigorously opposed the reform efforts of Pope Paul III.

Corvinus dedicated the majority of his professional life to the practical administration of the new evangelical (Lutheran) church. He paid special attention to preaching and composed numerous expository *postillae*. He followed his first *Postilla* on the Gospels (1535; prefaced by Luther) with writings on the Epistles, *Psalms,* and *Genesis*. These widely disseminated sermon aids appeared in several low German dialects, as well as in Danish, Polish, and English, and contributed greatly to the early success of the evangelical movement in these regions.

Both city councils and territorial rulers esteemed the organizational abilities of Corvinus. From his parish in Witzenhausen, Hesse (1529–1542), he served Landgrave Philipp of Hesse by leading a disputation against the imprisoned Anabaptists in Münster, by participating in the adoption of the Schmalkald Articles (1537), and as a delegate to the Regensburg Colloquy (1541).

Corvinus was directly responsible for several influential north German church orders. He composed orders for the territorial city of Northeim (1539), the Braunschweig duchies of Calenberg (1542) and Wolfenbüttel (1543), and the episcopal city of Hildesheim (1544, with Johannes Bugenhagen). While serving princes in their organizational efforts, he advocated church autonomy and even sought to develop new patterns for church discipline independent of the territorial sovereign. Consequently, he opposed the policies of his own prince, Duke Erich of Braunschweig, and was imprisoned (1549). Although Corvinus died shortly after his release, he had already established the initial framework for the new church in northwestern Germany.

BIBLIOGRAPHY

Primary Sources

Sehling, Emil, et. al, eds. *Die Evangelischen Kirchenordnungen des XVI. Jahrhunderts.* Leipzig and Tübingen, 1902–. Vols. 6 and 7 contain church orders by Corvinus.
Tschakert, Paul. *Antonius Corvinus Leben und Schriften.* Quellen und Darstellungen zur Geschichte Niedersachsens, vol. 3. Hannover, 1900. Brief biography and samples of pastoral writings.

Secondary Sources

Bailey, Teresa. *From Piety to Politics, Elizabeth of Braunschweig and the Introduction of the Reformation in Braunschweig-Calenberg, 1540–1545.* Ph.D. diss., Stanford University, 1987. Details the organizational work of Corvinus during the regency of Duchess Elizabeth.
Uhlhorn, Gerhard. "Antonius Corvinus, ein Märtyrer des evangelisch-lutherischen Bekenntnisses." *Schriften des Vereins für Reformations-Geschichte* 9 (1892), 1–38. Thorough biographical account highlighting the tensions between reformer and sovereign.

JEFFREY P. JAYNES

COUNCIL OF TRENT. *See* Trent, Council of.

COUNTER-REFORMATION. *See* Catholic Reformation.

COUNTS' WAR. Conflicting Danish and Lübeckese ambitions, as well as a bitter dispute over the royal succession within Denmark itself, resulted in the Counts' War (*Grevefejden*) of 1534–1536. At the death of King Frederick I (r. 1523–1533), the succession to the throne of Denmark was uncertain. Frederick's eldest son, Duke Christian of Holstein, was Lutheran and therefore unpopular with the Danish nobility and clergy. Jurgen Wullenwewer, the ambitious and aggressive burgomaster of Lübeck, appeared before the Diet of Copenhagen (June 1533) to demand an alliance against the Habsburg Netherlands. He secretly offered his support to Duke Christian in attaining the throne of Denmark. Christian refused the offer, and the Danish council of state refused the alliance.

The war began when Lübeckese troops under the command of Count Christopher of Oldenburg invaded Holstein in May 1534. Christopher was a devout Lutheran who introduced the evangelical faith by force throughout Denmark; since Lutheranism had already had some impact, and since the peasants and burghers were in widespread, open rebellion against their noble landlords, Christopher was greeted as a liberator. Cities like Copenhagen and Malmö opened their gates willingly to the invaders. Christopher soon gained control of much of Jutland, Fyn, and Sjælland.

To save Denmark from rebellion and invasion, the Danish

clergy and nobility decided to sacrifice the Catholic faith, electing the Lutheran Duke Christian as King Christian III (r. 1534–1559). Christian, with the aid of his lieutenant Johann Rantzau, was able to turn the tide of the war. After arranging a temporary cease-fire with Lübeck (Stockelsdorf, December 1534), Christian sent Rantzau into Jutland, where he took Ålborg by storm; Rantzau defeated the armies of Christopher and Duke Albrecht of Mecklenburg at Øksnebjerg (June 1535), thereby controlling the island of Fyn; Norway fell immediately thereafter. Simultaneously, a Danish fleet under Peder Skram destroyed the Lübeckese fleet near Bornholm, allowing Rantzau to ferry his troops to Sjælland and invest Copenhagen. Lübeck sued for peace, recognizing Christian III as king in return for the restoration of its old commercial privileges (Hamburg, January 1536); Copenhagen, however, held out for an entire year, capitulating in July 1536.

The impact of the Counts' War, particularly within Denmark, was profound. Christian III's election and military victory allowed him not only to establish a Lutheran church, thereby consolidating the gains of the Reformation in Denmark, but also to reduce the power of the nobility significantly. For Lübeck, the defeat precipitated the collapse of the Wullenwever regime and ended the city's brief period of predominance in Scandinavian and Baltic affairs.

BIBLIOGRAPHY

Paludan-Müller, Caspar. *Grevens Fejde.* 2 vols. Copenhagen, 1853–1854. Still the only extensive treatment of the Counts' War in any language. It is unfortunate that nothing has come along to supersede this venerable work, not even in Danish. It has been reprinted recently by the Selskabet for Udgivelse af Kilder til dansk Historie, Copenhagen, 1971.

PAUL DOUGLAS LOCKHART

COURTS. [*This entry comprises two articles. The first discusses the types of church courts that developed within Protestant territories, their relationship to the secular government, and their practices, as well as the changes in the role and practices of church courts in Roman Catholic territories consequent to the Catholic Reformation; the second surveys the types of marriage courts established in Protestant areas, the types of cases they heard, and the sorts of family policy they established.*]

Church Courts

Never exclusively ecclesiastical, church courts both before and after the Reformation were an integral part of a broader legal system. Concerned primarily with religious, moral, and social behavior as well as tithes, church property and personnel, and wills and legacies, their principal task was both to protect the church and to enforce rules of conduct derived chiefly from canon law and in some instances from local customs. Ecclesiastical courts adjudged the validity of marriages, punished fornicators and adulterers, and dealt with the condition of church buildings, the proper administration of the sacraments, ministerial conduct, and lay attendance at church services. On the eve of the Reformation the ecclesiastical tribunals were hierarchically structured, extending upward from the archidiaconal courts; each diocese usually had two or more of these, and they in turn sometimes had subordinate bodies of their own. Above the archidiaconal courts were the consistories of the bishops, the archbishops' tribunals, and ultimately the papal curia. Appeals from archiepiscopal courts to the pope could be facilitated by the latter's appointment of judges delegate to hear cases and render verdicts, though the latter could be appealed to the curia. At the archidiaconal, episcopal, and archiepiscopal levels, officials undertook periodic visitations to perform the work of supervision and correction throughout their respective jurisdictions. Private parties, ecclesiastical judges, or lesser officials acting on behalf of third parties could initiate cases.

Because church courts intruded into so many areas of life, and because the tribunals were used to repress religious dissidents, complaints against them were legion. Many were directed against archdeacons and help explain why a common subject of debate in the schools was whether an archdeacon could be saved. Yet recent research demonstrates that the courts performed many worthwhile tasks, such as the probate of wills and the peaceful resolution of conflicts, and often enjoyed lay cooperation and support. States and territories that abolished the traditional courts in the context of their break with Rome transferred many of their functions to civil tribunals and established marriage courts. Yet these states and territories or the Protestant churches within them soon found it necessary to supplement the work of civil courts with consistories to supervise morality and to discipline the wayward. Even separatist congregations deemed it essential to monitor and, as necessary, punish the behavior of their members.

The repudiation of papal authority had profound implications for the ecclesiastical courts. Generally speaking, the states or territories that broke with Rome responded in one of three ways: by introducing consistories whose members were appointed by the secular authority, as in most Lutheran and some Reformed lands; by replacing the traditional church courts, in whole or in part, with essentially democratic bodies, as did many Reformed territories; or by placing traditional institutions under royal control, as was the case in England.

The consistorial system of church government in Lutheran lands grew out of the visitations conducted in electoral Saxony commencing in 1527 at the behest of Elector John. Following the third of these, in 1532, the visitors proposed the revival of a revised form of episcopal consistorial courts in which the prince, exercising *jus episcopale*, would appoint a permanent tribunal comprising clerics and lawyers to hear ecclesiastical cases, including especially those involving matrimony. This proposal eventually led to the creation of the Wittenberg Ecclesiastical Consistory by Elector John Frederick in 1539; when it achieved permanence three years later, comparable consistories were founded at Zeitz and Zwickau, all of them resting on secular authority. These consistorial courts, which employed revised principles of canon law and had the power of excommunication, dealt with offenses that ranged from unorthodox doctrine and irregularities in worship to adultery and other forms of immorality. Each consistory comprised two lawyers, two theologians, and assorted minor officials and had the task of conducting annual visitations. A number of other northern and central German princes established similar consistories concerned primarily with matrimony but sometimes involving administrative tasks, such as the examination of prospective ministers.

As it developed in Württemberg, the consistorial system (*Konsistorialverfassung*) differed from the Saxon consistories. As in electoral Saxony, the Württemberg consistory grew out of visitations, in this case those initially appointed by Duke Ulrich in connection with the new church order of 1536. But whereas the Saxon consistories were analogous to secular courts, the Württemberg consistory was similar to the duke's privy council, a primarily administrative body. At its institution by Duke Christoph in 1553, the Württemberg consistory was called the visitation council (*Visitationsrat*), and shortly thereafter the church council (*Kirchenrat*); only in 1590 was the clerical bench of the church council referred to as the consistory. The Württemberg consistory functioned generally as an administrative body, for example, by managing ecclesiastical property and income, but it could also serve as a court and exercise the power of excommunication. Owing largely to the work of Johannes Brenz, the Württemberg consistorial system spread to the Neuburg Palatinate (1553) and parts of the Rhenish Palatinate (1556–1558). Ulm and Reutlingen (1554), Baden-Durlach (1556), Oettingen, (1557), Braunschweig-Wolfenbüttel (1569), and Saxony and Brandenburg-Ansbach (1580) were among the cities and territories that followed suit. Despite its success in financial administration and ecclesiastical government, the Württemberg system was ineffective in disciplining morals because of dissension between clergy and laity.

Attempts to introduce a consistory in Strasbourg were controversial. Its magistrates had long been interested in reducing the power of church courts and treating the clergy like citizens, and the Reformation provided the occasion to eliminate such tribunals. The city itself enforced legislation governing morality and the sabbath but not with sufficient zeal to satisfy Protestant ministers (who became subject to secular courts when they took out citizenship). As early as 1533 churchwardens were empowered to monitor morality, but six years later the Council of XXI and the Senate found

it necessary to deal with obstinate persons who refused to heed the churchwardens' admonitions. When even this measure proved inadequate, the Church Assembly, a council of the clergy, began exercising a role in disciplinary cases, hoping to recover some of the jurisdiction once possessed by the episcopal and archidiaconal tribunals. But the lay magistrates were not inclined to surrender such authority, granting the Church Assembly (in the 1598 church ordinance) only the right publicly to shame miscreants summoned by the churchwardens. There would be no consistory in Strasbourg, where ministers were denied seats on the marriage court (1529) and the morals board (1548).

In Zurich the erosion of the authority of ecclesiastical courts had begun well before the Reformation as the city councils adjudicated matrimonial and spousal abuse cases that technically should have been referred to the diocesan court at Constance or, for appeals, to the archiepiscopal tribunal at Mainz. The marriage ordinance of May 1525 that Zwingli drafted and the Great Council approved was therefore not a radical departure from previous practice, though it established a special court, consisting of two beneficed clerics, two lay members of the Great Council, and two from the Small Council, to hear matrimonial cases. The mayor or his delegate sat with the court when it heard cases from other districts or cantons, and the court periodically called on knowledgeable persons to assist in its deliberations. Despite its name, the marriage court rapidly expanded its jurisdiction to include offenses dealing with lay morality (formerly handled by the episcopal court at Constance) and violations of sumptuary legislation (hitherto the province of the councils). The court had the power not only to punish prostitutes but also to close bordellos, and by 1526 it could excommunicate adulterers. A few of the responsibilities of the medieval church courts became the province of the (Reformed) synod, founded in 1528. Composed of all ministers in the canton and two lay representatives from each congregation, it adjudicated clerical offenses and reported on marital problems. Although never popular because of its oversight of domestic life, Zurich's matrimonial court became a model for similar institutions in St. Gall, Bern, Basel, Schaffhausen, and various German cities, and in part for the consistory in Geneva.

In Geneva on the eve of the Reformation the responsibility of supervising morality rested primarily with the city council. Aided by the "official," one of the bishop's officers, the council could punish morals infractions, though its verdict could be reviewed in the diocesan court. Disturbed, like others, with the moral tone of Geneva, Calvin persuaded the council to establish a consistory in 1541. Like its Lutheran namesakes, it included both clerical and lay members, but it differed in its size and selection. Its members included the ordained ministers in the city (initially five) as well as twelve lay elders chosen annually by the city's voters. In selecting candidates, the Small Council had to consult with the ministers, giving the latter an opportunity to influence the consistory's lay composition. One of the syndics (lay magistrates), though not Calvin except on rare occasions, presided at the consistory's weekly meetings. The range of cases handled by the consistory embraced immorality, blasphemy, recusancy, Catholic or superstitious practices, impiety, and occasionally heresy. Charged to "oversee the life of everyone, admonish amicably those whom they see to be erring or living a disordered life, and, where it is required, enjoin fraternal correction," the consistory had a limited range of punishments at its disposal, including admonition, exclusion from the Lord's Supper, and excommunication (a power formally secured in 1555 after considerable debate). The consistory could also turn an offender over to the Small Council, which could use torture and impose a range of punishments extending from public humiliation to execution. The council also had the right to overturn or mitigate the consistory's sentences. According to the Ordinances of 1541, which included provisions for the establishment of the consistory, the latter was not a court, though in practice it essentially functioned as one; in 1556, for instance, it won the right to compel witnesses to testify under oath.

As the Reformed movement spread, two types of polity were evident, distinguished in part by the means for selecting members of the consistory. The Calvinist churches of western Europe, the Lower Rhine, and East Friesland selected members of the consistory democratically, whereas in the Palatinate, Hesse-Kassel, and most of Wetterau, secular officials continued to appoint the consistory, as they had under Lutheranism. Nor did these consistories, unlike that in Geneva, have the power to excommunicate. In urban Calvinist communities on the Continent and in Scotland, presbyteries composed of popularly elected elders and pastors played an important role in supervising morality and as such functioned in a quasi-judicial capacity. They could censor inappropriate behavior, mediate family disputes, and castigate doctrinal deviancy, but their efforts to alter behavior depended largely on voluntary compliance.

Reformed consistories in France were initiated by a national synod at Paris in May 1559, with François Morel presiding and an emissary from Calvin present. Composed of the minister and elected lay elders of a congregation, a French consistory supervised members of a single church. Each consistory had the authority to choose ministers, and, in the event of misconduct, it could dismiss pastors, elders, or deacons. Convicted parties could appeal to a provincial council or a synodal committee. Like the consistories, the synods included both clerical and lay representatives. Although synods had the authority to launch visitations, each congregation had the option of barring visitors.

Reformed churches in the Netherlands also operated in an environment unlike that of Geneva. Whereas the consistory in the latter exercised jurisdiction over all inhabitants, the Dutch and Flemish consistories (which date from the

1560s) had no authority over Lutherans, Mennonites, or even those who attended Reformed services without becoming members, though at least some consistories were empowered to deal with Catholics and especially Anabaptists after the revolt against Spanish rule was underway. Like their Geneva counterpart, the Dutch consistories were notable in disciplining even wayward magistrates, as at Dordrecht in 1574 and Enkhuizen in 1578/79. To avoid losing members by hasty excommunication, consistories in the Netherlands were slow to ban and required the approval of the appropriate classis (presbytery) before imposing this penalty. The imposition of discipline by consistories created tension with civil magistrates, some of whom argued in the late sixteenth century that consistories were necessary only when the church was undergoing persecution, not when Christian magistrates governed. But the Calvinists held firm, and by the early seventeenth century magistrates joined the Reformed congregations in growing numbers and served in the consistories.

In Scotland the parliamentary act of August 1560 abrogating papal authority cast doubt on the legality of the ecclesiastical courts, though they functioned intermittently after that date. The reformers considered transferring consistorial jurisdiction to the newly created superintendents, each of whom would act in conjunction with the church session of the principal town of his diocese. Several such courts operated for a few years, using the procedure and terminology of the medieval tribunals. Other cases that would have been adjudicated in consistorial courts went to the civil Court of Session. In 1564 the Privy Council vested the old consistorial authority in newly created commissary courts, which adjudicated cases involving morality, oaths, defamation, teinds (tithes), and testaments. Matrimonial cases could be heard only by the commissary court in Edinburgh.

Lords of the Session appointed the commissaries until 1609, when the bishops obtained that right, retaining it until 1640 and exercising it again between 1662 and 1690. Appeals could be made from regional commissaries to that in Edinburgh, and from it to the Court of Session. A degree of continuity was maintained with the medieval ecclesiastical courts when many judges in the latter received comparable positions in the new courts. The principal procedural changes involved the introduction of the vernacular and measures to expedite cases involving contumacious parties. The fact that the orientation of the traditional courts had become strikingly secular by the 1540s, when most officials were lawyers first and priests second, facilitated the changes.

The system of church courts in the Reformed Church of Scotland took decades to develop. Church sessions, which originated in the 1550s and were analogous to Huguenot consistories, performed disciplinary functions, but the more remote churches did not have them until the seventeenth century. Whereas elders had been elected annually under the terms of the *First Book of Discipline* (1560/61), the *Second Book of Discipline* (1578) called for elders to serve for life, though not all were willing to do so. Especially while the *First Book of Discipline* was in effect, deacons participated (with elders) in the disciplinary work of the church sessions; the *Second Book*, not altogether successfully, sought to terminate this aspect of the deacons' activities, perhaps because deacons typically came from a lower social order than the elders.

Not until 1579 did the General Assembly of the church determine that "exercises"—meetings of ministers and elders from different districts to study scripture—were presbyteries. The following year the assembly devised a plan to create approximately fifty presbyteries involving some six hundred parishes. Plans to eliminate church sessions were cancelled, leaving the Church of Scotland with a four-tiered system of courts: church sessions, presbyteries, synods, and the General Assembly. The first formal presbyteries, at Edinburgh and Stirling, began operating in 1581. Many laymen were reluctant to serve on the presbyteries, typically leaving them in the hands of clerics. Commencing in the 1560s, the supervision of ministers and congregations was vested in superintendents, commissioners, and bishops; twice a year these officials convened a synod in each diocese, with an elder or deacon from each parish participating. The synods served as courts of appeal from church sessions and, after their founding, presbyteries. The General Assembly was the highest court of appeal and had the authority to try and to depose clergy, superintendents, and bishops.

After the creation of the commissary courts, the competency of the Scottish church tribunals to deal with marriage and divorce was disputed and eventually rejected, though ecclesiastical courts continued to advise commissaries and to deal with immorality, slander, and minor assault. They typically admonished, fined, or excommunicated offenders. As in Geneva and the Netherlands, the courts sometimes referred offenders to the civil magistrates for appropriate punishment.

England avoided the need to create new church courts by retaining the medieval ecclesiastical tribunals while terminating final recourse to the papacy or its delegates by the Act in Restraint of Appeals (1533). Henceforth appeals from an archiepiscopal court went to the upper house of convocation if the case involved the Crown, or, commencing in 1534, to a specially appointed royal commission that came to be known as the High Court of Delegates. Although bishops and judges sometimes served as delegates along with ecclesiastical lawyers in the early years, in time the attorneys generally served alone. Each archbishop had a consistory court that handled both appeals and cases of first instance: the Court of Arches for Canterbury and the (archiepiscopal) Court of Chancery for York. Each archbishop also had a Court of Audience; originally intended as a rather informal tribunal in which the archbishop personally presided, by the late medieval period professional judges presided in the Courts of Audience and dealt with appeals. In addition, each archbishop had a Prerogative Court to handle testamentary cases involving property from more than one diocese. Below the archiepiscopal tribunals were the consistory courts of the bishops, the archdeacons' courts, and the courts of rural deans (necessary in sprawling, thinly populated archdeaconries). Courts of peculiars exercised jurisdiction in parishes exempt from episcopal jurisdiction.

The English also emphasized legal continuity by preserving canon law, though the Act for the Submission of the Clergy (1534) authorized the monarch to appoint a commission to determine, with royal approval, which canons would be retained, provided always that no canon could contravene the royal prerogative or the statutes and customs of the realm. Work on reforming the canon law began in Henry VIII's reign and was substantially completed by a commission appointed by Edward VI, though the result, published by John Foxe in 1571 as the *Reformatio legum ecclesiasticarum,* was never enacted by Parliament, probably because of opposition from Elizabeth I. English church courts used both canon law and statutes in their work, which now included the task of enforcing the religious changes initiated by the break with Rome. Although litigation in these courts declined between 1530 and 1570 because of the uncertainty occasioned by the break, it subsequently increased.

The roots of the Court of High Commission lie in the Act of Supremacy, passed by Parliament in 1534, which empowered the sovereign "from time to time to visit, repress, redress, reform, order, correct, restrain and amend" offenses and heresies. Henry VIII entrusted this authority to Thomas Cromwell as his vicegerent, but after Cromwell's fall in 1540 the crown issued commissions to bodies of bishops, civil attorneys, and laymen. In 1559 Parliament specifically authorized the Crown to exercise royal supremacy in the church by commission, and shortly thereafter the Court of High Commission for the province of York began functioning. So too, presumably, did a comparable commission in the province of Canterbury (whose authority extended throughout the country), though its early records have been lost. The history of the two courts was somewhat different. The influence of the northern commission, whose early importance derived from its role in checking the Catholic threat, declined after 1581, when Parliament empowered common law courts to try recusants. The High Commission in the southern province, which was concerned with both Protestant nonconformists and Catholic recusants, grew in significance during the Elizabethan period, especially after 1583 when John Whitgift became archbishop and used the court effectively in his campaign against Puritans.

The High Commissions could not adjudicate in cases involving property, including tithes, but their purview included virtually all other matters of a religious nature dealing with individuals. Although the commissions could not take cases on appeal from other courts, they periodically heard such cases as if the latter had never been pending or decided in other jurisdictions. The commissions could not impose capital punishment, but unlike the traditional church courts they could levy fines and imprison. Cases could be initiated by plaintiffs or on behalf of the commissioners, after which the accused was summoned and compelled to take the oath *ex officio*, promising to answer all questions concerning the allegations. Those who refused to take an oath that could compel self-incrimination faced incarceration for contempt of court. This aspect of the procedure, as well as the commissions' determination to punish religious dissent, made them unpopular in some circles, but many thought highly of the commissions because they could resolve disputes faster and with less expense than traditional ecclesiastical tribunals.

The Catholics opted to reform rather than to abolish the ecclesiastical courts. Pressure to reform them antedated the Protestant Reformation and was primarily the result of an inevitable conflict between the growing powers of state courts and clerical claims for exclusive judicial competency in all matters pertaining to the clergy (the *privilegium fori*). When church courts extended their reach to include all contracts confirmed by an oath and all matters involving sin (according to Pope Innocent III's decree *Novit*), their jurisdiction was pervasive. Secular authorities had introduced various expedients to restrict the activities of ecclesiastical courts, such as the demand of the French kings in the fourteenth century to have the final say in excommunication, or the use of writs of prohibition by secular courts in England to take jurisdiction of select cases in church courts (such as those involving real property or the right of presentation to benefices).

The Council of Trent introduced no major changes concerning the jurisdiction of diocesan courts, but it suppressed the unpopular archidiaconal tribunals. Essentially this decision marked the triumph of the bishops over the archdeacons in a centuries-old struggle that had seen the latter win the right to be the court of first instance for all but nobles and knights in many areas. When the bishops introduced "officials" to assist them with legal administration in the late twelfth century, the officials soon proved to be valuable in helping the bishops recover some of their lost juridical authority. The suppression of archidiaconal courts at Trent was the culmination of this campaign by the bishops as well as a manifestation of the council's commitment to strengthen the episcopate, administratively as well as morally. Henceforth the episcopal official exercised the bishop's juridical powers in the diocese, though that authority would decline in subsequent centuries in the face of the continued growth of state courts and the expansion of their jurisdiction. The council's decision to have the bishops conduct visitations every two years rather than triennially, as had often been the case, would have further increased the business of episcopal consistories, for the discovery of alleged offenses on visitations was tantamount to a formal accusation.

The Council of Trent also implemented measures designed to make the work of the church courts more efficient and effective. With the exception of matrimonial and criminal issues (which were reserved in the first instance for the bishops themselves to adjudicate) and matters pertaining to the papacy, all cases were to be handled initially by local ordinaries and resolved within two years; only after an initial verdict at this level could a case be appealed to a higher judge. Legates, nuncios, and ecclesiastical governors were barred from intervening in consistorial courts, even to proceed against wayward clerics, unless a bishop proved to be negligent. Other reforms expedited appeals and required appellants to bear a significant portion of the cost. The council's message was unmistakable: though in need of reform, the ecclesiastical courts performed a necessary function and must be preserved.

Because the primary concern of the Catholic states was the preservation and restoration of Catholic orthodoxy, they were more interested in using institutions of social control, including church tribunals, to obtain confessional uniformity than to police morality. This focus was in keeping with the spirit of a decree issued at Trent defining the "chief purpose" of visitations as the extirpation of heresy; "to guard good morals and to correct such as are evil" was subordinate in importance. To this end Bavarian secular and ecclesiastical officials, for instance, used commissions and visitations, giving the people the option of submission or exile. As in Protestant lands (except for the Separatist congregations), such activities marked the union of church discipline and state coercion.

[*See also* Law, *articles on* Canon Law *and* Roman Law.]

BIBLIOGRAPHY

Abray, Lorna Jane. *The People's Reformation: Magistrates, Clergy, and Commons in Strasbourg, 1500–1598.* Ithaca, N.Y., 1985. Discusses discipline and the work of the General Assembly.

Donaldson, Gordon. *Scottish Church History.* Edinburgh, 1985. Chapter 5, "The Church Courts," provides an excellent overview.

Duke, Alastair. *Reformation and Revolt in the Low Countries.* London, 1990. Contains substantive discussions of consistories, classes, and discipline.

Duncan, G. I. O. *The High Court of Delegates.* Holmes Beach, Fla., 1986. The history of England's highest appellate court for religious matters.

Estes, James Martin. *Christian Magistrate and State Church: The Reforming Career of Johannes Brenz.* Toronto, 1982. Particularly strong on the development and significance of the consistorial system in Württemberg.

Franz, Günther. *Die Kirchenleitung in Hohenlohe in den Jahrzehnten nach der Reformation: Visitation, Konsistorium, Kirchenzucht und die Festigung des landesherrlichen Kirchenregiments, 1556–1586.* Stuttgart, 1971. Analyzes the role of visitations and the consistory in maintaining church discipline in the Franconian district of Hohenlohe.

Helmholz, R. H. *Roman Canon Law in Reformation England.* Cambridge, 1990. Examines the history of the canon law and the church courts in the period 1485 to 1625, showing a decline in litigation during the Reformation years (1529–1570), followed by recovery in the ensuing decades.

Hofmann, Karl. "Die kirchenrechtliche Bedeutung des Konzils von Trient." In *Das Weltkonzil von Trient: Sein Werden und Wirken*, edited by Georg Schreiber, vol. 1, pp. 281–296. Freiburg, 1951. Discusses the reform decrees pertaining to the church courts, including the diocesan consistory.

Houlbrooke, Ralph. *Church Courts and the People During the English Reformation, 1520–1570*. Oxford, 1979. Discusses judicial procedure, matrimonial causes, testamentary issues, tithes disputes, and the role of the courts in maintaining religious uniformity.

Hsia, R. Po-Chia. *Social Discipline in the Reformation: Central Europe, 1550–1750*. London, 1992. Chapter 7, "The Moral Police," argues that the disciplinary institutions of the Lutheran, Reformed, and Catholic territories operated in essentially similar ways, using a combination of clerical and secular personnel to supervise moral conduct and enforce confessional conformity.

Ingram, Martin. *Church Courts, Sex and Marriage in England, 1570–1640*. Cambridge, 1990. Takes a positive view of the work of late Elizabethan and early Stuart church courts.

Kingdon, Robert M. "The Control of Morals in Calvin's Geneva." In *The Social History of the Reformation*, edited by Lawrence P. Buck and Jonathan W. Zophy, pp. 3–16. Columbus, Ohio, 1972. Discusses the work of the consistory in Geneva.

Köhler, Walter. *Zürcher Ehegericht und Genfer Konsistorium*, 2 vols. Leipzig, 1932, 1942. A classic account of discipline in Zurich (vol. 1) and Geneva (vol. 2).

Lander, Stephen. "Church Courts and the Reformation in the Diocese of Chichester, 1500–58." In *Continuity and Change: Personnel and Administration of the Church of England, 1500–1642*, edited by Rosemary O'Day and Felicity Heal, pp. 215–237. Leicester, 1976. Contrasts the effectiveness of the pre-Reformation consistory in the diocese of Chichester with its weakening after 1530.

Marchant, Ronald A. *The Church Under the Law: Justice, Administration and Discipline in the Diocese of York, 1560–1640*. Cambridge, 1969. Places the church courts of the diocese of York in their legal framework and the context of secular administration.

Monter, William. "The Consistory of Geneva, 1559–1569." *Bibliothèque d'Humanisme et Renaissance: Travaux et Documents* 38 (1976), 467–484.

Ollivant, Simon. *The Court of the Official in Pre-Reformation Scotland*. Publications of the Stair Society, vol. 34. Edinburgh, 1982.

Safley, Thomas Max. *Let No Man Put Asunder: The Control of Marriage in the German Southwest; A Comparative Study, 1550–1600*. Kirksville, Mo., 1984. Examines the legal process pertaining to marital issues in Constance, Freiburg, and Basel.

Wunderli, Richard M. *London Church Courts and Society on the Eve of the Reformation*. Cambridge, Mass., 1981. Illustrates the process of secularization as it affected the church courts in London, which saw commoners increasingly seek justice in secular courts in the four decades preceding the break with Rome.

RICHARD L. GREAVES

Marriage Courts

As they appeared during the Reformation, marriage courts were tribunals charged with the adjudication of marital disputes and related morals offenses. Therefore, they are distinguished from consistories, omnicompetent courts that addressed broader questions of moral and religious discipline.

Like consistories, however, marriage courts were staffed by a collegium of secular and religious officials and drew their inspiration both from theological considerations of the spiritual nature of human behavior and from legal concerns regarding civil jurisdiction. As such, marriage courts were a unique creation of the Reformation.

Religious reformers were particularly interested in the institution of marriage and wrote many pamphlets and sermons that recognized its importance for the propagation of order and piety. Civil magistrates shared these concerns and creating marriage courts and drafting marriage ordinances were among the first acts of their religious reform.

Nonetheless, the antecedents of these institutions predated the sixteenth century. Early modern governments incorporated marriage courts in their determination to extend their competence and to limit immunities within their jurisdictions. Marriage was traditionally recognized to be subject to canon law and ecclesiastical authority, especially as regarded the *substantia vinculi*, the bond between husband and wife, but canonists also recognized a civil competence in problems pertaining to conjugal property and morality. Beginning in the late fourteenth century, however, magistrates began to insist on their unique authority over marriage as part of their *ius commune*, reserving for their adjudication a growing number of disputes and creating specialized tribunals for the purpose.

In Zurich, for example, the city court exercised police authority over the property and morality of married couples. As early as 1366, an agreement between the city and the bishop of Constance confirmed the *privilegium fori*, the established division of legal competence in marital affairs between religious and secular authorities, suggesting the existence of questions and tensions in this regard. By 1496 the city council sought to restrict the appeal to the officials' court in Constance of marital disputes involving its subjects. In 1519, three years before appointing Zwingli as *Leutpriester* ("the people's priest"), the magistrates of Zurich violated the bishop's competence by granting a *divortium quoad thorum et mensam* ("a separation from bed and board"). The arrogation of diocesan legal competence in matters of marriage began well before the Reformation in Zurich.

The same course of events obtained in other cities. Civil authorities began to assume direct control over aspects of marriage and morality before the Reformation, avoiding or opposing the competence of Catholic church courts within their jurisdictions.

The marriage courts and marital laws that appeared in the 1520s not only incorporated local, judicial, and organizational traditions but also borrowed freely from one another. The marriage court of Zurich was the first of its kind, founded in 1525, and provided a model for nearly all those that followed. Magistrates in many Swiss and German cities borrowed directly from the ordinances of Zurich. For example, the authorities in Basel and Bern copied broad sections verbatim and referred to the magistrates and clergy of Zurich as experts in marital law. In fact, the constitution and competence of most marriage courts differed insubstantially from those of Zurich.

Marriage courts in the sixteenth century relied on collegia of judges to examine problems placed before them and to arrive at legal solutions. In Zurich a college of six judges, composed of two members of the city's clergy, two members of the Small Council, and two members of the Large Council presided over the twice-weekly meetings of the marriage court, on Mondays and Thursdays at 1:00 p.m. Other cities adopted the same basic constitution but utilized different arrays of councillors and clergymen and selected other times and dates. In this they followed a pattern long established for civic tribunals, where the judges were not professional jurists but public officials, appointed or otherwise selected to serve, who divided their time between the court and other duties. A chair, which rotated annually among the members, directed proceedings and read verdicts. The chair was assisted in his duties by a messenger and a secretary, thus completing the regular staff.

The procedures of a marriage court also followed a pattern common to most civic courts. The judges rarely initiated proceedings on behalf of the state or community, waiting instead for private parties to bring complaints or suits to their attention. They gathered evidence, heard all testimony, and examined witnesses. The entire process could extend over weeks or even months. When all testimony had been heard, the judges arrived at a verdict by majority vote, and their decision was read in public.

Two basic issues formed the bulk of litigation brought before the newly founded marriage courts: valid marital agreements and legal marital behavior. Some marriage courts gradually became omnicompetent like consistories. From 1526 the marriage court of Zurich extended its purview to such issues of nonmarital morality as gambling, cursing, and blasphemy. Injuries to personal honor and allegations of nonattendance at church were also prosecuted before this bench. In all marriage courts, however, disputed marital agreements constituted the overwhelming majority of all litigation; enforcing acceptable standards of behavior was a secondary concern that grew over time.

As for the validity of specific marriages, marriage courts assumed matters that had been reserved to the competence of church courts and changed them in the process. Consistent with Protestant and Reformed reliance on scriptural justification in all matters pertaining to religious life, they swept aside the complex array of canonical impediments to marriage and replaced them with the single impediment of consanguinity within the Levitical degrees. More important in the marriage courts was a new emphasis on publicity as a means of establishing acceptable and valid marriages. Or-

dinances drafted in the sixteenth century universally affirmed the necessity of parental consent for the valid marriage of minors. Also required were the presence of two witnesses, a public announcement from the chancel, and a consecration in church. Beyond divorce, these regulations may have been the most significant innovation attempted by marriage courts.

The range of legitimate marital behavior changed, too, under the scrutiny of marriage courts. Reformed tribunals rejected the Catholic practice of separations, which dissolved the communality between spouses but left the legal and spiritual relationship intact, in favor of a substantial divorce. Given specific grounds spouses could now divorce and remarry. Yet marriage courts hedged this potentially revolutionary innovation with so many limitations and safeguards that it exercised little influence until the eighteenth century. Most courts permitted only adultery and impotence as grounds for divorce; marriage would continue to be the only licit setting for human sexuality. Cases of abuse, abandonment, disease, or fraud, which had hitherto been causes for a separation from bed and board, were now left to the judges' discretion and rarely found their way into court. Furthermore, most ordinances allowed only the innocent or injured party to remarry after a divorce and then only after a waiting period of at least one year. As a result, marriage courts heard surprisingly few divorce cases, with the practical consequence that the range of tolerated behavior between spouses probably increased.

This situation must have worked to the immediate disadvantage of married women, all of whom were subject to their husbands' authority and many of whom were subject to their husbands' violence. They had recourse to fewer legal means to protect themselves. Despite this fact, the vast majority of plaintiffs were unmarried women, most of whom sued to enforce marital agreements. This is all that is known with certainty about the litigants before marriage courts, but it permits a noteworthy conclusion. Given the lack of legal personality that increasingly limited their public stature in the sixteenth century, women turned to the courts to secure the status and protection that only married life offered them. Early modern society assumed that all women required male governance and accordingly viewed unmarried women, and especially those not situated in a household, with increasing antagonism. By increasing the legal means to enforce marriage and decreasing the legal means to escape it, marriage courts must have amplified the already considerable patriarchal quality of marriage.

Marriage courts did not work a sea change in married life. Legal and social conservatism curbed their reforming impulses. By introducing publicity and divorce, innovations that would eventually have broad consequences, these new tribunals did little more than place a centuries-old tradition of marital litigation in secular hands.

[*See also* Family; Marriage; *and* Women.]

BIBLIOGRAPHY

Helmholz, R. H. *Marriage Litigation in Medieval England.* Cambridge, 1974. A concise discussion of Catholic marriage law and courts in England.

Houlbrooke, Ralph A. *Church Courts and the People during the Reformation, 1520–1570.* Oxford, 1979. A study of litigation before ecclesiastical courts in England that assesses the social consequences of the Reformation.

Ingram, Martin. *The Church Courts, Sex, and Marriage in England, 1570–1640.* Cambridge, 1987. Extends the analysis undertaken by Houlbrooke into the Stuart period to the beginning of the English Civil War.

Kingdon, Robert M. "The Control of Morals in Calvin's Geneva." In *The Social History of the Reformation*, edited by Lawrence P. Buck and Jonathan Zophy. Columbus, Ohio, 1972. A first attempt to examine the workings of the Genevan consistory and the early creation of Calvinism.

Köhler, Walther. *Zürcher Ehegericht und Genfer Konsistorium.* Leipzig, 1932–1942. The classic study of marriage courts and consistories throughout continental Europe during the Reformation.

Safley, Thomas Max. *Let No Man Put Asunder: The Control of Marriage in the German Southwest; A Comparative Study, 1550–1600.* Kirksville, Mo., 1984. Concise study of marital litigation in ecclesiastical and secular courts and the impact of Reformed legislation on marriage and the family.

Stone, Lawrence. *Road to Divorce: England, 1530–1987.* Oxford, 1990. Monumental study of divorce in England from its introduction to the present that offers an excellent assessment of marriage courts and law.

Watt, Jeffrey R. *The Making of Modern Marriage: Matrimonial Control and the Rise of Sentiment in Neuchâtel.* Ithaca, N.Y., 1992. Study of marriage courts and litigation in Neuchâtel offers conclusions on the long-term effects of Reformation marriage courts on marriage and the family.

THOMAS MAX SAFLEY

COVENANT. For the major reformers of the early sixteenth century, the use of the term *covenant* was a commonplace—as it had been in the Middle Ages—used to preach the promise of salvation through grace found in the Gospels that had replaced the condemnation of the law, though not its obligations. These obligations are important in the covenant theology of Heinrich Bullinger as is clear from his exposition on the eternal covenant (*De Testamento seu Foedere Dei unico et aeterno*, 1534) or from Melanchthon's insistence against the antinomians on the necessity of the "new" obedience. But these reformers saw God less as the one who "fettered" (from Hebrew *bĕrîth*, "bond"; e.g., *Jer.* 11:10ff., 32:31–40) his chosen than as the one who bound himself freely or as the testator who "bequeathed" (from the Greek *diathēkē*, "testament"; e.g., *Heb.* 7:22, 8:6, 9:16ff.) eternal life and who sent the Holy Spirit, who helped the believer do the spiritual works of the law.

Both *bĕrîth* and *diathēkē* are basic elements of the Christian concept of *covenant.* Many of the reformers of the late sixteenth century developed a systematic covenant theology in which the Old Testament "covenant of [the] works [of the law]" was a major component.

The distinction between law and gospel is an essential aspect of Luther's theology. The German word for "gospel" or "good news" is *Evangelium*, which is derived from a Greek word related to another Greek term meaning "promise". The association of these two concepts is central to the thought of Luther's associate Melanchthon, whose theology, although usually passed over by covenant students, has been called a "theology of the promise" by Ernst Bizer. Melanchthon wrote: "For the word 'testament' the Hebrew language uses this word, 'covenant,' or 'promise,' or 'obligation' and the Old Testament, or the Old Covenant, properly speaking, is the promise in accordance with which God gave a certain country to the stem of Israel. . . . [to be the setting of] the divine promises of the Savior Christ" (*Melanchthon on Christian Doctrine: Loci communes 1555*, edited and translated by Clyde L. Manschreck, New York, 1965, p. 192). The term "God's covenant" carries with it the notion of a "chosen people," which to the reformers meant the church, to whom this covenant, or promise of salvation, is given. This was not an arcane idea in a Latin treatise for theologians but a consolatory message in Melanchthon's most famous handbook for the laity. Similar definitions of covenant and its synonyms were given in most treatises on the subject, for example by Bullinger and Ursinus.

The word *covenant* (*bĕrîth*) and its New Testament synonyms *promise*, even "promise of the covenant," and *testament* occur frequently in the Bible. In the second century Irenaeus gave an early treatment of covenantal theology in a work that Erasmus edited again in the early sixteenth century. The Old Testament sometimes also refers to a treaty between relative equals (*Gn.* 26:29ff., 31:43ff.), one of whose purposes was the maintenance of peace (*Jer.* 16:5; *Is.* 54:10ff.), and this concept is important in the ideas justifying political resistance developed by Protestants. But for the reformers God's (self-)binding covenant, for example, the covenant made with Abraham (*Gn.* 15, 17, and especially 22:16ff.), becomes in the New Testament the promise given to Abraham (*Gal.* 3:14; *Heb.* 6:13). Similarly Melanchthon used *Isaiah* 51:16, where God reaffirms Israel as his chosen people, as one of the promises of Christ becoming man "so that we know that there is an eternal covenant between him and us" (in *Philippi Melanchthonis Opera*, edited by Karl G. Brettschneider, p. 847. *Corpus Reformatorum* [hereafter *CR*], vol. 11. Halle, 1834ff.).

Medieval scholars, whose preparatory education in Latin included collecting lists of synonyms and antonyms as well as examples to be used in arguments, also seized upon *sponsum*, from *spondeo* ("to pledge, to give a pledge, to contract for a marriage") as a synonym for "God's promise." This language introduced the marriage metaphor of bridegroom (*sponsus*, Jesus) and bride (*sponsa*, Church). The old Germanic words *Ee* or *ewe* ("law" and "contract," a word that looks similar to *Ehe*, "marriage") as well as the French word *alliance* ("treaty," "betrothal") carry most of the biblical meanings. *Alliance* also means "engagement ring," a covenantal token. The ring became the "ring of faith," a phrase that goes back to Wessel Gansfort (physician of the bishop of Utrecht) in the fifteenth century, to the poet Walther of Châtillon in the twelfth century, and to Isidore of Seville in the seventh century. Isidore develops the metaphor in an exposition on *Genesis* 38, where Judah gave his (seal) ring to Tamar, the ancestress of Christ as a pledge.

In an exposition on the marriage at Cana (*Jn.* 2) Melanchthon explains Christ's presence there as signifying "that he is the bridegroom who begins the covenant with our [human] nature and who binds himself to the church, who sanctifies and liberates it and gives it eternal life" (*CR*, vol. 24, pp. 286–287). Melanchthon returns to this idea in an exposition on the promise of the Holy Spirit (*Jn.* 16): "Whom St. Paul has called a token of our inheritance. . . when the Holy Spirit descends eternal life begins. . . . The Holy Spirit is the token of grace, as the bridegroom gives the bride a ring. . . . Among the Greeks *sponde* means *libation* and *covenant* [*foedus*] because one made covenants with libations" (*CR*, vol. 24, p. 821). These expositions too were not learned theology but more or less spontaneous ramblings in his Sunday morning sermons for foreign students, most of whom he refers to as "adolescents."

The church as the "bride of Christ" was also a commonplace in art and literature, for example, in connection with the mystical marriage of Christ with the church in the person of the Virgin Mary, or of Saint Catherine of Alexandria or Saint Agnes. The Philadelphia Museum of Art (Johnson Collection) has a small, anonymous painting from about 1420 showing the Madonna and Child surrounded by representatives of the church, including Catherine and Agnes, his legendary brides. But the infant holds a ring in one hand and reaches over with the other to Mary Magdalene. Perhaps the most complete example of this theme can be found in the Memlinc triptych (1476) in the Hospital of Saint John in Brugges. It is based on *John* 3:29, where John the Baptist says, "He who has the bride is the bridegroom." The right wing of the triptych depicts the life of the Baptist. On the center panel the Madonna and Child are surrounded by several of his brides. The infant Christ places the ring on Catherine's finger, while the Baptist, who stands behind her with his attribute, the lamb, points at the ring. John the Evangelist stands on the other side. The left panel shows the apostle John on Patmos. Above him is his vision of the book on the throne that can be opened only by the lamb who had been slaughtered (*Rv.* 5). On the reverse of this panel stands Saint Agnes, patroness of one of the donors. The saint holds between her fingers a ring from which a chain, as if it is a leash, descends to her attribute, the lamb. This chain is still more clearly visible in an anonymous painting done at about the same time in Utrecht or surroundings (Museum St. Ca-

tharijnenconvent, Utrecht). Here the infant places the ring on the finger of Saint Agnes and the chain links the ring with her lamb that lies on a table, an obvious reference to the lamb of God that was led to the slaughter (*Is.* 53:7; *Acts* 8:32). This anonymous painter and writers like Wessel Gansfort (who promoted the veneration of Saint Agnes) anticipated Melanchthon's reflections on the marriage of Cana cited earlier.

Such applications in art and mystic writings of the covenant idea and its consolatory consequences made it more accessible to the devout than the debates among late medieval professors. In fact, these applications seem to respond to Robert Holkot's admonition that one ought to speak of the questions that arose in the context of covenant theology "with greater piety than logic" ("*magis pie quam logice*," in his *Super libros sapientiae*, lect. 145b).

Among the important questions raised was whether God, once he freely bound himself to effect the salvation of believers, was then obligated to do so, a question that was part of the debate on grace and justification. In this debate a further question was whether the sinner could cooperate in that salvation, that is, through being disposed to receive God's grace. This was summed up as "doing what one has in oneself" (*facere quod in se est*). The substitution of *pactum* ("contract") for *foedus* ("covenant"), with its implications of mutual obligations, obscured the self-binding of God and evoked the specter of salvation through good works. But even this ability to do what one can is made possible by the God who bound himself to save those who use this gracious gift.

The scholastic debate remains important. For example, whatever affinity Luther felt with Wessel Gansfort or Gabriel Biel, he was by training familiar with academic scholasticism (see, for example, Bengt Hägglund, *Theologie und Philosophie bei Luther und in der occamistischen Tradition*, Lund, 1955).

Most modern scholarship on the covenant in Christian theology has been teleological because it is primarily concerned with finding the roots of the system of "federal theology" (from the Latin *foedus*, "covenant") developed at the end of the sixteenth century and perfected by Johannes Koch (Cocceus, 1603–1669), the Dutch Reformed professor of theology at Leiden. Following the by then commonplace Protestant doctrine of justification by grace, in his *Summa doctrina de foedere et testamento Dei* (The Doctrine of God's Covenant; 1648) Koch based his system of salvation history on the repeatedly renewed covenant, standard examples of which are the promise to Adam and Eve that the seed of the woman would tread on the snake; the institution of the rainbow as a sign of the promise made to Noah after the Flood; the promise made to Abraham; the Sinaitic covenant; and the renewal announced in *Jeremiah* 31. These instances were so widely used by mystics and theologians alike that Koch could have encountered them anywhere. But as he received his early education in Bremen, his birthplace, he may have found the ideas in Christopher Pezel's edition of the *Postillae Melanchthonianae* (*CR*, vol. 24) that were dedicated to the Dutch governors Maurits and William II van Nassau. There he could have found not only most of the instances but also his main idea of the frequent renewal of the covenant as God's gathering of his church in Melanchthon's remarks on the parable in *Matthew* 20:1–16: "This parable signifies [also] the numerous restitutions and instorations [renewals] of the church" (*CR*, vol. 24, p. 380). The parable compares the kingdom of heaven to a landowner who sends his workers to the vineyard. "Kingdom of heaven" is one of the metaphors for God's promise in covenant theology (e.g., Augustine) because it was this kingdom that was promised.

Modern students of federal theology like David Weir also distinguish a creation covenant established in paradise with the prohibition to eat from the Tree of Life. Both the expression *creation covenant* and the parallel expression *covenant of works* were not defined until the end of the sixteenth century. They are particularly Reformed contributions to covenant theology, attributed by Weir and others to Palatinate theologians of the late sixteenth century. As Michael McGiffert has usefully demonstrated ("From Moses to Adam: The Making of the Covenant of Works," *Sixteenth Century Journal* 19 [1989], 131–156), it has been difficult to trace the origin of the term "covenant of works" in the writings of the late sixteenth century, although he has apparently found it in the writings of such English divines as Dudley Fenner (1558–1587) and Thomas Cartwright (1535–1603) and their English as well as Continental contemporaries. One of these divines defined the "covenant of works" as "God will be our God, if we keep his commandments." Although the law was fulfilled by Christ, who has initiated the "covenant of grace" for the elect, the "covenant of works" remained in force for others, a distinction that reflects the double predestinarian thought of Calvinism. This phraseology differs somewhat from that expressed earlier by Melanchthon or later by Koch, for they stressed the promise of salvation as already implied in the covenantal statements of the Old Testament as well as the continued demand that the elect do the works of the law (which they can do because the Holy Spirit works in them).

All the writers cited by McGiffert appropriated ideas from the great reformers of the first generation, among whom Heinrich Bullinger's were most prominent and well known in England, though the works of Melanchthon should be added to the antecedents. Some of these work covenanters dealt with the possible misinterpretation of their insistence on doing the works of the law, namely, that obedience conferred merit. Their rejection of this "popish error" sounds similar to Melanchthon's defense of the doctrine that good works, or "the new obedience," are necessary for salvation but do not confer merit-earning justification.

But if medieval writers did not use the concept "covenant of works," the idea that the commands of the law must be done was common nevertheless. A fifteenth-century mystic writer like Hendrik Mande could write (see Gerard Visser, *Hendrik Mande*, The Hague, 1899, pp. 48 and 103) that obedience is made possible by "the Holy Spirit promised by God," for the law (*die ewe*) of God is in the heart of the believer (*Is*. 51:16). Mande's contemporary, the much better known Thomas à Kempis, wrote that grace was the gift of God, "the seal of His Chosen and the pledge of salvation," without which one can achieve nothing nor carry out any good work (*Imitatio Christi*, edited by Leo Sherley-Price, Hammondsworth, England, 1952, pp. 133 and 171). Wessel Gansfort wrote several decades later that because one (unlike Christ in *Eph*. 5) "cannot make something clean [the bride of *Eph*. 5 and of *Sg*. 4] out of the unclean," even God's commands are promises, for only God through his Son secures their fulfillment (*De Incarnatione* in *Opera*, Groningen, 1614). This standard imagery survived the Reformation, in part because of its use by Luther and Melanchthon. When the Dutch Calvinist pastors met in a national synod (Middelburg, 1581), they wrote in the preface to the *Acta* that God elected out of the human race a people as his church on which he bestowed freely, "as on the immaculate bride of his son Jesus Christ, unmerited eternal salvation."

The covenantal texts cited by Koch and his predecessors were already much used by medieval exegetes. Their typology of "foreshadowing events" traditionally divided salvation history into three periods: before the law (before Moses received the Ten Commandments or Sinaitic covenant), under the law, and under grace (initiated by the sacrifice of Christ but to be completed in his second coming). This tripartite typology determined the decorations on the well-known Klosterneuburg altar by Nicholas of Verdun of the late twelfth century. It was repeated later in the so-called *Biblia Pauperum* of the fifteenth century.

Luther's law and gospel concept, or Irenaeus's old and new covenant, were traditionally represented in crucifixion scenes by a synagogue and a church. In such scenes a woman representing the church stands on the right side of the cross and often receives the blood of Christ's wounds in a chalice. The synagogue, at the left side, has her head bent and turned away. Typical examples can be seen in the former altar front by Benedetto Antelami in Parma Cathedral and on the left tympanum of the abbey church of Saint Giles in Nîmes, both of the late twelfth century. In Luther's own day the theme was frequently taken up again by Lucas Cranach the Elder and others in paintings that show the Fall and the Decalogue on the right side and the resurrected Christ on the left.

The covenant as theological commonplace was given still greater currency through the use of the covenant concept in treatises on politics and ethics. For example, Melanchthon wrote in *Philosophia Moralis Epitome* (1546) that among friends "some covenant" must exist, as among two spouses, neither of whom can tyrannically oppress the other (*CR,* vol. 16, p. 159).

The political usage of the covenant idea accorded with the medieval feudal contract and with much of sixteenth-century application of contract law to political theory as developed during the religious wars, for example, the monarchomach (antimonarchist) literature summed up in the *Vindication Against Tyrants* (1579); it is also reflected in the Scottish National Covenant (1637), whose framers are known as "Covenanters." (It is perhaps ironic that in the Netherlands Anabaptists, derided by most theologians, sometimes also called themselves "Covenanters.") Political contracts between a people and the ruler are subject to the one imposed by God, to whom one owes obedience before anyone else. The apparent legal equality of the covenanting parties was most real only in their equality before God: kings too must obey him.

The political appropriation of covenant by "rebels" with a reformed persuasion was facilitated perhaps by theologians like Bullinger, who had explained God's covenant in terms of existing political structures (*The Decades of Henry Bullinger,* edited by Thomas Harding, vol. 5, pp. 231ff., Cambridge, 1848). But Bullinger had already stated that magistracies are subject to God and must make their own laws in conformity with God's law (*Decades,* vol. 3, p. 280 and elsewhere).

The formulation of a systematic Protestant covenant theology, of which the covenant of works became an integral part, probably began in the late sixteenth century as a response to the need to reorder the Christian polity. This polity was to be organized according to the precepts of the reformed or evangelical religion. Canon law was rejected as suspect, and civil law was to be brought into harmony with God's law. In this context it remains interesting that covenantal theology was worked out by English Calvinist theologians who often wrote in the Low Countries and who, with some of their Dutch colleagues, struggled in their polemics against their respective governments that preferred an Erastian arrangement of the ecclesiastical establishment.

The Anabaptists saw baptism as the symbol of one's personal covenant with God to live a holy life of obedience. In fact, the term *Bondgenooten* ("covenanters") was much used in northwest Germany and the Low Countries. The origin of such Anabaptist usage undoubtedly lies with Thomas Müntzer, who, in the early years of the Reformation, used the term extensively, calling for a *Bund* ("covenant") of the truly committed Christian.

BIBLIOGRAPHY

Bacq, Philippe. *De l'ancienne à la nouvelle alliance selon S. Irénée.* Paris, 1978. Introduction provides illuminating insight into the context of the polemical uses made of covenant theology in the early church, much of which recurred in the sixteenth century.

Bierma, Lyle Dean. *The Covenant Theology of Caspar Olevian.* Ph. D. diss., Duke University, 1980. Important study of one of the earlier systematic expositions of covenant theology in the Palatinate by the possible coauthor of the Heidelberg Catechism.

Greschat, Martin. "Der Bundesgedanke in der Theologie des späten Mittelalters." *Zeitschrift für Kirchengeschichte* 81 (1970), 44–63. Useful treatment of covenant ideas in the century before the Reformation.

Hamm, Berndt. *Promissio, Pactum, Ordinatio: Freiheit und Selbstbinding Gottes in der scholastischen Gnadenlehre.* Tübingen, 1977. Important study of thirteenth- and fourteenth-century ideas of the covenant as God's voluntary commitment to save his chosen people (the church).

Johnston, Charles F. "Covenant and Kingdom of God in Augustine." In *A Covenant Challenge to Our Broken World,* edited by Allen O. Miller, pp. 98–114. Atlanta, 1982. Interesting essay that incidentally suggests antecedents for Bullinger's concept of the covenant as basis for the Christian polity.

Klassen, William. *Covenant and Community: The Life, Writings and Hermeneutic of Pilgram Marpeck.* Grand Rapids, Mich., 1968. Shows the importance of the covenental theme to the Anabaptist Pilgram Marpeck.

Klooster, Fred H. "Covenant, Church and Kingdom of God in the New Testament." In *A Covenant Challenge to Our Broken World,* edited by Allen O. Miller, pp. 84–94. Atlanta, 1982. Refreshing approach that must be read before Johnston.

McCarthy, Dennis J. *Treaty and Covenant.* Rev. ed. Rome, 1981. Completely rewritten edition, a useful survey of the origin of the terms and their use in ancient Near Eastern texts.

McCoy, Charles S., and J. Wayne Baker. *Fountainhead of Federalism: Heinrich Bullinger and the Covenantal Tradition.* Louisville, Ky., 1991. Meritorious work by longtime covenant scholars.

McGiffert, Michael. "Grace and Works." *Harvard Theological Review* 75 (1982), 463–502. One of the best treatments of the development of the "covenant of works" in the late sixteenth and early seventeenth century; especially helpful for its use of sources.

Preus, James S. *From Shadow to Promise: Old Testamental Interpretation from Augustine to Young Luther.* Cambridge, Mass., 1969. Useful as a survey of the typology of salvation history in which God's covenant is central.

Schiller, Gertrud. *Ikonographie der Christlichen Kunst.* 5 vols. Gütersloh, 1966–. *Der Kirche,* vol. 4, is relevant. General introductions helpful, with descriptions of many representative works reproduced in black and white.

Steele, Margaret. "The 'Politick Christian': The Theological Background to the National Covenant." In *The Scottish National Covenant in its British Context,* edited by John Morill, pp. 31–67. Edinburgh, 1990. Fine discussion of the subject, but errs on the sixteenth-century antecedents of continental covenant theology (see McGiffert citation).

Visser, Derk. "The Covenant in Zacharias Ursinus." *Sixteenth Century Journal* 18 (1987), 531–544. Analyzes the explanation of the term and the use of the concept in Ursinus's writings, especially his *Expositiones* of the Heidelberg Catechism. Argues against attributing origins of the "covenant of works" doctrine to Ursinus.

Weir, David A. *The Origins of Federal Theology in Sixteenth Century Reformation Thought.* Oxford, 1990. Thorough survey of the roots of covenantal concepts. Useful bibliography.

DERK VISSER

COVERDALE, Miles

COVERDALE, Miles (1488–1568), zealous English Protestant, Bible translator, and bishop. Coverdale was exposed to Lutheran ideas during the 1520s while he served as an Austin friar. He joined a circle of Cambridge scholars who engaged in seminal discussion of religious reform at the White Horse tavern. They included outstanding members of the first generation of English Protestants such as William Tyndale, Thomas Cranmer, Hugh Latimer, and Robert Barnes. After leaving religious orders, Coverdale moved within Protestant circles on the Continent during most of the period between 1528 and 1535.

He prepared the first complete printed text of the English Bible, which was produced abroad at an unknown location, possibly Cologne, in 1535. This landmark publication coincided roughly with the 1534 appeal by the convocation of the Church of England for an authorized Bible translation. Although Coverdale's work was not authorized, his dedication to Henry VIII and a title-page portrait of the king disseminating the Bible imply the existence of official support for the volume.

Coverdale then received patronage from Thomas Cromwell, Henry VIII's vicegerent for religious affairs. Like other Protestant publicists, the translator worked under the auspices of the king's chief minister during the early stages of the English Reformation. On Cromwell's behalf, Coverdale went to Paris to supervise production of the officially sponsored Great Bible of 1539, a task that he completed in London after French authorities withdrew permission for continuation of the project. Passage of the punitive Act of Six Articles in 1539 and Cromwell's execution during the following year cut short Coverdale's English sojourn, and he returned to the Continent for the remainder of Henry's reign.

Upon his return from exile in March 1548, Coverdale gained entrée at the royal court under the auspices of Thomas Cranmer, archbishop of Canterbury, with whom he had associated at Cambridge. Appointments that he received as almoner to Henry VIII's widow, Catherine Parr, and as chaplain to Edward VI (r. 1547–53) were consistent with the radical phase of the English Reformation at that time. Coverdale contributed to the first *Book of Common Prayer* (1549) and preached against the Mass and Anabaptism. He edited the second volume of Erasmus' *Paraphrases* on the New Testament (1549) under the patronage of the duchesses of Somerset and Suffolk. Edward Seymour, duke of Somerset and one-time protector of the realm, called for the publication of Coverdale's translation of Otto Werdmueller's *Spiritual and Most Precious Pearl* (1550). Coverdale served as bishop of Exeter from 1551 until King Edward's death in 1553.

Deprived from episcopal office by the government of Mary Tudor, he again went to the Continent, where he contributed to the Geneva Bible of 1560. He returned to England some months before its publication, at the outset of Queen Elizabeth I's reign, but he was never restored to episcopal office. Coverdale's high standing among the Elizabethan Puritans may be attributed to his religious zeal, his many translations, his contribution to the Vestiarian Controversy of the 1560s, and his popularity as a preacher.

BIBLIOGRAPHY

Coverdale, Miles. *Writings and Translations*. Edited by George Pearson. Parker Society, vols. 13–14. Reprint, New York, 1968. Edition of Coverdale's writings.

Mozley, J. F. *Coverdale and His Bibles*. London, 1953. Still the basic study.

Watson, George, et al., eds. *The New Cambridge Bibliography of English Literature*. Vol. 1, cols. 1097–1098, 1814–1815, 1832–1833, 1897–1898. Cambridge, 1974. Contains lists of Coverdale's publications.

JOHN N. KING

COX, Richard (1500–1581), English reformer and bishop of Ely. Cox was one of the first generation of English intellectuals to respond to the Continental Reformation. In the 1520s he was expelled from the newly formed Cardinal College at Oxford for heretical views. Thereafter he pursued a career as headmaster of Eton and chaplain to the king with sufficient distinction to be selected as senior tutor to the young Prince Edward. Edward's commitment to advanced Protestantism seems to have owed much to his instruction. When the prince succeeded to the throne, Cox remained a close mentor, but he also received ecclesiastical promotion as dean of Christ Church (the former Cardinal College) and vice-chancellor of Oxford. At Oxford he assailed "Romish" practices with great vigor. His major doctrinal contribution was his work on the two prayer book commissions. At Mary's accession he was imprisoned, escaping to the Continent in 1554. There he became a leader of the English congregation at Frankfurt and played a key role in defending the use of the Edwardian *Book of Common Prayer* against the more Genevan form of service espoused by John Knox and William Whittingham. His protection of the English liturgy, as well as his past services to the Crown, earned him the senior bishopric of Ely after Elizabeth's succession.

In the first years after the Elizabethan Settlement, Cox was one of a small coterie of bishops consulted on religious changes and ecclesiastical discipline. He often resided in London although he was also a conscientious diocesan, visiting his see in person and concerning himself with the instruction of the laity. By 1570, however, he was less active, and his last years were overshadowed by pessimistic fears for the security of the Elizabethan Settlement and by conflicts over the possession of his episcopal lands. The latter so depressed him that he planned to resign in 1580, though death intervened before a satisfactory agreement had been reached with the Crown. He was a gifted religious leader and administrator, with a passionate commitment to the royal supremacy and the English church, but was an aggressive controversialist who sometimes deserved Calvin's stinging observation that he had "an immoderate fervour for meddling."

BIBLIOGRAPHY

Haugaard, William P. *Elizabeth and the English Reformation.* Reprint, Cambridge, 1968.

Heal, Felicity. "The Tudors and Church Lands: Economic Problems of the Bishopric of Ely." *Economic History Review* 2d ser. 26.2 (1973), 198–217.

Knappen, M. M. *Tudor Puritanism.* Reprint, Chicago, 1966.

FELICITY HEAL

CRANACH, Lucas the Elder

CRANACH, Lucas the Elder (1472–1553), German painter, draftsman, engraver, and designer of woodcuts in Wittenberg. One of the pivotal figures in early sixteenth-century German art, Cranach the Elder was the Reformation artist *par excellence.* A close friend and follower of Martin Luther (they were godfathers to one another's children), Cranach collaborated with Luther in producing numerous single-sheet woodcuts and book illustrations that were crucial for the spread of the new evangelical theology in the early years of the Reformation in Germany. The "Passional Christi et Antichristi" (Wittenberg, 1521), for example, contrasts the holy life of Christ with the decadent life of the pope and the venal customs of the Curia Romana in thirteen antithetical pairs of woodcuts, with brief texts from the Bible and papal decretals composed by Philipp Melanchthon and Johann Schwertfeger. The epilogue was perhaps written by Luther himself. In 1529 Cranach created the quintessential new Reformation image, the "Allegory of Law and Grace," contrasting mankind's damnation under the law of Moses with his hope of salvation under the New Testament's offer of grace in Luther's interpretation. The allegory was typically produced both as a woodcut (London, British Museum) and as a panel painting (Gotha, Schloßmuseum) and was often copied. Portraits by Cranach and his son, Lucas the Younger, of Luther (Weimar, Schloßmuseum), Melanchthon (Frankfurt am Main, Städel), and the other reformers (Toledo Museum of Art), as well as the many copies and variants made from them by workshop assistants, have determined our perception of the reformers to the present day.

Cranach took his name from the town of his birth, Kronach, near Bamberg. He was probably trained by his father, the painter Hans Maler. By 1503 he was working among a circle of humanists at the University of Vienna. His earliest known works, created at this time, were characterized by a religious and spiritual intensity and an emphasis on man's relationship to nature and constituted the beginning of the stylistic movement known as the Danube School.

In 1504 Cranach was called to Wittenberg by Elector Frederick the Wise of Saxony. There he developed the smooth, linear style that became the standard form of ex-

pression of his large and productive workshop and that determined the appearance of painting in Saxony throughout the sixteenth century. Until his death Cranach served as court artist to Frederick the Wise and successors John the Steadfast and John Frederick the Magnanimous, decorating the elector's favorite residences, such as the Veste Coburg and Torgau castles, but no traces of his mural paintings survive. In addition to the many portraits of members of the Saxon nobility, produced as woodcuts or painted on panel, Cranach served their more private tastes with small paintings of a tantalizing, mildly erotic nature, showing nude Venuses or Lucretias. After 1508 he used a winged serpent as a signature on his own work and on the products of his workshop. In Wittenberg he was one of the two wealthiest citizens, the result of earnings not only from the workshop but also from the pharmacy, wine store, bookstore, and printer's shop he owned.

From 1519 to 1545 he served on the Wittenberg city council and was elected burgomaster on three occasions. After Charles V took John Frederick prisoner at the Battle of Mühlberg in 1547, Cranach followed him into exile at Augsburg and Innsbruck, and after the elector's release in 1552, he accompanied him to Weimar, where the artist died in 1553.

BIBLIOGRAPHY

Andersson, Christiane. "Religiöse Bilder Cranachs im Dienste der Reformation." In *Humanismus und Reformation als kulturelle Kräfte in der deutschen Geschichte: Ein Tagungsbericht,* edited by Lewis W. Spitz, pp. 43–79. Berlin, 1981. Summarizes Cranach's Reformation-inspired paintings and prints.

Friedländer, Max J., and Jakob Rosenberg. *The Paintings of Lucas Cranach.* Rev. ed. New York, 1978. Expanded but uncritical new version of the 1932 first edition.

Jahn, Johannes. *Lucas Cranach d.Ä., 1472–1553: Das gesamte graphische Werk mit Exempeln aus dem graphischen Werk Lucas Cranachs d.J. und der Cranachwerkstatt.* Munich, 1972. Lavishly illustrated source for Cranach's influential drawings, engravings, and woodcuts.

Koepplin, Dieter, and Tilman Falk. *Lukas Cranach. Gemälde, Zeichnungen, Druckgraphik: Ausstellung im Kunstmuseum Basel, 15. Juni-8. Dezember 1974.* Exhibition catalog, Kunstmuseum Basel. 2 vols. Basel, 1974–1976. Exhaustive, well-illustrated study of all aspects of Cranach's work, including the workshop and contemporaries.

Schade, Werner. *Cranach: A Family of Master Painters.* New York, 1980. Focuses on the family tradition, including the work of sons Lucas and Hans, who carried on the entrepreneurial workshop activity.

CHRISTIANE ANDERSSON

CRANACH, Lucas the Younger

CRANACH, Lucas the Younger (1515–1586), German painter, draftsman, and designer of woodcuts in Wittenberg. The only son of Lucas Cranach the Elder who lived to maturity and followed in his artistic footsteps, Lucas the Younger was one of the foremost portrait painters of the late Renaissance in Germany. This talent, inherited from his father, expressed itself in particular in portraits of the Wittenberg reformers and of members of the ruling families of Saxony and Anhalt, such as the powerful likeness of Elector Joachim II of Brandenburg (c.1555; Berlin, Jagdschloss Grunewald). Married to Barbara Brück, daughter of the Saxon chancellor Gregor Brück, Lucas played a role in the political events of his time, being elected to various municipal offices. He was burgomaster of Wittenberg from 1565 to 1568.

Having taken over his father's workshop after his departure from Wittenberg in 1550, Lucas continued the traditions of painting Reformation-inspired themes established by his father. The "Allegory of Law and Grace," for example, forms the central image of Lucas's monumental high altarpiece of 1555 in the Collegiate Church (Herderkirche), Weimar. The three huge panels include portraits of Martin Luther, Lucas Cranach the Elder, and Elector John Frederick with his family. Much less active than his father in the medium of woodcut, Lucas nonetheless created a number of memorable woodcut portraits of Luther, Philipp Melanchthon, and Saxon nobles. He developed several new image types in his paintings, some of them as epitaphs, such as the Baptism of Christ observed by members of the princely donor's family, an image preserved in the painting of 1556 in Berlin (Jagdschloß Grunewald). His "Last Supper" shows Luther and the other reformers in the guise of apostles in the large altarpiece of 1565 at Dessau-Mildensee. The servant pouring wine in the central image is a self-portrait of the artist. Lucas's paintings of the conversion of Saul emphasize the conversion experience so central to evangelical theology.

BIBLIOGRAPHY

Schade, Werner. *Cranach: A Family of Master Painters.* New York, 1980. The best source on the work of the Cranach sons, Lucas and Hans.

Zimmermann, Heinrich. "Beiträge zum Werk Lucas Cranachs des Jüngeren." *Zeitschrift des deutschen Vereins für Kunstwissenschaft* 7 (1953), 209–215.

CHRISTIANE ANDERSSON

CRANMER, Thomas (1489–1556), English reformer as well as archbishop of Canterbury from 1533 to 1556. Born at Aslockton (Nottinghamshire) to a minor gentry family, Cranmer went to Jesus College, Cambridge, in 1503, crowning his succession of university degrees with a doctorate of divinity in 1526. In 1515 or 1516 he relinquished his fellowship at Jesus College in order to marry, taking a lesser post as reader at Buckingham College, but his wife, Joan, soon died in childbirth. After this he regained the Jesus fellowship and was ordained priest by 1520 at the latest. There is no evidence that during the 1520s he was involved in the radical discussions over church reform taking place at the university, and his annotations in his copy of John Fisher's *Asser-*

tionis Lutheranae Confutatio (1523; British Library C.81.f.2) express disapproval of Luther's criticisms of the papacy. John Foxe, however, is probably reliable in his assertion that, as university examiner in divinity at this time, he was unusually conscientious in examining candidates in their biblical knowledge, indicating that Cranmer's was the orthodoxy of a moderate humanist with an enthusiasm for the biblical text.

His worthy but unspectacular academic career abruptly changed direction in the summer of 1529; Cranmer joined the team producing propaganda for Henry VIII's first "divorce," which was to clear the ground for a marriage to Anne Boleyn. In January 1530 he accompanied the embassy to Holy Roman Emperor Charles V and Pope Clement VII led by Anne's father, Sir Thomas Boleyn, earl of Wiltshire. He remained in Rome until September to act as grand penitentiary for England and then helped to collect favorable opinions for the divorce in Italy; probably while in Rome he was granted the benefice of Bredon (Worcestershire) by the absentee bishop of Worcester, Jerome Ghinucci. After his return in October 1530—by now closely associated with the Boleyn interest—his literary contributions to the royal cause included an English translation of the major tract arguing the King's case, *Gravissimae. . . Academiarum Censurae. . . .* From January 1532 and continuing for the rest of the year, Cranmer, by now archdeacon of Taunton, went on an embassy to Charles V. While at Nuremberg he was married to his second wife, Margaret, niece by marriage of the Lutheran theologian Andreas Osiander. This rejection of his clerical vow of celibacy was the first sign of his move toward reformist religious views.

Cranmer was recalled in late 1532 as the king's surprise choice to fill the vacant archbishopric of Canterbury; apparently reluctant to accept the honor, he delayed his return and was not provided to the see until 21 February 1533, being consecrated on 30 March. Although not informed of Henry and Anne's secret marriage in January 1533 until after the event, he was responsible for pronouncing the subsequent divorce from Catherine of Aragon, and he presided over Anne's coronation in May 1533. As archbishop he carried out his administrative and pastoral duties scrupulously; he endeavored loyally to conform to Henry's wishes, while doing his best to further the reformed cause if the king would allow it and promoting reformist clergy wherever he could. He granted two further royal divorces—from Anne Boleyn in 1536, and from Anne of Cleves (Henry's fourth wife) in 1540—and showed no open opposition to the passage of the conservative Six Articles Act (1539), despite his strong disapproval of its theological stance and coercive character. He left most political maneuvers to his ally Thomas Cromwell. After Cromwell's fall in July 1540, Cranmer was more vulnerable, being forced to take a higher political profile. In November 1541 it was he who revealed to Henry the news of Queen Catherine Howard's adultery, a severe blow to the religious conservatives. During 1543 tensions in his own diocese and cathedral culminated in conservative attempts to discredit him and his circle with the king (the so-called Prebendaries' Plot), but Henry did not withdraw his support, and Cranmer survived this and the other religious instabilities of the king's last years.

Under the regimes of Edward Seymour (from 1547 duke of Somerset) and John Dudley (from 1551 duke of Northumberland) during the reign of Edward VI (1547–1553), Cranmer became a chief architect of religious change. He played a major part in writing the first English Eucharistic liturgy (1548)—the two versions of *The Book of Common Prayer* (1549 and 1552), and the Ordinal of 1550—as well as presiding over the construction of the Forty-two Articles (published in 1553) and the abortive revision of English canon law, the *Reformatio Legum Ecclesiasticarum* (under active consideration 1551–1553). He oversaw the publication of the collection of official sermons, the *Book of Homilies* (1547), himself writing those on scripture, faith and good works, and "An Exhortation on the Fear of Death." He also encouraged leading Continental theologians to take refuge in England, continuing his long-standing tradition of personal hospitality to foreign scholars. Two in particular, Martin Bucer and Peter Martyr Vermigli, proved to hold views close to his developing theological outlook, and Bucer contributed much to the 1552 revision of *The Book of Common Prayer.* Cranmer also became involved in controversial writing, producing with Vermigli a rather hectoring answer to the demands of the conservative rebels of Devon and Cornwall in 1549. His *Defence of the True and Catholic Doctrine of the Sacrament. . .* (published in 1550) provoked Stephen Gardiner, bishop of Winchester, to reply, in turn eliciting a detailed and abusive *Answer Unto a Crafty and Sophistical Cavillation. . .* (1551) from Cranmer.

Cranmer's relations with the duke of Northumberland became strained; he disapproved of the regime's continuing depredations on church lands and of the imprisonment and deprival (1550–1553) of his old friend Cuthbert Tunstall, the conservative bishop of Durham. In July 1553, however, he acquiesced in Northumberland's unsuccessful attempt to put Lady Jane Grey on the throne in place of the Catholic Mary Tudor. After Mary's successful coup d'état, he remained at liberty until September; he was arrested after his declaration against the restoration of the Mass had been made public. Convicted of treason on 13 November 1553, Cranmer was not pardoned but spared a traitor's death so that his theological views—along with those of his friends and fellow prisoners Nicholas Ridley and Hugh Latimer—could be examined at Oxford in April 1554. He was tried for heresy in September 1555, providing the formal evidence for a condemnation by Rome (December 1555). Demoralized by his imprisonment and isolated after the burning of Ridley and Latimer, he signed six progressively more abject recantations in February and March 1556 but was still con-

demned to burn at the stake at Oxford. Realizing that no mercy would be shown to him, he made a final and unexpected statement of his Protestant faith at the service before his burning (21 March), and at the stake he ostentatiously thrust his right hand (the one he used to sign the recanting documents) into the flames to emphasize his rejection of the recantations. His wife, Margaret, and his children were provided for with the help of friends in the printing and publishing trade; she subsequently married first Cranmer's publisher, Edward Whitchurch, and then in 1564 Bartholomew Scott, an associate of Whitchurch.

Cranmer changed his mind cautiously and piecemeal on theological questions, which has left much scope for subsequent argument about his views and his moral status—both important issues in constructing a distinctive identity for the Church of England. Anglican scholars in the Anglo-Catholic tradition have often been as quick as Roman Catholics to condemn him for exhibiting cowardice and a slippery conscience. Certainly he had no interest in defending the traditional privileges of the church against Henry VIII's attacks, and like other prelates he submitted to large-scale losses of diocesan estates at Henry's order. Moreover, his witness for reform was equivocal; he had to conceal the existence of his wife for the first fifteen years of their marriage, sending her away to Germany after the passage of the Act of Six Articles, and he complied with the disciplining of other married clergy. Yet even under Henry VIII Cranmer could show more courage than most others at Court, attempting some defense of both Anne Boleyn and Cromwell at the moment of their falls and when revising the *Bishops' Book* in 1538, attempting aggressively but unsuccessfully to convince Henry of the central importance of the doctrine of justification by faith. He genuinely believed in the royal supremacy as the agency of divine will, which made it easier for him to accept Henry VIII's often murderous inconsistencies but caused him great agony in the wake of the Lady Jane Grey fiasco. Much of his hesitation in his last months under Mary can be attributed to an acute sense of guilt in having betrayed her over Jane Grey and to a reluctance to abandon his high view of royal authority, despite the queen's misuse of it in restoring England to papal obedience.

Cranmer's eucharistic views have given rise to especial controversy. During the 1530s he was willing to preside over the burning of John Frith (1533) and John Lambert (alias Nicholson; 1538), who denied the real presence; in summer 1537 he rebuked Joachim Vadian for the memorialist views expressed in his treatise of 1535–1536 on the Eucharist. As late as 1543 his annotations to depositions in the Prebendaries' Plot show that he found attacks on requiems and prayer for souls departed erroneous and offensive, and his handwritten commonplace books of the 1530s and early 1540s criticize Zwinglian statements, favoring instead Luther's pronouncements, which retain a strong belief in the real presence.

At his trial in 1555, Cranmer denied that he had held three different positions on the Eucharist; but then, he did not consider that his eucharistic views had materially changed until about 1546, when his chaplain, Nicholas Ridley (initially influenced by the ninth century theologian Ratramnus), persuaded him to think afresh. It is likely that he regarded his earlier shift from strict belief in transubstantiation to a less closely defined realist position sometime in the 1530s as not nearly as important as this later conversion to the idea of spiritual presence and receptionism. By December 1548, in the Lords' Debate on the sacraments, he openly defended the idea of a purely spiritual eucharistic presence and rejected the idea of *manducatio impiorum* implied by real presence ideas.

Perhaps in the interests of episcopal unity with conservative colleagues, Cranmer's 1549 *Book of Common Prayer* used realist language in dealing with the Eucharist; similarly, in 1548 he had issued an English translation of the Lutheran Justus Jonas catechism, which despite minor modification was probably more conservative than he intended and which later caused him embarrassment. The 1552 prayer book, however, was much more radical: its view of the nature of the eucharistic elements is so far from being realist that the minister officiating at a Communion is enjoined to take unconsumed bread and wine home for his own domestic use (a rubric not altered until the more Catholic revisions of 1637 and 1662). A similar attitude, springing from uncompromising hostility to transubstantiation, dominated Cranmer's controversial eucharistic writings of the 1550s. They argue for a spiritual presence in the Eucharist, available only to recipients with faith. He was perhaps unaware of how much his continuing use of realist language with purely figurative meaning confused the issues at stake in his debates with Gardiner.

Too fair-minded and cautious to be a ready-made hero in Reformation disputes, Cranmer was an impressively learned, if unoriginal, scholar who, together with his religious opponent John Fisher, can be seen as one of the first exponents of humanist patristic study in England. He was ready in his liturgical constructions to draw on the work of an ecumenically wide range of thinkers, including Cardinal Francisco de Quiñones, Hermann von Wied (the reformist archbishop of Cologne), and his friend Martin Bucer. His 1552 prayer book, though still more elaborate than any other Protestant liturgy, revealed its liturgical radicalism not only in eucharistic theology but also in its treatment of the funeral rite, which became little more than a service of reassurance for the mourners. Among Cranmer's lasting liturgical innovations were the establishment of a twofold pattern of Mattins and Evensong as offices for regular congregational devotional use (by both the laity and the clergy) and, in the 1549 marriage service, the introduction of the idea of "the mutual society, help and comfort that the one ought to have of the other" as one of the liturgically expressed justifications for marriage. His abiding legacy is his accidental gift of nature: a genius for formal prose, displayed in the two prayer books and in the *Book of Homilies*, which through liturgical repetition has left a lasting mark on the development of the English language.

BIBLIOGRAPHY

Ayris, Paul, and David Selwyn, eds. *Thomas Cranmer: Churchman and Scholar*. Woodbridge, England, and Rochester, N.Y., 1993. A very useful collection of thematic essays.

Bond, Ronald B., ed. *"Certain Sermons or Homilies" (1547) and "A Homily against Disobedience and Wilful Rebellion" (1570): A Critical Edition*. Toronto, 1987.

Bromiley, Geoffrey W. *Thomas Cranmer, Theologian*. London, 1956.

Brooks, Peter Newman, ed. *Cranmer in Context: Documents from the English Reformation*. London, 1989. Much consists of extracts from the Cox edition, but some material is new, embedded in the editor's commentary.

———. *Thomas Cranmer's Doctrine of the Eucharist*. 2d ed. Basingstoke, England, 1992. Sets out the development of Cranmer's thought with reference to his unpublished commonplace books.

Buchanan, C. "What Did Cranmer Think He Was Doing?" *Grove Liturgical Studies*, no. 7. Bramcote, England, 1976. A concise study of Cranmer's developing Eucharist thought as expressed in his liturgies of 1548, 1549, and 1552.

Cox, J. E., ed. *The Works of Thomas Cranmer*. 2 vols. 1844, 1846. Overall, a reliable text, omitting little but the literature of Henry VIII's first divorce.

Foxe, John. *Acts and Monuments. . . .* 8 vols. Edited by G. Townsend and S. R. Cattley. London, 1837–1841; reprint, New York, 1965. Vol. 8, pp. 1–101, is still the basic source on Cranmer's life, though substantially dependent on Nicholas's edition.

Loades, D. M. *The Oxford Martyrs*. London, 1970. Deals with Cranmer's experiences in Mary's reign.

———. *Cranmer and the English Reformation*. Bangor, Wales, 1991. A useful brief overview of recent research.

MacCulloch, Diarmaid. *Thomas Cranmer*. New Haven, forthcoming. Biography in preparation.

Nichols, John Gough. *Narratives of the Days of the Reformation*. Camden Society, 1st ser., 77 (1859), 218–275. Narratives of Cranmer's life by his secretary Ralph Morice and by an anonymous author (possibly Stephen Nevinson) who probably also edited and amplified for publication Cranmer's notes on unwritten verities: cf. the edition by Cox, vol. 2, pp. 1–67.

Pocock, Nicholas, ed. *Records of the Reformation: The Divorce, 1527–33*. Oxford, 1870. Vol. 2, pp. 334–399, covers the tract *Articuli duodecim* (possibly by Cranmer) in favor of Henry VIII's first divorce, now thought to date from winter 1533.

Ratcliff, E. C. "The Liturgical Work of Archbishop Cranmer." *Journal of Ecclesiastical History* 7 (1956), pp. 189–203.

Ridley, Jasper. *Thomas Cranmer*. Oxford, 1962. A careful biography, although it predates much modern discussion, particularly of Tudor politics.

Smyth, C. H. *Thomas Cranmer and the Reformation under Edward VI*. Cambridge, 1926; reprint London, 1973. Still a highly useful and perceptive study, despite its invention of a theology of the Eucharist, "Suvermerianism," which Smyth later admitted was a mistaken idea.

Surtz, Edward J., and Virginia Murphy, eds. *The Divorce Tracts of Henry VIII*. Angers, 1987. The first critical edition of Cranmer's translation of the *Censurae* of 1531, containing both invaluable commentary and notes.

DIARMAID MACCULLOCH

CRATANDER, Andreas

CRATANDER, Andreas (Ger., Hartmann; d. 1540), Basel printer and bookseller. Of Cratander's early life little is known. He studied at the University of Heidelberg, earning his baccalaureate in 1503. The next years he moved between Basel and Strasbourg. By 1513 he was working in Strasbourg for the printer Michael Schürer. In 1515 he returned to Basel, still working in the print trade. For a time he was a corrector in Adam Petri's printshop.

Soon he set up his own business, which included a press as well as a bookshop. It was apparently a small press that focused on pamphlets and publications for university students. The first work to appear was Johannes Oecolampadius's Greek grammar in September 1518. In all, Cratander printed some two hundred titles. Oecolampadius lived in his home for a time and worked for him, and Cratander later became the Basel reformer's primary publisher. He published reform works as early as 1520, including *Julius Exclusus* and Lorenzo Valla's critique of the *On the Donation of Constantine*. Among other important works that appeared from his press were a 1526 Latin edition of Hippocrates and Sebastian Münster's early cosmographical works. He also printed German editions of several of Desiderius Erasmus's works, including the *Paraclesis*.

In 1536 Cratander sold his printing business to a group that included the famous Basel diarist Thomas Platter. After that, he and his son focused their efforts on bookselling.

BIBLIOGRAPHY

Meier, Eugen, et al. *Andreas Cratander: Ein Basler Drucker und Verleger der Reformationszeit.* Basel, 1967.

D. JONATHAN GRIESER

CRATO, Adam.

CRATO, Adam. *See* Krafft, Adam.

CRATO VON KRAFFTHEIM, Johannes

CRATO VON KRAFFTHEIM, Johannes (born Krafft; 1519–1585), Silesian Reformed Protestant, medical humanist, and personal physician to Ferdinand I, Maximilian II, and Rudolf II. A native of Breslau (Wrocław, Poland), Crato lodged with Martin Luther while a student at Wittenberg University. Johannes Aurifaber used Crato's notes as a source for his edition of Luther's *Tischreden* (1566). Thinking Crato lacked the temperament needed to be a pastor, Luther suggested he study medicine. Crato moved to Leipzig and then Padua, where he served as an assistant to the medical humanist Giovanni Battista da Monte (Montanus). After taking his doctorate, Crato resettled in 1550 in Breslau, where he became city physician (*Stadtartz*). Responding to an outbreak of the plague, he wrote a tract (1555) that has been hailed as the first German work that clearly asserts the plague's contagiousness. He also composed summaries of the works of Hippocrates and Galen and edited the medical *consilia* of da Monte. Theologically, his denial of the real presence in the Eucharist created problems in Breslau, and the city council removed him from his position. From 1560 to 1581 the Habsburg emperors employed Crato as personal physician. Although the Jesuits at court were suspicious of Crato, Maximilian II favored him, ennobling him and granting him the title count palatine.

Although imperial service limited the number of his academic publications, Crato exercised a wide-ranging influence through his correspondence. He encouraged Andreas Dudith—the Hungarian humanist, imperial ambassador, former bishop of Pécs (Fünfkirchen), and delegate to the Council of Trent—to return to Protestantism after a flirtation with antitrinitarianism. Crato stirred the Heidelberg physician Thomas Lüber to refute the medical philosophy of Paracelsus. He also prompted his Silesian protégé, Zacharius Ursinus, to write against the Gnesio-Lutherans. As students of Melanchthon who adopted a Reformed interpretation of the Lord's Supper the two represent a bridge between north German Philippism and the Calvinist Second Reformation.

BIBLIOGRAPHY

Primary Sources

Crato von Krafftheim, Johannes. *Isagoge medicinae.* Venice, 1560.
———. *Perioche methodica in libros Galeni.* Basel, 1563.
———. *De morbo gallico commentarius.* Frankfurt a.M., 1594.

Secondary Sources

Evans, R. J. W. *Rudolf II and His World: A Study in Intellectual History, 1576–1612.* Reprint, New York, 1984. Best introduction to late sixteenth-century Habsburg court life.
Gillet, J. F. A. *Crato von Crafftheim und seine Freunde: Ein Beitrag zur Kirchengeschichte, nach handschriftlichen Quellen.* 2 vols. Frankfurt a.M., 1860–1861. Highlights Crato's significance in church history. A valuable source for Crato's intellectual circle (including Andreas Dudith and Zacharias Ursinus).
Helmich, Egon. *Die Briefe Konrad Gesners an Crato von Krafftheim.* Düsseldorf, 1938.
Jantsch, Marlene. "Crato von Krafftheim." In *Gestalten und Ideen um Paracelsus: Salzburger Beiträge zur Paracelsusforschung,* edited by Sepp Domandl, vol. 11, pp. 99–108. Vienna, 1972. Focuses on Crato as a physician and why he opposed Paracelsus.

CHARLES D. GUNNOE, JR.

CRAUTWALD, Valentin

CRAUTWALD, Valentin (1465?–1545), German humanist colleague of Kaspar von Schwenckfeld; spiritualist co-author of the distinctive Christology of the Silesian Schwenkfelders. Crautwald came to the attention of leading European reformers in the late 1520s as the scholarly and reflective colleague of Schwenckfeld in Legnica (Liegnitz), Silesia. In his position as cathedral canon and lector from 1524 to 1537, Crautwald promoted a vision of inward spiritual renewal that reflected his reading of Erasmus, but he opposed Lutheran sacramentalism and clerical religion, earning him Luther's rebuke in a letter dated 14 April 1526. Crautwald was initially influential among local clergy and people through his lectures and writing, and on occasion Duke Frederick II looked to him for counsel. After the duke began suppression of Schwenkfeldianism in 1530, Crautwald's influence continued as his numerous writings and letters circulated among the conventicles of Schwenkfelders scattered throughout Silesia and southern Germany. Noteworthy among these are two works completed in 1529, *De Cognitione Christi* and *Novus Homo* (*Corpus Schwenckfeldianorum* [hereafter *CS*] vol. 8, pp. 46–79).

Immersed as he was in the writings of the Fathers, Crautwald joined other sixteenth-century reformers in citing the works of Augustine, whom Crautwald called *magnus Augustinus* ("the great Augustine"). He was especially impressed by Augustine's notion that the true eating of Christ was a spiritual partaking by faith, and by Augustine's views on Christian nurture and catechism.

Shortly after Crautwald's death, Schwenckfeld described him as "the true lover of the glory of Christ" (*CS* vol. 8, p. 673). The designation is apt, for the centerpiece of Crautwald's thought was his unique Christology, not fully developed until 1538. Crautwald taught an incarnation in reverse: just as God assumed flesh in the earthly Christ, so the flesh was gradually deified, culminating in the glorified Christ. Crautwald probably anticipated Schwenckfeld in affirming the "non-creaturehood" of Christ's earthly body, dependent as it was on the Father's generation. In this way Crautwald put Christ beyond all creaturely forms and sacraments and explained how Christ's body could be shared directly with believers for their salvation. In Zwinglian or humanist fashion Crautwald valued the Lord's Supper for its symbolic and educative role. The Schwenckfeldian Christology took on new life in the "celestial flesh" doctrine of Melchior Hoffman and various Dutch Anabaptists.

BIBLIOGRAPHY

Primary Source

Corpus Schwenckfeldianorum. 9 vols. Edited by Chester D. Hartranft and Elmer Johnson. Leipzig, 1907–1928. Includes some fourteen Crautwald works that Schwenckfeld edited and published. The majority of Crautwald's works and letters circulated in manuscript and are extant in manuscript books in archives in Munich (CLM 718) and Wolfenbüttel (Cod. Aug. 45.9.2 and 37.27.2).

Secondary Sources

Erb, Peter C. "Valentin Crautwald." In *Bibliotheca Dissidentium,* edited by André Séguenny, vol. 6, pp. 1–70. Baden-Baden, 1985. A complete bibliographical listing of primary and secondary literature relating to Crautwald.
Shantz, Douglas H. *Crautwald and Erasmus: A Study in Humanism and Radical Reform in Sixteenth Century Silesia.* Baden-Baden, 1992. The only book length study of Crautwald, highlighting his intellectual and social context, theological contributions, and influence on Schwenckfeld. Also contains a translation of Crautwald's key christological treatise, *De Cognitione Christi.*
Weigelt, Horst. *The Schwenkfelders in Silesia.* Translated by Peter C. Erb. Pennsburg, Pa., 1985. Best overview of the Silesian reform movement; valuable for placing Crautwald in the context of Silesian politics and the larger Schwenckfeld circle.

DOUGLAS H. SHANTZ

CRESPIN, Jean (1520?–1572), printer-publisher and martyrologist of Geneva. Born into a high patrician family of Arras, then under the rule of Emperor Charles V, Crespin was educated as a humanist and studied both civil and canon law at the University of Louvain. Afterward he became secretary to the French jurist Charles Du Moulin in Paris. Returning to Arras, he married Madeleine Le Cambier in 1544, who was to bear him seven children. In 1545 he was banished from Arras under suspicion of being a Lutheran.

Crespin planned to found a publishing house with Théodore de Bèze and moved to Geneva in 1548. Bèze did publish some of his work through Crespin, as did John Calvin, but by 1550 Crespin had associated with Conrad Badius (1510–1562), subsequently with Nicolas Barbier (1554–1558), and finally with Eustache Vignon, husband of his only surviving child, Marguerite.

With four presses, Crespin was one of the major publishers of Geneva. He had a variety of fonts accommodating several foreign languages. He published grammars for Latin, Greek, Italian, and Hebrew, as well as French. Ten percent of his titles were in Italian, Spanish, and English. He was the publisher of the Geneva Bible of the Marian Exiles from England. Crespin marketed more titles through the Frankfurt book fair than any other Genevan printer. For that international market he touted his books in Latin and Greek. He also published ancient classics such as the *Iliad* and the *Odyssey*, but mostly he printed religious books. Sixty percent of his titles, and half his printed pages, consisted of Bibles, biblical commentaries, catechisms, liturgical manuals, and polemical theology. He published the only two editions of the theologians of the early church produced in Geneva before 1570: Augustine, and a theological study that included extracts from many of the church fathers.

Crespin helped make the works of Martin Luther and Philipp Melanchthon available in French, although theologically he was a disciple of Calvin. He published attacks on Lutherans in the Lutheran-Reformed debate over the Lord's Supper. He printed the works of other German lanuage authors such as Johannes Sleidanus and Heinrich Bullinger. A leader for his time, Crespin printed contemporary history in French.

A successful printer, Crespin was also an author. His most famous work was his book of martyrs, *Histoire des Martyrs persécutez et mis à mort.* It came off the press for the first time in 1554 and saw more than fifteen editions in twenty years. When he died, his successors carried on the work through 1619. The martyrology continued to be identified in the public mind with Crespin and became a classic of the Reformed tradition. It is one of the eminent martyrologies of the Reformation period. The stories of Crespin's Protestant martyrs were recounted from the pulpit and read aloud, providing the Huguenots of seventeenth- and eighteenth-century France with inspiration under persecution.

In Geneva Crespin maintained ties with the Low Countries and helped immigrants. His daughter and wife died in 1570. In 1572 he remarried and shortly thereafter died of the plague, leaving his wife pregnant with a son, Samuel.

BIBLIOGRAPHY

Primary Sources

Crespin, Jean. *Histoire des martyrs persécutez et mis à mort pour la vérité de l'évangile, depuis le temps des apostres iusques à présent* (1619). 3 vols. Introduction and notes by Daniel Benoît. Toulouse, 1885–1889. This is the most readily accessible edition of Crespin's book of martyrs.
———. *Histoire des vrays tesmoins de la verité de l'evangile, qui de leur sang l'ont signée, depuis Jean Hus iusques au temps present. Comprinse en VIII livres contenans actes memorables du Seigneur en l'infirmité des siens, non seulement contre les forces et efforts du monde, mais aussi à l'encontre de diverses sortes d'assauts et heresies monstrueuses* (1570). Liège, 1964. Large folio edition. This is a facsimile with a modern index.

Secondary Sources

Gilmont, Jean-François, ed. *Bibliographie des éditions de Jean Crespin, 1550–1572.* 2 vols. Verviers, Belgium, 1981. This carefully researched and annotated bibliography includes facsimiles of the title pages of the works.
———. *Jean Crespin, un éditeur réformé du xvie siècle.* Geneva, 1981. A detailed and well-documented biography of Crespin.
Olson, Jeannine. "Jean Crespin, Humanist Printer among the Reformation Martyrologists." In *The Harvest of Humanism in Central Europe: Essays in Honor of Lewis W. Spitz,* edited by Manfred Fleischer, pp. 317–340. Saint Louis, 1992. This essay summarizes in English the life and works of Crespin and provides a description of the contents of his book of martyrs.
Piaget, Arthur, and Gabrielle Berthoud. *Notes sur le livre des martyrs de Jean Crespin.* Neuchâtel, 1930. This product of the seminar on the history of the Reformation of the University of Neuchâtel reveals some of the errors of fact and repetition of documents in Crespin's martyrology.

JEANNINE E. OLSON

CREUTZIGER, Caspar. *See* Cruciger, Caspar.

CROMWELL, Thomas (c.1485–1540) earl of Essex, chief minister in state and church to Henry VIII, king of England, was the son of a clothworker and alehouse keeper of Wimbledon (Surrey). In his teens he left England to travel all the way down to southern Italy, serving there briefly in the French army. He returned by way of Rome and Antwerp, having acquired both a knowledge of languages and an understanding of international trade and finance; in about 1512 he settled, newly married, at London. Here he acquired formal skills in the law and less formal ones in business. For close to twenty years he practiced as a solicitor and moneylender in the capital, making the acquaintance of the circle of Thomas More and establishing contacts with the leading commercial interests in the city. In 1517 he revisited Rome to secure a license for the setting up of a religious guild in Boston (Lincolnshire); on the journey he is reported to have learned the New Testament by heart, using Erasmus's recently published translation into Latin. However, from about 1514 he was formally in the service of Thomas, Cardinal Wolsey, the lord chancellor who governed England under the king, and by the mid-1520s he was in fact Wolsey's chief lay councillor. He organized the dissolution of some small monastic institutions and the transfer of their endowments to fulfill Wolsey's dreams of founding a school at Ipswich and a college (later Christ Church) at Oxford, and he remained loyally in Wolsey's service when the cardinal fell from power in October 1529.

Cromwell now needed to reconstruct his career, and though he waited till Wolsey had died (November 1530), he then managed to transfer to the king's service. He had prepared the move by entering the Parliament called in November 1529 which Henry hoped might be able to assist him in securing an end to his first marriage. Cromwell's move bore unsuspected significance. He had sat in the Parliament of 1523 and come to understand the role that that institution should play in the running of the realm; once in charge, he was in effect to transform the king's high court of Lords adjudicating on petitions brought up by the Commons into the legislative sovereign, the king-in-Parliament, with unchallenged powers in all matters touching the English nation—that body which ever since has been the center of English constitutional government. Cromwell gained his ascendancy in the king's council in part by his phenomenal powers of concentrated work and in part by taking up Henry's half-formed beliefs in his sovereign independence of Rome in matters spiritual. It was Cromwell who turned those aspirations into political reality by means of acts of Parliament that he drafted and saw passed through both houses: by 1534, the king was acknowledged supreme head of the Church of England and had been freed of his first marriage. This revolution in church and state rested on law traditional in its essence, augmented by statutes and enforced in the ancient courts of the realm.

Though Cromwell was undoubtedly the king's chief minister from 1532 to 1540, he was never in the position of unrivaled ascendancy that Wolsey had enjoyed: an upstart of such lowly origins was bound to excite personal hostilities of an often fierce kind, the more so because he used his years of power to transform or at least reform every aspect of the scene that came under his eye. He superintended the total abolition of monastic institutions and the distribution of their wealth between crown and individual grantees (1536–

1540); he reorganized the finances and financial offices of the Crown; he elevated the hitherto very secondary office of the king's principal secretary into that secretaryship of state which for centuries thereafter was the main executive agency of royal government; and he made a reality of the reorganization of the king's large and diffuse council into the small and efficient Privy Council which had been spoken of before but never carried through. He also opened up a new and energetic phase in attending to the social and economic problems of the commonwealth, diagnosed and complained of often enough for the best part of a century but never before systematically subjected to legislative reform. None of the things undertaken—including the royal supremacy in the Church—came entirely out of the blue; the difference in the Cromwell era lay in the fact that the chief minister collected a program, added his own contributions, and turned proposals into reality. Given a bare eight years of by no means always free action, he could not be expected to bring all the matters tackled to a conclusion, especially as the primary tasks of creating the unitary state/church of England and seeing to the transfer of monastic property necessarily absorbed an enormous amount of time. Many of Cromwell's initiatives were taken up again later in the century, so that the impetus of incisive action which he imparted to the system was never quite lost. That is to say, he launched the realm upon its transformation into the modern state.

In the way he tackled problems Cromwell tended to observe certain guidelines. In the first place, though himself devoid of any formal education, he valued the help of trained minds and respected the purveyors of thought-out ideas. His office archive became the repository of proposals reduced to writing—his own and those of many others—and he held the advanced thinkers of the day in considerable regard, the more so because the peculiar experiences of his youth had freed him of that body of instinctive convictions which tends to tie men to the preservation of things as they are. Second, he believed in preparing the ground for any reform by a careful investigation of the existing scene, a systematic attitude which, for instance, opened the attack on ecclesiastical property with a complete census of the church's wealth (Valor Ecclesiasticus, 1535). The propaganda campaign by means of which he brought the new order to the attention of the nation depended on establishing contacts with writers and printers, even as the production of an English Bible called for preparatory work with translators and book publishers. The confusion of rights to property and inheritance, deeply embedded in the law and the interests of lawyers, called for the introduction of parish registers of births, marriages, and deaths (1538) if order was ever to be established; the even more urgent provision of a register of land transactions, which Cromwell planned, was defeated by the lawyers who preferred the uncertainties profitable to themselves. All Cromwell's moves tended to be very well pre-

pared, and he rarely faced the common administrator's experience of groping in the dark. And last, Cromwell proved to be exceptionally efficient and incisive in the carrying out of policies: he worked remarkable hours but also knew how to use the time and labor of others to get things done.

These characteristics of the man—his attitudes to the task and his unfailing desire for improving things—naturally enough, in that age of the Reformation, called for a positive reaction to the problems of the church and the faith, the more so because in 1535–1536 Cromwell was appointed vicar-general and vicegerent to Henry VIII. He thus ruled the church as the supreme head's deputy, and it fell to him to resolve problems of the faith quite as much as to attend to problems of administration. At one time he was thought to have been entirely "secular," concerned only with power and the creation of a strong, perhaps despotic, kingship; but this view, which derived from the accusations of personal enemies and a curious desire to cleanse Henry VIII of all traces of guilt in the savageries of his reign, can no longer be maintained. So far from trying to build a Tudor despotism, Cromwell organized the reformed state around the rule of the common law and the legislative sovereignty of the king-in-Parliament. So far from confining himself to a nonreligious secularism, he quite consciously undertook to introduce the religious Reformation into England. Even the dissolution of the monasteries was meant to serve both the economy of the state and the spiritual health of the church.

Cromwell's most manifest contribution to the move away from past orthodoxy lay in his promotion of an English Bible: by 1539, an officially endorsed version, derived in great part from the work of William Tyndale (whom Henry VIII abominated) was available for purchase by the parishes. Cromwell not only supervised its production but contributed to the financing of it. But the Great Bible was only the most obvious indicator of his position in the disputes over the truth of religion. Throughout his years of power, and indeed before he achieved power, he had been in touch with the London brethren—those remnants of Lollardy who eagerly embraced the onset of Lutheran influence—and promoted leading reformers to the high places in the Church. He worked very much hand-in-hand with Thomas Cranmer, the first archbishop of what became the Protestant Church of England; influential reforming preachers like Hugh Latimer looked to him as patron; for a long time he protected men like Robert Barnes, personal friend to Luther, and employed a German Lutheran, Christopher Mont, as his agent in dealing with continental Protestants. It is true that he cannot be simply assigned to any of the reformed positions that grew up in the 1530s. Though he once told some Lutheran envoys that in his heart he shared their views but, as the world stood, would have to believe even as his master the king believed, he was never a straightforward Lutheran; and he was definitely hostile to the more radical ideas, especially touching the Eucharist, that were coming out of Switzerland. His injunctions of 1536 and 1538, his contributions to the debates that produced the formulary called the Bishops' Book in 1537, his comments on Thomas Starkey's endeavor to find a position between the extremes, and his address to the House of Lords in 1540 indicate two things: he wished to see the English church pursue an eirenic middle way (*via media*) that would prevent clashes of intolerance with fanaticism, and he wished to put down the high clericalist pretensions of what he regarded as a priest-ridden church. In other words, in alliance with Cranmer he was mapping out the moderate line of reform that in the end was to characterize the Church of England after it had overcome both Calvinist radicalism and high-church pretentiousness within its own ranks. In the church and religion, as in the state and its guiding principles, Cromwell pointed to the future.

However, this moderation did not save Cromwell from enemies who hated both the man and his true intentions, and who were to find it possible to charge him with extremer views that set the king against him. In 1538, Cromwell began to neglect the caution that had hitherto marked his actions and indeed began to ignore the very point he had made to those Lutheran envoys. The need to find a fourth wife for Henry VIII and the threat of an anti-English alliance between the Empire and France led Cromwell into pursuing a virtually independent foreign policy of his own, aimed at a great Protestant alliance with northern Europe and parts of Germany. Even if he had found a consort more acceptable to Henry than Anne of Cleves, these moves would have seriously endangered his position. He failed to see in time that sacramentarian heresy was establishing a hold on the English outpost of Calais, and he misread Henry's mind when the king decided to use the Parliament called in 1539 to restore Catholic orthodoxy by the savage act of Six Articles. Though by the spring of 1540 Cromwell appeared to have recovered his position, he was in fact living on borrowed time, a situation disguised by his elevation to the earldom of Essex. He had been in part responsible for putting his king into a most uncomfortable corner at home and abroad, saddled with an unwanted wife and needlessly maneuvered into a possible state of war with the Catholic powers. Whenever Henry found himself in such difficulties he escaped at one bound by locating a convenient scapegoat: persuaded that his vicegerent was a sacramentary heretic, he threw him to the wolves, that is, to the duke of Norfolk and Bishop Gardiner of Winchester. Cromwell was arrested on 10 June 1540 and executed on 28 July under a parliamentary act of attainder, without trial, on totally trumped up charges of treason and totally misconceived charges of heresy. His death condemned the next twenty years to much aimless futility and indeed deprived the realm of an outstanding guide. The master he had served so well soon recognized this. Henry's own verdict on the fall of Cromwell may stand, provided we add his own folly to the causes he spoke of: within a few

months of the event, he accused his present councillors of having by a pretense of imaginary misdeeds and lying accusations "caused him to put to death the most faithful servant he had ever had."

BIBLIOGRAPHY

Brigden, Susan. *London and the Reformation*. Oxford, 1989. Documents Cromwell's involvement with the reformers.

Dickens, A. G. *Thomas Cromwell and the English Reformation*. London, 1959. Brief Cromwell life history emphasizing his religion.

Elton, Geoffrey R. *The Tudor Revolution in Government: Administrative Changes in the Reign, of Henry VIII*. Cambridge, 1953. Deals at length with Cromwell's work as the king's chief minister and reformer.

———. *Policy and Police: The Enforcement of the Reformation in the Age of Thomas Cromwell*. Cambridge, 1972. Deals at length with Cromwell's work as the king's chief minister and reformer.

———. *Reform and Renewal: Thomas Cromwell and the Common Weal*. Cambridge, 1973. Deals at length with Cromwell's work as the king's chief minister and reformer.

———. *Studies in Tudor and Stuart Politics and Government*. 4 vols. Cambridge, 1974–1992. Collection of articles, several of them central to an understanding of Cromwell.

———. *Reform and Reformation: England, 1509–1558*. London and Cambridge, Mass., 1977. The most recent full treatment of the period, with a full bibliography.

Guy, J. A. *Tudor England*. Oxford, 1988. Most recent treatment of the period not by G. R. Elton, with an enormous bibliography.

Lehmberg, Stanford E. "Thomas Cromwell." In *Leaders of the Reformation*, edited by Richard De Molen. London, 1984. Cautious evaluation of Cromwell's religion.

Mayer, Thomas F. *Thomas Starkey and the Commonweal: Humanist Politics and Religion in the Reign of Henry VIII*. Cambridge, 1989.

Scarisbrick, J. J. *Henry VIII*. London, 1968. A necessary antidote to Cromwell worship.

GEOFFREY R. ELTON

CROTUS RUBEANUS (Ger., Johannes Jäger; 1480–1545), German humanist. Born in Thuringia, he entered the University of Erfurt in 1498 (B.A. 1500, M.A. 1507). He became a leader of the young Erfurt poets and a friend of Conrad Mutianus Rufus and Ulrich von Hutten, accompanying Hutten to Cologne in 1505. After working as a tutor, he became director of the abbey school at Fulda (1510–1516) and also Latin secretary to the abbot. Enraged by the attacks of the Cologne Dominicans on Johannes Reuchlin, Crotus, Hutten, and Hermann von dem Busche produced anonymously the famous satire *Epistolae virorum obscurorum* ("Letters of Obscure Men," 1515–1517). Modern studies have shown that he wrote nearly all of part 1 (while Hutten wrote most of the rest and Busche arranged publication). His portion, though the least violent in tone, is acknowledged as the most effective part of one of history's most famous satires. In 1517 Crotus traveled to Italy and took a doctorate in theology at Bologna.

In 1519, impressed by Luther's early tracts, Crotus wrote to him from Bologna, recalling their student days at Erfurt and welcoming his reforms. When Luther passed through

Erfurt in April 1521 en route to the Diet of Worms, Crotus was serving as rector and welcomed him to the university. In 1524 he became chancellor to Albert of Brandenburg, grand master of the Teutonic Knights, and assisted in transforming Prussia into a secular Protestant duchy. In 1530, however, he left for the service of the archbishop of Mainz and became a cathedral canon at Halle and later (1537) at Halberstadt. In 1531 he wrote an *Apologia* justifying his repudiation of the Reformation. This work elicited bitter denunciations by many former friends, but he refused either to respond to attacks or to write any more books.

BIBLIOGRAPHY

Becker, Reinhard Paul. *A War of Fools: The Letters of Obscure Men*. Bern, 1981.

Brecht, Walther. *Die Verfasser der Epistolae obscurorum virorum*. Strasbourg, 1904. The definitive discussion of the authorship of the *Letters of Obscure Men*, demonstrating Crotus's leading role. Later scholarship has revised some of its conclusions, but basically the book has held up.

Forstreuter, Kurt. "Johannes Crotus Rubianus in Preussen." In *Festschrift für Hermann Heimpel*, edited by the Max-Planck-Institut für Geschichte, Göttingen, vol. 2, pp. 293–312. Göttingen, 1972. Clarifies Crotus's role in creating a Protestant Prussia and his eventual return to Catholicism.

Holborn, Hajo. *Ulrich von Hutten and the German Reformation*. Reprint, Westport, Conn., 1978. Chapter 4 provides an excellent English-language account of the Reuchlin controversy and Crotus's role in it.

Kleineidam, Erich. *Universitas studii Erffordensis*. 3 vols. Leipzig, 1969–1983. Vol. 2 contains the definitive account of humanism at the University of Erfurt, including Crotus's role.

Stokes, Francis Griffin. *Epistolae Obscurorum Virorum: The Latin Text with an English Rendering, Notes, and an Historical Introduction*. London, 1909. The most convenient edition for English readers. The introduction gives a clear account of the work and its authors, but its interpretation of scholasticism, humanism, and the early Reformation is badly outdated. The English text only was reprinted with a new introduction by Hajo Holborn under the title *On the Eve of the Reformation: Letters of Obscure Men*, New York, 1964.

CHARLES G. NAUERT, JR.

CROWLEY, Robert (1518?–1588), English Protestant controversialist and clergyman. This fervid editor, bookseller, and propagandist for religious and social reform had a prolific career as a satirist during the early years of Edward VI's reign (1547–1551). That brief interval marked the most radical phase of the English Reformation. Under the probable influence of Hugh Latimer, Crowley appealed to King Edward and Parliament for a thoroughgoing program of commonwealth reform that would eradicate religious and social abuses. He satirized clerics for holding multiple benefices and misappropriating tithes and attacked property owners for increasing poverty by enclosing arable land, raising rents, and driving up the price of food.

Crowley's chief contribution as an editor was his publication of the first printed editions of *The Vision of Piers Plow-

man* (1550; attributed to William Langland). Attracted chiefly by the erroneous association of that poem with Lollardy, he added a preface and marginal glosses that convert an orthodox religious work into a powerful attack against monasticism and the Roman Catholic hierarchy. Deeply imbued with the densely scriptural style favored by the Edwardian "gospellers," Crowley modeled his own prophetic poems on that medieval masterpiece. The most interesting of those works, *Philargyrie of Greate Britayne* (1551), appeals to Edward VI to fulfill reforms that his father had blocked. In Crowley's view, Henry VIII's dissolution of monastic houses and disestablishment of the Roman church had failed because redistribution of ecclesiastical wealth to the king and royal favorites simply perpetuated the oppression of the poor common people.

After going into exile to escape persecution under Mary Tudor, he returned under Elizabeth I to enjoy a long career as a Puritan clergyman, pamphleteer, and arbiter of public morality. His Elizabethan reputation owed much to his tracts against clerical vestments during the initial outburst of Puritan controversy in the 1560s.

BIBLIOGRAPHY

Primary Source

Crowley, Robert. *The Select Works of Robert Crowley*. Edited by J. M. Cowper. Early English Text Society, extra series, vol. 15. Reprint, Millwood, N.Y., 1987. Edition of Crowley's tracts.

Secondary Sources

King, John N. *English Reformation Literature: The Tudor Origins of the Protestant Tradition*. Princeton, 1982. Contains a full treatment of Crowley's career and a critical bibliography of his publications.

———. "*Philargyrie of Greate Britayne* by Robert Crowley." *English Renaissance Literature* 10 (1980), 46–75. A critical edition of an important satire against religious and social abuses.

Norbrook, David. *Poetry and Politics in the English Renaissance*. London, 1984. Considers Crowley as a radical prophetic poet.

JOHN N. KING

CRUCIGER, Caspar (Ger., Creutziger; 1504–1548), German humanist, Lutheran theologian, and ally of Philipp Melanchthon. Born 1504 in Leipzig, Cruciger received his early humanist education from Georg Helt and at age twelve entered his hometown university, where he studied with the humanist Peter Mosellanus. Cruciger witnessed the 1519 Leipzig Disputation between Martin Luther and Johann Eck. The outbreak of the plague in 1521 drove him to Wittenberg, where he began Hebrew studies, soon working with Luther on the Old Testament translation. As the Reformation continued, Cruciger leaned toward Philipp Melanchthon's theology, and later, in 1537, drew Conrad Cordatus's fire on the doctrine of justification. Cruciger echoed Melanchthon's interests in such subjects as natural science, mathematics, and astronomy. Melanchthon's attempt to keep him in Wittenberg to lecture on Quintilian did not succeed, and Cruciger left in 1525, presumably under pressure from another Melanchthon critic, Nikolaus von Amsdorf. He became rector of the Johannisschule in Magdeburg.

With Wittenberg theologians frequently absent to work on reform elsewhere, Cruciger returned in 1528 to lecture for both the philosophy and theology faculties, to preach in the castle church, and to write faculty opinions on theological and practical matters. He received his doctorate in theology from Wittenberg in 1533 and continued teaching in exegesis and dogmatics and editing a series of instructional materials. Luther valued his service on the Bible translation. In 1539 Cruciger helped introduce reform to his hometown. In subsequent years he served as a delegate to theological colloquies at Hagenau, Worms, and Regensburg. During the Schmalkald War, when others fled Wittenberg, Cruciger remained, serving as rector until his death. Johannes Bugenhagen preached his funeral, and Melanchthon delivered an oration at the academic ceremony.

Although theologically akin to Melanchthon, Cruciger generally maintained good relations with Wittenberg colleagues. Luther thought highly of his student. The relative quiet of academic life suited his temperament, and his careful secretarial work also drew praise from his Roman Catholic colloquy counterparts. His close association with Melanchthon caused historians in later centuries to attribute many of Cruciger's orations, essays, and books to his likeminded friend. Cruciger also launched the Wittenberg edition of Luther's works.

BIBLIOGRAPHY

Leder, Hans-Günter. "Luther's Beziehungen zu seinen Wittenberger Freunden." In *Leben und Werk Martin Luthers von 1526 bis 1546*, edited by Helmar Junghans, vol. 1, pp. 419–440; vol. 2, pp. 863–870. Göttingen, 1983. Includes a brief look at Cruciger's Wittenberg years and literary efforts.

Pressel, Theodor. *Caspar Cruciger*. Elberfeld, 1862.

Schmidt, Oswald Gottlob. *Caspar Crucigers Leben für christliche Leser insgemein: Aus Quellen erzählt*. Leipzig, 1862. There being no modern biography, Pressel and Schmidt continue to serve as standard treatments of Cruciger's life and thought.

Wengert, Timothy. "Caspar Cruciger, 1504–1548: The Case of the Disappearing Reformer." *Sixteenth Century Journal* 20 (1989), 417–441. A careful rehabilitation of Cruciger's literary reputation, noting how subsequent generations attributed much of Cruciger's work to Melanchthon.

ROBERT ROSIN

CRUSIUS, Arnoldus. *See* Corneliszoon, Arend.

CUENCA. Many aspects of the Catholic Reformation in Spain, particularly its impact on local institutions, are relatively unknown. The experience of an average-sized, central Castilian diocese such as Cuenca tests prior assumptions and fills in several lacunae in an understanding of the process of religious change during the Reformation era.

The bishopric of Cuenca was founded in 1183 shortly after the reconquest of the region by Alfonso VIII. In the late sixteenth century, the diocese boasted a population of about 300,000, who were served by 1,405 secular priests, 773 religious, and 479 nuns. The diocese's 282 communities supported 354 parishes, some 80 religious houses, 850 rural chapels, and 1,000 confraternities. The cathedral was complemented by one collegiate church, founded in 1460 in the town of Belmonte. The city of Cuenca was also home to a local tribunal of the Spanish Inquisition, established in 1489.

Although it is commonly assumed that the pre-reform under Cardinal Francisco Jiménez de Cisneros effectively improved conditions in the Spanish church, those reforms did not reach the local level in Cuenca. Eyewitness reports on religious conditions sent to the 1566 diocesan synod underscored the low level of pastoral care and lack of popular compliance with the church's precepts. Concerted efforts to improve clerical discipline, teach doctrine and morals, and introduce reformed religious orders did not take hold in the diocese until after the mid-sixteenth century.

When change came, it was rapid. Bishop Bernardo de Fresneda (1562–1571) oversaw the initial implementation of the Tridentine reforms. In 1566 the diocesan clergy accepted the rulings of the Councils of Trent and Toledo: 1569 witnessed the first full-scale Tridentine episcopal visitation; 1571 brought the publication of the 1566 synodal constitutions and 1572 the first inspections of female convents. The years between 1555 and 1575 also marked the beginning of consistent record keeping by the bishop and parish priests as ordered by the Council of Trent.

Central to reform efforts was the education and disciplining of the parish clergy. Five Jesuit colleges were established in the diocese between 1554 and 1620, and a conciliar seminary was founded in 1584. These foundations, coupled with the boom in university enrollments during the sixteenth century, resulted in marked improvement in the clergy's education. Although according to the episcopal visitations of 1569, 1579, and 1589, only 24 percent of the secular clergy born before 1540 had earned a university degree, 45 percent of those born after 1540 had done so. Among the parish curates, 87 percent of the Tridentine-era men were university trained, the majority of them having received their degrees in theology. Discipline came through visitations, both extraordinary and ordinary, regular examination and licensing of priests, and less frequently, recourse to the episcopal and inquisitorial courts. Although abuses did continue to occur, cases of gross ignorance or dishonesty, absenteeism, and concubinage in the late sixteenth century were relatively rare, particularly among priests charged with pastoral duties.

Officially, the only theological changes that came to the diocese were those approved by the Council of Trent. Dogma having been reconfirmed by the council, it was up to local ecclesiastical authorities to ensure that all Catholics knew it. Mass religious indoctrination in Cuenca began in earnest in the 1550s. Within a generation, the majority of laypeople questioned by the Inquisition could recite the required prayers and claim to have done their Easter duty. The local tribunal of the Inquisition enforced doctrinal purity by singling out for prosecution the converted descendants of Muslims and Jews, arresting foreigners, censoring literature, and conducting extensive visitations of the district. The visitations served to teach the local population how to recognize the principal forms of heresy but also sought to correct common errors, such as blasphemy, popular sayings influenced by vestiges of Judaism or Islam, superstition, and magic. The vast majority of the several thousand individuals called before the tribunal during the forty-year period following Trent were not heretics but ordinary Catholics guilty of relatively minor transgressions against the faith.

Via the diocese's ubiquitous confraternities, religious authorities introduced several cults typical of the Catholic Reformation: the Rosary, Name of Jesus, Christ's Blood, Immaculate Conception, and the Blessed Sacrament. Chapel cults continued to serve the traditional function of insurance against disease and crop failure, and during the Catholic Reformation, the cults of the Virgin Mary, Sebastian, and Roch reigned paramount.

The Catholic Reformation in Cuenca also brought the complete triumph of the cult of the souls in purgatory. Although pre-Tridentine testators in the city of Cuenca made reasonable provisions for the well-being of their souls, bequests rarely exceeded more than one hundred masses and more typically consisted of one requiem mass, one novena, and a trental, altogether a total of forty masses. By the early seventeenth century, the city's parish death registers and notarial protocols record an extraordinary rise in the quantity of suffrages ordered by all citizens, regardless of their social status, and well in excess of the period's rampant price inflation. The medieval novenas and trentals were replaced by large numbers of low masses and special services at privileged altars, a shift in devotions that seems to have been particularly promoted by the diocese's various Franciscan orders, who invaded the diocese en masse in the latter part of the sixteenth century.

Given the still limited knowledge of the Catholic Reformation in the Spanish dioceses, it is not possible to state to what degree the experience of Cuenca was typical. While Cuenca's history resembles that of the neighboring archdiocese of Toledo, it bears no comparison to Galicia or Catalonia, where reforms appear to have come later and less dramatically. Both regions were characterized by widely dispersed populations, which made the parish-based reforms and devotions of the Counter-Reformation more difficult to implement. Even in Cuenca, communities smaller than four hundred inhabitants could not support the necessary network of priests and parochial institutions, and lagged behind in catechization. In larger communities, however, the Catholic Reformation ushered in a new regime of faith that would be felt for centuries to come.

BIBLIOGRAPHY

Christian, William A., Jr. *Local Religion in Sixteenth-Century Spain.* Princeton, 1981.
Kamen, Henry. *The Phoenix and the Flame: Catalonia and the Counter Reformation.* New Haven, 1993.
Nalle, Sara T. *God in La Mancha: Religious Reform and the People of Cuenca, 1500–1650.* Baltimore, 1992.

SARA T. NALLE

CULT OF SAINTS. *See* Saints, *article on* Cult of Saints.

CURIA ROMANA. In the broadest sense the Curia Romana—the arm of papal government that administered routine business of the papacy—could be said to comprise the papal household (including its honorary members in other lands) and the numerous *Romanam Curiam sequentes*: lawyers, agents, suppliers, artists, and so on; in a narrower sense it was made up of the college of cardinals and the papal judicial and administrative authorities. Founded in the high Middle Ages, it was an organization of a markedly patrimonial, if unstable, nature, even well into the sixteenth century; from a modern standpoint its structure appears both clumsy and impenetrably complex. For its time, however, the Curia was very efficient. Its rational structure initially gave it the edge over other administrative bodies, although this advantage was lost in the seventeenth century. When the reformer Sixtus V strengthened the principle of collegiality and reorganized the responsibilities of the various departments, the Curia was able to maintain its position as the most advanced administrative apparatus in Europe.

The Curia constantly attracted criticism because its members received preferential treatment in the allocation of benefices (thanks to the pope's plenary power over the church), and because considerable extra costs were incurred for the "services" of the papal administration. Benefices that were bestowed directly from Rome were subject to taxes (*servitia* and *annates*). Charges (*compositiones*) that were imposed on privileges and papal graces *in foro externo*, such as indulgences and dispensations, were extended when other income from the church decreased. It was almost impossible to reform the structure of this fiscal system. The income derived from it was needed to finance the administrative apparatus; at the same time, most members of the Curia had legally purchased their offices and therefore had a right to their privileges. Rescinding this right would automatically wreck the papal credit—and in fact the extension of papal credit, with the price of the office being the capital invested and the income from office covering the payment of annuities, had been the reason behind the expansion of the venal offices in the first place. The papacy, like all other monarchies, was entirely dependent upon credit and could not have functioned without it. Because the resultant revenues were so indispensable to the papacy, it was found impossible in 1569 to reform the apostolic penitentiary (responsible for cases of conscience) by abolishing certain widely detested financial transactions connected with its business; the only solution was to transfer them to the chancery. The Curia, however, became ever more financially dependent as well upon the taxes and duties levied in the Papal States, the Roman authorities being responsible for church *and* state.

From the earliest days of the papacy the cardinals in the consistory formed the papal council. Apart from this, the oldest institutions were the chancery, the chamber, and the Rota. The apostolic chancery, with its many and various functionaries headed by the cardinal–vice-chancellor, could be said to be the typical office in the age of charters, and was the executive body responsible for enacting the pope's decrees in the form of papal bulls. However, even during the late Middle Ages, between the chancery, the chamber, and the pope himself a number of apostolic secretaries were established to deal with less solemn documents, the briefs. The apostolic chamber under the cardinal-chamberlain was in the broadest sense the economic authority; that is, its responsibilities included the administration of the Papal States. However, financial matters were actually dealt with by the independent *Thesaurarius Generalis*, while the *Auditor Camerae*, originally the highest judge in fiscal matters, became responsible for all trials involving members of the Curia. The *Sacra Romana Rota*, on the other hand, was the supreme court, with overall responsibility for the church and the Papal States. In the *Signatura justitiae* legal cases were given a preliminary examination by a referendary before they went to court or were referred to the pope for his personal judgment. The *Signatura qratiae* dispensed graces. During the sixteenth century the referendaries of both *Signaturae* became the stepping-stone to a career in the higher prelature. The datary was formed in the late Middle Ages to act as the papal court of grace *in foro externo*, and acted for the pope in matters relating to petitions for simple benefices, the purchase of offices, marriage dispensations, indulgences, etc. Because these fell within the expanding financial domain of the *compositiones*, where a certain degree of flexibility was possible, the pope always chose the *Datarius* from among the most trustworthy members of his entourage. For the same reason, Rome's critics were particularly assiduous in their denunciations of the datary. The penitentiary, under the cardinal–grand-penitentiary, was responsible for the *forum internum*, which represented the pope in such matters as the absolution of sins and penances.

With the arrival of the age of files, correspondence developed into an important instrument of government. Accordingly, from the fifteenth century onward the pope's personal secretariat, headed by a *Secretarius domesticus* chosen from the ranks of the apostolic secretaries, became increasingly powerful. This secretariat handled the correspondence between Rome and the European courts, particularly that of the papal nuncios appointed to those courts and that of the governors of the diverse provinces of the Papal States. In the sixteenth century the cardinal-nephew took over formal or actual control of this office, but the chief secretary, who in the seventeenth century was given the title secretary of state, also dealt directly with the pope. Subordinate to the chief secretary were secretaries for correspondence with princes, for Latin correspondence, and for ciphered letters. In addition, there was a secretary of briefs through whose office appointments and decrees were processed.

Following the establishment of both the Inquisition in 1542 and the Congregation of the Council of Trent in 1564, permanent commissions (congregations) of the college of cardinals were formed, with responsibilities for specific aspects of policy. Sixtus V's papal bull *Immensa aeterni Dei* transformed these congregations into the backbone of the curial organization. He created fifteen congregations, each made up of three cardinals or more, headed by a cardinal known as the prefect, with a prelate as secretary. Nine of these were responsible for the Universal Church, led by the Inquisition (*Sanctum Officium*) and the congregation of the council, and six for the Vatican State; of these, the supervisory body, the *Consulta*, was the most important. Subsequent popes added others to the list, and on occasion formed *ad hoc* congregations as required to deal with pressing problems. These measures, however, rendered the consistory's appointed role as the "senate" of the church permanently obsolete, and meant that the cardinals, once partners in papal government, were now little more than senior bureaucrats.

[*See also* Papacy *and* Sixtus V.]

BIBLIOGRAPHY

Färber, Konrad M. "Der Brevensekretär Cesare Gloriero: Ein Beitrag zur Geschichte der kurialen Sekretariate in der zweiten Hälfte des 16. Jahrhunderts." *Quellen und Forschungen aus italienischen Archiven und Bibliotheken* 67 (1987), 198–220. A typical career of a sixteenth-century official.

Hofmann, Walter von. *Forschungen zur Geschichte der kurialen Behörden vom Schisma bis zur Reformation* (1914). 2 vols. Reprint, Tübingen, 1975. Fundamental; includes lists of officeholders.

Kraus, Andreas. "Die Geschichte des päpstlichen Staatssekretariats im Zeitalter der katholischen Reform und der Gegenreformation als Aufgabe der Forschung." *Römische Quartalschrift* 84 (1989), 74–91. Summary of modern research on the secretariat of state, including the important contributions of the author.

Moroni, Gaetano. *Dizionario di erudizione storico-ecclesiastica.* 109 vols. Venice 1840–1879. Very old-fashioned, but a mine of important information collected by an insider.

Pásztor, Lajos, ed. *Guida delle fonti per la storia dell'America Latina negli archivi della Santa Sede e negli archivi ecclesiastici d'Italia.* Vatican City, 1970. The former official of the Vatican archives and professor of history of the Curia Romana at the Gregorian University has converted the guide to Latin American sources into a general guide to the Vatican Archives containing abundant information on the institutions of the Curia Romana.

Rapp, Francis. "La Cour de Rome a l'époque de Luther." *Revue de théologie et philosophie (Lausanne)* 119 (1987), 171–194. An excellent overview.

Re, Niccolò del. *La Curia romana: Lineamenti storico-giuridici.* 3d ed. Rome, 1970. Study of the Curia after the reform of Paul VI in 1967 but contains abundant information on the history of all institutions, abolished ones included, an extensive bibliography, and an appendix of some key documents, including *Immensa aeterni Dei.*

Storti, Nicola. *La storia e il diritto della Dataria Apostolica dalle origini ai nostri giorni.* Naples, 1969. Basic information on one of the most crucial offices.

WOLFGANG REINHARD

CURIONE, Celio Secondo (1503–1569), Italian heterodox reformer and writer. Born in Cirié (near Turin) in 1503 of Jacomino and Carlotta Montrotier, he became acquainted with the first writings of the reformers through the Augustinians of Turin, and this soon led him to attempt to flee to the Protestant countries, but he was easily turned back and punished. He then traveled through Italy before settling down for a few years in Salò and in Pavia, where he taught for a three-year period from 1536 to 1539. Again suspected and sought for further charges of antiecclesiastical polemics, he began to wander through Italy; he went to Venice, Ferrara, and Lucca, all of which were cities that, between the end of 1530s and the beginning of the 1540s were important centers for the elaboration and dissemination of Protestant teaching. The contacts he had there with Giulio da Milano, Renata di Francia, Olimpia Morata, Peter Martyr Vermigli, Oalso Martinengo, and others also identified Curione as a member of the pro-Protestant group in Italy, and he was therefore known to the various heterodox circles of north-central Italy. His fame must have been particularly widespread, as he appears among the first people prosecuted by the Roman Inquisition, which at that time had just been reorganized (1542). Even the duke of Florence, Cosimo I de' Medici, was on his trail, although in those years he was anything but eager to support the repressive work of the Inquisition.

Sensing the danger, Curione promptly left Italy, taking refuge in Switzerland, from where he returned a few months later to retrieve his family (around 1529–1530 he had married Margherita Isacchi, who bore him eight children) and to deliver to Duchess Renée of Ferrara *Commentarii in Matthaeum* (Commentaries on [the Gospel of] Matthew) by Heinrich Bullinger. After returning again to Switzerland and settling in Lausanne as prefect of studies, he published in 1544 *Pasquillorum tomi duo* (Two Volumes of Lampoons), which were destined to enjoy long popularity because of their biting as well as easily and widely understood, antiecclesiastical wit; moreover, they reflected a long-standing Italian tradition. The second of the two volumes contains the first version of his *Pasquillus exstaticus* (Ecstatic Lampoon), which was reedited in separate editions in Geneva and Basel. A translation in Venice by Francesco Strozzi was commissioned by Pietro Carnesecchi. Shortly before leaving Lausanne for Basel, on account of the tension caused by the rigid Calvinist orthodoxy, Curione published *Pro vera et antiqua Ecclesiae Christi auctoritate in Antonium Florebellum Mutinensen Oratio* (Oration to Antonio Fiorbello Mutinense for the True and Ancient Authority of the Church of Christ), in which he was one of the first to advance the theme of tolerance, particularly toward the Anabaptists. In Basel he was warmly received by Bonifacius Amerbach and obtained there a respectable and stable position by succeeding J. Hospinianus in the chair of rhetoric at the University of Basel.

Thus relieved of economic worries, he was able to make his house available to Italians exiled for religious reasons who were passing through Basel, and he even made it into an active, albeit cautious, center for antirigorist polemics. It was not by chance after the execution of the Spanish antitrinitarian Michael Servetus in Geneva that Curione was accused of being one of the secret authors of *De haereticis an sint persequendi,* (Heretics: Should They Be Persecuted), published by Sébastien Castellion (under the assumed name of Martinus Bellius) in Basel in 1554. In this same year he also anonymously published *De amplitudine beati regni Dei* (Of the Breadth of the Blessed Kingdom of God), in which an ancient traditional Italian religious theme, the immense mercy of God, is once again used in an anti-Calvinist polemic. It stirred up debates and accusations, which made it necessary for him to defend himself before the senate of Basel. These were not the only cases in which he risked dangerous disciplinary measures, for he was, in fact, also accused of failing to exercise proper preventative censorship against the *Triginta Dialogi* (Thirty Dialogues) by Bernardino Ochino, who, while residing in Zurich, had had the volume published illegally in Basel and was therefore expelled from Zurich. Nevertheless, Curione did not incur any legal sanctions and was able to continue teaching in Basel until his death in November 1569.

BIBLIOGRAPHY

Benrath, K. "Curione Celio Secondo." In *Realencyclopaedie für protestantische Theologie und Kirche,* vol. 4, pp. 353–357. Leipzig, 1898.

Biondi, A. "Curione, Celio Secondo." In *Dizionario Biografico degli Italiani,* vol. 31, pp. 443–449. Rome, 1981.

Cantimori, Delio. *Eretici italiani del cinquecento.* 3d ed. Edited by Adriano Prosperi. Turin, 1992. An earlier edition is available in English translation: *Italian Heretics of the Sixteenth Century,* Cambridge, Mass., 1979.

Kutter, Marcus. *Celio Secondo Curione: Sein Leben und seine Werke, 1503–1569.* Basel, 1955.

Stupanus, J. N. *De Coeli Secund: Curionis vita atque obitu oratio.* Basel, 1570.

Trechsel, Fr. *Die protestantischen Antitrinitarier vor Faustus Socinus.* Vol. I, *Michael Servet und seine Vorgänger.* Heidelberg, 1839.

Williams, George H. *The Radical Reformation.* 3d ed. Kirksville, Mo., 1992.

PAOLO SIMONCELLI
Translated from Italian by Robert E. Shillenn

CUSPINIAN, Johannes (Ger., Spießheimer; 1473–1529), humanist, poet, physician, librarian, and rector at the University of Vienna. Cuspinian also served as the historian of the Habsburgs and of Austria and as a diplomat in the court of the Habsburg emperor Maximilian I. In the latter position he undertook diplomatic missions to Hungary, Bohemia, and Poland. His *Tagebuch* ("diary") from the years 1502–1527 is thus an important source of Austrian and imperial history. A significant center of northern humanism, Vienna's *Sodalitas litteraria Danubiana* (a learned society dedicated, among other things, to the promotion of the three sacred languages: Latin, Greek, and Hebrew) met in Cuspinian's home. This sodality counted among its members many influential humanists, including Conradus Celtis.

Perhaps hoping to gain his support, Luther wrote warmly to Cuspinian in 1517 on the evening following his first appearance before the Diet of Worms, assuring him that he would not recant his books. Initially sympathetic, Cuspinian later apparently opposed the Reformation following the social unrest at Wittenberg in the early 1520s and the Peasants' War.

His appreciative modern biographer, Hans Ankwicz von Kleehoven, styles him a practitioner of sixteenth-century *Realpolitik*, who, in contrast to the impatience of an Ulrich von Hutten or a Luther, devoted himself to a life of learning and public service and became in the process a true Renaissance man worthy to be counted among the most significant figures of his day. Whether that judgment shall hold, the case of Cuspinian is a reminder of the significance of those lesser figures who, though they did not occupy center stage in the dramas of the Reformation, nevertheless made lasting contributions to the course of sixteenth-century European history.

BIBLIOGRAPHY

Ankwicz-Kleehoven, Hans. "Das Tagebuch Cuspinians." *Mitteilungen des Instituts für österreichische Geschichtsforschung* 32 (1911), 274–293.
———. *Der Wiener Humanist Johannes Cuspinian: Gelehrter und Diplomat zur Zeit Kaiser Maximilians I.* Graz, 1959.
Aschbach, Joseph. *Die Wiener Universität und ihre Humanisten im Zeitalter Kaiser Maximilians I.* Vienna, 1877.

MICKEY L. MATTOX

D

DANEAU, Lambert (Lat., Lambertus Danaeus; 1530?–1595), French Calvinist pastor, theologian, and writer. Born in Beaugency-sur-Loire, France, Daneau came from a family of minor nobility. In 1547 or 1548 he was sent to Paris, where he took courses in the newly founded royal college. It was doubtlessly at this time that he was introduced to the classical languages and critical methods in philology and that he acquired his considerable knowledge of grammar, logic, rhetoric, physics, history, and geography that he would later put to extensive use in his work as a theologian. From 1553 to 1559 he studied law in Orléans and then in Bourges, which culminated in a doctorate and which led him to practice law in Orléans. In the course of his studies of law, he was influenced by two famous teachers, François Hotman, whom he was later to join in Geneva after the Saint Bartholomew's Day Massacre, and Anne du Bourg, whose martyrdom in Paris in December 1559 fostered his own religious vocation. During the time he was in Geneva in 1560–1561, he was won over by John Calvin's preaching and teaching. He decided to devote himself to theology and became one of the best advocates of the Calvinist "model," which had captivated him because of its doctrinal, ethical, ecclesiastical, and political coherence.

Daneau was one of the many pastors sent into France by the Compagnie des Pasteurs (Company of Pastors) of Geneva to establish the Reformation in the French kingdom. From 1562 he exercised pastoral ministry in Gien. Despite the frustrations the Wars of Religion imposed on him—temporary exile, loss of library, and imprisonment—during this period Daneau acquired an astounding knowledge of patristics and in particular of Augustine. He published several works, including translations of the polemical and moral treatises of Tertullian and Cyprian, that revealed his interest in the moral and apologetic application of the word of God.

The Saint Bartholomew's Day Massacre put a brutal end to the career of this pastor, who had become justly famous among the Reformed churches of France. After taking refuge in Geneva in September 1572, he was appointed pastor in Vandoeuvres in the Genevan countryside and was assigned to teach theology at the academy of Geneva as an assistant to Théodore de Bèze. In 1574 he became a pastor in the city of Geneva. Daneau was encouraged by Bèze, who wished to find worthy spokesmen for Calvinism. Despite his weak health and lack of self-confidence, Daneau displayed amazing intellectual energy by publishing twenty-seven books in less than eight years—from 1573 to the beginning of 1581. Among them are treatises on morality (*Les sorciers, Remonstrance sur les jeux de sort*), editions of Augustine with commentary (*Enchiridion commentariis illustratus* [1575] and *De haeresibus ad Quodvultdeum* [1578]), a commentary (1580) on the first book of the *Sentences* of Peter Lombard, works on methodology (such as the *Elenchi haereticorum* [1573] and the *Methodus tractandae sacrae Scripturae* [1573]), a commentary (1577) on the first letter to Timothy (which was a veritable treatise on Calvinist ecclesiastical discipline), and a series of polemical works against the papists and against the ubiquitarians Andreas Osiander, Martin Chemnitz, and Nicholas Selnecker. Through this profuse literary production, which revealed his mature theological thought, Daneau made an international place for himself in the theological realm of the Reformation. So it is not surprising that as early as 1579 he was considered for the chair of theology at the new University of Leiden. In January 1581 Daneau received authorization to leave Geneva for the Netherlands.

Daneau's stay in Leiden was difficult and came to an end by 1582. Since he was committed to Reformed ecclesiastical discipline, Daneau came into conflict with the magistracy of Leiden, which had Caesaro-papist leanings and opposed the Genevan model, comparing it to the Spanish Inquisition. The troubled circumstances of his stay did not prevent Daneau from publishing his important commentary (1582) on the Lord's Prayer or from preparing the first volume of his major theological work, the *Christianae Isagoges ad christianorum theologorum locos communes libri II* (Christian Introduction to the Common Sources of Christian Theologians—Two Books; 1583).

After a brief stay (May 1582–May 1583) in Ghent, which was Calvinist at the time, Daneau was summoned to teach theology at the academy of Orthez in the region of Béarn, which enjoyed the support of Henry of Navarre (the future Henry IV). Daneau, serene and circumspect, spent seven years at Orthez, during which he finished his *Isagoge* (*De salutaribus Dei donis erga Ecclesiam* [On the Salutary Gifts of God to the Church], 1586, and *De homine*, 1588). In particular he published a commentary (1586) on the minor prophets and an explanation (1587) of the Apostles' Creed. In 1591 he followed the academy, which was moved to Lescar. In the following year he left the region of Béarn to become the pastor of Castres, where he wrote his *Politice christiana*, published posthumously in 1596, and a refutation of Roberto Bellarmino, published in 1596 and 1598. In 1595 he once more synthesized his thought in his *Compendium sacrae theologiae*, which was published in Montpellier. Daneau died in 1595 in Castres.

As a typical representative of the beginning of Reformed academic teaching, Daneau was concerned with passing on in the most synthetic manner possible the theological thought of his teachers, Calvin and Bèze. He also strove to show the implications of this thought for all areas of knowledge. Thus, he attempted to ground the traditional Aristotelian sciences of physics, ethics, and politics in sacred scripture as interpreted by the Calvinist Reformation. This design led him to borrow theoretical patterns of thought from such theologians as Andreas Hyperius and Niels Hemmingsen. Through the scope of his work and because of his all-encompassing curiosity, Daneau contributed to the creation of a veritable Scholasticism that promoted the stabilization of Reformed orthodoxy.

BIBLIOGRAPHY

Desplat, C. "Lambert Daneau, l'Académie d'Orthez et les superstitions." *Revue de Pau et du Béarn* 12 (1984).

Fatio, Olivier. *Nihil pulchrius ordine: Contribution à l'étude de l'établissement de la discipline écclésiastique aux Pays-Bas ou Lambert Daneau aux Pays-Bas, 1581–1583.* Leiden, 1971.

———. *Méthode et théologie: Lambert Daneau et les débuts de la scolastique réformée.* Geneva, 1976.

———. "Lambert Daneau, 1530–1595." In *Shapers of Religious Traditions in Germany, Switzerland and Poland, 1560–1600,* edited by Jill Raitt. New Haven and London, 1981.

Félice, P. de. *Lambert Daneau (de Baugency-sur-Loire), pasteur et professeur en théologie, 1530–1595: Sa vie, ses ouvrages, ses lettres inédites.* Paris, 1882.

Perrottet, Luc. "Un exemple de la polemique religieuse à la fin du XVIe siècle: La défense de la tradition par Robert Bellarmin (1542–1621) et la réplique calviniste." *Revue de théologie et de philosophie* 114.4 (1982), 395–414.

Ridderkhoff, Cornelia M. "Lambert Daneau, juriste et théologien." *Bulletin de la Société archéologique et historique de l'Orléanais,* n.s., vol. 9.68 (1985).

Sinnema, Donald. "The Discipline of Ethics in Early Reformed Orthodoxy." *Calvin Theological Journal* 28 (1993), 10–44.

OLIVIER FATIO
Translated from French by Robert E. Shillenn

DATHENUS, Petrus

DATHENUS, Petrus (also Pieter Datheen of Daeten; c.1531–1588), Dutch Calvinist preacher and author. Around 1551, during his studies for the priesthood in the Carmelite monastery at Ieper, Dathenus joined the Reformation and settled in London as a printer's apprentice. He received religious instruction in the congregation of Jan Łaski.

After the accession of Mary Tudor, he fled in 1554 to Emden and afterward to Frankfurt am Main, where he became pastor to the Netherlandish refugees in 1555. Here he met John Calvin, with whom he corresponded regularly until 1562. He waged vigorous disputes with the Lutherans, who made his stay in Frankfurt impossible. With the support of Elector Frederick III of the Palatinate he founded the Netherlandish congregation at Frankenthal near Worms. He translated the Heidelberg Cathechism into Dutch. He also wrote, after the French model of Clément Marot, his own rhymed translation of the *Psalms De Psalmen ende ander Lofsanghen wt den Francoyschen Dichte in Nederlandschen overghesett* (The Psalms and Other Songs of Praises Translated into Dutch from the French Versification; 1566).

In 1566 he returned to his native land in order to support the Reformation there. As pastor of the Calvinist congregation in Ghent following the wave of iconoclasm, he pushed for the organization of armed resistance. By the spring of 1567 he was back in Frankenthal. He presided over the Colloquy of Wesel (1568), where the foundation was laid for the organization of the Dutch Reformed church. In 1570 Frederick III of the Palatinate named Dathenus to be his court preacher in Heidelberg. After the capture of Den Briel (1572), William of Orange commissioned him to organize the Reformed church in the provinces of Holland and Zeeland. As a confidant of William, Dathenus was also entrusted with diplomatic missions to England and Germany. He was president of the Synod of Dordrecht (1578), which undertook the organization of the Reformed church in all the provinces of the Netherlands.

As the foremost pastor in Ghent, he openly supported the strong anti-Catholic course of the revolutionary government of Jan van Hembyze. He quickly set about organizing the Reformed church and religious instruction in most Flemish cities and towns. His zealous campaign against Catholics led to an open break with William of Orange. In August 1579 Dathenus moved back to Frankenthal accompanied by Hembyze. Numerous attempts by the Synod of Middelburg (1581) failed to reconcile Dathenus with William. In 1583 Dathenus and Hembyze were called back to Ghent. When it appeared that the radical government had no future prospects, however, Dathenus supported the betrayal of Hembyze (1584). After a short time of incarceration in Vianen and Utrecht as a coconspirator, Dathenus permanently left the Netherlands, where he could play no further role. For three years he wandered around Lutheran north Germany. Disheartened and the victim of religious doubts, he adhered for a while to the libertinism of the followers of David Joris. He died in Elbing in East Prussia, where he was a secondary school teacher.

Dathenus, the exponent of unbending and pugnacious Calvinism in the Netherlands and beyond, did not disdain the use of the sword. His Calvinist exclusivism and his open support of intolerance at Ghent were disastrous for the cause of William of Orange and the States-General. This did not hinder him from bringing to the church his exceptional qualities in organization and instruction. Of special significance were his *Psalms* translation and his liturgical writings, which strongly determined Calvinist piety and liturgy in the Netherlands from 1566 until the late eighteenth century.

BIBLIOGRAPHY

Bremmer, R. H. *Reformatie en Rebellie: Willem van Oranje, de calvanisten en het recht van opstand; Tien onstuimige jaren; 1572–1581.* Franeker, 1984. Studies the political and liturgical role of Petrus Dathenus, as well as his relations with William of Orange between 1571 and 1584.

Crew, Phyllis Mack. *Calvinist Preaching and Iconoclasm in the Netherlands, 1544–1569.* Cambridge, 1978. Sheds light on the significance of Dathenus in the religious and political realms.

JOHAN DECAVELE
Translated from Dutch by Jeff Bach

DÁVID, Francis (Hung., Ferenc; Ger., Franz Hertel; Lat., Franciscus Davidis; c.1520–1579), successively a superintendent (bishop) of the Hungarian Lutherans, the Reformed, and the Unitarians in Transylvania. Born of a well-to-do Saxon artisan family in Transylvania, Dávid started his studies in his hometown of Kolozsvár (Klausenburg). Concerning his further education, scholarly opinion differs, and he is reported to have attended schools in Transylvania, the chapter school in Gyulafehérvár (Karlsburg), the municipal school in Brassó (Kronstadt), and, abroad, the universities of Wittenberg and Frankfurt an der Oder. Upon returning home around 1551, Dávid held the positions of rector and then cleric in several places until he became the town pastor of Kolozsvár in 1556. He would remain in this city until his imprisonment at Déva (Diemrich) in 1579.

Dávid's spiritual odyssey, however, was complex and led from Roman Catholicism, to Lutheranism, to Helvetic Reformed views, and ultimately to Unitarianism. The date of his conversion to Lutheranism is unknown. Until 1558 he was one of the ruling spirits of the struggles of the Hungarian Lutherans in Transylvania against other religious inclinations, and he drafted the articles adopted by several synods. In 1559, however, he was an advocate of Swiss Reformed views and drafted a resolution on the Eucharist in accordance with these views. Eight years later, in 1567, he joined the antitrinitarian, or Unitarian, movement, subsequently publishing his most important and influential works. After 1575 he started preaching against the "true divinity" of Jesus Christ and thus against the invocation of his name in prayer. These changing views of Dávid, which were manifested also by many others in Transylvania, indicate the spiritual atmosphere of the principality during the third quarter of the sixteenth century. Freethinkers and radicals from all of Europe found shelter and toleration there.

Dávid must have been an able, forceful, and personable figure, for he was elected to high offices in each of the religious communities to which he belonged. In 1557 he was elected a superintendent of the Hungarian Lutherans in Transylvania. Abdicating this position, but not his pastorate, two years later, he became the superintendent of the Calvinists in 1564. From 1571 he was the superintendent of the Unitarians. From 1564 until the death of John II Sigismund, Dávid served as the court chaplain of the prince and helped influence the ruler's open conversion to antitrinitarianism at the religious colloquy at Nagyvárad in 1569. Dávid lost his position in the court when the Catholic Stephen Báthory succeeded John II Sigismund.

Dávid was an energetic ecclesiastical organizer and a fierce disputant. His adversaries accused him of both violence and superciliousness. Yet he must have demonstrated spiritual integrity, since the repeated, conspicuous changes of his religious persuasion did not generate great hostility among his contemporaries. Only in 1578, after a further radicalization of his views, did Dávid lose the support of the Unitarians, and he was delivered up to the state authorities. He was accused of violating the law by repudiating the legally sanctioned tenet that God shared his divinity with Christ. At a public hearing before the diet in June 1579, Dávid, ill and unable to speak up anymore, held onto his newly acquired belief that God shared only the power of his divinity with Jesus. Dávid was convicted "as a warning to others" and hauled to the fortress of Déva, where he died in November of the same year.

The opposition to Dávid—led by his former antitrinitarian colleague, the courtier and physician Giorgio Biandrata—occasioned fierce debates among Unitarians both at home and abroad. The defenders of Dávid published a widely read book, the *Defensio Francisci Davidis in negotio de non invocando Jesu Christo in precibus*, issued in several editions and including many documents. Modern Unitarianism would come to regard him as one of the founders of this movement.

Dávid's outward life was as variegated as his spiritual world. Although he was of Saxon origin and had excellent contacts with the Germans in Transylvania, Dávid did not compose a single work in his native tongue. All of his writings are in Hungarian or Latin. He married twice. His first wife was perhaps of Polish origin, as well as the mother of his daughter and two sons that survived to maturity. He married his second wife, Katherine Münich-Barát, in 1572 and divorced her four years later. Dávid is the only sixteenth-century ecclesiastic who is known to have divorced.

BIBLIOGRAPHY

Primary Sources

Dávid, Francis. *Az Szent Irásnak fundamentumából vött magyarázat az Jesus Christuról és az ó igaz istenségéről* (Explanation Founded on the Bible Regarding Jesus Christ and His True Divinity). N.p., n.d.

———. *Elsó része az Szent Irásnak kölen-külen részeiből vött prédiká-*

cióknak az Atya Istenról, ennek kedig az ó fiáról, az Jézus Christusrul és a mi örökségünknek pecsétiról, az Szt Lélekról (First Part of the Sermons from Various Parts of Bible on God the Father, His Son Jesus Christ, and the Seal of Our Heritage the Holy Spirit). Albae Juliae, 1569. There is no second part.

———. *Rövid magyarázat miképpen az Antichristus az igaz Istenról való tudományt meghomályosította* (Short Explanation that the Antichrist obscured the Knowledge of the True God). Albae Juliae, 1567. Facsimile edition, Kolozsvár, 1910. Excerpts appear in Latin translation in *De falsa et vera unius Dei patris filii et spiritus sancti cognitione. . . .* Albae Juliae, 1568.

———. *Theses de non invocando Jesu Christo in precibus.* In *Defensio Francisci Dávidis. . . .* Krakow, 1581. Facsimile edition, introduced by Mihály Balázs, Budapest and Leiden, 1983.

Secondary Sources

Dán, Róbert, and Antal Pirnát, eds. *Antitrinitarianism in the Second Half of the Sixteenth Century.* Proceedings of the International Colloquium held on the Four-Hundredth Anniversary of Ferenc Dávid's Death. Budapest and Leiden, 1982.

Dávid Ferenc, 1579–1979. Cluj-Napoca, 1979. Several important studies.

Jakab, Elek. *Dávid Ferencz emléke* (The Memory of Francis Dávid). Budapest, 1879. Contains an extensive bibliography and some of Dávid's minor writings; although it must be used with caution in the light of later research, this book is regarded even today as the basic work on Dávid.

KATALIN PÉTER

DEATH. The Reformation violently disrupted late medieval religious life and practices and affected Christian attitudes toward death. Johan Huizinga observes, in *The Waning of the Middle Ages* (New York, 1965), how "an everlasting call of *memento mori*" sounds through late medieval life. According to Philippe Aries's survey, *Western Attitudes Toward Death* (Baltimore, 1974), a new tradition arose in the twelfth century that focused on the individual's death (*la mort de toi*, "one's own death") and displaced the older tradition (*et moriemur*, "and we all shall die"), which viewed death as "the collective destiny of the species."

Cult of the Dead. This new emphasis on the individual is expressed in various ways in the latter Middle Ages, especially in the portrayal of the Last Judgment, in the displacement of this judgment to the moment of death, in the rise of macabre themes in literature and art, such as the portrayal of physical decomposition, and in the return to funeral inscriptions and other ways to personalize tombs. It is what A. N. Galpern (*The Religion of the People in Sixteenth-Century Champagne*, Cambridge, 1976) recognizes in French Catholicism as "in large part a cult of the living in service of the dead." The ubiquitous influence of the cult of the dead, however, was also a way for the living to order their community; when the reformers attacked the cult of the dead it was, as Duffy suggests, an attempt to redefine the

boundaries of human community and to limit the claims of the past.

The medieval Dance of Death (*danse macabre, Totentanz*), a procession of representatives of all social ranks and groups, each accompanied by a corpse-like figure representing Death, emphasized in the late Middle Ages a realistic treatment of the physical aspects of dying and death. Verses on death appear as explanatory legends for illustrations of the dance and emphasize the suffering of the dying person's sickness and agony; yet, medieval poetry on death is characterized by a collective acknowledgment of death's universality.

In observing the depiction of the Dance of Death at Saint Paul's Cathedral (*De Quatuor Novissimis* [Four Last Things], 1522), Thomas More notes that "we shall feel ourself stered and altered by the feeling of that imagination in our hearts." The dance and visual representations in cadaver tombs (*transi*) that portrayed the deceased as a dying corpse reminded people of their mortality and inescapable fate. When Death can come at any time, one must focus on last things—death, judgment, hell, and heaven—and the need for good works to ensure salvation.

Fifteenth-century guides suggested well-defined attitudes and gestures expected by the dying in the final deathbed struggle for the Christian's soul. It was a communal event at which the dying Christian, by making a will, not only disposed of property but also put his or her spiritual house in order. This included making bequests for prayers and supplications interceding for the departed soul (e.g., by requiem masses, Evensong, or Matins for the dead), and providing alms for the poor who would pray for the dead and encircle the body with lighted candles (to banish demons). One also arranged for secular bequests such as the upkeep of roads and bridges, or having one's name included on the bede-roll, a list of deceased parishioners to be remembered for their devotion and for whose soul prayers were offered. Some left bequests to the high altar of the parish church for forgotten tithes and offerings.

Catholics offered prayers for departed souls suffering in purgatory. Devotional literature pictures the sufferings of the damned as a warning to the living, whose prayers, like indulgences and requiem masses for the dead, could hasten the dead soul's removal to heaven. Books providing advice on the "art of dying," or *ars moriendi* (*Kunst zu starben, l'art de mourir*), were popular works of consolation and personal devotion meant to help the Christian die well and to overcome the fear of death. These works, often illustrated with woodcuts and explanatory verses, were commentaries on the texts of the services for visitation of the sick and for burial, and included such instructions as having the priest hold the Crucifix before the eyes of the dying person and interrogate the dying to reject heresy, die in the faith, repent, and trust in Christ's passion. The final step was the anointing of the sick (the sacrament of Extreme Unction), which completes the effects of the sacrament of Penance. Such works proliferated during the sixteenth and seventeenth centuries among both Catholics and Protestants, preparing the Christian mentally for death.

Reformers Assault Tradition. The Reformation effected a major shift in thinking about the dead. Reformers eliminated the last rites as a sacrament and displaced the hope of purgatory as allowing sin to be too easily expiated in the afterlife. Late medieval Catholicism obligated the living to provide services for the dead and the souls in purgatory. The reformers denounced the doctrine of purgatory to insist, as Calvin does, that "the blood of Christ is the sole satisfaction for the sins of believers, the sole expiation, the sole purgation" (*Institutes*, 3.5.6). Luther rejects the pardoning power of the pope, the validity of indulgences for the dead, and the Roman theory of abundant merits from the saints that supplement Christ's merits as the basis for the forgiveness of sins. If Catholics prepared for death through the sacraments, each of which helped in some way to prepare for death, and through participation in the liturgy, the reformers found less need for the sacraments. Luther substitutes a new conception of faith and justification in place of the sacrament of repentance with its meritorious works, for example, yet talks about how baptism renders "all afflictions, and especially, death useful and helpful" ("Sermon on Baptism," 1519).

Medieval people assumed they were being defeated by death, but their attitude of extreme humility seems to disappear in the early sixteenth century, when Renaissance poets, for example, dwell on fame and immortality rather than death. Yet, in later sixteenth-century England, poems appeared anticipating the poet's own death or responding to the death of another; elegies, epitaphs, and ornate monuments and tombs became popular, perhaps because of the religious uncertainty of the times. There was also a steady stream of books representative of early Puritan and late sixteenth-century English attitudes toward death, which often adopt the *ars moriendi* tradition to a Calvinistic theology. These include such popular works as Thomas Becon's *Sick Man's Salve* (1561), William Perkins's *A Salve for a Sick Man* (1595), and Nicholas Bayfield's *Cure of the Fear of Death* (1618). Perkins characteristically claims that the life of a Christian "is nothing else but a meditation of death," echoing Calvin's observation that our lives are "enveloped" in death (*Institutes*, 1.17.10).

Rather than providing for the sale of masses and privileged mortuary devotions, the Reformed doctrine of predestination and the belief that the living can do nothing for the dead assaulted traditional masses for the dead and the endowment of religious houses. Protestant wills often provided for Christian charities or found substitutes for earlier obligations such as, in England, building elaborate monuments. Alterations in conventional phrasing used in wills may offer clues to shifts in religious belief and attitudes toward death, or reflect accommodation to theological and political realities of the time. Reformers scoffed at the physical presence of demons at death, the ringing of bells, and the leaving of holy bread on the windowsill to counteract Satan and denounced pardons and other traditional Catholic practices surrounding dying Christians and their families and friends. Yet it was important to attend to the dying person. Calvin recognized that God's judgment cannot be felt without evoking the dread of death (*Institutes* 2.8.3.), and Luther advocates, in his "Von der Bereitung zum Sterben" (Sermon of Preparation for Dying; 1519), the custom of praying with a dying person to avoid loneliness in the hour of death. Christians are emboldened to die when they know they are not alone, although "we should think about death while we are alive." Death is the death of our sin and the end of our imperfections; it is unnatural and God's punishment for sin. It is a matter of faith for Luther that death brings life; the gospel and faith allow one to see in the midst of death, and it is a paradox that death causes the soul to become well and slays sin.

The Deathbed and Funeral. Writing against the fear of death, Calvin says no one "has made progress in the school of Christ who does not joyfully await the day of death and final resurrection" (*Institutes* 3.9.5), while Luther frequently talks about how one is to "venture joyously" (*fröhlich wagen*) in the face of death. Deathbed rituals, especially surrounding the dying person with family members, became important for reformers. Luther observes in a sermon on preparing for death (1519) that at death we should have before us only life, grace, and salvation; we should brood over our sins during our lifetime, not on our deathbed. Moreover, the true preparation for death, Luther explains in his comments on *Isaiah* 38.10, is the exercise of faith, which knows that death is vanquished through Christ.

While the medieval funeral service eulogized the deceased, the core of the reformers' funeral service was the sermon, an exposition of a scriptural text, with a focus on the primacy of the gospel for salvation. Luther's own funeral sermons for the electors Frederick III and John, which view the deceased as models of Christian behavior in life and death, may be the model for later exempla of holy living and holy dying. By mid-sixteenth century collections of Protestant funeral sermons appeared, and other model lives and deaths became available. These included the widespread accounts of Luther's death and those of other reformers, and such works in England as John Foxe's *Book of Martyrs* (London, 1563), accounts of Protestant martyrs, and later works such as Thomas Fuller's *Abel Redevivus, or The Dead Yet Speaking* (1651), which offered "a Magazeen of religious patterns for their Imitation," and Puritan divine Samuel Clarke's *The Lives of Sundry Eminent Persons* (1683), which emphasized the saints' courage and lack of fear of death. Religious literature and sermons directed at the young, who often associated death with old age, warn against death and urge them to tend to their salvation.

BIBLIOGRAPHY

Beaty, Nancy Lee. *The Craft of Dying: A Study in the Literary Tradition of the Ars Moriendi in England.* New Haven, 1970. Discusses some of the early literature on death, with particular emphasis on Jeremy Taylor's *The Craft of Dying.*

Davis, Natalie Z. "Some Tasks and Themes in the Study of Popular Religion." In *The Pursuit of Holiness in Late Medieval and Renaissance Religion,* edited by Charles E. Trinkhaus and Heiko A. Oberman, pp. 307–336. Leiden, 1974.

Doering-Hirsch, E. *Tod und Jenseits im Spätmittelalter.* Berlin, 1927. Careful documentation of how contemporary religious literature emphasized the soul's fate while secular art and literature were also concerned with the process of dying.

Duffy, Eamon. *The Stripping of the Altars: Traditional Religion in England, c.1400–c.1580.* New Haven, 1992. A detailed examination of beliefs and practices of late medieval parishioners and of their dismantling and destruction under the Tudors.

O'Connor, Mary Catherine. *The Art of Dying Well: The Development of the Ars Moriendi.* New York, 1942.

Stannard, David E. *The Puritan Way of Death: A Study in Religion, Culture, and Social Change.* New York, 1977.

Thomas, Keith. *Religion and the Decline of Magic.* New York, 1971.

ANDREW M. MCLEAN

DECIUS, Johannes. *See* Diaz, Juan.

DEDEL, Adriaan Floriszoon. *See* Adrian VI.

DEFENESTRATION OF PRAGUE. This dramatic act of rebellion, by which two principal lieutenants of the absentee Habsburg ruler of Bohemia were thrown out of a high window in Prague Castle on 23 May 1618, inaugurated not only the Bohemian Revolt but the whole Thirty Years' War in Europe. It was provoked by the attempts of the royal authorities to implement the Counter-Reformation in the kingdom and to ignore the freedoms secured for non-Catholics by the Letter of Majesty nine years earlier. Two particular cases were at issue: at Broumov (Braunau) and Hroby (Klostergrab) Protestants sought to erect new churches on lands belonging, respectively, to a Benedictine monastery and the archbishopric of Prague.

Resentment at the religious policies of the Crown caused the Protestant estates to assemble for a dietal session, despite royal prohibition. Their anger focused on two zealously Catholic aristocrats who were regarded as the chief culprits, Jaroslav Martinic and Vilém Slavata. A small group of radical dissidents decided to impose the same summary and condign punishment on them as had been meted out in Hussite times. But the tactic failed of its real purpose: both

officials, together with their secretary, survived the long drop into the grassy castle moat and were able to flee abroad.

Although halfhearted attempts at last-minute compromise were made, the defenestration precipitated a civil war in Bohemia between parties divided on mainly religious lines. The Protestants issued an apology to justify their action, raised troops, and sought foreign allies. In 1619, on the death of King Matthias, they deposed his designated heir, the militantly Catholic Ferdinand II, and elected the Calvinist Elector Palatine, Frederick V. But Ferdinand, who could call on military support from Bavaria and Spain, prevailed at the Battle of White Mountain and thereby sealed the fate of Protestantism in Bohemia.

[*See also* Bohemia *and* White Mountain, Battle of.]

BIBLIOGRAPHY

Gindely, Anton. *Geschichte des Dreißigjährigen Kriegs.* 4 vols., Prague, 1869–80. Classic account, not superseded, of the Bohemian Revolt and its aftermath. Despite the title, not to be confused with the general *History of the Thirty Years War* 2 vols. which appeared under Gindely's name.

Kavka, František. *Bílá Hora a ceské dejiny.* Prague, 1962. Studies the place of the Revolt in Bohemian history.

Polienský, Josef V., *The Thirty Years War.* London, 1971. Narrative and analysis, from the Bohemian perspective, of the whole conflict unleashed by the Defenestration.

Sturmberger, Hans. *Der Aufstand in Böhmen. Der Beginn des Dreißigjährigen Kriegs.* Munich, 1959. A useful short account of the central-European context.

Tapié, Victor-Lucien. *La Politique étrangère de la France et le début de la guerre de Trente ans, 1616–21.* Paris, 1934. Major study of the European context of the Bohemian Revolt, which draws on Czech sources.

R. J. W. EVANS

DELLA CASA, Giovanni (1503–1556), Italian ecclesiastical careerist, inquisitor, writer, and poet. Della Casa was born to a Florentine patrician family and studied law and letters, including Greek. His intellectual style and personal morality were those of a Renaissance *letterato* (learned author) belonging to the social elite. His most famous work is *Galateo,* a treatise on manners.

Though Della Casa had no religious vocation, he did have the patronage of the Farnese, the family of Pope Paul III (1534–1549), and so took holy orders in 1537, receiving the rich archbishopric of Benevento in 1544. Della Casa expected to be made a cardinal in 1549 but was disappointed. He was papal nuncio to Venice (1544–1549), and was energetic and effective in carrying out diplomatic and other functions, including that of inquisitor. But Della Casa was often frustrated by Venice, the Italian state most jealous of its own jurisdiction, in his attempts to arrest, try, punish, or extradite individuals accused of spreading Protestant heresy. The Venetian inquisition was a uniquely mixed tribunal, being composed of Venetian lay patricians who represented the state and held ultimate power, as well as the nuncio and other clerics. In April 1547 it was reorganized, and repressive action against those spreading Protestant ideas increased.

Della Casa's most notorious case was that of Pier Paolo Vergerio, bishop of Capodistria, at first a reformer and critic of the church, but in 1549 a fugitive heretic. Though Della Casa handled this case with moderation, he was made the target of Vergerio's literary revenge. Della Casa supervised, in collaboration with the Venetian state, the publication in 1549 of the first Index of Prohibited Books to appear in Italy. It was used as Protestant propaganda by Vergerio, who republished it in the north with a sarcastic commentary, making note of many Protestant works that had been omitted by the compilers.

BIBLIOGRAPHY

Primary Source

Della Casa, Giovanni. *Correspondenza di Giovanni Della Casa.* Rome, 1986.

Secondary Sources

Bujanda, J. M. de. *Index des livres interdits.* Vol. 3, *Index de Venise 1549, Venise et Milan 1554.* Sherbrooke, Que., 1987. Text and full analysis of the contents of the Venetian Index of Prohibited Books of 1549, with a historical introduction by Paul F. Grendler that updates the relevant sections of his 1977 book on Venetian censorship.

Mutini, C. "Della Casa, Giovanni." In *Dizionario biografico degli Italiani*, vol. 36, pp. 699–719. Rome, 1988. A detailed summary and evaluation of his life, with complete bibliography.

Santosuosso, Antonio. "The Moderate Inquisitor: Giovanni Della Casa's Venetian Nunciature 1544–1549." *Studi Veneziani*, n.s. 2 (1978), 119–210. A full account in English of Della Casa as inquisitor, undercutting the myth of Venice as a haven of freedom.

———. *Vita di Giovanni Della Casa.* Rome, 1979. A valuable biography, despite debatable psychological and cultural explanations of the personality and writings of Della Casa.

WILLIAM MCCUAIG

DENCK, Hans (c.1500–1527), early leader of the Anabaptist movement in south Germany. He is one of the most important sources for the distinctive spiritualist form of Anabaptism that spread in south Germany in the 1520s. During his short life he came into contact with most of the important leaders of the radical brand of reform in the south. The intellectual life of Johannes Bünderlin, Ludwig Hätzer, Jacob Kautz, and even Sebastian Franck developed under the influence of Denck. Given the brief span in which he was active, his impact is indicative of the seminal nature of his ideas.

Denck's life and thought were shaped by a variety of influences. He was trained in the humanistic languages. In Basel (c.1523) he came under the influence of Erasmus and Oecolampadius. Later he resided in Nuremberg (1524–1525) and came into contact with the theologies of Andreas Bodenstein von Karlstadt and Thomas Müntzer, as well as with proto-Anabaptist ideas. He was eventually examined by the town council and expelled from Nuremberg in January 1525 because of his unorthodox views. For the remainder of his life Denck led a peripatetic existence, residing for a time in Augsburg, Strasbourg, and Worms. It was in this period he published his written works and came to have such a major influence in shaping the ideas of south German Anabaptism. He was witness to the beginning of sectarian organizing and to the violence exercised against the Anabaptist movement by the authorities. He died a victim of the plague in 1527.

Denck put forward in his writings a number of key ideas that challenged the nascent orthodoxies of the evangelical movement. Denck's thought—shaped by the medieval mysticism of Johannes Tauler and the *Theologia Deutsch*, as well as the sacramentarian theology of Müntzer and Karlstadt—came to question the utility of outward forms and authorities as mediating God's revelation or grace. Denck posited as the true religious authority an inward seed or image of God within the soul. Outward forms, he thought, are of use only as witnesses to the inwardly revealed truth, to substantiate and strengthen what is already known within. Scripture and the sacraments serve as secondary witnesses to a truth first grasped inwardly. The outer witness, not the inward enlightenment, is ultimately dispensable. Christ himself is understood as an exemplar of what God desires from us. He has shown the way God wishes humans to go—to be resigned and empty so that God may work within us.

Denck allowed a limited free will: humans can choose to permit God's spirit to work within them and conform them to his image. The sure sign of this inward enlightenment is outward obedience to God's law and thus a pure and spotless life. In putting forward this theology, Denck set himself sharply at odds with the theology of Luther, as he denied the bondage of the human will, the primacy of the scriptures for faith, and the spoken word as the avenue through which God communicates. For most of his short career Denck espoused adult baptism as an outward sign of the inward penetration of God's word, a sign of the covenant formed in one's conscience. At the very end of his life, Denck, disillusioned by the excesses of the early Anabaptist movement and the violence exercised against it by the authorities, came to imply that outward forms should be left completely to convention and thus divisive sectarianism avoided. With this he anticipated the thoroughgoing spiritualism of Sebastian Franck.

Denck's writings inspired many others, who subsequently worked out the implications of these ideas. One strand of the Anabaptist movement clearly has its roots in the spiritualizing theology of Denck. His emphasis on inward enlightenment formed the basis for most radical challenges to the movement to institutionalize the newly reformed religion, which came from such figures as Johannes Bünderlin, Christian Entfelder, Johannes Kautz, and most prominently Sebastian Franck. Later free-spirit movements, such as the Family of Love and the spiritualist Anabaptism of Dirk Philips, stand in a line of development that in part goes back to Denck. One can see in Denck a basic response to the challenge of reform—the inner world of the spirit becomes the arena in which God first works to purify his church, after which the outer world will come to conform itself as an imperfect witness to what can only be realized within.

BIBLIOGRAPHY

Primary Sources

Bauman, Clarence. *The Spiritual Legacy of Hans Denck: Interpretation and Translation of Key Texts.* Leiden, 1991. Bauman seeks a close faithfulness to the German and publishes the original text on the facing page, with extensive biographical discussion and interpretation plus a useful bibliography.

Denck, Hans. *Schriften I: Bibliographie.* Edited by G. Baring. Gütersloh, 1955.

———. *Religiöse Schriften.* Edited by W. Fellmann. Gütersloh, 1956.

———. *Exegetische Schriften.* Edited by W. Fellmann. Gütersloh, 1960.

Furcha, E. J., ed. and trans. *Selected Writings of Hans Denck, 1500–1527.* Lewiston, NY, 1989. Contains Denck's major works in English translation. Furcha's translation aims at an idiomatic English text.

Secondary Sources

Bautz, Friedrich Wilhelm, ed. *Biographische-Bibliographisches Kirchenlexikon.* Hamm, 1970–. See vol. 1, pp. 1256–1257.

Ozment, Steven. *Mysticism and Dissent.* New Haven, 1973. Contains a chapter on Denck important for understanding the intellectual context into which Denck fits.

Packull, Werner O. *Mysticism and the Early South German-Austrian Anabaptist Movement, 1525–1531.* Scottdale, Pa., 1977. Puts Denck into the context of early Anabaptism in South Germany.

Verzeichnis der im deutschen Sprachbereich erschienenen Drucke des XVI. Jahrhunderts. Stuttgart, 1983–. See vol. 5, nos. 555–573.

Weis, F. L. *The Life, Teachings and Works of Johannes Denck.* Strasbourg, 1924. An old, straightforward, and reverent treatment of Denck's life.

PATRICK HAYDEN-ROY

DENIS THE CARTHUSIAN (also Denys van Leeuwen; Denys of Rijkel/Ryckel; 1402/03–1471), encyclopedic, theological, and spiritual writer known as "Doctor ecstaticus." Born at Saint Truiden (Saint Trond) in Limburg (Belgium), Denis was educated at Saint Truiden and Zwolle before gaining a Thomist and Albertist education at the University of Cologne (M.A., 1424). He entered the charterhouse of Roermond in Limburg (Netherlands) in 1425 and spent most of his life in a spiritual and scholarly retirement that was unusually strict even by Carthusian standards. Largely self-taught in scholastic theology, he was best known as a spiritual and devotional writer and received local veneration for sanctity.

Denis the Carthusian's massive oeuvre offers students of the Reformation era an encyclopedia of late medieval theology that has remained largely unexploited since Johann Huizinga drew on it for his *Waning of the Middle Ages*. The Carthusian's scope was comprehensive: he wrote commentaries on each book of the Bible and covered topics in dogmatic theology, Mariology, monastic reform, general church reform and conciliarism, contemplative and mystical theology, vices and virtues, discretion of spirits, theological aesthetics, and the Christian life of merchants, soldiers, princes, prelates, and others. His method was compendious: he produced successful abridgments of the Pauline epistles, scholastic philosophy, Thomas Aquinas's *Summa Theologiae*, and of some of the scholastic commentaries on Peter Lombard's *Sentences*. Yet his most popular writings were devotional in nature: *De contemptu mundi, Speculum animae peccatricis,* and *De quatuor novissimis.* Ten of these devotional works were published before 1500, and several were translated into various vernaculars. Four sermon sequences contain about seven hundred sermons.

Early Protestants made little use of Denis's writings, although his collected works did find their way into the library of the Geneva academy by the 1570s. The Cologne Carthusians' edition (1530–1540) of Denis's entire oeuvre permitted Denis to leave a clear impress on the Catholic Reformation. Responding to Protestant theology, the Cologne editors placed Denis's commentaries on the Pauline epistles in one of the first volumes. Individual volumes were dedicated to leading Catholic figures from Germany to England; in 1532 and 1533, before the tide turned against the London Carthusians, two volumes were dedicated to Henry VIII and Thomas Cromwell. Ignatius of Loyola may have drawn on several of Denis's works. Many of the ascetic and devotional writings and some of the scripture commentaries were republished in the sixteenth and seventeenth centuries. The works of scholastic philosophy and theology sustained less interest.

BIBLIOGRAPHY

Primary Sources

Doctoris ecstatici Dionysii Cartusiani Opera Omnia. 42 vols. Montreuil-sur-Mer, Tournai Parkminster, 1896–1913, 1935. A noncritical, slightly corrected reissue of the sixteenth-century Cologne edition, produced under the stimulus of the neo-Thomist revival of Leo XIII, who thought highly of Denis's spiritual teachings. See Chaix.

Emery, Kent, Jr. *Dionysii Cartusiensis Opera Selecta.* Corpus Christianorum, Continuatio Mediaevalis 121, 121A. Turnhout, Belgium, 1991. A thorough study of questions of authorship and of the manuscript transmission of Denis's writings.

Secondary Sources

Chaix, Gerald. *Réforme et contre-réforme catholiques: Recherches sur la Chartreuse de Cologne au XVIe siecle.* 3 vols. Analecta Cartusiana 80.1–3. Salzburg, 1981. Vol. 1, pp. 211–233, 241; vol. 2, pp. 443–507, 773–778 offer a thorough bibliography of sixteenth- and seventeenth-century editions of Denis's *corpus* of writings.

Emery, Kent, Jr. "Twofold Wisdom and Contemplation in Denys of Ryckel (Dionysius Cartusiensis, 1402–71)." *Journal of Medieval and Renaissance Studies* 18 (1988), 99–134. The best scholarly overview in English.

Spaapen, B. "Karthuizer-Vroomheid en ignatiaanse spiritualiteit." *Ons aeesteliik Erf* 30 (1956), 337–366; 31 (1957), 129–149.

Steinmetz, David C. *Luther in Context*. Bloomington, Ind., 1986.

Stoelen, Anselme. "Denys the Carthusian." In *Spirituality through the Centuries*, edited by James Walsh, pp. 220–232. New York, 1964.

DENNIS D. MARTIN

DENMARK. In the sixteenth century Denmark and Norway were united, and together they also included the provinces of Scåne, Halland, and Blekinge (which now belong to Sweden); the Faroe Islands; Iceland; Gothland; and the island of Rygen (the latter however only in an ecclesiastical sense because secularly it belonged to the duchy of Pomerania). Between Germany in the south and Denmark were the duchies of Schleswig and Holstein, which stood in personal union with the kingdom of Denmark because the king was also the duke of Schleswig and Holstein. Schleswig was a fief under the Crown, but Holstein (until 1548) was also a fief under the German emperor. In 1544 the duchies were divided among King Christian III and his younger brothers Hans and Adolf. Norway had been a country with its own national council and royal governor until 1536, but that year Christian III abolished Norway as an independent country. He dissolved the national council and made Norway into a province of Denmark. This Danish-Norwegian monarchy lasted until 1814.

The crisis that had dominated the late Middle Ages—falling prices for agricultural products, rising costs, and population decline—changed about 1500 into economic and demographic growth, and it is assumed that Denmark's population was then about five hundred thousand. There were some eighty market towns, but most of them had less than a thousand inhabitants. Copenhagen had a population of about ten to fifteen thousand. Economic progress and population growth took place mainly in the large trading cities. By 1600 Copenhagen had about twenty thousand inhabitants. Malmö, Odense, and Ribe had about five thousand. Norway was almost completely a farming community. In Oslo there were approximately a thousand inhabitants, and the city of Bergen had about five thousand.

Until 1536, when the Lutheran Reformation was officially introduced, the church owned 30 to 40 percent of the country's land, which gave it extensive economic and legal privileges. The clergy made up only a small percentage of the population. The king owned 20 percent of the land, and the nobility, which made up one quarter of 1 percent of the population and consisted of about two hundred fifty noble families, owned 40 percent of the cultivated land, which was tax free. Farmers represented 80 percent of the population, but only 10 to 15 percent of them owned their own land.

The citizens of the market towns made up approximately 10 to 12 percent of the population. With the introduction of the Reformation, all bishopric estates were confiscated by the Crown, and the king's ownership rose to about 60 percent of the cultivated land.

On the eve of the Reformation, the country was ruled by the king and the national council, which consisted of representatives of the most well-to-do landed nobility, the country's bishops, and some of the abbots and cathedral chapter representatives. The clergy ranked highest, and the archbishop was the chairman of the national council, which consisted of fifty members. Denmark was a free electoral monarchy, but in electing the king the national council usually elected the king's eldest son, who was to rule on the basis of a coronation charter. When the Reformation began, all the clergy were removed from the national council, the size of which was reduced to about twenty members. The king had to obtain the national council's agreement on, among other things, legislation and the levying of extraordinary taxes. The members also acted as judges in the king's "court of justice," the highest instance of appeal. In this way the national council members wore two hats. They were selected by the king and stood in his service, but, at the same time, they exercised control over royal power.

As was the case with Martin Luther's work on the Bible, the Bible translation of the Danish Reform church (Christian III's Bible, 1550) was of inestimable significance for the development of the Danish language. It was the first complete translation of the Bible into Danish, and it was based on the work of the humanist Christian Pedersen, whose work a Bible commission brought into agreement with Luther's German Bible of 1545. This Bible became the standard model for written Danish.

Among the most important preconditions for the Reformation in Denmark was the reform development in the duchies of Schleswig and Holstein, where evangelical sermons were given as early as 1522. At the diets of Rendsburg (1525) and Kiel (1526), pressure from the evangelical movement aggravated the economic and political conflict between the nobility and the clergy. The highest secular authority, King Frederick I of Denmark and Norway, who was in economic difficulties and faced political problems, mediated between the religious camps, but in reality the evangelical movement was allowed to spread. Against this background the king's eldest son, Duke Christian (later Christian III), was able in 1528 to introduce the Lutheran Reformation in his principality around Haderslev in the duchy of Schleswig, including some sixty parishes. With the help of two German theologians, Eberhard Weidensee and Johann Wendt, who were both educated, among other places, in Wittenberg, he created the first Lutheran territorial church in Scandinavia. The duchy's ministers, appointed by the duke, were bound to him by a loyalty oath. They had to attend a reeducation course at a newly established seminary for evangelical ministers in Haderslev and conduct evangelical services. They were checked by the superintendent during regular visits. A brief church ordinance, *Artickel vor de Kerckheren vp den Dorpern* (Articles for the Clergy in the Villages; 1528), which was not discovered until 1888, gives the impression of a conservative Wittenberg system. In spite of his modest territorial holdings, Duke Christian's pronounced Lutheran position and church policy had great importance. As early as 1527 evangelical sermons were being given in all the market towns throughout the duchy of Schleswig, and "fallen" monks traveled from the kingdom of Denmark to study in the Haderslev seminary for ministers.

Another precondition for the Reformation in Denmark was the development in the early 1520s of humanism and reform Catholicism. A typical representative of humanism was Christian Pedersen (c.1480–1554), who was born in Helsingør and held a master's degree from Paris. He left a large body of writings consisting of devotional and "secular" humanistic books, including a Latin-Danish dictionary, a collection of proverbs, an edition of Saxo Grammaticus's *Gesta Danorum* from the 1200s, and a book of sermons in which both the scripture texts and the sermons were written in Danish. Several other young Danish men promoted the new ideas they had obtained at foreign universities. The Carmelite provincial Paul Helie (c.1480–c.1534) had the greatest influence. He was well educated in philosophy and theology and taught in Copenhagen in a biblical-humanist manner, with the main emphasis on the study of the New Testament. He had a critical attitude toward Scholasticism and certain aspects of ecclesiastical life. Like his teacher Desiderius Erasmus of Rotterdam, he stressed human free will and its ethical responsibility, but, in spite of his criticism, he did not want to break with the official church position. His ideal was a unity of pious (theological) erudition and an erudite piety (*et pia Eruditio et erudita Pietas*). At first he looked positively upon Luther's piety and church criticism, but he disagreed sharply with him after reading his *De captivitate Babylonica ecclesiae praeludium*.

In about 1520 humanistic ideas, furthered by King Christian II (r.1513–1523), gained a footing at the University of Copenhagen. Married to Emperor Charles IV's sister Elizabeth (Isabella), Christian was a typical ruler of the time, who tried brutally to limit the economic and political power of the high nobility and the high clergy. His harsh conduct in Stockholm—where, despite promising amnesty after an attempted rebellion, in 1520 he had executed almost eighty people, among whom were some clergy—awoke terror throughout Europe (the Stockholm Bloodbath). At the same time he planned a large-scale change in Danish society with a reform of law. In 1523 he was forced into exile. When he attempted a reconquest in 1531, he was arrested and held in prison until his death in 1559.

Accusations of heresy had played a role in Christian II's conflict with the high nobility and clergy, and his successor,

Frederick I, had to swear in his coronation charter never to allow Lutheran heresy in Denmark and Norway. Nevertheless, the evangelical movement spread in all of the country's market towns during Frederick's reign. Denmark was a crisis-filled community with violent tensions between all the classes. Again and again expensive military security measures were necessary because of the danger of attack from the exiled King Christian II. In addition, there was religious unrest everywhere. Frederick I, whose personal confessional position is hard to determine, mediated between the parties to the advantage of the reformers. At two meetings of the council of nobles in Odense (1526 and 1527), Denmark broke with the Holy See and gave freedom to the reformers to preach and to have their own parishes. Frederick did not want to be the "king of souls" and believed each person should stand responsible before God. Moreover, he also spoke of a final settlement of the contested issues at a prospective ecumenical council.

The following ten years were a time of conflict between Catholicism and evangelical Christianity, and the Reformation became a market-town movement. At the beginning of the 1530s, there were evangelical churches in all the larger market towns. The movement's leaders, many of whom were former monks who had been pupils of Helie, called themselves "preachers." Unlike him, however, they took the full step, left reform Catholicism, and became Protestants. A series of writings shows that the polemical tone between them was unusually personal and bitter. Whereas scholars used to assume that the preachers were solidly Lutheran in their theology, studies of their confessional writings, the Confessio Hafniensis (1530) and other books, indicate that they were closer to the south German and north German humanist-evangelical movement. It is not known how committed Frederick I was to the goal of a national reform-Catholic church or whether he actually wanted a Protestant, possibly Lutheran, church. His policy of suppression of the archbishop and the bishops shows at any rate that his goal was a royally directed church.

After his death in 1533, the Catholic majority tried in the national council to pass a Catholic response and create a republic ruled by the nobility, but things got out of hand, foreign powers entered the picture, and from 1534 to 1536 Denmark was devastated by civil war, the so-called Count's War. The victor was the Lutheran Duke Christian from Schleswig, Frederick I's eldest son. Even though many of the national council members belonged to the country's Catholic nobility, they supported him because he guaranteed their economic and political privileges.

Christian, who reigned as Christian III from 1534 to 1559, carried out the legal settlement in such a way that he made the Catholic bishops responsible for the civil war. He removed them from office, put them in prison, and confiscated church property for the Crown. At a public meeting of the council of nobles in Copenhagen (October 1536), the judgments were proclaimed. At the same time, the king carried out an organizational change in the relationship between the church and the state, declaring that only evangelical Christianity and a reformed church would in the future be allowed in the country.

In August and September 1537 four ceremonies in Copenhagen marked the official implementation of the Lutheran Reformation in church and society. Christian III had appointed Johannes Bugenhagen from Wittenberg for a two-year period (1537–1539) in Copenhagen, and he became the leader of the reorganization. Bugenhagen crowned the king and queen using the old medieval ritual, which was changed to a Protestant orientation. He ordained the seven new Lutheran bishops (superintendents), and with this Denmark lost the apostolic succession. The king signed the Latin church ordinance, and the University of Copenhagen was reopened using the University of Wittenberg as a model for organization and for courses of study.

Christian III's official implementation of the Reformation brought about great changes in the laity and the church. A basis was created for a new national administration. Church and state were separated in such a way that the church leaders—the bishops—lost direct political influence because they were no longer members of the national council. The medieval state was eliminated, and a modern monarchy was established. The nobility had retained and extended its privileges, and the new national administration, developed by the king and the landed nobility in the national council, lasted with various changes until the introduction of the absolute monarchy in 1660.

Even church administration took on a strongly secular character, as the king in practice became the supreme head of the church. He was in agreement with Philipp Melanchthon's idea of the prince taking responsibility for both the secular and spiritual well-being of his subjects. He approved the bishops, who were elected by the ministers. The clergy had to pledge obedience to him. The bishops' visitations took place with the king's authority, and the king had authority over church legislation and discipline.

The principle of tithing was maintained just as it had been in the Middle Ages. The proceeds went to church, preacher, and bishop, but the bishop's tithe was changed to the "king's tithe." The nobility maintained its former exemption from tithing, and members could get back goods that had been given to the church for requiem masses if they could document the gift. Nobility and Crown maintained their former patronage rights. Besides payments in kind, the Lutheran bishops received a regular salary from the king, and the incumbent vicars kept their vicarages and former incomes.

The church's offices and institutions were organized in such a way that the old diocesan divisions and the former parishes were maintained. The new Lutheran bishops had to occupy themselves exclusively with proclaiming the gospel in the widest sense. They were both royal civil servants and church shepherds, and they had to reeducate the ministers and laymen to Lutheranism, make inspections, teach in the cathedral city (Zealand's bishop, with a residence in Copenhagen, became at the same time a professor of theology at the University of Copenhagen), advise the king, and supervise the diocese's school system and social work. From 1536 all Catholic priests continued in their offices as Lutherans, and the government allowed the former cathedral chapters to continue, with the proviso that they be reformed. The monasteries and those living in them were treated just as carefully and mildly. Those who wished could continue living in the monasteries until their death. They could wear the habit but not the tonsure, and they were to be taught to understand Lutheran Christianity. The monasteries themselves were placed under the supervision of the king and the national council—that is, they were secularized. The monasteries were generally not dissolved until the last monk or nun was dead. On the other hand, the mendicant monks were treated mercilessly. They were explicitly forbidden throughout the country, and many of their monasteries were closed even before 1536. For example, of the country's twenty-eight Franciscan monasteries, only seven remained in 1532.

The close relationship that existed in Catholic times between the church and the educational system was changed in such a way that the king now made the rules and issued the regulations. He ordered the market towns to establish and maintain schools, but here, too, tradition played an important role. Education was still considered to be a church task, and the legal provisions were written in the church ordinance. The main supervision was shared by the bishop and the king's minister. To be sure, the university now formally became a state institution, but it did not lose its ecclesiastical stamp. In organization, courses of study, and doctrine, Melanchthon's instructions from the University of Wittenberg became the model.

After the extensive Catholic welfare work had ceased, the lay authorities acknowledged, but only to a certain extent, their responsibility in this regard. The king's main principle was that the care of the poor should be at least as extensive as before. Hospitals were to be built in market towns. Begging should be limited. Only those truly in need could beg after they had received a beggar's permit from the secular authorities. Following the German model, a "poor chest" was established in every parish. The main idea in the care of the poor was therefore regular almsgiving, but it was difficult for the people to understand that the theological motivation had changed. Tradition played a large role in this regard as well, and the lay authorities and clergy worked together. The poor were scarcely worse off after the Reformation.

In legal practice there were also significant changes. The old legal system, which had been established according to canon law, was eliminated. Christian III made great efforts from the very beginning to restore a sense of legal security and a consciousness of law in the people, and in the first years he availed himself of ecclesiastical cooperation when cases previously belonging to the church courts had to be handled by the royal courts. After some years of uncertainty, special marriage courts in the individual parishes were established in which members of the cathedral chapters cooperated.

Whereas the first Protestant ministers (those before 1536) had represented a biblical-humanist Protestantism, Christian III demanded that Luther's and Melanchthon's theology—the "Wittenberg theology"—form the basis for the Danish Reform Church. This is evident, for example, in the church ordinance of 1537 to 1539. Christian III was a committed Lutheran, a typical "praying prince" who was interested in theology and led an active religious life. He demanded uniformity in doctrine and liturgy and forbade doctrinal controversies. The most influential theologians were Bishop Peder Palladius, Bishop Hans Tausen, and Bishop Niels Palladius, all trained in Wittenberg, as well as Bishop Jørgen Jensen Sadolin and Professor Niels Hemmingsen.

Christian III's extensive correspondence with Luther, Melanchthon, Bugenhagen, and the other Wittenberg theologians gives an insight into his relationship with German Lutheranism. In addition, he was a practical politician and though associated with the Schmalkald League, entered into a friendship agreement with Emperor Charles V in 1544. He tried to tie himself to the emperor for dynastic-political reasons. He therefore refused to help the German Lutheran princes in the Schmalkald War with the emperor. His son and successor, Frederick II (r.1559–1588), was so diligent in following his father's example that in 1579 he dismissed Hemmingsen from the university because of suspected crypto-Calvinism. Fear of doctrinal conflicts made him refuse to sign the *Book of Concord* (1580).

BIBLIOGRAPHY

Andersen, Niels Knud. *Confessio Hafniensis: Den kobenhavnske Bekendelse af 1530.* Copenhagen, 1954. The first large study of the early evangelical ministers' theology. It is defined here as humanist-reform, not Wittenbergian.

———. "The Reformation in Scandinavia and the Baltic." In *The New Cambridge Modern History,* edited by G. R. Elton, 2d ed., vol. 2, pp. 134–160. Cambridge, 1990.

Dunkley, E. H. *The Reformation in Denmark.* London, 1948.

Elton, G. R. *Reformation Europe, 1517–1559.* London, 1963. See pp. 124–131.

Grane, Leif, ed. *University and Reformation.* Leiden, 1981. Lectures from the University of Copenhagen symposium. Six studies in English and German that describe Copenhagen's university during the time of the Reformation by Lewis W. Spitz, Bernd Moeller, Olaf Pedersen, Ditlev Tamm, Richard Stauffer, and Martin Schwarz Lausten.

Grane, Leif, and Kai Hørby, eds. *Die dänische Reformation vor ihrem international Hintergrund.* Göttingen, 1990. The Danish Reformation is explained in studies in English and German by a respected group of scholars.

Kidd, B. J., ed. *Documents Illustrative of the Continental Reformation.* Oxford, 1967. Included are the Ordinance of the Diet of Odense, 1527 (in English), no. 100; the Seizure of the Bishops of Denmark, 12 August 1536 (in English), no. 131; the Recess of the Diet of Copenhagen, 30 October 1536 (in Latin), no. 132; Ordinatio Ecclesiastica, 2 September 1537 (in Latin), no. 132a; the Manifesto of Christian III, 30 October 1536 (in English), no. 133.

Lausten, Martin Schwarz. *Religion og politik: Studier i Christian IIIs forhold til det tyske rige i tiden, 1544–1559.* Copenhagen, 1977. Contains a summary in German. Studies the relationship between the Danish Reformation king's confession and his foreign policy toward the Protestant German princes and Emperor Charles V.

———. "Dänemark." In *Theologische Realenzyklopädie,* vol. 8, pp. 300–317. Berlin and New York, 1981. Contains an extensive bibliography.

———. *Biskop Peder Palladius og kirken, 1537–1560.* Copenhagen, 1987. Investigates his work as a bishop, professor, and royal adviser.

———. *Christian d.3. og kirken, 1537–1559.* Copenhagen, 1987.

———. *Reformationen i Danmark.* 2d ed. Copenhagen, 1992. The most recent account of the Reformation; assumptions, course, content, and the consequences for Danish society.

———. "The Early Reformation in Denmark and Norway, 1520–1559." In *The Scandinavian Reformation: From Evangelical Movement to Institutionalisation of Reform,* edited by Ole Peter Grell, pp. 12–41. Cambridge, 1995.

Lausten, Martin Schwarz, ed. *Kirkeordinansen, 1537–1539.* Copenhagen, 1989. Publication of preliminary work on the church ordinance; contains the Latin and the Danish texts as well as commentary.

Palladius, Peder. *Peder Palladius' Danske Skrifter.* 5 vols. Edited by Lis Jacobsen. Copenhagen, 1911–1926.

Petersen, E. Ladewig. *Dansk social historie.* Vol. 5, *Fra standssamfund til rangssamfund, 1500–1700.* Copenhagen, 1980.

Severinsen, P., et al., eds. *Skrifter of Paulus Helie.* 7 vols. Copenhagen, 1932–1948.

Wittendorff, Alex. *På Guds og Herskabs nåde.* Edited by Olaf Olsen. Danmarkshistorie, vol. 7. Copenhagen, 1989.

MARTIN SCHWARZ LAUSTEN

DENTIÈRE, Marie (d. 1561?), chronicler and reformer. As an Augustinian prioress in Tournai (Belgium), she adopted Luther's doctrines in 1521 and left for Strasbourg, where she married another convert, Simon Robert. From Strasbourg the couple moved to Aigle (Switzerland) where Simon Robert was pastor until his death in 1532/33. Marie Dentière then married the French itinerant minister Antoine Froment (1509–1581) and accompanied him to Geneva in 1535. A year later she published anonymously the first favorable account of the events leading up to the adoption of the Reformation in Geneva. The chronicle is entitled *La Guerre et deslivrance de la ville de Genesve.* No copies of the original printing are known to survive; the two nineteenth-century editions of the work (1863 and 1881) are based on eighteenth-century manuscript copies.

A fervent supporter of Guillaume Farel and John Calvin, Marie was happy to comply in 1539 with the wish of Marguerite d'Angoulême, queen of Navarre (who sympathized with the Reformation), to be enlightened as to the reasons for the two reformers' expulsion from Geneva. The result was the only "feminist" theological treatise to issue from Calvin's Reformation. Published anonymously in 1539 "by a Christian woman of Tournai," the *Epistre tresutile. . . contre les Turcs, Juifs, Infideles, faulx Chrestiens, Anabaptistes et Lutheriens* contains a passionate defense of Calvin and Farel as well as a plea for greater involvement of women in the church. The entire printing was confiscated by the Geneva authorities, and only two copies are known to be extant today. After Calvin's return to Geneva (1541), relations between him and the Froments deteriorated. However, it seems that in 1561 Marie wrote a preface to Calvin's *Sermon ou il est montré quelle doit estre la modestie des femmes en leurs habillemens* (Sermon on Female Apparel) adding to it an extract from the North African church father Cyprian, translated into French.

BIBLIOGRAPHY

Backus, Irena. "Marie Dentière. Un cas de féminisme théologique à l'époque de la Réforme?" *Bulletin de la Société de l'Histoire du Protestantisme Français* 137 (1991), 177–195.

Douglass, Jane Dempsey. "Marie Dentière's Use of Scripture in Her Theology of History." In *Biblical Hermeneutics in Historical Perspective.* Studies in Honor of Karlfried Froehlich on His Sixtieth Birthday, pp. 227–244. Grand Rapids, Mich., 1991.

Head, Thomas. "The Religion of the 'Femmelettes'". In *That Gentle Strength,* edited by L. Coon, K. Haldane, and E. Sommer. London, 1990, pp. 149–175.

Rilliet, Albert, ed. *La Guerre et deslivrance de la ville de Genesve.* Mémoires de la Société d'Histoire et d'Archéologie de Genève, vol. 20. Geneva, 1881.

IRENA BACKUS

DENYS OF RIJKEL. *See* Denis the Carthusian.

DERING, Edward (c.1540–1576), English preacher.
He was a prototype of the "godly" divines who personified the Puritan tendency in the Elizabethan and post-Elizabethan English church; and more especially those preachers and pastors whose "Puritanism" was defined less by legalistic scruples about outward forms than by an all-consuming concern to assure themselves of their own salvation and to convey the same experience to others. Politically, but in no other respect, these were moderate Puritans.

Dering, who came from good and ancient Kentish gentry stock, attended Christ's College, Cambridge, early in Mary's reign. He was a fellow of the college from 1560 to 1570, years of heated academic and religious controversy in Cambridge. Dering helped to lay the foundation of a tradition of godly, pastorally oriented learning in Christ's College that was later transplanted to the new foundation of Emmanuel College.

With his Kentish pedigree, Dering could expect preferment from Archbishop Matthew Parker and a successful ecclesiastical career. But in 1570 he put paid to these worldly prospects by playing the prophet Nathan to Queen Elizabeth's David in a bold court sermon that held Elizabeth accountable for the neglected state of the church and called her "an untamed and unruly heifer." This offense was compounded by equally outspoken letters to Parker and William Cecil, who was chancellor of the university.

Dering devoted the last years of his short life to a powerful and popular preaching ministry in Saint Paul's cathedral, protected in his nonconformity by influential friends. His letters reveal him as a "physician of the soul," with a practice cultivated among aristocratic and pious ladies. He married Anne Locke, the widow of a wealthy London mercer and the close friend and companion in exile of John Knox. Dering died, affectingly, of consumption on 26 June 1576.

BIBLIOGRAPHY

Collinson, Patrick. "A Mirror of Elizabethan Puritanism: The Life and Letters of 'Godly Master Dering.'" In *Godly People: Essays on English Protestantism and Puritanism,* edited by Patrick Collinson. London, 1983.

———. *The Elizabethan Puritan Movement.* Reprint, Oxford, 1990.

Lake, Peter. *Moderate Puritans and the Elizabethan Church.* Cambridge, 1982.

Porter, H. C. *Reformation and Reaction in Tudor Cambridge.* Cambridge, 1958. Porter and Lake together provide the best account of religion in Elizabethan Cambridge.

PATRICK COLLINSON

DEUTSCH, Niklaus Manuel. *See* Manuel, Niklaus.

DÉVAY, Mátyás Bíro (also Matthias Bíro Dévai; c.1500–1545), theologian and reformer in Hungary. A Magyar born in Transylvania, Dévay studied in Kraków (1523–1526) and had entered the Franciscan order before traveling to Wittenberg in 1529, where he was briefly one of Luther's table companions. By 1531 he had returned to Hungary and began to preach reformist doctrines in Buda. Here he prepared his discussion of basic Christian doctrines in fifty-two theses, *Rudamenta salutis.* Later that year, Dévay was preaching in Košice in northeastern Upper Hungary (Slovakia), where he was arrested in November on the orders of Thomas Szlakay, bishop of Eger, and taken to Bratislava (Poszony, Pressburg). The citizens of Košice appealed for his release in 1532. The following year he was interrogated in Vienna by its bishop, Johann Fabri. He escaped from captivity in 1533, possibly with the help of some citizens of Košice. He returned to Buda but was arrested once again, this

time by János Zápolya. After his release from this second incarceration Dévay journeyed to Nuremberg in 1536, where he visited Veit Dietrich and sought relief from an eye disease, and then visited Wittenberg in the spring of 1537. While in Wittenberg, he received a letter of recommendation from Melanchthon addressed to Thomas Nádasdy, one of the first Hungarian magnates to support the Reformation.

In the fall of 1537, in the company of Janos Sylvester (Erdösi), the noted Hungarian humanist and translator of the New Testament into Hungarian, Dévay returned to Hungary via Leipzig and Kraków, where his *Orthographica Hungarica* was published. He taught at the school established by Nádasdy in Uj-Sziget near Sárvár and then was rector-chaplain at the court of the Hungarian magnate, Péter Perény, one of the most ardent supporters of the Reformation among the Hungarian nobility. Then he served briefly in Szikszó on the lands of Gáspár Serédi. But once again he had to flee because of the hostility of the bishop of Eger. In the summer of 1541 he was again in Wittenberg, visited Margrave George of Brandenburg-Ansbach and also Johann Jacob Grynaeus in Basel, where three of his works, including his *Disputatio de statu in quo sint beatorum animae post hanc vitam, ante ultimi indicil diem* (Discussion on the State of Souls after Death and before the Day of Judgment), probably were published in 1537. The *Disputatio* was a response to the work of a Hungarian Franciscan, Gregor Szegedi, *Censurae in propositiones erroneas Mathiae Dévai Biro*(1538), the first Counter-Reformation work in Hungary.

After his return to Hungary in late 1541, Dévay was in Miskolc and then on the estates of Gáspár Drágffy. He also attended the pastoral conferences held in Oradea Mare (Nagyvárad, Grosswardein) in Siebenbürgen, or Transylvania, in July 1544 and in Debrecen early the following year, probably in March.

During the 1540s, Dévay came under attack for his interpretation of the real presence in the Lord's Supper. His theology was closer to that of Melanchthon and even the Helvetic reformers than to that of Luther. Leonard Stöckel chastised Dévay for having forsaken Lutheranism. Dévay probably also left the service of Perényi because of his views. The controversy soon came to the attention of Luther, who was disturbed by reports concerning the theological position of Dévay. In 1544 he wrote to the city of Prešov in eastern Slovakia deploring the emergence of sectarian views in the region and expressing astonishment at the reports concerning Dévay. While Dévay was warmly regarded in Wittenberg, he certainly did not learn there the teachings he was promulgating.

Dévay was an ardent if enigmatic reformer. Called the "Hungarian Luther," he had more in common with the theology of Melanchthon and other humanist evangelicals than with the more uncompromising positions of Luther. He demonstrated his independence in theological formulation in his view of the real presence and of the soul sleep of the saints. He had no fixed abode, changing his residence frequently in the face of danger and hostility. The record of his activities and views is difficult to reconstruct from the evidence available. Nevertheless, Dévay was one of the leading native Hungarian advocates of reform. He was not only a popular preacher who promulgated Reformation doctrines among the Magyars, but he also contributed to the development of Hungarian as a literary language.

BIBLIOGRAPHY

Primary Sources

Dévay, Mátyás Biro. *Disputatio de statu in quo sint beatorum animae post hanc vitam, ante ultimi iudicii diem. Item de praecipuis articulis christianae doctrinae, per Matthiam Dévay Hungarum. His addita est expositio examinis quomodo a Fabro in carcere sit examinatus.* N.p., n.d.
———. *Az tiz parantsolatnac, ah hit agazatinac am mi at[y]áncnac, aes ah hit petsaetinec röviden valo mag[y]arázatt[y]a.* Kraków, 1549.
———. *Orthographia Ungarica, azaz igaz iraz modiarol valo tudoman[y] mag[y]ar n[y]eluenn irattatott.* Kraków, 1549.

Secondary Sources

Botta, István. *Dévai Mátyás, a magyar Luther: Dévai helvét irányba hajlásának problémája.* Budapest, 1990.
Odön, Miklos. "Dévai Bíro Matyas, mint Debrecen papja," *Református Egyház* 6.14 (1954), 21–23; 6.15, (1954), 22–23.
Révész, Imre. *Dévai Biró Mátyás tanításai.* Klausenburg, 1915.
Sólyom, Jenó. "Dévai Mátyás tiszántúli múkodési." *Egyhaztörtenete* 2 (1959), 193–217.

DAVID P. DANIEL

DEVOTIONAL PRACTICES. Discrete religious acts generally performed in words and gestures, devotional practices demonstrate, build, and nurture the devotee's relationship with God or a holy person. Throughout the Middle Ages, it was devotional acts, rather than knowledge of doctrine *per se*, that defined the everyday practice of Christianity for people of all social classes. Beginning in the early sixteenth century, humanist and Protestant critiques of popular Christianity successfully challenged the privileged status of devotional practice in relation to religious knowledge. By the late sixteenth century, Protestants and reformed Catholics had codified separate theologies, distinctive modes of religious practice, and an ethos concerning use of the body and material objects for religious purposes.

Traditional devotional practices articulated implicit but rich theologies that were often culturally or locally specific in character. Thus it would be possible to write an ethnography of lived Christianity based on an examination of practices such as prayer; veneration of images and relics; the cult of saints; pilgrimage; penitential and ascetic acts; almsgiving; and the use of books, images, and objects for devotional purposes. While this article cannot claim to be such an ethnography, it does attempt to suggest the spiritual vision behind devotional acts.

Varieties of Devotional Practice in Late Medieval Christianity and Early Modern Catholicism. The logic and function of devotional practices derived from contemporary understandings of God and the process of salvation. The spiritual world in which God and human beings interacted was generally thought to be a polity and an economy. God was the omnipotent, eternal king residing in heaven together with the saints—human friends, servants, and kin whom he had rewarded for their faithful service on earth by granting them a place in his royal court of heaven. In the spiritual world, as in the earthly one, a royal court functioned according to a system of hierarchy, patronage, and intercession. All supernatural-human relationships were reciprocal. Human beings acknowledged, honored, and served God, expecting in return his attention, protection, and favor. From their privileged position in the heavenly court, saints might intercede with God on behalf of individuals and communities that appealed to them for assistance. Praying to saints, venerating their relics and images at shrines, dedicating oneself to their honor: all these devotional practices constituted participation in a system of spiritual patronage that devotees fervently hoped would ultimately support their entrance into heaven.

The meaning of devotional practices for late medieval and early modern Christians stemmed from this vision of divine-human relations. The highest goal of human life was to attain salvation—eternal life in the heavenly court following one's life on earth. Salvation was normally gained through the performance of religious acts (also termed "good works," and usually identified with devotional practices). Within this economy of salvation, sin was understood to create a debt to God, even if the sin had been forgiven by a priest (acting as God's agent). Human beings who died in God's debt could not enter heaven immediately, but rather spent time in purgatory, the debtor's prison of the spiritual world. Hence the aim was to acquire enough spiritual merit to enter heaven. Praying, going on pilgrimage, and giving alms to the poor gained spiritual merit for human beings. Here we can see how apt the metaphor of economy is. Excess merit earned by especially saintly human beings could be banked in the so-called "treasury of merit," a kind of community savings bank from which needier Christians might borrow. Church authorities (bishops, and increasingly, the pope) claimed control over the treasury of merit through the granting of indulgences in exchange for specific devotional acts, or sometimes—by the late fifteenth century—money.

Since the Reformation, theologians, historians, and practicing Christians have felt free to denigrate this religious system, labeling it materialistic, "superstitious," and even "childish." However, it is important to acknowledge that in fifteenth- and sixteenth-century terms, the polity and economy of salvation were rational, expansive, and open to individual initiative. In performing devotional acts devotees intended to create closer, warmer relationships with God and the saints, as well as to redeem their own souls and those of their family and friends.

Prayer. The most basic of devotional practices is prayer. A wide variety of source material is available about the practice of prayer: numerous surviving manuscripts and printed books of religious instruction; individually owned collections of prayers (many of them books of hours); and artistic representations in panel paintings, altarpieces, stained glass, and manuscript illuminations. Although it would be impossible to demonstrate how many ordinary Christians prayed on a regular basis, and in precisely what manner, it is clear from these sources that the practice of prayer played a central role in the lives of late medieval women and men.

Prayer might be defined as a discourse, spoken or silent, expressed in the first person (singular or plural), that establishes a relationship with a person or persons believed to have supernatural power. For late medieval devotees these persons were God, the Virgin Mary, and saints. Perhaps not surprisingly, most forms of discourse and relationship people used in prayer mirrored those they knew in their wider social world. God was addressed as creator, but also as king, lord, father, and master. The Virgin Mary became mother, mistress, mediator, and advocate (the last two being quasi-legal terms). In late medieval prayers she is often commended not only for her motherly comfort but also for the mercy she shows in interceding on behalf of devotees. Saints were most commonly addressed as patrons by their human clients, but also on occasion as lords, masters, friends, and godparents. Not only the forms of address but also the modes of relationship familiar from everyday life characterized prayer. Devotees offered praise, service, and donations to their lords, patrons, and advocates, and in return expected protection, assistance, and material and spiritual benefits. To pray was to participate in a system of spiritual patronage in which all relationships and transactions were reciprocal.

Prayer was so imbedded in the practice of everyday life that people prayed at special times of day (upon rising, at meals, before retiring), special seasons (holy days, saints' feast days), family occasions (births, marriages, deaths, anniversaries), and for special intentions (illness, childbirth, travel, financial crisis, war, famine). These kinds of prayers tended to differ in aim and length from the more strictly disciplined, meditative, or mystical prayer practiced by monks, nuns and other religious women, and—increasingly by the later Middle Ages—leisured and literate lay people. People also prayed on liturgical, sacramental, and other ritual occasions such as Mass, baptism, sacramental confession, public days of feasting or fasting, and processions.

Spoken prayers were normally accompanied by physical acts—kneeling, removing one's hat, bowing the head, lowering the eyes, raising folded hands—that signaled respect, deference, and humility in the gestural code of the period. Wealthy and literate men and women might have prayed with the aid of a book or before a private devotional image portraying the crucified Jesus, the Virgin Mary, or a saint. But like less prosperous or illiterate devotees, they would also have recited informal or memorized prayers, perhaps kneeling before painted or sculpted images housed in churches.

Shrines and pilgrimage. Journeys to holy places have a long and venerable history in western Christianity. Since late antiquity men and women had traveled from near and far to visit sites of important events in Christian history, burial places of saints and martyrs, and locations where miracles and supernatural apparitions had taken place. The idea of traveling to a holy place to pray was so deeply imbedded in the piety of this era that even ordinary devotional literature evoked the image of pilgrimage to help the devotee approach God or a saint.

Most pilgrims in western Europe visited shrines housing either relics or images. There is evidence that by the late Middle Ages shrines holding images, especially statues and paintings of the Virgin Mary, had overtaken relics in popularity among pilgrims. Although the universal appeal of Rome, Jerusalem, and Santiago de Compostela (Spain)—all of which featured relics of early Christian saints—did not wane, other relic shrines seem to have fallen out of favor. Local communities continued to pride themselves on their relic collections, which they enclosed, maintained, and honored in small chapels. But the largest crowds of foreign and domestic visitors descended upon Marian shrines at Montserrat (Catalonia), Le Puy (France), and Altötting (Bavaria). In German-speaking lands miraculous consecrated hosts vied with Mary for popularity. These developments probably reflect the increased devotion to the Virgin Mary, the Eucharist, and religious images that characterized late medieval piety.

Pilgrims who traveled a long way generally brought personal problems to the object of their journey, and once there, performed relatively standard devotional acts at the shrine. They attended Mass, received the sacraments, consulted priests, gave alms to the poor, and prayed in the cathedral or chapel. They acquired souvenirs—badges, amulets, pamphlets. Local and papal authorities sometimes granted partial or plenary indulgences for specific devotions performed by pilgrims. Back home, pilgrims might join local confraternities made up solely of returned pilgrims, where they continued their devotion to the spiritual person they had visited.

Despite the popularity of cults like Compostela, most pilgrims probably visited local shrines. In fact, images and relics were scattered throughout most rural and urban landscapes. Studies of Castile and Grenoble reveal a multitude of locally frequented chapels, each with its own local saint or Virgin, each with its own history and spiritual specialty.

Florence boasted three major Marian images at Impruneta, Orsanmichele, and Santissima Annunziata. Although less popular with foreign pilgrims, local shrines tended to attract devotees who prayed there regularly and probably thought of their saint or Virgin as part of the local community.

Devotional images and objects. Visual images performed several closely related functions in devotional practice. They presented to the viewer a supernatural person who might be available for a relationship with a human devotee. They also provided a visual reminder of God, the Virgin Mary, or a saint. And finally, they sometimes represented an individual or group kneeling in prayer before a supernatural person, thereby providing a model for the viewer's prayer.

Devotees often prayed before or to artistic representations of a supernatural person. There were many varieties of this basic practice, but what they shared was the belief that the image in some way made present—or better, embodied—a supernatural figure. The notions of representation and embodiment implicit in this form of devotional practice were related to the logic underlying the concepts of transubstantiation and Jesus' incarnation. For centuries theologians and churchmen had debated in subtle ways the ontological status of images, as M. Camille has shown in *The Gothic Idol* (Cambridge, 1989). It is questionable, however, whether such learned debates and instructions about the "proper" understanding of religious images affected popular belief and practice in any substantial way. Devotees believed Our Lady of Le Puy and Our Lady of Montserrat to be individual manifestations of the Virgin Mary, embodied in small, archaically designed black statues, each possessing her own unique history of arrival and activity at the shrine. For pilgrims at Conques (France), the jeweled silver reliquary-statue that housed Saint Foy's relics literally "was" Saint Foy. Contemporary descriptions reveal how profoundly the images were thought to be animated, even sentient persons. Devotees spoke to images in prayer and expected a reply; rituals of scorning or defiling images also testify eloquently to popular beliefs about the personhood and personality of images. Such beliefs survived through the early modern period even in Protestant cultures, as Robert Scribner shows in his study of miraculous images of Luther.

The crucifix—a carved or sculpted representation of Jesus crucified on the cross—was another commonly venerated image. In this form, the suffering Jesus was present in every parish church and cathedral, ready to receive the prayers of the faithful. Ignatius Loyola acknowledged the imaginative power of this devotional image by including in his *Spiritual Exercises* (composed 1530s) model colloquies for the exercitant to conduct with Jesus hanging on the cross. Such devotion evoked an emotional response to the present Jesus, leading the devotee into a closer relationship with him. Church authorities sometimes awarded indulgences to devotions addressed to images.

Devotionally related to the crucifix were the various images of the suffering, dying, or dead Jesus available in paintings and statues housed in churches and owned by individuals, and woodcuts, engravings, and paintings bound into devotional books and pamphlets. These images included iconic representations like the Man of Sorrows, the Mass of Saint Gregory, and Veronica's veil, as well as scenes of the Crucifixion itself. Sometimes these images included a devotee kneeling in adoration before the suffering Jesus, thereby providing a model for the devotee's own relationship to him. Well-known examples of the latter are the frescoes in the Dominican convent of San Marco in Florence painted by Fra Angelico and his assistants.

Just as the religious use of images expresses widespread confidence in the ability of supernatural persons to manifest themselves bodily, so also devotional practices employing objects like rosaries and amulets reveal the spiritual value this religious culture assigned to contact with and use of material objects. The rosary—a string of small beads that a devotee fingered as she recited aloud a series of standard prayers—reached the height of its popularity in the late fifteenth and early sixteenth century. Practices such as saying the rosary and wearing or holding an amulet reveal that for late medieval Christians, use of objects wove intimate ties between body and soul.

Penitential acts. A similar spiritual function and meaning were assigned to penitential acts such as fasting, chastity, flagellation, and other forms of ascetic deprivation or punishment. The penitential practices of the late Middle Ages were grounded in the desire to imitate the suffering Jesus and in the value granted to bodily discipline for the purpose of redemption. The practice of voluntary suffering or deprivation was believed to help devotees purify their lives and clarify their religious commitment. As with other devotional practices, devotees might on occasion gain papal or episcopal indulgences for specific penitential acts. Such indulgences were generally announced or advertised by parish priests or traveling mendicant friars.

Fasting and abstinence from certain foods was obligatory for all Christians on particular days, especially during Lent. Fasting marked these days as special, set apart from ordinary business, and dedicated such time to God's service. Such food practices also provided a bodily means of sympathetic identification with the suffering Jesus, especially for women, as C. Bynum has shown (*Holy Feast and Holy Fast*, Berkeley, 1987). Most other forms of penitence were widely practiced by priests and members of religious orders, and somewhat less by lay people. For example, chastity was required of monks, nuns, and priests. Lay people might withdraw voluntarily from sexual relationships, even within marriage; notable examples can be found in the lives of Margery Kempe, Thomas More, and uncloistered religious women.

More severe—and to modern sensibilities, dramatic or objectionable—forms of penance such as flagellation, sleep deprivation, hair shirts, and ritual mutilation were occasionally practiced by individuals in private or as part of monastic communities or confraternities. Ignatius Loyola's *Spiritual Exercises* and Teresa of Ávila's autobiography testify to the spiritual significance of such practices. Confraternity members performed penance on behalf of themselves, their families, and fellow members. From the mid-thirteenth through the sixteenth century, northern Italian flagellant confraternities conducted processions in time of plague, war, and famine. Such theatrical displays of public penance evoked sorrow and repentance in viewers and contributed to the physical and spiritual well-being of the urban community.

The Impact of Protestant and Catholic Reform. Christian humanists and Protestants criticized what they saw as abuses in traditional religious practice. But new Protestant theologies went beyond condemning abuses and formulated doctrines of salvation that essentially eliminated the salvific value of devotional practices. Erasmus's wish to see a closer identification between exterior devotion and interior piety led him to bitter attacks on the "hypocritical" practice of pilgrimage, prayer to saints, the rosary, and asceticism in *Enchiridion militis Christiani* (1501) and the *Colloquia* (1518–1530s). It is important to note that Erasmus did not object to devotional practices *per se*, but simply called for them to be more expressive of interior dispositions. Luther opposed Rome's teaching that human beings could contribute to their own salvation through performing good works. In *Von der Freiheit eines Christenmenschen* (1520) he argued that human beings are saved solely through God's gift of faith. Additionally, he issued a fundamental challenge to the commonly accepted value of devotional practices: "It does not help the soul if the body is adorned with the sacred robes of priests or dwells in sacred places or is occupied with sacred duties or prays, fasts, abstains from certain kinds of food, or does any work that can be done by the body and in the body." Luther did allow some disciplinary function to penitential practices. But this does not soften the death blow he and other Protestant reformers such as Zwingli and Calvin dealt to the traditional structure of religious practice, in which Christians prayed, fasted, and gave alms expecting to strengthen their reciprocal relations with God and the saints and to add to the spiritual merit they accumulated on earth.

Consequently, Protestant theologies could be said to devalue the religious meaning of the human body and the religious use of the material world. Theory and practice of Protestantism could diverge, as work by P. Joutard and Robert Scribner has shown. It remains true, however, that through the doctrine of salvation by faith, Protestant reform privileged religious belief as opposed to religious practice. In response to Protestant challenges, the Catholic church reiterated its teaching that human beings are saved both through having faith and performing good works. Early modern Catholics continued the devotional practices of the late Middle Ages, though pastors claimed new authority

480 DIACONATE

over that practice. Yet even sixteenth-century Catholic theologians gradually presented doctrine and belief, rather than practice, as the foundation of the "proper" exercise of Christianity. As a result of the Reformation, western Christianity began to evolve into a religious system grounded more in codes of belief than in patterns of practice.

[*See also* Festivals; Flagellants; Liturgy; Piety; Pilgrimages; Popular Religion; Sacramentals; Sacraments; *and* Saints, *article on* Cult of Saints.]

BIBLIOGRAPHY

Bossy, John. *Christianity in the West, 1400–1700.* Oxford, 1985. Attention to both religious belief and practice; focus on sacramental and devotional life.

Bynum, Caroline Walker. "The Female Body and Religious Practice in the Later Middle Ages." In *Fragmentation and Redemption: Essays on Gender and the Human Body in Medieval Religion*, pp. 181–238. New York, 1991. Welcome study of women's religious practice, with original and persuasive argument about "somatic piety."

Chase, Mary Jane. "Popular Piety in Sixteenth-Century Picardy: Amiens and the Rise of Private Devotions, 1500–1540." Ph.D. diss., Columbia University, 1992. Ownership and use of devotional books, objects, images; based on wills and inventories in the Amiens municipal archives.

Chiffoleau, Jacques. *La comptabilité de l'au-delà: Les hommes, la mort et la religion dans la région d'Avignon à la fin du moyen âge.* Rome, 1980. Regional study of prayers and rituals surrounding death and dying. Best explication of the cultural meaning of indulgences and of the multiple, repetitive devotions so commonly practiced in the late Middle Ages.

Christian, William A., Jr. *Local Religion in Sixteenth-Century Spain.* Princeton, 1981. Imaginatively conceived ethnography of peasant religion, by an anthropologist. Special focus on saints, shrines, vows.

Davis, Natalie Zemon. "From 'Popular Religion' to 'Religious Cultures.'" In *Reformation Europe: A Guide to Research*, edited by Steven E. Ozment, pp. 321–341. Saint Louis, 1982. Judicious review of literature on the history and anthropology of early modern religious life.

Duffy, Eamon. *The Stripping of the Altars: Traditional Religion in England, c.1400–1580.* New Haven and London, 1992. Exhaustively documented, profusely illustrated treatment of lay Christianity and the impact of government-imposed reform.

Joutard, Philippe. "Protestantisme populaire et univers magique: Le cas cévenol." *Le monde alpin et rhodanien* 5 (1977), 145–164. Questions Protestant ability to eliminate traditional sacramentality from religious practice.

Luria, Keith P. *Territories of Grace: Cultural Change in the Seventeenth-Century Diocese of Grenoble.* Berkeley, 1991. Innovative local study of the Counter-Reformation in rural France; discusses clerical efforts to transform and discipline lay religious practice. Attention to local shrines, pilgrimages, and festivals.

Marrow, James H. "Symbol and Meaning in Northern European Art of the Late Middle Ages and the Early Renaissance." *Simiolus* 16 (1986), 150–172. An art historian discusses the devotional use and meaning of various forms of religious art.

Moeller, Bernd. "Piety in Germany around 1500." In *The Reformation in Medieval Perspective*, edited by Steven E. Ozment, pp. 50–75. Chicago, 1971. Pioneering study; argues that late medieval Christians were increasingly conscientious in devotional practice, in contrast to previous historians' formulations of the relationship between popular religion and the advent of the Reformation.

O'Neil, Mary R. "*Sacerdote ovvero strione*: Ecclesiastical and Superstitious Remedies in Late Sixteenth-Century Italy." In *Understanding Popular Culture*, edited by Steven L. Kaplan, pp. 53–84. Berlin and New York, 1984. Subtle study of sixteenth-century clerical judgments concerning magic, superstition, and "proper" devotion, focusing on Modena.

Rapp, Francis. *L'église et la vie religieuse en Occident à la fin du moyen âge.* Paris, 1971. Judicious overview of late medieval religious history; begins chronologically where Vauchez (below) stops.

Reinburg, Virginia. *Practices of Prayer in Late Medieval and Reformation France.* Ithaca, N.Y., forthcoming. Discusses prayer in the context of religious practice; attention to use of devotional books and images.

Scribner, Robert W. *Popular Culture and Popular Movements in Reformation Germany.* London, 1987. Exposes the sacramental character of late medieval and early modern religious practice, both Protestant and Catholic.

———. "The Impact of the Reformation on Daily Life." In *Mensch und Objekt im Mittelalter und in der frühen Neuzeit: Leben, Alltag, Kultur*, edited by Gerhard Jaritz, pp. 315–343. Vienna, 1990. Innovative approach to the question of how Protestant reform reshaped popular religious practice, especially in the German countryside.

Trexler, Richard C. "Florentine Religious Experience: The Sacred Image." *Studies in the Renaissance* 19 (1972), 7–41. Investigates popular religion through study of one form of behavior: veneration of a public cult image in Florence.

Vauchez, André. *La spiritualité du moyen âge occidental, VIIe–XIIe siècles.* Paris, 1975. Succinct account of early medieval religious history.

Wilkins, Eithne. *The Rose-Garden Game: The Symbolic Background to the European Prayer-Beads.* London, 1969. Includes history of the rosary.

VIRGINIA REINBURG

DIACONATE. This term is used to refer to the collective entity of deacons and deaconesses, as well as to the general social welfare responsibility of the church. Reformation leaders attempted to restore deacons to the early church model. By that the reformers meant to recur to the model of the *Acts of the Apostles* (chapter 6), in which Stephen and six others were chosen to take care of widows. The reformers, therefore, felt that the correct role for deacons was that of social welfare and not, as had become normative in the Western church in the centuries before the Reformation, as a transitional office (to include teaching, preaching, and liturgy) to the priesthood. Deaconesses, in turn, had moved from their service role in congregations into convents and had become nuns. The reformers criticized the medieval understanding of the role of deacons for neglecting the poor.

In some Lutheran regions those responsible for poor relief were called deacons. Johannes Bugenhagen (1485–1558) incorporated the diaconate into the various church orders he wrote or edited for the Lutheran churches in north Germany and Scandinavia. Deacons tended to be officials as much of local government as of the church. In some instances Lutheran usage of *deacon* in the sixteenth century also referred to ordained clergy serving as curates, or assistants, to the rector of a parish. By the seventeenth century, *deacon*, as a title, generally applied to assistant pastors.

In Reformed Zurich, Huldrych Zwingli (1484–1531) did

not call those in charge of social welfare deacons. The Zurich city council took over the welfare system (1524–1525). The 1525 Zurich liturgy retained the use of the terms *deacon* and *lector* to refer to assistants in liturgy, as did other liturgies of the early Reformation, perhaps an echo of the terminology of the Catholic Mass. Zurich served as a model for Reformed cities, such as Bern.

Martin Bucer (1491–1551) included deacons in his concept of ministry and church office, although welfare officers in Strasbourg were not so-called. John Calvin (1509–1564) may have perfected his ideas of the diaconate while in Strasbourg (1538–1541). Returning to Geneva, he included deacons in the ecclesiastical ordinances for the city (1541) as the fourth order of church office, alongside pastors, doctors (teachers), and elders. At this time he considered deacons in Geneva to be the directors of the city hospital and its welfare program. Calvin described a two-part division of the diaconate: those who "receive, dispense and hold goods for the poor" (the procurators, or trustees, of the hospital) and those who "tend and care for the sick and administer allowances to the poor" (those who ran the hospital). Calvin found the basis for this "double diaconate" in *Romans* 12:6–8 and provided a place for women in the care of the poor, advocating the revival of the ancient Christian office of "widow" as a female diaconate. There were no deaconesses in Geneva in the sixteenth century.

After the Ecclesiastical Ordinances of 1541 were written, French-, Italian-, English-, and German-speaking refugees in Geneva raised funds for their poor compatriots flocking to the city. The administrators came to be called deacons. The French fund (*Bourse française*) also paid to record Calvin's sermons and helped send colporteurs and ministers to evangelize France. This Genevan model spread with Reformed churches to France, the Low Countries, and England. In Scotland the first *Book of Discipline* (1561) included the office of deacon. The Church of England retained deacons on the transitional model despite Puritan prodding toward a reformed diaconate. The same position was taken by the Council of Trent, which also maintained the diaconate as transitional to the priesthood.

BIBLIOGRAPHY

Calvin, John. "Draft Ecclesiastical Ordinances." In *Calvin: Theological Treatises*, edited and translated by J. K. S. Reid, pp. 64–66. Reprint, Philadelphia, 1977. Contains a description of deacons in Geneva and Calvin's views on the diaconate.

Kingdon, Robert M. "Calvin's Ideas about the Diaconate: Social or Theological in Origin?" In *Piety, Politics and Ethics: Reformation Studies in Honor of George Wolfgang Forell*, edited by Carter Lindberg, pp. 167–180. Kirksville, Mo., 1984. Argues that Calvin was influenced by the contemporary organization of social welfare in the world around him in developing his theory of the double diaconate even though he appealed to scripture to support his point of view.

Krimm, Herbert, ed. *Quellen zur Geschichte der Diakonie*. 2 vols. Stuttgart, 1960–1963.

Lindberg, Carter. "'There Should Be No Beggars among Christians': Karlstadt, Luther, and the Origins of Protestant Poor Relief." *Church History* 46.3 (September 1977), 313–334. Karlstadt's and Luther's views and influence on poor relief.

McKee, Elsie Anne. *John Calvin on the Diaconate and Liturgical Almsgiving*. Geneva, 1984. An exegetical and liturgical approach to Calvin's ideas on the diaconate.

Olson, Jeannine E. *Calvin and Social Welfare: Deacons and the Bourse Française*. Selingsgrove, Pa., 1989. Describes the diaconate in Geneva, especially the French Fund, and social welfare there and elsewhere in Europe and the British Isles.

———. *Deacons and Deaconesses through the Centuries: One Ministry/Many Roles*. Saint Louis, 1992. The most up-to-date detailed study on the diaconate. See chap. 3, "The Reformation," and chap. 4, "The Protestant Reformation through the Nineteenth Century," pp. 97–194.

"Ordonnances ecclésiastiques." In *Registres de la Compagnie des Pasteurs de Genève au temps de Calvin*, vol. 1, *1546–1553*, edited by Jean-François Bergier. Geneva, 1964.

Pettegree, Andrew. *Foreign Protestant Communities in Sixteenth-Century London*. Oxford, 1986. Describes deacons in the Stranger Churches of London and elsewhere in England.

Thiersch, Heinrich W. J. *Über das Diakonenamt*. Lüdenscheid, Germany, 1990.

JEANNINE E. OLSON

DIAZ, Juan (also Diazius, Decius; 1515?–1546), Spanish Protestant theologian and martyr. Born in Cuenca in central Spain, Diaz left his homeland as a youth to study theology in Paris, where he stayed about fourteen years. He was persuaded into evangelical views by Francisco de Enzinas's brother, Diego, and in 1545 went with Matthieu Budé and Jean Crespin to Geneva, where Calvin was impressed by his character and approved his views. With two Swiss friends, Louis and Claude de Senarclens, he went via Neuchâtel and Basel to Strasbourg, where he established himself so well that, when Martin Bucer was sent as that city's representative to the Colloquy of Regensburg, he asked for Diaz and Claude Senarclens as his deputies. Diaz also was commissioned by Cardinal Jean du Bellay to report on religious conditions in Germany.

In Regensburg, the Catholic Pedro Maluenda tried to convince Diaz of his errors. When he saw he had made no impression, he sent information to the emperors's confessor, Domingo do Soto, who further informed Juan's brother, Alfonso, a lawyer at the Roman Rota. Alfonso rushed off to Regensburg, to find Juan had gone to Neuburg on the Danube, where he was supervising the printing of a work by Bucer and of his own *Christianae religionis summa* (1546), an independent work of unexceptional Protestant ideas. After failing to persuade Juan to return to the Roman Catholic fold, Alfonso feigned interest in the evangelical faith. He plotted his brother's murder with an accomplice, who, bringing a letter, was able to sink an ax into Juan's skull, after which both fled to safety. A work by Diaz, *Annotationes theologicae*, left in his will to Francisco de Enzinas, was never printed and has disappeared.

The fratricide scandalized the Protestant world, particularly since both Charles V and Pope Paul III refused to take action against the culprits. Bucer and Philipp Melanchthon produced pamphlets about the event, which were widely circulated both in Latin and in German translation and then incorporated into several well-known Protestant martyrologies. This story became a powerful component in the propaganda that eventually produced the Black Legend.

BIBLIOGRAPHY

Bautz, Friedrich Wilhelm, ed. *Biographische-Bibliographisches Kirchenlexikon* Hamm, 1970–. See vol. 1, p. 1280.
Boehmer, Eduard. *Bibliotheca Wiffeniana: Spanish Reformers of Two Centuries.* Vol. 1. London, 1874. See pp. 185–216.
Senarclens, Claude. "Historia vera de morte Joan. Diazii Hispani." In *Miscellanea Groningana,* edited by Daniel Gerdesius, vol. 8, pp. 389–465. Groningen, 1763.
Verzeichnis der im deutschen Sprachbereich erschienenen Drucke des XVI. Jahrhunderts. Stuttgart, 1983–. See vol. 5, nos. 1377–1379.

A. GORDON KINDER

DIDYMUS. *See* Zwilling, Gabriel.

DIET. Although the German Reformation did not succeed on the level of the Holy Roman Empire, it did succeed in most cities and some territories. Therefore all imperial diets (*Reichstage*) between 1521 and 1555 were confronted with it. The diet was a prominent forum for Martin Luther and later for the Protestant estates. The religious question (*causa Lutheri*) initially divided the diet. After a number of short-term settlements, however, a permanent political compromise emerged in the Peace of Augsburg.

Apart from the emperor, the diet as an assembly of all imperial estates was one of the few institutions that kept the early modern empire together. Electors, princes, counts, prelates, and their representatives, as well as the delegates of the free imperial cities, took part in its meetings. Here they discussed the affairs of the empire with the emperor and his counselors. The religious conflict was never the central concern of the gatherings, but again and again it seemed to overshadow all other problems: for example, the maintenance of domestic peace, the elaboration of the legal and judicial system, the provision of social and economic regulations, and the task of persuading the estates to contribute increasingly toward the costs of the empire. In spite of the religious conflicts, however, the estates reached consensus on many other questions.

Nature of the Diet. In its early modern form the Diet developed in the late fifteenth century. Its organization was consolidated in the 1520s, when Emperor Charles V was not present. There is debate about whether the late medieval assemblies should be called diets or simply enlarged royal court assemblies. In the same way, the assemblies of estates without the king and the gatherings of the electors were also precursors. The highly privileged electors were able to transfer their traditional preeminence to the diet and formed its core. They met in a separate chamber, so they could not be outvoted by the mass of princes or other estates.

The free imperial cities were obliged to participate in the royal court assemblies and in the diets and to guarantee a rapid and harmonious implementation of the decisions. Since they depended on the emperor's protection, their attendance was a duty, not a privilege. Although they had their own chamber, their influence was limited.

The princes' chamber was considerably more important. Apart from many less powerful estates, it united those princes, counts, and prelates who had only sporadically attended the royal court assemblies. Although the chamber of the princes soon became the counterpart of the electors chamber, it did not threaten their preeminence. Even though not all the invited estates appeared—because they were not interested in the empire or because they did not wish to be obliged toward emperor and empire—the development of the diet is an element in the diffuse attempts around 1500 to introduce statelike structures into the empire.

Maximilian I ultimately established himself as arbitrator between the estates and as a representative of the empire above the estates. He convened the diet, set the agenda, and gave his assent to the estates' decisions before they were published as imperial decrees. A presiding emperor was the center of the diet, although the archbishop of Mainz as *Kurerzkanzler* was responsible for internal proceedings, as were the *Reichserbmarschälle* of Pappenheim for external organization.

In the three chambers voting was indirect. Each delegation declared its view according to the order dictated by the seating arrangement. The votes were not counted but assessed by the chairman. Although the estates sought consensus, the proceedings favored the powerful princes. Yet the pressure to give in and to compromise kept the diet viable. If no clear conclusion could be reached, the issue was tabled or referred to a committee. As soon as the views of the separate chambers were clear, electors and princes attempted to reach an agreement. If they did not, the deliberations continued.

The early modern diet was an assembly of estates that participated by virtue of their positions as legitimate sovereign rulers. For this reason, and because there was no written constitution, some procedural questions were never solved (e.g., the binding force of majority decisions on absent or protesting estates).

Place of the Diet in the Constitution of the Holy Roman Empire. The diet increasingly became an assembly of German estates: the estates of northern Italy, Burgundy, and the Swiss Confederation showed their indifference by absence. The diet could not integrate the peripheral areas of the Holy Roman Empire; it thus helped consolidate the German nation. As the membership of the diets clearly shows, this political system was initially concentrated in south Germany. North Germany slowly became more integrated after 1555.

Although the diet dealt with all issues, imperial decrees were implemented by the estates themselves. Despite this particularity however, both diet and emperor symbolized the concept of unity, the homeland of the "German Nation." The diet owed much of its significance to its function as a moneylender to the emperor. It also discussed and ratified all imperial taxes.

The Diet and the Reformation. The first time the diet became a forum for religious conflicts was in 1518, when Martin Luther was examined by Cardinal Cajetan in Augsburg, but only a few of the imperial estates were involved. Three years later things had changed radically. Luther's journey to Worms became a triumph. His refusal to recant made him even more popular. The religious conflict became an issue for the diet because Charles V did not automatically outlaw Luther after the papal ban against him. Emperor and empire had claimed the right to confirm a papal sentence—an exorbitant violation of tradition, even if the Edict of Worms condemned Luther and his followers to the imperial ban and prohibited the dissemination of his teachings. But the edict failed. Because of the long absence of the emperor the diet occupied the decisive position in the German constitutional system. In a sense it replaced the national council.

Because neither emperor nor pope accepted the demand for a free and ecumenical council, the Diet of Nuremberg (1524) transferred the decision to a national council. Meanwhile the estates had to obey the Edict of Worms insofar as possible. For the first time the diet offered a way out to all estates that were under pressure from the Reformation movement. The solidarity of the princes turned the religious problem to a political question: excluding no one and reaching an agreement became the central goal.

The Peasants' War and its evident close connection with the Reformation, which brought great difficulties to the ruling system of the German princes, showed urgently the necessity for an agreement. The Decree of Speyer (1526) included the promising article that until the decision of a church council every estate should proceed in religious matters as it considered justified before God and the emperor. Thus a generally accepted compromise according to the estates theory of the empire seemingly had been found. For the princes accepting the Reformation the agreement became a charter of the princely territorial church regime, which underlined their sovereign rights.

In this way the first Diet of Speyer marked a turning point for the constitutional system of the empire and for the breakthrough of the Reformation. The development could no longer be halted in a peaceful manner. According to the constitution of the empire the Reformation definitively fell un-

der the control of the imperial estates. Furthermore, two factions formed whose fundamental religious disagreement could not be overcome even at the diet. This confrontation dominated the second Diet of Speyer (1529). Under the leadership of Ferdinand I the Catholic majority forbade any religious innovation and nullified the religious stipulation of 1526. The evangelical estates protested officially. Appealing solemnly to emperor and council, they declared that they did not accept the majority decision because it abolished the unanimous agreement of a former diet and, more generally, because the settlement of religious matters could not be determined by a majority vote.

At the Diet of Augsburg in 1530 Charles V was present and willing to come to a compromise on the religious questions. But the confessional texts, such as the Augsburg Confession and Tetrapolitan Confession, showed only that the various positions were incompatible. Charles V implemented the Edict of Worms; a religious war seemed imminent. But as in 1521 the edict failed once more. A new round of discussion began which resulted in a temporary toleration of Protestants until a church council could take place.

Characteristically this agreement was neither reached at a diet nor confirmed at the following Diet of Ratisbon (1532). There the estates decided that if a free church council did not take place, the next diet should install itself as a national council and try to settle the religious dispute. For this reason the next diet did not occur until 1541, and then under different circumstances. Like the preceding series of religious colloquies, the following diets achieved only brief temporary religious truces, but there emerged a variation in the procedural system of the diet: the Protestant estates began to act as a caucus in order to break the Catholic majority in the upper chambers.

Although the emperor was victorious in the Schmalkald War, at the Diet of Augsburg (1547/48) he could realize only some of his aims. Even in times of crisis the diet supported the status quo. While the Protestants had to accept the Augsburg Interim, Catholics refused. For this reason the religious division was not healed. Moreover, Charles V failed in his ambition to transform the constitutional system of the empire into a more monarchical one. On this matter all the estates could unite in resistance.

After the Princes' Rebellion there was no possibility of establishing a monarchical system or of settling the religious conflict, which meant a modified return of the old church. A lasting agreement had to take account of the ideas and plans of the estates. The Treaty of Passau (1552), discussed by Moritz of Saxony and King Ferdinand I, was successful in this regard. It continued the toleration without imposing a time limit, and both Protestants and Catholics were able to secure their possessions, especially the secularized church properties.

The Diet of Augsburg in 1555 integrated the Treaty of Passau into a new general peace. It was a religious peace concluded by and in favor of the estates. For the first time two different confessions coexisted in one political system. The phrase "cuius regio, eius religio," which was coined later, described the situation exactly. With the exception of the free imperial cities every government received the right to decide about the religion of its subjects. The Peace of Augsburg became the "Magna Carta" of the German territorial princes and their states.

The religious conflict helped both to establish the rights of government of the estates and to institutionalize the diet. The diet became the representative institution of the German nation and protected the development of the territorial states without threatening the unity of the German nation. Thus in a sense the Catholic estates also profited from the advancing Reformation. The success of the Reformation and the rapid stabilization of the diet were closely interrelated.

[*See also* Augsburg, Peace of; Augsburg Confession; Charles V; Ferdinand I; Habsburg, House of; Maximilian II; *and* Protestantism.]

BIBLIOGRAPHY

Aulinger, Rosemarie. *Das Bild des Reichstages im 16. Jahrhundert: Beiträge zu einer typologischen Analyse schriftlicher und bildlicher Quellen.* Göttingen, 1980. This book also describes all organizational problems at the banquets and other festivities during the time of a diet.

Hughes, Michael. *Early Modern Germany, 1477–1806.* Basingstoke, England, 1992.

Moraw, Peter. "Versuch über die Entstehung des Reichstags." In *Politische Ordnungen und soziale Kräfte im Alten Reich,* edited by Hermann Weber, pp. 1–36. Wiesbaden, 1980. This famous essay was the beginning of a debate regarding whether the late medieval assemblies should be called diets or not.

Neuhaus, Helmut. *Reichstag und Supplikationsausschuß: Ein Beitrag zur Reichsverfassungsgeschichte in der ersten Hälfe des 16. Jahrhunderts.* Berlin, 1977. A detailed study of a special committee in the first half of the sixteenth century.

Oestreich, Gerhard. "Zur parlamentarischen Arbeitsweise der deutschen Reichstage unter Karl V., 1519–1556." *Mitteilungen des Österreichischen Staatsarchivs* 25 (1972), 217–243. This essay sheds light on how the diet functioned, but it rather overestimates the parallels with our modern parliaments.

Press, Volker. "Die Reformation und der deutsche Reichstag." In *Martin Luther: Leistung und Erbe,* edited by H. Bartel et al., pp. 202–215. Berlin, 1986. A short but very important essay showing how closely the success of the Reformation and the stablization of the diet were interrelated.

Rauch, Karl, ed. *Traktat über den Reichstag im 16. Jahrhundert: Eine offiziöse Darstellung aus der kurmainzischen Kanzlei.* Weimar, 1905. Studies the procedural organization of the diet.

Schmidt, Georg. *Der Städtetag in der Reichsverfassung: Eine Untersuchung zur korporativen Politik der Freien und Reichsstädte in der ersten Hälfte des 16. Jahrhunderts.* Wiesbaden, 1984. Studies the organization and politics of the free and imperial cities during the Reformation.

Schubert, Friedrich Hermann. *Die deutschen Reichstage in der Staatslehre der frühen Neuzeit.* Göttingen, 1966. A detailed study of the position of the diet in German public law during the early modern period.

Schulze, Winfried. "Majority Decision in the Imperial Diets of the the Sixteenth and Seventeenth Centuries." *Journal of Modern History* supp. 58 (1986), s46–s63.

GEORG SCHMIDT

DIETENBERGER, Johann

DIETENBERGER, Johann (c.1475–1537), German Dominican theologian and anti-Luther polemicist, best known for his Catholic catechism and German Bible based on the Vulgate. Dietenberger was born in Frankfurt am Main and entered the Dominican order as a young man. He studied theology in Cologne, Heidelberg, and Mainz, where he earned a doctorate in 1515. He became a respected scholar, educator, and administrator, serving as prior at Dominican institutions in Frankfurt, Trier, Coblenz, and Mainz, where he died in 1537.

Called into service against the Reformation, Dietenberger brought his extensive biblical knowledge to bear with a sharp and witty pen. Two of his fifteen extant polemical writings remain exemplary defenses of Catholic doctrine on the efficacy of good works. While not denying their worthiness, Dietenberger warned against taking personal credit for good works, as they issue from God's grace and mercy, and have merit only if grounded in faith. In the mid-1520s Dietenberger defended monasticism against Luther's attack on monastic vows and the cloistered life. Tracts published in 1524 and 1526 countered Luther's views on aural confession and the Holy Sacrament respectively. In 1530, arguing strictly from scripture, he justified the Catholic position on the major points of contention not resolved at the Augsburg Diet. A strong polemic covering similar ground appeared in Latin in 1532 (*Phimostomus Scripturariorum*) not only to meet the Protestant challenge but to accuse Luther personally of defaming the emperor, princes, and estates in a manner reserved for the "lowliest prostitutes." The strong language used here as elsewhere was justified as "paying back Luther in his own coin."

Dietenberger's two major contributions to German Catholicism, free of anger and contentiousness, were intended as guides to piety and understanding for the faithful: his catechism (1537) and his German-language Bible (first published in 1534). By his own admission the new Bible was largely a composite of earlier translations, Luther's most prominent among them, although the reformer was not acknowledged by name and specifically Protestant interpretations were deleted. Doctrinally true to the Vulgate, stylistically true to Luther's prose, Dietenberger's Bible went through fifty-eight editions, remaining the most widely used German Catholic text for over two centuries.

BIBLIOGRAPHY

Bautz, Friedrich Wilhelm, ed. *Biographische-Bibliographisches Kirchenlexikon* Hamm, 1970–. See vol. 1, p. 1296.

Iserloh, Erwin. "Dietenberger, Johann." In *Lexicon für Theologie und Kirche*, vol. 3, p. 382. Freiburg, 1965.

Paulus, Nikolaus, *Die deutschen Dominikaner im Kampf gegen Luther*. Freiburg, 1903. Based on the Wedewer biography.

Schottenloher, Karl, ed. *Bibliographie zur deutschen Geschichte im Zeitalter der Glaubensspaltung*. Stuttgart, 1957.

Stupperich, Robert. "Dietenberger, Johann." In *Die Religion in Geschichte und Gegenwart*, vol. 2, p. 194. Tübingen, 1986.

Verzeichnis der im deutschen Sprachbereich erschienenen Drucke des XVI. Jahrhunderts. Stuttgart, 1983–. See vol. 5, nos. 1476–1506.

Wedewer, Hermann, *Johannes Dietenberger 1475–1537: Sein Leben und Wirken*. Freiburg, 1888. The lone biography.

KARIN BRINKMANN BROWN

DIET OF ———. *See under latter part of name.*

DIETRICH, Veit

DIETRICH, Veit (1506–1549), Martin Luther's amanuensis and Nuremberg reformer. The world of Veit Dietrich revolved around two centers of the German Empire—the imperial city of Nuremberg and the university town of Wittenberg. He invested roughly half of his adult life ministering in each community. In 1522 Dietrich left his hometown of Nuremberg for Wittenberg, where Luther insisted he pursue theology instead of medicine. After his master's promotion, he taught in the university arts faculty and later was named its dean.

Dietrich developed a particularly strong relationship with Luther, whom he served as personal secretary. He accompanied Luther to the Marburg Colloquy (1529) and to Coburg castle during the Diet of Augsburg (1530). While at Coburg castle, Dietrich supervised Luther's correspondence with the reformers in Augsburg and took dictation in preparation for future commentaries. In Wittenberg Dietrich resided in the former Black Cloister which now served as Luther's home. His early transcriptions of the *Tischreden* (Table Talk) have provided arguably the most accurate accounts of these exchanges.

A call to the pastorate at Saint Sebaldus in Nuremberg prompted Dietrich to return home in 1535. Although he still edited works of Luther (notably his *Hauspostille*) and Philipp Melanchthon, Dietrich began to focus on his own work as preacher and church administrator. He published preaching aids, catechetical literature, and an influential chapter-by-chapter summary of the Old and New Testaments. To combat residual anticlericalism, Dietrich assembled a prototype pastor's manual, the *Agend-Büchlein*, which offered encouragement and simple instruction to village pastors.

Controversy filled the later years of Dietrich's career. His support of Melanchthon's efforts to initiate reform in Regensburg led to a vehement struggle with the local cathedral chapter concerning the practice of the Lord's Supper. The arrival of the victorious Charles V resulted in Dietrich's sus-

pension from his office at Saint Sebaldus (1547). He lost council support but remained in the city, where he boldly criticized the provisions of the Interim (1558–1552). Although Dietrich died a renegade, his efforts had altered the religious situation in Nuremberg for both clergy and laity.

BIBLIOGRAPHY

Primary Sources

Luther's Works. American ed., vol. 54. Philadelphia, 1967. Samples the "Table Talk" of Luther transcribed by Dietrich. For complete record see Weimar ed., ser. 4, vol. 1, pp. 1–309.

Secondary Sources

Bautz, Friedrich Wilhelm, ed. *Biographische-Bibliographisches Kirchenlexikon* Hamm, 1970–. See vol. 1, pp. 1302–1303.

Grimm, Harold. *Lazarus Sprengler: A Lay Leader of the Reformation*. Columbus, Ohio, 1978. Presents the relationship between Dietrich, Luther, and the reformers in Nuremberg.

Klaus, Bernard. *Veit Deitrich: Leben und Werke*. Nuremberg, 1958. Comprehensive biographical account and analysis of Dietrich's theological contributions.

Verzeichnis der im deutschen Sprachbereich erschienenen Drucke des XVI. Jahrhunderts. Stuttgart, 1983–. See vol. 5, nos. 1548–1689.

JEFFREY P. JAYNES

DIODATI, Jean

DIODATI, Jean (Ital., Giovanni; 1576–1649), Genevan ecclesiastic and translator of the Bible. Diodati was born into one of the Luccan (Italian) banking families that emigrated to Geneva and Zurich for religious reasons. Educated at the Geneva academy, then under the influence of Théodore de Bèze, he was a gifted linguist and became a doctor of theology at the age of nineteen and professor of Hebrew at twenty. He retained the chair of Hebrew until 1618 and was professor of theology from 1599 to 1645. It is from this time that the teaching of Hebrew in Geneva became more theological and less humanist.

He worked for the success of Protestantism in the Venetian republic as one of a group including Paolo Sarpi, the English ambassador Henry Wotton, and George Bedell (later bishop of Kilmore). These efforts were ultimately unsuccessful, but it was for this work that Diodati translated the Bible into Italian. He also translated Sarpi's *Histoire del Concile Tridentini* into French. The biblical translation was done at great speed and was reedited in 1640–1641. He published a complete French translation of the Bible in 1644 despite opposition from French Protestants who had found that Catholic (notably Jesuit) controversialists were using the variety of Protestant versions to ridicule claims of the primacy of scripture. The Italian version continued to be published into the twentieth century and has remained the standard Bible of Italian Protestantism.

Diodati represented the Genevan church at the Synod of Dordrecht in 1618–1619, where he and his fellow representative, Benedict Turrettini, maintained the same dogmas as the other delegations but with a different theology—notably as regards the death of Christ.

Diodati was part of a group of Reformed theologians who, at the beginning of the Thirty Years' War, were experiencing the regression of European Protestantism both territorially and theologically. He was doctrinally orthodox, though his biblical annotations had a pietistic aspect, suggesting that propositional revelation was of less importance to him. He was a translator rather than a systematic theologian at a time when Geneva was already experiencing the constraints of Reformed orthodoxy.

BIBLIOGRAPHY

Primary Source

Diodati, Jean. *Glossa in Sancta Biblia.* Geneva, 1644.

Secondary Sources

Bautz, Friedrich Wilhelm, ed. *Biographische-Bibliographisches Kirchenlexikon.* Hamm, 1970–. See vol. 1, p. 1314.
McComish, William A. *The Epigones.* Allison Park, Pa., 1989. Biography and bibliography of Jean Diodati with a study of his theology.

WILLIAM A. McCOMISH

DISCOVERIES IN THE NEW WORLD.

The European discovery of new lands and new peoples in the Americas challenged the visions of world history and of the salvation of the infidel accepted by both Roman Catholics and Protestants alike. The results were a revival of apocalyptic history with the New World at its center, a wide debate about the possibility of the salvation of non-Christian peoples, and the creation of new missionary strategies to effect their conversion, often under the impact of the evangelical success of the Catholic Reformation both in Europe and in America. Catholic and Protestant reformers reached similar conclusions about the New World's place in providential history but diverged sharply in their assessment of the possibility of the natives' salvation, and hence the effort which should be put into their evangelization.

The discovery of America and the Reformation have been linked in history since at least the end of the sixteenth century. For example, the Franciscan apocalyptic historian Gerónimo de Mendieta, in his *Historia Eclesiástica Indiana* (1596), drew a parallel between the careers of Martin Luther and of the conquistador Hernán Cortés: at the same time that Luther destroyed the foundations of the Roman church in Europe, Cortés conquered new lands and opened the way for the conversion of new souls across the Atlantic. The comparison of Luther and Cortés was a commonplace in Spanish historical thought, and it resembled two strains of reform thought, one earlier, Roman, and Catholic, the other later, English, and Puritan. In the papal court in the early decades of the sixteenth century, the ideal of reform was extended to include a worldwide *renovatio* encompassing the New World discoveries. Just as thinkers like Mendieta saw the New World as a compensation for the losses suffered by the Roman church at the hands of Protestant reformers, so papal reformers saw the new lands of the Americas as compensation for territory lost to the Turks. This would herald an expansion of the bounds of the church beyond anything even the Roman empire had known, as part of a new golden age of Christian peace during which the gospel would go "out to the ends of the earth" (*Ps.* 19:4). By contrast, in English Protestant thought of the seventeenth century (as earlier in French Huguenot thought during the late sixteenth-century Wars of Religion), America was seen as revealed by God as a refuge for those persecuted by the forces of Counter-Reformation. As the English radical Tom Paine put it in 1776, "the Reformation was preceded by the discovery of America—as if the Almighty graciously meant to open a sanctuary to the persecuted in future years." Renewal would not be general, however, but would be confined to those groups of the reformed who made the regenerative errand into the wilderness of America.

Both Catholic and Protestant reformers placed America within the context of apocalyptic history. There was a *translatio religionis*—a westward movement of religion, from its cradle in Israel, as well as a *translatio imperii*, a westward course of empire—that would be fulfilled in the Americas. For the Franciscans in particular, as indeed for Christopher Columbus, the discovery of the New World affirmed the universal claims of the church, the imminence of the last days, and the necessity of evangelization. For English Protestants, the New World became both the battleground for the fight against the forces of the Roman church and the arena in which the final preparatory drama of the last days would be played out.

The role of the salvation of the natives of the New World in these apocalyptic histories was perhaps the major distinction between Roman Catholic and Protestant thought occasioned by the discoveries in America. Though both the Spanish and the English colonial enterprises were authorized by an evangelical intent (the Spanish through the papal bulls confirming their rights in the New World, the English by their royal charters, for example), Protestant missionary activity lagged far behind the Franciscan, Dominican, and Jesuit missions in the New World. Few of the first generation in the magisterial Reformation were concerned about the peoples of the newfound lands. If they were interested in the question of the salvation of non-Christian peoples at all, their interest was in the Turks and the Jews, not the native peoples of America. The Lutheran insistence on justification by faith alone and scriptural authority "tended to restrict rather than enlarge the scope of salvation," as George Huntston Williams put it. Only the beliefs of the Radical Reformers, in universal salvation and ecumenism, and the missionary fervor of their lay apostolate, encouraged the evangelization of non-Christians. The later Calvinist emphasis on doctrines of election and the necessity of testimony to conversion, however, further restricted Protestant evangelization in the New World. In contrast to the Catholic missions, the first generations of English Protestants were also constrained by their ministry of the elect, their belief in the necessity of civilization (that is, acculturation and settlement) before Christianization, and their refusal to temper their message to the culture and practices of the native Americans. ("By [Puritan] principles, no Nation can or could ever be converted," complained an Anglican visitor to New England in 1642.) The apparent success of the Catholic missions in the New World inspired the parallel efforts of Catholic reform and conversion (in Italy, for example) in the sixteenth century. It would take the forces of Protestant reform in the New World until the turn of the eighteenth century to realize that if they were to imitate that success and follow fully the Gospel's exhortations to universal evangelization, they would have to abandon the restrictions imposed by the theology of the magisterial reformers and take up the mission approved by both Catholic and radical Reformations alike. Only then could all the peoples of the Old and New Worlds become potentially a part of salvation history.

[See also America and Missions.]

BIBLIOGRAPHY

Axtell, James. The European and the Indian: Essays in the Ethnohistory of Colonial North America. New York, 1981. Especially important on the missionary practice of the English Protestants in North America up to the eighteenth century.

DeJong, J. A. As the Waters Cover the Sea: Millennial Expectations in the Rise of Anglo-American Missions, 1640–1810. Kampen, Netherlands, 1970.

Hanke, Lewis. "The Theological Significance of the Discovery of America." In First Images of America: The Impact of the New World on the Old, edited by Fredi Chiappelli, vol. 1, pp. 363–374. Berkeley, 1976. Mostly on Spanish reception of the New World; good for comparison with the different idiom of northern European reception of America.

Lestringant, Frank. Le Huguenot et le Sauvage: L'Amérique et la controverse coloniale, en France, au temps des Guerres de Religion, 1555–1589. Paris, 1990. The best account of sixteenth-century French Protestant views of America.

McShane, F. "America, Theological Significance of." In Catholic Dictionary of Theology, edited by H. Francis Davis et al., vol. 1, pp. 69–70. London, 1962. A brilliant short description of theories of salvation in relation to the New World.

O'Malley, John W. "The Discovery of America and Reform Thought at the Papal Court in the Early Cinquecento." In First Images of America: The Impact of the New World on the Old, edited by Fredi Chiappelli, Vol. 1, pp. 185–200. Berkeley, 1976. Convincingly places attitudes to the New World in the context of theories of worldwide renovatio.

Phelan, John Leddy. The Millennial Kingdom of the Franciscans in the New World. 2d rev. ed. Berkeley, 1970.

Prosperi, Adriano. "'Otras Indias': Missionari della Contrariforma tra Contadini e Selvaggi." In Scienze, Credenze Occulte, Livelli di Cultura, edited by Giancarlo Garfagnini, pp. 205–234. Florence, 1982.

Details the impact of American Jesuit missions on parallel enterprises in Europe (especially Italy).

Williams, George Huntston. "Erasmus and the Reformers on Non-Christian Religions and Salus Extra Ecclesiam." In Action and Conviction in Early Modern Europe: Essays in Memory of E. H. Harbison, edited by Theodore K. Rabb and Jerrold Seigel, pp. 319–370. Princeton, 1969. The best account of the reformers' diverse attitudes to non-Christian peoples.

Wright, A. D. The Counter-Reformation: Catholic Europe and the Non-Christian World. London, 1982. Chapter 4 gives a brief but dense summary of the activities of the orders during the age of the Catholic Reformation.

DAVID ARMITAGE

DISPUTATIONS. The Reformation, understood as a datable historical event, began with a disputation. It is a matter of controversy, to be sure, whether Luther's famous Ninety-five Theses, Pro declaratione virtutis indulgentiarum, of 31 October 1517 achieved the goal of serving as a topic of discussion at a disputation at the University of Wittenberg. Possibly the event never took place. It is well known, however, that these theses represent a kind of rudimentary text for the protest of the reformer against the medieval theology and church, and that as such they have had an enormous influence.

This did not occur by accident. By making public his insights in the form of disputation theses, Luther made use of a medium which was important and characteristic in the context of his vocation as professor. Both in academic instruction and the discussion of controversial questions, disputations had been common practice at medieval universities, where they represented nothing short of the peculiar spirituality and erudition of the Middle Ages. This was based on the notion of "truth" as given, present in the teaching statements handed down from antiquity. It was assumed that, with the help of a dialectic process of understanding, through artful questions and answers to these questions, through the confrontation of assertion and repudiation, through orderly use of authorities and other arguments, and finally by harmonizing contradictions, it would be possible to "find the truth again."

Luther held certain axioms of this conception of knowledge not only in 1517 but during his whole life, and they were authoritative for his followers as well: that there was truth, and indeed only one truth, and that one finds access to it through an ancient document. Thus the dialectic process of ascertaining truth had, in a way, a natural plausibility also for the Reformation. It was understood that one authority surpassed all others and preceded them: the "word of God" as set down in the gospel. Existential meaning was ascribed to it, since salvation itself, the eternal fate of man, depended on the correct interpretation of this authority. Thus disputations gained new status and meaning in the Reformation, their social context expanded, and various forms developed. After 1517, too, disputations played a significant role in Luther's theological development. In the context of these events (Heidelberg, 1518; Leipzig, 1519) Luther achieved his most important insights, and he later urged that disputations be maintained at the University of Wittenberg for the purpose of instruction, indeed for the disclosure of truth. Consequently they remained valid at Protestant universities everywhere—in some areas to the present day.

Political Disputations. Another development had even greater meaning for the Reformation. The form of the disputation was carried over from the universities into completely different settings, especially urban communities, where it acquired a political function and became an element in the religious and political success of the Reformation.

Zurich, 1523. Huldrych Zwingli must be considered the "inventor" of these municipal disputations. Not only was he a leading voice in determining the course of the first two meetings of this kind in Zurich in January and October of 1523, but he also may have devised the guiding concept. This was done in close cooperation and agreement with the council of Zurich, which emerged as the organizer of the disputations, set the objectives, and provided the setting for them. In each case it had to do with an effort to quell the conflict that had broken out in the city during the course of reform preaching and the public dissent of the preachers. The official responsibility to preserve the peace was advanced as the legal argument for the meeting. The council saw itself as authorized to undertake altogether unusual measures, summoning the clergy of the city and province of Zurich to the city hall. Already in the announcement of the first disputation it was stipulated that only argumentation from the Bible was to be permitted. The council claimed the right to determine which of the two disputing parties had carried the day, and according to which rules preaching would take place in Zurich in the future. It was a radical move, one on which the earlier legal basis of the secular authorities' relationship to the church was challenged.

In the January disputation, Zwingli offered with his *67 Schlußreden* ("conclusions") the *materia disputandi* and gave direction to the discussion. As a result the guidelines of university disputations were adopted. This was even more clearly the case in the October meeting. The disputation offered the invaluable advantage of clarifying disputes methodically and bringing religious disagreements to a decision. In many respects, however, the Zurich disputations were different from ordinary university disputations. The deliberations were held in German, and moreover the sessions were held in the city hall and before the council. The subject matter was the whole of the Protestant-Catholic disagreement, indeed, the whole of Christian truth. The January meeting differed greatly from the university model. Thus, on the whole, the Zurich disputations were innovations, and this was especially true of the outcome: the instruction of the city council on 29 January 1523 that Zwingli continue his reform preaching according to the word of God, and the subsequent inclusion of all other clergy in city and country in this instruction. This meant that the civic community of Zurich acting as religious community had accepted the Reformation and had broken off the connection to the church governed by Rome; it was the first establishment of a new church within Protestantism.

Significance of the Zurich disputations. The events in Zurich exerted a great impact. It was extraordinary that, even in that time of literary feats and mass publication success, the extensive transcript of the first disputation saw no fewer than seven editions in 1523, and Zwingli's *Schlußreden* were printed a total of twenty-six times in the course of two years. The Zurich proceedings seemed to influence many who were faced with similar decisions—with respect not only to religion or theology, but to politics as well—for the proceedings would be imitated in subsequent years in numerous places in German-speaking areas and beyond. They proved to be one of the most effective means to create in the cities a basis of legitimation for the Reformation that met the need of city councils to clarify the religious situation and to preserve peace, not to mention the burghers' desire for information and involvement.

The authorities of the established church and the empire that sought to stave off the Reformation were virtually defenseless in the face of disputations whenever they were resolutely taken in hand by reform-minded authorities and church people. Neither the scholastic principle that one should not argue questions of faith before the laity nor the argument that an authoritative ecclesiastical judgment was necessary had persuasive power under the circumstances: they could be easily refuted by the invitation to participate in the discussion inherent in the idea of the disputation and the Reformation scripture principle. The most effective countermeasures on the part of the old church were therefore refusing to participate and official prohibition. The imperial Edict of Burgos of 15 July 1524 prohibited disputations concerning the Christian faith in the empire. Accordingly, they were labeled in Germany, as a rule, a "dialogue," "hearing," or "collation," without, however, essentially changing the format. In the Swiss Confederation they remained "disputations."

According to twentieth-century scholarship, the first disputations to follow the pattern conceptualized by Zwingli took place far from Zurich—in 1523 in Altenburg (Saxony) and in April 1524 in Breslau (Wrocław). In both instances the champions of the Reformation (with the exception of Zwingli, who held only a master of arts degree) had doctorates in theology (in Altenburg, Wenceslaus Linck, in Breslau, Johann Hess). In at least the second instance the practices conformed more clearly than in Zurich to university customs.

In 1524 and the early months of 1525 an additional series

of political disputations took place or were planned, all in close proximity to Zurich (Appenzell, Strasbourg, Mulhouse, Schlettstadt, Constance, Memmingen, Kaufbeuren). In south German and Swiss cities, disputations of this kind seem already to have become rather commonplace before the Peasants' War.

A major disputation of extraordinary and vastly influential significance took place in the imperial city of Nuremberg in March 1525. This eclipsed even the Zurich models in the care of preparation and the stringency of execution and was a central event in the Reformation history of Nuremberg. In Nuremberg as in Zurich the establishment of the Reformation by the city council was the immediate consequence of the disputation.

The first phase of dynamic expansion of the Reformation ended in 1525 with the Peasants' War and the beginning of the dispute over Communion. The political attractiveness of the Reformation had lessened, and the scriptural principle had lost its clarity. Thus, in the spring of 1526 the opponents of change appropriated the idea in direct confrontation with its originator and mobilized disputations for their own cause. After a trial run in Ilanz (Graubünden), the disputation of Baden (Aargau) took place from 21 May to 8 June 1526. It was perceived and executed as a general meeting of the Swiss Confederation. The spokesman for the Catholic faction, Johann Eck, embarrassed his main antagonist, Oecolampadius, over the issues of biblical authority and also over the Lord's Supper. This Catholic victory had notable consequences, however, only in the Catholic areas of Switzerland.

With the Baden disputation, political disputations reached for the first time beyond the boundaries of a given city. In the same year, Landgrave Philipp of Hesse seized the opportunity to obtain for himself and for his territorial diet a basis for legitimating the planned change of his territory to the new faith: at the Synod of Homberg, the debate between two Franciscans, François Lambert and Nikolaus Herborn, ended with the declaration of the authorities that the representative of the new faith had been able to prove his case on the basis of the Bible.

The disputation at Bern of January 1528 was an important event in the Swiss Confederation whereby the reformed towns attempted to offset the Baden disputation and the defeat that had been suffered there. A kind of Swiss national council took place that included many participants from south Germany as well. Lasting twenty days and bringing together 350 clergy as well as an unknown number of politicians and citizens of Bern, it was the largest and most spectacular of all disputations in the cities. Zwingli took a prominent part. The most important result was the introduction of the Reformation into the city and territory of Bern and with it the crucial stabilization of Swiss Protestantism.

The Bern Disputation also had the effect of furnishing proof of the usefulness of disputations to Protestantism. In

subsequent years a wave of similar events occurred in German-speaking areas, mostly in cities. In the Swiss Confederation a disputation was held in Frauenfeld (Thurgau) in December 1529 and others were planned for Basel in 1529 and for Solothurn in 1530; others were held in the southwest German cities of Ulm (July 1531) and Esslingen (November 1531) and in the north German cities of Hamburg (April 1528), Lüneburg (September 1532), and Münster (August 1533); finally, still others were planned for the north German cities of Lübeck, Minden, and Lippstadt (1530), Göttingen and Soest (1531), and Osnabrück (1532). In each instance a disputation launched, accompanied, or prepared the change of the city to the new faith.

The political disputationen entered the last phase of their history in connection with the Reformation in western Switzerland. Large gatherings took place along well-established lines in Geneva (March 1535) and Lausanne (October 1536) and justified the introduction of the Reformation in those cities. Here ended the usefulness of Zwingli's fruitful "invention." Attempts were made to revive the institution by Martin Bucer at the reform of the archbishopric of Cologne 1542–1543, and Théodore de Bèze and his associates in the presence of the French court at the Colloquy of Poissy 1561, but these came to nothing.

Historical Significance of Political Disputations. Alongside the political disputations mentioned here, a large number of other debates, discussions, and colloquies took place that in many instances took the form of the disputation. The upheaval of the period created in many places the desire for certainty and for accountability, delimitation, and confrontation in direct intellectual exchange. The historical significance of political disputations, however, lies in the fact that the decisions that were made there entailed—as was intended—ecclesiopolitical consequences. In them, as a rule, all ecclesiastical-theological differences of opinion were debated. However, the point was hardly to reach agreement, but to prove the superiority—indeed, the exclusive right—of a particular confessional position, as a rule that in accordance with Reformation doctrine (the exception was Baden in 1526). These disputations may well have been the most important element in the cities for introducing the Reformation and avoiding the appearance of arbitrariness in the legal decree of *jus reformandi* that was used to support the action.

[*See also* Cities *and* Clergy.]

BIBLIOGRAPHY

Backus, Irene. *The Disputations of Baden (1526) and Berne (1528): Neutralizing the Early Church.* Princeton, 1993.

Ebeling, Gerhard. *Lutherstudien.* Vol. 2, *Disputatio de homine.* Tübingen, 1971–1989.

Kaufmann, Georg Heinrich. *Geschichte der deutschen Universitäten.* Stuttgart, 1896. See vol. 2, p. 369ff.

Moeller, Bernd. "Zwinglis Disputationen: Studien zu den Anfängen der Kirchenbildung und des Synodalwesens im Protestantismus."

Zeitschrift der Savigny-Stiftung für Rechtsgeschichte 87 (1970), 275–324, and 91 (1974), 213–364.

Oberman, Heiko A. *Werden und Wertung der Reformation: Vom Wegestreit zum Glaubenskampf.* Tübingen, 1977. See especially pp. 241–303.

BERND MOELLER

Translated from German by Susan M. Sisler

DISSIDENTS. *See* Nonconformity.

DIVINE RIGHT. *See* Secular Magistrate, Office of.

DIVORCE is the formal dissolution of the contract and union between a husband and wife, enabling one or both of them to enter a new marriage. One must distinguish carefully between the juristically sanctioned procedure that emerged during the Reformation of the sixteenth century and both the popularly recognized renunciation that had long been common practice throughout premodern Europe and the Catholic separation that parted a couple but preserved their spiritual and legal relationship. A renunciation usually involved nothing more than the spontaneous abandonment of one spouse by another, frequently serving as the only readily available means to escape an inconvenient or unhappy marriage. A separation required a canonical examination of the relationship between husband and wife, determining whether their communality could be preserved without risk of physical or spiritual injury to either but not altering their spiritual union. A divorce differed from both of these by insisting on complex legal procedures to establish the cause and culpability of violations that sundered the bonds of marriage entirely and made remarriage possible. It was an attempt to reform married life by assuming that marriage was not indissoluble.

Divorce was strictly prohibited by the Catholic church, a notion founded directly on its understanding of the nature of marriage. Not a purely religious state, marriage was a stable, contractual relationship entered freely by a man and a woman in order to bear children and to establish a household. Only insofar as it provided a setting for the service of God did it achieve religious significance; marriage received a new meaning in the Christian revelation as a work of God yielding grace—that is, as a sacrament. In 1159 Pope Alexander II ruled that persons marrying by free and mutual consent, the *sponsalis per verba de praesenti* ("espousal by words of present context"), and observing local ceremonial custom (an inessential element, nonetheless) were sacramentally united whether or not their union was ever consummated. Contract and sacrament were indistinguishable because the signs of consent were also the symbols of the sacrament. This mutual, free, and true *consensus* was the essential element that made a marriage indissoluble.

Canonists recognized, however, that some persons were unable to give consent to a marriage by virtue of age or infirmity. Moreover, the institution of marriage required protection to uphold its religious, moral, and social significance. From these more practical considerations developed the entire spectrum of marital impedimenta, those conditions that rendered a marriage invalid *ab initio* and left the unaffected parties free to remarry, and those that made valid marriages illegal and left the parties liable to sanctions. An invalidating impediment constituted grounds for an annulment, a ruling in canon law that no marriage ever existed because the parties had been unable or unwilling to give their mutual, free, and true consent. A prohibiting impediment resulted in the imposition of legal penalties but left the marriage bonds intact. As a remedy for crime within a marriage, canonists had recourse to the *divortium quoad thorum et mensam* ("separation from bed and board"), the legal separation. This judgment dissolved the communality between husband and wife, relieving them of the burdens of cohabitation but maintaining the spiritual union between them and making remarriage impossible.

Yet the strict prohibition of divorce and remarriage by the Catholic church was observed only in the breach during the Middle Ages. Roman and Germanic law allowed both, and repudiation and abandonment were popular extralegal means of achieving the same end. Not until Gratian (d. before 1159), did the Catholic principle achieve its final form; the *matrimonium perfectum* was indissoluble.

Religious reformers in the sixteenth century reconsidered the nature of marriage and arrived at conclusions that made divorce not only a possibility but a necessary option. Though they generally rejected the notion of marriage as a sacrament—a divinely ordained institution through which Christians might obtain grace and, ultimately, salvation—they understood it to be a religious state, created specifically by God as a remedy for human concupiscence. Marriage constituted a refuge for human nature made weak and imperfect by original sin. As a result, reformers rejected the Catholic glorification of celibacy. Only those few saints called by God to an austere life could hope to practice it without danger to their immortal souls. By the same token, marriages in which husband and wife failed to comfort and support one another physically, materially, or emotionally might lead them to violate their conjugal union and thus pose a threat both to their immortal souls and to the social order. Divorce and remarriage proved the solution of choice for sixteenth-century reformers because marriage was a human institution, essential to salvation and society.

Nearly all Protestants affirmed the legitimacy of divorce. Catholics, too, recognized that scripture apparently sanctioned divorce under certain circumstances. Jesus responded to the question of a Pharisee by saying that any husband who divorces his wife for reasons other than adultery and remarries commits adultery himself despite the fact that husband and wife are one flesh and inseparable in the eyes of God (*Mt.* 19:6–9). Yet the Bible also offered contradictory testimony. Paul prohibited divorce altogether but permitted a heathen spouse to separate from a Christian mate as a matter of human law (*1 Cor.* 7:10–15). The unanimity of sixteenth-century theologians and jurists dissolved over the correct interpretation of these passages.

With the Bible to guide them, all Protestants affirmed that adultery was a cause for divorce. Beyond this point, however, their opinions diverged considerably, especially over the two issues of licit grounds for divorce and the possibility of remarriage.

In his early treatise on married life, *Vom ehelichen Leben* (On the Married State; 1522), Martin Luther advocated divorce and remarriage for both spouses in cases of adultery, abandonment, or impotence. Marriages marked by these problems no longer protected husband and wife from sin. Two of his most influential disciples, Johannes Brenz and Johannes Bugenhagen, were more conservative. While accepting divorce on the grounds of adultery and impotence, they argued that abandonment could lead to divorce only when one spouse was absent over a period of time, could not be located despite the most diligent efforts, and might reasonably be presumed dead. Were a divorce granted, the innocent spouse could remarry; neither Brenz nor Bugenhagen granted remarriage for the guilty party.

Swiss reformers tended to be more liberal than their Lutheran counterparts in the matter of divorce, allowing more grounds for it and permitting remarriage to one or both parties. Huldrych Zwingli and Johannes Oecolampadius extended the legal causes of divorce to include not only adultery, abandonment, and impotence but also contagious disease and insisted that in all cases, except those in which physical infirmity prevented marriage from fulfilling its essential purpose, both spouses should be allowed to seek new partners and marry again.

Beyond the two major reformed confessions, attitudes toward divorce could be even more latitudinarian. For example, Martin Bucer believed that marriage required continual affection and cohabitation and that the union dissolved if that communality ceased for any reason. In short, divorces required no more cause than the mutual consent of the spouses. Radical reformers seem to have agreed with the possibility of a consensual divorce as a consequence of their notion of covenantal marriage, that is, a union in which the bond between man and woman resembled that between Christ and his church. Divorce and remarriage might be required when spouses were not both covenanting members of the church and were permissible between members of the church, in cases, such as adultery, where the marriage posed spiritual danger to a believer or to a believer's children. This was the thrust of an anonymous tract

attributed to Michael Sattler in 1527. In either instance, the civil authority appeared superfluous.

Unlike theologians considering divorce in terms of its implications for the souls and salvation of individual Christians, magistrates had to translate reform ideals into legal practice. They sought workable guidelines for dissolving marriages, punishing the guilty, protecting the innocent, and preserving order. The marriage ordinance of Zurich, promulgated in 1525, provided an outline for divorce in many reformed communities. Certainly the first and arguably the most influential, it was quoted verbatim in the ordinances of other Swiss Reformed cantons, most notably Basel, Bern, and St. Gall, and influenced marital legislation in the duchy of Württemberg and the free imperial cities of Ulm, Strasbourg, and Augsburg. In all these states, the magistrates viewed those circumstances that violated the monogamy and harmony of married life as grounds for divorce. For example, the marriage court in Zurich regularly granted divorces in all proven cases of adultery and impotence, but conviction of a capital crime, contracting a contagious disease, committing deadly assault, or maliciously abandoning a spouse could become grounds, too, at the discretion of the court. Other marriage courts followed Zurich's lead in granting divorce, differing only in matters of detail.

Zurich's magistrates treated remarriage after divorce as the necessary means to prevent the sin and disorder associated with extramarital sexual relations. Thus they made it relatively easy for both parties to contract new unions. Once the divorce was granted, innocent spouses could remarry without further ado; guilty spouses could remarry only after they demonstrated moral behavior over a period of time. Reformed communities usually developed their own guidelines for remarriage, but most adopted some form of Zurich's strategy of immediate remarriage for the innocent and a waiting period for the guilty.

Though they were prepared to admit the possibility of divorce and remarriage, reformers never encouraged it. Divorce was a last resort only. Protestant theologians and magistrates alike sought to preserve marriage wherever possible, preferring reconciliation and using every means at their disposal to accomplish it. They limited the grounds for divorce to a few objective, verifiable circumstances. They pressured spouses to forgive their errant mates and frequently ordered extended negotiations involving friends, relatives, and officials to resolve the conflict rather than dissolve the union. They deliberately prolonged hearings, increasing procedural expense and inconvenience and encouraging parties to consider alternatives. Finally, if the circumstances of a case offered any hope of reconciliation or any doubts regarding the complaint, they flatly refused the divorce and ordered the estranged couple to resume cohabitation as husband and wife. Magistrates shared the conviction of theologians that marriage was the preferred state for a moral existence and hence sought to limit instances of divorce and remarriage solely to those situations in which marriages had clearly and irremediably ceased to exist.

And yet legal divorce was not rare in the period of the Reformation. Complaints covered the entire range of permissible grounds, but abandonment, adultery, and impotence were the most frequently cited causes. For example, the Zurich marriage court heard seventy-two petitions for divorce from 1525 to 1531; an average of twelve per year in a city of somewhat less than six thousand souls. That divorces were regular but infrequent seems to indicate that they did not find too ready acceptance among married couples, a testimonial either to their own private scruples or to the magistrates' legal stratagems.

As a result, the consequences of divorce were private rather than public, limited to those few families that experienced them. Within the circle of the early modern family, however, it must have had a shattering impact. It greatly complicated the bonds of affection, compromised the patriarchal authority, prejudiced the social standing of a family, and, most obviously, dissolved the material communality of husband and wife. In short, the immediate consequences of divorce during the Reformation were not much different from those in the present.

Divorce failed to alter the nature of married life in preindustrial Europe. Marriage united families and fortunes for the dual purposes of bearing the next generation and of establishing a new household. Thus families had a stake in preventing divorce and preserving these unions. Only as industrialization changed the role of the family, separating its productive and affective functions, weakening the solidarity and collective interest of its members, and dissolving the physical unity of workshop and household could divorce become an engine of change.

[See also Courts, article on Marriage Courts; Family; Marriage; and Women.]

BIBLIOGRAPHY

Carter, Hugh, and Paul C. Glick. *Marriage and Divorce.* Cambridge, Mass., 1970. Reliable and accessible overview of divorce as a historical problem.

Kitchen, Shepherd B. *A History of Divorce.* London, 1912. An early though still useful overview of the subject despite the author's dated biases.

Lottin, Alain, et al. *La désunion du couple sous l'Ancien Régime: L'exemple du Nord.* Paris, 1975. A study of civil divorce in eighteenth-century France with useful background and comparisons for the earlier period.

Noonan, John T. *The Power to Dissolve: Lawyers and Marriage in the Courts of the Roman Curia.* Cambridge, Mass., 1972. A collection of six case studies of divorces before the Sacra Romana Rota in Rome.

Ozment, Steven E. *When Fathers Ruled: Family Life in Reformation Europe.* Cambridge, Mass., 1983. A too-positive assessment of family life in the sixteenth century; though biased by its dependence on prescriptive materials, offers a concise section on divorce and the Reformation.

Phillips, Roderick. *Putting Asunder: A History of Divorce in Western So-ciety.* Cambridge, 1988. A recent, largely derivative overview of divorce that offers reliable but disappointingly cautious conclusions.

Safley, Thomas Max. *Let No Man Put Asunder: The Control of Marriage in the German Southwest; A Comparative Study, 1550–1600.* Kirksville, Mo., 1984. Concise study of marital litigation in ecclesiastical and secular courts with particular attention to divorce during the Reformation.

Stone, Lawrence. *Road to Divorce: England, 1530–1987.* Oxford, 1990. Monumental study of divorce, its antecedents, and its consequences from its introduction through the twentieth century in England.

THOMAS MAX SAFLEY

DOBNECK, Johann. *See* Cochlaeus, Johannes.

DOLET, Étienne (1508–1546), French humanist, publisher, and editor of evangelical literature. Born at Orléans, Dolet began his university studies at Paris and continued them at Padua (1527), where he came under the influence of Paduan Aristotelianism and Ciceronianism, especially through contact with Christophe de Longueil and Simon Villanovanus. After two years as secretary to Jean Langeac, the French ambassador in Venice, he returned to France to study law at the University of Toulouse (1532). Disappointed as a contestant in the city's annual poetry contest, Dolet created a scandal as university orator by denouncing the religious bigotry of the city, which he decried as a threat to humanistic learning. Forced to flee (1534), he moved to Lyon, where he soon found employment as a corrector and later established himself as one of the most important printers in the city. The publication of his *Commentariorum linguae latinae* (Commentaries on the Latin Language; 1536) made him famous and gained him the friendship of the most celebrated humanists of the city; however, he soon quarreled with many of his friends, ran afoul of the other printers in the city, and was forced to seek the pardon of the king for the murder of a painter with whom he had quarreled.

Between 1540 and 1542 his printing business flourished, and he committed himself to a vast program of publication entailing the translation of the best of modern and ancient literature into the French vernacular. The embellishment of the French language, among other reasons, impelled him toward the publication of evangelical literature, including Pierre Robert Olivétan's Bible, Clément Marot's psalms, and Jacques Lefèvre d'Étaples's *Les Epitres et Evangiles des Cinquante et Deux Dimenches de l'An.* Arrested on suspicion of heresy in 1542, Dolet was released by a second royal intervention (June 1543). He was arrested again soon thereafter (January 1544) because of the seizure of a shipment of heretical books in Paris bearing his name. Escaping to Piedmont, he returned briefly to Lyon and then fled to Troyes, where he was seized and brought to Paris for trial. Condemned by the Parlement of Paris for blasphemy, sedition, and trafficking in prohibited books, he was consigned to the flames in the Place Maubert on 3 August 1546.

Dolet illustrates the complexity of the interaction between humanism and reform in the development of the French Reformation. In particular, the relationship between his philosophical opinions and his increasing interest in heretical literature has perplexed scholars. In 1534 Dolet attacked Erasmus for mingling philosophy and religion, holding Erasmus responsible for the spread of heresy and even atheism. Dolet preferred the Ciceronianism of his Paduan masters, which strictly separated matters of faith and philosophy. Current scholarship has established that in his *Commentariorum linguae latinae*, Dolet denied the Christian idea of the immortality of the soul and of a personal God in favor of the classical notions of fame and Stoic resignation to fate.

The weight of scholarly opinion holds that Dolet maintained these opinions to the end of his life despite his growing interest in evangelical writing. Explanations vary from those who believe that Dolet promoted evangelical literature for mercenary reasons or to curry favor with his political masters to those who hold that he did so because he felt that the evangelical position, although flawed, was the more enlightened.

BIBLIOGRAPHY

Primary Sources

Dolet, Étienne. *L'Erasmianus sive Ciceronianus.* Introduction by Emile Telle. Geneva, 1974. Telle's excellent introduction to this facsimile edition explores the relationship between Erasmus and Dolet, elucidating the significance of the latter's Ciceronianism.
———. *Préfaces Françaises*, edited by Claude Longeon. Geneva, 1979. Dolet's prefaces to his French vernacular editions. Provides an insight into Dolet's program for the French language and the place of evangelical literature in it.

Secondary Sources

Christie, Richard Copley. *Étienne Dolet: The Martyr of the Renaissance.* 2d ed. London, 1899. Still the essential work and standard biography.
Longeon, Claude. *Bibliographie des oeuvres d'Étienne Dolet.* Geneva, 1980.
Mayer, C. A. "The Problem of Dolet's Evangelical Publications," *Bibliotheque d'humanisme et renaissance* 17 (1955), 405–414. Reviews various theories on Dolet's religious and philosophical opinions, emphasizing the political context of Dolet's evangelical publications.
Weber, Henri. "La pensée d'Étienne Dolet et le combat humaniste." In *Actes du colloque sur l'humanisme lyonnaise au 16e siècle*, pp. 339–368. Grenoble, 1974. Dolet's philosophical opinions are elicited through study of his *Commentariorum linguae latinae.*

HENRY HELLER

DOMINICANS. As with Christendom itself, the Order of the Friars Preachers, also called Dominicans, at the be-

ginning of the sixteenth century presented different faces that varied greatly from region to region and from nation to nation according to the degree of observance (reformed or unreformed) in the various provinces and congregations, and even according to the temperament of its individual members, who had diverse reactions to the Protestant Reformation. Their formation was certainly imbued with the Thomistic tradition, which still flourished in Paris and in Italy, but biblical humanism and patristics also counted many followers among the Dominicans. The reformers relied on the work of a Dominican, Sante Pagnini, one of the best Hebrew scholars of his time. By contrast, the scandal of the Dominicans in Bern who had organized false apparitions of the Virgin Mary in 1507 no doubt contributed to the unpopularity of the Roman church in that region.

Luther presented his Ninety-five Theses to refute a Dominican preacher with limited theological depth, Johann Tetzel, subcommissioner general of the archbishop of Mainz, who was preaching on indulgences at Jüterbog, not far from Wittenberg. What are called the counter-theses of Tetzel are propositions that Luther drew from the Dominican's sermons on indulgences.

In terms of their attitudes to the onslaught of the Lutheran Reformation one can contrast two Dominicans: Cajetan and Martin Bucer. Cajetan was a personality of the first rank. At the time he met Luther in October 1518 at the Diet of Augsburg, one of the decisive steps in the developing schism, he had been master general of the Dominican order a few months before and was now a cardinal and papal legate. After 1527 Cajetan devoted himself to writing biblical commentaries that were judged to be rather audacious, particularly in that he proposed making distinctions within the biblical canon. It was not without some irony that Luther remarked that his former censor had become "Lutheran." This opinion was shared by the Dominican Ambrogio Catarino Politi, who denounced Cajetan in 1533 at about the same time that he attacked Bernardino Ochino.

Martin Bucer had entered the Dominican order in 1506 at Sélestat in Alsace. In 1518 he began to correspond with Luther, whom he had heard at the disputation of Heidelberg, where Bucer attended the university as a student while holding the office of "magister studentium," a position of trust, in the Dominican priory. He applied for and obtained a dispensation from his vows in 1521. His knowledge of Thomistic theology that he had acquired in his years as a Dominican made itself felt in his activity as a reformer, in his refutations, and in his various works

With this twofold example, one may divide the Dominicans into adversaries and followers of the reformers. The latter left the order at various points. Among the most active opponents of Protestantism was Sylvester Mazzolini Prierias, "master of the sacred palace," an office always entrusted to a Dominican. In 1518 he initiated a debate with

Luther. In the faculty of theology at Cologne, Dominicans such as Conrad Köllin, Jakob van Hoogstraeten, Johann Dietenberger, and Johannes Host, who had refuted Johannes Reuchlin, fought against Luther and the other reformers. Bernard of Luxembourg drew up a *Catalogus haereticorum,* of which there were successive editions between 1522 and 1537. After at first expressing some understanding of Luther, Johannes Augustanus Faber began to fight against him. In the generation that followed, the fight was joined by men such as Johannes Fabri and Ambrosius Pelargus, who took part in the interconfessional Colloquy of Worms as well as that of Regensburg. Sometimes the reformers faced less able opponents; that is at least what Guillaume Farel suggested about Guy Furbity in Geneva in 1534. Later the Dominicans in charge of the Inquisition had the responsibility of prosecuting heretics; for example, Jean de Roma prosecuted the Waldensians of Italy.

But some Dominicans went over to Protestantism: for example, Aimé Maigret, who preached the Reformation in Lyon, and Thomas Malingre in the region of the Vaud. But in no other area was there such a massive defection as in England after 1534, although a number of Dominicans had already left the country. Obedience to the orders of Henry VIII was insured by John Hilsey, appointed by the king as provincial of England and then bishop of Rochester to replace John Fisher, and also by Richard Ingworth, who became suffragan bishop of Dover in 1537.

Although the documentary evidence is lacking, to complete the picture of the relationship of the Dominican order to the Protestant Reformation one should take into account the attitude of the cloistered nuns and the lay tertiaries. For example, Bucer had to contend with the resistance of the Sisters of Saint Margaret in Strasbourg. Overall the scholastic formation of the Dominicans, stemming as it did from Thomas Aquinas, who ascribed an important role to the thought of Aristotle, as well as their ecclesiology, should have made them adversaries of Protestantism. In addition, it is important to emphasize their role in the Catholic Reformation, both because of the part they played in the Council of Trent (Melchior Cano, Pietro Bertano, Domingo de Soto) and in the preparation of the Roman catechism, as well as their pastoral influence, of which Bartholemew of the Martyrs, archbishop of Braga in Portugal, is a primary example. The Order of the Friars Preachers thus contributed to the reform and renewal of preaching, which was, in the church of the sixteenth century, a common effort that transcended all divisions.

BIBLIOGRAPHY

Jarrett, Bede. *The English Dominican Province, 1221–1921.* Rev. ed. London, 1938.
Lauchert, Friedrich. *Die italienischen literarischen Gegner Luthers.* Freiburg, 1912.
Mortier, Antonin. *Histoire des maîtres généraux de l'ordre des frères prêcheurs.* Vol. 5. Paris, 1911.
Paulus, Nikolaus. *Die deutschen Dominikaner im Kampfe gegen Luther, 1518–1563.* Freiburg, 1903.
Quétif, Jacques, and Jacques Echard. *Scriptores Ordinis Praedicatorum* (1719–1721). 2 vols. Louvain, 1961.
Walz, Angelo. *I Domenicani al concilio di Trento.* Rome, 1961.

GUY BEDOUELLE
Translated from French by Robert E. Shillenn

DON JUAN OF AUSTRIA.   *See* John of Austria.

DONTECLOCK, Reynier (Lat., Reginaldus, Regnerus, Reinerus; dates unknown), Calvinist minister and polemicist in the doctrinal controversies during the Dutch Reformation. Donteclock is familiar to students of the Dutch Reformation primarily through his polemical writings in defense of the strictest doctrinal form of Calvinism. Little biographical information about Donteclock exists.

A native of Ieper in western Flanders, Donteclock became associated with the Reformed religion in Brielle, where he played a role, albeit an indeterminate one, in Calvinist activity in 1566. With the arrival of the king of Spain's heavy-handed captain general, Fernando Álverez de Toledo, duke of Alba, in 1567, Donteclock fled Brielle. In 1570 he was a seminary student at the University of Heidelberg and in 1577 began service as a minister in Delft. Donteclock served in the Reformed church in Delft until 1590, during which time he worked closely with his colleague Arend Corneliszoon.

In this interval Donteclock established his reputation as a strident Calvinist and outspoken opponent of Pelagian theological strains in the Dutch Reformation. In particular, he targeted the ideas of the noted humanist Dirk Volkertzoon Coornhert. In collaboration with Corneliszoon, Donteclock published three treatises that supported strict adherence to the Belgic Confession and dealt with such issues as original sin and predestination. Regarding the latter, Donteclock believed that a more moderate stance, sublapsarianism, was a better strategy to combat Coornhert's charges that predestination made God the author of sin. According to the sublapsarianist position, God permitted the Fall to occur but did not will it. Nonetheless, Donteclock and Corneliszoon encountered nothing but criticism from more extreme Calvinists on one side and from opponents of predestination on the other.

On the practical level, Donteclock lacked the diplomatic skills of Corneliszoon and provoked the hostility of Delft magistrates by his stridency. With the encouragement of the city council, he resigned his post at Delft in 1590, and shortly thereafter he accepted the call of the Reformed congregation in Voorschoten. Conflict continued to follow Donteclock, and his proclivity to make enemies ensured that he would be a much-traveled controversialist. His only subsequent posts were in Brielle as a pastor from 1592 to 1599 and as the rector of the Latin school from 1604 to 1605. His last published work dates from 1612.

Despite his lack of official appointments, Donteclock continued to participate in the theological disputes within the Dutch Reformed church. As the theological divisions in the church became increasingly polarized over the issue of predestination after 1605, Donteclock abandoned his moderate sublapsarianism for the stricter position on predestination. Accordingly, he supported the supralapsarian view of the Leiden theologian Franciscus Gomarus and attacked the free will doctrine of Jacobus Arminius. Donteclock considered Arminianism a dangerous novelty that endowed humans with an autonomy reserved only for the godhead. Donteclock contributed to the ongoing theological disputes in the Dutch Reformation as an enthusiastic supporter of the stringent brand of Calvinism that eventually triumphed at the Synod of Dordrecht in 1618.

BIBLIOGRAPHY

"Donteclock, Reynier." In *Biographische woordenboek van protestantsche godgeleerden in Nederland*, edited by J. P. De Bie, L. A. van Langeraad, and J. Loosjes, vol. 4, pp. 537–547. The Hague, 1919. Brief overview of Donteclock's life and thought. While Donteclock figures in most monographs on the Dutch Reformation, there is no single published treatment of him beyond reference material in Dutch.

CHARLES H. PARKER

DOOPSGEZINDEN. This term is now the official description in the Netherlands of those Protestants who are known elsewhere as Mennonites (literally those of the baptism persuasion). The term was first used in the late sixteenth century: William of Orange, for example, referred in a letter of 1578 to those who are called *Doopgesindt* (baptism-minded). Dutch radical sectaries employed this comprehensive description in the first half of the seventeenth century as a substitute for the pejorative *wederdoper* or *herdoper* (Anabaptist) and as an inoffensive common denominator for the various sects, whose spiritual ancestors included Melchior Hoffman, Menno Simons, and Hans de Ries.

The mid-1540s marked a watershed in the history of the radical Reformation in the Low Countries. By then the followers of Jan van Batenburg, who had kept alive certain aspects of Munsterite Anabaptism, had been effectively marginalized. More significantly, persecution forced David Joris, widely regarded as the leading Anabaptist in the Low Countries in the aftermath of Münster, to seek refuge in 1544 at Basel. At the same time the influence of his rival, Menno Simons, began to be felt, first in Friesland, where the authorities put a price on Joris's head in 1542. Shortly before 1544 his *Dat Fundament des Christelycken Leers* (Foundation of Christian Doctrine) was printed in Antwerp

for distribution in Holland and Friesland. About the same time a "Mennonite" congregation came to light in Amsterdam, and by 1550 Mennonites were active in Antwerp and Flanders.

Dutch Anabaptism was made up of freestanding congregations. "Teachers" or "exhorters," usually lay preachers with no formal training, conducted the simple services; "deacons," sometimes women, distributed relief; and *weet-doeners* made known the time and place of the secret meetings. Charismatic and largely autonomous "elders" or "bishops" exercised substantial but ill-defined authority over the congregations; they administered baptism to believers, arbitrated in the case of disputes, and enforced discipline. Several of the elders exercised a roving commission: Leenaert Bouwens traveled throughout the western Low Countries between 1554 and 1582, visiting congregations from Flanders and Tournai in the south to East Friesland in the north, during which time he baptized more than ten thousand persons.

The occupational profile of Dutch Anabaptism was quite distinctive. Whereas priests, schoolmasters, printers, and lawyers took a prominent part in the evangelical gatherings in the 1520s and subsequently in Reformed circles, such groups were less well represented among the Anabaptists. Though several of the most prominent elders had been Catholic clerics, notably Menno Simons, Dirk Philips, Gillis van Aken, and Adam Pastor, most preachers gained their living from manual work. This circumstance may explain the suspicion in Anabaptist circles about academic training and dogmatic theology. Contemporaries, too, remarked on the humble background of Dutch Anabaptists. Recent studies of Anabaptists at Amsterdam and Antwerp show that "mechanics," often recent immigrants, formed the mainstay of these urban congregations. But if Dutch Anabaptists were, as a rule, not wealthy or well educated, neither were they destitute nor altogether cut off from the bookish culture of their day. Menno Simons urged parents to teach their children to read and write, and many indeed owned works of edification and read the scriptures.

Though Dutch Anabaptists under Simon's guidance distanced themselves from the events at Münster, the doctrinal break was not absolute. In particular Hoffman's incarnational doctrine, according to which Christ did not acquire his human nature from Mary, continued to command widespread allegiance. This doctrine followed from Hoffman's soteriology. As a result of Adam's sin, humanity belonged by right to Satan, and redemption depended on a Saviour who shared nothing with Adam's accursed seed. The desire for the restitution of the New Testament church can be represented as the counterpart to this concern for the regeneration of the Christian. It found expression in the endeavor to form and maintain a congregation that was both "without spot or wrinkle" and at odds with the world. The preservation of the purity of the "holy congregation" required the exclusion of sinners. The rigorists among the elders insisted that not only the congregation but even the spouse should shun the excommunicant.

Such severity provoked controversy and contributed to the process of fragmentation of Dutch Anabaptism. This process began in 1556 when the Waterlanders, led by Jacob Janszoon Scheedemaker, separated; another rupture in 1567 led to the split between the Frisians and the Flemings; and there were further schisms in the 1580s. Doctrinal differences played a significant part in these controversies, but the growing power and forceful personality of the elders exacerbated these difficulties, which, in the absence of an "objective" source of authority (the first Anabaptist confession of faith was drawn up only in 1577 and had no binding authority) often led to the formation of new congregations. Seven separate Anabaptist congregations existed at Haarlem about 1620. Though the intensity of persecution slackened somewhat after 1544, martyrdom and suffering remained a continuing part of Anabaptist experience and reinforced their sense of being strangers in the world; suffering became a mark of the true Christian and of the church. The *imitatio Christi* found fullest expression in the conduct of those witnesses to the faith, the martyrs. Their spiritual testimonies were treasured by the brethren and formed the basis of the first Dutch Anabaptist martyrology, *Het Offer des Heeren* (The Sacrifice of the Lord; 1562).

With the success of the Revolt of the Netherlands, Anabaptists in the northern Netherlands no longer needed to fear for their lives. After 1579 freedom of conscience was guaranteed; in practice Dutch Anabaptists, unlike Catholics, usually enjoyed freedom of worship. In some parts the civil authorities, aware of Mennonite objections to oath taking, made alternative arrangements. Mennonite artists like Karel van Mander, the Dutch Vasari, and Salomon van Ruysdael, the landscape painter, contributed to contemporary Dutch culture. But if the Mennonites in the towns of Holland in the seventeenth century attained a social respectability unknown to their forebears, they did not live at ease with the world. Rembrandt's double portrait of the wealthy merchant and Mennonite preacher Cornelis van Anslo and his wife conveys the tension between, on the one hand, their material prosperity and elevated social station and, on the other, their sobriety and biblical piety. Mennonites kept alive the memory of past sufferings by reading the numerous martyrologies in the seventeenth century, notably Thieleman Janszoon van Bragt's *Het Bloedig Toneel of Martelaersspieghel* (The Bloody Theater or Martyrs' Mirror; 1660).

In the late sixteenth and early seventeenth century Reformed ministers and synods waged a bitter polemical offensive against the Mennonites. Though the fissiparous tendencies of Dutch Anabaptism were tempered in the seventeenth century, the movement had ceased to expand. In Friesland and in some parts of Holland (Waterland, Zaanstreek) Anabaptists still constituted a significant proportion of the population; their discipline and piety could exert an attraction locally on discontented Calvinists. Statistical information about the *Doopsgezinden* is not available. Van der Zijpp estimates that there were about 150,000 *Doopsgezinden* in the mid-seventeenth century, of whom by far the greater part belonged to either the Waterlanders or the United Flemish, Frisian, and High German congregations; the conservative congregations constituted only a small fraction of the total.

[*See also* Batenburg, Jan van; Joris, David; Menno Simons; Philips, Dirk; Philips, Obbe; *and* Ries, Hans de.]

BIBLIOGRAPHY

Braght, Thieleman Jansz. van. *The Bloody Theater or Martyrs' Mirror of the Defenseless Christians . . . who suffered and died for the Testimony of Jesus, . . . to the year A.D. 1660*. 15th ed. Scottdale, Pa., 1987.

Decavele, Johan. *De dageraad van de reformatie in Vlaanderen, 1520–1565*. Brussels, 1975. An exhaustive study based throughout on archival sources; gives close attention to the socioeconomic background of the religious dissidents in Flanders.

Deppermann, Klaus. *Melchior Hoffman: Social Unrest and Apocalyptic Visions in the Age of the Reformation*. Edinburgh, 1987. Important because of the abiding influence of Melchiorite theology on later Dutch Anabaptism.

Keeney, William E. *The Development of Dutch Anabaptist Thought and Practice from 1539–1564*. Nieuwkoop, Netherlands, 1968. This volume is an examination of the writings of Menno Simons and Dirk Philips.

Krahn, Cornelius. *Dutch Anabaptism: Origin, Spread, Life and Thought, 1450–1600*. 2d ed. Scottdale, Pa., 1981. A useful survey, though dated in many particulars.

Krahn, Cornelius, et al., eds. *The Mennonite Encyclopedia*. 4 vols. Scottdale, Pa., 1955–1959. Especially strong on Dutch Anabaptism with many entries by N. van der Zijpp.

Kühler, W. J. *Geschiedenis der nederlandsche doopsgezinden in de zestiende eeuw*. Reprint, Haarlem, Netherlands, 1961. Though his interpretation of Munsterite Anabaptism is no longer accepted, his analysis of the tensions among individual, congregation, and elder retains its value.

Marnef, Guido. "Antwerpen in Reformatietijd: Ondergronds Protestantisme in een internationale handelsmetropool, 1550–1577." Ph.D. diss., Katholieke Universiteit Leuven, 1991. English translation forthcoming from Johns Hopkins University Press. The most comprehensive treatment of the Reformation in Antwerp, the center of Anabaptism in the southern Netherlands.

Mellink, Albert F. *Amsterdam en de wederdopers in de zestiende eeuw*. Nijmegen, 1978. This volume represents reflections on the sources that the author has also edited in the series *Documenta Anabaptistica Neerlandica*.

Verheyden, A. L. E. *Anabaptism in Flanders, 1530–1650*. Scottdale, Pa., 1961. Retains its usefulness, but those with Dutch should consult Decavele.

Voolstra, Sjouke. *Het woord is vlees geworden: De Melchioritisch-Menniste incarnatieleer*. Kampen, 1982. Demonstrates the fundamental and continuing importance for Dutch Anabaptism of Hoffman's doctrine of the incarnation. Also examines the treatment of this topic by Rothmann, Menno, and later Mennonites.

Zijpp, N. van der. *Geschiedenis der doopsgezinden in Nederland*. Delft, 1980. Useful chapters on the piety of the martyrs and on the life of the congregations.

ALASTAIR C. DUKE